ELEMENTS OF

Writing

REVISED EDITION

Complete Course

James L. Kinneavy

John E. Warriner

The Senior Class
of
Central High School
announces the commencement exercises
Friday evening, May twenty-eighth
at eight o'clock
Central Stadium

English Research
Paper
(Works Cited)

HOLT, RINEHART AND WINSTON
Harcourt Brace & Company

Austin • New York • Orlando • Atlanta • San Francisco
Boston • Dallas • Toronto • London

Critical Readers

Requests for permission to make copies of any part of the work should be mailed to: Permissions Department, Holt, Rinehart and Winston, Inc., 6277 Sea Harbor Drive, Orlando, Florida 32887-6777.

Portions of this work were published in previous editions.

Acknowledgments: See page 1188, which is an extension of the copyright page.

Printed in the United States of America

ISBN 0–03–050888–6   1 2 3 4 5 6 7   040   00 99 98 97

James L. Kinneavy, the Jane and Roland Blumberg Centennial Professor of English at The University of Texas at Austin, directed the development and writing of the composition strand in the program. He is the author of *A Theory of Discourse* and coauthor of *Writing in the Liberal Arts Tradition.* Professor Kinneavy is a leader in the field of rhetoric and composition and a respected educator whose teaching experience spans all levels—elementary, secondary, and college. He has continually been concerned with teaching writing to high school students.

John E. Warriner developed the organizational structure for the Handbook of Grammar, Usage, and Mechanics in the book. He coauthored the *English Workshop* series, was general editor of the *Composition: Models and Exercises* series, and editor of *Short Stories: Characters in Conflict.* He taught English for thirty-two years in junior and senior high school and college.

Writers and Editors

H. Edward Deluzain has a Ph.D. in English Education from Florida State University. He teaches at A. Crawford Mosley High School in Panama City, Florida. He is a writer of educational material in literature and composition.

Mary Hynes-Berry has a Ph.D. in English from The University of Wisconsin-Madison. She is an educational consultant for public schools in Chicago, Illinois. She has been a writer of educational materials for over fifteen years.

Beverly A. Grossman has an M.A. in English as a Second Language from The University of Texas at Austin. She has written extensively for educational publications. Currently she is an educational consultant.

Sylvia Teague has an M.A. in economics from the University of Texas, where she also taught economics for two years. She has been writing educational materials in composition and literature for ten years.

Glenda A. Zumwalt has an Ed.D. in Teaching Composition and Rhetoric from East Texas State University. She teaches composition at Southeastern Oklahoma State University. She is a writer of educational material in composition and literature.

Elizabeth McGonigal has an M.A. in English from Vanderbilt University. She teaches at Round Rock High School in Round Rock, Texas. She is a trainer with the New Jersey Writing Project in Texas.

Staff Credits

Associate Director: Mescal K. Evler

Managing Editor: Steve Welch

Senior Editors: Lynda Abbott, Richard Blake, Suzanne Thompson

Editorial Staff: *Editors:* Cheryl Christian, Adrienne Greer, Scott Hall, Colleen Hobbs, Eileen Joyce, Ginny Power, Laura Cottam Sajbel, Elizabeth Smith, Stephen Wesson; *Copyeditors:* Joel Bourgeois, Roger Boylan, Mary Malone, Michael Neibergall, Copyediting Supervisor; *Editorial Coordinators:* Susan Grafton Alexander, Amanda F. Beard, Rebecca Bennett, Wendy Langabeer, Marie Hoffman Price; *Support:* Ruth A. Hooker, Senior Word Processor, Christina Barnes, Kelly Keeley, Margaret Sanchez, Raquel Sosa, Pat Stover

Editorial Permissions: Catherine J. Paré, Janet Harrington

Production: *Pre-press:* Beth Prevelige, Simira Davis, Sergio Durante

Manufacturing: Mike Roche

Media: Belinda Barbosa

Page Production: Preface, Inc.

Design: Richard Metzger, *Art Director;* Lori Male, *Designer*

Photo Research: Peggy Cooper, *Photo Research Manager;* Mavournea Hay, Mike Gobbi, Victoria Smith, *Photo Research Team*

Acknowledgments

We wish to thank the following teachers who participated in field testing of pre-publication materials for this series:

Susan Almand-Myers
Meadow Park Intermediate School
Beaverton, Oregon

Theresa L. Bagwell
Naylor Middle School
Tucson, Arizona

Ruth Bird
Freeport High School
Sarver, Pennsylvania

Joan M. Brooks
Central Junior High School
Guymon, Oklahoma

Candice C. Bush
J. D. Smith Junior High School
N. Las Vegas, Nevada

Mary Jane Childs
Moore West Junior High School
Oklahoma City, Oklahoma

Brian Christensen
Valley High School
West Des Moines, Iowa

Lenise Christopher
Western High School
Las Vegas, Nevada

Mary Ann Crawford
Ruskin Senior High School
Kansas City, Missouri

Linda Dancy
Greenwood Lakes Middle School
Lake Mary, Florida

Elaine A. Espindle
Peabody Veterans Memorial High School
Peabody, Massachusetts

Joan Justice
North Middle School
O'Fallon, Missouri

Beverly Kahwaty
Pueblo High School
Tucson, Arizona

Lamont Leon
Van Buren Junior High School
Tampa, Florida

Susan Lusch
Fort Zumwalt South High School
St. Peters, Missouri

Michele K. Lyall
Rhodes Junior High School
Mesa, Arizona

Belinda Manard
McKinley Senior High School
Canton, Ohio

Nathan Masterson
Peabody Veterans Memorial High School
Peabody, Massachusetts

Marianne Mayer
Swope Middle School
Reno, Nevada

Penne Parker
Greenwood Lakes Middle School
Lake Mary, Florida

Amy Ribble
Gretna Junior-Senior High School
Gretna, Nebraska

Kathleen R. St. Clair
Western High School
Las Vegas, Nevada

Carla Sankovich
Billinghurst Middle School
Reno, Nevada

Sheila Shaffer
Cholla Middle School
Phoenix, Arizona

Joann Smith
Lehman Junior High School
Canton, Ohio

Margie Stevens
Raytown Middle School
Raytown, Missouri

Mary Webster
Central Junior High School
Guymon, Oklahoma

Susan M. Yentz
Oviedo High School
Oviedo, Florida

Contents in Brief

Table of Contents

PROFESSIONAL ESSAYS

T6

CHAPTER 2 UNDERSTANDING PARAGRAPH STRUCTURE

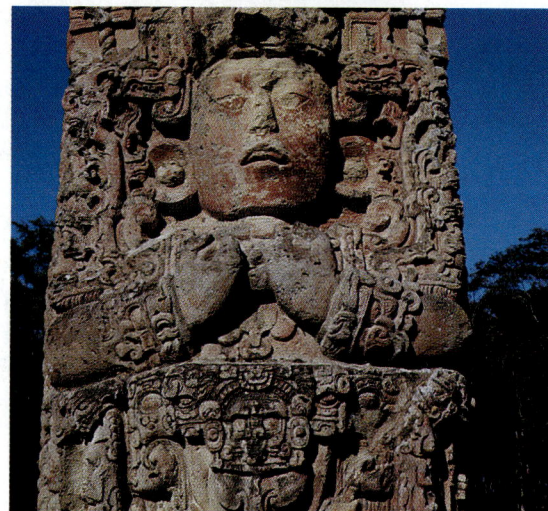

► CHAPTER 3 UNDERSTANDING COMPOSITION STRUCTURE

CHAPTER 4 EXPRESSIVE WRITING: NARRATION

► CHAPTER 6 WRITING TO INFORM: EXPOSITION

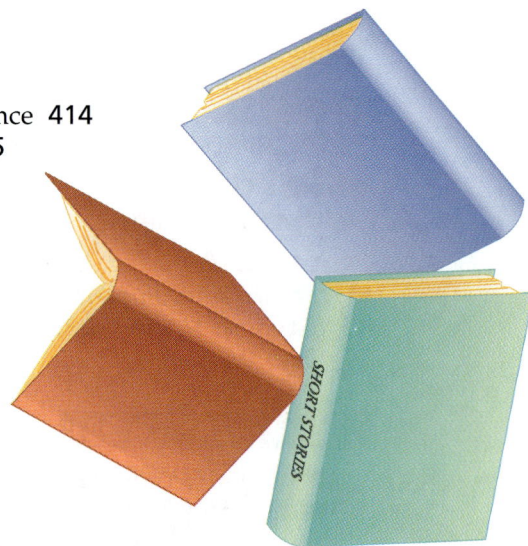

SHORT STORIES

The Granger Collection, New York

CHAPTER 14 WRITING CLEAR SENTENCES

PART TWO HANDBOOK

CHAPTER 17 THE PARTS OF SPEECH   598

Identification and Function

► CHAPTER *18* THE PARTS OF A SENTENCE   629

Subject, Predicate, Complement

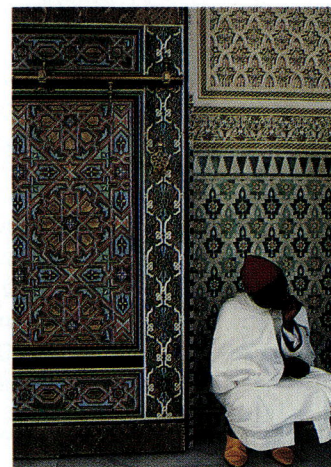

CHAPTER 21 AGREEMENT 698

Subject and Verb, Pronoun and Antecedent

CHAPTER 22 CORRECT PRONOUN USAGE 726

Case Forms of Pronouns; Special Problems

Satoshi Yabuuchi/Courtesy of Gallery Kitano,
Tokyo, Japan

CHAPTER 23 CLEAR REFERENCE 752

CHAPTER 24 CORRECT FORM AND USE OF VERBS 764

► CHAPTER 25 CORRECT USE OF MODIFIERS 811

Forms of Adjectives and Adverbs; Comparison

CHAPTER 31 SPELLING 962

Improving Your Spelling

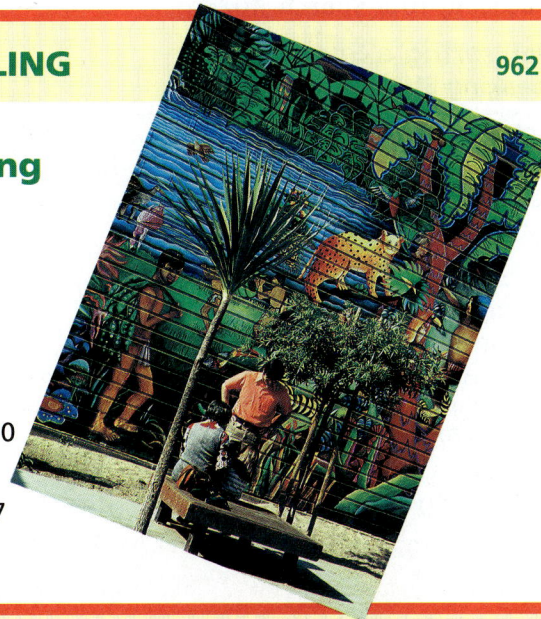

CHAPTER 32 CORRECTING COMMON ERRORS 990

Key Language Skills Review

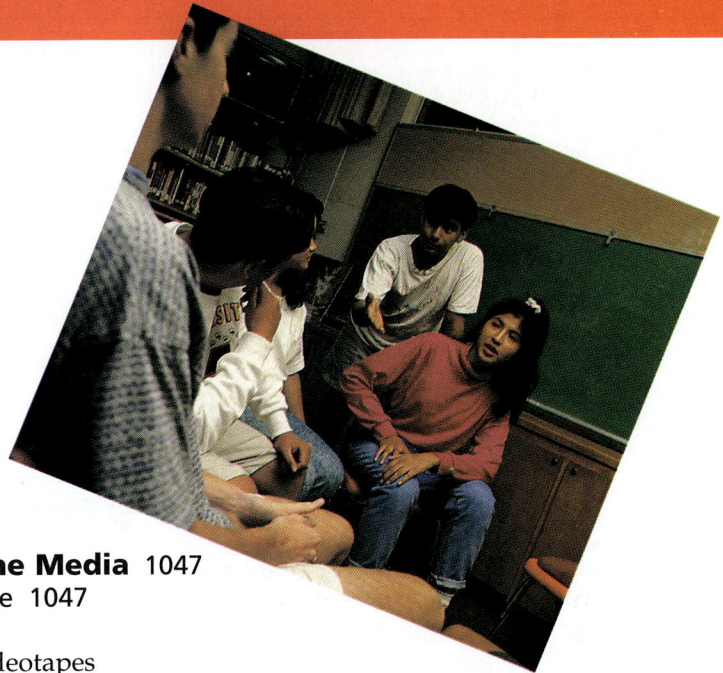

CHAPTER **35** THE LIBRARY/MEDIA CENTER 1051

Finding and Using Information

Fiction

Elizabeth Bowen, "The Demon Lover," *The Collected Stories of Elizabeth Bowen*

Truman Capote, "A Christmas Memory," *Breakfast at Tiffany's*

Lewis Carroll, *Through the Looking-Glass*

Eugenia Collier, "Marigolds," *Negro Digest*

Manuela Williams Crosno, "The Precious Stones of Axolotyl," *Sudden Twists*

Richard Erdoes and Alfonso Ortiz, "Why the Owl Has Big Eyes," *American Indian Myths and Legends*

William Faulkner, "Spotted Horses," *Uncollected Stories of William Faulkner*

F. Scott Fitzgerald, *The Great Gatsby*

Ernesto Galarza, *Barrio Boy*

Nadine Gordimer, "The Soft Voice of the Serpent," *Selected Stories*

Egyirba High, "The Lion Sleeps Tonight," *Tight Spaces*

Langston Hughes, "Thank You M'am," *The Langston Hughes Reader*

Gus Lee, *China Boy*

Beryl Markham, *West with the Night*

Paul Theroux, "Dengue Fever," *The Consul's File*

Maurice Walsh, "The Quiet Man"

Jessamyn West, "Then He Goes Free," *Cress Delahanty*

Hisaye Yamamoto, "Reading and Writing," *Seventeen Syllables*

Nonfiction

Diane Ackerman, "Last Refuge of the Monk Seal"

Maya Angelou, *Singin' and Swingin' and Gettin' Merry Like Christmas*

Isaac Asimov, "The Villain in the Atmosphere," *Past, Present, and Future*

Margaret Atwood, "An End to Audience?," *Second Words*

Tim Baer, *How to Teach Your Old Dog New Tricks*

Melinda Beck, "The Lost Worlds of Ancient America," *Newsweek*

Jane Brody, "Heat Disorders: When the Body Gets Too Hot," *Jane Brody's The New York Times Guide to Personal Health*

Art Buchwald, "The Killers," *I Think I Don't Remember*

Rachel Carson, *The Sea Around Us*, *Silent Spring*

Judith Ortiz Cofer, *Silent Dancing*

Sam Connery, "Taking Liberties with an American Goddess"

"Dog Tales," *Country*

Ralph Ellison, "An Extravagance of Laughter," *Going to the Territory*

Louise Erdrich, "The Names of Women"

Linda Flower, *Problem-Solving Strategies for Writing*

Hugh Gallagher, "The Wonder Years," *Literary Cavalcade*

Merwyn S. Garbarino and Robert F. Sasso, *Native American Heritage*

Emily Gaul, "Vitreography: Making Prints with Glass Plates"

Marcia Ann Gillespie, "Oseola McCarty"

Frederic Golden, "Clever Kanzi," *Discover*

James Gorman, "Man, Bytes, Dog"

Susan Shown Harjo, "I Won't Be Celebrating Columbus Day," *Newsweek*

August Heckscher, "Doing Chores," *Short Essays*

Jamake Highwater, *Native Land: Sagas of the Indian Americas*

Jeanne Wakatsuki Houston and James D. Houston, *Farewell to Manzanar*

Zora Neale Hurston, "How It Feels to Be Colored Me"

"I wish I could give my son a wild raccoon.", ed. Eliot Wigginton

Bruce E. Johansen, *Forgotten Founders*

LeRoi Jones, *Blues People: Negro Music in White America*

Martin Luther King, Jr., "I Have a Dream," "Letter from Birmingham Jail," *Why We Can't Wait*

Stephen King, "Now You Take 'Bambi' and 'Snow White'—That's Scary!," *TV Guide*

Harold Krents, "Darkness at Noon," *Short Essays: Models for Composition*

William Langewiesche, "The World in Its Extreme," *The Atlantic*

"Large Pizza, Hold the Microchips," *Discover*

William Least Heat-Moon, *Blue Highways*

Connie Leslie, et al., "Classrooms of Babel," *Newsweek*

Abraham Lincoln, "The Gettysburg Address"

Barry Lopez, *Arctic Dreams*

Meg Lukens, "Skiing a Formidable Course," *Sports Illustrated*

Jay Mathews, *Escalante: The Best Teacher in America*

Steve Nadis, "Road Show," *Omni*

V. S. Naipaul, *India: A Wounded Civilization*

Madeleine Nash, "A Bumper Crop of Biotech," *Time*

Katharine Payne, "Elephant Talk," *National Geographic*

David Roberts, "The Decipherment of Ancient Maya," *The Atlantic*

Paul Robeson, *The Whole World in His Hands*

Carl Sagan, "Nuclear War and Climatic Catastrophe: A Nuclear Winter," *Reading Critically, Writing Well* by Rise B. Axelrod and Charles R. Cooper

Steve H. Scheuer, review of "Back to the Future," *The Complete Guide to Videocassette Movies*

Wolf Schneider, "Film Preservation: Whose responsibility is it?" *American Film*

David M. Schwartz, "Snatching Scientific Secrets from the Hippo's Gaping Jaws," *Smithsonian*

"Scourge of the South May Be Heading North," *National Geographic*

Joanna L. Stratton, "Days of Valor," *Pioneer Women: Voices from the Kansas Frontier*

Amy Taubin, "He Did It," *The Village Voice*

Paul Theroux, *Riding the Iron Rooster: By Train Through China*

Dylan Thomas, *A Child's Christmas in Wales*

Susan Trausch, "Out, out, telltale spot!" *The Boston Globe*

Joyce L. Vedral, "Life Is Not a Television Show," *My Teacher Is Driving Me Crazy*

Booker T. Washington, "Up from Slavery," *African American Literature*

E. B. White, "Dog Training," *One Man's Meat*

Lindsey Williams, "Our Fascinating Past," *Charlotte Sun Herald*

Zheng Zhensen and Alice Low, *A Young Painter*

Poetry

Jimmy Santiago Baca, *Martín and Meditations on the South Valley*

Elizabeth Bishop, "One Art," *The Complete Poems*

Nina Cassian, "The Bear," *Lady of Miracles: Poems by Nina Cassian*

Henry Wadsworth Longfellow, *The Song of Hiawatha*

William Shakespeare, "Sonnet 29," "Sonnet 33"

Percy Bysshe Shelley, "Ozymandias"

George A. Strong, "The Modern Hiawatha," *Parodies: An Anthology from Chaucer to Beerbohm—and After*

Alfred, Lord Tennyson, "The Eagle"

Nguyen Thi Vinh, "Thoughts of Hanoi"

Drama

Bernard Shaw, *Pygmalion*

A Teacher's Guide to

ELEMENTS OF WRITING

CONTENTS

DONALD MURRAY

KAREN GREENBERG

Lee Odell

Barbara Shade

Maxine Hairston

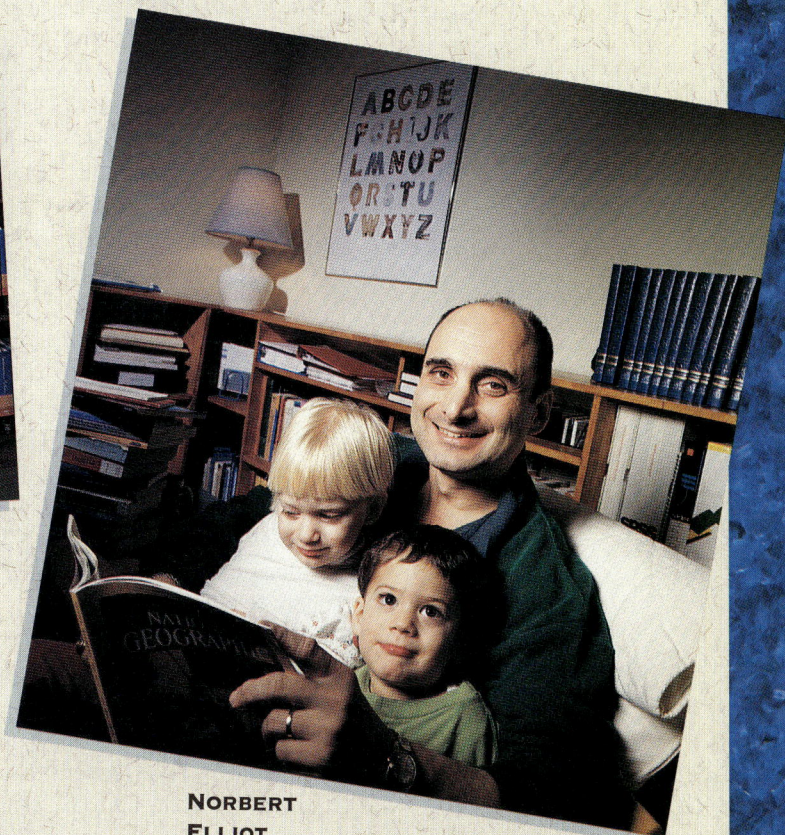

Norbert Elliot

Wanda Schindley

HOW DARE THEY?

. . . IN THE SPIRIT OF MAINTAINING THE LASTING VALUES AND STANDARDS OF THE SERIES . . .

Certainly when teachers saw a new name listed on *Elements of Writing* as a coauthor with John E. Warriner, some must have said, "How can the editors dare do this?" Warriner has been a legendary name in high school English composition and grammar books since 1941, the year of the first edition of his series. His high school textbooks have changed somewhat through the decades, but they have stood the test of half a century—despite many educational trends and fashions—because they have incorporated important values and standards. Warriner's texts have assumed an almost biblical authority.

But even the Bible is translated anew for different generations. So it is in the spirit of maintaining the lasting values and standards of the series that this new edition of the series is published with a new coauthor. I was properly flattered when Holt, Rinehart and Winston asked me to be the consultant for the composition sections of the books in the new series. But I was also in awe of this long tradition of excellence and can only hope that this tradition can be upheld.

Like John E. Warriner, I have a long and varied experience as a teacher. He taught in junior high, high school, and college. I have taught in elementary school, high school, and college. He taught for many years; I have been teaching since 1941 and continue to teach today. For the past twenty-five years I have given workshops to high school students involved in statewide competition in extemporaneous writing. Like Warriner, I have attempted to keep up with the profession and to reflect in my writings what we have learned and continue to learn about teaching the language arts. I have trained students to teach at all grade levels from elementary school through graduate school. I have also observed student teachers for years at the high school and college levels.

You will find in this series, therefore, an attempt to maintain the best values of the Warriner series and to add to it a few new features that teachers, administrators, and scholars think will make it an even better set of books.

THE TEACHER'S EDITION IS A *GREAT* HELP

I know that teaching school is incredibly time consuming: You're there at 8:00 and leave at 4:00; then you take on extra professional chores in the evening, and spend weekends correcting papers, read to keep up professionally, work on extracurricular activities, and attend conventions. Clearly you need all of the timesavers you can find.

You will find help in this series. On each page you will find that your objectives, your lesson plan, and your resources are involved with the student text. Questions for the students are provided with answers. Vocabulary items are defined. Adaptations for more-advanced students, less-advanced students, and ESL students are suggested. Opportunities for critical thinking and for cooperative learning are continually provided.

So, before spending hours looking up supplementary materials for a class, look in your teacher's edition. Someone else may have done your work already and saved you hours

Also, beginning teachers should exploit these thorough materials to avoid some all-too-common problems in the classroom.

RELATIONSHIP BETWEEN COMPOSITION AND GRAMMAR

Elements of Writing demonstrates the same close relationship between composition and grammar that has characterized the Warriner's series since its inception. You can see this by simply looking at the table of contents, which makes quite clear that primary attention is given to writing, and that grammar is a support to writing. Yet both are covered extensively.

Given the increasing importance of rhetoric in public schools and in college, you will find more depth in the composition section of this textbook. Lesson plans add more discernible structure to the chapters on writing. The chapters cover the kinds of writing students need to succeed in school and in life. Thus, there is a chapter devoted to each of the major purposes of writing—to inform or explain, to persuade, to entertain, and to express oneself. Strategies or modes of writing, such as narration, description, classification, and evaluation, are also discussed at each grade level.

In each chapter, the close relationship between composition and grammar is maintained. A relevant grammatical issue is covered in each writing chapter. Thus, a chapter on persuasion may consider fragments and a chapter on description may consider adjectives and adverbs. Finally, the composition chapters refer to the grammar chapters for coverage of issues that relate to the kind of writing under consideration.

Studies at all levels, from elementary school through college, confirm that grammar is learned best when taught in conjunction with composition, as well as with speaking and listening and literature. For instance, consistent fragments in a student's paper suggest a need for a lesson in the parts of the sentence. A mini-lesson about fragments should increase students' awareness of sentence structure. The mini-lesson would be followed with an activity in which students read peers' papers,

WHAT THIS TEXTBOOK DOES NOT WANT TO DO IS TO ENCOURAGE THE ISOLATED TEACHING OF GRAMMATICAL SKILLS IN A ROTE MANNER.

identify fragments, and resolve them with the writer. You will have reinforced a grammatical point and, more importantly, integrated grammar and composition. This textbook does not want to encourage the isolated teaching of grammatical skills in a rote manner. Most of the time, the grammar is linked to a writing assignment and even motivated by it.

THE PROCESSES OF COMPOSING

Elements of Writing consistently focuses on the processes of writing in every writing chapter. The stress on process is evident in the structuring of the chapters by the stages of the writing process—prewriting, writing, evaluating, revising, publishing, and finally reflecting.

A COOPERATIVE ATMOSPHERE

The idea that writing is a solitary, sedentary process, as a poet once said, is not at all adhered to in this textbook. Rather writing is viewed as a collaborative and cooperative action. Working cooperatively enables students to receive support from one another and from the teacher.

The students who work in *peer groups* of three or four help each other turn out better work. The members plan the papers, critique drafts, and provide a real audience for the final paper. The members of the group are like a team working toward a common goal.

The *teacher* moves from group to group, helping in the planning and discussing problems. Like the members of the peer groups, the teacher fulfills different functions:

at times the teacher is a motivator, a problem solver, a careful listener, a constructive critic, a sympathetic reader, and above all, a fellow writer.

With this view of the writing process, the teacher with a *heavy paper load* can be assisted by students. The teacher now is not the only person who reads and evaluates a student's paper. The support group also provides useful feedback to the author about mechanics, word choice, organization, ideas, and style. If the teacher trains peer groups to be constructively critical, a good deal of the drudgery of grading papers can be avoided.

The writing process often results in some kind of *publication*, such as a public speech, a performance, a class newspaper, or placement in a permanent portfolio that the student keeps of his or her progress as a writer.

The general structure of *Elements of Writing* places the composition chapters before grammar, usage, and mechanics chapters, thus mirroring the process in which students write rapidly and enthusiastically in their first plans, sketches, and drafts, without stopping to check spelling, word choice, or grammatical purity. The idea is to support the writing process as a creative surge in the beginning. The mechanical and stylistic matters are better addressed in revision with peers.

THE AIMS OR PURPOSES OF WRITING AND DIFFERENT LANGUAGE STYLES

Different levels of formality are suggested with the different pur-

poses of writing presented in *Elements of Writing*. In the chapters on expressive writing, a casual, personal, and familiar style is suggested. At the other extreme, in the chapters on information and proof, a more formal sense of grammar and word choice is expected. This is true in real life and in the classroom. In between self-expression and these types of expository writing, there are various shades of formality in persuasive, creative, and exploratory writing.

The model adopted here is that of Martin Joos, whose book *The Five Clocks* distinguishes five different levels of formality that nearly all of us use, depending on the circumstances. Joos calls these the intimate, the colloquial, the consultative, the formal, and the ritual levels. We speak to our family members in a familiar language. We speak to our friends in an ordinary conversation on the colloquial level. We adopt the consultative tone usually when we are teaching class. We use a formal level when we are giving speeches at a convention. And we use the ritual level of formality when we are at church or are graduating or are being initiated into a society.

But teachers are not the only people who have their five levels of formality. Teenagers also have their own colloquial, consultative, formal, and ritual levels as do middle-aged adults and older people.

WRITING AND LITERATURE

This series is permeated with reading and literature. Each writing chapter includes models of the type of writing that is being studied. Many samples are drawn from

the literary canon. In one grade level, for instance, an excellent poem by William Stafford illustrates the aims of writing. Nearly every writing chapter in the student's edition contains similar material. Of course, all of these selections used as writing models are annotated. Further, in the teacher's edition, are **Literature Links,** which take common literary selections and relate them to the material being studied.

Some writing chapters are almost completely devoted to literary writing, especially the chapters on creative writing, narration, and description. Thus writing and literature are highly integrated by a common underlying philosophy of language.

WRITING AND THE OTHER LANGUAGE ARTS

In addition to being highly integrated with literature, *Elements of Writing* is also integrated with reading, speaking and listening, and viewing.

Each chapter contains several reading samples of the type of writing being studied. These are carefully analyzed by the students by means of questions after each selection. These questions may be answered orally. The oral emphasis continues throughout the chapter as each stage of the writing process is carried out by means of peer discussion groups. Frequently, the publication of the paper takes an oral form as persuasive speeches are delivered to the class.

The peer group is also clearly a speaking and listening group. Students must learn to listen carefully to each other in order to make constructive suggestions for improvement.

Thus the four language arts are carefully interwoven into the structure of each chapter at each stage of the writing process.

WRITING AND NEW TECHNOLOGIES

Whenever possible, teachers should take advantage of the new technologies that are increasingly becoming available at the high school level. Consequently, throughout this edition there are continual reminders of these possibilities.

Networking with Computers

Many schools have computers available for use in teaching writing. Some are even networked to allow student interactions with each other, either with the entire class or with selected groups. The simultaneous writing reactions of all members of the class to a common reading assignment is one of the most effective methods to ensure one hundred percent participation in group discussions, especially if the right questions are asked. And the use of computers to set up small support groups for the different stages of the writing process is also an exceptionally efficient technique of using small groups in teaching writing.

Revising and Computers

Even without networking, however, the use of computers is to be commended whenever possible, particularly because of the manner in which revising is accomplished on computers. Students who formerly hated to revise now see revision as an easy and enjoyable manner to improve their work, not just at the level of vocabulary or mechanics, but even at the level of full discourse changes.

Computers also bring substantial help to the poor speller and to the student having trouble finding the right word. Nearly all word-processing programs have some type of spell-check feature that shows students which words are incorrectly spelled. Thus each student can keep a list of his or her own problem words. This is acknowledged by nearly all spelling research as the single best way to improve spelling. Most spell-check programs are accompanied by programs that properly hyphenate words at the end of a line. This is an additional bonus for students who use computers.

In addition, most word-processing programs now come with a thesaurus and grammar program. The first enables students to look for options in vocabulary, even while working at the computer.

The grammar programs can check tense, case, subject-verb agreement, fragments, and so forth.

Publishing and Word Processors

It is possible to use a computer as a desktop publisher to enable students to see some of their writings in elegant print and format. These can be put into portfolios for permanent records. Throughout the annotated teacher's edition there are reminders of this option of publishing.

A FINAL WORD

Possibly after reading this essay, which brings together many of the rather complex tasks of the writing teacher, you may be worried about the size of the task. But luckily you don't have to solve all of these problems overnight. The teaching of writing is a slow and cumulative process. Each chapter of this textbook focuses on a very specific issue and tries to address just that particular skill. Subsequent chapters build on the skill just learned. The students then slowly build up a range of abilities.

Just remember that your predecessors have worked with the students whom you now face, just as your colleagues will pick up where you leave off. And you are not alone at the present time: Your current colleagues are working with the same students in other classes.

In other words, just as writing is a cooperative endeavor for your students, so also is it a cooperative endeavor for you with the teachers from year to year and among a group of teachers one year at a time.

No One Does A More Important Job

Finally, you should be assured that your task is at the top of educational priorities. No one does a more important job than the teacher of writing. Such a person is also teaching students how to read, think, listen, and speak in ways that will enable them to contribute to a complex modern society as educated communicators.

BY DONALD M. MURRAY, PROFESSOR EMERITUS OF ENGLISH, THE UNIVERSITY OF NEW HAMPSHIRE

USE GENRE AS LENS

WE WRITE ABOUT WHAT WE DON'T KNOW ABOUT WHAT WE KNOW.

Students are usually introduced to each genre—essay, narrative, poem—in isolated units, as if one form of writing would contaminate another. But each genre is a lens, a way to observe, record, and examine the world. Students should be encouraged to use each genre to explore a single important experience.

Student writers and their teachers should begin the exploration with a personal experience—an event, a person, a place—that holds a significant mystery for them. Mystery is the starting place for most writing, what Grace Paley described when she said, "We write about what we don't know about what we know." Invite your students to explore a moment in their lives to which they keep returning in memory, the way the tongue seeks the missing tooth.

Encourage your students to play with the fragments of language connected with that experience in their minds and on paper to discover a line, a phrase, or a word that contains a tension or conflict within the experience. The "line" might be a word—*Christmas*—that might have special implications for a student with a Catholic mother and a Jewish father. It might be a phrase—*the debts of Christmas*—to a person whose family spends too much money to make up for their true family feelings. The "line" could be a sentence—"Each Christmas I remember my sister who will never grow old."—for someone who lost a sister years before. Each "line" has a tension and mystery the writer needs to understand by writing.

Before your students begin, it is important to remind them that all writing is experimental, that experimentation implies failure, and that failure is instructive. It is not possible they will fail; it is imperative that they fail. We do not improve our writing by avoiding failure, but by making use of it.

To guarantee failure, urge students to write the first draft fast. Velocity is as important in writing as it is in bicycle racing. Speed will produce the accidents of language, connection, and insight that will propel the draft forward towards meaning. And velocity allows students to escape, for the moment, the censor that demands premature correctness.

They should allow their drafts to instruct them. The evolving text will take its own course, exploring the experience as it is relived. If they are patient, receptive, and open to surprise, the text will tell them what they have to say. You may want to write two statements by E. M. Forster on the chalkboard:

Think before you speak is criticism's motto; speak before you think creation's.

and

How do I know what I think until I see what I say?

Students should write out loud, hearing the text as they write it. They may actually do this—it is your classroom—or read silently but *listen* to the text. As they tune their voices to the story being told, the voice—angry, nostalgic, humorous, sad, analytical, instructive, argumentative, poetic, even narrative—will reveal the meaning of the draft to the writer.

I invite you to stand beside me at my workbench and to observe me as I use genre to explore an experience of mine.

THE ESSAY

I prefer the term *reflective essay* to *personal essay* because the writer reflects on personal experience, or on a topic of personal interest. The essay is neither a simple narrative of experience nor of thought unanchored by experience, but a combination of thought and experience, an effort to discover and share meaning in experience. The essay is a demonstration of critical thinking.

Some notes on the craft of the essay.

• Narrow the territory to be explored so you can achieve depth.

• Be specific. The specific will instruct. The more specific you are, the more universal your audience will be.

• Work locally; the paragraph you have just written contains the seed of the next paragraph. For example, if you have said the experience was important, show how it was important in the next paragraph.

• Answer the reader's questions. Writing is a conversation between reader and writer.

• When the draft surprises you, pay attention. Develop the surprise to discover its meaning.

On April 21, while visiting a daughter and her husband in their new home, I got up early without the alarm, as is my habit, and ended up sitting at the top of the stairs waiting for my family to wake, and I found mystery in the experience. It was a moment full of emotion, and I needed—not wanted, but needed—to explore that moment through writing.

I made a few notes in my daybook:

I can remember myself as a small boy in Doctor Denton's trying to be quiet sitting at the head of the stairs (night) waiting for the family to get up

I can remember my own daughter's impatient waiting

Sunday morning I sit at the head of the stairs a good place to read, a good place legs waiting, wife, behind me in the room, my wife

It is 8 AM and they plan on rising 9 AM, I've been up at 5:33, explored town, coffee, read Sunday NY Times

The next day I wrote the column that was published in *The Boston Globe*, April 30, 1991:

I am, once again a small boy in Dr. Denton's sitting at the top of the stairs waiting for the snoring to stop and another day to begin.

I am, at the same time, an old man sitting at the top of the stairs in the new home of a daughter and her husband, waiting once more for the snoring to stop and a new day to begin.

Minnie Mae and I, on our first visit, have taken their bed, and they sleep on the hide-a-bed in the living room. They work in the theatre and have agreed to get up early—at 9 o'clock on Sunday morning—because the old folks are here.

But I followed the custom of many old men and was up at 5:33 A.M. I tiptoed downstairs, went out to the car, explored Mount Kisco, sipped a cup of coffee at Dunkin Donuts—yes, and had a doughnut, and yes, juice to get down my six pills I take because of previous doughnuts—bought the Sunday *New York Times*, sat in the car reading it, and now, at 8 A.M. sit at the head of the stairs where I can stretch my legs, flex my football knee, and read my book and wait.

It has been a good morning, and I feel little guilt that I have not been able to sleep in. They will laugh at my compulsion to be up and doing, and I will tease them for their laziness, but they will not understand the joy I, like many over sixties, experience when I am up in the lonely hours of dawn.

I ruminate—early morning is ideal for rumination—on the fact that as a child I was always up early when I could lose myself in a book —no TV then—explore the backyard or the vacant lot where the morning glories grew.

Awake before the grown-ups, I could be what I needed to be: Lindbergh crossing the Atlantic

WE DO NOT IMPROVE OUR WRITING BY AVOIDING FAILURE, BUT BY MAKING USE OF IT.

alone, Admiral Byrd isolated in his tiny room under the Antarctic ice, the unnamed Indian scout watching the palefaces land on the Maine coast

As a teenager I bicycled my route for Gallagher's News Agency in Quincy finishing before the sun was up, drove Miller's grocery truck to market in Boston or cleaned the vegetables and laid them out in rows on the boxes balanced in front of the small store on Beach Street.

Only now I confess that when I nicked myself trimming the lettuce that was packed in ice, my hands numb and clumsy, I would turn that lettuce head so the blood did not show. I was apprentice to Miller's game: profit through deceit.

I still remember playing grown-up early in the morning, the grocer's apron twice tucked so it did not sweep the sawdust strewn floor. The profit would be Miller's not mine, but I anticipated the

customers who might, this Depression Saturday, pay cash. That anticipation would last until midnight when Mr. Miller would go out and scan the street right and left and reluctantly, when no one was on the street, give the command to close.

In combat I preferred the early morning patrols, guard duty when I was alone to watch the theatre of morning's change from dark to light, the promise of a new day even when the landscape was littered with last night's dead.

After college I worked for a morning newspaper and liked the mystery and companionship of the night worker, enjoyed the coming home at dawn. Eventually I returned to days, and morning became my best writing time as it is for most writers.

Goethe advised, "Use the day before the day. Early morning hours have gold in their mouth." John Hersey testified that "To be a writer is to sit down at one's desk in the chill portion of every day, and to write." A few years ago poet Donald Hall said, "In summer I'll be up at 4:30, make coffee, let out the dog, go pick up *The Boston Globe*. Then I write."

In retirement I, like so many other over sixties, still get up early when there are no cows to milk, no

commuter train to meet, no factory shift to join. It is habit, but for me a habit built not from compulsion but delight.

Sitting at the top of the stairs waiting for the young—and the not-so-young Minnie Mae—to wake, I try to define the strange emotion I feel. At last it comes to me. I am, after a lifetime of chasing the carrot, content.

I have another day to celebrate. Sitting here alone, I can enjoy the feeling of this house that is turning so quickly into a home. I am comfortable in this home and know that soon my wife will wake with a groan and a smile, and downstairs I will hear conversation and music, smell coffee and we will all make plans for the day not too far off when a grandchild will sit where I sit, perhaps beside me, waiting for another day to begin.

The grandchild has arrived. His name is Joshua. I have not yet sat beside him at the top of the stairs but I will.

THE NARRATIVE

There are many wonderful ways to tell stories, but I suggest student fiction writers begin with the scene. Conrad is supposed to have said that a novel is a series of scenes of confrontation. The writer experienced in nonfiction tells *about* the story; the fiction writer *reveals* the story. That is an enormous difference, and the writing of a scene is the best way to cross the divide. Students can draw on their experiences with TV and film. The reader observes a room with the fourth wall removed; the action within the room tells the story and the reader discovers its meaning. As the short-story writer Becky Rule points out, students think that fiction has no rules, but the rules come from the story, and they are established early; if Hamlet is an indecisive prince he can suddenly become a king but not a decisive one.

Some notes on the craft of narrative.

• Start with character, not theme. The story and its meaning are revealed through the interaction of the characters.

• Write in the third person. It gives you more room and detachment.

• Dialogue is action, what the characters do to each other. Joan Didion says, "I don't have a very clear idea of who the characters are until they start talking."

• Point of view is where the camera is positioned to record the scene. In the beginning, stick with one point of view, perhaps entering into one head but not jumping in and out of every head. If you are in one sister's head, you don't know Frank is in the freezer; in the other sister's head, you do.

• Kurt Vonnegut counsels, "Don't put anything in a story that does not reveal character or advance the action."

In writing a draft of my novel, I found myself stealing the experience from my own essay and began a scene:

Melissa found Iain sitting in the shadows at the top of the stairs, "It's 5:30 in the morning."

He nodded.

"On guard duty?"

"In a way. I often sit here in winter, watch the light just before dawn, the woods, the field that goes down to the lake."

She thought for a moment of what it would be like to be a spy to your life, always on guard and asked, "You said last night that wherever you are, you see a field of fire, are aware of where to dig in, put the machine guns, even after all these years?"

"I'm not proud of it, Melissa. It's just my geography, an infantryman's geography."

"Do you always see a geography of war?"

"Always first, then I can make it go away. Most times.

It's natural, just the way I see things. The doctor sees you as kidney or a colon; I'm an old soldier, I see a field of fire, where the attack would come from."

"That's sad."

"Tedd's a soldier too, Melissa."

They hear the key probe for the lock, at last find it, and hurried down the stairs....

That is just a small fragment of narrative, and yet you can see

how the story is revealing itself dramatically to the writer and the reader.

THE POEM

Poetry is the most disciplined and difficult form of writing. It is also the most fun. Experience is distilled by the writing of poetry. Poetry is always play—play with image and language so that meaning is revealed directly without rhetoric getting between the writer and reader or between experience and reader. Inexperienced poets often write with adjectives and adverbs, trying to describe their own feelings. The experienced poet writes with information, revealing specifics, provocative details, and compelling images that make the reader feel and think. The meaning is rarely stated but always there. In the poem, even more than fiction, the meaning is implied. The poem is the stimulus to the reader's thinking.

Some notes on the craft of poetry.

• Forget, for the moment, rhyme, meter, and traditional verse forms.

• Brainstorm images and other specifics, creating a list that may become a poem.

• Draft lines—not sentences but fragments of language—that capture an event, person, or place.

• Rearrange the lines until they reveal a meaningful pattern.

• Pay attention to the line breaks, trying to end on a strong word that causes the reader to read on.

The morning I wrote the column, I also wrote, on the computer, what might become a poem for my poetry group that was meeting that Thursday evening. I pasted this in my daybook:

Sitting at the top of the
stairs
    I listen to the silences
    to understand Grandma's
war with Mother

Sitting at the top of the
stairs
    I tune
                train myself to 1
eliness

Later that day I made a hand-written note I also cut out and pasted in the daybook:

I lived at the top of the
stairs, behind the living room
couch, under the dining room
table, the tent of tablecloth—
in the apple tree, under the
porch,

And still later I drafted a poem that went through one radical and three or four extensive revisions (periods of word play) until it became the following completed poem:

Childhood Espionage

Spy to my life, I lived at the
top of the stairs, recorded
silence, mapped how hurt was
done. Under the porch, at the
bedroom door, behind living
room

sofa, I filled notebooks with
what was not said, not done,
escaped to the sidewalk, tried
to read the shades drawn
against my life. It must be
Mother's shadow

sitting on the edge of the
double bed, must be father's
kneeling to pray. I cannot be
sure, circle the block,
listen to the neighbor's opera
of argument, stand under

an open window where
conversation will pour over me
Once I saw my friend's older
sister. She never pulled the
shade. The dogs learned my
smell

and let me patrol back yard,
alley, vacant lot, in silence. I
found the room where the
Beckers kept the boy with the
enormous head, watched
comfort flow

from a priest's dancing hands
as he gave the last rites to
Vinnie's grandma, swayed to
the rhythm of the Mitchells'
bedroom dancing, lying down.
Late, I returned to the home

of closed doors where we
passed each other without
touching. We never raised our
voices, never stood between
light and shade, never let a
secret fall out a window.

Students should be encouraged to take central experiences from their lives—Willa Cather said, "Most of the basic material a writer works with is acquired before the age of fifteen"—and explore them with an array of genre, using each lens—essay, narrative, poem—and then examining the subject through other genre, perhaps argument, report, screenplay, or news story, to discover the many meanings in their lives. ❧

POETRY IS THE MOST DISCIPLINED AND DIFFICULT FORM OF WRITING. IT IS ALSO THE MOST FUN.

❧❧❧❧❧

Sources quoted include Grace Paley, Joan Didion, and Kurt Vonnegut cited in the following work: Donald M. Murray, *Shoptalk: Learning to Write with Writers*, Boynton/Cook Publishers, Inc., 1990.

By James L. Kinneavy

Meet the Aims and Modes of Writing

The place to start (and end) the teaching of writing is to have students see what written language can do for them.

WHY WRITE? WHERE DO I BEGIN?

Writing is a very complex activity, and so is the teaching of writing. I admit these facts, and I have been teaching writing for fifty years. You may be teaching your first class this year, and you probably have the same problem: In the face of this complex process, where do you start?

Some teachers recommend what may seem to be a very simple and logical approach: Start with the simple building blocks of writing and gradually work up to more complex blocks. In other words, teach students some elementary things about words, then move up to phrases, afterwards teach sentences, eventually work up to paragraphs, and finally, have students write full themes. Some say this is how children learn to use language orally. At first blush this theory has a kind of plausible simplicity to it. Years of research, however, have shown that it doesn't work and that it isn't the way children learn language.

LANGUAGE GETS THINGS DONE

Babies see the family members around them accomplish things by using language, and they quickly learn to use it themselves to get food, drink, or attention. This is the motivation behind all language acquisition and usage, from cradle to grave—language gets things done.

Consequently, if we can keep this elementary driving force behind our attempts to teach writing (or any language art for that matter), we can draw on a basic incentive that even babies understand. But when language teaching is divorced from getting things done, students rightly find it boring and uninteresting.

For this reason, the place to start (and end) the teaching of writing is to have students see what written language can do for them. What can writing do? In one introductory chapter, we attempt to get students to look around and see what language is getting done. We call language-users the hidden agents behind many of the miracles of our age, we say that language is where the action is, and we call language-users the movers and shakers of the world.

Using very concrete examples, we focus the student's attention on the different kinds of things that language accomplishes. But the principle is the same at every grade-level and on into the college educations, careers, and adult lives of our graduates: The central concept in the teaching of writing at every level is an awareness of the aims or purposes of writing.

THE FOUR MAJOR AIMS OR PURPOSES OF WRITING

Luckily for you as well as for the students, these aims are not infinite, unpredictable, and unmanageable. They can be reduced to a few basic categories, and both you and the students have a good deal of practical experience with the categories in general. For example, one kind of language experience with which you are very familiar has to do with attempts to explain to or inform an audience about something of which it is partially or totally ignorant. You do this daily in the classroom and the students are the targets of this use of language. Other examples of this kind of writing are news stories in newspapers and magazines, encyclopedia articles, reports, textbooks, discussions, proposed solutions to problems, and research studies. *The emphasis is always on the subject matter, considered more or less objectively.* This kind of writing is generically referred to as **expository writing.**

As a teacher, you are only too aware of a second kind of writing that places more emphasis on the writer. In this case, the writing reveals the feelings of the writer, allows the writer to voice his or her aspirations or reactions to something in a quite personal way, or gives the writer a chance to articulate important beliefs. Examples of this kind of writing are journals, diaries, myths, prayers, credos, and protests. Of course, some of this writing may also overlap with other kinds. *The major emphasis in this kind of writing is on the writer.* This kind of writing is often called **expressive writing.**

As a teacher, you often try to convince your students of the importance of an education and of their duties as citizens. As a matter of fact, in our culture we are bombarded with attempts to get readers

to vote a certain way, to change attitudes or beliefs, to buy certain products, to switch allegiances, etc. Examples of such writing are advertising, political speeches, legal oratory, editorials, and religious sermons. In all of these cases, *the focus of the use of language is on the receiver of the message.* Usually, this kind of writing is called rhetorical or **persuasive writing.**

A fourth kind of writing, probably your favorite, is literature. This type of writing is given an honored place in English classes. We read selections of literature. They are intended to delight us and sometimes to teach us lessons. Examples of literature range from simple jokes, funny stories, ballads, small poems, and TV sitcoms to serious dramas, movies, novels, and epics. We try to get students to write this way when we teach creative writing. *Although all writing involves originality, we usually reserve the term* **creative writing** *for this kind of writing.*

THE COMMUNICATION BASIS OF THE AIMS OF WRITING

As a perceptive reader, you may have noticed as we went through the four major aims of writing that each one emphasized a different element of the communication process. It is not accidental that the

major purposes of writing generally can be reduced to four. The structure of the written communication process is based on a writer, a reader, a language, and the subject matter.

To assist you to get students to see the different roles of each aim, the relationship between the elements of the communication process and those of the aims of discourse is expressed graphically below. (The major aims of writing and the main parts of the communication process).

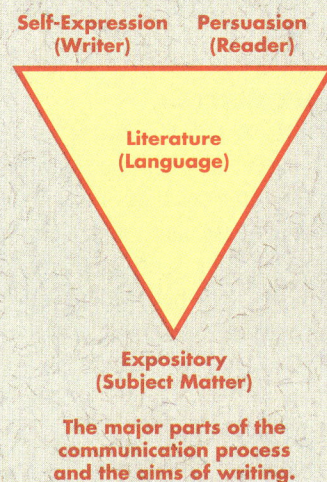

Self-Expression (Writer)   **Persuasion** (Reader)

Literature (Language)

Expository (Subject Matter)

The major parts of the communication process and the aims of writing.

Consequently, from aim to aim, there is a continual shifting of roles in the communication process. The lead role determines the major purpose of the writing and the other roles become subordinate. Many teachers have found this simple diagram enables students to grasp the changing dynamics of language use.

DOMINANT AIMS AND OVERLAP

As a teacher, you have probably written one or two of these different kinds of writing, but you may not have written all of them. In your own writing you are certainly aware that most writing does not

attempt to achieve all of these aims at the same time. A specific piece of writing usually has a single dominant aim, subordinating the others to avoid conflicts and confusion. Though subordinate, the other aims are still present. Thus, movie ads in the newspaper contain important information about actors, actresses, directors, titles, and show times, but the information is there to persuade people to come to the movies.

Indeed, all the aims overlap each other.

WHY ARE THE BASIC AIMS IMPORTANT?

Despite overlaps, however, it is quite important to distinguish the various aims. As a teacher, you are very aware that the criteria by which one kind of discourse is judged are different from the criteria by which another kind of discourse is judged. You try to impress upon your students that expository writing is judged on the basis of objective evidence; the appeal of the writer as such is not relevant to the final proof or explanation, nor is the use of emotion or humor. For this reason, you know that when you teach expository writing, it is important to discourage the use of these other kinds of appeal—they are, in fact, considered inappropriate in news stories, scientific reports, or textbooks. Thus the pedagogy of expository writing follows from the nature of this kind of writing.

But when you teach other kinds of writing, these other appeals are important. In persuasion, for example, the emphasis is on the appeal of the writer and the appeal to the interests of the audience. **The differences among exposi-**

AS A TEACHER YOU OFTEN TRY TO CONVINCE YOUR STUDENTS OF THE IMPORTANCE OF AN EDUCATION . . .

tion, **persuasion, literature, and self-expression force you to emphasize different criteria when teaching these different kinds of writing.** There is no single criterion of aim which makes all writing good. That is why the different aims are taught separately.

THE MODES OF WRITING

After all this talk about the aims of writing, you, as a teacher, might ask, "Are you maintaining that if I get students to pay attention to the aims of their writing, all other problems will disappear? There are many other facets of the process of writing to which we teachers have to pay attention. Grammar is clearly a persistent concern, as are spelling, vocabulary, sentence structure, paragraphing, genres of writing (letter, report, story, poem, speech, ad, etc.), subject matter, and last but not least, the modes. What do you propose to do with all of these issues?"

I recognize all of these concerns and reply that they will be given close and continuous attention throughout the entire course, but I would like to stress the last dimension, that of the modes of writing.

JAMES L. KINNEAVY
AUTHOR OF
ELEMENTS OF WRITING

This dimension bridges the two mentioned just before it—genre and subject matter, and it implicates a major concern of all writing teachers—organization. More than any other aspect of writing, modes determine overall organization. This particular essay, for example, is a series of classifications and definitions.

At times in the history of writing, modes have been given almost as much attention as the aims, but most of the time they have been a serious second candidate. The modes are listed differently in various books. In this textbook we call narration, description, classification, and evaluation the modes. They could be called the genres of writing, and they could be called ways of looking at subject matter.

When I want to introduce students to the modes, I use a newspaper. I ask students to find examples of news stories (narratives). I ask them to find classifications, especially in the classifieds, as they are called. I ask the students to examine individual items within each section of the classifieds and to tell me what the details are. It becomes clear to them that there are specific descriptions of cars, houses, lost dogs, or jobs in the classifieds. Finally, I have students check reviews of books, movies, television programs, or concerts. These are all evaluations.

Like the aims, the modes have to be taught separately. **What makes a good narrative is not what makes a good evaluation or a good description or a good classification.** Consequently, the modes are given careful consideration in this textbook. ❧

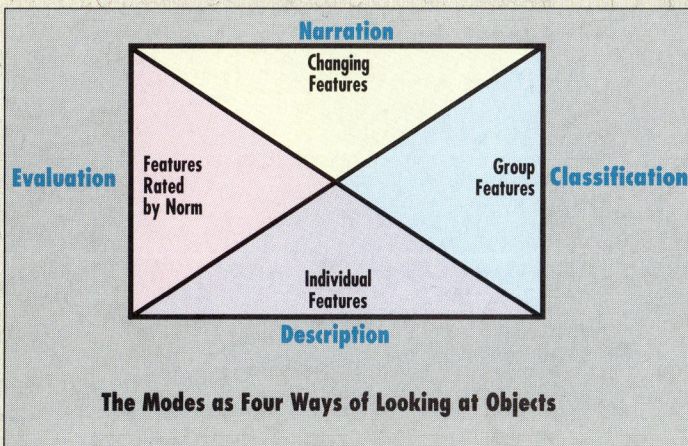

The Modes as Four Ways of Looking at Objects

Narration — Changing Features

Evaluation — Features Rated by Norm

Group Features — Classification

Individual Features

Description

BY DR. LEE ODELL, RENSSELAER POLYTECHNIC INSTITUTE

MODELING

MAKE US SEE WHAT YOU'RE TALKING ABOUT.

For some time now, teachers of writing have made a point of exhorting students to make their writing "show, not tell." Don't just tell us your reactions or opinions, we say to them. Make us see what you're talking about. If you're trying to describe a person, let us see facial expressions, details of clothing, mannerisms, actions; let us hear exactly what the person says. Or, if students are trying to write persuasively, we insist: Don't just give us your generalized conclusions. Give us some specific information that lets us see what you base your judgment on and that lets us decide for ourselves whether your judgement makes sense.

This advice is not an infallible, inflexible rule. Writers can't elaborate on everything. Furthermore, readers sometimes let a generalization pass unchallenged because it seems to ring true or because writers have sufficient authority for us simply to take their word on the matter. But if we are judicious in asking students to "show, not tell," the phrase constitutes good advice for writers and excellent advice for teachers. If we want students to make significant progress as writers, we will have to show them—not just tell them, *show*

Lee Odell opens his classroom door at Rensselaer Polytechnic Institute.

them—what we mean. In effect, we need to make sure they have models, not just of the kinds of writing they will do but of the writing processes.

There is, of course, a long history to the practice of working with models. For centuries, teachers of rhetoric and writing have required students to study the works of great writers, sometimes having students copy model texts word for word or asking students to imitate the sentence structures they found in these works. Indeed, a version of this practice persisted through the middle 1980's in the form of sentence combining. This system did not ask students to emulate one specific writer, but it did show them frequently used sentence patterns in the works of highly admired professional writers so students could construct their own sentences based on a wide variety of these patterns.

Traditional approaches to using models have their uses, but these approaches are not what I'm talking about here. I'm suggesting that we depart from traditional practice in several ways. For one thing, the model should come not solely from famous authors but rather from books and magazines students read willingly and have readily accessible. Also, teachers don't have to provide all the models; students should be asked to bring in articles or excerpts from books that they personally find engaging and effective. Finally, these models should not be treated as though they are sacred; they are, instead, objects for analysis—for criticism as well as for praise. We and our students need to examine entire models where writers

have used successful strategies that students might incorporate into their own writing, as the occasion warrants. But we and our students also need to identify things that don't work and maybe even to collaborate on devising ways to improve the model.

There are several ways we might use models, but my favorite is to use them to help students solve their own writing difficulties. For example, a number of my students can't figure out how to begin a piece of writing, what Donald Murray would refer to as a "lead." When this is a problem, I ask students to bring in copies of the first pages of articles that they somehow found themselves reading,

I DON'T WANT STUDENTS TO THINK THERE IS JUST ONE WAY TO BEGIN A PIECE OF WRITING.

❦❦❦❦❦

even though the topics might not normally have concerned them.

For example, one student brought in an article entitled "Hell on Wheels," which began this way:

Almost from the time the downtown No. 4 subway train began its 21-mile run below New York City at 11:38 p.m. on the night of Tuesday, Aug. 27, something seemed amiss. Heading from the Bronx to Manhattan, the train overshot the platform at a couple of stations. At times it slowed to a crawl and then accelerated to breakneck speeds. The conductor contacted the motorman, Robert Ray, 38, several

times on the intercom to find out if everything was all right. Ray replied that he was fine. But that was clearly not the case....

This article begins of course, with a claim about a specific event ("something seemed amiss") and then illustrates this claim with a series of incidents. It mentions specific, troubling things that happened (for example, the train "slowed to a crawl and then accelerated to breakneck speeds"); it reports what people said to each other; and then it challenges what one of the people said ("But that clearly was not the case...."). In this last sentence, the author creates a conflict that engages the reader and lets the reader know

what the rest of the article will be about (i.e., it will show how the driver's claim was "not the case").

Other articles brought in by the students began quite differently—by citing troubling statistics, for example, or by describing general trends in society that a reader was almost certain to know and be concerned about. These differences are important. I don't want students to think there is just one way to begin a piece of writing. Consequently, I photocopied a variety of examples and asked students to talk them through to identify the strategies writers had used to engage readers. My goal was to

help students recognize some of the options that are open to them in doing their own writing.

In addition to bringing in models written by professionals, it can be extremely useful for us to bring in copies of our own efforts to do the same kind of writing students are working on. And once we have developed an atmosphere of trust, it can be useful to bring in effective examples of student work, continually asking such questions as these: What did the writer do here? How did he or she go about capturing our interest and letting us know what to expect in the rest of the text? Is there anything that this writer is doing that you might profitably do? Again, the goal is not to provide recipes or rules chiseled on tablets of stone but to get students to see what is possible.

MODELING THE COMPOSING PROCESS

Thus far, I have been describing ways we might use written products as models. In addition, we also need models of the composing processes of writers. This modeling can be as sophisticated or as rudimentary as our students need. It can focus on the work of an individual writer as Donald Murray shows in his "Use Genre as Lens" essay or on the efforts of peers as they revise their initial drafts. That is, we need to let students see the processes professional writers and students go through in doing their own writing and even in responding to classmates' writing.

There are several activities teachers can use that allow students to observe their peers' writing processes. For example, a colleague was concerned that her tenth-graders would have difficulty passing the state basic competency test that is required for high school graduation. Knowing that one of the questions on that test was likely to require students to report information in a well-organized form, she could have concentrated on paragraph form and the proper use of transitions. But suspecting that her students' difficulties were more profound than that, she decided that her students weren't paragraphing because they did not understand that certain kinds of expository paragraphs require writers to group facts by setting up categories that the paragraphs would be about.

Consequently, she asked students to watch a videotape of a movie that she was fairly certain they would find moving, an account of the difficulties encountered by a child who had been classified as mentally retarded but who had, nonetheless, a number of good traits and who was personally likable. After students had watched the videotape, she asked them to write down every fact they could remember from the movie and to collaborate as a class to make the list as complete as possible. That night she typed a complete list of facts, made an overhead transparency of them, and then cut the transparency into strips, each strip containing one fact.

The next day, she asked students to collaborate on ways to group these facts. For instance, students noticed that many of the facts pertained to ways people reacted to the young boy, while others could be grouped under such headings

as the boy's reactions to other people or his abilities. As students discussed ways of grouping facts, the teacher reflected what they were saying by moving the transparency strips around on the overhead projector. She was showing, not telling, her students about the basic process they needed to create one type of organized paragraph.

Another approach to modeling the composing process comes from a ninth-grade teacher concerned that her students' descriptive writing was bland. She believed their real problem was not a lack of descriptive adjectives and adverbs but that students weren't really looking closely at the people or objects they were describing.

She also knew that television programs routinely provide excellent examples of the process of observing. That is, as a rule, television cameras do not stay in one spot to observe everything from the same angle and distance. Instead, the cameras change position to vary the angles and the distances from which they view things. For example, one detective program began with a close-up shot of a ringing phone. Then the camera moved back so that the viewers could see a well-dressed man hurrying across an elegant apartment toward the phone. Next the camera moved in to focus on the man's trembling hands as he nervously dried his sweaty palms on his handkerchief before picking up the phone. Finally, the camera shifted focus again, to show the head and shoulders of a burly, unshaven man speaking into a pay phone. These shifts in focus set the scene for the entire episode.

To help students understand this process of observing by shifting focus, the teacher asked students, as part of their homework, to watch one of their favorite TV programs and to count the number of times the camera shifted its focus in a two-minute period. She also asked them to make notes about the different things they saw every time the camera shifted focus. The next day they discussed these episodes and concluded that a program in which the camera did not shift focus would almost certainly be dull.

To help students see how this process applied to writing, the teacher gave students the following description:

She probably has false teeth and wears glasses. She wears her hair up in a bun and wears dresses from the 1930's. She has a habit of tapping her pencil on her desk.

Students readily agreed that this passage was uninteresting. To help them see why, the teacher asked students to think of the grammatical subject of each sentence as the visual focus of the sentence. (In response to the predictable question, the teacher told students that, for this passage, they could think of the grammatical subject as "how the writer begins each sentence.") Students saw readily that this writer's "camera" was standing in one place, not shifting at all. So the teacher asked students to work in groups to revise the passage so that the grammatical focus reflected changes in visual focus.

As one group collaborated on revising the passage, the following discussion took place:

"OK. Let's start with her false teeth—yeah—write that down."

She has false teeth.

"No, dummy. We gotta start the sentence with 'her false teeth'."

Her false teeth

"OK, now what?"

"Oh, no. If we start with that we gotta add stuff. Like.... 'Her false teeth look funny'."

"Yeah, put that down."

"No, you gotta tell what 'funny' means. She'll [the teacher] only ask 'What's funny mean?'"

"I got it." Her false teeth look yellow. "My grandma's are."

"Yeah, 'cause they're old, like her."

"Hey. Who's writing?"

"I am." Her false teeth are yellow because they're old.

"That's good."

"OK, now the stuff on glasses. Oh, gosh. We're gonna have to add stuff to everything!"

Indeed, they would. And that was just the point. Their teacher wanted them to see that as they shifted visual focus, they would have to explore their subject further. Not only was their teacher showing these students a fundamental process of observing, but also she was showing them how the process of observing translated into the process of writing.

In addition to modeling the writing process, we also need to model the process of responding to writing. It is true that students can learn to make very helpful comments about their peers' writing. But the important phrase here is *learn to.* As Karen Spear has pointed out in her excellent book *Sharing Writing,* working in response groups is a complex process. It requires that students be able to go beyond uninformative, global comments ("Yeah, it's pretty good." "I guess it's OK.") and do two things: pay attention to specific words, phrases, or ideas and explain why and how they personally react to those things. The ninth-grade class I've just described illustrates one way to model the process of responding. When the teacher asked students to revise the bland description, she was showing them a process they could use in responding to each other's drafts. That is, she was helping them see that when they responded to a classmate's descriptive writing, they might consider whether the student had shifted focus and whether the shifts in focus helped give the reader a clearer visual picture of the person, object, or place being described. Indeed, the teacher made sure students worked as a class to give this sort

of response to one or two students' subsequent drafts.

But modeling the response process may not be enough. It may also be necessary to model the processes of listening to and using those responses. Listening can be especially difficult when the response implies that a writer's work is unclear or in need of further effort. In such cases, any writer—and students are no exception—may well become defensive, more eager to prove that responses are invalid or irrelevant than to listen to those responses and consider the uses they might have. In other words, students may need to learn how to respond to responses.

If so, teachers may need to model the way we want student writers to react to their classmates' comments. Specifically, we should bring in our own efforts to do some of the same writing students are doing and ask students to respond to it. Where is it clear or unclear? What sort of personality or attitude is our writ-

ing conveying? At what points have we said things that seem appropriate or inappropriate for the audience we are addressing? My experience in doing this sort of work with students is that if they trust us, they can be very perceptive and painfully direct. If they don't get it, they can tell us so in no uncertain terms. In doing so, they give us a chance to show how a writer listens to readers, not by arguing but by attempting to find out why readers react as they do and then using that information to revise a subsequent draft.

❧

The process of modeling is, like everything else about teaching writing, a slow business. One example rarely does the trick. But if we are persistent in showing students what is involved in producing good writing through the writing process, we can usually count on results. But if we don't model, we should expect our distinction between *showing* and *telling* to fall on deaf ears. If we don't follow our own advice, why should they? ❧

*I*N ADDITION TO MODELING
THE WRITING PROCESS,
WE ALSO NEED TO MODEL
THE PROCESS OF RESPONDING
TO WRITING.

❧❧❧❧❧

BY DR. MAXINE HAIRSTON, FORMER DIRECTOR OF FRESHMAN ENGLISH, THE UNIVERSITY OF TEXAS

THE JOY OF WRITING

STUDENTS NEED TO GET SOME FUN OUT OF WHAT THEY'RE DOING.

MAXINE HAIRSTON TAKES A BREAK FROM CLASSES.

In recent years I have come to believe that the most important job I can do as a writing teacher is to help my students enjoy writing. I say this because I am convinced that unless students find some pleasure in their writing classes, most of them will not be willing to invest the time and energy required to turn out work that they—and we, as their teachers—can be proud of. Few adults are disciplined and determined enough to drudge away at some project—whether it's exercising or learning Spanish verbs—simply because someone else tells us that it will be good for us in the long run. We just won't stay with some projects unless there's some satisfaction in the process itself. How much harder it is, then, for youngsters to whom college or even next fall seems light years away to subject themselves to the hard work of learning to write if they get no pleasure from it at the time. Deficit motivation, working to avoid penalties or simply for a passing grade, isn't enough; students need to get some fun out of what they're doing. Fortunately, given what we now know about teaching the writing process, it's quite possible to create a writing classroom in which many students work from growth motivation; that is, they work at their writing because they enjoy doing it for its own sake.

Cognitive studies, ethnographic studies about writing, and the national projects argue that four characteristics define the congenial writing classroom, the kind in which students are likely to enjoy writing and to flourish as writers.

First, teachers provide a low-risk environment that encourages students to write without fear. Second, teachers have students develop their papers through a series of drafts and revisions. Third, teachers honor the students' right to their own writing, allowing students to choose their own topics and encouraging them to write about their interests. Fourth, teachers create and support a collaborative learning environment.

ESTABLISHING A LOW-RISK CLASSROOM

Creating a low-risk environment in the writing classroom may seem like a formidable challenge, and indeed it can be at the beginning of a new term when many students are as wary as stray cats. They're nervous for fear someone is going to try to trap them. In the first week of a writing class sometimes I feel as if I want to wear a banner across my chest, emblazoned with "Trust me! It's going to be all right!" But I can understand students' anxiety. Students who have come from writing courses with a heavy emphasis on rules and form, courses in which they did badly, have good reason to see a composition course as a high-risk situation. No wonder they start out by trying to stay in the safety zone of rules and formulas.

The humanistic psychologist Abraham Maslow theorizes that all people have two sets of forces operating within them: a need for safety and a fear of risk on one hand and an urge toward growth

and autonomy on the other hand. Maslow also believes that every individual has an innate urge to create, to grow, to discover new abilities and talents. I agree; I think all children want to communicate, to write something that catches the interest and attention of others, but most will hesitate if they think they will be punished for

*I*N THE FIRST WEEK OF A WRITING CLASS SOMETIMES I FEEL AS IF I WANT TO WEAR A BANNER ACROSS MY CHEST, EMBLAZONED WITH "TRUST ME! IT'S GOING TO BE ALL RIGHT!"

breaking rules. As Maslow points out, "Safety needs are prepotent over growth needs.... [and] in general, only a child who feels safe dares to grow forward healthily" (49). He adds, "Only the [teacher] who respects fear and defense can teach; ..." (53).

The writing teacher's challenge is to foster the low-risk environment that will encourage creativity and expression but at the same time to work toward helping students master the writing conventions that they must know to be accepted as writers. There are several ways teachers can do this. First, of course, is to emphasize that we write in stages; we plan, we draft, we read and reread, and we revise. Final details matter when a writer gets ready to publish, but the most-productive writers learn how to suspend their error monitors in the early stages.

I have found it helps me to suspend my own error monitor when reading early drafts if I can put down my pencil and force myself to read strictly for content, good practice for trying to become a courteous reader. I ask myself, what is this writer trying to express? Why? How? Then I make only a large-scale response, focusing on being positive and on asking questions that could help the next draft. I emphasize that I hope to see substantial change and development in that draft. It would waste time even to mention error at this stage. When students realize that I really am not looking for mistakes in their drafts, they begin to relax and become more venturesome.

On second drafts, I still try to avoid writing on the paper, but focus on more specific suggestions for improvement. I also make checks in the margins to indicate potential trouble spots that the writers need to be aware of when they begin to polish their papers, sometimes adding a comment that the writer should be alert for problems with commas, subject-verb agreement, or whatever area seems most troublesome. This gives the writer specific areas to concen-

trate on at proofreading/editing time.

Probably one of the best ways to reduce risk in the writing classroom is to set up a portfolio system that allows students to draft a variety of papers over a period of time and then to choose a limited number to develop fully and submit for final evaluation. This method has become increasingly popular for a number of reasons. For one, student writers can work more as adult working writers do. They can attempt different kinds of writing, can stay with those projects that go well and, putting the others aside, they can invest as much as they like in them. It also gives students more control over the evaluation process. They decide which pieces they want evaluated; the teacher doesn't even have to see the others. There is considerable literature on the portfolio system if you find it an attractive option. (See also Elliot and Greenberg's essay "The Direct Assessment of Writing: Notes for Teachers.")

A final specific suggestion for reducing your students' anxieties is to establish a hierarchy of errors. We know from research that not all errors are created equal. Some are truly damaging: for instance, wrong verb forms, egregious sentence fragments, double negatives and faulty parallelism. Errors like these set off alarms for most readers. Others, such as split infinitives, comparison of absolutes, or misusing *lie* and *lay* cause scarcely a riffle with most audiences. We should be lenient about such lapses and reduce the number of things our students have to worry about.

We should also remember that the more a writer attempts, the more mistakes he or she is likely to make. But if we are encouraging growth, we need to let student writers know that we regard such mistakes as the natural accompaniment of growth and as less important than the students' fresh ideas.

TEACHING THE WRITING PROCESS THROUGH A SYSTEM OF DRAFTS

Because this textbook so strongly emphasizes that drafting, evaluating, and revising are essential parts of the writing process, I don't feel I need to build an elaborate case for having students develop their papers in drafts. Fortunately, with most writing teachers and curriculum supervisors embracing the concept of writing as a process, students accept drafting as a routine practice. I hope so, because students write more freely and more confidently when they know that their readers view their drafts as "work in progress," not as finished products to be critiqued and judged. Under such a system, knowing they're not irrevocably committed to what they've written, writers can afford experiments. Writing tentatively, they can count on getting help from their readers to help them work out their ideas. That's very reassuring, particularly to students who haven't written much and aren't sure they have anything to say.

The less articulate, inexperienced writers are probably those who get the most out of numerous drafts because they have the opportunity to improve first attempts substantially before they must submit the papers for evaluation. They also have the chance to get feedback *during* the writing process, feedback that is far more valuable than comments on a paper that has already been graded. We know that many students, perhaps even most, pay scant attention to comments written on graded papers, especially negative comments. But when they get comments—both written and oral—on drafts, they are likely to pay attention because they use them to real advantage.

Good students also benefit from drafts, although sometimes they may resist doing them because the system requires more work than they've usually had to do in order to get good grades. But for some good writers, developing a paper through drafts can be a heady experience as they tap into talent they didn't know they had and then earn new recognition from their peers. Writing can become a genuine joy for good writers working at their peak.

In my opinion the worst possible system for having students write papers is to give a fresh assignment each week, have everyone write the paper only once and turn it in for a grade, and then return the graded papers and repeat the process. Under such circumstances the anxiety level skyrockets for all but the most able

WRITING CAN BECOME A GENUINE JOY FOR GOOD WRITERS WORKING AT THEIR PEAK.

•••••

students, writers get no help during the process (when they need it most), and teachers never learn what most students can really do. Even when students write in class, those papers should be drafts that they can work on again during the next class periods. Only then are students likely to develop their potential.

LETTING STUDENTS CHOOSE THEIR OWN TOPICS FOR WRITING

After several years of having students choose their own writing topics, I am committed to the practice because it has several invaluable benefits. First, most students have never had an opportunity to write about matters they're genuinely interested in and can write about with authority. Too often they see traditional assignments that ask everyone to write on the same topic as meaningless exercises in which the teacher seems to be forgetting that students are individuals.

Second, students are more likely to put time and energy into their writing when they can explore topics that interest them. When students are writing on their own topics, they may also discover a potent truth: Writing is a powerful tool for learning, one that will serve them well.

Third, when students choose their own topics, a rich diversity can develop as they write about their own special interests. Some students may write about family rituals that come from their ethnic heritages or about unusual people in their families; others may write about living in another country or on a military base; others may write about hobbies—bicycling or scuba diving or canoeing. The possibilities are almost endless. In many schools, a rich multicultural tapestry can emerge as students from diverse backgrounds and cultures read each other's work and share stories.

Fourth, students will become more confident as writers because they have more control over their writing. As they develop their expertise in some area, they begin to realize how much they know about something, whether it's car stereos or cooking hamburgers. They can take on a new identity in the class and find that people pay attention to what they have to say. That's good for all of us.

Finally when students choose their own writing topics, the class simply becomes more interesting for everyone. Students may cover a remarkable range of subjects, and even those writing on similar topics bring different perspectives to them. Boredom drops quickly because everyone is constantly learning directly from other people's experiences. Perhaps the greatest bonus is to teachers, who not only garner a wealth of information about their students, but also over a period of years become mini-experts on numerous topics. Furthermore, they are spared trying to think up a good writing topic and then having to read fifty papers on that topic.

I BELIEVE STRONGLY IN PEER GROUPS AND COLLABORATIVE LEARNING IN WRITING CLASSES.

It does take considerable class time to help select topics, since many students will protest that they have nothing to write about, but such obstacles can be overcome in a few days of brainstorming and group work in class. As teacher, you can come in with a list of possible topics and then work with the class to generate subtopics. Or ask everyone to bring in a list of fifteen things to write about, encouraging the concrete and specific rather than large, abstract categories.

I have had good success with asking students to choose a general topic to write on for the whole term and then to pick subtopics for individual papers. That way they get into their topics in some depth and eliminate the process of having to work through choosing a fresh topic for each paper. You may want to specify the kinds of papers students write within their topics—informative, expressive, persuasive, and so on—to focus the class within the formats they're learning from the textbook.

ESTABLISHING A COLLABORATIVE-LEARNING CLASSROOM

I believe strongly in peer groups and collaborative learning in writing classes. Perhaps their greatest advantage is that they give students an immediate sense of audience, something that's hard to achieve when the teacher is the only reader for the drafts. Usually they respect each other's opinions; in fact, they may take their peers' responses more seriously than they do the teacher's because they feel closer to peers and they genuinely want to communicate.

Students also begin to see how useful collaboration can be for generating ideas. Most students in writing groups readily admit how much their classmates have contributed to the final versions of their papers. Each class period when I hand back graded papers, I pick two or three of the best ones to read aloud and then ask the writer and the writer's group to comment on how the paper developed through drafts. Their accounts are revealing, and the investment they feel in each other's work is truly gratifying.

I favor randomly chosen groups of at least four students so if someone is absent, the discussion doesn't break down. I reorganize groups to allow working with as many writers as possible. This arrangement also enhances every student's exposure to diverse cultural experiences as they get to know other students more closely. Managing groups in the classroom may not be easy, although I suspect trained secondary teachers know considerably more about it than most college teachers do. For the teacher who doesn't feel comfortable with groups, there is considerable literature on the concept.

Ultimately, groups help to establish the whole class as a community of writers who work together, feel a common sense of purpose, and see writing as a shared enterprise that's important to everyone. We all know intuitively that the most important element for achieving a congenial writing classroom is the teacher's attitude, and for that reason it's important for the teacher to be a part of that community, not to be an outside authority and a judge. Teachers need to write with students during writing workshops and share writing with them—its joys and frustrations. With luck and time, I am convinced that both teachers and students will enjoy being in a writing classroom more than they might have thought possible. ❦

References

Maslow, Abraham. Toward a Psychology of Being, 2nd ed. New York: D. Van Nostrand Company. 1968.

TEACHERS NEED TO WRITE WITH STUDENTS DURING WRITING WORKSHOPS AND SHARE WRITING WITH THEM —ITS JOYS AND FRUSTRATIONS.

By Dr. Barbara J. Shade, Professor and Dean, School of Education, The University of Wisconsin–Parkside

TEACHING FOR LEARNING'S SAKE

THIS APPROACH TO TEACHING WILL EMPOWER STUDENTS AS LEARNERS.

Helping students incorporate ideas, skills, and concepts that will improve their ability to perform tasks and to solve problems is the ultimate goal of teaching. Teachers who achieve this goal effectively find ways to accommodate students' different learning styles so that the teaching-learning process works more efficiently.

What do we mean by *learning styles?* Over the years, researchers have identified three dimensions in which students have specific learning preferences: (1) their preferences for various environmental factors that influence the learning climate; (2) their preferences about the ways they choose to engage in the learning process (motivational style); and (3) their preferences for the various ways in which they process information (cognitive style).

ENVIRONMENTAL PREFERENCES

Individual environmental preferences focus on the lighting, temperature, and furniture used in the learning process. For example, some individuals might prefer bright light while others prefer it muted; some might prefer a warm room while others like it cool. A variation in studying postures has also been noted, with some individuals preferring to sit in a traditional classroom desk while others prefer to stand or recline when engaged in a learning task.[1]

MOTIVATIONAL STYLE

The second dimension of learning style focuses upon the extent to which students take responsibility for their own learning. Teachers often incorrectly assume that students' desire to engage in work is inherent. As with other aspects of learning, the extent to which individuals become involved in work depends upon how they have been socialized to respond to work. Some students, for example, have been taught to rely on others for assistance, to follow directions as given, and to perform the task as modeled. Others have been made more independent of others and have been taught to work alone, to find their own solutions, and to decide whether or not they can complete the work before asking for assistance. Corno and Mandinach refer to this stylistic dimension as a preference for resource management, and students tend to use the approach that makes them feel the most comfortable and the most competent.

The teaching-learning process involves human interaction, and students prefer different levels of involvement with others, depending upon the social and personality development that emanates from their families and communities. Families stressing prosocial behavior encourage children to help, to share, and to work toward benefiting others.

These students are more likely to give and receive assistance in the learning process and to like cooperative-learning ventures. Children trained to be highly individualistic and self-oriented are less likely to cooperate

---

[1]For a more detailed description of the social and physical environment preferences of students, the reader should examine the writings of Kenneth and Rita Dunn.

and offer help. Learners with this orientation function well in a competitive setting because they prefer to work alone and are less likely to enjoy cooperative-learning activities unless there is a reward or a method of accommodating their need for individuality.

COGNITIVE STYLE

The least discussed dimension of learning style—that of cognitive style—represents individually preferred ways of perceiving, organizing, and evaluating information so that it can be learned.

Three cognitive processes influence the way individuals acquire and produce knowledge. These are the perceptual, the conceptual, and the evaluative processes.

1. Perceptual Processes: The most recognized area in learning-style literature, this area focuses on the sensory modalities. Through cultural socialization, learners develop a preference for either the visual modality (photographs, graphs, art, texts); the aural modality (records, tapes, lectures); the haptic/kinesthetic modality (group discussions, interactive debates, drama); or some combination of these. Instruction delivered through the preferred modality establishes an instant rapport that allows students to process information more easily.

Different cultures socialize their children to attend to different cues in the environment; therefore, students have selective attention. Some students focus their attention on the task or idea being presented. For others, the people, their peers, their self-evaluation, or even the teacher's reaction to them are the most important

elements on which to focus. How children choose to attend to cues is an important dimension of learning, and teachers who wish to ensure cognitive engagement find ways to influence the perceptive focus of the students.

2. Conceptual Processes: Having focused on an idea that must be learned, students must then classify it based upon prior experiences. The techniques involved include assessing similarities and differences to prior knowledge, as well as determining how best to define or describe the concepts. Again, the extent to which students can manipulate various concepts depends upon whether or not the ideas can be communi-

cated to them using a common language with commonly accepted images.

Some students prefer to have ideas presented in a hierarchical manner, beginning with the big picture followed by the details involved (whole to part). Other

students prefer to have the information presented in a more sequential approach, beginning with the minute details and building toward the larger concept (part to whole). Regardless of the technique used, teachers must include methods of helping learners make connections with prior knowledge.

3. Evaluative Processes: The third aspect of cognitive style focuses on the processes of thinking about the information. *Thinking* is difficult to define, but many researchers define it as "comprehension monitoring." The major focus of thinking centers on the individual's ability to plan, monitor, and evaluate his or her learning and understanding about the information he or she is seeking to learn.

Again, teachers should look for variations in the way individuals approach thinking. On one hand, individuals may spend time using their imaginations to create ideas based upon personal views or

*T*HE KEY TO A GOOD GROUP DISCUSSION IS A TEACHER WHO IS AN EXCELLENT QUESTIONER, WHO IS REFLECTIVE, WHO CAN LEAD STUDENTS TO REFLECT AND INQUIRE . . .

✦✦✦✦✦

beliefs. On the other hand, some individuals will engage in a more formal logic, which requires familiarity with the rules in order to select the correct problem-solving strategies. In the first type of information processing, individuals seem to arrive at their decisions rather intuitively, using a process that seems to be generated from an internalized logic. In the second type, the one most influenced by instruction, students learn to organize and review their approach to information or problems through an analytical process.

ACCOMMODATING VARIATIONS IN LEARNING STYLES

When teachers are first introduced to the concept of learning styles, they immediately conjure up visions of having to construct thirty different learning plans to accommodate their students. *Learning styles* is not another euphemism for individually guided education. Instead, it is an entreaty to teachers to provide different approaches and strategies that individuals can use as they work at learning.

In today's classrooms, there are basically *two distinct modes of learning:* the *traditional orientation,* the one to which most instruction is geared; and the *community orientation,* the one more likely to be displayed by African American, Hispanic American, Native American and immigrant Asian students who identify closely with the culture of their ethnic communities.

Particular suggestions to enhance the instructional process for the community-oriented students

who are often ignored in instructional delivery system include the following ones:

Environment Style Accommodation: For the community-oriented students, the classroom should become inviting and supportive as an experiential setting in which students can use various media to explore concepts that may be foreign to them because they are not prevalent in their communities or because their economic situation does not permit the type of travel or involvement in enrichment activities that is true of the more successful, economically affluent students. Being able to see an enlarged picture of the Eiffel Tower in the classroom can provide an important conceptual image that might be needed to foster comprehension. Because learning centers permit self-exploration, they should also become important aspects of the classroom design for all levels of students in all types of classes.

Motivational Style Accommodation: Having the opportunity to participate in a good class discussion on lesson content motivates community-oriented students, satisfying their needs to share information with others and to obtain feedback. Moreover, it provides them an opportunity to listen to different perspectives. Teachers should note, however, that group discussion is not the same as class recitation in which students are asked to recite facts and information to the teacher from a textbook. For example, it is not enough to discuss nouns as a part of speech without leading students through the concept of a complete sentence and the purpose of using nouns

within sentences and paragraphs. Moreover, students need to be able to identify nouns within the framework of their own speech and written narratives as well as to determine how and why they have used a particular word as a noun.

The key to a good group discussion is a teacher who is an excellent questioner, who is reflective, who can lead students to reflect and inquire, and who has an excellent understanding of the broad structure and relationships within the lesson content.

Information Processing Style Accommodation: Teachers can facilitate the processing of information by students through the use of some of the following techniques:

1. Present concepts with multimedia using a variety of modalities.

2. Assist the students in identifying the relationships of concepts through cognitive mapping, brainstorming, or reciprocal teaching.

3. Take time to ensure there is a common understanding of words, concepts, or ideas. Bilingual students should be encouraged to interpret the words in their languages. Students should also be encouraged to develop art projects and to use new words orally.

4. Model the thinking processes needed to complete tasks successfully. Provide students time to think about a problem or to complete an assignment. Students learn best when they can perform when the teacher is available for feedback.

Teachers must remember that students have different perceptions of the world and teach to these perceptions. Assisting students in learning requires lots of talking— talking between students and

teachers and between students.

When considering the use of learning styles, teachers must confront three important perceptions. First, teachers should understand that the identified style preference should not and cannot be used as evidence of deficiencies. Second, teachers should not think that the community-oriented style reflects all members of a group. It is merely behavior that is most likely to be found within the community. Third, teachers who use the concept of learning styles should do so as indicators of approaches to lesson design and to the selection of methods of instruction, not as the basis for judging intellectual potential.

A FINAL CAVEAT

Developing a successful learner is the ultimate goal of a successful teacher, and ensuring that children become successful learners requires that teachers see themselves not as the ultimate purveyors of knowledge, but as guides through the learning process. This approach to teaching will empower students as learners and will permit them to approach the learning process in their own words. When learners grasp the ideas, their sense of self-worth and confidence and their intellectual strength improve tremendously. It is at this point teachers know they, too, have been successful. What a great sense of accomplishment! ✿

MULTIPLE INTELLIGENCES AND THE WRITING CLASSROOM

WHAT ARE THE MULTIPLE INTELLIGENCES?

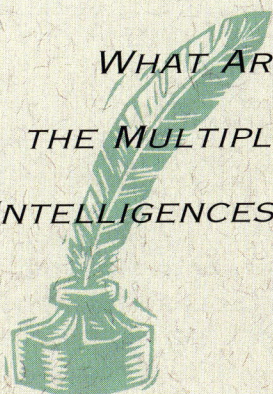

The theory of multiple intelligences was developed by Harvard psychologist Howard Gardner, who, in researching the function of the human brain in trauma, discovered that damage to one area of the brain, such as the speech center, does not necessarily incapacitate other areas of intelligence, such as appreciation of music or artistic ability. This discovery led to the proposal that the human brain does not operate with one single intelligence, but with seven.

Gardner labeled the seven intelligences logical-mathematical, linguistic, musical, bodily-kinesthetic, interpersonal, intrapersonal, and spatial.

Each intelligence operates both independently and cooperatively with the others in every human brain. Gardner contends that even though a certain intelligence may not be fully developed or even apparent in every person, the potential for that development exists and its expansion depends in large part on the environment in which the person lives or works.

IDENTIFYING STUDENTS' MULTIPLE INTELLIGENCES

The most immediate challenge for teachers is to identify students' intelligences and then to apply strategies and to create opportunities for students that will allow them to use and develop all their intelligences in the classroom. Discovering students' intelligences should

An overview of the seven intelligences

Intelligence	Characteristics	Possible vocation using this intelligence
Linguistic	Uses language effectively, orally or in writing	Writer, storyteller, editor
Logical-Mathematical	Uses numbers and figures effectively, reasons, identifies patterns, has organizing skills	Accountant, lawyer, journalist
Spatial	Observes or perceives relationships between real or imaginary objects	Artist, architect, nature guide
Bodily-Kinesthetic	Has sense of ease in movement of one's body to express ideas or to create or transform something	Dancer, mechanic, surgeon
Musical	Perceives and/or creates music, rhythm, pitch, or harmony	Musician, composer, disc jockey
Interpersonal	Interacts with the outside world, is sensitive to the feelings, actions and motivations of others	Social worker, politician, parent
Intrapersonal	Is sensitive to one's own thoughts, feelings, ideas, and place in the world	Poet, artist, singer

not be a time-consuming process. But it does require that teachers become better acquainted with their students so that they can learn **how students perform, what students prefer to do,** and **how students perceive themselves.**

Thomas Armstrong, the author of *Multiple Intelligences in the Classroom,* suggests several approaches.
• Consider preparing a questionnaire or checklist of the characteristics of the multiple intelligences for students and ask them to choose the items that apply to them.
• Give students an informal, oral survey that, with general questions about their likes and dislikes and talents, identifies which intelligences dominate the class.
• Use journal entries or personal narratives as an opportunity to evaluate the intelligences of students.

Keep in mind, though, that students usually have strengths in several areas. Armstrong also suggests that teachers identify their own intelligences and mention them to students as a way to explain their approaches to the subject matter so that students can see how their intelligences are compatible with their teachers'.

INSTRUCTIONAL STRATEGIES THAT TARGET THE MULTIPLE INTELLIGENCES

The next step for teachers is to target the kinds of strategies that facilitate students' multiple intelligences and to include those in their instruction. The following list gives samples of some strategies for each learning style. However, you should try to develop some of your own adaptations to address the needs of your classroom.

Stage of the Writing Process	Activities and Multiple Intelligences
Prewriting	**Brainstorming:** Linguistic, Interpersonal **Cluster/Diagramming:** Spatial, Intrapersonal, Interpersonal **Freewriting/Journaling:** Intrapersonal **Researching/Asking questions:** Logical-Mathematical **Observing/Imagining:** Spatial, Musical, Bodily-Kinesthetic **Reading with a Focus:** Linguistic, Logical-Mathematical, Intrapersonal **Listening with a Focus:** Musical, Interpersonal, Logical-Mathematical
Drafting	**Expressive/Creative Writing:** Interpersonal, Musical, Linguistic, Bodily-Kinesthetic **Informative Writing:** Logical-Mathematical **Writing to Explain:** Spatial, Logical-Mathematical, Interpersonal **Writing to Explore:** Logical-Mathematical **Writing about Literature:** Musical, Bodily-Kinesthetic, Spatial **Writing a Research paper:** Logical-Mathematical (depends also on the subject researched)
Evaluating and Revising	**Peer revision:** Interpersonal **Attention to details and organization:** Logical-Mathematical **Organization of text:** Bodily-Kinesthetic **Attention to images:** Spatial
Proofreading and Publishing	**Peer revision, public reading, performance:** Interpersonal **Polishing manuscript:** Intrapersonal **Reflecting:** Interpersonal, Linguistic

• **Spatial learners** benefit from watching videotapes or from drawing on overhead transparencies, a chalkboard, or a computer screen.
• **Interpersonal learners** thrive in discussion groups, especially if given opportunities to act as the group leader.
• **Intrapersonal learners** need individual goal-setting sessions and time for reflection in personal journals or portfolios.
• **Bodily-Kinesthetic learners** benefit from acting out concepts alone or in front of the class and from being able to physically manipulate things, such as a puzzle pieces, flashcards, index cards, or sections of a written draft.
• **Musical learners** are more productive if music is played during discussion sessions or while reading or writing, particularly if the music reflects the emotional content of the work.

• **Logical-mathematical learners** need a set of direct questions to work on and independent time to explore and research answers.
• **Linguistic learners** do well using tape recorders to record oral brainstorming sessions and having opportunities to discuss their ideas with their teacher or their peers.

It is important to remember that the activities mentioned here engage more than one intelligence at a time. Consider experimenting with different activities, and ask for student feedback.

APPLYING MULTIPLE INTELLIGENCES TO THE WRITING PROCESS

Being flexible and recursive, the writing process allows student writers to use their multiple intelligences at each of the four stages—prewriting; drafting; evaluating and revising; and proofreading, publishing, and reflecting.

Writing projects draw heavily on linguistic and intrapersonal intelligences, but consider the chart above for other possible intelligences that can be addressed at each stage in the writing process.

References
Armstrong, Thomas. *Multiple Intelligences in the Classroom.* Alexandria, VA: Association for Supervision and Curriculum Development. 1994.
Gardner, Howard. *Frames of Mind: The Theory of Multiple Intelligences.* 1983. NY: Basic Books. 1985.
Grow, Gerald. "Writing and Multiple Intelligences." June 1996. Online. Internet. 18 July 1996. Available HTTP://www.famu.edu/sjmga/ggrow/7In/7IntelIndex.html

DR. WANDA B. SCHINDLEY, NORTHEAST TEXAS COMMUNITY COLLEGE

INTEGRATING THE LANGUAGE ARTS

INTEGRATING THE TEACHING OF THE LANGUAGE ARTS CREATES THE MAGIC THAT HELPS STUDENTS LEARN.

Thirty-five years ago in a rural classroom, a creative woman integrated the teaching of reading, writing, speaking, listening, and even math. Her second-graders built a playhouse-size cardboard post office, made block-letter signs, wrote and read letters, counted tokens to buy and sell stamps, and spoke and listened as postmaster and customer. That teacher had not read research on the integration of skills or on using whole-language methodologies, but she knew intuitively what worked. I don't remember much about my experiences in kindergarten, first grade, third grade, or even fourth grade, but I remember well that second-grade classroom; I remember the magic of learning.

Integrating the teaching of the language arts creates the magic that helps students learn. It creates a context for developing language proficiency and relevancy for reading, writing, speaking, and listening activities. Students grow through active participation in language activities. Although categorizing the language arts may be necessary for describing curricula, in the classroom language skills are best learned through doing— through seeking meaning from texts, through writing and revising, and through sharing ideas and opinions.

WANDA SCHINDLEY IS A SPECIALIST FOR THE WORKPLACE PARTNERSHIP.

SUGGESTIONS FOR INTEGRATING THE LANGUAGE ARTS

• Involve students in prereading activities such as discussion, writing, research, and sometimes, vocabulary development. Creating a context for reading involves discussing themes and related issues, making predictions, recalling prior knowledge and related experiences, and searching out related information.

• Involve students in prewriting activities such as discussion of possible topics and details, reading model essays, searching out and reading informative pieces, reading literary writing, interviewing others, and sentence-combining or sentence-revision activities. Like the writing process itself, development of language proficiency involves a recursive practice in reading, writing, thinking, speaking, and listening.

• Make writing assignments relevant by having students write for and share with real audiences for meaningful purposes. Have students share their writing with peers.

• Relate correctness—development of conventional usage, spelling, grammar, and punctuation—

to the revising and proofreading stages of the writing process. Correctness becomes important to students when it helps them communicate their ideas clearly. Class review of grammar, usage, and mechanics can be done with sentences from student papers and with sentence-combining, sentence manipulation, and vocabulary activities.

• Approach standard usage in speech as appropriate for use in business and academic situations, not as a replacement for all vernacular expression.

• Encourage student involvement in class discussion, team study groups, cooperative research projects and presentations, group creative writing, and role playing.

• Foster an atmosphere in which students feel free to respond to, to evaluate, and to critique literature.

• Act as facilitator in students' discovery processes through activities that encourage creative and critical thinking—decision making and problem solving—and allow students to take more responsibility for their own learning.

Create an atmosphere of cooperation, caring, and high expectations.

*L*IKE THE WRITING PROCESS ITSELF, DEVELOPMENT OF LANGUAGE PROFICIENCY INVOLVES A RECURSIVE PRACTICE IN READING, WRITING, THINKING, SPEAKING, AND LISTENING.

USING THE TEXTBOOK IN AN INTEGRATED APPROACH

Literature selections are provided in each chapter to give students opportunities to read before writing. However, this book can be used in a literature-driven approach as the springboard to writing by incorporating into the study of each chapter ample readings from literature anthologies, magazines, and student papers. The features in each chapter of the *Teacher's Edition* contain suggestions for integrating additional literature selections (**Integrating the Language Arts: Literature Link**), using a variety of group activities (**Cooperative Learning**), and encouraging students to use higher-level thinking skills to contribute to class discussion (**Critical Thinking**).

The **Common Error** and **Integrating the Language Arts** features in each chapter of the *Teacher's Edition* contain suggestions for integrating the teaching of grammar, usage, and mechanics into the stages of the writing process, as do the suggestions for integrating the language arts in the introduction of each composition chapter.

Sample Integrated Lesson Plan

A lesson on creative writing might begin with a class discussion about stories and poems.

Guiding questions encourage students to share attitudes: What kinds of stories/poems do you like?

—to recall prior knowledge about the structure of stories: What happened toward the end of a favorite story? How did you feel as you

read? What name do we use for the most exciting or scary part of the story?

—to synthesize knowledge about fiction: What characteristics do stories and poems have in common? What other forms might a writer use to tell about an event or to express an idea?

Teachers can use group stories and poems as guided practice and as a non-threatening introduction to creative writing. A group activity in which students write noun poems might begin informal grammar instruction. Small groups can then choose from the list of topics for noun-metaphor poems.

Example: Dreams are
  Envelopes of hope,
  Fluffy clouds that
    disappear in daylight,
  Stars to reach for.

As groups begin to revise and proofread their poems for class presentation, teachers might focus on the use of commas and end marks.

When students begin the creative writing assignments, they are again given opportunities to write, discuss, read, think, talk, revise, and so on. Instruction in usage and mechanics can be provided to the class as the need arises, to partners as they debate an issue of correctness, and to individuals in one-on-one conferences.

Finally, students share their work with the class—perhaps anonymously at first, but eventually as accomplished and proud authors who share a firsthand knowledge of the creation of literature and a greater understanding of language. ❦

DR. JUDITH IRVIN, FLORIDA STATE UNIVERSITY

BECOMING A STRATEGIC READER

BECOMING A PROFICIENT READER AND WRITER IS A LIFE-LONG PROCESS.

In the past, reading was viewed as a simple task of decoding words. Educators generally emphasized the strategies of sounding out words, recognizing words out of context by sight, and reproducing content by answering comprehension questions. Research has led to a new conceptualization of the reading process—that, as writing is, reading is a complex learning process. In this new view, readers construct meaning from a text, not simply by decoding words, but by using reading strategies that incorporate and expand their prior knowledge. Prior knowledge includes not only readers' knowledge of the definition of a word, but also their responses to the context of the word—the entire text. Careful reading of a text using strategies like those explained in the following pages will allow readers to use their prior knowledge to create meaning and to extend their understanding of a text. As students become more involved in developing and reflecting on their reading and learning processes, meaning may now be defined as "something that is actively created rather than passively received" (Buehl, 1995, p. 8).

As will be explained, the process of constructing meaning both in writing and in reading is not linear, but recursive and interactive and helps to create a richer, more productive experience.

THE READER

Former models of reading focused on whether or not students had acquired specific skills. Recent models of reading allow that students come to learning with previous information about particular topics, with definite attitudes about reading, writing, and school in general, and with varying motivations for reading and learning. It is the interaction of what is in reader's minds with what is on the page within a particular context that helps them to comprehend what they read.

SCHEMA THEORY

It is impossible for readers to learn anything new without making connections to their prior knowledge or schemata. The schemata are like the components of an elaborate filing system inside every reader's head. If the reader's mind is the filing system, the schemata, then, are the ideas contained in the file folders within the system. For example, you probably have a schema for a computer, a mental picture of what a computer is and what it does. You probably also bring to that basic picture many other associations, ideas, and feelings. If you use computers regularly, your schema may include positive feelings about their limitless applications. If the computer revolution has left you yearning for the days of yellow note pads and typewriters, then you may have feelings of anxiety as you approach a computer manual. For teachers, it is important to remember that readers encountering new ideas must often be shown how the new material fits into their existing filing system.

THE TEXT

The content, format, and organization of a text are factors that make a text easy or difficult for students to understand. If students' schemata tell them that a particular assignment will be difficult or un-related to their personal experi-ences, they will probably be reluc-tant to read it and will most likely not make much meaning of it. The students know with one look that they will read and respond to a poem differently than they will to a chapter in a science book. A teacher should be prepared to ex-ercise flexibility and sensitivity in presenting the text so as to en-courage students to use their schemata to enhance their reading experiences.

THE CONTEXT

Readers and writers approach texts differently, and they also vary their processes according to their purposes. If they are reading for pleasure, students may skip over a difficult word or read an exciting passage more than once. But if they are reading for class, skipping a word might mean not under-standing an important concept needed in class the next day. A reader's purpose for reading also dictates how attentive he or she is to details and how much effort will be put into remembering what is read. Similarly, when and where the reading is done affects the reading process. Readers will make less meaning from texts they read on the bus or with thoughts of a sick relative in the backs of their minds than they might make if they had a quiet space and clear thoughts.

STRATEGIC LEARNING

Suppose that during a racquet-ball game you hit a straight shot down the right side of the court, and your opponent misses the ball. The point is yours. This well-

placed shot may have been a lucky one, or it may have been the result of a strategy. Before you hit the ball, you may have noticed that your opponent was standing in the middle of the court, and you re-membered that she is left-handed with a weak backhand. You hit the ball to exactly the right spot delib-erately and strategically. The analo-gy of planning your shots in a game can be applied to learning.

Strategic learning involves ana-lyzing the reading task, establishing a purpose for reading, and then selecting strategies for making meaning. A strategy is a conscious effort by the reader to attend to comprehension while reading. Weinstein explains that "learning strategies include any thoughts or behaviors that help us to acquire new information in such a way that the new information is inte-grated with our existing knowl-edge" (Weinstein, p.590). Strategies occur before reading when readers activate prior knowledge by think-ing and discussing the title and topic and by identifying a purpose for reading. They also occur during reading as readers use context to figure out unknown words and monitor their understanding, and beyond the reading when readers summarize or evaluate the main ideas of the text.

METACOGNITION

Reading is often referred to as a cognitive event. It is also a meta-cognitive event. Cognition refers to a person's using the knowledge and skills he or she possesses; metacognition refers to a person's awareness and understanding of that knowledge and conscious control over those skills. It is

essentially, thinking about one's way of thinking. Metacognition, then, is knowing how and when to use strategies to solve problems in understanding. It develops as a reader matures, usually during ado-lescence, but it can be taught and strengthened by explicit instruc-tion and practice.

Becoming a proficient reader and writer is a life-long process. Accepting the premise that mean-ing is constructed in the mind of the learner implies that metacog-nitive abilities must be operational for learning to occur. Adolescents are just beginning to be able to consider their own thinking in relation to the thoughts of others. The middle and high school level years are an ideal time to develop the metacognitive abilities that will serve them throughout life.

STRATEGIC READING

Good readers are strategic, and being strategic involves the meta-cognitive abilities to think, plan, and evaluate their understanding of a text.

Adolescence is partially charac-terized by a new capacity for thought. Students are moving from the concrete stage (able to think logically about real experiences) to the formal stage (able to consider "what ifs," think reflectively, and reason abstractly). This intellectual change is gradual and may occur in different contexts at different times for different students.

Formal thinking is just develop-ing during the middle school years,

so concrete examples and step-by-step modeling are necessary to move students to the more abstract metacognitive thinking. The follow-ing concepts help students to focus on their own reading strategies:

- activating schema (prior knowl-edge) and building background information
- predicting and confirming
- organizing information
- drawing conclusions
- making inferences
- text differences
- retelling/summarizing

As strategic readers, before they read, students use their prior knowledge by making predictions about the content of a selection, to establish a clear purpose for read-ing, and to think about reading strategies they might use as they read. During the reading process, students use context to connect what they are reading with what they already know and to continue to monitor and evaluate their com-prehension. And after completing their reading, students review their reading through peer discussion, class discussion, preparing entries in Reader's Logs, and using graphic organizers.

New research and practice in literacy learning reflects a more holistic view of understanding text. Students need opportunities to apply reading strategies to a variety of texts in a meaningful manner. ❧

References

Buehl, D. *Classroom Strategies for Interactive Learning*. Schofield, WI: Wisconsin State Reading Association, 1995.
Weinstein, C.E. "Fostering Learning Autonomy Through the Use of Learning Strategies." *Journal of Reading* 30 (1987): 590-595.

JOYCE ARMSTRONG CARROLL, DIRECTOR, THE NEW JERSEY WRITING PROJECT IN TEXAS

SHOW DON'T TELL: THE ORIGINAL VIRTUAL REALITY

GOOD WRITING THAT SHOWS TAKES US THROUGH THE EXPERIENCE . . .

Perhaps one of the oldest pieces of advice offered by master writers to neophytes is "show don't tell." Likewise, one of the most frequent pieces of advice offered by teachers to fledgling student writers is "show don't tell."

The truth is the old "show don't tell" adage lives as the original virtual reality and makes sense to students if presented that way. Think about it. Our brains receive and process sensory signals from our environment through our five senses in order to make sense of our world, our experiences. Good writing that shows takes us through the experience; it excites the brain by wrapping pictures and sounds, tastes, smells and movements around its readers and immersing their senses in such a way that the writing actually creates another world. Catherine Drinker Bowen, biographer and writer on musical subjects, puts it more poetically, "Writing, I think, is not apart from living. Writing is a kind of double living."

Phrased in the positive, this "showing," this "going through the experience" causes the reader to feel an immediacy, a vitality, and an authenticity. When we're finished reading writing that shows, we often think, "I wish this wouldn't end." Flip-flopping to the negative, writing devoid of this "showing" reads flat, seems plastic, and bores the brain. If we even finish reading writing that tells, we find ourselves yawning and asking, "What did I just read?"

But there's an irony in "show don't tell." The maxim itself tells. It's right up there with "develop your writing" and "liven those verbs." There is no doubt about it—the advice is sound—it's just too abstract. Therein lies the rub. What can we teachers do to make "show don't tell" more concrete, more understandable for students? I'd like to share five ways to involve students in learning this concept. Students

• Analyze the work of published authors

• Compare telling writing to showing writing

• Identify telling parts in their own writing

• Replace the telling parts of their writing with showing passages

• Recognize and use "show don't tell" as an elaboration technique

ANALYZING THE WORK OF PUBLISHED AUTHORS

When examining the work of published authors, I start with Mark Twain's words, "Don't say the old lady screamed. Bring her on and let her scream." It's a great quote that begs great questions, "What does Twain mean?" "How might we describe her?" "Where is she?" "What words could we use to hear her scream?" "Why is she screaming?" It's fun to divide the room—half tells about the old lady, while the other half shows. Students of all ages delight in the comparison and begin their move toward understanding.

Will Hobbs, noted YA author, says it this way, "Let's say I almost drowned last summer, when a rip tide was taking me out to sea, and I'm trying to tell a reader what it was like: 'I was drowning. It was really bad. I thought I was going to die...' Now, is my writing coming to life? Does the reader feel what it was like? Not really. Did I tell, or did I show? I told. I didn't use the five senses. Where's the taste of salt water, the powerful tug of the rip tide, the voices at the shore dimming, the squawk of a gull?" (Hobbs, 19).

Now what Hobbs suggests is pure virtual reality. No one really wants to experience drowning, but if the writer crafts the experience by showing not telling then the reader experiences the virtual reality of drowning. It works this way because of the sensory signals the words conjure; the brain makes a connection and consequently makes meaning. Since our senses are the primary information gatherers, constantly sending signals to the brain, Hobbs invites student writers to stimulate all five senses through the power of words. That way, after the brain has reconstructed and synthesized the signals, it makes an identification and the reader understands. Helping that connection equals good writing.

Once students awaken to "show don't tell" in their writing it becomes an excellent technique for literary analysis. Imagine students quibbling over colonist Edward Winslow's letter to a friend in England, pointing out how much more powerful it would have been had he taken his friend through the experience of the "harvest being gotten in" instead of just telling him. Or picture a group of students eagerly identifying examples of showing not telling in *The Red Badge of Courage.* After reading, "One of the wounded men had a shoeful of blood. He hopped like a schoolboy in a game. He was laughing hysterically…" (Crane, 44), it is unlikely they would settle for, "One man was shot in the foot. He was in pain."

COMPARE TELLING WRITING TO SHOWING WRITING

One of the attributes of showing writing is specificity and concern for detail. Using comparisons of different versions of the same story helps students see this. For example, take the passage that first describes Baba Yaba in the Russian, Romania, Yugoslavian, Polish folktale called by titles such as "The Doll," "The Doll in Her Pocket," "Vasalisa the Wise," "Vassilisa the Wise," "Vasilisa the Beautiful," "Baba Yaga and Vasilisa the Brave," or simply "Vasilisa."

Version One: "When they had entered the hut the old witch threw herself down on the stove, stretched out her bony legs and said…" (Sierra, 97).

Version Two: "When Vasilisa entered the hut, Baba Yaga was already sitting in her chair by the fire. Her black eyes sparkled as she fixed them on the girl" (Mayer).

Version Three: "Suddenly the forest was filled with a terrible noise, and Baba Yaga came flying through the trees. She was riding in a great iron mortar and driving it with a pestle, and as she rode, she swept away her trail with a kitchen broom" (Winthrop, 17).

Finally we come to Version Four. This version is embedded in the penetrating psychological study *Women Who Run With the Wolves: Myths and Stories of the Wild Woman Archetype* by Clarissa Pinkola Estes.

Now the Baba Yaga was a very fearsome creature. She traveled not in a chariot, not in a coach, but in a cauldron shaped like a mortar which flew along all by itself. She rowed this vehicle with an oar

shaped like a pestle, and all the while she swept out the tracks of where she'd been with a broom made of long-dead persons' hair.

And the cauldron flew through the sky with Baba Yaga's own greasy hair flying behind. Her long chin curved up and her long nose curved down, and they met in the middle. She had a tiny white goatee and warts on her skin from her trade in toads. Her brown-stained fingernails were thick and ridged like roofs, and so curled over she could not make a fist (Estes, 77).

Juxtaposing these versions (or versions of other literary pieces) illuminates the power of "show don't tell." While the first three versions, taken from children's literature, rely on pictures to convey most of the detail, even the slowest student will see how ably Estes crafted her showing of Baba Yaga from the opening, somewhat telling statement, through the layers of detail, calling upon each of the reader's senses to prove Baba Yaga's fearsomeness.

Again, after an exercise such as this, students no longer write, "She was ugly." They are no longer satisfied with "She was a witch." Their journey into the lushness of writing and literature is enriched.

IDENTIFYING TELLING PARTS IN THEIR OWN WRITING

Armed now with clearly concrete experiences between telling and showing in writing, the students are better able to assess their own writing with new eyes and finding parts to improve is an awesome cognitive task, especially for adolescents.

As students reread their work,

they simply highlight the telling statements, share and discuss them with peers or teacher, and ultimately decide if each is fine as it is (some telling is inevitable in any piece of writing) or if it needs reworking. This process not only invites higher-level thinking and decision-making, but it also paves the way by patterning the brain for the day-to-day coping of considerations based on importance, need, aptness, and priority.

REPLACE THE TELLING PARTS OF THEIR WRITING WITH SHOWING PASSAGES

This represents the pith of the showing/telling dichotomy. When students become facile enough to enliven their writing with powerful passages that show not tell, they have learned the concept. Following is an example from Adrian's writing. He highlighted his first three sentences:

I stayed over at Robert's house last Friday. We were going camping. That was our favorite thing to do even though we only pretended.

On his next draft he replaced those telling with this showing passage:

I was spending Friday night at Robert's house, so our camping gear was strewn across the backyard. We pretended we had pitched camp in the outback of Australia, so we called each other "mate" alot.

"Ay, mate," I'd call even though we were pretty close to each other in that backyard. "Let's take a walkabout." (I had seen a movie about that.)

"Ay, mate," he'd call back louder. "Let's throw some shrimp on the barbee," (I knew he saw that commercial on T.V.)

Finally, we went to bed. Robert had asthma and was lying in the tent on his cot wheezing like a water pump gone dry. My buddy did many things better than me, but I envied his asthmatic wheeze the most. That night he wheezed out a little tune in his sleep and I accompanied him on the drums by playing my stomach and cot.

While Adrian did some throat clearing first, the passage about Robert's asthma takes us through what Adrian went through. It shows promise and a grasp of the "show don't tell" concept.

RECOGNIZE AND USE "SHOW DON'T TELL" AS AN ELABORATION TECHNIQUE

I opened the novel in full view of the class. "Take out some paper and write down these sentences," I invited.

I remember the day Claire Louise started first grade. . . . She had on a red dress. . . . Mother made all our clothes. . . . She had a book satchel my grandmother bought for her. . . . That was a Saturday (Arnold, 7–8).

"What do you think about that writing?" I asked.

Students, who typically want to please the teacher, began by tenta-tively, and without much enthusi-asm, saying, "It's O.K." But then they quickly pulled the turn-about and asked, "Who is Claire Louise?" "Why are you reading this?"

I continued to probe. "She's a character in this novel, but I really want to know what you think of the writing."

Eventually a brave soul admit-ted, "It sounds dull." Another agreed and collectively they deter-mined it was definitely telling not showing.

At this point I wrote ELABORA-TION on the board. I explained how showing helps the writer achieve an elaborated piece, one that reveals depth of thought. Under "elaboration" I wrote D.I.D. I told the students that although there are many ways to achieve this depth, these letters stood as a mnemonic device to remember at least three of them.

Their first response was "dia-logue," which we had worked on previously and which is one way to achieve elaboration. We talked about that, but I wanted them to explore further. After some nudges and discussion, they came up with DESCRIPTION, ILLUSTRATION, DETAIL.

Together we defined DESCRIP-TION by comparing it to a camera shot in movies. It's the long shot as in "the gray house sitting way up on the hill in the distance." Following that analogy, we defined DETAIL as a close-up as in "the run-down gray house squatted on a crumbling foundation. Its paint puckered and peeled as one shut-ter banged against the wood like some large, slow-witted wood-pecker. Weeds marked flower beds and masked a stone walkway lead-ing to the discolored, stained back door." ILLUSTRATION gave us a tussle. What finally worked was in-serting the phrase "for instance" as a reminder that an illustration serves as an example, a support for a telling sentence.

Then I told them I would read the passage from the novel exact-ly as it was written and cautioned them to listen for D.I.D.

I remember the day Claire Louise started first grade. Everyone claims I'd have been too young to remember that, that at two years old I couldn't possi-bly remember Claire Louise starting school. But I do remember. She had on a red dress. Red was always my favorite color, still is for that matter. The dress was red checks and had a starched white collar and puffy white sleeves with white cuffs on them. And the belt that went with the dress my mother bought from the store to go with it, the dress she made herself. Mother made all our clothes. Mostly she made Claire Louise's clothes and I wore them four years later. And Claire Louise even had red socks to go with her dress and she wore her black and white saddle oxfords that my mother bought to be her school shoes. She had a book satchel my grandmoth-er bought for her, and all the school supplies the drugstore had printed on the first-grade list on the lowest shelf. She had those in the book bag. She had carefully printed her name on everything that went in her bag. We watched her do it, my mother and me. I sat in my mother's lap and watched Claire Louise get ready for her first day at school. That was a Saturday, I'm sure, because I can remember the sound of the lawn mower as Claire Louise carefully wrote her name, and my father only mowed on Saturday morning.

The students caught the big picture, the description of the nar-rator on her mother's lap. They rev-eled in all the details of color of collar, belt, and satchel. They real-ized the moving proved to be an illustration, a proof. (This tech-nique can be used with any rich piece of writing.)

They were ready, once again, to reenter their writing. They added some description and lots of detail. One young man asked, "Now what's illustration again?" I told him to find a telling sentence in his writing. He offered, "My little broth-er loves me." I asked him to insert "for instance" and give me an ex-ample. After some thought, he said, "For instance, he runs down the sidewalk to meet me after school and gives me a high-five."

"Perfect," I said. Although none of us really saw his little brother running to meet him, hand ex-tended, we did see it in the virtual reality of writing that shows. ❦

References

Arnold, Janis. *Daughters of Memory.* Chapel Hill, NC: Algonquin Books, 1991.

Crane, Stephen. *The Red Badge of Courage.* New York: W.W. Norton & Co., 1962.

Estes, Clarissa Pinkola. *Women Who Run With the Wolves: Myths and Stories of the Wild Woman Archetype.* New York: Ballantine Books, 1992.

Hobbs, Will. "Bringing Your Words to Life." *R & E Journal.* (Spring, 1996): 19–21.

Mayer, Marianna. *Baba Yaga and Vasilisa the Brave.* New York: Morrow Junior Books, 1994.

Sierra, Judy. *The Oryx Multicultural Folktale Series: Cinderella.* Phoenix, AZ: The Oryx Press, 1992.

Winthrop, Elizabeth. *Vasilissa the Beautiful.* New York: Harper Collins, 1991.

BLOCK SCHEDULING

A BLOCK

SCHEDULE

ARRANGES

CLASSES INTO

LONGER TIME

PERIODS...

WHAT IS BLOCK SCHEDULING?

A block schedule arranges classes into longer time periods of approximately ninety minutes. Classes may meet every day for one semester—called the A/B or the rotating block. Or, they may meet every other day for a full year—called the 4 x 4 or semester block.

WHAT ARE ITS BENEFITS?

There are several advantages to implementing block scheduling, both for the teacher and for the students. Block scheduling

- Is economical, allowing teachers to teach more students and requiring fewer textbooks and other materials.
- Allows more time for instruction and for more personalized student-teacher interaction.
- Promotes teaching a concept or skill in more depth.
- Affords more time for teachers to identify and respond to student needs and performances.
- Provides the opportunity for structuring interdisciplinary coordination.

- Provides for greater opportunities for multiple and creative teaching strategies and for use of more resources during a given class period (library resources, laboratory space, computers).
- Allows for varied assessment strategies.
- Reduces the number of classes students must prepare for each day.
- Allows students to earn more credits each year.
- Decreases the number of teachers students must adjust to.

HOW DOES BLOCK SCHEDULING AFFECT TEACHING?

In preparing for a block scheduling classroom, teachers should carefully examine their curriculum and be prepared for adjustments. Consider the following guidelines:
- Pare down the curriculum rather than padding it to fill an extended teaching period. Don't try to teach twice as much. This practice will frustrate you and your students. Covering less material can actually be more effective in block scheduling classes. The key phrase has been "more is less" because teach-

ers have taught fewer concepts but have taught them in more depth.
- Concentrate on a few key skills or concepts that you want students to master at the end of the course and plan your units and lessons around these skills.
- Think about the class period in terms of smaller time segments. Most adults can maintain focus for only twenty to thirty minutes. The average students are no different, so plan to their advantage—base your lessons on shorter, attention-getting activities and allow students to work in groups on longer, more enriching assignments.
- Use authentic assessments such as portfolios; peer groups and peer evaluation; and displays of student products. Allow students to learn and demonstrate mastery of their learning in ways that are successful for them.

HOW DOES A TYPICAL BLOCK-SCHEDULE CLASS PERIOD WORK?

The following is a general format that suggests the flexibility and variety that a teacher can explore in a block scheduling classroom.

By varying activities, a teacher can maintain students' attention, increase students' motivation, and create an environment that encourages learning.

HOW DOES BLOCK SCHEDULING AFFECT THE LANGUAGE ARTS CLASSROOM?

Block scheduling is particularly conducive to the teaching of language arts.

• The ninety-minute class period allows for a more seamless blending of reading, writing, language, and speaking and listening.

• Because the lessons are less fragmented, the connections between the strands can be seen more readily. For example, if literature is used as a springboard for writing, there is an opportunity for a more immediate shift from literature to writing.

• Also, for teaching the writing process in a block schedule, a watchful teacher can tailor the time spent on each stage of the process to fit the needs of the students. If students need more time revising than they do brainstorming, that is figured into a schedule that allows for more flexibility. If students need periodic mini-lessons on the uses of quotation marks, the block schedule allows for that, too.

EXPECTATIONS FOR TRANSITION/ TROUBLESHOOTING

Achieving a successfully balanced learning experience in a block schedule may take some time. However, keeping careful records of planning and daily activities and a file of ideas for varying instruction can help. Consider establishing a support group with other teachers. Sharing common problems and success stories will help the transition.

In the classroom, some regularity will help students adjust to the longer time period. Consider the following ideas for instruction:

- Begin class quickly.
- Deliver short lectures only.
- Allow some student movement/ interaction.
- Monitor student responses well.
- Vary activities every 15-20 minutes on average.
- State expectations very clearly before students begin any activity.

For classroom management, try some of the following suggestions:

• Devote a portion of team meetings to discussion of the block.

• Color code class rosters, student files, gradebook by day.

• Keep a notebook to record after class the basics of each lesson.

• Fill in only the dates in your gradebook on which classes actually meet to help avoid confusion regarding dates students were in class.

• Consider allowing students a short break from time to time during a longer class period.

CONCLUSION

Although it is a fairly new concept in education, block scheduling seems to be popular with educators because it provides them with the opportunity to control the time factor in learning. In schools that have instituted block scheduling, no longer are students racing from one 50-minute class to another, attending as many as seven classes in a single day. Teachers are not having to rush to get through the period's objectives before the bell.

In general, teachers and students seem to like longer classes. According to John O'Neil in his article "Finding Time to Learn," most teachers don't want to return to traditional scheduling—not because things are easier in block scheduling, but because they think they have been more successful in working with their students. ✿

BLOCK SCHEDULING SEEMS TO BE POPULAR WITH EDUCATORS BECAUSE IT PROVIDES THEM WITH THE OPPORTUNITY TO CONTROL THE TIME FACTOR IN LEARNING.

By Hilve Firek, College of Education and Allied Professions, University of North Carolina at Charlotte

Technology in the Language Arts Classroom

If we've learned one thing from technology, it is that we exist in a state of flux.

If we've learned one thing from technology, it is that we exist in a state of flux. What is cutting-edge today may be obsolete tomorrow. What the following day will bring is anybody's guess. But regardless of the frenetic changes, the need to communicate effectively in writing remains constant.

So, how do we teach composition in the glare of the bright lights, pulsating sounds, and moving images that are everywhere in today's technologically-fascinated society? Simple. We use the lights, sounds, and images to build bridges between popular culture and the culture of the classroom. We use what is familiar to teach what is new. *In essence, we use technology to inspire students to want to learn to write.*

TELEVISION AND VIDEOS

Let's begin with a technology your students know extremely well— television. If you doubt the intimate relationship our young people have with TV, listen to them talk about the characters and situations on the latest sitcoms, soaps, or prime-time dramas. Or eavesdrop on a discussion of the most popular music videos on MTV or BET. Without their even knowing it, these young adults have developed for themselves a rather complex understanding of plot, characterization, symbolism, and other literary devices used by the most skilled writers. The challenge for educators is to help students span the distance between what television has already taught them and what we, as facilitators of the language arts, are attempting to teach them.

Let's examine ways we might use television to reach students in teaching the writing process. If you spend an hour or two watching the shows your students watch, chances are you will encounter any number of situations that reflect the human condition. In a single segment, a program may explore the emotions of love, hate, jealousy, and desire through the dramatic elements of conflict and complications or through such devices as irony and satire. For the most part, the plot has a discernible beginning, middle, and end. Of course, setting plays a critical role in establishing tone; for example, a love affair set against the backdrop of a hospital emergency room differs from a summer romance on the beaches of California. Further, devices common in television, such as laugh and music tracks, steer viewers to specific responses.

The problem is that adolescents process this information that they see on TV without necessarily being cognizant of how each part contributes to the whole. Using this popular medium, teachers can help students recognize the numerous means by which messages are conveyed. Once they learn the tools that are utilized on television, students can build on this learning to understand the tools writers employ in their craft. In essence, by becoming critical viewers, students may more readily learn to see themselves as critical writers. For instance, if your students decide to change the format of a popular show from a situational comedy to a dramatic miniseries, what writing devices would they utilize? How would the dialogue change? How would the setting change? Would the characters develop differently?

By envisioning what they might see on the small screen, students can envision what they must put down on paper or key into their word-processing programs.

WORD PROCESSING AND DESKTOP PUBLISHING

Though most of us tend to think of word-processing software as an elementary tool that permits us to correct typos easily, most programs now offer features that serve to engage spatial learners in the written word. Simply by changing font styles and sizes and by incorporating such options as bold, italics, and underline, students can add a visual flair to their compositions impossible with a blue ballpoint pen. Additionally, many word-processing programs interface easily with desktop publishing software, thus providing users with the means to import clip art, digitized photos, charts, and graphs into their documents. The paintbrush feature found on many programs allows students to create their own illustrations, giving spatial learners the opportunity to express their thoughts in visual terms before embarking on the writing process.

The ample features of today's desktop publishing software encourage writers to experiment with eclectic blends of text and images to create new and ever-changing forms of communication where style conveys every bit as much as content. The increasing popularity among adolescents of alternative publications, known as *zines*, reflects this interest in multi-layered combinations of words, type styles, and graphics. Armed with computers, printers, and copiers, students turned off by the rigid structure of the five paragraph essay are using zines to experiment with voice, to share ideas, and to create unique products via a medium heretofore available only to professional writers (Williamson). By utilizing software commonly loaded on computers, young adults can begin to understand the connection between how messages are presented and how they are received. We teachers of the language arts can help our students incorporate this understanding.

AUTHENTIC COLLABORATION AND PUBLICATIONS: THE INTERNET

Netzines

As more and more schools across the country obtain Internet access, teens are establishing for themselves a writing-centered subculture that revolves around electronic versions of alternative publications, or *netzines*. Traditionally a forum for free expression, the Internet provides adolescents with the opportunity to share ideas through a creative blending of words, art, animation, sound, and video with little or no interference, or criticism, from adults. Jon Katz, in his article "The Rights of Kids in the Digital Age," asserts that America's youth is finding its identity tied inextricably to the digital world and the information age (122). Netzines created by and for kids are everywhere on the World Wide Web, and their often-uncensored formats may concern some parents and teachers.

Still, Internet access has ignited in many young people a desire, even a compulsion, to write. Since they have the freedom to play with words, young adults take risks with expression, experimenting with style, spelling, diction, capitalization, and punctuation in ways that proclaim a message of artistic experimentation. For example, young women who create electronic publications often refer to their creations as *gurl-* or *grrrl-zines;* in doing so, they have used alternative spellings to define themselves in a way other teens immediately recognize.

Netzines also give adolescents a chance to explore, in writing, topics of their own choosing, topics that are rarely addressed in the language arts classroom. Of course, kids discuss among themselves the issues frequently considered taboo in schools, but they also write untiringly about topics that may be considered too frivolous for the academic classroom or too embarrassing to share with a teacher, such as friends, dating, parents, fashion, cars, skating, and music.

Traditional Writing and Netzines

The idea of students writing and publishing their own magazines via computer technology is exciting, but most language arts teachers are expected, if not required, to teach standard methods of composition using standard rules of the English language. Describing a potential date as a wAy2KoOl chick may be acceptable in the underground press, but a similar statement on a job application might give a potential employer an excuse to join the education bashing that is so popular in this country. How then, might caring educators teach the rigors of composition without crushing the fervor teens show for writing?

The answer may reside in the zines themselves. If language arts teachers use zines, either the electronic or paper variety, to introduce written communication, they offer their students a chance to begin their writing journeys by learning to express themselves honestly and for real purpose. Interestingly, at least one study suggests that the writing young people do for their peers via the Net is often actually better than the writing they produce in traditional classroom assignments. In 1989, two researchers from the University of California at San Diego compared compositions written for teachers with those addressed to peers in other countries linked by the Internet. The compositions written and transferred by way of the Internet received distinctly better grades than those written for the teachers (Leslie 20).

EDUCATIONAL MULTIMEDIA PROGRAMS

There is also a whole new world of CD-ROM programs that address a variety of needs in the language arts classroom. These multimedia products capture the imaginations of even the most reluctant learners because of their dynamic nature and visual appeal. For example, Holt, Rinehart and Winston's CD-ROM software *Writer's Workshop* uses an environmental interface to engage students who might otherwise be completely disinterested in writing. It also includes music, a media center, author interviews, video clips, graphic organizers, photos, and online chat features to inspire students during prewriting, writing, or revising.

To involve students when teaching grammar, usage, and mechanics, Holt, Rinehart and Winston also offers *Language Workshop.* This award-winning CD-ROM program offers interactive instruction with options for on-screen self-assessment through performance-based practice. Along with these features for the student, *Language Workshop* has monitoring and assessment features exclusively for the teacher.

ON-LINE RESOURCES

Those of us who have attempted to teach research writing know that the struggle to engage young people in a systematic process of research can be tough. The Internet not only offers students the means by which they can publish their work, but also serves as a resource tool on topics of interest and on writing itself. Students who wouldn't be caught dead with a copy of Strunk's *Elements of Style* might not think twice about accessing the online version of the book.

Also, Net aficionados form a community of people, so that there is always an expert to be found on any subject, including composition. If students have World Wide Web access from home, they can do a keyword search for grammar and find a site that lists a state-by-state Grammar Hotline Directory. Or if they are too shy to speak aloud in class, they can post questions to tutors at several writing labs available through e-mail. Teachers just need to be aware that because these resources are sometimes public forums, the content on them can be unpredictable.

The Internet also serves as a resource for those of us who teach composition. If you access any major search engine, you will find a link to education-related sites; from there you can narrow your search as needed. On the World Wide Web teachers can find lesson plans, collaborative project ideas, supplementary materials, and even a netzine or two. And since teaching is all too often an isolated activity, many educators find reward in discussing their chosen field with colleagues in chat groups or on such e-mail discussion lists as the Dead Teachers Society.

Regardless of the position we take on the humans versus machines conflict, we cannot deny that technological innovations are now a part of everyday life. What still seems magical to us is commonplace to children who grow up expecting more than a hundred channels on their television sets and instant information from their computers. As concerned teachers, we can use technology to our own advantages—to incite interest, to simulate reality, and to open the world to our students. And if one of our goals as teachers of composition is to instill a love of writing—a need to write—then we owe it to our students to foster this love using all the tools we can find. ❦

References

Katz, Jon. "The Rights of Kids in the Digital Age." *Wired* July 1996: 120+
Leslie, Jacques. "Connecting Kids: On-line Technology Can Reform Our Schools." *Wired* Nov. 1993: 20–23.
Williamson, Judith. "Engaging Resistant Writers through Zines in the Classroom." College Composition and Communication Conference. Nashville, TN. March 1994.

BY DR. NORBERT ELLIOT, WRITING PROGRAM DIRECTOR, NEW JERSEY INSTITUTE OF TECHNOLOGY &
DR. KAREN GREENBERG, ASSOCIATE PROFESSOR, HUNTER COLLEGE OF THE CITY UNIVERSITY OF NEW YORK

THE DIRECT ASSESSMENT OF WRITING:

Notes For Teachers

> *HOW CAN ASSESSMENT STRATEGIES BE MODIFIED TO HELP BOTH TEACHERS AND STUDENTS?*

Teachers spend a great deal of time assessing students' writing: They correct errors, offer suggestions, and assign grades. This process can be exhausting to teachers and discouraging for students. How can assessment strategies be modified to help both teachers and students?

Instruction and assessment can be aligned so that the two work together. To enable instruction and assessment to complement each other, teachers have turned to two relatively new methods of direct assessment: holistic scoring and portfolio assessment.

HOLISTIC SCORING

One of the most common methods of scoring writing samples is holistic scoring, a procedure based on the responses of concerned readers to a meaningful whole composition. Holistic scoring involves reading a writing sample for an overall impression of the writing and assigning the sample a score based on a set of consistent scoring criteria. Most holistic scoring systems use a scoring scale, or guide, that describes papers at six or eight different levels of competence.

Holistic scoring has many advantages:

1. It communicates to students that writing is a process leading to a unified, synergistic piece of writing.

2. Writing samples that have been holistically scored provide students with clear information about the quality of their writing, but they are less intimidating than grades or written critiques.

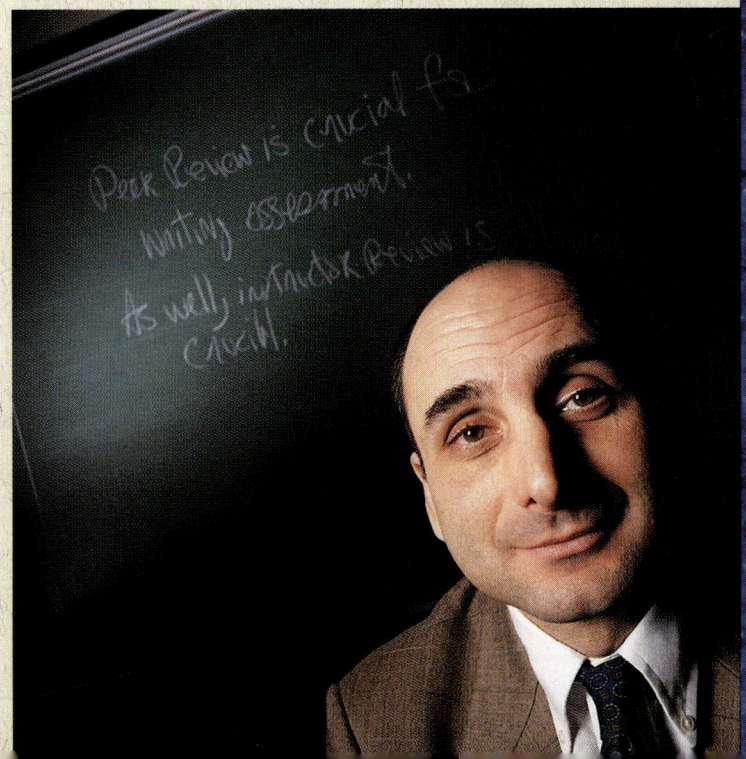

Peer Review is crucial for writing assessment. As well, instructor Review is crucial.

NORBERT ELLIOT, DIRECTOR OF THE WRITING PROGRAM AT THE NEW JERSEY INSTITUTE OF TECHNOLOGY.

3. Holistic scoring is rapid. Readers spend only minutes judging the total effect of a paper.

4. The criteria on a holistic scoring scale give teachers a vocabulary to use in discussing essays with students and their parents.

5. The process of developing holistic scoring guides and scoring writing samples enables teachers to share their unique responses to writing, as well as their evaluative criteria. If an entire department uses the same scoring guide, students will realize that effective writing has definable features upon which all of their English teachers agree.

Nevertheless, there are weaknesses to this method. It alone cannot, for instance, provide diagnostic information about specific writing proficiencies and deficiencies. The score cannot substitute for a teacher's detailed responses to an essay—the provocative notes in the margin, the encouraging comments at the end, etc. This weakness, however, can be overcome if teachers review papers with their students in light of the scoring criteria.

Another weakness is more serious. Using holistic scoring, teachers often consider only one piece of writing during assessment. If only one sample of writing is evaluated, then teachers may not get a representative idea of students' writing ability, because this ability does not exist in a vacuum but varies from day to day and across the aims and modes of writing. In response to this concern, teachers have investigated a second method of direct assessment.

KAREN GREENBERG, DIRECTOR OF THE NATIONAL TESTING NETWORK IN WRITING.

PORTFOLIO ASSESSMENT

Portfolio assessment allows writing teachers to evaluate various samples of students' work, taken at various times under various conditions. Consequently, portfolio assessment can provide a fuller portrait of writing abilities.

To begin portfolio assessment, teachers develop a series of writing assignments that express the goals of a course. For instance, a group of teachers might require their students to write papers based on each of James Kinneavy's aims: expressive writing (a journal entry), informative writing (a summary of a news article), literary writing (a short story), and persuasive writing (an editorial). Over time, students work on these papers both at home and in class. Portfolios can include other forms of communication that students have produced, such as artwork, audio recordings, or videotapes.

Teachers need not assess everything that is included in a portfolio. In fact, it is often preferable not to evaluate every piece of a student's writing. This strategy allows teachers to separate instruction and response from formed evaluation. Portfolio assessment, therefore, can be based on samples that the teacher, the student, or both consider to be the student's best writing.

Clearly, there are advantages to this method:

1. Because multiple samples are assessed, portfolio assessment is a valid, authentic evaluation.

2. Because the authenticity of the assessment is increased, the curriculum becomes enriched.

As teachers plan tasks, they debate curricular values and strategies, devise workable instructional schemes for the classroom, and design thoughtful evaluative criteria for assignments.

With portfolio assessment, students gain a more positive attitude toward writing. Because they invest in their writing, students seek both teacher and peer response, create multiple drafts, and revise for their readers. Over time, a school's entire writing program can become an exciting adventure in communication and critical thinking.

CONCLUSION

There is still much to be investigated about the evaluation of writing. What kind of assessment best suits the multiple literacies on which our democratic society rests? What kind of local assessments will best supplement large-scale assessment? How can assessment reveal more about effective teaching? Answers will have to come from those who know students best: their teachers. ❧

*P*ORTFOLIO ASSESSMENT ALLOWS WRITING TEACHERS TO EVALUATE VARIOUS SAMPLES OF STUDENTS' WORK, TAKEN AT VARIOUS TIMES UNDER VARIOUS CONDITIONS.

❧❧❧❧❧

To the Teacher

A new feature in the Annotated Teacher's Edition *for* Elements of Writing *is the Chapter Planning Guide. Located at the beginning of each of the writing chapters, this four-page guide includes the features listed below. Within each guide, we have included lesson plans for you to use in customizing your instruction. The instructional choices and lesson pacing in these plans are* only suggestions. *We recognize that any determination of lesson planning must be based on the needs of your individual classrooms.*

Objectives
Identifies the major objectives covered in the chapter.

Writing-in-Process Assignments
Provides an overview of the cumulative writing assignments that culminate in the main writing assignment of the chapter. Also outlines the developmental skills addressed in the chapter exercises.

Cross-Curriculum feature
Workplace Writing feature
Vary with each writing chapter in the Pupil's Edition. These features suggest ways to tailor the writing instruction addressed in the chapter to either a cross-discipline writing activity or to a form of writing used in the workplace.

Integrating the Language Arts Chart
Offers a convenient overview of the different strands of the language arts curriculum as they are incorporated in the activities provided in the Pupil's Edition.

Suggested Integrated Unit Plan
Appears only with chapters that address a particular kind of writing, such as a personal narrative or the research paper. Provides teachers with a unit plan that addresses reading; writing; listening and speaking; and language.

Chapter Planning Guide—Pupil's Edition
Suggests lesson plans and pacing for the instructional material, writing assignments, and exercises in each writing chapter in the Pupil's Edition. Outlines plans for students at three levels of learning—**developmental, core, and accelerated**.

Suggested pacing can be used to develop lesson plans for either a block or a traditional schedule.

Chapter Planning Guide— Program Resources
Provides an overview of the many program resources that support the instruction for each segment of the chapter.

These resources include various blackline masters for practice and assessment, transparencies for reinforcement, and writing and language CD-ROMs for instruction and practice.

Elements of Writing: Curriculum Connections
Identifies the activities at the end of each writing chapter that incorporate a cross-disciplinary approach.

Assessment Options
Identifies the assessment materials that accompany *Elements of Writing*. Addresses summative, portfolio, on-going, and self-assessment opportunities for evaluation.

ELEMENTS OF *Writing*

THE WRITING PROCESS COMES *Alive!*

If you're going to teach writing, *Elements of Writing* is *the* program to use. With *Elements of Writing,* students explore the writing process through unique lessons that take the puzzle and perplexity out of the experience and put the excitement of discovery back in.

A Pupil's Edition that Shows *and* Explains

This student book opens up the process of writing with an easy-to-follow, interactive style that hones students' writing skills and that talks to students in a friendly, encouraging tone. The program includes

- Brief, accessible segments of instruction immediately followed by practice
- Four writing models in *every* chapter to accommodate different learning styles
- Specific revision strategies for each major chapter
- A superb grammar handbook for reference and practice
- **NEW TO THIS EDITION!** More workplace writing; more grammar, usage, and mechanics; more student models; and even more attention to the revision process.

A Teacher's Edition at Work for You

In addition to pacing charts, program managers, and ideas for integrating workplace writing and reading skills, the *Elements of Writing Annotated Teacher's Edition* includes

Instructional Strategies to help you meet the needs of your students in efficient, effective, and creative ways.

- *Visual Connections*
- *Meeting Individual Needs*
- *Using the Selection*
- *A Different Approach*
- *Timesaver*
- *Critical Thinking*
- *Integrating the Language Arts*
- *Cooperative Learning*

Lesson Plans that provide clear and easy suggestions for managing the program at each step in the lesson.

- *Objectives*
- *Teaching the Lesson*
- *Guided* and *Independent Practice*
- *Assessment*
- *Reteaching*
- *Closure*
- *Motivation*
- *Extension*

Elements of Writing Supplements— The *joy* of Following Through

Every teacher knows the importance of following through. With *Elements of Writing,* you get a comprehensive array of support materials to help students follow through with a piece of writing and succeed in the writing process. Practice sheets, technology, instructional transparencies, activity booklets, and a whole lot more let your class discover just how joyful and relevant the writing process can be.

Teaching Resources
Outstanding materials reinforce concepts and strategies for students and provide teachers with support for reteaching and assessment. Supplements include

Academic and Workplace Skills

Practice for Assessment in Reading, Vocabulary, and Spelling

Practicing the Writing Process

Strategies for Writing

Word Choice and Sentence Style

Language Skills Practice and Assessment

Holistic Scoring: Prompts and Models

Portfolio Assessment

Fine Art and Instructional Transparencies
Transparencies for each major writing chapter, including teacher's notes and graphic organizers, prompt students to generate and organize ideas.

Available separately are other invaluable resources that will add an extra dimension to your instruction. These include **Merriam-Webster Middle School** and **High School Dictionaries, Holt Complete School Atlas, English Workshop,** and **Vocabulary Workshop.**

Multimedia and Technology

HRW Multimedia and Technology opens doors, expands options, and turns possibilities into realities. Connections that begin in the textbook move to a new level— a level that motivates students to get involved, to look farther, deeper, and beyond the page. **HRW Multimedia and Technology** also gives you the flexibility to teach the way you want, whether you have only a few computers or a writing lab for 30 students.

TEST GENERATOR A software package that allows you to revise, edit, or re-sort existing worksheets, quizzes, or tests for each grammar, usage, and mechanics chapter in the *Pupil's Edition.*

LANGUAGE WORKSHOP CD-ROMs for Macintosh® and Windows® A software program for your students that gives additional instruction and practice with grammar, usage, and mechanics, while engaging students with lively, interactive examples, prompts, and exercises.

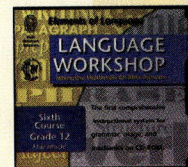

WRITER'S WORKSHOP 1 AND 2 CD-ROMs for Macintosh® and Windows® Writing process software that provides visual and spoken prompts to guide students through the eight most common assignments, such as writing a story, an informative report, or a persuasive essay.

HOLISTIC SCORING WORKSHOP An effective teacher-tutorial program in integrated performance assessment that instructs you in the use of holistic scoring of student reading and writing and that gives you practice with actual student papers.

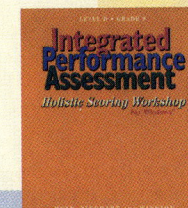

ELEMENTS OF

Writing

REVISED EDITION

Complete Course

James L. Kinneavy

John E. Warriner

The Senior Class
of
Central High School
announces the commencement exercises
Friday evening, May twenty-eighth
at eight o'clock
Central Stadium

English Re
Pap
(Wor

HOLT, RINEHART AND WINSTON

Harcourt Brace & Company

Austin • New York • Orlando • Atlanta • San Francisco
Boston • Dallas • Toronto • London

Critical Readers

Grateful acknowledgment is made to the following critical readers who reviewed pre-publication materials for this book:

Anthony Buckley
East Texas State University
Commerce, Texas

Elaine A. Espindle
Peabody Veterans
  Memorial High School
Peabody, Massachusetts

Barbara Freiberg
Louisiana State University
Laboratory School
Baton Rouge, Louisiana

Martha Morrow
Clements High School
Athens, Alabama

Vincenza Pentick
Kingston City School District
Kingston, New York

Carol Piper
Eldorado High School
Albuquerque, New Mexico

Linda E. Sanders
Jenks High School
Tulsa, Oklahoma

Janet Sanner
Berkeley County School
  District
Moncks Corner, South
  Carolina

Robert Sinclair
Brooklyn Technical
  High School
Brooklyn, New York

Virginia Tincher
Chardon High School
Chardon, Ohio

Brena Walker
Anderson College
Anderson, South
  Carolina

Staff Credits

Associate Director: Mescal K. Evler
Executive Editors: Kristine E. Marshall, Robert R. Hoyt
Managing Editor: Steve Welch
Editorial Staff: Editors, Cheryl Christian, A. Maria Hong, Constance Israel, Kathryn Rogers Johnson, Karen Kolar, Christy McBride, Laura Cottam Sajbel, Patricia Saunders, Michael L. Smith, Amy Strong, Suzanne Thompson, Katie Vignery; *Copyeditors,* Michael Neibergall, Copyediting Supervisor; Katherine E. Hoyt, Carrie Laing Pickett, Joseph S. Schofield IV, Barbara Sutherland; *Editorial Coordinators,* Amanda F. Beard, Senior Editorial Coordinator; Rebecca Bennett, Susan Grafton Alexander, Wendy Langabeer, Marie Hoffman Price; *Support,* Ruth A. Hooker, Senior Word Processor; Christina Barnes, Kelly Keeley, Margaret Sanchez, Raquel Sosa, Pat Stover
Permissions: Catherine J. Paré, Janet Harrington
Production: Pre-press, Beth Prevelige, Simira Davis; *Manufacturing,* Michael Roche
Design: Richard Metzger, *Art Director;* Lori Male, *Designer*
Photo Research: Mavournea Hay, Kris Hook, Jeannie Taylor, Tim Taylor

Authors

James L. Kinneavy, the Jane and Roland Blumberg Centennial Professor of English at The University of Texas at Austin, directed the development and writing of the composition strand in the program. He is the author of *A Theory of Discourse* and coauthor of *Writing in the Liberal Arts Tradition*. Professor Kinneavy is a leader in the field of rhetoric and composition and a respected educator whose teaching experience spans all levels—elementary, secondary, and college. He has continually been concerned with teaching writing to high school students.

John E. Warriner developed the organizational structure for the Handbook of Grammar, Usage, and Mechanics in the book. He coauthored the *English Workshop* series, was general editor of the *Composition: Models and Exercises* series, and editor of *Short Stories: Characters in Conflict*. He taught English for thirty-two years in junior and senior high school and college.

Writers and Editors

John Algeo is Professor of English at the University of Georgia. He is coauthor with Thomas Pyles of *The Origins and Development of the English Language*.

Ellen Ashdown has a Ph.D. in English from the University of Florida. She has taught composition and literature at the college level. She is a professional writer of educational materials and has published articles and reviews on education and art.

Norbert Elliot has a Ph.D. in English from the University of Tennessee. A Professor of English at New Jersey Institute of Technology, he is a specialist in test development and writing assessment.

Phillis Goldenberg has an A.B. in English from the University of Chicago. She has been a writer and editor of educational materials in literature, grammar, composition, and critical thinking for over thirty-five years.

Alice M. Sohn has a Ph.D. in English Education from Florida State University. She has taught English in middle school, secondary school, and college. She has been a writer and editor of educational materials in language arts for seventeen years.

Glenda A. Zumwalt has an Ed.D. in Teaching Composition and Rhetoric from East Texas State University. She teaches composition at Southeastern Oklahoma State University. She is a writer of educational materials in composition and literature.

PART ONE

WRITING

INTRODUCTION TO WRITING

The Movers and the Shapers

WRITING HANDBOOK

AIMS FOR WRITING

LANGUAGE AND STYLE

PART ONE: WRITING

The following **Teaching Resources** booklets contain materials that may be used with this part of the Pupil's Edition.

WRITING HANDBOOK

- *Practicing the Writing Process*
- *Portfolio Assessment*
- *Practice for Assessment in Reading, Vocabulary, and Spelling* (for Ch. 3)

AIMS FOR WRITING

- *Strategies for Writing*
- *Holistic Scoring: Prompts and Models*
- *Portfolio Assessment*
- *Practice for Assessment in Reading, Vocabulary, and Spelling*

LANGUAGE AND STYLE

- *Word Choice and Sentence Style*
- *Portfolio Assessment*

OBJECTIVES

- To explore the ways that writers and writing affect the world
- To identify and analyze the aims of writing
- To compare and contrast the aims of writing

INTRODUCTION TO WRITING

THE MOVERS AND THE SHAPERS

James L. Kinneavy

ANNOUNCING

Author
Maya Angelou
Reading selections from

I know why the caged bird sings

Central Library
May 27   8:00 p.m.

VOTING
RIGHTS
NOW!

END
SEGREGATED
RULES
IN
PUBLIC
SCHOOLS

USING THE INTRODUCTION TO WRITING

This introduction to writing is just that—an introduction. It starts by talking briefly about the power of writing in people's lives. Next it touches upon the two central focuses of the writing chapters in the textbook—the "how" of writing (modes) and the "why" of writing (aims).

The communication triangle graphically reflects the four major aims of James Kinneavy's theory of discourse. For more information, refer to the essay in the front of this book, "Meet the Aims and Modes of Writing," or to Dr. Kinneavy's two books, *The Theory of Discourse* and *Writing in the Liberal Arts Tradition.* ∎

Take any area of life, and it's not hard to put your finger on people who **move** the world's wheels and **shape** its future.

Government: Abraham Lincoln, whose courageous decisions helped unite our divided country.

Work and business: Bill Gates, who helped transform the computer software business into a billion-dollar industry.

Entertainment and art: Oprah Winfrey, actor, producer, and talk-show host, who is recognized for her dedication to high standards and helping others.

Humanitarianism: Jane Addams, winner of the Nobel Prize for peace, who championed—against all odds—the causes of the poor and burdened.

But now try to put your finger on what these movers and shapers have in common.

Lincoln, Gates, Winfrey, Addams: Their spheres of life are so different. Is it possible that success in Washington, in a corporate boardroom, on a television sound stage, and in a Chicago settlement house are related in any way? Do all movers and shapers share a crucial skill? Yes. And they share it with you.

Clockwise from top left: Roberto Clemente, Connie Chung, Gloria Steinem, Theodor Seuss Geisel, Sequoyah, Martin Luther King, Jr., and Maya Angelou.

3

What's Common to All Uncommon Leaders?

Leaders, no matter what their fields, actually share many qualities and abilities. You can probably suggest several: drive, intelligence, vision. But there's something else absolutely essential to any leader who influences followers: communication. After all, if word doesn't get out, heartfelt beliefs, hard work, innovative ideas, and creative talent have no effect. Leaders have to let people know.

Using words well is common to people who get things done. Abraham Lincoln, Bill Gates, Oprah Winfrey, and Jane Addams have had a tremendous impact on life in the United States. And they couldn't have done it without their abilities to speak their minds, prepare speeches, entertain through words, and write proposals, contracts, and books.

But famous figures aren't the only ones who use words to move people and shape ideas. Think of your city's mayor, the manager of your favorite restaurant, a popular local singer, the head of a homeless shelter. Would they be where they are if they couldn't communicate? Think of any important goal you have for your life. What role could words play in making you a standout?

It doesn't matter where your interests lie. In the worlds of politics, business, art, and social service, communication is crucial. Movers and shapers put words to work.

The Power of Communication

Making an impact with words is a special, liberating power, but it's one that is accessible to all of us. All communication requires is someone who wants to communicate (a *writer*) about something (a *subject*), someone to say it to (an *audience*), and a way to say it (a *language*). Visualize these elements as a communications triangle. Language—both written and spoken—is at the center.

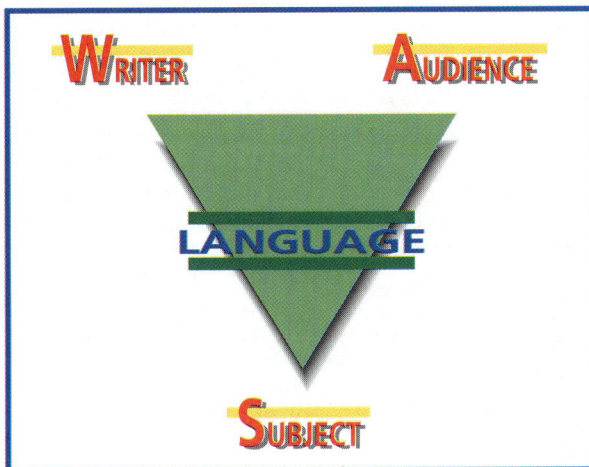

WRITER   **AUDIENCE**

LANGUAGE

SUBJECT

How Do They Communicate?

The Writing Process

Besides effective communication, all movers and shapers have something else in common: the way they go about that communication. They, like all writers, use the stages of the *writing process* to go from first idea to final realization in words. As you would expect, each writer can use the process differently. Thought, language, and *people* will never be confined in rigid steps, but the stages below are basic elements in leading yourself from rough thought to clear expression.

Prewriting	Thinking and planning: thinking about your purpose and audience; determining what you're going to write about; collecting ideas and details; creating a plan for presenting ideas
Writing	Writing a first draft: expressing ideas and details in sentences and paragraphs; carrying out the writing plan
Evaluating and Revising	Reviewing the draft to decide what works well and what doesn't; changing the draft to improve it
Proofreading and Publishing	Finding and correcting mistakes; writing or printing out a final copy; sharing it with an audience

Why Do They Communicate?

The Aims of Writing

Consider Bill Gates and Oprah Winfrey, and you might conclude that people write for limitless reasons. While it's true that each piece of writing has its own individual purpose, the aims of writing as a whole aren't infinite. Writers actually have four basic *aims,* or reasons, for writing.

Expository	**Informative:** Writers sometimes want to give facts or other kinds of information. **Explanatory:** Writers may want to explain something in detail. **Exploratory:** Writers may also investigate in depth a complex idea or seek an answer to a question.
Persuasive	Writers often want to convince others to accept an idea or take a specific action.
Self-Expressive	Sometimes writers simply want to express personal feelings or thoughts.
Literary	Writers also create imaginative works— novels, short stories, poems, plays, songs.

The models that follow all relate to the same topic, but each is written by a different writer and illustrates a different basic aim. As you read, think about each writer's purpose.

EXPOSITORY WRITING

Local College Students Uncover Archaeological Find

Seven Westhaven College students may have uncovered a more than 3,000-year-old Egyptian statue. The students, under the direction of Professor Ramón Arcaro, made the discovery Tuesday while digging on the east bank of the Nile River, between Karnak and Luxor in Egypt.

The students were completing the final week of a six-week exploratory dig when Li Kwan and Ivan McAfee uncovered what appears to be the foot of a sandstone statue. "We were about four feet down in the sand when we hit it," said Kwan. "The excitement was indescribable."

Arcaro says there is every reason to believe they have uncovered one of the hundreds of statues constructed by Ramses II, an Egyptian pharaoh of the 19th dynasty (1304–1237 B.C.). If so, the statue could be 30 to 50 feet in height and is considered a major archaeological find.

The college has filed a declaration of the find with the Egyptian government. The students continue logging data and photographing the site, but will return home later this week to await approval from Cairo to continue the dig. In the meantime, the college will begin fund-raising for the statue's excavation.

READER'S RESPONSE

1. What are you most curious about after reading this report? What one question would you like to ask Li Kwan or Professor Arcaro?
2. Does the writer of this article stick to the facts about the incident, or include personal opinions and feelings? Explain.

PERSUASIVE WRITING

Dear Westhaven College Alumni:

Westhaven College has a once-in-a-lifetime opportunity to contribute to the world's understanding of the past <u>and</u> to enhance its academic reputation. On December 3, Professor Ramón Arcaro of the Westhaven Archaeology Department and his students uncovered a portion of a statue on the east bank of the Nile River. They believe the statue may have been constructed by the Egyptian pharaoh Ramses II over three thousand years ago.

Unfortunately, Professor Arcaro and his students made the discovery during the final two days of their six-week dig. About $500,000 is needed to complete the excavation and authenticate the find. The Archaeology Department does not have this money, and all the hard work and the credit for it are in danger of being lost.

But that's where you can help. By making a contribution to the final excavation, you can give Westhaven students a unique educational experience. Your gift will also keep giving back to the college, as Westhaven's discovery attracts international attention.

Time is short; Professor Arcaro must make a commitment to the Egyptian government by January 31. Please write your check and use the enclosed envelope to mail it today. Your gift will truly make a difference.

Sincerely,

Annette Kaufman

Annette Kaufman, Director
of Alumni Giving

READER'S RESPONSE

1. What do you think of the role of history and archaeology? Has a knowledge of history ever been significant for you?
2. Would this letter convince you to make a contribution? What did the writer say that was most convincing? least convincing?

Dec. 3

Today I think I hit the high point and t
low point of my life. Around three P.M. I
working with two students who were remo
and from around a piece of sandstone. T
probably

EXPRESSIVE WRITING

Today I think I hit the high point and the low point of my life. Around three P.M. I was working with two students who were removing sand from around a piece of sandstone. Think it's the foot of a huge statue, probably one of the statues Ramses II built to honor himself. What a find! My first thought was that it could make my career and the careers of my students. Could do a lot for Westhaven, too. But now that I've had time for a second thought, I'm panicked. How will I ever get the money to go on with the excavation?

To give up now—when we're so close. Let someone else, some other university, take the credit for the find because they had the money and we didn't? Don't think I could stand it. What can I do? Get a corporate sponsor? Call the college president? Would she support a fund-raising campaign for this? Call tomorrow, soon as she's in her office.

Later. Had to go out and take one more look at the foot we uncovered. The moon was bright, so I could see. I had a thought—Ramses II looked at the same moon. I wonder what he was really like. All that ego, hundreds of statues. Where did they get him?

READER'S RESPONSE

1. From this journal, what can you tell about Professor Arcaro? How would you describe his personality?
2. How would you feel if you found a 3,000-year-old statue?

ANSWERS
Reader's Response

1. Students should cite examples from the journal entry to support their conclusions about Professor Arcaro.

2. Look for responses in which students discuss emotions.

LITERARY WRITING

The "antique land" in this poem is Egypt, where over three thousand years ago, the pharaoh Ramses II built hundreds of palaces, temples, and monuments commemorating his own greatness. Ramses II is referred to here as "Ozymandias," perhaps another version of "User-Maet-Re," the name used for Ramses at the temples at Abu Simbel.

OZYMANDIAS

BY PERCY BYSSHE SHELLEY

I met a traveller from an antique land
Who said: Two vast and trunkless legs of stone
Stand in the desert . . . Near them, on the sand,
Half sunk, a shattered visage lies, whose frown,
And wrinkled lip, and sneer of cold command,
Tell that its sculptor well those passions read
Which yet survive, stamped on these lifeless things,
The hand that mocked them, and the heart that fed:
And on the pedestal these words appear:
"My name is Ozymandias, king of kings:
Look on my works, ye Mighty, and despair!"
Nothing beside remains. Round the decay
Of that colossal wreck, boundless and bare
The lone and level sands stretch far away.

READER'S RESPONSE

1. The phrase "colossal wreck" sums up the irony many readers see in this poem: Ramses/Ozymandias is conquered by sand. But could you write a poem about this broken statue that would celebrate the king's power through the ages? How would you do it?
2. Besides "colossal wreck," what other words of Shelley's stand out vividly for you in this poem? Is there any place in the poem where meaning is not as clear to you as in the sentences of the other models? Where? How do you interpret the passage?

ANSWERS
Reader's Response

Responses will vary.

1. Students might note that although the statue is broken, it reminds people of the power once wielded by Ramses/ Ozymandias, thereby giving him immortality.

2. Students should each cite at least one word or phrase from the poem that is striking. You may want to specify whether you expect a paraphrase of the poem or a brief summary.

Writing and Thinking Activities

1. Get together with two or three other students to discuss the following questions.
   a. Which model persuades readers to do something? How?
   b. Which one provides facts and details to inform readers about an event?
   c. Which writer used words in a way that is different from ordinary speech? What's the effect of these differences?
   d. Which model is mostly about the writer's thoughts and feelings?
2. You are a constant communicator, and your own communication patterns may surprise you. How much of your communication is expository: informing, explaining, or exploring? How much is persuasive? How much is self-expressive? How much is literary? Research yourself. Jot down all your uses of language—writing, reading, speaking, listening—during a typical day. Then meet with two or three classmates to discuss what you've learned.

3. Bring a copy of a magazine or newspaper to class. Work with two or three other students to find examples of all four types of writing: expository, persuasive, self-expressive, literary. (Look at *all* the writing, not just articles.) Analyze the mix. Is one aim more common than the others? Do all the publications have the same mix of the four aims for writing?

4. Choose a radio or TV station to listen to or watch for a period of three hours—6 to 7 P.M. on a week night, 8 to 9 P.M. on a week night, and 3 to 4 P.M. on Saturday or Sunday. Categorize all programs, as well as short features and ads, according to the aim. Then get together with another student who studied a different station and compare the two.

5. Can you take the idea from a poem and convert it to a news story, a persuasive piece, or an expressive piece? Look for a poem in your literature book or the library and try to write another piece on the same topic, but with a different aim.

WRITING AND THINKING

OBJECTIVES

- To analyze writing as personal, creative, and imaginative
- To use brainstorming, clustering, and the *5W-How?* questions in prewriting
- To write for a specific audience and purpose
- To use prewriting notes to write a first draft
- To evaluate and revise an essay
- To proofread and publish an essay

cross CURRICULUM

Using Writing Skills to Investigate a Potential Career

Have students investigate career possibilities by using the writing process for standard or e-mail inquiries to request career information. Have students begin by brainstorming a list of questions and appropriate people to ask. Invite teachers from appropriate disciplines to direct brainstorming sessions.

- **Prewriting** Divide interpersonal learners into small groups based on a common interest in a profession. Have students brainstorm a list of questions to ask an expert. Students may wish to begin with *5W-How?* questions like the following:

Profession: Politician

- **Who** would you recommend as a mentor or role model for someone wishing to enter politics?
- **What** degree would most benefit a student interested in politics?
- **Why** would this course of study be useful?
- **Where** would you recommend I study to meet my goals?
- **When** would you suggest I start to get hands-on experience? Is after college graduation too late to start?
- **How** can I use my writing skills to help as a volunteer working in a political campaign?

Intrapersonal learners may prefer imagining a conversation with an appropriate person, or they might want to freewrite possible questions in a journal that they could submit to an appropriate teacher for input.

- **Writing** Appoint one group member to draft an e-mail message or letter that includes the prepared questions. Suggest that students read about writing business letters on pp. 1088–1095 before they begin drafting.

- **Evaluating and Revising** As group members evaluate the draft, remind them to consider whether the questions have stuck to the purpose and if the tone is an appropriate one for a professional inquiry.

- **Proofreading and Publishing** Remind students that some computer programs will not permit them to use a spelling check for e-mail. In that case, students may want to prepare the material in a word-processing program and copy the material into the e-mail format. Each member of the group should be made responsible for checking specific items on the Guidelines for Proofreading chart on p. 49 of *Elements of Writing.*

INTEGRATING THE LANGUAGE ARTS

SELECTION	READING AND LITERATURE	WRITING AND CRITICAL THINKING	LANGUAGE AND SYNTAX	SPEAKING, LISTENING, AND OTHER EXPRESSION SKILLS
• from *An End to Audience?* by Margaret Atwood pp. 16–18 • from "**Scourge of the South May Be Heading North,**" *National Geographic* p. 33 • Letter to the Editor by Albert Morelli pp. 33–34 • from *Escalante: The Best Teacher in America* by Jay Mathews p. 36	• Responding personally to literature p. 18 • Reading for specific information pp. 28–29 • Evaluating a paragraph pp. 46–47	• Responding personally to literature p. 18 • Writing a journal entry pp. 18, 23 • Relating personal experience to literature p. 18 • Applying interpretive and creative thinking pp. 18, 23, 25, 26, 27–28, 30, 36, 39, 52, 55 • Freewriting p. 23 • Brainstorming and clustering pp. 25, 36, 51 • Creating *5W-How?* questions p. 26 • Observing and imagining pp. 27–28 • Making inferences and drawing conclusions pp. 28–29, 39 • Analyzing a topic p. 30 • Analyzing purpose, audience, and tone p. 34 • Using tone to achieve an effect p. 34 • Arranging order of details pp. 36, 39, 41 • Classifying information p. 39 • Writing a first draft p. 41 • Evaluating and revising a paragraph pp. 46–47 • Proofreading a paragraph pp. 49–50 • Reflecting on writing for portfolio selections p. 50 • Researching potential publishers p. 52 • Exploring the writing process p. 54 • Researching multimedia software p. 55	• Proofreading for errors in grammar, usage, and mechanics pp. 49–50 • Using a dictionary pp. 49–50	• Discussing creative writing pp. 18, 54 • Working with a classmate to brainstorm topics p. 25 • Working with classmates to compare *5W-How?* questions p. 26 • Working with classmates to compare research pp. 28–29 • Working with a classmate to analyze a topic p. 30 • Creating a chart to classify information p. 39 • Working with classmates to compare charts p. 39 • Working with classmates to evaluate a paragraph pp. 46–47 • Working with classmates to compare revisions pp. 46–47 • Working with classmates to brainstorm publishing ideas p. 52 • Compiling information and creating a computer database p. 52 • Interviewing a professional and sharing findings with the class p. 54 • Preparing and presenting oral reports on multimedia authoring programs p. 55 • Adding audiovisual enhancements to writing p. 55

CHAPTER 1: WRITING AND THINKING

Use this guide for creating an instructional plan that addresses the individual needs of your students. Assignments accompanied by the following symbol (*) may be complete out of class. Times given for pacing lessons are estimated.

CHAPTER PLANNING GUIDE—PUPIL'S EDITION

| LESSONS | LITERARY MODEL pp. 16–18 from *An End to Audience?* by Margaret Atwood | PREWRITING pp. 21–39 | |
		Generating Ideas	Gathering/Organizing
DEVELOPMENTAL PROGRAM	20–25 minutes • Read model aloud in class and answer questions orally on p. 18	60 minutes • Main Assignment: Looking Ahead p. 18 • Aim/Process pp. 19–20 • Finding Ideas for Writing pp. 21–29 • Exercises 1–4 pp. 23–28	30–35 minutes • Considering Purpose, Audience and Tone pp. 31–32 • Critical Thinking pp. 32–34* • Arranging Ideas pp. 35–38 • Exercise 6 p. 36*
CORE PROGRAM	15–20 minutes • Assign student pairs to read the model and answer questions on p. 18	30–35 minutes • Main Assignment: Looking Ahead p. 18 • Aim/Process pp. 19–20 • Finding Ideas for Writing pp. 21–29* • Exercises 1*, 2–3, 4* pp. 23–28 • Critical Thinking pp. 29–30*	20–25 minutes • Considering Purpose, Audience, and Tone pp. 31–32 • Critical Thinking pp. 32–34, 38–39* • Arranging Ideas pp. 35–38 • Exercise 6 p. 36*
ACCELERATED PROGRAM	15 minutes • Assign students to read model independently on pp. 16–18	20–25 minutes • Main Assignment: Looking Ahead p. 18 • Aim/Process pp. 19–20 • Chart p. 21 • Exercise 5 pp. 28–29 • Critical Thinking pp. 29–30*	10–15 minutes • Considering Purpose, Audience, and Tone pp. 31–32 • Critical Thinking pp. 32–34, 38–39* • Chart p. 35

CHAPTER PLANNING GUIDE—PROGRAM RESOURCES

	LITERARY MODEL	PREWRITING
PRINT	• Reading Master 1, *Practice for Assessment in Reading, Vocabulary, and Spelling* p. 1	• Freewriting and Brainstorming; Clustering and the *5W-How?* Questions; Purpose, Audience, and Tone; Arranging Details in Order, *Practicing the Writing Process* pp. 1–4 • The Writing Process, *English Workshop* pp. 1–18
MEDIA		• Graphic Organizers 1–2, *Transparency Binder*

WRITING pp. 40–41	EVALUATING AND REVISING pp. 42–47	PROOFREADING AND PUBLISHING pp. 48–52

🕐 **30–35 minutes**
• Writing a First Draft
  pp. 40–41
• Exercise 7 in pairs p. 41
	🕐 **45–50 minutes**
	• Evaluating and Revising
	  pp. 42–45
	• Chart p. 42
	• Guidelines pp. 43, 44
	• Critical Thinking in pairs
	  pp. 46–47
		🕐 **60–65 minutes**
		• Proofreading and
		  Publishing pp. 48–50
		• Guidelines pp. 49, 51
		• Exercise 8 in pairs
		  pp. 49–50
		• Critical Thinking
		  pp. 50–51
		• Symbols p. 53

🕐 **20–25 minutes**
• Writing a First Draft
  pp. 40–41
• Exercise 7 p. 41
	🕐 **20–25 minutes**
	• Chart p. 42
	• Guidelines pp. 43, 44
	• Critical Thinking
	  pp. 46–47*
		🕐 **30–35 minutes**
		• Guidelines pp. 49, 51
		• Exercise 8 pp. 49–50*
		• Critical Thinking
		  pp. 50–51*
		• Exercise 9 p. 52
		• Symbols p. 53

🕐 **10–15 minutes**
• Writing a First Draft
  pp. 40–41
• Exercise 7 p. 41*
	🕐 **15–20 minutes**
	• Chart p. 42
	• Guidelines pp. 43, 44
	• Critical Thinking
	  pp. 46–47*
		🕐 **25–30 minutes**
		• Guidelines pp. 49, 51
		• Critical Thinking
		  pp. 50–51*
		• Exercise 9 p. 52
		• Symbols p. 53

💾 Computer disk or CD-ROM   📠 Overhead transparencies

WRITING	EVALUATING AND REVISING	PROOFREADING AND PUBLISHING

• Writing a First Draft,
  *Practicing the Writing
  Process* p. 5
	• Evaluating a Peer,
	  Revising: Adding and
	  Cutting, Revising:
	  Replacing and Reorder-
	  ing, *Practicing the
	  Writing Process* pp. 6–8
		• Proofreading Your Work,
		  Proper Manuscript Form,
		  *Practicing the Writing
		  Process* pp. 9–10

	• Revision Transparencies
	  1–2, *Transparency
	  Binder* 📠
		• *Language Workshop:*
		  Lessons 5–10, 15, 31–32,
		  42–58 💾

ELEMENTS OF WRITING: CURRICULUM CONNECTIONS

Making Connections
• Exploring the Writing Process p. 54
• Multimedia Projects p. 55

ASSESSMENT OPTIONS

Portfolio Assessment
Portfolio forms, *Portfolio Assessment* pp. 5–25

Summative Assessment
Review—The Aim and Process of Writing,
Practicing the Writing Process p. 11

Reflection
Self-assessment Record, *Portfolio Assessment*
p. 19

OBJECTIVES

- To analyze personal, creative, and imaginative writing
- To examine how writing personalizes experiences
- To write personal responses to literature

MOTIVATION

On the chalkboard put the following question: "Does a writer have to experience something in order to write well about it?" Then discuss how Margaret Atwood describes writing as becoming personal through imagination, and, therefore, why it is not necessary to live through an experience to be able to write about it.

PROGRAM MANAGER

CHAPTER 1

- **Computer Guided Instruction** *Writer's Workshop 2 CD-ROM* Applied instruction about specific types of writing is cross-referenced where appropriate, in subsequent chapters, beginning with **Chapter 4.**

- **Practice** To help less-advanced students who need additional practice with concepts and activities related to this chapter, see **Chapter 1** in *English Workshop, Complete Course,* pp. 1–18.

- **Reading Support** For help with the reading selection, pp. 16–18, see **Reading Master 1** in *Practice for Assessment in Reading, Vocabulary, and Spelling,* p. 1.

VISUAL CONNECTIONS
Interior with a Girl Drawing

About the Artwork. This painting is done in the cubist style pioneered by Picasso and Georges Braque. Like other cubist paintings, *Interior with a Girl Drawing* shows multiple perspectives. For example, Picasso shows both of the girl's eyes although she is in a profile pose. Relate this concept to writing by explaining that to understand their subjects, writers must also see from many viewpoints. Then point out the use of

continued on next page

1 WRITING AND THINKING

After students read the introductory paragraphs and Atwood's essay, point out that although the writer tells them writing is more than self-expression, writing is based on our individual perceptions of the world and our experiences, real or imagined. Illustrate this idea to students by placing an object in the center of the room and asking each student to write a brief description of it. Ask students to share descriptions and compare similarities and differences in their perceptions.

Using your own writing as a model, write a paragraph detailing your ideal home. Then describe to students which details are ☞

Looking at the Process

Have you heard of "automatic writing"? It's a **process** of "ghost writing" in the truest sense: an unseen force supposedly pushes the pen while the "writer" merely watches. Unbelievable? Yes; but it's unbelievable for more reasons than our doubts about unseen forces.

Writing and You. When was your writing ever totally unconscious, with words filling the page while you remarked, "Why, look at that!"? Never! When you write, your brain is engaged before, during, and after putting words on paper. Planning, judging, and just mentally doodling are indispensable, because the writing process involves more than a moving hand; it takes a working brain, too. But that doesn't make writing *un*mysterious. Since writing is thinking, it is always a process of discovery; it often surprises the person holding the pen.

As You Read. Writer Margaret Atwood believes writing is about as automatic a process as brain surgery. Her comparison is a joke, but she's serious, too. Why does she say many people misunderstand writing?

Pablo Picasso, *Interior with a Girl Drawing.* (Paris February 1935) Oil on canvas, 51¼"x 64¾". The Museum of Modern Art, New York. Nelson A. Rockefeller Bequest.

geometrical shapes and bold colors as characteristics of the cubist style.

Ideas for Writing. Suggest that keeping a writing journal can be like drawing a self-portrait. Have students create brief writing journal entries responding to this painting and to consider what their responses tell them about themselves.

QUOTATION FOR THE DAY

"I don't wait to be struck by lightning and don't need certain slants of light in order to write." (Toni Morrison, 1931–   , American novelist)

Copy the quotation on the chalkboard and explain that good writing is as much hard work as it is inspiration and involves active thinking at every stage of the process.

MEETING *individual* NEEDS

LEP/ESL

General Strategies. Atwood's article relies for its meaning on several unusual, idiomatic, and figurative expressions that might be difficult for some of your English-language learners to understand: *honorable, expressing yourself, caricaturing, spinning out his entire work, solipsism, self-enclosed monads, garland of clichés, literalists, invest interest, identify with, feel a thing, diminishes me, neurotic, lets us off the hook, Heaven forefend, human . . . partake, more and other.* You may wish to read the article aloud in class and explain these concepts as you do so.

based on personal experiences and which are based on material you have read, seen, or heard.

Students are responsible for creating a writing journal entry for **Reader's Response** in reaction to Atwood's essay. Encourage them to use specific examples of stories, songs, or movies.

ASSESSMENT

Assess comprehension of Atwood's essay by asking students to respond to **Reader's Response** orally or on paper.

MEETING *individual* NEEDS

ADVANCED STUDENTS

Ask advanced students to engage in a library activity to discover why it is especially appropriate that Atwood includes words from John Donne and Adrienne Rich in her work. Have students write a paragraph explaining why Atwood chooses these quotations and what proof students have found to show that Donne and Rich share Atwood's attitude toward writing.

AT-RISK STUDENTS

At-risk students who do not have extensive vocabularies or appropriate reading skills might have difficulty reading and interpreting Atwood's essay. Help students by paraphrasing in your own words what they will read in Atwood's essay. This previewing and purpose-setting will guide students in their reading and keep them from feeling overwhelmed.

16

from Second Words

from

An End to Audience?

by Margaret Atwood

RETEACHING

Ask each student to write a paragraph discussing a friend's exciting experience from the first-person viewpoint of the friend; point out to students that this is what Atwood means in her essay when she states that writers do not have to live through an experience to imagine what it would be like.

CLOSURE

Close this lesson by discussing the following questions as a class:

1. Why does Atwood think writing is more than mere self-expression?
2. How does writing involve thinking?
3. How can experiences personalize writing? ■

A friend of mine told me once that when she'd been in France a man, upon hearing she was a writer, commented, "It is an honorable profession." In Canada we don't—even now—think of writing as an honorable profession. We don't think of it as a profession at all. We think of it, still, as something called "expressing yourself." I'm sure you've all heard the one about the writer and the brain surgeon who met at a cocktail party. "So you write," said the brain surgeon. "Isn't that interesting. I've always wanted to write. When I retire and have the time I'm going to be a writer." "What a coincidence," said the writer, "because when I retire I'm going to be a brain surgeon."

Deep down inside, most people think that writing is something anyone can do, really, because after all it's only expressing yourself. Well, it's probably true that anyone can write. Anyone can play the piano too, but doing it well is another thing. If writing is merely and only self-expression, then all the <u>philistine</u> reactions to it I've been <u>caricaturing</u> above would be, in my opinion, quite justified.

Readers and critics both are still addicted to the concept of self-expression, the writer as a kind of spider, spinning out his entire work from within. This view depends on a solipsism, the idea that we are all self-enclosed <u>monads</u>, with an inside and an outside, and that nothing from the outside ever gets in. It goes hand in hand with that garland of clichés, the one with which women writers in particular are frequently decorated, the notion that everything you write *must* be based on personal experience. *Must*, because those making this assumption have no belief in the imagination, and are such literalists that they will not invest interest in anything they do not suppose to be "true." Of course all writing is based on personal experience, but personal experience is experience—wherever it comes from—that you identify with, *imagine* if you like, so that it becomes personal to you. If your mother dies and you don't feel a thing, is this death a personal experience? "If a clod be washed away by the sea, Europe is the less," said John Donne; or, to paraphrase him as Adrienne Rich does, "Every woman's death diminishes me."

We like to think of writing as merely personal, merely self-expression, and hopefully neurotic, because it lets us off the hook. If that's all it is, if it is not a true view of the world or, Heaven <u>forefend</u>, of a

> *"I happen to believe that at its best writing is considerably more and other than mere self-expression."*

USING THE SELECTION
from Second Words

1
What does Atwood mean by this bit of humor? [Writing is not a casual or easy process; Atwood believes it involves more than self-expression.]

2
philistine: narrow-minded; lacking in and indifferent to cultural and aesthetic values

3
solipsism: the theory that the self can be aware of nothing except its own experiences and states

4
John Donne, 1572–1631, was an English metaphysical poet who wrote, among other things, "Death Be Not Proud."

5
neurotic: characterized by anxiety

What does Atwood mean by this statement? [Writing involves more than just deciding to put thoughts on paper; writing is an intellectual process that takes skill.]

ANSWERS
Reader's Response
Answers will vary.

1. Students' writing journal entries should include specific examples from stories, songs, or movies to support their opinions agreeing or disagreeing with Atwood's essay.

2. Students should analyze at least three or four pieces of their own writing to discover the experiences that have become personal as a result of reading, watching, listening, or dreaming.

3. Students might say that Atwood's *more* and *other* include the skills she has acquired to become a good writer.

SELECTION AMENDMENT
Description of change: excerpted
Rationale: to focus on the concept of writing and thinking presented in this chapter

---

human nature of which we ourselves partake, we don't have to pay any serious attention to it. I happen to believe that at its best writing is considerably more and other than mere self-expression.

READER'S RESPONSE

1. Margaret Atwood usually writes fiction and poetry, and in this essay, she uses the term *writing* to mean creative writing. Do you agree with Atwood that most people think imaginative writing is "something anyone can do"? that it's always "based on personal experience"? or that it's something you "don't have to pay any serious attention to"? What is your own opinion about creative writing? Before you answer, have a group discussion, using specific examples of stories, songs, or movies. Then write your opinion in your journal.

2. Atwood says an experience becomes personal when you can imagine or identify with it, not necessarily live it. Look back at the last three or four pieces of writing you have done for school. What "experiences" played a part in the writing that became personal to you through reading, watching, listening, or imagining?

3. The last sentence says "at its best writing is considerably more and other than mere self-expression." Explain what you think Atwood means by the words *more* and *other* and whether you agree with her.

LOOKING AHEAD

In this chapter, you'll look at a general approach to writing that you can use with many types of writing. You will learn about some specific writing techniques, experiment with them, and decide how they work for you. As you read, write, and explore, remember that

- writing and thinking are inseparable
- the writing process isn't a set of rigid steps, a straight line, or the same for everyone every time
- topic, purpose, and audience always shape each other

THE "WHY" AND "HOW" OF WRITING

TEACHING STRATEGIES

Explain to students that the aims in writing are also known as purposes, and that the modes in writing are the tools they will use to achieve the aims. Briefly define each mode for students and give examples to explain how each mode achieves the aims (modes are narration, description, classification, and evaluation). To assess students' comprehension, ask them to give examples of writing prompts that could be used for the possible combinations of aims and modes:

1. expressive/narrative
2. persuasive/classificatory

☞

Aim—The "Why" of Writing

Writing gets things done. It has purpose. This is true not only for instruction manuals, congressional bills, news bulletins, and articles explaining medical discoveries, but for *any* writing: a cereal ad, a cartoon script, a secret entry in your journal, a note to a friend.

A person who puts words on a page is communicating, even if only privately in a personal journal. This active, purposeful aspect of writing is one to keep in mind as you write, because it unites you with all other writers and readers. It may appear that the reasons for writing are limitless. Still, no matter what the specific intent for a particular piece of writing (and each is different), it will usually fall within four basic purposes.

WHY PEOPLE WRITE	
To express themselves	To understand themselves better; to find some kind of meaning in their own lives
To inform, to explain, or to explore	To provide knowledge, facts, or data to other people; to make something clear or understandable; to investigate an idea or problem
To persuade	To convince other people to do something or believe something
To create literary works	To be creative with language; to say something in a unique way

Of course, communicating is as multifaceted as people are—that is, any one piece of writing can have more than one side, or purpose. In fact, you are more likely to combine purposes than to have one simple, pure purpose—like writing "Danger! Keep out!" For example, you may want to write a suspenseful short story and also explore the idea of loyalty. You may want to explain organic pesticides and at the same time urge people to use them.

? CRITICAL THINKING

Synthesis. Ask students to look through their literature books and find examples of each writing aim. Ask students to write explanations of the aims and to identify the modes used to achieve the aims.

COOPERATIVE LEARNING

Have students work together in groups of four to fill in titles or subjects for a chart that shows the possible combinations of the aims and modes. You can use the following example or create one of your own:

	Desc.	Narr.	Classif.	Eval.
Express				
Inform				
Persuade				
Create				

3. informative/descriptive
4. expressive/descriptive
5. informative/narrative

Close this lesson by discussing the following questions as a group:

1. What does all writing have in common?
   [a purpose]
2. Give an example of each writing aim. ■

Process—The "How" of Writing

If you view the writing process as a general way of thinking and writing that is common to all writers and all writing, you are right. But you also need to think of the writing process as something that is tremendously flexible, a process that can be individualized to fit your working style and whatever you are trying to write at the moment. That's the beauty of the writing process; once you've learned the basic thinking skills, strategies, and techniques, you can manipulate them to suit your own needs.

The following diagram illustrates the flexibility of the writing and thinking process. At any point in the process, you can stop and spend more time, go back to an earlier stage, or retrace your steps.

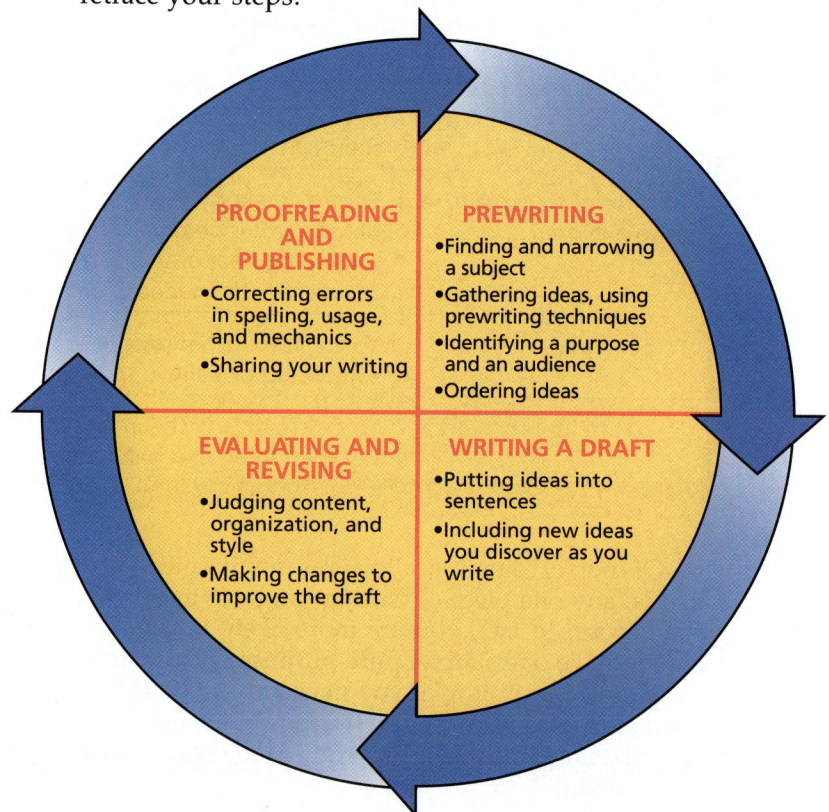

PROOFREADING AND PUBLISHING
- Correcting errors in spelling, usage, and mechanics
- Sharing your writing

PREWRITING
- Finding and narrowing a subject
- Gathering ideas, using prewriting techniques
- Identifying a purpose and an audience
- Ordering ideas

EVALUATING AND REVISING
- Judging content, organization, and style
- Making changes to improve the draft

WRITING A DRAFT
- Putting ideas into sentences
- Including new ideas you discover as you write

PREWRITING

OBJECTIVES

- To freewrite from a writing journal entry
- To use brainstorming and clustering as prewriting
- To ask the *5W-How?* questions to generate ideas
- To gather prewriting information by observing and imagining
- To read and listen for specific information
- To arrange the order of details

☞

Prewriting

Finding Ideas for Writing

All writers face two beginning challenges: coming up with a good idea and gathering the information needed to put that idea across. Like any art, however, writing is a very individual matter. A prewriting technique that works well for another writer may not work for you.

Still, over the years, many writers have found the following techniques useful. In the following pages you have the opportunity to test them and determine which ones feel natural to you and which ones fit well with certain writing tasks.

PREWRITING TECHNIQUES		
Writer's Journal	Recording personal experiences and observations	Page 22
Freewriting	Writing for a few minutes about whatever comes to mind	Pages 22–23
Brainstorming	Listing ideas as quickly as they come to mind	Pages 23–24
Clustering	Using circles and lines to show connections between ideas	Page 24
Asking Questions	Using the reporter's *5W-How?* questions	Page 25
Observing	Observing details of sight, sound, smell, taste, touch	Page 26
Imagining	Probing your imagination for ideas, often using a "What if?" approach	Page 27
Reading with a Focus	Reading to find specific information	Page 28
Listening with a Focus	Listening to find specific information	Page 28

PROGRAM MANAGER

PREWRITING

- **Heuristics** To help students generate ideas, see **Freewriting and Brainstorming** and **Clustering and the *5W-How?* Questions** in *Practicing the Writing Process*, pp. 1–2.

- **Analyzing** To help students analyze and organize ideas, see **Purpose, Audience, and Tone** and **Arranging Details in Order** in *Practicing the Writing Process*, pp. 3–4.

- **Instructional Support** See **Graphic Organizers 1** and **2.** For suggestions on how to tie the transparencies to instruction, review teacher's notes for transparencies in *Fine Art and Instructional Transparencies for Writing*, pp. 53, 55.

QUOTATION FOR THE DAY

"A moment's thinking is an hour in words." (Thomas Hood, 1799–1845, English poet and humorist)

Write the quotation on the chalkboard and ask students to freewrite for a few minutes about its meaning. Then remind students that thinking before writing will help them to gather ideas for their work. Explain that this lesson includes many prewriting tools and techniques writers use to collect ideas, gather information, and plan their work.

Ask students to name the procedures they would go through if they were going to build a home. Where would they get their ideas? How would they know what the house would look like both inside and out? Write responses on the chalkboard and lead students to understand that the process of writing a paper, like the process of building a home, has to have a creating and a planning stage before the product starts to take shape.

Keeping a Writer's Journal

A *writer's journal* can be kept in almost any form: a notebook, three-ring binder, scrapbook, file folder, or computer. You can use your journal to record your dreams and beliefs, your disappointments, your hopes, and your happy times. You can also include anything that catches your attention: newspaper and magazine clippings, quotations, song lyrics, poems, cartoons, or photos. Stocked with material that's important to you, your journal can become a great source for writing ideas. Here are some tips for keeping a writer's journal.

1. Find time each day to write a dated entry in your journal. You may set aside a specific time for writing, or you may carry your journal with you for spontaneous entries.
2. Concentrate on getting your thoughts down. Perfect grammar and punctuation aren't necessary for a journal entry.
3. Be imaginative. Create song lyrics and poetry; draw or sketch; recast an event in your life as a dramatic scene in a movie script. (Change the ending, if you wish!)
4. Jot down notes beside your entries, reacting to and reflecting on what you write and include. Why was this important? Why did you choose it?

AH, MY NEW JOURNAL!... FULL OF FRESH, CLEAN BLANK PAGES TO RECORD MY THOUGHTS AND FEELINGS ON.

HMMM...LET'S SEE, HOW DOES ONE BEGIN?...HOW DOES ONE ADDRESS ONE'S JOURNAL?

Hi there!

THIS MAY BE AWKWARD AT FIRST...

Kudzu by Doug Marlette. By permission of Doug Marlette and Creators Syndicate.

Freewriting

To *freewrite,* quickly write down your first thoughts on any given subject.

1. Write for three to five minutes without stopping.
2. Start with any topic or word—such as *pollution* or *diets* or *Shakespeare* or *treason.*

1. Journal writing helps writers to keep track of good ideas and to sharpen their powers of observation.
2. Freewriting lets writers' first ideas or feelings come forth.
3. Brainstorming helps to get a fresh approach to a subject and helps overcome writers' block.
4. Clustering helps writers see connections and patterns for organizing or expanding their writing.
5. Asking questions and observing helps writers view their subjects clearly and objectively.

☞

3. Write down any ideas, images, details, or associations that come into your head without worrying about grammar or punctuation.
4. If you become "stuck," just copy your last word until a fresh idea strikes, or write questions to yourself about why you're temporarily out of ideas.
5. As a variation, try *focused freewriting,* or *looping.* Select one word or phrase from your freewriting and use it as a starting point to "loop" to more writing.

HERE'S HOW

Special Olympics. National finals televised. Celebrities, etc. Started by whom? A good way for these kids to build achievement and self-esteem. It really works! I know this from last summer—volunteering there was the best experience of my life. Everyone came away a winner. I remember Kathy didn't walk until she was 5 (she's 10 now) but was in a race. When they put the ribbon around her neck, her head was high!

EXERCISE 1 ▶ **Freewriting from a Journal Entry**

Evaluate for completion.

If you don't keep a journal yet, start by answering one of these questions: *What new thing did I learn yesterday? Which of yesterday's experiences would I like to undo or do over, and why?* After writing your journal entry, select one word or topic from it as your subject for freewriting. Freewrite for three or four minutes.

Brainstorming

Brainstorming, which helps you generate a free flow of ideas on any given subject, can be used either to find a topic or to gather information. Although you can brainstorm alone, the process works even better with a partner or in a group.

1. Write down one specific subject or topic on your paper or on the chalkboard.

LESS-ADVANCED STUDENTS

Suggest to students that they work on developing their skills of observation by actually taking a picture of the place or event they wish to describe. This process will allow students to refer to the pictures when they are writing their descriptions. If students have cameras, suggest that they carry their cameras for a day and take pictures of events or scenes that would be interesting subjects for writing.

LEARNING STYLES

Auditory Learners. Ask auditory learners to freewrite by dictating their thoughts into a tape recorder. Later they can listen to what they have said and record their thoughts on paper.

Visual Learners. To help visual learners sort out clustering exercises, allow them to use different-colored markers for each new series of connecting ideas. This color-coding will allow students to use each group of colored ideas as the basis for a paragraph.

6. Imagining allows for exploring ideas more freely and encourages divergent thinking.
7. Both reading with a focus and listening with a focus help writers gain productive ideas and can give them a head start in the writing process.

Encourage students to try each prewriting technique, even though they may initially have a preference for a particular technique. Reinforce the idea that it is possible to use several techniques for one paper. Explain to students how the *5W-How?* questions are used in journalism to develop news stories. Suggest that students read the paper or watch a newscast to see how the questions are used to develop accurate, organized information.

2. Record every word or phrase that comes to mind. In a group, brainstorm out loud and ask one person to write down all responses.
3. Work quickly. Don't stop to evaluate your ideas; just continue until your ideas run out.

Clustering

Like brainstorming, *clustering* can help you make associations or break down a topic. But with clustering, you create a diagram that helps you discover relationships among ideas.

1. Write down a subject or topic on your paper and circle it.
2. Around the subject, quickly write down and circle all related ideas that come to mind. Draw lines connecting the new ideas either to your original subject or to one another.
3. Keep associating and connecting as long as you can.

Clustering is sometimes called *webbing* or *making connections*. Your finished cluster may not make perfect sense to someone else, but you'll understand your own connections.

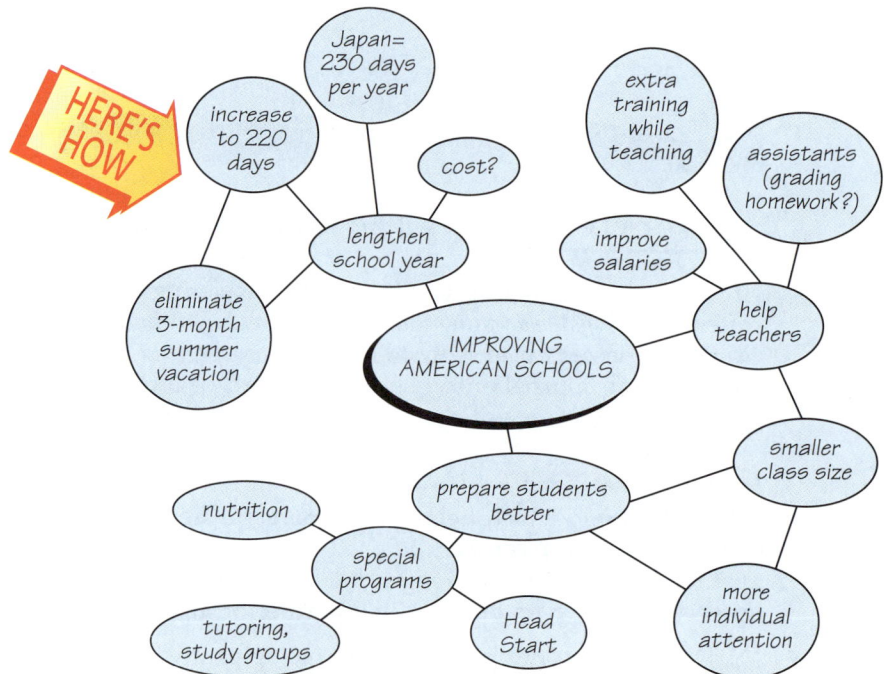

HERE'S HOW

Japan= 230 days per year
increase to 220 days
cost?
extra training while teaching
assistants (grading homework?)
lengthen school year
improve salaries
eliminate 3-month summer vacation
help teachers
IMPROVING AMERICAN SCHOOLS
smaller class size
nutrition
prepare students better
special programs
tutoring, study groups
Head Start
more individual attention

MEETING *individual* NEEDS

LEARNING STYLES

Kinetic Learners. When students are employing the looping technique, have them write each new starting point and loop on a separate card. After completing three loops, students should choose the card that focuses their ideas the best.

INTEGRATING THE LANGUAGE ARTS

Literature Link. Show students how writing journal entries can be adapted to learning about literature by giving students focused freewriting on words or phrases from particular works of literature. For example, suggest that students focus on Shakespeare's *Macbeth* by freewriting or looping on the topics of evil, fate, or morality.

Students can also apply literature to this lesson by allowing their imaginations and observations to place them in the literature and then to visualize what the characters are experiencing through the five senses. For example, ask students to pretend they are the mariner in *The Rime of the Ancient Mariner* by Samuel Taylor Coleridge. Ask students to freewrite by focusing on the sensory details that describe their environment after their crew has risen and is sailing the ship.

Discuss with students the chart on p. 19 to identify the purposes of writing. Stress that the aim, purpose, and tone work together, not independently, to create an essay. Therefore, if the purpose is to persuade, a writer must use a convincing tone.

When presenting **Arranging Ideas** on p. 35, ask students to engage in activities that will help them remember each type of order. For example, ask students to illustrate chronological order by writing a time line highlighting major events in their lives, or ask them to illustrate logical order by making two separate columns on a piece of paper, labeled *SIMILARITIES* and *DIFFERENCES*, to use in comparing themselves with a best friend.

☞

EXERCISE 2 ▶ Using Brainstorming and Clustering

Test the theory that two heads are better than one. Working with a partner, list as many ideas as you can about one of the following topics, or choose your own.

computers	nuclear power
favorite vacation spots	television comedians
national monuments	women athletes

Next, work together to choose a second topic for clustering, but work individually to create your clusters. Compare the two webs when you finish. Where did your minds travel similar paths? Where did they diverge?

Asking Questions

One of the best ways to gather information is to ask questions. But what questions? The reporter's *5W-How? questions* (*Who? What? Where? When? Why?* and *How?*) are a good place to start. Like many other prewriting techniques, this one is flexible. You don't have to use a question word if it doesn't apply to your topic, and you can use the same question word many times. The following questions about the topic "the history of the Academy Awards" are just some of the questions that are possible.

HERE'S HOW

WHO?	*Who began the Academy Awards? Who won the first awards for best actor, actress, and director? Who has won the most Academy Awards?*
WHAT?	*What are the significant changes in the awards over the years? What were some famous, or amusing, acceptance speeches?*
WHERE?	*Where were the first and last year's ceremonies held?*
WHEN?	*When is the deadline for nominations? When was the ceremony first televised?*
WHY?	*Why are the awards important to a winner's career? Why is the little golden statuette called "Oscar"?*
HOW?	*How are winners chosen?*

ANSWERS
Exercise 2

Students should work with partners to list ideas about topics. For example, computer ideas might include computers in classrooms, computers for artwork, computers to improve motivation in the classroom, computer time as a reward, learning basic word processing, beginning a series of computer classes at school, writing computer programs, playing computer games to learn new things, and playing computer games to improve hand-eye coordination.

COOPERATIVE LEARNING

Ask students to work in groups of four to brainstorm, cluster, and ask *5W-How?* questions about topics you have given them. Give each group a different topic and a large piece of paper. Ask group members to work together on the floor or in a large area to complete all three prewritings on these papers. After students have finished, display their work in the classroom and discuss how prewriting techniques can be used to plan different topics.

GUIDED PRACTICE

Guide students through as many of the prewriting techniques as you can. Demonstrate freewriting on the chalkboard; brainstorm with the class; use the overhead projector to do clustering; and probe world issues with "What if?" questions.

INDEPENDENT PRACTICE

Students will work independently to freewrite in writing journals for **Exercise 1** (p. 23), to observe and imagine using "What if?" questions in **Exercise 4** (p. 27), to read and listen for specific information in **Exercise 5** (p. 28), and to arrange order of details in **Exercise 6** (p. 36).

ANSWERS

Exercise 3

Students should ask the *5W-How?* questions and compare lists with peers.

CRITICAL THINKING

Synthesis. As students gather ideas by using "What if?" questions, ask them to expand on this approach by brainstorming for answers to another question—"Then what?"

EXERCISE 3   **Asking the *5W-How?* Questions**

Where will you be at this time next year? Since finding the right school or job may depend on asking the right questions, identify a particular university, college, training program, apprenticeship, or job and ask as many good *5W-How?* questions as you can. Compare your list with those of others.

Observing

Think about the best meal you've ever had. Can you remember the smell and taste of the food? Can you almost hear the background sounds? Can you picture who you were with? If you were going to write about that special event, you would need to bring all your senses into play—touch, sound, smell, taste, and sight.

Using all five of your senses will increase your ability to observe and improve your writing. Here are details recorded from a first snow-skiing experience.

HERE'S HOW

TOUCH:	softly falling snow on eyelashes; warmth of ski suit; tightly buckled boots; trembling hands grasping ski poles; face covered with snow after fall; chapped lips
SOUND:	whisper of snow under skis; moaning wind on mountain; ski pro shouting out instructions
SMELL:	sharp pine; wet clothes drying; coffee brewing in ski shack; crisp, fresh mountain air
TASTE:	waxy lip salve; buttery hot chocolate in front of fire
SIGHT:	mountains soaring above clouds; neon skiers streaking down slope; ski lifts dangling high above the ground

To assess **Exercises 1–6,** lead a class discussion of the answers. You may also want to ask a few students to write their answers for each exercise on overhead transparencies and to discuss the responses as a class.

Assess student comprehension by asking students to determine an appropriate audience and tone for the following subjects:

1. collecting baseball cards
2. teen runaways
3. the impact of video games on the current generation.

☞

Imagining

Who asks "What if?" questions? The scientist trying to develop a new cure asks, "What if we synthesized these compounds?" The scriptwriter asks, "What if a passenger falls off a cruise ship?" The store manager trying to attract more business asks, "What if we offered a preferred-customer bonus?"

Anyone trying to solve a problem or to create literary works needs to be imaginative. Asking ***"What if?" questions*** like the following ones can stimulate your imagination.

- *What if I could change the past?* (What if the Vietnam War hadn't happened? What if a woman had written all of Shakespeare's plays?)
- *What if something we take for granted were totally different?* (What if eating meat were against the law? What if all people could speak a common language?)

You can ask "What if?" questions about specific topics, too. Writing about the homeless, for example, you could ask, *What if the government paid people to house the homeless?*

EXERCISE 4 ▶   **Observing and Imagining**

Use careful observation along with your imagination to develop ideas about life among American Indians a hundred years ago. Begin by looking at the following photograph of a Sioux camp in South Dakota around 1880.

1. Identify three things you can tell about life in this Native American camp by looking at this picture.
2. What if you were one of the people in this picture? List at least ten things you might see, hear, feel, smell, or taste.

Ed Bodein (1879). From Collection of Lynda Abbott.

ANSWERS
Exercise 4

Answers will vary. Here are some possibilities:

1. All members of the camp had to work together; life was dependent on hunting and gathering; American Indians had to produce shelter that would shield them from harsh environments.

2. Students might say they would see mountains, horses, snow, trees; hear birds, running creeks, and rivers; feel pottery, firewood, and animal skins; smell food cooking and smoke; and taste freshly cooked meat, berries, vegetables, special dishes, and fresh water from streams or rivers.

3. What if I were there and was allowed to go on a hunting trip? What if the community was low on firewood and facing a terrible winter snowstorm? What if the community never had to work for their food again?

To reteach this lesson, show students writing samples and work with them to determine what prewriting techniques could have been used by the authors. Writing samples might include a student essay, letters to the editor, an advertisement, or a poem.

Close this lesson by asking students to describe an advantage of each prewriting technique. Then ask students to volunteer some of the questions writers use when addressing an audience. [Sample questions are given on p. 31.]

Cont. on p. 31

INTEGRATING THE LANGUAGE ARTS

Listening Link. To help students practice listening with a focus, have them listen to a famous speech or political debate. Then ask students questions to test their listening skills. Suggest that students take notes to remember key names, dates, and points.

Library Link. Suggest to students that a logical place to continue prewriting after freewriting is the library. Encourage students to verify or expand information by reading about their freewriting topics in the library.

TIMESAVER

To save time grading all six exercises for this lesson, ask students in groups of five to write answers on the chalkboard. This approach will allow you to monitor student progress; you may want to assign participation points to reward student involvement.

3. Imagine that the photograph on page 27 is the opening setting of a short story you're writing, and write three "What if?" questions about what might happen next.

Reading with a Focus

Since gathering information often involves reading, reading efficiently can save you both time and trouble. When you've found a possible source of information, keep the following tips in mind.

1. Preview the material by glancing through the table of contents, headings and subheadings, index, illustrations, and charts. Be alert for material related to your topic.
2. Skim until you find information about your topic; then read carefully. Take notes on main ideas and relevant details, and be sure to keep track of your sources.

Listening with a Focus

Think of all the ways you can *listen* to learn: videotapes and audiotapes, radio and television programs, conversations with experts, recordings on CD-ROM discs and other online sources, and live speeches and performances. To collect the details you need from these sources, prepare yourself for concentrated listening.

1. Because familiarity with your topic will make understanding easier, do some background investigation first.
2. Create a list of the main information you need to gather or questions you want to ask, and keep the list.
3. Take notes even when you are also recording, and plan your note-taking method so you aren't trying to write every word. Use phrases and abbreviations, and try circling or underlining key points to make them stand out.

☞ **REFERENCE NOTE:** For information on interviewing, see pages 1040–1042.

EXERCISE 5 ▶ **Reading and Listening for Specific Information**

According to some trend watchers, the yo-yo is enjoying a resurgence in popularity. When was it popular before? Do a little reading about amusement fads, and see if you can find answers to the following questions.

TEACHING *ANALYZING A SUBJECT*
Explain to students that they can use several prewriting techniques to help them determine if their subjects are too broad or too narrow. For example, if a student is clustering and cannot develop very many branching ideas, his or her subject is probably too narrow. If a student cannot stop branching, then his or her subject is

1. What was an amusement fad from the 1950s? from the 1920s?
2. What are two dance fads from the past, and when were they popular?
3. What's something that began as a fad but became part of the mainstream culture?

After reading about past fads, use listening to discover what's popular today. For the next few days, listen to the radio (perhaps call-in shows and National Public Radio), television (sitcoms, commercials, and "entertainment news"), and the conversations of students at your school. What fads are people following today? What might they be doing tomorrow? Compare your answers with those of classmates.

CRITICAL THINKING

Analyzing a Subject

You're told, "Write about what interests you." But maybe the interests that first occur to you—perhaps *dance*, *history*, *windsurfing*, or *movies*—are likely to be too broad for any paper, even a full-blown research report.

probably too broad. Encourage students to develop topics that are both timely and interesting for their intended audience. To guide students in this mini-lesson, narrow a topic on the chalkboard by using the technique in the textbook. Then allow students to try developing charts on their own to narrow a topic. Assess students' comprehension by asking volunteers to write their charts on the chalkboard. Close this lesson by asking students to explain how they know when they have adequately narrowed a topic. ⚡

CRITICAL THINKING

Evaluation. Give students copies of letters to the editor from a variety of newspapers. Ask students to analyze each letter to determine if the letter contains a topic that is too broad or too narrow, or a topic that is just right. Ask students to write their opinions and two supporting reasons.

In writing, your first step after deciding on a subject that interests you is usually *analyzing:* breaking the subject down into parts or aspects. This is necessary to develop a better understanding of the broad subject and to find a manageable topic for the length of the paper you plan. For example, if you were interested in the Supreme Court, you could analyze it to discover specific aspects of the Court you might write about.

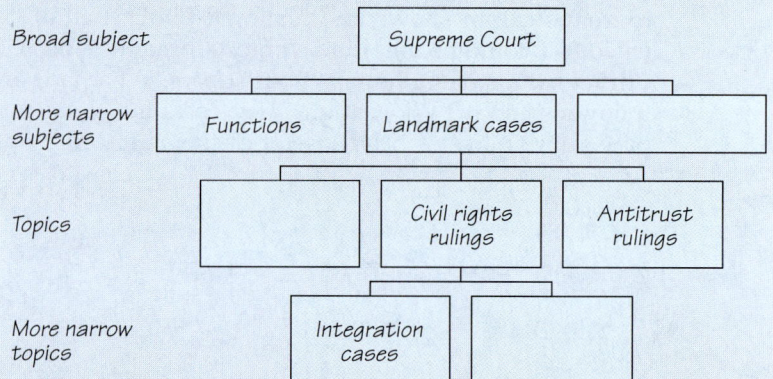

Broad subject	Supreme Court		
More narrow subjects	Functions	Landmark cases	
Topics		Civil rights rulings	Antitrust rulings
More narrow topics		Integration cases	

⚡ CRITICAL THINKING EXERCISE:
Analyzing Subjects and Topics

Practice your analytical thinking skills by working with a partner to answer the following questions. If your knowledge of the Supreme Court is limited, you may have to do some research.

1. You will notice empty "boxes" in the diagram. At every level of the analysis, there could be additional or different subdivisions. Under *civil rights rulings*, what topics could you add to *integration*? Under *landmark cases*, can you identify topics other than *civil rights* and *antitrust*?
2. What narrower aspect of the final topic, *landmark integration cases*, could you focus on?
3. Perform an entirely different analysis. Instead of *landmark cases*, analyze *functions* through all the levels shown, or think of another first-level subdivision and analyze it fully.

ANSWERS
Critical Thinking Exercise

1. Possible topics added to *integration* could be *affirmative action, busing,* or *equality in public school;* under *landmark cases* other topics could be *school funding, labor regulations,* and *minimum wage.*
2. Possibilities might include focusing on state-by-state cases or rulings of landmark cases and the explanations behind them.
3. One level under *functions* is *final rulings;* another first-level subdivision could be *history.*

Cont. from p. 28
ENRICHMENT

Ask students to try taking the same subject through two different writing techniques. You can use the following examples:

1. a recent movie you saw—looping and asking questions

2. school problems—freewriting and imagining

3. a sports figure that inspires you—reading with a focus and looping ■

Prewriting

Considering Purpose, Audience, and Tone

Purpose.   As you read earlier in this chapter, all writing generally has one of four *purposes* (page 19). But within those purposes, you have a broad range of writing forms to use, including the following possibilities.

MAIN PURPOSE	FORMS OF WRITING
Self-Expressive	Journal, letter, personal essay
Literary	Short story, poem, play
Expository: Informative, Explanatory, Exploratory	Science and social science writing, news articles, biography, autobiography, travel essay, industry newsletters, office memos
Persuasive	Persuasive essay, letter to the editor, advertisement, political speech

Audience.   To understand the importance of *audience,* think about yourself. You *are* an audience, and writers who want your attention must write in a style that grabs your interest, make their subject appealing to you, and use language that doesn't lose you. When you write, you have the same goal; asking yourself these questions will help accomplish that goal.

■ Who is my audience? (Am I writing for a teacher? a friend? classmates? younger students? newspaper readers?)
■ What does my audience already know about the topic?
■ What background or technical information do I need to provide? Do I need to define technical terms?
■ What topic, details, or approach will interest my audience?
■ What level of language should I use—formal or informal? Should I use simple or complex words and sentences?

CRITICAL THINKING
Evaluation. Ask students to evaluate three of their own textbooks by determining how well the publisher has appealed to its audience, shown its purposes, and used a tone to attract readers. Ask students to explain which textbook has accomplished its goal of satisfying an audience through purpose and tone.

TEACHING *ANALYZING PURPOSE, AUDIENCE, AND TONE*

Remind students that because vocabulary complexity and choice of topic should suit an audience, writers must know their audiences before they write. Students may need an additional explanation of tone. Read the explanation in the textbook and give examples of words that connote tone.

32 | WRITING HANDBOOK | *Process*

Tone. Words carry feeling as well as meaning. *Tone,* your attitude toward your topic and readers, comes through in the choice of words and details and even in the rhythm of your sentences. Many times you will want to have a knowledgeable, somewhat serious tone, especially if you are explaining something or trying to persuade. But tone is always tied to topic, purpose, and audience. There are many times when some other tone—funny, sympathetic, indignant—is called for.

◈ **INTEGRATING THE LANGUAGE ARTS**

Listening Link. Have each student make two columns on a piece of paper. Then ask them to listen to you or a student volunteer read the informative article and letter to the editor. As they listen, they should write details. Students should listen for key terms, dates, and points. After they finish, ask students questions about each article to determine comprehension.

⚡ **CRITICAL THINKING**

Analyzing Purpose, Audience, and Tone

The critical thinking skill of **analysis** is essential when you begin to plan any piece of writing. Unless you analyze your purpose, your audience, and your own attitude toward your topic, you will be unable to control the tone—and indirectly the effect—of what you are writing. To understand the difference tone can create, read the following examples, both of which are about the kudzu plant.

The first example is from an informative article in a national magazine with a general audience. Its tone is objective.

You can assess students' comprehension of the informative article and letter to the editor by discussing the following questions with the class:

1. Although the author of the informative article clearly realizes the harms of kudzu, what information is given to show that the attitude toward kudzu was not always negative? [The writer states that kudzu has lush green leaves and beautiful flowers, and it halts erosion.]

2. How does the tone of the informative article differ from that of the letter to the editor? [The informative article relies mostly on facts to present an objective opinion of the positive and negative aspects of kudzu; the letter to the editor is more passionate and conveys a desperate tone.]

Kudzu, a vine with lush green leaves and beautiful purple flowers that originated in Japan, first appeared in the U.S. at the 1876 Centennial Exposition in Philadelphia. It became popular in the Southeast in the 1930s, when soil conservationists urged farmers to plant it to halt erosion.

They succeeded—too well. Kudzu is now a common weed from East Texas to Florida and as far north as southeastern Pennsylvania. It can grow a foot a day and covers roadsides, trees, utility poles, and anything else in its path. Kudzu is tough, too: It takes repeated doses of strong and expensive herbicides to eradicate it.

"Scourge of the South May Be Heading North,"
National Geographic

The second example is a letter to the editor of a newspaper.

To the Editor:

Our city is being taken over by kudzu! Known to grow a foot a day, this jungle-like eyesore has become a real hazard. In many locations, it has taken over utility poles, threatening cables and electrical wires. In some cases, it shorts out or corrodes electrical utility boxes and transformers, disrupting power supplies and communications. It is also strangling trees that have grown in our city and surrounding farms and woods for decades.

As concerned citizens, we must find a way to stop the growth of this dangerous plant. Right now our only defense

COOPERATIVE LEARNING

You may want to have students work in groups of four to determine possible audiences and tones for the following subjects:

1. expressing your concerns about world hunger
2. telling how to plant trees to prevent erosion
3. describing the pleasures of skiing
4. discussing the growing number of teenagers who are illiterate

SELECTION AMENDMENT
Description of change: excerpted
Rationale: to focus on the concept of audience, purpose, and tone presented in this chapter

Close this lesson by asking students to explain the connection between purpose, audience, and tone. ⚡

⟨?⟩ CRITICAL THINKING

Synthesis. Ask students to read a newspaper to find a controversial issue about their neighborhood or town. Then have students each write an informative paragraph that introduces the controversial issue to a group of concerned citizens in a tone that will convince the group to support a position on the issue. Have each student then write a second paragraph in a tone that will convince the group not to support the position.

ANSWERS
Critical Thinking Exercise

Students will have successfully completed this exercise when each has used his or her knowledge of purpose, audience, and tone to write a passage called "The Attack of the Killer Kudzu." Students should have used the information they learned from reading about kudzu.

against this dangerous pest is repeated blasts of killer chemicals. Money should be given to our state university immediately so that researchers there can find a way to get rid of the kudzu safely and inexpensively before it takes over the entire city!

Albert Morelli

Here the writer is addressing a local audience and urging them to take action. The tone is more informal and decidedly anti-kudzu. Much of the same information is conveyed in the article and in the letter, but the differences in tone help to achieve very different effects.

⚡ CRITICAL THINKING EXERCISE:
Analyzing Purpose and Audience

You are a summer camp counselor entertaining your seventh-grade charges with a short before-bedtime campfire story, "The Attack of the Killer Kudzu." Analyze your purpose and audience, as well as your attitude toward the topic. Then write a passage from the story, controlling the tone to achieve the effect you want. Will you go for goose bumps?

SELECTION AMENDMENT
Description of change: excerpted
Rationale: to focus on the concept of audience, purpose, and tone presented in this chapter

Prewriting

Arranging Ideas

After collecting information for a paper, a moment of confusion isn't unusual. *Where will I begin? And besides that, where will I stop?* Deciding on the flow of your ideas is an important part of planning, and with practice it is a manageable one. The following chart shows four common methods of ordering information.

TYPE OF ORDER	DEFINITION	EXAMPLES
Chronological	Narration: Order that presents events as they happen in time	Story; narrative poem; explanation of a process; history; biography; drama
Spatial	Description: Order that describes objects according to location	Descriptions (near to far; left to right; top to bottom; etc.)
Importance	Evaluation: Order that gives details from least to most important or the reverse	Persuasive writing; description; explanations (main idea and supporting details); evaluative writing
Logical	Classification: Order that relates items and groups	Definitions; classifications; comparisons and contrasts

The specific order you use in a paper can depend on your subject as well as on earlier decisions you've made. For example, in the following paragraph, Jay Mathews is introducing his subject, math teacher Jaime Escalante, who was depicted in the film *Stand and Deliver*. He's writing for a general audience of readers, and he wants both to describe Escalante and to convey his charisma and style. Mathews uses order of importance.

CRITICAL THINKING

Evaluation. Ask students to read newspapers and magazines to find an example of each type of order. Then ask students to write a short paragraph explaining why that type of order is or is not the best type of order to use for that particular piece of writing.

MEETING *individual* NEEDS

STUDENTS WITH SPECIAL NEEDS

Students who have difficulty with motor skills and students with limited attention spans might find it tedious to write in a journal daily. Allowing such students to tape-record their writing journals will probably significantly increase their participation. If students have visual materials, such as drawings or photographs, to include in their writing journals, they could make scrapbooks to complement their tape recordings.

I noticed his hands first. His thick brown fingers swept the air when he lectured and ground chalk into the blackboard with an audible crack. He had a stocky build, a large square head with prominent jaw, and a widening bald spot covered with a few stray hairs, like a threadbare victory wreath on a Bolivian Caesar. He looked oddly like the school mascot, a gruff bulldog, and exuded a sense of mischief that made me and, I discovered later, many others want to keep a close eye on him.

Jay Mathews, *Escalante: The Best Teacher in America*

However, if Mathews were describing his subject for an audience who had to pick Escalante out in a crowd, he might have chosen spatial order (top to bottom) for his details and begun with the "widening bald spot covered with a few stray hairs." And if he wanted to relate how Escalante's students changed from hating math to liking it and winning scholarships, a natural order would have been chronological.

Often your material suggests a natural order, but you have choices, too. Decide what you want your writing to *do,* and create a sensible order to guide your readers smoothly through your ideas.

EXERCISE 6   **Arranging the Order of Details**

Like most people, you probably spend about one third of your time in your bedroom. First, brainstorm and list details of this familiar place. Next, arrange these details for a paragraph describing your room to someone who has never seen it. What order best does that job? Then, reorder your details for a paragraph telling how you clean up your room (or how you *would* if you did). What order did you use? Last, write both paragraphs.

Using Charts

Charts offer a visual way to arrange ideas, allowing you to display several pieces of information at once and map their relationships. Here's a chart one writer developed for a paper on the accomplishments of the Harlem Renaissance, a period of great artistic activity in America during the 1920s and 1930s.

HERE'S HOW

ART FORMS	REPRESENTATIVE ARTISTS	EXAMPLES OF WORK
Music	W. C. Handy	"St. Louis Blues" "Beale Street Blues"
	Fats Waller	"Honeysuckle Rose" "Ain't Misbehavin'"
Literature	Claude McKay	Harlem Shadows (poems) Home to Harlem (novel)
	Zora Neale Hurston	Their Eyes Were Watching God (novel) Mules and Men (folklore)
	Jean Toomer	Cane (poetic novel)
	Countee Cullen	Color (poems) Copper Sun (poems)
	Langston Hughes	The Weary Blues (poems) Not Without Laughter (novel)
Theater	Nobel Sissle and Eubie Blake	Shuffle Along
	Paul Robeson	roles in Shuffle Along, All God's Chillun Got Wings, and The Emperor Jones

Paul Robeson

Countee Cullen

Langston Hughes

Zora Neale Hurston

VISUAL CONNECTIONS
Exploring the Subject. Countee Cullen was only twenty-two years old when he published his first volume of poems, *Color,* in 1925. Cullen's lyric poetry, rich in imagination and intellectual content, made him one of the major poets of twentieth-century America.

Langston Hughes brought his wide traveling background and great talent to his poetry. Hughes, having lived in Mexico, Africa, and Europe, combined his cosmopolitan outlook with his personal feelings to produce deeply moving verses about racial pride.

Paul Robeson was a singer, actor, and political activist who performed on the stage and on radio and made many motion pictures and phonograph records. He gained international fame for his performances in such plays as *Othello* and *The Emperor Jones.*

Zora Neale Hurston was a prominent writer, and her works were widely published in the 1930s. Though largely forgotten at the time of her death, she is now recognized as an important interpreter of the African American experience.

TEACHING *CLASSIFYING* *INFORMATION*

Teach this lesson by stressing to students that classifying information is one form of organization. Explain that classifying information for writing is like classifying students by grade level. Working with the class, classify information on the chalkboard to guide students in their thinking. Classify music by

---

A paper answering the question "What factors helped to nurture the Harlem Renaissance?" might have used a fishbone chart showing causes and results.

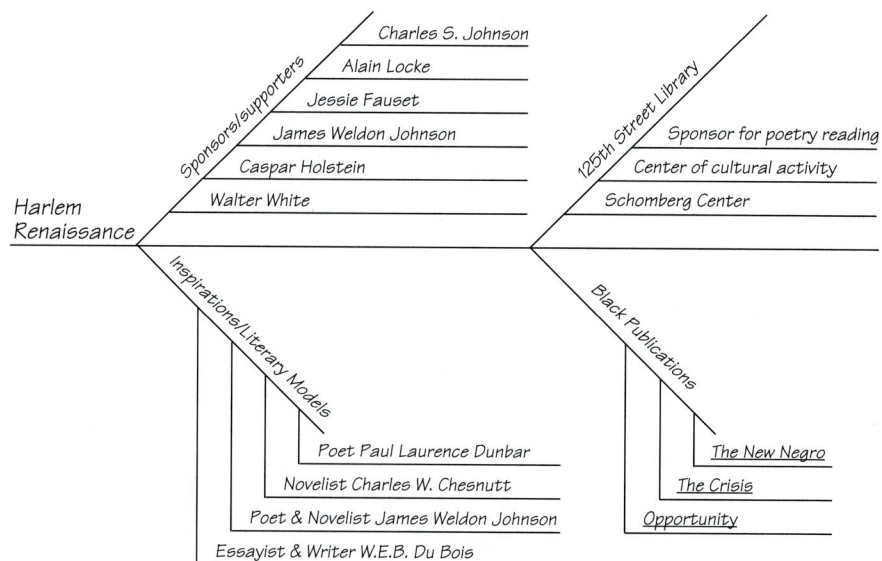

MEETING *individual* NEEDS

LEARNING STYLES

Visual Learners. Ask visual learners to classify ideas and details by grouping like ideas together in boxes or circles on their papers.

COOPERATIVE LEARNING

Adapt the critical thinking exercise to a cooperative learning activity by copying the notes about diamonds on paper and then cutting the notes apart. Arrange students in groups of three and give each group the strips of information and two envelopes. Ask students to put the appropriate strips that answer question 1 in an envelope marked *1* and appropriate strips that answer question 2 in an envelope marked *2*. After students have finished, work together as a class to discuss questions 3 and 4.

⚡ **CRITICAL THINKING**

Classifying Information

For many types of charts, you group together ideas or details that are similar in some way: you *classify* your information. The following questions are useful when you attempt to classify material.

- Which items have something in common? What heading describes this common trait?
- Are any items subdivisions of other items? Which ones?
- Are any items left over? Should a new heading be created for them? Should they be discarded?

types and musicians, classify sports by rules and regulations, or classify television shows by audiences. Assess students' comprehension by discussing the critical thinking exercise as a group. Close this lesson by asking students to explain three advantages to classifying information by grouping ideas and details that are similar.

CRITICAL THINKING EXERCISE:
Classifying Information

Read these notes for a paper on diamonds, looking for similarities among the items. Then answer the questions that follow.

a. Used for rings, earrings, bracelets, pins, and necklaces
b. Hardest material found in the natural world
c. Most diamonds sold at monthly "sights"
d. Koh-i-noor diamond once possessed by Indian and Persian rulers; now one of England's crown jewels
e. Top mining nations: Australia, Botswana, the former Soviet Union, Zaire
f. Doctors use diamond-edged knives during surgery
g. Found in meteorites from space
h. Minerals formed from carbon within igneous rock
i. Found in subsurface rock formations called "pipes"
j. Hope Diamond: world's largest blue diamond on view in Washington, D.C., at Smithsonian Institution
k. Jewelers use diamonds to cut other gem stones
l. Uncut stones used in automobile and airplane manufacturing and electronics
m. Found in river gravel and coastal sand dunes
n. Most form about 100 miles beneath the earth's surface
o. Cullinan Diamond largest single rough diamond ever found: 1905, in South Africa; weighed 3,106 carats
p. Diamond-studded rotary bits used to drill oil wells and bore tunnels in solid rock

1. One obvious heading for items in the list is *Uses*. Which items fall under this heading?
2. Decide on at least two other classifications for items in the list, and create a simple three-column chart that includes your headings as well as *Uses*.
3. *Uses* can include other classifications, or subheadings. What are they? Rearrange, or rechart, the *Uses* column to show the new subgroupings and their items visually.
4. Compare your charting with other students' work. Did you use the same classifications? Are your charts visually alike or different? What, if any, items did not fit into your classifications?

ANSWERS
Critical Thinking Exercise

1. Items under *Uses* are a, f, k, l, p
2. Answers will vary. Here is a possibility:

Uses	Famous Diamonds	Geological Info
a f k l p	d j o	b g h i n

3. The two possible subgroupings are ornamental uses and utilitarian uses.
4. You may want students to share their responses with the class so you can discuss any questions or problems they may have had.

WRITING A FIRST DRAFT

OBJECTIVE

- To use given prewriting notes to write a first draft

TEACHING THE LESSON

After a volunteer reads the introductory paragraphs of this lesson, tell students that they need to write first drafts using techniques that work best for them. Emphasize that this stage of the writing process is a first draft and can be changed later if students decide to include additional details or to take details out.

PROGRAM MANAGER

WRITING YOUR FIRST DRAFT

- **Instructional Support** For suggestions on developing prewriting notes into a first draft, see **Writing a First Draft** in *Practicing the Writing Process,* p. 5.

QUOTATION FOR THE DAY

"I'm always in a dither when starting a novel—that's the worst time. It's like going to the dentist, because you do make a kind of appointment with yourself." (Sir Kingsley Amis, 1922–1995, English novelist)

Share the quotation with the class as students begin writing their first drafts. Remind them that just as a dentist appointment sometimes requires a follow-up visit, a first draft is not the finished product.

MEETING *individual* NEEDS

LESS-ADVANCED STUDENTS

Explain that transitions tie sentences back to the topic sentence and show how these sentences are related to the controlling idea. Share the following list with students so that they can use it to complete **Exercise 7:**

continued on next page

Writing a First Draft

A first draft is simply a way to get your thoughts down on paper. Professional writers usually write several drafts; they add new ideas, delete weak details, rearrange information, and improve wording until they are satisfied with their work.

As you write your first draft, keep these thoughts in mind.

- Follow your prewriting plan, but don't hesitate to include additional thoughts or details that occur to you.
- Write freely, but try to present your ideas clearly.
- Don't overedit. You can evaluate, revise, and proofread later.

Here is a draft of a short paper about genealogy.

The British royal family can trace its ancestors back through fifty generations and nearly twelve hundred years. Genealogists warn that it is almost impossible for most people to track down their family histories very far. They also say that each generation's number of direct ancestors--parents, grandparents, great-grandparents, and so on--doubles. And think about when relatives have remarried and started a second set of kids. Over a time span of thirty generations, everyone has more than one billion ancestors. [check number] It can get complicated!

If you are going to take on the job of tracing your inheritance [right word?], genealogists suggests that you begin with public records. These can be birth, death, and marriage registrations. You can also obtain what you need to know from census returns, wills, and parish registers. [something else?] A great deal of family history can usually be uncovered just by talking with older people.

Demonstrate how to write a first draft of a paragraph by analyzing the paragraph about genealogy on p. 40.

Students will work independently to write a first draft of their own essays for **Exercise 7.**

Close this lesson by discussing the following questions as a class:

1. What should not be your main concern when writing a first draft?
2. What are the purposes of writing a first draft? ■

Writing a First Draft **41**

1. To Show Order
   first, second, then, next, finally
2. To Add Details
   also, in addition, another
3. To Introduce Illustration
   for example, for instance
4. To Show Conclusion
   so, thus, therefore

TECHNOLOGY TIP

Remind students that it isn't necessary to know in advance which words and sentences they want to mark for later revision. They can highlight text as they read it on the screen and click on the feature (boldface, italics, etc.) they wish to use to mark the text for later revision.

ANSWERS
Exercise 7

Answers will vary. Here is a possibility:

Today we register births, marriages, and other important events by using government documents. Before people kept documents, they passed down genealogical information by word of mouth, or oral history. Oral family histories have traditionally fostered family pride and have helped establish inheritance claims. The longest oral history known, seventy generations, is told by Indonesians living on an island off the coast of Sumatra. In Africa some Gambian tribes have *griots*—old men who memorize centuries of clan histories. Oral tradition is still alive and well in some countries; for example, oral history is still used by some African, Indonesian, and Pacific Island tribes.

EXERCISE 7 ▶ **Writing a First Draft**

Using the following prewriting notes, write another paragraph concerning genealogy, adding or dropping details as needed. Arrange the information and then start drafting.

Before written records many peoples kept track of ancestry through oral history

In Africa some Gambian tribes have *griots*—old men who memorize centuries of clan histories

Oral family histories fostered family pride, established inheritance claims

Longest oral history known (seventy generations) told by Indonesian living on an island off coast of Sumatra

Ancient Scandinavians, Irish, Scots, and Welsh kept oral histories (bards or storytellers)

Some African, Indonesian, and Pacific Island tribes still use oral history

Late 1960s, Alex Haley (*Roots*) traced his African ancestry to 1700s—consulted a *griot*

Recently, a Polynesian chieftain recited 34-generation history, proving claim to a piece of territory—took three days!

COMPUTER NOTE: When you're writing a draft, use boldface, italic, or underline styling or a different color to mark words and sentences you plan to replace or revise later.

EVALUATING AND REVISING

OBJECTIVE

- To evaluate and revise a first draft

TEACHING THE LESSON

Because students will spend most of this lesson working in groups to evaluate writing models and their own writing, stress the importance of including constructive comments in evaluations. Post the writing etiquette rules from the textbook and add any others you feel are needed.

PROGRAM MANAGER

EVALUATING AND REVISING

- **Reinforcement/Reteaching** See **Revision Transparencies 1** and **2.** For suggestions on how to tie the transparencies to instruction, review teacher's notes in *Fine Art and Instructional Transparencies for Writing,* pp. 95, 97.

- **Ongoing Assessment** To help students apply peer evaluation techniques and identify four ways to revise, see **Evaluating a Peer; Revising: Adding and Cutting;** and **Revising: Replacing and Reordering** in *Practicing the Writing Process,* pp. 6–8.

- **Assessment/Reflection** To assess student work and evaluate progress, see **Portfolio Forms** in *Portfolio Assessment,* pp. 5–21.

QUOTATION FOR THE DAY

"A work of art is not a matter of thinking beautiful thoughts or experiencing tender emotions (though those are its raw materials) but of intelligence, skill, taste, proportion, knowledge, discipline and industry; especially discipline." (Evelyn Waugh, 1903–1966, English novelist, travel writer, and biographer)

Ask students in small groups to complete the sentence, "A disciplined writer is someone who . . ." Explain that

continued on next page

Evaluating and Revising

Although closely connected, *evaluating* and *revising* are two separate steps within the writing process. First you judge what can be improved, and then you execute needed changes.

Evaluating

Since evaluating your writing is one of the most important steps in the writing process, don't allow yourself to cut corners. To evaluate, you must look critically at what you have written. Are you saying what you mean to say? Will your audience understand it? Will it accomplish your purpose?

Self-Evaluation.   It's never easy to evaluate your own work objectively, but the following techniques will help.

TIPS FOR SELF-EVALUATION

1. **Reading Carefully.** Read your draft several times, with a different purpose in mind each time. Read first for *content* (what is said), then for *organization* (arrangement of ideas), and finally for *style* (the way you use words and sentences).
2. **Listening Carefully.** Read your paper aloud, listening for confusing statements and awkward wording. Besides forcing you to slow down and pay attention to each word, reading aloud gives you a good sense of your paper's flow, its movement from sentence to sentence and idea to idea.
3. **Taking Time.** Gain some distance from your writing by setting it aside for awhile and going back to it later. This will help you see it fresh, and you will be more objective.

Peer Evaluation.   It's often helpful to have a classmate or a group of peers read your draft and comment on it; others may see strengths and weaknesses in your writing that you miss. In peer evaluation, you benefit both from receiving evaluations of your work and from evaluating the work of others. The following guidelines will help you in both roles.

To model evaluation and revision for students, discuss the sample paragraphs on p. 45 with the class. Point out to students where the writer has made evaluations and decided to add, cut, replace, or reorder information. Discuss why the changes are an improvement in the writing.

Students should work independently to evaluate and revise the paragraphs they have written for **Exercise 7.** Students should refer to the **Guidelines for Evaluating and Revising** chart on p. 44.

Assess comprehension of evaluation and revision by asking students to label their changes *add, cut, replace,* or *reorder* in the right margin next to their revisions. This procedure will allow you to see readily what

☛

PEER-EVALUATION GUIDELINES

Guidelines for the Writer
1. Tell your evaluator your concerns. Where do you think you need the most help?
2. Accept the evaluator's comments gracefully, without becoming defensive or argumentative.

Guidelines for the Evaluator
1. Point out strengths as well as weaknesses.
2. Offer specific, positive solutions to the problems you identify. A criticism without a suggestion for a remedy may leave a writer feeling lost.
3. Be sensitive to the writer's feelings. It's true that it's not *what* you say as much as *how* you say it.
4. Focus your comments on content, organization, and style. Because proofreading comes later, ignore mechanical errors, such as spelling and punctuation, unless they interfere with your understanding.

Luann reprinted by permission of United Feature Syndicate, Inc.

Revising

Every problem you have uncovered in the evaluation stage can be corrected by applying one or more of four basic revising techniques: **add, cut, replace,** and **reorder.** This simplicity is good to keep in mind, because revision—let's be honest—is a tough part of writing for many people.

The following chart gives you some overall guidelines for evaluating and revising your writing using the four revision techniques. Other chapters will supply charts for particular types of writing.

evaluation and revision are essential steps to disciplined writers.

MEETING *individual* NEEDS

LESS-ADVANCED STUDENTS
Give students an opportunity to evaluate and revise in a different way. Ask students to color-code revision strategies by using a different colored marker for each strategy. For example, students could circle with a blue marker all words that are to be deleted.

TECHNOLOGY TIP
Ask students to evaluate and revise their essays on computers at home or school. Students should focus on using the cut, copy, and paste functions.

INTEGRATING THE LANGUAGE ARTS
Listening Link. Though reading their own papers to themselves might help, students might also benefit from hearing their work read aloud by peers.

43

changes were made and if the changes have improved the essay.

Ask students to discuss the advantages of peer evaluation and the importance of revision and evaluation to the writing process.

EXTENSION

Give students an opportunity to apply their evaluating and revising skills to journalism. Explain to students that often news stories must be cut due to space constraints, and the editor's job is to add, cut, replace, or reorder information without losing too much content. Ask students to reduce a newspaper article by half by using the evaluating and

![icon] **COOPERATIVE LEARNING**

Students could work together in groups of four to complete peer evaluations. Each student in each group would be responsible for evaluating each group member's paper. To add organization to this activity, ask that each group member use the following questions:

1. Name two writing strengths in this paragraph.
2. Name two writing weaknesses in this paragraph.
3. What solutions can you offer for the writing weaknesses?
4. Do you see any places where the writer should have added, cut, replaced, or reordered information? If so, specify the location and give a suggestion for improvement.
5. What one word or phrase do you remember most? (This choice is often a good selection for a title.)

GUIDELINES FOR EVALUATING AND REVISING

EVALUATION GUIDE	REVISION TECHNIQUE
CONTENT	
1. Is the writing interesting?	**Add** examples, an anecdote, dialogue, and additional details. **Cut** or **replace** repetitious or boring details.
2. Does the writing achieve the intended purpose?	**Add** explanations, descriptive details, arguments, or narrative details.
3. Are ideas given sufficient support?	**Add** more details, facts, and examples to support your topic.
4. Are all ideas or details related to the topic or main idea?	**Cut** irrelevant or distracting information.
5. Are unfamiliar terms explained or defined?	**Add** definitions or other explanations of unfamiliar terms. **Replace** unfamiliar terms with familiar ones.
ORGANIZATION	
6. Are ideas and details arranged in the most effective order?	**Reorder** ideas and details to make the meaning clear.
7. Are connections between ideas and sentences logical and clear?	**Add** transition words or phrases (such as *therefore, for example,* and *because*) or sentences to link ideas.
STYLE	
8. Is the meaning clear?	**Replace** vague or unclear wording with precise words and phrases.
9. Is the writing style fresh and interesting?	**Cut** clichés, or **replace** with specific details and fresh comparisons.
10. Is the level of language appropriate for the audience and purpose?	**Replace** formal words with more conversational words and phrases to create an informal tone. To create a more formal tone, **replace** slang, contractions, and colloquial language.
11. Do sentences read smoothly?	**Reorder** to vary sentence beginnings. Reword to vary sentence structure.

The following paragraphs on genealogy illustrate the use of all four revision techniques. You may want to check the chart of Symbols for Revising and Proofreading on page 53 to understand the changes. Notice that the questions noted in the first draft (page 40) are answered here.

Although
The British royal family can trace its   **add**

ancestors back through fifty-three

generations and fifteen hundred years.   **add**

Genealogists warn that it is almost im-

possible for most people to track down their

(much past three or four generations)
family histories very far. They also say that   **replace**

each generation's number of direct

ancestors--parents, grandparents, great-

grandparents, and so on--doubles. And   **cut**

This is especially true
think about when relatives have remarried   **replace/reorder**

children
and started a second set of kids. Over a time   **replace/cut**

span of thirty generations, everyone has

two
more than one billion ancestors. [check   **replace/cut**

number] It can get complicated!

planning to
If you are going to take on the job of   **replace**

e   *ancestry*
tracing your inheritance [right word?],   **replace**

genealogists suggests that you begin with   **cut**

These
public records. This can be birth, death,   **replace**

and marriage registrations. You can also

obtain what you need to know from census

(military records.)
returns, wills, and parish registers,   **reorder/add**

[something else?] A great deal of family   **cut**

history can usually be uncovered just by

members of your family
talking with older people.   **replace**

CRITICAL THINKING

Evaluation. Ask each student to write a paragraph evaluating his or her performance up to the evaluation and revision steps on the new paragraphs about genealogy. Ask students to include strengths they encountered in their writing when evaluating and revising and the weaknesses they revised. Ask students to describe what they will do to avoid the same weaknesses the next time they write.

TEACHING *REFLECTING ON YOUR WRITING*

Tell students that improvement in writing is a slow process and that growth can sometimes only be seen over a long period. The portfolio is a means whereby they will be able to look back over months of work to see their growth. Also tell students that reflections are ways of becoming aware of

Many high school students find it real hard to choose a college major. This problem should not have no affect on a student's decision to attend college, however. Tanya and her teacher, Mrs. Jackson, discussed her feelings about Junior College. Tanya said, "My parents and me agree that this would be a good way to save on tuition while I contemplate my future and in the meantime, I will be completing my first two years of college. Mrs. Jackson said that Tanya had chose a good option.

Publishing

Publishing is often just a matter of sharing your writing with an audience beyond your teacher. Here are a few ideas.

- Submit an article to your school newspaper or magazine.
- Write a letter to the editor of your local newspaper.
- Submit an essay, poem, or short story to a magazine. Check professional writers' publications, such as the current year's *Writer's Market*, for magazines, journals, and publishers that are interested in receiving material from new writers.
- Look for writing contests to enter. Some offer prizes; others will publish your writing.
- Mail or e-mail an essay on a contemporary subject to governmental representatives.
- Organize a forum, presenting class essays as speeches.

ANSWERS
Exercise 8

Many high school students find it hard to choose a college major. This problem should not affect a student's decision to attend college, however. Tanya and her teacher, Mrs. Jackson, discussed her feelings about junior college. Tanya said, "My parents and I agree that this would be a good way to save on tuition while I contemplate my future; in the meantime, I will be completing my first two years of college." Mrs. Jackson said that Tanya had chosen a good option.

MEETING *individual* NEEDS

AT-RISK STUDENTS

To help students accomplish their publishing goals, ask that they publish their essays by reading them to younger students, or by asking their friends and relatives to attend a reading of essays held in your classroom, in the auditorium, or outdoors. This activity should help students become more confident in their writing and allow them to experience success through writing.

Reflecting on Your Writing

Sharing your writing with others is often rewarding, but taking the time to reflect on your writing by yourself can be just as important. One way to make reflection a regular part of your writing process is to create a portfolio.

A **portfolio** is a collection that reflects the diversity of your writing skills and interests. As you complete writing assignments throughout the year, you can build your portfolio by selecting pieces to add to it. You may also use the reflecting questions in each chapter to spur thoughts about how you what they've learned. The more effort they put into writing reflections, the more useful the reflections will be.

You can have students address all of the questions in the **Critical Thinking Exercise** individually, or you can have them answer the questions in one or two paragraphs. The form of the reflection is less important than its content.

developed each piece of writing. Remember to date each portfolio selection, so that you and other people reading your work can monitor your progress over time.

Your portfolio will function as a useful resource to draw upon when you need writing samples for college or job applications. It should also help you improve your writing skills. One of the challenges of being a writer is learning how to evaluate your work without being overly critical. By learning how to assess your writing as an objective but sympathetic observer, you can become an effective editor of your own work.

When you make writing a regular habit, it resembles a cycle, with the beginning of one project following the completion of another. If you move from one assignment to another without thinking about your writing process, you may repeat old patterns that could be improved. The beauty and the burden of writing is that you can endlessly tinker with a poem, short story, or essay—deleting a phrase here, adding a metaphor there. By making reflection a part of the writing process, you can focus your energy on areas that really need improvement and learn when to recognize that something is good enough to leave alone.

CRITICAL THINKING EXERCISE:
Reflecting on Your Writing

Reread some of your recent writing, including previous writing assignments. Then, reflect on your writing process by answering the following questions. Date your answers and save them in your portfolio.

1. Which part of the writing process generally goes most smoothly for you? Which part do you find the most challenging? Why?
2. Do you notice any patterns in your writing? Which types of writing do you most enjoy doing?
3. What have you discovered about yourself by reflecting on your writing? How would you describe your general attitude toward the process of writing?

TEACHING NOTE

If students have written reflections on their writing in the past, and if these are available in their portfolios, ask them to reread some of their previous reflections. Ask them to jot down areas in which they notice the greatest improvement in their writing.

As students write their present reflections, ask them to pay particular attention to the third question and to give it special thought. Then ask them to formulate a goal for themselves, with regard to their writing, for the current school year. They can write the goal in a place in their portfolios where they are most likely to see it from time to time.

ANSWERS
Critical Thinking Exercise
Answers will vary.

1. Students should use the items that are used in the textbook for the stages of the writing process. They should give specific reasons why they find a particular part challenging.
2. Students should focus on patterns that deal with actual writing, not with patterns of errors.
3. Students should give specific details about what they have discovered about themselves and about their general attitude toward the writing process.

As you make a final copy of your paper for publication, follow these guidelines for a clean, professional look.

GUIDELINES FOR MANUSCRIPT FORM

1. Use only one side of a sheet of paper.
2. Write in blue or black ink, or type.
3. If you write, do not skip lines. If you type, double-space the lines.
4. Leave margins of about one inch at the top, sides, and bottom of a page.
5. Indent the first line of each paragraph.
6. Number all pages (except the first page) in the upper right-hand corner, about one-half inch from the top.
7. All pages should be neat and legible. You may make a few corrections with correction fluid, but they should be barely noticeable.
8. Follow your teacher's instructions for placement of your name, the date, your class, and the title of your paper.

EXERCISE 9 **Publishing Your Writing**

With your classmates, brainstorm for other publishing ideas. Work in teams to follow up on each suggestion. For example, find and list names and addresses of potential publishers, types of materials accepted, manuscript requirements, deadlines, and awards. As you compile information, you might want to use spreadsheet software to create a database for students seeking publishing information. You may share this database with students in other writing classes.

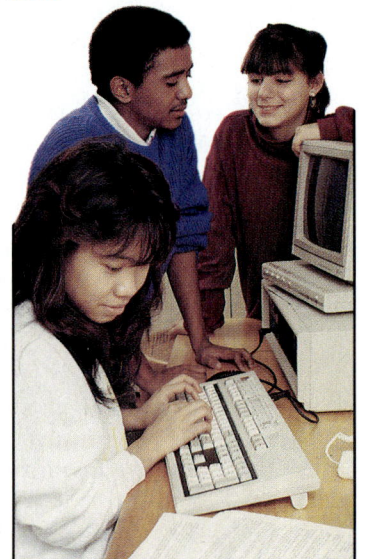

Close this lesson by discussing the following questions as a class:

1. Which proofreading guidelines were most helpful to you? Explain.

2. When you proofread, what type of errors are you mainly looking for? [errors in grammar, usage, and mechanics]

3. What types of writing do the questions under **Guidelines for Proofreading** apply to? [almost any type of writing] ■

SYMBOLS FOR REVISING AND PROOFREADING

SYMBOL	EXAMPLE	MEANING OF SYMBOL
cap ≡	805 Linden avenue	Capitalize a lowercase letter.
lc /	the First of May	Lowercase a capital letter.
∧	one my friends (of)	Insert a missing word, letter, or punctuation mark.
∧	appear (a)	Change a letter.
⌐	at the beginning (in)	Replace a word.
ℓ	Give me a a number	Leave out a word, letter, or punctuation mark.
⌒	a misstake	Leave out and close up.
⌒	a touch down	Close up space.
∩	beleive	Change the order of letters.
tr	He walked (slowly) forward.	Transfer the circled words. (Write (tr) in nearby margin.)
¶	¶"Yes," she answered.	Begin a new paragraph.
⊙	Follow me⊙	Add a period.
∧	Oh, not now!	Add a comma.
#	upper atmosphere	Add a space.
⊙	the following items⊙	Add a colon.
∧	Columbus, Ohio; Orlando, Florida and Seattle, Washington	Add a semicolon.
=	one=third portion	Add a hyphen.
∨	Juans idea	Add an apostrophe.
stet	A faster method	Keep the crossed-out material. (Write (stet) in nearby margin.)

A DIFFERENT APPROACH

You may want to invite local writers, newspaper reporters or editors, or television anchorpersons to speak individually or as a panel on their writing and publishing experiences. Prior to the guest experts' visit, students might collaborate in groups of three or four to brainstorm for questions tailored to the visitors' occupations. The groups should take turns asking questions.

Groups should also brainstorm and choose unique ways to publish what they learn. For example, one group might videotape the interview for other classes; others might write a synopsis to report to the school board or local newspaper, present a slide presentation at a school assembly, or take photos and write captions for a bulletin board display.

**EXPLORING THE
WRITING PROCESS
OBJECTIVE**

• To explore the writing process

EXPLORING THE WRITING PROCESS

Teaching Strategies

Discuss proper interviewing techniques with students before they speak with a professional. Suggest that students consider the following advice to ensure smooth interviews:

1. Call before visiting to set up a time that is convenient for your subject.
2. Explain to your interview subject why you wish to interview him or her.
3. Prepare to record the interview in some way—through note taking or a tape recorder. If you use a tape recorder, get permission beforehand.

COOPERATIVE LEARNING

If the equipment is available, suggest that students work in pairs to produce videotapes of their interviews that include introductions of the guest speakers by their student interviewers.

GUIDELINES

Suggest that each student include the interviewee's name, place of business, and job title in the notes that he or she shares with classmates.

MAKING CONNECTIONS

EXPLORING THE WRITING PROCESS

What would you like to be doing five or ten years from now? Will you be writing? You may be surprised at the answer! Professional writers and editors are not the only ones who spend the majority of their day composing. One research scientist estimates that he spends 30 percent of his time doing experiments and 70 percent writing letters, grant proposals, reports, and articles.

To explore the importance of writing, find someone working in a profession you're considering. Ask him or her the questions that follow. Take notes on the answers, and share your findings with classmates. Is there writing in your future?

What types of writing do you do?
Do you make lists? write memos?
Do you take notes in meetings? while you're on the telephone?
Do you write up proposals? estimates? bills? receipts? diagnoses? summaries? reports? messages?
What writing technique that you learned in school or have developed is most helpful to you now?

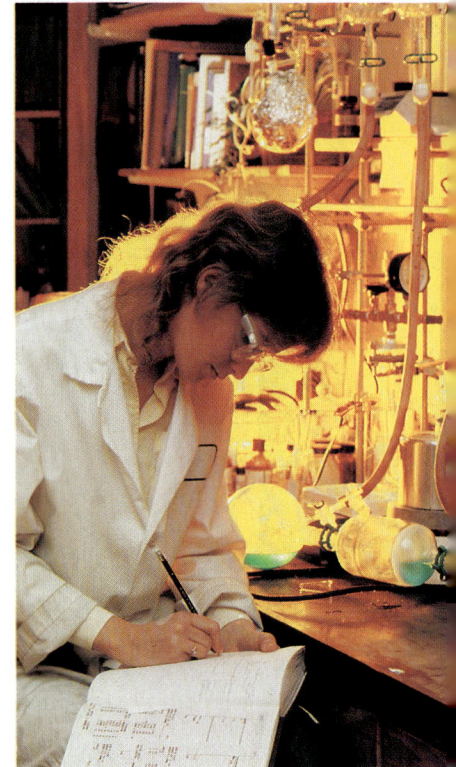

WRITING AND COMPUTERS
OBJECTIVES

- To research and deliver an oral report
- To create a multimedia project

WRITING AND COMPUTERS

Multimedia Projects

The Wizard of Oz was a multimedia pioneer. In the film, although he's really a kind man, he hides behind a curtain and uses a machine to create sound and visual effects to present himself as "the great and powerful Oz," a frightening apparition. Even after his hiding place is revealed, the Wizard tries to maintain the illusion. He hopes Dorothy and her friends will think it is the apparition that orders them to "pay no attention to that man behind the curtain." They are no longer intimidated, though, because they can see that he, the real speaker, is just a timid man. Stripped of special effects, his words cannot frighten them.

The Wizard of Oz would have found many uses for today's computers and for special computer programs, called *multimedia authoring applications* or *presentation applications,* that allow a computer user to combine words and audiovisual effects to present anything from a simple on-screen slide show to a fully interactive project.

A multimedia writer, like all other writers, starts with text—a report, story, or script, for example. The writer then uses a presentation or authoring program to integrate the text with illustrations, movies, animation, music, and sound effects that enhance the information in the text. The finished product is a multimedia project.

If you've never used multimedia software or don't have access to it, do some research to find out what kinds of presentation and multimedia authoring programs are available, what they do, and how much they cost. Then, prepare an oral report, and present it to the class.

If you do have multimedia software, take something you've written and create a project that integrates the text of your paper with audiovisual enhancements. Because users will probably best remember the project's beginning and ending, you should use sounds and images to make them as interesting as possible.

MULTIMEDIA PROJECTS
Teaching Strategies

Point out to students that most software programs include extensive help files that they should consult when they create multimedia presentations. Some programs also include tutorials, wizards, and templates that offer assistance. Remind students that they probably won't remember all of the fine points of using software unless they use it very frequently. However, an important part of being computer literate is knowing how to take advantage of the information about the software that the software itself has to offer.

Encourage students who are giving reports to consult reviews of the software they're reporting on. These reviews, much like book and movie reviews, can be found in many magazines that specialize in computers.

Chapter 2

UNDERSTANDING PARAGRAPH STRUCTURE

OBJECTIVES

- To identify different uses of a paragraph
- To identify the main ideas and topic sentences in a paragraph
- To identify and analyze supporting details in paragraphs
- To understand and apply the strategies of description, narration, classification, and evaluation for paragraph development

CROSS CURRICULUM

Fine Arts and Language Arts: How Is a Paragraph Like a Picture?

Use visuals, such as the fine art transparencies from the *Transparency Binder,* photographs, CD covers, comic strips, or posters to reinforce the different strategies of developing paragraphs explained on pp. 79–87. Consider asking a volunteer to work with you to model the process for the class. Then, work through the various types of paragraph development using graphic arts examples.

- **Narration** For example, to demonstrate the narrative strategy, ask the class to examine Lois Mailou Jones's *The Ascent of Ethiopia,* Transparency 2, and to discuss what sequence of development of civilization the painting suggests. Then, divide the class into small groups to discuss the sequence behind other narrative pictures. If students have difficulty with this concept, offer them comic strips as an example. To help students stretch their imaginations, ask them to imagine a sequence of events that led the scene in Pablo Picasso's *The Tragedy,* Transparency 1. Have group members freewrite their ideas and compare notes.

- **Description** To demonstrate that a piece of art can suggest more than one type of development, have students look again at *The Tragedy* and consider descriptive elements such as color, composition, and mood. Then, lead students to discuss if considering these elements changed the way they looked at the painting.

- **Classification** Have students find examples of art filled with objects to be classified. If you anticipate that students will need guidance with this concept, begin by having them work together to examine Larry Rivers's *History of the Russian Revolution: From Marx to Mayakovsky,* Transparency 8 in the *Transparency Binder,* to find ways to group the picture's various components. Let students freewrite their initial responses to see how many types of groupings they create.

- **Evaluation** Have students examine *The Lady of Shalott* by William Holman Hunt, Transparency 7; *Government Bureau* by George Tooker, Transparency 5; or *For Ishmael Tiller: The Ledgy Rocks* by David Blackwood, Transparency 4. Pair students so that one takes notes as the other responds to the art orally. Then, reverse the roles. Reserve time at the end of the exercise for a group discussion.

- **Extension** To extend the lesson, have students bring favorite art works to class to share in small groups. Allow group members to examine each work and freewrite for two minutes. Record how each student responded to the art. Use this list to emphasize that each person has a valid personal way of viewing art; similarly two students might choose the same subject for a paragraph but may approach it through different styles of development.

INTEGRATING THE LANGUAGE ARTS

SELECTION	READING AND LITERATURE	WRITING AND CRITICAL THINKING	LANGUAGE AND SYNTAX	SPEAKING, LISTENING, AND OTHER EXPRESSION SKILLS
FROM • "How It Feels to Be Colored Me" pp. 58–60 • "Dog Tales" p. 62 • *Problem–Solving Strategies for Writing* p. 64 • "Letter from Birmingham Jail" p. 65 • *A Young Painter* p. 66 • *Singin' and swingin' and gettin' merry like Christmas* pp. 67–68 • "The World in Its Extreme" p. 68 • *My Teacher Is Driving Me Crazy* p. 69 • *Pioneer Women: Voices from the Kansas Frontier* p. 69 • *Arctic Dreams* p. 70 • *Farewell to Manzanar* p. 71 • *A Wounded Civilization* pp. 71–72 • *The Sea Around Us* pp. 72–73 • "Marigolds" pp. 79–80 • *How To Teach Your Old Dog New Tricks* p. 82 • *Blues People* p. 82 • *Native Land: Sagas of the Indian Americas* pp. 83–84 • "Vitreography: Making Prints with Glass Plates" pp. 84–85 • "Dog Training" p. 85 • *The Complete Guide to Videocassette Movies* pp. 86–87	• Responding personally to literature p. 61 • Finding the main idea pp. 61, 65–66 • Analyzing paragraphs p. 61 • Locating different types of paragraphs p. 63 • Identifying topic sentences pp. 65–66 • Identifying direct references and transitional expressions p. 78	• Writing a journal entry p. 61 • Using literature as a catalyst for personal expression p. 61 • Making inferences and drawing conclusions pp. 61, 65–66, 73 • Evaluating paragraph function pp. 61, 63 • Analyzing a variety of paragraphs pp. 61, 63 • Identifying main ideas and topic sentences pp. 61, 65–66 • Applying interpretive and creative thinking pp. 63, 65–66, 83, 86, 93 • Writing topic sentences pp. 65–66, 90, 92, 93 • Identifying different types of supporting details p. 70 • Analyzing notes for unity p. 73 • Identifying direct references and transitional expressions p. 78 • Developing sensory details p. 80 • Ordering information within a paragraph p. 80 • Developing supporting details pp. 80, 87, 88–89, 92, 93 • Using description as a writing strategy pp. 80, 93 • Using narration as a writing strategy p. 83 • Using classification as a writing strategy p. 86 • Writing opinion statements p. 87 • Using evaluation as a writing strategy p. 87 • Writing an expressive paragraph pp. 88–89 • Evaluating and revising pp. 89, 90, 92, 93 • Writing an expository paragraph pp. 90–91 • Using appropriate order pp. 90, 92 • Writing a persuasive paragraph pp. 91–92 • Writing a literary paragraph p. 93 • Reflecting on writing for portfolio selections p. 93	• Identifying direct references and transitional expressions p. 78 • Proofreading for errors in grammar, usage, and mechanics pp. 89, 90–91, 92, 93 • Using precise words p. 93	• Working with classmates to identify uses of paragraphs p. 63 • Discussing different types of supporting details p. 70 • Working with classmates to analyze notes for unity p. 73 • Drawing a sketch of a character p. 93

CHAPTER 2: UNDERSTANDING PARAGRAPH STRUCTURE

Use this guide for creating an instructional plan that addresses the individual needs of your students. Assignments accompaied by the following symbol (*) may be completed out of class. Times given for pacing lessons are estimated.

CHAPTER PLANNING GUIDE—PUPIL'S EDITION

LESSONS	LITERARY MODEL pp. 58–60 from *How It Feels to Be Colored Me* by Zora Neale Hurston	THE USES OF PARAGRAPHS pp. 62–70
DEVELOPMENTAL PROGRAM	⏱ **20–25 minutes** • Read model aloud in class and answer questions orally on p. 61	⏱ **60–65 minutes** • Main Assignment: Looking Ahead p. 61 • The Uses of Paragraphs pp. 62–63 • Exercises 1, 2*, 3 pp. 63, 65–66, 70 • Paragraphs That Develop a Main Idea pp. 63–69
CORE PROGRAM	⏱ **15–20 minutes** • Assign student pairs to read the model and to discuss the questions on p. 61	⏱ **25–30 minutes** • Main Assignment: Looking Ahead p. 61 • Paragraphs That Develop a Main Idea pp. 63–69* • Exercises 2*, 3 pp. 65–66, 70
ACCELERATED PROGRAM	⏱ **15 minutes** • Assign students to read model independently and take notes in their Reader's Logs	⏱ **20–25 minutes** • Main Assignment: Looking Ahead p. 61 • Location of a Topic Sentence and model p. 64 • Models pp. 67–70* • Exercise 3 p. 70

CHAPTER PLANNING GUIDE—PROGRAM RESOURCES

	LITERARY MODEL	THE USES OF PARAGRAPHS
PRINT	• Reading Master 2, *Practice for Assessment in Reading, Vocabulary, and Spelling* p. 2	• The Uses of Short Paragraphs, Main Idea and Topic Sentence, Supporting Sentences, Clincher Sentences *Practicing the Writing Process* pp. 15–18 • Uses of Paragraphs, *English Workshop* pp. 19–20
MEDIA		• Graphic Organizer 3, *Transparency Binder*

UNITY AND COHERENCE pp. 71–78	STRATEGIES OF DEVELOPMENT pp. 79–87
🕐 **50–55 minutes** • Unity pp. 71–73 • Exercise 4 p. 73 • Coherence pp. 74–77 • Exercise 5 in pairs p. 78	🕐 **60–65 minutes** • Strategies of Development pp. 79–87 • Exercise 6 in pairs p. 80 • Exercise 7 #2 p. 83 • Exercises 8–9 pp. 86–87
🕐 **25–30 minutes** • Unity pp. 71–73* • Exercise 4 p. 73 • Coherence pp. 74–77* • Exercise 5 p. 78*	🕐 **20–25 minutes** • Strategies of Development pp. 79–87* • Exercise 6 p. 80* • Exercise 7 #3 p. 83 • Exercises 8–9 pp. 86–87*
🕐 **20–25 minutes** • Models pp. 71–73, 74–77* • Charts pp. 74, 76 • Exercise 5 p. 78*	🕐 **20–25 minutes** • Chart p. 79 • Models pp. 81–82, 83–85, 86–87* • Exercise 7 #1 p. 83 • Exercise 9 p. 87*

ELEMENTS OF WRITING: CURRICULUM CONNECTIONS

Making Connections
Writing Paragraphs for Different Purposes pp. 88–93

ASSESSMENT OPTIONS

Portfolio Assessment
Portfolio forms, *Portfolio Assessment* pp. 6–25

Summative Assessment
Review: Transitional Words and Phrases, *Practicing the Writing Process* p. 23

Reflection
Self-assessment Record, *Portfolio Assessment* p. 19

📽 Overhead transparencies

UNITY AND COHERENCE	STRATEGIES OF DEVELOPMENT
• Achieving Unity, Achieving Coherence, *Practicing the Writing Process* pp. 19, 20 • Unity, Coherence: Order of Ideas, Coherence: Connections Between Ideas, *English Workshop* pp. 21–26	• Using Description and Narration, Using Classification and Evaluation, *Practicing the Writing Process* pp. 21, 22 • Using Description, Using Evaluation, Using Narration, Using Classification, *English Workshop* pp. 27–32
• Revision Transparency 3, *Transparency Binder* 📽	

LESSON 1 *(pp. 56–61)*
LOOKING AT THE PARTS

OBJECTIVES

- To record personal responses to a literary model
- To identify the main idea of a paragraph
- To analyze the possible reasons for varying paragraph lengths in writing

MOTIVATION

Write the word *paragraph* on the chalkboard and challenge students to define it in a way that applies to all paragraphs. Encourage class discussion of suggested definitions. Students may discover that *paragraph* is a difficult word to define because paragraphs can vary so much.

PROGRAM MANAGER

CHAPTER 2

- **Practice** To help less-advanced students who need additional practice with concepts and activities related to this chapter, see **Chapter 2** in *English Workshop, Complete Course,* pp. 19–32.

- **Reading Support** For help with the reading selection, pp. 58–60, see **Reading Master 2** in *Practice for Assessment in Reading, Vocabulary, and Spelling,* p. 2.

VISUAL CONNECTIONS
Union Mixer

About the Artist. Colleen Browning was born in Ireland in 1929 and immigrated to the United States when she was twenty. Browning soon gained public recognition, and she has exhibited work frequently at galleries such as the Whitney Museum of Modern Art. Browning paints in a realistic style, and her subject matter ranges from New York street scenes to her garden on the island of Grenada in the Caribbean.

Ideas for Writing. You could relate this painting to the study of paragraphs by pointing out to students how each of the squares in the painting is like a paragraph in a piece of writing. Each square tells its own story and these stories combine in the painting to tell a larger story.

continued on next page

2 UNDERSTANDING PARAGRAPH STRUCTURE

Tell students that by discussing specific uses for paragraphs and the most effective organizations for paragraphs, this chapter will help them better understand what a paragraph is.

Looking at the Parts

You wouldn't look for paragraphs in most poems, plays, or song lyrics. However, you will find them in almost every other kind of writing—ads, articles, books, short stories, lab reports. They are the **parts** that make up the whole.

Writing and You. Paragraphs are difficult to define because they come in so many shapes and sizes. A paragraph may be as short as a single word or as long as many pages. It may be structured around a main idea, provide a transition from one idea to the next, or show emphasis. A paragraph may stand alone or may be part of a long, unified piece of writing that has been divided to make it easier to read. How do you use paragraphs?

As You Read. In the following selection, notice how the writer uses paragraphs to organize and relate her ideas about being an African American.

Colleen Browning, *Union Mixer* (1976). Lithograph, 20″ × 33″.

Have students freewrite in their writing journals about the thoughts and feelings this painting evokes in them.

Use the literary model to explore these characteristics with students. You may want to use the **Reader's Response** questions to initiate a class discussion.

As guided practice for the **Writer's Craft** questions, work with students to identify the suggested main idea of the second paragraph of the literary model, and discuss what Hurston accomplishes in this lengthy paragraph. Why is it so long? [The implied main idea of the paragraph is that slavery is in the past and that the writer (Hurston) sees

USING THE SELECTION
from **How It Feels to be Colored Me**

1

Hurston (c. 1891–1960) was a novelist, folklorist, and anthropologist. She was born in Eatonville, Florida, where her father was a minister and a mayor. In the 1930s she studied with Franz Boas, a distinguished anthropologist at Columbia University. Hurston's work captures the African American culture and dialect of her time. Her second novel, *Their Eyes Were Watching God,* is generally considered her best.

2

The terms *colored* and *Negro* were commonly used until the mid-1960s. You may want to discuss the connotations that the words hold today and their decreasing use after the civil rights movement of the 1960s.

3

Hurston is alluding to the saying "The world is my oyster." The saying compares the world to an oyster, which can be opened to reveal a pearl, and suggests that everything is accessible—it's just a matter of going after whatever is desired.

4

In these lines Hurston is probably referring to the Civil War and the Emancipation Proclamation, which freed enslaved people.

5

The Reconstruction (1865–1877) was the reorganization of the states that had seceded during the Civil War and their reestablishment into the Union.

58

from

how it feels to be colored me

1 by Zora Neale Hurston

2 But I am not tragically colored. There is no great sorrow dammed up in my soul, nor lurking behind my eyes. I do not mind at all. I do not belong to the sobbing school of Negrohood who hold that nature somehow has given them a low-down dirty deal and whose feelings are all hurt about it. Even in the helter-skelter skirmish that is my life, I have seen that the world is to the strong regardless of a little pigmentation more or less. No, I do **3** not weep at the world—I am too busy sharpening my oyster knife.

Someone is always at my elbow reminding me that I am the granddaughter of slaves. It fails to register depression with me. Slavery is sixty years in the past. The operation was successful and the **4** patient is doing well, thank you. The terrible struggle that made me an American out of a potential slave said "On the line!" **5** The Reconstruction said "Get set!"; and the generation before said "Go!" I am off to a flying start and I must not halt in the stretch to look behind and weep. Slavery

her future as an exciting adventure. In this long paragraph Hurston uses a succession of metaphors to get her point across, perhaps because she feels that readers will not be easily convinced of the point she is trying to make.]

Assign the **Writer's Craft** questions as independent practice.

"Even in the **helter–skelter skirmish** that is my life, I have seen that the world is to the **strong** regardless of a little **pigmentation**. . . ."

6 is the price I paid for civilization, and the choice was not with me. It is a bully adventure and worth all that I have paid through my ancestors for it. No one on earth ever had a greater chance for glory. The world to be won and nothing to be lost. It is thrilling to think—to know that for any act of mine, I shall get twice as much praise or twice as much blame. It is quite exciting to hold the center of the national stage, with the spectators not knowing whether to laugh or to weep.

7 The position of my white neighbor is much more difficult. No brown <u>specter</u> pulls up a chair beside me when I sit down to eat. No dark ghost thrusts its leg against mine in bed. The game of keeping what one has is never so exciting as the game of getting.

8 I do not always feel colored. Even now I often achieve the unconscious Zora of Eatonville before the <u>Hegira</u>. I feel most colored when I am thrown against a sharp white background.

9 For instance at Barnard. "Beside the waters of the Hudson" I feel my race. Among the thousand white persons, I am a dark rock surged upon, and overswept, but through it all, I remain myself. When covered by the waters, I am; and the <u>ebb</u> but reveals me again.

Sometimes it is the other way around. A white person is set down in our midst, but the contrast is just as sharp for me. For instance, when I sit in the drafty basement that is The New World Cabaret with a white person, my color comes. We enter chatting about any little nothing that we have in common and are seated

6
bully: excellent, first-rate

7
What "brown specter" is Hurston referring to here? [Responses will vary. Students might say that she is referring to the white neighbors' fears of losing their jobs, money, or power to African Americans.]

8
Eatonville, where Hurston was born, was the first incorporated city in the United States to consist solely of African Americans. The Hegira was Islamic prophet Mohammed's flight from Mecca to Medina in 622 A.D. The term *Hegira* can be used to refer to any journey or exodus.

9
Barnard: Barnard College in New York City

Ask students to discuss what important facts about paragraphs were revealed through their examination of the literary model. [Students should note that paragraphs can have stated or suggested main ideas and can vary greatly in length.]

You could have interested students present brief oral reports about Hurston's life and writings or encourage students to read and report on one of her novels—*Jonah's Gourd Vine, Their Eyes Were Watching God,* or *Moses, Man of the Mountain.*

60

10
Hurston uses a metaphor that likens the orchestra to a fierce animal and uses specific verbs to convey a sense of frenzied activity.

11
How does the imagery here contrast with Hurston's description of the orchestra? [Responses will vary. The words *rest, creep, slowly, motionless,* and *calmly* create a sense of stasis and inactivity.]

12
It is ironic that the man seems to be responding to the music with only his fingertips while Hurston responds with her entire being and spirit.

13
This is possibly a reference to the distance that separates Africa and the United States.

SELECTION AMENDMENT
Description of change: excerpted
Rationale: to focus on the concept of paragraph structure presented in this chapter

by the jazz waiters. In the abrupt way that jazz orchestras have, this one plunges into a number. It loses no time in <u>circumlocutions</u>, but gets right down to business. It constricts the thorax and splits the heart with its tempo and narcotic harmonies.
10 This orchestra grows rambunctious, rears on its hind legs and attacks the tonal veil with primitive fury, rending it, clawing it until it breaks through to the jungle beyond. I follow those heathen—follow them exultingly. I dance wildly inside myself; I yell within, I whoop; I shake my assegai [a light spear used by tribesmen in southern Africa] above my head, I hurl it true to the mark yeeeeooww! I am in the jungle and living in the jungle way. My face is painted red and yellow and my body is painted blue. My pulse is throbbing like a war drum. I want to slaughter something—give pain, give death to what, I do not know. But the piece ends. The men of the orchestra wipe their lips
11 and rest their fingers. I creep back slowly to the <u>veneer</u> we call civilization with the last tone and find the white friend sitting motionless in his seat, smoking calmly.
12 "Good music they have here," he remarks, drumming the table with his fingertips.
Music. The great blobs of purple and
13 red emotion have not touched him. He has only heard what I felt. He is far away and I see him but dimly across the ocean and the continent that have fallen between us. He is so pale with his whiteness then and I am *so* colored.

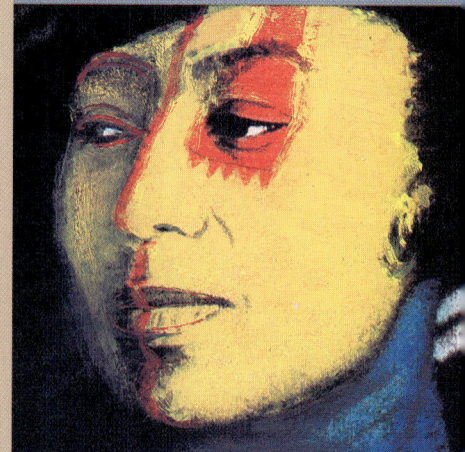

"The great blobs of **purple** and **red** emotion have not touched him. . . .

He is so **pale** with his **whiteness** then and I am *so* **colored**."

Some of the views expressed by Hurston in the literary model could provide excellent topics for debate. Allow students to participate in choosing topics to debate by asking them which of Hurston's statements seemed most controversial. Guidelines for debates can be found in **Chapter 33: "Formal Speaking and Debate."** ■

READER'S RESPONSE

1. Hurston wrote this piece more than sixty years ago. Do you feel that music divides ethnic and racial groups today, or do you think it helps to unify them? Explain your answer in a short journal entry.
2. Hurston says that life since slavery "is a bully adventure and worth all that I have paid through my ancestors for it." How is this comment similar to or different from what you know or what you have heard about the black experience? Do you think that opportunities can grow out of hardships? How?

WRITER'S CRAFT

3. Paragraphs are often structured around a main idea. What is the main idea of Hurston's first paragraph? Does she state the main idea in a sentence, or does she just suggest it?
4. Hurston's paragraphs vary in length from one sentence to seventeen. Why does the length of her paragraphs vary so much? What does she accomplish in her longer paragraphs? in her shorter ones?

LOOKING AHEAD

In this chapter, you will study some of the principles of form and structure in paragraphs. As you work through the chapter, keep in mind that

- an important use of paragraphs is to develop a main idea
- paragraphs have many uses
- the strategies of description, narration, classification, and evaluation are ways of developing paragraphs
- sensory details, facts and statistics, examples, and anecdotes are ways to support or prove the paragraph's main idea

ANSWERS

Reader's Response
Responses will vary.

1. Students should provide specific examples in their explanations.
2. Responses should cover all three questions presented. For the first question, students should clearly explain what they know or have heard about the experiences of African Americans. Students should give reasons to explain their opinions about whether or not opportunities can grow out of hardships.

Writer's Craft
Answers may vary.

3. The main idea could be stated as, "I (Zora Neale Hurston) am not bothered by being 'colored.'" The main idea is suggested.
4. The paragraphs vary so much because their purposes vary. The longer paragraphs develop main ideas (stated or implied). Among the shorter paragraphs, the fourth paragraph provides a transition, the fifth paragraph makes an important point, and the seventh paragraph shows dialogue.

THE USES OF PARAGRAPHS

OBJECTIVES

- To identify different uses of paragraphs
- To identify main ideas and topic sentences of paragraphs
- To write topic sentences for paragraphs
- To identify supporting details and to analyze and discuss why particular kinds of details were used

---

The Uses of Paragraphs

A paragraph is usually defined as a group of sentences that develop a main idea. Sometimes, however, you will find brief paragraphs—perhaps just one sentence in length—that are used in a different way by sources such as newspapers, magazines, advertising copy, and instruction manuals. Here, for example, are eight short paragraphs that make up a magazine article. What do you think is the purpose of these paragraphs?

Dog Tales

What's good for the goose may be good for the gander . . . but it's not always good for an Australian shepherd.

"Ginger," owned by Bill and Helen Gerdes of Burlington, Iowa, spent a busy day roaming around the fields and meadows on the Gerdeses' farm.

To her surprise, when she returned to her doghouse at the end of the day, an uninvited tenant had moved in and claimed squatter's—err, setter's rights.

"A large African goose had moved in and made a nest out of the straw in the house," says Helen, "and she wasn't about to give in to the previous tenant.

"She not only made herself at home, she eventually laid eight eggs there.

"Ginger's been pretty cooperative and a little confused by all this. One day when the goose was out of the house, Ginger went in and laid on the eggs without disturbing them.

"Our other dog and our cat get curious enough to come close now and then, and the goose lets them know with no uncertainty that they're to stay away from her nest.

"But Ginger and the goose seem to have come to some sort of coexistent agreement that's working."

from *Country*

PROGRAM MANAGER

THE USES OF PARAGRAPHS

- **Practice/Reteaching** For practice and reinforcement, see **The Uses of Short Paragraphs, Main Idea and Topic Sentence, Supporting Sentences,** and **Clincher Sentences** in *Practicing the Writing Process,* pp. 15–18.

- **Instructional Support** See **Graphic Organizer 3.** For suggestions on how to tie the transparency to instruction, review teacher's notes for transparencies in *Fine Art and Instructional Transparencies for Writing,* p. 57.

QUOTATION FOR THE DAY

"People are used to reading in blocks, and the idea that one sentence has any meaning, as opposed to a paragraph, escapes them." (Gore Vidal, 1925–   , American writer)

As students begin to think about some of the reasons writers use paragraphs, have them monitor themselves the next time they read a story or an article. Do they read in blocks? Have students report their findings to the class.

SELECTION AMENDMENT
Description of change: excerpted
Rationale: to focus on the concept of paragraph structure presented in this chapter

You may want to begin this lesson by calling students' attention to the **Writing Note** on this page. Tell students to remember as they study paragraphs that paragraphs are usually parts of longer written works.

After such an introduction, you could use the explanations and examples in the textbook to present and discuss these uses for paragraphs:

1. to make an article attractive to readers
2. to call attention to an important point
3. to provide a transition between ideas in other paragraphs
4. to develop a main idea

☞

Paragraphs That Develop a Main Idea **63**

All but one of the paragraphs in "Dog Tales" have only one sentence each. These one-sentence paragraphs make the article attractive to readers; it looks easy to read. Short paragraphs can also call attention to an important point or provide a transition between the ideas in longer paragraphs. Reread the following paragraph from the opening selection.

> I do not always feel colored. Even now I often achieve the unconscious Zora of Eatonville before the Hegira. I feel most colored when I am thrown against a sharp white background.

This paragraph does not develop an idea: It provides a transition between the paragraphs that explain the advantages she sees in being colored and the paragraphs that explain how she is sometimes very conscious of her color.

EXERCISE 1 ▶ **Surveying the Uses of Paragraphs**

Work with a few classmates to survey the many different uses of paragraphs in the "real" world. Check ads, CD notes, letters, bulletins, postings to newsgroups, and magazine articles. Make a list of the different uses, noting where you found each type. Share your results with other groups that have researched the uses of paragraphs.

Paragraphs That Develop a Main Idea

Paragraphs in essays and other types of nonfiction, including workplace writing, often develop main ideas. Each of these paragraphs is a kind of "mini-composition": Each one usually— but not always—has a topic sentence and several supporting sentences.

WRITING NOTE

It is important to remember that all of the paragraphs in this chapter were written as part of longer works. The paragraphs are taken out of context so that you can study their form and structure.

COOPERATIVE LEARNING

You could have students work in groups of three or four to find examples of paragraphs used to call attention to important points, paragraphs that provide transitions between ideas, and paragraphs that develop main ideas. Students could look for paragraphs in newspapers, magazines, short stories, novels, or textbooks. Each group member should look for examples of each type of paragraph, and then the group should discuss which examples are the best. Each group could then read its paragraphs to the class.

ANSWERS
Exercise 1

Responses will vary. Students should try to find examples of paragraphs that develop main ideas, that make articles attractive to readers, that call attention to important points, and that provide transitions between the ideas in longer paragraphs.

Point out to students that paragraphs written for the first three purposes are generally short, while paragraphs written to develop main ideas are often longer.

Then, use the explanations and model paragraphs in the textbook to instruct students about the components of paragraphs.

Before you begin to discuss the model paragraphs, you may want to read the paragraphs aloud to your class. As a result, students will have overall impressions of the paragraphs before they begin to analyze them. You could take this opportunity to discuss the synergistic nature of good writing—the whole is greater than the sum of the parts.

SELECTION AMENDMENT

Description of change: excerpted
Rationale: to focus on the concept of paragraph structure presented in this chapter

The Topic Sentence

A *topic sentence,* which specifically states the paragraph's main idea, is one of the many options writers have when they are creating paragraphs.

Location of a Topic Sentence. The topic sentence is often the first or second sentence of the paragraph, but you can find it in other parts of the paragraph as well. A topic sentence at the end of a paragraph may create surprise, or it may summarize or reinforce the main idea. In the following paragraph, the writer states her topic—that recognizing the "needs of the reader is often crucial to your success as a writer"—in the first sentence. She goes on to support that idea, the topic, with an extended example.

> The ability to adapt your knowledge to the needs of the reader is often crucial to your success as a writer. This is especially true in writing done on a job. For example, as producer of a public affairs program for a television station, eighty percent of your time may be taken up planning the details of new shows, contacting guests, and scheduling the taping sessions. But when you write a program proposal to the station director, your job is to show how the program will fit into the cost guidelines, the FCC requirements for relevance, and the overall programming plan for the station. When you write that report your role in the organization changes from producer to proposal writer. Why? Because your reader needs that information in order to make a decision. He may be *interested* in your scheduling problems and the specific content of the shows, but he *reads* your report because of his own needs as station director of that organization. He has to act.
>
> Linda Flower, *Problem-Solving Strategies for Writing*

Model **Exercise 1**, p. 63, for students by surveying the wide variety of paragraphs found in this textbook and by discussing their uses. You may want to work with students to analyze one of the three paragraphs in **Exercise 2**, p. 65. Work with students to state the paragraph's main idea and to identify or write its topic sentence. To prepare students for **Exercise 3**, p. 70, look through this textbook with your class for examples of paragraphs that include each of the types of supporting details and discuss why each type of detail might have been chosen.

☞

Importance of a Topic Sentence. Many paragraphs don't have topic sentences at all. In some paragraphs, for example, the main idea is implied, or suggested, rather than directly stated. In other paragraphs, a sequence of events or actions keeps the paragraph focused.

However, stating your main idea in a topic sentence can help you avoid straying from the topic when you are writing. A topic sentence can also help focus the main idea in the reader's mind.

COMPUTER NOTE: Use your word-processing program's Cut and Paste commands to find the best location for your topic sentence and to revise other sentences accordingly.

EXERCISE 2 ▶ **Identifying Main Ideas and Topic Sentences**

Now, apply the explanation you have just read to three paragraphs. Each paragraph has a main idea, but not all of them have a topic sentence. State the main idea of each paragraph in your own words. If the paragraph has a topic sentence, identify it. If it doesn't, write a sentence that states the topic.

1. The First Amendment may be considered the foundation of the democratic process in the United States. The amendment keeps Congress from passing laws that limit freedom of speech, of peaceful assembly, of the press, and of petition. It also makes it illegal for Congress to pass laws that would restrict religious freedom or form a state religion. Civil rights leaders, such as Martin Luther King, Jr., have often referred to the First Amendment's guarantees when asserting their rights to peaceably assemble and protest as citizens of the United States.

Amendment 1
Congress shall make no law respecting an establishment of religion, or prohibiting the free exercise thereof; or abridging the freedom of speech, or of the press; or the right of the people peaceably to assemble, and to petition the government for a redress of grievances.

TECHNOLOGY TIP
Point out to students that some word-processing programs also allow writers to move text by highlighting it, clicking on it, and dragging it to a new location. In most cases, this is as simple as selecting the text they want to move, holding down the mouse button, and moving the block of text to a new location.

ANSWERS
Exercise 2

Wording of main ideas and possible topic sentences will vary.

1. Main idea: By ensuring important rights, the First Amendment provides a democratic foundation for the United States.
    Topic sentence: "The First Amendment may be considered the foundation of the democratic process in the United States."

AMENDMENTS TO SELECTIONS
Description of change: excerpted
Rationale: to focus on the concept of paragraph structure presented in this chapter

INDEPENDENT PRACTICE

Assign **Exercise 1,** the remaining two paragraphs in **Exercise 2,** and **Exercise 3** for independent practice.

ASSESSMENT

Use students' responses to **Exercise 2** and **Exercise 3** to assess students' ability to identify the main ideas, topic sentences, and supporting details of paragraphs, as well as their ability to write topic sentences for paragraphs with implied main ideas.

2. Main idea and possible topic sentence: She [Wang Yani] prefers times when her life is quieter and she has more time to herself.

3. Main idea: Care must be taken when canoeing, but it's worth it.
Topic sentence: "Canoeing requires vigilance, but the rewards far outweigh the effort it takes to do it safely."

2.   When she [Wang Yani] is touring, she is always surrounded by reporters, with all their questions. She says she prefers a quieter life, with more time for painting. She looks forward to having time to herself so that she can do things on her own, rather than having everything arranged for her. And, she says, she would like to see more of the countryside wherever she goes, to see animals, mountains, and fields.

Zheng Zhensun and Alice Low, *A Young Painter*

3.   Tree stumps, floating debris, rocks, white water, swimmers, and other canoers can all be hazards on a river. You can't canoe responsibly without keeping a sharp eye out, but the feeling you get from moving silently through beauty is unequaled. The perspectives are new and always changing. And there's the feeling of being in the open air and sometimes sharing the adventure with like-minded friends. Canoeing requires vigilance, but the rewards far outweigh the effort it takes to do it safely.

SELECTION AMENDMENT
Description of change: excerpted
Rationale: to focus on the concept of paragraph structure presented in this chapter

Give students copies of a paragraph that develops a main idea and that includes a topic sentence. Have students highlight the paragraph's topic sentence in one color and its supporting details in another color. Then work with students to analyze the supporting details and to identify them as sensory details, facts and statistics, examples, or anecdotes. You may want to repeat this process several times until you feel that students are grasping the material.

☞

Supporting Sentences

What is your reaction to these statements? Do you believe them?

> Most of those huge ferocious dinosaurs weren't carnivores—they ate "veggies."
> American students' standardized test scores show that our educational system is on the decline.
> Americans are killing themselves with their forks.

You probably want more details, in **supporting sentences,** before you decide whether or not the statements are responsible ones. Supporting sentences may consist of sensory details, facts and statistics, examples, or anecdotes. They are used to develop the main ideas found in topic sentences. You can develop a paragraph with one type of detail or with a combination of types.

Sensory Details

When you describe the sounds on a football field or the smell of hot popcorn, you are using **sensory details.** These are words that describe what you know through your five senses: sight, hearing, touch, taste, and smell. In the following paragraph, the writer uses the sense of hearing to describe singers preparing for a performance and the senses of sight and touch to describe her own preparations for a dance performance.

> They took no notice of me, but I couldn't do the same with them. I had never been so close to trained singers and the reverberations shook in my ears. I left the room and walked down the corridor to find my place in the wings. Sounds came out of each door I passed. One baritone roared like a wounded moose, another wailed like a freight train on a stormy night. The tenors yelped in high screeches. There were whines and growls and the siren of an engine on its way to a four-alarm fire. Grunts overlapped the high-pitched "ha ha ho ho's" and the total cacophony tickled me; I could have laughed outright. These exquisite singers who would soon stand on the stage delivering the most lovely and liquid tones had first to creak like rusty scissors and wail like banshees. I remembered that before I could lift my torso and allow my arms to wave as if suspended in water, I had to bend up and down, sticking my

Ask students to recall four uses of paragraphs [to make writing attractive to readers, to call attention to a point, to provide a transition, and to develop a main idea]

Have students evaluate the model paragraphs in this lesson. First, work with students to develop a set of criteria by which to evaluate the paragraphs. Then, instruct students to reread the paragraphs, and have them choose the model they think best meets the criteria. After students have made their selections, call on students to tell which

INTEGRATING THE LANGUAGE ARTS

Speaking Link. You may want to have some students prepare oral readings of paragraphs containing especially effective sensory details, as in the excerpt from Maya Angelou's *Singin' and swingin' and gettin' merry like Christmas.* You could assign paragraphs to be read by students or you could allow students to choose paragraphs that appeal to them. Good sources for paragraphs rich with sensory details are "In the Shadow of War" by Ben Okri and "Games at Twilight" by Anita Desai.

AMENDMENTS TO SELECTIONS
Description of change: excerpted
Rationale: to focus on the concept of paragraph structure presented in this chapter

---

behind in the air, plié and relevé until my muscles ached, arch-roll and contract and release until my body begged for deliverance. The singers were not funny. They were working. Preparation is rarely easy and never beautiful. That was the first of many lessons *Porgy and Bess* taught me.

Maya Angelou, *Singin' and swingin' and gettin' merry like Christmas*

Facts and Statistics

The main idea of a paragraph can also be supported by *facts* and *statistics.* A **fact** is a statement that can be proved true by concrete information: *The first wave of women's movements in the United States focused on obtaining the right to vote for women.* A **statistic** is a fact based on numbers: *On September 6, 1995, Cal Ripken, Jr., broke Lou Gehrig's 1939 record by playing 2,131 consecutive major league baseball games.* You can check the accuracy of facts and statistics in reference sources. In the following paragraph, the author uses facts and statistics to describe the climate of the Sahara desert.

The Sahara is hot because it is sunny. In Adrar out of some 4,400 hours of annual daylight there are 3,978 hours of direct sun, on average. (Paris, home of the great Saharan colonizers, gets 1,728 hours of sun.) Elsewhere in the desert the count is equally high. And this is steep-angle sunlight, powerful stuff. In the winter, air temperatures can drop to freezing at night and rise to 90 by noon; soil temperatures can fluctuate so brutally that rocks split, a process called insolation weathering. In the summer the Sahara is the hottest place on earth. The record, 136° Fahrenheit, is held by al Azizia, Libya. Airborne dust makes things worse. It traps heat radiated by the hot soil, and is why in Adrar the desert does not cool much on summer nights.

William Langewiesche, "The World in Its Extreme"

paragraphs they think are best and to cite specific reasons for their selections. You could lead a discussion of elements not included in the set of criteria developed by the class that may have influenced students' decisions. ■

Examples

Sometimes the best way to support a main idea is to give examples of it. *Examples* are specific instances or illustrations of a general idea. In the following paragraph, the writer gives examples of goal-oriented (but often boring) activities that face people.

> You probably have more experience in goal-oriented activity than you think. Didn't you read the boring driver's manual in order to pass the road test, or bring your grades up to qualify for a school team, or do that humdrum clerical work last summer to buy the stereo system you wanted? People sometimes put up with a lot in order to reach their goals. They memorize all sorts of facts for job advancement or a higher salary, they read complicated instruction booklets in order to find out how to operate certain machinery, and on and on. So when a teacher assigns a book to read, just think of it as good training for life and get on with the job.
>
> Joyce Vedral, *My Teacher Is Driving Me Crazy*

Anecdotes

When writers support a main idea by using an extended example or telling a little story, they are using *anecdotes*. Notice how, in the following paragraph, the writer uses an anecdote to show that Mother was plucky and resolute.

> "Mother has always been the gamest one of us. I can remember her hanging on to the reins of a runaway mule team, her black hair tumbling out of its pins and over her shoulders, her face set and white, while one small girl clung with chattering teeth to the sides of the rocking wagon and a baby sister bounced about on the floor in paralyzed wonder. I remember, too, the things the men said about 'Leny's nerve.' But I think, as much courage as it took to hang on to the reins that day, it took more to live twenty-four hours at a time, month in and out, on the lonely and lovely prairie, without giving up to the loneliness."
>
> Joanna L. Stratton, *Pioneer Women: Voices from the Kansas Frontier*

A DIFFERENT APPROACH

Give your class the following topic sentence: "The weather in this part of the state has been unusual recently."

Instruct each student to write two short paragraphs—one using the topic sentence (stated main idea) and another developing the topic sentence but not using it (implied main idea). Tell students to label the types of supporting details (sensory details, facts and statistics, examples, or anecdotes) they use in each paragraph. Students can use real or imaginary details for their paragraphs.

AMENDMENTS TO SELECTIONS
Description of change: excerpted
Rationale: to focus on the concept of paragraph structure presented in this chapter

ANSWERS
Exercise 3

Responses will vary. Students should clearly identify the main ideas and supporting details of paragraphs they've chosen. You may want to circulate around the classroom as students discuss their paragraphs.

CRITICAL THINKING

Analysis. Have students look at advertisements in newspapers and magazines to find paragraphs with supporting sentences that use sensory details, facts and statistics, examples, and anecdotes. You may want students to find appropriate ads, to label supporting sentences, and to post the ads on a bulletin board in the classroom. You could then initiate a discussion of which types of supporting sentences are used in which types of advertisements. For example, students might find that sensory details are often used in advertisements for food. Have students posit theories as to why certain types of supporting sentences are used in certain types of advertisements. This could lead into a discussion of the advertisers' purpose for writing—to persuade.

SELECTION AMENDMENT
Description of change: excerpted
Rationale: to focus on the concept of paragraph structure presented in this chapter

EXERCISE 3 ▶ **Identifying Supporting Details**

Get together with two or three classmates and some magazines. Then have each person choose a different one of the following types of supporting details: sensory details, facts and statistics, examples, or anecdotes. Each of you should then look through the magazines to find at least two paragraphs that use the kind of supporting details you chose. When you have identified the paragraphs, share them within your group. Discuss what main idea was developed in each paragraph and why the writer selected a particular type of supporting detail.

The Clincher Sentence

A *clincher sentence* can be used at the end of a paragraph to wrap it up with a final thought, summarize supporting sentences, or draw a conclusion. In the following paragraph, Barry Lopez uses a clincher sentence to give a slightly different twist to the point he makes in his topic sentence, the first sentence of the paragraph.

A Yup'ik hunter on Saint Lawrence Island once told me that what traditional Eskimos fear most about us is the extent of our power to alter the land, the scale of that power, and the fact that we can easily effect some of these changes electronically, from a distant city. Eskimos, who sometimes see themselves as still not quite separate from the animal world, regard us as a kind of people whose separation may have become too complete. They call us, with a mixture of incredulity and apprehension, "the people who change nature."

Barry Lopez,
from *Arctic Dreams*

LESSON 3 *(pp. 71–78)*

UNITY AND COHERENCE

OBJECTIVES

• To analyze notes and to decide which ones would work together to create a unified paragraph

• To identify direct references and transitional words and phrases in a paragraph

☞

Unity

To be clear and effective, a paragraph must have *unity:* All of the sentences must relate to and develop one main idea. This need for unity exists whether the main idea is stated in a topic sentence, implied, or inherent in a sequence of events and actions.

All Sentences Relate to the Main Idea in the Topic Sentence. In the following paragraph, the first sentence states the main idea—that the silver wedding anniversary of the writer's parents was the high point of the years preceding World War II. Each of the remaining sentences provides details to show how grand the event was.

> If any single event climaxed those prewar years, it was, for me at least, the silver wedding anniversary we celebrated in 1940. Papa was elegant that day, in a brand-new double-breasted worsted suit, with vest and silk tie and stickpin. He was still the dude, always the dude, no matter what, spending more money on his clothes than on anything else. Mama wore a long, crocheted, rose-colored dress. And I see them standing by our round dining room table, this time heaped not with food but with silver gifts—flatware, tureens, platters, trays, gravy bowls, and brandy snifters. The food was spread along a much larger table, buffet style, in glistening abundance—chicken teriyaki, pickled vegetables, egg rolls, cucumber and abalone salad, the seaweed-wrapped rice balls called *sushi,* shrimp, prawns, fresh lobster, and finally, taking up what seemed like half the tablecloth, a great gleaming roast pig with a bright red apple in its mouth.
>
> Jeanne Wakatsuki Houston and
> James D. Houston, *Farewell to Manzanar*

All Sentences Relate to an Implied Main Idea. The following paragraph lacks a topic sentence, but all the sentences provide details about an implied main idea: overpopulation in Bombay, India.

> It is said that every day 1,500 more people, about 350 families, arrive in Bombay to live. They come mainly from the countryside and they have very little; and in Bombay

---

PROGRAM MANAGER

UNITY AND COHERENCE

■ **Analyzing** To help students analyze and organize ideas, see **Achieving Unity** and **Achieving Coherence** in *Practicing the Writing Process,* pp. 19–20.

■ **Reinforcement/Reteaching** See **Revision Transparency 3.** For suggestions on how to tie the transparency to instruction, review teacher's notes in *Fine Art and Instructional Transparencies for Writing,* p. 99.

QUOTATION FOR THE DAY

"We're always connecting, trying to make our lives seem logical." (Richard Ford, 1944– , American novelist)

Write this quotation on the chalkboard and ask students if they ever make connections between events in their lives. Explain that if students use this ability to make connections when writing, their writing will become more logical, clear, and effective.

SELECTION AMENDMENT
Description of change: excerpted
Rationale: to focus on the concept of paragraph structure presented in this chapter

Find or create a paragraph that has very little unity or coherence. Read the paragraph to students and ask them if they think it is a well-written paragraph. Ask students what the paragraph is lacking [unity and coherence] and tell them that in this lesson they will learn how to avoid writing paragraphs like the one you just read to them.

MEETING individual NEEDS

LEARNING STYLES

Visual Learners. You may want to have students outline this lesson under the title *Qualities of Good Paragraphs*. Students could use *Unity* as one main heading and *Coherence* as another main heading in their outlines. Here is a sample outline:

I. Unity
   A. Topic sentence
   B. Implied topic sentence
   C. Sequence of events or actions
II. Coherence
   A. Order of ideas
     1. Chronological
     2. Spatial
     3. Order of importance
     4. Logical order
   B. Connections between ideas
     1. Direct references
     2. Transitional words and phrases

Auditory Learners. You may want to read aloud three or four paragraphs into which you've inserted sentences that don't relate to the paragraphs' main ideas. Have students listen to identify those sentences that don't belong in the paragraphs. Have students explain why the sentences break the unity of the paragraphs.

SELECTION AMENDMENT
Description of change: excerpted
Rationale: to focus on the concept of paragraph structure presented in this chapter

there isn't room for them. There is hardly room for the people already there. The older apartment blocks are full; the new skyscrapers are full; the small, low huts of the squatters' settlements on the airport road are packed tightly together. Bombay shows its overcrowding. It is built on an island, and its development has been haphazard. Outside the defense area at the southern tip of the island, open spaces are few; cramped living quarters and the heat drive people out into such public areas as exist, usually the streets; so that to be in Bombay is always to be in a crowd. By day the streets are clogged; at night the pavements are full of sleepers.

V. S. Naipaul, *India: A Wounded Civilization*

All Sentences Relate to a Sequence of Events. You won't find a topic sentence in the following paragraph, but you will find a main idea—the formation of the island of Bermuda. The paragraph has unity because all the sentences relate to the sequence of events involved in the formation of the island.

Millions of years ago, a volcano built a mountain on the floor of the Atlantic. In eruption after eruption, it pushed up a great pile of volcanic rock, until it had accumulated a mass a hundred miles across at its base, reaching upward toward the surface of the sea. Finally its cone emerged as an island with an area of about 200 square

Tell students that in this lesson they'll analyze paragraphs to examine the relationship of sentences to main ideas (unity) and to each other (coherence). You may want to take one day to discuss unity by referring to the textbook explanations and examples. Go through each sample paragraph sentence by sentence and discuss how each sentence relates to the paragraph's main idea. Be sure that students understand how unity is achieved in the different types of paragraphs—paragraphs with stated main ideas, paragraphs with implied main ideas, and paragraphs that relate sequences of events or actions.

The next day you could discuss coherence. You may want to provide students ☞

Unity **73**

miles. Thousands of years passed, and thousands of thousands. Eventually the waves of the Atlantic cut down the cone and reduced it to a shoal—all of it, that is, but a small fragment which remained above water. This fragment we know as Bermuda.

Rachel L. Carson, *The Sea Around Us*

EXERCISE 4 ▶ **Analyzing Notes for Unity**

How much do you know about lightning? Here is a cluster diagram of notes for a paragraph with the topic sentence "Although all lightning has a common origin, it appears in many different forms." Get together with two or three classmates, and try to decide which of the notes in the diagram will work together to create a unified paragraph and which should be discarded.

HERE'S HOW

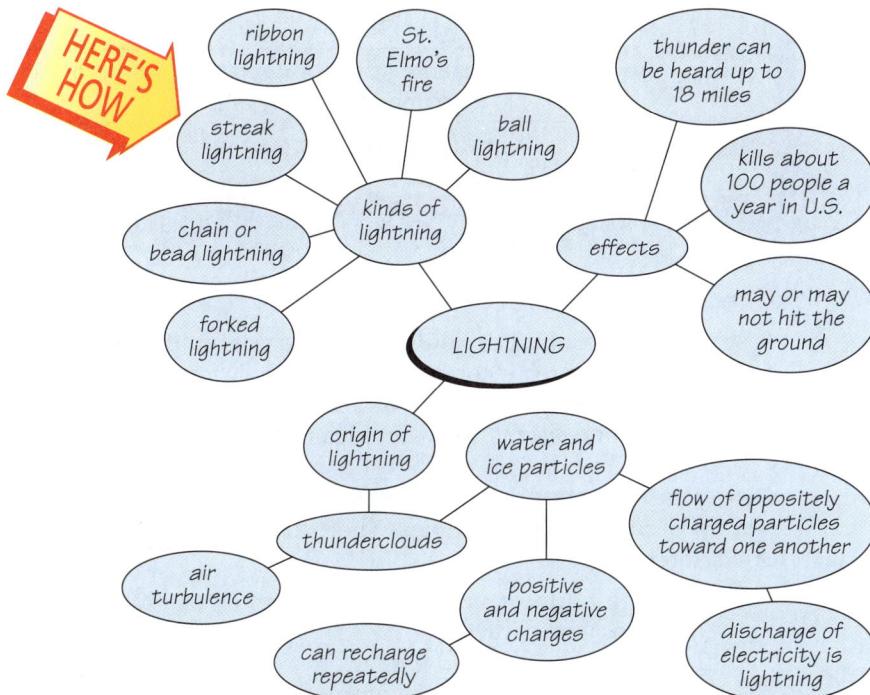

ANSWERS
Exercise 4

The cluster of notes around "effects" should be discarded.

TEACHING NOTE

Evaluating Group Work. After students complete the activity in **Exercise 4**, have them briefly evaluate their group's work. Student evaluations should answer the following questions: Who participated in the group? What was the group's task? Did the group stay on task? Did every member contribute to the group? What was the group's greatest strength? Each student should also address his or her own participation and effectiveness in the group.

You may want to have students use the forms **Evaluating Group Participation** on pp. 40–42 in the Teaching Resources booklet *Portfolio Assessment.*

SELECTION AMENDMENT
Description of change: excerpted
Rationale: to focus on the concept of paragraph structure presented in this chapter

with examples of paragraphs that order ideas in each of the ways described in the **Ways of Ordering Ideas** chart.

When presenting **Connections Between Ideas,** go through the sample paragraphs with your class and discuss direct references and transitional words and phrases. Caution students that the words in the list of transitional expressions aren't

always used as such. Explain that transitional expressions are most often used at the beginnings of sentences or between clauses.

INTEGRATING THE LANGUAGE ARTS

Test-Taking Link. You may want to emphasize that students should keep these ways of ordering ideas in mind when deciding how to answer essay questions on tests. Tell students that choosing the best method of ordering ideas can help make their answers clearer and more effective.

You could ask students to analyze two or three essay questions in one of their textbooks and to decide which way of ordering ideas would be best for answering each question.

MEETING *individual* NEEDS

LEARNING STYLES

Kinetic Learners. Copy the sentences of well-written paragraphs onto separate strips of paper and give the strips to students. Challenge the students to piece the strips together in a logical order to reform the paragraphs. Assess students on the basis of whether or not the new paragraphs are coherent, rather than on the basis of whether the new paragraphs are exactly the same as the original paragraphs.

Coherence

Unity is one quality of a good paragraph; *coherence* is another. When a paragraph has *coherence,* the ideas are arranged in an order that makes sense, and the reader knows how the ideas are related to each other. Two things can help you to make paragraphs coherent: (1) the order you use to arrange ideas, and (2) the connections you make between ideas.

Order of Ideas

The chart below lists four basic ways of arranging ideas to make their relationships clear. You will learn more about how ideas can be organized in the section **Strategies of Development,** on pages 79–87.

WAYS OF ORDERING IDEAS	
Chronological Order	Arrange events in the order they happen.
Spatial Order	Arrange details in the order that the eye sees them.
Order of Importance	Arrange ideas or details according to how important they are.
Logical Order	Arrange ideas or details into related groups.

Connections Between Ideas

A sensible order of ideas helps to make a paragraph coherent, but you can also create coherence by using *direct references* and *transitional expressions.* These words and phrases help readers understand connections between ideas.

Direct References.   *Direct references* are words that refer to a noun or pronoun used earlier. There are three ways to make direct references:

(1) Use a noun or pronoun that refers to a noun or pronoun used earlier.
(2) Repeat a word used earlier.
(3) Use synonyms to recall words or phrases used earlier.

Before students work with partners on **Exercise 4**, p. 73, model the activity. Write on the chalkboard the following notes and topic sentence and work with students to decide which notes should be included to create a unified paragraph:
Topic sentence: In the 1920s a new, antifeminist image of women appeared in the media.

Notes: housewives were glamorized, working women pictured as having given up privileges, women gained right to vote in 1920, women shown as devoted to family life and beauty. [The note "women gained right to vote in 1920" does not belong in a unified paragraph.]

For **Exercise 5**, p. 78, you could use the paragraph from *The Sea Around Us*, by ☞

The following paragraph has examples of the three types of direct references. Superscript numbers indicate which of the three types the writer is using.

> Juano Hernandez, born in Puerto Rico in 1896, was *one*[1] of the most highly regarded black *actors*[1] in the history of the movies. As a *young man*[1], *he*[1] worked in vaudeville and did other stage work that led to *acting*[1] on Broadway, where *he*[1] established a reputation as a fine *dramatic actor*[2]. *Hernandez*[2] was one of the first *black*[2] *thespians*[3] to be featured in *stage*[2] and *cinema*[3] roles. *His*[1] most famous *screen*[3] *portrayal*[3] is as the intended lynching victim in the 1949 *film*[3] *Intruder in the Dust*. *Hernandez*[2] read extensively, and spoke four languages fluently. *His*[1] aversion to the prejudice *he*[1] encountered in everyday life in the United States caused *him*[1] to keep his home in *Puerto Rico*[2] until his death in 1970.

Transitional Words and Phrases.   Words and phrases that connect by showing transitions between ideas are called *transitional expressions.* They include prepositions that show chronological or spatial order and conjunctions that connect

INTEGRATING THE LANGUAGE ARTS

Grammar Link. Because pronouns are frequently used as direct references, you may want to have students review the different classifications of pronouns: personal, reflexive, intensive, relative, interrogative, demonstrative, and indefinite. Tell students that all of these pronouns can be used as direct references. You could have students identify the types of pronouns used as direct references in the sample paragraph about Juano Hernandez.

Rachel L. Carson (pp. 72–73), to model identifying direct references and transitions.
Assign **Exercises 4** and **5** as independent
practice.

ASSESSMENT

Use students' answers to **Exercises 4**
and **5** in conjunction with your evaluations
of students' writing to assess their understanding of unity and coherence.

MEETING *individual* NEEDS

LEP/ESL

General Strategies. Transitional words
and phrases can be a problem for some
English-language learners because the
meanings of transitional expressions are
abstract and thus difficult to understand.
Transitional expressions may not translate easily into students' native languages, and their positions in English
sentences may differ. Also, the transitional words and phrases often have
multiple meanings in English (such as
since, which means both "because" and
"from a time in the past until now").
Give students sentences that include
transitional words and phrases to show
students how the transitions are used.

INTEGRATING THE LANGUAGE ARTS

Mechanics Link. Transitional expressions often join independent clauses;
therefore, you may want to give students a review of the use of semicolons
between independent clauses. Tell students to use a semicolon between independent clauses joined by such words as
therefore, moreover, likewise, nevertheless,
and *however.*

ideas and show relationships. The following chart lists some
transitional expressions, grouped according to the relationships they usually indicate. The chart also shows the type of
writing in which the expressions are likely to be used.

TRANSITIONAL WORDS AND PHRASES

Comparing Ideas/Classification and Definition

also	just	moreover
and	like	similarly
another	likewise	too

Contrasting Ideas/Classification and Definition

although	in spite of	on the other hand
but	instead	still
however	nevertheless	yet

Showing Cause and Effect/Narration

accordingly	consequently	so
as a result	for	so that
because	since	therefore

Showing Time/Narration

after	finally	next
at last	first	then
at once	immediately	thereafter
before	lately	until
early	later	when
eventually	meanwhile	while

Showing Place/Description

above	beside	inside
across	between	into
around	beyond	next
before	down	over
behind	here	there
below	in	under

Showing Importance/Evaluation

first	mainly	then
last	more important	to begin with

CLOSURE

Ask students to discuss briefly how unity is achieved in a paragraph [all sentences should relate to main idea] and to identify the two ways to make paragraphs coherent [order of ideas and connections between ideas].

EXTENSION

Have each student choose a paragraph of at least five sentences to evaluate for unity and coherence. Students could find paragraphs in textbooks or in magazines and newspapers. Here are some criteria students could use for evaluation:

☛

Coherence   **77**

Notice how the writer uses transitional words in the following paragraph to show how the ideas in her description are connected.

> <u>In</u> 1990, the Television Decoder Circuitry Act was passed, which said that, <u>after</u> 1993, new television sets with 13-inch screens or bigger must have built-in closed caption decoders. Closed captions show the dialogue being spoken as written words that appear <u>at the bottom</u> of the TV screen. <u>As a result</u> of this law, more people who are deaf or hard of hearing have greater access to TV programming. <u>In addition,</u> closed caption programming benefits people learning to speak or read English. <u>However,</u> some people have pointed out that TV viewers who are deaf or hard of hearing may still miss much of a show's content, <u>since</u> they have to focus on rapidly rolling captions. <u>In order to</u> address this problem, several people have established TV networks dedicated to creating programs that serve children and adults who are deaf or hard of hearing.

A DIFFERENT APPROACH

To reinforce the importance of coherence, create or find a "how-to" paragraph. Rearrange some of the sentences, omit any transitional expressions, and hand out copies of the paragraph to students. Ask students if they think they could follow the procedure described in the paragraph. Then have students revise the paragraph by putting the information in the order that makes the most sense and by adding transitional expressions. Ask for volunteers to read their revised "how-to" paragraphs aloud.

I'M SORRY, EVERYBODY.

77

1. Do all the sentences relate to the main idea?
2. Are ideas arranged in a particular order?
3. Are there direct references?
4. Are there transitional words or phrases? ■

EXERCISE 5 ▶ **Identifying Direct References and Transitional Expressions**

Most paragraphs have coherence because writers use both direct references and transitional words and phrases. As you read through this paragraph, list as many of each as you can find. **Answers may vary.**

Today Vincent van Gogh is one of the most appreciated artists who ever lived, but during his lifetime virtually no one even liked his art. When he was young, he didn't intend to be an artist, although between the ages of sixteen and twenty-three he worked in art galleries and studied art. Then, for the next four years, he studied for the ministry. At the end of the fourth year, van Gogh decided to devote his life to art. From then until his death ten years later, he produced more than fifteen hundred paintings and drawings. Unfortunately, he was able to sell only one during his lifetime. Eventually, people realized the importance of his art, and it has continued to increase in popularity and value.

VISUAL CONNECTIONS
Self-Portrait

Ideas for Writing. Students could use this image as a prompt for writing a descriptive paragraph. Suggest that students brainstorm lists of sensory details. Students can then use the sensory details to support topic sentences that state their overall impressions of the image. Tell students to use direct references and transitional expressions to lend coherence to their paragraphs.

Vincent van Gogh, *Self-Portrait*. Oil on canvas. Paris, Musee d'Orsay/ Giraudon/Art Resource, New York.

STRATEGIES OF DEVELOPMENT

OBJECTIVES

- To list sensory details to use in a paragraph of description and to decide how they should be arranged
- To use narration to tell a story, to explain a process, and to explain causes and effects
- To classify by dividing, defining, and comparing and contrasting
- To give opinions of four topics and to give supporting reasons for each opinion

☞

Strategies of Development

Paragraphs are written for different purposes, and different purposes call for different strategies of development. There are four basic strategies writers use for developing paragraphs: description, narration, classification, and evaluation.

STRATEGIES OF DEVELOPMENT	
Description	Looking at individual features of a person, place, or thing
Narration	Looking at changes in a subject over a period of time
Classification	Looking at a subject in relation to other subjects
Evaluation	Looking at the subject's value

Description

What does your driver's license photo look like? How could you describe the place where you live so that someone else could recognize it?

When you describe someone or something, you use sensory details—details of hearing, sight, smell, taste, and touch—to create a verbal picture. Descriptions of places and objects are frequently organized by *spatial order;* in other words, the details are arranged by location in space. Descriptions of people are more likely to be organized in the *order of importance,* starting or ending with the detail the writer wants to emphasize.

> Miss Lottie's house was the most ramshackle of all our ramshackle homes. The sun and rain had long since faded its rickety frame siding from white to a sullen gray. The boards themselves seemed to remain upright not from being nailed together but rather from leaning together like a house that a child might have constructed from cards. A brisk wind might have blown it down, and the fact that it was still standing implied a kind of enchantment that was stronger than the elements. There it stood, and as far as I

Ask students if they have ever formulated a strategy. For example, a student may have formulated a strategy for winning a game or for getting a date. Tell students that in this lesson they will learn strategies for developing effective paragraphs.

Begin by writing the **Strategies of Development** chart (p. 79) on the chalkboard so students can refer to it throughout the lesson. Then focus on individual strategies. Make sure that students understand the ways of ordering ideas usually associated with each strategy.

MEETING *individual* NEEDS

LEP/ESL

General Strategies. Because of cultural differences, you may want to allow English-language learners to choose alternative topics for writing in **Exercises 6–9**. For example, students who have not read a Shakespearean play or a Greek myth (**Exercise 7**) can recount the plot of any story or folktale they have heard or read.

A DIFFERENT APPROACH

After students have read the model paragraph excerpted from Eugenia W. Collier's **"Marigolds,"** have them write expressive paragraphs that describe a place. Instruct students to fill their paragraphs with sensory details and to use order of importance or spatial order to organize their paragraphs. Give students time to freewrite about possible places and to make lists of sensory details. You may want to call on volunteers to read their paragraphs aloud.

ANSWERS
Exercise 6

Responses will vary. Look for a minimum of five sensory details and for clear arrangement of details. You could have students use their lists to write descriptive paragraphs.

SELECTION AMENDMENT
Description of change: excerpted
Rationale: to focus on the concept of paragraph structure presented in this chapter

know is standing yet—a gray rotting thing with no porch, no shutters, no steps, set on a cramped lot with no grass, not even any weeds—a monument to decay.

Eugenia W. Collier, "Marigolds"

EXERCISE 6 ▶ **Using Description as a Strategy**

Choose one of the following subjects and list at least five sensory details that you could use to describe it. Try to use as many different senses as possible. When you have finished your list, decide how you would arrange the details in a paragraph so that the description would be clear to a reader.

1. a summer night in your back yard
2. your school the minute you return after summer vacation
3. the last second of a tied championship basketball game
4. yourself—the first time you drove alone
5. a concert, dance, or jam session you attended

Narration

What happens when Romeo finds Juliet in the tomb? How does the water cycle work? What caused the United States to get involved in the Persian Gulf Conflict?

When you answer questions like these, you are using the strategy of *narration* to explain changes over time. Narration can take several forms. You can use it to tell a story (what happens to Romeo), explain a process (how the water cycle works), or explain causes and effects (U.S. involvement in the Persian Gulf Conflict). Writers often use *chronological order,* telling events or actions in the order they occur, to arrange the details in paragraphs that are developed through the strategy of narration.

Read the model paragraphs aloud as students follow in their textbooks. Discuss with students how each strategy is applied in the corresponding textbook model. You may want to enlist students' help to analyze the methods of ordering ideas in the model paragraphs.

Before assigning **Exercises 6–9**, model the necessary processes. For **Exercise 6**, p. 80, you could list and arrange sensory details that describe an alternative subject; for **Exercise 7**, p. 83, list causes and effects of a recent event; for **Exercise 8**, p. 86, classify something other than cars; and for **Exercise 9**, p. 87, give your opinion ☞

Telling a Story. Whenever you tell a story—whether it's fiction or nonfiction—you use narration to tell about events and actions that occur over a period of time. In the following paragraph, the writer uses narration to tell the story of an encounter with a rattlesnake.

> When Bill was a teenager, he loved to read westerns. One of his favorites had a hero so tough, he'd even pick up a rattlesnake by the tail and snap its head off by cracking it like a whip. Bill was fascinated by the concept—he read the book over and over, and then went to find a rattlesnake. He found one sunning itself on a rock, grabbed it by the tail, and raised his arm in a whip-snapping gesture. The snake, much heavier and wilier than anticipated, had other plans. It twisted to face Bill, and began wrapping itself around his arm. The book hadn't mentioned this possibility. The furious struggle ended only when Bill was finally able to hold the snake's head under his boot while he, bent double, uncoiled the rest from his arm. After he staggered home, Bill burned the book and gave up reading westerns for a long time.

Explaining a Process. When you explain a process—how something works or how to do something—you are also using narration. The steps or events in the process change over time,

COOPERATIVE LEARNING
Divide your class into small groups, and give each group a general topic about which they can brainstorm sensory details. Students should think of as many sensory details as possible and record all acceptable ideas. Then have each group organize its details and read its organized lists to the class.

MEETING individual NEEDS

LESS-ADVANCED STUDENTS
You may want to work with students to make a time line of the main actions, steps, or events in the three models of narration. Here is a sample list of events to include in a time line for the **Telling a Story** model: **1.** Bill read westerns; **2.** Bill found rattlesnake; **3.** Bill grabbed snake by tail; **4.** Bill raised arm; **5.** snake twisted to face Bill; **6.** snake wrapped itself around Bill's arm; **7.** the two struggled; **8.** Bill held snake under his boot; **9.** Bill uncoiled the snake; **10.** Bill staggered home; **11.** Bill burned book and stopped reading westerns.

Point out to students the cause-and-effect relationships inherent in this narration, and make clear that the forms of narration often overlap.

about a topic and then give three reasons to support your opinion. Assign **Exercises 6–9** as independent practice.

Students' responses to the four exercises in this lesson should give you a good gauge for measuring students' understanding of the four strategies of paragraph development.

INTEGRATING THE LANGUAGE ARTS

Literature Link. Students could consider the narration strategy as it is used to develop a short story. Nadine Gordimer's "Once Upon a Time," Elizabeth Bowen's "The Demon Lover," or Doris Lessing's "No Witchcraft for Sale" are good choices. After students read the story, lead a class discussion by first examining the order of events and then the cause-and-effect relationships in the story. You may want to list the story's principal events on the chalkboard. You could use arrows to show the relationships between causes and effects in the story.

MEETING *individual* NEEDS

LEARNING STYLES

Kinetic Learners. Have students create time lines to represent the actions or processes described in the three model paragraphs for narration. You could suggest that students use arrows to indicate cause-and-effect relationships.

AMENDMENTS TO SELECTIONS
Description of change: excerpted
Rationale: to focus on the concept of paragraph structure presented in this chapter

82

just like the events or actions in a story. In the following paragraph, the writer uses the strategy of narration to explain how to teach a dog to crawl.

> A crawl is easily achieved by first giving your dog the command "*Down.*" Position yourself on the floor next to and slightly ahead of her. Use her name followed by the command, "*Come, crawl.*" The come command will help communicate to her that she should move toward you. Hold a piece of food in your hand and tempt her into stretching forward for it. Use your other hand to gently keep her in the *down* position if she attempts to get up. Allow her to succeed in reaching the food, but require her to reach a little farther each time. In the *crawl,* she needs to shift her front paws to move forward and scoot her hindquarters along. If necessary, you can help her by moving one paw at a time so that she gets the idea and also the food reward! She should be crawling on her first lesson.
>
> Ted Baer, *How To Teach Your Old Dog New Tricks*

Explaining Causes and Effects.   Whenever you explain causes and effects, you also use the strategy of narration to look at the way things change over time. To make cause-and-effect connections clear, you often need to arrange them in chronological order, cause before effect. In the following paragraph, the writer explains how the Civil War helped to cause the development of the form of music known as the blues.

> Primitive blues-singing actually came into being because of the Civil War, in one sense. The emancipation of the slaves proposed for them a normal human existence, a humanity impossible under slavery. Of course, even after slavery the average Negro's life in America was, using the more ebullient standards of the average American white man, a shabby, barren existence. But still this was the black man's first experience of time when he could be alone. The leisure that could be extracted from even the most desolate sharecropper's shack in Mississippi was a novelty, and it served as an important catalyst for the next form blues took.
>
> LeRoi Jones, *Blues People*

RETEACHING

After briefly reviewing each of the four strategies of paragraph development, show students a documentary film or video that includes examples of each strategy. You may want to stop the film or video periodically to discuss which strategy is being used at that time.

CLOSURE

Ask students to identify the four basic strategies writers use to develop paragraphs [description, narration, classification, and evaluation].

Strategies of Development **83**

EXERCISE 7 ▶ **Using Narration as a Strategy**

As you have seen, narration is a flexible strategy for developing paragraphs. It lets you tell a story, explain a process, or explain causes and effects. Now try it out on these subjects. Just follow the directions. Responses will vary. Students' explanations should follow chronological order.

1. What Shakespearean play or Greek myth do you remember best? Briefly tell (in a talk or in writing) what happens in one of the plays or myths.
2. You are teaching a four-year-old how to ride a bike. Write out the basic steps and major points of bike riding.
3. Write down at least three causes that made you decide to go or not to go to college. Then list at least three effects your decision is likely to have.

Classification

Which states are doing the most to control pollution? What is a Shakespearean sonnet? What's the difference between jazz and blues?

If you answer any of these questions, you are using the strategy of *classification.* You are examining a subject and its relationship to other subjects. When you classify, you can divide a subject (the fifty states) into its parts, you can define it (Shakespearean sonnet), or you compare and contrast it (jazz and blues).

Writers usually use *logical order* to arrange ideas in paragraphs that classify. Logical order groups related ideas together.

Dividing. Often you need to discuss a subject by looking at the parts that make it up. For example, if you are writing about the National League pennant race, you will probably need to divide the league into its teams and discuss each one. In the following paragraph about the social system of the ancient American civilization of the Mayas, the writer divides the society into three groups and then discusses each group.

> Maya society displayed a rigid structure based on class distinction. The most dominant persons were *almehen*—nobles—a hereditary elite, with close association to the priesthood. But the Maya appear to have lived in a secular society despite the austerity and authority of their religion.

TIMESAVER

Exercises **7, 8,** and **9** contain multiple parts. If you feel that your students understand the use of some or all of the strategies, you may want to assign only one or two parts of these exercises.

CRITICAL THINKING

Analysis. Ask each student to list ten subjects that are of interest to her or him. Then ask students to discuss whether the subjects in which they are interested could be best classified by dividing, by defining, or by comparing and contrasting.

EXTENSION

Tell students that visual artists also use strategies of development in their creations; they describe, tell stories, classify, and offer evaluations through their art. Some students may enjoy creating paintings or drawings that use the developmental strategies discussed. Or students may want to find pictures of artwork that they think show use of these strategies. ■

◆◆ INTEGRATING THE LANGUAGE ARTS

Vocabulary Link. After students read the paragraph by Emily Gaul, you may want to point out that *vitreography* comes from the Latin word *vitreus,* meaning "glass." Tell students that several English words trace their origins to this word. Challenge students to guess the meanings of the following words: *vitreous, vitrine,* and *vitriol.*

SELECTION AMENDMENT
Description of change: excerpted
Rationale: to focus on the concept of paragraph structure presented in this chapter

84

The nobility possessed private lands and held the most important offices—ranking warriors, merchants, and clergy. Peasants were free workers. Slaves were mainly commoners taken in war (ranking prisoners of war were sacrificed). Slavery was hereditary, but menials could buy their freedom. Under the authority of the Maya nobility, the life of the peasant and slave was entirely devoted to cultivating the soil, to constructing and repairing public spaces, and to the strict observation of religious life: prayer, offerings, homage, and sacrifices.

Jamake Highwater, *Native Land: Sagas of the Indian Americas*

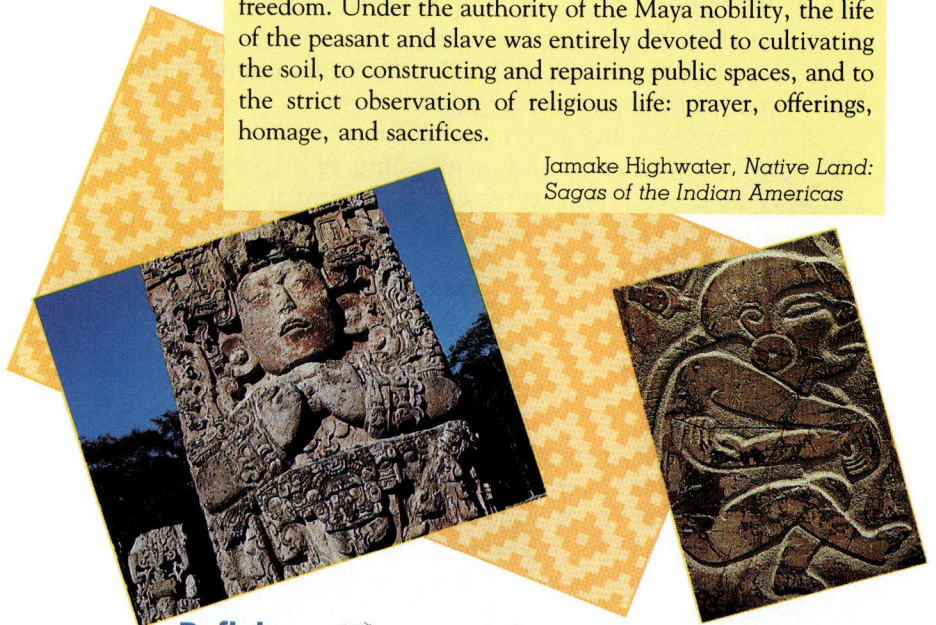

Defining. When you define a new term or idea, you help the reader understand your meaning by first identifying the large group or class to which it belongs (A *democracy* is "a form of government . . ."). Then you identify features that make the term or idea different from all the others in that class (". . . under which the people rule directly or through elected representatives"). In the following paragraph, the writer defines *vitreography* as a type of printmaking process and then elaborates on its unique features and history.

Vitreography is a printmaking process that utilizes etched glass as the printing plate. Originally developed in 1790 in Europe as a way of engraving currency, the process was demonstrated at the 1860 Crystal Palace Exhibition in London. It fell out of favor, however, because the glass produced at that time (called "barn" glass, it was blown in a molten state and then rolled flat) had an uneven thickness, and the etched plates would often crack when rolled through an etching press. Vitreography wasn't seriously considered a viable art form until Harvey Littleton rediscovered the process in 1972. He reasoned that modern technology made it possible to produce glass of uniform thickness, reducing the likelihood of breakage.

Emily Gaul, "Vitreography: Making Prints with Glass Plates"

Comparing and Contrasting.   A third way of classifying is by *comparing*—telling how things are alike—and *contrasting*—telling how things are different. In the following paragraph, the writer contrasts dog ownership today with dog ownership at the turn of the century.

The possession of a dog today is a different thing from the possession of a dog at the turn of the century, when one's dog was fed on mashed potato and brown gravy and lived in a doghouse with an arched portal. Today a dog is fed on scraped beef and Vitamin B_1 and lives in bed with you.

E. B. White, "Dog Training"

A DIFFERENT APPROACH

Because writers often use similes and metaphors when making comparisons, you may want to review these two types of figurative language with students. After you have defined *simile* (a figure of speech that makes a comparison between two seemingly unlike things by using a connective word such as *like, as, than,* or *resembles*) and *metaphor* (a figure of speech that makes a comparison between two seemingly unlike words without using a connective word), have students write similes and metaphors to compare any two objects.

AMENDMENTS TO SELECTIONS
Description of change: excerpted
Rationale: to focus on the concept of paragraph structure presented in this chapter

ANSWERS
Exercise 8

Responses will vary. Students' classifications should be clear and detailed.

CRITICAL THINKING

Analysis. Because evaluations call for opinion statements, you may want to discuss the difference between facts and opinions with students. Point out to students that a single sentence can contain both facts and opinions. Challenge students to find such sentences in the model paragraph of evaluation and to identify parts of the sentences that are facts and parts that are opinions.

EXERCISE 8 ▶ **Using Classification as a Strategy**

How can you divide it, define it, compare and contrast it? For practice, try classifying cars. Use the following directions.

1. Based on the advertising you have seen and the cars you are familiar with, what kinds of cars are available? Try to classify them into four or five categories (such as sports, luxury, and so on). Give examples of cars in each category, and then tell about their characteristics in each category.
2. What's your dream car? Define it by describing its individual features and telling how it is different from other cars.
3. How do you think the cars of today might be similar to the cars people will drive in fifty years? How might they be different? Compare and contrast cars of today with cars fifty years in the future.

Evaluation

Should everyone over eighteen be allowed to vote? What kind of Hamlet did Mel Gibson make?

These questions call for an *evaluation,* or judgment, of the value of some idea or thing. Writers use evaluation to inform readers or to persuade them to think or act differently. An effective evaluation is always backed up with reasons to support the writer's evaluation. Writers often use *order of importance* to arrange reasons and information when they are evaluating. With order of importance, you can emphasize something by listing it first or last in the paragraph.

In the following paragraph, the writer evaluates the 1985 movie *Back to the Future.* At the same time the reviewer gives his opinion of the film, he also gives reasons for his opinion.

Director Robert Zemeckis's hip tale of time travel is a witty blend of comedy, manic characterizations, and special effects that pumps new life into the familiar time-travel genre. Every-teenager Marty McFly (Michael J. Fox) is transported back to 1955 and meets his nerdy father and lascivious mother as young adults. It's up to Marty to attract these two opposites to one another, or he will cease to exist before he can get "back to the future." Even though the movie telegraphs its plot twists, Zemeckis vigorously works around his self-imposed barriers to create one of the wackiest, most original science-fiction films in recent years—a picture that mixes nuclear-powered DeLoreans, Libyan terrorists, sock hops, and malt shops. It's obvious that everyone loves the material they're working with—especially Christopher Lloyd as the maddest scientist since Dr. Frankenstein. *Back to the Future* is an irresistibly enthusiastic film made in the Spielberg tradition, and produced by the master himself.

Steven H. Scheuer, *The Complete Guide to Videocassette Movies*

EXERCISE 9 ▶ Using Evaluation as a Strategy

What is your opinion? Write a sentence giving your opinion of each of the following topics. Then write three reasons to support each of your opinions. Responses will vary but should demonstrate carefully considered opinions and reasoning.

1. the value of a high school diploma
2. the importance of being popular in high school
3. the quality of public transportation in your city or state
4. the quality of the last movie you saw

SELECTION AMENDMENT

Description of change: excerpted
Rationale: to focus on the concept of paragraph structure presented in this chapter

WRITING A SELF-EXPRESSIVE PARAGRAPH
OBJECTIVE

• To write a self-expressive paragraph

WRITING A SELF-EXPRESSIVE PARAGRAPH

Teaching Strategies

It might be helpful to emphasize the prewriting stage of this assignment. Tell students to spend as much time as they need in freewriting and identifying their thoughts and feelings. Tell them not to be surprised if thoughts and feelings they hadn't previously been aware of come to the surface.

MEETING *individual* NEEDS

LEARNING STYLES

Visual Learners. You may want to create a cluster diagram on the chalkboard to model the prewriting stage of this assignment. Select a topic about which you know many of your students have strong feelings. The topic might be related to recent news stories. Write that topic on the chalkboard and then ask students to tell you their thoughts and feelings about the topic. Write key words in cluster fashion around the topic. (For an example of a cluster diagram, refer to p. 73.) Tell students that they can use a cluster diagram to brainstorm for their self-expressive paragraphs.

88

MAKING CONNECTIONS

WRITING PARAGRAPHS FOR DIFFERENT PURPOSES

In this chapter, you have studied some principles of the form and structure of paragraphs. Now it's time to apply what you have learned by writing paragraphs for the four basic purposes of writing: self-expression, exposition, persuasion, and literature.

Writing a Self-Expressive Paragraph

You write to express yourself when you write about your thoughts and feelings—perhaps in a letter, a journal entry, or even song lyrics. Self-expressive writing is useful because it helps you to sort out confusing thoughts and feelings and, sometimes, to understand yourself better.

Self-expressive writing can be completely personal—your own thoughts in your own way—and doesn't have to be seen by any other person. Or, it can be directed toward an audience. Using one of the following sentences as a starting point, write a paragraph expressing your thoughts and feelings.

Starter Sentences for Expressive Writing

The thing I would like most to change in the world is _____.
What I like best about myself is _____.
It scares me to think that _____.
The one thing I'd most like to do in the next five years is _____.
_____ is a real concern of mine because _____.

Prewriting. Getting started is often the hardest part of writing. To help you get started with your self-expressive paragraph, quickly jot down some words and phrases that immediately come to your mind when you think about your starter sentence. These can be used to jog your memory when you develop your ideas into a paragraph.

Writing, Evaluating, and Revising. If you are writing the paragraph for yourself, just say what you want and then stop. However, if you have struggled with a problem or developed a special insight that others in your situation might find useful, you might want to share your paragraph with others. If so, revise your paragraph for this wider audience.

Proofreading and Publishing. If you intend to share your self-expressive paragraph, proofread it and then correct any grammar, usage, or mechanics errors. You might want to include it in a scrapbook, along with photographs and other keepsakes. In later years, the paragraph will be a kind of verbal photograph, a reminder of "the inner you" of the past.

Writing an Expository Paragraph

Many of the paragraphs that you write, especially in school, have an expository aim. And one type of expository paragraph is informative—the writer shares information with the reader. When you write this type of exposition, your purpose is to present the information as accurately and as clearly as possible.

Here is some information about tourism and its impact on the environment. Use the information to write an expository paragraph about the pros and cons of tourism as it relates to environmental concerns. You might want to start the paragraph with the following topic sentence.

Topic Sentence: Tourism may help protect endangered habitats worldwide, but it can also cause environmental problems.

TOURISM AND THE ENVIRONMENT

Tourism can provide alternative income to subsistence farmers living in endangered forests, who would otherwise have to cut down trees so they could farm the land.

Tourism is expanding at a rate of 4 percent per year worldwide.

Ecological tours conducted by conservation groups like The Nature Conservancy help to increase membership and generate money for education and other conservation efforts.

(continued)

WRITING AN EXPOSITORY PARAGRAPH
Teaching Strategies

You may want to begin by pointing out that informative paragraphs are the paragraphs students commonly find in news articles, reports, textbooks, summaries, and encyclopedia articles. Emphasize that the primary aim or purpose of these paragraphs is always to inform—not to persuade or evaluate.

Instruct students to adhere to the stages of the writing process as presented in the textbook. Tell students to be sure to present both the pros and cons of the topic.

A DIFFERENT APPROACH

You may want to discuss the ordering of information in students' expository paragraphs in more detail. You could discuss two traditional methods of arranging the information in a comparison/contrast paragraph—the block method and the point-by-point method. Explain that the block method presents all the ideas about one aspect of the topic first, and then all the ideas about another aspect of the topic second (such as all the pros first and all the cons). Point out that the textbook suggests using the block method. Explain that in the point-by-point method, each feature of the topic is discussed individually (such as the pros and cons of one feature of tourism, followed by the pros and cons of another feature of tourism).

TOURISM AND THE ENVIRONMENT (continued)

According to the World Bank, each lion in Kenya's Amboseli National Park is worth $27,000 per year in tourist revenue. Rapidly increasing tourist activity can cause problems in natural areas, such as soil compaction and erosion, litter, and the introduction of new types of viruses and bacteria.

Prewriting. Before you begin to write, make sure that you understand the information. Since the topic is the pros and cons of tourism (a form of comparison/contrast), you will probably want to use logical order to arrange your ideas. You might begin by jotting down two lists of ideas, one for pros and one for cons. Which seem to be more significant—the pros or the cons?

Writing, Evaluating, and Revising. Use the information from the chart or from your own research to develop the main idea in the topic sentence. However, don't copy the information just as it appears here; put it into your own words. Once you have grouped pros and cons together in a logical order, you might use order of importance to arrange information within each group. Maintain this order by discussing the most important pro (or con) first, the next most important pro (or con) next, and so on. When you evaluate and revise, be certain that each supporting sentence develops the main idea in the topic sentence.

Proofreading and Publishing. Accuracy is very important in expository writing, so be certain that the facts and statistics you've taken from the chart have been copied accurately. If you have done some research on your own, double-check to be sure

91

that your sources are trustworthy and that your information is accurate. Publish your paragraph by sharing it with a friend. Ask your friend to tell you whether the information is clear and logical.

Writing a Persuasive Paragraph

When you write to convince someone to think or act in a certain way, you are writing persuasion. The ability to write persuasively will be useful long after you leave school. You will use it to get a job or raise, to convince friends to go to the restaurant you prefer, or to convince people of ideas that you think are important.

To begin working on your ability to persuade, choose an issue that you think is important—one at school, on your part-time job, in your community, or for the nation as a whole. You might, for example, choose an issue like one of these:

- changing the school year from a nine-month to a twelve-month calendar
- raising the minimum wage
- regulating the cost of car insurance for teenagers
- increasing the amount of federally funded college loans

WELCOME FRESHMEN

Write a paragraph that states your conviction about an issue and gives reasons to support it. Remember that you are trying to persuade readers to support your view.

Prewriting. Jot down notes about why you feel the way you do. If possible, do some research to find facts, examples, and other specific evidence that will support your viewpoint. Think about the biggest single objection that readers might have to your position, and be prepared to refute that objection.

In presenting this assignment, appeal to one aspect of human nature that most of your students undoubtedly share—the desire to convince others of the importance of one's own ideas and beliefs. Tell students that this assignment is giving them a forum to express opinions about an issue.

You may want to emphasize that a persuasive paragraph not only presents a strong conviction but also gives reasons to support that conviction. Tell students that because it is the strength of the reasons they present that will persuade others, they should gather sufficient facts and other evidence to support their opinions.

- To write a literary paragraph that describes an imaginary character in a famous painting

INTEGRATING THE LANGUAGE ARTS

Vocabulary Link. You may want to remind students to use connotative words in their persuasive paragraphs. Explain that an emotional appeal is a statement that arouses a strong feeling, such as anger or sadness, and that connotative words can be used to make emotional appeals.

VISUAL CONNECTIONS
Nighthawks

About the Artist. Edward Hopper (1882–1967) is noted for his realistic depiction of ordinary scenes of American life. He was born in Nyack, New York. The use of light to create a sense of isolation is characteristic of his work. Other famous Hopper paintings are *Early Sunday Morning, House by the Railroad,* and *Second-Story Sunlight.*

Writing, Evaluating, and Revising. Begin your paragraph with a strong topic sentence that states your opinion. Then support your opinion with reasons, including specific facts and examples. Consider arranging your reasons in order of importance, ending with the most important one.

When you finish your first draft, evaluate the paragraph to decide how convincing you have been. Do your reasons make sense? Do your facts and examples support your position? Revise your paragraph to make it more persuasive by adding reasons, facts, and examples.

Proofreading and Publishing. Proofread your paragraph for errors in grammar, usage, and mechanics. Then consider publishing your paragraph by using it as the basis for a letter to the editor of your school or community newspaper or to another appropriate publication.

Writing a Literary Paragraph

Another purpose of writing is to create a work of art—a piece of literature. Just as a composer uses notes to create music, a writer can use language to create a poem, a story, a play, or even a simple paragraph.

Try out your knowledge of paragraphs and your artistic skills by writing a paragraph. Start by looking at the following piece of visual art—the painting *Nighthawks* by Edward Hopper.

The people in this painting seem to be caught in the midst of life, as though they had been somewhere, doing something, before Hopper painted them. Use your imagination to create a description of another person to be put into this painting. The following questions should help trigger your imagination.

1. Who are the people in the painting?
2. What brings the people in the painting to this diner?
3. What other person might be in this diner? How would the new person you are creating be dressed? What kind of facial features and hairstyle would this person have?
4. Is this new person sad, angry, or amused?

Prewriting. Examine the painting carefully, jotting down notes that help answer the questions. Think about the kind of person who might fit into the mood that you see in the painting.

Writing, Evaluating, and Revising. Begin your paragraph with a statement that introduces the person or that grabs your readers' attention. Then, describe the features that make this person unique. Use specific details to show your readers what the person looks like, but also try to reveal your subject's personality. When you revise your paragraph, replace vague words with precise details that will help readers "see" the person.

Proofreading and Publishing. Review your paragraph for errors in grammar, usage, and mechanics. Draw a sketch of the person you have created, or ask a classmate to draw a sketch based on your paragraph. Ask classmates how well the verbal description and the sketch match. Post the sketches on a bulletin board under the heading "Nighthawks."

Reflecting on Your Writing

You may decide to include some of these paragraphs in your **portfolio.** If so, include a brief reflection using these questions.

- How did you decide which details to include or discard to support your topic sentence?
- Which of your paragraphs did you enjoy most? Why?
- Did you feel that you needed to write more than one paragraph? Explain.

WRITING A LITERARY PARAGRAPH
Teaching Strategies

To help students who are uncomfortable with producing their own literary creations, you could tell them to imagine that they are writing a paragraph about a new character that is about to debut on a television series based on Hopper's painting. Have students ask themselves:

1. Who is this person?
2. Where did he or she come from?
3. What is his or her basic attitude about life?
4. Why is this person here?

GUIDELINES

Students' paragraphs should reflect the instructions. If you decide to look at the self-expressive paragraphs, check for expression of thoughts and feelings. Expository paragraphs should present both the pros and cons in a clear, organized way. In persuasive paragraphs, look for strong statements of opinion supported by solid reasoning. For the literary paragraphs, accept any reasonable responses in which students describe new characters for the painting.

TEACHING NOTE

After students have written their reflections, ask volunteers to share their answers to the first question with the class. Make a list on the chalkboard of methods for deciding which details to keep and which to discard.

Chapter 3

UNDERSTANDING COMPOSITION STRUCTURE

OBJECTIVES

- To analyze the structure of a composition
- To analyze and write thesis statements
- To make an early plan and formal outline
- To analyze and write introductions
- To write effective conclusions

CROSS CURRICULUM

Is Writing Instruction Just for the Language Arts Teacher?

As students study the construction of a composition, remind them that a paper with a beginning, middle, and end is not the exclusive property of the language arts department. Remind them that they may use this structure for reports in their jobs and for writing for other disciplines in high school and in college. To reinforce this concept, get together with teachers from other disciplines and hold a composition sharing session.

Traditionally, teaching writing has been considered the domain of the language arts teacher. In reality, though, every teacher in every subject area teaches communication. After all, students use both oral and written language to reveal what they know and understand in every class. However, for several reasons, teachers of subjects other than language arts are usually hesitant to teach writing.

One reason these teachers are not comfortable teaching writing is that they may not have been trained in the differences between purposes and forms of writing. They may also feel that they are not qualified to evaluate the writing once students have turned it in.

To help with these two areas, first reassure your team members that they are experts in the use of language in their fields. They just need a plan for instructing students as they write for each discipline and assessment tools to use for evaluation. You could help teachers create their own plans or use a form like the following one:

- **Grade level:** 12th grade
- **Purpose/form for writing:** To inform in essay questions
- **Procedures/strategies for using the writing process**

   Prewriting: Group brainstorming, creating a thesis statement

   Writing: Graphic organizer for structure

   Evaluating and Revising: Read drafts aloud to peers

   Proofreading and Publishing: Peer groups

- **Ideas for Evaluating Student Papers:** Rubric based on content, style, and mechanics

So that teachers understand how to set up a rubric, work through creating one for an essay question like "Explain the role immigration has played in United States' politics in this decade." You might also want to share other evaluating ideas with the team, such as a rating scale.

INTEGRATING THE LANGUAGE ARTS

SELECTION	READING AND LITERATURE	WRITING AND CRITICAL THINKING	LANGUAGE AND SYNTAX	SPEAKING, LISTENING, AND OTHER EXPRESSION SKILLS
• "Road Show" pp. 96–97 • from "Clever Kanzi" p. 111 • "Taking Liberties with an American Goddess" p. 112 • from "A Bumper Crop of Biotech" p. 112 • from *Riding the Iron Rooster* pp. 112–113 • from *Blue Highways* p. 113 • "Last Refuge of the Monk Seal" pp. 113–114, 120 • from "The Lost Worlds of Ancient America" p. 114 • from "I Won't Be Celebrating Columbus Day" p. 115 • from "Oseola McCarty" pp. 115–116 • from "Large Pizza, Hold the Microchips," *Discover* p. 116 • from "Skiing a Formidable Course" p. 118 • from "The Decipherment of Ancient Maya" p. 119 • from "Class-rooms of Babel" p. 120	• Responding personally to literature p. 98 • Finding the main idea pp. 98, 115–116, 118 • Analyzing a conclusion pp. 98, 121 • Analyzing thesis statements p. 102 • Analyzing introductions pp. 115–116 • Analyzing tone pp. 115–116 • Analyzing supporting details p. 118 • Identifying transitional words and phrases p. 118 • Identifying direct references p. 118	• Responding personally to literature p. 98 • Applying interpretive and creative thinking pp. 98, 102, 103, 116, 121, 122–123 • Supporting an opinion pp. 98, 122–123 • Finding the main idea pp. 98, 103, 115–116, 118 • Analyzing a conclusion pp. 98, 121 • Making inferences and drawing conclusions pp. 98, 102, 103, 106–107, 115–116, 118 • Analyzing and revising thesis statements pp. 102, 116 • Writing a thesis statement pp. 103, 116, 122–123 • Making an early plan and a formal outline pp. 106–107, 122–123 • Analyzing introductions pp. 115–116 • Analyzing tone pp. 115–116 • Writing an introduction p. 116 • Analyzing organization p. 118 • Writing a conclusion pp. 121, 122–123 • Writing an informative composition pp. 122–123 • Reflecting on writing for portfolio selections p. 123	• Rewriting phrases to create parallel structure pp. 106–107 • Identifying transitional words and phrases p. 118 • Identifying direct references p. 118 • Proofreading for errors in grammar, usage, and mechanics pp. 122–123	• Working with a classmate to make an early plan and create a formal outline pp. 106–107 • Working with classmates to compare revised introductions p. 116 • Working with classmates to evaluate and revise an informative composition pp. 122–123

CHAPTER 3: UNDERSTANDING COMPOSITION STRUCTURE

Use this guide for creating an instructional plan that addresses the individual needs of your students. Assignments accompanied by the following symbol (*) may be completed out of class. Times given for pacing lessons are estimated.

CHAPTER PLANNING GUIDE—PUPIL'S EDITION

LESSONS	LITERARY MODEL pp. 96–97 "Road Show" by Steve Nadis	THE THESIS STATEMENT pp. 100–103	EARLY PLANS AND OUTLINES pp. 104–110
DEVELOPMENTAL PROGRAM	⏰ **20–25 minutes** • Read model aloud in class and answer questions 1–2 orally on p. 98	⏰ **50–55 minutes** • Main Assignment: Looking Ahead p. 98 • The Thesis Statement pp. 100–101 • Hints Chart pp. 100–101 • Exercises 1–2 in pairs pp. 102, 103	⏰ **50–55 minutes** • Early Plans and Formal Outlines pp. 104–106 • Exercise 3 pp. 106–107 • Read Writer's Model aloud pp. 107–110
CORE PROGRAM	⏰ **15–20 minutes** • Assign student pairs to read the model and answer questions 3–4 on p. 98	⏰ **20–25 minutes** • Main Assignment: Looking Ahead p. 98 • Hints Chart pp. 100–101 • Writing Note p. 101 • Exercises 1–2 pp. 102–103*	⏰ **20–25 minutes** • Early Plans and Formal Outlines pp. 104–106 • Exercise 3 pp. 106–107* • Writer's Model pp. 107–110*
ACCELERATED PROGRAM	⏰ **15–20 minutes** • Assign students to read model independently and then discuss in small groups questions 1–4 on p. 98	⏰ **15–20 minutes** • Main Assignment: Looking Ahead p. 98 • Hints Chart pp. 100–101 • Writing Note p. 101 • Exercise 2 p. 103*	⏰ **15–20 minutes** • Early Plans and Formal Outlines pp. 104–106 • Exercise 3 pp. 106–107* • Writer's Model pp. 107–110*

CHAPTER PLANNING GUIDE—PROGRAM RESOURCES

	LITERARY MODEL	THE THESIS STATEMENT	EARLY PLANS AND OUTLINES
PRINT	• Reading Master 3, *Practice for Assessment in Reading, Vocabulary, and Spelling* p. 3	• The Thesis Statement, *Practicing the Writing Process* p. 27 • The Thesis Statement, *English Workshop* pp. 33–34	• Early Plan, Formal Outline, *Practicing the Writing Process* pp. 28, 29 • Planning a Composition, *English Workshop* pp. 35–36
MEDIA		• Graphic Organizer 4, *Transparency Binder*	

THE INTRODUCTION pp. 111–116	THE BODY pp. 117–118	THE CONCLUSION pp. 119–121

🕐 **40–45 minutes**
• The Introduction
  pp. 111–115
• Exercise 4 in pairs
  pp. 115–116
	🕐 **20–25 minutes**
	• The Body p. 117
	• Exercise 6 as a class
	  p. 118
		🕐 **30–35 minutes**
		• The Conclusion
		  pp. 119–120
		• Writing Note p. 121
		• Exercise 7 in pairs p. 121
		• Framework p. 121

🕐 **25–30 minutes**
• The Introduction
  pp. 111–115
• Exercises 4, 5
  pp. 115–116*
	🕐 **5–10 minutes**
	• The Body p. 117
	• Exercise 6 p. 118*
		🕐 **15–20 minutes**
		• Techniques for Writing
		  Conclusions pp. 119–120
		• Writing Note p. 121
		• Exercise 7 p. 121*
		• Framework p. 121

🕐 **15–20 minutes**
• The Introduction
  pp. 111–115
• Exercise 5 p. 116*
	🕐 **5–10 minutes**
	• The Body p. 117
	• Exercise 6 p. 118*
		🕐 **10–15 minutes**
		• Techniques for Writing
		  Conclusions pp. 119–120
		• Writing Note p. 121
		• Exercise 7 p. 121*
		• Framework p. 121

Overhead transparencies

THE INTRODUCTION	THE BODY	THE CONCLUSION
• An Effective Introduction, *Practicing the Writing Process* p. 30 • Writing Introductions, *English Workshop* pp. 37–40	• Achieving Unity and Coherence, *Practicing the Writing Process* p. 31 • Writing Conclusions, *English Workshop* pp. 41–44	• An Effective Conclusion, *Practicing the Writing Process* p. 32
		• Revision Transparency 4, *Transparency Binder*

ELEMENTS OF WRITING: CURRICULUM CONNECTIONS

Making Connections

• Writing an Informative Composition pp. 122–123

ASSESSMENT OPTIONS

Portfolio Assessment
Portfolio forms, *Portfolio Assessment* pp. 5–25

Summative Assessment
Review: Revising and Proofreading, *Practicing the Writing Process* p. 33

Reflection
Self-assessment Record, *Portfolio Assessment* p. 19

LOOKING AT THE WHOLE

OBJECTIVES

- To analyze a composition's structure
- To respond personally to a composition
- To identify the thesis of a composition
- To analyze a composition's conclusion

TEACHING THE LESSON

Because this material is more a review than new information, you may want to begin with a class discussion of what should be included in any composition. Record the students' answers for review and revision at the end of the study of this chapter.

PROGRAM MANAGER

CHAPTER 3

- **Practice** To help less-advanced students who need additional practice with concepts and activities related to this chapter, see **Chapter 3** in *English Workshop, Complete Course*, pp. 33–44.
- **Reading Support** For help with the reading selection, pp. 96–97, see **Reading Master 3** in *Practice for Assessment in Reading, Vocabulary, and Spelling*, p. 3.

VISUAL CONNECTIONS
Oriental Poppies

About the Artist. Georgia O'Keefe was one of the foremost American painters of the twentieth century. She was born in 1887 and grew up on a farm in Wisconsin where she began drawing as a child. She studied at the Art Institute of Chicago and at the Art Students League of New York. She then taught art at various schools in Texas and throughout the South from 1912 to 1916. At that time her drawings were discovered and exhibited by the photographer Alfred Stieglitz, whom she later married. After Stieglitz died in 1946, O'Keefe moved to New Mexico. She worked there until she was in her eighties. Georgia O'Keefe lived to be ninety-eight years old.

3 UNDERSTANDING COMPOSITION STRUCTURE

GUIDED PRACTICE

After students read "Road Show," (p. 96) you could answer the **Writer's Craft** questions with them. Then you can lead a discussion of the **Reader's Response** questions to elicit as many responses as possible.

INDEPENDENT PRACTICE

Students could each find a newspaper editorial or an informative magazine article to bring to class. Ask students to read the article and to create questions similar to the ones on **"Road Show."** Then have students exchange papers to analyze other compositions. ☞

Looking at the Whole

What do you think of when someone says, "Picture your school in your mind"? Do you think of isolated parts—the science lab, the second floor hall, your locker, the principal's office? Or do you see the building as a whole—as if you were viewing it through a wide-angle lens? A composition is a little like your image of the school; you can look at its parts, or you can look at it as a **whole.**

Writing and You. In *Sports Illustrated* you find an interesting editorial on professional athletes and the Olympics. In *Time* magazine you read a review of the new movie you think you would like to see. And in English class, you write a persuasive essay on preserving our environment. Have you noticed that all these pieces of writing have something in common? They use a standard composition form.

As You Read. In the following article, Steve Nadis uses standard composition form. How do the parts come together to create a whole piece of writing?

Georgia O'Keeffe, *Oriental Poppies* (1928). Oil on canvas, 30" × 40⅛". Collection University Art Museum, University of Minnesota, Minneapolis. © 1997 The Georgia O'Keeffe Foundation/Artists Rights Society (ARS), New York.

QUOTATION FOR THE DAY

"Language grows out of life, out of its needs and experiences. . . . *Language* and *knowledge* are indissolubly connected; they are interdependent. Good work in language presupposes and depends on a real knowledge of things." (Anne Sullivan Macy, 1866–1936, American educator of the visually and hearing impaired)

Share the quotation with the class. Then lead a discussion about some ways composition or language is connected to knowledge. Lead the class to understand that knowledge of composition structure allows writers to create essays that seem to flow spontaneously.

MEETING individual NEEDS

LEP/ESL

General Strategies. The article contains idiomatic vocabulary that may be problematic. Write the following terms on the chalkboard and discuss their meanings:

1. couch potato
2. project/beam
3. virtual
4. device
5. fitted
6. outlawed

Use the terms in simple contexts in complete sentences on the chalkboard.

ASSESSMENT

Students will demonstrate comprehension both by creating appropriate questions for **Independent Practice** and by answering their peers' questions. You could let the author of each set of questions evaluate the responses.

RETEACHING

Find a composition with a well-defined introduction, body, and conclusion and cut the composition apart by separating it into its three major sections. Then help students analyze the contents of the three sections so they can put the composition back together in the correct order.

USING THE SELECTION
Road Show

1

This first sentence states the thesis.

2

This paragraph gives the background of Schiffman's invention.

3

This paragraph explains how the device works.

96

96

ROAD SHOW

BY STEVE NADIS

"... couch potatoes of the future won't be confined to the living room sofa — they'll be able to watch their favorite TV shows while driving their cars."

1 If Jay Schiffman has his way, couch potatoes of the future won't be confined to the living room sofa—they'll be able to watch their favorite TV shows while driving their cars.

2 Schiffman, an electrical engineer, got his idea 15 years ago while designing head-up display (HUD) systems for military aircraft. HUD systems project images into a space in front of the pilots, allowing them to check their instruments without taking their eyes off the sky. Schiffman realized that a similar projection scheme would enable drivers to watch a TV show without taking their eyes off the road.

3 His AutoVision device, recently patented by AutoVision Associates in Ferndale, Michigan, is a miniature projector located on the roof inside the car. It beams a picture

CLOSURE

Ask volunteers to describe what most compositions have in common. Then you could ask other students to list the kinds of writing they will need in their lives.

ENRICHMENT

Have students research further information on head-up displays as used by the military. They may also want to check to see if HUD systems have been employed in other industries. After students have finished their reports, have them present their findings to the class. ■

through a small mirrorlike lens on the windshield, which reflects a "virtual image" that appears to float above the road, about 15 feet in front of the car. The device has been tested for six years, with some 300 drivers logging more than 200,000 miles "without so much as a scratched fender," according to Schiffman.

Paul Green, an associate research scientist at the University of Michigan's Transportation Research Institute, has driven a car fitted with the device and discovered that "it's not as outlandish as you might think. But that doesn't mean that it's safe." He says that independent experiments are now needed to determine the conditions, if any, under which AutoVision could be used.

Car radios, which were introduced 60 years ago, may serve as a precedent: The devices were outlawed in many areas of the country because lawmakers feared they would distract drivers. But recent tests by Green and his colleagues have shown that radios help keep drivers alert. Car TVs may serve the same function, Green says, "or you might be better off with just a radio."

4

5

6

"...'it's not as outlandish as you might think. But that doesn't mean that it's safe.'"

projector
mirror
projected virtual image

image as perceived by driver

4

Here the author includes expert testimony, a direct quotation from an authority in the field.

5

This paragraph addresses probable criticism about the safety of the device.

6

As a final comment, the conclusion compares the negative reaction to Schiffman's new device to the negative reaction to the radio when it was introduced.

98

Reader's Response

Answers may vary.

1. Students might argue that the invention would be useful in certain driving situations such as a long trip or a daily commute. Other students might suggest that the additional visual images are unnecessary because drivers have enough to observe already. Other responses might be that drivers would enjoy the TV and would therefore be more relaxed and better drivers.

2. Because all students have been raised in a technological age, they may feel that people will not fear technology because they are used to having so much of it in their lives.

Writer's Craft

3. The thesis statement is the first sentence.

4. The author is demonstrating that the public reaction to something new is often negative. He compares the initial reaction to car radios with the initial reaction to car TVs. The comparison relates to the main idea by showing how drivers could learn to appreciate car TVs as they have come to appreciate car radios.

READER'S RESPONSE

1. What do you think of Jay Schiffman's invention? Do you think you could drive safely with AutoVision operating? What do you think the effect on traffic would be if everyone had it?
2. Do you believe that people tend to fear and resist new technology? Why or why not?

WRITER'S CRAFT

3. What is the thesis statement—the sentence that states the main idea—in this article?
4. In the conclusion of the article, what is the author demonstrating by pointing out the reaction of the public sixty years ago to the car radio? What does the author compare this to? How does this comparison relate to the main idea?

LOOKING AHEAD

In this chapter, you'll study the structure of a composition. You'll learn that

- most compositions have a thesis statement
- most have an introduction that catches the reader's attention
- the paragraphs of the body are unified and coherent
- most compositions have a conclusion that ties ideas together and brings the composition to a satisfying close

What Makes a Composition

You've already written a lot of compositions—you've probably called them *essays* or *reports*. And you'll continue to write compositions even after you're out of school. College and job applications usually involve writing short compositions, and many jobs require the ability to use the principles of composition form in memos, letters, and reports. In later chapters, you'll use what you learn in this chapter to write expository essays, persuasive essays, and problem-solution essays. You'll also use principles of composition form in writing about literature and in writing a research paper.

Peanuts reprinted by permission of United Feature Syndicate, Inc.

MEETING individual NEEDS

LEP/ESL

General Strategies. You may want to introduce students to composition form through group discussion. Bring the material to a more familiar level by asking students if they have ever written personal letters. Emphasize that a personal letter is an example of composition. Ask the following questions: Do most personal letters have a beginning, a middle, and an end? Why is it important to follow this sequence? What objectives should a writer keep in mind when writing a letter? The idea is to build on an experience (letter writing) that is likely to be familiar to English-language learners and other students developing English proficiency.

THE THESIS STATEMENT

OBJECTIVES

- To analyze thesis statements
- To write thesis statements

TEACHING THE LESSON

After students have read **Hints for Writing and Using a Thesis Statement,** use a sample essay, perhaps from a previous year, to reinforce the text material. Ask questions such as "Is the thesis statement clear and specific?"

PROGRAM MANAGER

THE THESIS STATEMENT

■ **Analyzing** To help students analyze and organize ideas, see **Thesis Statement** in *Practicing the Writing Process,* p. 27.

QUOTATION FOR THE DAY

"Only the thinking man lives his life, the thoughtless man's life passes him by." (Marie, Freifrau von Ebner-Eschenbach, 1830–1916, Austrian writer and literary figure)

Students might write journal entries that respond to the quotation by explaining how a "thinking man" might differ from a thoughtless person. Then ask students how a paragraph without a thesis statement is like a thoughtless person.

The Thesis Statement

When you write a composition, you usually have a *thesis,* or main idea, in mind. Your thesis is not your topic, but what you want to say about it. The expression of this thesis, or main idea, in one or two sentences is the ***thesis statement.***

The thesis statement often appears somewhere in the introduction, where it introduces and summarizes the main idea (or ideas) of the composition. However, some writers may put their thesis statements later in their compositions. Their thesis statements may even be implied, rather than directly stated.

Thesis statements vary according to your aim for writing. When your aim is to give information, the thesis statement may simply announce the topic: "Computers are widely used in elementary and high school classrooms." When your aim is to explain or to persuade, the thesis statement may tell what you intend to prove in the composition: "Unless there are drastic changes in public education, this country won't be able to compete in the world market of the future."

Your thesis statement can be long or short, one sentence or more than one. What's important is that it lets readers know about the main ideas of your composition.

HINTS FOR WRITING AND USING A THESIS STATEMENT

1. **Develop your thesis statement from your prewriting notes.** Look over the facts and details that you have gathered during prewriting. What's the most important idea?
2. **Identify both your limited topic and your main ideas about it.** A thesis statement should identify your topic and state the points you wish to make about it. For example, here's a thesis statement about classroom computers: "Computers have brought new dimensions to classrooms everywhere by opening up worlds of information and help for students and teachers, but they're not without problems." The limited topic is computers in the classrooms. The main idea is that computers help students and teachers, but may cause some problems.

(continued)

GUIDED PRACTICE

Work with the class to complete **Exercise 1** on p. 102. You can discuss each proposed topic to help students see what is good or bad about each statement.

INDEPENDENT PRACTICE

Students can complete **Exercise 2** on p. 103 either individually or in pairs.

HINTS FOR WRITING AND USING A THESIS STATEMENT *(continued)*

3. **Make your thesis statement clear and specific.** Notice the difference between the thesis statement you've just read and this one that's too vague: "There are good and bad things about computers in the classrooms."
4. **Be guided by your thesis statement as you plan and write.** As you plan your composition, set aside ideas or details that don't support or develop your thesis statement. Later, you might decide to revise your thesis statement to include them. If not, discard them. Remember, your composition should support and develop the central ideas expressed in your thesis statement.

WRITING NOTE

As you're planning your composition, you'll develop a preliminary thesis statement that will guide your first draft. Later, during revision, you can revise your thesis statement to make it more interesting. Here are examples of a preliminary and a revised thesis statement. Notice how much more interesting the revised statement is.

PRELIMINARY   Many critics believe that the SAT doesn't measure critical thinking skills or students' true potential.

REVISED   In a yearly ritual, millions of high school students suffer the anguish of the SAT; many critics, however, believe the exam fails to measure students' critical thinking skills or their true potential.

MEETING *individual* NEEDS

LEP/ESL

General Strategies. You may want to reinforce what is introduced in the text by writing the following criteria on the chalkboard:

A thesis statement
a. is usually found in the introductory paragraph
b. states the main idea
c. can be one or more sentences in length

ADVANCED STUDENTS

Encourage students who already write clear thesis statements to examine professional writing samples to see how the placement and choice of a thesis statement can be varied. Students can collect examples, highlight the thesis statements, and make a bulletin board featuring their findings.

INTEGRATING THE LANGUAGE ARTS

Literature Link. Try using a nonfiction selection or two from your literature textbook to illustrate further that good writers often include thesis statements. For example, you might refer students to Richard Steele's essay "Alexander Selkirk" or to the excerpt about James Boswell's first meeting with Samuel Johnson from *The Life of Samuel Johnson.*

ASSESSMENT

Assess quickly by giving the class a general topic and by asking each student to write two thesis statements on that topic, one for an informative paper and one for a persuasive paper.

RETEACHING

Students who write a fact instead of a thesis idea may benefit from working in small groups to practice writing thesis statements. When a student reads a proposed thesis to the others, another group member will ask how this statement can be supported. If the student doesn't know, the thesis might need work.

ANSWERS
Exercise 1

The third statement does not have a specific topic or a clear main idea. This thesis statement needs to be more specific so that it is clear which direction the composition will take. For example, the student might choose to state more clearly what makes Colin Powell well known. Is it for his service in the military? his writings? other activities?

EXERCISE 1 ▶   **Analyzing Thesis Statements**

Now you'll have an opportunity to check out what you have learned about thesis statements. Four of the following five thesis statements have specific topics and clear main ideas. Find the one that doesn't. Then rewrite it to make it more effective.

1. Despite being confined to a wheelchair by the crippling effects of motor neuron disease, British physicist Stephen Hawking expands our understanding of the universe through his brilliant writing.
2. When you're ready to study subjects in both Spanish and English, two-way immersion may prove to be a beneficial alternative to bilingual education.
3. Colin Powell, who has a military background, is a well-known American.
4. Robots don't perform experiments, but they do carry out many precision tasks in today's laboratories.
5. Would you like to interpret your dreams? Here are keys that will unlock the mysteries.

E X E R C I S E 2 ▶   Writing Thesis Statements

The ability to write clear and specific thesis statements comes with practice; here's your chance to get some of that practice. Following are two limited topics with ideas and details. Decide what main idea is central to each list of ideas and details. Then write a thesis statement for each limited topic that clearly expresses the topic and main idea.

1. Limited topic: effect of houseplants on indoor air pollution
   Ideas and details:
   - EPA reports health risks from indoor pollution greater than risks from outdoor pollution
   - examples of indoor pollutants: formaldehyde from plywood, carpeting, some household cleaners; benzene from paints, tobacco smoke, detergents; trichloroethylene from paints, varnishes, dry cleaning
   - reports that one houseplant per 100 square feet of floor space removes over 85 percent of indoor pollutants

2. Limited topic: coping with the rising costs of colleges
   Ideas and details:
   - college costs—average increase more than 6 percent annually
   - parents and students—both need to plan ahead for college costs; save money
   - many students eligible for financial aid—scholarships, low-interest loans, work-study programs
   - information through Foundation Center about tuition assistance from foundations

ANSWERS
Exercise 2

Answers may vary. Here are some possibilities:

1. People can reduce serious health risks from indoor air pollution by placing house plants in their homes.

2. Because of the rising costs of college, parents and students need to plan ahead by saving money and by finding out about financial aid possibilities.

MOTIVATION

Have volunteers describe typical school activities in which they participate (a game or a performance). Next have students compare the time spent preparing for the event and the actual time spent in the event. Explain to students that writing, like other activities, requires much preparation.

PROGRAM MANAGER

EARLY PLANS AND FORMAL OUTLINES

■ **Analyzing** To help students analyze and organize ideas, see **Early Plan** and **Formal Outline** in *Practicing the Writing Process*, pp. 28–29.

QUOTATION FOR THE DAY

"Sometimes, I think, the things we see are shadows of the things to be; that what we plan we build. . . ." (Phoebe Cary, 1824–1871, American poet)

You may wish to write the quotation on the chalkboard and ask students to freewrite for a few minutes about how the quotation might relate to the building of a bridge, a student's graduating from high school, or the writing of a good composition. Explain that early plans and formal outlines help writers see the work they want to complete.

TECHNOLOGY TIP

If students use the outline view in a word-processing program, they will have to enter information in outline form, rather than in paragraph form. Encourage students to experiment with the outline view function.

Early Plans and Formal Outlines

In the prewriting stage (see pages 21–38), you gather information to support your thesis, the unifying idea of your composition. Sometimes, the information comes from your own knowledge or experience. Other times, you go "outside" for the information—to reference materials, to films or recordings, to experts on your topic. Organizing all this information is easier if you make an *early plan* or a *formal outline*. Either one helps you to identify major ideas and to group and order information under these major ideas.

The Early Plan

An *early plan*, or informal outline, is very simple—you don't need to worry about Roman numerals or letters of the alphabet. It just gives you a rough idea of how you want to group the information.

Grouping. You group things all the time. Your tapes or CDs, for example, may be grouped together according to performer or type of music. The following steps can help you group ideas for your composition.

- Put each piece of information on a separate note card.
- Sort through the cards. Set aside details that don't seem to support your thesis for later use.
- Sort the cards into stacks, putting related details together.
- Give each stack of cards a label.

COMPUTER NOTE: Use a stand-alone outlining program or your word-processing program's outline view to organize your prewriting notes into an outline for your first draft.

Here's how a writer grouped and labeled details in an early plan for a composition on classroom computers. (Remember that an early plan, like a rough draft, may change.)

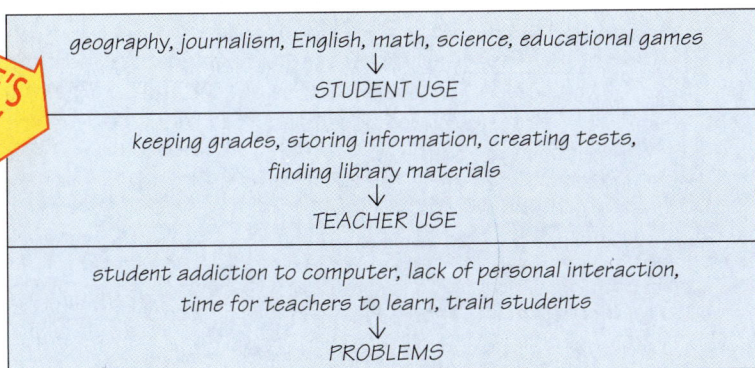

HERE'S HOW

> geography, journalism, English, math, science, educational games
> ↓
> STUDENT USE
>
> keeping grades, storing information, creating tests, finding library materials
> ↓
> TEACHER USE
>
> student addiction to computer, lack of personal interaction, time for teachers to learn, train students
> ↓
> PROBLEMS

Ordering.   *Ordering* makes your ideas easy to follow so that readers can understand them easily. In a composition, two kinds of order are important: the order of paragraphs and the order of details within each paragraph.

The topic for your composition may lend itself to a certain order. For example, *chronological order* is a natural way to describe a sequence of events, a cause and effect, or a step-by-step process. Writers often use *spatial order* to describe a place or an object in detail. To point out similarities and differences between two subjects, you'd use *logical order* to compare and contrast features. For a persuasive composition, you might use *order of importance,* arranging ideas from the least to the most important, or vice versa.

☞ REFERENCE NOTE: For more information on arranging details, see pages 74 and 79–87.

The Formal Outline

An early plan puts your notes roughly in order. A *formal outline* uses Roman numerals, letters, and numbers to organize your headings and subheadings. There are two types of formal outline: a *topic outline,* which has single words or short phrases, and a *sentence outline,* which has all complete sentences.

☞ REFERENCE NOTE: For more information on formal outlines, see pages 460–461.

You can model **Exercise 3** for the class by creating some notes on a subject that interests you. Write these notes on the chalkboard; then beside them write an outline.

You may want to allow students to work in small groups for **Exercise 3**. First, however, let students work alone for a few minutes to create ideas to share with the group. You can ask groups to share by having them prepare their outlines to display on a transparency.

COOPERATIVE LEARNING

Divide the class into groups of three or four. Ask a student in each group to select a familiar topic (or you may assign topics) and to write a thesis statement for that topic and to list a dozen ideas or details about that topic. Have students pass their papers to the students on their right. Those students should use the thesis statements and the lists to create early plans before passing the papers on. The third student in each group should read the work already done and then create a formal outline from the early plan. After the papers have been passed on a third time, ask students to evaluate the prewriting as you review the requirements for each step.

Here's a formal topic outline for the composition on computers in the classroom, pages 108–110. (Notice that the introduction and conclusion aren't part of the outline.)

Title: Computers: The New Kids in Class
Thesis Statement: Computers have brought new dimensions to classrooms everywhere by opening up worlds of information and help for students and teachers, but they're not without problems.

    I. Student use of computers
       A. Geography
          1. Maps
          2. Games
          3. Growth and weather patterns
       B. English and journalism
          1. Essays
          2. Lessons and games
          3. Desktop publishing
       C. Math
       D. Science
          1. Dry labs
          2. Physics labs
          3. Animal dissection

   II. Teacher use of computers
       A. Grades
       B. Image production and projection
       C. Tests
       D. Professional growth

  III. Problems
       A. Student addiction
       B. Noninteraction
       C. Teacher time

EXERCISE 3 ▶ **Making an Early Plan and a Formal Outline**

Here are some notes about jumping rope as aerobic exercise. Working with a partner, organize the notes into an early plan and then into a formal topic outline. [Hint: You will probably have three headings, or major ideas.] You may add to, delete, or combine any of the information. When you write the formal outline, you may need to rewrite phrases so that items are parallel.

Jumping Rope to Keep Fit

leather or beaded ropes
easier on body than running
equipment inexpensive
strengthens muscles
variety of surfaces
cross-training or aerobic
   shoes
improves coordination
rotate wrists and forearms,
   not shoulders
feet together or alternate feet
improves circulation
do 3–5 times a week for 20
   minutes
burns calories
stand straight
keep elbows at sides
wood, carpet, or asphalt
   surface
improves heart and lung
   health

A WRITER'S MODEL

Here's the final draft of a composition that follows the outline on page 106. You'll see that the writer has added information since the early plan. Much of the information in the composition comes from the writer's own knowledge and experience, but some comes from outside sources—interviews with a student and a teacher. Notice what the parts of the paper are and how they are put together to create a *whole* piece of writing.

You may want to lead a brief discussion of the reasons for careful planning before writing. Explain that prewriting is sometimes not written down for very short papers.

Ask each student to select a chapter from some other class—social studies or science, for example—and to take notes in the form of a formal outline. Tell students to use the subtitles found in the text to denote main ideas and supporting details. You may want to work with teachers in other departments to require this type of note taking for

MEETING *individual* NEEDS

ADVANCED STUDENTS

Ask each student to bring a magazine article or a newspaper editorial to class and to list the information and ideas found in the compositions, but not in the original order. Tell students to underline the thesis statement or to write it out if it is implied. Then ask students to exchange lists and organize these notes into logical early plans and formal outlines. Finally, let each student compare the original piece of writing with his or her plan. In discussion of the similarities and differences of the final plans, point out that there is more than one viable way to organize a piece of writing effectively. The students may even prefer their own plans.

LEARNING STYLES

Kinetic Learners. Because so much of planning a composition entails thinking and writing, you may want to have students experiment with making cards and moving the cards around to organize the information. Some students will be especially responsive to this technique; others may prefer the more common method of listing and grouping information on a single sheet of paper.

Computers: The New Kids in Class

INTRODUCTION

Seventeen-year-old Wyatt Pierce attends high school in a very small town in Oregon, but through classroom computers, he has access to a much wider world. He can see up-to-date maps, browse through the online catalog of the state library, even design shelves for the ranch where he lives. Computers have brought new dimensions to classrooms everywhere by opening up worlds of information and help for students and teachers, but they're not without problems.

BODY
Major idea:
Student use of
computers

Experts see computers as one way of remedying the poor geography skills of most high school and elementary school students. Geography students use computer software featuring world, country, and state maps that include physical features, population statistics, and economics of each area. Students also play geography games that require research in encyclopedias, atlases, travel guides, and almanacs. In addition, geography software is available that shows students the changing patterns of growth in population areas as well as weather patterns.

In English classes, computers make the dreaded essay a little easier to swallow. Students write papers using word-processing software with thesauruses, spelling checkers, dictionaries, and even grammar-and-style checkers. Other types of software feature vocabulary, spelling, and grammar lessons and games. Some schools even have desktop publishing systems that enable students to write and print the school newspaper or to produce professional versions of their essays.

Math and science classes have also benefited from classroom computers. Students in math classes use computers at every level from early arithmetic to the most advanced math. User interactive software "watches" students' attempts to solve math problems and gives them help when they need it. "Nice try. Why don't you try this?" is becoming a familiar computer refrain to many students.

ENRICHMENT

To help students improve their reading skills, use the reading comprehension portions of old SAT tests and ask students to write brief outlines of the reading selections before they try to answer the questions. In this way, they can learn to notice small supporting details as well as to determine main ideas and thesis statements. Students can ☞

A Writer's Model   **109**

In science classes, computers make possible "dry labs" where experiments and tests are carried out without physical contact with hazardous materials such as toxins or carcinogens. They simulate situations and act as precise stopwatches in physics labs, and allow animal dissection without animals in biology.

**Major idea:
Teacher use of
computers**

Teachers' lives have been affected by computers, too. Many teachers now keep grades on spreadsheets instead of in grade books and use the computers to calculate grades. With sophisticated computers, teachers can hook an overhead projector into a computer screen. Whatever image the teacher calls up on the screen is then projected to the students on the overhead screen. When enough classroom computers become available, teachers may finally be freed from the hassle of dusty chalkboards and messy duplicating masters.

Teachers are also finding that computers offer another boon--test generators. With the right software, teachers can select from, or key in, items for an objective test. The teacher can then use the computer to arrange the items in a different order for each class.

Finally, computers help teachers in their professional growth. In most school districts, teachers are required to update their credentials continually with new courses. In smaller districts, it is often difficult for teachers to find the library materials they need. Computers can allow teachers to search through sources such as the Readers' Guide, newspaper indexes, and the online catalogs of

TIMESAVER

To save time collecting resources, ask each student to bring one magazine or copies of five articles or editorials to class. These materials can provide resources for all parts of this lesson.

MEETING *individual* NEEDS

LEARNING STYLES

Visual Learners. A Writer's Model could be analyzed by using different-colored markers to highlight the thesis, main ideas, supporting ideas, and transitions. Suggest that students follow the same marking procedures to analyze their own compositions.

increase their learning by working on these SAT questions first in small groups; then they can discuss, using their analytical skills, until the group agrees on an answer for each question. ■

CRITICAL THINKING

Analysis. A Writer's Model (pp. 107–110) can serve as a writing sample for students to analyze by using the organizational knowledge just practiced in this lesson. Ask students to read **"Computers: The New Kids in Class"** and then have them write brief analyses of its organization. Have them point out the thesis and its placement, the main ideas and transitions between ideas, and the order of the ideas. Students can work individually or in small groups.

COOPERATIVE LEARNING

Divide the class into small groups and ask each group to use a magazine article or an editorial to write a formal outline of that composition and to write the outline on a sheet of overhead film. Volunteers from each group can explain the composition's organization to the rest of the class. These outlines can then be taped to blank sheets of paper and displayed on a bulletin board.

Major idea: Problems with classroom computers

large libraries. To get the materials they need, teachers may be able to send inter-library loan requests over the Internet.

Classroom computers aren't without their problems, however. Students can sometimes become addicted to them, especially to the games. In addition, some students tune out all but computer teaching. In classrooms where each student has a computer and work is geared to the student's own pace, very little human interaction takes place. Why talk to a person when the computer knows it all?

Another problem is that although computers save teachers time in some ways, they require more time in others. Software takes hours to evaluate and order and then many more hours to train students to use it. Sometimes, teachers must write their own programs for obsolete systems. Then, too, teachers may find it a time-consuming challenge to stay ahead of students who have grown up using computers.

CONCLUSION

No one doubts that computers in the classroom are here to stay. They open doors into vast new worlds, and students and teachers can benefit from them enormously. Concerns about classroom computer use are real, but they are minor compared with the

Outside source— interview

benefits computers offer. Robert Halfhill, who teaches both English and computers, sums up the advantages of computers this way: "Computers are the most valuable tool to be introduced into the classroom in the last two hundred years. They remove the walls and allow students and teachers to expand the learning experience far beyond the limits of the classroom."

THE INTRODUCTION

OBJECTIVES

- To analyze introductions
- To write an introduction

MOTIVATION

You could read aloud several introductions from different aims of writing. Ask the class whether or not it wants you to read on. Point out that the introduction is important; it often determines whether or not the rest of the writing is read.

☞

The Introduction

An *introduction* can be as short as one sentence or as long as several paragraphs. But regardless of its length, an introduction should do these three things:

- get the readers' attention (so they'll read on)
- set the tone (humorous, friendly, critical, casual, and so on)
- state the thesis (usually at the end of the introduction)

Techniques for Writing Introductions

Experienced writers have many options they use in writing an interesting introduction. Following are eight techniques they sometimes use. Try one or more of them yourself—they can be combined—when you write an introduction.

1. **Start with a question.** An intriguing question or a question readers will apply to their own lives can be an effective "hook." Notice how this introduction begins with a question.

> Can an ape master anything like human language? Although primatologists have reported such abilities, the high priests of linguistics have scoffed. The animals, they said, displayed a gift for mimicry, reinforced by rewards of food and play, rather than true understanding.
>
> Frederic Golden, "Clever Kanzi"

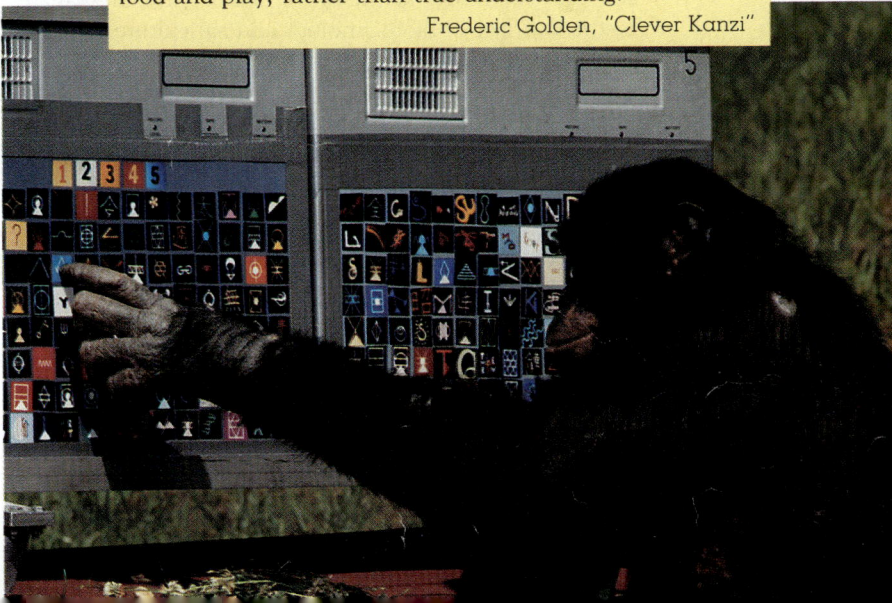

PROGRAM MANAGER

THE INTRODUCTION

- **Analyzing** To help students analyze and organize ideas, see **An Effective Introduction** in *Practicing the Writing Process,* p. 30.

QUOTATION FOR THE DAY

"To know when one's self is interested, is the first condition of interesting other people." (Walter Pater, 1839–1894, English writer)

First, ask students how Pater's quotation from *Marius the Epicurean,* iv (1885) applies to the writing of a composition. [They might say that a composition will probably be more appealing to the reader if its topic interests the writer.] Then have students list several topics that interest them, and have them suggest ways to introduce those topics to others.

SELECTION AMENDMENT
Description of change: excerpted
Rationale: to focus on the concept of writing an introduction presented in this chapter

After examining the three qualities of a good introduction—gets the reader's interest, sets the tone, and states the thesis—ask students to read about the eight techniques often used in writing an introduction. Then, using the formal outline written for **Exercise 3** (p. 107), work with students to create eight different introductions using the different techniques. Ask volunteers from each group to give their ideas. You might even want to write out the eight introductions that are developed on a piece of poster paper and display it in the room.

MEETING individual NEEDS

LEP/ESL

General Strategies. Dividing the writing process into a step-by-step method will benefit students with less sophisticated writing styles. Short-term, rather than long-term goals, also make the composition process seem less insurmountable. The introduction is a good place to begin. Have students work with partners to create eight introductory paragraphs that reflect each of the techniques presented on pp. 111–115. Students can choose whatever topics are most interesting or meaningful to them.

LESS-ADVANCED STUDENTS

The numerous types of introductions can be overwhelming to some students. You may want to teach them only three or four of the most common at this time and gradually add more during the year.

AMENDMENTS TO SELECTIONS
Description of changes: excerpted
Rationale: to focus on the concept of writing an introduction presented in this chapter

112

---

2. **Open with an anecdote or example.** An *anecdote,* a brief story, or an extended example can also hook readers. This introduction relates an anecdote about the inauguration of the Statue of Liberty.

> It was, one reporter wrote, like a "hundred Fourths of July"—the air ringing with tugboat whistles, shouts, and marching bands. A speech by New York's Senator William Evarts could hardly be heard; when he paused, an impatient crowd burst into applause. Perched high above, inside his 302-foot masterpiece, French sculptor Frédéric-Auguste Bartholdi heard the cheers and prematurely let loose a tricolor veil from the stern face of his creation, *Liberty Enlightening the World.*
>
> Sam Connery, "Taking Liberties with an American Goddess"

3. **Open with a startling or unusual fact, idea, or opinion.** This technique makes people want to read on to learn more. In this introduction, for example, the author depicts some unusual possibilities.

> Imagine a cow that produces skim milk, a canola seed rich in sperm-whale oil, or a naturally decaffeinated coffee bean. Such curios may sound like science fiction, but they are real possibilities in the brave new world being created by the marriage of biotechnology and agriculture. In scores of experiments, scientists are changing the genetic endowments of plants and animals, and the results could spawn a revolution in farm fields, feedlots, and dairy barns.
>
> J. Madeleine Nash, "A Bumper Crop of Biotech"

4. **Address the reader directly.** By addressing the reader directly, the writer immediately involves the reader and sets a friendly, informal tone, as in this introduction to a writer's story about his travels through China.

> The bigness of China makes you wonder. It is more like a whole world than a mere country. "All beneath the sky" (*Tianxia*) was one Chinese expression for their empire, and another was "All between the four seas" (*Sihai*). These days

You could use **Exercise 4** (p. 115) to model the skills for students before they write introductions. Answer the questions on the first paragraph for the class, and then ask a volunteer to do the same for the second paragraph.

INDEPENDENT PRACTICE
Students can complete **Exercise 5** (p. 116) on their own. Ask volunteers to share their introductions with the class.

☞

The Introduction **113**

people go there to shop, or because they have a free week and the price of a plane ticket. I decided to go because I had a free year. And the Chinese proverb *We can always fool a foreigner* I took to be a personal challenge. To get to China without leaving the ground was my first objective. And then I wanted to stay for a while—in China, on the ground, going all over the place.

Paul Theroux,
*Riding the
Iron Rooster*

INTEGRATING THE LANGUAGE ARTS

Literature Link. Students could analyze introductions to nonfiction or semifictional works in their literature textbooks. For example, they might look at some or all of the following selections: "Of Studies" or other essays by Sir Francis Bacon, "Shakespeare" by John Dryden, *The Life of Samuel Johnson* by James Boswell, "A Modest Proposal" by Jonathan Swift, *A Journal of the Plague Year* by Daniel Defoe, "Dream Children: A Reverie" by Charles Lamb, or "The Death of the Moth" by Virginia Woolf.

5. Simply state your topic or thesis. Often, a well-worded statement of the topic or thesis is interesting in itself. Here's an introduction that uses this technique. The writer goes on to describe the barrenness of a desert landscape.

There's something about the desert that doesn't like man, something that mocks his nesting instinct and makes his constructions look feeble and temporary. Yet it's just that inhospitableness that endears the arid rockiness, the places pointy and poisonous, to men looking for its discipline.

William Least Heat-Moon, *Blue Highways*

6. Describe a person, object, or place. If your composition involves a person, object, or place that's unusual or especially interesting, you can start with a description.

In daydreams I have seen the monk seal's face: a bulbous head covered in silvery fur, with black buttonhook-shaped eyes, a snout on which springy nostrils open full

AMENDMENTS TO SELECTIONS
Description of changes: excerpted
Rationale: to focus on the concept of writing an introduction presented in this chapter

ASSESSMENT

Evaluate the introductions written for **Exercise 5** (p. 116) or give students a piece of writing with the introduction omitted and have them write appropriate introductions. You might also ask students to analyze their own introductions.

RETEACHING

For further investigation of good introductions, present students with examples of the different types of introductions—possibly from magazines or newspapers. Identify the types of introductions used in the samples.

INTEGRATING THE LANGUAGE ARTS

Writing and Usage. To help students identify tone in writing, ask them to work with you to change the tone of an introduction in this lesson. You may want to model the process by writing an introduction on an overhead transparency and changing words and phrases as students suggest them. For example, you might use the sample introduction for technique 1 from **"Clever Kanzi"** by Frederic Golden. Discuss the indignant tone used about linguistic experts; then ask students to edit the piece to show more respect for these people, probably by changing the words "high priests of linguistics" and "scoffed."

CRITICAL THINKING

Analysis. Have students brainstorm as many different tones for writing as they can while you write these ideas on the chalkboard. The list might include such tones as angry, disdainful, mocking, or funny. Then narrow the list to two or three tones and give students about ten common, neutral words or phrases. Ask the students to provide synonyms for those words that will convey each of the tones listed. Neutral words and phrases might include *walked, spoke, passed the test, smiled, ate lunch,* or *bought a car.*

AMENDMENTS TO SELECTIONS
Description of changes: excerpted
Rationale: to focus on the concept of writing an introduction presented in this chapter

like quotation marks, tiny slot-shaped ears, a spray of cat's whiskers, and many doughy chins. On land, it drags itself with excruciating effort, or ripple-gallops like a 400-pound slug. But the water sets it free to swivel and race. Powered by twin flippers at the rear, its torpedo body can outmaneuver a shark. Books say it grows as long as seven and a half feet, but the photographs show distant and indistinct creatures. There are no cozy details—the touch, the smell, the sound, the expressions.

Diane Ackerman, "Last Refuge of the Monk Seal"

7. **Begin with interesting, specific details.** These may often be sensory details that help readers see, hear, taste, smell, and touch the subject. This introduction is to an article about the civilizations that existed in the "New World" long before Columbus.

In his explorations of the New World, Columbus found only primitive inhabitants—"a very poor people . . . without weapons or laws." He didn't go far enough. In Mexico there were towering temples and a teeming city as big as any in Europe. In Peru stretched the vast Incan empire, resplendent in silver and gold. In the Guatemalan jungles—and in the great plains of America—lay the ruins of other civilizations that had thrived centuries before.

Melinda Beck,
"The Lost Worlds of
Ancient America"

For a quick review, read several introductions to the class and ask students to identify the techniques used. Then ask for an evaluation of these introductions by using the questions in **Exercise 4**.

EXTENSION

You could ask students to tabulate the types of introductions found on the editorial page of a newspaper. They may conclude that the type of introduction depends on the type of composition or that today's writers prefer some types of introductions. ■

8. **Begin with your stand on an issue.** A direct statement of your stand on an issue can often be the most effective introduction for a persuasive essay. This introduction is from an article about the harmful effects of European explorations on Native Americans. It was written shortly before the five hundredth anniversary of Columbus's voyage to the "New World."

> Columbus Day, never on Native America's list of favorite holidays, became somewhat tolerable as its significance diminished to little more than a good shopping day. But this next long year of Columbus hoopla will be tough to take amid the spending sprees and horn blowing to tout a five-century feeding frenzy that has left Native people and this red quarter of Mother Earth in a state of emergency. For Native people, this half millennium of land grabs and one-cent treaty sales has been no bargain.
>
> Suzan Shown Harjo, "I Won't Be Celebrating Columbus Day"

EXERCISE 4 ▶ Analyzing Introductions

What makes a good introduction work? Analyze the following introductions to find out. Answer these questions about each introduction.

- What technique or combination of techniques does the writer use?
- Does the technique work well? Does it make you want to read the article?
- What's the tone of the writing? What's the topic?

1.
> Oseola McCarty never finished the sixth grade, never made more than poverty wages, never had many material possessions, and never expected that in her 87th year she'd be the center of so much attention. But from the moment news spread that this longtime resident of Hattiesburg, Mississippi, had bequeathed $150,000—much of her life's savings—to the local university, this shy woman has been in the spotlight. With her gift, McCarty affirmed her love of

A DIFFERENT APPROACH

For further work on developing tone in introductions, ask each student to copy one of the sample introductions and then to change the tone to angry. When students have finished, tell them to pass their writing to someone else. For the second step, ask each student to read what has been written and then to change the tone of the introduction a second time, perhaps to a skeptical one. Have students create as many different tones as you have time for.

ANSWERS
Exercise 4

1. The introduction begins with a series of interesting details and then in the second sentence states a startling fact. In the third sentence, the writer states the topic sentence of the paragraph.

    The tone is casual and reflective. The topic is stated in the title, "Oseola McCarty."

2. The introduction begins by addressing the reader and also includes unusual facts.

    The tone is casual and humorous ("socially responsible robotics"). The topic is robots enabling handicapped people (a quadriplegic) to work in a pizzeria in Pittsburgh.

AMENDMENTS TO SELECTIONS
Description of changes: excerpted
Rationale: to focus on the concept of writing an introduction presented in this chapter

young people, her belief in education, and her hope for the future, and she reminded a country caught up in a mean-spirited season what our national priorities should be.

Marcia Ann Gillespie, "Oseola McCarty"

2.   If you walk into a pizzeria in Pittsburgh this spring, don't be surprised if the person running the place is a quadriplegic. And don't be surprised if he calls out your order to a robot, which then whips together your pizza. It's just the latest experiment in socially responsible robotics.

"Large Pizza, Hold the Microchips," *Discover*

Bill Redic/©1991 Discover Magazine

E X E R C I S E 5 ▶ **Writing an Introduction**

The introduction to "Road Show" (page 96) takes the reader right into the topic. Read that introduction again, and then write a new introduction for the "Road Show" composition, using one or more of the techniques you've just read about. Be sure you include the thesis statement and set the tone. When you finish your rewrite, compare your new introduction with the introductions of other students. What different techniques were used?

ANSWERS
Exercise 5

The new introductions will vary. An introduction should be acceptable if it uses one or more of the techniques described in this lesson, includes a thesis statement, and sets the tone for the piece.

AMENDMENTS TO SELECTIONS
Description of changes: excerpted
Rationale: to focus on the concept of writing an introduction presented in this chapter

OBJECTIVE

- To analyze unity and coherence in a piece of writing

You could divide the class into groups of three and ask each member to choose one characteristic—unity, coherence, or emphasis—to teach to the others. Have groups use **"Road Show"** (p. 96) for examples. After modeling the paragraph analysis from a sample essay, you could let groups complete **Exercise 6**, p. 118. ☞

The Body

The *body* of a composition develops the major points that support the thesis. One or more paragraphs develop each point and support, or prove, it with details. Readers can follow these points clearly and easily if the body of the composition has these characteristics:

- unity—all paragraphs and details relate to the main idea set out in the thesis statement
- coherence—relationships between ideas are obvious
- emphasis—important ideas stand out more than ideas that are less important

☞ REFERENCE NOTE: For strategies of paragraph development, see pages 79–87.

Unity

Unity is the condition of being "one." For a composition to have unity, all the major points must relate to the main idea in the thesis statement. In addition, all the details in each paragraph must relate to the point expressed in the topic sentence of that paragraph.

Coherence

Coherence describes an orderly relationship. In a coherent composition, ideas are clearly connected. Readers get the sense that sentences and paragraphs flow smoothly and sensibly from one to the other. You can use three techniques to make a composition coherent: (1) transitional words and phrases, (2) direct references, and (3) in a longer composition, a short paragraph that acts as a transition between the paragraph before and the one after.

☞ REFERENCE NOTE: For more about the use of direct references and transitional words and phrases, see pages 74–77.

Emphasis

When you *emphasize* something, you stress it. In a composition, you can emphasize ideas by giving them extra space and attention. That is, you'll write more about one main point than another. If you want to give equal emphasis to two main points, you'll give each about the same amount of space.

PROGRAM MANAGER

THE BODY

- **Instructional Support** To help students identify and use transitional expressions and direct references and reorder and delete sentences to support paragraph topics, see **Achieving Unity and Coherence** in *Practicing the Writing Process,* p. 31.

- **Instructional Support** See **Graphic Organizer 4.** For suggestions on how to tie the transparency to instruction, review teacher's notes for transparencies in *Fine Art and Instructional Transparencies for Writing,* p. 59.

QUOTATION FOR THE DAY

"The discipline of the writer is to learn to be still and listen to what his subject has to tell him." (Rachel Carson, 1907–1964, American naturalist and science writer)

You might have students discuss how the quotation relates to writing the body of a composition. Lead students to understand that the body of the composition develops the major points that support or prove the thesis.

ASSESSMENT

You can assess students' progress by examining their efforts on **Exercise 6**.

CLOSURE

Close the lesson by asking for definitions of *unity* and *coherence*. You could also ask students to identify how unity and coherence are important to the thesis statement. ■

MEETING *individual* NEEDS

LEP/ESL

General Strategies. On the chalkboard, draw a large circle with a point in the middle. Draw several spokes, as one would find in a wagon wheel, expanding out from the middle point. Explain that each of the spokes signifies a major point made in the body of the composition. Each of these must be directly connected to the center point, or thesis, for the composition to be effective.

EXERCISE 6 ▶   **Analyzing Unity and Coherence**

How do professional writers achieve unity and coherence in their compositions? Read the following paragraph from an article about Diana Golden, an accomplished athlete who skis on one leg. Then answer these questions about the paragraph.

- What's the (main idea) of the paragraph? Do all the details in the paragraph support that main idea?   yes
- How is the paragraph organized? What order do most of the ideas follow? (See pages 74 and 79–87 for more about order of ideas.)   chronological
- What transitional words or phrases and what direct references does the writer use to connect ideas?   Answers may vary.

Golden's record as a disabled champion will not, however, stand as her greatest legacy to skiing. (She will be most significantly remembered as the woman who, perhaps more than any other athlete, brought crossover credibility to the disabled-sports movement.) Golden was among the first to persuade sponsors and the public to perceive disabled athletes as *athletes*, period. She was awarded numerous titles never before granted to a disabled person. In 1986, for instance, she won the U.S. Ski Association's (USSA) Beck Award, given to the best American racer in international skiing. *Ski Racing* magazine named her the 1988 U.S. Female Alpine Skier of the Year. And the U.S. Olympic Committee stunned the international sports community when it bypassed all of 1988's two-legged competitors and named Golden the Female Skier of the Year. Not disabled skier. No asterisk. Just Skier of the Year.

Meg Lukens, "Skiing a Formidable Course"

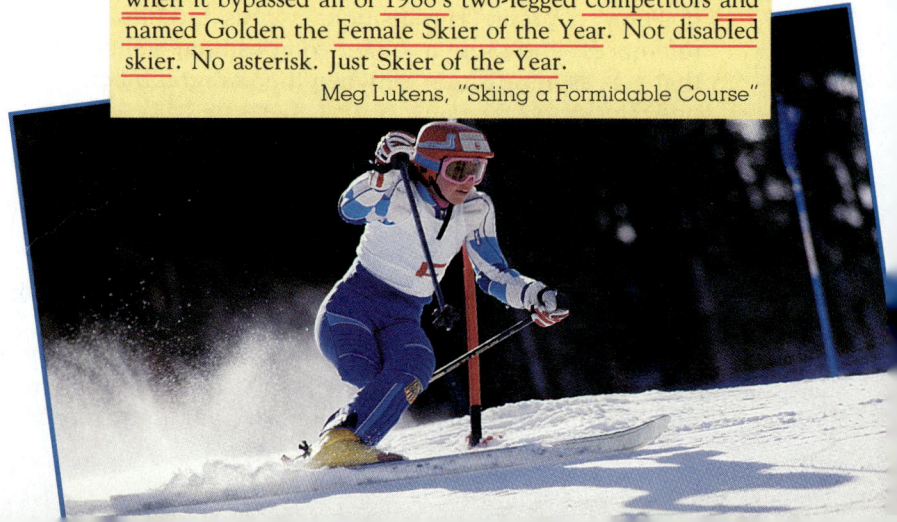

THE CONCLUSION

OBJECTIVE

• To write a conclusion

You may want to review by asking students about thesis statements, plans, introductions, and bodies. Explain that students will make use of all the information they have generated to develop their conclusions. Then you can go on to the six techniques given for writing conclusions. Read the descriptions and examples together. ☞

The Conclusion

Readers usually remember longest what they read last. The *conclusion* of your composition should leave readers with a final thought and a sense of closure—it should clearly say THE END. Note the following techniques.

Techniques for Writing Conclusions

1. **Restate your thesis.** To be sure your main idea hits home, say it again in a different way. The model composition on pages 108–110 has this kind of conclusion, combined with a final comment.

2. **Summarize your major points.** This type of conclusion helps to reinforce what you've said.

3. **Direct your readers' attention to consequences or future directions.** The following conclusion ends with a look at the possibilities for future research in Native American languages.

> Maya was long considered the only true writing system to have developed in the New World. Now we know that another written language, perhaps belonging to the Olmec people, developed more or less independently. Some 400 glyphs are discernible on the stela. Simply on the basis of their variety Grube speculates that the La Mojarra language may have fewer signs than Maya, and may thus represent an even more phonetic, less logographic system. But unless many more carved stones are found in Veracruz, the glyphs will probably never be read.
>
> David Roberts, "The Decipherment of Ancient Maya"

4. **Close with a call to action.** Writers often ask readers to take action in persuasive essays and articles, but a call to action also suits other types of compositions. The following conclusion is from a composition urging people to conserve fuel.

> Do you really need the vehicles you have? Why not take inventory? How often do you use that gas-guzzler, and when you do, would a smaller, more economical vehicle do the job as well? Every person who switches to a more envi-

---

PROGRAM MANAGER

THE CONCLUSION

■ **Instructional Support** To help students identify techniques used to write conclusions, see **An Effective Conclusion** in *Practicing the Writing Process,* p. 32.

■ **Review** For a review of revising and proofreading symbols, see **Review: Revising and Proofreading** in *Practicing the Writing Process,* p. 33.

■ **Reinforcement/Reteaching** See **Revision Transparency 4.** For suggestions on how to tie the transparency to instruction, review teacher's notes in *Fine Art and Instructional Transparencies for Writing,* p. 101.

QUOTATION FOR THE DAY

"Well, I've gotten to the end of the subject—of the page—of your patience and my time." (Alice B. Toklas, 1877–1967, American writer and companion to Gertrude Stein)

An ideal conclusion does more than signify that the writer has reached the end of a page or said all there is to say about a subject. Explain that conclusions should leave readers with a final thought and a sense of closure.

AMENDMENTS TO SELECTIONS
Description of changes: excerpted
Rationale: to focus on the concept of writing a conclusion.

MEETING individual NEEDS

LEP/ESL

General Strategies. The final technique for creating conclusions is to refer to the introduction. You may want to point out that many movie directors use this technique in bringing their films to a close. Ask students to suggest movies that they have seen in which this technique is implemented. Have the students briefly describe the introduction and conclusion. This type of activity encourages students to tap into their firsthand knowledge and, in doing so, stimulates interest in the topic.

COOPERATIVE LEARNING

After dividing the class into groups of four or five, ask each group to find one or two examples of each type of conclusion and then to mount and number them on a poster. Pass the posters from group to group and ask each group to label the technique of each conclusion on a sheet of paper.

AMENDMENTS TO SELECTIONS
Description of changes: excerpted
Rationale: to focus on the concept of writing a conclusion presented in this chapter

ronmentally sound vehicle becomes a part of the solution instead of contributing to the pollution. It's our earth and our air and our ozone layer. And it's the pollution from our vehicles that's destroying them. Let's change our ways now.

5. **End with an appropriate quotation.** A quotation that sums up your main point or that's particularly striking can make a strong ending. This technique concludes "Road Show," page 97, and is used in the following conclusion.

Being a stranger in a strange land is never easy. "All the English-speaking kids should learn a foreign language. Then they'd know how hard it is for us sometimes," says 17-year-old Sufyan Kabba, a Maryland high-school junior, who left Sierra Leone last year. But here they are, part of the nation's future, young Yankees who in the end must rely on the special strength of children: adaptability.

Connie Leslie, Daniel Glick, and Jeanne Gordon, "Classrooms of Babel"

6. **Refer to the introduction.** Bring your composition full circle by mentioning something in your introduction. Diane Ackerman begins and concludes her article (pages 113–114) by describing monk seals.

Standing at the stern as the boat gathers speed, I watch until the crescent island grows shorter, the shining monk seals become indistinguishable from smooth wet stones, and all that's left are the indecipherable gestures of the sea.

Diane Ackerman, "Last Refuge of the Monk Seal"

Ask each group to read its best conclusion aloud to the class. Require each member of the class to evaluate each conclusion based on these points: Is it strong? Does it leave you with a sense of closure? The groups could then look at these peer evaluations.

You could review quickly what a conclusion should do and why it is important. Try demonstrating the point by ending the class in several different ways—for example, with a summary, a final comment, or a quotation. ■

The Conclusion   **121**

WRITING NOTE

The title of your composition is your first chance to grab your reader's attention. And it can also act as a very short summary, pointing your reader toward your main ideas. Go for a title that's both catchy and pointed. Writers often give their compositions a tentative title as they're writing and then revise the title once they're finished. Even then, it usually takes several drafts before they're satisfied with the results. Here are some examples of titles for the composition on pages 108–110. What's your choice for the most effective title?

Computers in the Classroom
Computers: The New Kids in Class
Computers: The New Way to Teach

EXERCISE 7 ▶ **Writing a Conclusion**

Working with a small group, reread the conclusion to Steve Nadis's "Road Show" (page 97) or the conclusion to the Writer's Model (page 110). Then write a new conclusion for one of these compositions, using one or more of the techniques you've just read about. (Don't be afraid to experiment!)

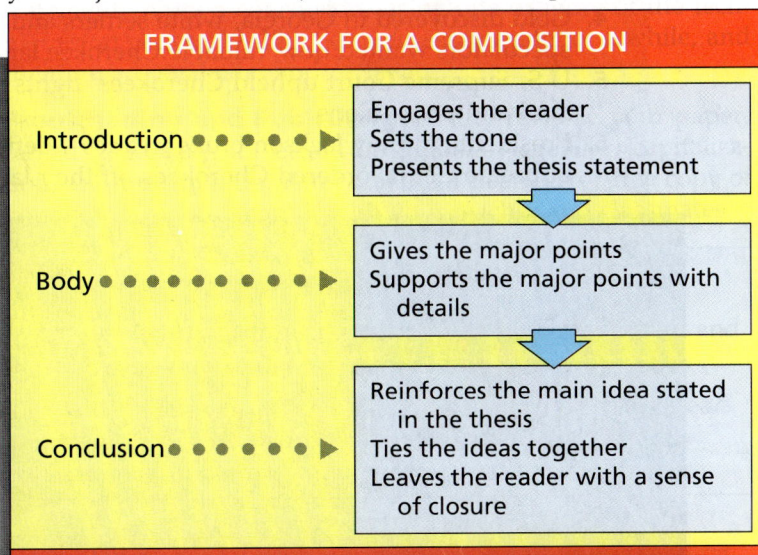

FRAMEWORK FOR A COMPOSITION

Introduction • • • • • ▶ | Engages the reader
Sets the tone
Presents the thesis statement

Body • • • • • • • • • ▶ | Gives the major points
Supports the major points with details

Conclusion • • • • • • ▶ | Reinforces the main idea stated in the thesis
Ties the ideas together
Leaves the reader with a sense of closure

EXPRESSIVE WRITING: NARRATION

OBJECTIVES

- To select an appropriate reflective experience as the topic for a reflective essay
- To recall details and to explore the meaning of a reflective experience
- To organize and draft a reflective essay
- To analyze a writer's revisions
- To evaluate and revise the content and organization of a reflective essay
- To proofread and publish a reflective essay

WRITING-IN-PROGRESS ASSIGNMENTS

Major Assignment: Writing a reflective essay
Cumulative Writing Assignments: The chart below shows the sequence of cumulative assignments that will guide students as they write a reflective essay. These Writing Assignments form the instructional core of Chapter 4.

PREWRITING
WRITING ASSIGNMENT
- Part 1: Choosing an Experience for a Reflective Essay p. 131
- Part 2: Recalling Details and Exploring Meanings p. 136
- Part 3: Organizing Details p. 138

WRITING YOUR FIRST DRAFT
WRITING ASSIGNMENT
- Part 4: Writing a Draft of Your Reflective Essay p. 147

EVALUATING AND REVISING
WRITING ASSIGNMENT
- Part 5: Evaluating and Revising Your Reflective Essay p. 150

PROOFREADING AND PUBLISHING
WRITING ASSIGNMENT
- Part 6: Proofreading and Publishing Your Essay p. 152

In addition, exercises 1–3 provide practice in freewriting about in speaking and listening, analyzing a reflective essay, and analyzing revisions.

WORKPLACE writing

Expressive Writing on Job Applications

Job applicants are often asked to identify and discuss a meaningful event in their lives. Have students use the material in Chapter 4 to practice writing a reflective essay for a job application.

- **Reflection and Brainstorming** After students have reviewed pp. 132–136 and had time to brainstorm, consider the following exercise. Have students retell to a partner the experience they would like to write about. After a retelling, the listener should complete in writing the statement "I think that this experience was meaningful to you because _____." The speaker should write a similar statement; "I think that this experience was meaningful to me because _____." Have students switch roles and write statements about the second student's experience. After both students have retold their experiences and written statements, ask students to compare the statements their partners wrote with their own.

  Students may decide after this exercise that the experience they described does not lend itself to a reflective essay. Allow students to repeat the exercise with a different experience. If students still have trouble, have them do the exercise with you.

- **Troubleshooting** If students find that they have trouble writing the first draft of their essays, suggest that they return to the prewriting stage and read excerpts from journals or autobiographies of people they admire. Suggest that they answer questions like the following about their reading:
  - Why does this person consider this experience meaningful?
  - Can I identify with the writer's experience?
  - What did the writer learn from his or her experience? Encourage students to apply similar questions to their own essays.

INTEGRATING THE LANGUAGE ARTS

SELECTION	READING AND LITERATURE	WRITING AND CRITICAL THINKING	LANGUAGE AND SYNTAX	SPEAKING, LISTENING, AND OTHER EXPRESSION SKILLS
• from "I Have a Dream" by Martin Luther King, Jr. pp. 126–128 • from *Silent Dancing: A Partial Remembrance of a Puerto Rican Childhood* by Judith Ortiz Cofer pp. 140–143 • "Out, out, tell-tale spot!" by Susan Trausch pp. 153–155	• Responding personally to literature pp. 128, 143 • Determining an author's purpose p. 128 • Reading for specific details pp. 128, 143 • Analyzing an introduction p. 143 • Finding the main idea p. 143	• Making inferences and drawing conclusions pp. 128, 143, 150 • Choosing an experience p. 131 • Analyzing details and the meaning of experiences pp. 134, 136, 143 • Organizing details pp. 138, 155 • Analyzing a writer's revisions p. 150 • Evaluating and revising, and proofreading and publishing an essay pp. 150, 152 • Reflecting on writing for portfolio selections p. 152 • Using exaggeration to create humor in an essay p. 155 • Applying interpretive and creative thinking pp. 155, 158–159 • Writing an autobiographical sketch pp. 158–159	• Proofreading for errors in grammar, usage, and mechanics pp. 152, 155 • Using sentence fragments effectively p. 152	• Working with a classmate to refine details for clarity p. 134 • Working with classmates to analyze the meaning of experience pp. 136, 143 • Working with classmates to analyze a writer's revisions p. 150 • Working with classmates to evaluate and revise a reflective essay p. 150 • Working with classmates to evaluate a humorous essay p. 155

SUGGESTED INTEGRATED UNIT PLAN

This unit plan gives suggestions on how to integrate the major strands of the language arts with this chapter.

If you begin with this chapter expressive writing or with the suggested literature selections, you should focus on the common characteristics of expressive writing. You can then integrate speaking/listening and language concepts with both the writing and the literature.

Common Characteristics

- Frequent use of first person—*I, me, us, we*
- Figurative language that evokes a mood and appeals to the senses
- Content that is self-expressive and conveys emotion and attitudes
- Usually chronological organization
- Possible use of dialogue

Writing
Reflective Narrative

Speaking/Listening:

- Retelling an experience to a partner
- Discussing the meaning of an experience with a partner

UNIT FOCUS
EXPRESSIVE WRITING

Language
Mechanics, Style

- Apostrophes
- Sentence fragments
- Voice, tone, and mood

Literature
Nonfiction such as

- "Shooting an Elephant" George Orwell
- "The Death of a Moth" Virginia Woolf
- "Zagreb: A Letter to My Daughter" Slavenka Drakulíc

CHAPTER 4: EXPRESSIVE WRITING: NARRATION

Use this guide for creating an instructional plan that addresses the individual needs of your students. Assignments accompanied by the following symbol (✱) may be completed out of class. Times given for pacing lessons are estimated.

CHAPTER PLANNING GUIDE—PUPIL'S EDITION

LESSONS	LITERARY MODEL pp. 126–128 from "I Have a Dream" by Martin Luther King, Jr.	PREWRITING pp. 130–138	
		Generating Ideas	Gathering/Organizing
DEVELOPMENTAL PROGRAM	🕐 25–30 minutes • Have students read model aloud to partners and discuss questions on p. 128	🕐 40–45 minutes • Main Assignment: Looking Ahead p. 129 • Choosing a Personal Experience pp. 130–131 • Writing Assignment: Part 1 p. 131	🕐 55–60 minutes • Planning Your Reflective Essay pp. 132–138 • Exercise 1 p. 134 • Critical Thinking pp. 134–136 • Writing Assignment: Parts 2–3 pp. 136, 138
CORE PROGRAM	🕐 20–25 minutes • Assign student pairs to read the model and answer questions on p. 128	🕐 30–35 minutes • Main Assignment: Looking Ahead p. 129 • Choosing a Personal Experience pp. 130–131 • Writing Assignment: Part 1 p. 131✱	🕐 45–50 minutes • Planning Your Reflective Essay pp. 132–138 • Writing Note p. 134 • Exercise 1 p. 134 • Critical Thinking pp. 134–136 • Writing Assignment: Parts 2–3 pp. 136, 138✱
ACCELERATED PROGRAM	🕐 15–20 minutes • Assign students to read model independently and take notes in their Reader's Logs	🕐 20–25 minutes • Main Assignment: Looking Ahead p. 129 • Choosing a Personal Experience pp. 130–131 • Writing Assignment: Part 1 p. 131✱	🕐 40–45 minutes • Planning Your Reflective Essay pp. 132–133 • Writing Note p. 134 • Exercise 1 p. 134 • Critical Thinking pp. 134–136 • Organizational Chart p. 137 • Writing Assignment: Parts 2–3 pp. 136, 138✱

CHAPTER PLANNING GUIDE—PROGRAM RESOURCES

	LITERARY MODEL	PREWRITING
PRINT	• Reading Master 4, *Practice for Assessment in Reading, Vocabulary, and Spelling* p. 4	• Prewriting, *Strategies for Writing* p. 2 • Expressing Yourself, *English Workshop* pp. 45–54
MEDIA	• Fine Art Transparency 1: *The Tragedy, Transparency Binder* 💾	• Graphic Organizers 5–6, *Transparency Binder* 💾 • *Writer's Workshop 2:* Reflective Essay 💾

WRITING pp. 139–147	EVALUATING AND REVISING pp. 148–150	PROOFREADING AND PUBLISHING pp. 151–153
⏱ **40–45 minutes** • The Elements of a Reflec-tive Essay pp. 139–140 • A Basic Framework p. 144 • Read aloud A Writer's Model pp. 144–146 • Framework Chart p. 147 • Writing Assignment: Part 4 p. 147*	⏱ **45–50 minutes** • Evaluating and Revising p. 148 • Evaluating and Revising Chart p. 149 • Exercise 3 p. 150 • Writing Assignment: Part 5 p. 150	⏱ **45–50 minutes** • Proofreading and Publishing p. 151 • Grammar Hint p. 151 • Writing Assignment: Part 6 p. 152 • Reflecting p. 152 • Student Model p. 153
⏱ **45–50 minutes** • The Elements of a Reflec-tive Essay pp. 139–140 • A Passage pp. 140–143 • Exercise 2 p. 143 • A Basic Framework p. 144 • Framework Chart p. 147 • Writing Assignment: Part 4 p. 147*	⏱ **40–45 minutes** • Evaluating and Revising p. 148 • Evaluating and Revising Chart p. 149 • Exercise 3 p. 150 • Writing Assignment: Part 5 p. 150	⏱ **35–40 minutes** • Proofreading and Publishing p. 151 • Grammar Hint p. 151 • Writing Assignment: Part 6 p. 152 • Reflecting p. 152 • Student Model p. 153
⏱ **40–45 minutes** • The Elements of a Reflec-tive Essay pp. 139–140 • A Passage pp. 140–143 • Exercise 2 p. 143 • Framework Chart p. 147 • Writing Assignment: Part 4 p. 147*	⏱ **35–40 minutes** • Evaluating and Revising Chart p. 149 • Exercise 3 p. 150* • Writing Assignment: Part 4 p. 150	⏱ **30–35 minutes** • Grammar Hint p. 151 • Writing Assignment: Part 6 p. 152 • Reflecting p. 152

WRITING	EVALUATING AND REVISING	PROOFREADING AND PUBLISHING
• Writing, *Strategies for Writing* p. 3	• Evaluating and Revising, *Strategies for Writing* p. 4	• Proofreading Practice, *Strategies for Writing* p. 6 • *English Workshop* pp. 93–94
	• Revision Transparencies 5–6, *Transparency Binder* 📽	• *Language Workshop:* Lesson 31 💾

ELEMENTS OF WRITING: CURRICULUM CONNECTIONS

Writer's Workshop
• A Humorous Personal Essay pp. 154–156

Making Connections
• Writing a Brief Autobiography pp. 157–158
• Self-Expression and the Future: Setting Goals pp. 158–159

ASSESSMENT OPTIONS

Summative Assessment
Holistic Scoring: Prompts and Models pp. 3–8

Portfolio Assessment
Portfolio forms, *Portfolio Assessment* pp. 5–25, 44–48

Reflection
Self-assessment Record, *Portfolio Assessment* p. 19
Writing Process Log, *Strategies for Writing* p. 1

Ongoing Assessment
Proofreading, *Strategies for Writing* p. 5

Performance Assessment
Assessment 1 and Assessment 3, *Integrated Performance Assessment, Level G* For help with evaluation, see *Holistic Scoring Software.* 💾

💾 Computer disk or CD-ROM

📽 Overhead transparencies

DISCOVERING YOURSELF

OBJECTIVES

- To analyze the expressive qualities of a literary model
- To write an expressive journal entry
- To write personal responses to literature

MOTIVATION

Ask students to freewrite for five minutes in response to this question:

If you could have anything in the world, what would you wish for?

Then classify on the chalkboard the dreams of students who do not mind sharing their dreams with the class and then initiate a class discussion about types of dreams. How

PROGRAM MANAGER

CHAPTER 4

- **Computer Guided Instruction** For a related assignment that students may use for additional instruction and practice, see **Autobiographical Incident** in *Writer's Workshop 2 CD-ROM.*

- **Practice** To help less-advanced students who need additional practice with concepts and activities related to this chapter, see **Chapter 4** in *English Workshop, Complete Course,* pp. 45–54.

- **Summative Assessment** For a writing prompt, including grading criteria and student models, see *Holistic Scoring: Prompts and Models,* pp. 3–8.

- **Performance Assessment** Use **Assessments 1** and **3** in *Integrated Performance Assessment, Level G.* For help with evaluating student writing, see *Holistic Scoring Workshop, Level G.*

- **Extension/Enrichment** See **Fine Art Transparency 1,** *The Tragedy* by Pablo Picasso. For suggestions on how to tie the transparency to instruction, review teacher's notes in *Fine Art and Instructional Transparencies for Writing,* p. 3.

- **Reading Support** For help with the reading selection pp. 126–128, see *Reading Master 4* in *Practice for Assessment in Reading, Vocabulary, and Spelling,* p. 4.

4 EXPRESSIVE WRITING: NARRATION

many want money or success? Tell students that Martin Luther King, Jr., had a special and unselfish dream for America.

Discovering Yourself

All your life you have been **discovering things about yourself**—that music brings you joy, that relationships can bring pain. Those discoveries help you understand yourself; but more than that, they help you understand being human.

Writing and You. In a published speech, Sandra Cisneros recalls her experience making tortillas and then reflects on her accomplishments as a woman and a writer. In an essay, E. B. White expresses his feelings about the death of his pet pig. When have you written to discover something about yourself?

As You Read. In the following speech, a man reflects on his dreams for the future. What are they?

Donald Crowley, *The Critics* (1990). Oil on canvas, 48" × 60". Courtesy of the artist.

Response and Writer's Craft questions to involve students in the discovery process—theirs and King's.

GUIDED PRACTICE
Have students share their responses to the first question as you give your responses. Model freewriting by showing students the ideas you would address for the second question. For the analytical questions, share one example of images from King's speech with the class.

USING THE SELECTION
from I Have a Dream

1

First-person point of view is an important characteristic of expressive writing.

2

What is the American dream? [The American dream includes personal freedom, equality, and economic opportunity.]

3

The allusion to the Declaration of Independence relates King's dream to the dreams and beliefs of the founders of the United States.

4

What does this facet of King's dream symbolize? [To share food symbolizes a familiar relationship of love and acceptance.]

5

Repetition of the phrase at the start of each paragraph is one example of King's effective use of parallel structure.

6

The use of a one-sentence paragraph emphasizes the urgency of King's dream and the fact that his hope for freedom is still just a dream.

7

In this paragraph, King alludes to the Biblical prophet Isaiah and makes a connection between enslaved Israelites and African Americans.

8

What example of parallel structure do you find in this paragraph? [Students may list introductory prepositional phrases and infinitive phrases.]

126

from

I HAVE A DREAM

by MARTIN LUTHER KING, JR.

1 **2** I SAY TO YOU TODAY, my friends, that in spite of the difficulties and frustrations of the moment, I still have a dream. It is a dream deeply rooted in the American dream.

3 I have a dream that one day this nation will rise up and live out the true meaning of its creed: "We hold these truths to be self-evident: that all men are created equal."

4 I have a dream that one day on the red hills of Georgia the sons of former slaves and the sons of former slave owners will be able to sit down together at the table of brotherhood.

5 I have a dream that my four little children will one day live in a nation where they will not be judged by the color of their skin but the content of their character.

6 I have a dream today.

7 I have a dream that one day every valley shall be exalted, every hill and mountain shall be made low, the rough places will be made plains, and the crooked places will be made straight, and the glory of the Lord shall be revealed, and all flesh shall see it together.

8 This is our hope. This is the faith with which I return to the South. With this faith we will be able to hew out of the mountains of despair a stone of hope. With this faith we will be able to transform

INDEPENDENT PRACTICE

Question 2 of **Reader's Response** asks students to write journal entries about their personal dreams. Have students write their entries independently. Also ask students to answer the **Writer's Craft** questions independently.

ASSESSMENT

You will want to be sure that students respond in their writing journals, but you may want to give students the option of keeping their dreams private. Tell students that you will read and respond to their entries if they wish, but that if they do not want you to read their writing journals, they can simply fold and staple the page. Ask ☞

127

the jangling discords of our nation into a beautiful symphony of brotherhood. With this faith we will be able to work together, to pray together, to struggle together, to go to jail together, to stand up for freedom together, knowing that we will be free one day.

This will be the day when all of God's children will be able to sing with new meaning, "My country, 'tis of thee, sweet land of liberty, of thee I sing. Land where my fathers died, land of the Pilgrim's pride, from every mountainside, let freedom ring."

And if America is to be a great nation, this must become true. So let freedom ring from the prodigious hilltops of New Hampshire. Let freedom ring from the mighty mountains of New York. Let freedom ring from the heightening Alleghenies of Pennsylvania. Let freedom ring from the curvaceous peaks of California!

Let freedom ring from Stone Mountain of Georgia!

Let freedom ring from every hill and molehill of Mississippi. From every mountainside, let freedom ring.

9

". . . my four little children will one day live in a nation where they will not be judged by the color of their skin but the content of their character."

9
A positive image contrasts effectively with a negative image.

10
Repetition produces strong emotional response toward love of freedom.

VISUAL CONNECTIONS

Exploring the Subject. Martin Luther King, Jr., was a Baptist minister with a doctorate in theology from Boston University. Influenced by Henry David Thoreau and Mohandas Gandhi of India, King used nonviolent resistance to advocate social and political change. King's crusade for civil rights began in December of 1955 in Montgomery, Alabama, where Rosa Parks, an African American woman who had refused to give up her bus seat to a white person, was arrested. Under King's leadership, African Americans organized and boycotted the transit system. King's house was dynamited and his family threatened, but eventually the city of Montgomery desegregated its buses. On August 28, 1963, King presented his famous "I Have a Dream" speech to a quarter of a million Americans who had marched peacefully to Washington, D.C. to ask for civil rights legislation.

students to share their responses to the **Writer's Craft** questions orally. You can assess mastery as you listen to the students' answers.

CLOSURE

Ask volunteers to explain how people can use expressive (reflective) writing. [Expressive writing helps people make discoveries about themselves.] ∎

When we let freedom ring, when we let it ring from every village and every <u>hamlet</u>, from every state and every city, we will be able to speed up that day when all of God's children, black men and white men, Jews and Gentiles, Protestants and Catholics, will be able to join hands and sing in the words of that old Negro spiritual, "Free at last! Free at last! Thank God almighty, we are free at last!"

READER'S RESPONSE

1. Imagine that you are in Washington, D.C., on August 28, 1963, listening to King's speech. It is a glorious day of deep blue sky and sunshine glinting off the Washington Monument. What thoughts and feelings do you have as King speaks?
2. Think of who you are and the future ahead of you. What do you dream? In a journal entry, freewrite about your dreams, trying to envision specific images for the future as King does in his speech.

WRITER'S CRAFT

3. Reflective writing usually begins with a specific incident or idea that triggers broader reflections. Read over the first few paragraphs of King's speech (page 126). What experiences or ideas might have triggered the speech?
4. King uses many specific images to depict his dream, including "a beautiful symphony of brotherhood." Which images most appeal to you? Why?

⬦ CRITICAL THINKING

Analysis. Although King's speech is an excellent example of expressive writing, it also has qualities of persuasion. Explain that persuasion uses one or more of these techniques to convince an audience: an appeal to the emotions, an appeal to reason, or an appeal based on the authority or personality of the speaker.

Ask students to analyze King's speech to determine which of these three appeals is the strongest.

ANSWERS

Reader's Response

Responses will vary.

1. If possible, play an audiocassette or videotape of King's speech. Students may experience a variety of feelings.
2. Encourage students to use specific images in writing about one or two specific dreams.

Writer's Craft

Responses will vary.

3. The first four paragraphs suggest that recent experiences of prejudice and discrimination were sources of King's speech.
4. Specific images will vary, but King's most effective images have strong sensory appeal.

SELECTION AMENDMENT
Description of change: excerpted
Rationale: to focus on the concept of expressive writing presented in this chapter

WAYS TO EXPRESS YOURSELF

TEACHING THE LESSON

Begin your lesson by reading aloud the introductory paragraph. You may also want to ask students what forms of expression they use at football or basketball games (cheers, school songs) and what forms of popular expression they like (popular songs).

Tell students that writers use four basic methods of development: narration, description, classification (which includes comparison and contrast), and evaluation. Students will use two methods, narration and evaluation, to write essays for this chapter. ■

129

Ways to Express Yourself

You don't have to search far to find examples of expressive writing. You find it in greeting card stores, where you search for a card that says exactly what you feel. You find it in the lyrics of the tapes and CDs that "speak" to you. And you read it in letters, journals, and articles or essays in magazines. Here are some specific examples of writing used for self-expression.

- in your journal, describing how you feel about the senior prom
- in an e-mail message, telling a friend about a frightening experience
- in a personal essay, writing about old mementos, photos, and letters you discovered in the attic of your house
- in a song, describing the pain of lost love
- in a letter, comparing your current dreams and plans for yourself with what they were two years ago
- in a job application, explaining your three main goals in life
- in an editorial, giving your opinion about a new curfew for teenagers
- on a World Wide Web page, expressing your favorite band's significance to you
- in a review, stating what you liked about a movie
- in your journal, exploring your thoughts about the college application process

INTEGRATING THE LANGUAGE ARTS

Literature Link. Have your students read the speech about ambition in Act I of Shakespeare's tragedy *Macbeth*. Then ask students to explain in journal entries or in a class discussion how the speech employs the four qualities of expressive, reflective discourse given at the bottom of this page.

Be sure students give specific examples from the literature to support their analyses.

LOOKING AHEAD

In the main assignment in this chapter, you will use narration and evaluation to write a personal, reflective essay. As you work through the writing assignments, keep in mind that a personal, reflective essay

- begins with a concrete experience
- weaves in personal thoughts and feelings to convey a theme or main idea
- moves from a personal to a universal level gradually reveals the full significance of the experience

OBJECTIVES

- To select a personal experience as the topic for a reflective essay
- To recall narrative and descriptive details of a personal experience by working with a partner
- To analyze the meanings of an experience
- To prepare an organizational plan for a reflective essay about an experience

---

PROGRAM MANAGER

PREWRITING

- **Self-Assessment** Before beginning instruction of the writing process, see **Writing Process Log** in *Strategies for Writing*, p. 1.

- **Heuristics** To help students generate ideas, see **Prewriting** in *Strategies for Writing*, p. 2.

- **Instructional Support** See **Graphic Organizers 5** and **6.** For suggestions on how to tie the transparencies to instruction, review teacher's notes in *Fine Art and Instructional Transparencies for Writing*, pp. 61, 63.

QUOTATION FOR THE DAY

"A writer uses what experience he or she has. It's the translating, though, that makes the difference." (John Irving, 1942–   , American author)

Discuss that "translating" an experience involves describing the experience's impression on the participant. Tell the class to choose as subjects personal experiences that are significant and to record what they saw, heard, did, felt, and thought.

Writing a Reflective Essay

Prewriting

Choosing a Personal Experience

At first, you may notice that some people are always late for class or that they always park in front of "No Parking" signs. Then you take your thinking a step further and apply what you have noticed to your own life, wondering why you sometimes want to rebel against limits, like tardy bells and "No Parking" zones. Once again you look outward, observing that other people also feel rebellious at times. Just noticing the actions of a few people has led you to reflect about human nature in general.

That's an example of what you can do in a reflective essay—use a specific incident as a springboard to reflect about your feelings and behavior, then those of other people, then the human condition. You do not have to be involved in the "triggering" incident; you may be just an observer. Nor do you have to observe or participate in a single incident: There may be a series of incidents that inspire you to write.

You can begin your search for an experience for reflection by brainstorming for memories of incidents that have moved you to explore broader meanings. You might also do some brainstorming or freewriting to explore what those meanings are. Following is the freewriting one writer did while deciding on a topic for a reflective essay.

After asking students if they have ever kept diaries or writing journals, initiate a discussion about the purpose of a diary or writing journal. Some students will explain that they have recorded daily events, personal experiences, and their thoughts and feelings in their diaries or writing journals. Point out that the assignment in this lesson is similar in some ways to writing a journal.

Prewriting **131**

HERE'S HOW

> Watching Tamara, 7-year-old niece, get ready for party. She's wearing party dress—ruffles, bows, everything—but other kids wearing jeans. She doesn't care—willing to be different. But am I? Are any of us?

> Sitting in my room with the window open. Reading a magazine, feeling sort of lonely and sad. Then saw something fly by my shoulder—looked up and saw a little yellow bird. It flew out the window, then came in again and landed on my computer. Amazed me and made me think life can be surprising. Do we ever know what will happen next? Is it possible that during bad times we just need to remember that things are always changing?

> Went snorkeling for the first time. Water was sort of a dirty gray and I expected underwater to be like on top. Didn't expect the bright colors—fish and coral. Like a different world underneath. I'd judged the ocean based on its surface. Do I do that with people—make judgments based on outward appearances? Is that what leads to bigotry and prejudice?

WRITING ASSIGNMENT

PART 1:
Choosing an Experience for a Reflective Essay

What has happened to you that's made you wonder about your own thoughts and actions, about those of other people, about what it means to be human? What has affected your view of yourself and of others? Choose one of these experiences as the "anchor" for your reflective essay. Remember that the experience may actually have been a series of experiences and that you may have been just an observer.

MEETING individual NEEDS

LEP/ESL

General Strategies. One of the steps suggested in the prewriting process, the step of working with a partner to clarify details, is invaluable to students and should not be overlooked. If possible, pair your English-language learners with partners from the same language background. This type of partnership fosters a level of safety in sharing and exploring personal information. Although it is preferable that students exchange ideas in English, it is not imperative, and they should not be discouraged from using their native languages if doing so facilitates the creative process. Clarification of thought and intention can be accomplished in any language. Students can make the switch to English in the following stage, when writing actually begins.

As you begin this lesson, help students to understand the overall purpose of a reflective essay by writing on the chalkboard *personal experience* and *your reflections about it.* To be complete, a reflective essay must contain both of these elements.

When you assign **Writing Assignment: Part 1,** p. 131, warn students not to select topics for their essays too quickly. Explain that if they choose experiences with little meaning for themselves and little universal significance, they will lose valuable time and effort.

Model on the chalkboard the prewriting procedures explained in this lesson. Select a topic for group discussion, brainstorm for supporting details, and use the four

MEETING *individual* NEEDS

AT-RISK STUDENTS

The opportunity to write about their personal experiences should help students understand that their personal lives are important. In your responses to the essays that students write, you will want to praise and encourage them, but you will also want to avoid giving too much personal advice.

LEARNING STYLES

Visual Learners. Encourage students to bring to class photographs or other memorabilia. Give students the opportunity to study the visuals before they select their topics and as they are collecting details.

Kinetic Learners. Some students are likely to choose tactile objects—perhaps stuffed animals from their childhood or trophies that represent important achievements. Allow students to keep such objects with them as they write about their experiences.

Auditory Learners. Although it will be more difficult for students to bring to class objects that directly relate to their learning style, some may be able to bring personal or commercial tapes that remind them of experiences. If possible, make available tape players with earphones for students.

Prewriting

Planning Your Reflective Essay

When you write a reflective essay, you are taking readers on a guided tour through a personal experience and your reflections about it. To make certain the tour is a memorable one, you need to plan your essay carefully.

Thinking About Purpose, Audience, and Tone

Your main *purpose* in writing a reflective essay is to explore and discover the significance of an incident or experience. You'll want to show how and why the incident was significant for you.

When you start your essay, you might not know what "truths" you will discover. That's okay. Uncovering layers of meaning in personal experience is part of the process of writing a reflective essay. Your first *audience,* then, is yourself. But you'll also want to broaden the experience to show why others might find significance in it, so you will need to consider other readers, too. Think about the kinds of details they will need in order to understand the significance of the experience.

A reflective essay has an informal *tone,* almost as if the writer is thinking out loud. You can achieve this tone by using the first-person point of view and conversational language. A reflective essay is effective when your readers feel they can trust you, when they feel you are being honest with them.

Recalling Details

A reflective essay is based, first of all, on a personal experience. In some essays that experience is mentioned only briefly before the writer moves on to a reflection on it, but in other essays the experience may be more important. The following two examples show how writers might treat experiences differently.

- One writer briefly tells about the experience of seeing the first buds of spring on an apple tree. The writer then quickly moves into a reflection on how it is almost always possible to make a new start in life.

questions on p. 135 to explore the meaning of the experience. You can use the **Here's How** chart of an organizational plan (p. 138) as a model to guide students as they complete **Writing Assignment: Part 3** on page 138. Monitor students as they select the topics for their essays and complete their organizational plans. Provide additional guidance as necessary.

INDEPENDENT PRACTICE

After you have modeled the various prewriting stages discussed in this lesson, allow students to complete **Exercise 1** and **Writing Assignment: Parts 1–3** independently. Because these assignments are based on personal memories and reflections, students

Cont. on p. 136

■ Another writer relates the experience of an agonizing defeat in the last moments of a championship basketball game. Enough of the experience is described so that readers understand the pain of defeat for the writer. Then the writer reflects on the difficulty of learning to lose.

COOPERATIVE LEARNING

After they have selected experiences for their reflective essays, students should write their topics on paper. The very act of writing helps to reinforce the choice and triggers other associations. Have students share their choices in small groups. This sharing will generate more ideas and can help students to confirm or revise their choices at this early stage.

Whatever the experience, you need to recall details that will set the stage for your reflections. There are two types of details to think about: *narrative* and *descriptive*. **Narrative details** tell specifically about actions and events: "My seven-year-old niece flounced into the room. My sister glanced over at her and groaned." **Descriptive details**, both factual and sensory, describe important people, places, and objects: "Tamara's party dress was all over ruffles, lace, and bows. Lace stockings and shiny white patent leather shoes completed the outfit."

Other types of details you might use include these:

■ *Your thoughts and feelings.* What are your thoughts and feelings about the events you're narrating? Do they help to trigger ideas that expand the meaning of the experience?

■ *Examples.* What examples can you cite from other people or other experiences that might illustrate your own thoughts and reflections?

■ *Anecdotes.* What anecdotes (brief, illustrative stories) about other people might show how the meaning of the experience expands to include them?

☞ **REFERENCE NOTE:** For more information about narrative and descriptive details, see pages 67–68 and 179–180.

OBJECTIVE

- To use questions to analyze the meaning of an experience

TEACHING *ANALYZING AN EXPERIENCE FOR MEANING*

The questions on p. 135 provide helpful guidelines for analyzing an experience for its meanings. However, students may need additional modeling of this complex process. Therefore, you may want to use additional questions to guide students through the

ANSWERS
Exercise 1

Responses will vary. However, all responses should include both factual and sensory details of various types. You may want to ask each pair of students to use blank sheets of paper to prepare grids with two columns: narrative and descriptive. You may want to have pairs of advanced students prepare other grids with three columns: thoughts and feelings, examples, and anecdotes. As the first partner relates details, the second partner should record them.

MEETING *individual* NEEDS

LEP/ESL

General Strategies. Because some students generally perform more effectively and are more comfortable with an assignment that has tangible, specific objectives, you may want to lend further structure to the **Critical Thinking Exercise** on p. 136. Instead of having students merely *discuss* the meanings inherent in the five incidents listed, have groups of three or four each choose one incident on which to focus. Using the four questions on p. 135, each student should record her or his response. Then have students share their responses with the group.

134

---

134 *Expressive Writing*

WRITING NOTE

As you try to recall your experience, your memory may be a little vague, but keep digging for details and recording them until you can see the experience clearly. Select only those details that will focus the experience for readers. Don't, for example, take time to describe unimportant people, places, and objects. Since you will be sharing your reflections on the experience, not just telling about it, try to choose details that will sharpen its meaning for readers.

EXERCISE 1 ▶ **Speaking and Listening: Recalling Details**

Can you clearly remember the experience you'll be writing about? To test your recall, work with a partner and take turns relating the narrative and descriptive details of your experience. Prompt each other by asking for more details in areas that seem unfocused or vague. Keep talking until your partner is satisfied that he or she can "see" your experience clearly.

Exploring the Meaning of an Experience

Once you have recalled the details of your experience, you are ready to explore its meaning. Even though you may have some initial ideas, you should spend some time studying the experience to identify further levels of meaning.

⚡ **CRITICAL THINKING**

Analyzing an Experience for Meaning

Analysis is a thinking skill you use whenever you need to examine something in detail, to understand something fully. Analyzing an experience to find its meaning is like studying the impact of a stone tossed into a pond, watching as its impact makes a circle, then another and another until the ripple has exhausted itself. First, you consider the impact of the experience on yourself. Then, you look outward to see what other example. Or you may want to use the questions to model the process with one of the sample experiences on p. 136. When you believe students understand the questioning process that they are to use in analyzing experiences for meaning, assign the **Critical Thinking Exercise.** Encourage students to work in groups to compare their personal responses. Emphasize that there are no right and wrong answers in this exercise and that the goal is to use the thinking process itself. After students complete the exercise, review the lesson by having volunteers write on the chalkboard the four guiding questions. ⚡

ripples of meaning the experience might have in the larger world. In other words, you move from the center outward— from yourself to the human condition, from the personal to the universal.

As the example below shows, you can use the following types of questions to guide an analysis of the meaning of an experience.

1. What does the experience mean to me?
2. What does the experience show me about myself—about what I believe, the way I act, what I think is important?
3. What ideas about people in general can I form from my own reactions to the experience?
4. What are some related experiences that show these ideas?

> *Experience: Watching my seven-year-old niece Tamara get dressed for a birthday party.*
>
> 1. *The experience impressed me because Tamara didn't care if she dressed differently from all the other kids. I was a little surprised by her reaction.*
>
> 2. *I always worry about how I dress. Clothes are important to me— I like to feel accepted.*
>
> 3. *Here are some ideas about people: clothes can make a person fit in; people like to be part of groups; it's scary to be different; it's easy and safe to be part of a crowd.*
>
> 4. *Related experiences: being afraid to take shop because no other girls do; watching my dad mow the grass because neighbors do; hearing my mom worry about what to wear.*

MEETING *individual* NEEDS

LESS-ADVANCED STUDENTS

The example about seven-year-old Tamara's dressing for a party should be a clear model for most students. However, some students may not take the time to work through the writer's mental process. Therefore, you may want to monitor students' processes by asking these follow-up questions:

1. Why was the writer surprised? [Most kids don't want to be different, but Tamara didn't care.]
2. Why are clothes important to the writer? [She wants to be accepted.]
3. How are clothes related to being part of a group? [The right clothes help people fit in. People don't want to be different but want to be part of the crowd.]
4. What other experiences show people being afraid to be different? [Some examples are the writer being afraid to take a shop class because other girls don't, her father mowing when neighbors do, and her mother still worrying about what to wear.]

Cont. from p. 133
will need to work on them alone before getting feedback from classmates or from you.

No formal grade is required for this lesson. However, you can assess students' selection of details in **Exercise 1** through individual conferences. You may want to collect and respond to students' organizational plans from **Writing Assignment: Part 3.**

ANSWERS
Critical Thinking Exercise

Responses will vary.

1. Students might consider whether the two students grumbling about the new coach's record are fans or players. If the students are players, the experience will be much more important to them—perhaps a winning season might help them to obtain college scholarships.

2. Some people might think that the half-starved animal was not their responsibility or that it might be dangerous; other groups might feel responsible for it and want to feed it and take it home. To most groups, it would make a difference whether the animal was a kitten or a wolf.

3. To most people, having to respond to a telephone machine before getting to speak to a real person is frustrating.

4. To most people, winning even a twenty-five cent prize inside a cereal box means that they are somehow special because they won.

5. People usually like to help others if they will only take the time to do it.

Going through such a questioning process will give you some ideas to consider about the meaning of your experience. Later on, though, as you write and revise, you may discover different meanings.

CRITICAL THINKING EXERCISE:
Analyzing Experiences for Meaning

Now, you decide. Get together in a small group and practice analyzing the meanings of experiences. There are no "right" and "wrong" answers that your group must discover, just possible meanings about the human condition. Use the four questions you have just read to guide your discussion.

1. overhearing two students grumbling about a new coach's win/loss record
2. finding a half-starved animal by the side of the road
3. calling an office or a department store and getting recorded messages that direct you to push different buttons before you can speak to a human being
4. getting excited because you win a twenty-five-cent prize inside a cereal box
5. spending a Saturday with other volunteers who are cleaning up the side of a highway

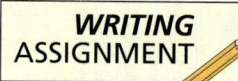

WRITING ASSIGNMENT

PART 2:
Recalling Details and Exploring Meanings

Now see what you can do with your own experience. To recall the details, brainstorm or talk to people who shared the experience. After you have listed a number of narrative and descriptive details, use the questions on page 135 to analyze the meanings of the experience. Don't censor yourself at this point; write down all your ideas.

Organizing Ideas and Details

Depending upon the type of expressive writing you do, you might use *chronological order, spatial order, order of importance,* or

CLOSURE

Ask students to comment briefly about the value of writing personal essays. Do such essays help them learn more about themselves? Do such essays help them learn more about others and the world at large? Why?

EXTENSION

Tell students to pretend that they have the ability to move backward in time to observe and experience such events as Neil Armstrong's walk on the moon or the assassination of Abraham Lincoln or John Kennedy. (Actually, through television, students may have already had many such experiences.) Tell students to use the **Critical Thinking** ☞

Prewriting   **137**

logical order. The following chart shows how different types of expressive writing might be organized.

ORGANIZATIONAL PATTERNS IN EXPRESSIVE WRITING	
Personal narrative or reflective essay on an event	Chronological order to relate series of events or series of actions within a single event, sometimes adding flashbacks to recall events that happened earlier in time or a flash-forward to look at what may happen in the future
Personal or reflective essay on a place or person	Spatial order to show details from left to right, near to far, and so forth; order of importance to show what characteristics of the person are most important to the writer; or chronological order to trace the history of the relationship between this person and the writer
Personal or reflective essay of definition	Logical order, such as general to specific or specific to general, to show how the definition has been developed
Personal or reflective essay of evaluation	Logical order, such as best to worst, or order of importance to show criteria used and judgment made

Often you may need to use a combination of two or more organizational patterns. For example, in a reflective essay about an event, you might use chronological order in the beginning, to discuss the event itself. Then you might use logical order or order of importance as you discuss your thoughts about the event's meaning, how it affects other people, and what it says about life in general. For more information on organizational patterns, see pages 74 and 79–87.

As with any other kind of writing, the most important thing is to make sure you don't jump around from point to point and confuse your readers. Following is one writer's organizational plan for a reflective essay about clothes and people.

MEETING individual NEEDS

LEARNING STYLES

Visual Learners. Have students visualize the ripples that an experience makes by creating an Experience Wheel based on the image of concentric circles. Have students draw—or reproduce for them—the following diagram.

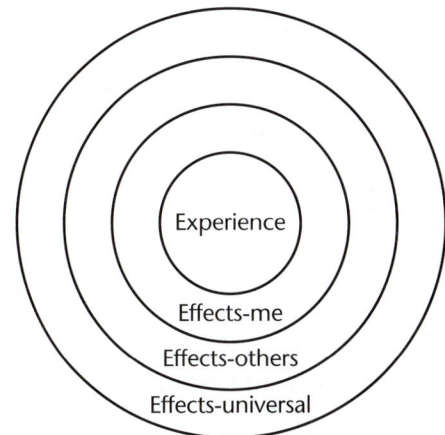

Then have each student fill each circle with the specifics of his or her experience and its effects.

137

questions on p. 135 to write responses to
one of these "time machine" experiences. ∎

INTEGRATING THE LANGUAGE ARTS

Literature Link. Tell students that frequently a lyrical poem will begin with a concrete, sensory experience and then will move to a reflective statement about the universal significance of the experience. Illustrate this point with one or more lyric poems by Shakespeare, Wordsworth, or Shelley. Shakespeare's "Sonnet 73" and Shelley's "Ozymandias" are especially good choices.

COOPERATIVE LEARNING

After students complete the organizational plans called for in **Writing Assignment: Part 3,** have them work in groups of three or four to evaluate one another's plans. Encourage students to make positive comments and suggestions for improvement. Remind students that each plan should include three elements: the event itself, reflections about self and others, and a return to the event.

HERE'S HOW

The event itself, what Tamara did	chronological order—Tamara comes into room; my sister groans about her dress; Tamara doesn't worry; she goes happily off to party
My reflections about self and others	logical order would be to start with me; give specific examples of others—Mom, Dad; go to discussion for what this says about all of us
Return to event	go back to time of Tamara's return from party; connect her actions to earlier reflections

Reminder

To plan a reflective essay

- think of a meaningful experience you had or witnessed
- explore the layers of meaning and significance—as they apply to you, to other people you know, and to life in general
- take notes on the details of the experience and your thoughts and feelings (reflections) about the experience
- look for a way, or a combination of ways, to organize the details and ideas so they will make sense to your readers

WRITING ASSIGNMENT

PART 3:
Organizing Details

Begin by looking over your notes from Writing Assignment, Part 2 (page 136) to decide how you might want to arrange them. Remember that you might use a combination of organizational patterns. Make a plan like the one at the top of this page and save it to use as a guide for your first draft.

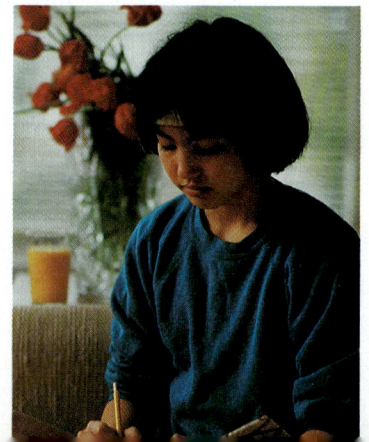

LESSON 4 *(pp. 139–147)*
WRITING YOUR FIRST DRAFT

OBJECTIVES
- To analyze the style and content of a reflective essay
- To write a draft of a reflective essay

MOTIVATION
To capture students' interest, read aloud the introduction to a well-written reflective essay, such as the essay by Judith Ortiz Cofer (pp. 140–143), **A Writer's Model** (pp. 144–146), or a reflective essay by another professional writer such as E. B. White, Annie Dillard, or Joan Didion.

Writing Your First Draft

The Elements of a Reflective Essay

As you begin to draft your essay, you might still be fuzzy on the significance of the experience you have chosen. Don't worry. Writing a reflective essay is a discovery process, and you might find that writing a first draft unlocks the significance of the experience for you. As you draft, keep in mind the following tips:

- **Create an interesting beginning.** A reflective essay, like any other essay you might write, needs a strong beginning to grab the reader's interest. You could "set up" the experience by beginning with its most important moment and then giving a hint or two concerning the overall significance of the experience. Just remember not to announce your theme as you would in a thesis statement for an expository or persuasive essay.

- **Use dialogue and vivid, realistic details.** Your essay may use very little dialogue, but make sure any dialogue is effective. Capturing exact words isn't as important as creating dialogue that conveys the meaning and mood of the experience. Use vivid and realistic details in the same way—to show, not tell.

- **Interweave events and reactions.** As you relate your experience, mix your thoughts and comments in with the events. Relating all the events first and then concluding with your reflections may make your essay seem forced or artificial.

- **End well.** By the time readers get to the end of your essay, they should already understand the significance of your experience. Avoid a pat *And that's what my experience meant to me.* Try, instead, to end in a fresh way by referring to the beginning, relating one final example, or asking a question that sums up your reflections.

PROGRAM MANAGER

WRITING YOUR FIRST DRAFT
- **Instructional Support** For help with writing an essay introduction, see **Writing** in *Strategies for Writing*, p. 3.

QUOTATION FOR THE DAY
"The man who writes about himself and his own time is the only man who writes about all people and about all time." (Bernard Shaw, 1856–1950, British playwright, critic, and essayist)

Working with partners or small groups, students might use this quotation as the focus to brainstorm a list of problems, themes, or events that are similar for people living in modern times and for people living a hundred years ago. Remind students that it is not usually the uniqueness of an event that makes it interesting to read about, but the meaningful details and the significance of the event to the writer.

Begin your lesson by reviewing with students the four tips for writing effective drafts (p. 139.) Then analyze and discuss in detail Judith Cofer's essay. After reading the first paragraph, ask students if they can predict where the essay is leading and what its theme will be. Explain that this paragraph contains clues to the essay's theme, but like most reflective essays, it develops its meaning rather than stating it bluntly at the beginning. Continue through the essay by using the side glosses to discuss narrative and descriptive details. Point out that the two concluding sentences give the clearest indication of the theme of the essay.

Before you assign all of **Exercise 2** on p. 143, you may want to give students a few

140   *Expressive Writing*

In the following reflective essay, the writer remembers her first day of school and then reflects on the strong feelings that day aroused. Notice how the passage exhibits the techniques you have just read about and also presents a *flashback,* a return to earlier events and thoughts.

A PASSAGE FROM AN AUTOBIOGRAPHY

from Silent Dancing: A Partial Remembrance of a Puerto Rican Childhood
by Judith Ortiz Cofer

INTRODUCTION

1   **M**y mother walked me to my first day of school at La Escuela Segundo Ruiz Belvis, named after the Puerto Rican patriot born in our

2   town. I remember yellow cement with green trim. All the classrooms had been painted these colors to identify them as government property. This was

Sensory details   3   true all over the Island. Everything was color-coded, including the children, who wore uniforms from first through twelfth grade. We were a

4   midget army in white and brown, led by the hand to our battleground. From practically every house in our barrio emerged a crisply ironed uniform

Hint of meaning   inhabited by the wild creatures we had become over a summer of running wild in the sun.

BODY   At my grandmother's house where we were staying until my father returned to Brooklyn Yard in New York and sent for us, it had been complete chaos, with several children to get ready for school. My mother had pulled my hair harder than

Event   usual while braiding it, and I had dissolved into a
Feelings   pool of total self-pity. I wanted to stay home with her and Mamá, to continue listening to stories in

140

minutes to freewrite in response to the first question. Let students share these responses in small groups before proceeding to questions 2–5.

Emphasize that students are writing drafts, not final versions. Relate the word *draft* to its original meaning of "pulling" or "drawing" and explain that at this point students are pulling ideas out of their minds.

Explain that they will have opportunities to revise, edit, and proofread later.

the late afternoon, to drink _café con leche_ with them, and to play rough games with my many cousins. I

5 wanted to continue living the dream of summer afternoons in Puerto Rico, and if I could not have that, then I wanted to [go] back to Paterson, New Jersey, back to where I imagined our apartment waited, peaceful and cool for the three of us to

6 return to our former lives. Our gypsy lifestyle had convinced me, at age six, that one part of life stops and waits for you while you live another for a while—and if you don't like the present, you can always return to the past. Buttoning me into my stiff blouse while I tried to squirm away from her, my mother tried to explain to me that I was a big girl now and should try to understand that, like all the other children my age, I had to go to school.

"What about him?" I yelled pointing at my brother who was lounging on the tile floor of our bedroom in his pajamas, playing quietly with a toy car.

"He's too young to go to school, you know

7 that. Now stay still." My mother pinned me between her thighs to button my skirt, as she had learned to do from Mamá, from whose grip it was impossible to escape.

"It's not fair, it's not fair. I can't go to school here. I don't speak Spanish." It was my final argument, and it failed miserably because I was shouting my defiance in the language I claimed not to speak. Only I knew what I meant by saying in Spanish that I did not speak Spanish. I had spent my early childhood in the U.S. where I lived in a

8 bubble created by my Puerto Rican parents in a home where two cultures and languages became one. I learned to listen to the English from the television with one ear while I heard my mother and father speaking in Spanish with the other. I thought I was an ordinary American kid—like the children on the shows I watched—and that everyone's parents spoke a secret second language at home. When we came to Puerto Rico right before I started first grade, I switched easily to Spanish.

Unfolding meaning

Narrative details

Dialogue/ Descriptive and narrative details

Event

Feelings

Flashback

Narrative details

5
The Ortiz family had immigrated to the United States in 1956, when Judith was four years old; Paterson is an industrial city in northeastern New Jersey.

6
Cofer's father was in the U.S. Navy.

7
"Pinned me between her thighs" creates a sensory image.

8
The image of a bubble suggests that Cofer has been protected in an unrealistic environment.

Using the class topic selected in the prewriting lesson, model for students the drafting process for a reflective essay. Elicit class suggestions for the introductory paragraph, and then write the paragraph on a transparency as the students watch. Discuss the details that could be included in the body of the draft. Finally, return to the transparency to draft a conclusion based on class suggestions. Lead students to understand that in a reflective essay, the writer lets the theme develop naturally, perhaps by stating or suggesting it clearly in the conclusion.

INTEGRATING THE LANGUAGE ARTS

Vocabulary Link. Discuss and analyze the effective use of vivid verbs in Cofer's reflective essay. For example, she says she "tried to squirm away" instead of get away, and her mother "pinned" her rather than held her. Explain to students that vivid verbs help create specific images for the reader. To encourage effective use of vivid verbs, give your students several overused verbs and ask the students to think of more specific and vivid synonyms. You could use the following examples:

1. talked [squealed, mumbled, stuttered]
2. walked [ambled, shuffled, strutted]

Literature Link. The difference between a formal tone and an informal tone is one of the major characteristics that distinguishes formal and informal essays. You can illustrate these different forms by asking your students to read and analyze Francis Bacon's essay "Of Studies" for characteristics of formal tone and Richard Steele's essay "Remembering the Dead" for a characteristic of informal tone. Bacon's essay employs a third-person, objective point of view, is dignified in style, and is tightly organized. In contrast, Steele's essay uses a first-person, subjective point of view and a conversational, digressive style.

142

---

142   *Expressive Writing*

Unfolding meaning

Event

Narrative details

Meaning expanded

It was the language of fun, of summertime games. But school—that was a different matter.

I made one last desperate attempt to make my mother see reason: "Father will be very angry. You know that he wants us to speak good English." My mother, of course, ignored me as she dressed my little brother in his playclothes. I could not believe her indifference to my father's wishes. She was usually so careful about our safety and the many other areas that he was forever reminding her about in his letters. But I was right, and she knew it. Our father spoke to us in English as much as possible, and he corrected my pronunciation constantly—not "jes" but "y-es." Y-es, sir. How could she send me to school to learn Spanish when we would be returning to Paterson in just a few months?

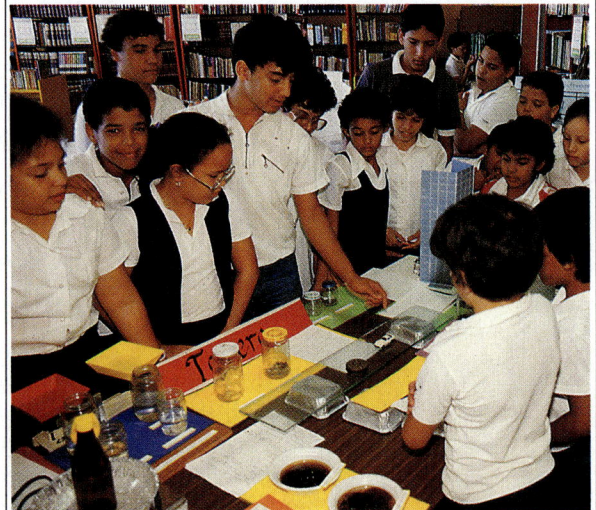

But, of course, what I feared was not language, but loss of freedom. At school there would be no playing, no stories, only lessons. It would not matter if I did not understand a word, and I would not be allowed to make up my own definitions. I would have to learn silence. I would have to keep my wild imagination in check. Feeling locked into my stiffly starched uniform, I only sensed all this.

Allow students to answer the questions in **Exercise 2** independently and then have students share their answers in small groups. Students can also write their drafts independently.

You will not want to grade students' drafts, but you may want to check to make sure that each draft includes a clear, detailed narrative and a clear suggestion of significance or theme.

☞

Writing Your First Draft   **143**

Movement from personal to universal

I guess most children can <u>intuit</u> their loss of childhood's freedom on that first day of school. It is separation anxiety too, but mother is just the guardian of the "playground" of our early childhood.

CONCLUSION Narrative and descriptive details

The sight of my cousins in similar <u>straits</u> comforted me. We were marched down the hill of our barrio where Mamá's robin-egg-blue house stood at the top. I must have glanced back at it with yearning. Mamá's house—a place built for children—where anything that could be broken had already been broken by my grandmother's early batch of offspring (they ranged in age from my mother's oldest sisters to my uncle who was six months older than me). Her house had long since been made child-proof. It had been a perfect summer place. And now it was September—the cruelest month for a child.

Full meaning completed   9

9
This is an allusion to the line in T. S. Eliot's "The Waste Land": "April is the cruellest month, breeding/Lilacs out of the dead land,/mixing memory and desire . . ."

ANSWERS
Exercise 2

1. Responses will vary. Students may recall their own fears on this day.

2. Cofer gives an interesting narrative beginning that engages the reader's interest. She also includes vivid descriptive details.

3. Narrative events include Cofer's mother's walking her to school, her mother's dressing her for school, and Cofer's argument with her mother about going to school.

4. The theme of Cofer's essay is that she began to lose the freedom of childhood on the day she started school. This main idea is suggested in the first paragraph by the confinement of each child's "crisply ironed uniform."

5. Narrative details include Cofer's being walked to school by her mother, being buttoned into a stiff blouse to prepare for school while her brother played on the floor, and arguing with her mother about attending school. Descriptive details include the comparison of the children to an "army in white and brown," the children's stiff uniforms, and the grandmother's "robin-egg-blue" house. The confining images of an army and stiffly starched uniforms contrast with images of freedom.

EXERCISE 2 ▶ **Analyzing a Reflective Essay**

Do you remember your first day of school as vividly as Cofer does hers? After you have finished reading her reflections (pages 140–143), meet with two or three classmates to discuss these questions.

1. What memories of your first day of school did this essay evoke?
2. What technique does Cofer use in her introduction to get her reader's attention?
3. Although Cofer uses mostly chronological order to organize her essay, there are not many events that actually happen. What are the few events that do take place?
4. In between events, Cofer reflects on her feelings. What is the theme, or main idea, expressed in these reflections? Where is the main idea expressed most directly in the essay?
5. Cofer uses narrative and descriptive details to describe how her mother gets her ready for school. What are some of the details? How do they contribute to the overall feelings of loss that Cofer suggests?

Some students who are used to writing essays with stated theses in the introductions may have trouble understanding the concept of developing meaning. Reread and label the first and the last two paragraphs in **A Writer's Model** to show how the writer leads up to her theme, with the clearest hints

of the theme coming in the next-to-the-last paragraph.

MEETING *individual* NEEDS

LEP/ESL

General Strategies. In discussing the relevance of dialogue in a reflective essay (p. 139), you may want to emphasize that use of nonstandard speech, when used to record speech as it actually occurred, is not only acceptable in this kind of essay, but is necessary to paint a realistic picture of one's experience, and, therefore, to achieve the expressive aim. Underscore the fact that there are certain types of expression—the expressive essay being one—in which nonstandard usage is sanctioned (in this case, as it pertains to dialogue). Information such as this, neither implied nor directly stated in the text, needs to be presented. Otherwise, some students may draw back from a uniquely creative expression.

144

---

144   *Expressive Writing*

A Basic Framework for a Reflective Essay

Judith Ortiz Cofer's reflections about the first day of school are organized as a narrative; she uses the events and conversations of that day to reflect on why she dreaded school. If you are writing about a milestone experience, you might want to follow a similar narrative structure in your essay. However, if your experience is merely the starting point, rather than the focal point, you might want to spend less time describing the experience and more time reflecting, as the writer in the following essay does. As you read, notice how the writer uses a brief, seemingly insignificant experience to reflect on the importance of fitting in.

A WRITER'S MODEL

Fitting In

INTRODUCTION
Descriptive details

My seven-year-old niece, Tamara, flounced into the room in her best dress, a dress covered with ruffles, lace, and bows. Lace stockings and shiny white patent leather shoes completed the outfit. "I'm ready," she announced.

Dialogue

My sister glanced over at her. "Tamara, you're not wearing <u>that</u>. This is an outdoor birthday party, sweetie. All the other kids will have on shorts and tennis shoes."

"But I won't," Tamara said.

After a few more tries to get Tamara to change, my sister gave up, and Tamara went off to the party.

Hint of meaning

I admired her spunk and her determination to be different. I wondered how long it would last.

BODY

I thought about the way I act. Before I go anywhere, I go through a mental checklist to make

Related example

sure I've worn the "right" thing. Sometimes I don't trust my judgment, so I call my best friend, María, to see what she's wearing. She doesn't mind; usually she's just about to call me to ask the same thing. Like most other girls in our group, María and I spend hours thinking about our clothes.

CLOSURE

Ask students to list the four helpful tips for writing a reflective essay discussed in this lesson. Call on a few students to share their answers to allow all students to participate in the review. When students finish, ask four volunteers to list the tips on the chalkboard.

EXTENSION

Make available to your students copies of E. B. White's reflective essay "Death of a Pig." Have students work in groups to annotate this essay. Tell them to use the annotations of Cofer's essay and of **A Writer's Model** as guides.

☞

Writing Your First Draft   **145**

Related example

It isn't just the girls who are concerned about clothes. The guys at school have a dress code, too. Otherwise, athletic shoes that cost as much as $150 wouldn't be so popular, and there wouldn't be a certain way to tie the shoes. For a few months, you could walk down the hall and almost never see the laces tied at the top. The "proper" style was to leave them untied and dangling. And then there are the same clothing labels that you see on almost every teenage boy's clothes--on the outside of their shirts and jeans.

Descriptive details

Related example

Adults haven't outgrown this concern about clothes and fitting in, either. Just the other day I overheard my mother on the phone discussing a school meeting. "Do you think slacks will be all right?" she asked her friend. She sounded just like my friends and I do. And when my father leaves the house, he looks just like every other adult male in our neighborhood. Their "uniform" consists of jeans and a short-sleeved shirt for casual wear, slacks and a tie for dressier times.

Dialogue

Descriptive details

Reflection on previous examples

What all this tells me is that fitting in is important, not just to me, not just to teenagers, not just to one sex or the other. But why? Maybe it is because we're all scared to be alone. I can understand why we feel scared, though. The truth is, it's risky to stand alone. It's risky to wear jeans when everyone else is

MEETING *individual* NEEDS

LESS-ADVANCED STUDENTS

Some students may have difficulty with this assignment because they usually perform better with structured models such as the traditional five-paragraph theme. Without a clear structure, less-advanced students may lose sight of the significance of the experience and lapse into mere narration. Monitor the work closely to be sure each student includes the significance of the experience. You might even want students to state this significance rather obviously at the beginning of their essays.

A DIFFERENT APPROACH

Before students write their drafts, have them work in groups to role-play scenes that they plan to use in their essays. Each group should role-play one scene from each group member's essay. Remind students to include dialogue and vivid, realistic details.

MEETING *individual* NEEDS

LEARNING STYLES

Visual Learners. To help visual learners see the structure of a reflective essay more clearly, make a poster of the **Framework for a Reflective Essay.** Or have a group of visual learners make the poster.

INTEGRATING THE LANGUAGE ARTS

Speaking Link. Have individual students select reflective, lyrical poems from their literature textbooks to prepare for oral reading. Students can read their poems to the class or to a small group of classmates.

TECHNOLOGY TIP

Have students with access to word-processing programs use them to write their drafts. Have students use the comments command to jot down notes as they are drafting their papers. Be sure the students know how to use the delete and block-and-move functions to recast their notes into essay form.

Focus on universal meanings

wearing something dressier. It's risky to take shop when everyone else is taking typing. It's risky to study and make good grades when everyone else is thinking of partying. You might get noticed. Then you might get laughed at. Worst of all, you might get excluded, banished forever by the unwritten code of "the group." Alone.

Thoughts and feelings

It's a scary thought. I know I need the security of a group. I want to feel loved, accepted, even approved of by someone. And I don't think I'm unusual. Let's face it. It takes courage to stand alone.

Extended meaning

Details

Some people do have that courage. They are trendsetters and innovators who aren't afraid to be different. Think of the Wright brothers, who clung to the dream of flight through years of disappointment until that day in Kitty Hawk that changed history. Think of Rosa Parks, who defied tradition and rules by refusing to give up her seat on a Montgomery bus. And think of the immigrants to the United States who often endured poverty and hard work to make better lives for themselves and a better country for us all.

CONCLUSION

Return to introduction

I was still thinking about these trendsetters when my niece Tamara returned from the party. "What were the other kids wearing?" my sister asked. Tamara looked puzzled. "I don't know," she shrugged. Spoken like a true trendsetter. Maybe one day I will sound like one, too.

For Better or For Worse copyright 1991 Lynn Johnston Productions, Inc. Reprinted with permission of Universal Press Syndicate. All rights reserved.

The following framework for a reflective essay shows how the Writer's Model is developed. Notice how it includes the characteristics of a reflective essay—thoughts, feelings, dialogue, and so forth—that you studied earlier in the chapter. You might want to use this framework in your own essay.

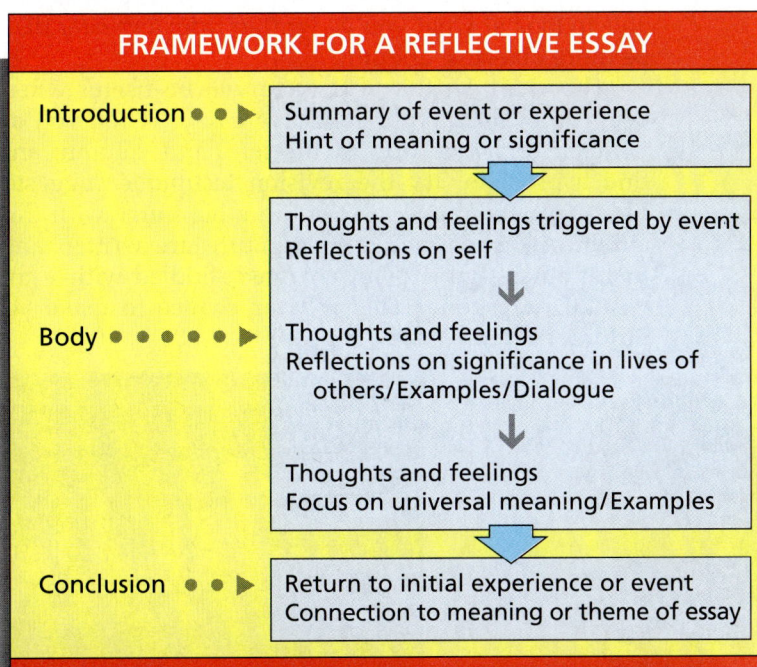

FRAMEWORK FOR A REFLECTIVE ESSAY

Introduction ▶
Summary of event or experience
Hint of meaning or significance

Body ▶
Thoughts and feelings triggered by event
Reflections on self

Thoughts and feelings
Reflections on significance in lives of others/Examples/Dialogue

Thoughts and feelings
Focus on universal meaning/Examples

Conclusion ▶
Return to initial experience or event
Connection to meaning or theme of essay

WRITING ASSIGNMENT

PART 4:
Writing a Draft of Your Reflective Essay

Your reflective essay is a journey, one that may be taking you to ideas that surprise you. Continue on the most exciting and demanding part of your journey by writing a first draft. Start with all the ideas and details you collected and organized in Part 2 and Part 3 of the Writing Assignment, and then let your reflections unfold as you write. Don't worry about creating the perfect essay now; you will evaluate and revise later.

TIMESAVER
After students have completed their drafts, have each student use a colored highlighter to mark the phrases and sentences that explain the events themselves and another colored highlighter to mark the sentences that show the meaning or significance of the experience. Then scan the highlighted material to be sure students are actually writing reflective essays rather than simple narratives.

EVALUATING AND REVISING

OBJECTIVES

- To analyze the revisions of a reflective essay
- To evaluate and revise the content and organization of a reflective essay

TEACHING THE LESSON

Explain to students that an essay that needs revising isn't necessarily wrong or bad. Emphasize that because writing is discovery, writers often discover meaning in their drafts. That process means that revisions are necessary for writers to clarify meaning and to polish style.

PROGRAM MANAGER

EVALUATING AND REVISING

■ **Reinforcement/Reteaching** See **Revision Transparencies 5** and **6.** For suggestions on how to tie the transparencies to instruction, review teacher's notes in *Fine Art and Instructional Transparencies for Writing,* p. 103.

■ **Ongoing Assessment** For a rubric to guide assessment, see **Evaluating and Revising** in *Strategies for Writing,* p. 4.

■ **Assessment/Reflection** To assess student work and evaluate progress, see **Portfolio Forms** in *Portfolio Assessment,* pp. 5–21.

QUOTATION FOR THE DAY

"I think the writer ought to help the reader as much as he can without damaging what he wants to say; and I don't think it ever hurts the writer to sort of stand back now and then and look at his stuff as if he were reading it instead of writing it." (James Jones, 1921–1977, American novelist)

Share the quotation with students as they begin to evaluate and revise their work. Explain that it's especially important to evaluate personal narratives from a reader's point of view because writers might not have included enough information to make their work clear.

---

148   *Expressive Writing*

Evaluating and Revising

After you have written a first draft, let it rest a while before you attempt to evaluate and revise it. As time passes, you will be able to look at what you've written from a greater distance and be more objective about it.

The chart on the next page will be useful when you do begin to evaluate your reflective essay. When you use it, ask yourself each question in the left-hand column; and, if you find a problem, try the revision technique suggested in the right-hand column. Don't get in a big hurry with this process either. All great pieces of literature are written and revised many times—gone over, changed, fiddled with—until all the wrinkles are gone. This is your chance to make your essay unforgettable.

Review with students the **Evaluating and Revising Reflective Essays** chart on this page. Explain that in revising their papers, students should focus on each question separately because it is difficult to keep in mind several items at once. Suggest that students read through their essays completely after each question and then make revisions for one question or problem before proceeding to the next.

Prepare a transparency of a paragraph that needs revision—perhaps an unrevised version of the paragraph on p. 150. Then, before you assign **Exercise 3**, p. 150, ask students how they would revise the paragraph. Guide students through a revision of the paragraph by making revisions on the transparency. ☞

EVALUATING AND REVISING REFLECTIVE ESSAYS

EVALUATION GUIDE	REVISION TECHNIQUE
1 Is the theme, or main idea, of the writer obvious? Does it grow out of the experience in a natural way?	**Add** to your introduction a sentence or two hinting at the significance of the experience. **Cut** any statement that treats the theme like a moral.
2 Are events, people, and places vividly and realistically portrayed?	**Add** narrative and descriptive details. **Add** dialogue to show what people think and say. **Cut** any details that do not contribute to a realistic, vivid portrayal.
3 Does the organization of details and ideas make sense?	**Reorder** details and ideas in chronological order, spatial order, order of importance, or logical order.
4 Is the tone appropriate for a reflective essay?	**Add** first-person pronouns to create a consistent first-person point of view. **Replace** formal language with conversational language.
5 Do the writer's reflections move outward from the experience to its universal significance?	**Add** anecdotes, examples, and dialogue to illustrate the significance to yourself, to other people you know, and to people in general. **Add** your thoughts and feelings, interweaving them throughout the essay.
6 Does the essay come to a satisfactory close?	**Cut** any direct statement of the theme (or a moral). **Add** details that reconnect the theme with the significance of the original experience.

MEETING *individual* NEEDS

LEARNING STYLES

Visual Learners. Prepare a chart that shows the organization and content of a reflective essay so students can use it to evaluate the content of their essays. You could use the following example.

Event:

	Sensory Details	Dialogue
FEELINGS, SIGNIFICANCE-SELF		
FEELINGS, SIGNIFICANCE-OTHERS		
FEELINGS, SIGNIFICANCE-UNIVERSAL		

LESS-ADVANCED STUDENTS

Some students may need help in leading up to the significance of their essays. You may want to help them reduce obvious statements of meaning in introductory paragraphs by moving such statements to the end of their essays.

CLOSURE

Ask students to freewrite for a few minutes about the helpfulness of the revision chart on p. 149. Which questions were the most helpful? Which were the least helpful? Discuss students' responses. ■

EXERCISE 3 ▶   **Analyzing a Writer's Revisions**

The paragraph below shows changes in the first draft of the Writer's Model on pages 144–146. With a classmate, discuss why the writer made the changes and answer the questions that follow.

> Adults haven't outgrown this concern
> about ~~their apparel~~ *clothes* and ~~the necessity of a~~   **replace/cut**
> fitting in, either. Just the other day I
> overheard my mother on the phone
> *"Do you think slacks will be all right?"*
> discussing a school meeting. She asked her   **add**
> friend ~~whether slacks would be all right.~~ She   **cut**
> sounded just like my friends and I do. And
> when my father leaves the house, he looks
> just like every other adult male in our
> neighborhood. *Their "uniform" consists of jeans*   **add**
> *and a short-sleeved shirt for casual wear,*
> *slacks and a tie for dressier times.*

1. How do the changes in the first sentence affect the tone?
2. Why did the writer change the third sentence so that it became a direct quotation?
3. Why did the writer add the last sentence? How does the word *"uniform"* help focus the meaning of the experience?

COMPUTER NOTE: If your word-processing program has a function that allows you to insert annotations, try using it to add your comments to the next essay you evaluate.

WRITING ASSIGNMENT

PART 5:
Evaluating and Revising Your Reflective Essay

Use the chart on page 149 to evaluate your essay, and then ask one or more classmates to evaluate it. After thinking about these evaluations, make the changes you think will improve your essay.

ANSWERS
Exercise 3

1. Both changes make the tone more informal. "Their apparel" and "the necessity of" sound much less conversational.
2. The mother's exact words are more vivid and direct than the indirect quotation.
3. The last two sentences clarify and extend the idea that people like the writer's father also follow fashions or trends.

TIMESAVER

Ask students to highlight hints or statements of meaning in their papers. Read the highlighted material for both content and placement in the essay. Make suggestions for further revision if such statements are not clear enough or if they are too obvious. Suggest that some statements be moved toward the end of the essays if such revision is necessary.

TECHNOLOGY TIP

To make it possible for students to use the annotations feature, they will have to work with a computer file rather than a printed copy of another student's work. Remind students to use the Help file if they need assistance in using the annotations feature.

PROOFREADING AND PUBLISHING

OBJECTIVES

- To proofread a reflective essay
- To prepare a reflective essay for publication

TEACHING THE LESSON

Refer students to the **Grammar Hint,** and spend some time discussing effective as well as ineffective uses of fragments.

Continue your lesson by having students work with partners to proofread their reflective essays.

You may want to assess not only the completed papers, but also the processes ☞

Proofreading and Publishing

Once you have revised your essay, you need to look at it in a different way. Appearances are important to your readers, even in a personal essay, so you need to carefully proofread for mistakes in mechanics and usage. Then you might try one of the following suggestions for publishing your essay:

- If your essay is too private to share with a wider audience, consider starting a collection of private reflections. These would be similar to journal entries, but more finished and organized. Add to the collection as you write other reflective essays.

- With classmates who wish to share their thoughts, organize a booklet of essays. Title it "Reflections on ____" and then make a table of contents page that lists the subject of each essay. See how many different ideas and topics are represented.

GRAMMAR HINT

Using Sentence Fragments Effectively

A personal essay has a more relaxed, informal tone than many other types of essays. That informality extends to the essay's sentence structure. Sentence fragments are usually considered a glaring error, but there are times in an informal essay when they can be used deliberately and effectively. Dialogue is one such place because people often talk in phrases, not complete sentences.

ORIGINAL: Jake couldn't believe what Gina had just said. "That's what you'd see in your dreams," he growled.

REVISED: Jake couldn't believe what Gina had just said. "In your dreams," he growled.

PROGRAM MANAGER

PROOFREADING AND PUBLISHING

- **Instructional Support** For a chart students may use to evaluate their proofreading progress, see **Proofreading** in *Strategies for Writing,* p. 5.

- **Independent Practice/ Reteaching** For additional practice with language skills, see **Proofreading Practice: Using Sentence Fragments Effectively** in *Strategies for Writing,* p. 6.

- **Assessment/Reflection** To assess student work and evaluate progress, see **Portfolio Forms** in *Portfolio Assessment,* pp. 22–25.

- **Computer Guided Instruction** For additional instruction and practice with sentence fragments as noted in the **Grammar Hint,** see **Lesson 31** in *Language Workshop CD-ROM.*

- **Practice** To help less-advanced students who need additional practice with sentence fragments, see **Chapter 8** in *English Workshop, Complete Course,* pp. 93–94.

QUOTATION FOR THE DAY

"Of all the needs a book has the chief need is that it be readable." (Anthony Trollope, 1815–1882, English author)

that students have followed.

Ask each student to compare his or her first draft to the final draft and to share one change that has taken place during the writing process. ■

INTEGRATING THE LANGUAGE ARTS

Literature Link. If the work is available in your literature textbook, read to your class the poem "Fern Hill" by Dylan Thomas. Explain that poems as well as essays can be reflective. You may want to have your students make a class collection of reflective poems from their literature textbook and other sources.

TIMESAVER

Before students prepare their papers for publication, have students highlight each sentence fragment in a color different from any previous highlighting. Review these fragments and discuss any that are questionable.

TEACHING NOTE

Remind students that reflection is essential to learning and that time spent on reflection now will be useful to them in the future. Ask students to focus on the first two questions under **Reflecting on Your Writing.** They can even highlight their answer to the first question to make it easier to find when they might need techniques to spur their memories in future writing assignments.

Fragments may also be used to emphasize a point or repeat a theme. Notice how the writer of the essay on fitting in, pages 144–146, uses a sentence fragment in the fourth paragraph from the end.

Alone.

This fragment helps to focus the writer's meaning—it emphasizes the most important reason for fitting in. The next-to-the-last sentence of the essay is also a fragment. "Spoken like a true trendsetter" calls attention to the writer's last point. It also reinforces the reflective nature of the essay by mimicking the writer's thoughts and reactions to the experience. Use sentence fragments cautiously in informal writing and not at all in formal essays with a more serious tone.

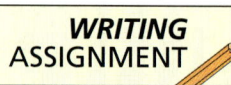

WRITING ASSIGNMENT

PART 6:
Proofreading and Publishing Your Essay

Put the finishing touches on your essay by proofreading it and correcting all mistakes. Make sure that any sentence fragments are confined to dialogue or used in another effective way. Then, using the second suggestion on page 151 or an idea of your own, share your work with others.

Reflecting on Your Writing

Your reflective essay will make an interesting addition to your **portfolio.** To include the essay, date it and write a brief reflection responding to the questions below. Remember to attach your reflection to your essay.

- Which techniques did you use to spur your memory about specific details? Which of these techniques did you find most helpful?
- Were you able to strike the right tone for this essay? How would you adjust the tone to make it more appropriate?
- Did you learn anything surprising about your subject in the process of writing the essay?

A STUDENT MODEL

Here is a paper by Sandrine Shelton, a student from Ellison High School in Killeen, Texas. Notice how she begins with the most important moment and hints at the overall significance of the experience.

The Victory in Defeat
by Sandrine Shelton

I will never forget that image—the picture of the tennis ball hitting the net tape and sliding down. I still remember how it hit the top of the net and paused for a split second, keeping me and the crowd in suspense. Then, finally the ball rolled down our side in slow motion. In many ways, though, that image and the disappointment it created have made me a stronger and better person.

I was a sophomore, and it was the district playoffs. My partner Cheryl and I were in the most influential tennis match of our lives. It was late in the day, and the humidity clung to our skins like a heavy, wet towel. We played on the first court by a stadium filled with rambunctious fans. I remember the roar of the crowd between points and the dead silence during points.

"Right here!" Cheryl urged. "This is ours! Come on, Sandrine! Fight!"

"All right! We can do it! Let's go, Cheryl!" I replied trembling. The match was so close, and if we won it, we would go on to regionals. However, on their match point, I hit a backhand volley into the net. I wanted to scream and cry, but I focused myself on the path to future victory.

Still angry from that loss, we played our next fall season, losing one match. We continued working harder and harder, eagerly awaiting the tournament that would avenge the loss and give us our break—the district playoffs. Finally, our day came.

In the semifinals we met the third-ranked team. The match went three sets, but our desire to win was much greater than theirs, and we prevailed. We had qualified for regionals. We had proved we were good enough to go to the next step. It was then I realized that losing the year before had made us stronger and had taken us farther, not only in tennis but also in life.

A STUDENT MODEL
Evaluation

1. Sandrine introduces her main idea at the end of the first paragraph, and the rest of the details lead to its restatement at the end.
2. Sandrine effectively creates realistic events, people, and places. Her dialogue with her partner contributes to her realistic presentation.
3. Sandrine uses chronological order effectively.
4. Sandrine's tone, which is a mixture of excitement and reflection, is appropriate for her subject matter.
5. The statement of the universal significance at the end of the essay brings the composition full-circle to the ideas introduced in the first paragraph and provides a satisfactory closing for the paper.

WRITING WORKSHOP

OBJECTIVES
- To analyze a humorous personal essay
- To use the writing process to write a humorous personal essay

TEACHING THE LESSON
To pique your students' interest in Susan Trausch's essay, read aloud the first sentence. Ask students what they expect to follow this sentence. Then let students test their expectations as you continue reading.

Because students have already used the writing process to write reflective essays, they should be able to work independently

WRITING WORKSHOP

A Humorous Personal Essay

A reflective personal essay examines the meaning of an experience that was important to the writer, but with just a little twist, these same experiences might take a humorous turn. In the following essay, for example, Susan Trausch reflects on an experience most people have had—getting spots on clothing. To make her point, Trausch relies heavily on *exaggeration*, a form of humor that stretches reality.

As you read the essay, notice that the writer grabs your attention in the beginning with a humorous statement that also summarizes her main idea. Trausch also supports her main idea with a series of comic experiences and concludes with a humorous reflection. Where does the title of the essay come from? Why is it appropriate for the essay?

Out, out, telltale spot!
by Susan Trausch

It must be nice to be a slob.

There is a magnificence to people who can walk around all day with egg salad on a jacket and not care.

"Oh yeah," they say when people point, "that's my egg salad."

Most of us will never achieve such cool. We splotch up an outfit and want to go home. A spot becomes a billboard advertising our ineptitude, an all-points bulletin announcing that we are not the professionals we pretend to be.

"Some big-shot lawyer—can't even eat soup."

I remember lunching with a psychologist who, in the middle of an interview on societal stress, began screaming obscenities at his tie.

"Look at this," he shouted, whipping off the offending accessory and dunking it into his water glass. "Salad dressing! On silk!"

He gripped the tie in a stranglehold. The dirty little traitor! He'd have to buy a new one after lunch, drive back to his

QUOTATION FOR THE DAY
"There are several kinds of stories, but only one difficult kind—the humorous." (Mark Twain, 1835–1910, American humorist and author)

Use the quotation as a basis for discussing the difficulties in producing humorous writing. Do your students agree with Twain?

MEETING *individual* NEEDS

LEARNING STYLES
Auditory Learners. You may want to read Trausch's essay to the class. In addition, allow your auditory learners to work in pairs to talk-write their prewriting and perhaps their rough drafts.

USING THE SELECTION
Out, out, telltale spot!

1

The title alludes to Act V, Scene I of *Macbeth,* in which Lady Macbeth rubs at what she perceives to be a spot of blood on her hands and cries, "Out, damned spot! Out, I say!"

to write humorous personal essays. Allow students to work in small groups to share ideas in the prewriting stage and to make suggestions for revision and proofreading.

To give students credit for creativity and cleverness, as well as for using the writing process, consider giving three grades for this assignment: one grade for creative and entertaining content; one grade for following the steps of the writing process; and one grade for organization, coherence, editing, and proofreading.

Encourage students to reflect on their essays and to try to determine why some people find something humorous and others don't.

---

apartment and change, or try to do something creative with his tie clip.

He decided on a fourth option—wearing his jacket buttoned, even though the temperature was near 90.

Desperation transcends logic on such occasions. We wrap ourselves in sweaters, turn collars under, raise belts, or try to roll up the sleeves of a blazer. Sometimes we keep our hands over the spot and tell people we have heartburn.

2 I once wore a raincoat to hide the ink stain on a skirt. Then I spilled ice cream on the coat and covered it by holding a large brown envelope strategically over the chocolate. By the time I got home I needed an appointment with the psychologist.

There is probably a long name for this neurotic behavior, but **3** I think of it as The Lady Macbeth Syndrome.

4 "Out, out!" we cry, working over our garments in the company **5** washroom, usually making the problem worse. A tomato splatter on a white shirt becomes a smeared tomato splatter on a drenched white shirt.

And when we get back to our desks, the boss calls us in for a strategy session.

"Why are you carrying that magazine, Benson?"

6 "Interesting article in here . . . on spot metals."

The only thing worse than a stain front and center is one behind.

"You sat in something," says an observer, with that note of superiority clean people have when speaking to the soiled. "Looks like blueberries. You remember sitting in blueberries?"

One of the more inane questions of all time, but it is invariably asked. I always want to say, "Yes, I remember it well. It was 1:15 at **7** the Ritz. I asked the waiter to bring over a big bowl of blueberries and dump them on my chair."

Who knows how half the stuff that we get on us gets there? Maybe it comes from God to keep us humble. It just appears, that's all, telling the world that here is a person who cannot control his fettuccine.

A fortune could be made with the invention of a solution guaranteed to remove stains instantly. We'd carry small vials of it with us everywhere, discreetly spritzing ourselves and eliminating spot shame forever.

8 I bet the president of the United States has it already. The Pentagon probably developed it years ago as a national security measure.

2
Exaggeration builds as attempts to hide the ink stain pile up.

3
In her sleepwalking and her visions of spots that do not physically exist, Lady Macbeth is also neurotic.

4
Food spots, the humorous subject of this essay, are trivial compared to the spot or stain of guilt for murder that Lady Macbeth feels in her heart and conscience.

5
Trying to rub out a food spot often makes it worse, just as Lady Macbeth's obsession with her own spot of guilt leads to her own death.

6
"Spot metals" is a pun on the food spot that Benson obviously has.

7
The Ritz is a common name for an elegant hotel.

8
Humorous exaggeration to support writer's case for the existence of a top-secret spot remover.

Make copies of a humorous personal essay such as "The Night the Bed Fell" or "The Night the Ghost Got In," both by James Thurber. Highlight exaggeration in blue and surprise in pink, and work with students to label these characteristics of humor.

Have volunteers tell why they think Susan Trausch's essay is or is not humorous. Then have students discuss their conclusions. ■

156

9
paisley: colorful woven or printed swirled pattern resembling an enlarged comma

After students have brainstormed about funny or embarrassing experiences they have had and are comfortable revealing, tell each of them to list three of these experiences on a sheet of paper. Then have students meet in groups of three to exchange lists. Tell each student to put a check by the topic that sounds the funniest and most interesting. Students can then use this feedback in selecting their subjects.

Speaking Link. Have students read their humorous personal essays to the class. Give students the following guidelines on how to read aloud:

1. Practice reading aloud.
2. Alter the pitch and volume of your voice.
3. Change the rate of your reading to fit the content.
4. Use gestures for emphasis.
5. Make eye contact.
6. Pronounce words distinctly.

"If the prez stands there with beet juice on his suit, everybody will think we're a second-class power," said the generals. "Nuke that sucker."

Has the president or any other head of state ever been seen in public looking like the rest of us do after eating a submarine sandwich? Of course not. I rest my case.

But until the stuff is marketed to the public, we'll simply have to try harder to be slobs. With a little discipline and practice, we could learn to relax with our dirt.

9   On the other hand, maybe we should just wear more paisley.

The Boston Globe

Trausch's essay is an example of gentle humor. Instead of making biting, cruel fun of people, she is laughing at human nature, including herself in the crowd.

Writing a Humorous Personal Essay

Prewriting. Think of a human frailty you have noticed, perhaps one you have experienced yourself. What is so embarrassing about the experience? What might the situation reveal about human nature? What's funny about it? Brainstorm examples or anecdotes of the experience happening to people, and jot down some specific details.

Writing, Evaluating, Revising. Relax while you write, but allow your imagination to work overtime. If you think of any way to add humor by exaggerating details and dialogue, do it. Before revising, share your draft with some classmates or friends. Find out what parts make your readers laugh, and go back to work on the parts they find dull.

Proofreading and Publishing. Check your essay for mistakes and correct them. Read your essay aloud to the class or to a friend. Your humorous essay might make someone's day!

You may also want to put your essay in your **portfolio.** If so, date the essay and attach a note of reflection. Did you find it difficult to write a humorous personal essay? Why or why not? What did you learn about writing this type of essay by sharing it with others?

• To write a brief autobiographical sketch in a serious or a humorous tone

WRITING A BRIEF AUTOBIOGRAPHY OBJECTIVES

• To read and study a humorous autobiographical sketch

157

MAKING CONNECTIONS

Writing a Brief Autobiography

Autobiography is a prevalent form of self-expression. As a senior in high school, you may soon be asked to write a brief autobiographical statement on an application for a job or college. When you work on it, remember to use the skills you have learned in writing your reflective essay.

The following essay is a humorous reply to a standard college application, written by an eighteen-year-old student named Hugh Gallagher. Gallagher's lighthearted approach worked well for him. His essay was published and won first prize in the humor category of a writing contest.

The Wonder Years
by Hugh Gallagher

QUESTION: ARE THERE ANY SIGNIFICANT EXPERIENCES YOU HAVE HAD, OR ACCOMPLISHMENTS YOU HAVE REALIZED, THAT HAVE HELPED TO DEFINE YOU AS A PERSON?

I am a dynamic figure, often seen scaling walls and crushing ice. I have been known to remodel train stations on my lunch breaks, making them more efficient in the area of heat retention. I translate ethnic slurs for Cuban refugees, I write award-winning operas, I manage time efficiently. Occasionally, I tread water for three days in a row.

I woo women with my sensuous and godlike trombone playing, I can pilot bicycles up severe inclines with unflagging speed, and I cook Thirty-Minute Brownies in twenty minutes. I am an expert in stucco, a veteran in love, and an outlaw in Peru.

Using only a hoe and a large glass of water, I once single-handedly defended a small village in the Amazon Basin from a horde of ferocious army ants. I play bluegrass cello, I was scouted by the Mets. I am the subject of numerous documentaries. When I'm bored, I build

WRITING A BRIEF AUTOBIOGRAPHY
Teaching Strategies

Read Hugh Gallagher's humorous essay to your students. Discuss with them any allusions that are not immediately clear (the length of *Paradise Lost, Moby Dick,* and *David Copperfield,* or the location of Sri Lanka, for example).

Compare the techniques Gallagher uses with some of the same techniques found in Susan Trausch's essay. Students should recognize that Gallagher makes even greater use of exaggeration than does Trausch. Then ask students to comment on the effect of the final sentence. This sentence comes as a surprise and makes a tongue-in-cheek jab at college: What else can college teach this paragon?

Bring to class a variety of college catalogs, college application forms, and job announcements. Let students look through these materials and, if they wish, write autobiographical sketches that meet the requirements of one of the applications or announcements. Thus, if students choose, this assignment can be the beginning of their application process.

GUIDELINES

Whether students create original autobiographical sketches or share examples they find, be sure students can identify the expressive qualities in the works.

SELF-EXPRESSION AND THE FUTURE: SETTING GOALS

Teaching Strategies

To give students some direction in setting their goals, suggest that they set one goal in each of these areas:

1. personal life
2. career
3. community, church, social, or political life

After they have drafted their goals, give students an opportunity to share these goals in groups. After group discussions, allow students to revise their goals.

SELECTION AMENDMENT
Description of change: excerpted
Rationale: to focus on the concept of expressive writing presented in this chapter

large suspension bridges in my yard. I enjoy urban hang gliding. On Wednesdays, after school, I repair electrical appliances free of charge.

I am an abstract artist, a concrete analyst, and a ruthless bookie. Critics worldwide swoon over my original line of corduroy evening wear. I don't perspire. I am a private citizen, yet I receive fan mail. I have been caller number nine and have won the weekend passes. Last summer I toured New Jersey with a traveling centrifugal-force demonstration. I bat .400. My deft floral arrangements have earned me fame in international botany circles. Children trust me.

I can hurl tennis rackets at small moving objects with deadly accuracy. I once read *Paradise Lost, Moby-Dick,* and *David Copperfield* in one day and still had time to refurbish an entire dining room that evening. I know the exact location of every food item in the supermarket. I have performed covert operations for the CIA. I sleep once a week; when I do sleep, I sleep in a chair. While on vacation in Canada, I successfully negotiated with a group of terrorists who had seized a small bakery. The laws of physics do not apply to me.

I balance, I weave, I dodge, I frolic, and my bills are all paid. On weekends, to let off steam, I participate in full-contact origami. Years ago I discovered the meaning of life but forgot to write it down. I have made extraordinary four-course meals using only a Mouli and a toaster oven. I breed prizewinning clams. I have won bullfights in San Juan, cliff-diving competitions in Sri Lanka, and spelling bees at the Kremlin. I have played Hamlet, I have performed open-heart surgery, and I have spoken with Elvis.

But I have not yet gone to college.

Harper's Magazine

Try writing your own autobiographical sketch. It can be serious or humorous—just be sure that it illustrates how a significant experience has affected you.

Self-Expression and the Future: Setting Goals

Exploring the meaning of a past experience is just one way to learn about yourself through writing. Another way is to think about how you might affect the future. What dreams do you have for yourself? for others? for the world around you?

One way to shape your future is to create a statement of goals. Look ahead to your life five years from now. What kind of person do you want to be? What kind of relationships do you want to have with others? And how do you want the world around you to be? Using these three questions, write a statement of goals for yourself, as in the following example. Notice that the writer lists ways to meet each goal.

1. Five years from now I want to be the kind of person who is *intellectually curious*. How will I get there?

   I'll continue to read newspapers, books, and magazines that broaden my knowledge.
   I'll take courses that challenge me, like science.
   I'll try not to be obsessed with grades and getting a job.

2. Five years from now, I want people to see me as the kind of person who is *a leader*. How will I get there?

   I'll speak out about issues I believe in.
   I'll look for ways to show leadership—in school and at work.
   I'll follow through on commitments.

3. Five years from now, I want the world to be *environmentally safer*. How will I help to make this happen?

   I'll make a serious effort to recycle as much as possible.
   I'll register and vote for candidates who support this issue.
   I'll talk to people about doing their part.

   Save your statement of goals, and read it again in six months to see whether you need to make any adjustments.

> "...I always try to write on the principle of the iceberg. There is seven-eighths of it under water for every part that shows."
>
> *Ernest Hemingway*

GUIDELINES

Because most expressive writing is addressed to the writer, you may not want to evaluate students on grammar, usage, or mechanics errors. Emphasize that students should be as specific as possible in their goals.

SELECTION AMENDMENT
Description of change: excerpted
Rationale: to focus on the concept of composition presented in this chapter

Chapter 5

CREATIVE WRITING: NARRATION

OBJECTIVES

- To develop an idea, conflict, plot, characters, setting and point of view for a story
- To analyze a model of a short story
- To write a draft of a short story
- To evaluate, revise, proofread, and publish a draft of a short story
- To write and analyze a scene from a play or a poem

WRITING-IN-PROGRESS ASSIGNMENTS

Major Assignment: Writing a short story

Cumulative Writing Assignments: The chart below shows the sequence of cumulative assignments that will guide students as they write a short story. These Writing Assignments form the instructional core of Chapter 5.

PREWRITING

WRITING ASSIGNMENT
- Part 1: Finding a Story Idea p. 170
- Part 2: Developing Your Conflict and Plot p. 172
- Part 3: Exploring Your Setting and Characters p. 174
- Part 4: Completing a Plan for Your Story p. 178

WRITING YOUR FIRST DRAFT

WRITING ASSIGNMENT
- Part 5: Writing a Draft of Your Story p. 195

EVALUATING AND REVISING

WRITING ASSIGNMENT
- Part 6: Evaluating and Revising Your Story p. 197

PROOFREADING AND PUBLISHING

WRITING ASSIGNMENT
- Part 7: Proofreading and Publishing Your Story p. 199

In addition, exercises 1–4 provide practice in speaking and listening, in analyzing a short story, in writing Tom Swifties, and in analyzing revisions.

cross CURRICULUM

The Story of A Community: A Historical Narrative

The elements that are essential to a good story, such as plot, description, setting, character, and point of view are also important in writing history. History is more than simply names and dates; it is a narrative of people's lives and the events that shape them. Offer students an opportunity to work in groups to research, write, and present a narrative of a historical event, such as the founding of their town, city, or community.

- **Researching** Research may be conducted in a local library and by interviewing local residents, such as older citizens, historians or members of a local historical society. (See pp. 1040–1041 for help with interviewing guidelines.) If possible, allow students to conduct interviews on audiotape or videotape. Students may use excerpts from the tapes later in their presentations. Remind students to add maps, photographs, or photocopies of historical records, if they are available, to their narratives.

- **Writing or Scripting a Presentation** Offer students options for the format of their narratives. Students may prepare a formal presentation of their research by writing and giving an oral report, complete with audiovisual support, or they may be creative and write and act out a script that depicts several important scenes from the history of their community. If students are familiar with video technology, they may script and edit a video documentary of their research. (You may want to work out with students criteria for evaluating each format before students begin their projects.) Encourage students to present their completed projects to the local library, historical society, or town or city council.

INTEGRATING THE LANGUAGE ARTS

SELECTION	READING AND LITERATURE	WRITING AND CRITICAL THINKING	LANGUAGE AND SYNTAX	SPEAKING, LISTENING, AND OTHER EXPRESSION SKILLS
• "The Precious Stones of Axolotyl" pp. 162–167 • from "Spotted Horses" p. 176 • from *China Boy* p. 180 • "The Lion Sleeps Tonight" pp. 183–187 • from *Pygmalion, Act III* pp. 201–203 • "The Bear" p. 207	• Identifying conflict and details pp. 167, 188, 203, 207 • Finding the main idea p. 167 • Analyzing point of view p. 188 • Evaluating dialogue pp. 188, 204 • Identifying themes in literature p. 188 • Analyzing the elements of a short story p. 188 • Analyzing a scene from a play p. 204 • Reading a poem for rhythm, imagery, and symbolism p. 208	• Finding a story idea pp. 170, 204 • Developing conflict and planning plot pp. 172, 204 • Exploring setting and characters pp. 174, 176, 182, 188, 204 • Experimenting with point of view p. 176 • Considering audience, purpose, tone, and point of view pp. 178, 188 • Evaluating and revising dialogue p. 182 • Analyzing a short story p. 188 • Reflecting p. 199 • Analyzing and writing a scene from a play p. 204 • Analyzing and writing a poem p. 208	• Creating verb-adverb puns p. 195 • Proofreading for errors in grammar, usage, and mechanics pp. 199, 208 • Following an established format for dialogue and stage directions p. 204 • Using figurative language pp. 208, 209 • Using sound devices in a poem p. 208	• Working with classmates to explore setting and characters p. 174 • Reading a revised paragraph aloud p. 176 • Working with classmates to evaluate dialogue p. 182 • Working with classmates to analyze the elements of a short story p. 188 • Working with classmates to create verb-adverb puns p. 195 • Performing a dramatic scene p. 204 • Reading poetry aloud p. 208

SUGGESTED INTEGRATED UNIT PLAN

This unit plan gives suggestions on how to integrate the major strands of the language arts with this chapter.

If you begin with this chapter on writing a short story or with the suggested literature selections, you should focus on the common characteristics of a short story. You can then integrate speaking/listening and language concepts with both the writing and the literature.

Common Characteristics

- Content choices that are consistent with choice of form and style and that involve presentation, climax, and resolution of a conflict
- Chronological organization with basic units of sentences and paragraphs
- Content and language entertains the readers
- Effective choice and use of point of view

Writing
Short Story

Speaking/Listening
- Reading a revised paragraph aloud
- Identifying a point of view with a group
- Reading a poem aloud

UNIT FOCUS SHORT STORY

Language Usage
Grammar, Mechanics, and Style
- Verbs
- Quotation marks
- Sentence combining

Literature
Short stories such as
- "The Demon Lover" Elizabeth Bowen
- "The Rocking-Horse Winner" D. H. Lawrence
- "Araby" James Joyce

CHAPTER 5: CREATIVE WRITING: NARRATION

Use this guide for creating an instructional plan that addresses the individual needs of your students. Assignments accompanied by the following symbol (∗) may be completed out of class. Times given for pacing lessons are estimated.

CHAPTER PLANNING GUIDE—PUPIL'S EDITION

LESSONS	LITERARY MODEL pp. 162–167 "The Precious Stones of Axolotyl" by Manuela Williams Crosno	PREWRITING pp. 169–178	
		Generating Ideas	Gathering/Organizing
DEVELOPMENTAL PROGRAM	🕐 20–25 minutes • Read model aloud in groups and discuss questions on p. 167 as a class	🕐 35–40 minutes • Main Assignment: Looking Ahead p. 168 • Exploring Story Ideas pp. 169–170 • Writing Assignment: Part 1 p. 170	🕐 55–60 minutes • Planning Your Story pp. 171–178 • Writing Assignment: Parts 2, 3 pp. 172, 174∗ • Point of View Chart p. 175 • Exercise 1 p. 176 in pairs • Writing Assignment: Part 4 p. 178∗
CORE PROGRAM	🕐 15–20 minutes • Assign student pairs to read the model aloud and answer questions on p. 167	🕐 30–35 minutes • Main Assignment: Looking Ahead p. 168 • Exploring Story Ideas pp. 169–170 • Writing Assignment: Part 1 p. 170	🕐 50–55 minutes • Planning Your Story pp. 171–178 • Writing Assignment: Parts 2, 3 pp. 172∗, 174∗ • Point of View Chart p. 175 • Exercise 1 p. 176 • Writing Assignment: Part 4 p. 178∗
ACCELERATED PROGRAM	🕐 15 minutes • Assign students to read model aloud to a partner and discuss questions 4–6 on p. 167	🕐 15 minutes • Main Assignment: Looking Ahead p. 168 • Writing Assignment: Part 1 p. 170	🕐 30 minutes • Charts pp. 171, 175 • Writing Assignment: Parts 2, 3 pp. 172∗, 174∗ • Exercise 1 p. 176∗ • Thinking About Purpose pp. 177–178 • Writing Assignment: Part 4 p. 178∗

CHAPTER PLANNING GUIDE—PROGRAM RESOURCES

	LITERARY MODEL	PREWRITING
PRINT	• Reading Master 5, *Practice for Assessment in Reading, Vocabulary, and Spelling* p. 5	• Prewriting, *Strategies for Writing* p. 9 • Creative Writing, *English Workshop* pp. 55–66
MEDIA	• Fine Art Transparency 2: *The Ascent of Ethiopia,* *Transparency Binder*	• Graphic Organizer 7: Planning a Plot, *Transparency Binder* • Graphic Organizer 8: Exploring Story Ideas, *Transparency Binder*

WRITING pp. 179–195	EVALUATING AND REVISING pp. 196–198	PROOFREADING AND PUBLISHING pp. 199–200
🕐 **50–55 minutes** • Combining Elements pp. 179–181 • Critical Thinking pp. 181–182 • A Writer's Model pp. 188–193 • Framework p. 194 • Exercise 3 p. 195 • Writing Assignment: Part 5 p. 195*	🕐 **45–50 minutes** • Evaluating and Revising pp. 196–198 • Exercise 4 in pairs pp. 196–197 • Writing Assignment: Part 6 p. 197 • Evaluating and Revising Chart p. 198	🕐 **45–50 minutes** • Proofreading and Publishing p. 199 • Writing Assignment: Part 7 p. 199 • Reflecting p. 199 • A Student Model p. 200
🕐 **40–45 minutes** • Combining Elements pp. 179–181 • Critical Thinking pp. 181–182 • Short Story pp. 183–187* • Exercises 2, 3 pp. 188, 195* • Framework p. 194 • Writing Assignment: Part 5 p. 195*	🕐 **40–45 minutes** • Evaluating and Revising pp. 196–198 • Exercise 4 pp. 196–197* • Writing Assignment: Part 6 p. 197 • Evaluating and Revising Chart p. 198	🕐 **25 minutes** • Proofreading and Publishing p. 199 • Writing Assignment: Part 7 p. 199* • Reflecting p. 199 • A Student Model p. 200*
🕐 **30–35 minutes** • Critical Thinking pp. 181–182 • Short Story pp. 183–187* • Framework p. 194 • Writing Assignment: Part 5 p. 195*	🕐 **35–40 minutes** • Writing Assignment: Part 6 p. 197 • Evaluating and Revising Chart p. 198	🕐 **20–25 minutes** • Writing Assignment: Part 7 p. 199* • Reflecting p. 199

WRITING	EVALUATING AND REVISING	PROOFREADING AND PUBLISHING
• Writing, *Strategies for Writing* p. 10	• Evaluating and Revising, *Strategies for Writing* p. 11	• Proofreading Practice, *Strategies for Writing* p. 13
	• Revision Transparencies 7–8, *Transparency Binder* 📽	• *Language Workshop:* Lessons 49–50 💾

ELEMENTS OF WRITING: CURRICULUM CONNECTIONS

Writing Workshop
• A Scene pp. 201–204
• A Poem pp. 205–208

Making Connections
• Creating a Storyboard p. 209

ASSESSMENT OPTIONS

Summative Assessment
Holistic Scoring: Prompts and Models
pp. 9–14

Portfolio Assessment
Portfolio forms, *Portfolio Assessment*
pp. 5–25, 44–48

Reflection
Writing Process Log, *Strategies for Writing*
p. 8
Self-assessment Record, *Portfolio Assessment*
p. 19

Ongoing Assessment
Proofreading, *Strategies for Writing* p. 12

💾 Computer disk or CD-ROM

📽 Overhead transparencies

IMAGING OTHER WORLDS

OBJECTIVES

- To write personal responses to a short story
- To identify conflict, symbol, and theme in a short story
- To compose a writing journal entry about a personal experience

PROGRAM MANAGER

CHAPTER 5

- **Additional Instruction** To help less-advanced students who need additional practice with concepts and activities related to this chapter, see **Chapter 5** in *English Workshop, Complete Course,* pp. 55–66.

- **Summative Assessment** For a writing prompt, including grading criteria and student models, see *Holistic Scoring: Prompts and Models,* pp. 9–14.

- **Extension/Enrichment** See **Fine Art Transparency 2,** *The Ascent of Ethiopia* by Lois Mailou Jones. For suggestions on how to tie the transparency to instruction, review teacher's notes in *Fine Art and Instructional Transparencies for Writing,* p. 9.

- **Reading Support** For help with the reading selection, pp. 162–167, see **Reading Master 5** in *Practice for Assessment in Reading, Vocabulary, and Spelling,* p. 5.

5 CREATIVE WRITING: NARRATION

MOTIVATION

Motivate students to read Manuela Williams Crosno's story by asking them to identify their favorite stories and to tell why they like the stories. Lead students to realize that the primary purpose of most stories is to entertain.

TEACHING THE LESSON

Have a student read aloud the introductory paragraphs and then use the question at the end of the introduction to prepare students to read the story. After students read the story silently, ask for questions and use the annotations as the basis for a discussion.

You may want to identify the ☞

Imagining Other Worlds

It has been said that what distinguishes human beings from animals isn't reason at all, but imagination. The ability to **imagine other worlds** is a remarkable, rather mysterious gift, isn't it?

Writing and You. You use your imagination so often that you probably take it for granted. For example, a novelist lets you live among a fantastic race of trolls. A scriptwriter puts you on the streets of St. Louis or on a mountain in Colorado, no matter where you really live. The combination of language and imagination in stories, films, plays, and comic strips gives all of us opportunities to experience other lives, other times, other places. What imaginative world have you inhabited recently?

As You Read. Some characters in the following story fail to find what they're searching for. Is there a message here about imagination?

Doug Webb, *American Dream* (1986). Serigraph, 29" × 35".
© 1986 Martin Lawrence Limited Editions.

QUOTATION FOR THE DAY

"In [fiction] we find, in imagination, not only the pleasure of recognizing the world we know and of reliving our past, but also the pleasure of entering worlds we do not know. . . ." (Robert Penn Warren, 1905–1989, American author)

Use the quotation to prompt a discussion of why people read.

VISUAL CONNECTIONS
American Dream

About the Artist. Doug Webb follows many of the traditions of the surrealist movement and then adds techniques of his own to create a hyper-surrealist style. Surreal art usually combines a realistic painting style with imaginary subject matter that results in a dreamlike effect. Webb rearranges size and context in his paintings, and he often uses commonplace settings for his uncommon scenes. These juxtapositions challenge the viewer to see creatively.

Ideas for Writing. Have students work as a class to tell a funny story. Each student should take a turn and add a sentence or two. Encourage students to use incongruity to create humor. Then, allow each student to evaluate and revise a copy of the story. After volunteers share their revised drafts with the class, point out that evaluating and revising often require as much creativity as prewriting and writing.

161

elements in this short story that are its strengths. One way to present these elements effectively is to put on an overhead transparency a chart headed "Story Elements." Then, ask for specific examples from **"The Precious Stones of Axolotyl"** that illustrate how the story has addressed each element.

You could include the following elements in the chart:

1. fast-paced beginning to arouse the reader's interest
2. conflict established quickly
3. interesting plot to keep reader's interest
4. effective descriptions of setting
5. clear order of events
6. believable characters

USING THE SELECTION
The Precious Stones of Axolotyl

1

An axolotyl is a dark salamander found in Mexico. In the wild, axolotyls are found in certain lakes around Mexico City. This fact helps fix the setting of the story.

2

The first three words of the story, the equivalent of *once upon a time,* identify the story as a folktale.

3

A special stick or staff is often a tool of power for wizards or sorcerers.

4

An aged person is often associated with wisdom or knowledge in the folktale tradition.

The Precious Stones of Axolotyl
by Manuela Williams Crosno

Once long ago, there was an old woman who lived near the village of Agua Clara, which means "clear water." Although she was to live for many years more, she seemed older than anyone in the village. No one could remember where she came from or when.

She lived in a small lean-to built against a great rock. Among her few possessions were a herd of goats and an oddly shaped stick on which it was her custom to lean heavily as she went about her work.

She was so wrinkled one could not see her eyes to tell what color they were. Her skin was deep brown, like pine cones when they fall to the ground. And when she laughed she showed just two teeth. Because no one knew her name, and because she seemed to have lived in the

7. effective dialogue
8. consistent point of view
9. conflict brought to a climax
10. satisfying and original ending

GUIDED PRACTICE

Model answers to **Reader's Response** and **Writer's Craft** questions by using a traditional fairy tale that you briefly recount. To be useful, this fairy tale must have an old, wise person, symbols, a theme, and an unexpected reward. "Toads and Diamonds" is a possible choice.

☛

mountains from their very beginning, she was called "La Vieja de las montañas"—the old woman of the mountains.

5
6 Now there resided in the village of Agua Clara three small boys whose names were Anselmo, Felipe, and Guillermo. They lived in separate houses built of adobe. The houses were almost as alike as the boys, who were the same age and were constant companions.

7 One time when they went toward the mountains, they came upon the goats of La Vieja, unwatched, and eating peacefully at the sparse gramma grass that grew about. Guillermo began to throw stones at the animals. Anselmo howled like a coyote. Felipe gave the weird cry of the mountain lion. The goats, in a panic, began to run in all directions.

8 Suddenly, the voice of La Vieja called to them. The goats stopped where they were and again ate grass in a peaceful manner. The boys turned homeward, but standing in their pathway and leaning on her stick was La Vieja.

Shaking her stick in his direction, she said to Anselmo, "You howled like a coyote to frighten my goats. You are unwise." And to Guillermo, "You threw stones to hurt my goats. You are unkind." Then to Felipe, "You cried like the lion of the mountains to make my goats run away. You have little understanding." To all three she said, "When you have learned wisdom, kindness, and understanding, then I will show you the precious stones of axolotl."

5
The use of the number three is common in folktales. Name some other tales that use the number three. ["Three Little Pigs," "Goldilocks and the Three Bears," and "The Three Sillies"]

6
At this point all the main characters have been introduced.

7 6
The next three paragraphs introduce the first major conflict of the story—the conflict between the three boys and La Vieja.

8 7
La Vieja's ability to calm the animals suggests that she has magical powers.

INDEPENDENT PRACTICE

Have students work independently to complete the **Reader's Response** and **Writer's Craft** questions, or use the questions to generate discussion of the story.

164

Stepping aside, she disappeared behind a rock, leaving the boys somewhat frightened. For many days they thought about this meeting with La Vieja, and they *never forgot* the words of the old woman.

Many years passed and Guillermo, Anselmo, and Felipe grew to manhood. Anselmo was judge of all disputes in the village and was considered to be very wise. However, if anyone had a story to tell and needed a sympathetic ear, he went to Felipe who could always be counted upon for understanding. Guillermo was the one to call when a child was hurt, for he ministered to the ill and needy. It was well known in the village that no one was as kind and as gentle as Guillermo.

9   Now when Otero became governor, he sent his soldiers about the country to seize any possessions of value which they might discover. They had heard of the precious stones of axolotyl which were said to belong to La Vieja, and although the soldiers thought this talk was probably just a fable, they went to the old woman.

"We have come for your jewels!" they said.

She was silent for a long moment. Then she smiled—a smile they could not interpret. It showed her two teeth, but since they could not see her eyes, they did not know whether or not she was angry.

"They are the jewels of axolotyl, the water dog," she said, finally. "Come with me and I will show them to you."

The soldiers followed La Vieja past the place where the goats were corralled, and beyond her house into the wooded foothills. She walked slowly and leaned heavily on her stick. Finally, she came to a

8 Here the second major conflict—between the authorities and La Vieja—is introduced.

ASSESSMENT

You can use students' written or oral responses to the questions at the end of the short story to judge how well the students have responded to the short story and whether they have correctly identified the symbolism, conflict, and themes in the selection.

RETEACHING

To review concepts, use the chart on the next page and work with students to identify the elements of another well-known fairy tale or folktale.

☞

165

pool beyond a waterfall where it seemed the waters, after their noisy dash over the rocks, had stopped to rest. There was no movement in the still depths of the pool. Glistening far below the surface were rocks of many colors.

"See the green one?" she asked, pointing to a green pebble near the bottom of the pool. "See the scarlet one," she said, selecting a red pebble still farther in the clear depths. "See the perfectly white one?" she asked, thrusting the stick toward the deepest part of the pool. The soldiers nodded and looked at one another.

"Those," she cried, laughing triumphantly, "are the precious stones of axolotl!"

10   Now axolotl is a water dog and is reported to be poisonous. Long ago, it is said, he took the soul of one of the people. So the soldiers were afraid of him or the mention of his name. They looked at the rocks shining in the pool. They looked at La Vieja.

> **When you have learned wisdom, kindness, and understanding, then I will show you the precious stones of axolotl.**

"She is a foolish old woman," they whispered together. "These are not precious stones, they are but rocks."

Since she had no jewels, and because they felt that she had attempted to deceive them, the soldiers took La Vieja to Agua Clara. There she was locked in a small room where she was to remain for many days. After some time, there was a knock at her door and Felipe stood outside. He had heard that she was ill and had come with food. She would accept nothing, however. Instead, she said these words which she repeated many times:

"You understand, amigo, you understand."

Still later, there was a voice at her window in the dark and

11   Guillermo whispered, "La Viejita, I have cared for your goats and brought you your walking stick which I found near the corral."

9

10
Axolotl is identified as a powerful spirit.

11
The diminutive -ita ending on *La Viejita* makes the name a term of endearment.

Title:	
Theme	
Conflict	
Symbols	

CLOSURE

Ask students to write down the titles of their favorite stories and to identify the conflict, main theme, and symbolism of each story.

She remembered where the soldiers had thrown her stick and she accepted it gratefully. For a long time she looked at Guillermo in the darkness until she recognized who he was. Then she said, "Amigo, you are kind—very kind."

Finally, Anselmo pleaded with the governor to let the woman go because she was old and owned no precious stones. The governor would not permit La Vieja to be freed until Anselmo had promised him many pesos to help pay for the soldiers.

The old woman of the mountains thanked Anselmo for her release, and said to him, "Amigo mio, I see that you are one who is very wise. Tomorrow, bring Felipe and Guillermo with you and come to see me."

Since he wished to please her, Anselmo called his friends the next day. Together they went to the place where La Vieja was tending her goats. She smiled when she saw the three friends and said, "You have indeed learned wisdom and kindness and understanding. Come with me."

Slowly she led them to the pool which was bathed in sunlight and shadow. It was the pool she had shown the soldiers. Pointing to the three stones shining within it, she said, "These are the precious stones of axolotl."

Now she took the long stick on which she had always leaned so heavily, and turned the knob outward. They saw that it was a cup which swiveled, and that when the stick was turned about, it resembled a large dipper. Thus, she thrust the stick into the pool once and

10

12

An unexpected reward for kindness is a common theme in folktales.

166

12

brought up the white stone, and gave it to Anselmo saying, "For wisdom." In the same manner she dipped the stick into the pool again, and gave the green stone to Guillermo, telling him only that he had become very kind. Again the stick went into the water, and this time the red stone was placed in the hand of Felipe, "For understanding."

Soon after this, La Vieja died, but she was never forgotten. Felipe, Guillermo, and Anselmo carried the stones in their pockets for some time before they learned that one was a diamond, another an emerald, and the third one, a ruby. Yet they never considered them as priceless as the real jewels of axolotyl.

READER'S RESPONSE

1. Did you believe the stones were jewels when La Vieja showed them to the soldiers? Why or why not?
2. Why do you think a very old, mysterious person—whether wise or sinister—figures in so many stories, from ancient times to today? What examples can you think of besides La Vieja?
3. What reward have you received that you didn't expect or that came from a surprising source? Why was it unexpected, and what did you learn from it? Write about the experience in your journal.

WRITER'S CRAFT

4. A story without tension isn't a story. There's always a conflict or problem that someone faces and must resolve. What conflicts do you find in "The Precious Stones of Axolotyl"?
5. From the very first, we have a sense of La Vieja's mystery and power. Through what specific details does the writer convey these qualities?
6. Crosno used her imagination to create a story with a message, or theme. If you removed the imaginary world and simply stated the theme, what would you say?

ANSWERS
Reader's Response
Answers will vary.

1. Students who answer yes will probably refer to their knowledge of the genre or hints in the story, although some may just have guessed. All students should explain their answers.
2. Students' answers will vary, depending on the particular works students have in mind.
3. Students should include why their experiences were unexpected and what they learned from their experiences.

Writer's Craft
4. Students should mention the conflicts between the boys and La Vieja and between the authorities and La Vieja.
5. Students should note some of the following points: her age, her unknown origins, her stick, her hidden eyes, her lack of a name, her nickname, her ability to calm the goats, her prophetic remarks to the boys, her apparent guardianship of the precious stones, her disappearance, and the boys' fright.
6. Students should make the point that some things are more valuable than material riches. Some students may consider these jewels to be wisdom, kindness, and understanding. Others may think that the men themselves have become jewels to others.

Write the words *narration, description, classification,* and *evaluation* on the chalkboard. Point out that classification can include comparison/contrast. Tell students that the terms on the chalkboard identify four ways of writing creatively. Then, ask students to read the examples in the textbook and to suggest additional examples. Next, have students read the **Looking Ahead** box as a way of making a transition to the rest of the chapter. ■

CRITICAL THINKING

Synthesis. Ask students to invent titles for each of the works described in the examples in the textbook. Explain that the title should give a clue as to the content of the work and to which method of development was used in the work's creation. Have volunteers share their ideas with the class, and lead the class in a discussion about why each title would be appropriate.

COOPERATIVE LEARNING

Divide the class into groups of three or four and ask them to develop additional examples for each of the methods of development. Ask a reporter from each group to share the group's examples. You might consider awarding bonus points or a prize for the cleverest or most unusual suggestions.

Ways to Write Creatively

Writers whose purpose is to be creative—to use language in an original, imaginative way—may write stories, poems, novels, movie and TV scripts, even comic strips and song lyrics. Here are some examples of ways to write creatively.

- in a movie script, telling about scientists shrunk to the size of molecules for a journey inside the human body
- in a company newsletter, telling a fable about the value of hard work
- in a short story, telling about a boy who wakes up one day to find himself turned into a giant guinea pig
- in a script for a computer game, describing a strange palace, cavern, forest, and river
- in a play, having a character describe the teacher who taught him to read
- in a poem, cataloging several different kinds of work and workers
- in a children's story, showing a fish swimming through five oceans in search of her lost brother
- on a World Wide Web page, contrasting two movies by the same director
- in a novel, showing how ambition and pride can lead to evil deeds
- in a television script, having a character decide how to handle a problem with a new roommate

LOOKING AHEAD

In this chapter, you will use narration and description to create a short story, a scene, and a poem. As you work through the chapter's main assignment, which is to write a story, keep in mind that a good short story

- holds the reader's attention with believable characters and an interesting plot
- involves the main character in a problem or conflict that must be resolved
- may communicate some insight about life

PREWRITING

OBJECTIVES

- To brainstorm for and to choose an idea for a short story
- To develop conflict and plot
- To create a plot plan for a story

- To use prewriting strategies to develop characters and setting
- To rewrite the point of view of a passage
- To share point-of-view revisions in a group
- To make judgments about audience, tone, and point of view
- To create a plan for a short story

☞

Writing a Short Story

Prewriting

Exploring Story Ideas

You can start small when looking for a story idea. Just a glimpse of some person, place, or situation may be the seed your imagination can water.

- A computer that runs a spaceship decides to take control from the human crew.
- An old fisherman, alone in his small boat, hooks an enormous fish.
- An ambitious general hears a mysterious prophecy that he will be crowned king.

PROGRAM MANAGER

PREWRITING

- **Self-Assessment** Before beginning instruction of the writing process, see **Writing Process Log** in *Strategies for Writing*, p. 8.

- **Heuristics** To help students generate ideas, see **Prewriting** in *Strategies for Writing*, p. 9.

- **Instructional Support** See **Graphic Organizers 7** and **8**. For suggestions on how to tie the transparencies to instruction, review teacher's notes in *Fine Art and Instructional Transparencies for Writing*, pp. 65 and 67.

QUOTATION FOR THE DAY

"The trouble with the average human being is that he never goes on mountain journeys. He stops at the first way station and refuses to believe there is country beyond." (Agnes Sligh Turnbull, 1888–1982, American writer)

Write the quotation on the chalkboard and explain to the class that finding ideas and planning a creative story require a writer to go beyond the first stop. Remind students that sometimes an entire story may begin with a person the writer has seen only once.

Because this lesson is long, you may want to present the material in five sections. Assign independent reading and then review the material for each section in class. The following list gives the titles of the sections:

1. **Exploring Story Ideas**
2. **Developing Conflict and Plot**
3. **Exploring Characters and Setting**
4. **Choosing a Point of View**
5. **Thinking about Purpose, Audience, and Tone**

These divisions are natural to the lesson because each one ends with an exercise, a writing assignment, or both.

Discuss the three methods for getting story ideas and ask students to consider their observations, memories, and imaginings.

MEETING *individual* NEEDS

LESS-ADVANCED STUDENTS

Use the mnemonic acronym AMI (*ami* is French for "friend") to encourage recall of the three ways to find story seeds: attention, memory, imagination.

ADVANCED STUDENTS

Some students may want to try writing stories by using the stream-of-consciousness approach. You may want to show students how a published author applies this technique in his or her short stories. If it is in your literature textbook, have students read James Joyce's story "Araby" and then work with them to analyze how it reveals the characters' random thoughts, mental images, and emotions. Guide students to tell the stories of characters not through external events but through the drama that unfolds through the stream of thoughts in the characters' minds. Be sure to reinforce that these thoughts should paint portraits of their characters.

---

170   *Creative Writing*

Do these seeds sound familiar? Even the fascinating, full-blown stories of *2001: A Space Odyssey, The Old Man and the Sea,* and *The Tragedy of Macbeth* sprang from something particular—and not yet complete. To begin your search for a story idea, be alert to anything and everything that captures your attention, sticks in your memory, or turns your imagination on high.

Observing and Reading. Keep your antennae out. Watching television, reading a magazine, or even sitting on a bench may bring something into your vision that could grow into a story—a fire in a high-rise, a man who keeps twenty dogs in his house, a young girl who is training for a marathon.

Remembering. Brainstorming or freewriting can help you pluck kernels of story ideas from memories of people you have known or from situations you have experienced. Do you have a recurring dream of coming to school in pajamas? Does your eight-year-old cousin do fantastic things with computers?

Imagining. Because some of your best ideas come from letting your imagination go, try asking yourself "What if?" questions. What if the President of the United States were a teenager? What if a tornado hit your neighborhood?

Calvin & Hobbes copyright 1988 Watterson. Distributed by Universal Press Syndicate. Reprinted with

WRITING ASSIGNMENT

PART 1:
Finding a Story Idea

You have looked at several methods—observing and reading, remembering, and imagining—that you can use to identify a story idea. Try one or more of these methods now; and when you have your story idea, write it in a few sentences.

Then, ask volunteers to offer the class any insights they have into the methods—good spots for observations, memory cues or jogs, or stimuli for the imagination. If you wish, you could model the brainstorming process for students.

Explain to students that **Planning Your Story** has four parts: **Developing Conflict and Plot, Exploring Characters and Setting,** **Choosing a Point of View,** and **Thinking About Purpose, Audience, and Tone.** Story planning can occur in any order, and in fact, because the writing process is recursive, much of it often occurs while the writer is writing.

After students have read **Developing Conflict and Plot,** pp. 171–172, have them reconsider the **Types of Conflict** chart. Work with the class to generate at least one ☜

Prewriting

Planning Your Story

Where is your story idea leading you? Who will be in your story? What will happen? It is some distance (and discovery) from first idea to finished story, but the rest of this chapter will help you find your way. And it will be *your* way: You'll use basic short-story elements to tell your unique tale.

Developing Conflict and Plot

The *plot*, or events, of your story offers you much freedom but has one indispensable part: a *conflict,* or problem, that the main character (or characters) faces. The character can cause a crisis or be confronted with one, can hunger for something or fear a terrible decision. The possibilities are endless, but the reader must wonder, "How will this turn out?"

TYPES OF CONFLICT	
A character struggles against another character, a group, or society's rules.	Josh and his best friend are competing for the same scholarship.
A character struggles against a force of nature.	The car carrying the wrestling team stalls in a blinding blizzard.
A character struggles with personal feelings, values, or needs.	Suzette regrets leaving home but feels she can't go back.

With a conflict established, your job is to decide (1) how to solve that conflict and (2) how to keep the story moving forward and readers interested until the solution is reached.

Most story writers use a basic shape to drive their plots and draw in readers. After the conflict sets events in motion, *complications* may arise. These setbacks or additional conflicts make the outcome less sure. What you're always leading to,

MEETING individual NEEDS

LESS-ADVANCED STUDENTS

Students who need a simpler approach to developing plot can do what many other authors do—copy a plot. Because you need to differentiate this concept from plagiarism, you may want to begin by pointing out the similarities among many plots of detective stories or among many romance plots. Work with students to identify the common factors. Tell students that they, too, can use these common factors without infringing on anyone's rights. Encourage students to look for appropriate models.

example for each specific kind of conflict. Then, have students name stories (any type) that use each kind of conflict. Be sure students explain their answers.

Ask students to consider how the setting and characters of a story with an external conflict might differ from those of a story with an internal conflict. [A story with an internal conflict might have a more confined setting and fewer characters because it focuses more on a single consciousness.]

To reinforce the importance of the flow of the plot, reproduce the **Timesaver** graph on p. 173 for the whole class.

Draw attention to several important elements of the **Here's How** plan: two conflicts—one external, one internal; use of colloquial language; use of abbreviation;

though, is a *climax:* a scene of keen interest when the conflict will be settled. The climax may be a small gesture (sharing a plate of food), or it may be action-packed excitement (roping a runaway horse). (Another name for climax is **high point,** and that's the image to keep in mind.)

After the climax, or high point, of the action, you need to "resolve" the problem or conflict for your readers. This ending of a story is the ***resolution,*** the final details that show how everything works out and that bring the story to a satisfying close.

Here's one writer's plan for the plot of her story.

COOPERATIVE LEARNING

Divide the class into pairs. Each student should brainstorm five conflicts that each fit a different category and exchange the conflicts with a partner. Students must then identify whether each conflict is internal or external and the kind of conflict it is; for example, a fistfight (external—character), a tornado hitting a town (external—nature), a compulsion to steal (internal—values), trespassing to protest (internal and external—personal values and society's rules).

Help students understand that some conflicts (like getting fired or breaking a leg) might have or might lead to both internal and external components.

A DIFFERENT APPROACH

Studying resolutions can help students to avoid dull or trite endings and to be aware of the wide variety of possible endings.

Have students study endings of familiar stories to come up with a categorization scheme of kinds of resolutions. You may want to have students decide what kinds of endings are possible and what kinds work best before thinking about their own endings.

HERE'S HOW

Conflict:	<u>External</u>—Myung Hee is going away to college, but her best friend, Julia Billings, is not. <u>Internal</u>—Myung's feelings of happiness, sadness, and guilt are all mixed up.
Plot Events:	Julia calls Myung to go to mall. Everything there makes Myung talk about going away to college. Finally Julia gets really upset and tells her to be quiet. Major fight. M. and J. stop speaking, and M. hangs out with other girls going to college. They make fun of Julia.
Climax:	Myung faces Julia in store, starts to speak. Julia's still angry. M. apologizes.
Resolution:	They're friends again. Julia has plans, too.

WRITING ASSIGNMENT

PART 2:
Developing Your Conflict and Plot

You may have already identified a conflict when you chose a story idea for Writing Assignment, Part 1. Now check that idea and expand it if necessary to make sure your main character has a struggle against someone or something else, or a struggle within himself or herself. Then brainstorm for complications and decide how the conflict will be resolved. Pull it all together in a plot plan like the one shown above.

foundation for development of setting, characters, and theme.

To prepare students to complete **Writing Assignment: Part 2,** model answering the questions and creating an outline like the one in the **Here's How** by using a story idea of your own.

As students begin to consider their characters, make sure that they understand that real characters do not necessarily have to be realistic. A real character is a unified being whose motivations and actions are consistent (unless there's a good reason for them not to be) and understandable.

As students focus on the section on setting, it is important to point out that many stories have multiple settings; otherwise ☞

Exploring Characters and Setting

Characters. Like Frankenstein's monster, your *characters* are entirely your own creation; but if you make them real enough, they may eventually start acting on their own. Plan to give each one a distinct personality, appearance, and history. You may create characters that are totally imaginary, or you may combine traits from real-life people. For example, you could create a main character with the humor of Eddie Murphy, the strength of Arnold Schwarzenegger, and the looks of your Uncle John. Collect enough details to develop a full sense of who your characters are—even though you may not use all the details you invent. Here are some questions to use.

- How old are the characters? What do they look like (height, weight, eye color, skin color, hair color and style, clothing)?
- How do they move (clumsily, gracefully, sneakily) and speak (tone of voice, accent, expressions)?
- What are some important personality traits (bossy, angry, arrogant, timid, kind, confident, sneaky)?
- What do they think about (wishes, hopes, worries)?
- How do they get along with other characters?

"YOU CAN'T START WITH HOW PEOPLE LOOK & SPEAK & BEHAVE AND COME TO KNOW HOW THEY FEEL. YOU MUST KNOW EXACTLY WHAT'S IN THEIR HEARTS & MINDS BEFORE THEY EVER SET VISIBLE FOOT ON THE STAGE."

EUDORA WELTY

TIMESAVER
Give students a chart with spaces for answers as they complete **Writing Assignment: Part 2.** Using this will save time for both you and the class and will also give students a clear, neat record of their plans. You can use the following example:

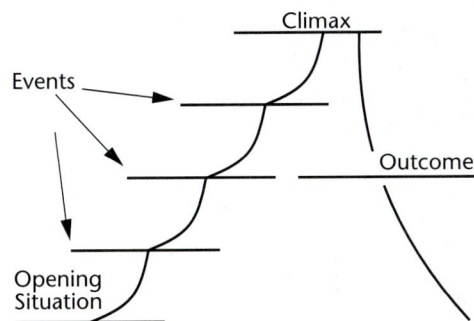

Events · Climax · Outcome · Opening Situation

SELECTION AMENDMENT
Description of change: excerpted
Rationale: to focus on the concept of characterization presented in this chapter

students may get the idea that they must have only one.

To prepare students for **Writing Assignment: Part 3**, continue planning the story you modeled for **Writing Assignment: Part 2** by using the questions on character and setting. Then, write separate paragraphs about characters and setting on an overhead transparency as you talk through your ideas.

Model sharing with a classmate by asking for and incorporating responses from the class.

Choosing a point of view is a problem that may require some experimentation before a good solution can be reached. Begin by reviewing the **Point of View** chart to make sure that students understand and can distinguish first-person point of view and the third-person limited and omniscient

Setting. A story's setting can be as ordinary as Saturday morning in a kitchen or as strange as a space colony a thousand years from now; it can be crucial to the development of the story or only a minor element. *Setting* includes the time and place, weather and season—even the objects in a room.

Sensory details of place and time often help create a story's *mood,* or general feeling. The testing room at a shampoo factory, for instance, can be scary or funny, depending on the sounds, smells, and sights the writer describes. As you think about your setting, ask yourself these questions:

- Where and when will my story take place?
- What sensory details about time, place, or weather could contribute to the story's mood?
- What details of setting could reveal information about the characters or plot?

COMPUTER NOTE: Use the multiple-window feature of your word-processing program to view several documents, such as your prewriting notes about characters and setting, at one time.

WRITING ASSIGNMENT PART 3:
Exploring Your Setting and Characters

Can you imagine your setting clearly? Can you picture your characters and predict their behavior? Using the questions on characters and setting (page 173 and above), freewrite paragraphs describing each setting and important character in your story. If freewriting doesn't seem to work, try clustering or brainstorming. Share your descriptions with a classmate, and ask: *What other details do you "see" in such a setting? What else would you like to know about the characters?*

Choosing a Point of View

In a book about fiction writing, Robert Newton Peck refers to choosing a point of view as "nailing down the camera." *Point of view* refers to the vantage point, the camera angle, from which your readers will see the events of your story. Remember that it is not your personal viewpoint: You are the writer, *not* the narrator.

MEETING individual NEEDS

ADVANCED STUDENTS

Clever authors build unwritten resolutions into their endings. For example, in *Brighton Rock* by Graham Greene, it is clear, though it is not stated, that sooner or later, the record will be played, probably with devastating results. You may wish to have some students explore the idea of books that, so to speak, extend beyond their own endings. Encourage students to experiment in their own writing with the techniques they find.

TECHNOLOGY TIP

When students use multiple windows in a word-processing program, they might find it useful to remove temporarily tool bars, rulers, and other menu items from the top of the screen. They then will be able to see larger windows when they open more than one folder or document.

points of view. Students should be able to identify examples of each in their literary anthologies or in stories they know well.

You may wish to have students practice this skill by orally retelling a traditional fairy tale from a different point of view. This could be done by assignment or choice. First, model telling "The Three Little Pigs" from the wolf's point of view in first person. Then, encourage students to talk about how this change affected the story. Did it improve? Did it detract from the story? Next, discuss the possible point of view for the story plan shown in **Here's How,** p. 172.

Before students begin **Exercise 1,** p. 176, make sure they understand the sequence of events in the passage and the cause-and-effect relationships.

☞

A basic choice in point of view is whether to use a first-person or third-person narrator. A first-person narrator communicates immediacy and a distinct personality, while a third-person narrator (either limited or omniscient) is a more distant and faceless reporter. Each point of view has some advantages and disadvantages, but whichever you choose, be consistent. You'll confuse readers if you switch the point of view from a first-person narrator to a third-person narrator.

POINT OF VIEW	
First-person: This point of view can make a story personal and build strong response to a character, but the reader can be told only what the character sees, hears, knows, and believes.	"It was partly her own fault, of course. How was I to know? She was pretty clever about it. And she never once came out and admitted she was illiterate. It took me years to catch on, and by then it was much too late." Hisaye Yamamoto, *Reading and Writing*
Third-person limited: This outside point of view focuses on one character's perspective. The narrator can enter that character's mind without being restricted to the character's actions or location.	"She felt so much the change in her own face that she went to the mirror, polished a clear patch in it and looked at once urgently and stealthily in." Elizabeth Bowen, "The Demon Lover"
Third-person omniscient: *Omniscient* means "all-knowing." This outside narration, the most flexible, can enter the mind of *any* character. It gives a wider view, presenting any detail or viewpoint—even revealing the future.	"She had a white nape to her neck and short red hair above it, and Shawn liked the color and wave of that flame. . . . Ellen, her heart desolate, lay on her side, staring into the dark, grieving for what she had said and unable to unsay it." Maurice Walsh, *The Quiet Man*

MEETING individual NEEDS

LEARNING STYLES

Visual Learners. Rather than using only the verbal explanation of plot, you may want to show students a visual demonstration of plot development.

Plot Plan

Conflict(s):
Events: 1. 2. 3. 4. 5.
Outcome: 1. Climax 2. Resolution

You may want to have students practice applying this model to familiar stories. Or, you may want to allow students to develop their own methods of modeling plot development.

AMENDMENTS TO SELECTIONS
Description of change: excerpted
Rationale: to focus on the concept of point of view presented in this chapter

Tell students that a theme is not just a moral stuck on at the end. The story should reveal the theme. Remind students that they all have basic, critical issues in their lives—fear of failure, a yearning for security, sadness over losing a friend. These events and feelings are the starting blocks for stories and for themes.

Tone may be the single most difficult literary concept for students to understand. Teaching this concept will require many examples and repeated exercises in identification and creation of different tones.

Exercise 1 prepared students to choose a point of view in **Writing Assignment: Part 4**, p. 178. To model choosing audience,

ANSWERS
Exercise 1

Responses will vary. Each student should use a consistent point of view; the events should be unchanged in sequence or nature, although events may be added; and the rewritten passage should have a sense of unity.

MEETING *individual* NEEDS

LEP/ESL

General Strategies. A brief discussion regarding Faulkner's use of nonstandard English is necessary prior to assigning **Exercise 1**. English-language learners, far more than their English-proficient counterparts, need standard models of English to follow and are likely to be confused by Faulkner's style. You can compensate for this situation by photocopying the excerpt and replacing instances of nonstandard grammar with blanks. Assign the paragraph handouts as a grammar exercise. Pair students and ask them to fill in the blank spaces with standard grammatical forms.

EXERCISE 1 ▶ **Speaking and Listening: Experimenting with Point of View**

Read the following passage, which is told by a first-person narrator. Then rewrite the passage from another point of view—as a different first-person narrator (one of the Tulls), as a third-person limited narrator, or as an omniscient narrator. After you have finished writing, read what you've written aloud to the members of your class and ask them to identify the point of view you are using. If you have done a good job, they will be able to identify it correctly.

> That horse. It ain't never missed a lick. It was going about forty miles a hour when it come to the bridge over the creek. It would have had a clear road, but it so happened that Vernon Tull was already using the bridge when it got there. He was coming back from town; he hadn't heard about the auction; him and his wife and three daughters and Mrs. Tull's aunt, all setting in chairs in the wagon bed, and all asleep, including the mules. They waked up when the horse hit the bridge one time, but Tull said the first he knew was when the mules tried to turn the wagon around in the middle of the bridge and he seen that spotted varmint run right twixt the mules and run up the wagon tongue like a squirrel. He said he just had time to hit it across the face with his whip-stock, because about that time the mules turned the wagon around on that ere one-way bridge and that horse clumb across one of the mules and jumped down onto the bridge again and went on, with Vernon standing up in the wagon and kicking at it.
>
> William Faulkner, "Spotted Horses"

purpose, and tone, continue with the story you have been using in modeling previous assignments.

CLOSURE

Ask students to name the major elements of a short story and then lead a discussion based on the answers. [Possible answers include conflict, plot, theme, tone, audience, purpose, characters, setting, mood, and climax.] ■

Thinking About Purpose, Audience, and Tone

Purpose and Audience. When you write a story, your main *purpose* is to be creative, to exercise your imagination through words. That purpose includes entertaining your *audience*, but "entertaining" doesn't necessarily mean amusing them or making them happy. It means keeping them interested, compelling them to turn the page, and creating *any* effect you want to achieve. Depending on how you tell it, a story about a seventy-year-old woman who collars a robber in a bodega (grocery store) can move your readers to tears, white knuckles, or tender smiles.

Part of your purpose may also be to communicate an idea, or *theme*. Perhaps your story about the bodega has a message about elderly people or desperately poor people or city barrios (districts). Usually you don't state the theme directly, as you might state an idea in an essay (*we often underestimate old people*), but you can show it through characters and events.

Tone. *Tone* plays a part in the effect you create because it expresses your attitude toward characters, plot, and readers. You can create a serious, silly, romantic, or ironic tone with your choice of events, details, and language. Point of view, the narrator who "speaks," affects tone, too. Notice how the tone changes in these two descriptions of the same scene. The first tone is matter-of-fact, clear and simple, and informal. The second is poetic and dramatic.

> I bought six cartons of umbrellas and got stampeded the day I set up on Eighty-fifth Street. It poured so hard the $3.98 specials were gone by noon.

TECHNOLOGY TIP

Some students may find that a database is a convenient place to store character information. They may wish to use the words in the questions on p. 173 as cues to their column titles. The database can keep the information neat and accessible and also will allow easy comparison across categories to prevent characters from being too similar.

Your school's computer-resource person can help students with the details of creating their databases.

INTEGRATING THE LANGUAGE ARTS

Literature Link. To help students understand the importance of the choice of point of view, have them read parts of *Beowulf* followed by the parallel sections of the novel *Grendel* by John Gardner. After students have read both excerpts, lead a discussion on how the choice of point of view influences the two works. Lead to a discussion of students' own choices of point of view.

Like a tide of ants attacking a chocolate bar, buyers swarmed around the umbrella seller. Crimson, black, and polka-dot umbrellas billowed into the wind-whipped rain, with their new owners struggling beneath them.

Reminder

To plan your story

- put a main character into a conflict and decide how the conflict will end
- map plot events that move steadily, with possible complications, to a climax and resolution
- sketch details of main characters and setting
- decide on point of view
- think ahead about what you want readers to feel and whether you want them to reflect on an idea or theme

WRITING ASSIGNMENT

PART 4:
Completing a Plan for Your Story

To complete the planning for your story, take time to think about your audience, purpose, and tone. Do you want your audience to laugh, cry, reflect on some idea about life? This is also the time to decide on your point of view. Remember that your choice of point of view will determine how close your readers feel to the characters, as well as how much flexibility you'll have as a writer. When you have finished your plan, save it for later use.

WRITING YOUR FIRST DRAFT

OBJECTIVES

- To analyze the principles of organization and the basic elements in short stories
- To write dialogue tags in the form of puns
- To write a draft of a short story

☞

Writing Your First Draft

Combining the Basic Elements of Stories

A good story suspends reality. No matter how fantastic—a smooth crystal planet with stick-fast, rubber inhabitants—we believe in it as a living world. How do writers do it? They combine the basic elements of stories—characters, plot, setting—with specific techniques that bring both the characters and the story to life.

Creating Living, Breathing Characters.   Telling readers about a character is fine; it's a direct, to-the-point technique of defining character: *Eddie really cared about other people, at least when he took the time to think about them.* But if you overuse this direct-statement approach, you will lose all the life in your characters. Instead, develop characters by showing their

- **appearance, actions, and thoughts:** *Eddie bounced his way down the street, glancing in every store window to check out his new black jeans. He was definitely looking good—in fact, he was looking better every day.*
- **effects on other characters:** *This time Sara had had it with Eddie. She wasn't going to forgive being stood up for the third time in a week.*
- **speech (dialogue):** *"Aw, Sara," Eddie wheedled, "what you want? I'm supposed to stop going to practice? Coach ran us so hard I slept all afternoon. I didn't forget—I just wasn't awake."*

Creating Vivid Descriptions.   You can also create a world that seems real by using vivid, concrete details. This means using words that are as precise as possible (*kayak,* not *boat; slithered,* not *moved*) and *images,* details that create sights, sounds, smells, tastes, and textures for readers. *Figures of speech* (unusual comparisons) such as *metaphors* and *similes* are another way your language can be vivid and surprising—for example, comparing steam shovels to yellow dinosaurs or garden hoses to green snakes.

In the following passage, look for all three of these descriptive strategies. The narrator is describing his martial-arts instructor practicing on the YMCA roof.

PROGRAM MANAGER

WRITING YOUR FIRST DRAFT

- **Instructional Support** For help with writing a scene from a short story, see **Writing** in *Strategies for Writing,* p. 10.

QUOTATION FOR THE DAY

"With me, a story usually begins with a single idea or memory or mental picture. The writing of the story is simply a matter of working up to that moment, to explain why it happened or what caused it to follow." (William Faulkner, 1897–1962, American author)

Before students begin writing their drafts, share the quotation with the class and ask students to discuss other methods they use or know to get their stories down on paper.

TEACHING THE LESSON

After reading over the introductory paragraphs with your students, you may want to practice writing dialogue and showing the action as opposed to telling the reader something. Give students a sentence or two about a character, and work with the class to create better ways of showing the character's personality. **Cont. on p. 182**

MEETING individual NEEDS

LEARNING STYLES

Visual Learners. Students could use a time line to check the organization of their plots. Remind students that even though a time line shows the events of a plot in chronological order, a writer may decide not to tell the events in that order. You can use the following example:

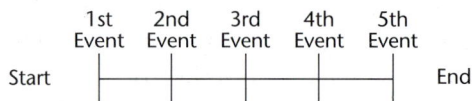

	1st Event	2nd Event	3rd Event	4th Event	5th Event	
Start						End

INTEGRATING THE LANGUAGE ARTS

Vocabulary Link. Point out that too many specific, technical words (jargon) make a passage seem pretentious. Explain that using only the right words can make a passage ring true. This means that students should use specialized language in their writing only when it's appropriate.

SELECTION AMENDMENT
Description of change: excerpted
Rationale: to focus on the concept of description presented in this chapter

180

180   *Creative Writing*

Then he did *katas*, attacking the head, stabbed, and punctured the dummy with kicks, then with punches, and then with combinations. He was unbelievably quick, his hands, feet blurs in the high roof wind. He had a turn kick, rotating his body like a 78 rpm record, his back horizontal to the ground as his free leg punched into the dummy, making it bend on its stake and crack back. He cried, "Keee-YAT!" as he did his work. It was like watching Victor Mature kill the lion, or Big Willie do Kai Ting. This was *wu-shu*, the combat of my ancestry. Uncle Han knew how to do this, in China.

Gus Lee, *China Boy*

Did Gus Lee's descriptive techniques make this scene seem real to you? Can you see the blur of the man's hands and feet? Does the comparison between the man's turn kick and a rotating record create a vivid image in your mind? If you can see the man's actions in your mind, the writer made these techniques work.

👉 **REFERENCE NOTE:** For more about figurative language, see page 534.

WRITING NOTE

Make your descriptions work for you, not overwhelm readers. An avalanche of descriptions, no matter how vivid, will clutter the story path for readers. Give them sensory experiences that make a difference in a story, as the description of the *wu-shu* practice helps to reveal character, build mood, and prepare for later action.

OBJECTIVES
- To use three important qualities of dialogue to evaluate a sample dialogue
- To revise a sample dialogue by using guidelines

TEACHING *EVALUATING DIALOGUE*

Begin by discussing the difficulty of writing convincing dialogue. Tell students that realistic dialogue sounds like natural conversation and fits the personalities and backgrounds of the characters talking. It often requires unusual spellings to mirror the sounds of the words as they are spoken and unique punctuation to show the pace of the

Building a Tight Plot.   There is one way in which your story can't be *too* much like real life: It can't be as messy—as full of random, accidental, inconsequential events. To keep your readers interested, the plot can't wander or change direction on whim. Keep your story in line and your readers involved with the following techniques:

- **Arouse interest immediately.** Open with sharp dialogue, a mood-setting description, a puzzle, or fast action.
- **Establish conflict quickly, and never forget it.** Get to the main problem as soon as possible, and make sure all events and details are important to it. This doesn't mean you can't provide background and colorful details—just make them *count* in the plot.
- **Keep current action clear but the future uncertain.** Create suspense or curiosity about what may happen, but don't pull tricks (like old boyfriends or erupting volcanoes) out of a hat. Even a surprise ending should be believable. Keep events in chronological order (see pages 74 and 80–82) unless you must give a *flashback,* a memory or a scene of important past events.
- **Resolve the conflict in a satisfying, original way.** After the climax of the conflict, the reader needs to see that the loose ends are tied up—and that's all. This is not the time to drag things out; and unless you are writing a fable, it isn't the time to announce a moral or theme. Instead, try showing the main character in a final moment of action, thought, or dialogue.

CRITICAL THINKING
Evaluating Dialogue

Evaluating means judging the quality or effectiveness of something. How do you judge the dialogue in a story? Isn't it the writer's decision what characters say? Yes, the writer decides what to say, but *readers* decide whether the speech sounds forced, fake, or forgettable. Here are some important qualities of effective dialogue in stories.

INTEGRATING THE LANGUAGE ARTS

Library Link. If there is any setting, equipment, or background in their stories that they do not have firsthand familiarity with, students may need to do research to make their writing realistic. It would be fairly easy to write a passage about a fight without actually having been in such a fight. But a passage about a martial art written by someone unfamiliar with it would never pass. Have students identify in the passage by Gus Lee every piece of information that requires special knowledge of martial arts or other areas. Help students see that checking to get the facts right is worth the effort.

conversation. Model the exercise by applying the three qualities on this page to the model. ⚡

Cont. from p. 180
For example, you might begin with "Bruce was not the best athlete trying out, but he really wanted to be on the team" or "Jana was upset when her dog destroyed her homework assignment." Students might use dialogue or action to better characterize the people involved. Emphasize showing, not telling.

MEETING individual NEEDS

LEP/ESL

General Strategies. Students may need assistance to complete this **Critical Thinking Exercise.** The ability to identify faulty use of dialogue and to rewrite it correctly is a skill one expects from English-proficient speakers. Students may benefit from working in peer-tutoring situations to complete this assignment.

ANSWERS
Critical Thinking Exercise

Responses will vary.

1. Some of the language does not fit the characters.
2. Kate's expostulations do not fit the circumstances.
3. Burton's diction changes from sentence to sentence, as does his syntactic style. There is no unity in his speech.
4. Burton's speech switches from formal (in the first four sentences) to informal.
5. The purpose and meaning of some of Burton's dialogue is obscure.

---

1. **Dialogue is speech: spoken language, not written language.** You should try to write the way people talk, using contractions, slang, and fragments when necessary. (Think of your own conversations or those you overhear in public places.)
2. **Dialogue fits the character.** Teenagers and grandparents don't usually talk the same way; neither do Russian immigrants and midwestern farmers. Choose a character's words and sentence structure carefully. In some cases, you might want to change spellings to show *dialect,* special speech characteristics.
3. **Dialogue serves a purpose.** Make your dialogue contribute to the story. Does it reveal character, move the plot forward, add background information?

⚡ CRITICAL THINKING EXERCISE:
Evaluating and Revising Dialogue

Work with one or two of your classmates to evaluate the dialogue in the following passage. It's definitely ineffective, but *why*? Keep in mind the three important qualities of effective dialogue: It should sound like spoken language; it should fit the character; and it should serve a purpose. Then rewrite the passage to create more effective dialogue for each character. Your group might enjoy comparing your revisions with another group's work.

> Kate was so mad she was talking to herself. "Fiddlesticks and rats," she said. She'd been waiting for Burton for two hours. He was supposed to bring her homework and visit for a while. Didn't he know she was sick of being at home with two broken legs, one broken arm, and the mysterious ear rash? "Some compatriot you have shown yourself to be," she muttered. "Slime bag bozo."
>
> When Burton arrived, he came in apologizing. "Whew, a tad late. Are you especially irritated? Forgive me, dear heart. Where do the hours fly? I dunno, I dunno. I believe I'll park it in this chair today." He continued with a grin, "But then, where was ya gonna go? Out dancing?"
>
> Kate said that she would like to hit him with her crutch if she could reach it.

When discussing vivid description, you may want to share other examples with your students. For example, you could analyze the mood-setting description of the sea in Joseph Conrad's story "The Secret Sharer." Conrad reinforces a threatening mood with details such as *fishlike, cadaverous,* and *corpse.* You may want to show some photographs or pictures to the class and have students vividly describe the images presented. Emphasize that description need not include every minute detail to etch a picture and create a scene for the reader.

The guidelines in **Building a Tight Plot** on p. 181, though brief, are extremely important. Students may need help to see that there often needs to be a difference between what an author knows about a ☞

Looking at a Short Story

Now you will see how one writer combines the basic story elements into a unique short story. As you read, notice especially how Egyirba High immediately focuses your attention on an unforgettable character who always stirs things up.

A SHORT STORY

The Lion Sleeps Tonight
by Egyirba High

Attention grabber/Song

1   In the jungle
the mighty jungle
the lion sleeps tonight . . . .

First-person point of view

Eloise Carter wasn't my blood relative. She was just Aunt Eloise.

In the jungle
the mighty jungle
the lion sleeps
tonight.

She was the odd one.

2   A weema way, a weema way
A weema way, a weema way
A weema way, a weema way
A weema way, a weema way . . . .

Conflict

At least that's what the folks wanted us to believe — that Aunt Eloise was crazy or something.

Character developed/ Appearance and responses of others

Bright orange or yellow caftans flowing, purple and brown and green turbans sitting stately upon her head. She was regal. Her face was not extraordinary, but bathed and dressed in Africa, she was exquisite. She was all Africa. She was out of step. She embarrassed them.

Setting/Sensory images

Flashbacks

Sometimes, after church on Sundays, we'd go to her home. I remember once smelling something good in the kitchen and then jumping back ten feet when I peeked in and saw a large cow tongue in

USING THE SELECTION
The Lion Sleeps Tonight

1

These lyrics are from "The Lion Sleeps Tonight," a Zulu lion-hunting song. The lion is thought to represent the government of South Africa.

2

"A weema way" means "the lion sleeps tonight."

character and what the readers need to know. For example, if you were writing about a martial-arts instructor, you might know that he starts his day with a shower, eats whole-grain toast and grapefruit for breakfast, and enjoys going to the opera. These are character elements you could well have formulated in planning your story. But when it comes to writing the story, none of this information may be of any use to the reader in following the causality of plot development, in which case you should leave out the information.

You may want to introduce the term *in medias res* to help students learn one way to establish conflict quickly. The detective fiction of P. D. James has excellent examples of introducing the conflict quickly and

3
Headcheese or brawn is a jellied meat dish resembling pâté.

MEETING *individual* NEEDS

AFRICAN AMERICAN

The short story by Egyirba High is an excellent opportunity for emphasizing the important contributions made by individuals of African descent to all aspects of American life, including literature, music, and medicine. The challenge in presenting and discussing the content of this short story is to de-emphasize the schism between cultures and to underscore instead the central, universal theme: Remain true to your own beliefs and aspirations, even in the face of peer pressure or ridicule.

the pot. I grabbed my throat and wondered how painful it must be not to be able to talk.

3 Then there was the time when she cooked hogshead cheese. I looked at the finished product and tried to figure out what the head of the hog must have looked like.

Characters developed/ Dialogue

"Go on and taste it."

"It looks ugh, Aunt Eloise."

"Come on, take this little, bitty cracker and put some cheese on it, just a little itsy-bitsy."

I looked at her intently to see if she was serious. Her face bore a deadpan expression.

Sensory detail

"Okay, just a little." My mouth turned up, imagining the worst, as I bit into the jelly-like substance.

"It's still ugh."

Characters developed/Actions and dialogue

And peals of laughter came bellowing out of her mouth.

"Well, good, then. More for me."

"You can have it."

***End of Flashback*/ Background details**

"You know, Michelle, that's how Negroes had to survive in slavery times – with what they had."

Characters developed/ Actions, dialogue, others' responses

Those conversations happened on her more subdued days. She was a teacher and always teaching me and my sisters when we came to visit. But the most curious, exciting times had to do with African dancing.

Aunt Eloise would sit and chat for a while and then, as if by cue, she would glide over to the

colorfully, and you may want to use some of her opening lines as models.

Students may need some help in distinguishing a legitimate surprise at the ending from an unjustified *deus ex machina* to save a feeble plot. One way to present this point is to say that something that is essential to the ending should be either mentioned or at least hinted at in the preceding text—not sprung on an unsuspecting reader at the very last.

Coming up with a resolution that is appropriate and satisfying is hard enough. You may want to explain to students that the important rule about endings is to avoid the banal, trite, and clichéd. In the right setting, the prince marrying the princess could be an excellent resolution. ☞

record player. This was the signal that there was about to be a show. Stef or Lisa would giggle, "Uh oh, she's getting ready to start," and I'd turn towards the grownups to catch their reactions. Mama and Daddy would sigh a big here-we-go-again sigh, and the voice of Miriam Makeba filled the room.

Sensory detail   **4**

She danced. My sisters, Stefanie and Lisa, stood by and watched her with great curiosity. None of us had ever seen dancing like it before, and nobody did it except Aunt Eloise.

All the time the music played, Aunt Eloise danced. And danced. And then as she danced, she remembered us.

"Come dance, girls."

Conflict building

Timidly, Stef and I would get behind her and try to copy her steps. Lisa hid in the corner.

The grownups, Mama and Daddy, her husband, Uncle John, and their daughter, Brenda, were always ashamed.

Dialogue/Feelings and plot details

"Woman, sit down. Don't nobody wanna see all that spook stuff."

No response.

"Eloise, come on over here and talk to your company. You can't leave these people just sitting here."

Sensory images

Still no response. Only the beat of drums growing louder in the room as the silence of discomfort grew, and Uncle John quit trying to reason with his wife. He'd look back at Mama and Daddy, and then they'd play the eye game, which was also known as the what-can-I-say-you-know-how-she-is look.

Mama would pick up his cue, glance back at Uncle John with "I-know-but-you-have-to-let-her-be," while my daddy just grunted, to no one in particular, his feelings of disgust. Brenda, who had no patience with her mother's shenanigans, would sigh loudly, turn on her heels, and walk quickly out of the room.

Dialogue/ Character development and background

"Ahwoo! Ahwoo! Ah! Ah! Uhn! Ah! You have to feel it, Michelle. Feel the beat. See the drummer

4
Miriam Makeba is a recording artist from South Africa who settled in the United States in 1959. Her personal favorite of all her songs is "Mbube," known as "Wimoweh" in the United States. A verse of the song is included at the beginning of this story.

As students read the short story by Egyirba High, ask them to pay close attention to the description and the character portrayals.

The story demonstrates many of the fine points that were only hinted at in the **Prewriting** section—the first-person narration in which the narrator is not the major character and an external conflict that creates internal conflict. To ensure that all important points are covered, you could use the following chart to outline the main points of characterization in **"The Lion Sleeps Tonight."**

5

'Legba, Yemaya, and Oshun are three West African gods. 'Legba is the messenger and interpreter of the gods. Yemaya is the offspring of the sky god and Earth mother, and Oshun is the river goddess.

6

Benjamin Banneker (1731–1806) was a surveyor and self-taught mathematician. He published an almanac from 1792 until his death. The almanac included his own astronomical calendar and weather predictions.

Joe Louis (1914–1981), born Joseph Louis Barrow, was the world heavyweight boxing champion from 1937 to 1949.

Phillis Wheatley (c. 1753–1784), whose birthplace, African name, and exact date of birth are unknown (it is suspected that she may have been born in what is now Senegal or Gambia), was the first important African American woman poet. She came to America as a slave when she was about eight years old.

Mary McLeod Bethune (1875–1955) was an American educator and government official. She founded the school that later became Bethune-Cookman College, and she also served as its president.

Jesse Owens (1913–1980), born James Cleveland Owens, is one of the most famous athletes in sports history. He won the 100-meter and 200-meter dashes and the long jump at the 1936 Olympics in Berlin.

Charles Richard Drew (1904–1950) was a surgeon known for his research on blood preservation. He became chief surgeon at Freedman's Hospital in Washington, D.C., in 1944 and became the hospital's medical director in 1946.

Description/ Images

Character developed/ Thoughts and actions
Complication
Suspense

playing there. Feel it. You can see the blood spilled across centuries. Feel and know all things."

Dancing. Bending and stretching to the earth, her right foot touched down, and she'd swoon in place. Then her left foot, her body yielding to African gods. Somewhere inside I knew it wasn't really funny. I felt awkward trying to dance. Something stirred in me, though it would not be named. I would dance with her until I became conscious of the stares again, and the silent reprobations would stop me cold.

Climax

Confused, I'd look back at Aunt Eloise, who never stopped dancing. She had greeted 'Legba and was now possessed by Yemaya. Or caught up in Oshun. I wasn't sure. I wanted to know . . . to dance . . . but they were looking. Their stares would reach into my awkwardness. And I'd freeze, aching to go where she was. Then suddenly, the drumming ended.

Even when the music stopped, the feeling didn't. Aunt Eloise, with new gusto, would go on talking about Africa, the beauty of Black people, how Cleopatra was Black and Elizabeth Taylor could only wish she was. She immortalized our heroes in the poems she wrote, and her stories left me curious and hungry for more. The walls were **Setting/Character development** covered with pictures of Benjamin Banneker, Joe Louis, Phillis Wheatley, Mary McLeod Bethune,

Believable Characters	Vivid Descriptions
1. appearance– actions– thoughts–	1. precise diction–
2. effects on other characters–	2. sensory images–
3. speech (dialogue)–	3. figures of speech–

As students read **"The Rest of Her Life"** on p. 188, they should pay close attention to the plot development and the use of dialogue. Use the basic framework on p. 194 to analyze the pattern and elements of **"The Rest of Her Life."** Note especially the use of the flashback in the beginning. Be sure students can give the details that parallel each element in the framework. You may want to ☞

Writing Your First Draft   **187**

7 Jesse Owens. On every spare shelf were African carvings of animals, goddesses and gods.

"Michelle, did you know that Charles Drew invented blood plasma?"

"No, Aunt Eloise."

"He did. And guess what?" she'd say, pointing to his picture on the wall. "He died needing blood, because he was turned away from a white hospital."

"Ohhhh." I'd nod my head, not because I knew **8** this but as a sign for her to go on. I was young and overwhelmed by the essence of her. She was <u>ambrosia</u> to my spirit, ever sustaining her image by the charms and magic she brought to my life. She whirled endlessly in her dreams. I drank of her. I tasted her. I savored it.

Aunt Eloise wasn't crazy. She was a sleeping lion ready to spring on cue to the moment. She was life and she was music. We only had to wonder. She knew and hoped we'd care. It was years later, after her death, that I realized I had received her legacy of love. She gave me Africa, and I love it passionately. When I hear her notes now, I sing her praises loudly, skin oiled in red earth, body dressed in the blackness of my people, soul moving to the rhythms of talking drums. She smiles, my ancestor, <u>placated</u> by my gifts, and returns to her throne, content, awaiting her invitation to the next celebration of life.

Direct explanation, narrator

Resolution

Theme expressed

Sensory images

7
Students may notice that there are no references to contemporary African Americans. Ask the students whom they would mention if asked to name living African Americans who could serve the same function in the story.

8
How does the writer use the narrator's view of Aunt Eloise as a contrast to the other characters' views of Aunt Eloise? [The narrator's sympathetic view of Aunt Eloise counteracts and eventually overcomes the views of the other characters.]

show students models of stories in which different order is used.

As students read the **Usage Hint** on p. 194, point out that in extended dialogue between only two people, tags are often dropped. The dialogue does not become difficult to understand because readers are guided by indentations and quotation marks to know when the speaker changes. In addition, writers work to individualize each character's speech so that readers can easily distinguish the characters even without tags.

Exercise 3, p. 195, may be a welcome distraction from the students' short stories. You could give more practice with dialogue by using an additional exercise. One way to do this is to have students revise their rewrites in the **Critical Thinking Exercise**

ANSWERS
Exercise 2

Responses will vary.

1. Students may feel that having Eloise win over the narrator is an effective strategy to elicit sympathy from the reader.

2. Students' interpretations of both the external and internal conflicts may vary. Some students may say that there is a conflict between Aunt Eloise and the rest of the community. They may say that Michelle's internal conflict is between wanting to be like Aunt Eloise and wanting to be ordinary like her blood relatives. The climax is on p. 186.

3. Students should mention at least some of the following examples of Aunt Eloise's teaching: She taught about slavery times—surviving with what you had; she taught Michelle to dance African dances; she taught Michelle to follow her own inclinations to overcome the influence of other people's opinions.

   Students' answers to the question about Michelle will vary, but they should support their statements about Michelle's character with information from the story.

4. Some students may talk about the importance of history in discovering who they are; some about doing what they believe in despite others' opinions; others about the importance of heritage.

5. Students may state that the characters other than Aunt Eloise and the setting are fairly weak, while the portrayal of the main character is the strongest element.

E X E R C I S E 2 ▶   **Analyzing the Elements of a Short Story**

With a partner or small group, discuss the following questions.

1. As the preceding story shows, a first-person narrator is not always the main character. What is the effect of telling the story from Michelle's, not Aunt Eloise's, point of view?
2. The main conflict in this story—the one that starts the plot—is an external one. What is it? This external conflict causes an internal conflict in Michelle. What is it, and how does it come to a climax in the story?
3. The narrator says that Aunt Eloise was "always teaching me and my sisters." Find examples of dialogue, events, and details of setting that *show*, not *tell*, what Aunt Eloise taught. Michelle is an important character, too. How does the writer let you know what she is like?
4. One theme of the story is labeled on page 187. Do you find other messages or ideas? Explain.
5. Do some elements of the story—plot, characters, setting, description—seem stronger to you than others? What has the writer done to make these elements stand out?

Using a Framework for a Short Story

"The Lion Sleeps Tonight" (pages 183–187) gives a vivid portrait of a strong character, but the plot is actually subdued. The pattern of a whole life, not a few specific events, is the writer's concern. In the following story, "The Rest of Her Life," the writer takes a more usual approach to plot—the two main characters definitely have important events to deal with. You may want to use this story's framework as a model. Notice especially how the writer uses dialogue to develop conflict and plot.

A WRITER'S MODEL

The Rest of Her Life

Main character
Third-person,
Myung's thoughts

Every night Myung thought about what college would be like. She couldn't wait. She'd be away from her nosy little brother and nagging parents. She'd

GUIDED PRACTICE

To model **Exercise 2**, p. 188, adapt the questions and use them to reanalyze **"The Precious Stones of Axolotyl,"** p. 162.

To prepare students for **Exercise 3**, p. 195, use an overhead transparency to show how to construct a Tom Swifty. Many people start with the pair of punning words, and you can show how you reject and choose ☞

make cool new friends, meet boys, go to parties. And, of course, she'd study. She didn't intend to blow away her hard work in high school and have to come <u>home</u>.

Characters developed/ Dialogue and setting

The phone next to Myung's bed squealed. Without even a hello, her best friend's voice rushed out, "I feel like I've been let out of prison!"

"Julia," Myung laughed, "what's going on?"

"Dad says he can handle the store and I can leave. Want to go to the mall? Please!"

"Have I ever said no to hanging out? I am ready to get out of here <u>immediately</u>. Meet you at the bus stop in fifteen minutes."

Flashback

Julia, Myung thought, was one of a kind--and not because of frantic mall calls. As she hung up, Myung's mind was going back to another phone call from Julia, one she'd actually cried over. "I'm not going to the university," Julia had pronounced flatly.

Conflict

Dialogue/Plot details

It still seemed unreal. Unfair. Julia came out on top in every test, every essay contest. "You won a scholarship!" Myung protested. But Julia said it wasn't enough, not now. "Mother's too sick," she explained, "and Dad needs me in the store. I can't go."

Internal conflict

And that was it. Julia just dropped it. For a while Myung was afraid to talk about college at all with Julia, but now she'd relaxed. Julia acted fine, as if nothing had changed. She was something else.

End of flashback

Characters developed/ Actions, appearance, and setting details

At the mall, the two friends started their usual stroll around the food court, Julia leading with her typical long stride and tiny Myung chattering and constantly pushing her dark bangs out of her eyes. Julia finished her frozen yogurt and sighed, "Freedom. Sometimes I'm so sick of that hardware store I feel like throwing the hammers. It's--"

Description

"Yeah, I baby-sat my brother <u>every day</u> last week, and it was worse than prison." Myung spun around. "The record store! Let's go there."

Julia was right behind her. "Look," she pointed. "That tape I've been wanting is on sale!"

Myung kept going. "Uh, in a minute. I want to look at the posters. You know, for my dorm room.

❓ CRITICAL THINKING

Analysis. Explain to students that readers should be able to understand the reasoning behind a character's choices. Ask students to use the following questions to analyze the character motivation in **"The Rest of Her Life"**:

1. Why does Myung start talking about college at the mall? [The things Myung was seeing reminded her of the needs she'd have in her dorm room, and she didn't hold back because Julia seemed to be okay.]

2. Why does Julia get angry? [She has made an extraordinary effort to not let Myung's future prospects come between them and feels that Myung is being particularly insensitive.]

3. What makes Myung decide to go see Julia in the store? [She is motivated by her feeling that she hadn't behaved well toward Julia, by her realization of what it would mean to Julia not to go to college, and by the other girls' insensitivity.]

a combination and then draft and revise the sentences in which they are to fit.

Model **Writing Assignment: Part 5,** p. 195, by writing your own version of part of the story of Julia and Myung.

INDEPENDENT PRACTICE

Have students write the answers to **Exercise 2,** p. 188, independently. The primary independent practice for this lesson, however, is **Writing Assignment: Part 5,** in which students write their drafts. At this stage, you can allow students to work on their own unless they ask for help.

◆ INTEGRATING THE LANGUAGE ARTS

Vocabulary Link. When the writer writes "It was weird not sitting together in the cafeteria, but Myung started meeting Annella and Patty," the first part of the sentence is indirect discourse. Students should notice how the writer has employed Myung's vocabulary even in giving indirect thoughts. Have students look through the story for other examples [the first paragraph is one], and talk about the effectiveness of this technique of adding to characterization.

Conflict built/ Actions and dialogue

Annella got the coolest one last week."

Julia was sitting on a bench outside the store when Myung got finished. "Tired?" Myung asked.

"No, just waiting. Let's go to Lane's. I need a lipstick."

"Sure," Myung agreed, but then she ran to another window. "Look at those bulletin boards! I didn't even think of that. I can't take my old beat-up one. It'll just take a minute."

"I don't want to," Julia said, too loudly.

"What?" Myung stood still.

Characters and conflict developed/ Dialogue

"I don't want to. I don't want to go there. I don't want to follow you. Can't you talk about anything but college, college, college?"

"What's that supposed to mean?"

"What does it sound like?" Julia snapped. Myung had never heard this voice. "Don't you ever think about my feelings?"

Sensory image

Myung felt her temper rising, too. Her black eyes burned. "Sure. Of course. But that doesn't mean you have to take them out on me. I'm not keeping you from college. Am I supposed to pretend I'm not going so you'll feel better? You're jealous!"

Assess students' mastery of story elements through class discussion. You will not, however, want to make a formal assessment of drafts because students should not be overly concerned with errors at this stage. It is a good idea to read students' drafts and to make suggestions to prevent students from completing their own evaluations and

revisions and then discovering that you have suggestions for major changes. Suggestions at this point should be kept to a general level—the plot development, characterization, dialogue, setting, mood, and theme. Do not at this time make any minor suggestions.

The most difficult task in assessing fiction is to keep a balance between your idea and the student's idea of what the short ☞

Descriptive detail

It was said before she thought.

"Jealous!" Julia stepped so close Myung could see her shaking. "Well, you're selfish, and that's worse." Julia paused. "And you're not much of a friend." She walked away without looking back.

Character and plot developed/ Thoughts and actions

Myung's phone didn't ring that night, and she couldn't call either. Had she done something so terrible? Did she deserve to be yelled at? The days at school were bad at first. She and Julia had most of the same classes, and it wasn't easy always looking the other way. Or she'd see Julia ahead of her in the hall, long brown hair streaming down her blue jacket, and slow down so they wouldn't meet.

Description

Complication

It was weird not sitting together in the cafeteria, but Myung started meeting Annella and Patty. She didn't have to worry about what she said to them. They liked to talk about college. Why have friends if you can't share things?

One day Myung, Annella, and Patty walked after school to the post office. As usual, they were talking about college--freedom, fun, fraternities--when Myung saw they were going right by Billings Hardware. Patty nodded at Julia behind the counter. "Look. How would you like to do that for the rest of your life? She always thought she was so smart."

Complication Dialogue/ Reactions to character

Annella barely turned her head. "Well, brains don't do everything," she said. "She'll get over it. Lots of people don't go to college."

Preparation for climax/Thoughts and feelings

Myung stared at them. Did they have to put Julia down? Did they think they were better than Julia? They didn't know what she was like! Myung saw Julia hand a customer change and then turn to the next one. The rest of her life? Myung turned back to her friends. She couldn't think of anything to say. She felt disoriented, as if she were waking up in a strange place.

Dialogue/Action

Now they were staring at her. "Why are you stopping?" Annella and Patty waited nervously.

Myung realized she was standing frozen. Her mind churned. "Look, I don't feel so hot. I'd better go back." Before they could ask questions, she turned.

◆ INTEGRATING THE LANGUAGE ARTS

Speaking Link. One of the best ways to evaluate dialogue in a story is to read it aloud. You may want to have students try saying dialogue in different ways to get it to sound right. But if nothing they do makes it sound right, tell them to try changing the words, syntax, or sentence length so the dialogue sounds more natural.

Style Link. The writer of Myung's story has made a stylistic choice to use very brief flashbacks to illuminate the present situation. Sentences such as "Myung had never noticed how much it sagged" don't distract from the present moment in the story, but cast light on the present so that the reader gains understanding. Suggest that this is a technique students might want to employ in their stories.

story should be like. You need to balance respect for the student as an artistic creator with the standard demands of the genre and your own taste.

RETEACHING

If students do not understand story elements after discussing the professional and writer's models, have them analyze a different medium of storytelling. Bring in a videotaped adaptation of a short story and work with students to identify its major story elements and story structure.

A DIFFERENT APPROACH

You may want to make copies of the **Framework for a Story** chart on p. 194 for students to refer to as they finalize their story plans. This visual representation will help students make sure that their plans are complete, as well as provide an outline for students to work from.

Setting details

All the customers in the hardware store were gone, but it still seemed crowded and cramped. Julia turned around as Myung walked in. She looked surprised for only a moment and then her face hardened.

Complication (anger)

Myung searched for words. She really did feel sick now. "Julia, I know it's been a long time--"

"Well, what a surprise! We just got in new bulletin boards. You must have heard."

Sensory detail, figurative language, suspense

Julia's icy voice knotted Myung's stomach more. What was she doing here? She stepped back toward the door.

Climax
Conflict outcome/ Dialogue and action

"I just saw you through the window," Myung began again, faintly. Julia glared. "I thought . . ." Julia's hands fidgeted over the counter display. "Look, Julia," Myung blurted out. "I'm sorry. I don't blame you for hating me. I was really stupid and blind, but I thought you were okay! It's," she fought for words, "hard to admit you think only your life

CLOSURE

Ask students to label in different colors the story elements and structural elements they have included in their drafts. Then, ask volunteers to share their analyses with the class.

EXTENSION

Show students a movie version of a work of literature they've read. Ask them to evaluate how well the director has adapted, changed, or reworked story elements and structures found in the written text.

Writing Your First Draft   **193**

counts." Myung looked very small as she turned back to the door.

Julia exhaled as if she were letting something go. "I <u>was</u> jealous." She came out from behind the counter. "Myung, I'm sorry too. And I was just as blind! I didn't know how disappointed I was. Really, I know you didn't mean to hurt me." She raised her eyes to Myung's. "But--the terrible things I said!"

Neither moved or spoke, but both knew something had ended. Julia touched Myung's arm. "Come to the back. I can put the <u>Closed</u> sign up for a minute."

Setting details/ Mood

They sat together on a torn plaid sofa where Julia's mother used to rest. Myung had never noticed how much it sagged. "Julia," she whispered, "right now I don't even want to go to college."

Resolution

"Of course you do!" Julia almost sounded angry. "I do, too. And I'm not giving up. Our fight woke me up in some ways. So what if my plans didn't work out? Can't I make new ones? I found out they'll hold my scholarship for one year, and Dad is trying to get his cousin to buy into the store." She seemed to run down. "Things can happen."

Characters deepened/Actions, dialogue, and thoughts

Myung brightened. "It might work out. It might be the same as we planned."

Julia looked at her. She plucked at a tear in the couch. "Maybe. Maybe not quite the same. But we're friends. <u>That's</u> the same."

Myung smiled. She'd never felt so close to Julia. She liked sitting on the lumpy couch and wanted to stay there forever. She closed her eyes and was still for once.

"So," Julia broke the silence, "about those bulletin boards!" She was already rising.

When Myung looked up, Julia's face seemed miles away. She laughed, "Okay, I see it's back to business." Then she said with no laughter, "I'll remember today, Julia, no matter where I am."

Julia turned the sign to <u>Open</u> and stood staring out into the street.

"Yes, we do have some memories, don't we?"

194   *Creative Writing*

A basic framework for a short story, similar to the pattern of the Writer's Model, follows. You may want to use it for your own story.

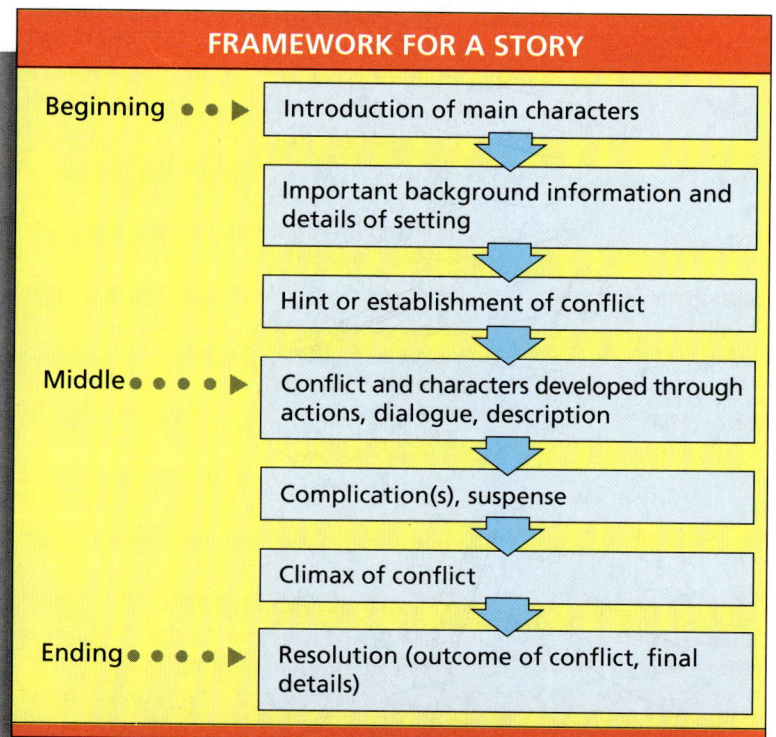

FRAMEWORK FOR A STORY

Beginning ● ● ▶ Introduction of main characters

Important background information and details of setting

Hint or establishment of conflict

Middle ● ● ● ● ▶ Conflict and characters developed through actions, dialogue, description

Complication(s), suspense

Climax of conflict

Ending ● ● ● ● ▶ Resolution (outcome of conflict, final details)

In addition to varying functional verbs with precise verbs and adding descriptive adverbs to their dialogue tags, students can also vary the location of the tags. Tags can come at the beginning of the sentence to introduce the dialogue, at the end to conclude it, or in the middle to break up parts of dialogue. Tags that break up dialogue are often placed at natural pauses in the speech—at a comma or period, for example. But tags can also be used to create a little suspense by holding off the end of a sentence or thought for just a moment. Have students experiment with the wide variety of ways in which they can employ tags.

USAGE HINT

Using Verbs and Adverbs in Dialogue Tags

Most dialogue has a *tag* that identifies the speaker: "Get your feet off the couch," **Dad said.** *Said* is a perfectly functional verb in dialogue tags, and sometimes its plainness is best. But also consider using precise verbs. They can vividly show a speaker's mood, tone of voice, or intention.

> **"Get your feet off the couch,"** Dad (*yelled, pleaded, murmured, repeated, whined, coaxed, sighed, threatened*).

You can also combine a verb and an adverb in dialogue tags to sharpen description. While this technique can be effective, too many verb-adverb tags can make your dialogue seem overdone and monotonous.

> **"Get your feet off the couch,"** Dad said (*firmly, pleadingly, impatiently*).
> **"I didn't mean it,"** Joshua whispered *piteously*.

EXERCISE 3 ▶   **Writing Tom Swifties**

Tom Swift was the hero in a series of adventure novels begun in the 1910s. In those novels, the writer used so many verb-adverb dialogue tags that readers created a form of *puns*—wordplay—called Tom Swifties. In Tom Swifties, the adverb in the dialogue tag creates a humorous pun on the action, as in the following examples:

> "We're stuck in this glacier," Monica intoned icily.
> "So you can't stand a little pain?" challenged the surgeon cuttingly.
> "I wasn't sleeping on the job!" the guard said uprightly.

With a partner or small group, make up five Tom Swifties to share with the class.

WRITING ASSIGNMENT

PART 5:
Writing a Draft of Your Story

The professional short story and the Writer's Model give you examples of ways to begin a story, develop its characters and conflict, and bring the plot to an end. They may even have given you ideas for *changing* your story plan. Don't hesitate to try out new ideas whenever you have them. As you write your first draft, use your prewriting notes, but don't lock your imagination in a closet.

ANSWERS
Exercise 3

Students' Tom Swifties should each include a pun created by using a verb-adverb dialogue tag. Frequently the adverb is a synonym or antonym of a concept expressed by the speaker.

OBJECTIVES
• To analyze a writer's revision
• To evaluate and revise a short story

TEACHING THE LESSON
Although the **Evaluating and Revising Short Stories** chart is placed after **Exercise 4** in this chapter, it will be worthwhile to review it with students before they complete the assignment. Point out that the chart covers the specific concepts concentrated on earlier in the chapter.

PROGRAM MANAGER

EVALUATING AND REVISING

■ **Reinforcement/Reteaching** See **Revision Transparencies 7** and **8.** For suggestions on how to tie the transparencies to instruction, review teacher's notes in *Fine Art and Instructional Transparencies for Writing,* p. 107.

■ **Ongoing Assessment** For a rubric to guide assessment, see **Evaluating and Revising** in *Strategies for Writing,* p. 11.

■ **Assessment/Reflection** To assess student work and evaluate progress, see **Portfolio Forms** in *Portfolio Assessment,* pp. 5–21.

QUOTATION FOR THE DAY
"Your audience gives you everything you need. They tell you. There is no director who can direct you like an audience." (Fanny Brice, 1891–1951, American comedienne and singer)
After sharing the quotation with the class, explain that a reader is to a writer what an audience is to a performer. Tell students that readers' responses to the students' work might indicate what needs to be changed in, added to, or deleted from their stories.

196

196 *Creative Writing*

Evaluating and Revising

Like many writers, you may have a tendency to fall in love with what you have written. When you first read it over, you can't find anything that should be changed. But if you allow some time to pass before rereading your draft, you'll find you are more objective.

It's also a good idea to test your story on other readers: What part do they think is really good? What parts seem to need a jolt of life? Both you and your readers can use the chart on page 198 to pinpoint strengths and weaknesses. Then you can use the suggested revision techniques to solve the problems you have identified.

EXERCISE 4 **Analyzing a Writer's Revision**

Here's how the writer of "The Rest of Her Life" (pages 188–193) revised two paragraphs of her story. After studying the changes she made, answer the questions that follow.

One day Myung, Annella, and Patty walked after school to the post office. ~~They were now spending almost every afternoon together.~~ **cut** As usual, they were talking about college, *freedom, fun, fraternities* when Myung saw they were going **add** right by Billings Hardware. Patty ~~said,~~ *nodded at Julia behind the counter.* "Look. **replace** How would you like to do that for the rest of your life? ~~I'm sure I wouldn't want to.~~ *She always thought she was so smart."* **replace** Annella barely turned her head. ~~It was obvious that she had no feelings for Julia and didn't even care what happened to her.~~ *"Well, brains don't do everything," she said. "She'll get over it.* **replace** ~~She knew that~~ lots of people don't go to college."

1. Why is the entire second sentence cut?
2. What details and information does the writer add to the third sentence? How does that change improve the paragraph?
3. What is the replacement for *said* in the fourth sentence? Why is it an improvement?
4. What is the effect of the replacement sentence at the end of the first paragraph? What does it contribute to character development?
5. The writer changed the last two sentences to dialogue. What other changes were necessary to do this? How does this change make the story more effective?

His was a story that had to be told.

Well, maybe not.

© 1985 United Feature Syndicate, Inc.

Peanuts reprinted by permission of United Feature Syndicate, Inc.

WRITING ASSIGNMENT

PART 6:
Evaluating and Revising Your Story

Use the chart on page 198 and your classmates' suggestions to evaluate and revise the first draft of your story. Remember that a story is a *streamlined* and *heightened* version of life. Cut wordy parts that go nowhere, jazz up characters, and increase the tension in your plot. Aim to rivet your readers.

ANSWERS
Exercise 4

1. The words "As usual" at the beginning of the third sentence express the same idea.

2. Specific details about college life are added to show the contrast between Julia's future and the other girls' futures.

3. The words *nodded at Julia behind the counter* replace *said*. They point to the focus of Patty's next words. It is an improvement because it is a very minimal gesture that shows Patty's disdain for Julia.

4. The original sentence has some measure of sympathy in it. The replacement sentence indicates jealousy or ill will. The change affects the characterization of Patty by making her seem unreasonably harsh and cruel. It helps make Myung's return to Julia understandable.

5. The writer must insert proper punctuation to create dialogue. The change makes the story more effective because it shows rather than tells Annella's attitude toward Julia.

A DIFFERENT APPROACH

Have students focus on questions 7 and 10 of the **Evaluating and Revising Short Stories** chart. Ask the class to consider whether formal language is always inappropriate in a short story and to explain its answers. Then, ask what advice students would give a writer who had written an unsatisfactory or trite ending.

INTEGRATING THE LANGUAGE ARTS

Vocabulary Link. Explain to students that actions can tell a great deal about the people who commit them. This fact makes it very important for students to use vivid, specific verbs in their stories. One way to revise weak verbs is to use metaphorical verbs. To create these, a writer thinks of a comparison that involves the person committing the action and then uses a verb that completes the comparison. For example, if a person were compared to a bird, the writer could use a verb such as *bobbed, pecked,* or *hatched* to explain the character's actions.

198   *Creative Writing*

EVALUATING AND REVISING SHORT STORIES

EVALUATION GUIDE	REVISION TECHNIQUE
1 Is the reader's interest aroused immediately?	**Replace** a slow-paced beginning with sharp dialogue, a mood-setting description, fast-paced action.
2 Is the conflict established quickly?	Early in the story, **add** a hint of the conflict that the main character faces.
3 Does the plot keep the reader's interest or create suspense?	**Cut** events and details that slow down the story or wander away from the main conflict. **Add** details that create complications and uncertainty for the main character.
4 Are descriptions of setting effective?	**Cut** references to setting that do not contribute to mood or action. If your setting affects the conflict, **add** details that heighten the tension of the conflict.
5 Is the order of events clear?	**Reorder** events in chronological order. **Add** a flashback if you need to refer to earlier events. **Cut** any flashback that occurs during an exciting or dramatic event.
6 Are the characters believable?	**Cut** sentences that *tell* what a character is like. **Add** realistic dialogue, actions and thoughts, and details *showing* other characters' reactions.
7 Is dialogue used effectively?	**Replace** formal language with conversational language—contractions, slang, fragments—if appropriate. **Add** dialogue to reveal characters' personalities or move action forward.
8 Is the story told from a consistent point of view?	**Cut** details that shift from the first-person to the third-person point of view, or vice versa.
9 Is the conflict in the story successfully brought to a climax, or high point?	**Add** a scene of high interest that determines how the conflict will be resolved.
10 Is the ending of the story satisfying and original?	**Replace** unnecessary details and discussion with pointed description and dialogue that show how the conflict is resolved.

PROOFREADING AND PUBLISHING

OBJECTIVE
- To proofread and publish a short story

TEACHING THE LESSON
Suggest that students read through their stories once to check dialogue mechanics and once to check for other types of errors. Also suggest that students work in groups or pairs for more thorough proofreading. Have students use different colors of ink for each proofreading they do of their papers. ■

Proofreading and Publishing

Before proofreading, you may want to review the rules for punctuating, capitalizing, and paragraphing dialogue (see pages 935–938). The rules are important because they prevent confusion about who is speaking and when she or he stops. Once you have corrected each error, your story will be ready to publish. Here are some ideas:

- Adapt your story into a comic book. If you don't like to draw, collaborate with someone who does.
- Choose five stories from your class that would appeal to junior high or middle school students. Create a booklet of these stories, and distribute it in the junior high or middle school. If you have access to a computer, use it to make the booklet as inviting and professional-looking as you can.

WRITING ASSIGNMENT

PART 7:
Proofreading and Publishing Your Story

Proofread your story first; then, decide how you can publish it. Do you have an idea of your own, or do you want to try the comic book or collaborative booklet described above?

Reflecting on Your Writing

If you plan to include your story in your **portfolio,** date it and use the following questions to write a brief reflection to accompany your story.

- What was difficult about using the point of view you chose?
- How did you develop a plot for your story? Were you pleased with the way you resolved the story's conflict?
- Does the dialogue you wrote seem natural to you? What could you do to make the dialogue more realistic?
- Which aspect of the story are you most satisfied with? Was writing a creative piece more or less challenging than doing other types of writing?

PROGRAM MANAGER

PROOFREADING AND PUBLISHING

- **Instructional Support** For a chart students may use to evaluate their proofreading progress, see **Proofreading** in *Strategies for Writing,* p. 12.

- **Independent Practice/ Reteaching** For additional practice with language skills, see **Proofreading Practice: Using Verbs and Adverbs in Dialogue** in *Strategies for Writing,* p. 13.

- **Assessment/Reflection** To assess student work and evaluate progress, see **Portfolio Forms** in *Portfolio Assessment,* pp. 22–25.

QUOTATION FOR THE DAY
"Trifles make perfection, and perfection is no trifle." (Michelangelo Buonarroti, 1475–1564, Italian Renaissance sculptor, painter, and poet quoted by C. C. Colton in *Lacon*)

TEACHING NOTE
When students work on their reflections, encourage them to think seriously about each question before they answer it. Point out that their reflections will not only help them become better writers but also will help make them better readers by helping them understand how an author works.

A STUDENT MODEL
Evaluation

1. Colleen arouses the reader's interest from the very beginning of the excerpt, and she implies the conflict (characters versus the environment of the stalled elevator) by the end of the second paragraph.
2. Colleen's dialogue is very realistic, and she uses aspects of syntax to convey the anxiety of the characters. For example, run-on sentences in the second paragraph show the pregnant mother's uneasiness.
3. Colleen's characters are very well developed in such a short excerpt. Both are very believable, and readers are sympathetic toward them from the beginning of the story.
4. The point of view isn't entirely consistent. It shifts from third-person objective to third-person omniscient at the end. Otherwise, though, the conclusion is satisfying.

A STUDENT MODEL

In the following passage, an expectant young mother and an elderly man are trapped in a hospital elevator. Through skilled use of dialogue, Colleen Corkery, a high school senior in St. Louis, Missouri, reveals the feelings of the two characters.

A Brief Exchange
by Colleen Corkery

"Would you prefer to sit?"

"Maybe that's a good idea. My feet are really tired, and I didn't eat breakfast, I know I should have, I mean for the baby. Any little thing can weaken her—or what if I fall? She's so fragile. Everyone has had a healthy baby, taken care of their children, why am I so nervous? I mean, I'm just like every other mother out there, right? I . . ." Her voice trailed off at the realization that she had been babbling to a complete stranger, but she lifted her head to find him listening intently. "I'm sorry. This elevator is making me nervous. What should we do?"

"There's nothing to do but wait. My wife's on the twelfth floor."

"That's ICU, isn't it?"

"Yes, but we can pull through this one." He forced a smile.

"I know we're strangers," she began, "but would you like to talk? It eased my nerves a little to get that off my chest."

"This is the third one, third stroke, I mean, and I just don't know how much more Dorothy's poor body can take. All of our children live out of town and can't drop everything every time she gets sick. My son is a lawyer. He sent his mother a business card the other day: John Mardune, Attorney at Law. I am so proud of him! I just hope that the doctor has something encouraging to say." He looked down and folded his hands. She didn't know what to say except, "I understand." And she did.

In both of their hearts, they felt responsible for those most in need of them, most a part of them. And in this time when they should have felt trapped, for a moment they felt freed. Their burdens had been shared and weighed much lighter on their shoulders.

WRITING WORKSHOP

OBJECTIVES

- To analyze creative elements in a dramatic script
- To apply the writing process to create a dramatic script

TEACHING THE LESSON

After a student reads the introduction, discuss how a dramatic script differs from a short story. Besides the fact that a dramatic script relies primarily on dialogue, what difference might exist in handling of mood, setting, plot, and so forth?

Make sure that students understand the technical terms before they read the ☛

WRITING WORKSHOP

A Scene

Drama is another way of writing creatively and telling a story. Writers of movies, plays, and TV shows, however, must use only dialogue and onstage action to reveal plot, character, setting, and theme. Dramatic works are meant to be performed for an audience, rather than just read.

Besides the words the characters speak, a dramatic script contains stage directions, usually italicized and enclosed in brackets or parentheses. They provide directions for the actors as well as for the staging (sound effects, props, costumes, and so on) of the play.

Most plays are divided into separate acts, with distinct breaks between them. Scenes, which are smaller parts of acts, usually focus on a single place and time.

As you read the following scene from *Pygmalion*, think about how the dialogue and stage directions work.

from Pygmalion, Act III
by Bernard Shaw

MRS. HIGGINS: [*Dismayed*] Henry! [*Scolding him*] What are you doing here today? It is my at-home day: you promised not to come. [*As he bends to kiss her, she takes his hat off, and presents it to him.*]

HIGGINS: Oh bother! [*He throws the hat down on the table.*]

MRS. HIGGINS: Go home at once.

HIGGINS: [*Kissing her*] I know, mother. I came on purpose.

MRS. HIGGINS: But you mustn't. I'm serious, Henry. You offend all my friends: they stop coming whenever they meet you.

HIGGINS: Nonsense! I know I have no small talk; but people don't mind. [*He sits on the settee.*]

MRS. HIGGINS: Oh! don't they? Small talk indeed! What about your large talk? Really, dear, you mustn't stay.

QUOTATION FOR THE DAY

"The theatre has given me a chance not only to live my own life but a million others. In every play there is a chance for one great moment, experience or understanding." (Margo Jones, 1913–1955, American director, producer, and actress)

Use the quotation to initiate a discussion of drama. Ask students to brainstorm similarities and differences between a performed drama and a written story.

MEETING individual NEEDS

LESS-ADVANCED STUDENTS

You may want to allow your students to use the short stories they have created earlier in this chapter as the bases for their scenes. Remind students that they will need to incorporate description and explanations into either the dialogue or the stage directions.

scene. Before you have them read the model independently, explain the connection between *Pygmalion* and *My Fair Lady*. Then, have students discuss the questions in small groups. If students' literature textbook contains the play, use it to provide background on the play. Students should at least know who Colonel Pickering is before they read the scene because there is an unexplained reference to him on p. 203.

Also explain that because a play is meant to be performed, students will better grasp what is meant to happen if they visualize the action in their minds. If possible, show scenes or stills from the movie *My Fair Lady*.

INTEGRATING THE LANGUAGE ARTS

Literature Link. After students have read the play *Pygmalion* and viewed the movie *My Fair Lady,* encourage them to reflect on the similarities and differences between Bernard Shaw's work and Lerner and Loewe's production.

You may also want to have students talk about where this scene fits in the plot development of the entire play—what aspects of conflict or characterization is the scene supposed to emphasize, make clear, or bring to light?

Another idea is to provide a videotape of the play so that students can see the connection between the words on paper and what actually happens on the stage.

HIGGINS: I must. I've a job for you. A phonetic job.

MRS. HIGGINS: No use, dear. I'm sorry; but I can't get round your vowels; and though I like to get pretty postcards in your patent shorthand, I always have to read the copies in ordinary writing you so thoughtfully send me.

HIGGINS: Well, this isn't a phonetic job.

Audrey Hepburn as Eliza Doolittle and Rex Harrison as Professor Higgins in *My Fair Lady,* based on *Pygmalion.*

MRS. HIGGINS: You said it was.

HIGGINS: Not your part of it. I've picked up a girl.

MRS. HIGGINS: Does that mean that some girl has picked you up?

HIGGINS: Not at all. I don't mean a love affair.

MRS. HIGGINS: What a pity!

HIGGINS: Why?

MRS. HIGGINS: Well, you never fall in love with anyone under forty-five. When will you discover that there are some rather nice-looking women about?

HIGGINS: Oh, I can't be bothered with young women. My idea of a lovable woman is somebody as like you as possible. I shall never get into the way of seriously liking young women: some habits lie too deep to be changed. [*Rising abruptly and walking about, jingling his money and his keys in his trouser pockets*] Besides, they're all idiots.

To complete the assignment of writing scenes that might come in the middle or at the end of a conflict, students need to be especially aware of what the audience knows and doesn't know. Early peer review to determine what elements in the scene need further explanation can be a great help to the writers.

Another aid to writers is to have them read their scripts aloud. This practice will help bring to light stilted dialogue or characters who sound too much alike. This exercise can help students decide if they need more or clearer stage directions and whether the physical interplay of the characters works.

☜

MRS. HIGGINS: Do you know what you would do if you really loved me, Henry?

HIGGINS: Oh bother! What? Marry, I suppose.

MRS. HIGGINS: No. Stop fidgeting and take your hands out of your pockets. [*With a gesture of despair, he obeys and sits down again.*] That's a good boy. Now tell me about the girl.

HIGGINS: She's coming to see you.

MRS. HIGGINS: I don't remember asking her.

HIGGINS: You didn't. *I* asked her. If you'd known her you wouldn't have asked her.

MRS. HIGGINS: Indeed! Why?

HIGGINS: Well, it's like this. She's a common flower girl. I picked her off the kerbstone.

MRS. HIGGINS: And invited her to my at-home!

HIGGINS: [*Rising and coming to her to coax her*] Oh, that'll be all right. I've taught her to speak properly; and she has strict orders as to her behavior. She's to keep to two subjects: the weather and everybody's health—Fine day and How do you do, you know—and not to let herself go on things in general. That will be safe.

MRS. HIGGINS: Safe! To talk about our health! about our insides! perhaps about our outsides! How could you be so silly, Henry?

HIGGINS: [*Impatiently*] Well, she must talk about something. [*He controls himself and sits down again.*] Oh, she'll be all right: don't you fuss. Pickering is in it with me. I've a sort of bet on that I'll pass her off as a duchess in six months. I started on her some months ago; and she's getting on like a house on fire. I shall win my bet. She has a quick ear; and she's easier to teach than my middle-class pupils because she's had to learn a complete new language. She talks English almost as you talk French.

MRS. HIGGINS: That's satisfactory, at all events.

HIGGINS: Well, it is and it isn't.

MRS. HIGGINS: What does that mean?

HIGGINS: You see, I've got her pronunciation all right; but you have to consider not only how a girl pronounces, but what she pronounces . . .

A DIFFERENT APPROACH

You could have students research the myth of Pygmalion in Ovid's *Metamorphoses* to see how Shaw altered the myth to create his play. Then, students could select other myths as the bases for their dramatic scripts. Explain to students that they must consider who their characters will be, what the setting will be, and what the conflict will be. You will probably need to remind students to update the elements to make them contemporary.

If students have props they want used in their productions, encourage them to bring the props in. Make sure everyone's possessions are carefully labeled.

As students reflect on their writing, ask them to pay particular attention to how they felt about the scene when they saw it performed. Have them comment on what they would do differently.

CLOSURE

Have students discuss how they revise and proofread differently for a dramatic script than for a short story. Encourage students to examine the sample script and its format before they reply.

Then, ask students what they think are the key factors in writing a good script. ■

ANSWERS
Writing Workshop Questions

Any answer that may vary is indicated by an asterisk.(*)

1. The basic conflict is between Higgins's determination to have Eliza at the at-home, and Mrs. Higgins's reluctance to have either Higgins or Eliza there. The dialogue reveals that Henry's mother would rather not have him present at her at-homes because they live such different lives. For example, she says, "You offend all my friends. . . ."

2. The time is sometime in the afternoon at Mrs. Higgins's home.

*3. Each student should accurately identify a stage direction and give solid evidence supporting the explanation.

*4. Higgins is an acerbic, single-minded man with a mission. He just is not aware that others may have different points of view from his, and so he makes no plans for and takes no account of their reactions to his projects. The decisions he makes with no regard to his mother's wishes or plans and the way he argues with her reveal his personality.

1. What is the basic conflict in this scene? How does the dialogue reveal it?
2. What is the time and place of this scene?
3. Choose any stage direction, and explain why you think Shaw wanted to specify it. Why is it important?
4. How would you describe Higgins's personality? What details in the script created this impression?

Writing a Scene

Prewriting. Since you are going to be writing a single scene, you'll need to think of a conflict that can take place in a single place and time. Brainstorm, scan the news headlines, ask "What if?" questions. You'll need at least two characters, but more than three or four will be unmanageable. Flesh out your characters and setting by answering the questions on pages 173 and 174. Finally, make a brief plan of what will happen at the beginning, middle, and end of your scene.

Writing, Evaluating, and Revising. Your two tools are dialogue and action, so put yourself in your characters' places and start talking. Jot down any actions or mannerisms that come to your mind, as well as what the characters say.

The best way to evaluate your script is to ask friends to read it aloud and act it out. Do they need more stage directions? dialogue more in keeping with the characters? a clearer conflict? Make any changes you feel are needed.

Proofreading and Publishing. Follow the format for dialogue and stage directions used in the scene from *Pygmalion*. Then, cast the parts, rehearse the actors, and schedule a performance for your class.

To add your scene to your **portfolio,** date it and attach a note of reflection. Which methods could you use to research the background and details of the scene if you rewrote it? What did you learn about the scene by having it rehearsed and performed?

WRITING WORKSHOP

OBJECTIVES

- To analyze creative elements in a literary model of a lyric poem
- To apply the writing process to create a lyric poem

TEACHING THE LESSON

Before you begin, consider whether you want to have students complete both **Writing Workshops** or only one.

Then, you need to consider whether the lyric poem is the most appropriate task for your students. Less-advanced students, at-risk students, and students with special needs may more easily write narrative poems ☛

WRITING WORKSHOP

205

A Poem

Poetry, like fiction (stories, drama, novels), is a form of literary writing; your purpose in writing is to use language imaginatively to create a work of art. But when you write poetry, you are more concerned with emotions, with the musical sounds of language, and with the images you create in your readers' minds.

Poetry can be divided into two basic types—narrative and lyric. Narrative poems, such as Samuel Taylor Coleridge's *The Rime of the Ancient Mariner*, tell whole stories. Characters are involved in conflicts, and we as readers look forward to seeing how the conflicts are finally resolved. Lyric poems, on the other hand, may suggest glimpses of stories, but they don't tell a whole story. Rather, they capture the essence of an important moment, a feeling, an object, or a person.

Often, what makes a poem work is the use of figurative language and special sound devices. The following chart has examples of the various kinds of figurative language and sound devices you can use when you write poetry.

FIGURATIVE LANGUAGE AND SOUND DEVICES

Imagery: concrete details that appeal to the senses of sight, hearing, smell, taste, or touch	Listen! you hear the grating roar
	Of pebbles which the waves draw
	     back, and fling,
	At their return, up the high strand
	          Matthew Arnold, "Dover Beach"

Simile: comparison of two unlike things using *like, as, than, resembles,* etc.	My heart is like a singing bird Christina Rossetti, "A Birthday"

(continued)

QUOTATION FOR THE DAY

"Writing is an act of sharing a gift that doesn't always come *from* you—it's more like something comes *through* you." (Rita Ariyoshi, American travel author and editor)

Share the quotation with your class and initiate a discussion of the difference between writing coming "from you" and writing coming "through you." Lead students to see that poetry requires an author to instill his or her feelings into the words.

MEETING *individual* NEEDS

AT-RISK STUDENTS

Because some students may find the concepts involved in poetry very difficult, an alternative assignment may be more successful. Allow students to present or tape a rap performance as their work for this lesson. Rap is a highly demanding form that requires a specialized vocabulary, rhythm, meter, and plot.

AMENDMENTS TO SELECTIONS
Description of change: excerpted
Rationale: to focus on the concept of figurative language presented in this chapter

because of the resemblance to a short story. Consider a narrative poem as an alternative for some or all of your students. Much of the material in this **Writing Workshop** can be adapted for teaching a narrative poem, and students can brainstorm plots, conflicts, characters, and settings as they did for their short stories.

In teaching the lyric poem, be sure to leave enough time to teach both figurative language and sound devices adequately. You might want to supplement the instruction and examples provided with additional examples from literature textbooks.

Before students attempt to answer the questions about **"The Bear,"** have pairs

MEETING *individual* NEEDS

LEP/ESL

Spanish. Introduce students to poetry that is, in some way, personally and culturally relevant. You could visit the poetry section of your library and select several volumes by noted Hispanic poets such as Pablo Neruda and Jorge Luis Borges. You will want to look for those editions that have Spanish on the right side with an English translation on the left. Ask your students to peruse these books in class and to select a short poem. Then, make the following assignment:

1. Read the Spanish entry first, then the English.
2. Identify the similes and metaphors.
3. Does the poet use personification? In what way(s)?
4. Is the Spanish free-verse or rhyme? Does the translation follow the same technique?
5. Feel free to use a bilingual dictionary. Do you agree with the translation?
6. What is your favorite part of the poem? Why?

AMENDMENTS TO SELECTIONS
Description of change: excerpted
Rationale: to focus on the concept of figurative language presented in this chapter

FIGURATIVE LANGUAGE AND SOUND DEVICES *(continued)*	

Metaphor: comparison that equates two unlike things	The crowds upon the pavement
	   Were fields of harvest wheat.
	      W. H. Auden, "Song: As I
	      Walked Out One Evening"

Personification: giving human qualities to something nonhuman	The sullen wind was soon awake,
	It tore the elm-tops down for spite,
	   And did its worst to vex the lake
	      Robert Browning, "Porphyria's
	      Lover"

Rhyme: repetition of an accented vowel and end sound in words that are close together	So long as men can breathe, or eyes
	   can see,
	So long lives this, and this gives life
	   to thee.
	      William Shakespeare, "Sonnet 18"

Alliteration: repetition of initial consonant sounds	O wild **W**est **W**ind
	      Percy Bysshe Shelley, "Ode
	      to the West Wind"

Assonance: repetition of vowel sounds	Awake ye muses nine, sing me a strain
	   divine,
	Unwind the solemn twine, and **tie** my
	   Valentine!
	      Emily Dickinson, *The Complete
	      Poems of Emily Dickinson*

Onomatopoeia: a word's sound that imitates its meaning	And full-grown lambs loud **bleat**
	   from hilly bourn
	      John Keats, "To Autumn"

Rhythm: Beat made by accented and unaccented syllables. *Metrical verse* has *meter,* a regular pattern of beats. *Free verse* does not have meter.	Ĭ wándĕred lónelў ás ă clóud
	Thăt flóats ŏn high o'er váles ănd hílls
	      William Wordsworth, "I
	      Wandered Lonely as a
	      Cloud"

of students share their personal responses and then work together to identify examples of figurative language and sound devices in the poem. You may also want to have students work in pairs or small groups to answer the questions.

ASSESSMENT

This genre requires a combination of a literary purpose and an expressive purpose, a combination that makes the poetry very personal. One way to handle assessment is to evaluate the poems using plus and minus signs only. You could use the following aspects when considering the effectiveness of the poems: ☞

The following poem is written in *free verse,* a form that uses repetition, pauses, and the natural beats of speech to create rhythm. Like other free verse poems, "The Bear" does not have meter. Read the poem aloud. What "music" do you hear? What images engage your senses?

The Bear
by Nina Cassian, translated by Laura Schiff

The bear paces the cage for hours
the four bars in the four corners
drip with his saliva and sniffs
the bear's snout up and down on
the four bars, only the four bars
a frenzy for four sides.
If the cage were completely round
he'd stand in the center for hours
feeling all points narrowing tight
to a prison and at last he'd lose
the tragic illusion of a road along
one side and from there again along
another side and from there again along
another side and from there, again . . .

INTEGRATING THE LANGUAGE ARTS

Speaking Link. The models of figurative language and sound devices, as well as the model poem, must be read aloud to be effective. In addition, students should be encouraged to read aloud a wide variety of lyric poems before beginning their own writing so they can get a feel for the genre.

Grammar, Usage, and Mechanics Link. Have students study the model poem in terms of the requirements of prose writing. They will find that the writer both ignores and violates prose rules in constructing the poem. Ask students to consider what rules are ignored and what effects are achieved. Finally, have students consider how they might incorporate similar techniques in their poetry.

1. Compressed images (includes eliminating unnecessary words)
2. Strong, clear word choice
3. Arrangement of lines to help the images, the meaning, or both
4. Fluent, pleasing rhythm
5. Obvious meaning or purpose
6. Suitable images

CLOSURE

Have students discuss their specific purposes in writing their poems. Then, have students compare the experience of writing a poem to the experience of writing a short story. ∎

ANSWERS
Writing Workshop Questions

Any answer that may vary is indicated by an asterisk. (*)

*1. The mood is almost, but not quite, hopeless in a situation in which despair is warranted. The description of the cage as it is and as it might have been if it were round creates this mood.

2. There are several examples of alliteration: *saliva, sniffs,* and *bear's snout.* The repeated sounds suggest the bear's repeated actions. Cassian uses assonance in several lines: "drip with his . . . sniffs." Assonance helps the rhythm. Repetition also helps the poem's rhythm and reinforces the bear's repeated actions.

3. Be sure students support their answers with reasons.

*4. The bear might be a symbol, perhaps of the human situation (that people are all in cages) or perhaps of a common human reaction to any bad situation, which is to look for hope.

A DIFFERENT APPROACH

You could have students use current events as the bases of their poetry. First, you'll want to share published poetry in which the authors have responded to public events (such as Walt Whitman's "When Lilacs Last in the Dooryard Bloom'd") and then have students select articles from current newspapers or magazines to use as the subjects of their poems. Explain that they can explain, describe, commemorate, or criticize the events.

1. How would you describe the mood or feeling of this poem? What words and sounds create this effect?
2. What sound devices can you find in this poem? What meaning or emotion do they suggest?
3. What single image from the poem do you remember when you close your eyes? Why?
4. A symbol is an object, place, person, or event that represents something beyond itself. Could the bear in this poem be meant as a symbol? Why?

Writing a Poem

Prewriting. You are going to be writing a lyric poem describing an object or a moment in time, and the first thing you need to do is free your imagination. Brainstorm or look for ideas in your writer's journal. Think of an intense moment in your life—one of total gloom, pure excitement, or blissful peace. Or picture an object that fascinates you or frightens you. Once you capture the basic idea, you can begin to flesh it out. Jot down words, phrases, and figures of speech that you might use.

Writing, Evaluating, Revising. Before you start, review the chart of techniques on pages 205–206. Then, decide whether you'll use rhyme and meter or free verse. In a poem, each word counts, so use specific nouns, lively verbs, and many sensory details. Try to include at least one metaphor or simile. After you write your draft, read your poem aloud, listening for the precision of descriptions and rhythms of the language. Let your ear guide you to changes.

Proofreading and Publishing. Before you write your final copy, check your spelling and punctuation. Practice reading your poem aloud, and plan a poetry-reading session with the class. Use a camcorder or tape recorder to record all the readings. If you want to add your poem to your **portfolio,** remember to date it and include a note of reflection. Which figures of speech and sound devices did you use? Which of these do you think worked the best and why? How could you change the poem to make the rhythm seem more natural?

MAKING CONNECTIONS

CREATING A STORYBOARD
OBJECTIVE

- To create a storyboard for a scene for the screen

MAKING CONNECTIONS

CREATING A STORYBOARD

When you write a script for film or video, you have to consider the possibilities of the medium. It's not as intimate as a theater production, but you can change scenes with ease and you can focus on a close-up of a pebble or a bird's-eye view of a whole valley. You're probably familiar with several visual techniques used in videos and films: fade in and out; close-ups and long shots; panning (moving) shots and zooms; cuts and dissolves.

A television or movie script includes written directions for the visual and sound effects, but sometimes a storyboard is created as well. As you can see from the following example, a storyboard is a visual plan of what will be filmed.

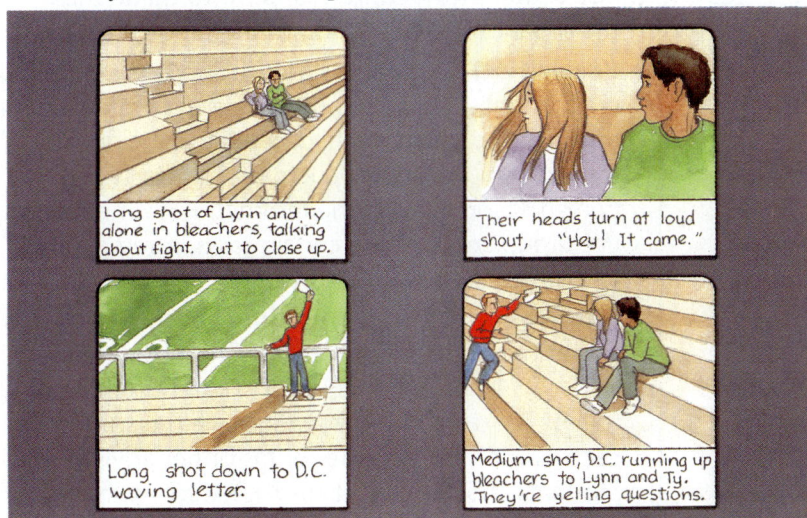

Long shot of Lynn and Ty alone in bleachers, talking about fight. Cut to close up.

Their heads turn at loud shout, "Hey! It came."

Long shot down to D.C. waving letter.

Medium shot, D.C. running up bleachers to Lynn and Ty. They're yelling questions.

Now, try creating a storyboard for the scene you wrote in the scenewriting workshop (pages 201–204), or for a scene from any play you've read. Remember to write directions for action, camera work, special effects, music, props, and so forth. Sketch a storyboard of at least six panels, beginning a new panel whenever there's a significant visual shift in the scene.

CREATING A STORYBOARD
Teaching Strategies

Use a video recording to demonstrate the various visual techniques mentioned in the textbook. *Citizen Kane* is a good demonstration model for its camera and sound techniques. The movies *Who Framed Roger Rabbit* and *Mary Poppins* are good demonstration models because they both combine animation with live action and use many special effects.

Remind students that, unlike a dramatic scene on stage, a film uses dialogue sparingly. The emphasis is on what is seen, not on what is heard, because the images convey much of the story. For example, there is no need for dialogue such as "Are you in pain?" if the images include a shot of a girl wincing and clutching her arm.

Other elements students may want to add to their storyboards are notations about camera distance, angle, movement, and time of run.

GUIDELINES

Students should have at least six panels. Evaluate storyboards for the accuracy of directions, inclusion of correct elements, and proper shifting of scenes.

Chapter 6

WRITING TO INFORM: EXPOSITION

OBJECTIVES

- To choose a subject for a feasibility report
- To gather information and develop a thesis statement for a feasibility report
- To write a draft of a feasibility report
- To evaluate, revise, proofread and publish a draft of a feasibility report

WRITING-IN-PROGRESS ASSIGNMENTS

Major Assignment: Writing a feasibility report

Cumulative Writing Assignments: The chart below shows the sequence of cumulative assignments that will guide students as they write a feasibility report. These Writing Assignments form the instructional core of Chapter 6.

PREWRITING
WRITING ASSIGNMENT
• Part 1: Choosing a Subject and Considering Alternatives p. 220
• Part 2: Gathering Information p. 223
• Part 3: Establishing Criteria for Your Report p. 225
• Part 4: Organizing Information p. 227

WRITING YOUR FIRST DRAFT
WRITING ASSIGNMENT
• Part 5: Writing a First Draft p. 236

EVALUATING AND REVISING
WRITING ASSIGNMENT
• Part 6: Evaluating and Revising Your Feasibility Report p. 239

PROOFREADING AND PUBLISHING
WRITING ASSIGNMENT
• Part 7: Proofreading and Publishing Your Feasibility Report p. 241

In addition, exercises 1–4 provide practice in speaking and listening, analyzing a feasibility report, and analyzing revisions.

cross CURRICULUM

Feasibility Reports in Government

Ask students to think of some important decisions made in American government. Then, ask students how they think history might have been altered if the decision makers had chosen a different course of action.

- **Assignment** Have students work in groups of four to choose one decision made by a government official in American history or current events. Then, ask them to imagine that they work for the person who made the decision and that they have been asked to write a feasibility report about other possible decisions and their outcomes. For example, suppose students were examining the decision of the Commissioner of Public Safety in Birmingham, Alabama to deny Martin Luther King, Jr., and his followers a permit to demonstrate in April 1963. Students would need to investigate 1) why he made his decision and what the results of it were, 2) what other options he might have pursued, and 3) what the results of following those other options would have been. Students should use the instruction provided in Chapter 6 to guide them in the organizing and writing of the report.

- **Prewriting** Students in groups should work together to establish criteria and consider recommendations that need to be researched. Students should use resources in the library, such as periodicals and first person accounts, and the Internet. Each member of the group should have certain tasks in researching, and all students should contribute to the writing.

- **Publishing** Ask students to present their reports by acting out an imagined scene from history. Ask a fellow teacher, your principal, or a parent to play the role of the decision maker and have the students in each group play the roles of his or her advisers. Students should present their findings (with visuals, if possible) to the decision maker. After each presentation, the decision maker should make a decision and explain why. Take an informal poll of the class to see if students agree with the decision.

INTEGRATING THE LANGUAGE ARTS

SELECTION	READING AND LITERATURE	WRITING AND CRITICAL THINKING	LANGUAGE AND SYNTAX	SPEAKING, LISTENING, AND OTHER EXPRESSION SKILLS
• "Man, Bytes, Dog" by James Gorman pp. 212–214 • "Doing Chores" by August Heckscher pp. 243–245 • from *Farewell to Manzanar* by Jeanne Wakatsuki Houston and James D. Houston p. 248	• Responding personally to literature pp. 215, 245–246, 249 • Identifying elements of a feasibility report pp. 216, 228	• Identifying elements of a feasibility report pp. 216, 228 • Choosing subjects for a feasibility report pp. 218–220 • Gathering and arranging information pp. 221–223, 226–227 • Establishing criteria pp. 223–225 • Analyzing the organization of a feasibility report p. 223 • Developing a recommendation p. 225 • Evaluating, revising, proofreading, and publishing pp. 237–242, 246, 250 • Analyzing and writing an extended definition pp. 243–246 • Writing a comparison/contrast essay pp. 247–250 • Writing using analogy p. 251	• Proofreading for errors in grammar, usage, and mechanics pp. 241, 250 • Using analogy p. 251	• Working with classmates to find subjects for a feasibility report p. 220 • Survey students for information p. 221 • Using a chart to organize information p. 222 • Working with classmates to analyze a feasibility report p. 233 • Working with classmates to analyze the organization of a feasibility report p. 237 • Working with classmates to evaluate and revise p. 239 • Making a class dictionary to extend definitions p. 246

SUGGESTED INTEGRATED UNIT PLAN

This unit plan gives suggestions on how to integrate the major strands of the language arts with this chapter.

The suggested selections include a discussion of film as an extension of literature and an ironic plan for improving the human condition. If you begin with this chapter on writing a feasibility report or with the suggested selections, focus on the common characteristics of a feasibility report. Then integrate speaking/listening and language concepts with both the writing and the literature.

Common Characteristics

- Content that is comprehensive
- Precise language
- Documentation of facts or events
- Use of third person for objectivity or use of first person for authenticity of experience or observation
- Organization of ideas or examples usually from least to most important

Writing
Feasibility Report

Speaking/Listening
- Giving a speech
- Conducting a student survey

UNIT FOCUS
NONFICTION: INFORMATIVE WRITING

Language
Grammar and Usage
- Transitions
- Infinitive phrases
- Degrees of comparison

Literature
Selections such as
- "Film as Literature: More Than Meets the Eye" William Costanzo
- "A Modest Proposal" Jonathan Swift

CHAPTER 6: WRITING TO INFORM: EXPOSITION

Use this guide for creating an instructional plan that addresses the individual needs of your students. Assignments accompanied by the following symbol (*) may be completed out of class. Times given for pacing lessons are estimated.

CHAPTER PLANNING GUIDE—PUPIL'S EDITION

LESSONS	LITERARY MODEL pp. 212–215 "Man, Bytes, Dog" by James Gorman	PREWRITING pp. 217–227	
		Generating Ideas	Gathering/Organizing
DEVELOPMENTAL PROGRAM	⏱ **20–25 minutes** • Students read model aloud in pairs and discuss questions on p. 215	⏱ **45–50 minutes** • Main Assignment: Looking Ahead p. 216 • Exploring a Course of Action pp. 217–220 • Writing Notes pp. 217, 219 • Exercises 1–2 p. 220 • Writing Assignment: Part 1 p. 220	⏱ **50–55 minutes** • Planning a Feasibility Report pp. 221–227 • Writing Assignment: Part 2 p. 223* • Critical Thinking pp. 223–224 • Writing Assignment: Parts 3, 4 pp. 225, 227
CORE PROGRAM	⏱ **15–20 minutes** • Have students read the model independently and answer questions on p. 215 in small groups	⏱ **30–35 minutes** • Main Assignment: Looking Ahead p. 216 • Exploring a Course of Action pp. 217–220 • Writing Notes pp. 217, 219 • Exercises 1–2 p. 220* • Writing Assignment: Part 1 p. 220*	⏱ **40–45 minutes** • Planning a Feasibility Report pp. 221–227 • Writing Assignment: Part 2 p. 223* • Critical Thinking pp. 223–224 • Writing Assignment: Parts 3, 4 pp. 225, 227*
ACCELERATED PROGRAM	⏱ **15 minutes** • Assign students to read model independently and take notes on questions 3 and 4 on p. 215 in Reader's Logs	⏱ **20 minutes** • Main Assignment: Looking Ahead p. 216 • Exploring a Course of Action pp. 217–220 • Writing Notes pp. 217, 219 • Writing Assignment: Part 1 p. 220*	⏱ **30–35 minutes** • Planning a Feasibility Report pp. 221–227 • Writing Assignment: Part 2 p. 223* • Critical Thinking pp. 223–224* • Writing Assignment: Parts 3, 4 pp. 225, 227*

CHAPTER PLANNING GUIDE—PROGRAM RESOURCES

	LITERARY MODEL	PREWRITING
PRINT	• Reading Master 6, *Practice for Assessment in Reading, Vocabulary, and Spelling* p. 6	• Prewriting, *Strategies for Writing* p. 16
MEDIA	• Fine Art Transparency 3: *Sun and Moon,* *Transparency Binder* 📽	• Graphic Organizers 9–10, *Transparency Binder* 📽

WRITING pp. 228–236	EVALUATING AND REVISING pp. 237–239	PROOFREADING AND PUBLISHING pp. 240–242
🕐 **55–60 minutes** • The Structure of a Feasibility Report p. 228 • A Basic Framework/ A Writer's Model pp. 232–235 • Writing Note p. 236 • Writing Assignment: Part 5 p. 236*	🕐 **50–55 minutes** • Evaluating and Revising p. 237 • Evaluating Chart p. 238 • Exercise 4 p. 239 in pairs • Writing Assignment: Part 6 p. 239	🕐 **45–50 minutes** • Proofreading/Publishing pp. 240, 241 • Grammar Hint p. 240 • Writing Assignment: Part 7 p. 241 • Reflecting p. 241 • A Student Model p. 242
🕐 **45–50 minutes** • The Structure of a Feasibility Report/ Feasibility Report pp. 228–231 • Exercise 3 p. 232 • A Basic Framework p. 232 • Writing Note p. 236 • Writing Assignment: Part 5 p. 236*	🕐 **40–45 minutes** • Evaluating and Revising p. 237 • Evaluating Chart p. 238 • Exercise 4 p. 239 • Writing Assignment: Part 6 p. 239	🕐 **30–35 minutes** • Proofreading/Publishing pp. 240, 241 • Grammar Hint p. 240 • Writing Assignment: Part 7 p. 241* • Reflecting p. 241 • A Student Model p. 242*
🕐 **40–45 minutes** • Feasibility Report pp. 229–231 • Exercise 3 p. 232 • A Basic Framework p. 232 • Writing Note p. 236 • Writing Assignment: Part 5 p. 236*	🕐 **30–35 minutes** • Evaluating Chart p. 238 • Writing Assignment: Part 6 p. 239	🕐 **20–25 minutes** • Grammar Hint p. 240 • Writing Assignment: Part 7 p. 241* • Reflecting p. 241

Overhead transparencies

WRITING	EVALUATING AND REVISING	PROOFREADING AND PUBLISHING
• Writing, *Strategies for Writing* p. 17	• Evaluating and Revising, *Strategies for Writing* p. 18	• Proofreading Practice, *Strategies for Writing* p. 20 • Coherence, *English Workshop* pp. 25–26
	• Revision Transparencies 9–10, *Transparency Binder*	

ELEMENTS OF WRITING: CURRICULUM CONNECTIONS

Writing Workshop
- An Extended Definition pp. 243–246
- Writing a Comparison/Contrast Essay pp. 247–250

Making Connections
- Test Taking: Using Analogy p. 251

ASSESSMENT OPTIONS

Summative Assessment
Holistic Scoring: Prompts and Models pp. 15–20

Portfolio Assessment
Portfolio forms, *Portfolio Assessment* pp. 5–25, 44–48

Reflection
Writing Process Log, *Strategies for Writing* p. 15
Self-assessment Record, *Portfolio Assessment* p. 19

Ongoing Assessment
Proofreading, *Strategies for Writing* p. 19

MOTIVATION

Ask how many students in the class have dogs. Have a few volunteers tell how they chose their dogs. Then, ask the same questions about computers. Point out that the essay in this lesson evaluates both a dog and a computer by comparing them. Tell students that this is a humorous example

WORKPLACE writing

6 WRITING TO INFORM: EXPOSITION

of a feasibility report and that they will learn how to write a more serious version of a feasibility report in this chapter.

TEACHING THE LESSON

Begin the lesson by asking a student volunteer to read aloud the introductory material on the first page of the chapter. Before reading the essay **"Man, Bytes, Dog"** by James Gorman, tell the class that the tone of the essay is ironic. Then, read the essay, or have a student who has practiced read it to the class. ☞

Making Decisions

Where should a day-care business locate its new center? What's the most efficient checkout system for the school library? How should the local recreation center expand its programs? When we ask questions like these, we're seeking information; when we respond to them, we're providing information to help people **make decisions.**

Writing and You. Writers often try to provide readers with information they need to evaluate options and choose a course of action. An advice columnist tells teenagers to consider location, size, and cost when choosing a college. The manager of a newspaper wants to explore the possibility of introducing more efficient delivery routes. A market research firm reports on four possible sites for a store's expansion. Do you have a question or idea that you could answer or act on if you had more information?

As You Read. In the following passage, a writer provides information about the comparative advantages of a dog and a computer. What criteria, or standards, does he use to evaluate each?

Kurt Mitchell, *Thumbs Up and Thumbs Down* (1990). Watercolor, 14" × 12".

QUOTATION FOR THE DAY

"If I could but describe in simple words the immensity of simple knowledge." (Patrick White, 1912–1990, Australian author)

Ask students to describe their experiences with evaluating options. Students could freewrite in their writing journals, or volunteers could relate their experiences to the class.

VISUAL CONNECTIONS

Exploring the Subject. After a student volunteer has read aloud the introductory material on this page, ask students to think about what Kurt Mitchell's watercolor *Thumbs Up and Thumbs Down* suggests about decision making. Ask students to consider why "thumbs up" is characterized as the point of a pencil, while "thumbs down" is characterized as an eraser.

GUIDED PRACTICE

You can guide students in their work on the **Reader's Response** questions by answering the first question yourself and reading your answer to the class. You can guide their work on the **Writer's Craft** questions by answering the first question orally with the whole class.

MEETING *individual* NEEDS

LEP/ESL

General Strategies. Some students may not be familiar with some of the terms that are used in James Gorman's essay. You might begin with the title and explain that it is a takeoff on a familiar American expression that indicates something unusual or out of the ordinary. Also, point out that Gorman introduces the computer by using the computer term *bytes*. Similarly, you can explain that a Macintosh is a kind of computer. You may want to find a photograph of Toto from *The Wizard of Oz* so that students have some idea of what a Cairn Terrier looks like.

You may find it useful to spend a few moments discussing the concept of criteria. Point out to students that they regularly use criteria in making decisions, even if they are unaware of doing so. Every time they choose a product or an activity, they do so for a particular reason. Tell them that these reasons are their personal criteria.

212

MAN, BYTES, DOG

BY JAMES GORMAN

Many people have asked me about the Cairn Terrier. How about memory, they want to know. Is it IBM compatible? Why didn't I get the IBM itself, or a Kaypro, Compaq, or Macintosh? I think the best way to answer these questions is to look at the Macintosh and the Cairn head on. I almost did buy the Macintosh. It has terrific graphics, good word-processing capabilities, and the mouse. But in the end I decided on the Cairn, and I think I made the right decision.

Let's start out with the basics:

Macintosh	Weight (without printer):	20 lbs.
	Memory (RAM):	128 K
	Price (without printer):	$3,090
Cairn Terrier	Weight (without printer):	14 lbs.
	Memory (RAM):	Some
	Price (without printer):	$250

Just on the basis of price and weight, the choice is obvious. Another plus is that the Cairn Terrier comes in one unit. No printer is necessary, or useful. And—this was a big attraction to me—there is no user's manual.

Here are some of the other qualities I found put the Cairn out ahead of the Macintosh.

Portability: To give you a better idea of size, Toto in *The Wizard of Oz* was a Cairn Terrier. So you can see that if the young Judy Garland was able to carry Toto around in that little picnic basket, you will have no trouble at all moving your Cairn from place to place. For short trips it will move under its own power. The Macintosh will not.

212

INDEPENDENT PRACTICE

Students can practice independently by answering the second and fourth of the **Reader's Response** and **Writer's Craft** questions on their own.

ASSESSMENT

Monitor students' responses to the **Reader's Response** and **Writer's Craft** questions. Students should demonstrate an understanding of how Gorman employs criteria in evaluating the Cairn and the Macintosh.

Reliability: In five to ten years, I am sure, the Macintosh will be superseded by a new model, like the Delicious or the Granny Smith. The Cairn Terrier, on the other hand, has held its share of the market with only minor modifications for hundreds of years. In the short term, Cairns seldom need servicing, apart from shots and the odd worming, and most function without interruption during electrical storms.

Compatibility: Cairn Terriers get along with everyone. And for communications with any other dog, of any breed, within a radius of three miles, no additional hardware is necessary. All dogs share a common operating system.

Software: The Cairn will run three standard programs, SIT, COME, and NO, and whatever else you create. It is true that being microcanine, the Cairn is limited here, but it does load the programs instantaneously. No disk drives. No tapes.

Admittedly, these are peripheral advantages. The real comparison has to be on the basis of capabilities. What can the Macintosh and the Cairn do? Let's start on the Macintosh's turf—income tax preparation, recipe storage, graphics, and astrophysics problems:

	Taxes	Recipes	Graphics	Astrophysics
Macintosh	yes	yes	yes	yes
Cairn	no	no	no	no

At first glance it looks bad for the Cairn. But it's important to look beneath the surface with this kind of chart. If you yourself are leaning

MEETING individual NEEDS

LESS-ADVANCED STUDENTS

Some students might benefit from seeing writing that evaluates alternatives. Bring to class several letters from advice columns on a variety of subjects, such as etiquette, home improvement, and personal relationships. Have students read the letters and then discuss with them how the columnists use criteria to help their readers make decisions.

ADVANCED STUDENTS

Have students work in groups of three or four to generate lists of pairs of items that can be evaluated through unlikely comparisons. Ask each group to choose one of the topics generated and to write an introductory paragraph for a humorous essay.

LEARNING STYLES

Visual Learners. Clip from magazines photographs of a variety of items and places. Ask students to match pairs of pictures that they think could be discussed in an essay such as "Man, Bytes, Dog." Encourage them to be creative in their comparisons. Ask students to explain to the class their selections and how they would develop an essay on the objects or places in the photographs.

214

toward the Macintosh, ask yourself these questions: Do you want to do your own income taxes? Do you want to type all your recipes into a computer? In your graph, what would you put on the x axis? the y axis? Do you have any astrophysics problems you want solved?

Then consider the Cairn's specialties: playing fetch and tug-of-war, licking your face, and chasing foxes out of rock cairns (eponymously). Note that no software is necessary. All these functions are part of the operating system:

	Fetch	Tug-of-war	Face	Foxes
Cairn	yes	yes	yes	yes
Macintosh	no	no	no	no

Another point to keep in mind is that computers, even the Macintosh, only do what you tell them to do. Cairns perform their functions all on their own. Here are some of the additional capabilities that I discovered once I got the Cairn home and housebroken.

Word Processing: Remarkably, the Cairn seems to understand every word I say. He has a nice way of pricking up his ears at words like "out" or "ball." He also has highly tuned voice recognition.

Education: The Cairn provides children with hands-on experience at an early age, contributing to social interaction, crawling ability, and language skills. At age one, my daughter could say "Sit," "Come," and "No."

Cleaning: This function was a pleasant surprise. But of course cleaning up around the cave is one of the reasons dogs were developed in the first place. Users with young (below age two) children will still find this function useful. The Cairn Terrier cleans the floor, spoons, bib, and baby, and has an unerring ability to distinguish strained peas from ears, nose, and fingers.

Psychotherapy: Here the Cairn really shines. And remember, therapy is something that computers have tried. There is a program that makes the computer ask you questions when you tell it your problems. You say, "I'm afraid of foxes." The computer says, "You're afraid of foxes?"

The Cairn won't give you that kind of echo. Like Freudian analysts, Cairns are mercifully silent; unlike Freudians, they are infinitely sympathetic. I've found that the Cairn will share, in a nonjudgmental fashion, disappoint- ments, joys, and frustrations. And you don't have to know BASIC.

This last capability is related to the Cairn's strongest point, which was the final deciding factor in my decision against the Macintosh—user-friendliness. On this criterion, there is simply no comparison. The Cairn Terrier is the essence of user-friendliness. It has fur, it doesn't flicker when you look at it, and it wags its tail.

READER'S RESPONSE

1. Did this evaluation of dog versus computer surprise you? Is it funny? Explain your response.
2. Review what the Cairn can do that the Macintosh cannot. How would you summarize the differences?

WRITER'S CRAFT

3. What are the criteria the writer uses to evaluate the Cairn and the Macintosh?
4. What do the charts contribute to the essay? How do they rein- force the writer's message?

ANSWERS
Reader's Response

Responses will vary.

1. Students might say that the essay is funny because a comparison between a dog and a computer is not one most people would make.
2. The Cairn can play fetch and tug-of- war, lick a person's face, and chase foxes out of rock cairns. The dog can also understand words, educate children, clean floors, and provide psychotherapy. In summary, Cairns can interact with people and the computer can't.

Writer's Craft

Answers may vary.

3. The criteria are weight, memory, price, portability, reliability, compatibility, and software. He also evaluates the dog and the computer on the performance of certain tasks: word processing, educating, cleaning, and providing therapy.
4. The charts serve to reinforce the humorous, ironic tone of the essay. Ordinarily, charts of this type would be used to summarize information. By using them, the writer maintains a humorous tone.

WAYS TO INFORM

TEACHING THE LESSON

Explain to students that informative writing can be developed in several ways, including narration, description, classification, and evaluation. Then, ask them to read and study the examples in the textbook to determine which method of development is best suited for each. Assess students' comprehension of the methods by asking them to give their own examples of what they might write for each of the methods. ■

COOPERATIVE LEARNING

Ask students to work in groups to develop three examples of topics that involve writing to inform. Then, ask each group to pass its topics to another group. The second group should select one of the topics and write a thesis statement that is appropriate to it. Then, have the groups that generated the topics evaluate the thesis statements.

A DIFFERENT APPROACH

Students may express their confusion over the different types of expository writing. You could recreate this chart on the chalkboard to illustrate how writing to inform, writing to explain, and writing to explore are all related. You then could select a topic and describe how it might be presented in three different expository writing assignments.

INFORMING
- Gives the facts
- Focuses on these facts

↓

EXPLAINING
- Explains the facts
- Focuses on the meaning of these facts
  (draws a conclusion)

↓

EXPLORING
- Gives the facts
- Explains the facts
- Asks questions about these facts
- Focuses on some problem created by the facts

216

Ways to Inform

When your purpose is to inform, *evaluation*—judging something against a set of criteria—is one approach you can take. But you can inform in other ways. Here are some examples:

- on a history test, detailing the events leading up to the firing on Fort Sumter
- in a sports article, reporting on the highlights of a high school soccer game
- in a business report, describing a new telephone system in enough detail so decision makers will have the information to decide whether to purchase it or not
- in an oral report for a world literature class, describing the treasure of the Anglo-Saxon ship found at Sutton Hoo
- in a memo to an employer, comparing and contrasting two systems for tracking inventory in a hardware store
- in a personal narrative, defining what freedom means to you
- in a voiceover script for a video, describing the paintings of Jacob Lawrence
- in a letter to a friend, explaining why you enjoy reading mystery novels more than historical fiction
- in an article for the school newspaper, writing a review of last night's rock concert
- in a science report, comparing and contrasting cells seen through a microscope

LOOKING AHEAD

In the main assignment in this chapter, you will write a feasibility report to inform your readers about alternatives to a current state of affairs. As you work through the assignment, keep in mind that a feasibility report

- identifies the need for a new course of action
- establishes criteria to evaluate possible courses of action, or alternatives
- uses those criteria to determine the best course of action

OBJECTIVES

- To work in groups to identify a need for improvement
- To choose a subject for a feasibility report, identify a related need, and select alternatives that address the need
- To gather information about a need and about alternative solutions to that need
- To develop criteria for evaluating alternatives
- To organize information

☞

Writing a Feasibility Report

Prewriting

Exploring a Course of Action

Feasibility reports usually grow out of a need. For example, someone sees a need to improve upon or replace the *status quo*—the way things are normally done—and wants to explore whether a new idea is feasible. (The word *feasible* means possible, or capable of being done.) The idea for improvement usually involves a new product or procedure: a new high-strength part for an aircraft, for example, or a medical procedure for early diagnosis of cataracts. A feasibility report tells whether the product or procedure is *effective, practical,* and *desirable.* Its purpose is to give decision makers the information necessary to choose a course of action.

In everyday life, you make feasibility judgments all the time, usually without realizing that you're doing so. Which college or training program to attend, whether to buy a new bicycle, even whether to participate in an extracurricular activity—all these can be considered feasibility questions. In each case, you are weighing the pros and cons of one choice against the alternatives. In business and industry, workers frequently conduct feasibility studies; when the decision involved is a major one for the company, they usually write feasibility reports.

In this chapter, your writing assignment is to write a feasibility report about some new product or procedure for your school, home, neighborhood, or community. Your report is supposed to answer these questions: "Is it effective?" "Is it possible?" and "Is it desirable?"

WRITING NOTE

In this chapter, note that the word "product" is used broadly: For example, it can be a service (overnight shipping), it can be a thing or place with a specific function (a community garden); or it can be a facility (a university).

PROGRAM MANAGER

PREWRITING

- **Self-Assessment** Before beginning instruction of the writing process, see **Writing Process Log** in *Strategies for Writing,* p. 15.
- **Heuristics** To help students generate ideas, see **Prewriting** in *Strategies for Writing,* p. 16.
- **Instructional Support** See **Graphic Organizers 9** and **10**. For suggestions on how to tie the transparencies to instruction, review teacher's notes in *Fine Art and Instructional Transparencies for Writing,* pp. 69, 71.

QUOTATION FOR THE DAY
"He who does not expect a million readers should not write a line." (J. W. Goethe, 1749–1832, German poet, dramatist, and thinker)
Write the quotation on the chalkboard and ask students to freewrite about the importance of audience when choosing a subject for a paper.

MEETING *individual* NEEDS

LEP/ESL

General Strategies. It may be helpful to review what an essay is and does. Once students have chosen their topics, ask each student to write a one-sentence statement of purpose. "I am writing to persuade my reader to . . ." or "I am writing to explain to my reader how . . ." are two examples of such a statement. Then, explain that this is not the thesis statement because it is written in the first person. This statement serves to clarify the topic and objective in the student's mind.

LESS-ADVANCED STUDENTS

Some students might benefit from additional criteria for determining whether or not they have found appropriate subjects for a feasibility report. Tell students that if there are not at least three alternatives that meet the need, the topic is too narrow. If more than four alternatives meet the need, the topic is too broad.

Thinking About Purpose, Audience, and Tone

The *purpose* of the feasibility report is to give readers the information they need when choosing between two or more courses of action. This information is provided in the form of an objective evaluation of each alternative you have decided to consider. Remember: Your report ultimately answers the questions "Is the product (or procedure) effective?" "Is it possible?" and "Is it desirable?"

Depending on your *audience,* your purpose may also include recommending a course of action. Supervisors in business and industry may ask employees for reports that evaluate alternatives but do not make a recommendation. However, feasibility reports assigned to consultants outside a company usually do recommend one alternative. For the assignment in this chapter, your report should include a recommendation.

Audience also affects your purpose in that readers may have differing perceptions about a particular need. For example, some members of your neighborhood may see a great need for a play area for small children, while others may see no such need at all. You will have to take these different points of view into account as you describe the need and consider the alternatives to meet it.

In addition, your audience will affect your purpose in terms of how much information you provide. Just as you need to be aware of what your readers know about the need you have identified, you should be aware of how much they know about the alternative solutions you are evaluating. That way, you can gauge how much information to include in your report.

A confident *tone* will help persuade your readers to take your recommendation seriously. Feasibility reports usually contain objective, somewhat formal language. The resulting tone conveys a sense that the writer has carefully considered both the need and the course of action being recommended.

Choosing Your Subject

Can you see a better way of doing something? Start with a subject that interests you, and think about a related opportunity or need. For example, if acting is your special interest, you might investigate whether your school's theater facilities can be upgraded. If your family is considering a major purchase—a car or

Since students probably have not had experience writing feasibility reports, you might consider working through the **Prewriting** lesson more slowly than you might otherwise. One way to summarize the information in the chapter so that students can see all of it at a glance is to make an outline on the chalkboard or on a piece of poster board. In either case, the outline should be available for students to use as they work on the exercises and the parts of the writing assignment.

You may want to remind students that their topics must also interest their audience. Explain that readers are better able to process information when it is clear, interesting, and objective. ☞

a home computer, for example—you might prepare a feasibility report to help make a decision. If you want to help out in your community, you might work with your neighborhood association on a proposal to develop an underused public area.

Once you have an issue in mind, you will want to determine whether others agree with you that it presents a need. In some cases, the need will be apparent: If a family's car requires weekly repairs, everyone will probably agree that it should be replaced. But there may not always be consensus that a need exists. For example, suppose you want to investigate the feasibility of starting an incentive program to reduce tardiness to class. Before you start planning your report, you will want to find out from teachers or administrators how serious a problem tardiness really is. If no one thinks tardiness is a significant issue, you might want to find another topic to pursue.

WRITING NOTE

If other people disagree with you about the need for a new course of action, that doesn't mean you should automatically abandon your subject. It could be that others simply haven't thought about the issue or don't have as much information as you do. If you decide to write on this subject, make sure that your introduction justifies the need or opportunity that you see.

Choosing Alternatives to Consider

Chances are that as you considered subjects and needs, you were also imagining possible courses of action, or alternatives. For example, if you determined that your family needs a new car, you were probably considering an obvious course of action: buying another car. But there are other alternatives, such as leasing; even repairing the car might be a reasonable alternative in some circumstances. The alternative of buying another vehicle

Encourage students to follow the **Here's How** example for gathering information (p. 222). As they begin using the block method and the point-by-point method to organize their prewriting notes, encourage students to experiment with both methods to find the one that works best for their essays. You could also present a graphic organizer such as a Venn diagram. Tell students that clear organization will make their papers more effective.

TEACHING NOTE

Evaluating Group Work. After students complete the activity in **Exercise 1,** have them briefly evaluate their group's work. Student evaluations should answer the following questions: Who participated in the group? What was the group's task? Did the group stay on task? Did every member contribute to the group? What was the group's greatest strength? Each student also should address his or her own participation and effectiveness in the group.

The forms **Evaluating Group Participation** on pp. 40–42 in *Portfolio Assessment* may encourage students to fully answer these questions.

itself involves options: whether to purchase a new or used one; what type, model, and year to select; and so on.

As the above example suggests, you may be able to brainstorm several ways to meet the need you identified. For the writing assignment in this chapter, you will have to narrow down the alternatives you consider to two or three—knowing that one of your alternatives will always be to leave things as they are.

EXERCISE 1 ▶ **Speaking and Listening: Identifying a Need**

With two or three classmates, discuss improvements that could be made at your school or in your community. Then, list your ideas as needs. Some areas you might consider include the following:

1. School curriculum: Are there courses or activities (such as field trips, festivals, art exhibits, or assembly programs) that could be introduced or changed?
2. Extracurricular school activities: Are there clubs, activities, or sports that students would enjoy but that aren't available at your school? Are there problems with scheduling the use of some facilities, such as the gymnasium or auditorium, that a change in procedures might solve?
3. Community projects: Can you think of groups of people in your neighborhood or community whose needs are not being met? (Think about young children, teenagers, older citizens, people with disabilities, and so on.)

EXERCISE 2 ▶ **Speaking and Listening: Identifying Alternatives**

Choose one need from the list you have generated, and work with two or three other students to discuss and list alternatives that would meet that need.

WRITING ASSIGNMENT PART 1: **Choosing a Subject and Considering Alternatives**

What subject would you like to explore? Choose a subject you would like to write about, and identify a related need. Then, brainstorm several alternatives that would address the need.

Prewriting

Planning a Feasibility Report

Taking time to plan your feasibility report before you begin writing can save time and effort later on. Through careful planning, you can decide what's feasible and what isn't before it's time to write.

Gathering Information

You will want three types of information for your report. First, you will want information about the need you have identified. Second, you will want information about the alternatives you've chosen to evaluate. Third, you will want information that will help you establish criteria for evaluating your alternatives.

Gathering Information About a Need. To start collecting information about the need you have identified, think about what information is *relevant*. For example, if you have decided that your school needs a site on the Internet's World Wide Web in order to publicize activities and generally inform the public about the school, you might do a computer search to determine how many schools in your city or state already have such sites and how often the sites are accessed. You could also survey students on how often they would access a school Web site and whether they think it would be worthwhile. Of course, there might be general agreement at school that a Web site is desirable. In that case, you wouldn't have to devote as much energy to collecting information to prove the need exists.

Gathering Information About Alternatives. Once you've collected information to document your need, you'll have to collect information about alternatives to meet the need. Depending on your topic, you may want to consult print and nonprint sources in your library or media center, or on computer. People who are knowledgeable about your subject also can be good sources of information. As you gather information, you may come up with alternatives you hadn't previously thought of. Keep an open mind. The better your alternatives are, the stronger your report will be.

MEETING *individual* NEEDS

LESS-ADVANCED STUDENTS

Some students will have difficulty organizing the three types of information required for the feasibility report. To help them as they gather information, you may want to have students use different-colored index cards for each type of information. For example, students can use blue cards for information about the needs they have identified, yellow cards for their chosen alternatives, and orange cards for the criteria they have established. Students can list one piece of information on each appropriately colored index card.

Students can use the cards to help them organize their essays. They might want to lay the index cards out on their desks and rearrange them to find the most effective order.

Students will practice choosing subjects, gathering information, writing thesis statements, and organizing information in either the block method or point-by-point method of organization when they complete **Writing Assignments: Parts 1–4.**

Ask students to hand in **Writing Assignments: Parts 1–4** together to be assessed holistically. You may want to use a scale from 1 to 3 and to write your suggestions for improvement. For example, if a student receives a rating of 2 for **Writing**

Cont. on p. 224

◆ INTEGRATING THE LANGUAGE ARTS

Literature Link. Ask students to apply the concept of needs and alternative solutions to conflicts they find in literary works. For example, they could state the conflict between the Danes and Grendel in *Beowulf* in terms of a need, and then they could suggest alternatives that would meet that need, including calling in Beowulf and his men. Ask individuals or small groups to select a literary work and create statements of needs and alternatives for at least one of the conflicts in the work.

Vocabulary Link. Suggest that students use conjunctive adverbs to flow smoothly from one focus to the other. Students might want to use such words as *however, moreover, nevertheless,* and *therefore.* Remind students that a semicolon is used between clauses joined by a conjunctive adverb.

222   *Writing to Inform*

Collecting Information About Criteria.

As you discuss alternatives with people, they will unconsciously apply criteria as they form opinions and make choices. You can find out what some of these criteria are by asking people to explain why they prefer one alternative to another. Make notes of these reasons; you'll use them later as you develop criteria to show why one alternative is superior to another.

The following chart shows how one writer gathered reasons for and against two ways to use undeveloped parkland as a recreation area for children, teenagers, and adults.

HERE'S HOW

POSSIBLE LAND USES	BUILD A PUBLIC SWIMMING POOL	BUILD BASKETBALL AND TENNIS COURTS
Reasons in favor	with lifeguard supervision, could be used by people of all ages a place to stay cool in summer no equipment necessary (besides suit and towel!) good way for neighbors to meet	cost of construction relatively low both sports quite popular can be used most of the year cost of maintenance low
Reasons against	cost of maintenance high could be used only in summer traffic and parked cars might be a nuisance to neighbors safety issues	would be used only by people who knew how to play and had the equipment not likely to be used by very young or very old night lights and noise might disturb neighbors players might not limit their length of play, thus keeping others from playing

TEACHING *DEVELOPING CRITERIA*

Ask students to list all of the factors they would take into consideration in shopping for a new or used car. Then, after students read the material in the **Critical Thinking** feature, have them organize their criteria. Ask students to make charts with the ☞

Prewriting **223**

WRITING ASSIGNMENT

PART 2:
Gathering Information

Now it's time to start gathering information for your feasibility report. You will probably have to do research and talk to several people about the need you've identified and the alternative solutions you want to explore. You might find it helpful to use a chart like the one on page 222. Allow one column for each alternative course of action you plan to consider in your report.

Establishing Criteria
You now have information on needs and alternative solutions, and you may have notes on why the people you've interviewed favor one alternative over another. You no doubt have assessed the pros and cons of the alternatives you're considering. Now it is time to analyze those reasons to discover the underlying criteria.

CRITICAL THINKING

Developing Criteria

Criteria (the singular form is *criterion*) are standards we use to evaluate, or make judgments. They are tools for judging whether a course of action is feasible. Feasibility criteria usually fit into four categories that answer the following questions:

1. *Will it work?* If our school adopts block scheduling, will it really improve academic performance? If our company installs a new computer system, will it succeed in making our word-processing department more efficient?
2. *Can we do it?* Do scheduling conflicts or other factors prohibit block scheduling? Can the wiring in our building support a new computer system?

MEETING individual NEEDS

LEP/ESL
General Strategies. If there are significant numbers of English-language learners with similar language and cultural backgrounds, allow the students to work together to come up with a need and alternatives. Then, ask them to develop criteria. When subject matter is relevant to personal interests and experiences, and when students are given the autonomy to explore information that has relevance to their daily lives, they are more likely to perform successfully.

CRITICAL THINKING
Analysis and Synthesis. Challenge students to apply the skills they have gained in this lesson to analyze a need of state, national, or international significance. They should find out about the issue by reading articles in newspapers and magazines or on the World Wide Web. Then, have them write a statement of need, propose several alternatives to meet that need, and develop criteria to evaluate the proposals.

four general categories of criteria as headings and to list under the appropriate heading the factors to consider when buying a car.

Assess students' comprehension by giving students a criterion, such as "The software should improve productivity," and by asking them to identify which of the general categories it fits into [Will it work?]. ⚡

Cont. from p. 222
Assignment: Part 1, you could give the following suggestions:

1. Choose a need that you know something about.
2. Choose a need that others recognize.
3. Need should be appropriate for audience.

---

3. ***Can we afford it?*** Can the cost of implementing block scheduling be covered by the school budget? How will our company pay for a new computer system?

4. ***Is it desirable?*** What might be the negative effects of block scheduling? Will having to learn a new computer system disrupt the work of our word-processing department so much that business will suffer?

⚡ CRITICAL THINKING EXERCISE:
Defining Criteria for an Issue

With two or three other students, discuss the following reasons for and against extending the school year; then, rank them in order of importance. Use your ranked list to develop four criteria for evaluating several alternative proposals to extend the school year. (One criterion might be that a proposal should maintain or improve academic performance.) Hint: You may decide that some of the reasons do *not* translate into viable criteria.

1. Students need time off to relax and spend with their families.
2. School buildings are idle too much of the time.
3. American students don't perform as well on some academic tests as do students in countries with longer school years.
4. The summer vacation is too long, and students get bored.
5. Voters may oppose the tax increases necessary to pay teachers and other school employees for extra work time.
6. A longer school year would enable teachers to cover more material in greater depth.
7. Community businesses that depend on having students as summer employees would object.
8. Parents would have to spend less money on day care for younger children.
9. Maintenance of school buildings would decline.
10. There is no proof that a longer school year is the most important reason why students from other countries sometimes outscore American students.

ANSWERS
Critical Thinking Exercise

Answers may vary. Here are some possibilities:

1. An extended school year should maintain or improve academic performance. [Will it work?]
2. An extended school year should occupy students' time with worthwhile activities. [Will it work?]
3. An extended school year should enable school facilities to be put to maximum use and still allow for necessary maintenance. [Can we do it?]
4. An extended school year should not be a significant economic burden on the community. [Can we afford it?]
5. An extended school year should not interfere with admissions to college or training programs. [Can we do it?]
6. An extended school year should satisfy the public's need for accountability. [Is it desirable?]

If students have difficulty developing workable alternatives to meet the need they identify, encourage them to interview people at school or in the community who may be in a position to have an opinion about the need. Tell students to ask these people what they would do to solve the problem.

Ask students to discuss the following questions:

1. What is the purpose of a feasibility report?
2. How does the audience of a feasibility report affect its contents? ■

WRITING ASSIGNMENT

PART 3:
Establishing Criteria for Your Report

Now it is time to develop criteria for evaluating the alternatives you plan to explore in your report. Brainstorm criteria that would be appropriate for your topic. Then, use the list of categories on pages 223–224 to create a list of three to five criteria.

Developing a Recommendation

Your criteria are the tools you'll use to evaluate the alternatives you've come up with. The main body of your feasibility report will consist of this evaluation; it will provide your readers with the information necessary to make an informed decision. Even though decision makers can draw their own conclusions based on your evaluation, they usually will want to know what your recommendation is. They know that, because you have considered the issues thoroughly, you are the person best qualified to answer the question, "What action should we take?"

Your recommendation should be stated in the introduction to your report and again in the conclusion. At this point, you can write a preliminary statement of your recommendation. (You may decide to rework it when you draft the actual feasibility report.) Here is an example of a recommendation statement made in the introduction to a feasibility report. Notice that the writer has also summarized how the recommended site meets the criteria.

COOPERATIVE LEARNING

Students can work on **Writing Assignment: Part 3** in groups of three or four. The groups can brainstorm to find criteria for each group member, and then the members can help one another to create their lists according to the categories on pp. 223–224.

HERE'S HOW

> To determine the best site for a new branch of DollarOne Savings, I have considered four sites: Rolling Hills, Fargo Branch, Essex, and Diver's Cove. Of these four sites, I recommend the first one, Rolling Hills. The Rolling Hills area includes a large population of potential customers; we can lease the necessary office space; the costs are reasonable; and a branch at that site is consistent with our corporate objectives.

MEETING *individual* NEEDS

LEARNING STYLES

Visual Learners. Draw a balance on the chalkboard. Explain to students that in the block method there must be relevant features for the first subject followed by relevant features for the second subject. Ask students to visually place the first subject and its information on one side of the balance and the second subject and its information on the other side of the balance. Explain to students that they should seek an equal amount of information for each subject. The image of the scale can also illustrate the point-by-point method.

Kinetic Learners. Have students copy their prewriting information on large pieces of poster board. Some students can use the posters for the block method, and other students can use the posters for the point-by-point method. Students should tape their relevant features to the correct posters in logical order. Students can easily rearrange their features as they work to complete this activity.

Organizing Information

After developing criteria and deciding on your recommendation, your next step is to arrange your information so that your evaluation is presented clearly to your readers. Here are two common ways to organize a feasibility report.

- The *block method.* With the block method, you evaluate the first alternative by all your criteria, then evaluate the second alternative by each criterion, and so on. If you use this method, which is more suitable for brief reports than for long ones, be sure to apply the criteria in the same order, when examining each alternative.
- The *point-by-point method.* With this method, you organize the report by criteria. You discuss each alternative as it relates to the first criterion, then each as it relates to the second criterion, and so on. This method works well with long reports, but be sure to present the alternatives in the same order for each criterion.

The chart that follows shows both methods. The subject is whether to build a swimming pool or basketball and tennis courts in a neighborhood park.

BLOCK METHOD	POINT-BY-POINT METHOD
Alternative 1: Swimming pool Criterion 1: Will it work? Criterion 2: Can we do it? Criterion 3: Can we afford it? Criterion 4: Is it desirable? **Alternative 2: Basketball/ tennis courts** Criterion 1: Will it work? Criterion 2: Can we do it? Criterion 3: Can we afford it? Criterion 4: Is it desirable?	**Criterion 1: Will it work?** Alternative 1: Swimming pool Alternative 2: Basketball/ tennis courts **Criterion 2: Can we do it?** Alternative 1: Swimming pool Alternative 2: Basketball/ tennis courts **Criterion 3: Can we afford it?** Alternative 1: Swimming pool Alternative 2: Basketball/ tennis courts **Criterion 4: Is it desirable?** Alternative 1: Swimming pool Alternative 2: Basketball/ tennis courts

Reminder

When you plan your feasibility report, you should

- identify a topic and a related need
- identify one or more alternatives, or ways of meeting that need
- determine criteria for judging the feasibility of alternatives
- apply your criteria, then decide which alternative you will recommend
- organize your information by using either the block method or the point-by-point method

---

WRITING ASSIGNMENT

PART 4:
Organizing Information

Now that you have established the criteria you'll use for evaluating feasibility, evaluate your alternatives, and decide which one you will recommend in your report. Then, organize your information according to the method—block or point-by-point—you plan to use in drafting your paper.

WRITING YOUR FIRST DRAFT

OBJECTIVES

- To analyze a feasibility report
- To write a first draft of a feasibility report

MOTIVATION

Ask students what causes them to lose the most time when they try to accomplish a task. Consider all the responses, but gradually help students realize that a lack of organization is probably the basic cause of their wasting time.

WRITING YOUR FIRST DRAFT

■ **Instructional Support** For help with organizing details in a paragraph, see **Writing** in *Strategies for Writing*, p. 17.

QUOTATION FOR THE DAY

"How many good books suffer neglect through the inefficiency of their beginnings!" (Edgar Allan Poe, 1809–1849, American short-story writer and poet)

Use the quotation to emphasize the importance of creating interesting introductions. You may want to ask students to share strategies for grabbing the readers' attention.

MEETING *individual* NEEDS

LEP/ESL

General Strategies. Before students begin the drafting process, meet with each student to monitor his or her progress. Conferring will allow you to review all notes that students have compiled. Be prepared to make recommendations. Students may need encouragement to convince them that they can successfully complete the assignment.

228

Writing Your First Draft

Once you have completed the prewriting stage for your feasibility report, you are ready to shape the results into your first draft. As you write, keep in mind that if you discover you need more information about one of the alternatives you are considering, you may have to go back and forth between the drafting and prewriting stages. This kind of movement is natural and will strengthen your report.

The Structure of a Feasibility Report

Your aim in a feasibility report is to present information about alternatives that meet a need. The most important quality of your writing is clarity, and the structure of your report can enhance this quality. Most feasibility reports consist of an introduction, a body, and a conclusion.

Introduction
- describes the need you have identified
- briefly describes any alternatives you considered but rejected
- identifies the one or two alternatives your report will evaluate
- makes a recommendation about which alternative is superior
- briefly summarizes how the recommended alternative meets criteria

Body
- explains the need in more detail, if necessary
- describes the criteria that will be used to evaluate each alternative
- evaluates alternatives according to each criterion

Conclusion
- brings the report to a clear, definite close
- restates the recommendation first stated in the introduction

If you need more information about structuring your report, review the material in the chapter **Understanding Composition Structure,** pages 99–121.

The feasibility report that follows evaluates a plan to expand a health-care network by building a new center. Before you read, scan the report's headings to see how the writers organized their presentation.

TEACHING THE LESSON

Read over both models with students first. Before students complete **Writing Assignment: Part 5** on p. 236, provide a sample report written by you or by a former student or a report obtained from another source. Place this report on a transparency and review it with the class. Call on students to help you annotate the report. ☞

A FEASIBILITY REPORT

INTRODUCTION

Need established

Alternative to be evaluated

1   Langer Healthcare Network has identified a need for a medical services center in the northern part of Marburger County. At present, our patients who live in this area have to travel a significant distance for comprehensive health-care service. This report evaluates a proposed facility, Langer North, which is intended to meet the needs of patients in northern Marburger County.

Recommendation

Recommendation

2   Based on our feasibility study, which is summarized below, we recommend proceeding with the Langer North project. Patient surveys suggest a strong demand for the facility. We have a suitable site on which to build and adequate funding for the project. The long-term projected financial return of the facility meets corporate standards. Finally, the ability of the Langer Healthcare Network to continue to be competitive with other health-care providers is dependent upon its ability to provide geographically accessible, high-quality services.

Documentation of Need

BODY
Explanation of need

3   In developing its health-care system, Langer has identified certain medical services that patients want to have close to where they live. Identified needs include a primary-care center; a rehabilitation and sports medicine center; a facility for minor surgery and other outpatient procedures; and office space for pediatricians, surgeons, and other specialists.

Criteria

We used the following criteria to evaluate the Langer North project.

Description of criteria

■ The center should meet the needs identified by network patients in northern Marburger County.
■ Construction must be practicable in light of zoning regulations, environmental restrictions, and other geologic and geographic factors.

USING THE SELECTION
A Feasibility Report

1
What does the opening sentence imply about the audience of this feasibility report? [It implies that the audience is familiar with the area and with the types of services the Langer Healthcare Network provides.]

2
The recommendation section in the introduction summarizes how the recommendation meets the criteria that are used in the report.

3
How does this paragraph expand the introduction? [It lists the specific patient needs Langer discovered in the development of its health-care system.]

4

What do these elements imply about the relationship of the new facility to a larger hospital? [The larger hospital would still be needed to serve patients with more severe medical problems than those that will be addressed at Langer North.]

5

Why might Langer have already purchased this land? [It may have foreseen the need for a new facility prior to the preparation of this report. A feasibility report prior to this one may have been written—one to purchase the land at the intersection of Highway 30 and Walker Road in the expectation of a growing need for and profitability in health-care facilities.]

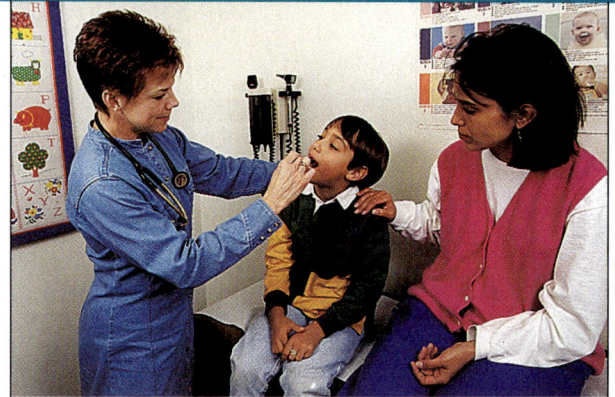

- Adequate funding for land purchase and construction must be available.
- The facility should be consistent with Langer Healthcare's overall goals and financial objectives.

Evaluation

Criterion 1

The Langer North plan was conceived to meet the identified needs of northern Marburger County patients. The current proposal includes the following elements.

4

(1) Physician offices. This space would include a family care center with family practice physicians, pediatricians, and other specialists

(2) Outpatient surgery and recovery center

(3) Outpatient rehabilitation, including a sports medicine facility

(4) Other services, including a pharmacy

Criterion 2   **5**

The facility will be located on fifteen acres of land that Langer already owns in the northeast quadrant of the intersection of Highway 30 and Walker Road. Plans are under way to create an option to purchase adjacent land to allow for the possible future expansion of the facility.

The land upon which Langer North is to be built is considered environmentally sensitive and thus must meet certain building restrictions with regard to geologic/geographic factors. Costs related to land developing and special zoning permits have been built into the total estimated construction costs.

Criterion 3

The total estimated cost of the project is $20,000,000, as detailed below.

Students might work independently on **Writing Assignment: Part 5** on p. 236 after they have examined **A Writer's Model** on pp. 232–235. Tell students to pay particular attention to the organization of their drafts. Point out that feasibility reports are different from other kinds of writing and that readers expect feasibility reports to follow a specific organizational plan. Call students' attention to the annotations in the two models as a guide for organizing their own reports.

☞

Writing Your First Draft   **231**

	Cost
Land	$3,000,000
Building	9,000,000
Professional Fees	1,000,000
Equipment	6,000,000
Administration/Other	1,000,000
Total	$20,000,000

Of the total project cost, it is expected that $5,000,000 will be from a capital building fund. The rest will be funded through a bond offering.

Criterion 4

6

The proposed Langer North center is consistent with the network's strategic goal of providing comprehensive health care to Marburger County patients. The center's estimated earnings are consistent with the network's financial goals: Projected financial statements show the facility achieving profitability in the sixth year of operation. Both net income and return on investment will meet or exceed the company's requirements.

Summary

CONCLUSION

To sustain itself as the medical provider of choice, Langer Healthcare Network must establish a significant physical presence in northern Marburger County. Since the proposed plan for Langer North meets all the criteria established for a network facility, we conclude that the risks of not undertaking this project outweigh the risks of proceeding. We therefore recommend proceeding with the Langer North project.

Restatement of recommendation

6

A bond offering is a way for a government or business to raise money. Such an organization issues the buyer (the bondholder) a certificate, or bond, and promises to return to the buyer the sum borrowed when the bond matures on a specific date. Most bonds pay interest as well as return the principal, the sum borrowed.

TECHNOLOGY TIP

Encourage students who have access to computers at home or at school to create bar graphs or pie charts to illustrate information they are presenting in their reports. Point out to students that a pie chart in the professional model could have shown readers the percentage of the total cost of the new health center that will be spent for each item in the list noted in Criterion 3. Remind students to use bar graphs and pie charts only where they will enhance understanding and illustrate important points for their audiences.

ASSESSMENT

Ask students to use margin notes to identify and label the following features in their papers: description of need and alternatives, recommendation, criteria, evaluation of alternatives by criteria, and restatement of recommendation.

CLOSURE

Conclude the lesson with a class discussion of the following question: What should each of the three basic parts of a feasibility report contain? Write responses on the chalkboard until the basic outline of the contents of the introduction, body, and conclusion has been filled in.

ANSWERS
Exercise 3

1. The report addresses a need for a new medical facility for primary-care and outpatient services.
2. Criterion 1: Will it work? Criterion 2: Can we do it? Criterion 3: Can we afford it? Criterion 4: Is it desirable? and Can we afford it?
3. Yes. The writer gives reasons for his or her evaluation with respect to each criterion.
4. The tone is serious and businesslike. Yes, the tone is appropriate.

MEETING *individual* NEEDS

LESS-ADVANCED STUDENTS

Have students use one color of ink or highlighter to mark the criteria they use, and a different color or highlighter to mark the reasons they give in support of the criteria.

EXERCISE 3 ▶ **Analyzing a Feasibility Report**

After reading the feasibility report on pages 229–231, think about how the report accomplishes its purpose. Then, with two or three classmates, discuss your answers to the following questions.

1. What is the need addressed in the report?
2. Review the criteria used to evaluate the feasibility of the new center. How do they correspond to the criteria guidelines listed on pages 223–224?
3. Does the writer adequately evaluate the proposed center according to each of the criteria?
4. What tone does the opening paragraph set for the feasibility report? Is the tone appropriate?

A Basic Framework for a Feasibility Report

The feasibility report on a proposed health-care center uses the block method of organization. That is, it evaluates the proposed course of action by each criterion. In the following feasibility report, the writer uses the point-by-point method by organizing the body of the report according to the four criteria. The writer evaluates each alternative with respect to the first criterion; then, to the second; and so on.

A WRITER'S MODEL

A Commons Area for Westbank High

INTRODUCTION

Need established

For the last several years, students at Westbank High School have expressed the need for a place where they can study, talk, and relax during periods when they are not in class. At present, students tend to congregate close to classrooms; as a result, students in class are distracted by the conversation and activity. Other places are outside, and so can't be used in cold or rainy weather. Since there is general agreement among students, teachers, and administrators

Writing Your First Draft   **233**

that the current situation is not satisfactory, the Student Council Special Projects Committee has decided to consider several courses of action.

Alternatives to be evaluated

Three options the committee has explored are (1) encouraging students to use the cafeteria during their free time; (2) allowing students to leave campus during the day; and (3) creating a commons area out of part of the old theater building.

Alternative dismissed

We rejected the first alternative because the cafeteria is off-limits to students during much of the day, when the staff is setting up for lunch.

Recommendation

Of the remaining two alternatives, the last one—creating a commons area on campus—is the best because it will work, we can do it, it is affordable, and it would be a desirable addition to our school.

Criteria

BODY

Creating a commons area on campus meets four criteria established by the Special Projects Committee.

Description of criteria

Any good plan must meet all of the following standards:

1. It has to be for a place on or near the school campus where students would opt to go during their free time.
2. It has to be possible and practical, and in keeping with school district policies.
3. It has to be affordable.
4. It has to result in an overall improvement in the school environment.

MEETING *individual* NEEDS

ADVANCED STUDENTS

Ask students to contact local businesses, industries, and public agencies to solicit copies of feasibility reports they may be willing to share. Ask students to analyze at least one of these reports to determine the extent to which the report follows the organizational pattern of a feasibility report described in this lesson.

Evaluation

Criterion 1

With respect to the first criterion, a commons area on the school grounds would be accessible to all students. If a commons area were created out of the old theater building's rehearsal hall and courtyard, it would be large enough to accommodate all students who wanted to use it; it would also combine the advantages of indoor and outdoor space. In a survey of over half the students in each grade, 80 percent said they would use a commons area at least once a week.

Allowing students to leave campus would meet the first criterion in that many students would take advantage of the option; but there are few, if any, restaurants or other businesses near campus that would allow students to spend time without making a purchase. Moreover, the closest places are a ten- to fifteen-minute walk from school—not easily accessible, in our view.

Criterion 2

On the question of whether creating a commons area is physically possible and in accord with district policies, the answer is yes. According to school administrators, there are currently no plans for the old theater building. Westbank High's buildings and grounds supervisor says the space could be converted into a commons area with a minimal amount of construction.

There are no district rules prohibiting a commons area. However, with regard to the alternative of leaving campus, district rules do prohibit anyone except seniors leaving during the school day. Consequently, this alternative does not meet the second criterion.

Criterion 3

With respect to affordability, a commons area would obviously require money for construction. According to Principal Daniel Price, next year's construction budget would cover the cost of creating a commons area. On the other hand, the option of allowing students to leave campus would not cost the school any money.

Criterion 4

With regard to the fourth criterion, the creation of a commons area would make Westbank

High School a better learning environment. If the school had such an area, students would not be inclined to congregate in the halls and near classrooms; as a result, hall congestion and classroom disruption would be reduced. Furthermore, a commons area would give students the opportunity to practice using their time responsibly—a necessary skill for college and adult life.

Allowing students to leave campus during the day, on the other hand, would probably not improve the school environment. It is likely that the parking lot would be congested at the beginning and end of each class period; in addition, the number of tardies would probably increase.

The only alternative that meets all four criteria is the creation of a commons area on school grounds. The following table shows how the two alternatives measure up against the four criteria.

CRITERION	CREATE A COMMONS AREA	ALLOW STUDENTS TO LEAVE CAMPUS
Can all students get to it, and will they use it?	Yes; yes	No; yes
Is it possible?	Yes	Not for all students
Is it affordable?	Yes	Yes
Will it improve the school environment?	Yes	No

Summary

CONCLUSION

Restatement of recommendation

The Student Council Special Projects Committee recommends that we create a commons area for Westbank High School. Although its construction will involve some cost, it is clearly superior to the other alternatives. A commons area will create a better learning environment for all students.

WRITING NOTE

Graphics—like the chart on page 235—are an effective way to present certain kinds of information. Consider using a chart, table, graph, or other visual when you need to summarize data or emphasize important points.

WRITING ASSIGNMENT

PART 5:
Writing a First Draft

Now you can make use of your careful planning and thinking as you attempt to get a rough draft down on paper. Use the information you have gathered as a guide, but don't let it be a straitjacket. For example, you may need to stop and look for more information, or you may decide to change or refine your criteria. It is important that you not be too critical at this point: Allow yourself the freedom to experiment a little.

OBJECTIVES

- To analyze a writer's revisions
- To evaluate and revise a feasibility report

MOTIVATION

Have students respond to the following questions:

1. What would newspapers be like if there were no editors?

2. How does evaluating and revising help the reader of an essay?

☜

Evaluating and Revising

If you saw an original manuscript by nearly any great writer, you'd probably be surprised. In most cases, you'd find it to be a mass of handwritten changes. An experienced writer is usually a careful self-editor.

But experienced writers also know that there are advantages to having someone else read and evaluate their work. They often ask professional editors, family members, or friends to evaluate their manuscripts. In the business world, it is not uncommon for supervisors to ask to see any written document that deals with important topics, and they often pass preliminary drafts around among several people for comments.

The chart on page 238 can help you, and anyone you have asked to evaluate your report, to be a better editor. The first step is to read over the report as objectively as possible, asking the evaluating questions in the left-hand column. If the answer to any question is no, try correcting the problem with the revision technique suggested in the right-hand column.

"*must you* cor*r*ect *every thing* i ~~said~~ *say?*"

By permission of George Dole.

PROGRAM MANAGER

EVALUATING AND REVISING

- **Reinforcement/Reteaching** See **Revision Transparencies 9** and **10.** For suggestions on how to tie the transparencies to instruction, review teacher's notes in *Fine Art and Instructional Transparencies for Writing,* p. 111.

- **Ongoing Assessment** For a rubric to guide assessment, see **Evaluating and Revising** in *Strategies for Writing,* p. 18.

- **Assessment/Reflection** To assess student work and evaluate progress, see **Portfolio Forms** in *Portfolio Assessment,* pp. 5–21.

QUOTATION FOR THE DAY

"We write frankly and freely, but then we 'modify' before we print." (Mark Twain, 1835–1910, American writer and humorist)

After sharing the quotation with students, ask them to consider Twain's use of the word *modify.* How might a piece of writing be altered in the evaluating and revising stage? Would the alteration or modification ever change the tone of the writing? Have students volunteer both positive and negative experiences they have had in the evaluating and revising stage of the writing process.

Use the edited paragraph from **A Writer's Model** on p. 239 to give students examples of adding, deleting, replacing, and reordering words. As students evaluate their reports by using the chart below, suggest that they work with only one revision strategy at a time to avoid overlooking any needed corrections.

Guide students through **Exercise 4** on p. 239, and point out where the author has made revisions. Ask students to analyze the excerpt carefully to see if they would make additional revisions.

MEETING *individual* NEEDS

LEP/ESL

General Strategies. The seventh entry in the **Evaluation Guide** suggests that students replace tentative or vague words, informal words, and emotional language. These instructions may prove frustrating for English-language learners. Many students bring limited vocabulary to an assignment that demands a broad vocabulary base. Students may need continual exposure to high-interest reading materials and correct models of the language (both oral and written forms). Additionally, students should have access to a thesaurus and should know how to use it effectively.

INTEGRATING THE LANGUAGE ARTS

Listening Link. Adapt **Writing Assignment: Part 6**, p. 239, to a listening activity. Rather than having students work in pairs, place students in groups of four to listen to each paper being read by its author. Students should take notes about suggested revisions. This activity will encourage students to listen attentively and will give them practice evaluating writing.

238

---

238   *Writing to Inform*

EVALUATING AND REVISING FEASIBILITY REPORTS

EVALUATION GUIDE	REVISION TECHNIQUE
1 Does the introduction contain a statement or an explanation of the need?	**Add** a statement that tells why the feasibility report was written.
2 Does the introduction contain a recommendation which is restated in the conclusion?	**Add** a recommendation statement at the beginning and end of the report.
3 Are criteria described early in the report?	**Add** information on criteria.
4 Is the body organized clearly?	**Reorder** the information in the body by moving sentences and paragraphs to follow block or point-by-point organization.
5 Are the relevant features (alternatives or criteria) discussed in the same order for each subject?	**Reorder** sentences so that the relevant features are discussed in the same order for each subject.
6 Is the conclusion definite, and does it restate the recommendation?	**Cut** needless sentences. **Add** sentences that restate or summarize the reasons for your recommendation.
7 Is the report's tone confident, objective, and somewhat formal?	**Replace** tentative or vague words with direct, specific words. **Replace** informal words and phrases with more formal language, and emotional language with objective language.

CLOSURE

Discuss the following questions with the class:

1. What revision technique did you use most frequently? How will you avoid having to use this technique in the future?

2. What are three ways that evaluating and revising improved your essay? ■

EXERCISE 4 ▶ **Analyzing a Writer's Revisions**

The original draft of the Writer's Model on pages 232–235 required some changes, as all first drafts do. Below is a revision of part of the introduction to that report. Study the writer's revisions, and then answer the questions that follow.

For the last several years, students at West-bank High School have expressed the need for a place where they can *(study, talk, and relax)* ~~hang out~~ during periods **replace**
when they are not in class. At present, students *(close to classrooms; as a result,)* tend to congregate. Students in class are dis- **add**
tracted by the conversation and activity. Other places are outside, and so can't be used ~~all the~~ *(in cold or rainy weather)* **replace**
~~time.~~ The Student Council Special Projects Com- **reorder**
mittee has decided to consider several courses of action. *(Since)* There is general agreement among **add**
students, teachers, and administrators that the current situation is not satisfactory. **add**

1. How does the revision in the first sentence affect the tone of the paragraph?

2. Why did the writer insert "close to classrooms; as a result" between the second and third sentences?

3. How did changing "all the time" to "in cold or rainy weather" improve the fourth sentence?

4. Why did the writer reorder the last two sentences?

WRITING ASSIGNMENT

PART 6:
Evaluating and Revising Your Feasibility Report

Evaluate your own essay, using the chart on page 238 for reference. What changes would strengthen your essay? Then, exchange papers with another student, and use the questions from the chart to evaluate his or her report.

ANSWERS
Exercise 4

1. The revision improves the formality of the tone, makes the ideas more appealing to the audience, and provides more specific information about how the commons area will be used.

2. The inserted clause explains why students in class are distracted.

3. The change makes the sentence more specific by stating precisely the times when outside locations can't be used.

4. The reordering makes explicit the cause-and-effect relationship between the present condition and the recommendation.

COOPERATIVE LEARNING
Students could peer edit in groups of four for **Writing Assignment: Part 6.** Ask students to answer the following questions for all papers:

1. What are two writing strengths and two writing weaknesses in this essay?

2. What solutions can you offer for the writing weaknesses?

3. Did the writer consistently conform to the organizational structure of a feasibility report?

PROOFREADING AND PUBLISHING

OBJECTIVE

- To proofread and publish a feasibility report

TEACHING THE LESSON

Ask students to brainstorm at least five common errors to watch for in proofreading an essay. Write responses on the chalkboard to remind students to check their reports for these errors.

Ask volunteers each to write a paragraph from their reports on the chalkboard.

PROGRAM MANAGER

PROOFREADING AND PUBLISHING

- **Instructional Support** For a chart students may use to evaluate their proofreading progress, see **Proofreading** in *Strategies for Writing,* p. 19.

- **Independent Practice/ Reteaching** For additional practice, see **Proofreading Practice: Using Transitions to Show Cause and Effect** in *Strategies for Writing,* p. 20.

- **Assessment/Reflection** To assess student work and evaluate progress, see **Portfolio Forms** in *Portfolio Assessment,* pp. 22–25.

QUOTATION FOR THE DAY

"How long a time lies in one little word!" (William Shakespeare, 1564–1616, English playwright and poet)

You may wish to use the quotation to discuss the proofreading and publishing stages of the writing process. Explain to students that once work is published, any errors that remain in the paper are subject to judgment by the reader. Challenge the class to use this stage of the writing process to polish their work and to share their informative essays with others.

Proofreading and Publishing

Proofreading.   You wouldn't think of going out on a date without taking one last look in the mirror before heading for the door; likewise, your feasibility report needs one last check. It is always important to look for mistakes in spelling, capitalization, punctuation, grammar, and usage. (See page 49 for **Guidelines for Proofreading**.)

GRAMMAR HINT

Using Transitions to Show Cause and Effect

Although transitional words and phrases are not unique to feasibility reports, you may have noticed several in the Professional Model and the Writer's Model.

> "We *therefore* recommend proceeding with the Langer North project."
> "Some of those areas are close to classrooms; as a *result,* students in class are distracted . . ."
> "*Since* there is general agreement among students, teachers, and administrators . . ."

These transitional expressions show cause and effect. These expressions, along with others such as "accordingly," "because," "for," and "so that," are frequently used in feasibility reports, because they help show the connection between information presented in a report and the conclusions drawn from that information.

> The company's incentive program increased carpooling by 30 percent; *consequently,* the program met the criterion of conserving scarce resources. *Because* of the test results summarized above, we recommend the new fire-resistant roof shingle over all other currently available types.

REFERENCE NOTE: For more information about transitional expressions, see pages 75–77, 686–687, and 928–929.

With the class, proofread the paragraphs for errors in spelling, capitalization, punctuation, grammar, and usage. Then, have students work independently to complete **Writing Assignment: Part 7**. You can then assess students' final drafts.

CLOSURE

First, ask students to describe the errors they have encountered while proofreading. Then, ask someone to explain why proofreading is an important part of the writing process. ∎

Publishing. Your feasibility report deals with a real need in your school, neighborhood, or community, and you wrote your report with a specific audience in mind. It's time to make your work available to your audience. Here are two ways you can publish your report.

- Submit your feasibility report to your school or community newspaper as a letter or an article. The newspaper staff may ask you to shorten the report or make other adjustments to it before they publish it.
- Deliver copies of your report to people who would be interested in your recommendation. Depending on what need you address, you may want to distribute copies to administrators, teachers, neighborhood or community committees, or city council members.

COMPUTER NOTE: If your school has an Internet Web site or electronic bulletin-board service, you may consider submitting your report to the webmaster or sysop for electronic distribution.

WRITING ASSIGNMENT

PART 7:
Proofreading and Publishing Your Feasibility Report

Read your report over carefully one last time, looking for any remaining errors in spelling, capitalization, punctuation, or usage. Be on the alert for words left out and for words used incorrectly (*there* for *they're*, for example). Make any necessary corrections, and create a final copy. Then, share your report with others, using one of the publishing ideas suggested above or an idea of your own.

Reflecting on Your Writing

Add your feasibility report to your **portfolio** by dating it and writing a brief reflection based on these questions.

- How did you identify the need you addressed?
- What was the greatest help in coming up with alternatives to meet your need?
- What steps should now be taken to implement the alternative you recommended?

MEETING *individual* NEEDS

LEP/ESL

General Strategies. One way to publish reports that would be advantageous for English-language learners is to have students privately record their reports on tape. On the same audiocassette, you should record the report as well in clear, standard speech. Ask students to listen carefully to compare the two versions and then to make written notes on any discrepancies in expression. They should then record a third and final version in which they correct their pronunciation. Check this final version and make appropriate suggestions for practice in areas that are particularly troublesome for students.

TEACHING NOTE

As students write reflections on their writing, remind them that they may be called upon to write feasibility reports at work, for extracurricular organizations, or for community services. The most difficult part of writing a feasibility report, but also the most important part, is coming up with alternatives to meet the needs they identify. Encourage students to be as specific and as precise as possible when they address the second question in **Reflecting on Your Writing**.

A STUDENT MODEL
Evaluation

1. Billie Jean's introduction describes the need in a concise statement.
2. The introduction also contains a recommendation, and Billie Jean refers to it in the second paragraph.
3. Billie Jean states the criteria in the second paragraph. Since this report is only the introduction, she would show how the proposed alternative meets these criteria later in the report.

A DIFFERENT APPROACH

If students are having difficulty proofreading their work, try working with students one-on-one or allowing students to work with peer tutors. For example, you could set up desks labeled *spelling, capitalization, punctuation, grammar,* and *usage.* Ask advanced students to sit at the desks and let students who are having problems consult the appropriate student.

TECHNOLOGY TIP

Have students use presentation software to create presentations based on the introductions to their feasibility reports. The presentation slides can include a summary outline of the contents of the introductions and clip art and other visual images to enhance the information students are presenting.

A STUDENT MODEL

Here is part of a feasibility report by Billie Jean Murray, from Moncks Corner High School in Moncks Corner, South Carolina. She felt that the most difficult thing about writing a feasibility report "was organizing the ideas to a concise form."

A Recycling Plan for the Workplace
by Billie Jean Murray

In the billing department of the company where I work, one hundred pounds of paper is discarded every week. Because we are conscious of the environmental problems with waste, my co-workers and I have tried to come up with a solution to this wastepaper problem. We considered two recycling alternatives to help our company do its part to help the environment. For both alternatives, trash receptacles for paper would be placed at each workstation. In the first alternative, the paper would be picked up once a week after work by people from the recycling center. They would charge $10 a week for this service. The center would then pay us for the paper. In the second alternative, an employee-volunteer from the billing department would collect and transport the paper once a week to the recycling center, and would collect the money.

After weighing the alternatives, we decided to recommend the second one because it meets the three criteria we believe a plan must meet:
1. The process must be convenient; it cannot interfere with business transactions.
2. The process must be affordable.
3. The results of the process must be favorable and beneficial.

WRITING WORKSHOP

OBJECTIVE

• To write an extended definition

MOTIVATION

Ask students to classify the following subjects into subgroups: pets, dogs, Dachshunds, parrots, Siamese cats. Explain that writing an extended definition requires being able to place parts of a subject into smaller and smaller categories.

☞

243

WRITING WORKSHOP

An Extended Definition

In your feasibility report, you used evaluation to inform: You identified alternatives and evaluated them in terms of specific criteria. Another way to inform is through classification. For example, you use classification when you define a word. First, you identify the general category the word belongs to (a *chore* is a type of job or work). Then, you identify its relationship to other words in the same category by examining characteristics that distinguish the word from those other words. (A *chore* is a type of job or work that's assigned to be done on a regular basis, especially around the home.)

An *extended definition* may begin with the basic definition of the word, or the writer may assume that readers already know the basic definition. The extended definition goes beyond the basic definition by adding details such as examples, facts, word origins, quotations, anecdotes, descriptions, and opinions. For example, following is an extended definition of *chores*. As you read, notice the kinds of details the writer uses to explain what chores are.

Doing Chores
by August Heckscher

I have been doing chores, being for a brief spell alone in a house that recently was astir with bustle and echoed with the voices of a gathered family. For those who may be in some doubt as to the nature of chores, their variety, their pleasures and their drudgery, I am prepared to deliver a short disquisition.

The first point about chores is that they are repetitive. They come every day or thereabouts, and once done they require after a certain time to be done again. In this regard a chore is the very opposite of a "happening"—that strange sort of event which a few years back was so much in fashion. For a happening was in essence unrepeatable; it came about in ways no one could predict, taking form from vaporous imaginings or sudden impulse. Chores, by

QUOTATION FOR THE DAY

"A definition is the enclosing a wilderness of idea within a wall of words." (Samuel Butler, 1835–1902, English novelist and scholar)

Ask students to freewrite about what they think Butler's quotation means. [Some students might say that once something is defined, imaginative powers are no longer necessary.]

MEETING *individual* NEEDS

LEP/ESL

General Strategies. Some students may need vocabulary assistance to comprehend "Doing Chores" fully. Write the following words on the chalkboard:

1. (for a brief) spell	**10.** dote on
2. bustle	**11.** spouse
3. disquisition	**12.** mundane
4. presumptuous	**13.** expeditious
5. evanescent	**14.** (the divine) muse
6. appease	**15.** domain
7. a stir	**16.** evoke
8. drudgery	**17.** insuperable
9. (the same small) round	**18.** devotee
	19. intersperse

Ask the class to volunteer definitions along with original sentences using the words in context. Students should enter the vocabulary words in their writing journals along with a definition and a simple sentence using each word in context.

Explain to students that an extended definition can be subjective because it can rely on personal anecdotes, descriptions, or opinions. Remind students that an extended definition must be written with the audience in mind and that an extended definition must serve a purpose.

Guide students through the professional model of extended definition. After students have finished reading, work with them to answer the questions that follow the essay. Then, develop a subject for an extended definition.

Students will work independently to complete extended definition essays by using the stages of the writing process.

USING THE SELECTION
Doing Chores

1

evanescent: tending to fade from sight, vanishing

2

obligatory: legally or morally binding

244

contrast, can be foreseen in advance; for better or worse, I know that tomorrow I must be re-enacting the same small round of ritualistic deeds; and they arise, moreover, from practical necessities, not from poetic flights.

A second point about chores is that they leave no visible mark of improvement or progress behind them. When I am finished, things will be precisely as they were before—except that the fires will have been set, the garbage disposed of, and the garden weeded. In this, they are different from the works which optimistically I undertake. Ozymandias may have been presumptuous, but he was essentially right when he looked about him and said: *"See how my works endure!"* A work, once achieved, leaves a mark upon the world; nothing is ever quite the same again. The page of a book may have been printed or a page of manuscript written; a sketch, a poem, a song composed; or perhaps some happy achievement reached in one of the more **1** evanescent art forms like the dance or cooking. All of these have an existence of their own, outside of time, and at least for a little while live on in the mind of their creator and perhaps a few of his friends.

For Better or For Worse copyright 1989 Lynn Johnston Productions, Inc. Reprinted with permission of Universal Press Syndicate. All rights reserved.

The well-meaning wife, seeing her husband about his chores, will miss the character of his performance. "Henry loves to cut wood," she will say; "he positively dotes on controlling the flow of waste from dinner-table to compost heap." The wife is perhaps trying to appease an unnecessary sense of guilt at seeing her spouse engaged in mundane efforts. The fact is, he doesn't love doing chores. But neither does he feel humiliated or out of sorts for having to do them. The nature of a chore is that it is neither pleasant nor unpleasant in itself; it is entirely neutral— **2** but it is obligatory.

Assess students' comprehension by examining the completed assignments. You may want students to summarize their extended definitions by having them draft outlines of the essays before they begin writing. If students choose to include these papers in their portfolios, have them attach reflections.

Ask volunteers to give a brief extended definition of one of the following subjects: *honor, fear, holidays,* or *teenagers.*

245

Neutral—and yet I must confess that with their repetition, and perhaps because of their very inconsequence, chores can in the end evoke a mild sort of satisfaction. Here, as in more heroic fields of endeavor, a certain basic craft asserts itself. To do what

3 must be done neatly, efficiently, expeditiously—"without rest and without haste"—lights a small fire deep in the interior being and puts a man in good humor with the world. Santayana de-

4 scribed leisure as "being at home among manageable things"; and if he was right we who are the chore-doers of the world are the true leisure classes. At least one can be sure that no chore

5 will defeat us; none will raise insuperable obstacles, or leave us deflated as when the divine muse abandons her devotee.

A man I know became seduced by the minor pleasure of doing chores—or at any rate by the absence of pain which they involve—and could be seen from morning till nightfall trotting about his small domain, putting everything in order, setting everything to rights that the slow process of time had disturbed. He was perhaps going too far. To season chores with work, and to intersperse them with a few happenings, is the secret of a contented existence. Fortunate the man or woman who achieves a just balance between these three types of activity—as I have been able to do by good chance, and for a little space of time.

3
expeditiously: speedily, promptly

4
Santayana, George (1863–1952) Spanish-born American philosopher and writer

5
insuperable: cannot be overcome or passed over, insurmountable

For Better or For Worse copyright 1989 Lynn Johnston Productions, Inc. Reprinted with permission of Universal Press Syndicate. All rights reserved.

1. In the second, third, fourth, and fifth paragraphs, the writer gives important characteristics of chores. What characteristic does he describe in each paragraph?
2. What do you think the writer means by "happenings" in the essay's second paragraph? by "work" in the third

ANSWERS
Writing Workshop Questions

1. second paragraph—chores are repetitive; third paragraph—chores do not make improvements or progress; fourth paragraph—a chore is neutral and obligatory; fifth paragraph—chores can lead to feelings of satisfaction

2. *Happenings* can be defined as "events that happen spontaneously." Works are tasks that leave a lasting impression, although *work* in the sixth paragraph describes a job to be done. Chores are different from "happenings" because chores are repetitive and "happenings" are exciting and spontaneous; chores are different from work because work leaves a lasting impression.

ENRICHMENT

Ask students to rewrite their extended definitions in poetic form. Students can begin their poems with the subject and the verbs *is* or *are.* For example, a poem might be titled "Honor is . . ." Encourage students to illustrate their extended definitions. ■

3. The writer uses anecdotes in the first and fourth paragraphs, explanation and opinion in the second paragraph, quotations in the third and fifth paragraphs, and example in the sixth paragraph.

4. Chores are described in a more general way. Rather than giving specific details about how to iron, do laundry, or straighten up, the author tells the reader why people do chores.

5. A definition in expressive or persuasive writing may use analogies or anecdotes to compare and contrast events that the writer has experienced with knowledge that the reader should have.

paragraph? According to the writer, how are chores different from "happenings"? from "work"?

3. What kinds of details (example, quotation, anecdote, and so on) does the writer use to extend the definition?

4. Informative writing should provide new information. In this piece, what information about chores is new to you or makes you see chores differently?

5. This writer uses a definition to inform. How might you use a definition to express yourself? to persuade?

Writing an Extended Definition

Prewriting. Choose an idea or term that interests you and that can't be easily defined in a single sentence. Here are some suggestions:

the ideal job	blues music	fun
true love	winning and losing	success
"street-smart"	fairness (justice)	adult

Think of examples, quotations, facts, anecdotes, comparisons, contrasts, or other kinds of details to extend the definition. Gather details from dictionaries, encyclopedias, magazines, or friends. Keep your audience in mind as you decide what information to use.

Writing, Evaluating, and Revising. In your first paragraph, write one or two sentences briefly identifying the general class to which the subject belongs and telling how it is different from other items in this general class. Then, extend your definition with the details (examples, quotations, facts, and so on) you have gathered. Since this is an essay, don't forget to include a concluding paragraph.

Exchange papers with a partner, and ask for comments. Is the definition informative? Have you provided enough specific details? Revise your essay as necessary.

Proofreading and Publishing. Proofread your paper to correct errors in spelling, grammar, usage, and punctuation. Then, get together with classmates to decide how to publish your essay—for example, by creating a dictionary of extended definitions. If you would like to add your essay to your **portfolio,** date it and write a brief reflection in response to this question: How did thinking about details shape your ideas about the term you defined?

TEACHING THE LESSON
Make sure students understand that a comparison/contrast essay can deal with similarities, with differences, or with both. Point out that while some comparison/contrast essays deal with subjects that are completely different from one another, most comparison/contrast essays deal with subjects ☞

WRITING WORKSHOP

247

QUOTATION FOR THE DAY
"Good order is the foundation of all things." (Edmund Burke, 1729–1797, British statesman, orator, and writer)
Share this quotation with your class and ask the students to discuss the relationship between order and classifying subjects, especially by comparing and contrasting them.

Writing a Comparison/Contrast Essay

Defining is just one way to classify information. Another way to present information is through *comparison/contrast*.

You make comparisons every day of your life. For example, you think about the plot, the actors, and the reviews you have read; and then you decide to see a Mel Gibson movie instead of a Tom Cruise movie. You have made your decision on the basis of comparisons and contrasts. Comparing and contrasting is a common thought process, so familiar that you hardly think about it; but it is a valuable technique for both decision making and writing.

When your purpose is to inform, comparison/contrast enables you to give your audience new information or a new way of looking at old information. For example, the differences between Ronald Reagan and Bill Clinton are obvious; but if you can point out some similarities between them, you may be able to help your audience perceive these two leaders in a new way.

In a comparison/contrast essay, you will be doing three things:

- examining two or more subjects
- pointing out relationships or patterns
- focusing on the subjects' similarities or differences or both

In the following excerpt, the writer is sharing information about an experience common to many Japanese Americans during World War II. Soon after the Japanese bombing of Pearl Harbor and the United States's entry into the war, more than 110,000 Japanese Americans were placed in internment camps. One of these camps, located in California, was called Manzanar. As you read, notice how the writers use the block method to contrast warm and loving mealtimes at home with the starkness of mealtimes in camp.

247

GUIDED PRACTICE

After students read the excerpt from *Farewell to Manzanar* and answer the questions that follow it, develop a subject as a model for a comparison/contrast essay. Provide enough details to include in the body of the essay.

USING THE SELECTION
from **Farewell to Manzanar**

1

Why do the writers give these details about the size of the table and the connection between the dining room and the kitchen? [The details emphasize the family unity of their meals before internment.]

2

What advantages does the seating arrangement have? [Since they are more likely to be interested in adult topics of conversation, the older children are seated closer to the parents. The younger children are seated at the table so the parents can keep an eye on them. The younger children can also interact with each other.]

3

Why don't the parents insist that all the children eat with them? [Answers will vary. Some students might say the parents want their children to be as happy as possible under the circumstances, so they don't try to interfere with the children's plans.]

248

from Farewell to Manzanar
by Jeanne Wakatsuki Houston and James D. Houston

1 Before Manzanar, mealtime had always been the center of our family scene. In camp, and afterward, I would often recall with deep yearning the old round wooden table in our dining room in Ocean Park, the biggest piece of furniture we owned, large enough to seat twelve or thirteen of us at once. A tall row of elegant, lathe-turned spindles separated this table from the kitchen, allowing talk to pass from one room to the other. Dinners were always noisy, and they were always abundant with great pots of boiled rice, platters of home-grown vegetables, fish Papa caught.

2 He would sit at the head of this table, with Mama next to him serving and the rest of us arranged around the edges according to age, down to where Kiyo and I sat, so far away from our parents, it seemed at the time, we had our own enclosed nook inside this world. The grownups would be talking down at their end, while we two played our secret games, making eyes at each other when Papa gave the order to begin to eat, racing with chopsticks to scrape the last grain from our rice bowls, eyeing Papa to see if he had noticed who won.

3 Now, in the mess halls, after a few weeks had passed, we stopped eating as a family. Mama tried to hold us together for a while, but it was hopeless. Granny was too feeble to walk across the block three times a day, especially during heavy weather, so May brought food to her in the barracks. My older brothers and sisters, meanwhile, began eating with their friends, or eating somewhere blocks away, in the hope of finding better food. The word would get around that the cook over in Block 22, say, really knew his stuff, and they would eat a few meals over there, to test the rumor. Camp authorities frowned on mess hall hopping and tried to stop it, but the good cooks liked it. They liked to see long lines outside their kitchens and would work overtime to attract a crowd. . . .

My own family, after three years of mess hall living, collapsed as an integrated unit. Whatever dignity or feeling of filial strength we may have known before December 1941 was lost, and we did not recover it until many years after the war, not until after Papa died and we began to come together, trying to fill the vacuum his passing left in all our lives.

INDEPENDENT PRACTICE
Students can work in pairs or on their own to develop their essays. You might want to consider having students create outlines to help them organize their essays.

ASSESSMENT
Examine students' completed essays to determine if students understand the process of comparison/contrast.

1. Before the war, the family ate together as a unit. How does this behavior at mealtime contrast with mealtimes in the camp? How does it compare with what happened after the family left the camp?

2. Why do you think the writers chose the block method rather than the point-by-point method for organizing their material? How does this method help to stress the writers' main point?

Writing a Comparison/Contrast Essay

Prewriting. Choose subjects to write about that lend themselves to comparison/contrast. You might use the following criteria to help you select subjects.

- The two subjects should have something in common. For example, Japanese and Chinese porcelain are both Asian, and they are both types of ceramics.
- The two subjects should have some significant differences. There is no point in comparing two identical subjects.
- Your subjects should interest you.
- Information about your subjects should be fairly accessible.

You may already know enough about some subjects to write without further research. Perhaps you will just need to do a little brainstorming or freewriting to start your thinking. For subjects that are not as familiar, you will need to look for additional information. Remember to restrict the information you provide to what is relevant to your subject.

ANSWERS
Writing Workshop Questions

1. Before internment, family meals are the center of family life. Family members communicate and interact, and the children can be near their parents. At the camp, the family splinters and stops eating together. As a consequence, the family can no longer maintain the closeness and support that it once had. After the camp, it takes a long time for the family to regain its sense of unity.

2. The block method helps the writers set the tone by describing an idyllic time followed by a period of unwelcome change. This method helps to stress the writers' main point by showing how life was before internment. This information is necessary to understand the profound and lasting destruction of the family unit after internment.

SELECTION AMENDMENT
Description of change: excerpted
Rationale: to focus on the concept of writing a comparison/contrast essay presented in this chapter

CLOSURE

Close this lesson by discussing the following questions as a class:

1. Why should the subjects have something in common, yet have significant differences?

2. Why should the paper have a straightforward introduction, body, and conclusion?

3. Did you choose the point-by-point method or the block method for your paper? Why did you choose that particular method? ■

MEETING *individual* NEEDS

LEARNING STYLES

Visual Learners. Have students use two different colors of ink or two highlighters to mark the two subjects they are addressing. For example, if students are using the point-by-point method of organization, they should highlight information for subject 1 of feature 1 in a given color and subject 2 of feature 1 in another color. This activity will allow students to differentiate information and will reinforce the organizational format.

Your essay may focus on similarities, differences, or both. The thesis statement, which is usually a one- or two-sentence summary of your main idea, should indicate that focus. (For more information about the thesis statement, see pages 100–101.)

As a last step in planning your paper, organize your information so that patterns and relationships are clear for your readers. Most comparison/contrast papers are organized by either the block method or the point-by-point method.

Writing, Evaluating, and Revising. To help readers follow your ideas, your essay should have a fairly straightforward introduction, body, and conclusion. When you have finished your first draft, exchange papers with a classmate and ask for comments. Is the main idea clear? Is the body well organized? Does the essay have enough specific, relevant information? Revise your essay to clarify ideas and add information.

Proofreading and Publishing. Proofread your paper for mistakes in spelling, usage, and mechanics, and make a clean copy of it. If you choose to add your essay to your **portfolio,** include a reflection on your work that briefly describes the most difficult aspect of writing a comparison/contrast essay. Be sure to date your reflection.

· APPLES and ORANGES ·

EDIBLE
WARM COLOR
ROUND SHAPE
SIMILAR SIZE
CONTAIN SEEDS
GROW ON TREES
GOOD FOR JUICE
NAMES BEGIN WITH VOWEL
SIMILAR PESTICIDE TREATMENT
UNSUITABLE FOR MOST SPORTS

Drawing by Jonik; © 1991 The New Yorker Magazine, Inc.

USING ANALOGY
OBJECTIVE

- To write an analogy

251

MAKING CONNECTIONS

cross CURRICULUM

TEST TAKING

Using Analogy

An *analogy* is a special kind of comparison—it points out the similarities between two basically unlike subjects. You can often create an analogy which will explain a complex subject by comparing it with something familiar. To explain how the human heart works, for example, you might compare it with a pump.

How is voting like taking an exam? That's the analogy used in the following introduction to an essay about voting.

> Voting is much like taking an important exam. Both require preparation, and both can have long-lasting effects. Pulling just any lever or punching any hole is as foolish as randomly marking every answer on a test. Chances are that you'll make more bad decisions than good ones. It's just as important to study the candidates and their positions on issues as it is to learn the material that will be covered on a test. It's even better if you've been actively involved in both processes all along so that you don't make last-minute decisions. More than one election has been won or lost by just one vote, just as tests have been passed or failed by a single point.

Try writing a paragraph using analogy to explain a complex idea or subject. You might want to adopt one of the following suggestions or think up two subjects of your own. Just be certain that the subjects are basically not similar, but share enough characteristics to make the analogy meaningful.

1. first date—first day of school
2. army ants—human army
3. the game of chess—war
4. green plant during photosynthesis—a factory
5. running a marathon—baby-sitting a two-year-old for a day

USING ANALOGY
Teaching Strategies

Explain to students that analogies are also used in everyday conversation to explain information. For example, explaining that the body is like a machine will help people understand why good nutrition is important. You may want to ask students to think of three analogies they have read, heard, or used recently to share with the class.

As they are writing analogies, suggest that students form visual images of the subjects being compared. For example, students might benefit from visualizing an army of ants and a human army.

GUIDELINES

Assign grades based on the complexity of the analogy, its degree of creativity, and the amount of effort it required.

Chapter 7

WRITING TO EXPLAIN: EXPOSITION

OBJECTIVES

- To choose a subject for a cause-and-effect essay
- To identify causes and effects about a topic and to gather supporting information and evidence
- To formulate a thesis statement, to create an organizational map, and to write a draft of a cause-and-effect essay
- To evaluate, revise, proofread, and publish a draft of a cause-and-effect essay

WRITING-IN-PROGRESS ASSIGNMENTS

Major Assignment: Writing a cause-and-effect essay

Cumulative Writing Assignments: The chart below shows the sequence of cumulative assignments that will guide students as they write a cause-and-effect essay. These Writing Assignments form the instructional core of Chapter 7.

PREWRITING

WRITING ASSIGNMENT
- Part 1: Choosing a Topic p. 259
- Part 2: Planning Your Cause-and-Effect Explanation p. 265
- Part 3: Organizing Your Information p. 267

WRITING YOUR FIRST DRAFT

WRITING ASSIGNMENT
- Part 4: Writing Your First Draft p. 278

EVALUATING AND REVISING

WRITING ASSIGNMENT
- Part 5: Evaluating and Revising Your Essay p. 280

PROOFREADING AND PUBLISHING

WRITING ASSIGNMENT
- Part 6: Proofreading and Publishing Your Essay p. 283

In addition, exercises 1–3 provide practice in speaking and listening, analyzing a cause-and-effect essay, and analyzing revisions.

cross CURRICULUM

Causes, Effects, Chemistry, and Television

So that students can see that cause-and-effect relationships are also important in chemistry, allow your students to focus their cause-and-effect writing on the properties of solutions that contain ions.

- **Assignment** Have students work in groups to write a script for a science segment of a television news show that explains the effects that an imbalance of electrolytes and electrolytic solutions in the body has on the functioning of nerves and muscles.

- **Prewriting** Students can use much of the prewriting instruction on pp. 260–267 of this chapter. To generate ideas and information, students should interview the chemistry teacher at school for suggestions on where to start their research. Chemistry textbooks and books and articles on physiology and sports medicine are good resources. If possible, have students talk to medical doctors and nutritionists and use the Internet to find information.

- **Writing** Refer students to the graphic organizers on pp. 265–267 for suggestions on organizing their information. Because understanding complex chemical processes can be difficult, encourage students to include diagrams to illustrate their explanations.

- **Presenting** Students will need to work out details on how they will present their scripts—who speaks first, who plays what roles, and so forth. Remind students to credit their sources at the end of the presentation to show the audience where they got their information. You may want to videotape these presentations to show to other classes.

INTEGRATING THE LANGUAGE ARTS

SELECTION	READING AND LITERATURE	WRITING AND CRITICAL THINKING	LANGUAGE AND SYNTAX	SPEAKING, LISTENING, AND OTHER EXPRESSION SKILLS
• "Why the Owl Has Big Eyes" pp. 254–255 • "Darkness at Noon" pp. 269–272 • from *Jane Brody's "The New York Times" Guide to Personal Health* pp. 285–286 • from "**Gaining on Fat**" p. 289	• Reading for specific details pp. 256, 272, 286 • Analyzing the effects of repetition p. 256 • Responding personally to literature pp. 256, 272 • Evaluating a cause-and-effect essay p. 272 • Identifying supporting evidence pp. 277, 286 • Identifying the main idea p. 272 • Analyzing a process explanation p. 287	• Analyzing repetition p. 256 • Making inferences and drawing conclusions pp. 256, 259, 264–265, 267, 272, 279 • Brainstorming a topic pp. 259, 286 • Organizing information pp. 267, 287, 289 • Analyzing a cause-and-effect essay pp. 272, 280 • Analyzing the validity of generalizations pp. 277–278 • Analyzing and writing a process explanation pp. 286–287 • Writing a scientific cause-and-effect report p. 289	• Proofreading for errors in grammar, usage, and mechanics pp. 283, 287 • Using transitional words and phrases p. 287 • Using library resources to research a topic p. 289	• Working with classmates to gather and discuss information about causes and effects pp. 264–265 • Working with classmates to analyze the validity of generalizations pp. 277–278 • Working with classmates to analyze a writer's revisions p. 279 • Working with classmates to create a process encyclopedia p. 287 • Working with classmates to research, write, and present an oral report p. 289

SUGGESTED INTEGRATED UNIT PLAN

This unit plan gives suggestions on how to integrate the major strands of the language arts with this chapter.

The suggested literary selections are fiction and nonfiction examples of writings that illustrate, in some way, cause-and-effect relationships. The fictional pieces listed below will not contain all the common characteristics. If you begin with this chapter on writing a cause-and-effect essay or with the suggested selections, you should focus on the common characteristics of cause-and-effect essay. You can then integrate speaking/listening and language concepts with both the writing and the literature.

Common Characteristics

- Content that is comprehensive
- Precise language
- Documentation of facts or events
- Use of third person for objectivity or use of first person for authenticity of experience or observation
- Organization of ideas or examples usually from least to most important

Writing
Cause-and-Effect Essay

Speaking/Listening
- Presenting an oral report
- Thinking aloud in groups

UNIT FOCUS
NONFICTION: CAUSE AND EFFECT

Language
Grammar and Usage
- Subordinate clauses
- Verb tense
- Active voice and passive voice

Literature
Selections such as
- "Old English: Where English Came From" John Algeo
- "The First Day of the Great Fire of London" Samuel Pepys
- from *A Journal of the Plague Year* Daniel Defoe

CHAPTER 7: WRITING TO EXPLAIN: EXPOSITION

Use this guide for creating an instructional plan that addresses the individual needs of your students. Assignments accompanied by the following symbol (*) may be completed out of class. Times given for pacing lessons are estimated.

CHAPTER PLANNING GUIDE—PUPIL'S EDITION

LESSONS	LITERARY MODEL "Why the Owl Has Big Eyes" pp. 254–255	PREWRITING pp. 258–267	
		Generating Ideas	Gathering/Organizing
DEVELOPMENTAL PROGRAM	🕐 **20–25 minutes** • Read model aloud and have students discuss in pairs questions on p. 256	🕐 **40–45 minutes** • Main Assignment: Looking Ahead p. 257 • Considering Topic, Purpose, and Audience pp. 258–259 • Writing Note p. 259 • Writing Assignment: Part 1 p. 259	🕐 **55–60 minutes** • Planning a Cause-and-Effect Explanation pp. 260–267 • Exercise 1 pp. 264–265 • Writing Assignment: Parts 2, 3 pp. 265, 267
CORE PROGRAM	🕐 **15–20 minutes** • Have students read the model aloud to partners and answer questions on p. 256	🕐 **30–35 minutes** • Main Assignment: Looking Ahead p. 257 • Considering Topic, Purpose, and Audience pp. 258–259 • Writing Note p. 259 • Writing Assignment: Part 1 p. 259	🕐 **40–45 minutes** • Planning a Cause-and-Effect Explanation pp. 260–267 • Exercise 1 pp. 264–265 • Writing Assignment: Parts 2, 3 pp. 265, 267*
ACCELERATED PROGRAM	🕐 **15 minutes** • Assign students to read model independently and take notes in Reader's Logs	🕐 **25–30 minutes** • Main Assignment: Looking Ahead p. 257 • Purpose and Audience p. 259 • Writing Assignment: Part 1 p. 259*	🕐 **30–35 minutes** • Reminder p. 264 • Exercise 1 pp. 264–265 • Writing Assignment: Part 2 p. 265* • Organizing Information pp. 265–267 • Writing Assignment: Part 3 p. 267*

CHAPTER PLANNING GUIDE—PROGRAM RESOURCES

	LITERARY MODEL	PREWRITING
PRINT	• Reading Master 7, *Practice for Assessment in Reading, Vocabulary, and Spelling* p. 7	• Prewriting, *Strategies for Writing* p. 23
MEDIA	• Fine Art Transparency 4, *Transparency Binder* 📠	• Graphic Organizers 11–12, *Transparency Binder* 📠 • *Writer's Workshop 2:* Cause and Effect 💾 📠

WRITING pp. 268–278	EVALUATING AND REVISING pp. 279–281	PROOFREADING AND PUBLISHING pp. 282–284
🕐 **45–50 minutes** • The Structure of an Explanation p. 268 • Framework p. 272 • A Writer's Model pp. 273–275 • Framework Chart p. 275 • Writing Assignment: Part 4 p. 278*	🕐 **45–50 minutes** • Evaluating and Revising p. 279 • Exercise 3 in pairs p. 279 • Writing Assignment: Part 5 p. 280 • Evaluating and Revising Chart p. 281	🕐 **35–40 minutes** • Proofreading/Publishing pp. 282, 283 • Grammar Hint pp. 282–283 • Writing Assignment: Part 6 p. 283 • Reflecting on Your Writing p. 283 • A Student Model p. 284
🕐 **40–45 minutes** • The Structure of an Explanation p. 268 • An Essay pp. 269–272* • Exercise 2 p. 272* • Framework p. 272 • Framework Chart p. 275 • Critical Thinking pp. 276–278 • Writing Assignment: Part 4 p. 278*	🕐 **40–45 minutes** • Evaluating and Revising p. 279 • Exercise 3 p. 279* • Writing Assignment: Part 5 p. 280 • Evaluating and Revising Chart p. 281	🕐 **25–30 minutes** • Proofreading/Publishing pp. 282, 283 • Grammar Hint pp. 282–283 • Writing Assignment: Part 6 p. 283 • Reflecting on Your Writing p. 283 • A Student Model p. 284*
🕐 **30–35 minutes** • The Structure of an Explanation p. 268 • An Essay pp. 269–272* • Framework p. 272 • Framework Chart p. 275 • Critical Thinking pp. 276–278 • Writing Assignment: Part 4 p. 278*	🕐 **30–35 minutes** • Exercise 3 p. 279* • Writing Assignment: Part 5 p. 280 • Evaluating and Revising Chart p. 281	🕐 **20–25 minutes** • Grammar Hint pp. 282–283 • Writing Assignment: Part 6 p. 283 • Reflecting on Your Writing p. 283

WRITING	EVALUATING AND REVISING	PROOFREADING AND PUBLISHING
• Writing, *Strategies for Writing* p. 24	• Evaluating and Revising, *Strategies for Writing* p. 25	• Proofreading Practice, *Strategies for Writing* p. 27
	• Revision Transparencies 11–12, *Transparency Binder* 📽	• *Language Workshop:* Lessons 10, 12 💾

ELEMENTS OF WRITING: CURRICULUM CONNECTIONS

Writing Workshop
• A Process Explanation pp. 285–287

Making Connections
• Using Cause and Effect in Persuasion p. 288
• Cause and Effect in Science p. 288

ASSESSMENT OPTIONS

Summative Assessment
Holistic Scoring: Prompts and Models pp. 21–26

Portfolio Assessment
Portfolio forms, *Portfolio Assessment* pp. 5–25, 44–48

Reflection
Writing Process Log, *Strategies for Writing* p. 22
Self-assessment Record, *Portfolio Assessment* p. 19

Ongoing Assessment
Proofreading, *Strategies for Writing* p. 26

Performance Assessment
Assessment 2, *Integrated Performance Assessment, Level G* For help with evaluation, see *Holistic Scoring Software.* 💾

💾 Computer disk or CD–ROM

📽 Overhead transparencies

MAKING THINGS CLEAR

OBJECTIVES

- To complete a writing journal entry
- To compare examples of myths
- To evaluate and analyze a literary model

TEACHING THE LESSON

You may want to have a volunteer read the introductory paragraphs aloud to give the class an overview of the material in this chapter. Because these paragraphs send students' thoughts in many directions, you could expand on the **As You Read** paragraph to focus students' attention.

PROGRAM MANAGER

CHAPTER 7

- **Computer Guided Instruction** For a related assignment that students may use for additional instruction and practice, see **Cause and Effect** in *Writer's Workshop 2 CD-ROM.*

- **Summative Assessment** For a writing prompt, including grading criteria and student models, see *Holistic Scoring: Prompts and Models,* pp. 21–26.

- **Performance Assessment** Use **Assessment 2** in *Integrated Performance Assessment, Level G.* For help with evaluating student writing, see *Holistic Scoring Workshop, Level G.*

- **Extension/Enrichment** See **Fine Art Transparency 4,** *For Ishmael Tiller: The Ledgy Rocks* by David Blackwood. For suggestions on how to tie the transparency to instruction, review teacher's notes in *Fine Art and Instructional Transparencies for Writing,* p. 21.

- **Reading Support** For help with the reading selection, pp. 254–255, see **Reading Master 7** in *Practice for Assessment in Reading, Vocabulary, and Spelling,* p. 7.

7 WRITING TO EXPLAIN: EXPOSITION

Have students read the selection independently first. Then, use your annotations to guide students by emphasizing the important points in the myth. Help students answer the **Writer's Craft** questions. Then, have students independently write responses to the **Reader's Response** questions.

SEQUENCE OF EVENTS

1. (lower right) The acrobat on stilts balances on a catapult using a pole handed to him by an assistant.
2. (lower right corner) Two men leap from a platform onto the catapult, propelling the acrobat on stilts high into the air.
3. (center) The acrobat, still wearing the stilts, does a somersault in the air.
4. (lower left) The acrobat lands, balanced on his stilts, which bow slightly from the impact.

Making Things Clear

Why has the grizzly bear become almost extinct? How will you be affected by attending a small college? a large university? Questions like these abound in your everyday life. In an attempt to **make things clear,** you look for explanations. "A huge star collapses into itself and causes a black hole." "Serious bone changes can result from a lack of vitamin D, produced by sunlight."

Writing and You. Writers often try to explain things. An environmentalist explains the effects of the 1989 *Valdez* oil spill in Alaska. A reporter for the school newspaper explains why a school policy has been changed. What questions do you have that explanations might make clear?

As You Read. In prescientific ages, people sought explanations for natural phenomena from folk tales and myths. What explanation does the following Native American myth give for the characteristics of the rabbit and the owl?

Dr. Harold E. Edgerton, *Moscow Circus* (1963). Photograph. © The Harold E. Edgerton 1996 Trust. Courtesy of Palm Press, Inc., Concord, Massachusetts.

VISUAL CONNECTIONS
Moscow Circus

About the Artist. Dr. Harold Edgerton, an Institute Professor at M.I.T., invented the stroboscopic flash in the early 1930s. His invention revolutionized photography by making possible stop-motion photographs and slow-motion cinematography. Dr. Edgerton also invented flash equipment used in night aerial photography, in deep-sea photography, and in sonar equipment.

QUOTATION FOR THE DAY

"How do I know what I think until I see what I say?" (E. M. Forster, 1879–1970, English novelist)

Write the quotation on the chalkboard and ask each student to write a restatement of the quotation and to explain how the quotation might relate to writing.

MEETING individual NEEDS

LEP/ESL

General Strategies. As often as possible, create a link between the literature being presented and students' daily reality. Use the three themes featured in this story that relate to the human condition: anger (the Everything-Maker), fear (Rabbit), and disobedience (Owl). Have students produce brief writing journal entries that each describe a recent event in which anger, fear, or disobedience affected the student personally.

WHY THE OWL HAS BIG EYES

**An Iroquois Myth
retold by Richard Erdoes
and Alfonso Ortiz**

▼▼▼

"I want nice long legs
and long ears
like a deer,
and sharp fangs and claws
like a panther."

▼▼▼

1 Raweno, the Everything-Maker, was busy creating various animals. He was working on Rabbit, and Rabbit was saying: "I want nice long legs and long ears like a deer, and sharp fangs and claws like a panther."

"I do them up the way they want to be; I give them what they ask for," said Raweno. He was working on Rabbit's hind legs, making them long, the way Rabbit had ordered.

Owl, still unformed, was sitting on a tree nearby and waiting his turn. **2** He was saying: "Whoo, whoo, I want a nice long neck like Swan's, and beautiful red feathers like Cardinal's, and a nice long beak like Egret's, and a nice crown of plumes like Heron's. I want you to make me into the most beautiful, the fastest, the most wonderful of all the birds."

Raweno said: "Be quiet. Turn around and look in another direction. Even better, close your eyes. Don't you know that no one is allowed to watch me work?" Raweno was just then making Rabbit's ears very long, the way Rabbit wanted them.

Owl refused to do what Raweno said. "Whoo, whoo," he replied, "nobody can forbid me to watch. Nobody can order me to close my eyes. I like watching you, and watch I will."

ENRICHMENT
Have each student choose a scientific occurrence and write a myth to explain this occurrence. ∎

Then Raweno became angry. He grabbed Owl, pulling him down from his branch, stuffing his head deep into his body, shaking him until his eyes grew big with fright, pulling at his ears until they were sticking up at both sides of his head.

"There," said Raweno, "that'll teach you. Now you won't be able to crane your neck to watch things you shouldn't watch. Now you have big ears to listen when someone tells you what not to do. Now you have big eyes—but not so big that you can watch me, because you'll be awake only at night, and I work by day. And your feathers won't be red like cardinal's, but gray like this"—and Raweno rubbed Owl all over with mud—"as punishment for your disobedience." So Owl flew off, pouting: "Whoo, whoo, whoo."

Then Raweno turned back to finish Rabbit, but Rabbit had been so terrified by Raweno's anger, even though it was not directed at him, that he ran off half done. As a consequence, only Rabbit's hind legs are long, and he has to hop about instead of walking and running. Also, because he took fright then, Rabbit has remained afraid of most everything, and he never got the claws and fangs he asked for in order to defend himself. Had he not run away then, Rabbit would have been an altogether different animal.

3   As for Owl, he remained as Raweno had shaped him in anger—with big eyes, a short neck, and ears sticking up on the sides of his head. On top of everything, he has to sleep during the day and come out only at night.

"... I want a nice long neck like Swan's, and beautiful red feathers like Cardinal's, and a nice long beak like Egret's, and a nice crown of plumes like Heron's."
▼ ▼ ▼

3   Other creation stories include tales of disobedience and punishment; see Genesis 1–3.

ANSWERS

Reader's Response

Answers may vary.

1. Students' lists should include specific puzzling natural phenomena or even queries.

2. Students may be familiar with other Greek myths. They may also suggest myths from other cultures—American Indian, Asian. The myths should be explanatory, and each should focus on a natural phenomenon.

Writer's Craft

3. Rabbit has long ears and long hind legs, and he is perpetually fearful.

4. The results are that Owl has no neck, big eyes, ears that stick out, and nocturnal habits. Some students may think that the reiteration sums up the selection nicely. Others may think it an unnecessary addition.

5. Students might find that this particular myth focuses on the importance of a creator figure. Others may see this myth as an indication that the Iroquois culture gains a spiritual understanding of the world through an examination of nature.

READER'S RESPONSE

1. Folk tales and myths were created by people who wanted an explanation for natural phenomena they had observed. Modern science has provided many explanations, but many phenomena are still unexplained. In your journal, make a list of natural phenomena you would like to have explained.

2. What are some other myths that explain natural phenomena? For example, how does the Greek myth of Apollo driving his golden chariot explain the rising and setting of the sun? How does the myth of Demeter and Persephone explain the seasons?

WRITER'S CRAFT

3. What physical attributes of rabbits does this myth attempt to explain?

4. What were the effects of Everything-Maker's anger? The writers explain these effects twice. How does the repetition strengthen— or weaken—the telling of the story?

5. You may think of myths and folk tales as children's stories; but, in fact, they are generally stories created by adults for adults. As such, they reveal a great deal about the culture in which they originated. What does "Why the Owl Has Big Eyes" tell you about the Iroquois culture?

⟶ LESSON 2 *(p. 257)*
WAYS TO EXPLAIN
TEACHING THE LESSON
Students may not be clear on the distinction between explanatory and informative writing. Before beginning this lesson, read aloud the **Writing Note** on p. 259. Give additional examples to illustrate how writing with the same purpose might be different.

Assess students' understanding by asking them to use textbooks from other classes to identify examples of explanatory writing. ■

257

Ways to Explain

The preceding myth uses narration to explain how things happen, or change, over time. When you are writing to explain, you may also use description, classification, or evaluation to make your message clear. Here are some examples of ways to write to explain.

- in a history paper, recounting the causes of the Civil War
- in a written apology, explaining why your team was two hours late for a swimming meet
- in a research report, describing Finnish folk customs and how they are sustained today
- in a novel, describing the village a character lives in and how her environment affects her actions
- in a magazine article, defining the term *search engine* and using examples and facts to differentiate between types of search engines
- in a children's book, explaining the attributes of different kinds of sharks and using details to illustrate their differences
- in a letter, defending your choice of a new career to your parents and providing data to show that your reasoning is sound
- in a review, giving your opinion about a movie and backing it up with examples
- in a grant proposal, explaining the goals of a proposed mural project and how the grant would enable you to accomplish the project

LOOKING AHEAD

In the main assignment in this chapter, you will use narration in an essay to explain causes and/or effects. As you work, keep in mind that a cause-and-effect explanation

- focuses on a particular situation or event
- provides an answer to one or both of these questions: Why did it happen? (What caused it?) What were the effects?
- gives evidence to support the explanation

⟳ A DIFFERENT APPROACH
Students may be confused about the different types of expository writing. You could recreate the following diagram on the chalkboard to illustrate how writing to inform, writing to explain, and writing to explore are all related. You could then take a topic and describe how it might be presented in these three different expository writing assignments.

```
INFORMING
• Gives the facts
• Focuses on these facts
        ↓
EXPLAINING
• Explains the facts
• Focuses on the meaning of these
  facts (draws a conclusion)
        ↓
EXPLORING
• Gives the facts
• Explains the facts
• Asks questions about these facts
• Focuses on some problem created
  by the facts
```

OBJECTIVES

- To select an appropriate topic for a cause-and-effect paper
- To use speaking and listening skills to create and share causes, effects, and evidence for given questions
- To brainstorm or freewrite for causes and effects of a chosen situation or event
- To organize causes and effects and to write a thesis statement

PROGRAM MANAGER

PREWRITING

- **Self-Assessment** Before beginning instruction of the writing process, see **Writing Process Log** in *Strategies for Writing*, p. 22.

- **Heuristics** To help students generate ideas, see **Prewriting** in *Strategies for Writing*, p. 23.

- **Instructional Support** See **Graphic Organizers 11** and **12.** For suggestions on how to tie the transparencies to instruction, review teacher's notes in *Fine Art and Instructional Transparencies for Writing*, pp. 73, 75.

QUOTATION FOR THE DAY

"A writer's material is what he cares about." (John Gardner, 1933–1982, American author)

As the quotation suggests, students should select the topics they are particularly interested in or the subjects they most care about for their papers. Have students brainstorm lists of answers to complete these sentences: "I wonder why . . ." and "What would happen if . . . ?" Explain that students now have lists of subjects they care about to use as possible paper topics.

Writing a Cause-and-Effect Essay

Prewriting

Considering Topic, Purpose, and Audience

An Appropriate Topic.   You can take almost any idea or situation, apply a little curiosity to it, and come up with an appropriate *topic* for a cause-and-effect essay. Here are some examples to show how this works:

- One of the most popular books ever published is Margaret Mitchell's *Gone with the Wind*. Why? What caused it to be so popular?
- U.S students, many critics say, can no longer compete with students from Japan and other industrialized countries. If this statement is true, what caused the situation? What will the future effects be?
- Whales shouldn't be taken from their natural habitats, say many experts. Why? What happens when whales are put on display in gulfariums?

MOTIVATION

Think of a subject that interests you and that has at least one cause-and-effect relationship. For example, you might write the topic *global warming* on the chalkboard. Then, list everything that you know about this subject. Ask students to give you any suggestions about how you might find additional information on the subject.

Next, ask a volunteer to suggest another subject. Tell students that the subject must be something that can be explained and that it must be either a cause or an effect of something. Have the class suggest ways in which this subject might be further developed.

☛

As the examples on the previous page illustrate, an appropriate topic for cause-and-effect essays begins with a *situation* or *condition* (the popularity of *Gone with the Wind*, the decline in American education) and then asks *Why?* and/or *What's the result?*

If you are still bewildered about how to find a good topic, look for changes. Anything that represents **change**—a trend, an invention, a physical or political shift—necessarily has both cause and effect. Combine a changing situation with your own personal interest and you have a topic with potential.

Purpose and Audience. Your purpose in examining causes and effects could be to persuade, to express yourself, or to create a literary work. In this chapter, though, your main *purpose* will be to explain. When you explain anything, you try to clarify it and supply evidence that proves what you say. An explanation is not valid without sound evidence, such as facts, to support it. For now, your *audience* includes your teacher and classmates. As you begin your research and writing, look for information that appeals to their interests. Treat your readers as thoughtful, mature people who won't accept an explanation without sound evidence to back it up.

WRITING NOTE

Explaining is just one type of **expository** writing. The other types are informing and exploring. When you **explain,** you use facts and other forms of evidence to prove that your explanation is sound. When you **inform** (see Chapter 6), you share facts and ideas with your readers. When you **explore** (see Chapter 9), you attempt to discover facts and evidence.

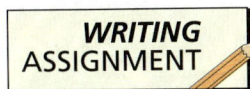

WRITING ASSIGNMENT

PART 1:
Choosing a Topic

What ideas do you have for cause-and-effect topics? Observe what is changing in your environment—home, school, or city. Brainstorm about pastimes and subjects you enjoy, looking for a change—a situation or event that makes you ask *Why?* or *What's the result?*

MEETING individual NEEDS

LEP/ESL

General Strategies. The **Identifying Sources** section (p. 261) lists interviewing as a possibility for gathering information. The interviewing process should be emphasized as a technique for accessing information. In an interview, the English-language learner practices all four basic skills: listening, speaking, writing, and reading. Interviewing also places the student in an interactive environment in which purposeful communication occurs. If the individual being interviewed is enthusiastic about the subject, this enthusiasm stimulates the student's involvement as well.

You might consider dividing the material in this lesson into the following four subsections:

1. **Considering Topic, Purpose, and Audience**
2. **Planning a Cause-and-Effect Explanation**
3. **Identifying Sources**
4. **Organizing Information**

When you begin teaching **Considering Topic, Purpose, and Audience,** pp. 258–259, you can refer to the example topic that you created on the chalkboard. Alternatively, you could suggest that students refer to their

MEETING individual NEEDS

LESS-ADVANCED STUDENTS

Explain to students that their chosen topics may turn out to be the cause of an effect, the effect of a cause, or the combination of both causes and effects. For example, if a chosen situation is an outbreak of a disease, the student might focus on the effects. If the chosen situation is the extinction of the passenger pigeon, the student might focus on the causes. If the chosen situation is a rise in unemployment, the student could focus on both causes and effects.

Prewriting

Planning a Cause-and-Effect Explanation

Your explanation won't be clear to your readers unless it is first clear to you. That means that you will have to form a *thesis,* or main idea; gather information about it; and decide how best to arrange your ideas for your readers.

Identifying Your Thesis

Writers sometimes decide on a thesis, or main idea, as soon as they have chosen a topic. For example, you hear that African elephants are in danger of becoming extinct, and you decide to write about the causes. Other times, writers may simply know that a situation exists—high insurance rates for teenage drivers, for example—and gather information about it before deciding on a thesis.

A cause-and-effect explanation may focus on causes, effects, or both. The *thesis statement,* which is usually a one-sentence summary of your thesis, should indicate the focus. The following thesis statements show three different focuses on the same situation:

Causes: Three major factors prompt teenagers to sign up for volunteer work in the community.

Effects: While the number of teenage volunteers may be small, the impact of their services is large.

Causes and Effects: Teenagers have different reasons for doing volunteer work, but the effects of their work are generally significant.

While students are working on **Planning a Cause-and-Effect Explanation**, p. 260, they are likely to need additional practice in formulating theses. For the practice to be worthwhile, you will want to suggest that they choose topics about which they are knowledgeable.

To help them begin the process, list the following topics across the top of the chalkboard:

1. attendance regulations
2. dances/parties
3. dress codes
4. graduation
5. school lunches

☞

Identifying Sources

For some topics, you will be your own best source of information. If you have done volunteer work yourself, for example, you can draw on your own personal experience and knowledge for information about the reasons why teenagers are volunteering for community work. For other topics, you may need to use some of the following techniques to gather information.

- Interview people to learn from their experience.
- Read magazines and newspapers to find facts and figures about current situations.
- Read reference books for background information.

COMPUTER NOTE: When using a computer-based card catalog or other database to find source listings, use mixed keywords or advanced searching language to limit or focus your search.

Investigating Causes and Effects

Before you can explain something, you have to discover the causes and effects of the situation or condition. It is important to identify and investigate *all* possible causes and effects. Otherwise, you may miss something very important.

Causes.   Why do birds rub ants on their backs? Why have historians begun using the term *Middle Ages* rather than *Dark Ages*? These are the kinds of questions to ask when you explore causes. You can start by asking *Why did this happen?* and listing every likely cause that you uncover. Later, when you have completed your investigation, you can select the causes that you think merit discussion. The following questions will help you thoroughly investigate causes:

- What are the obvious causes?
- Is there a main, or most important, cause? What is it?
- What is the most recent cause?
- What causes occurred in the distant past?

Effects.   What are the effects of not studying? One direct effect might be poor grades, but there may be other effects as well, ones that aren't as immediately obvious. You might not

A DIFFERENT APPROACH

To help students gain familiarity with the concept of the thesis statement, present the same topic used in the examples—teenage volunteerism—and have students work in groups to generate as many plausible thesis statements as possible. Suggest that students concentrate on factors such as age, places where they volunteer, hours per week, length of involvement, and other easily definable factors. [Sample answers: Teenagers volunteer more now than previously. Teenagers volunteer as much as older people. Teenagers stay longest in volunteer jobs of five or less hours per week.]

COMPUTER NOTE

Remind students that the suggestion about using mixed keywords for card catalogs and other databases is also applicable to the World Wide Web. Students can pinpoint their searches by using mixed keywords on the indexes and search engines that locate resources on the Web.

Have students spend a few minutes brainstorming about these topics, and then have students practice making up thesis statements that focus on causes and effects within these subject areas.

You can continue the exercise with the next section, **Identifying Sources** (p. 261), by asking students to identify appropriate sources for some of the thesis statements they have generated.

As students begin to investigate causes, you may need to distinguish between topics for which students would expect to find a definitive or complete set of causes and topics for which students would expect to have more tentative information.

(p. 261)

TECHNOLOGY TIP

A database can be used in prewriting both to record and to organize information. Students can create the categories *cause, effect, situation,* and *cause/effect.*

INTEGRATING THE LANGUAGE ARTS

Literature Link. A variation on false cause and effect can be examined by referring students to poems such as Christopher Marlowe's "The Passionate Shepherd to His Love" and Sir Walter Raleigh's "The Nymph's Reply to the Shepherd." In the first poem, the shepherd claims that the nymph's acceptance of his offer of marriage will result in a rich and privileged life for her (in addition to all the natural beauty and happiness of the pastoral life). The nymph in reply exposes the unlikeliness of those effects and reveals effects that are far more likely to occur. Encourage students to discuss the necessity of proving links between effects and causes.

COOPERATIVE LEARNING

Brainstorming causes and effects in a group allows students to take advantage of one another's ideas at the earliest stages of thought. Students should name possible causes and effects for given topics while their fellow group members take notes.

---

get into college, or you might not get a scholarship. When you investigate effects, ask yourself, *What are the results?* and list every possible effect you can think of. As with causes, wait until you have completed your investigation and then discard any effects that seem to be unrelated or unsupportable. These questions will help you investigate effects:

- What are the most obvious effects?
- Are there any hidden effects? What are they?
- What was (or will be) the first effect?
- What might be the future effects?

Cause-and-Effect Chains. During your investigation of the situation, you also need to look for a possible *cause-and-effect chain.* In such a chain, one event or situation causes an effect, then that effect becomes a cause for an additional effect, and so on. For example, a fire produces dangerous gases that cause health problems. The health problems cause people to move away, and their moving in turn causes a recession in the local economy. If such a chain exists, it may become an important part of your explanation.

Machine for Washing Dishes

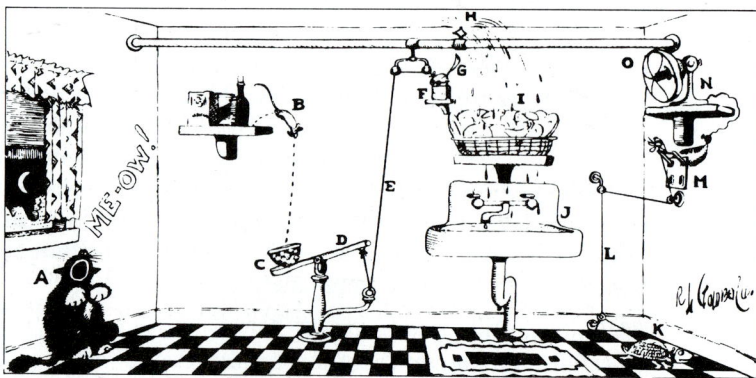

Rube Goldberg reprinted with special permission of King Features Syndicate, Inc.

The professor turns on his think-faucet and dopes out a machine for washing dishes while you are at the movies.

When spoiled tomcat (**A**) discovers he is alone, he lets out a yell which scares mouse (**B**) into jumping into basket (**C**), causing lever end (**D**) to rise and pull string (**E**) which snaps automatic cigar-lighter (**F**). Flame (**G**) starts fire sprinkler (**H**). Water runs on dishes (**I**) and drips into sink (**J**). Turtle (**K**), thinking he hears babbling brook babbling, and having no sense of direction, starts wrong way and pulls string (**L**), which turns on switch (**M**) that starts electric glow heater (**N**). Heat ray (**O**) dries the dishes.

If the cat and the turtle get on to your scheme and refuse to cooperate, simply put the dishes on the front porch and pray for rain.

Tell students that topics in the natural sciences or topics in which there are only physical causes are those that writers can discuss most confidently.

Students might need some assistance in learning how to research hidden causes and effects. Explain that they can look for causes or effects that are far removed in space or time from the focus situation or that are not obviously connected to the focus situation.

You may want to have students turn immediately to the maps on pp. 265–267 so that they can see in graphic form what information a paper on a causal chain might contain.

You can use the acronym *EAR* to help students remember the criteria for ☞

WRITING NOTE

When you are exploring causes and effects, you need to avoid an error in thinking called *false cause and effect.* You can't assume that a cause-and-effect relationship exists just because one thing precedes another; there must be a valid connection between them.

FALSE CAUSE AND EFFECT

My computer broke the day after I bought those new disks. The disks must have caused the problem.

The only connection here is sequence, or timing, of the events. A more likely cause might be moisture or crumbs in the keyboard.

Providing Believable Support

According to one study, parts of the east coast of North America and Europe could actually grow cooler in response to global warming. Do you believe that statement? An important part of an explanation is the support, or evidence, that proves your explanation is valid. You won't stand a chance of supporting your explanation unless you have sufficient, accurate, and reliable evidence.

☞ **REFERENCE NOTE:** For more on evidence, see pages 302–303.

Sufficient Evidence. What is *enough* evidence? The answer is, "Whatever it takes to prove your point." Sometimes one example may be enough; at other times, you may need some statistics as well as two or three examples to prove that a certain cause or effect exists. Your task is to be sensitive to your audience's doubts and to make sure that you have a reasonable amount of support. Your evidence may consist of facts, statistics, examples, or anecdotes, but you need to have enough of it.

Accurate Evidence. Whether you are quoting an expert or a magazine article, citing statistics, or giving an example, you need to be accurate. If you mean to say that the average American throws away five pounds of trash a day and instead say fifty pounds, your audience will begin to question your entire explanation. Take notes accurately, and be sure you get both the numbers and the words right.

MEETING individual NEEDS

LEARNING STYLES

Kinetic Learners. Students might benefit from writing each step in their cause-and-effect chains on index cards and arranging these cards in order on a bulletin board.

SUFFICIENT EVIDENCE

You may wish to expand on the explanation given in the textbook. Tell students that a variety of types of evidence (for example, an interview, a newspaper article, and a periodical article) may sometimes be more convincing than sources of only one type. Sometimes just using a quotation rather than a paraphrase can make evidence more convincing.

ACCURATE EVIDENCE

Conflicting evidence can present problems for the student researcher. When evidence does not agree, students should check the dates of the sources. It is possible for evidence to differ because new information has come to light. Students should also note whether the evidence is an established fact, an estimation, or a deduction.

RELIABLE EVIDENCE

Reliable evidence not only needs to come from an expert (or at least a well-informed) source, but it also must be stated in a convincing way to be of use.

Convincing can mean different things in different situations. Scientific experts sound more reliable if their technical evidence is clearly presented and documented. A person whose expertise comes from experience, however, can provide convincing evidence by providing examples he or she has experienced.

264

Reliable Evidence.   Reliable evidence comes from a "trustworthy" source. You or your neighbor, for example, may speak reliably about the effects of your neighborhood street becoming one-way, but unless you are scientists, you would not be reliable sources for an explanation of how climatic changes led to dinosaur extinction. And don't assume everything that is printed is reliable. Make sure that any magazine or newspaper you use, for example, has a reputation for using trustworthy sources.

Reminder

To plan for a cause-and-effect essay

- identify a thesis that focuses on causes, effects, or both
- record information about secondary sources so you can cite them in your paper
- look for multiple and/or hidden causes and effects
- look for evidence to prove that the cause or effect exists

EXERCISE 1   **Speaking and Listening: Gathering Information About Causes and Effects**

Mr. and Mrs. Smith have died and left each of the one thousand residents of Nowhere, U.S.A., one million dollars. What caused the Smiths to make this donation? What might be the effects of this sudden wealth on the residents of this town? Get together with a small group of your classmates and discuss possible answers to these questions. Try to think of at least two likely causes of the Smiths' generosity and two effects the

To model the activity in **Exercise 1**, p. 264, provide statistics from a local animal shelter and have students ponder the causes and effects of the figures. Alternatively, you might use information from a local hospital on a specific subject and have students speculate on the causes of each effect you identify.

You may want to have students discuss their progress with you while they complete **Writing Assignment: Part 2** on this page. You can then advise students who have chosen inappropriate topics.

The section **Organizing Information**, below, suggests that a cause-and-effect essay may concentrate on causes, effects, or both. The three possibilities are presented in graphic form to make it easier to compare ☞

money might have on the residents of the small town. Then identify information that would support each cause and each effect. When you finish, share your causes and effects and supporting evidence with other groups.

WRITING ASSIGNMENT

PART 2:
Planning Your Cause-and-Effect Explanation

You are now ready to begin planning your own cause-and-effect explanation. If you are using the topic you chose in Writing Assignment, Part 1, you probably already have some idea about the answers to one or both of these questions about your topic: *Why? What's the result?* Brainstorm or freewrite (see pages 22–24) to find additional possible causes or effects, and look for others in sources such as books, magazines, tapes, or interviews. At the same time, look for evidence that supports each cause or effect. At some point, identify your focus—causes, effects, or both—and write your thesis statement.

Organizing Information

The focus of your essay—causes, effects, or causes and effects—helps to determine how to organize your information. A map that shows the relationship between causes and effects is a useful organizational aid at this point, and the following example shows one writer's map for an essay on the causes of a dangerous intersection.

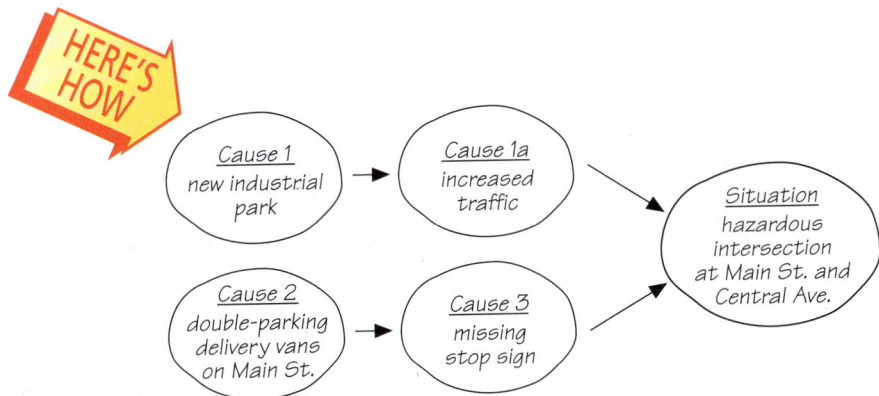

HERE'S HOW

Cause 1
new industrial park → Cause 1a
increased traffic →

Situation
hazardous intersection at Main St. and Central Ave.

Cause 2
double-parking delivery vans on Main St. → Cause 3
missing stop sign →

and contrast the organization that the finished essay might have.

Try creating actual text so that students see the connection between the planning charts and a written product. Then, you might try organizing this text as a model for **Writing Assignment: Part 3**, p. 267.

ASSESSMENT

You may want to have students work in pairs to evaluate each other's writing maps. Remind them to check for a focus on causes, effects, or both; a logical ordering of the elements; and a group of causes or effects that seems reasonably complete and accurate.

266   *Writing to Explain*

The following examples illustrate mapping for essays with other focuses.

Focusing on Effects

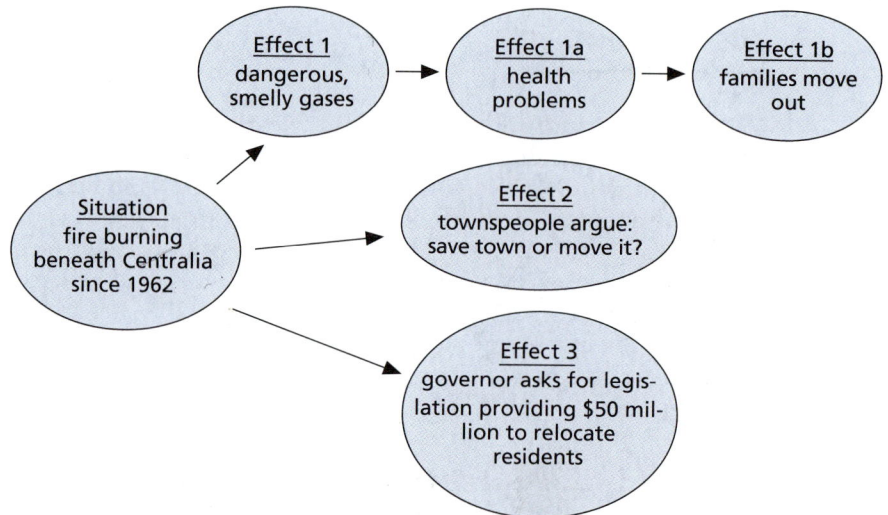

Focusing on Causes and Effects

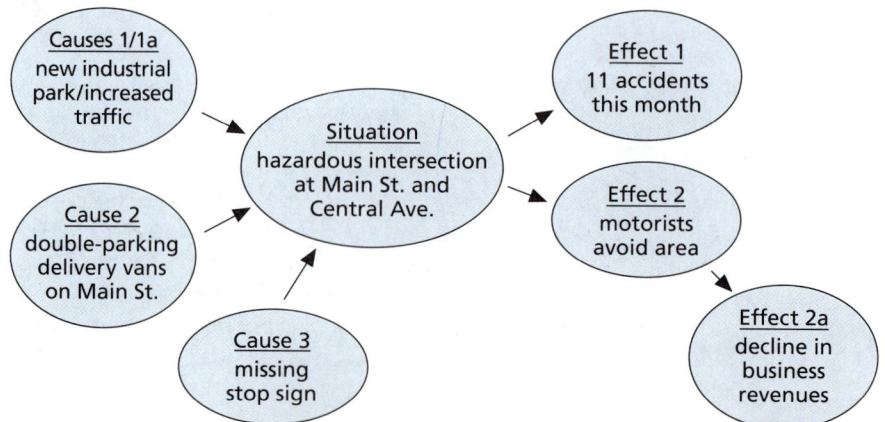

CLOSURE

When students have finished **Writing Assignment: Part 3,** conduct a survey by asking the following questions:

1. Who focused only on causes? Who focused only on effects? Who focused on both?
2. Who used a causal chain?

3. Who organized the information by order of importance? Who used chronological order?

Record the answers and briefly discuss the results. ∎

Focusing on a Chain of Causes and Effects

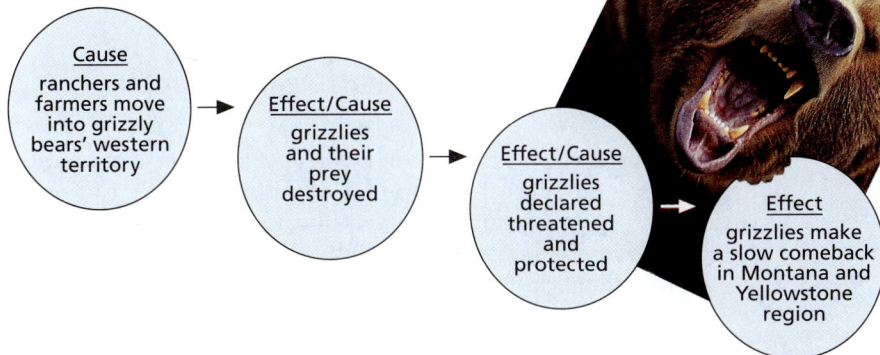

Cause
ranchers and farmers move into grizzly bears' western territory

→ **Effect/Cause**
grizzlies and their prey destroyed

→ **Effect/Cause**
grizzlies declared threatened and protected

→ **Effect**
grizzlies make a slow comeback in Montana and Yellowstone region

Arranging Causes and Effects. Naturally, it only makes sense to discuss causes before effects, but which cause do you list first when you have two or three causes? Out of three effects, which do you list first and which last? In most cases, use *order of importance,* listing the least important cause or effect first and building up to the most important one at the end. However, when a situation has developed over a long period of time, producing one effect after another, it's often best to use *chronological order.* The fire in Centralia, Pennsylvania, is such a topic. And when you are putting your causes and effects in order, remember to discuss the supporting evidence for each cause or effect before moving on to the next cause or effect.

👉 **REFERENCE NOTE:** See pages 74, 79–82, and 86–87 for more information on order of importance and chronological order.

WRITING ASSIGNMENT

PART 3:
Organizing Your Information

When you completed Writing Assignment, Part 2, you had a thesis statement and a great deal of information about causes and effects, probably jotted down on note cards or paper in no certain order. The next step is to arrange that information in an order that will make sense to readers. Depending on your focus—causes, effects, or causes and effects—use one of the patterns on pages 265–266 to make a map that you will use as a guide for writing your essay.

A DIFFERENT APPROACH

Advanced students may benefit from attempting to create their own written products for each map on pp. 265–267. You may want to have students work in pairs or in small groups. The groups can compare and contrast their different products.

In explaining the last chart, you could point out that the original situation that gave rise to the cause-and-effect chain shown might have been any of the four entries on the chart.

WRITING YOUR FIRST DRAFT

OBJECTIVES

- To analyze the structure and content of a model cause-and-effect essay
- To write a draft of a cause-and-effect essay

MOTIVATION

Ask students to visualize a multi-colored puzzle cube. Explain that the objective of the puzzle is to have all of the same colors on the same side. Tell students that their goal is similar. They should place all similar information, such as causes, together.

PROGRAM MANAGER

WRITING YOUR FIRST DRAFT

- **Instructional Support** For help with writing an introductory paragraph, see **Writing** in *Strategies for Writing*, p. 24.

QUOTATION FOR THE DAY

"That writer does the most, who gives his reader the *most* knowledge, and takes from him the *least* time." (C. C. Colton, 1780–1832, American author and clergyman)

MEETING individual NEEDS

LEP/ESL

General Strategies. Some students will need extra help in developing research skills. Plan a trip to the public library and pair students with peer tutors. Instruct peer tutors to assist their partners with hands-on practice in using the online catalog, accessing and copying articles on microfiche, and navigating successfully through the stacks.

SELECTION AMENDMENT.
Description of change: excerpted
Rationale: to focus on the concept of writing to explain presented in this chapter

---

Writing Your First Draft

The Structure of a Cause-and-Effect Explanation

You will find the structure of a cause-and-effect explanation comfortably familiar; it isn't much different from that of other essays you have written. The typical cause-and-effect explanation includes

an **introduction** that

- captures your reader's attention
- identifies the situation or event you're explaining
- provides important background information
- identifies your thesis

a **body** that

- explains the causes and/or effects of the situation
- uses facts, examples, anecdotes, and statistics to support, or prove, each cause or effect
- has a clear organization

a **conclusion** that

- sums up the explanation
- possibly, refers to the introduction
- possibly, predicts future changes or effects

In the essay on the next page, Harold Krents writes about a situation he knows well—his blindness—and its effects on the sighted members of society. Krents moves from the "nuisance" effects to a more serious effect: the belief that a blind person can't practice law.

"I'm not sure I understand the process of writing.... The brain slowly begins to function in a different way, to make mysterious connections."

Elizabeth Hardwick

TEACHING THE LESSON
Have students read the first section independently, and then review the main points with the whole class before the students read the model essay. Point out that the essay does not deal with causes of the focus situations, but only with various effects.
Krents's essay will be especially useful for students whose topics are closely linked

to their own experiences. The essay contains examples of both irony and personal anecdote.

After discussing **Exercise 2**, p. 272, you may introduce **A Writer's Model**, p. 273, as a more formal, objective essay. Point out that while there is some use of first person in the first paragraph, this point of view is included more for informational reasons than to personalize the entire essay. ☞

Writing Your First Draft   **269**

A CAUSE-AND-EFFECT ESSAY

Darkness at Noon
by Harold Krents

INTRODUCTION
Attention grabber

1   Blind from birth, I have never had the opportunity to see myself and have been completely dependent on the image I create in the eye of the observer. To date it has not been narcissistic.

BODY
Effect 1

    There are those who assume that since I can't see, I obviously also cannot hear. Very often people will converse with me at the top of their lungs, enunciating each word very carefully. Conversely, people will also often whisper, assuming that since my eyes don't work, my ears don't either.

Evidence—example

Evidence—anecdote

2   For example, when I go to the airport and ask the ticket agent for assistance to the plane, he or she will invariably pick up the phone, call a ground hostess and whisper: "Hi, Jane, we've got a 76 here." I have concluded that the word "blind" is not used for one of two reasons: Either they fear that if the dread word is spoken, the ticket agent's

269

As in the section on arranging evidence, the **Framework for a Cause-and-Effect Explanation** on p. 275 is a simplified presentation of the possibilities for presenting this kind of an essay. Allow students to create alternative forms of organization, if they like.

GUIDED PRACTICE

You may want to model the analysis of the cause-and-effect essay by discussing **Exercise 2** on p. 272 with students. Volunteers can answer question 3 aloud before you continue to discuss questions 4 and 5 with the class.

3

Krents continues his ironic tone as a kind of punch line to his anecdote. This method serves as evidence for effect 2.

4

Without stating it explicitly, Krents provides evidence to prove his point that many people think blindness indicates some kind of mental disability.

270

---

270   *Writing to Explain*

retina will immediately detach, or they are reluctant to inform me of my condition of which I may not have been previously aware.

**Effect 2
Evidence—
examples**

3

On the other hand, others know that of course I can hear, but believe that I can't talk. Often, therefore, when my wife and I go out to dinner, a waiter or waitress will ask Kit if "*he* would like a drink" to which I respond that "indeed *he* would."

**Evidence—
anecdote**

This point was graphically driven home to me while we were in England. I had been given a year's leave of absence from my Washington law firm to study for a diploma in law degree at Oxford University. During the year I became ill and was hospitalized. Immediately after admission, I was wheeled down to the X-ray room. Just at the door sat an elderly woman — elderly I would judge from the sound of her voice. "What is his name?" the woman asked the orderly who had been wheeling me.

4

"What's your name?" the orderly repeated to me.

"Harold Krents," I replied.

"Harold Krents," he repeated.

"When was he born?"

"When were you born?"

"November 5, 1944," I responded.

"November 5, 1944," the orderly intoned.

This procedure continued for approximately five minutes at which point even my saint-like disposition deserted me. "Look," I finally blurted out, "this is absolutely ridiculous. Okay, granted I can't see, but it's got to have become pretty clear to both of you that I don't need an interpreter."

"He says he doesn't need an interpreter," the orderly reported to the woman.

**Effect 3
Evidence—
examples**

The toughest misconception of all is the view that because I can't see, I can't work. I was turned down by over forty law firms because of my blindness, even though my qualifications included a cum laude degree from Harvard College and a good ranking in my Harvard Law School class.

Because students have seen several examples of cause-and-effect essays, they may have some new ideas about presentation. Give students the opportunity to review the maps they created in **Prewriting** and to rethink the arrangement they will use for writing a first draft.

Writing Assignment: Part 4 provides an opportunity for students to write their rough drafts.

☞

The attempt to find employment, the continuous frustration of being told that it was impossible for a blind person to practice law, the rejection letters, not based on my lack of ability but rather on my disability, will always remain one of the most disillusioning experiences of my life.

*Future effect/
cause*

Fortunately, this view of limitation and exclusion is beginning to change. On April 16 [1976], the Department of Labor issued regulations that mandate equal-employment opportunities for the handicapped. By and large, the business community's response to offering employment to the disabled has been enthusiastic.

*Future effect
anticipated*

5   I therefore look forward to the day, with the expectation that it is certain to come, when employers will view their handicapped workers as a little child did me years ago when my family still lived in Scarsdale.

*Evidence—
anecdote*

I was playing basketball with my father in our backyard according to procedures we had developed. My father would stand beneath the hoop, shout, and I would shoot over his head at the basket attached to our garage. Our next-door neigh-

5
Here Krents shifts his focus from an account of his experiences to his prognostications for the future.

You could have students work independently following the class discussion to write answers to all the questions in **Exercise 2** as homework.

To assess **Writing Assignment: Part 4,** have students create annotations for their essays that are similar to the annotations in Krents's essay. Each student should identify the introduction, body, and conclusion, as well as the use of causes, effects, and evidence.

You can then assess whether students have matched the appropriate terms with the parts of their essays and whether they have chosen appropriate arrangements for their topics.

---

bor, aged five, wandered over into our yard with a playmate. "He's blind," our neighbor whispered to her friend in a voice that could be heard distinctly by Dad and me. Dad shot and missed; I did the same. Dad hit the rim: I missed entirely: Dad shot and missed the garage entirely. "Which one is blind?" whispered back the little friend.

I would hope that in the near future when a plant manager is touring the factory with the foreman and comes upon a handicapped and nonhandicapped person working together, his comment after watching them work will be, "Which one is disabled?"

CONCLUSION

Prediction about future

ANSWERS

Exercise 2

Answers may vary.

1. Krents explained only a narrow range of the effects of being blind, but he did it very well. The most convincing anecdote was the one about playing basketball with his father.

2. Krents ascribes the change to the equal-employment regulations passed in 1976.

3. The main idea is that people should be judged by their capabilities, not by their so-called disabilities.

4. He uses order of importance and ends with the most important effect, probably both because this effect was the focus of his essay and because he wanted to use it as the basis for his comments about the future.

5. Krents's personal examples and anecdotes are sufficient because in this particular case they indicate stereotypes that would not apply only to Krents. This makes his conclusion—that some people stereotype people with disabilities—believable.

EXERCISE 2 ▶ **Analyzing a Cause-and-Effect Essay**

After you have finished reading Harold Krents's essay, meet with two or three classmates to discuss these questions.

1. How well do you think Krents explained the effects of being blind? What examples or anecdotes did you find particularly convincing?
2. Krents says that the effects of blindness might be different in the future. What cause does he give for this change?
3. In your own words, explain the main idea of the essay.
4. Does Krents use chronological order or order of importance to present the effects in his essay? Why do you think he chooses the order he does?
5. Most of Krents's evidence consists of examples and anecdotes drawn from his own experience. Do you think this type of evidence is sufficient to support Krents's explanation? Explain your answer.

A Framework for a Cause-and-Effect Essay

In writing about his blindness, Krents makes use of several writers' options—extended anecdotes, witty quips, dialogue, and concise descriptions of scenes and people. The following essay, which focuses on causes, is written in a simpler, more straightforward fashion. You may wish to use this model when you write your own essay.

Try using a visual example of an explanation to help students identify the structure that their essays will include. A nature show on PBS or a science film from the media center would be appropriate. Guide students in taking notes about causes and effects that are found in the program. After viewing the program together, work with students to arrange the information into the categories of introduction, body, and conclusion.

☞

A WRITER'S MODEL

Why Teenagers Volunteer

INTRODUCTION
Attention grabber

Situation

Typical teenagers have no interest in helping others. That is what some people believe, but it is not true. According to a Gallup survey, more than 12 million teenagers volunteer an average of 3.2 hours per week. Why do teenagers donate their time? As a teenage volunteer myself, I had some ideas, but I decided to find out what other teenage volunteers think.

Thesis statement

The three major reasons teenagers I interviewed in our school had for volunteering were to help people, to do something they enjoyed, or to learn new skills.

BODY
Cause 1

Over half (51 percent) of the volunteers enlisted simply because they wanted to help other people. The teenagers in this group became aware that certain needs or problems existed, and they realized they could make a difference. For the most part, the needs the volunteers discovered involved people--including disabled, poor, young, and elderly individuals. Sometimes, the volunteers had direct contact with the people they helped. They ran errands, helped with housework, mowed yards, and so on. Other times, the work involved community

Evidence—
examples

A DIFFERENT APPROACH

In **A Writer's Model,** first person is used in the first paragraph as an attention grabber. You may choose to have students use the first-person point of view if it is appropriate for their topics. Have each student include a personal anecdote that will catch the reader's attention.

Ask students to describe the structure of a cause-and-effect essay. Then, ask for volunteers to discuss if they found that writing one part of the rough draft (for example, the introduction) was easier than writing another. ■

MEETING *individual* NEEDS

LESS-ADVANCED STUDENTS

The statistics in **A Writer's Model** may puzzle some students. The writer reports that 51 percent of volunteers want to help others; 45 percent volunteer because they enjoy the work; and 33 percent want to learn new skills. This adds up to 129 percent. Point out that although the writer did not clearly state this, it is clear that some of those interviewed must have given more than one answer. This explains why there is more than 100 percent.

You may want to use this discussion to point out the necessity of clarity when using statistics.

improvement, such as removing graffiti or turning an ugly vacant lot into a neighborhood garden.

Cause 2

Another common reason (45 percent) for volunteerism was enjoyment of work. Most students began volunteering in order to help others, but they continued to volunteer because they discovered along the way that they really enjoyed what they were doing. One girl, a junior, said, "I didn't realize

Evidence—quotes

how bored I was until I started working with the Youth Volunteer Corps. I help out in a soup kitchen for the homeless, and the time flies. I know I would be bored again if I quit volunteering." A sophomore boy said, "I started volunteering in the first place because my parents insisted on it. Then I found I really liked it. I work in a daycare center, and the kids really like me. I'd feel terrible if I had to give it up now."

Cause 3

A third reason for volunteering, given by 33 percent of the teenagers interviewed, was a desire to learn new skills and to grow as a person. One junior boy said that he felt he needed to develop better skills in working with other people. Working as a part of a team to clean and maintain the town's beaches was one way he could gain useful experience. A senior girl volunteered to work in the gift shop of the local art museum. She wanted to help

Evidence—examples and quote

the art museum in a time of severe budget cuts, but she also wanted to learn more about the arts. She said, "I know what I'm learning at the museum will help me as I study to be a sculptor."

CONCLUSION
Restatement of
thesis

As these interviews show, teenage volunteers are enthusiastic about their work. The main reason they volunteer is to help others and to help their communities, but many also volunteer because they feel a need to do interesting work or develop their

Reference to
introduction

own skills and abilities. But whatever their motivation, these young men and women are destroying the myth of the self-centered teenager; they are showing the world that they care.

The essay you've just read focuses on causes only and adheres to the following simple framework for a cause-and-effect essay.

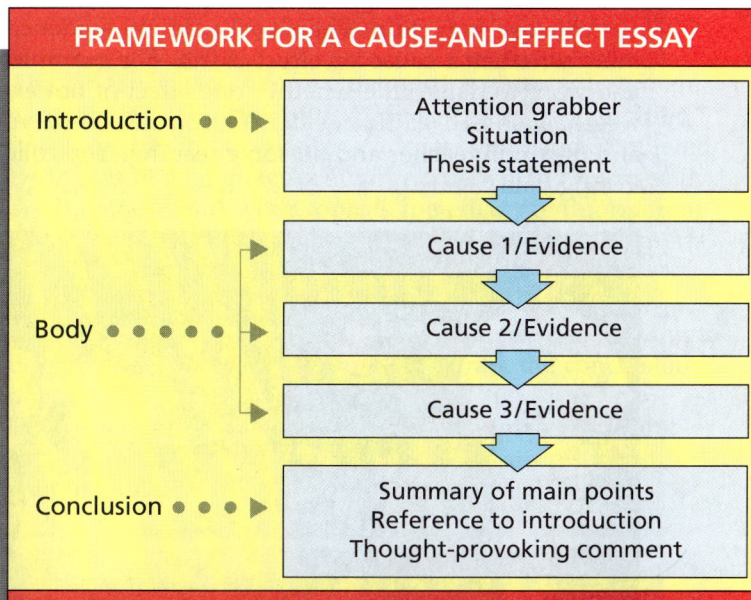

FRAMEWORK FOR A CAUSE-AND-EFFECT ESSAY

Introduction ● ● ▶	Attention grabber / Situation / Thesis statement
	⬇
	Cause 1/Evidence
	⬇
Body ● ● ● ● ● ▶	Cause 2/Evidence
	⬇
	Cause 3/Evidence
	⬇
Conclusion ● ● ● ▶	Summary of main points / Reference to introduction / Thought-provoking comment

If your essay focuses on effects only, or on both causes and effects, you can use the same framework. Just substitute effects (or causes and effects) for causes in the body of the framework.

LEARNING STYLES

Visual Learners. Many students may benefit from actually seeing different frameworks, rather than just reading about how they can be constructed. You may wish to put the following examples on the chalkboard or on a poster:

BODY
situation
cause
cause
cause
effect
effect
effect

BODY
situation
effect
effect
effect

BODY
situation
cause
cause
cause

BODY
effect
effect
effect
cause/situation

BODY
situation
cause
effect/cause
effect/cause
effect

valid. What kind of research is needed? What sources might be trustworthy? When you have finished your analysis, exchange ideas with other students in your class.

1. *Topic:* "the effects of the senior prom"
   John spent $210 last year on the prom.
   I spent a lot, too.
   Generalization: Everybody spends too much money on the senior prom.

2. *Topic:* "the effects of teenagers' driving"
   Three drivers in the senior class had accidents last month.
   My car insurance costs $100 a month.
   Generalization: Teenagers have more accidents than drivers in almost any other category.

WRITING ASSIGNMENT

PART 4:
Writing Your First Draft

With your preparations complete, you now are ready for the actual writing of a first draft. Try using some of your options as a writer—inserting a personal anecdote to explain a cause or using a vivid example or shocking statistic to boost your audience's interest. You don't have to start your draft at the beginning—you may choose to begin with the body, then go back and add the introduction and conclusion later.

EVALUATING AND REVISING

OBJECTIVES

- To analyze a writer's revision
- To evaluate a peer's paper
- To revise an essay

TEACHING THE LESSON

Discuss the chart on p. 281 and point out that the evaluation guide questions require students to judge their essays as if they were members of the intended audiences. Tell students that keeping the audience in mind—and perhaps even keeping a particular audience member in mind—is a technique some people find helpful as they revise their work. ☞

Evaluating and Revising

After finishing your draft, let it sit for a few days. Then use the chart on page 281 to identify and correct weaknesses in your draft. Answer each question in the left-hand column, and use the revision techniques in the right-hand column to correct any weaknesses.

EXERCISE 3 ▶ Analyzing a Writer's Revisions

With a partner, study the changes the writer made in the first draft of a paragraph from the model, pages 273–275. Answer the questions that follow to analyze the revisions.

> Over half (51 percent)
> ~~Many~~ of the volunteers enlisted ~~for~~   **replace**
> simply because they wanted to help other people.
> ~~another reason.~~ The teenagers ~~throughout~~   **replace**
> in this group became
> ~~the country are~~ aware that certain needs or   **replace**
>   ed   d   could
> problems exist, and they realize they ~~can~~   **add/replace**
>
> make a difference. For the most part, the
>
> needs the volunteers discovered involved
>
> people--including disabled, poor, young,
>
> and elderly individuals. Sometimes, the
>
> volunteers had direct contact with the
>
> people they helped. They ran errands,
>
> helped with housework, mowed yards, and
>
> so on. Other times, the work involved
>   ↑ such as removing graffiti or turning an
> community improvement, ugly vacant lot into   **add**
>   a neighborhood garden.

1. Why did the writer change *Many* to *Over half (51 percent)*?
2. How does the replacement at the end of the first sentence make the explanation clearer?
3. What is the reason for the changes in the second sentence? [Hint: Review inductive thinking, pages 276–277.]
4. Why did the writer add additional information to the last sentence? How does this information make the explanation more acceptable to the audience?

PROGRAM MANAGER

EVALUATING AND REVISING

- **Reinforcement/Reteaching** See **Revision Transparencies 11** and **12.** For suggestions on how to tie the transparencies to instruction, review teacher's notes in *Fine Art and Instructional Transparencies for Writing,* p. 115.

- **Ongoing Assessment** For a rubric to guide assessment, see **Evaluating and Revising** in *Strategies for Writing,* p. 25.

- **Assessment/Reflection** To assess student work and evaluate progress, see **Portfolio Forms** in *Portfolio Assessment,* pp. 5–21.

ANSWERS
Exercise 3

1. The statistic is more specific and more accurate.
2. Without the change at the end of the first sentence, the reader does not reach the reason until line four of the paragraph. By moving the information up, the writer makes the paragraph clearer.
3. It changed the generalization from an all-inclusive one to one focused on a smaller section of the population. This makes the claim more believable.
4. The specific examples of the work students did further explain the topic.

Work through **Exercise 3, p. 279**, with the class as a model for the independent practice that is involved in **Writing Assignment: Part 5.**

If you choose to grade students' revisions, you may want to focus on whether there have been improvements from the previous drafts as your evaluation criterion.

CLOSURE

Using the idea of a suggestion box, encourage students to make suggestions about how the evaluation and revision process could be improved for them. Suggest that they focus on the **Evaluating and Revising Cause-and-Effect Essays** chart and the writing assignment as they brainstorm. ■

QUOTATION FOR THE DAY

"Careful consideration is the best known defense against change." (John C. Burton, 1932–   , American educator)

Use the quotation to approach the evaluation and revision stages of the writing process. Lead students to understand that the art of revision involves knowing what to delete, what to add, what to change, and what not to change.

MEETING *individual* NEEDS

LEP/ESL

General Strategies. Although the textbook recommends that students exchange essays, you may want to work individually with students in revising their first drafts. Because cultural identity is so closely tied to written expression, sensitivity is needed to guide students toward standard usage. Try to reinforce the notion of replacing nonstandard usage, rather than correcting mistakes. Have students make written notations concerning those aspects of their essays that need further work.

WRITING ASSIGNMENT

PART 5:
Evaluating and Revising Your Essay

Reread your essay and, with the help of the evaluating and revising chart on page 281, decide what changes are needed. Mark the spots that need improving. What might you add, cut, reorder, or replace? Then, exchange papers with a classmate and use the chart once more to evaluate each other's essays. Finally, revise your essay, using both your classmate's and your own observations to improve it. Make the changes on either your hard copy or word processor.

EVALUATING AND REVISING CAUSE-AND-EFFECT ESSAYS

EVALUATION GUIDE	REVISION TECHNIQUE
1 Does the introduction capture the reader's attention?	**Add** an interesting anecdote or details. Ask a startling question.
2 Does the introduction clearly present the situation to be explained? Does it contain a clear thesis statement?	**Add** information that presents the situation. **Add** a sentence (or **replace** an existing sentence) that states the topic and main idea, including the focus: causes, effects, or both.
3 Does the essay provide a sufficiently complete answer to at least one of these questions: *What are the causes? What are the effects?*	Do more research to find additional causes or effects. (Look for hidden causes and effects.) **Add** them to the essay.
4 Is the explanation supported, or proved, with evidence?	**Add** facts, quotations, examples, and statistics from reliable sources to support each cause and effect you have identified.
5 Are all generalizations valid? Is evidence solid?	**Cut** any generalization for which you don't have enough evidence or for which the evidence is contradictory. **Cut** any evidence that is from an untrustworthy source. **Add** words such as *many* or *most* to any generalization stated as an absolute.
6 Is the information organized in a clear, easy-to-follow way?	**Reorder** causes or effects in order of importance or chronological order.
7 Does the essay have a strong conclusion?	**Add** a summary of the explanation. **Add** a thought-provoking comment about the future.

A DIFFERENT APPROACH

You may prefer to have students evaluate their essays by focusing on the three criteria for evidence (enough, accurate, and reliable) and the criteria for the three parts of a cause-and-effect essay (introduction, body, and conclusion).

PROOFREADING AND PUBLISHING

OBJECTIVE

- To proofread and publish a cause-and-effect essay

TEACHING THE LESSON

Write the following sentence on the chalkboard:

More than 500 people marched to the capitol this morning.

Ask students how the importance of this fact might differ if one zero were added or dropped. Explain that students should

PROGRAM MANAGER

PROOFREADING AND PUBLISHING

- **Instructional Support** For a chart students may use to evaluate their proofreading progress, see **Proofreading** in *Strategies for Writing*, p. 26.

- **Independent Practice/ Reteaching** For additional practice with language skills, see **Proofreading Practice: Using Verb Tenses Effectively** in *Strategies for Writing*, p. 27.

- **Assessment/Reflection** To assess student work and evaluate progress, see **Portfolio Forms** in *Portfolio Assessment*, pp. 22–25.

QUOTATION FOR THE DAY

"So let great authors have their due, as time, which is the author of authors, be not deprived of his due, which is further and further to discover truth." (Francis Bacon, 1561–1626, English essayist)

Before students begin proofreading and publishing their essays, you may wish to assign the quotation as a writing journal topic. Students might write about how their essays would have been different if written fifty or a hundred years in the past or in the future, or they might write general explanations of the quotation.

282

---

282   *Writing to Explain*

Proofreading and Publishing

Proofreading.   Errors in spelling, punctuation, and grammar can detract even from an essay that's beautifully written. If you have quoted sources, proofread for the accuracy of quotations and the spelling of names and titles.

GRAMMAR HINT

Using Verb Tenses Effectively

To explain causes and effects, you use the strategy of narration, looking at what happens over the course of time. An effect is always a change, and it always happens later than the cause. In your cause-and-effect essay, you will probably need to change verb tenses to show the changes in time.

Use *past* and *present* tenses to explain past causes that have led to present effects.

Last year, the average American **threw** away more than 1500 pounds of trash. More than 8 percent of it **was** plastic. This trash **creates** a monumental disposal problem.

always recheck spelling of proper nouns, wording of quotations, and the numerals in figures they mention.

You could proofread for one aspect, such as spelling, by using a sample essay as your model. Students can then proofread for other mechanical problems independently.

CLOSURE

Ask students to respond to the following questions:

1. How do you feel about sharing your work with a wider audience as opposed to sharing it with only your teacher and classmates?
2. What are the differences and what are the similarities? ■

Use *present, present progressive,* and *future* tenses to explain present causes that may lead to future effects.

> Garbage **is piling** up around us. Each American **throws** out between four and five pounds of trash each day. This **includes** everything from empty bottles to old refrigerators. At this rate, our landfills **will be** full within a few years.

☞ **REFERENCE NOTE:** For more information about verb tenses, see pages 788–799.

Publishing.   Here are some suggestions for sharing your writing with an audience beyond your teacher.

- Send or e-mail your essay to an expert on the topic you have explained.
- Convert your written essay to a speech, and present it to your class, an assembly or club in your school, or a community group that would be interested in your topic.

| WRITING ASSIGNMENT | PART 6: **Proofreading and Publishing Your Essay** |

Proofread your essay carefully, and correct any errors you find. Then, make a final clean copy, and share what you have written with at least one other person. Use the suggestions you've just read or an idea of your own for finding an audience.

Reflecting on Your Writing

If you want to add your essay to your **portfolio,** date it and write a note of reflection that answers the following questions.

- Does your introduction explain your subject clearly? How could you clarify your points?
- Was it more difficult to think of causes and effects for your essay or to think of a good way to organize your ideas?
- How did you know that you had enough information to write your essay? Do you feel that you did too much or too little research?

MEETING individual NEEDS

LEP/ESL

General Strategies. Students will likely use past and present tenses to show causes in their cause-and-effect essays. Students may have a tendency to omit the *–ed* marker for past-tense regular verbs, as in "The Vietnam War seem unjust to many citizens in the 1960s." You may want to have students scan their compositions specifically for this omission. After the forms are corrected, ask students to underline the past-tense markers.

ADVANCED STUDENTS

Some students may wish to create multimedia presentations from their cause-and-effect essays. Encourage students to incorporate videotapes, slide shows, or computer-generated graphics in their presentations, and help them find the resources they need.

TEACHING NOTE

Encourage students to jot down notes about their reflections before they begin working on the answers to the questions. Since the point of the reflecting activity is to encourage students to think about their writing, in some instances these notes can serve as the reflection. The notes can be dated and attached to students' essays before they are placed in the students' portfolios.

A STUDENT MODEL
Evaluation

1. The introduction captures the reader's interest with an anecdote, and it also contains a thesis statement that tells what the rest of the essay is about.
2. Cheryl's essay deals with the effects of running cross country, and she provides good details that spell out what these effects are.
3. Cheryl provides excellent support for the effects she claims. Specifically, she provides evidence of the condition that existed before she started running and evidence of the condition that exists at present.
4. The essay is clearly organized and easy to follow. It doesn't contain a conclusion because this is only a part of the whole essay.

A STUDENT MODEL

The following passages are from a cause-and-effect essay by Cheryl Flugan, a student in Mayfield Heights, Ohio. Notice her opening anecdote.

What Are the Effects of Running?
by Cheryl Flugan

I hovered in the doorway, waiting. Jenni was crazy, I was sure. It was the end of our eighth-grade year, and Jenni had decided to join cross country. She asked me to do the same, and I bluntly turned her down. Me run three miles? Absurd. At that moment my friend was sealing her fate by speaking to the cross country coach. Impatient to leave, I peered into the classroom. A piercing gaze captured my own.

"You running?" he inquired in a booming voice, his tone making the question seem more akin to a command. He pressed me for my answer while Jenni looked on, amused. I squeaked out an "Um, yeah," being too afraid to answer no. The man looked satisfied. Jenni looked shocked. I was certain I had signed myself up for five months of torture. Only recently have I realized that that day was a turning point for me, marking not only the birth of my athletic career, but also a major landmark in my growth as a person. For I have benefited greatly from the many positive effects running has had on my life.

I was shy and unassertive coming out of the eighth grade. Running changed that. My improvement in self-confidence, I believe, is the result of many different elements of running. For one thing, being part of a team forced me to meet new people. Through cross country I have formed many precious friendships. Running has also given me the confidence to be a leader and mentor for younger runners. More than anything else, however, I think my improvement in self-confidence has been based on learning to have the courage to succeed. Often I see girls who are reluctant to display their talents for fear of intimidating, and possibly losing, friends. A runner cannot think like that. I have learned not to apologize for being successful in running or in any other aspect of life.

WRITING WORKSHOP

OBJECTIVES

- To analyze process elements in a literary model
- To apply a writing process to create a process analysis

TEACHING THE LESSON

After students read the introduction, point out that the terms *how-to* and *how* are subpoints of process explanations. Ask students to predict what kind of organization is used in process explanations [chronological].

Have students read the model and then discuss the questions with the class. ☞

WRITING WORKSHOP

A Process Explanation

While a cause-and-effect essay uses narration to explain *why*, a process explanation, or *analysis*, uses narration to explain *how* or *how to*. Instructions of any sort are examples of one type of process explanation. They explain how to *do* something: how to cook a great meal, how to make yourself glamorous, how to get into the college of your choice, how to prepare a résumé. A second type of process explanation explains how a process *works*: how your body digests food, how a car speedometer clocks speed, how snakes shed their skins.

As the name implies, a **process analysis** breaks down a process into steps or stages and then explains each one in the order the steps occur (or should occur). The following excerpt is a good example of writing that explains how something works. It is part of an article on heat disorders, and it tells how the human body regulates its temperature.

The body temperature of warm-blooded animals is regulated by a tiny control center in the brain called the hypothalamus. When a person's blood rises above 98.6 degrees Fahrenheit, the hypothalamus sends chemical messages that prompt the heart to pump more blood and dilate the blood vessels, especially the tiny capillaries in the upper layers of the skin. More blood flows through these surface vessels so that excess heat will drain off into the cooler atmosphere by heat conduction. At the same time water diffuses through the pores of the skin (called insensible perspiration because the water evaporates before you see it and the skin remains dry).

If this is not adequate to cool the blood, the hypothalamus signals the sweat glands to pour out larger amounts of water and heat in what is called sensible perspiration, or sweating. When perspiration evaporates, heat energy is

Make the connection between the explanatory nature of cause-and-effect writing and the explanatory nature of process-analysis writing. Point out that the similarities between the two should make the writing process for the process analysis fairly easy to follow.

Ask students to tell the similarities and differences they found between cause-and-effect writing and process writing. ∎

needed to change the liquid to vapor. This heat comes from your skin; that is why sweating helps to cool your body.

Jane E. Brody, *Jane Brody's "The New York Times" Guide to Personal Health*

1. What changes (or stages) does the writer describe, and when do they occur?
2. How does the writer make the sequence clear?
3. What supporting details does the writer include, and how do these help the reader understand the process?

Writing a Process Explanation

Prewriting. What process can you explain? Have you learned about a process in social studies or science class—how a prime minister is elected in England? how mitosis occurs in cells? Perhaps you have learned about a process while working at a part-time job or participating in a sport—how a retail franchise works, how to interview prospective employees, how a sail catches the wind and powers a sailboat. Choose a process you know something about and, to avoid boring yourself and your readers, one that you think is interesting.

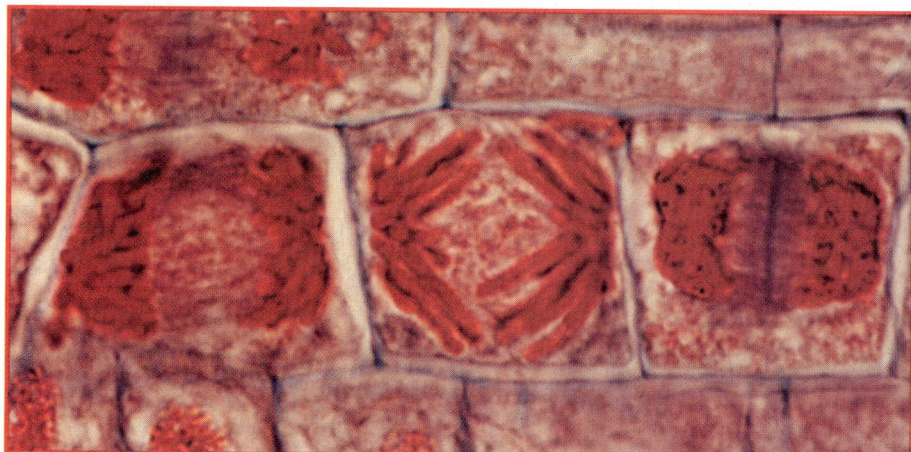

ANSWERS
Writing Workshop Questions

1. The writer describes two stages of response to overheated blood. The first, insensible perspiration, occurs when the blood temperature rises above 98.6 degrees Fahrenheit. The second is sensible perspiration, and it occurs when insensible perspiration is insufficient to cool the blood.

2. The writer makes the sequence clear by using transitional words (*when, so that, at the same time, if*), chronological order, and sequence of tenses.

3. She includes definitions of *insensible perspiration* and *sensible perspiration* and clearly worded explanations in the first and last lines of the essay to help the reader understand.

TEACHING NOTE

Remind students that in school, and especially in the workplace, writing is often a collaborative effort. When students reflect on their writing, ask them to pay particular attention to the help they received from someone else who read their essays and made suggestions for improvement.

Begin to analyze the process involved, breaking it down into separate stages or steps and putting them in the order in which they occur. If you aren't positive about all the stages and their sequence, do some research. Talk to an expert, search the Internet, or find an article on your topic. Think about the terms you will need to define and a visual diagram or chart that would help your readers.

Writing, Evaluating, and Revising. Write a first draft that opens with an attention-grabbing statement or detail. Include in your introduction any important background information. Then explain the steps or stages of the process in order, providing supporting details. To make the order of the process clear, use transitional words such as *first*, *second*, *next*, *then*, and *finally*.

After writing, ask some classmates to read your first draft and give you feedback. Are there any parts where they became lost or confused? Use your classmates' responses to help you revise your essay.

Proofreading and Publishing. Proofread the spelling, grammar, and punctuation in your revised draft. (See the guidelines for proofreading on page 49.) To share your essay, you might work with your classmates to create a "process encyclopedia," a booklet including all of your process analyses, with appropriate diagrams and illustrations. The high school or middle school media center might keep your booklet as reference material for younger students. You may also want to put your essay in your **portfolio.** If you do so, remember to date it and write a reflection. Does your essay seem interesting as well as informative? How could you make the explanations more lively? How helpful was it to have someone else read the essay?

MEETING *individual* NEEDS

LEP/ESL

General Strategies. Writing a process-explanation essay is an ideal exercise because it offers students the chance to describe things they know well. This type of essay also allows students to bring their own prior knowledge to the assignment, an important element in building self-esteem. As a warm-up, have the class brainstorm for other topics that fall into the "how-to" category and write these topics on the chalkboard. Emphasize that no process is too simple to consider as a topic. Explain to students that a familiar topic will help a writer create a clearly written paper.

LEARNING STYLES

Kinetic Learners. As students organize the steps in their process analyses, encourage all students who are writing about processes they know personally to walk through the processes or to act them out as a technique for recalling all the important details. This activity will also help students with various learning styles not to skip steps.

MAKING CONNECTIONS

USING CAUSE AND EFFECT IN PERSUASION
OBJECTIVE

- To analyze how cause and effect can be used to persuade

CAUSE AND EFFECT IN SCIENCE
OBJECTIVE

- To work with others to write a report that explains the causes and effects of some scientific topic

---

USING CAUSE AND EFFECT IN PERSUASION
Teaching Strategies

You may want to provide editorials or letters to the editor and have students explore the causes and effects found in these examples of persuasive writing. Or, you could work with students as a class to create an outline for a cause-and-effect persuasive essay on the chalkboard. Choose a pertinent topic such as "Students should be allowed to leave campus at lunch." Then, ask students to supply the causes and effects necessary to write this persuasive essay.

GUIDELINES

Assessment can be based on students' answers to the questions in the textbook. If you give students an alternative writing sample, you can evaluate whether or not they can identify the causes and effects found in that writing sample.

CAUSE AND EFFECT IN SCIENCE
Teaching Strategies

Remind students of the link between cause and effect and the narrative strategy. Point out that cause and effect is an important element in much scientific writing.

Have students read the introduction and the model. Then, discuss other scientific issues that are of concern, such as global warming, pollution, or destruction of ecosystems such as the rainforest. Help each student determine a subject of interest that can be researched.

288

MAKING CONNECTIONS

USING CAUSE AND EFFECT IN PERSUASION

Your main assignment in this chapter was to write an explanation of causes and effects; it was an attempt to explain and prove objectively, rather than an attempt to persuade—to change the attitudes or behavior of your audience. However, an explanation of causes and effects is often a significant part of a persuasive argument. Many persuasive editorials and letters to the editor, for example, base their arguments on causes that need to be remedied or on the effects of a policy or situation.

How often do writers and speakers identify causes and effects in order to persuade? Get together with a partner and conduct a survey. Find five persuasive pieces—speeches, letters to the editor, editorials, or ads. Read each example and answer the following questions:

- How many of the examples refer to causes and effects in order to support an opinion or position?
- Do the references to causes and effects strengthen the argument? Why or why not?
- Of the five examples you studied, which is the most persuasive? the least persuasive? Why?

CROSS CURRICULUM

EXPLANATIONS ACROSS THE CURRICULUM

Cause and Effect in Science

What are the effects of acid rain? What caused the dinosaurs to die out? What causes cancer? How will advanced robotics and computers affect our lives? What would be the effects of a large-scale nuclear war?

Much of scientific research is concerned with an investigation of causes or effects, and many scientific reports explain the results of those investigations. For example, scientists have recently conducted investigations into the causes and effects of obesity as a growing health problem in wealthy countries. As you read the following excerpt from an article focusing on this research, think about how the author's questions could uncover possible causes of obesity.

> Armed with powerful new tools in molecular biology and genetic engineering, scientists are seeking physiological explanations for some of the most puzzling aspects of the fattening of industrial society. Why is obesity on the rise, not just in the U.S. but in nearly all affluent countries? How is it that some individuals remain fat despite constant diets, whereas others eat what they want without gaining a pound? Why is it so hard to lose a significant amount of weight and nearly impossible to keep it off? Perhaps most important, what can be done to slow and eventually reverse this snowballing trend? The traditional notion that obesity is simply the well-deserved consequence of sloth and gluttony has led to unhelpful and sometimes incorrect answers to these questions. Science may at last offer better.
>
> W. Wayt Gibbs, from "Gaining on Fat"

Whether or not you go into one of the scientific professions, scientific research will be important in your life. Research will, or may, find cures for life-threatening diseases, discover how to protect the environment for your children, identify ways to feed the fast-growing population of our world. What scientific issues are important to you, and what have scientists already learned about their causes and effects?

Get together with two classmates, and select one scientific issue or phenomenon you all find interesting and think is important. Using library and community resources (see pages 440–441), research the topic to determine what experts say are the causes and/or effects of this issue or phenomenon. Then, prepare a three-part report: Part 1, explanation of the phenomenon or issue; Part 2, the causes and/or effects that have been identified by experts; and Part 3, a summary and projection of future actions to be taken. Finally, share what you've learned in an oral presentation to your class or an interested community organization, with each member of your group taking responsibility for one of the three parts.

Chapter 8

WRITING TO PERSUADE

OBJECTIVES

- To choose a topic for a persuasive essay and to write a position statement about the topic
- To assemble reasons and evidence that support an opinion statement
- To organize and draft a persuasive essay
- To evaluate, revise, proofread, and publish a draft of a persuasive essay

WRITING-IN-PROGRESS ASSIGNMENTS

Major Assignment: Writing a persuasive essay
Cumulative Writing Assignments: The chart below shows the sequence of cumulative assignments that will guide students as they write a persuasive essay. These Writing Assignments form the instructional core of Chapter 8.

PREWRITING
WRITING ASSIGNMENT
- Part 1: Choosing a Topic p. 300
- Part 2: Identifying and Organizing Support p. 309

WRITING YOUR FIRST DRAFT
WRITING ASSIGNMENT
- Part 3: Writing a First Draft p. 324

EVALUATING AND REVISING
WRITING ASSIGNMENT
- Part 4: Evaluating and Revising Your Essay p. 330

PROOFREADING AND PUBLISHING
WRITING ASSIGNMENT
- Part 5: Proofreading and Publishing Your Persuasive Essay p. 332

In addition, exercises 1–5 provide practice in speaking and listening, identifying appeals, choosing effective appeals, analyzing elements of a persuasive article, and analyzing revisions.

cross CURRICULUM

Paper Proposals for Social Studies

If you team teach with a social studies teacher who requires students to write research papers, consider tailoring the instruction in this chapter to a format that students may use to propose paper topics and research ideas in their social studies class. Students' proposals may include the following sections.

- **A statement of subject and purpose** Having to state clearly why a topic is worth exploring will help students choose topics that engage them. Also, students must use persuasive strategies in this section in order to convince the teacher that the proposed topic will stand up to the examination of a research paper.

- **A list of resources** Students will need to do preliminary research on their topics. A prepared list of sources shows the teacher that students have investigated their topics.

- **A schedule of work** Schedules should include the date to complete research, the date for the first draft, the date for peer evaluation, and the final due date. Working on this section as a class may help some students better organize their time.

- **Students' credentials for writing** Requiring students to examine their own interests and expertise will make them more aware of themselves as writers. The purpose of this section is for students to let the teacher know that they are qualified and able to do the kind of research and writing that they propose. Have students work in pairs to evaluate each other's proposals. Invite students to present their proposals so that all students know what their classmates are researching. Encourage students working on similar projects to collaborate on research and to work together in the evaluation and revision stages.

INTEGRATING THE LANGUAGE ARTS

SELECTION	READING AND LITERATURE	WRITING AND CRITICAL THINKING	LANGUAGE AND SYNTAX	SPEAKING, LISTENING, AND OTHER EXPRESSION SKILLS
• from **"Now You Take 'Bambi' or 'Snow White'—That's Scary!"** by Stephen King pp. 292–296 • **"Film Preservation: Whose responsibility should it be?"** by Wolf Schneider pp. 313–317 • **"The Killers"** by Art Buchwald pp. 336–337	• Responding personally to literature pp. 296, 318–319 • Identifying the main idea p. 296 • Identifying and analyzing supporting evidence pp. 296, 318–319, 338 • Responding to satire p. 338 • Analyzing satire p. 338	• Analyzing a persuasive essay pp. 296, 318–319 • Analyzing word choice p. 296 • Researching a topic p. 300 • Writing a position statement p. 300 • Identifying and analyzing logical, emotional, and ethical appeals pp. 306, 318–319, 340 • Choosing effective appeals pp. 306–307, 338 • Exploring resources p. 309 • Anticipating opposing arguments p. 309 • Identifying and correcting logical fallacies p. 328 • Evaluating and revising p. 330 • Reflecting on writing p. 332 • Writing a satire pp. 338–339 • Analyzing persuasion in an advertisement p. 340 • Writing a letter to the editor p. 343	• Analyzing word choice pp. 296, 340 • Identifying and analyzing stylistic techniques pp. 296, 318–319, 338, 340 • Using stylistic techniques p. 324 • Proofreading for errors in grammar, usage, and mechanics pp. 332, 339 • Analyzing verbal irony p. 338 • Using satirical tone and language pp. 338–339	• Discussing a persuasive essay p. 296 • Identifying issues and opposing positions in non-print media p. 300 • Working with classmates to evaluate and revise persuasive essays p. 330 • Working with classmates to analyze and present an oral report on advertising p. 340 • Working with classmates to organize and present a debate p. 342

SUGGESTED INTEGRATED UNIT PLAN

This unit plan gives suggestions on how to integrate the major strands of the language arts with this chapter.

The suggested literary selections are two examples of ironic persuasive writings and a scene in which one character persuades another. If you begin with this chapter on writing a persuasive paper or with the suggested selections, you should focus on the common characteristics of persuasive essay. You can then integrate speaking/listening and language concepts with both the writing and the literature.

Common Characteristics

- Content that is mainly evidence and explanation mixed with emotional appeal
- A purpose that is to convince a specific audience
- Language that appeals to the intended audience
- Organization that can vary with purpose—from most to least important idea or the systematic addressing of opposing points

Writing
Persuasion

Speaking/Listening
- Planning a rebuttal
- Presenting an oral report

UNIT FOCUS NONFICTION: PERSUASION

Language
Mechanics and Style

- Commas with parenthetical expressions
- Punctuation of interrupters
- Sentence combining by inserting clauses and coordinating ideas

Literature
Selections such as

- "A Modest Proposal" Jonathan Swift
- "Shakespeare's Sister" from *A Room of One's Own* Virginia Woolf
- *Macbeth* Act 1, Scene 7 William Shakespeare

CHAPTER 8: WRITING TO PERSUADE

Use this guide for creating an instructional plan that addresses the individual needs of your students. Assignments accompanied by the following symbol (*) may be completed out of class. Times given for pacing lessons are estimated.

CHAPTER PLANNING GUIDE—PUPIL'S EDITION

LESSONS	LITERARY MODEL pp. 292–296 "Now You Take 'Bambi' or 'Snow White'... by Stephen King	PREWRITING pp. 298–309	
		Generating Ideas	Gathering/Organizing
DEVELOPMENTAL PROGRAM	🕐 25–30 minutes • Read model aloud to class and discuss questions 1 and 2 on p. 296	🕐 45–50 minutes • Main Assignment: Looking Ahead p. 297 • Choosing an Issue pp. 298–300 • Exercise 1 p. 300 in pairs • Writing Assignment: Part 1 p. 300	🕐 60 minutes • Developing Support pp. 301–309 • Exercises 2–3 in groups pp. 306–307 • Writing Assignment: Part 2 p. 309
CORE PROGRAM	🕐 15–20 minutes • Have students read the model independently and discuss questions on p. 296 as a class	🕐 35–40 minutes • Main Assignment: Looking Ahead p. 297 • Choosing an Issue pp. 298–300 • Writing Note p. 300 • Exercise 1 p. 300 • Writing Assignment: Part 1 p. 300*	🕐 45–50 minutes • Developing Support pp. 301–309 • Writing Notes pp. 305, 308 • Exercises 2–3 pp. 306–307 • Writing Assignment: Part 2 p. 309*
ACCELERATED PROGRAM	🕐 15 minutes • Have students read the model independently and jot down in Reader's Logs answers to questions 3–6 on p. 296	🕐 30–35 minutes • Main Assignment: Looking Ahead p. 297 • Choosing an Issue pp. 298–300 • Writing Note p. 300 • Exercise 1 p. 300* • Writing Assignment: Part 1 p. 300*	🕐 25–30 minutes • Developing Support pp. 301–309 • Writing Notes pp. 305, 308 • Exercise 3 pp. 306–307* • Writing Assignment: Part 2 p. 309*

CHAPTER PLANNING GUIDE—PROGRAM RESOURCES

	LITERARY MODEL	PREWRITING
PRINT	• Reading Master 8, *Practice for Assessment in Reading, Vocabulary, and Spelling* p. 8	• Prewriting, *Strategies for Writing* p. 30 • Persuading Others, *English Workshop* pp. 77–86
MEDIA	• Fine Art Transparency 5, *Transparency Binder*	• Graphic Organizers 13–14, *Transparency Binder* • *Writer's Workshop 2:* Controversial Issue

WRITING pp. 310–324	EVALUATING AND REVISING pp. 325–330	PROOFREADING AND PUBLISHING pp. 331–334
🕐 **60–65 minutes** • The Basic Elements pp. 310–312 • A Basic Framework p. 319 • A Writer's Model in groups pp. 319–323 • Framework Chart p. 324 • Writing Assignment: Part 3 p. 324	🕐 **60–65 minutes** • Critical Thinking as a class pp. 325–328 • Evaluating Chart p. 329 • Exercise 5 p. 330 • Writing Assignment: Part 4 p. 330	🕐 **50–55 minutes** • Proofreading/Publishing pp. 331, 332 • Mechanics Hint p. 331 • Writing Assignment: Part 5 p. 332 • Reflecting p. 332 • A Student Model pp. 333–334
🕐 **50–55 minutes** • The Basic Elements pp. 310–312 • Writing Note p. 312 • A Persuasive Essay/ Exercise 4 pp. 313–319 • A Basic Framework/Chart pp. 319, 324 • Writing Assignment: Part 3 p. 324*	🕐 **45–50 minutes** • Critical Thinking in pairs pp. 325–328 • Evaluating Chart p. 329 • Exercise 5 p. 330* • Writing Assignment: Part 4 p. 330	🕐 **40–45 minutes** • Proofreading/Publishing pp. 331, 332 • Mechanics Hint p. 331 • Writing Assignment: Part 5 p. 332 • Reflecting p. 332 • A Student Model pp. 333–334*
🕐 **30–35 minutes** • The Basic Elements pp. 310–312 • A Persuasive Essay/ Exercise 4 pp. 313–319* • Framework Chart p. 324 • Writing Assignment: Part 3 p. 324*	🕐 **30–35 minutes** • Critical Thinking pp. 325–328* • Evaluating Chart p. 329 • Exercise 5 p. 330* • Writing Assignment: Part 4 p. 330	🕐 **20–25 minutes** • Mechanics Hint p. 331 • Writing Assignment: Part 5 p. 332* • Reflecting p. 332

WRITING	EVALUATING AND REVISING	PROOFREADING AND PUBLISHING
• Writing, *Strategies for Writing* p. 31	• Evaluating and Revising, *Strategies for Writing* p. 32	• Proofreading Practice, *Strategies for Writing* p. 34 • Commas with Other Interrupters, *English Workshop* pp. 305–306
	• Revision Transparencies 13–14, *Transparency Binder* 📽	• *Language Workshop:* Lesson 44 💾

ELEMENTS OF WRITING: CURRICULUM CONNECTIONS

Writing Workshop
• A Satire pp. 335–339

Making Connections
• Analyzing Persuasion in an Advertisement p. 340
• Speaking and Listening: Persuasion and Debate pp. 341–342
• Writing a Letter to the Editor pp. 342–343

ASSESSMENT OPTIONS

Summative Assessment
Holistic Scoring: Prompts and Models pp. 27–32

Portfolio Assessment
Portfolio forms, *Portfolio Assessment* pp. 5–25, 44–48

Reflection
Writing Process Log, *Strategies for Writing* p. 29
Self-assessment Record, *Portfolio Assessment* p. 19

Ongoing Assessment
Proofreading, *Strategies for Writing* p. 33

💾 Computer disk or CD-ROM

📽 Overhead transparencies

OBJECTIVES

- To write personal responses to literature
- To identify and analyze characteristics of persuasive writing
- To identify supporting examples in a persuasive essay

MOTIVATION

Bring to class two or three newspaper editorials that each take a stand on a particular issue. Read these editorials to the class and then have the class identify the issue discussed and the stand taken in each editorial.

PROGRAM MANAGER

CHAPTER 8

- **Computer Guided Instruction** For a related assignment that students may use for additional instruction and practice, see **Controversial Issue** in *Writer's Workshop 2 CD-ROM*.

- **Practice** To help less-advanced students who need additional practice with concepts and activities related to this chapter, see **Chapter 7** in *English Workshop, Complete Course,* pp. 77–86.

- **Summative Assessment** For a writing prompt, including grading criteria and student models, see *Holistic Scoring: Prompts and Models,* pp. 27–32.

- **Extension/Enrichment** See **Fine Art Transparency 5,** *Government Bureau* by George Tooker. For suggestions on how to tie the transparency to instruction, review teacher's notes in *Fine Art and Instructional Transparencies for Writing,* p. 27.

- **Reading Support** For help with the reading selection, pp. 292–296, see **Reading Master 8** in *Practice for Assessment in Reading, Vocabulary, and Spelling,* p. 8.

8 WRITING TO PERSUADE

After you have introduced the idea of taking a stand on an issue, point out that the audience that King is addressing in *TV Guide* includes many parents. Next, read the first paragraph aloud. Before reading the next three paragraphs aloud, tell your students to see if they can predict the horror tale that King is narrating. Give students an opportunity to guess what tale King has just retold. Then tell students to finish reading the article independently.

When students finish reading the article, use the annotations and the **Writer's Craft** questions to guide a class discussion of the article.

☛

Taking a Stand

We all have pet peeves, little things that bother us but are not worth getting upset about. Every now and then, though, an issue comes up that we feel we just can't let slip by. We decide we have to say something, to let others know our opinion. We have to **take a stand.**

Writing and You. Writers often take a stand. Powerful columnists pressure lawmakers to take action or to change their positions on sensitive issues. Critics build or threaten artists' careers with their reviews. People just like you argue, complain, encourage, and urge others on in letters to newspapers and magazines. On what issue are you ready to take a stand?

As You Read. In the following article, writer Stephen King tackles an issue personally important to him in more ways than one: children's exposure to horror on TV. As you read, look especially at the examples he uses to persuade readers that his opinion has merit.

Ben Shahn, *For All These Rights We've Just Begun to Fight* (1946). Lithograph in colors (poster), $28\frac{1}{4}$" × $38\frac{3}{4}$". Collection of the New Jersey State Museum, Trenton, New Jersey. Gift of Mr. and Mrs. Michael Lewis, FA1969.156. © 1998 Estate of Ben Shahn / Licensed by VAGA, New York, N.Y.

VISUAL CONNECTIONS
For All These Rights We've Just Begun to Fight

About the Artist. Ben Shahn (1898–1969) expressed through his art his opinions about issues that were important during his lifetime. Part of the Social Realist tradition, Shahn chronicled the American political scene and sought to inspire his viewers to support the causes he believed in. This poster, for example, supports workers' rights. In addition to graphics such as the lithograph shown here, Shahn was engaged in drawing, painting, printmaking, and the design and production of murals, tapestries, and stained glass.

Ideas for Writing. Discuss with the class how purpose, audience, and tone apply to art. Then have students write paragraphs about this print by identifying its purpose [to persuade], audience [eligible voters], and tone [answers may vary].

QUOTATION FOR THE DAY
"When I saw something that needed doing, I did it." (Nellie Cashman, Irish adventurer)

Ask students to freewrite for a few minutes about what needs to be done to improve or change negative circumstances. Explain that in this chapter, students will consider current issues and will argue points about these issues in persuasive compositions.

MEETING *individual* NEEDS

LEP/ESL

General Strategies. Students' oral language skills are usually more developed than their written language skills. Stephen King's article and the **Reader's Response** activity provide an opportunity for student involvement in oral debate and in role-playing. Have students assume the role of parents debating among themselves the very issue that King has raised. Or have students play the roles of a parent and child taking opposite views. Encourage students to draw upon their experiences to justify statements and opinions.

USING THE SELECTION

from Now You Take 'Bambi' or 'Snow White'—That's Scary!

1

What fairy tale does this story remind you of? ["Hansel and Gretel"]

292

from **"NOW YOU TAKE 'BAMBI' OR 'SNOW WHITE'—**

THAT'S SCARY!"

by Stephen King Read the story synopsis below and ask yourself if it would make the sort of film you'd want your kids watching on the Friday- or Saturday-night movie:

A good but rather weak man discovers that, because of inflation, recession and his second wife's fondness for overusing his credit cards, the family is tottering on the brink of financial ruin. In fact, they can expect to see the repossession men coming for the car, the almost new recreational vehicle and the two color TVs any day; and a pink warning-of-foreclosure notice has already arrived from the bank that holds the mortgage on their house.

1 The wife's solution is simple but chilling: kill the two children, make it look like an accident and collect the insurance. She browbeats her husband into going along with this homicidal scheme. A wilderness trip is arranged, and while wifey stays in camp, the father leads his two children deep into the Great Smoky wilderness. In the end, he finds he cannot kill them in cold blood; he simply leaves them to wander around until, presumably, they will die of hunger and exposure.

The two children spend a horrifying three days and two nights in the wilderness. Near the end of their endurance, they stumble upon a back-country cabin and go to it, hoping for rescue. The woman who lives alone there turns out to be a cannibal. She cages the two children and prepares to roast them in her oven as she has roasted and eaten other wanderers before them. The boy manages to get free. He creeps up behind the woman as she stokes her oven and pushes her in, where she burns to death in her own fire.

RETEACHING

Duplicate copies of an editorial from a newspaper or magazine. Using the **Writer's Craft** questions as a guide, design an exercise to give students practice in analyzing an editorial. Work with students to highlight the thesis statement and to underline the support statements.

CLOSURE

Have students list in their writing journals some basic persuasive elements that King and other writers use. Ask two or three volunteers to read their lists. [clear stand, reasons, factual examples, logic, emotion, and effective style]

293

You're probably shaking your head no, even if you have already recognized the origin of this bloody little tale (and if you didn't, ask your kids: they probably will) as "Hansel and Gretel," a so called "fairy tale" that most kids are exposed to even before they start kindergarten. In addition to this story, with its grim and terrifying images of child abandonment, children lost in the woods and imprisoned by an evil woman, cannibalism and justifiable homicide, small children are routinely exposed to tales of mass murder and mutilation ("Bluebeard"), the eating of a loved one by a monster ("Little Red Riding-Hood"), treachery and deceit ("Snow White") and even the specter of a little boy who must face a black-

2 hooded, ax-wielding headsman ("The 500 Hats of Bartholomew Cubbins," by Dr. Seuss).

I'm sometimes asked what I allow my kids to watch on the tube, for two reasons: first, my three children, at 10, 8, and 4, are still young enough to be in the age group that opponents of TV violence and horror consider to be particularly impressionable and at risk; and

3 second, my seven novels have been popularly classified as "horror stories." People tend to think those two facts contradictory. But . . . I'm not sure that they are.

Three of my books have been made into films, and at this writing, two of them have been shown on TV. In the

4 case of "Salem's Lot," a made-for-TV movie, there was never a question of allowing my kids to watch it on its first run on CBS; it began at 9 o'clock in our time zone, and all three children go to

"I watched, appalled, dismayed and sweaty with fear, as Snow White bit into the poisoned apple while the old crone giggled in evil ecstasy."

VISUAL CONNECTIONS

Exploring the Subject. Born in 1947 in Portland, Maine, Stephen King had an impoverished childhood. His father, who had himself been interested in macabre writing, deserted the family when King was two or three years old. Lonely and introverted, King enjoyed listening to horror tales on the radio, watching science fiction and monster movies, and reading stories from his father's paperback collection of fantasy-horror fiction. King began writing when he was seven years old. He graduated from the University of Maine at Orono in 1970 with a degree in English. He taught English at Hampden Academy until his writing turned into a full-time career. He lives with his wife and children in a rambling Victorian house in Bangor, Maine.

2
In this book, published by Theodore Seuss Geisel (Dr. Seuss) in 1938, Bartholomew doffs his hat to the king only to find it replaced again and again by other hats; his life is in danger for not respecting the king until the king himself trades Bartholomew's life for the last elegant hat.

3
Since this article was written in the early 1980s, King has written several other novels—bringing his total to well over twenty.

4
Salem's Lot was a successful TV miniseries in 1979.

EXTENSION

Let students work in groups of four or five to rewrite fairy tales into scripts for modern horror films. Suggest that the best source for tales is probably the retellings of Jakob and Wilhelm Grimm. Give students simple guidelines for selecting characters, writing dialogue, costuming, acting, and filming their script on videocassette.

ENRICHMENT

Have students search for articles that refute King's stand on horror movies. Once the articles are found, have students analyze them to find the reasons the authors use to convince readers that this genre of movies is harmful to children. ■

294

5
Ironically, King almost scrapped the partial manuscript of *Carrie,* his first successful novel, but his wife retrieved it and encouraged King to finish it.

6
Made into a successful movie (1976) with Sissy Spacek, William Katt, and John Travolta, this book tells of how a girl avenges the humiliation her teenage schoolmates have brought her by telekinetically destroying them and the entire town.

7
Perhaps King is suggesting that the curious blend of fantasy and reality in Walt Disney's films *Snow White, Bambi, Fantasia,* and *101 Dalmatians* can be a cause of childhood fear.

bed earlier than that. Even on a weekend, and even for the oldest, an 11 o'clock bedtime is just not negotiable. A previous *TV GUIDE* article about children and frightening programs mentioned a 3-year-old who watched "Lot" and consequently suffered night terrors. I have no wish to question any responsible parent's judgment—all parents raise their children in different ways—but it did strike me as passingly odd that a 3-year-old should have been allowed to stay up that late to get scared.

But in my case, the hours of the telecast were not really a factor, because we have one of those neat little time-machines, a videocassette recorder. I taped the program and, after viewing it myself, decided my children could watch it if they wanted to. My daughter had no interest; she's more involved with stories of brave dogs and loyal horses these days. My two sons, Joe, 8, and Owen, then 3, did watch. Neither of them seemed to have any problems either while watching it or in the middle of the night—when those problems most likely turn up.

"Like their elders, children have a right to experience the entire spectrum of drama. . . ."

5 I also have a tape of "Carrie," a theatrical film first shown on TV about two and a half years ago. I elected to keep this one on what my kids call "the high shelf" (where I put the tapes that are **6** forbidden to them), because I felt that its depiction of children turning against other children, the lead character's horrifying embarrassment at a school dance and her later act of matricide would upset them. "Lot," on the contrary, is a story that the children accepted as a fairy tale in modern dress.

Other tapes on my "high shelf" include "Night of the Living Dead" (cannibalism), "The Brood" (David Cronenberg's film of intergenerational breakdown and homicidal "children of rage" who are set free to murder and rampage), and "The Exorcist." They are all up there for the same reason: they contain elements that I think might freak the kids out.

Not that it's possible to keep kids away from everything on TV (or in the movies, for that matter) that will freak them out; the movies that terrorized my own nights most thoroughly as a kid were not those through which Frankenstein's monster or the Wolfman **7** lurched and growled, but the Disney cartoons. I watched Bambi's mother shot and Bambi running frantically to escape being burned up in a forest fire. I watched, appalled, dismayed and sweaty with fear, as Snow White bit into the poisoned apple while the old <u>crone</u> giggled in evil ecstasy. I was similarly terrified by the walking brooms in "Fantasia" and the big, bad wolf who chased the fleeing pigs from house to house with such grim and homicidal intensity. More recently, Owen, who just turned 4, crawled into bed with my wife and me. "Cruella DeVille is in my room," he said. Cruella DeVille is, of course, the villainess of "101 Dalmatians," and I suppose Owen had decided that a woman who would want to turn puppies into dogskin coats might also be interested in little boys. All these films would certainly get G-ratings if they were produced today, and frightening excerpts of them have been shown on TV during "the children's hour."

Do I believe that all violent or horrifying programming should be banned from network TV? No, I do not. Do I believe it should be telecast only in the later evening hours, TV's version of the "high shelf"? Yes, I do. Do I believe that children should be forbidden all violent or horrifying programs? No, I do not. Like their elders, children have a right to experience the entire <u>spectrum</u> of drama, from such warm and mostly unthreatening **8** programs as *Little House on the Prairie* and *The Waltons* to scarier fare. It's been suggested again and again that such entertainment offers us a <u>catharsis</u>—a chance to enter for a little while a scary and yet controllable world where we can express our fears, aggressions and possibly even hostilities. Surely no one would suggest that children do not have their

8
The television programs *Little House on the Prairie* and *The Waltons* were popular family shows in the 1970s.

ANSWERS

Reader's Response

Responses will vary.

1. Students might agree that parents have more responsibility for deciding what their children watch. Encourage students to set up an imaginary family with children of specific ages.

2. Students might list several horror movies that were exceptionally scary, such as *The Shining* and *Friday the 13th.*

Writer's Craft

3. In his last two paragraphs, King states his thesis that "children have a right to experience the entire spectrum of drama," but that "a child's intake of violent or horrifying programs should be limited" by parents.

4. King gives the example of his own children watching *Salem's Lot* without disturbing effects. His example from "Hansel and Gretel" is emotional. In the essay, he emphasizes that a child has to face fears and dark feelings anyway, so books and films may be psychologically helpful.

5. Students should support their responses with specific examples from the essay.

6. King concedes that a limited number of programs should be telecast only in the later evening. But he argues that horror and fear are already present in accepted children's fare.

SELECTION AMENDMENT
Description of change: excerpted
Rationale: to focus on the concept of persuasive writing presented in this chapter

---

own fears and hostilities to face and overcome; those dark feelings are the basis of many of the fairy tales children love best.

Do I think a child's intake of violent or horrifying programs should be limited? Yes, I do, and that's why I have a high shelf. But the pressure groups who want to see all horror (and anything smacking of sex, for that matter) arbitrarily removed from television make me both uneasy and angry. The element of Big Brotherism inherent in such an idea causes the unease; the idea of a bunch of people I don't even know presuming to dictate what is best for my children causes the anger. I feel that deciding such things myself is my right—and my responsibility.

TV Guide

READER'S RESPONSE

1. Do Stephen King's arguments convince you that only parents have the right to decide what their children are allowed to watch on TV? Why or why not? Discuss in class how you would feel, and act, as a *parent*.

2. What movie or TV show has frightened you badly or kept you from sleeping? What about it frightened you? How old were you? Did this affect the type of movies or TV shows you watched afterward?

WRITER'S CRAFT

3. Not until late in the essay does King explicitly state his opinion, or stand. What (and where) is this statement?

4. Before this, you implicitly know King's position because he's advancing support for it—reasons, especially in the form of factual examples. What are these examples? Do they have a logical or emotional impact? At the end of the excerpt, what reasons does King hammer home?

5. Where in the essay do you think King's writing—his word choice or style—is an effective part of his persuasion?

6. How well does King answer people on the other side of the issue—people who want to further restrict or ban horror on television? What arguments of theirs does he meet, and how? Are there any strong opposing arguments that he does *not* address?

WAYS TO PERSUADE

TEACHING METHODS OF DEVELOPMENT

You may want to help students understand the various methods of development by giving examples of each as used in Stephen King's article. For example, King uses narration to tell his modern version of "Hansel and Gretel," description in recreating frightening scenes from Disney films, classification in categorizing movies as appropriate or not appropriate ("high shelf") for children, and evaluation in criticizing parental behavior that allows three-year-old children to stay up late to watch frightening movies. ■

297

Ways to Persuade

Like Stephen King, writers who persuade want to change people's minds and, sometimes, their actions. In order to reach the right audience for this issue, King chose to publish his essay in the popular magazine *TV Guide*. Persuasive writing, however, shows up in many different forums and forms: books, newspapers, speeches, advertisements, editorials, sermons, business proposals, and résumé cover letters. There are many ways to develop a persuasive message. Here are some examples.

- in an e-mail message, describing how popular a band has become in order to persuade a friend to buy her concert ticket early
- in a note, describing an artist's paintings to persuade a parent to go to an exhibit with you
- in a speech, telling about your experiences tutoring fifth-graders in math to convince other high school students to become tutors
- in an editorial, comparing two methods of lawn care to convince readers that one is safer for residents and the environment
- in a school magazine article, defining the term *individualism* to persuade school officials rot to require school uniforms
- in a business proposal, telling about your experience as a chef to convince investors to finance your restaurant
- in a letter to a senator, considering the pros and cons of lowering the voting age, and either supporting or opposing this action
- in a review, evaluating a book to convince readers to buy it

LOOKING AHEAD

In this chapter, you will write a persuasive essay using evaluation in your main writing assignment. Keep in mind that persuasive essays

- state the writer's position, or opinion, about an important issue
- provide convincing support for the writer's stand
- refute significant opposing positions

INTEGRATING THE LANGUAGE ARTS

Literature Link. If it is available in your literature textbook, have students read George Orwell's essay "Shooting an Elephant." Orwell is trying to persuade his readers to gain and keep individual freedom in thought and action and not to give in to institutional or mob pressures as he had when, as a young man, he shot an elephant. Ask students to search the essay for examples of narration (paragraphs 4–13), description (paragraphs 11–12), classification (paragraph 9), and evaluation (last paragraph). Remind your class that each of these methods of development can occur in combination—even in the same paragraph—with one or more of the other methods.

COOPERATIVE LEARNING

Organize students into small groups and give each group three or four advertisements from newspapers or magazines. Ask students to analyze the advertisements to determine what methods of persuasion the advertisers have employed. Ask students to draw a conclusion about the most common methods of persuasion used in advertising.

OBJECTIVES

- To use speaking and listening skills to select an issue for a persuasive paper and to write a position statement
- To analyze examples of persuasion for audience and for use of logical, emotional, and ethical appeals
- To find and organize support for a persuasive essay

PROGRAM MANAGER

PREWRITING

- **Self-Assessment** Before beginning instruction of the writing process, see **Writing Process Log** in *Strategies for Writing*, p. 29.
- **Heuristics** To help students generate ideas, see **Prewriting** in *Strategies for Writing*, p. 30.
- **Instructional Support** See **Graphic Organizers 13** and **14**. For suggestions on how to tie the transparencies to instruction, review teacher's notes in *Fine Art and Instructional Transparencies for Writing*, pp. 77, 79.

QUOTATION FOR THE DAY

"The world is not run by thought, nor by imagination, but by opinion . . ." (Elizabeth Drew, 1887–1965, English literary critic and writer)

Have students brainstorm a list of current opinions. Explain that persuasive writing provides students the opportunity to select issues about which they feel strongly.

VISUAL CONNECTIONS

Exploring the Subject. Derived from the court dances of Renaissance Italy, ballet reflects its courtly origins in its elegant movements.

Pioneers of the modern dance

continued on next page

Writing a Persuasive Essay

Prewriting

Choosing an Issue

Look around. What's going on in your life? in your community? in the world? Chances are you are surrounded by many *issues*, topics about which people have opposing opinions.

How do you feel about the government guaranteeing everyone a free college education? Should the manufacturing of items be banned if they can't be recycled? Should animal experimentation be abolished? There are at least two sides to each of these questions. Any one of them would make a good topic for a persuasive essay.

The issue you choose to write about, however, should also mean something to you personally. You need to get fired up, or you won't be able to fire up other people. Here are some points to keep in mind as you look for a topic that's right for you:

- Choose an issue that is important and interesting to you. It should be one you have a strong belief about, or at least a strong curiosity about.
- Make sure it's a real issue, not just your personal preference. You will have to be able to gather outside evidence to convince others. (You may think ballet surpasses all other dance forms, but you will never be able to persuade a modern dance lover that modern dance is an inferior art. It's a matter of taste.)

Bring to class examples of magazine advertisements that use different appeals to try to sell similar products—automobiles, for example. Ask students to brainstorm about the advertisers' purpose (to sell cars), audience (prospective buyers), and appeals (logical, emotional, ethical). You might begin with the advertisements described in the answers to **Exercise 2** on p. 306 and add an advertisement with an ethical appeal— the founder of a company speaking for her or his product, for example.

■ Be sure your issue is arguable, that many people can and will disagree about it. (You may feel strongly that teenagers shouldn't hitchhike, but few people are real proponents of hitchhiking.)

Identifying Your Thesis

In a persuasive essay, the *thesis* of your paper—the main point you want to get across—is your opinion, or position, on the issue. This thesis is called a *proposition* or *position statement.* Writing your position statement in a sentence or two is an important prewriting step. It helps you stay on track as you gather information and as you draft.

POSITION STATEMENTS

Schools should abolish grades as a way of judging performance.

Passive resistance is the only acceptable way to protest.

Mohandas Gandhi (center), proponent of passive resistance

No single country should control any part of the world's oceans.

Laws should limit violence on television.

movement believed that ballet movements were artificial and sought personal expression through dance.

MEETING individual NEEDS

LEP/ESL

General Strategies. To introduce the material and to provide a clear understanding of what is expected in the assignment, show segments taped from television that exemplify the persuasive techniques. Include ads from political campaigns or for cars, cereals, cosmetics, soft drinks, or hosiery. Encourage class discussion about the questions posed in this exercise: Who is the probable audience? Which appeal (logical, emotional, or ethical) predominates? Why do you think each appeal was chosen? How well do you think it works? Why? Be sure to pinpoint concrete examples of the different kinds of appeals.

VISUAL CONNECTIONS
Exploring the Subject. Mohandas Karamchand Gandhi, called "Mahatma" or "Great Soul" by the people of India, is known as the father of modern India. He employed the method of nonviolent resistance based on courage and truth. Gandhi's dream of independence for India was realized in 1947, but the accompanying conflict between Hindus and Muslims resulted in Gandhi's assassination by an extremist Hindu who opposed Gandhi's program.

Before you assign **Exercise 3**, on p. 306, model the procedure of developing evidence with logical, emotional, and ethical appeals by answering the first question in class. Call on three different volunteers to provide the three kinds of evidence, and then ask the class which type of appeal should be emphasized.

You can provide further guided practice for your students by creating a group planning chart like the one on p. 308. At the top of a transparency, write the position statement "Penalties for oil spills should be more severe." Then elicit students' suggestions for reasons and supporting evidence, opposing arguments, and refutations. You might even write evidence for the various

MEETING *individual* NEEDS

LEP/ESL

General Strategies. A direct, well-reasoned, and logical approach is the standard of good persuasive writing in American culture. But not all cultures share this approach. Some cultures prefer indirect persuasion; others use passionate emotion; and many place much less importance on logic.

Many of your students may have already received instruction in persuasive writing in their native countries. When critiquing students' papers, acknowledge that other approaches are useful, but that mastering this method will help students to persuade others in American society.

302

Writing to Persuade

Using Logical Appeals

Logical appeals are appeals to reason, to clear thinking; and they are important in any persuasive essay. An ad, for example, may disregard logic entirely (many do!), but an essay can't. Readers expect you to have good *reasons* for your opinion; they expect to learn *why* you believe as you do.

Position Statement: Penalties for oil spills should be more severe.
Reasons: Oil spills may permanently damage the environment.
Oil companies will improve safety measures if their profits are threatened.

Most people also want *evidence*, or proof, to back up the reasons. Here are two basic forms of evidence:

- *Facts:* statements that can be proved by testing, personal experience, or verification from reliable sources. Some facts consist of *data,* or information that can help in reasoning to a conclusion. They may also consist of examples and *statistics,* or numerical information. *Anecdotes,* or brief stories often based on personal experiences, also may be used as factual evidence.

> It is estimated that for every million metric tons of oil transported annually, about one metric ton is lost to spillage.

> A study of spill effects in the Caribbean found that coral organisms were severely harmed.

Remind students that the text itself contains supporting evidence on this issue that appeals to an audience's logic and emotions.

Some companies that have paid large fines—especially in highly publicized cases—have released public statements of new procedures they will follow to prevent oil spills.

- *Expert Testimony:* statements by people who are recognized authorities on the issue.

In her book *Silent Spring,* Rachel Carson, marine biologist and environmentalist, wrote, "The most alarming of all man's assaults upon the environment is the contamination of air, earth, rivers, and sea with dangerous and even lethal materials. This pollution is for the most part irrecoverable; the chain of evil it initiates not only in the world that must support life but in living tissues is for the most part irreversible."

When you are gathering evidence from outside sources, make sure the source is reliable and not unfairly biased. Because your topic is inherently controversial, you should check facts and expert opinion in more than one source. If your sources aren't sound, your logical appeals can fail.

Using Emotional Appeals

People tend to make decisions with their hearts as well as their minds. Knowing what your audience cares about gives you a chance to appeal to their emotions. For example, there is a good reason why advertisers so often use children in their commercials. What better way to sell long-distance telephone service than by showing a grandparent receiving a call from an adorable grandchild?

You usually don't have to look far to find an idea with *emotional appeal.* In fact, because some examples and details appeal to the emotions as well as to reason, you will probably discover some emotional appeals when you are looking for logical appeals. For example, the following details about an Alaskan oil spill are factual, but they also arouse strong feelings.

VISUAL CONNECTIONS
Exploring the Subject. Marine biologist, author, and teacher Rachel Carson (1907–1964) dates her love of nature back to her childhood. She says that her mother introduced her to the wonders of the outdoors and its creatures, and she admits that she was fascinated by the sea long before she ever saw it.

Of her many books about the sea, *The Sea Around Us,* which won a National Book Award in 1951, is probably the most popular and critically acclaimed. Carson's most famous book, however, is *Silent Spring* (1962). This book captured the attention of the public in general and of President John F. Kennedy in particular, resulting in a federal investigation into the indiscriminate use of pesticides.

SELECTION AMENDMENT
Description of change: excerpted
Rationale: to focus on the concept of prewriting presented in this chapter

After completing **Exercises 1–3** and after analyzing the model that you have provided, students should be able to complete **Writing Assignment: Parts 1** and **2** on their own.

ASSESSMENT

Exercises 1 and **2** need no formal assessment, but you may want small groups of students to compare and discuss their answers for **Exercise 3**. Assess the position statements elicited from **Writing Assignment: Part 1** informally to make sure that each position statement focuses on a real, arguable issue and that the position is clearly

---

Following the oil spill, the beaches were littered with thousands of otters and birds, slowly freezing to death after their protective fur and feathers were drenched with the black, foul-smelling oil.

This example shows you another potent emotional tool in persuasion: *language.* Words can have great power, especially those with **connotative meanings:** the feelings or attitudes that a word suggests. If you are calling for stronger penalties against those responsible for oil spills, you will want to gather data and statistics about environmental effects, but you will bring those facts to frightening life when you describe feathers "drenched" (not just "covered") with "black, foul-smelling oil" (not just "oil") or otters "slowly freezing to death" (not just "dying"). Suddenly, the incident is real. People care.

Powerfully charged words such as these must be used carefully, however. Use them only to emphasize important points. It is okay to shock, but you don't want to overdo it. Your purpose is to appeal to your audience's emotions, but you want to be seen as credible, not extreme.

Using Ethical Appeals

Establishing your own credibility and character is also a specific type of appeal: the **ethical appeal.** If you are to convince people of anything, people must believe in you, the writer. They must believe that you can be trusted; that you are fair, that you know what you are talking about; that you are sensitive, responsible, and sincere. Rather than hoping readers will assume these qualities, the careful persuader exhibits them.

A DIFFERENT APPROACH

Refer students to the paragraph on this page that begins "Powerfully charged words such as these must be used carefully, however." Tell students that two unfair techniques are attacking the person and hasty generalization. Attacking the person elicits an automatically negative response from such emotional terms as "warmonger" or "rabble rouser." Hasty generalizations can elicit unearned positive responses from such phrases as "a loyal American" and "a fine, upstanding citizen." In both cases these emotional terms are often used to cover up for missing support. Ask students to identify each of the terms below as attacking the person, neutral, or hasty generalization:

1. a bleeding-heart liberal [attacking the person]
2. a conservative Democrat [neutral]
3. a heartless reactionary [attacking the person]
4. the American way of life [hasty generalization]
5. a courageous veteran [hasty generalization]

TIMESAVER

Ask students to highlight each different type of appeal in a different color. At a glance, you will be able to make sure that students have a variety of evidence.

RETEACHING

Use a documentary that you have recorded from PBS to provide a visual example of persuasion. Analyze this program for the class by pointing out such things as the issue (which may be implicit), the support, and the appeals that are used.

☛

For example, you help establish your sense of fairness by considering different sides of an issue. Let's say your essay calls for drastic cuts in the benefits members of Congress receive. Although some people might agree that legislators, as public servants, should work for minimum wage without special benefits, many business people and political insiders would consider this argument foolish. You may gain credibility with these audiences by writing:

> As we begin to bring Congressional expenditures into line, we must be careful not to go overboard. Members of Congress must be able to support their families, must be able to maintain homes in Washington as well as in their home states. But they cannot be allowed to become independently wealthy at taxpayers' expense.

In this way, you exhibit common sense and show that you are not calling for irresponsible or radical action.

A different ethical appeal might establish the moral basis for an argument, therefore engaging the readers' values. In his essay about film preservation, magazine editor Wolf Schneider appeals to the audience's sense of what is important in life as he quotes two well-known directors.

> At the launching of the Film Foundation last year, in the cool chamber of the Creative Artists Agency screening room, director Sydney Pollack warned that "a society that doesn't pay attention to its cultural heritage is not an interesting or pleasant society to live in." "Films tell us about our souls," [Martin] Scorsese says a year later. "No one can calculate that value."

WRITING NOTE

A persuasive essay differs from *formal argument,* a line of reasoning that attempts to explain or prove by logic. Research reports, business proposals, and some school essays require formal argument. They are strictly logical, thorough, and fair, looking at all available evidence, whether favorable or unfavorable. Most examples of persuasion in books, newspapers, and public speaking, however, aren't formal arguments. Their purpose is to persuade, not to prove by logic. In a persuasive essay you can select the most favorable evidence, appeal to emotions, and use style to sway your readers. Your single purpose is to be convincing.

SELECTION AMENDMENT
Description of change: excerpted
Rationale: to focus on the concept of ethical appeals presented in this chapter

You can conclude this lesson by asking students the following questions:

1. Define *position statement.* [sentence that states writer's position on issue]
2. What are the three types of appeals? [logical, emotional, ethical]

3. Define *refutation.* [answer to opposing arguments]

ANSWERS
Exercise 2

Have students work in mixed-ability groups of three or four students each. Have the groups present their reports to the whole class.

ANSWERS
Exercise 3

1. Emphasize emotional appeal.
Logical: Some poor families spend as much as 20 percent of their income on lottery tickets.
Emotional: Many people will buy lottery tickets with grocery money.
Ethical: The lottery has an effect on individuals and families.

2. Emphasize emotional appeal.
Logical: Less than half of today's school children know the national anthem.
Emotional: The national anthem is a badge of honor and pride.
Ethical: Three generations of my family have fought for the United States.

306

---

306   *Writing to Persuade*

EXERCISE 2 ▶ **Identifying Logical, Emotional, and Ethical Appeals**

Work with others as a team to analyze the appeals in different examples of persuasion. Collect a good sampling—advertisements, editorials, and letters—and pinpoint logical, emotional, and ethical appeals. (Don't forget to consider music and/or visuals in ads.) Prepare a group report by considering these questions for each example: Who is the probable audience? Which appeal(s) predominates? (Give examples.) Why do you think each appeal was chosen? How well do you think it works? Why?

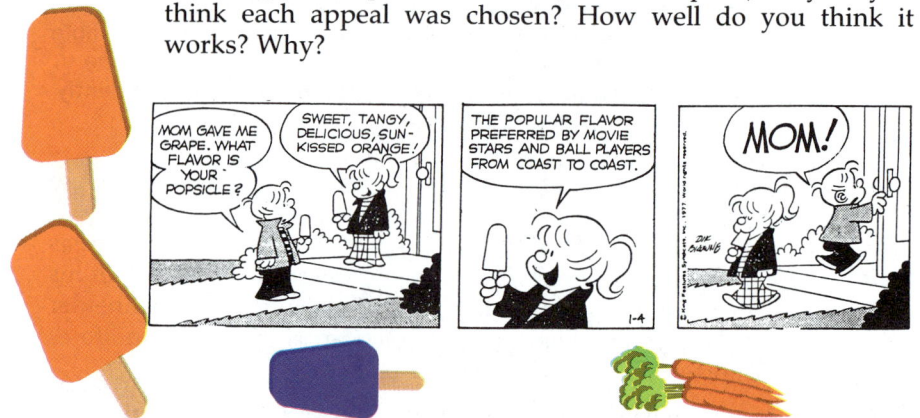

Hi & Lois reprinted with special permission of King Features Syndicate, Inc.

EXERCISE 3 ▶ **Choosing Effective Appeals**

The most effective appeals are the ones most persuasive to a particular audience. Study the four position statements that follow and the audience for each. In an essay, what particular support might convince these readers? Would you emphasize a certain type of appeal? For each position statement, develop at least one logical appeal (reason and evidence), emotional appeal (details/language), and ethical appeal (testimony to the writer's good character).

Have each student apply the principles of persuasion by planning and presenting a political speech—perhaps on the same topic as the paper he or she is planning. The class can then evaluate the speeches. Have students determine if each speech would convince them to change their minds about the issue.

If possible, take your students on a field trip to a civil court in your area. Ask students to listen for the types of persuasive appeals and methods of refutation used by the lawyers in the courtroom. When you return to the classroom, list on the chalkboard the various appeals and methods of refutation that your students identified. ■

1. **Position Statement:** State lotteries conducted for any purpose should be abolished.
   Audience: state legislators

2. **Position Statement:** Every school day should begin with students singing the national anthem.
   Audience: PTA members

3. **Position Statement:** The city should not build a new municipal building.
   Audience: city council

4. **Position Statement:** Fasting is a dangerous way to try to lose weight.
   Audience: students your own age

Identifying Opposing Positions

When you chose your issue, you knew others would disagree with you. And you have to be ready for that opposition. Before writing, you should anticipate strong opposing arguments and plan your response, called a *refutation.* Your audience analysis and research are two good sources of opposing reasons.

Although you are not required to cover all opposing positions in a persuasive essay, refutation is usually an important strategy. Addressing the strongest opposing views strengthens your own argument and helps you select the most convincing support possible. You may even find an opposing position that you believe has merit. Admitting this in your essay is called *conceding a point.* It won't hurt you. Sometimes, it even helps, because it shows your fairness and openness. (Remember that establishing your credibility with your readers is an important part of persuasive writing.) In effect, your concession is an ethical appeal.

One way to pull together your support for a position statement is to make a chart like the one shown on the following page. Notice that the writer has included a position statement and that the audience is clearly identified. Next, the reasons and supporting evidence for the writer's position are listed. Finally, the writer has anticipated the most significant opposition positions and has collected a number of arguments to counteract these opposing ideas.

3. Emphasize logical appeal.
   Logical: The old municipal building has adequate workspace for its employees, and it does pass recent safety codes.
   Emotional: The old municipal building is a work of art.
   Ethical: I spent one entire day inspecting the old building and talking to workers there.

4. Emphasize ethical appeal.
   Logical: Fasting affects the metabolism and can cause many health problems.
   Emotional: Don't risk your life by fasting.
   Ethical: After fasting for a week, I was hospitalized for dehydration and malnutrition.

MEETING *individual* NEEDS

LEARNING STYLES

Auditory Learners. Allow students to use radio advertisements and persuasive musical lyrics as the basis for answering **Exercise 2.**

Visual Learners. Tell students that humor is often used for persuasive purposes. This kind of humor, often called satire, is most common in political cartoons. Ask students to create persuasive cartoons to accompany the prewriting for their persuasive essays.

INTEGRATING THE LANGUAGE ARTS

Library Link. You may want to take students to the library to research various issues before the students select issues and write position statements. Explain that they may discover their position statements and plans on their own, or they may get ideas from secondary sources. If necessary, help students to use various indexes such as the *Readers' Guide.*

MEETING *individual* NEEDS

LEARNING STYLES

Visual Learners. If you do not ask your students to complete their prewriting on computers, encourage them to use a visual format to create the plans called for in **Writing Assignment: Part 2.** Use the textbook examples to illustrate the technique of mapping or branching on the chalkboard and tell students to try this method by listing the main idea first, branching down or out with major points, and finally adding branches of supporting evidence.

HERE'S HOW

Position statement: The United States should require mandatory national service of young people after high school graduation.

Audience: general public

Logical, Emotional, and Ethical Appeals:

Reasons	Evidence
• Public wants youth to help provide vital services.	Polls: majority want mandatory service Bills proposed for "national service" Nunn-McCurdy bill linking college aid to service
• All teenagers will receive benefits.	College-bound: more career choices; maturity; broader life perspective (emotional appeal) Work force: learn skills to get jobs; incentive to study
• Young people will become better citizens.	Serving others wherever assigned, they will see beyond narrow concerns, gain responsibility (emotional appeal) Joseph Duffey to World Future Society: summary of advantages

Opposing Positions	Refutations
• U.S. can't afford it.	Military—billions to recruit, reenlist Cold War and arms race money could be redirected; good for economy Teen unemployment statistics; chronic unemployment, crime more costly (emotional appeal)
• Young people are too self-centered; they will fight or avoid service.	Not "me generation": environmental and social concerns, Persian Gulf Conflict support (emotional appeal)
• Difficult to make workable.	Conceded, but concerned citizens can and must do it (ethical appeal)

WRITING NOTE

The types of appeals can overlap. A factual example may be emotionally persuasive. Evidence can show your reasonableness, or ethical stance. In fact, emotional appeals are possible *whenever* you use language, and ethical appeals are most often coupled with other support. In an essay the three types of appeals aren't always strictly separated.

Organizing Support

In a persuasive essay an effective, easy-to-follow plan of organization is to present your logical, emotional, and ethical appeals first, followed by opposing positions and refutations.

- **Order of Importance.** You can present your appeals by *order of importance,* beginning or ending with your strongest appeal—strongest in the eyes of *your audience.*
- **Chronological Order.** Sometimes, a *cause-and-effect chain,* or *chronological order,* works best—for example, to propose or attack a course of action.
- **Logical Order.** *Comparison and contrast* is often used to present opposing positions and refutations. You may present all objections first, then your refutations. Or, you may present and refute the positions one by one.

☞ **REFERENCE NOTE:** For more information on organization, see pages 35–36, 74, and 79–87.

Reminder

In planning and organizing your support

- identify logical appeals to support your position statement
- identify emotional and ethical appeals appropriate for your topic and audience
- identify significant opposing positions and plan your refutations
- select an order for your support that will be clear and convincing

WRITING ASSIGNMENT	PART 2: **Identifying and Organizing Support**

Brainstorming, clustering, and freewriting are all good ways to start building support for your opinion. Next, explore available resources. Keeping your audience in mind, remember to look for opposing arguments. Use your notes to make a chart like the one on page 308. Then, review: Do you have enough information? Are your appeals on target for the audience? Are your refutations realistic? Finally, decide how you will organize your support. What order will have the greatest impact?

TECHNOLOGY TIP
If computers are available for your class, encourage students to use word-processing programs to complete **Writing Assignment: Parts 1** and **2.** Students can save their notes, position statements, and plans to use when they write their drafts.

COOPERATIVE LEARNING
As they work on **Writing Assignment: Part 2,** you might ask students to work in pairs to take different sides of the same issue. Students could then debate the issue twice, arguing for one side of the issue and then the other. Having investigated both sides, your students should have a much more effective refutation.

WRITING YOUR FIRST DRAFT

OBJECTIVES

- To analyze a professional persuasive essay for its style and its use of appeals
- To write a draft of a persuasive essay

MOTIVATION

Read aloud to your students an example of effective persuasion. For example, you might read an editorial from a political magazine. After explaining that students will be adding style to their essays, point out elements of style found in your example.

PROGRAM MANAGER

WRITING YOUR FIRST DRAFT

■ **Instructional Support** For help with writing a body paragraph, see **Writing** in *Strategies for Writing*, p. 31.

QUOTATION FOR THE DAY

"Three foremost aids to persuasion which occur to me are humility, concentration, and gusto." (Marianne Moore, 1887–1972, American poet)

Write the quotation on the chalkboard and ask a few volunteers to tell about times when someone or something persuaded them to think or act a certain way. Lead the class to understand that putting power or gusto in their style is often a key to becoming effective persuasive writers.

VISUAL CONNECTIONS
Exploring the Subject. Cesar Chavez (1927–1993) was a Mexican American labor leader who organized the National Farm Workers Association (now called the United Farm Workers of America), the first major farm workers' union in the United States. Chavez, who had been a migrant worker all of his life, organized the union in 1962, and later initiated various strikes to protest the working conditions of farm workers.

Writing Your First Draft

The Basic Elements of Persuasion

In many ways, you make your own rules when you plan your persuasive essay. You can be in favor of something or against it. You can choose your evidence and kinds of appeals. You can refute a long list of opposing positions, just one or two, or none at all. It's up to you.

Yet you are working with basic elements that are easily incorporated into composition form (pages 99–121), with a clear introduction, body, and conclusion.

> **Introduction:** You begin by presenting your opinion, or position, and providing any background necessary for understanding the issue.
>
> ■ **Body:** You use logical, emotional, and ethical appeals to develop your support; and you present opposing positions with your refutations.
>
> ■ **Conclusion:** You end your essay by reemphasizing your position, perhaps summing up your most important ideas, repeating your strongest argument, or giving a *call to action*—something your audience should do.

Persuasion and Style

Language is a powerful tool for inspiring people to action. The labor leader César Chávez brought hope to migrant workers with words such as these: "We will win, we *are* winning, because ours is a revolution of mind and heart, not only of economics." And Paul Robeson, in his valedictorian speech at Rutgers University in 1919, attempted to persuade other African Americans to fight for the future with the following words.

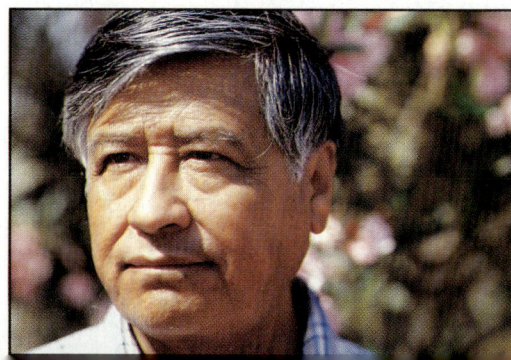

César Chávez

After an overview of the traditional essay structure (introduction, body, and conclusion), focus immediately on the stylistic elements of effective persuasion. If possible, expand the discussion in the text with additional examples of repetition, rhythm, and word choice taken from Stephen King's essay or from another effective piece of persuasion.

Introduce Wolf Schneider's essay with a brief discussion of old movies. Ask students if they have seen *Lawrence of Arabia, Spartacus,* or *Citizen Kane.* Create a list on the chalkboard of these or other classic films. Did they enjoy these movies? Why or why not? Would they have strong feelings if such films were no longer available for viewing? Why or why not? Before assigning Schneider's essay, you ☞

On ourselves alone will depend the preservation of our liberties and the transmission of them in their integrity to those who will come after us. And we are struggling on, attempting to show that knowledge can be obtained under difficulties; that poverty may give place to affluence; that obscurity is not an absolute bar to distinction and that a way is open to welfare and happiness to all who will follow the way with resolution and wisdom; that neither the old-time slavery, nor continued prejudice need extinguish self-respect, crush manly ambition, or paralyze effort; that no power outside of himself can prevent man from sustaining an honorable character and a useful relation to his day and generation. We know that neither institutions nor friends can make a race stand unless it has strength in its own foundation; that races like individuals must stand or fall by their own merit; that to fully succeed they must practice the virtues of self-reliance, self-respect, industry, perseverance, and economy.

Paul Robeson

It is not just Robeson's ideas that are stirring; it is also his *style* that makes his ideas persuasive. When used well, style can be a powerful component in persuasion. In other words, it's not just what you say, but how you say it. Following are three stylistic techniques that are effective in persuasion.

MEETING *individual* NEEDS

LEP/ESL

General Strategies. In terms of vocabulary comprehension, Wolf Schneider's article may present stumbling blocks for students. You may want to create a word list including the words *disintegration, restoration, spearhead, archivist, heritage, municipalities, calculate, savor, concurrent, scalpers, allocate, deterioration, assets, masthead, comprised, leverage, forefront,* and *priority.* Pair students with peer tutors. Make sure students have access to a dictionary. (English-language learners may use a bilingual dictionary, as well, and record definitions in their own languages.) Have students write definitions in their writing journals for each of these words and, with the help of their peer tutors, create simple, original sentences using this vocabulary.

SELECTION AMENDMENT
Description of change: excerpted
Rationale: to focus on the concept of writing presented in this chapter

Repetition.   Paul Robeson begins each of a series of clauses with *that*. The repetition creates a dramatic expectation, focuses attention on his ideas, and unites those ideas to make one major point: that no obstacles, no matter how great, can destroy the integrity of anyone determined to overcome them.

Rhythm.   Read the excerpt again, concentrating on its sound. The rhythm—the beat, or music—is rolling, stately, and formal. Robeson's audience was an academic one at a very formal occasion. At a different occasion with a different audience, his rhythm might have been faster and more informal, with drum bursts of words building in energy. You can create the rhythm you want through words' sounds and stressed syllables, their arrangement in phrases, the length of your sentences, and repetition.

Language.   You won't convince readers if you lose them or put them off—both of which can happen if you use inappropriate language. Robeson's speech is an example of persuasion using formal language; his audience expected this relatively formal word choice and style. However, when the audience doesn't have this set of expectations, informal language can have a positive appeal. Readers or listeners feel you are speaking directly to them in language they understand. That's one of the ways advertising reaches out to an audience. In persuasive writing, it is important to recognize what kind of language will make your audience feel comfortable and responsive to your ideas; in other words, talk their language!

WRITING NOTE

Sentence fragments used inadvertently or carelessly can interfere with communication; but—in the hands of a skilled writer—fragmented sentences can create an energetic rhythm and emphasize important points. They can be an effective stylistic device. However, before using fragments deliberately in school papers, be sure your teacher feels you are ready to experiment with sentence style.

The following essay, written by the magazine editor Wolf Schneider, addresses the subject of preserving films. As you read, pay attention to the essay's content, tone, and style. What do you expect the tone to be? Is your expectation accurate?

Work with the class to develop answers for **Exercise 4,** pp. 318–319. After you provide an answer for each of the questions, have a volunteer provide additional support. Students often have more difficulty in drafting their essays than in the other stages of the writing process. You may want to provide further guided practice by writing a model introduction on a transparency or on the chalkboard. Remind students to use the position statements that they formulated in the prewriting stage.

Writing Your First Draft **313**

A PERSUASIVE ESSAY

Film Preservation
Whose responsibility should it be?
by Wolf Schneider

Rudolf Klein-Rogge and Brigitte Helm in *Metropolis.*

INTRODUCTION

1 In my bookcase at home, behind the cut glass, a shelf holds the words of James Baldwin, Jorge Luis Borges, Lawrence Durrell, and C. S. Lewis. Most of these books are yellowing now; they emit that sour library scent of old age, and sometimes the pages fall loose from the binding when I scan them for a certain passage. Still, these volumes from my teenage years remain safe in my living room. And as disintegration takes further toll, I reassure myself that I can always call Book 2 Soup for a new copy of *The Screwtape Letters* (of course, now it will cost me more than the original ninety-five cents). Failing that—in sleepless moments, when worry treads through the skull— I tell myself I will *probably* be able to locate these books at the library. I hope to never lose touch with those thoughts on which I based so much of my own life philosophy so long ago.

VISUAL CONNECTIONS
Exploring the Subject. *Metropolis* (1926) is a classic silent film by the innovative German director Fritz Lang. Set in the future, the film features a mechanized society, a mad scientist and his creation, and a revolution by the workers who live underground. In 1984 Giorgio Moroder released an edited version of the film with tinted sequences and a rock music score.

USING THE SELECTION
Film Preservation: Whose responsibility should it be?

1
James Baldwin (1924–1987) American novelist and essayist; Jorge Luis Borges (1899–1986) Argentine writer and literary critic; Lawrence Durrell (1912–1990) British novelist, poet, and travel writer; C. S. Lewis (1898–1963) British writer

2
The Screwtape Letters (1942) is a satire by C. S. Lewis in which a young devil is advised in matters of temptation by an older devil.

313

3

Martin Scorsese (1942–   ) is an American film director. Some of his movies include *Alice Doesn't Live Here Anymore* (1974), *New York Stories* (1989), and *The Age of Innocence* (1993).

VISUAL CONNECTIONS

Exploring the Subject. Charlie Chaplin's 1931 film *City Lights* focuses on human feelings and suffering and on the destruction of the individual by social forces. Chaplin plays a tramp who, in better times, has generously helped a blind flower girl who recognizes the tramp as her benefactor just after giving him a flower out of pity. The little tramp remains mute throughout the film even though he is surrounded by sounds, by the talking of others, and even by sounds that he makes himself.

It's a Wonderful Life (1946) is a sentimental movie in which the main character, played by Jimmy Stewart, learns on Christmas Eve that his ordinary life has made a difference in the lives of many of the people of his town. Facing financial ruin and prison after his bumbling uncle loses a bank deposit, he wishes he had never been born. A comical angel grants his wish to show him how the world would have been different without him.

314

BODY
Background information

Statement of opinion

3

Conceding a point

Logical appeal

The same cannot be said about our films. With half of the pre-1950 films having crumbled into dust, with even the simplest film-restoration job costing $8,000 to $10,000, with more than four hundred new films coming out each year, most of us agree that some regular preservation effort needs to take place. But whose responsibility should it be? "It should be a joint responsibility between the studio/distributors—the owners of the film—and the government," assesses Martin Scorsese, the director who began spearheading a film-restoration movement in the early '80s and today is president of the Film Foundation, a filmmaker and archivist collective.

"It's a very complex question," considers Jean Firstenberg, director of the American Film Institute. "The copyright holder historically was concerned with the film in its first exhibition and didn't realize there was an afterlife, a library, a history of our culture, a heritage that would survive." To answer the question, she raises another: "Who preserves our libraries? Not the copyright holders. It's our cities, our universities, our municipalities, the Library of Congress. I think it's a national responsibility to save this art form, and the rights holders have to play a role."

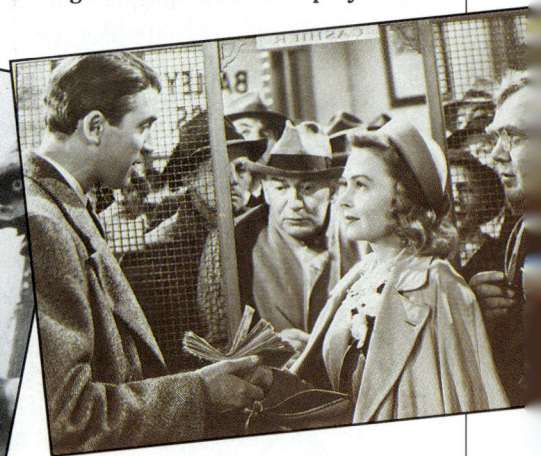

Charlie Chaplin (left) in *City Lights*; Jimmy Stewart and Donna Reed (above) in *It's a Wonderful Life*

Assess students' responses to **Exercise 4** on pp. 318–319 informally. The drafts produced for **Writing Assignment: Part 3** on p. 324 are not an end product, and you will not want to grade them, although you may want to award credit for each successfully completed stage of the writing process. Use student-teacher conferences if students need individual evaluation and help.

Writing Your First Draft   **315**

Peter O'Toole
and Omar Sharif
in *Lawrence of Arabia.*

VISUAL CONNECTIONS

Exploring the Subject. A sprawling epic about the adventures of T. E. Lawrence (1888–1935), *Lawrence of Arabia* is noted for its cinematic beauty. The film is based on Lawrence's book *The Seven Pillars of Wisdom* (1926).

Ethical appeals

At the launching of the Film Foundation last year, in the cool chamber of the Creative Artists Agency screening room, director Sydney Pollack warned that "a society that doesn't pay attention to its cultural heritage is not an interesting or pleasant society to live in." "Films tell us about our souls," Scorsese says a year later. "No one can calculate that value."

Emotional appeals

4 A lot has happened in the past two years. Some $600,000 were spent to restore *Lawrence of Arabia*, and director David Lean lived just long enough to savor it. This spring, we saw chart-topping per-screen averages for the con-
5 current rereleases of *Spartacus* and *Citizen Kane*. In New York, a friend of Firstenberg's went to see *Spartacus* and found it sold out and scalpers outside selling tickets. "I was in New York a couple of days later. The line for *Citizen Kane* was around the block, and there was a blind man in it," says Firstenberg. "I was stunned."

4
Lawrence of Arabia (1962) won seven Oscars and made Peter O'Toole a star in his first leading role.

5
Spartacus (1960) was a big-budget film featuring many Hollywood stars, including Kirk Douglas, Laurence Olivier, Jean Simmons, Charles Laughton, Tony Curtis, and Peter Ustinov. *Citizen Kane* (1941) is considered one of the most important American films ever made; Orson Welles wrote, produced, directed, and starred in the film.

315

VISUAL CONNECTIONS

Exploring the Subject. Focusing on the destructive childhood and resultant ambition of its main character, *Citizen Kane* is a gripping drama with elements of mystery. Perhaps the most intriguing aspect of the movie is the mysterious word which Kane whispers as he is dying: "Rosebud."

Directed by Stanley Kubrick, *Spartacus* is an excellent example of the epic genre of films made in Hollywood during the 1950s and 1960s. The movie is a fictionalized account of an actual slave who led a revolt against the forces of the Roman empire. A fully restored version of the film was released in 1991.

6

UCLA (University of California, Los Angeles). John Ford (1895–1973) directed over two hundred films during his long career and was the first director to win Oscars for four movies. In 1973 President Nixon awarded Ford the Presidential Medal of Freedom.

7

VistaVision was a wide-screen film process developed during the 1950s. The process resulted in a sharper picture than images shot with standard cameras.

8

Steven Spielberg (1947–   ) is a motion-picture director and producer. Several of his films are among the highest grossing movies in history. Some of his many hits are *Jaws* (1975), *Raiders of the Lost Ark* (1981), *E.T.: The Extra-Terrestrial* (1982), *Jurassic Park* (1993), and *Schindler's List* (1993). George Lucas (1944–   ) is a motion-picture

continued on next page

316

Orson Welles (left) in *Citizen Kane*; Kirk Douglas (above) in *Spartacus*.

Additional information

Emotional appeal

Logical appeal

6
7

8

Film Foundation coexecutive director Raffaele Donato (who is also Scorsese's private archivist) reports that Universal, which owns the largest library, is planning to <u>allocate</u> a yearly sum to preserve its titles. He says Warner Brothers, in a joint project with the Museum of Modern Art and UCLA, plans to restore John Ford's *The Searchers* to its original VistaVision. Donato says Fox intends to restore all the John Ford titles it owns and that Columbia has created a special committee to supervise preservation of its titles. Scorsese says former Paramount studio head Frank Mancuso understood the value of the film preservation so well that he built a state-of-the-art vault and vowed to restore practically every Paramount title.

"The first thing we tried to do, and we've succeeded almost, is to inform and alert the studios as to the deterioration of their own assets," says Scorsese. "The main thing with the Film Foundation is for me and Spielberg and Lucas and the other gentlemen on the masthead to constantly be dealing with the studios, to show our concern, and that's not meant as a criticism of the studios."

1. What are the three main parts of any essay? [introduction, body, conclusion]
2. What are three stylistic techniques often used in persuasion? [repetition, rhythm, appropriate language]

3. What is refutation? Why is it important to persuasion? [Recognizing and then refuting opposing arguments makes a position more valid.]

☞

Additional background

"Because the Film Foundation is comprised of working directors, they have some kind of leverage," adds Donato. "There have been some commitments to some degree, but the only common policy is to see what the others do first. They all follow their own policy in the end, though." In the forefront of the film preservation movement, according to Scorsese, are the five
9 archival organizations: the AFI, UCLA, MOMA, George Eastman House, and the Library of Congress.

John Wayne and Jeffrey Hunter in *The Searchers.*

CONCLUSION
Calls to action

Yes, a lot has happened in the past two years. But so much more needs to be done. Firstenberg says more projects, a greater priority, and a national campaign are needed. Scorsese reminds us that independent films need saving too. Donato points out that this October, one hundred films will be screened at the first International Film Preservation Festival in Paris. "I hope you can read French or someone can translate it for you," he writes on the FAX he sends me about it. Soon, perhaps, no translation will be necessary to follow the film-preservation movement.

American Film

producer, director, and writer. He wrote and directed *Star Wars* (1977), one of the all-time most popular science-fiction movies. Other Lucas films of note are *American Graffiti* (1973) and *Willow* (1988).

9
AFI (American Film Institute), MOMA (Museum of Modern Art)

VISUAL CONNECTIONS
Exploring the Subject. *The Searchers* (1956) is considered by many to be director John Ford's masterpiece. Based on Alan LeMay's novel and featuring John Wayne and Natalie Wood, the western saga is noted for its moving story and excellent cinematography.

Ask students to find short persuasive essays, perhaps from the *Newsweek* "My Turn" columns or from the *Time* "Essay" section. Then have students analyze these essays for their use of logical, emotional, and ethical appeals and for their use of effective stylistic techniques—repetition, rhythm, and appropriate language. Consider having students mount a copy of the essay on paper and then color-code the different categories. Then you can scan and evaluate student analyses more quickly.

VISUAL CONNECTIONS

Exploring the Subject. Ginger Rogers and Fred Astaire were popular movie actors in the 1930s and 1940s. They are most remembered as dazzling dance partners in films such as *The Gay Divorcee* (1934), *Top Hat* (1935), and *Swing Time* (1936).

Humphrey Bogart is famous for his rakish hat, his wry smile, and his husky, gravelly voice. He developed a distinctive screen persona as a tough but basically humane individualist. Some of the classic films in which Bogart starred are *Casablanca* (1942), *Key Largo* (1948), and *The African Queen* (1951).

ANSWERS
Exercise 4

Answers will vary.

1. Most students will not have thought seriously about this subject before reading the essay. However, many will be convinced by the writer's arguments.

2. The writer probably begins his essay with the description as a way of introducing the rest of the essay. The paragraph helps set up the rest of the essay by tying the writer's sense of preservation of books with movies and conveys the idea of the importance of preserving important artifacts.

3. The writer's references to prominent directors in the essay strengthen the arguments because these people are recognized authorities on movies.

318

318   *Writing to Persuade*

Ginger Rogers and Fred Astaire (left) in *Swing Time;* Katherine Hepburn and Humphrey Bogart (right) in *The African Queen.*

EXERCISE 4 ▶ **Analyzing the Elements of a Persuasive Essay**

Get together with two or three other students to discuss the following questions about the preceding essay.

1. Did you hold an opinion about the preservation of film before you read this essay? How do you feel about the issue now? Did the writer convince you that the opinions put forward in his article are correct? Why or why not?
2. Reread the introductory paragraph. Why do you think the writer begins his essay with this description? How does the paragraph help set up the rest of the essay? What main idea does it convey?
3. The writer quotes and mentions several prominent directors in this essay. How do these references strengthen the arguments advanced in the article?

4. Think of a few arguments that oppose the position of film preservation presented in the article. Do you think the essay would have been more convincing if the writer had addressed more opposing arguments? Why or why not?
5. Identify two anecdotes cited in this essay. How do these anecdotes add to the essay's style and effectiveness?

☞ **REFERENCE NOTE:** For more information on using anecdotes in persuasive writing, see page 302.

A Basic Framework for a Persuasive Essay

Wolf Schneider combines the elements of a persuasive essay in an unusual manner. He begins with a description that does not directly state his opinion and then uses a mixture of quotations, anecdotes, and facts to build his argument. The effect is somewhat subtle, appropriate for an audience of knowledgeable and receptive readers. Since your audience will be broader, your essay will probably be more straightforward.

The Writer's Model that follows provides a framework you can study and use. As you read, pay attention to your own responses. The topic discussed is one that directly involves you. Do you agree with the writer?

4. Arguments opposing film preservation will vary. Had the author addressed more opposing arguments, the essay might have seemed more convincing by showing the writer to be fair, open, and credible.

5. The writer relates an anecdote about his fears of losing his books and another about receiving a FAX. The anecdotes add to the essay's style and effectiveness by their informal tone that speaks directly to the reader.

A WRITER'S MODEL

Mandatory National Service for
America's Youth: The Time Has Come

INTRODUCTION

Sentence fragment used to grab attention

Graduation day--what high school student doesn't look forward to it? A handshake, a diploma, tears and laughter, and it's all over. It's time to move on, to grow up. Many graduates will go on to some type of higher education, some will enter the work force, and others will combine the two. A few will drift, trying to find their places in the world.

Style/Break in rhythm

Very few will be totally prepared for any of these challenges.

Transition from high school into the real world is one of the most significant periods in a young

A DIFFERENT APPROACH

Organize a classroom debate of this issue, in which four or five students argue for a mandatory national service for young people and four or five students argue against. Remind students that their purpose is to persuade their audience—the rest of their classmates. When the debate is over, have the audience decide which side had the more effective argument.

MEETING *individual* NEEDS

ADVANCED STUDENTS

You may want to allow advanced students more flexibility in the format of their drafts. For example, you can encourage students to use more original introductions and conclusions or to begin with opposing arguments.

Position statement

person's life, yet our society offers almost no help with this giant leap into maturity. One step in this direction is mandatory national service. All young people leaving high school should be required to serve the country either in the military or through community service.

Background information

Those going into community service might work in hospitals, jails, schools, or poor neighborhoods, or on conservation projects. They might help build shelters for the homeless, plant trees in parks, help the illiterate to read, work in soup kitchens, or organize games and activities in child-care centers or senior citizen centers.

Logical appeal

More and more, America's citizens want youth to help with these vital services. Public-opinion polls consistently show that most Americans support mandatory service of some type. In September 1994,

Data

President Bill Clinton launched a national service program called AmeriCorps, which encourages young people to contribute to their communities. The AmeriCorps program provides twenty thousand young people with a minimum-wage salary and a $4,725 yearly college-tuition credit in exchange for full-time public service work. AmeriCorps participants work in areas such as education, health care, and crime reduction, helping groups that wouldn't be able to afford to hire them without the program. Although AmeriCorps has been criticized by some

Statistics

politicians, a 1995 poll showed that 52 percent of the general public and 63 percent of younger voters (aged 18 to 34) felt that eliminating the program would be a step in the wrong direction. This support indicates that people believe that community service is important. However, although the national service program is a start, it will suffer the problems of all nonmandatory systems. It will not affect enough people.

Logical appeal

No matter how it is structured, mandatory national service could directly benefit young people, not just the country. All teenagers will gain. Those going on to college will be exposed to career choices they may not have considered. They'll also gain maturity and a perspective on life that goes beyond the four walls of a classroom. Those planning to go directly into the job market will learn valuable skills that may help them escape the trap of "no experience--no job; no job--no experience." They may even discover a field they want to study further.

Examples

Emotional appeal

Logical appeal

A last reason, though, is less material but perhaps more important: Teenagers will better understand the responsibilities and rewards of citizenship. By serving the people wherever help is needed, they'll be forced to see beyond their homes, their neighborhoods, their separate regions and cultures. They'll learn that serving others is what being a mature citizen is all about. National service will be an important, lasting life experience.

Emotional appeal

TIMESAVER

Tell students to underline their position statements and to highlight their reasons in blue, the opposing positions in yellow, and their refutations in pink. You can then check the content and organization of the essays more quickly and easily.

MEETING *individual* NEEDS

LEARNING STYLES

Auditory Learners. Some students might benefit from talk-writing their drafts. You may want to pair each student with another who will ask questions and record responses. Have one student question the other about supporting reasons, opposing arguments, and refutation.

◆ INTEGRATING THE LANGUAGE ARTS

Vocabulary Link. To help students achieve coherence in their persuasive essays, share the following list of transitions with your class. Explain that these transitions are helpful in signaling concession or contrast.

1. although	6. nevertheless
2. admittedly	7. nonetheless
3. despite	8. still
4. even though	9. while it is
5. however	true that

Logical appeal

Joseph Duffey, chancellor of the University of Massachusetts at Amherst, summed up these advantages in a speech to the World Future Society:

> At its best national service . . . offers young people a chance to grow and mature at a critical stage in their development that cannot be accomplished in the schoolhouse or the workplace. Youth Service--as opposed to all other kinds of service--can teach lessons that redound to personal success in work, as citizens of the community and as examples to the generations that follow.

Opposing position/ Refutations

Many opponents of national service don't see benefits, though; they see expense, just one more big government program the United States can't afford. Consider, however, that our military services spend a billion dollars a year trying to recruit new volunteers and another billion in reenlistment pay to keep them. And they are still falling short of their recruitment targets. National service would save some of this cost.

Logical appeals

Style/Repetition (*Consider*)

Consider, too, our changing world. The Cold War and arms race are not the priorities they once were. It's time to divert some of those defense dollars into labor and service programs. These are dollars that will be reinvested in our economy by those who benefit from them, both the young people and those they help.

Logical and emotional appeals

Consider, too, unemployed teens. In July of 1996, the U.S. unemployment rate was 5.4 percent. At the same time, teenage unemployment was 16.4 percent. If teens don't learn useful skills through experience, many could become chronically unemployed. They may become discouraged about the possibility of ever doing meaningful work. The resulting costs of welfare and crime are, ultimately, far greater than the costs of giving young people the challenge and opportunity to serve their country.

Opposing position/ Refutation

Some opponents reply that the challenge and opportunity aren't wanted: young people are too self-centered, too unconcerned to participate willingly in such a program. They'll fight it or shirk their duties. But the "me generation" was another generation, not this one. Young people today are open to being better citizens: They know the environment is threatened and only people can save it. They proved their patriotism in the Persian Gulf Conflict. They reject the fates of joblessness and drug addiction.

Logical and emotional appeal

Style/Repetition and rhythm

CONCLUSION Conceding a point/ Ethical appeal

Yes, setting up a workable program will be difficult. Congress and concerned citizens will have to work extremely hard to get past the politics, opposition, and bureaucracy. But it can, and must, be done.

Call to action

The time for mandatory national service for all young people is now. You can do your part by writing to your U.S. senators and representative. Let them know that you support national service and urge them to find a way to make it happen. Do you care about the future of our country and youth? Then act. It will be a national service.

No two persuasive essays are alike. The author of "Mandatory National Service for America's Youth: The Time Has Come" presented three main reasons and refuted two opposing arguments. Your essay may be different, depending upon your issue, the line of reasoning you develop, and the points you must refute. One way to put your thoughts in order is to use a basic framework like the one that follows.

A DIFFERENT APPROACH

Some students who are familiar with outlining might find it a more convenient way to organize their essays. You can refer students to the material on outlining in **Chapter 3: "Understanding Composition Structure."**

A DIFFERENT APPROACH

Another more complex structure for a persuasive essay is a framework called "straw man." In it the writer presents a weak argument so he or she may attack it and gain an easy, showy victory. The following diagram shows the structure:

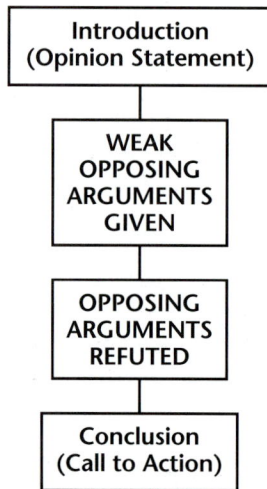

```
Introduction
(Opinion Statement)
        |
WEAK
OPPOSING
ARGUMENTS
GIVEN
        |
OPPOSING
ARGUMENTS
REFUTED
        |
Conclusion
(Call to Action)
```

FRAMEWORK FOR A PERSUASIVE ESSAY

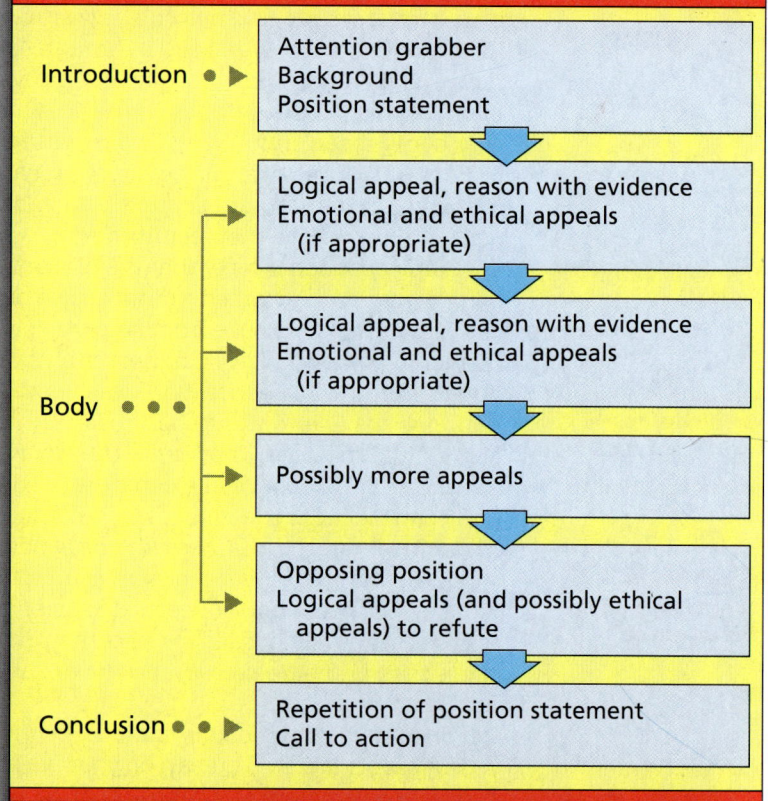

Introduction •▶
- Attention grabber
- Background
- Position statement

Body •••
- Logical appeal, reason with evidence
- Emotional and ethical appeals (if appropriate)

- Logical appeal, reason with evidence
- Emotional and ethical appeals (if appropriate)

- Possibly more appeals

- Opposing position
- Logical appeals (and possibly ethical appeals) to refute

Conclusion •••▶
- Repetition of position statement
- Call to action

WRITING ASSIGNMENT

PART 3:
Writing a First Draft

If you've chosen your topic well, you should be itching to give people a piece of your mind—in a way that will change their minds. But even if you are feeling some pre-draft dread of starting (it happens to everyone), you have only to follow the guides you have created: your position statement, chart of support, and plan of organization. Also repicture your audience: Speak directly to these readers as you write. And let your persuasive language flow. Try to put some power in your style.

↪ **EVALUATING AND REVISING**

OBJECTIVES
- To analyze a writer's revisions
- To evaluate and revise a draft of a persuasive essay

Cont. on p. 327

⚡ **CRITICAL THINKING**

(pp. 325–328)

OBJECTIVE
- To analyze and evaluate support to separate true reasoning from false reasoning or logical fallacies

---

Evaluating and Revising **325**

Evaluating and Revising

Becoming your own critic is the essence of evaluating and revising any paper, but for a persuasive paper, your role-playing of a reader is a little different. You have to become someone who *definitely* doesn't share your opinion, someone who may be ready to pick your argument to pieces. Will it hold up? In addition to evaluating other elements of your writing, you'll need to focus on logic, or reasoning.

⚡ **CRITICAL THINKING**

Evaluating Your Reasoning

When you are writing a persuasive essay, you don't have to be absolutely fair. You certainly aren't taking a neutral position—you're taking a stand. Some evidence may be one-sided; some emotion is allowed.

You must, however, provide logical support for your position statement because reasoning is essential to your essay. Avoid logical *fallacies* that look like reasons, but aren't. They are mistakes of logic, and you don't want them in your essay. While some readers may think hastily and be convinced by a fallacy, critical readers will not. They may decide you don't think well *or* are trying to fool them—and either opinion pokes holes in your persuasiveness. Watch out for these fallacies.

1. **Hasty Generalization.** A hasty generalization is a conclusion based on insufficient evidence or one that ignores exceptions. Sometimes broad generalizations can be made acceptable by using qualifying words like *many*, *most*, *generally*, and *some*.

   Hasty Generalization Television game shows exploit contestants by appealing to greed.

   Acceptable Generalization Many television game shows exploit contestants by appealing to greed.

⬆ **PROGRAM MANAGER**

EVALUATING AND REVISING

■ **Reinforcement/Reteaching** See **Revision Transparencies 13** and **14.** For suggestions on how to tie the transparencies to instruction, review teacher's notes in *Fine Art and Instructional Transparencies for Writing*, p. 119.

■ **Ongoing Assessment** For a rubric to guide assessment, see **Evaluating and Revising** in *Strategies for Writing*, p. 32.

■ **Assessment/Reflection** To assess student work and evaluate progress, see **Portfolio Forms** in *Portfolio Assessment*, pp. 5–21.

MEETING *individual* **NEEDS**

LEP/ESL

General Strategies. You may want to create small study groups to ensure that students focus on the material and participate fully. Suggest that each group select only one of the evaluation guidelines to focus on.

Bring to class several examples of the logical fallacies explained in the **Critical Thinking** section. You can obtain many examples of logical fallacies from advertising. Other excellent examples can be found in political speeches, especially during an election year.

Begin your lesson by discussing each fallacy separately with the class. Explain the fallacy, read and discuss the examples given in the textbook, and ask students to provide additional examples from their observations and experience. Before you assign the **Critical Thinking Exercise**, give students further practice with the examples brought to class.

MEETING *individual* NEEDS

LEP/ESL

General Strategies. Before students can be expected to differentiate between true and false reasoning, they need a clear understanding of what is specifically implied by *reasoning*. Checking a dictionary sends one into a circular tailspin. *Reasoning* means "the use of reason." What is reason? *Reason* means "the capacity for clear thought, for rational thought." But what is meant by *rational?* Rational means "having the ability to reason." To bypass this confusion, discuss the word in terms of how *reason* is manifested. Have the class suggest specific examples of how reasoning is used in daily life. In what situations do facts help form judgments or opinions? The more concrete and familiar the experience, the more likely students are to understand the concept of reasoning and to transfer this understanding to their essays.

2. **Attacking the Person.** This technique is formally called an *ad hominem* fallacy (Latin for "to the person"); informally, it's "name-calling." It avoids the real issue, attacking instead people who support the issue.

Attacking the Person	The only people who want television cameras in the courtroom are thrill-seeking busybodies.
Facing the Issue	Some people support television cameras in the courtroom because they believe that the public has a right to view all public trials.

3. **False Authority.** Just because a person is an authority in one field does not mean that person is an authority in all fields. Nor does a strong concern and opinion on an issue make someone an authority. Expert testimony is valuable only when it comes from someone knowledgeable about the topic in question.

False Authority	Michelle Van, president of the Downtown Merchants Association, says the proposed museum and auditorium will not interfere with traffic flow in the area.
Relevant Authority	City traffic engineers report that traffic on streets surrounding the proposed site is still far below maximum levels set in the city plan.

Cont. from p. 325
TEACHING THE LESSON

After students understand the reasons for revising their essays, review with the class the **Evaluating and Revising Persuasive Essays** chart on p. 329. You could use a sample essay and examine all ten parts of the chart, based on the model essay. ☞

4. **Circular Reasoning.** Reasoning is circular when the reason offered for an opinion is simply the opinion stated in different words.

Circular Reasoning	No one country should control the world's oceans because the oceans belong to all countries.
Acceptable Reasoning	The world's oceans must be accessible to all. International treaties guarantee all nations their fair share of the oceans' resources and their ships the right to unrestricted travel on the open seas.

5. **Either-Or Reasoning.** This fallacy assumes that every issue has only two possible sides. Usually, there are many different choices or positions that fall between the extremes.

Either-Or Reasoning	Either we limit population growth or we starve.
Realistic Reasoning	Unchecked population growth threatens the world's ability to adequately feed future generations.

6. **Non Sequitur.** In Latin, *non sequitur* means "it does not follow." In this fallacy, statements or ideas are presented as logically connected but in fact are not. One is not a logical consequence of the other.

Non Sequitur	Our increasingly mobile society demands a higher speed limit.
Logical Connection	A higher speed limit will aid commerce by allowing truckers to shorten delivery times and increase total deliveries.

ANSWERS
Critical Thinking Exercise

Answers may vary.

1. Either-or reasoning—Fewer government restrictions on new medicines may save the lives of some people who have not responded to medicines already on the market.

2. False authority—According to sociologist William Jones and physical therapist Carlos Torres, "Noncompetitive sports such as swimming, golf, and jazz dancing build the body without damaging social effects."

3. Circular reasoning—Our country needs a national health plan because many of its citizens cannot afford health insurance.

4. Non sequitur—Bingo should be made illegal since so many elderly people with small fixed incomes bet on bingo games with money that they need to use for food and clothing.

5. Hasty generalization—Each year, only a few participants in after-school sports receive injuries—although some of them might be serious; for example, last season one player on our football team had a broken leg and a dislocated shoulder.

6. Attacking the person—A higher sales tax will be a bigger burden on poor and middle-income people than on the rich.

7. Hasty generalization—Although those involved in the fur industry would lose income or even jobs if the fur industry were reduced or eliminated, many innocent animals would be saved.

8. Attacking the person/non sequitur— Only those who have actually lived in the big cities have a firsthand knowledge of urban problems.

CRITICAL THINKING EXERCISE:
Evaluating Reasoning

Here is a chance to test your ability to find errors in reasoning. Each of the following statements has a logical flaw. Identify which of the six fallacies each statement exhibits, and then write a logical statement to replace it.

1. Unless the government loosens its restrictions on new medicines, thousands of people will continue to die needlessly.

2. According to former state representative Isao, students should learn more noncompetitive sports, such as swimming, golf, and jazz dancing—sports that last a lifetime.

3. Our country needs a national health plan because a national system is the solution to our problems.

4. Bingo should be made illegal since so many elderly people are players.

5. After-school sports are becoming increasingly dangerous. Last season one player had serious injuries, which included a broken leg and a dislocated shoulder.

6. The advocates of a higher sales tax do not care that it will be a bigger burden on poor and middle-income people than on the rich.

7. No one will be harmed if the fur industry dies.

8. People who live in the suburbs don't understand the problems of our cities.

9. If this city doesn't reelect our mayor, everyone should just leave town on the next train because it just won't be worth living here anymore.

10. The driving age in this state should be raised to twenty-one. The governor was nearly run down by a reckless teenage driver last month.

or Non-sequitur

The following chart is an overall evaluation and revision guide for your essay. Ask yourself each numbered question in the left-hand column. If you find the weakness in your essay, use the revision technique suggested in the right-hand column to correct the problem.

ASSESSMENT

You can save time when evaluating final copies of students' essays by making notations about content and organization at this stage of the writing process. Be sure, however, that students have completed revisions before you read the papers.

CLOSURE

Ask students to describe some of the strengths and weaknesses of the essays they have read in their revision groups. Compile a list on the chalkboard and discuss with students ways to remedy or reduce weaknesses. ■

EVALUATING AND REVISING PERSUASIVE ESSAYS

EVALUATION GUIDE	REVISION TECHNIQUE
1 Does the introduction grab the reader's attention?	**Add** or **replace** existing information with an interesting fact, statistic, quotation, or anecdote.
2 Is the writer's opinion clear early in the essay?	**Add** a sentence or two stating your position on the issue.
3 Is necessary background information given?	**Add** information that helps your audience understand the issue.
4 Is logical support provided?	**Add** reasons backed by evidence: facts (examples, data, statistics, anecdotes) and expert opinion.
5 Is the reasoning sound?	**Cut** or revise logical fallacies.
6 Does the essay contain appropriate emotional and ethical appeals?	**Add** examples or details with emotional impact, connotative language, and statements that establish your character and credibility.
7 Does the essay present and respond to opposing positions?	**Add** the strongest positions on the opposing side and refute them with logical, emotional, or ethical appeals.
8 Is the organization clear and effective?	**Reorder** reasons in order of importance or chronologically; **reorder** information to present support for your own position before refuting opposing positions.
9 Is the style both suitable and persuasive?	**Add** effective rhythms or repetition. **Cut** overly formal language; **add** more direct, everyday speech.
10 Is the conclusion strong and effective?	**Add** a forceful restatement of opinion, a summary of reasons, and/or a call to action.

---

9. Either-or reasoning—The mayor has worked hard during his term to solve some major problems that faced our town.

10. Hasty generalization—Insurance studies have shown that older drivers have fewer accidents, and therefore the driving age should be raised.

MEETING *individual* **NEEDS**

LEARNING STYLES

Visual Learners. Prepare a transparency of a paragraph from a persuasive essay that needs revision and then model the revision for the class. Give students an opportunity for general response to the paragraph and then ask specific questions about supporting quotations and details. Use a marker to make actual revisions.

ANSWERS
Exercise 5

1. The intended audience is not "young people." The audience is general— primarily middle-aged or older, parents and taxpayers.

2. Although this sentence recognizes an opposing position, the writer doesn't refute that position at this point. Therefore, the sentence should be deleted.

3. The revision "the four walls of a classroom" is much more effective. The new image is vivid and expressed in everyday language; *school* is abstract, general, and dull.

4. The added information that young people will learn valuable skills from national service strengthens the writer's logical argument that such service may help these young people to get jobs; the qualifier "may help them" avoids a hasty generalization.

5. The last sentence is a logical fallacy— a non sequitur, with elements of either- or reasoning. A "nation of impractical or unemployed people" is not a natural and inevitable result of not having a national service. So the choice is not between a national service and such a nation. Many other possibilities exist.

EXERCISE 5 ▶   **Analyzing a Writer's Revisions**

Study the writer's revision of a paragraph of the essay on pages 319–323. Then answer the questions that follow.

> No matter how it is structured, manda-
> tory national service could directly benefit us,   *(young people)*   **replace**
> not just the country. All teenagers will gain, even   **cut**
> ~~though opponents argue the price is too high.~~
> Those going on to college will be exposed to
> career choices they may not have considered.
> They'll also gain maturity and a perspective
> on life that goes beyond ~~school~~. Those planning   *(the four walls of a classroom)*   **replace**
> to go directly into the job market will escape   *(learn valuable skills that may help them)*   **add**
> the trap of "no experience--no job; no job--
> no experience." They may even discover
> a field they want to study further. ~~If national~~   **cut**
> ~~service isn't begun, we'll produce a nation of~~
> ~~impractical or unemployed people.~~

1. From the replacement in the first sentence, what conclusion can you draw about the writer's intended audience?
2. What's the reason for the deletion in the second sentence?
3. Explain why *school* was replaced. Is the change effective?
4. The addition in the fifth sentence both strengthens a logical appeal and eliminates a logical fallacy. How?
5. Why did the writer cut the last sentence?

WRITING ASSIGNMENT

PART 4:
Evaluating and Revising Your Essay

Exchange essays with a classmate. Describe the audience you are writing for so that your reviewer can emulate a member of that audience. Review your partner's comments, and then evaluate and revise your own paper.

PROOFREADING AND PUBLISHING

OBJECTIVE

- To proofread a persuasive essay and to prepare it for publication

MOTIVATION

Ask students if they would believe the information in a newspaper, magazine, or textbook that was filled with errors in spelling and punctuation. Explain that a carefully proofread essay adds to the credibility—or ethical stance—of the writer.

☞

Proofreading and Publishing

Proofreading.   In a very real sense, careful proofreading can strengthen the ethical appeal of your paper. Readers aren't likely to see you as a thoughtful, concerned person if your paper is sloppy or peppered with mistakes. Always take time to make mechanics, usage, and grammar as sound as your reasoning.

MECHANICS HINT

Using Commas with Parenthetical Expressions

Some common expressions are particularly useful in persuasive writing because they draw the reader's attention to a logical, emotional, or ethical appeal: *I believe (think, know, hope, and so on); I am sure; in fact; naturally; in my opinion; for example; to tell the truth.* Most of the time these expressions are parenthetical: that is, they are not essential to the main idea of the sentence. They are included to qualify or to add emphasis. When you want the reader to pause when reading and to recognize that an expression is parenthetical, set it off with commas.

> In fact, the National and Community Service Act was passed in November 1990.

However, these expressions do not always have to be used parenthetically. When you want such expressions to be read as an essential part of the sentence, omit the commas.

> A bill to create a national service program was in fact passed in November 1990.

☞ **REFERENCE NOTE:** For more help with the use of commas in parenthetical expressions, see pages 914–915.

PROGRAM MANAGER

PROOFREADING AND PUBLISHING

- **Instructional Support** For a chart students may use to evaluate their proofreading progress, see **Proofreading** in *Strategies for Writing*, p. 33.

- **Independent Practice/ Reteaching** For additional practice with language skills, see **Proofreading Practice: Using Commas with Parenthetical Expressions** in *Strategies for Writing*, p. 34.

- **Assessment/Reflection** To assess student work and evaluate progress, see **Portfolio Forms** in *Portfolio Assessment*, pp. 22–25.

- **Computer Guided Instruction** For additional instruction and practice with using commas with parenthetical expressions as noted in the **Mechanics Hint**, see **Lesson 44** in *Language Workshop CD-ROM.*

- **Practice** To help less-advanced students who need additional practice with using commas with parenthetical expressions, see **Chapter 22** in *English Workshop, Complete Course*, pp. 305–306.

You may want to begin your lesson by showing students a paragraph from a persuasive essay that contains several errors in grammar, usage, and mechanics. Be sure that the paragraph contains errors in the punctuation of parenthetical expressions, the focus of the **Mechanics Hint** on p. 331. You could prepare the sample yourself or use a student paper from a previous class.

Refer students to the **Mechanics Hint** and briefly discuss the use of commas with parenthetical expressions. Then ask the class to help you proofread and correct the paragraph to make sure that students understand how to use commas to set off parenthetical

QUOTATION FOR THE DAY

"Things evidently false are not only printed, but many things of truth most falsely set forth." (Sir Thomas Browne, 1605–1682, English physician and author)

Share the quotation with the class and ask students to freewrite in their writing journals about possible misuse of persuasive writing.

MEETING *individual* NEEDS

LEP/ESL

General Strategies. The **Mechanics Hint** (p. 331) regarding parenthetical expressions could be difficult for students because such expressions require a refined understanding of the language. You might pair students with peer tutors, who can read through the essays to check for the proper use of commas.

TEACHING NOTE

Point out to students that much of the writing that is done in the workplace is persuasive, and remind them that one way to bring together all they have learned about writing to persuade is by serious reflection on the writing process. Emphasize that the better they understand their audiences, the more likely they are to be able to shape their writing to accomplish its purpose.

Publishing.   If you want to convince people that you are right, you have to put your essay out there for them to read. Here are three ideas for publishing.

- Send a copy of your essay to a magazine that deals with the issue you wrote about. Reference books such as *Writer's Market* explain how to submit articles to magazines.
- Create a poster on which you surround your essay with photographs or illustrations that highlight your major points. Ask permission to display your poster at a public location, such as a library or school lobby.
- Submit your essay to a listserv or newsgroup that focuses on your topic.

COMPUTER NOTE: Use your word-processing program's Border and Box tools to set off text and to create eye-catching pages.

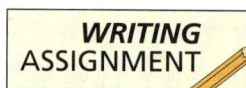

WRITING ASSIGNMENT

PART 5:
Proofreading and Publishing Your Persuasive Essay

Proofread and correct your paper so that its appearance and form give a clear message: Believe me. Then use one of the publishing ideas above, or an idea of your own, to distribute your essay to an audience whose belief in your ideas really matters.

Reflecting on Your Writing

Your essay will make a good addition to your portfolio. If you put your essay in your **portfolio,** remember to date it and include a note of reflection that answers the following questions.

- Did your opinion about your topic change as you wrote the paper? If so, how did you adjust your paper to reflect the change?
- How did you shape your supporting arguments to fit your audience?
- What did you learn about your ability to persuade by writing this essay?

expressions. After students have participated in this guided practice, they should be ready to proofread their own persuasive essays.

ASSESSMENT

You can assess not only the completed papers but also the processes that students followed. Check to be sure that students have taken group responsibilities seriously. They should have helped partners or group members evaluate, revise, and proofread. To check this, take up not only final versions but also drafts and written suggestions. ☞

A STUDENT MODEL

In the following persuasive papers, Martha Delgado and Greg Robertson, students at Valley High School in Albuquerque, New Mexico, express opposing opinions on an issue relevant to teens.

All Work and No Play
by Martha Delgado

It's nine o'clock when the front door opens. Another hard day of work has finally come to an end. "All work and no play" comes to mind as the working student climbs the stairs to his room. Since the student started working, there has been no time for anything besides work. He seems like a different person now that he has an after-school job. I believe that students should not have after-school jobs.

First of all, working has an effect on any student's social life. Having a job is too time-consuming, so students aren't able to enjoy life as teenagers. This is the time for students to live life fully and to be with friends. This is the time to take advantage of one's youth, not the time to spend life working when it's not really necessary.

Some people think that students should work because they begin to earn money. What's the rush? Why should students start working so soon when they're going to have the rest of their lives to earn money? Besides, when students do earn money, they usually end up spending it on things that are of no importance. About 83 percent of students surveyed said that they usually spend their money on entertainment. So what do students actually gain from earning their own money at such an early age? Students who don't work can manage just as well as students who do. This I know for a fact because I am one of the nonworking students.

Most important, working has an effect on grades. Many students' grades begin to drop because they don't have time to do homework. They arrive home from work too tired. The only thing on their minds is sleep. Many students usually

A DIFFERENT APPROACH

Encourage students to create their own magazine to publish student essays. Students could take turns serving as editor, copyeditor, illustrator, proofreader, and so forth. For each class writing assignment, the section editor could choose three or four essays to publish. Publication of any student's work should be limited to two essays per semester so that as many students as possible can see their work included.

A STUDENT MODEL
Evaluation

1. Martha uses an attention-grabber opening that includes specific examples of a working student's life. She follows it up with her thesis sentence that is her opinion.

2. There is logical support in this essay. Martha includes a fact that explains her statement that students spend their money on nonessential things.

3. Martha presents the opposing position by offering herself as an example that students don't need to work. She also offers the logical appeal that working has an effect on grades.

CRITICAL THINKING

Analyzing. Make copies of **A Student Model** of a persuasive essay. Have students work in groups to analyze and write annotations for this model in the style of **A Writer's Model** (p. 319). Then discuss students' analyses and add your own comments and observations.

Ask students to compare their first drafts to their final drafts and to note the changes that have taken place during the writing process. You may want to list some of the most common changes on the chalkboard. ■

A STUDENT MODEL
Evaluation

1. Greg clearly states his opinion in the first paragraph. He expresses the belief that working teenagers are showing that they are responsible.

2. He uses ethical appeals in the second paragraph by explaining that a paycheck helps to build self-esteem.

3. Greg presents and responds to an opposing opinion in the third paragraph. Here he uses a logical appeal.

4. The style is properly informal because Greg has recognized his audience as either his fellow students or adults such as parents or teachers.

arrive home at a late hour, so they really don't have time to do their homework. As a result, students don't work up to their full educational capacity.

Working after school is harmful as well as unnecessary. The high school years are not the years to work, but the years to enjoy life. If you agree, call or write your school board committee. If we--as people who care--take a stand, we can make a difference. Be one of these people.

"Get a Job!"
by Greg Robertson

Every week, many students give up their Saturday and Sunday afternoons to work and make money. Instead of sleeping late or "hanging out" with their friends, these youths are out in the working world getting a taste of how the real world works. I believe this shows responsibility. It also shows the community that not all young men and women are troublemakers with nothing to do.

A good reason for young men and women to have jobs is their self-esteem. When students have worked a couple of days a week and receive their paychecks, they feel good about themselves. They feel as though they have done a good deed, and they want to do it again!

Many people argue that when a person is young, a job consumes too much time. They say that young people waste the money they make on useless items. It is true that some of the weekly paycheck goes for recreation, but many students save money for school, use it to pay car insurance, or just put it in a savings account for future use. This is also a useful skill to learn because all people have to learn how to "pinch their pennies."

Students who have jobs are definitely doing themselves a favor. They are gathering experience for possible future jobs, and a good job is a wonderful thing to put on a résumé.

Having students in the workplace is a very good idea. It helps the student and the community. If YOU are a student who would like to be involved in the workplace, contact one of the agencies that help teens find jobs, such as "Dial-A-Teen" and "The Youth Employment Agency." Be part of the responsible (and richer) teens in your community. Go out and GET A JOB!

TEACHING THE LESSON

Students might be more successful if you allow them to work in pairs or groups. To begin, brainstorm and list on the chalkboard the various subjects that students would like to satirize. Then organize students into groups of three or four according to interests.

335

WRITING WORKSHOP

A Satire

Searching for persuasive issues showed you that people have a good many ideas about things that are wrong with our society and should be changed. In the main assignment in this chapter, you used logical, emotional, and ethical appeals to persuade. *Satire* is a form of persuasive writing that seeks to bring about change and reform through humor and wit. Satirists ridicule the failings of individuals, social and political institutions, and society in general in order to persuade people that reform—in thought or action—is needed.

Satirists often rely on distortion and exaggeration to get their points across. Their tone can be either gentle and smiling or biting and angry. They may use almost any form of writing—a poem, a novel, a short story, a song's lyrics, a play, an essay.

One of the most famous—and biting—satirists was Jonathan Swift. In his book *Gulliver's Travels*, Swift takes aim at many human failings, including the damaging inclination to fight over trivial matters. He describes two countries that were at war for three years. And for what? One country thought eggs should be cracked at the large end; the other thought they should be cracked at the small end. In the essay "A Modest Proposal," Swift ridicules those who complain about beggars yet offer no solution. He offers this satiric solution to the unpleasant sight of poor children begging in the street: Eat them!

Satire is still a flourishing and effective persuasive art, practiced by modern satirists such as Garry Trudeau, the creator of the *Doonesbury* comic strip; the writers and creators of the television series *The Simpsons*; essayist Fran Lebowitz; and a host of others. One well-known satirist is Art Buchwald, a syndicated newspaper columnist. As you read "The Killers," think not only about what he is satirizing but about the "support" he presents for his position.

MEETING *individual* NEEDS

LEP/ESL

General Strategies. It may be more beneficial to emphasize the recognition of satire rather than its creation. Bring visual examples of satire to the classroom, such as video segments from *Saturday Night Live*. Complement this with class discussion. Demonstrate how satire is uniquely suited to call attention to sensitive issues.

Before students work independently to write their satires, you can guide them toward an understanding of the form by answering the questions that follow the model.

After students have written their satires, ask them to read their creations aloud to the rest of the class. You might even have students prepare skits from their satires and videotape the skits for presentation.

ASSESSMENT

Assess students' satires informally as students read them orally or present them as skits. Consider audience reaction in your assessment and evaluation.

VISUAL CONNECTIONS
Exploring the Subject. Winner of the 1982 Pulitzer Prize for his commentary, Art Buchwald has delighted readers of his syndicated column for over three decades. His style is humorous and satirical, and his columns often make fun of national politics, American culture and customs, and human foibles. His columns have been published in several collections, including *You Can Fool All of the People All of the Time* (1985).

USING THE SELECTION
The Killers

1
This man becomes symbolic of the uncaring citizen who craves violence and sensationalism.

2
"Super-American" is ironic because superheroes such as Superman save the good and innocent.

3
Buchwald satirizes the man's lack of respect for property as well as for lives and slyly suggests a reason for higher insurance premiums.

4
The man is more interested in entertainment and action than in the lives of innocent people.

The Killers
by Art Buchwald

What fascinates me about films depicting so much violence is not the shooting, knifing, and garroting of the good guys as well as the bad guys, but the damage done to innocent people who just happen to be on the scene.

When I watch Sly Stallone, Clint Eastwood, Arnold Schwarzenegger, and Charles Bronson blowing up buildings, smashing cars, and spraying lead with submachine guns, the first thing that comes to mind is how much hurt they inflict on everyone else in the film.

The other night I said out loud in the theater, "Is this type of picture worth it?"

1 "Of course it's worth it," the man in the next seat said. "It teaches the audience that violence must be met with violence."

2 "But look at what's up on the screen. The Super-American has wrecked six cars and an orphanage to get the bad guy. He's driving like a madman. Who is going to pay for the wrecked automobiles and the buildings that the Super-American is senselessly destroying?"

3 "The Super-American's liability insurance company," the man said.

"But the Super-American didn't even stop to see if the bystanders were hurt."

4 "What would you want him to do, hold up the movie? You have to have continuous action in this kind of film. And when you do that, a lot of innocents are going to get hurt."

CLOSURE

Ask students to describe two techniques often used in satire [exaggeration, distortion, or humor]. Then ask students what two different tones are often found in satire [humorous and sarcastic].

EXTENSION

Have volunteers find another satire from the visual media. Some film examples are *Airplane* and *Naked Gun.* After viewing one of these films, students could write analyses of the satiric elements found in the film. If time permits, these analyses can be presented to the class. ■

337

"How about the Super-American's car going right through a fruit market and mowing down a Chinese laundry. Doesn't anyone in the theater care about the fruit dealer and the laundryman?"

5
6   The man said, "That's nothing compared to the Super-American wiping out some of the country's worst villains. The only reason the Super-American is pursuing evil is because the police have failed in their job."

"Good enough, but why did he blow up the Senior Citizens' apartment building with dynamite? The bad guy still got away and now twenty families have no place to live."

7   "It's just a movie," the man said.

"Then why are all the kids in the theater cheering?"

The man said, "Because they identify with the Super-American — a lone warrior fighting the battle to rid the world of rot."

8   "If you believe in law and order, how do you feel about the Super-American hitting the bad guy over the head with a fire extinguisher?"

"The Super-American won't do it for long. As soon as he can grab the Uzi submachine gun, he'll fill the bad guy's stomach full of lead."

"Why doesn't the Super-American just turn him over for trial?"

"How can he after what they did to his brother?"

"I didn't know they did anything to the Super-American's brother."

9   "It was in the coming attractions. They cut it out in the final version so that they could spend more time showing the Super-American setting the villain on fire."

I said, "I can't believe what I'm seeing. The Super-American just pushed a crowded bus off the pier so that he could improve his line of fire to the hospital ship."

"You really pick up on every little thing, don't you?" the man said.

"What must our children think? They probably believe that what they see on the screen is the real thing."

"When you have every top-grossing male star in Hollywood fighting to do one of these pictures, then you realize that vigilantism is here to stay," he said.

"Even if the Super-American doesn't care a fig about constitutional rights?"

10   "If the audience doesn't care, why should he?"

from *I Think I Don't Remember*

5

Buchwald satirizes the belief that the end justifies the means.

6

The man uses a logical fallacy—a non sequitur: The argument that a vigilante should use violent means to pursue evil when the police fail is not logical.

7

Although the man in the theater claims that "It's just a movie," Buchwald implies that this attitude pervades all life.

8

Ironically, action that Buchwald thought too violent is not violent enough for the man in the theater.

9

Ironically, motivation is omitted in favor of more violence.

10

Ironically, real life is often full of almost as much violence as that described in the movie.

1. Did you find this satire funny? Why or why not?
2. Clearly Art Buchwald is satirizing violence in the movies, but is that all? Read closely: What other aspects of America or American life are criticized through the actions of the "Super-American"? Explain your answer.
3. What details does Buchwald use to make his points? Are they realistic and believable or exaggerated? Explain.
4. Buchwald developed his satire as a dialogue between himself and another moviegoer. Why would he do this? [Hint: How does dialogue relate to an important part of your persuasive essay?] How else could he have developed this satire?
5. *Verbal irony,* saying one thing but meaning the opposite, is frequent in satire. Did Buchwald intend "It's just a movie" ironically? Explain.
6. Where in the satire does Buchwald try to include readers directly in the issues he's examining—to make them feel responsible? Is it effective?

Writing a Satire

Prewriting. What social or political situation seems to you unjust, harmful, or a threat to important values? What would you like others to think more about: the homeless? the power of the Supreme Court? the excessive amount of money students spend on proms? Then: How can you *make fun* of the situation? What elements lend themselves to ridicule? How can you use humor to persuade readers of the need for reform?

You have several choices for the form of your satire. For example, you could write an essay in which you make "serious" outrageous suggestions, a dialogue like Buchwald's (or one between two invented people), or a short comic story (for example, "The Unforgettable Prom Date").

Writing, Evaluating, and Revising. Remember that while your topic is serious, your tone should be humorous and tongue-in-cheek or sarcastic and biting. Use exaggeration, silly details, and unexpected points of view; use language that suits your purpose (and characters, if any), whether slangy, ridiculously formal, or deadpan. You don't have to make a direct position statement, but be sure action, details, or dialogue communicate your concerns. Think about whether you want to incorporate an indirect call to action: a suggestion of what readers can do.

Try your satire out on others. Do they get it? Are they amused? Ask them for suggestions for clarifying your targets or adding humor. After evaluating your satire, revise it as needed.

Proofreading and Publishing. Make a clean, corrected final copy. The school newspaper and the local paper's op-ed page are good forums for a satirical essay. Your satire might also be turned into a funny skit for the class (think of satiric television programs like *Saturday Night Live*). Satire is common on radio, too, so see if local stations are interested. Finally, start each class period with a different student's satire until all are read or performed.

If you want to include your satire in your **portfolio,** date it and write a note of reflection. How did you control the tone of your piece? Could you change the language you used to make the tone more effective? Did you enjoy writing satire? Why or why not?

"Satire should, like a polished razor keen, Wound with a touch that's scarcely felt or seen."

Lady Mary Wortley Montagu

INTEGRATING THE LANGUAGE ARTS

Literature Link. Assign your students Jonathan Swift's "A Modest Proposal" or part of *Gulliver's Travels.* Ask students to analyze Swift's satirical techniques.

A DIFFERENT APPROACH

Let students create their own *Saturday Night Live* program. Videotape readings or performances of skits based on students' satires and then play the tape for the class. If two or more classes are writing satires at the same time, they can trade videos for viewing. You might even have a contest to determine which satire is the most effective in persuading its audience.

TEACHING NOTE

Remind students that a satiric tone often depends on verbal irony, that is, saying one thing and meaning something entirely different, often the opposite of the statement's literal meaning. As students reflect on the tones of their essays, encourage them to focus on their use of verbal irony.

LESSON 8 (pp. 340–343)
MAKING CONNECTIONS

ANALYZING PERSUASION
IN AN ADVERTISEMENT
OBJECTIVE

• To work with a partner to analyze
  advertisements

ANALYZING PERSUASION IN AN ADVERTISEMENT

Teaching Strategies

To help students complete this assignment, bring to class several copies of old magazines that they can cut apart. Allow students to choose partners or to organize themselves into small groups to select two advertisements for analysis. Allow students ample time to discuss the answers to the questions on p. 340. Then ask students to mount their advertisements and typed or printed copies of their analyses on pieces of poster board to use as they present oral reports on their findings. You may want to ask three artistic students in the class to prepare humorous posters of the bandwagon appeal, snob appeal, and veiled threat to display with the advertisement analyses.

GUIDELINES

Evaluate students' advertising reports based on quality of analysis, completeness of analysis, visual support, and presentation.

340

MAKING CONNECTIONS

ANALYZING PERSUASION IN AN ADVERTISEMENT

We all know that advertising manipulates us. It isn't all logical. It plays on emotions—both desires and fears. And yet we respond to it, we enjoy it, we *buy things* because of it. Why? How do advertisers make us pick up a particular brand of deodorant? eat in a certain restaurant or see a certain movie? contribute to an organization or vote for a candidate?

With a partner or a group, become an advertising analyst. Choose two ads from different media: print, television, radio, and direct mail (the advertisements that come unsolicited in the mail). Then analyze, and give an oral report on, the persuasion you find, showing the ads or describing them thoroughly. Here are some guides for your investigation:

- What product, service, or cause is the ad selling? What *value or feeling* is being "sold"? How?
- Who seems to be the primary audience for the ad? How can you tell?
- What logical appeals are used (reasons, factual evidence, expert testimony)? How sound are they?
- How are emotional appeals made? Look at language, visuals (consider content, color, style), music, celebrities.
- Which, if any, of the following appeals are used?

  Bandwagon appeal—suggests that you should buy the product because everyone else is buying it.

  Snob appeal—appeals to your desire to be rich, brainy, famous, and generally better than other people.

  Veiled threat—hints that something bad will happen to you if you don't buy the product (you'll lose your girlfriend because of bad breath, for example).

- What ethical appeals do you find—ways that the advertiser shows fairness, good character, or concern for the audience?
- Does the ad work? Why or why not?

341

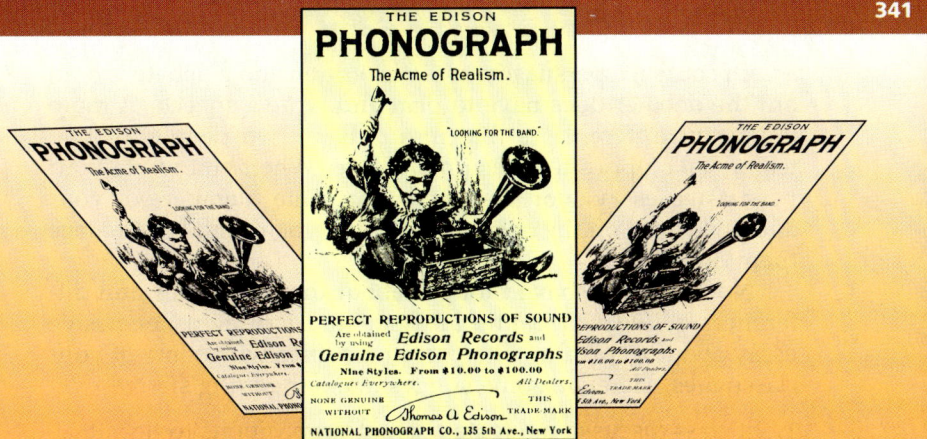

SPEAKING AND LISTENING

Persuasion and Debate

What does a debate have in common with a persuasive essay? The debater, like the writer of an essay, is taking a stand, trying to convince an audience to accept his or her position on an issue.

The proposition in a debate is much like the position statement in a persuasive essay. For example:

Position Statement:	All new urban road construction should include bicycle paths.
Debate Proposition:	Resolved, that all new urban road construction should include bicycle paths.

SPEAKING AND LISTENING
Teaching Strategies

Remind students that effective persuasion uses logical, emotional, and ethical appeals. You may even want to inform students that when Aristotle first described these appeals, he was thinking of how they would be used in speech rather than writing. Tell students that to be convincing, they must have specific supporting information for their debate proposition (logical appeal). You may want to suggest that students record this information on 3" x 5" note cards so that either partner or any member of the team can access the information during the actual debate. Point out also that they should be able to make even more effective use of emotional and ethical appeals in debate than in written compositions because they will be speaking directly to their audience.

GUIDELINES

Select three students to serve as judges for the debate. Suggest that students rate each debating team on (1) logical support, (2) fair and effective emotional appeal, (3) ethical credibility, (4) oral presentation, and (5) overall effectiveness in convincing the audience. Students may want to use a numerical scale. The team with the highest total score wins.

Of course, a persuasive essay is written and a debate is oral, but the debater does have to plan and write a speech. A more important difference is that in a debate, two people, or two teams, take opposite sides on an issue. When you wrote your persuasive essay, you assumed that some members of your audience were on the opposite side; but you didn't have to face them directly.

Now that you have thought about the similarities and differences between debating an issue and writing a persuasive essay about it, plan to take part in a debate with some of your classmates. Here are some suggestions for getting started:

1. In class discussion, create a list of propositions to debate (use the form in the example on the previous page). You could pick up some of the issues from the persuasive essays you wrote earlier in this chapter.
2. Decide whether you will debate in pairs or teams, and sign up for propositions. Your sign-up sheet should include an affirmative position and a negative position—that way you will have a pair or team on both sides of the issue.
3. Review the material on debating on pages 1031–1036, and plan your debate. After you have finished planning and rehearsing, hold the debate in your classroom.

PERSUASION AND THE MEDIA

Writing a Letter to the Editor

Sometimes, the editorial page of a newspaper or magazine is the most entertaining and interesting page in the publication. Letters to the editor are particularly interesting. People from all walks of life get their gripes and convictions off their chests, and usually they are trying to persuade others to agree with them.

They write for various reasons. They may be upset about an editorial; they may wholeheartedly agree or strenuously disagree with an article; they may want to start a debate; they may even be taking strong issue with a previous letter to the editor.

Have you ever written to a publication in response to something you read? If not, you now have a chance. Spend a few days looking over the letters to the editor in your local newspaper or a favorite magazine. Find a letter that stirs up your feel-

PERSUASION AND THE MEDIA
Teaching Strategies

When students have selected thought-provoking letters to the editor, have them read these letters to the rest of the class. Then initiate a class discussion about why these particular letters are so effective. Finally, ask students to write their own letters and to share the letters with one another.

GUIDELINES

Evaluate students' letters on their overall effectiveness. Consider publishing a few of the most interesting ones in a class newspaper or flier.

ings. Does it make you angry? Do you think the person is totally off base or right on target? Or do you have a different slant on the issue that you think readers should consider?

When you write your letter, think about everything you have learned in this chapter about persuasion. Remember, however, that this is just a letter—not an essay—so be brief. Many publications give requirements about form and submission. You have a much better chance of being published if you follow the guidelines. If your letter makes it into print, bring a copy of the publication to class. Then check out future issues of the publication. Someone else may respond to what you wrote.

Shoe reprinted by permission: Tribune Media Services.

Chapter 9

WRITING TO EXPLORE: EXPOSITION

OBJECTIVES

- To select a topic for a problem-solution essay
- To organize and draft a problem-solution essay
- To evaluate, revise, proofread and publish a draft of a problem-solution essay

WRITING-IN-PROGRESS ASSIGNMENTS

Major Assignment: Writing a problem-solution essay
Cumulative Writing Assignments: The chart below shows the sequence of cumulative assignments that will guide students as they write a problem-solution essay. These Writing Assignments form the instructional core of Chapter 9.

PREWRITING

WRITING ASSIGNMENT
- Part 1: Identifying and Investigating a Problem p. 353
- Part 2: Identifying Possible Solutions p. 355
- Part 3: Identifying Your Best Solution and Listing Necessary Steps p. 358
- Part 4: Planning Your Problem-Solution Essay p. 361

WRITING YOUR FIRST DRAFT

WRITING ASSIGNMENT
- Part 5: Writing a Draft of Your Essay p. 375

EVALUATING AND REVISING

WRITING ASSIGNMENT
- Part 6: Evaluating and Revising Your Essay p. 379

PROOFREADING AND PUBLISHING

WRITING ASSIGNMENT
- Part 7: Proofreading and Publishing Your Essay p. 381

In addition, exercises 1–3 provide practice in speaking and listening, analyzing a problem-solution essay, and analyzing revisions.

cross CURRICULUM

Problems and Solutions in Psychology

Have students apply the exploration techniques from this chapter to a topic studied in psychology class.

- **Assignment** Students often have problems with remembering information for tests. They may wonder why some people can recall more details than others or how they can improve their ability to remember information for tests. Have students work in groups to explore these questions and to propose solutions. Then, each group should present their findings in a self-help booklet.

- **Prewriting** Suggest that students investigate the following topics:
  - the four processes of memory
  - the theories explaining why people forget
  - the factors that help efficient learning
  - the levels-of-processing theory by Roberta Klatzky
  - the basic methods for measuring retention

  Besides doing research on the principles of efficient learning and thinking, students need to conduct some simple studies with their peers on the different theories of memory. Then, along with the research from printed sources, they can use their findings as support for their proposed solutions.

- **Writing** Because students will be presenting their findings in a booklet format, you may want to divide the body of the framework given on p. 375 into chapters. Then, one person in each group should be responsible for one chapter or part. Be sure students include a table of contents and a title for their booklets.

- **Publishing** Students can share their booklets with other classes or use the information from their booklets to give a presentation on how to improve memory for taking tests.

INTEGRATING THE LANGUAGE ARTS

SELECTION	READING AND LITERATURE	WRITING AND CRITICAL THINKING	LANGUAGE AND SYNTAX	SPEAKING, LISTENING, AND OTHER EXPRESSION SKILLS
• "Sonnet 29" by William Shakespeare p. 346 • "The Villain in the Atmosphere" by Isaac Asimov pp. 363–369 • from "An Extravagance of Laughter" by Ralph Ellison pp. 383–384	• Responding personally to literature pp. 347, 370, 384, 387 • Making inferences and drawing conclusions pp. 347, 350, 352–353, 355–356, 358, 370, 384, 387 • Identifying problems and solutions pp. 347, 370, 384, 387 • Reading for specific information pp. 347, 370, 384 • Finding the main idea p. 347 • Identifying causes and effects p. 347 • Analyzing an introduction p. 370	• Writing about personal experience pp. 347, 384–385 • Analyzing a problem pp. 352–353, 361 • Gathering information pp. 352–353 • Writing a summary paragraph pp. 352–353 • Brainstorming a topic problem p. 353 • Analyzing possible solutions pp. 355–356, 358, 361 • Choosing a solution and listing necessary steps pp. 358, 361 • Planning a problem-solution essay p. 361	• Proofreading for errors in grammar, usage, and mechanics pp. 381, 384–385	• Working with classmates to identify problem issues and gather information p. 350, 352–353 • Making a chart to evaluate possible solutions p. 358 • Working with classmates to evaluate and revise problem-solution essays p. 379 • Working with classmates to evaluate and revise self-explorations pp. 384–385 • Using questions to interview people p. 386 • Working with classmates to evaluate and share problem-solving techniques p. 386 • Working with classmates to analyze problem-solution structures across the curriculum p. 387

SUGGESTED INTEGRATED UNIT PLAN

This unit plan gives suggestions on how to integrate the major strands of the language arts with this chapter.

The suggested literary selections, which include fiction and nonfiction, are examples of writings that identify problems and pose solutions. If you begin with this chapter on writing a problem-solution essay or with the suggested literature selections, you should focus on the common characteristics of writing that explains a problem and proposes a solution. You can then integrate speaking/listening and language concepts with both the writing and the literature.

Common Characteristics

- Organization of ideas is usually linear
- Content includes a question, the search for an answer, and the proposal of a solution
- Language is usually objective, though evidence based on the writer's experience may be presented in first person
- Purpose is to explain and convince audience

Writing
Problem-Solution Essay

Speaking/Listening

- Presenting problems for discussion
- Listening critically at meetings

UNIT FOCUS: NONFICTION: EXPLORATIVE WRITING

Language
Mechanics, Grammar, and Usage

- Punctuation of subordinate clauses
- Infinitive phrases
- Pronoun references

Literature
Selections such as

- "A Modest Proposal" Jonathan Swift
- "Shooting an Elephant" George Orwell

CHAPTER 9: WRITING TO EXPLORE: EXPOSITION

Use this guide for creating an instructional plan that addresses the individual needs of your students. Assignments accompanied by the following symbol (*) may be completed out of class. Times given for pacing lessons are estimated.

CHAPTER PLANNING GUIDE—PUPIL'S EDITION

LESSONS	LITERARY MODEL p. 346 "Sonnet 29" by William Shakespeare	PREWRITING pp. 349–361	
		Generating Ideas	Gathering/Organizing
DEVELOPMENTAL PROGRAM	🕐 **20–25 minutes** • Read model aloud to class and discuss answers to questions on p. 347	🕐 **90 minutes** • Main Assignment: Looking Ahead p. 348 • Exploring Problems pp. 349–351 • Exercise 1 p. 350 • Critical Thinking pp. 351–353 • Exploring Solutions pp. 354–358 • Writing Assignment: Parts 1–3 pp. 353, 355, 358*	🕐 **35–40 minutes** • Planning Your Essay pp. 359–360 • Writing Assignment: Part 4 p. 361*
CORE PROGRAM	🕐 **15–20 minutes** • Have students read the model and answer questions on p. 347 in pairs.	🕐 **60 minutes** • Main Assignment: Looking Ahead p. 348 • Exploring Problems pp. 349–351 • Exercise 1 p. 350 • Critical Thinking pp. 351–353 • Exploring Solutions pp. 354–358 • Writing Assignment: Parts 1–3 pp. 353, 355, 358*	🕐 **30–35 minutes** • Planning Your Essay pp. 359–360 • Writing Note p. 361 • Writing Assignment: Part 4 p. 361*
ACCELERATED PROGRAM	🕐 **15 minutes** • Assign students to read model independently and answer questions 3–6 p. 347	🕐 **30 minutes** • Main Assignment: Looking Ahead p. 348 • Critical Thinking pp. 351–353 • Reminder p. 358 • Writing Assignment: Parts 1–3 pp. 353, 355, 358*	🕐 **20–25 minutes** • Planning Your Essay pp. 359–360 • Writing Assignment: Part 4 p. 361*

CHAPTER PLANNING GUIDE—PROGRAM RESOURCES

	LITERARY MODEL	PREWRITING
PRINT	• Reading Master 9, *Practice for Assessment in Reading, Vocabulary, and Spelling* p. 9	• Prewriting, *Strategies for Writing* p. 37
MEDIA	• Fine Art Transparency 6: *Self Portrait, Transparency Binder*	• Graphic Organizers 15–16, *Transparency Binder*

WRITING pp. 362–375	EVALUATING AND REVISING pp. 376–379	PROOFREADING AND PUBLISHING pp. 380–382
🕐 **50–55 minutes** • The Elements of an Essay p. 362 • Framework/A Writer's Model pp. 370–374 • Writing Note p. 374 • Framework Chart p. 375 • Writing Assignment: Part 5 p. 375*	🕐 **50–55 minutes** • Evaluating and Revising p. 376 • Evaluating and Revising Chart p. 377 • Exercise 3 in pairs pp. 378–379 • Writing Assignment: Part 6 p. 379	🕐 **50 minutes** • Proofreading and Publishing p. 380 • Mechanics Hint p. 380 • Writing Assignment: Part 7 p. 381 • Reflecting p. 381 • A Student Model p. 382
🕐 **60 minutes** • The Elements of an Essay p. 362 • An Essay pp. 363–369 • Exercise 2 p. 370 • Writing Note p. 374 • Framework Chart p. 375 • Writing Assignment: Part 5 p. 375*	🕐 **45–50 minutes** • Evaluating and Revising Chart p. 377 • Exercise 3 pp. 378–379 • Writing Assignment: Part 6 p. 379	🕐 **35 minutes** • Proofreading and Publishing p. 380 • Mechanics Hint p. 380 • Writing Assignment: Part 7 p. 381 • Reflecting p. 381 • A Student Model p. 382*
🕐 **40–45 minutes** • The Elements of an Essay p. 362 • An Essay pp. 363–364 • Framework Chart p. 375 • Writing Assignment: Part 5 p. 375*	🕐 **40–45 minutes** • Evaluating and Revising Chart p. 377 • Writing Assignment: Part 6 p. 379	🕐 **30 minutes** • Mechanics Hint p. 380 • Assignment: Part 7 p. 381 • Reflecting p. 381

💾 Computer disk or CD-ROM   🔦 Overhead transparencies

WRITING	EVALUATING AND REVISING	PROOFREADING AND PUBLISHING
• Writing, *Strategies for Writing* p. 38	• Evaluating and Revising, *Strategies for Writing* p. 39	• Proofreading Practice, *Strategies for Writing* p. 41 • *English Workshop* pp. 89–90, 303–304
	• Revision Transparencies 15–16, *Transparency Binder* 🔦	• *Language Workshop* Lessons 26–27, 42 💾

ELEMENTS OF WRITING: CURRICULUM CONNECTIONS

Writing Workshop
• Personal Exploration p. 383

Making Connections
• Speaking and Listening p. 386
• Problem Solving Across the Curriculum pp. 386–387

ASSESSMENT OPTIONS

Summative Assessment
Holistic Scoring: Prompts and Models pp. 33–38

Portfolio Assessment
Portfolio forms, *Portfolio Assessment* pp. 5–25, 44-48

Ongoing Assessment
Proofreading, *Strategies for Writing* p. 40

Reflection
Writing Process Log, *Strategies for Writing* p. 36
Self-assessment Record, *Portfolio Assessment* p. 19

- To evaluate the appropriateness of poetry as a means of exploring a nonpersonal problem

OBJECTIVES

- To respond to and analyze a literary model of exploratory writing

PROGRAM MANAGER

CHAPTER 9

- **Summative Assessment** For a writing prompt, including grading criteria and student models, see *Holistic Scoring: Prompts and Models,* pp. 33–38.

- **Extension/Enrichment** See **Fine Art Transparency 6,** *Self Portrait* by James Valerio. For suggestions on how to tie the transparency to instruction, review teacher's notes in *Fine Art and Instructional Transparencies for Writing,* p. 33.

- **Reading Support** For help with the reading selection, p. 346, see **Reading Master 9** in *Practice for Assessment in Reading, Vocabulary, and Spelling,* p. 9.

QUOTATION FOR THE DAY

"I am an explorer, then, and I am also a stalker, or the instrument of the hunt itself." (Annie Dillard, 1945–   , American writer)

Write the quotation on the chalkboard and discuss with students how Dillard's statement relates to writing. Ask students to consider how, as writers, they are instrument(s) of "the hunt itself."

9 WRITING TO EXPLORE: EXPOSITION

Have a volunteer read "**Sonnet 29**" aloud. Lead a discussion of why the sonnet can be considered an example of exploratory writing. Point out to students that the exploratory purpose coexists with the literary purpose in "**Sonnet 29.**" (For further explanation, see the **Teaching Note** on p. 346.)

Your class discussion may adequately prepare students to answer the **Reader's Response** and **Writer's Craft** questions.

If you feel that students will need additional guided practice to analyze the literary model, put "Sonnet 75" by Edmund Spenser on the chalkboard and use it to model answers to **Writer's Craft** questions 3 and 5. Then, have students complete the ☞

Asking Questions, Seeking Answers

On October 14, 1947, Chuck Yeager climbed into his X-1 plane and became the first human being to fly faster than the speed of sound. Both Yeager and the people watching this momentous event wondered: What will happen at supersonic speed? Will the plane vibrate to pieces, sending the pilot to his death? People always **ask questions** about the mysteries and problems around them. And as they do, they **discover** new answers, solutions.

Writing and You. Explorations may start in your mind, but often they turn into words on a page. For example, historian Barbara Tuchman asked questions about World War I and then wrote *The Guns of August*. What problems and solutions have you explored?

As You Read. Some people explore problems through poems. What problem does the following sonnet explore?

Julius Ciss, *Brainstorm on the Future*. Acrylic on canvas, 20" × 30". The Image Bank.

VISUAL CONNECTIONS
Brainstorm on the Future

About the Artist. Julius Ciss was born in Toronto, Canada, in 1951. He studied at the Ontario College of Art as well as the School of Visual Arts in New York. Ciss names Norman Rockwell and the music and art of the late 1960s as his main influences.

Ideas for Writing. Discuss with students how the technique of brainstorming can help them explore ideas for writing. You might have students explore a topic, such as challenges facing their generation, through brainstorming. Students could then discuss the results of their brainstorming.

This activity might give students some ideas for topics for their exploratory essays.

Reader's Response and Writer's Craft questions independently.

Use students' responses to Writer's Craft questions 3 and 5 to assess their ability to analyze a model of exploratory writing.

CLOSURE

Have students give brief descriptions of exploratory writing.

SONNET 29

Teaching Note. This sonnet can serve as a good example of how more than one literary purpose can coexist within one piece of writing. The sonnet exemplifies the literary purpose because its author obviously puts great emphasis on the language he uses. His words are carefully chosen and placed to create a poem that is entertaining and that bears reading again and again, not so much because of its message, but because of the elegance of its language.

However, "**Sonnet 29**" also exemplifies the exploratory purpose. In the first eight lines (the octet), the speaker of the poem presents and explores a problem. In the last six lines (the sestet) he resolves it—he discovers a new way to look at his situation.

MEETING *individual* NEEDS

LEP/ESL

General Strategies. Shakespeare's sonnet contains some word orders and meanings found rarely, if at all, in the English of today, (for example, "beweep," "like to," and "with friends possessed"). To help students, discuss the meanings of difficult words and phrases before students read the sonnet.

346

346

Sonnet 29

by William Shakespeare

When, in disgrace with fortune and men's eyes,
I all alone beweep my outcast state,
And trouble deaf heaven with my bootless cries,
And look upon myself, and curse my fate,
Wishing me like to one more rich in hope,
Featured like him, like him with friends possessed,
Desiring this man's art and that man's scope,
With what I most enjoy contented least;
Yet in these thoughts myself almost despising,
Haply I think on thee—and then my state,
Like to the lark at break of day arising
From sullen earth, sings hymns at heaven's gate;
For thy sweet love remembered such wealth brings
That then I scorn to change my state with kings.

You could have students write sonnets that explore personal problems. Suggest that students model their sonnets after **"Sonnet 29"**—exploring the problem in the first eight lines and resolving it in the last six lines. Remind students to choose topics they would not mind sharing with the class. ■

347

READER'S RESPONSE

1. When you're "down" or "depressed," is there someone or something that can raise your spirits? Explain.
2. Many people believe that part of Shakespeare's greatness lies in his exploration of timeless themes and feelings. Even though the sonnet was written about 400 years ago, do you understand and identify with the feelings it expresses? Why or why not?

WRITER'S CRAFT

3. When you write about a problem you've explored, you may describe the problem or explain a solution for it. In which lines of the sonnet does the speaker express his problem? In which lines does he identify a solution? What is the solution?
4. Part of exploring a problem may involve identifying its different causes and effects. What is causing the speaker's problem? What are its specific effects?
5. In this poem Shakespeare explores a personal problem. Would the poem work as well if he explored a problem that affected more people? Why?
6. Shakespeare's primary aim in creating this sonnet was, of course, to create literature. Exploring a problem was secondary. What other pieces of literature can you think of that show someone exploring a problem?

ANSWERS

Reader's Response

Responses will vary.

1. Students should mention people they turn to or techniques, practices, or habits they use to help them cope with difficult times.
2. Students should give reasons to explain their responses.

Writer's Craft

3. The speaker expresses the problem in lines 1–8, the octet. In lines 9–10, he identifies the solution—thinking about the person to whom the poem is addressed.
4. The speaker's problem is caused by economic and social disgrace. The effects are hopelessness, loss of friends, disquiet, and loss of self-esteem.
5. Students should give reasons to support their opinions.
6. Possibilities include "Meditation 17" by John Donne, "The Tyger" by William Blake, "When I Have Fears" by John Keats, and "The Death of the Moth" by Virginia Woolf.

347

WAYS TO EXPLORE

TEACHING THE LESSON

Explain to students that exploration often calls for a combination of methods of development. For example, an exploration of herbal remedies for the common cold might include a description of the various remedies, a narration of the history of such remedies, a comparison of herbal remedies to conventional medical remedies, and an evaluation of the efficacy of herbal remedies.

Show students examples of exploratory writing that use various methods of development, and work with students to identify the method or methods used in each example. ■

A DIFFERENT APPROACH

Show students a documentary film or videotape that explores an issue. Work with students to identify uses of the developmental methods—narration, description, classification, and evaluation—in the film or videotape.

Ways to Explore

Writers like William Shakespeare explore problems in many different ways. The exploration may be in writing, or it may take place entirely in the writers' minds. But once writers uncover an insight or develop a new idea, they usually want to share it with others and perhaps even convince them to share their way of thinking. Exploratory writing, combined with informative or persuasive writing, may appear in newspapers, magazines, speeches and sermons, business proposals, and books. Here are some examples of exploratory writing.

- in a research paper, tracing your family tree to learn about your forebears
- in an article, examining factors that might account for the decreasing crime rate in your city
- in a police report, describing your missing bicycle to help officers locate it
- in an application for an internship, describing your main goals in life and how the internship would help you achieve them
- in a letter to the editor, comparing and contrasting possible solutions to a local water shortage
- in a report, identifying both public and private sources of funding to facilitate getting new uniforms for a school volleyball team
- in an e-mail message, asking questions about candidates for local office before voting
- in a letter, explaining why you have decided to major in philosophy

LOOKING AHEAD

In the main writing assignment in this chapter, you will use narration and classification to explore a problem and its possible solutions in an essay. As you work, keep in mind that a problem-solution essay

- identifies and explores a problem
- identifies, explores, and evaluates solutions to the problem
- explains (and proves) how to solve the problem

OBJECTIVES
- To identify issues of concern by listening and reading for information and by speaking to classmates
- To decide whether issues affect large numbers of people
- To identify, investigate, and analyze a problem
- To identify possible solutions to a problem
- To analyze possible solutions to a problem and to list in chart form steps necessary to implement a solution
- To plan a problem-solution essay

Writing a Problem-Solution Essay

Prewriting

Exploring Problems

Although you may not be exploring new continents or theories, your daily conversations, thinking, and writing are still filled with exploration. In exploring a personal problem, you often write for yourself—in a journal entry, for example (or a sonnet!). But when you explore a problem that involves others, you often present your findings to an audience in the form of an essay. In this chapter you will study models of this type of exploration and write an essay exploring a problem and a solution.

Identifying a Problem

Like most people, you probably have your share of problems, but most personal problems are not appropriate for a problem-solution essay. When you are planning to share the results of your exploration with others, you need to identify a problem that is common to many people. For example, a quarrel with your kid brother is too personal, but many readers might be interested in the causes and effects of sibling rivalry.

As you consider possible problems for exploration, check the significance of each problem by asking

- Does it affect a number of people?
- Is it important to the people it affects?

HINTS FOR IDENTIFYING APPROPRIATE PROBLEMS

- **Address your concerns at the grass-roots level.** If you're concerned about environmental issues, you might explore a problem such as waste disposal or clean water in your community. Or, if you are worried about education, you might explore a problem such as falling test scores or student apathy in a local school.

(continued)

PROGRAM MANAGER

PREWRITING

- **Self-Assessment** Before beginning instruction of the writing process, see **Writing Process Log** in *Strategies for Writing*, p. 36.
- **Heuristics** To help students generate ideas, see **Prewriting** in *Strategies for Writing*, p. 37.
- **Instructional Support** See **Graphic Organizers 15** and **16.** For suggestions on how to tie the transparencies to instruction, review teacher's notes in *Fine Art and Instructional Transparencies for Writing*, pp. 81, 83.

QUOTATION FOR THE DAY
"The real questions are the ones that obtrude upon your consciousness whether you like it or not, the ones that make your mind start vibrating like a jackhammer, the ones that you 'come to terms with' only to discover that they are still there." (Ingrid Bengis, American writer)

Discuss with students the meaning of the quotation. Then, have students brainstorm in their writing journals lists of questions that fit Bengis's definition of a real question. Tell students that they may want to consider developing these questions as the topics for their problem-solution essays.

TEACHING THE LESSON

To motivate students, ask them to name problems that concern them, and record their responses on the chalkboard.

To prepare students for **Exercise 1**, model the process of identifying problems by showing a television news show or by bringing a local newspaper to class. Watch the news show or skim the newspaper with the class and note any problems that are presented. Then, work with students to decide which of the problems you have noted affect a number of people.

Have students complete **Exercise 1** independently. You may wish to have students work in pairs if they are attending public meetings.

Cont. on p. 353

MEETING *individual* NEEDS

LEP/ESL

General Strategies. You may want to suggest to students that they are welcome to explore problems concerning their countries of origin. This strategy will reinforce to students that their connections to their native countries are important, and such topics may prove more interesting to students.

ANSWERS
Exercise 1

Responses will vary. You could have students compile their lists of problems independently and then have students work in small groups to assess whether or not the problems affect large numbers of people.

HINTS FOR IDENTIFYING APPROPRIATE PROBLEMS *(continued)*

- **Address personal concerns that you share with others.** If you are worried about the crime rate and its effect on your family, you might explore a problem such as the rising crime rate or the understaffed police force. Or, if your concern is the worsening economy and its effect on your family, you might explore rising college costs or the lack of affordable housing.
- **Address problems that are solvable.** You probably can't make much progress in English class toward bringing peace to the Middle East or ending poverty in Central America.

EXERCISE 1 ▶ **Speaking and Listening: Identifying Problems**

What issues concern people in your school and community? One way to find out is by attending open meetings of groups such as the school board, the city council, and the local council on aging. Another way is to watch the broadcasts of such meetings on local cable TV. Or, you may gather information by reading the newspaper, following electronic bulletin board service discussions, or watching TV reports. Use these sources to identify and list three problems. With your classmates, decide which problems affect a large number of people.

OBJECTIVE

- To use the four methods of development of writing to generate information for an analysis of a problem

TEACHING *ANALYZING PROBLEMS*

Students may have had some experience with identifying methods of development. Here, however, students are being asked to use the methods to generate ideas. To help students, model the process several times. Using problems that the class is familiar with, answer each of the questions on this page. Then, have students ☞

Investigating a Problem

Before you can find a solution for your problem, you must first understand the problem itself. But problems aren't easy! They are, by definition, "complicated" or "difficult" situations. For this reason, they will require some careful study on your part.

Often when you look more deeply into a problem, you will discover that you need more information. You can use a variety of prewriting techniques to investigate your problem: brainstorming and asking yourself questions to discover what you already know; reading, listening, observing, and questioning to discover what other people think about the problem. You may have to go to the library or interview some people who are likely to be knowledgeable about the problem. (See pages 21–28 for more help with these techniques.) For example, if you were exploring the problem of rising costs of a college education, you might go to the library and look for recent newspaper or magazine articles on the topic. You might also talk to someone in your high school guidance office to find out whether rising costs are affecting local students.

MEETING *individual* NEEDS

LEARNING STYLES

Visual Learners. Exploration of problems and solutions often involves investigating chains of causes and effects. Work with students to draw a causal chain on the chalkboard. You could create a causal chain that relates to a problem you have been discussing in class, or you could create a causal chain to show the causes and effects of global warming, discussed in "**The Villain in the Atmosphere**," pp. 363–369. For examples of visuals that show chains of cause and effect, refer students to pp. 265–266.

CRITICAL THINKING

Analyzing Problems

One way to investigate a problem thoroughly is to analyze it using four different methods: description, narration, classification, and evaluation.

Description	What is the problem? How widespread is it?
Narration	What is its history? What are its causes? What are its effects?
Classification	How is the problem similar to other problems? How is the problem different from other problems? What are the major parts of the problem?
Evaluation	Is the problem important? Why?

To close, ask students to discuss which methods of development most helped them understand the problems. ⚡

COOPERATIVE LEARNING

Have students work in groups of three or four to generate more questions that could assist them in applying each method to a problem. This exercise may work more smoothly if students have specific problems in mind. For example, students might generate the following questions to explore the problem of air pollution in their city:

Description—What does the pollution look like?
Narration—How has the pollution changed over time?
Classification—How does the pollution vary in different parts of the city?
Evaluation—Is the problem solvable?

When they are finished, groups can pool their questions, and copies can be made so that each student has an additional resource to work with.

The following examples show how you might use these methods to gather information about the problem: the rising cost of college.

Description: Cost increasing faster than most consumers' ability to pay

Narration: Since 1980, the cost of tuition at most state universities has tripled or quadrupled. Average state-university tuition increased at least 10% a year between 1991 and 1994.
One cause, inflation; another cause, cuts in local and national funding for education
Students obviously affected; also long-range prospects for country—fewer college graduates

Classification: '90s, like housing and medical costs—increasingly unaffordable for many; government subsidies being cut
Parts of the problem—tuition, fees, housing

Evaluation: Importance—limits opportunities for many young Americans

⚡ CRITICAL THINKING EXERCISE:
Analyzing a Problem

Is student apathy a problem in your high school? Is there a parking lot or street near your school that's too congested? Do school buses have to pick some students up hours before classes begin? Select one of these problems (or a problem of

Cont. from p. 350
Using the problems that the class noted earlier from the news show or newspaper, model the skills necessary for completion of **Writing Assignment: Part 1.** With your class, evaluate the problems to decide which problem would make the best topic for an exploratory essay. Then, discuss what sources might help you to find out about the problem. Stress that exploratory writing must be based on facts.

Because **Writing Assignment: Part 1** incorporates all the skills taught so far, including those covered by the **Critical Thinking Exercise,** you may want to use it for assessment purposes.

Depending on the problems students choose, you may wish to limit the number of ☛

your own choosing) to analyze. Then, working with a partner, use each of the following approaches—description, narration, classification, evaluation—to gather information about the problem. In a short paragraph, summarize what you learn from your analysis.

ANSWERS
Critical Thinking Exercise

Paragraphs will vary. In evaluating the paragraphs, look for thorough analyses of the problems using each of the four methods of development. Keep in mind the applicability of this type of information-gathering to the scope of the chosen problem.

WRITING ASSIGNMENT

PART 1:
Identifying and Investigating a Problem

What are your concerns? Brainstorm a list of possible problems, including the ones you identified in Exercise 1 (page 350). The problems may affect your school or your community, or they may be of national and international significance. Then, evaluate the list to decide which problem would make the best topic for your essay (be sure that the problem is interesting and important to you). Once you've decided on a problem, use a variety of sources, and find out everything you can about it. Finally, use the methods that you read about in the Critical Thinking section (pages 351–352) to analyze the problem.

solutions they must consider. You could tell students to consider five different solutions thoroughly.

Discuss the **Strategies for Analyzing Possible Solutions** chart with your class. Point out that students should not hesitate, if necessary, to rephrase some of the questions to make them more applicable to particular problems. Before students begin **Writing**

Assignment: Part 2, use the chart to model the process of identifying possible solutions. You could return to a problem that has been the focus of a previous class discussion. Use this problem first to modify and then to answer the questions in the chart. Assign **Writing Assignment: Part 2** as independent practice. You will also want to model the process of finding the best solution.

INTEGRATING THE LANGUAGE ARTS

Test-taking Link. Point out that essay questions on tests in science, social studies, and other subjects may require or invite exploratory responses. For example, the essay question "Explore the possible effects on society of breakthroughs in increasing life expectancy" calls for an exploratory response that could be developed through narration, description, and evaluation. Tell students that as they progress through the chapter, they should look for ways to apply the strategies presented here to test-taking situations.

Prewriting

Exploring Solutions

Now that you are an expert on the problem you have chosen, it's time to turn your attention to the solutions. Most problems don't have easy solutions—if they did, they wouldn't be problems. Your job is to investigate all the possible solutions and then to decide which solution is the best one.

Identifying Possible Solutions

If your problem has been around for a while, somebody has probably already tried to solve it. One useful bit of exploration, then, is to investigate the solutions of others. But don't stop there—use freewriting, brainstorming, clustering, or imagining to create your own solutions. The following questions will help you get started.

STRATEGIES FOR ANALYZING POSSIBLE SOLUTIONS

Ideas of Others
1. What solutions to the problem have already been tried?
2. How effective have they been?
3. If the past solutions weren't effective, why not?
4. What solutions are currently being proposed?

Your Own Ideas
1. Can some of the causes of the problem be eliminated? How?
2. What can be done about the effects of the problem?
3. Is there any part of the problem that seems especially difficult to solve? Why?
4. Which part of the problem is simplest to solve? Why?
5. What is the strangest way you can think of to solve the problem? the easiest way? the most popular way?

It is possible to find creative solutions to problems that, on the surface, seem almost not to have a solution. For example, a college student named Wendy Kopp explored the problem of

Discuss the chart that shows one writer's analysis of solutions. Then, perhaps using the same problem you used to model **Writing Assignment: Part 2,** use the questions under **Finding the Best Solution** to analyze solutions. Have students help you generate and analyze some compromise solutions. Discuss whether different parts of the problem might warrant different solutions.

Once you have modeled the process of finding the best solution, move on to **Listing Necessary Steps,** pp. 357–358.

Ask students what the first step toward implementing the chosen solution might be. Write the response on the chalkboard and ask for the second step. Continue in this way until all the steps have been

☞

teacher shortages in inner cities and rural communities. As part of her senior thesis, she proposed the creation of a national teacher corps that would recruit, train, place, and support outstanding recent college graduates from all academic majors and backgrounds to commit a minimum of two years to teach in urban and rural public schools. Her solution became a reality with a program called Teach for America.

| WRITING ASSIGNMENT | PART 2: **Identifying Possible Solutions** |

Using the strategies on page 354, analyze the solutions others have proposed to the problem you investigated in Writing Assignment, Part 1 (page 353). Then explore your own ideas. Make a list of every possible way you can find or think of to solve the problem. At this point, don't censor any solutions, even those that may seem a bit ridiculous at first. Even the silliest solution can contain the germ of a good idea.

Finding the Best Solution

There are solutions, but there are rarely *perfect* solutions. And, in the absence of a perfect solution, you still need to make a decision about the best solution. Asking yourself questions like the following ones can help you find the best solution.

1. **What are the strengths and weaknesses of each solution?**
   Every solution will have some strengths and some weaknesses. Make a chart for yourself like the one on page 356, listing each solution and its strengths and weaknesses. Does any one solution seem to have more strengths and fewer weaknesses?

MEETING *individual* NEEDS

LESS-ADVANCED STUDENTS

You may want to break the **Writing Assignments** into discrete tasks. For example, to complete **Writing Assignment: Part 2** students will have to research and list solutions that others have proposed and brainstorm and list original solutions. Be sure that students have adequate time to complete each step of each assignment.

LEARNING STYLES

Kinetic Learners. Suggest that students write the advantages and disadvantages of solutions on note cards and that they arrange the cards on tables or on bulletin boards as they organize their ideas.

listed. Discuss with students whether the steps they have generated are practical.

Students should now be ready to begin **Writing Assignment: Part 3** (p. 358) independently. Use **Writing Assignment: Parts 2** and **3** to assess students' mastery of exploring solutions.

If students are not successful, use another topic to model identifying solutions, analyzing them, choosing the best solution, and listing the steps necessary to implement the solution. To close the lesson, have students list the stages of exploring a solution.

When addressing **Considering Purpose, Audience, and Tone** (p. 359), students might have difficulty understanding the distinction between the purpose of their exploratory essays and the purpose of a

A DIFFERENT APPROACH

An exercise in visualization may be helpful as students assess the practicality of the various solutions. Visualizing solutions can help students discover what it might actually be like to implement and live with the solutions.

TECHNOLOGY TIP

When students are dealing with large amounts of information that can be categorized—like the information that appears in the chart on this page—a database can be a convenient way to store the material. A database also has the advantage of allowing students to reshape material quickly and easily by adding, deleting, or changing information or by reorganizing material. If possible, consult the school's computer specialist for information on the best database available for this project and arrange for a presentation using the material in the chapter or an adaptation of your own.

2. **Which solution is the most practical?** Solutions may be impractical in terms of money or other resources that it would take to carry them out, in terms of time needed, or for many other reasons. Which solution would be the easiest to implement?

3. **Which solution has a comparative advantage?** A solution has a comparative advantage if it appears to offer more than other solutions do. For example, if a solution appears to be the fairest one or the one that will do the most good for the most people, then it has a comparative advantage over the others.

The following chart shows how one writer analyzed possible solutions for the problem of declining reading abilities.

HERE'S HOW

Possible Solutions	Advantages	Disadvantages
Hire additional teacher's aides to work one-on-one with students in the classroom.	Students would get more practice and help with reading skills.	Budgets are tight, and taxes are already high in the county.
Adopt a "book buddy" program, pairing older students with younger students.	Creates more opportunities to read, provides role models, promotes self-esteem of older students.	The students will not be able to identify and help each other with reading difficulties.
Library outreach program in day-care facilities or after-school programs.	Creates additional reading experiences; uses time spent in day-care facilities or after-school programs more effectively.	Library might need additional funding for staff; doesn't reach students who are at home.

Practicality
Providing more teacher's aides is not practical because it would cost more money. There just isn't any more money available in the school budget at this time.

Comparative Advantage
The "book buddy" system and library/day-care program are fairer because, used together, they will reach more children and they will not place an additional burden on the county's taxpayers.

persuasive essay. Explain that although students are recommending particular solutions to problems, their recommendations should be based on facts, and the language they use should be neutral and tentative. Remind students that persuasive essays, on the other hand, can be based on opinions, often include loaded language, and take the stance of being convinced the writer is right.

Use the questions provided to model analysis of an audience for a previously discussed topic.

Have a volunteer read the information under **Providing Support**, p. 360. As students search for support for their solutions, you may want to initiate a more detailed discussion of sources. Point out that sources such as *Time* and *Newsweek* are appropriate ☞

Prewriting   **357**

Developing a Compromise Solution.   What do you do if two solutions seem equally effective or if none of your solutions seem to work? First, check to see that you aren't falling into the either-or trap. With the problem of rising costs for college, for example, don't assume that a student either has to pay $20,000 a year to attend the state university or does not go to college. And don't assume that a student has to work full time. A compromise solution might be that a student could attend a community college, live at home, work part time for the first two years, and then transfer to the state university and take out government loans.

Finding Different Solutions for Different Parts of the Problem.   If your problem has several different causes or affects several different populations, you may need to think of several solutions. For example, if the problem is that you are getting a low grade in Spanish, a discussion with your teacher may reveal that the problem has two parts: (1) You aren't doing your homework regularly, and (2) you aren't participating in class discussion. One solution—writing down and remembering homework assignments—is not enough. You also need a solution for your lack of class participation.

COMPUTER NOTE: Create tables and charts within your word-processing program, and use them to organize your ideas about problems and solutions.

Listing Necessary Steps

Even the most brilliant solution won't automatically fall into place. You usually have to develop a plan, working toward a solution step by step. Decide exactly what has to be done, how it is to be done, and in what order it is to be done. For example, setting up a districtwide "book buddy" program to give younger children more role models for reading might involve the following steps:

1. Develop and conduct a short orientation for fifth- and sixth-graders at each school. Cover the program's goals and older students' roles and responsibilities.

? CRITICAL THINKING
Evaluation and Synthesis. Present students with several problem-solution essays. Have the students analyze the solutions presented in the essays by identifying the strengths and weaknesses. If students find the solutions given in any of the essays weak, have them suggest and support alternative solutions.

and reliable only for certain kinds of information. Problems that are highly technical or problems that are based on complicated local interactions may be better supported by data from other sources. Point out to students that their audience might prefer support from a variety of sources to support from only one kind of source.

Writing Assignment: Part 4 (p. 361) involves a synthesis of Writing Assignment: Parts 1–3. Model the process of pulling together and organizing these components. You may also want to model making decisions about gathering more evidence. Make sure you demonstrate links between your choices and the audience of the essay.

2. Set up the mechanics of the program: Pair each fifth-grade class with a kindergarten class, each sixth-grade class with a first-grade class. Have teachers create pupil pairs consisting of one older and one younger student, and schedule one half-hour meeting time per week for the program.

3. Monitor the program: Get feedback from teachers and students.

4. Evaluate the program's effectiveness. Monitor future test scores.

Reminder

When exploring solutions

- explore the solutions of others and create your own
- consider each solution's strengths and weaknesses, practicality, and comparative advantages
- identify the best solution(s) for the problem
- list the necessary steps to implement the solution

WRITING ASSIGNMENT

PART 3:
Identifying Your Best Solution and Listing Necessary Steps

Before you decide on the best possible solution to the problem you have explored, make a chart like the one on page 356, listing the possible solutions and their strengths and weaknesses. Analyze the solutions, also, for practicality and comparative advantage. On the basis of your analysis, choose the best solution to the problem. When you've identified the best solution, list the steps necessary to implement it.

Give students the three main titles— **Exploring Problems, Exploring Solutions,** and **Planning Your Problem-Solution Essay**—as cues to help them recall the necessary prewriting steps for this exploratory essay.

ENRICHMENT

Have students consider the Declaration of Independence as an example of problem-solution writing. You may want to read it to students. Point out that the Declaration describes a problem (the king's tyranny), discusses solutions that were tried unsuccessfully (petitions), and puts forth a solution (independence from Great Britain). ■

Prewriting

Planning Your Problem-Solution Essay

So far, you have been exploring a problem and its solutions—the focus has been on your own explorations. Now it's time to shift your attention to sharing what you have learned with others.

Considering Purpose, Audience, and Tone

Purpose.   Your purpose up to this point has been to explore a problem and solution. When you begin to write your essay, your *purpose* shifts to explaining and proving. You explain and prove what you've discovered in your exploration. You might explain, for example, the nature of the problem and the possible solutions. Readers will also expect you to prove that the problem is serious and the solution you have found is the best one.

Audience and Tone.   The exploration itself is as much for your own information as for that of your audience. However, when you begin to think about how to present what you have discovered, your *audience* now becomes very important. These questions will help you address their concerns.

- **What does your audience already know about this problem? How do they react to it?** If readers don't know about the problem or aren't affected by it, you may have to spend more time showing them that the problem really exists or that it is important to solve it.
- **What solutions might your audience favor?** Some readers may favor a solution you have rejected. In this case, you'll need to explain the disadvantages of your rejected solutions carefully.
- **What objections might your audience have to your solution?** Some readers may be quick to point out the flaws in your solution, so you'll need to explain its value thoroughly and attempt to answer their possible objections.

In writing your essay, use objective language that reflects your open, honest exploration of the problem—stay away from

INTEGRATING THE LANGUAGE ARTS

Literature Link. Have students read "A Modest Proposal" by Jonathan Swift. (Many twelfth-grade literature textbooks include this essay.) Afterward, ask students to identify the ways in which the essay is similar to the problem-solution essays they are writing. ["A Modest Proposal" includes the exposition of a problem, exploration of a solution, and a tentative tone. The essay also anticipates and addresses possible objections to the proposed solution and provides support for the solution.] Then, ask students how Swift's essay is different from the essays they are writing. ["A Modest Proposal" is a satire. Swift's proposal is not serious; rather, it ridicules society's treatment of the poor.] Ask students if they can identify the solutions that Swift would really like to see implemented. [Real solutions are introduced by "Therefore, let no man talk to me of other expedients."]

words that carry emotional overtones. However, because you are recounting a personal exploration, you may put yourself into your essay, referring to your own experience in the exploration. Another aspect of *tone* in exploratory writing is *tentativeness*. You may not always be certain that you've found the perfect solution, for example, and in that case you may use words like *appears*, *seems*, or *perhaps* to qualify your statements.

Providing Support

Evidence—in the form of facts, data, statistics, examples, and reasons—will help you explain and prove

- that a serious problem exists
- that the solutions you reject won't work
- that your solution is the best one

Readers usually require specific evidence before they are convinced. For example, suppose you want to prove that a problem exists with dumping garbage into a community lake. Readers tend to be suspicious of such vague statements as "A lot of garbage got dumped into Lake Osawaga last year." Instead, they prefer precise information: "The lake patrol office estimates that approximately a quarter of a ton of garbage was dumped in Lake Osawaga last year."

You have probably already collected some evidence through your analysis of the problem. When you analyzed possible solutions—their strengths, weaknesses, practicality, and comparative advantages—you found even more evidence. Now, to provide support, you may want to do some more research to find other facts, data, statistics, examples, and reasons. Be certain that the sources you use are reliable. A *reliable* source is trustworthy—the information you find there can usually be believed. Reliable sources are magazines like *Time* and *Newsweek*, major newspapers such as *The New York Times* and *The Washington Post*, and experts who have studied the problem carefully and objectively.

CRITICAL THINKING

Evaluation. As students evaluate evidence, you may wish to teach them the acronym EAR to help them remember three criteria they can use for evaluation. The acronym stands for *enough, accurate,* and *reliable.*

WRITING NOTE

If you are proposing a new solution, you may not have solid facts to prove its worth. But you can still provide reasons and, possibly, a model as proof. For example, for the problem of latchkey children, you may not know exactly how many such children will benefit from your proposed solution of an afternoon activity program. But you can offer readers this good reason: Organized recreational activities are better for young children than unsupervised TV viewing. You can also use a similar, successful program in another community as a model of how and why your solution will help to solve the problem.

WRITING ASSIGNMENT

PART 4:
Planning Your Problem-Solution Essay

First, plan your problem-solution essay by jotting down the evidence—facts, data, statistics, examples, reasons—that you will use to explain, and prove, the problem and its seriousness. Then, list each solution you are rejecting and a major disadvantage of each. Finally, list the evidence that helps to prove that your solution is the best one, and list the steps needed to implement it. If necessary, do more research to fill in gaps of evidence. And be sure to think about the objections your readers are likely to have. If they've never heard about the problem, for example, you may need more evidence that it exists.

WRITING YOUR FIRST DRAFT

OBJECTIVES

- To analyze the organization and content of an effective problem-solution essay
- To write a draft of a problem-solution essay

TEACHING THE LESSON

Read aloud and discuss **The Elements of a Problem-Solution Essay** before assigning **"The Villain in the Atmosphere"** by Isaac Asimov to be read independently. You can use the annotations in the margins to initiate class discussion of the structure and content of the essay.

PROGRAM MANAGER

WRITING YOUR FIRST DRAFT

- **Instructional Support** To help students write an introductory paragraph, see **Writing** in *Strategies for Writing*, p. 38.

QUOTATION FOR THE DAY

"Thou canst not stir a flower/ Without troubling of a star." (Francis Thompson, 1859–1907, English poet)

After students have read **"The Villain in the Atmosphere"** by Isaac Asimov, initiate a class discussion of how this quotation relates to the subject of Asimov's essay. Ask students if they think the quotation would make a good epigraph (a brief quotation at the beginning of a piece of writing that suggests its theme) for the essay.

Writing Your First Draft

The Elements of a Problem-Solution Essay

Problem-solution essays, like most other kinds of essays, may follow different patterns. Most problem-solution essays, however, have the following elements:

- an explanation of the problem
- evidence of the problem's seriousness
- a description of the proposed solution
- a list of steps to implement the solution
- discussion of the disadvantages of rejected solutions
- evidence to support the solution and to counter possible objections

The amount of space you devote to each of these parts can vary according to the concerns of your readers. If they have never heard of the problem, for example, you may spend more time discussing it. The nature of the problem and its solution(s) may also influence your presentation. For instance, if a fairly straightforward problem has a very complex solution, you may devote more time to discussing the solution than to discussing the problem. Regardless of the emphasis, however, the introduction should include an interesting opening that focuses the reader's attention on some aspect of the problem.

Blondie reprinted with special permission of King Features Syndicate, Inc.

The major emphasis in the following essay by Isaac Asimov is not the solution, but the problem itself—explaining its causes and effects and proving its significance. As you read "The Villain in the Atmosphere," think about why Asimov may have given the problem this amount of emphasis.

A PROBLEM-SOLUTION ESSAY

The Villain in the Atmosphere
by Isaac Asimov

**INTRODUCTION
Attention-grabbing statement of problem**

1   The villain in the atmosphere is carbon dioxide. It does not seem to be a villain. It is not very poisonous and it is present in the atmosphere in so small a quantity that it does us no harm. For every 1,000,000 cubic feet of air there are only 340 cubic feet of carbon dioxide — only 0.034 percent.

2   What's more, the small quantity of carbon dioxide in the air is essential to life. Plants absorb carbon dioxide and convert it into their own tissues, which serve as the basic food supply for all of animal life (including human beings, of course). In the process, they liberate oxygen, which is also necessary for all animal life.

BODY

Analysis of problem/ Examples

But here is what this apparently harmless and
3   certainly essential gas is doing to us:

The sea level is rising very slowly from year to year. The high tides tend to be progressively higher, even in quiet weather, and storms batter at breakwaters more and more effectively, erode the beaches more savagely, batter houses farther inland.

Possible future effects

In all likelihood, the sea level will continue to rise and do so at a greater rate in the course of the next hundred years. This means that the line separating ocean from land will retreat inland everywhere. It will do so only slightly where high land abuts the ocean. In those places, however, where there are low-lying coastal areas (where a large fraction of humanity lives) the water will advance steadily and inexorably and people will have to retreat inland.

Virtually all of Long Island will become part of the shallow offshore sea bottom, leaving only a

liberate some of the carbon dioxide dissolved in the ocean. With still more carbon dioxide, the temperature of the Earth will creep upward a little more and release still more carbon dioxide.

All this is called the "runaway greenhouse effect," and it may eventually make Earth an uninhabitable planet.

Clarification of problem

But, as you can see, it is not carbon dioxide in itself that is the source of the trouble; it is the fact that the carbon dioxide concentration in the atmosphere is steadily rising and seems to be doomed to continue rising. Why is that?

Causes

To blame are two factors. First of all, in the last few centuries, first coal, then oil and natural gas, have been burned for energy at a rapidly increasing rate. The carbon contained in these fuels, which has been safely buried underground for many millions of years, is now being burned to carbon dioxide and poured into the atmosphere at a rate of many tons per day.

Some of that additional carbon dioxide may be absorbed by the soil or by the ocean, and some might be consumed by plant life, but the fact is that a considerable fraction of it remains in the atmosphere. It must, for the carbon dioxide content of the atmosphere is going up year by year.

To make matters worse, Earth's forests have been disappearing, slowly at first, but in the last couple of centuries quite rapidly. Right now it is disappearing at the rate of sixty-four acres per minute.

Whatever replaces the forest—grasslands or farms or scrub—produces plants that do not consume carbon dioxide at a rate equal to that of forest. Thus, not only is more carbon dioxide being added to the atmosphere through the burning of fuel, but as the forests disappear, less carbon dioxide is being subtracted from the atmosphere by plants.

Final clarification of problem

But this gives us a new perspective on the matter. The carbon dioxide is not rising by itself. It is people who are burning the coal, oil, and gas,

10
Scientists estimate that Earth's tropical rain forests, which consume the greatest amount of carbon dioxide, are now disappearing at the rate of at least ninety acres per minute.

368

because of their need for energy. It is people who are cutting down the forests, because of their need for farmland. And the two are connected, for the burning of coal and oil is producing acid rain which helps destroy the forests. It is *people*, then, who are the villains.

What is to be done?

Solutions 12

First, we must save our forests, and even replant them. From forests, properly conserved, we get wood, chemicals, soil retention, ecological health—and a slowdown of carbon dioxide increase.

Second, we must have new sources of fuel. There are, after all, fuels that do not involve the production of carbon dioxide. Nuclear fission is one of them, and if that is deemed too dangerous for other reasons, there is the forthcoming nuclear fusion, which may be safer. There is also the energy of waves, tides, wind, and the Earth's interior heat. Most of all, there is the direct use of solar energy.

Comparative advantage

All of this will take time, work, and money, to be sure, but all that time, work, and money will be invested in order to save our civilization and our planet itself.

CONCLUSION 13

After all, humanity seems to be willing to spend *more* time, work, and money in order to support competing military machines that can only destroy us all. Should we <u>begrudge</u> *less* time, work, and money in order to save us all?

11
The real cause of the problem is revealed toward the end of the essay for greater rhetorical effect.

12
Asimov offers different solutions for different parts of the problem.

13
Where does Asimov suggest the resources to save the forests and develop alternative energy sources should come from? [Asimov suggests that the money should come from funds used for military purposes.]

ANSWERS
Exercise 2

1. In the first sentence of the essay, Asimov uses a surprising personification and a loaded word, *villain,* to get his readers' attention. He then seems to contradict himself in the sentences that follow. This apparent contradiction creates curiosity and expectation in the reader.

2. The problem probably was relatively unknown in 1968, so Asimov must alert his readers to the problem and stress its seriousness. Also, the causes and effects of the problem are complicated and require careful explanation.

3. Asimov also analyzes current effects and causes of the problem.

4. Asimov states that the real villains are people. He may have thought that the revelation would have greater effect toward the end of the essay because, after having read and become concerned about the problem, readers would be faced with the fact that they are partly responsible for it.

5. He proposes both saving and replanting forests and using alternative fuel sources. The comparative advantage is that the effort and money invested will contribute to the continuation of life on the planet.

EXERCISE 2 **Analyzing a Problem-Solution Essay**

You've probably heard the term *greenhouse effect* before. But did you realize the seriousness of the problem? Read and review Isaac Asimov's essay, and then, meet with two or three classmates to discuss these questions.

1. What does Asimov do in his introduction to get his readers' attention?
2. Most of the essay is devoted to an analysis of the problem. Why do you think Asimov spends so much time explaining the problem and so comparatively little time explaining the solution? [Hint: This essay was written in 1968.]
3. One approach Asimov takes to analyze the problem is to discuss possible future effects of carbon dioxide in the atmosphere. What else does Asimov do to analyze the problem?
4. In his opening sentence, Asimov states that carbon dioxide is the "villain," or problem, but later in the essay he clarifies the problem further. According to Asimov, who or what is the real villain? Why do you think he waits so long to make this clarification?
5. What solutions does Asimov propose to the problem? What is the comparative advantage of those solutions?

A Framework for a Problem-Solution Essay

Asimov's essay is a little unusual in that most of it is devoted to the problem. Problem-solution essays may follow many different patterns. The following Writer's Model illustrates a basic pattern that you may want to follow in your own essay.

A WRITER'S MODEL

Our Children Can't Read

**INTRODUCTION
Attention grabber**

Is Brown County's population less intelligent than it used to be? When I first saw headlines such as "Reading Scores Decline Fifth Year in a Row" or "Study Shows Average Reading Scores Drop Five

Statement of the problem

**BODY
Analysis of the problem**

Possible causes for lack of motivation

Points in Ten Years," I was tempted to answer yes. These reading scores, so widely reported in the newspaper and on television, are based on reading tests given to third- and fifth-grade students. The scores are, in fact, falling. Our children do not read as well as children did ten years ago. But it is not because the children are less intelligent.

What has caused this decline in reading abilities over the last ten years? Local elementary school teachers and administrators, as well as nationally recognized experts on the teaching of reading, say that the problem is not just in Brown County; it is a national one. Nor is it a problem with a single, clear-cut cause. Most educators agree that students are not as motivated to read as they once were, but the reasons for the lack of motivation are unclear.

Some educators cite statistics on two-career families and single-parent families and suggest that parents just don't have as much time to read to their children as they used to. Others tell me that what has changed is our society's perception of the importance of reading. Television and other electronic entertainment and information services are grabbing the attention and time of adults and children alike. Still other educators say that the demographics of our society are changing. Fewer adults are literate, and as a result, there are fewer parents who can serve as role models by reading to their children.

Whatever the reason, it seems that children who don't see others read and who don't read themselves

MEETING *individual* NEEDS

LESS-ADVANCED STUDENTS

Because **A Writer's Model** is less complicated than the professional model, you may wish to have some of your students concentrate on it. If you decide to make this adaptation, modify **Exercise 2** to relate to **A Writer's Model** so that students get the necessary practice analyzing an essay before they begin to write.

LEP/ESL

General Strategies. You may want to search for a problem-solution essay that is relevant to English-language learners' concerns, such as problems of learning a new language or of adapting to a new culture. Students may be more encouraged to understand the form for this kind of essay if they are interested in the material.

INTEGRATING THE LANGUAGE ARTS

Literature Link. Have students read "Shooting an Elephant" by George Orwell, which can be found in many twelfth-grade literature textbooks. In this essay, Orwell explores his ambivalent feelings about the role he plays in the imperial government in Burma. Begin by asking students to identify the narrator's obvious problem [the elephant]. Move from this to a discussion of how Orwell explores the more complicated problems facing him—his hatred of the imperial system he serves and of the Burmese who ridicule him.

Discussion of solutions

Practicality of solutions

Comparative advantage

Solutions for lack of role models

Necessary steps

Program model

Necessary steps

aren't very likely to realize the value of reading. This does appear to be the case in Brown County. Interviews with 20 local elementary-school teachers indicate that many of Brown County's young children today are not very interested in learning to read. If a lack of role models and experience is partially responsible for our students' declining reading abilities, then what are the solutions? In an ideal world with limitless funding, we can all think of many wonderful solutions. But budgets are tight and taxes already high here in Brown County, so the real question becomes "What solutions are possible within our existing institutions?" Fortunately, there seem to be several, relatively inexpensive remedies that might help solve the problem.

To provide more models of readers for young children, all the Brown County schools could adopt the "book buddy" program. Ms. Gladow's third-grade class at Horne Elementary already participates in this program, and according to Ms. Gladow, it is one of her students' favorite activities. The program works like this: each kindergarten and first-grade class is paired with a fifth- or sixth-grade class. Then each younger child is paired with an older one. Once a week for thirty minutes, the two classes meet, and the "book buddies" spend time reading and talking about books of their own choice. This program gives the younger children additional reading role models, and it gives the older children an important sense of self-esteem as well.

Marginally literate and illiterate parents might also become reading role models for their children. Our library, which already sponsors a literacy program, could expand its services to include an adult/child literacy program like one already operating in Indiana, Pennsylvania. According to a recent School Library Journal article, volunteer tutors in this program are trained to help parents learn to read with their children. Once a week, parents meet one-on-one with a tutor at the library and learn to read one easy-reading book. Then,

during the last fifteen minutes of class, each parent reads this book to his or her child or children.

Necessary steps

Many parents are too busy to read regularly for pleasure and so don't serve as role models for their children. Ms. Atkins, the reading specialist at Culvert Elementary, urges them to find other ways to be role models for reading. For example, she suggests that parents read recipes or directions aloud to children while fixing meals. Or, parents might read washing instruction tags aloud while sorting laundry.

Solutions for lack of experience

Children with more reading role models will also get more experience with reading. To create additional reading experiences, the library could modify and extend its services. For example, it could begin an outreach program for day-care facilities and providers. Rather than hold story hours only in the library, librarians could regularly visit day-care sites for story hours. In addition, the library could begin a special program for home day-care providers, creating specially prepared boxes of age-appropriate books for them to check out. Furthermore, if the library does begin the parent/child literacy program, the children of parents in the program could attend a story hour during the time their parents are being tutored.

Counter for possible objection

Experts may say that children who lack role models in reading and experience with reading also need extra instruction in reading skills. Teachers already provide this instruction, of course, but they often don't have the extra time that children with

MEETING *individual* NEEDS

LESS-ADVANCED STUDENTS

Some students may be overwhelmed by the length of the models in this segment. Explain to students that the length of a problem-solution essay often depends upon the number of solutions. Explain that each student may choose to focus on two well-written solutions rather than covering them all.

A DIFFERENT APPROACH

You may want to point out how the illustrations in the textbook help make some of the essay's points. Suggest that students may provide material to illustrate their writing. Students could find or create graphs, charts, photographs, or artwork to accompany their papers.

reading problems need. Using high school volunteers as tutors would solve that problem. High school students who have at least a C average could volunteer for thirty minutes each week, during their study hall or lunch period. Volunteer school-bus drivers would take the high school students to the elementary schools. A survey of two hundred high school students indicates that 80 percent of them would volunteer. And most of the elementary school teachers are enthusiastic about the prospect of more volunteers.

Statistic

CONCLUSION

The solutions aren't drastic. Adopt a "book buddy" program. Set up an adult/child literacy program. Create a library outreach program. Create a high school volunteer-tutor program. These programs cost almost nothing and ask of us only our time. Will they work? The children of this country are its most precious resource. Programs such as these might help us preserve that resource.

A DIFFERENT APPROACH

After students consider the **Writing Note,** have them look back at the model essay. Then, ask what this essay might gain from more rigorous acknowledgment of sources. Have students point out specific places in the essay where citation would have strengthened or clarified the points being made. [Students might say that the essay would be more effective if phrases such as "Some educators" and "most of the elementary school teachers" were replaced by more specific attributions.]

WRITING NOTE

Your facts and ideas will carry more weight with your readers if they know your information comes from reliable sources. Notice that "Our Children Can't Read" credits its information informally by naming sources within the paper. You might also use parenthetical citations and a list of Works Cited. Either method is acceptable as long as you acknowledge your sources. (For more help with crediting sources, see Chapter 11, **Writing a Research Paper.**)

Here is a framework you might use to develop your essay. "Our Children Can't Read" follows this framework.

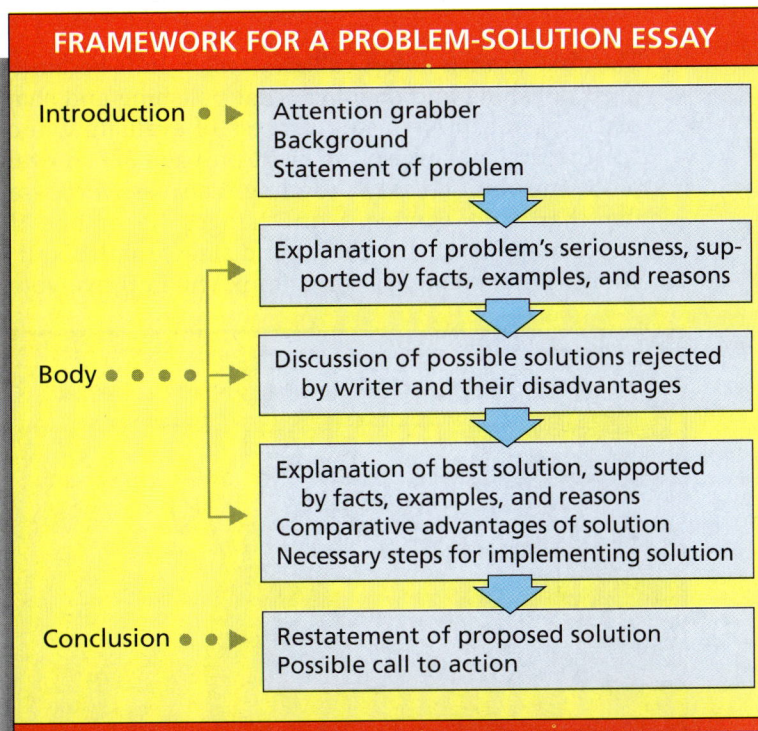

FRAMEWORK FOR A PROBLEM-SOLUTION ESSAY

Introduction ●▶
- Attention grabber
- Background
- Statement of problem

Body ●●●●▶
- Explanation of problem's seriousness, supported by facts, examples, and reasons

- Discussion of possible solutions rejected by writer and their disadvantages

- Explanation of best solution, supported by facts, examples, and reasons
- Comparative advantages of solution
- Necessary steps for implementing solution

Conclusion ●●▶
- Restatement of proposed solution
- Possible call to action

WRITING ASSIGNMENT

PART 5:
Writing a Draft of Your Essay

You have given some thought to planning your essay (in your work for Writing Assignment, Part 4, page 361). Now put your thoughts down on paper, using the framework above as a guide in writing your first draft. As you write, keep your readers in mind. Think about how you can best explain and prove to them that the problem is serious and that your proposed solution is both good and workable. Then, if possible, let your draft sit for a day or two before moving to the evaluating and revising stage.

LEP/ESL

General Strategies. As they write their first drafts, some English-language learners might spend so much time searching in their bilingual dictionaries for correct vocabulary and trying to write grammatically perfect sentences that they will become frustrated and give up. To preclude this possibility, you could allow students to write their drafts in their first languages. If possible, assign bilingual peers to assist students in rewriting their first drafts after they have finished writing. This strategy will allow students to concentrate on ideas and organization.

LESS-ADVANCED STUDENTS

For students who may have problems understanding the many parts of the problem-solution essay presented in the framework, you may want to simplify the assignment. This can be done by having each student write about only one solution and how to implement it. This streamlining will allow students who otherwise might be overwhelmed to be successful.

EVALUATING AND REVISING

OBJECTIVES

- To analyze a writer's revisions
- To evaluate a peer's problem-solution essay
- To evaluate and revise a problem-solution essay

QUOTATION FOR THE DAY

"A change of heart is the essence of all other change and it is brought about by a re-education of the mind." (Emmeline Pethick-Lawrence, 1867–1964, English suffragist)

Ask students if the exploration they have done while writing their problem-solution essays has changed any of their ideas. Then, ask volunteers to discuss how their ideas about writing have changed. For example, students might say that they thought a paper had to be perfect the first time, but now they know that first drafts are almost never perfect.

Evaluating and Revising

The first draft is often called a *rough* draft because the ideas need polishing and shaping. That polishing and shaping takes place during the two-step process of evaluating and revising. For the first stage, use the chart on page 377 to evaluate your problem-solution essay. You might also ask a classmate to use the chart and comment on changes he or she thinks will improve the draft. For the second stage, think about the evaluations: What changes do *you* think will improve your essay?

Drawing by Dan Krovatin.

You can use the following chart to evaluate and revise your problem-solution essay. Begin by asking yourself each question in the left-hand column. If the answer is no, then use the revision technique suggested in the right-hand column.

TEACHING THE LESSON

After reviewing the **Evaluating and Revising Problem-Solution Essays** chart with students, invite questions. Point out that students can also revise the tone of their essays by adding words that indicate tentativeness, such as *might, could, perhaps,* and *seems.*

Model the first question of **Exercise 3** for students. You may want to have some students work in groups to complete the exercise. To model **Writing Assignment: Part 6**, p. 379, use the **Evaluating and Revising Problem-Solution Essays** chart to analyze Asimov's essay or another problem-solution essay.

If you give a grade on the revision, focus on improvement from the previous draft as your evaluation criterion. ☞

EVALUATING AND REVISING PROBLEM-SOLUTION ESSAYS

EVALUATION GUIDE	REVISION TECHNIQUE
1 Does the introduction catch the reader's attention?	**Add** an interesting anecdote, facts, or a question. **Replace** dull material.
2 Is the problem clearly stated? Is its seriousness established?	Rewrite the explanation. **Add** facts, examples, and reasons that establish the seriousness.
3 Are other possible solutions discussed?	**Add** information about proposed solutions and their disadvantages.
4 Is the proposed solution clearly stated and supported?	**Add** a sentence or two (or **replace** existing ones) to clearly identify the solution you are proposing. **Add** relevant facts, examples, and reasons. **Cut** or **replace** evidence that is not accurate and reliable.
5 Are answers provided to possible objections to the proposed solution?	**Add** several sentences that answer possible objections.
6 Is the process for implementing the proposed solution clearly presented?	**Add** details to identify the steps in the process. **Reorder** steps in the order they're to be done.
7 Is the tone appropriate for a problem-solution essay?	**Replace** emotional language with objective language. **Add** references to your own role in the exploration.

A DIFFERENT APPROACH

Students who have been taught that essays should be objective and should not reveal any personal information may be surprised and confused by the advice to make references in their papers to their roles as writers. Explain that, increasingly, professional researchers and writers believe that when the writer identifies his or her position, it helps the reader to judge the credibility and accuracy of the data presented more clearly than when the writer presents his or her case in a seemingly objective way.

If students are interested, you may want to encourage discussion of this point because it raises interesting questions about the roles of writers and about objectivity and subjectivity in writing.

Have students discuss whether or not the **Evaluating and Revising Problem-Solution Essays** chart was useful to them, and ask them what they might add to the chart to make it even more useful. ■

EXERCISE 3 ▶ **Analyzing a Writer's Revisions**

Here's an early draft of two paragraphs from "Our Children Can't Read," pages 370–371. Study the changes that you see here, trying to figure out how they improve the paragraphs. Then answer the questions that follow.

(Is Brown County's population less intelligent than it used to be?)
I first saw

When headlines such as "Reading Scores   **add**

Decline Fifth Year in a Row" or "Study Shows

Average Reading Scores Drop Five Points in
I was

Ten Years," ~~appeared, some people may have~~   **replace**

~~been~~ tempted to answer yes. These reading

scores, so widely reported in the newspaper

and on television, are based on reading tests

given to third- and fifth-grade students.

The scores are, in fact, falling. Our children do not read as well as children did ten

~~There is a problem with these scores.~~ But it years ago.   **replace**

is not because the children are less

intelligent.

What has caused this decline in reading

abilities over the last ten years? Local

elementary school teachers and

administrators, as well as nationally

recognized experts on the teaching of
is not just in Brown County; it is a national one. Nor is it a problem with

reading, say that the problem ~~does not have~~   **replace**

a single, clear-cut cause. Most educators

agree that students are not as motivated to

read as they once were, but the reasons for

the lack of motivation are unclear.

1. Why did the writer add a question to the beginning of the first paragraph?
2. Why are the changes the writer made in the sentence about headlines appropriate for exploratory writing?

Exercise 3

1. The original first sentence obviously referred to a question.
2. It is appropriate to refer to the writer's role in the exploration.

3. Toward the end of the first paragraph, the writer replaced one sentence with two new ones. How does this change improve the essay?
4. How does the information the writer added in the second paragraph help to establish the seriousness of the problem?

WRITING ASSIGNMENT

PART 6:
Evaluating and Revising Your Essay

With your rough draft in hand and with a better understanding of what to look for when you evaluate and revise, take this time to reread your essay critically. Use the chart on page 377 as you evaluate; and if possible, exchange papers with someone else who will also evaluate your essay critically. Then, when you are satisfied you have identified your paper's serious problems, revise it using the suggestions in the evaluating and revising chart (page 377). Save your essay; you are nearly finished with it.

"Writing is not like painting, where you add. It is not what you put on the canvas that the reader sees. **WRITING IS MORE LIKE A SCULPTURE** where you remove, you eliminate in order to make the work visible."

ELIE WIESEL

3. The change clarifies the writer's meaning.
4. The change shows the scope of the problem.

MEETING individual NEEDS

LEP/ESL

General Strategies. Evaluating writing might be difficult for English-language learners. They might have trouble distinguishing emotional language and objective language and be uncertain as to what tone they have produced in English. You could help them by pairing them with English-proficient speakers who could go over their work with them and offer constructive criticism.

SELECTION AMENDMENT
Description of change: excerpted
Rationale: to focus on the concept of revision presented in this chapter

PROOFREADING AND PUBLISHING

OBJECTIVE

- To proofread and publish a problem-solution essay

TEACHING THE LESSON

You may want to provide a focus for students' proofreading. Ask your class to tell you the kinds of errors they should proofread for and write appropriate responses on the chalkboard. Tell students that they should always recheck spellings of proper nouns, the wording of quotations, and the numerals in figures they mention. A typing or

---

380   *Writing to Explore*

Proofreading and Publishing

Proofreading.   After you have worked hard on a paper, it would be a shame if your audience failed to appreciate your effort because of minor errors. What if they decide, fairly or unfairly, that you can't know much about the problem you have explored because you have misspelled words or made mistakes in subject-verb agreement? That's why it is always important to take the time to give your essay a shine and polish.

Publishing.   Solutions to problems do no good if no one knows about them. There are many ways to share a problem-solution essay with an audience, but here are two ideas you might try with your own paper.

- Use the desktop publishing features of a personal computer to create a broadside sheet (a sheet of paper printed on one or both sides and folded for distribution) from your essay. Distribute the broadside to people affected by the problem.
- Present your essay as an oral proposal before a group that has the power to solve the problem. Or, present it as a proposal before your classmates. Can you get them concerned about the problem?

MECHANICS HINT

Punctuating Subordinate Clauses

When explaining problems and their solutions, you need to make relationships between ideas clear. You may want to show, for example, that a problem has certain causes or that a solution has certain effects. You can do this by using subordinate clauses that begin with conjunctions such as *because, if, after, as long as, since, while*. Set off an introductory subordinate clause with a comma.

transcribing error can make an enormous difference.

An alternative publishing idea is to have students research state and federal legislative action to see if the problem they explored is under consideration. If it is, they might want to communicate their views to their representatives in government.

CLOSURE

Sometimes writers are satisfied to keep their writing to themselves. Other kinds of writing seem to need an audience for completion. Ask each student to respond to those observations in terms of his or her problem-solution essay: Does it seem to require an audience? Why? ■

EXAMPLES   **If a lack** of role models and experience is partially responsible for our students' declining reading abilities, **then** what are the solutions?
As long as children have models of readers and experience with reading, they will likely be interested in learning to read.
But it is not **because** the children are less intelligent.

☞ **REFERENCE NOTE:** For more information on punctuating introductory subordinate clauses, see page 913.

WRITING ASSIGNMENT   PART 7:
Proofreading and Publishing Your Essay

After carefully proofreading your essay and correcting any errors in grammar or spelling, make arrangements to share it with an audience. Use one of the suggestions mentioned earlier, or think of another way to distribute your essay, in printed form or electronically.

Reflecting on Your Writing

As an example of exploratory writing, your essay will round out your **portfolio.** If you choose to include the essay, remember to date it and write a note of reflection that answers the following questions.

- What was the most challenging part of writing this essay? What was the easiest part? Explain your answers.
- Did you let your first draft sit for a day or two before evaluating and revising it? If so, did the time away help you see your paper with a fresh eye? If not, how might you give yourself this extra time when writing your next essay?
- By writing this essay, what did you learn about your ability to explore a topic? Did you learn things about your topic that surprised you?

MECHANICS HINT

You may want to review the terms *clause, subordinate clause,* and *introductory subordinate clause.* Model correct punctuation by writing on the chalkboard some sentences that include subordinate clauses.

QUOTATION FOR THE DAY

"Proofreading is like the quality-control stage at the end of an assembly line." (John R. Trimble, American writer and teacher)

Write this quotation on the chalkboard, and remind students that proofreading allows them a final chance to catch errors in their work.

MEETING *individual* NEEDS

ADVANCED STUDENTS

Ask advanced students to present their papers in oratory style, with few or no notes to prompt them. Ask students to work on developing public-speaking skills by speaking without prompts.

TEACHING NOTE

Point out to students that writing reflections on their writing helps them explore their own thinking and learning processes. Just as writing exploratory essays can help students learn new information about a topic, so writing reflections can help them learn new information about themselves.

A STUDENT MODEL
Evaluation

1. Kerri's introduction catches the reader's attention by citing startling details about the amount of time it takes various pieces of trash to decompose.
2. Kerri states the problem clearly at the beginning of the second paragraph, and she names and discusses two alternate solutions for the problem.
3. The tone is serious and direct, and it is appropriate for a problem-solution essay.

A STUDENT MODEL

In the following introductory paragraphs from her essay, Kerri Pelz, a senior at Clearwater High School in Clearwater, Kansas, identifies a problem and tells why action must be taken to address it. Notice how she uses parenthetical citations, an option mentioned in the Writing Note on page 374.

Solid Waste in Sedgwick County
by Kerri Pelz

Each person in the United States throws away an average of 4.3 pounds of trash per day. Once thrown away, trash decomposes at varying rates: four weeks for a traffic ticket, five hundred years for an aluminum can, and up to one million years for a glass bottle (Wallace 14). At this rate, it is not surprising that our country's landfills are filling up. Over half of them could reach their capacities within the next ten years. This includes Brooks Landfill, which services most of the Wichita area.

We must decide what to do with solid waste in Sedgwick County. Forty-one states presently have comprehensive solid waste reduction laws in effect. There are forty-four that have legislated or announced goals for waste reduction of up to seventy percent. Kansas presently has neither reduction laws nor goals for the management of solid waste (Brown 5). In Sedgwick County, especially, we face the problem of too much trash and not enough space to dispose of it.

WRITING WORKSHOP

OBJECTIVES

- To analyze elements of personal exploration in a literary model
- To write a personal exploration

TEACHING THE LESSON

After students read the introduction, point out that personal exploration, unlike the problem-solution essay, focuses on personal matters.

Have a volunteer read the model aloud, and then allow students to discuss in small groups the questions that follow. Encourage students to make connections ☞

383

WRITING WORKSHOP

Personal Exploration

Exploring a problem and its possible solutions often leads to an outward exploration: to books, articles, videotapes, or other people. In contrast, a personal exploration requires an *inward* investigation into your own experiences, thoughts, and feelings.

In the following excerpt, Ralph Ellison explores an experience that brings him face-to-face with a personal dilemma. What does he discover about himself in his exploration?

from An Extravagance of Laughter
by Ralph Ellison

But for all their noise and tension, it was not the subways that most intrigued me. For although a pleasant way to explore the city, my rides in New York buses soon aroused questions about matters that I had hoped to leave behind. And yet the very fact that I encountered little on Northern buses that was distressing allowed me to face up to a problem which had puzzled me down South: the relationship between Southern buses and racial status. In the South you occupied the back of the bus, and nowhere *but* the back, or so help you God. So being in the North and encouraged by my anonymity, I experimented by riding *all* over New York buses, excluding only the driver's seat—front end, back end, right side, left side, sitting or standing as the route and flow of passengers demanded. *And,* since those were the glorious days of double-deckers, both enclosed and opened, I even rode *top*side.

Thus having convinced myself that no questions of racial status would be raised by where I chose to ride, I asked myself whether a seat at the back of the bus wasn't actually more desirable than one at the front. For not only did it provide more leg room, it offered a more inclusive perspective on both the interior and exterior scenes. I found the answer obvious and quite amusing, but then, as though to raise to consciousness more serious questions that I had too long ignored, the

QUOTATION FOR THE DAY

"People like definite decisions,/ Tidy answers, all the little ravelings/ Snipped off, the lint removed, they/Mop happily among their roughs/Calling what they can't clutch insanity/Or saintliness." (Gwendolyn Brooks, 1917–   , American poet)

Write these lines on the chalkboard and lead students in a discussion of what they mean. [Brooks seems to say that people don't like unanswered questions and things they don't understand.] Ask students if there are things that they don't understand about themselves, such as unexplained fears or desires. Point out that these would make excellent subjects for personal explorations.

WRITING ABOUT LITERATURE: EXPOSITION

OBJECTIVES

- To identify the literary aim and to analyze the characteristics of literary writing
- To select and read a story critically and analyze its literary elements
- To gather and organize supporting evidence for a critical analysis
- To write, evaluate, revise, proofread, and publish a critical analysis

WRITING-IN-PROGRESS ASSIGNMENTS

Major Assignment: Writing a critical analysis
Cumulative Writing Assignments: The chart below shows the sequence of cumulative assignments that will guide students as they write a critical analysis. These Writing Assignments form the instructional core of Chapter 10.

PREWRITING
WRITING ASSIGNMENT
• Part 1: Responding and Reading Critically p. 408
• Part 2: Finding a Focus and a Thesis p. 411
• Part 3: Gathering and Organizing Ideas p. 413

WRITING YOUR FIRST DRAFT
WRITING ASSIGNMENT
• Part 4: Writing the First Draft of Your Critical Analysis p. 419

EVALUATING AND REVISING
WRITING ASSIGNMENT
• Part 5: Evaluating and Revising Your Essay p. 421

PROOFREADING AND PUBLISHING
WRITING ASSIGNMENT
• Part 6: Proofreading and Publishing Your Essay p. 423

In addition, exercises 1–2 provide practice in sharing personal responses and analyzing a writer's revisions.

cross CURRICULUM

Government: Critical Analysis of a Political Debate

Have students practice their skills of critical analysis by judging a televised or live debate between political opponents and writing a brief critical analysis. Begin by reminding students that debate is a forum in which opposing sides of a single issue are presented for the purpose of determining which side is a stronger argument. Judges of a debate have two criteria for evaluation—which side gave a better argument and which side had better debaters.

- **Criteria** Analyzing a debate is similar to analyzing a piece of literature. Personal response is an important factor, but content-related issues must also be addressed. Work with students to create criteria they should attend to as they watch the debate. Students should consider the following:

Personal response to debaters: Did the speakers present themselves with confidence? Did they enunciate and use appropriate gestures?

Presentation: Did the debaters understand the issue they discussed? Did they address key points? Did they do thorough research? Did they anticipate and refute their opponent's arguments? Did they rebuild their cases after their opponent's attack?

Students should take notes on these points during the debate. After the debate, have students work in small groups to discuss their responses.

- **Writing** Ask students to review pp. 414–419 before writing their analyses. Remind students to include a thesis statement (an opinion statement of which argument was stronger or presented better), evidence from the debate to support the thesis, and a conclusion. Students should remember that their judgments may be affected by their own ideas about the issue and their personal responses to the debaters. Students may discuss these influences in the introductions to their analyses.

INTEGRATING THE LANGUAGE ARTS

SELECTION	READING AND LITERATURE	WRITING AND CRITICAL THINKING	LANGUAGE AND SYNTAX	SPEAKING, LISTENING, AND OTHER EXPRESSION SKILLS
• "He Did It" by Amy Taubin pp. 390–392 • "The Soft Voice of the Serpent" by Nadine Gordimer pp. 395–402 • from "The Song of Hiawatha" by Henry Wadsworth Longfellow p. 427 • "The Modern Hiawatha" by George A. Strong p. 427	• Responding personally to literature pp. 392, 402, 407, 428 • Identifying and analyzing supporting details p. 392 • Reading for specific information pp. 392, 413, 431 • Analyzing character, point of view, conflict, setting, and theme pp. 407, 408 • Identifying repetition in poetry p. 428 • Identifying and analyzing parody pp. 428–429	• Stating and supporting an opinion pp. 392, 402, 428, 430–431, 431–432 • Making inferences and drawing conclusions pp. 402, 407, 428–429, 433 • Analyzing short story elements pp. 407, 408 • Finding a focus and writing a thesis statement pp. 411, 431–432 • Organizing collected ideas into an early plan p. 413 • Reflecting on writing for portfolio selections p. 424 • Analyzing and writing parody pp. 428–429 • Writing a review pp. 430–431 • Writing a critical analysis of a poem pp. 431–432 • Evaluating poetry deductively p. 433	• Proofreading for errors in grammar, usage, and mechanics pp. 424, 429, 431–432	• Working with classmates to share personal responses to literature p. 402 • Discussing a literary analysis p. 407 • Discussing a writer's revisions p. 421 • Working with classmates to evaluate and revise p. 421 • Presenting a literary parody in performance p. 429 • Working with classmates to review a movie, play, or television special pp. 430–431 • Presenting an oral analysis of a poem pp. 431–432 • Working with classmates to evaluate poetry deductively p. 433

SUGGESTED INTEGRATED UNIT PLAN

This unit plan suggests how to integrate the major strands of the language arts with this chapter.

The suggested literary selections are examples of both prose and poetic literary criticism. If you begin with this chapter on writing a literary analysis or with the suggested selections, you should focus on the common characteristics of a critical analysis. You can then integrate speaking/listening and language concepts with both the writing and the literature.

Common Characteristics

- Content that is mainly factual and comprehensive
- Precise language that is neutral and unbiased
- Quotations as documentation of supporting ideas
- Technical terms with definitions
- Usually chronological organization (follows the organization of the literary text, i.e., by stanza or chapter)

Writing
Critical Analysis

UNIT FOCUS
SHORT STORY

Speaking/Listening

- Presenting reviews as a team
- Performing a parody
- Presenting an oral reading and an analysis of a poem

Language
Mechanics and Usage

- Quotations, ellipses, slashes
- Literary present tense

Literature
Selections such as

- "Preface to Fables Ancient and Modern" John Dryden
- "On the Knocking at the Gate in *Macbeth*" Thomas De Quincey
- "To the Memory of My Beloved Master, William Shakespeare" Ben Jonson
- "An Essay on Criticism" Alexander Pope

CHAPTER 10: WRITING ABOUT LITERATURE

Use this guide to create an instructional plan that addresses the individual needs of your students. Assignments accompanied by the following symbol (*) may be completed out of class. Times given for pacing lessons are estimated.

CHAPTER PLANNING GUIDE—PUPIL'S EDITION

| LESSONS | LITERARY MODEL pp. 390–392 "He Did It" by Amy Taubin | PREWRITING pp. 394–413 | |
		Generating Ideas	Gathering/Organizing
DEVELOPMENTAL PROGRAM	🕐 20–25 minutes • Have students read the model aloud to partners and answer questions on p. 392.	🕐 90–95 minutes • Main Assignment: Looking Ahead p. 393 • Reading and Responding pp. 394–395, 402–406 • A Short Story pp. 395–402 • Exercise 1 p. 402 • Writing Assignment: Part 1 p. 408*	🕐 35–40 minutes • Planning Your Critical Analysis pp. 409–412 • Writing Assignment: Parts 2, 3 pp. 411, 413* • Reminder p. 413
CORE PROGRAM	🕐 15–20 minutes • Have students read the model independently and answer questions on p. 392 in pairs.	🕐 50–55 minutes • Main Assignment: Looking Ahead p. 393 • Charts pp. 394, 403–406 • A Short Story pp. 395–402* • Critical Thinking p. 407 • Writing Assignment: Part 1 p. 408*	🕐 30–35 minutes • Finding a Focus/Developing Your Thesis pp. 409–410 • Writing Assignment: Parts 2, 3 pp. 411, 413* • Strategies Chart p. 412 • Reminder p. 413
ACCELERATED PROGRAM	🕐 15 minutes • Assign students to read model independently and take notes in Reader's Logs.	🕐 40–45 minutes • Main Assignment: Looking Ahead p. 393 • Charts pp. 394, 403–406 • A Short Story pp. 395–402* • Critical Thinking p. 407 • Writing Assignment: Part 1 p. 408*	🕐 25–30 minutes • Finding a Focus/Developing Your Thesis pp. 409–410 • Writing Assignment: Parts 2, 3 pp. 411, 413* • Strategies Chart p. 412 • Reminder p. 413

CHAPTER PLANNING GUIDE—PROGRAM RESOURCES

	LITERARY MODEL	PREWRITING
PRINT	• Reading Master 10, *Practice for Assessment in Reading, Vocabulary, and Spelling* p. 10	• Prewriting 1, *Strategies for Writing* pp. 44–45 • Prewriting 2, *Strategies for Writing* pp. 46–47
MEDIA	• Fine Art Transparency 7: *The Lady of Shalott*, *Transparency Binder*	• Graphic Organizers 17–18, *Transparency Binder* • *Writer's Workshop 2:* Evaluation

WRITING pp. 414–419	EVALUATING AND REVISING pp. 420–422	PROOFREADING AND PUBLISHING pp. 423–425
45–50 minutes • The Structure of a Critical Analysis p. 414 • Mechanics Hint pp. 414–415 • A Writer's Model pp. 415–417 • Framework p. 418 • Writing Note p. 419 • Writing Assignment: Part 4 p. 419*	**45–50 minutes** • Evaluating and Revising pp. 420–422 • Exercise 2 pp. 420–421 • Writing Assignment: Part 5 p. 421	**50 minutes** • Proofreading and Publishing p. 423 • Writing Note p. 423 • Writing Assignment: Part 6 p. 423 • Reflecting p. 424 • A Student Model pp. 424–425
25–30 minutes • Mechanics Hint pp. 414–415 • A Writer's Model pp. 415–417* • Framework p. 418 • Writing Note p. 419 • Writing Assignment: Part 4 p. 419*	**40–45 minutes** • Writing Assignment: Part 5 p. 421 • Evaluating and Revising Critical Analysis Essays Chart p. 422	**40–45 minutes** • Writing Note p. 423 • Writing Assignment: Part 6 p. 423 • Reflecting p. 424 • A Student Model pp. 424–425*
20–25 minutes • Mechanics Hint pp. 414–415 • A Writer's Model pp. 415–417* • Framework p. 418 • Writing Note p. 419 • Writing Assignment: Part 4 p. 419*	**30–35 minutes** • Writing Assignment: Part 5 p. 421 • Evaluating and Revising Critical Analysis Essays Chart p. 422	**35–40 minutes** • Writing Note p. 423 • Writing Assignment: Part 6 p. 423 • Reflecting p. 424

WRITING	EVALUATING AND REVISING	PROOFREADING AND PUBLISHING
• Writing, *Strategies for Writing* p. 48	• Evaluating and Revising, *Strategies for Writing* p. 49	• Proofreading Practice, *Strategies for Writing* p. 51
• *Language Workshop:* Lessons 50, 61	• Revision Transparencies 17–18, *Transparency Binder*	

ELEMENTS OF WRITING: CURRICULUM CONNECTIONS

Writing Workshop
• Parody pp. 426–429

Making Connections
• Speaking and Listening: A Critical Review pp. 430–431
• Evaluating Literature: Writing a Critical Analysis of a Poem pp. 431–432
• Evaluating Literature: Using Deductive Reasoning pp. 432–433

ASSESSMENT OPTIONS

Summative Assessment
Holistic Scoring: Prompts and Models pp. 39–44

Portfolio Assessment
Portfolio forms, *Portfolio Assessment* pp. 5–25, 44–48

Self-Assessment
Writing Process Log, *Strategies for Writing* p. 43
Self-assessment Record, *Portfolio Assessment* p. 19

Ongoing Assessment
Proofreading, *Strategies for Writing* p. 50

Computer disk or CD-ROM

Overhead transparencies

OBJECTIVES

- To read and respond to a movie review
- To analyze characteristics of critical analysis
- To determine the writer's opinion in a movie review
- To identify supporting examples in a movie review

VISUAL CONNECTIONS
Books

About the Artwork. This painting, an abstract composition of approximately six books haphazardly arranged on a table, has been interpreted as an autobiography of the artist, Bruce McGaw. From the top book, a copy of *Evergreen Review,* to the bottom work, a pamphlet representing the Oakland Art Museum catalog, all these books summarize the influences on McGaw's life in the early sixties.

10 WRITING ABOUT LITERATURE: EXPOSITION

MOTIVATION

Bring to class two recent movie reviews from a newspaper or from a magazine such as *Time.* Read the first paragraph or two of one of these reviews and ask students if they would like to see the movie. Tell them that they are going to read and analyze a movie review like this one.

TEACHING THE LESSON

Have a different volunteer read aloud each of the three introductory paragraphs. Direct students' attention to the picture of Gibson on p. 390 and ask them to tell what they know about Mel Gibson and his movies. Would they have cast him as Hamlet? Why or why not?

☞

Reading and Responding

Have you ever laughed at the words in a comic strip? ever gotten angry at the words in an editorial? Whenever you are **reading,** you are also **responding**—with pleasure, annoyance, anger, boredom, or in some other way. In a similar way, you respond to music, to movies, to everything you see and hear.

Writing and You. Sometimes, you move beyond a personal response to writing critically about a work. You look at the parts of the work—the book, poem, or play— to understand how it is put together and what it means. In the same way, a film reviewer analyzes a movie—the script, the acting, the direction—and writes a review of the movie. Has a movie (or book, play, concert) review ever helped to shape your opinion?

As You Read. The following review of the movie *Hamlet*, with Mel Gibson, focuses on the acting. After reading the review, would you want to see the movie?

Bruce McGaw, *Books* (1958). Oil on canvas, 11 $\frac{1}{16}$″ × 13 $\frac{5}{8}$″.
Courtesy of The Delman Collection, San Francisco.

QUOTATION FOR THE DAY

"Literature is an act of generosity—something that is going on in my head and I try to make happen in yours." (Elie Wiesel, 1928–   , Romanian-born American novelist and essayist, winner of the Nobel Peace Prize in 1986)

Write the quotation on the chalkboard and ask a few volunteers to share their thoughts about what Wiesel might have meant by "to make it happen in yours." Explain that writing about literature allows readers to respond to the author and his or her ideas and thoughts.

MEETING *individual* NEEDS

LEP/ESL

General Strategies. Some of your students might find the review of *Hamlet* difficult because Ms. Taubin assumes a familiarity with the play that they might not have and also because she uses several adjectives that the students might find unfamiliar, such as *brittle, girlishly, coy, fiercely, rotten,* and *doting.* You may want to give a brief idea of what the play is about and to point out the meanings of some of the adjectives used in the selection.

389

389

Read and discuss the first paragraph of the review with the class and explain that the writer of a review usually states the main point immediately. Ask students to find this main point in the first paragraph [sentence 2]. Have students read the remainder of the review independently and then you can guide a discussion of the review.

Students can answer the **Reader's Response** and **Writer's Craft** questions in small groups. After you have helped students begin their answers for question 3, allow them to finish question 3 and to answer questions 4 and 5 in their groups. Have one student in each group record the group's answers and turn in to you a group report.

VISUAL CONNECTIONS

Exploring the Subject. Mel Gibson was born in New York State in the mid-1950s, but his family emigrated to Australia during the Vietnam War. After graduating from high school, Gibson attended the National Institute of Dramatic Art in Australia, from which he graduated in 1977. His first film was *Summer City* (1977), but it was the international success of movies such as *The Road Warrior* (1982) that brought him into the public eye. Since then, Gibson has starred in numerous films, including *Tim, Gallipoli, The Bounty, The River, Bird on a Wire,* and *Forever Young.*

USING THE SELECTION
He Did It

1

Other famous actors who have played Hamlet are John Barrymore and Sir Laurence Olivier.

390

A review of Mel Gibson's Hamlet

He **did** it

by Amy Taubin

It may not be called *Mel Gibson Plays Hamlet*, but really, why would anyone go except to find out if "Mel" can pull it off. So it's a little like giving the plot away to say, yes he does, and very nicely too. Never less than forthright and well-spoken, Gibson's performance, once it gets going, is also witty, intelligent, and full of emotional surprises. Of the 30-odd Hamlets I've seen, his is certainly the most straight-talking. Gibson respects the verse without letting it overwhelm him; he has a way of making familiar lines sound not only spontaneous but effortlessly clear.

1

"Never less than forthright and well-spoken, Gibson's performance, once it gets going, is also witty, intelligent, and full of emotional surprises."

If you have students turn in one set of answers for each group, you can check responses quickly and easily. You may even want to facilitate further sharing of ideas by having groups exchange papers to check their own answers. Students can circle answers that differ for you to read and check.

RETEACHING

Use the overhead projector to display a recent movie review. Guided by **Writer's Craft** questions, design a model to give students practice analyzing a movie review. Highlight in blue the opinion statements; highlight in pink the support. Then, work with students to label the highlighted parts. ☞

391

No less admirable is the fact that Gibson refuses to rely on his glamour to get him through. This Hamlet is unremarkable physically: short, plain-faced, and pale-eyed. At a certain point, one even begins to wish that his body were more expressive—but the fault lies less with the actor than with his director, Franco Zeffirelli. **2**

Zeffirelli's overriding goal seems to involve cramming as many lines as possible into two hours. No one, including the star, is allowed on camera unless his/her lips are moving. The only exceptions take place in the scenes that Zeffirelli *adds* to the play—the funeral of Hamlet's father, the execution of Rosencrantz and Guildenstern—in some sort of desperate attempt at creativity. These are played in total silence—dumb, as it were.

If Zeffirelli has any concept of the play itself, it's not evident on the screen. For some inexplicable reason—perhaps it's cold in this medieval castle—the actors are constantly on the move. With the exception of Paul Scofield's fiercely exhausted Ghost and Stephan Dillane's ganglingly innocent Horatio, the other supporting roles are given short shrift by actors who are variously miscast, incompetent, or not bothering. In the last category are Ian Holm's Polonius and Alan Bates' smarmy but lethargic Claudius.

As for Glenn Close, her Gertrude is brittle, girlishly coy, and well-bred—i.e., a disaster. Without a Gertrude who's doting and sexually desirous, the familial intrigue makes

"... Paul Scofield's fiercely exhausted Ghost ..."

"As for Glenn Close, her Gertrude is brittle, girlishly coy, and well-bred—i.e., a disaster."

2

Franco Zeffirelli has also directed movie versions of Shakespearean plays *The Taming of the Shrew* and *Romeo and Juliet*.

VISUAL CONNECTIONS

Exploring the Subject. Paul Scofield was born January 21, 1922, in Hurstpierpoint, Sussex, England. He trained for the stage at the London Mask Theatre and Drama School. Scofield has portrayed many Shakespearean characters. His portrayal of Sir Thomas More in *A Man for All Seasons* won for him the Academy Award for best actor, the New York Film Critics Award, the London Film Academy Award, and the Saint Genesius Gold Medal of Rome, Italy, in 1966.

Glenn Close was born March 19, 1947, in Greenwich, Connecticut. She began acting in high school and graduated with a B.A. in drama from the College of William and Mary. A star of the stage and screen, Close has been nominated for five Academy Awards, a Tony Award, an Emmy Award, and several Golden Globe Awards for her acting. Close is also a singer and has been nominated for a Grammy Award.

Write on the chalkboard the words *response* and *analysis.* Ask students to explain the difference between the two processes. Then, remind students that it is important to react to a work of literature through both personal response and critical analysis. ■

392

3

The *he* refers to Gibson, not Hamlet. Gibson acted in the role because it challenged his acting skills.

ANSWERS

Reader's Response

Responses will vary.

1. Although some students will have difficulty watching even a modern film version of Shakespeare, most students who have seen the film will agree that Gibson gives a powerful performance.

2. Many students would go to see *Hamlet* just because they have liked Gibson's other movies. Also, Taubin is quite convincing in her praise of his performance.

Writer's Craft

Responses may vary.

3. Taubin obviously prefers Gibson's performance because he is "forthright and well-spoken," "witty, intelligent, and full of emotional surprises," and "straight-talking." She also praises his "way of making familiar lines sound not only spontaneous but effortlessly clear."

4. Although Taubin criticizes several performances, she seems to like that of Glenn Close least. She claims that Close's Gertrude is "brittle, girlishly coy, and well-bred."

5. Students will probably agree that Taubin includes sufficient support for her opinions about Gibson and Close. However, they may feel that she should have included more support for her criticism of minor characters.

392

absolutely no sense. And since Zeffirelli has stripped the text of its political content (if something is rotten in Denmark, its citizens don't seem to have noticed), it's hard to figure out what the fuss is about. Gibson, potentially, is Hamlet as undercover cop, feigning madness in order to gather evidence against his father's murderer. But since the performance happens in a vacuum, it never quite adds up.

3 If you have any doubts about why he did it, Shakespeare provides Gibson with several unique opportunities; not only does he speak in verse, he also dies.

The Village Voice

READER'S RESPONSE

1. If you have seen this movie, tell why you agree or disagree with the reviewer. If you haven't seen it, explain how you responded to another Shakespearean play or movie.
2. Suppose you have always disliked Shakespeare. Then you read this review. Would you go to see this movie? Why?

WRITER'S CRAFT

3. Whose performance does Taubin like best in the movie *Hamlet*? What reasons does she give to support her opinion?
4. Whose performance does Taubin like least? What reasons does she give to support that opinion?
5. Do you think the reviewer backs up her opinions with enough evidence? Give some examples to support your answer.

"Gibson, potentially, is Hamlet as undercover cop, feigning madness in order to gather evidence against his father's murderer."

PURPOSES FOR WRITING ABOUT LITERATURE

TEACHING THE LESSON

Write on the chalkboard the four purposes for writing and explain that in this chapter students will apply these purposes to literature. Read aloud but in random order the four examples and ask students to identify the purpose of each. For example, students should be able to identify "freewriting in your writing journal about a poem you especially like" as self-expressive. ∎

393

Purposes for Writing About Literature

The title of Taubin's review, "He Did It," shows that her purpose is partly informative, telling readers that Mel Gibson succeeds in his performance as Hamlet. But her purpose may also be partly persuasive—she's attempting to persuade you to accept her opinion of the film.

Here are examples of the purposes you might have when writing about literature or one of the other arts.

- in your journal, freewriting about a poem you especially like
- in an e-mail message to a friend, writing about the way you wish a novel had ended
- in an essay, analyzing Maxine Hong Kingston's style as demonstrated in the opening passage of *China Men*
- in a research paper, comparing ancient Roman and Greek poetry
- in a posting to an electronic bulletin board, contrasting Jane Austen's novel *Emma* with the film version
- in a letter to the author of a popular book, protesting his portrayal of female characters
- in a review, attempting to persuade other students to read Gabriel García Márquez's latest novel
- in a satire, writing a new ending to a play
- in a creative piece, writing a dialogue between you and a character in your favorite short story

LOOKING AHEAD

In this chapter, your main writing assignment will be a critical, or literary, analysis. Your purpose in writing this analysis will be to inform and to explain. As you work through the chapter, keep in mind that an effective critical analysis

- starts with a careful reading of the work
- identifies the writer's main idea, or thesis, about the work
- uses examples from the work to support, or prove, the main idea

COOPERATIVE LEARNING

After students have familiarized themselves with the storyline of *Hamlet* or *Macbeth*, discuss the possible purposes for writing about either play or about a particular scene. Divide students into groups of four and tell the groups to assign each student one of the purposes for writing. Then, direct each student to write a response according to the assigned purpose. Thus, one student will write a self-expressive response to the play; a second student will write an informative paragraph about plot or character; a third will write to persuade the reader to read or not read the play; and a fourth will write a new dialogue or a new ending for the play. Ask groups to share their responses with the class.

INTEGRATING THE LANGUAGE ARTS

Speaking and Listening Link. Ask students to read aloud their sentences or paragraphs illustrating different purposes. Then, ask the class to identify the purpose of each student's sentence or paragraph.

PREWRITING

OBJECTIVES
- To respond personally to a story and to share responses with classmates
- To analyze the literary elements of a story
- To select a story for independent personal response and critical analysis
- To select a focus and to write a thesis statement for a critical analysis
- To gather and organize supporting evidence for a critical analysis

PROGRAM MANAGER

PREWRITING

- **Self-Assessment** See **Writing Process Log** in *Strategies for Writing*, p. 43.

- **Analyzing** See **Prewriting** in *Strategies for Writing,* pp. 44–47.

- **Instructional Support** See **Graphic Organizers 17** and **18.** For suggestions on how to tie the transparencies to instruction, review teacher's notes in *Fine Art and Instructional Transparencies for Writing*, pp. 85, 87.

QUOTATION FOR THE DAY

"Who often reads will sometimes wish to write." (George Crabbe, 1754–1832, English poet)

MEETING individual NEEDS

LEP/ESL

General Strategies. Understanding an author's diction and the imagery he or she uses requires a knowledge of both meanings and connotations. Encourage English-language learners to ask questions about any diction and figures of speech they do not understand, and then give them an opportunity to work on these areas with peers who are proficient in English.

394

Writing a Critical Analysis

Prewriting

Reading and Responding to Literature

Your first reaction to what you have read is usually a personal response; perhaps you are puzzled by part of a poem, or you know you would like to read a story again. Your next reaction may be a feeling that you need, or want, to study the literature more critically and thoughtfully.

Starting with Personal Response

Maybe you are crazy about football games and reggae music and don't understand why your best friend prefers hockey and rap. It's the same with literature; people respond differently to everything they read. There is no right or wrong to personal response—it's as unique as you are.

To discover your own response, you need to become aware of your reactions, of the way a work of literature is affecting you. Any of the following strategies will help you identify your reactions or feelings about a piece of literature and respond to it.

STRATEGIES FOR RESPONDING TO LITERATURE

1. Freewrite in a journal about characters, ideas, and scenes that relate to your own experiences, knowledge, or memories.
2. Picture scenes in your mind. If you think in pictures rather than words, draw what the author describes.
3. Talk about your response with others who read the same work, discussing what you liked and disliked.
4. Respond creatively. Write a new ending to the work, or tell what happens to a character years later. Change the genre—make a poem into a short story, a play into a poem, and so on. Change the time and place—for example, rewrite a Renaissance poem as a modern poem.

Read to the class a short comic poem, a brief lyric poem that recreates a sense experience, and a brief poem that suggests a truth about life. (If you have trouble finding poems brief enough, use single stanzas from longer poems.) After you read each poem, ask students to respond briefly. Do they like or dislike it? Why? Then, ask how the last poem differs from the first poem. Explain that readers respond personally to all literature that they read but that some complex literature, such as the final poem, tempts readers to establish more than a personal response, such as interpretation and analysis. Tell students that in this lesson they will learn more about responding, reading critically, and analyzing literature. ☞

The following short story was written by Nadine Gordimer, a South African who won the 1991 Nobel Prize for literature. As you read the story, be aware of your personal response. Does the main character's experience remind you of any experience in your own life or the life of someone you know?

A SHORT STORY

The Soft Voice of the Serpent
by Nadine Gordimer

Nadine Gordimer displays her Nobel Prize.

1 **H**e was only twenty-six and very healthy and he
2 was soon strong enough to be wheeled out into
3 the garden. Like everyone else, he had great and curious faith in the garden: "Well, soon you'll be up and able to sit out in the garden," they said, looking at him fervently, with little understanding tilts of the head. Yes, he would be out . . . in the garden. It was a big garden enclosed in old dark, sleek, pungent firs, and he could sit deep beneath their tiered fringes, down in the shade, far away. There was the feeling that there, in the garden, he
4 would come to an understanding; that it would come easier, there. Perhaps there was something
5 in this of the old Eden idea; the tender human adjusting himself to himself in the soothing imper-

VISUAL CONNECTIONS
Exploring the Subject. A native of South Africa, Nadine Gordimer has published some twenty works of fiction, including ten novels. Four of Gordimer's works have in the past been banned by the government of South Africa because of their implicit criticism of apartheid. Gordimer has worked actively against the South African policy of apartheid, and many of her works focus on the difficult relationships between whites and blacks in contemporary South Africa.

USING THE SELECTION
The Soft Voice of the Serpent

1
The main characters in the story become universal because they are never named.

2
The word *wheeled* is the first clue that he is confined to a wheelchair.

3
Emphasis on the garden introduces it as an important image or symbol.

4
He seeks an understanding of his physical condition, but the word *understanding* also may suggest the knowledge gained in Eden.

5
Allusion to Eden confirms the significance of the garden image and foreshadows later actions and themes.

6

Images of sun and shade could suggest good and evil in the world; knowledge and reality may come in the garden.

7

Notice the metaphor of "slack, furled sail of himself" lifted by the wind of hope.

8

The character of the delicate wife is introduced along with the husband's sensitivity toward her feelings.

9

The stark description of the husband's amputated leg confirms earlier foreshadowing.

10

He denies reality of amputation.

sonal presence of trees and grass and earth, before going out into the stare of the world.

6 The very first time it was so strange; his wife was wheeling him along the gravel path in the sun and the shade, and he felt exactly as he did when he was a little boy and he used to bend and hang, looking at the world upside down, through his ankles. Everything was vast and open, the sky, the wind blowing along through the swaying, trembling greens, the flowers shaking in vehement denial. Movement . . .

7 A first slight wind lifted again in the slack, furled sail of himself; he felt it belly gently, so gently he could just feel it, lifting inside him.

8 So she wheeled him along, pushing hard and not particularly well with her thin pretty arms — but he would not for anything complain of the way she did it or suggest that the nurse might do better, for he knew that would hurt her — and when they came to a spot that he liked, she put the brake on the chair and settled him there for the morning. That was the first time and now he sat there every day. He read a lot, but his attention was arrested sometimes, quite suddenly and compellingly, by the sunken place under the rug where his leg used **9** to be. There was his one leg, and next to it, the rug flapped loose. Then looking, he felt his leg not there; he felt it go, slowly, from the toe to the thigh. He felt that he had no leg. After a few min-**10** utes he went back to his book. He never let the realization quite reach him; he let himself realize it physically, but he never quite let it get at *him*. He felt it pressing up, coming, coming, dark, crushing, ready to burst — but he always turned away, just in time, back to his book. That was his system; that was the way he was going to do it. He would let it come near, irresistibly near, again and again, ready to catch him alone in the garden. And again and again he would turn it back, just in time. Slowly it would become a habit, with the reassuring strength of a habit. It would become such a habit never to get to the point of realizing it, *that he*

Ask a different volunteer to read each of the three introductory paragraphs on pp. 395–396. Introduce the various ways to respond to a work of literature from the chart on p. 394. Use a recent movie as the basis for illustrating each type of response. For example, you could discuss with students their responses to one of the characters in *Dead Poets Society* or you could formulate a different ending for the movie.

Because Gordimer's **"The Soft Voice of the Serpent"** is a story of character rather than action, you may want to read the story to your students—perhaps with two good readers reading the dialogue for the man and the woman. Using the annotations and the questions from **Exercise 1** on p. 402, discuss ☞

Prewriting   **397**

never would realize it. And one day he would find that he had achieved what he wanted: *he would feel as if he had always been like that.*

11 Then the danger would be over, for ever.

12 In a week or two he did not have to read all the time; he could let himself put down the book and look about him, watching the firs part silkily as a

13 child's fine straight hair in the wind, watching the small birds tightroping the telephone wire, watching the fat old dove trotting after his refined patrician grey women, purring with lust. His wife came and sat beside him, doing her sewing, and sometimes they spoke, but often they sat for hours, a whole morning, her movements at work small and unobtrusive as the birds', he resting his head back and looking at a blur of sky through half closed eyes. Now and then her eye, habitually looking inwards, would catch the signal of some little happening, some point of colour in the garden, and her laugh or exclamation drawing his attention to it would suddenly clear away the silence. At eleven o'clock she would get up and put down her sewing and go into the house to fetch their tea; crunching slowly away into the sun up the path, going easily, empowered by the sun rather than her own muscles. He watched her go, easily . . . He was healing. In the static quality of his gaze, in the relaxed feeling of his mouth, in the upward-lying palm of his

14 hand, there was annealment . . .

11
The danger may be his emotions about reality.

12
He is gradually adjusting so that he doesn't need to escape through reading.

13
Images of boy and child in the story suggest innocence.

14
annealment: tempering to toughen and reduce brittleness

thoroughly students' personal responses and interpretations to the story and provide guidance when necessary. You will probably want to have students share their personal responses in small groups, but some students may need help from you in reading the story critically—especially in recognizing the allusion to the Garden of Eden and in interpreting the symbolism of the locust.

Selecting stories for analysis in **Writing Assignment: Part 1** on p. 408 is a crucial step in the prewriting process. If students have difficulty choosing stories, you might make suggestions. Possibilities are D. H. Lawrence's "The Rocking-Horse Winner," Katherine Mansfield's "The Doll's House," and Frank O'Connor's "My Oedipus Complex." When you introduce the skills of

15
The locust first approaches the wife as the snake first approached Eve in the Garden of Eden.

16
The wife's shuddering reaction takes on added significance when the locust is identified with her husband.

17
Personification of the locust prepares the way for the husband's identification with it.

18
The husband tries to enclose himself in psychological armor by not facing the reality of his condition, just as the locust is enclosed in armor.

15 One day a big locust whirred dryly past her head, and she jumped up with a cry, scattering her sewing things. He laughed at her as she bent about **16** picking them up, shuddering. She went into the house to fetch the tea, and he began to read. But presently he put down the book and, yawning, noticed a reel of pink cotton that she had missed, lying in a rose bed.

He smiled, remembering her. And then he **17** became conscious of a curious old mannish little face, fixed upon him in a kind of hypnotic dread. There, absolutely stilled with fear beneath his glance, crouched a very big locust. What an amusing face the thing had! A lugubrious long face, that somehow suggested a bald head, and such a glum mouth. It looked like some little person out of a Disney cartoon. It moved slightly, still looking up **18** fearfully at him. Strange body, encased in a sort of old-fashioned creaky armour. He had never realized before what ridiculous-looking insects locusts were! Well, naturally not; they occur to one collectively, as a pest — one doesn't go around looking at their faces.

The face was certainly curiously human and even expressive, but looking at the body, he decided that the body couldn't really be called a body at all. With the face, the creature's kinship with humans ended. The body was flimsy paper stretched over a frame of matchstick, like a small

19 boy's homemade aeroplane. And those could not be thought of as legs — the great saw-toothed back ones were like the parts of an old crane, and the front ones like — like one of her hairpins, bent in two. At that moment the creature slowly lifted up one of the front legs, and passed it tremblingly over its head, stroking the left antenna down. Just as a man might take out a handkerchief and pass it over his brow.

He began to feel enormously interested in the creature, and leaned over in his chair to see it more closely. It sensed him and beneath its stiff, plated sides, he was surprised to see the pulsations of a heart. How fast it was breathing . . . He leaned away a little, to frighten it less.

Watching it carefully, and trying to keep himself effaced from its consciousness by not moving,
20 he became aware of some struggle going on in the thing. It seemed to gather itself together in muscular concentration: this co-ordinated force then passed along its body in a kind of petering tremor, and ended in a stirring along the upward shaft of the great back legs. But the locust remained where it was. Several times this wave of effort currented through it and was spent, but the next time it ended surprisingly in a few hobbling, uneven steps, undercarriage — aeroplanelike again — trailing along the earth.

Then the creature lay, fallen on its side, antennae turned stretched out towards him. It groped with its feet, feeling for a hold on the soft ground, bending its joints and straining. With a heave, it righted itself, and as it did so, he saw — leaning for-
21 ward again — what was the trouble. It was the same trouble. His own trouble. The creature had lost one leg. Only the long upward shaft of its left leg remained, with a neat round aperture where, no doubt, the other half of the leg had been attached.

Now as he watched the locust gather itself again and again in that concentration of muscle, spend itself again and again in a message that was so puzzlingly never obeyed, he knew exactly what

19
Vivid similes compare "saw-toothed" back legs to cranes and front legs to the wife's hairpins.

20
Both the husband and the locust are undergoing a struggle.

21
In this climactic scene the husband recognizes similarity between his condition and that of the locust.

The example on p. 406 shows how a student reader who is planning a critical analysis of the story has used dialogue (questions and possible answers about the story) to produce critical reading notes for Nadine Gordimer's **"The Soft Voice of the Serpent."**

Continue to guide your students through a critical reading of Gordimer's story by working with the class to answer the questions for **Exercise 1**. Then, guide your students to an understanding of how these notes suggest the thesis statement on the bottom of p. 410 about the theme of illusion and reality in the story.

the creature felt. Of course he knew that feeling! That absolute certainty that the leg was there: one had only to lift it . . . The upward shaft of the locust's leg quivered, lifted; why then couldn't he walk? He tried again. The message came; it was going through, the leg was lifting, now it was ready — now! . . . The shaft sagged in the air, with nothing, nothing to hold it up.

22   He laughed and shook his head: He *knew* . . . Good Lord, *exactly* like — He called out to the house — "Come quickly! Come and see! You've got another patient!"

"What?" she shouted. "I'm getting tea."

"Come and look!" he called. "Now!"

". . . What is it?" she said, approaching the locust distastefully.

"Your locust!" he said. She jumped away with a little shriek.

23   "Don't worry — it can't move. It's as harmless as I am. You must have knocked its leg off when you hit out at it!" He was laughing at her.

24   "Oh, I didn't!" she said reproachfully. She loathed it but she loathed to hurt, even more. "I never even touched it! All I hit was air . . . I couldn't possibly have hit it. Not its leg off."

"All right then. It's another locust. But it's lost its leg, anyway. You should just see it . . . It doesn't know the leg isn't there. God, I know exactly how that feels . . . I've been watching it, and honestly, it's uncanny. I can see it feels just like I do!"

She smiled at him, sideways; she seemed suddenly pleased at something. Then, recalling herself, she came forward, bent double, hands upon her hips.

"Well, if it can't move . . ." she said, hanging over it.

"Don't be frightened," he laughed. "Touch it."

25   "Ah, the poor thing," she said, catching her breath in compassion. "It can't walk."

"Don't encourage it to self-pity," he teased her.

She looked up and laughed. "Oh you — " she parried, assuming a frown. The locust kept its

---

22
The husband increases his identification with the locust.

23
The husband's statement "It's as harmless as I am" is a conscious identification.

24
Because of the husband's clear identification with the locust, the wife's obvious loathing of the locust has ominous implications.

25
Perhaps the wife is more comfortable with creatures who require nurturing, like the locust and her husband.

solemn silly face turned to her. "Shame, isn't he a funny old man," she said. "But what will happen to him?"

"I don't know," he said, for being in the same boat absolved him from responsibility or pity. "Maybe he'll grow another one. Lizards grow new tails, if they lose them."

"Oh, *lizards*," she said. " — But not these. I'm afraid the cat'll get him."

"Get another little chair made for him and you can wheel him out here with me."

"Yes," she laughed. "Only for him it would have to be a kind of little cart, with wheels."

"Or maybe he could be taught to use crutches. I'm sure the farmers would like to know that he was being kept active."

"The poor old thing," she said, bending over the locust again. And reaching back somewhere into an inquisitive childhood she picked up a thin wand of twig and prodded the locust, very gently. "Funny thing is, it's even the same leg, the left one." She looked round at him and smiled.

"I know," he nodded, laughing. "The two of us . . ." And then he shook his head and, smiling, said it again: "The two of us."

She was laughing and just then she flicked the twig more sharply than she meant to and at the touch of it there was a sudden flurried papery whirr, and the locust flew away.

26

The reference to lizards suggests reptiles, which may be a subtle reference to snakes.

27

Note the detailed identification of the injured left legs of both locust and husband.

28

The wife initiates the event that brings knowledge to her husband just as Eve initiated the event that brought knowledge and death to humanity (succumbing to the snake's temptation to eat the fruit).

Assess students' responses to the questions in **Exercise 1** informally by circulating through the room as students are discussing their responses. If students have responded in their writing journals, you will want to read their responses. You might select one response from each student for a focused comment.

If students ask you to read and react to their notes for **Writing Assignment: Part 1**, you will want to do so. However, it is not necessary to read and respond to all students' work at this stage in the process. You will, however, want to check each student's focus and thesis statement carefully to avoid unnecessary problems in later stages of writing. Assess thesis statements informally for

---

29

The husband's irritability suggests that he has been forced to face reality and to accept the knowledge of his amputation.

30

The surprise ending is ironic; after his identification with the locust, the husband feels betrayed because it can escape through flight but he can't.

ANSWERS
Exercise 1

Answers will vary.

1. Because of the negative associations with serpents, most students will respond negatively to the word *serpent*. The title itself may have made students curious or uneasy.

2. Some students may describe personal experiences and observations. Others may describe books or movies focusing on a person who has a disability.

3. Because the story is told from the man's point of view, he will probably seem more real to students than the woman. Students might think they would behave as the man does.

4. The husband may retain his irritable mood, perhaps dwelling even more on his immobility since he has observed the locust flying away. Or, after truly facing the reality of his situation, he may try to make his life more productive than simply reading in a garden.

5. It is hard to imagine a better conclusion than Gordimer's ironic surprise ending. However, you should encourage students to use their imaginations.

402

---

402   *Writing About Literature*

> She stood there with the stick in her hand, half afraid of the creature again, and appealed, unnerved as a child, "What happened. What happened."
>
> There was a moment of silence.
>
> **29** "Don't be a fool," he said irritably.
>
> **30** They had forgotten that locusts can fly.

EXERCISE 1 ▶ **Speaking and Listening: Sharing Your Personal Responses**

How did you react to "The Soft Voice of the Serpent"? Get together with three or four classmates to share your personal responses to the story. You might use these questions to guide your discussion.

1. Think about the first time you saw the title, before you actually read the story. What is your response to the word *serpent*? How did the title as a whole make you feel?

2. Describe how you or someone you know copes with a disability.

3. How do you feel about the way the man and woman in the story relate to each other? How real do they seem to you? Suppose you were the man or woman. How do you think you would behave in his or her situation?

4. At the end of the story, the husband's mood suddenly changes. What do you think he might do the next day? Think up a dialogue between husband and wife that might take place the next day.

5. How do you like the way the story ends? If you don't like the ending, tell what would make a better ending.

Reading Literature Critically

When you read a piece of literature for pleasure, you often don't go beyond your personal response. But sometimes you may want, or even need, to take a more thoughtful look at the work so that you can compare your perceptions with those of others. Before you can thoughtfully discuss or write about literature, however, you have to read it more critically and understand its parts, or *elements*.

clear focus and make suggestions for improvement where necessary.

For **Writing Assignment: Part 3,** have students evaluate one another's plans in small groups by using a guide like this one:

1. Is the thesis clear and focused?
2. How many major points does the plan have? What are these points? If it has only one or two points, what other points could be added?
3. Does each major point have two or three pieces of supporting evidence? Which points need more evidence?

Understanding Literary Elements. *Literary elements* are the parts and characteristics of a poem, story, play, or other work of literature. The following charts identify the major elements of poetry and fiction and provide questions that you can use to analyze the writer's use of these elements.

ELEMENTS OF POETRY	
Diction—the poet's choice of words	What kinds of words does the poet use? Formal or informal? Concrete or abstract? One syllable or many syllables?
Figures of speech—words or phrases not meant to be taken literally	What kinds of imaginative comparisons (**similes** and **metaphors**) does the poet use? Does the poet use **personification** (giving human qualities to an animal or object)? Do the figures of speech suggest a mood? How do they affect the meaning of the poem?
Imagery—words or phrases that evoke sights, sounds, tastes, textures, and smells	What images are in the poem? Which images, or types of images, are repeated? What feelings do the images suggest?
Repetition—repeated consonant sounds, vowel sounds, words, or phrases	What words, phrases, or sounds are repeated? Why are they repeated? What effect does the repetition have on the meaning of the poem?
Rhyme—repetition of vowel sounds in accented syllables and all succeeding syllables	Does the poem have rhyme? How does the rhyme scheme add to the emotional effect or mood of the poem or reflect its meaning?

(continued)

MEETING *individual* NEEDS

LEARNING STYLES

Visual Learners. Reproduce the following story wheel and give it to students for generating ideas in prewriting. Explain that students are to answer the questions within each section. Each student can choose two aspects of the story as the basis of the thesis. For example, for style and theme, a thesis might read, "Emily Dickinson's use of symbols, imagery, and alliteration reinforces her theme that humankind's relationship with nature is tenuous."

PLOT
Retell the story.

STYLE
Explain how the author tells the story.

CHARACTERS
Describe the major people.

Title of the work

SETTING
Describe when and where the story takes place.

THEME
Explain the author's message.

403

Because the prewriting stage for writing a critical analysis is quite complex, some or all of your students may have difficulty with one or more major steps—responding personally, reading critically, note taking, selecting a focus and writing a thesis statement, or gathering and organizing evidence into a workable plan. You could repeat the steps with Gordimer's story or, if you feel a different example is needed, guide your students through the process with a simplified narrative such as an Aesopian fable.

A DIFFERENT APPROACH

To encourage visualization of the scenes in Gordimer's story, have students create a class mural of the story's various scenes after they finish reading. Encourage students to sketch scenes as they read or listen to the story.

TIMESAVER

If you have students write their responses to **Exercise 1** in their writing journals, you can save evaluation time by having each student circle the number of the one response which he or she wants you to read and respond to. In this way, you can respond to each student without taking the time to read complete journal entries.

MEETING *individual* NEEDS

AT-RISK STUDENTS

To motivate at-risk students, have each of them write a critical analysis of a movie—perhaps one available on videocassette—rather than of a story. Students are often media oriented, and if they have jobs after school, they may be more motivated to watch a movie when they get home than to read a story.

ELEMENTS OF POETRY *(continued)*

Symbol—a person, place, thing, or event that has meaning in itself but that also stands for something else	What person, place, thing, or event seems to stand for something else? How do the symbols relate to the meaning of the poem? Does the title suggest a symbol?
Theme—an underlying idea or insight that the poem reveals about life and people	Does the poem examine any common problem or life experience? What message, or theme, does the poem suggest?

ELEMENTS OF FICTION

Character—a person (sometimes an animal or thing) in a story or novel	What is the contribution of the characters to the development of the plot? How does the main character change during the story, and what does this change have to do with the theme? What do the characters' physical descriptions or the way they talk, act, or think suggest about their motivations and personifications?
Point of view—the perspective or vantage point from which a story is told	Does the story have a first-person or third-person (omniscient or limited) narrator? Through whose eyes do you see the events in the story? How much does the narrator know? What does the choice of narrator add to the theme or meaning of the story? How does it affect characterization?

(continued)

CLOSURE

Divide the chalkboard into three columns. At the top of each column, write one of these headings: "Strategies for Responding to Literature," "Strategies for Reading Critically," and "Strategies for Gathering Information." Then, ask your students to brainstorm various strategies for each task.

EXTENSION

To encourage students to look closely at the elements of character, setting, plot, and theme in the stories they have chosen for critical analysis, ask each student to illustrate one or two of these elements. For example, the illustrations of the garden setting and the characters of Nadine Gordimer's short story help readers to ☞

ELEMENTS OF FICTION (continued)

Plot—the events that follow each other and cause other events to happen	Is the plot predictable, or are there surprises along the way? What is the central problem, or **conflict**, of the story? How does the outcome of the story relate to *theme*, or meaning?
Setting—the time and place of the story	How do the time and place contribute to the plot and theme of the story? What details help you imagine the setting? Does the setting suggest a tone or mood?
Theme—an underlying principle, idea, or insight that the work reveals about life and people	Does the work reveal a lesson or insight about life? Who learns this lesson? What passages provide the clearest expression of the theme? To what extent does the theme seem "universal"?

Using Critical Reading Strategies.   One part of reading literature critically is knowing what to look for—the elements you have just read about. A second part of reading critically is knowing which strategies to use in order to read carefully and thoughtfully. You can use the following strategies along with your knowledge of literary elements to develop a good critical reading of a story or poem.

STRATEGIES FOR READING CRITICALLY

1. After you have read the story or poem once, go back and read it again. Each time you read it, you'll find something new.
2. Carry on a dialogue with the author by making notes to yourself as you read. Make a copy of the story or poem for yourself so you can mark it up or use self-sticking note papers to mark important details.

(continued)

CRITICAL THINKING

Analysis. Give students practice in analyzing poetry by asking them to identify examples of the various elements: formal or informal diction, concrete or abstract diction, simile, metaphor, personification, sense imagery, repetition, rhyme, symbol, and theme. Select examples from poems in your literature textbook or create examples. Here are some examples to get you started:

1. a sunrise like a roaring fire (comparison using *like*—simile)
2. a daisy lifting its face to the sun (personification)
3. rat-a-tat of the drum (onomatopoeia, repetition of sounds, sound imagery)
4. My dog has come home,/Never more will he roam (rhyme)

INTEGRATING THE LANGUAGE ARTS

Literature Link. Select a poem from your literature textbook for your students to analyze. You may have the entire class analyze the poem, or you could give this assignment to students who would rather analyze poetry. For example, students might analyze Tennyson's "The Lady of Shalott" (sound and sight imagery, repetition of sounds and words, rhyme, and theme) or Dylan Thomas's "Do Not Go Gentle into That Good Night" (diction, simile, repetition of words and sounds, rhyme, symbol, and theme).

visualize these elements. This assignment requires students to create mental pictures and to apply their story interpretations in these mental images. Students can publish their illustrations along with their critical analyses.

Cont. on p. 408

MEETING *individual* NEEDS

LEARNING STYLES

Visual Learners. Have each student make a copy of the story he or she has selected for analysis. Then, have students use different colors to highlight the five literary elements (example: character—pink; point of view—yellow; plot elements—blue; setting—green; theme—purple) on their copies. When they have highlighted the various elements, students will be able to organize the separate information more easily.

A DIFFERENT APPROACH

If students are going to focus on characterization in their analyses, they could use the following graphic organizer to gather or organize information:

Character	Traits	Supporting Actions	Supporting Words

STRATEGIES FOR READING CRITICALLY *(continued)*

3. Jot down notes about the elements in the work and underline or circle phrases or sentences that answer the questions in the elements charts (pages 403–405).
4. Look carefully at the title. Often it's like a piece of a puzzle: The words are a clue to the theme of the story.
5. Talk about the work with others who have read it. Exchange ideas and compare your understanding of the story with theirs. You don't have to agree with other people's interpretations, but you should be able to back up your ideas with quotations and other evidence from the story.

Here are critical reading notes that one writer made while reading the first part of "The Soft Voice of the Serpent." Notice how the writer carries on a dialogue with the author of the story.

He was only twenty-six and very healthy and he was soon strong enough to be wheeled out into the garden. Like everyone else, he had great and curious faith in the garden: "Well, soon you'll be up and able to sit out in the garden," they said, looking at him fervently, with little understanding tilts of the head. Yes, he would be out . . . in the garden. It was a big garden enclosed in old dark, sleek, pungent firs, and he could sit deep beneath their tiered fringes, down in the shade, far away. There was the feeling that there, in the garden, he would come to an understanding; that it would come easier, there. Perhaps there was something in this of the old Eden idea; the tender human adjusting himself to himself in the soothing impersonal presence of trees and grass and earth, before going out into the stare of the world.

What's wrong with him?

Third-person limited point of view.

Is the garden a symbol? What could it stand for?

Irony—"out . . . in the garden" he's not facing the world. Garden stands for safety, being protected from life?

What understanding? Related to the theme? Eden—could the serpent in the title be like the snake in Eden?

The world sounds mean, very different from life in the garden.

OBJECTIVE
• To apply the critical-thinking skill of literary analysis to a story

TEACHING *ANALYZING THE ELEMENTS OF A STORY*

Analysis means breaking an object, process, or work of literature into its various parts. To introduce students to the concept of analysis, bring to class a simple object or machine and show students how it can actually be separated into its various parts.

Prewriting   **407**

CRITICAL THINKING

Analyzing the Elements of a Story

Analyzing is a critical thinking skill that involves a careful study of a subject to see what it is like. It usually requires a study of the parts or pieces that make up the whole.

That's why the essay you are writing in this chapter is called a *literary analysis;* it involves a careful study of a work of literature. If you were analyzing your school, you might look at these parts: teachers, students, classrooms, instructional materials, and so on. The parts of a piece of literature are its basic elements, the ones in the charts on pages 403–405.

CRITICAL THINKING EXERCISE:
Analyzing a Story

In Exercise 1 you shared your personal responses to "The Soft Voice of the Serpent." Now practice the critical thinking skill of analysis by rereading the story and using the following questions to analyze its elements. You can also use the questions in the chart on pages 404–405 to analyze the story. After you have finished your analysis, get together with a small group and discuss your analyses.

1. How does the main character change during the story? What does this change have to do with the meaning of the story?
2. What is the point of view of the narrator? How does the choice of narrator affect the story?
3. What is the central conflict of the story? How does the outcome of the conflict relate to the meaning of the story?
4. How does the setting affect the plot and theme of the story?
5. What is the theme of the story? How does it apply to people other than the man in the garden?

TIMESAVER

Have each group clip together its separate answers to the five questions from the **Critical Thinking Exercise**. With a class of twenty-five, you will have only five sets of questions to check instead of twenty-five.

ANSWERS
Critical Thinking Exercise

Answers will vary.

1. At the beginning he is quite hopeful, as suggested by the "lifting inside him," and he "never let the realization (of his situation, of his amputated leg) quite reach him; . . . never quite let it get at *him.*" At the end, his irritability shows that he has realized the reality and finality of his situation.

2. The limited omniscient point of view, in which the narrator reveals actions and the thoughts of the main character, allows the reader to experience the character's change as it occurs.

3. The central conflict in the story is internal—a conflict between illusion and reality within the main character.

4. The garden setting alludes to the Garden of Eden, the archetypal setting for the loss of innocence (illusion) and the acceptance of knowledge (reality).

5. The theme of the story is that people often rely on illusion to avoid the harsh realities of life. Certainly many people, not just the man in the garden, prefer illusion to reality.

Cont. from p. 406
ENRICHMENT

The introduction of personal response to literature opens doors for personal response to other artistic forms. Return to the opening discussion about reading and responding personally to literature. Explain that these same principles of response apply to any work of art or music. Read to your class this explanation, adapted from p. 394:

Your first reaction to art or music is usually a personal response; perhaps you are puzzled, or you may want to experience the work again. Remember there's no right or wrong to personal response—it's as unique as you are. However, personal response

---

TIMESAVER

If you want to check your students' prewriting notes from **Writing Assignment: Part 1,** have them turn in their highlighted copies of their stories along with their other notes. You should be able to scan the highlighted information quickly to see if the stories are good choices for critical analysis and to see if students have been able to identify important literary elements.

A DIFFERENT APPROACH

Encourage students to work with partners to select stories that both students would like to analyze. Then, have each pair create a dialogue between a reader and the writer of the story. After writing the script for their dialogue, in which the reader asks questions about the story that the writer answers, students can present their dialogues to the rest of the class.

WRITING ASSIGNMENT

PART 1:
Responding and Reading Critically

Before you write a literary analysis of a story, you need to find a story you can work with. Browse through a literature anthology or short story collection to find a story that meets these criteria: (1) you won't mind reading it several times and (2) it appears to be well written and worth the time it will take to analyze it. After reading the story the first time, use one of the strategies for responding to literature on page 394. Then read the story critically, asking yourself the questions on the elements of fiction chart (pages 404–405). Jot down notes about your answers to the questions.

begins with involvement by keeping your mind focused as you experience the work.

Then, provide your students with two or three varied aesthetic experiences and ask each student to respond to at least one experience. You might show copies or slides of a great work of art; you could play part of a symphony by Wagner, Mozart, or Beethoven (or even a modern popular song); or you could show a clip from a ballet, an opera, or a play. Encourage students to respond in writing journal entries, drawings, discussions, or new versions of the work.

If time allows, you can also ask students to write critical analyses of the works of art to which they have responded. Ask students to identify a major theme or mood in the work and then to show how various ☞

Prewriting

Planning Your Critical Analysis

You could begin by writing down everything you know about your story, but your critical analysis will be more effective if you give some thought to planning. Think about why you are writing, who you are writing for, and what your main idea will be.

Thinking About Purpose, Audience, and Tone

When you write a critical analysis, your *purpose* is to write exposition—to explain the meaning of the work and to convince readers that your explanation is sound. Think about your *audience* as you plan your analysis. It's important to give readers enough information to understand your ideas about the story, without giving them information they already know.

The *tone* of a critical analysis is usually more formal than the reviews you might read in a newspaper or magazine. Try to avoid using first-person pronouns such as *I* and *we,* contractions, and colloquial expressions (such as "the *kids* in the story"). Focus on being objective and serious.

Finding a Focus for Your Analysis

In a short essay, it would be difficult to analyze all the elements of a story, so you should focus on the elements that seem the strongest. It is often useful to start with the theme of the story, because the theme is the key to the meaning of any literary work. Then you can add a discussion of other elements as they contribute to the development of theme. For example, you might

- analyze the role of plot and characters in developing the theme
- analyze how a particular point of view helps to bring out the theme
- analyze how setting or mood controls the plot and helps to develop the theme

TECHNOLOGY TIP

If computers are available for your class, encourage students to use word-processing programs to take notes (**Writing Assignment: Part 1**), to write their preliminary thesis statements (**Writing Assignment: Part 2**), and to create organizational plans (**Writing Assignment: Part 3**). Show students that they can record notes on a word processor and later add, delete, or rearrange notes just as they can when using index cards. Students can save their notes, thesis statements, and plans to use when they write their drafts.

elements (subjects, color, line, shape or tone, tempo, rhythm) contribute to this overall theme or mood. ■

A DIFFERENT APPROACH

Instead of using short stories or poems, students could base their critical analyses on Shakespeare's play *Hamlet* or *Macbeth* and focus their analyses on a specific image that recurs throughout the work. For example, students could chart the use of animal images in *Macbeth* or the use of clothing images in *Hamlet*. After they have finished the play, they can base their thesis statements on the pattern of the imagery. If, for example, animal images seem to reflect certain characters, then that idea could be the basis for a thesis. You could use the following chart or create one of your own for students to use as they keep track of the images they have chosen:

Type of imagery: animal

Act, Scene and Line	Quotation	Meaning/ Implication
II, i, 53	"Alarmed by his sentinel, the wolf,"	Macbeth— stalking

WE'VE BEEN READING POEMS IN SCHOOL, BUT I NEVER UNDERSTAND ANY OF THEM..

HOW AM I SUPPOSED TO KNOW WHICH POEMS TO LIKE?

10-21

SOMEBODY TELLS YOU

Peanuts reprinted by permission of United Feature Syndicate, Inc.

Developing Your Thesis Statement

A critical analysis, like other essays, has a main idea, or *thesis,* that is usually stated in one or two sentences—the *thesis statement.* The thesis statement that you write now will be a preliminary guide to your thinking and writing. As you collect evidence and draft your essay, you may find that your preliminary thesis statement is either too broad or too narrow; and if that happens, you will revise it.

The first step in developing a thesis (and a thesis statement) is to decide which elements you want to focus on in your critical analysis. The second step is to decide how those elements relate to the theme of the story and write a statement that summarizes this "interpretation." Here are some examples of thesis statements.

- In Julia Alvarez' story "Daughter of Invention," the theme—that old ways must give into new American ways—is brought out most clearly in the character of the mother, who changes dramatically. [focus on theme and character]

- The theme of Alice Walker's story "Everyday Use" is how people use their pasts. This theme becomes clear through the conflicts between two sisters and through the first-person point of view of the mother, who relates her own links to the past. [focus on theme, plot, and point of view]

- In Nadine Gordimer's story "The Soft Voice of the Serpent," the theme of illusion's being inevitably overthrown by reality is brought out primarily through characterization, setting, and plot. [focus on theme, setting, characterization, and plot]

WRITING ASSIGNMENT

PART 2:
Finding a Focus and a Thesis

It may seem early, at this point, to decide on a focus and a thesis for your analysis, but remember that you can always change your mind later. For now, decide which elements you want to focus on in the story you have selected. Then you will need to decide what main idea you want to explain and prove in your analysis, and write out that main idea in the form of a thesis statement.

Gathering Support for Your Thesis

In a literary analysis, your readers expect you to support, or prove, your thesis. Support for your thesis is comprised of (1) the major points you will make to explain the thesis and (2) the evidence or proof that you supply to demonstrate that your points are valid. The following example illustrates how this works.

> *Thesis Statement*: Nadine Gordimer reveals a theme of illusion versus reality through the setting, characterization, and plot of "The Soft Voice of the Serpent."

> *Major Point*: Gordimer's characterization of the man in the wheelchair contributes to the theme of illusion versus reality.

> *Evidence to Show Validity of Point*: The man in the wheelchair has the illusory hope that he "never would realize" (397) that he has lost his leg.

Which comes first—your sense of the major points you want to make or the evidence to back them up? That's rather like the chicken and the egg. Sometimes you'll have a sense of the major points and then go looking for the evidence. At other times, your search for evidence will lead you to the discovery of a point you want to make. Most of the evidence comes from the *primary source,* the work itself. However, you might also find evidence in *secondary sources,* reference materials such as books about authors and their works, encyclopedias, and periodicals.

👉 **REFERENCE NOTE:** For more information on secondary sources, see pages 448–449.

CRITICAL THINKING

Analysis. Most thesis statements have two primary elements: the subject or topic that the essay will be about and the focus that will be developed. Usually, the paper will be developed by analyzing either the subject or by dividing the focus into its component parts. For example, in the thesis statement "Nadine Gordimer reveals a theme of illusion versus reality through the setting, characterization, and plot in 'The Soft Voice of the Serpent,'" the subject is "theme of illusion versus reality." However, the focus "setting, characterization, and plot" provides the structure, or main divisions, of the paper. Ask your students to identify the subject and focus of each of the following thesis statements:

1. In H. G. Wells' "The Door in the Wall," the theme of the desire to escape reality is portrayed through plot, character, and setting.
2. The relationship between Paul and his mother in "The Rocking-Horse Winner" portrays the themes of the power of greed, the destructiveness of materialism in modern society, and the intense human need to be loved.
3. In Katherine Mansfield's story, "Miss Brill," Miss Brill's shattered perception of herself is shown symbolically through her actions and through her relationship to her fur piece.

CRITICAL THINKING

Evaluation. To give your students practice, ask them to evaluate the following evidence. How well does each piece of evidence support the thesis statement about Alice Walker's "Everyday Use" on p. 410?

1. Mama dreams about being on the Johnny Carson Show with Dee. [not related to theme of past]

2. To recognize her African past, Dee has chosen the name of Wangero Leewanika Kemanjo. [shows Dee's concept of her past]

3. Dee is used to getting her way with her mother. [Answers may vary: In one sense, this is not as clearly related to theme of past; however, it does show Dee's use of the past in terms of her relationship with her mother]

4. Dee wants to make objects from her past—a churn top, a dasher, and Grandma Dee's quilts—into artistic decorations for her home. [shows Dee's use of past]

5. Maggie remembers details about family keepsakes; for example, she remembers that Aunt Dee's first husband had whittled the churn dash that Dee wants but that Maggie and her mother use daily. [supports Maggie's relation to past]

6. Maggie offers to give the quilts up to Dee because she knows she can remember her grandmother even without having the quilts. [supports Maggie's relationship to past]

STRATEGIES FOR GATHERING INFORMATION

1. Reread the work of literature, thinking about the major points you will make in support of your thesis and looking for details and quotations to back them up.
2. As you read, make notes on note cards or sheets of paper.
3. Copy quotations exactly, and include the page numbers (for a story) or lines (for poetry) where the quotations appear.
4. Jot down information about the author, title, and place and date of publication so that you can give credit to your sources in your paper. (You want to avoid plagiarizing.)
5. Be certain that each piece of evidence is specific, not just a restatement of the thesis, and that it is related to the main idea.

Organizing Support

The evidence you gather may make sense to you, but it won't make sense to your readers unless it is organized in a sensible way. There are, however, several effective methods of organizing your material, and your choice of method will depend largely on the nature of your thesis.

For example, if you were writing about the symbolism of the garden in "The Soft Voice of the Serpent," you might divide your information into two groups—one group with points about the garden and another group with points about the real world. This is an example of *logical order;* related ideas are grouped together. On the other hand, if you were writing about the author's development of the main character, you might use *chronological* (time) *order* to organize examples that illustrate how the character changes during the course of the story. Yet another thesis might call for arrangement of information by *order of importance,* placing your most important point first or last. Then choose a method that works with your thesis.

REFERENCE NOTE: For more help with organizing ideas and details, see pages 35–38, 74, and 79–87.

Reminder

As you gather and organize your support

- identify your focus and keep it in mind
- find specific evidence to back up each major point you plan to discuss
- make sure your evidence is related to your thesis
- if necessary, find information about the author and/or the story in secondary sources
- arrange your ideas in a sensible order

WRITING ASSIGNMENT

PART 3:
Gathering and Organizing Ideas

Reread the story you have chosen, this time taking notes about the elements you intend to focus on and the points you want to make in your critical analysis. (For help, use the strategies for critical reading on pages 405–406.) Also, if you're using any secondary sources, take notes from them. Next, jot down your major points and their supporting evidence in the form of an early plan (see pages 104–105). If any part of the plan looks skimpy, go back to your sources to collect more evidence; then decide what order you will use to present your information.

INTEGRATING THE LANGUAGE ARTS

Library Link. After they have selected their stories, take students to the library to look for secondary sources about their stories. Explain that they may discover their thesis statements and plans on their own or they may get ideas from secondary sources.

A DIFFERENT APPROACH

If you do not ask your students to complete their prewriting on computers, encourage them to use a visual format to create the plans called for in **Writing Assignment: Part 3**. Illustrate on the chalkboard the technique of mapping and tell students to try this method by listing the main idea first, branching out with major points, and finally adding supporting evidence. The following diagram is an example:

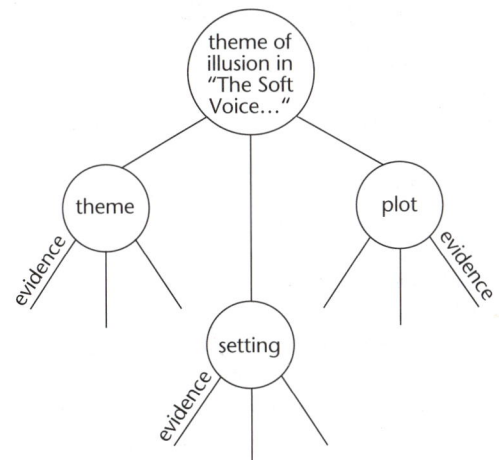

theme of illusion in "The Soft Voice…" — theme — evidence — setting — evidence — plot — evidence

413

WRITING YOUR FIRST DRAFT

TEACHING THE LESSON

Before students read **A Writer's Model**, refer them to the **Framework for a Critical Analysis** on p. 418. Because some students may have trouble applying the annotations directly to the model, you may want to discuss these annotations in class.

PROGRAM MANAGER

WRITING YOUR FIRST DRAFT

- **Instructional Support** See **Writing** in *Strategies for Writing*, p. 48.
- **Computer Guided Instruction** For additional instruction and practice with incorporating supporting evidence, as noted in the **Mechanics Hint**, see **Lesson 61** in *Language Workshop CD-ROM*.

QUOTATION FOR THE DAY

"What's a book? Everything or nothing. The eye that sees it is all." (Ralph Waldo Emerson, 1803–1882, American poet and essayist)

As students begin writing first drafts of their critical analyses, remind them that their papers should show evidence that they have read actively and analyzed the stories' literary elements.

MEETING individual NEEDS

LEP/ESL

Spanish. In Spanish, dashes are used to indicate quotations, and ellipses are used to indicate incomplete thoughts. You may want to give extra examples of the use of the punctuation rules in the **Mechanics Hint**.

Writing Your First Draft

The Structure of a Critical Analysis

When you write a literary analysis, you can use the basic structural pattern of a composition (Chapter 3), with a few special considerations:

- In your **introduction** you need to identify the work's title and author, as well as your thesis. You may also have to provide background information about the author or a brief summary of the work if it is essential to an understanding of your thesis.
- In the **body** of the essay, you need to state your major supporting points and the evidence (details and quotations from the work) you are using as proof. You will also need to explain the connection between each quotation and the major point it supports or proves. Typically, you will need one or more paragraphs to develop each major point.
- In your **conclusion** you can synthesize your ideas, perhaps summarizing your major points or restating your thesis.

MECHANICS HINT

Incorporating Supporting Evidence

The evidence you use to support your thesis statement often includes direct quotations. Follow these guidelines when quoting from a literary work or a secondary source.

1. Enclose direct quotations in quotation marks. Be sure the quotation appears in your paper exactly as it appears in the published work. Periods and commas usually go inside the closing quotation marks.
2. Use a slash (/), with a space before and after it, to indicate the end of a line of poetry.
3. Use ellipses (. . .) to indicate an omission.

Ask volunteers to read aloud the thesis statement, the first major point, and so forth.

To avoid overemphasis on mechanical aspects at this stage, reserve your discussion of the **Mechanics Hint** until after you have read and discussed **A Writer's Model** with your students.

GUIDED PRACTICE

A Writer's Model and the **Framework for a Critical Analysis** (p. 418) provide clear models for students. However, because students often have more difficulty getting started than anything else, you may want to provide further guided practice by writing a sample introduction on a transparency or on the chalkboard. Let students write drafts of ☞

Writing Your First Draft **415**

4. If the quotation is more than four typed or written lines, set it off by beginning a new line and indenting it ten spaces from the left-hand margin. Do not add quotation marks.
5. At the end of each quotation, place the page number in parentheses.

EXAMPLE **Gordimer makes the point explicitly in the opening paragraph:**

> Perhaps there was something in this of the old Eden idea; the tender human adjusting himself to himself in the soothing impersonal presence of trees and grass and earth. . . . (395–396)

☞ **REFERENCE NOTE:** For more information on using quotation marks and ellipses, see pages 935–939 and 941–943.

A Basic Framework for a Critical Analysis

The following Writer's Model is a critical analysis of "The Soft Voice of the Serpent" (pages 395–402). As you read it, see if you can identify the literary elements the writer focuses on to support the thesis statement.

A WRITER'S MODEL

A Locust in the Garden

INTRODUCTION
Title and author

Although the words <u>illusion</u> and <u>reality</u> never appear in Nadine Gordimer's "The Soft Voice of the Serpent," those two words accurately point to the theme of the story. Gordimer's "curiously human" (398) locust in the garden, with its "solemn silly face" (401), has lost a leg, just like the protagonist, but is not defeated. The locust's sudden flight from an Eden-like garden setting teaches the protagonist that he must abandon illusion and face reality. This theme

Reference to theme of story
Thesis statement

MEETING *individual* NEEDS

LESS-ADVANCED STUDENTS

Students may have difficulty incorporating quotations and examples into their critical analyses. Work closely with students by providing models that introduce quotations or that incorporate quotations smoothly into the text. Be sure that students understand that when using quotations they must keep the following points in mind:

1. You must introduce your quotation but not with an obvious phrase such as "As this quotation shows . . ."
2. Always interpret the quotation by showing how it supports your thesis or topic sentence.
3. Provide ideas to connect your quotation to other specifics.

Give examples to illustrate each of these points.

LEARNING STYLES

Auditory Learners. Students might benefit from talk-writing their drafts. Pair each student with another who will ask questions and record responses. Have one student question the other about major supporting points and about supporting quotations and details.

415

their introductions to discuss in small groups while you circulate through the room to make suggestions. Remind students to use the thesis statements that they have formulated in the prewriting stage.

INDEPENDENT PRACTICE

After you have modeled the writing of an introduction and guided students through the drafts of their introductions, give your class ample time to write the remainder of their drafts independently.

INTEGRATING THE LANGUAGE ARTS

Mechanics Link. The **Mechanics Hint** explains the use of quotation marks, the slash, and the ellipsis in quotations. However, in conjunction with your discussion of **A Writer's Model**, you may need to review with your students the use of quotations within quotations and the use of the colon to introduce quotations—especially long quotations (paragraph 2).

CRITICAL THINKING

Synthesis. The ability to paraphrase information requires students to use the critical-thinking skills of summarizing and formulating ideas in their own words. To give students practice in these skills, select several quotations from short stories and from literary criticism and ask students to paraphrase the information. Be sure to emphasize that the material must be fully paraphrased to avoid plagiarism. Encourage students to change not only vocabulary but also sentence structure and, where possible, the arrangement of ideas.

416

of illusion versus reality is brought out primarily through setting, characterization, and plot.

**BODY
Major point:
Setting**

The serpent in the story's title and the heavy emphasis on the garden setting suggest a parallel with the Old Testament story about Adam and Eve and their loss of innocence. Gordimer makes this point explicitly in the opening paragraph:

**Long quotation
from work**

> Perhaps there was something in this of the old Eden idea; the tender human adjusting himself to himself in the soothing impersonal presence of trees and grass and earth. . . . (395–396)

**Quotations from
work to support
interpretation of
garden as a
temporary shelter
from reality**

But such an Eden cannot last, either in the Bible or in the author's fictional setting, and the "tender human" (395) must eventually go "out into the stare of the world" (396).

The story alludes again and again to the sheltering comfort of the garden. The man tries to maintain an illusion that nothing serious has happened to him, that in time he will "feel as if he had always been like that" (397). The garden is his refuge against reality.

**Quotation from
work**

**Major point:
Character**

Gordimer's characterization of the man also contributes to the theme of illusion versus reality. In the garden setting, the man has plenty of time to think. What he tries to think about is anything <u>not</u> related to his missing limb. He reads to avoid considering his physical loss; and when his attention strays to "the sunken place under the rug where his leg used to be" (396), he represses the thought. His illusory hope is that he "never would realize" (397) he has lost his leg. Life will then be normal: the danger will be over.

**Quotation from
work to illustrate
how the character
is portrayed**

Paraphrase

**Quotations from
work to illustrate
character's illusions**

Throughout most of the story, the man focuses on mental avoidance. From childhood, the man remembers the flowers shaking "in vehement denial" (396). In the wheelchair, he feels the realization of loss "ready to burst" (396), but he always turns away, "just in time, back to his book" (396). He watches his wife "going" (not "walking") for tea. She is "empowered by the sun rather than her own muscles" (397). Only with the appearance

ASSESSMENT

These drafts are not final, so you will not want to grade them, although you may want to award credit for each successfully completed stage of the writing process. Use student-teacher conferences if students need individual help.

RETEACHING

You can help students to revise their thesis statements so that they suggest organizational structure by providing students with a model thesis statement such as this one:

The story _____ by _____ reveals the theme of _____ through its use of _____, _____, and _____. ☞

of the injured locust does the man begin to admit his plight. He identifies with the locust. "It's as harmless as I am," he says (400).

Major point: Plot

The twin illusions of the garden as sanctuary and of mental avoidance as therapy are shattered by the progress of the plot. Gordimer's locust in the garden (much like the Bible's serpent in Eden) is the central plot device. The maimed locust, seemingly so like the maimed man, does not give in to its apparent fate--"I'm afraid the cat'll get him," the wife says (401). The comparison fails suddenly and startlingly when the locust flies away. The reality is that the locust can still face "the stare of the world" (396). It is not fated to die or even languish because of its injury. Somehow the man in the wheelchair will have to find a way to gain the same assurance. When his wife asks him about the locust's flight, he says, "Don't be a fool," more to himself, perhaps, than to her. Reality has set in.

Quotations from work to show how reality replaces illusions

CONCLUSION Quotation from secondary source

The critic John Barkham, in reviewing Nadine Gordimer's first book of short stories, notes that "Miss Gordimer is a subtle writer who makes her points delicately and obliquely" (Barkham 176). That observation is certainly true of "The Soft Voice of the Serpent," the title story in the book Barkham is reviewing. Various interpretations of the story are possible. The one that seems the most logical is that the injured locust's whirring flight from the garden (of Eden?) shows the protagonist that he must face reality and give up his illusion of achieving wholeness without effort or pain.

Restatement of thesis

MEETING individual NEEDS

LEARNING STYLES

Visual Learners. Students might benefit from a visual representation of introductory and concluding paragraphs. The following examples are possibilities:

INTRODUCTORY PARAGRAPH

1st sent. = Author and some background

2nd sent. = Title, genre, and lead-in to thesis

3rd sent. = Thesis

1st sent. = Restatement of thesis idea

2nd sent. = Summary of three body points

3rd sent. = Generalization based on thesis

CONCLUDING PARAGRAPH

To conclude your lesson, ask five volunteers to write on the chalkboard the various elements of the **Framework for a Critical Analysis**. Ask the remainder of the class to use their textbooks to check the volunteers' work.

Instead of having students analyze short stories, you could have them apply their critical-analysis skills to poetry. They could compare two poems with the same theme (the theme of war in "The Rear-Guard" by Siegfried Sassoon and in "Dulce et Decorum Est" by Wilfred Owen), or they could show the same theme as presented by

TECHNOLOGY TIP

If computers are available, encourage students to write their drafts with word-processing programs so that they can revise and edit more easily later in the process. If students already have saved their prewriting on word processors, they can begin by fleshing out their organizational plans into complete—but not final—drafts.

TIMESAVER

Have students highlight their thesis statements and major supporting points (topic sentences) in blue and their supporting evidence (quotations, details) in yellow. You then can check their introductions, basic organizational structure, and conclusions quickly.

418   *Writing About Literature*

When you write your own literary analysis, you may wish to model your essay on this literary analysis of "The Soft Voice of the Serpent." After you have gathered and organized your critical reading notes about the literary work you plan to write about and are ready to write your own first draft, review the preceding essay's major points. You will find that it is based on the following framework.

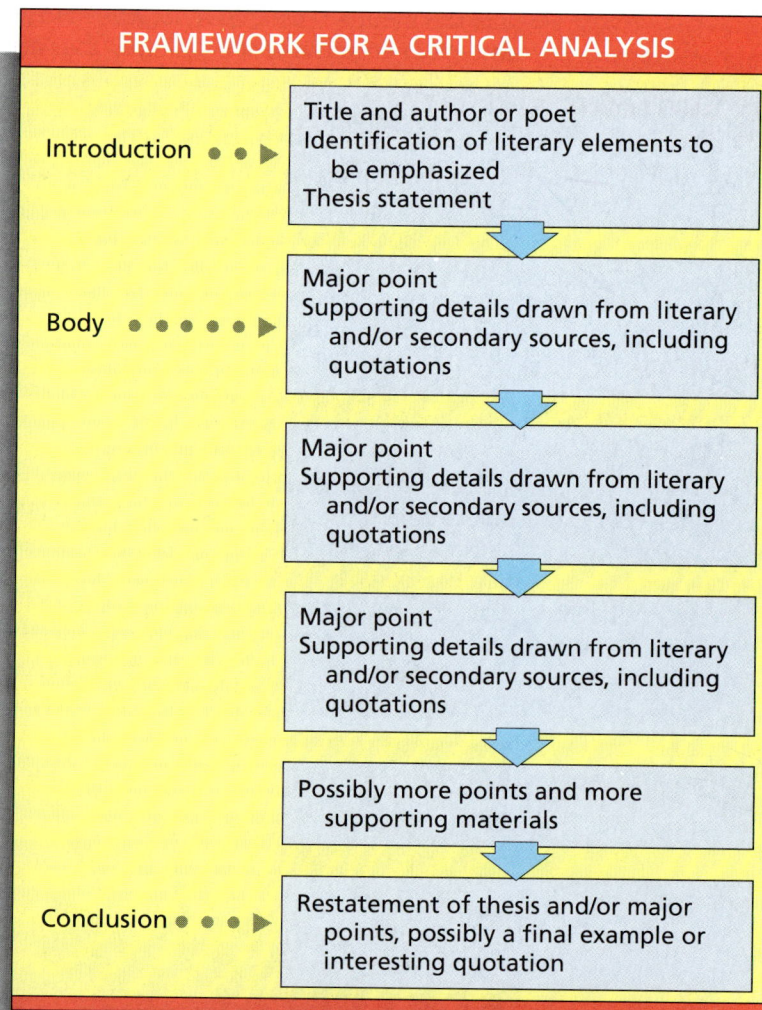

FRAMEWORK FOR A CRITICAL ANALYSIS

Introduction ● ● ▶
Title and author or poet
Identification of literary elements to be emphasized
Thesis statement

Body ● ● ● ● ● ▶
Major point
Supporting details drawn from literary and/or secondary sources, including quotations

Major point
Supporting details drawn from literary and/or secondary sources, including quotations

Major point
Supporting details drawn from literary and/or secondary sources, including quotations

Possibly more points and more supporting materials

Conclusion ● ● ● ▶
Restatement of thesis and/or major points, possibly a final example or interesting quotation

three authors (views of war as shown by Wilfred Owen, Siegfried Sassoon, and Rupert Brooke). ∎

WRITING NOTE

In writing a critical analysis of a short story, there is a strong temptation to summarize the plot of the story. Resist it. Your job is to analyze the story, not condense it. You may need some background information about the story or the author in your introduction, but you probably won't need a thorough plot summary.

It may have been dark...

It may have been stormy...

One thing, however, was for sure.. It was night.

SOMEHOW, I FEEL THAT COULD BE SHORTENED...

Peanuts reprinted by permission of United Feature Syndicate, Inc.

WRITING ASSIGNMENT

PART 4:
Writing the First Draft of Your Critical Analysis

You have the thesis statement, notes, and plan you worked on in Parts 2 and 3 of the Writing Assignment. Using those materials—as well as the pattern provided in the Writer's Model and framework—write your first draft. Don't let the task intimidate you, however. You will have a chance later to revise your draft.

? CRITICAL THINKING

Analysis. Prepare two paragraphs about a story that students have read recently. One paragraph should be a simple summary, whereas the other should be a critical analysis of one aspect of the story. Ask students to distinguish between the two types of writing and to analyze the critical analysis for its main idea and supporting evidence.

EVALUATING AND REVISING

OBJECTIVES

- To analyze a writer's revisions
- To evaluate a draft of a critical essay
- To revise a draft of a critical essay

MOTIVATION

Ask students if they have ever been in a restaurant that was so noisy they couldn't hear the people at their own table. Explain that a poorly written and poorly proofread essay includes the same interference.

PROGRAM MANAGER

EVALUATING AND REVISING

■ **Reinforcement/Reteaching** See **Revision Transparencies 17** and **18.** For suggestions on how to tie the transparencies to instruction, review teacher's notes in *Fine Art and Instructional Transparencies for Writing,* p. 127.

■ **Ongoing Assessment** For a rubric to guide assessment, see **Evaluating and Revising** in *Strategies for Writing,* p. 49.

■ **Assessment/Reflection** To assess student work and evaluate progress, see **Portfolio Forms** in *Portfolio Assessment,* pp. 5–21.

QUOTATION FOR THE DAY

"Just get it down on paper and then we'll see what to do with it." (Maxwell Perkins, 1884–1947, American editor, publisher, and journalist)

You may wish to share the quotation with the class to introduce the evaluation and revision stage of the writing process.

Evaluating and Revising

There comes a time when you have gone as far as you can go with thinking, planning, and getting your first draft on paper. And you've probably seen that drafting a critical, or literary, analysis has been like drafting any other kind of paper—you've pulled information, ideas, and details together without being overly concerned about having a perfect finished product. Now's the time, however, to think about the finished product.

No matter how good a writer you are, your first draft can be improved with revision. Use the chart on page 422 to guide your evaluation of your literary analysis. Ask yourself the questions in the left-hand column; then use the revision suggestions in the right-hand column.

EXERCISE 2 ▶ Analyzing a Writer's Revisions

Here is the first draft of the first paragraph of the writer's model on pages 415–416. In a small group, discuss the writer's reasons for making the handwritten changes shown here. Answer the questions that follow.

Although the words illusion and reality never appear in *Nadine Gordimer's* "The Soft Voice of the Serpent," those two words accurately point to *"curiously human" (398)* the theme of the story. Gordimer's locust in *"solemn silly" (401)* the garden, with its ~~funny~~ face, has lost a leg, just like the protagonist, but is not defeated. The locust's sudden flight from an Eden-like garden setting teaches the protagonist that he must abandon illusion and face reality. This theme of illusion versus reality is brought out *primarily through* ~~by the author~~ *setting, characterization, and plot* ~~all the way through the story. Illusion versus reality is an important theme.~~

                                        add

                                        add
                                        replace/add

                                        replace

                                        cut

After students understand the reasons for revising their essays, discuss the **Evaluating and Revising Critical Analysis Essays** chart on p. 422. Ask volunteers to read the questions and revision techniques. You might want to give an example to illustrate each point. After students have a clear understanding of the evaluation and revision techniques, proceed with **Exercise 2** and **Writing Assignment: Part 5**.

Although you will not want to give a final grade for students' critical analyses until they have been proofread and published, you can save time grading final copies by making notations in your grade book about content and organization.

☛

1. In the first sentence, why did the writer add the words *Nadine Gordimer's*?
2. In the second sentence, why did the writer add *"curiously human" (398)*? How does this addition help to strengthen the writer's explanation?
3. In the second sentence, why did the writer replace *its funny face* with *its "solemn silly face" (401)*?
4. In the next-to-the-last sentence, why did the writer replace the words *by the author all the way through the story* with the words *primarily through setting, characterization, and plot*?
5. Why did the writer cut the last sentence?

COMPUTER NOTE: When you print a draft to evaluate or revise, use double- or triple-spacing and a wide right margin to allow lots of space for handwritten corrections.

| WRITING ASSIGNMENT | PART 5: **Evaluating and Revising Your Essay** |

Exchange papers with a classmate to evaluate each other's first drafts. Using the chart on page 422 as a guide, make specific suggestions for changes and corrections. When you get your own paper back, think about your classmate's evaluations. Make whatever changes you think will improve your essay.

ANSWERS
Exercise 2

1. The introduction should state the complete name of the author and the title of the work. The unrevised paragraph gives only the last name of the author.

2. The added quotation helps to strengthen the writer's connection between the locust and the protagonist.

3. The quotation about the locust is more accurate and more clearly connected with the protagonist.

4. The addition of "primarily through setting, characterization, and plot" provides a clear structure for the development of the essay.

5. It is obvious and redundant. The theme has already been given.

TECHNOLOGY TIP

Remind students that they can change margins and line spacing at any time by selecting text and applying the commands that affect margins and line spacing. They don't have to worry about margins and spacing while they are busy writing their drafts.

Write on the chalkboard the following list that is based on the evaluation and revision chart:

1. Introduction
2. Thesis statement
3. Major points
4. Body
5. Organization
6. Conclusion

Ask students to explain briefly what aspects of each element should be evaluated and how these aspects can be revised. ■

A DIFFERENT APPROACH

To help students realize that revision is necessary for all writers, share with the class—perhaps on a transparency—a page or two of one of your own revised manuscripts. Point out that revising doesn't mean that the draft was wrong or that the writing was bad but that the process is not finished.

COOPERATIVE LEARNING

By evaluating their essays in pairs or small groups, students can get helpful feedback for their revisions. Organize groups so that each contains students of mixed abilities. Ask students to follow closely the revision chart but to give written evidence from the essays to support each answer. You may even make copies of the chart and have group members evaluate their classmates' papers on separate copies of the chart before discussing the revisions.

EVALUATING AND REVISING CRITICAL ANALYSIS ESSAYS

EVALUATION GUIDE	REVISION TECHNIQUE
1 Does the introduction identify the title and author and give necessary background information?	**Add** the title and author; add any interesting, relevant information about the author and work, as necessary, to help readers understand your analysis.
2 Does a clear and precise thesis statement appear in the introduction? Does it clearly state the main idea and the elements to be discussed?	**Add** a thesis statement or **replace** the existing one. **Add** the elements, or **reorder** them if they do not match the organization of the essay.
3 Does the essay identify major points that support the thesis?	**Add** statements identifying the relationship between the evidence you have gathered and your thesis about the story.
4 Does the body give ample supporting evidence? Is the evidence specific and relevant?	**Add** evidence from the literary work or from secondary sources. **Cut** useless or repetitious evidence.
5 Is the organization of the essay clear and consistent?	**Reorder** ideas and evidence to follow a sensible order, such as chronological order or order of importance.
6 Does the conclusion effectively reinforce the thesis of the essay?	**Add** a sentence or sentences to summarize the main points or restate your thesis about the work.

PROOFREADING AND PUBLISHING

OBJECTIVES
- To proofread a critical literary analysis
- To prepare a critical analysis for publication

TEACHING THE LESSON

You may want to begin your lesson by showing students a paragraph from a critical analysis that contains several errors in grammar, usage, and mechanics. Be sure to include errors in the use of tense. Ask students how effective such a paragraph published in a library source would be. ☞

Proofreading and Publishing

Proofreading.   Before you make the final, clean copy of your critical analysis essay, check for errors in spelling, capitalization, punctuation, grammar, and usage.

WRITING NOTE

To refer to events in a work of literature, you often use the *literary* (sometimes called *historical*) *present* tense. You use the present tense because a work of literature is considered to be alive, existing in the present. (See pages 791–792.)

EXAMPLE   Hamlet broods about what to do.

Publishing.   There are many ways to publish your paper so that it reaches a wider audience. Here are two possibilities:

- Ask your teacher to help you locate reading groups within your community. Many such groups are organized by places such as bookstores. Try getting in touch with one such group to see whether its members will consider reading the story you have analyzed. If the response is favorable, attend a meeting and share your analysis.
- Many online forums are devoted to discussions of works by different authors. Search the Internet for a listserv (e-mail list), newsgroup, or other discussion group that focuses on the author whose work you have analyzed, and offer to post your essay to the group.

WRITING ASSIGNMENT

PART 6:
Proofreading and Publishing Your Essay

Search diligently for errors. Reread your essay word for word, making sure you haven't left out any words or written the same word twice in a row—*the the*, for example. When you have corrected every mistake you can find, publish your essay, using one of the suggestions you have just read or an idea of your own.

PROGRAM MANAGER

PROOFREADING AND PUBLISHING

- **Instructional Support** For a chart students may use to evaluate their proofreading progress, see *Proofreading* in *Strategies for Writing,* p. 50.
- **Independent Practice/ Reteaching** See **Proofreading Practice: The Literary Present** in *Strategies for Writing,* p. 51.
- **Assessment/Reflection** See **Portfolio Forms** in *Portfolio Assessment,* pp. 22–25.

QUOTATION FOR THE DAY

"One has to dismount from an idea, and get into the saddle again, at every parenthesis." (Oliver Wendell Holmes, 1809–1894, American physician, professor, and man of letters)

MEETING individual NEEDS

LEP/ESL

General Strategies. You could help students by making initial contacts for them with appropriate groups, either directly or through the parents of students in your class.

INTEGRATING THE LANGUAGE ARTS

Speaking Link. Explain that to share their ideas and to earn promotions, college professors are often encouraged to read critical papers before groups of their colleagues. Panels of from three to five professional presentations are set up, with each separate presentation occurring within a prescribed time allotment of ten to twenty minutes.

Ask a group of students to serve as a planning committee to read student analyses and to select four or five of the best ones for a "professional" reading for the rest of the class. Then, help your committee to arrange the papers in the best order for presentation, to write acceptance letters and rejection letters politely explaining the choice, and to allot specific time limits to each presentation.

Before the reading, remind students to practice reading their papers, to time themselves, and to look up from their papers at the audience during the reading.

TEACHING NOTE

Encourage the class to spend time on their reflections, rather than dashing off quick answers to the prompts. Remind students that their reflections help to mark major milestones in the development of their writing.

Refer students to the **Writing Note** and spend some time discussing the use of the literary present tense. Then, ask the class to help you proofread and correct the paragraph. Make sure that students understand the reason for using the literary present and the importance of consistency in its usage.

You may want to assess not only the completed papers but also the processes that students have followed. That is, you may want to check to be sure that students have taken group responsibilities seriously in helping partners or group members evaluate, revise, and proofread. To do this, take up not only final versions but also drafts and written suggestions.

Reflecting on Your Writing

If you plan to put your essay in your **portfolio,** date it and include a note of reflection that answers the following questions.

- Was it more difficult to develop your thesis or to organize your ideas in an effective order? Why?
- Did you find it more challenging to write about literature than to write about a real-life issue or situation? Explain your answer.
- What did you learn about the story you analyzed when writing about it?

A STUDENT MODEL

Robert Browning, an English poet of the Victorian Period, mastered the dramatic monologue, a poem in which the speaker is clearly someone other than the poet. In the following essay, Kerry Cookson, who attends Oak Ridge High School in Orlando, Florida, analyzes the use of first-person point of view in Browning's "Porphyria's Lover."

"Porphyria's Lover"
by Kerry Cookson

The speaker in "Porphyria's Lover," by Robert Browning, is not of sound mind. Because of this, the first-person point of view is ideal for revealing the speaker's insanity. The speaker proves his psychosis through his actions, his motives, and his description of the weather.

First of all, the speaker is sitting in the dark and cold. He is doing absolutely nothing. Even when his lover walks through the door and embraces him, he doesn't move. However, because

Have students compare their first drafts to their final drafts and note the changes that took place during the writing process. You may want to list some of the most common changes on the chalkboard. ■

of Porphyria's embrace--her show of love--the speaker comes to the realization that Porphyria loves him. He says, "at last I knew / Porphyria worshiped me." To hold onto this moment, the speaker strangles Porphyria. These actions show clearly that he can't be in his right mind. The speaker's tone is so matter-of-fact and nonchalant that we see his madness clearly when he says, "and all her hair / In one long yellow string I wound / Three times her little throat around, / And strangled her." If the poem were written in the third person, this particular statement wouldn't reveal the speaker's true feelings.

The first-person point of view also allows the speaker to reveal that his motives are insane. He kills the woman he loves just so he can capture the moment. "That moment she was mine," he says, but he doesn't feel he can keep her love forever if she's alive. He wants to dominate Porphyria. His jealousy overtakes his being.

Finally, through his description of the weather, the speaker proves himself insane: "The rain set early in tonight, / The sullen wind was soon awake." His use of the word sullen depicts his brooding resentment. He resents Porphyria for not giving up her life to please and obey him. Describing the wind, he says, "It tore the elm-tops down for spite." The speaker's spite is his malicious ill-will to hurt others.

Throughout this poem, the speaker shows that he is quite psychotic. Because "Porphyria's Lover" is written in the first person, the speaker is able to prove his insanity in his actions, motives, and descriptions of the weather.

A STUDENT MODEL
Evaluation

1. Kerry's introduction includes the title, the author, interesting background, and a clear, precise thesis statement.

2. Kerry introduces each body paragraph with a topic sentence that directly relates to the thesis and that identifies each major body point.

3. In each body paragraph, Kerry gives specific, relevant evidence to support the thesis. For example, to support the idea that the weather description reinforces the speaker's psychosis, Kerry quotes, "The rain set early in tonight,/ The sullen wind was soon awake."

4. The essay's organization is clear and consistent; Kerry uses order of importance and ends with what she believes is her strongest body point.

"[The] most important tribute
any human being can pay
to a poem or a piece of prose
he or she really loves...
is to learn it by heart.

Not by brain, by heart;
the expression is vital."

GEORGE STEINER

SELECTION AMENDMENT
Description of change: excerpted
Rationale: to focus on the concept of literature responses presented in this chapter

TEACHING THE LESSON

Students will enjoy creating their parodies more—and will probably create better ones—if you allow them to work in pairs or groups. To get them started, conduct a class brainstorming session and list on the chalkboard the names of writers and works that have a distinctive style. For example, William Blake, T. S. Eliot, Edgar Allan Poe, Robert

QUOTATION FOR THE DAY

"Wit has a deadly aim and it is possible to prick a large pretense with a small pin." (Marya Mannes, 1904–1990, American essayist and journalist)

Share this quotation with your class and discuss the meaning and importance of wit for writing parodies. You might also ask your students if they agree with Mannes. Is it possible that wit has as much power as the quotation implies?

MEETING
individual
NEEDS

LEP/ESL

General Strategies. To write parodies successfully, students need to choose works suitable for being parodied. You can help English-language learners by suggesting works in English suitable for parody or by allowing students to parody in English works written in their native languages.

426

WRITING WORKSHOP

Parody

You have probably heard the truism "Imitation is the sincerest form of flattery." But the truth of that statement depends on the imitator's attitude: Is it genuinely respectful or comically mocking? In literature, a **parody** is a humorous imitation of a work or a style. Like a critical analysis, a parody is a response to literature, but it makes its point through ridicule—soft or sharp—and exaggerated mimicry.

Parody is an ancient form, going back at least to the Greek dramatist Aristophanes in the fifth century B.C. However, it's alive and well today: in *Saturday Night Live*'s and *Mad Magazine*'s parodies of commercials, sitcoms, and movies; in comedians' impressions of politicians, singers, and songs; in *The Naked Gun*'s parody of hard-boiled, hard-shooting cop movies. In all of these examples, the parodists make you laugh at their targets by exaggerating distinctive elements, whether language, mannerisms, characters, or subject matter.

A literary parody may imitate a particular work, writer, or school of writing. Miguel de Cervantes parodied courtly romances in *Don Quixote*. E. B. White parodied Ernest Hemingway's novel *Across the River and into the Trees* (and Hemingway's fiction in general) in "Across the Street and into the Grill." And in the following poem, George A. Strong parodies Henry Wadsworth Longfellow's well-known poem *The Song of Hiawatha*. Read aloud Longfellow's verse and then Strong's parody, and think about two questions: How does Strong make absolutely sure you'll "get" the parody? How does he make you laugh?

Frost, and Robert Burns all have distinctive styles. Especially distinctive works such as "The Love Song of J. Alfred Prufrock," "The Lamb," and "The Raven" are excellent choices for parody. (In fact, to get students started on a parody of "The Raven," you might read to them part of C. L. Edson's "Ravin's of Piute Poet Poe" from *The Brand-X Anthology of Poetry*.)

Guide students by duplicating a stanza of a poem to be parodied, but include blanks for several key words and phrases. Then, work with students to fill in the blanks with humorous words and phrases.

☞

from The Song of Hiawatha
by Henry Wadsworth Longfellow

He had mittens, Minjekahwun,
Magic mittens made of
    deer-skin;
When upon his hands he wore
    them,
He could smite the rocks
    asunder,
He could grind them into
    powder.
He had moccasins enchanted,
Magic moccasins of deer-skin;
When he bound them round
    his ankles,
When upon his feet he tied
    them,
At each stride a mile he
    measured!

The Modern Hiawatha
by George A. Strong

When he killed the Mudjokivis,
Of the skin he made him
    mittens,
Made them with the fur side
    inside,
Made them with the skin side
    outside,
He, to get the warm side inside,
Put the inside skin side outside;
He, to get the cold side outside,
Put the warm side fur side inside.
That's why he put the fur side
    inside,
Why he put the skin side outside,
Why he turned them inside
    outside.

◈ INTEGRATING THE LANGUAGE ARTS

Literature Link. You may want to use this opportunity to teach the qualities of parody in a mock epic such as *The Rape of the Lock* by Alexander Pope. Explain that a mock epic uses the traditional epic devices in a humorous way. You could show the following elements of an epic and ask your students to find how Pope has incorporated them into his mock epic:

1. invocation to a muse
2. statement of subject
3. gods' intervening
4. battles
5. hero or heroine reflecting society's values
6. elevated language

SELECTION AMENDMENT
Description of change: excerpted
Rationale: to focus on the concept of parody presented in this chapter

428

ANSWERS
Writing Workshop Questions

1. Longfellow repeats the words *mittens* and *moccasins,* the phrases "He had ____" and "He could ____," and clauses beginning with *when.* In addition, he alliterates the sound of *m.*

2. Hiawatha's magical mittens give him the power to "smite the rocks asunder" and "grind them into powder." Although Strong's emphatic repetition suggests something extraordinary about his subject, the mittens in his parody are quite ordinary. In fact, the repetition and reversal of "fur side" and "skin side," "inside" and "outside" becomes ridiculously comic—especially with the final pun "inside/outside."

3. Like many modern readers, Strong seems to read *Hiawatha* as exaggerated, sentimental, and romantic, but his parody is more amusing than interpretive. From this limited reading of *Hiawatha,* most students will probably agree with Strong; however, students who have studied *Hiawatha* more thoroughly may see more merit in the poem than is implied in the parody.

1. Since a parody has to be a close imitation, any good parody of a poem will duplicate its sounds. Besides copying *The Song of Hiawatha*'s singsong rhythm, Strong focuses on the many repetitions of words and phrases. What are some of Longfellow's repetitions? How does Strong exaggerate this style?

2. Often a parody's comedy involves applying the writer's style (recognizable but exaggerated) to a considerably "lowered" subject matter. How does Strong make fun of the *content* of *The Song of Hiawatha*?

3. What would you say is Strong's opinion of *The Song of Hiawatha*? Do you agree? Does Strong make you see this famous poem in a new way, or is his parody simply amusing and entertaining? Explain.

Writing a Literary Parody

Prewriting. Now, think of a writer or literary style that you could enjoy making fun of. Look through school texts and your own library. Perhaps you'll choose a favorite author, someone whose works and ways with words you know inside out or a form, like detective fiction, that seems full of comic possibilities.

Then, ask yourself (1) *What makes this work, writer, or form distinctive?* and (2) *How can I make these elements humorous?* The charts on pages 403–405 will help you focus on important literary elements. When you've settled on the main elements of your parody, plan your story, poem, or play, keeping it to a manageable length.

Writing, Evaluating, and Revising. Your dual goal, remember, is to imitate and be humorous. Whether you're focusing on prose or poetic style, characters, dialogue, or plot, you want readers to immediately recognize the original *but* see it in a new way. Use verbal exaggeration, laughable contrasts, and ridiculous twists. When you have a draft, definitely try it out on others, perhaps by reading it aloud. Do they instantly see the parody? Are they laughing? Use their suggestions and your own review to sharpen the comedy and mimicry.

Proofreading and Publishing. Correct errors, and make a clean copy of your parody. If several writers in your class have parodied brief poems, you could create a book with the original poems and parodies appearing on facing pages. Conduct live performances. You can emphasize the humor in a poem through your delivery: voice, gestures, facial expressions, and timing.

If you want to include your parody in your **portfolio**, remember to date it and write a reflection. Which aspects of the original work did you choose to parody? Why? What did you learn about writing parody by reading or listening to your classmates' work?

Shoe reprinted by permission: Tribune Media Services.

TIMESAVER

To save yourself time in looking up originals to check against students' parodies, have students turn in original works that they are parodying, along with their parodies.

A DIFFERENT APPROACH

You may want to allow students to apply the technique of parody to the lyrics of popular songs or to the style of popular movie or television characters such as E.T., Rocky, or Murphy Brown.

TEACHING NOTE

Ask students to write serious reflections on their parody assignments, but then offer them the opportunity to write parodies of the process of writing a parody, as well. Allow time for students to share their writing-process parodies with the class.

SPEAKING AND LISTENING

Teaching Strategies

To create your review teams, pair students and have each pair select a work to review. Each pair might list two or three movies that they would like to review and then discuss the list before making a final choice.

The six guidelines on the next page provide excellent guidance for your students. You may want to ask students to write out their reviews. Students who are nervous about oral reviews may want to have written scripts, but having each student use a simple outline or note cards promotes spontaneity.

Remind students that the tone of their reviews is to be more informal than that of their critical analyses. If possible, videotape the reviews and play them for other classes.

GUIDELINES

In evaluating your students' team reviews, you will want to be sure that the students in each team have contributed equally to the review and that they have kept their audience—their classmates—in mind in making their informal oral presentations.

430

MAKING CONNECTIONS

SPEAKING AND LISTENING

A Critical Review

What Amy Taubin did in this chapter's opening selection—discuss a movie and advise people whether to see it—is something you have no doubt done, too. You are offering at least a casual critical review whenever you say, "I kept my eyes closed through at least half of *A Teenage Nightmare Too Horrible to Watch.* Especially the anteater scenes. You've got to see it!"

In a real review, you do the same thing but more thoroughly: You combine a critical analysis of a work's elements— similar to the literary analysis you've done—with an evaluation, or judgment, about whether it's worth watching or reading. Readers also rely on you to give a brief summary or description of the work, without giving away too much.

Some movie critics like Joel Siegel do reviews on television or online. Because perceptions of and judgments about art frequently vary, some popular movie review programs on television feature two reviewers. For example, Roger Ebert and Gene Siskel review the same film independently and then surprise each other with their face-to-face reviews. Whether sparks fly or two thumbs go up or down harmoniously is part of the viewer's fun.

Joel Siegel

Gene Siskel and
Roger Ebert

**WRITING A CRITICAL
ANALYSIS OF A POEM
OBJECTIVES**

- To use the writing process to write a critical analysis of a poem
- To present an oral reading of a poem and a critical analysis

Work with a partner to do a team review of a movie, play, or television special. Use these guidelines:

1. Set a time limit of three to five minutes for each review.
2. Write your review in a more informal style than your critical analysis for this chapter. As a rule, reviews are more casual, using the first-person viewpoint and colloquial language.
3. In your introduction, identify the film, program, or play; the writer, director, and main actors; and the general plot or theme.
4. Make the analysis of elements the meat of your review, with as many supporting details and examples as possible.
5. Close with your overall judgment of the work, thumbs up or thumbs down, strong points and weak.
6. After both reviews, take thirty to forty-five seconds for a final comment, reacting to your partner's review.

EVALUATING LITERATURE

Writing a Critical Analysis of a Poem

Everything you've done in writing about a short story prepares you well for writing about a poem, but of course there are differences between prose and poetry. The two you may immediately think of (with either pleasure or a bit of anxiety) are poetry's *music* and its often *figurative, highly compressed language:* The sounds and syntax of poetry *are* unique. Here are two tips to add to your strategies for reading a poem.

- Read a poem aloud. Use the punctuation to hear its rhythm; let its sounds linger in your mouth. [Remember: Sound is physical.]
- Paraphrase passages to clarify meanings. You can put figures of speech into your own words or change unusual word order into everyday speech patterns. Your paraphrases will *not* be poetry, but they can help you unravel difficulties and come back to the poetry.

Try writing a critical analysis of a poem you have read and found interesting. Use the chart of poetry elements on pages 403–404 to study the poem, and then determine what you will

**WRITING A CRITICAL
ANALYSIS OF A POEM
Teaching Strategies**

Explain to your students that critical analyses of poems may be structured in several ways: structure, literary elements, or themes. For example, an analysis of the Shakespearean sonnet "That Time of Year" might be organized into five paragraphs—an introduction, a paragraph for each of the three stanzas, and a conclusion discussing the final couplet in relation to the remainder of the poem. A second analysis of this same poem could contain an introduction with a thesis statement about how various literary elements reveal the theme; separate paragraphs on the elements of diction, figures of speech, imagery, sounds, and symbolism; and a conclusion that reinforces how the poem reveals the theme. And a third analysis of this poem could move from an introduction to two or three body paragraphs developing different themes or interpretations and then to a conclusion.

Remind students to include specific quotations from the poems to support their interpretative points. Review methods of incorporating and punctuating lines of poetry. You also may want to model the technique of paraphrasing before students begin to write.

GUIDELINES

In evaluating each student's critical analysis of a poem, look for a clear thesis statement, a logical organization, and specific support (quotations and paraphrases).

USING DEDUCTIVE REASONING

Teaching Strategies

Use the examples on this page to illustrate the concepts of major premise, minor premise, and conclusion. You may want to work with the class to create an example of this reasoning process like the ones on this page.

TEACHING NOTE

Student Self-Evaluation

If you choose to have students give oral presentations of their critical analyses in class, you may want to follow up by asking them to write brief self-evaluations. Each student should rate his or her preparation and delivery based on the following items: topic and purpose, introduction, development, conclusion, verbal delivery, nonverbal delivery, and language.

Students may find the checklist format of **Evaluating a Speech** on p. 38 of *Portfolio Assessment* helpful in completing their self-evaluations.

---

focus on in your analysis. Your focus will, of course, be dependent on the poem you choose, but here are some examples:

- how sound effects create a specific tone
- what the images show you about the speaker's emotions
- how figurative language helps develop the poem's theme

After you have determined the focus of your analysis, you can follow the same process you used to write an analysis of a story—identify a thesis, find and organize support, write, evaluate and revise, proofread and publish. Since poetry is meant to be read aloud, you might want to combine an oral reading of your poem with an oral presentation of your analysis.

EVALUATING LITERATURE

Using Deductive Reasoning

At the beginning of this chapter you read a review of *Hamlet*, and in one of the other connections, you did a team review of a movie, play, or television show. One characteristic of a review is that it includes an evaluation, or judgment, of the work. Such evaluations are examples of **deductive reasoning.** (See pages 276–277, for information about inductive reasoning.)

In deductive reasoning, you start with a general rule or general knowledge, and then you apply it to a specific situation or instance. Finally, you draw a conclusion about that specific instance. A classic deductive argument is stated in the form of a *syllogism:*

Major Premise All seniors on the soccer team will receive a letter jacket.
Minor Premise Danielle is a senior on the soccer team.
Conclusion Danielle will receive a letter jacket.

Major Premise All animals need water.
Minor Premise Camels are animals.
Conclusion Camels need water.

Major Premise It is the duty of every American citizen eighteen and older to vote in every election.
Minor Premise Juan Rivera is an eighteen-year-old American citizen.
Conclusion It is Juan Rivera's duty to vote in every election.

When you evaluate something—whether it is a work of literature, a movie, or a CD player—you use a similar reasoning process. For example:

Major Premise A good short story has a tight plot and believable characters.

Minor Premise Eudora Welty's "A Worn Path" has a tight plot and believable characters.

Conclusion "A Worn Path" is a good story.

GUIDELINES

Evaluate students' examples of deductive reasoning on the basis of the validity of the major premises and the logic supporting those premises.

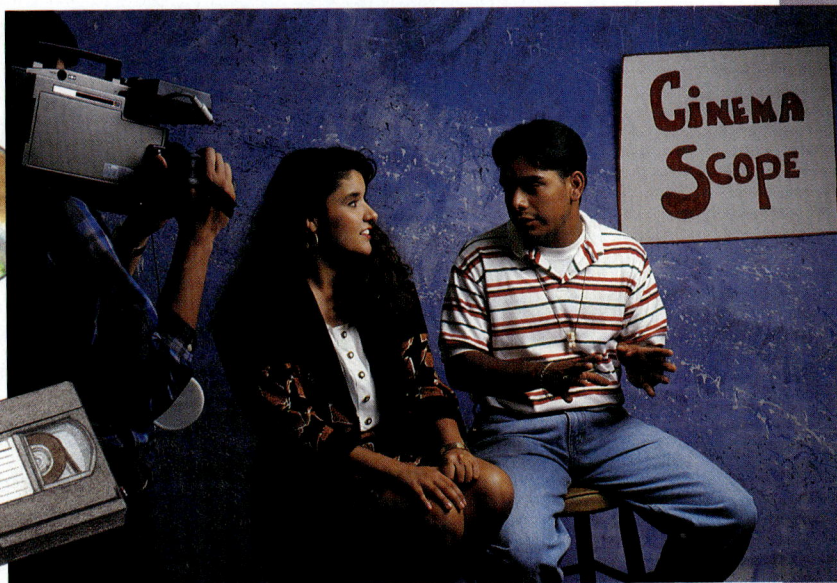

Keep in mind two important points about deductive thinking: (1) If your major premise is incorrect, your conclusion will be incorrect, and (2) if your readers don't agree with your major premise, they may not agree with your conclusion.

Now get together with two classmates and try some deductive thinking. Begin by selecting two poems to evaluate. Then review the elements of poetry on pages 403–404 and use them, as well as your own experience with poetry, to determine a major premise, or general rule, about the characteristics of good poetry. After you have agreed on your major premise, apply it to each poem, and then draw a conclusion about each poem. State your deductive thinking in the form of two syllogisms and share them with the rest of your class.

Chapter 11

WRITING A RESEARCH PAPER

OBJECTIVES

- To find and evaluate a research topic
- To develop research questions, take notes for a report, and evaluate and list sources
- To write a thesis statement and to create a working outline
- To write a draft of a research report complete with citations and a Works Cited page
- To evaluate, revise, proofread, and publish a research paper

WRITING-IN-PROGRESS ASSIGNMENTS

Major Assignment: Writing a research paper
Cumulative Writing Assignments: The chart below shows the sequence of cumulative assignments that will guide students as they write a research paper. These Writing Assignments form the instructional core of Chapter 11.

PREWRITING

WRITING ASSIGNMENT
- Part 1: Choosing a Limited Topic p. 443
- Part 2: Finding, Evaluating, and Listing Sources of Information p. 451
- Part 3: Taking Notes for Your Report p. 456
- Part 4: Writing a Thesis Statement and Outlining p. 461

WRITING YOUR FIRST DRAFT

WRITING ASSIGNMENT
- Part 5: Writing Your First Draft p. 476

EVALUATING AND REVISING

WRITING ASSIGNMENT
- Part 6: Evaluating and Revising Your Report p. 483

PROOFREADING AND PUBLISHING

WRITING ASSIGNMENT
- Part 7: Proofreading and Publishing Your Report p. 484

In addition, exercises 1–5 provide practice in evaluating topics for research, analyzing the audience for your report, taking notes, using sources, and analyzing a writer's revisions.

cross CURRICULUM
Video Research Project

Journalists who work for television news magazines use the research strategies presented in Chapter 11. They research and contact sources, conduct interviews, check their facts and references, and write scripts of their reports. Have students work in teams of four to research and report on a local event, personality, or problem. Students will have to set up and conduct interviews, record their findings, learn to record and edit videotape, and draft a five- to seven-minute script for a report that includes a Works Cited page.

- **Video Format Style** Have students watch excerpts from news reports on local or national television news programs. Students should pay attention to the information presented by the reporters, how reporters handle interviews, how pictures are used to capture a scene, how picture and voice are coordinated, and how the reporters speak.

- **Filming Interviews** Have students review pp. 1040–1041 for tips on interviewing. During the taping of the interviews, students should jot down any thoughts or questions that come to mind. Also, students may want to have a partner work the videocamera so that they can concentrate on conducting the interview.

- **Scripting** Students should review all the material they have gathered on videotape and in their notes. Then, they should begin to organize their information and script their reports. Suggest that students use a storyboard format to write their scripts and keep close watch of the time their scripts run. Students should review pp. 476–480 for instruction on preparing a Works Cited page.

- **Presentation** If students have access to a school or local television station, encourage them to submit their reports. Or have students present a mock news broadcast in class. Ask a journalism teacher or local newscaster to serve as the anchor for students' reports.

INTEGRATING THE LANGUAGE ARTS

SELECTION	READING AND LITERATURE	WRITING AND CRITICAL THINKING	LANGUAGE AND SYNTAX	SPEAKING, LISTENING, AND OTHER EXPRESSION SKILLS
• from **"Elephant Talk"** by Katharine Payne pp. 436–438 • from **Native American Heritage** by Merwyn S. Garbarino and Robert F. Sasso p. 453 • from **"Snatching Scientific Secrets from the Hippo's Gaping Jaws"** by David M. Schwartz pp. 454–456	• Responding personally to literature p. 438 • Reading for specific information pp. 438, 454–456 • Analyzing the content and organization of a report p. 438 • Identifying details pp. 454–456 • Researching and reading about a historical figure p. 493	• Locating, evaluating, and reading sources and taking notes pp. 451, 454–456, 458–459, 488–490 • Evaluating information to document pp. 458–459 • Analyzing graphs and charts pp. 458–459 • Organizing information and developing an outline p. 461 • Writing a first draft of a report, including parenthetical citations p. 476 • Preparing a Works Cited list p. 476 • Reflecting on writing for portfolio selections p. 484 • Writing a report on an unsolved mystery pp. 488–490 • Writing a report on experimental research pp. 491–492 • Researching the life of a historical figure p. 493	• Using direct quotations pp. 454–456, 475–476 • Proofreading for errors in grammar, usage, and mechanics pp. 456, 484, 490 • Using summaries, paraphrases, and parenthetical citations pp. 475–476 • Editing citations and a Works Cited list p. 484	• Discussing and evaluating topics p. 443 • Working with classmates to analyze audience p. 445 • Working with classmates to use source information correctly pp. 475–476 • Discussing unsolved mysteries pp. 488–490 • Presenting an oral report p. 490 • Working with classmates to conduct experimental research pp. 491–492 • Creating visuals p. 492 • Impersonating a historical figure p. 493

SUGGESTED INTEGRATED UNIT PLAN

This unit plan suggests how to integrate the major strands of the language arts with this chapter.

The suggested literary selections are examples of writing that required research. If you begin with this chapter on writing a research paper or with the suggested nonfiction selections, you should focus on the use of researched material in writing. You can then integrate speaking/listening and language concepts with both the writing and the literature.

Common Characteristics

- Content is factual and comprehensive
- Precise language that is neutral and unbiased
- Documentation of facts
- Quotations as documentation of supporting ideas
- Technical terms with definitions
- Use of third person to maintain objectivity
- Organization of ideas usually from least to most important

Writing
Research paper

UNIT FOCUS
RESEARCHED WRITING

Language
Mechanics and style

- Quotation marks
- Italicizing titles
- Parentheses
- Varied sentence style
- Bibliographic style

Speaking/Listening

- Presenting an oral report
- Role playing a historical character and answer interview questions
- Interviewing a historical character

Literature
Selections such as

- from *A History of the English Church and People* Bede, the Venerable
- "Shakespeare's Sister" Virginia Woolf
- *In Patagonia* Bruce Chatwin

CHAPTER 11: WRITING A RESEARCH PAPER

Use this guide to create an instructional plan that addresses the individual needs of your students. Assignments accompanied by the following symbol (*) may be completed out of class. Times given for pacing lessons are estimated.

CHAPTER PLANNING GUIDE—PUPIL'S EDITION

LESSONS	LITERARY MODEL pp. 436–438 from "Elephant Talk" by Katharine Payne	PREWRITING pp. 440–461	
		Generating Ideas	Gathering/Organizing
DEVELOPMENTAL PROGRAM	🕐 **20–25 minutes** • Read model aloud to students and answer questions on p. 438 as a class.	🕐 **90–95 minutes** • Main Assignment: Looking Ahead p. 439 • Finding a Topic pp. 440–442 • Exercises 1, 2 pp. 443*, 445 • Writing Assignment: Parts 1, 2 pp. 443, 451* • Developing a Plan pp. 444–450	🕐 **55–60 minutes** • Researching Your Topic pp. 452–461 • Exercise 3 pp. 454–456 • Writing Assignment: Parts 3, 4 pp. 456, 461* • Critical Thinking pp. 456–459* • Writing Note p. 459
CORE PROGRAM	🕐 **15–20 minutes** • Have students read the model in pairs and answer questions on p. 438.	🕐 **55–60 minutes** • Main Assignment: Looking Ahead p. 439 • Charts pp. 440–441, 442, 446–447 • Writing Assignment: Parts 1, 2 pp. 443, 451* • Guidelines p. 450 • Reminder p. 451	🕐 **40–45 minutes** • Guidelines p. 453 • Exercise 3 pp. 454–456* • Writing Assignment: Parts 3, 4 pp. 456, 461* • Critical Thinking pp. 456–459* • Writing Note p. 459 • Writing a Thesis Statement/Making an Outline pp. 459–461*
ACCELERATED PROGRAM	🕐 **15–20 minutes** • Assign students to read model independently and take notes in Reader's Logs	🕐 **45–50 minutes** • Main Assignment: Looking Ahead p. 439 • Charts pp. 440–441, 442, 446–447 • Writing Assignment: Parts 1, 2 pp. 443, 451* • Guidelines p. 450 • Reminder p. 451	🕐 **30–35 minutes** • Guidelines p. 453 • Writing Assignment: Parts 3, 4 pp. 456, 461* • Critical Thinking pp. 456–459* • Writing Note p. 459 • Writing a Thesis Statement/Making an Outline pp. 459–461*

CHAPTER PLANNING GUIDE—PROGRAM RESOURCES

	LITERARY MODEL	PREWRITING
PRINT	• Reading Master 11, *Practice for Assessment in Reading* p. 11	• Prewriting 1–2, *Strategies for Writing* pp. 54–55
MEDIA	• Fine Art Transparency 8: *Transparency Binder*	• Graphic Organizers 19–20, *Transparency Binder* • *Writer's Workshop 2:* Informative Report

WRITING pp. 462–480	EVALUATING AND REVISING pp. 481–483	PROOFREADING AND PUBLISHING pp. 484–487
⏱ **90–95 minutes** • Writing pp. 462–463 • Writer's Model pp. 463–469 • Using Quotations/Documenting pp. 470–475 • Exercise 4 pp. 475–476 • Writing Assignment: Part 5 p. 476*	⏱ **45–50 minutes** • Evaluating and Revising pp. 481–482 • Exercise 5 p. 481* • Writing Assignment: Part 6 p. 483	⏱ **50–55 minutes** • Proofreading and Publishing p. 484 • Writing Assignment: Part 7 p. 484 • Reflecting p. 484 • A Student Model pp. 485–487
⏱ **65–70 minutes** • Charts pp. 462, 473, 474, 477–480 • Writer's Model pp. 463–469* • Guidelines pp. 470–471, 475 • Exercise 4 pp. 475–476 • Writing Assignment: Part 5 p. 476*	⏱ **40–45 minutes** • Exercise 5 p. 481* • Guidelines p. 482 • Grammar Hint p. 483 • Writing Assignment: Part 6 p. 483	⏱ **35–40 minutes** • Writing Assignment: Part 7 p. 484 • Reflecting p. 484 • A Student Model pp. 485–487*
⏱ **55–60 minutes** • Charts pp. 462, 473, 474, 477–480 • Writer's Model pp. 463–469* • Guidelines pp. 470–471, 475 • Writing Note p. 474 • Writing Assignment: Part 5 p. 476*	⏱ **35–40 minutes** • Guidelines p. 482 • Writing Assignment: Part 6 p. 483	⏱ **30–35 minutes** • Writing Assignment: Part 7 p. 484 • Reflecting p. 484

WRITING	EVALUATING AND REVISING	PROOFREADING AND PUBLISHING
• Writing, *Strategies for Writing* p. 56	• Evaluating and Revising, *Strategies for Writing* p. 57 • *English Workshop* pp. 107–108, 181–182	• Proofreading Practice, *Strategies for Writing* p. 59
• *Language Workshop:* Lesson 61 💾	• Revision Transparencies 19–20, *Transparency Binder* 📽	• *Language Workshop:* Lesson 40 💾

CROSS CURRICULUM

ELEMENTS OF WRITING: CURRICULUM CONNECTIONS

Writing Workshop
• Informal Research: Investigating Unsolved Mysteries pp. 488–490

Making Connections
• Science: Experimental Research pp. 491–492
• History: Biography in Action p. 493

ASSESSMENT OPTIONS

Summative Assessment
Holistic Scoring: Prompts and Models pp. 45–51

Portfolio Assessment
Portfolio forms, *Portfolio Assessment* pp. 5–25, 40–45

Reflection
Writing Process Log, *Strategies for Writing* p. 53
Self-assessment Record, *Portfolio Assessment* p. 19

Ongoing Assessment
Proofreading, *Strategies for Writing* p. 58

💾 Computer disk or CD-ROM

📽 Overhead transparencies

GUIDED PRACTICE

You can use the **Reader's Response** questions as a class activity. Share your responses first so that students can see what types of things they could offer in the discussion.

USING THE SELECTION
from Elephant Talk

1

Notice that a research report may include some first-person narration if the writer chooses to include a personal experience relevant to the research topic.

436

from

ELEPHANT TALK

by
Katharine Payne

Spend a day among elephants, and you will come away mystified. Sudden, silent, synchronous activities— a herd taking flight for no apparent or audible reason, a mass of scattered animals simultaneously raising ears and freezing in their tracks—such events demand explanation, but none is forthcoming.

Some capacity beyond memory and the five senses seems to inform elephants, silently and from a distance, of the whereabouts and activities of other elephants.

1 I stumbled on a possible clue to these mysteries during a visit to the Metro Washington Park Zoo in Portland, Oregon, in May 1984. While observing three Asian elephant mothers and their new calves, I repeatedly noticed a <u>palpable</u> throbbing in the air like distant thunder, yet all around me was silent.

Only later did a thought occur to me: As a young choir girl in Ithaca, New York, I used to stand next to the largest, deepest organ pipe in the church. When the organ blasted out the bass line in a Bach chorale, the

"...I repeatedly noticed a palpable throbbing in the air like distant thunder, yet all around me was silent."

INDEPENDENT PRACTICE

After the discussion, have students answer question 4 of **Writer's Craft** independently.

ASSESSMENT

Use your evaluation of students' responses to **Reader's Response** and **Writer's Craft** to assess mastery of the concepts in this lesson.

☞

437

2 whole chapel would throb, just as the elephant room did at the zoo. Suppose the elephants, like the organ pipe, were the source of the throbbing? Suppose elephants communicate with one another by means of calls too low-pitched for human beings to hear?

3 Half a year later the World Wildlife Fund, the Cornell Laboratory of Ornithology, and friends in the Cornell biology department helped me, Bill Langbauer, and Liz Thomas return to the zoo to test this idea. We recorded near the elephants for a month. Then we made electronic printouts and saw that we had recorded 400 calls—three times as many as we'd heard.

Elephant sounds include barks, snorts, trumpets, roars, growls, and rumbles. The rumbles are the key to our story, for although elephants can hear them well, human beings cannot. Many are below our range of hearing, in what is known as infrasound.

4 The universe is full of infrasound: It is generated by earthquakes, wind, thunder, volcanoes, and ocean storms—massive movements of earth, air, fire, and water. But very low frequency sound has not been thought to play much of a role in animals' lives. Intense infrasonic calls have been recorded from finback whales, but whether the calls are used in communication is not known.

5 Why would elephants use infrasound? It turns out that sound at the lowest frequencies of elephant rumbles (14 to 35 hertz, or cycles per

2

The use of rhetorical questions heightens the interest of the reader and establishes the problem that the writer wishes to solve.

3

This is a research paper resulting from primary research—that is, not only from outside sources but also from the writer's own collection of data, experiences, and comments. This is another type of paper that advanced students may want to consider.

4

In this paragraph, and in other places as well, the writer obviously draws on outside sources for information without documenting the source because it is common knowledge—knowledge generally agreed upon by specialists in a field.

5

Again, the rhetorical question provides a good device to keep the reader involved by revealing the thought processes of the writer.

438

second) has remarkable properties—it is little affected by passage through forests and grasslands. Does infrasound, then, let elephants communicate over long distances?

Suddenly we realized that if wild elephants use infrasound, this could explain some extraordinary observations on record about the social lives of these much loved, much studied animals.

National Geographic

ANSWERS

Reader's Response

Answers may vary.

1. Be sure students give explanations and support for their responses.

2. This question has several parts; be sure students respond to each part. You may want to allow students time to look up ESP in encyclopedias or dictionaries.

Writer's Craft

3. They recorded sounds the elephants made and then studied the electronic printouts. Their reading informed them about known sources of infrasound in the universe.

4. A scientific report would probably be written, using more formal language, from an objective, third-person point of view. It would probably not use the first- or second-person point of view or the personal reference to Payne's experience as a choir girl. It might also include more technical information, such as the factual data collected by Payne and her associates.

READER'S RESPONSE

1. Sometimes a seemingly insoluble mystery has a perfectly reasonable explanation, such as the one here: the elephants' use of infrasound for communicating. Think of something that you once regarded as a mystery but later came to understand. Explain how you or someone else solved the mystery.

2. A different observer at the Metro Washington Park Zoo might have concluded that elephants have extrasensory perception (ESP). What are your views on ESP? Is there such a thing? Do you know anyone who seems to have ESP?

WRITER'S CRAFT

3. Katharine Payne's research began because she was observant: She noticed something she wasn't expecting. What kind of observing did she and her colleagues do during the research? What details in the article show that reading was also part of their research?

4. This article was written for *National Geographic,* a magazine for the general public. But Payne probably also wrote reports of the research for scientists or scientific groups such as the Cornell Laboratory of Ornithology, which helped fund the research. How might a report written for scientists be different from "Elephant Talk"? What information or details might Payne delete? What different kinds of information might scientists want?

SELECTION AMENDMENT
Description of change: excerpted and new ending added
Rationale: to focus on the concept of research presented in this chapter

WAYS TO DEVELOP RESEARCH

TEACHING THE LESSON

Begin by discussing informal and formal research papers. You could point out that most research articles in periodicals for the general public are informal. To show uses of different methods of development (narration, description, classification, and evaluation) in informative writing, use the literary model at the beginning of the chapter to identify the methods in each of the first three paragraphs [description and narration]. Point out that the majority of sentences are descriptive. Have the class identify and explain the methods used in the rest of the article. ■

439

Ways to Develop Research

The amount of information available on most topics is overwhelming. Businesses, government agencies, politicians, news reporters, and advertisers bombard you daily with facts and opinions and the results of research. Many of the reports you see are *informal*, like Katharine Payne's. An informal report doesn't use footnotes or provide a detailed list of sources. A *formal report*, like the one you'll be writing in this chapter, differs in that it always contains documentation, providing a detailed answer to the question "Where does this information come from?" Here are some examples of the various ways to develop research reports, whether formal or informal.

- in a news report, describing some of the dramatic events in a recent presidential campaign
- in a biographical report, recounting an important game in the career of your favorite athlete
- in a report for an art class, describing the murals created by the Mexican artist Diego Rivera
- in a history report, describing the construction of sod houses on the prairie frontier
- in a report for a physics class, describing the components in a telecommunications network
- in a civics report, comparing and contrasting the judicial systems of the United States and England
- in a report for a chemistry class, evaluating the methods used in the analysis of drinking water
- in a workplace report, explaining how your current job skills fit into your long-term career plans

LOOKING AHEAD

In this chapter, you will write a formal research report. At the end of the chapter, you'll have a chance to write other types of reports. To prepare your formal report, you'll create a research plan and organize information from the sources you find. Keep in mind that a formal research report

- gives factual information about a topic
- presents information from several sources
- documents its sources of information

INTEGRATING THE LANGUAGE ARTS

Literature Link. Students should understand that authors—those of fiction as well as of nonfiction—often bring some research to their subjects. If the works are available in your literature textbook, show students how research is used in works such as W. H. Auden's poem "Musée des Beaux Arts" or Thomas Gray's "Elegy Written in a Country Churchyard."

Tell students that the poems are primarily descriptive and that their purpose is literary rather than informative. However, like many writers, Auden and Gray may have done some research before writing their poetry.

After they've read the poems, ask students to speculate on what kinds of research and what sources the authors might have used to help develop their works. [Answers may vary. Auden obviously refers to Pieter Brueghel's famous painting of Icarus. He and Gray both may have consulted books on mythology. Gray also may have researched current history books or periodicals of his time.]

OBJECTIVES

- To evaluate and choose research topics
- To share a research topic and to role-play in a focus group
- To analyze an audience for a research paper
- To find and evaluate sources of information for a research topic
- To list sources of information for a research topic
- To take notes on a research topic
- To write a thesis statement and an informal outline for a research paper

PROGRAM MANAGER

PREWRITING

- **Self-Assessment** Before beginning instruction of the writing process, see **Writing Process Log** in *Strategies for Writing*, p. 53.

- **Heuristics** To help students generate ideas, see **Prewriting** in *Strategies for Writing*, pp. 54–55.

- **Instructional Support** See **Graphic Organizers 19** and **20**. For suggestions on how to tie the transparencies to instruction, review teacher's notes in *Fine Art and Instructional Transparencies for Writing*, pp. 89, 91.

QUOTATION FOR THE DAY

"Knowledge is of two kinds: we know a subject ourselves, or we know where we can find information upon it." (Samuel Johnson, 1709–1784, English lexicographer, essayist, and poet)

Share the quotation with your class and ask students to discuss what they think Johnson could be saying about generating ideas for writing.

Writing a Research Paper

Prewriting

Finding a Research Topic

To find a research subject, you may automatically think, "First stop: library." The impulse is natural. Libraries are repositories of research and information, and going to that bank of books is a strategy that won't fail you. But it's not your only option.

Discovering Subjects

Think for a minute about what's in a library and how it got there. *People* wrote, compiled, drew, filmed, or recorded all of it. They probably used a library at some point, but they didn't necessarily start there. Where were they when curiosity hit and wouldn't go away? At home, at work, at sea, at a movie? Where were they when they noticed something they had to know more about? In a courthouse, a desert, a gallery? The whole world is a repository of research ideas, and you have complete freedom to use it. The best idea for a research paper is one that grabs *you*. Following are some ideas for starting your search.

SOURCES FOR RESEARCH SUBJECTS

- **Everyday curiosity:** Have you ever wondered how something works or why it happened as it did? Would you like to understand animation? the Underground Railroad?
- **Personal experiences:** What have you seen, done, or accomplished that might provide a subject for research—a trip to the Everglades? a gymnastics competition?
- **Friends and relatives:** Does someone you know do something interesting or unusual? Is she a television director? Is he a dietitian for cancer patients?
- **Entertainment:** Don't think of television, radio, movies, and sports as just diversions. What draws your imagination and interest—reggae music? modern police methods? baseball legends?

(continued)

MOTIVATION

You may want to get the students into the spirit of research by asking them to brainstorm topics they would like to know more about. Review **Sources for Research Subjects** to help students realize the myriad possibilities for researching topics they care about. As they name possible topics, you can write those topics on the chalkboard.

SOURCES FOR RESEARCH SUBJECTS *(continued)*

- **Books, newspapers, magazines, documentary video-tapes:** What do you linger over when you go to the library? Browse through the card (or online) catalog, the *Readers' Guide to Periodical Literature,* or other indexes and see what catches your attention—women's rights? medicine? ballet?

Identifying a Suitable Topic

Your first idea may be quite general—for example, Jane Austen, the Super Bowl, folk music, Native American culture. Since a typical high school research report is five to ten typed pages (check with your teacher for specific requirements), you will have to limit your subject to a workable topic.

MEETING individual NEEDS

LEP/ESL

General Strategies. Some of your students may need assistance in choosing research topics. You may want to encourage English-language learners to write reports dealing with current events in their native countries. This strategy reinforces the important link between students and their native cultures, offers them a topic that most likely is of personal interest, and encourages them to interview family and community members regarding the issues at hand.

You may want to make sure students understand that they have already mastered, to some degree, most of the skills needed to write a good research paper. They probably have already written persuasive and informative papers, and they have already used the methods of writing. Now they are adding another component: Rather than base their writing on their personal experiences or knowledge, they will write on topics they know very little about. As a result, they will have to find the necessary information. After the information is gathered, they will continue to employ the same writing process they have been practicing for years.

The prewriting stage of the writing process is divided into several steps, which

MEETING individual NEEDS

ADVANCED STUDENTS

You may want to challenge students with well-developed writing skills by organizing debates and asking for debate briefs in research-paper form. Here are suggested steps to follow:

1. Divide the class into groups of four. Ask each group to decide on a current problem to be debated and to write a debate question that follows this form—"Resolved: That free health care should be available to all Americans." Then, ask each group to decide which two students will be for the proposal and which will be against it.

2. Each pair of students will then research the question and use their information to prepare a brief in the form of a research paper.

3. Finally, each question can be debated in class, with each student presenting a ten-minute speech. The second speaker on each team can also present a rebuttal.

Choose an aspect of the subject that can be thoroughly covered in a paper—not something so broad you'd need to write a book to deal with it well. To limit your subject, try looking for subtopics in library catalogs, encyclopedias, and the *Readers' Guide,* or use a World Wide Web search engine to find Internet sources containing keywords related to the subject. Keep pushing yourself to *be more specific.*

HERE'S HOW

Subject:	Native Americans
Be more specific!	Native Americans in the past
Be more specific!	the Iroquois League
Be more specific!	how the League worked as a government
Limited topic:	the influence of the Iroquois League on the form of the United States government

Besides being manageable and personally appealing, your topic must be appropriate for a research report. A good topic will meet all of the following requirements.

CHECKLIST FOR A SUITABLE TOPIC

1. Can you find at least five sources of information, including books, articles, and nonprint sources? Beware of topics that are too recent ("last month's high school dropouts") or too technical or unusual ("the incidence of rabies among wild dogs in India").
2. Is the topic an objective one? You cannot report on your personal experiences or opinions. You may, for example, write a paper about "triathlete training and competition" but not about your experiences in meets.
3. Can you make the topic appealing to your audience? Interest is important for readers, not just for you. If your topic is written about often ("crucial Civil War battles") or on first impression dry ("the invention and manufacture of squeeze tubes"), what approach will give it life for your audience?

should make it convenient for you to divide your teaching into those steps. Allow plenty of time to discuss the "how to's" of each step and gear your time to students' comprehension. Be sure that students understand how to apply each step to the preparation of their own research reports before proceeding to the next step.

Here are five divisions with textbook headings that you may want to use when teaching this lesson:

1. **Finding a Research Topic** (p. 440). This section involves choosing a subject and limiting it to a specific topic. Be sure students know the **Checklist for a Suitable Topic** before working on **Exercise 1.** You may want to stress that students should select ☞

Prewriting   **443**

E X E R C I S E 1 ▶ **Evaluating Topics for Research**

Which of the following topics are suitable for a five- to ten-page research report? Get together with a partner and discuss the merits of each topic. For each one that isn't suitable, explain why. Is it too broad? Does it fail a test in the checklist on page 442? Also suggest a more limited or usable topic.

1. urban renewal in Newark, New Jersey
2. the problem of slavery in America
3. how Labrador retrievers are trained to detect drugs smuggled as cargo
4. my year as an exchange student in Japan
5. a new immunological cancer treatment reported in the current issue of the *New England Journal of Medicine*

YES, I KNOW MY TERM PAPER IS DUE TOMORROW.

OH, YES, MA'AM, I'M ALMOST FINISHED...

THE TITLE?

... I CALL IT ... "WORK IN PROGRESS."

© 1990 Tribune Media Services, Inc. All Rights Reserved

Shoe reprinted by permission: Tribune Media Services.

WRITING ASSIGNMENT

PART 1:
Choosing a Limited Topic

Have you ever complained that you don't get to *choose* what to study in school? Well, whether the complaint's true or not, this is definitely one chance to choose, to study something that *you* want to learn. The source ideas on pages 440–441 give you ways to develop personal fascinations into research topics. The only director of this research project is you: Just remember to choose a topic that is specific and to satisfy the requirements on page 442. When you have chosen a topic, save it for later use.

ANSWERS
Exercise 1

Suggestions will vary for usable topics to replace the unsuitable topics. Accept any variation as long as it isn't too broad and it meets the criteria in the checklist.

1. unsuitable—five sources of information probably not available (unless you live in Newark) or limited appeal
2. unsuitable—too broad
3. suitable
4. unsuitable—not objective
5. unsuitable—too recent or too few sources

MEETING *individual* **NEEDS**

LESS-ADVANCED STUDENTS

An alternative to the typical research paper is a personal-quest paper in which the writer uses the narrative and descriptive methods to tell the story of his or her search for information.

Most of the research is from first-hand sources such as interviews, observations, phone calls, consultations, and shopping. The writer also keeps a diary or log to use as a basis for telling the story of the quest.

Students could choose to find out how to buy a certain car, how to get started in a modeling career, or what is involved in planning a trip to Hawaii. The paper is divided into four sections: "Why I Chose This Subject," "What I Needed to Know," "The Story of the Search," and "What I Gained."

subjects about which their school and local libraries have sufficient current information.

2. **Developing a Research Plan** (p. 444). This section includes considering purpose, audience, and tone, as well as asking research questions, getting an overview, finding sources, making source cards, and evaluating sources. Tell stu-

dents that these are important considerations in the early stages of prewriting.

3. **Researching Your Topic** (p. 452). This section includes guidelines for taking notes, making note cards, and conducting an interview. **Exercise 3** on p. 454 gives students practice taking notes. In **Writing Assignment: Part 3** (p. 456), students begin taking notes.

A DIFFERENT APPROACH

If your students have already learned to do library research, you may want to give them the opportunity to do primary research for this paper. They each will need to select a subject and make a plan. They might take polls (perhaps interview people who attend sports events), gather statistics (count items, such as the make and year of students' cars), or keep logs (perhaps record the kinds of responses teachers make to students' questions). The possibilities are limited only by time and resources. If you allow students to write this type of research paper, you will probably want to teach them good research procedures, such as how to do random samples and how to record information.

INTEGRATING THE LANGUAGE ARTS

Literature Link. If it's available in your literature textbook, refer students to an excerpt from *The Diary of Samuel Pepys.* Explain that this selection is an example of a primary source that could be used for a research paper on life in the 1660s. Ask students to read the selection and to pick out details that reveal differences between life then and life now.

Prewriting

Developing a Research Plan

Thinking of yourself as a project director is a good idea. Research—on any topic—is such a wide-open adventure that you have to have a plan, a direction. Since you don't want to go into the library and still be there when the paper's due, you need some solid methods for setting up and carrying out your research.

Considering Purpose, Audience, and Tone

Purpose.   What do you want to accomplish? You actually have a dual *purpose* in writing a research report—discovering information for yourself and sharing new information with an audience. What you'll give readers will not be a jumble of facts and ideas, or even an orderly list of them: It will be a synthesis, a bringing together of the pieces of information you uncover into a whole. So be ready to make sense of what you find.

Audience.   Your readers will usually be your teacher and your classmates, but don't limit yourself to that audience alone. You can plan your paper for a specific *audience* from the outset.

For example, if you are writing about educational methods in Japan, you may want the state legislature's education committee to read it. Whoever your readers are, they are looking for information, for a better understanding of the topic. You need to take them *beyond* what they already know. You also need to interest them: Look for surprising details or an unusual twist to old information.

4. Writing a Thesis Statement (p. 459). Use the textbook explanations and models to help students realize the importance of a clear, concise, thorough thesis statement to guide writing.

5. Making an Outline (p. 460). You'll want to tell students your requirements for outlining. You may want to let students choose the form of outlining that works best for them. Go over the outline example and then show students an alternative organizational method, perhaps mapping.

☞

Tone.   Adding interest to your report, however, doesn't mean using slang, exclamation marks, or flowery descriptions. The *tone* of a formal report should be serious but not stuffy: Think of yourself as an authority who really wants to communicate to others. To create this impression, you will have to sound objective. You can accomplish this by avoiding the use of the first-person pronouns *I, me,* or *my.* The use of *I* is appropriate in many kinds of writing, even in informal reports, but not in a formal research report.

EXERCISE 2 ▶ **Speaking and Listening: Analyzing the Audience for Your Report**

Companies, organizations, and even politicians often use a technique called *focus groups* to research a market before they put a new product, idea, or campaign before the public. The focus groups allow them to get the reactions of a small sample of people typical of the final audience. Form a focus group with five or six classmates, and test your topic. Tell the group briefly what your limited topic is and what you expect to cover in your report. If you have a special audience in mind, describe it, and have the others role-play its members. Ask them these questions, take notes on answers, and also let them question you. Take turns presenting and responding.

1. What do you know about this topic already? How did you learn it?
2. What interests you most about the topic? What questions about it would you like to have answered?
3. Does the topic seem boring to you? Why or why not?
4. If you were given this topic, how would you approach it?

Developing Research Questions

No matter how new to you a topic is, your mind isn't a blank about it. You chose it because you are curious, because you have questions about it, and those questions can guide you as you gather information. You can also generate research questions by brainstorming or by using the *5W-How?* questions: *Who? What? When? Where? Why?* and *How?* Remember that these questions are initial guides; you may ask others later. Following are some initial questions one writer brainstormed about the topic of the Iroquois League and the founding of the U.S. government.

MEETING *individual* NEEDS

LEARNING STYLES

Visual Learners. To help students who remember best what they see often, you may want to create posters to illustrate each step of the process of writing a research paper. Or, you could ask students to make the posters, perhaps for extra credit.

Subjects for posters might include such information as the **Checklist for a Suitable Topic** (p. 442), types and examples of research questions (pp. 445–446), **Sources of Information,** and the 4R test for evaluating a source (p. 448). You can add posters as the students progress through their research and writing.

446

446   *Writing a Research Paper*

HERE'S HOW

What was the Iroquois League? When and how did it begin? What was its purpose?

Besides being a confederation (union), did the League have other similarities to the United States?

What did our nation's founders know about the Iroquois League? Did any of the founders ever acknowledge Iroquois contributions to the new government?

Do historians think the Iroquois League influenced the founders' ideas? If so, how?

Getting an Overview and Finding Sources

Your actual research starts with a quick overview of your topic. You already know *something* about it, of course, or you couldn't have gotten this far; but you need a solid grasp of the basic shape of the topic before plunging into specifics. One way to get a quick overview is to read one or two articles in encyclopedias or other reference books about your topic or, if it is highly limited, about related topics. For example, when researching "recent drug therapies for mental illness," you could look up "psychiatry" or "schizophrenia." Sometimes a World Wide Web site or an expert (a teacher, librarian, parent, or neighbor) can give you a good overview, too. During this preliminary work, you may think of other research questions, and you may find good suggestions for other sources.

Once you have an adequate overview and are ready to look for specific sources of information, remember to explore both *print* and *nonprint* sources in your *library* and *community*.

SOURCES OF INFORMATION	
LIBRARY	
SOURCE	**WHAT TO LOOK FOR**
Card catalog or online catalog	Books, recordings, audiotapes, and videotapes (Print and audiovisual listings are in separate catalogs in some libraries.)

(continued)

You may want to give a process grade for the work from this lesson; that is, the students would receive credit for acceptable work.

Topic—5 points
Audience—5 points
Research Questions—10 points
List of Sources—10 points
Source Cards—50 points
Thesis—10 points
Outline—10 points

You could use this method of assessment or devise your own. This particular assessment adds up to 100 points, convenient for assigning grades.

☞

SOURCES OF INFORMATION *(continued)*	
LIBRARY	
SOURCE	**WHAT TO LOOK FOR**
Readers' Guide to Periodical Literature or an electronic index	Magazine and journal articles, indexed by subject and author (*InfoTrac*® is one well-known electronic index.)
Indexes to newspapers, essays, and articles	Articles from major newspapers, such as *The New York Times;* possibly local newspapers (Newspapers are frequently on microfilm.)
Specialized reference books and CD-ROMs	Encyclopedias of special subjects, such as the *Reference Encyclopedia of the American Indian;* almanacs; atlases; biographical references like *Current Biography*
Vertical file	Pamphlets and clippings
Microfilm, microfiche, or electronic databases	Indexes to major newspapers; back issues of some periodicals
COMMUNITY	
Colleges, historical societies, museums	Libraries, exhibits, experts, special collections, records
Local, state, and federal offices	Statistics, politicians' voting records, recent or pending legislation, surveys, reports, pamphlets, experts
World Wide Web and online services	Articles, interviews, bibliographies, pictures, videos, sound recordings

☞ **REFERENCE NOTE:** For more details on how to use library resources, online card catalogs, electronic databases, and the Internet to find information, see pages 1051–1058.

Evaluating Sources of Information. So many sources are available that it may be hard to know which ones to use. To evaluate the sources you find, apply the "4R" test.

COOPERATIVE LEARNING

Divide the class into groups of four to explore more about purpose, audience, and tone. Have students in some of the groups find articles from such popular magazines as *People,* the purpose of which is primarily to entertain, the audience of which is general, and the tone of which tends to be light, informal, and chatty. Have students in other groups obtain articles from such magazines as *Smithsonian, National Geographic,* or *Psychology Today.* These magazines are designed primarily to inform educated adults, and the tone tends to be formal or even scholarly.

Ask students in each group to identify words and details that illustrate the tone of the articles and publications. Then, have each group share its findings with the class.

Select a short (thirty-minute), interesting video to show to students. Then, ask students to discuss the following points about the video:

1. its broad subject
2. its limited topic and main idea (thesis statement)

3. its purpose and intended audience
4. its tone
5. possible sources used in researching the subject of the video (video credits should indicate some of these)

You also could require students to take notes while the video is being shown and then to make outlines of information contained in the video.

TIMESAVER

If you organize your class into groups for this project, you can make the groups responsible for checking each step of the writing process. The textbook usually provides guidelines, or you can make a detailed checklist for the students to use when checking one another's papers. Ask one student in each group to keep records for the group by checking off when the group has approved a student's work (for example, suitable topic, research questions, sources, source cards, note cards, thesis statement, and outline).

448   *Writing a Research Paper*

1. **Relevant.** The source must contain information *directly* related to your topic. You can check the table of contents and index of a book and skim articles. Videotapes and audiotapes sometimes provide a written summary; and for some books, useful summaries and excerpts of reviews will appear in *Book Review Digest*.
2. **Recent.** Always use sources that are as current as possible. In many fields, research findings change rapidly. Even for a topic that doesn't rely on data and experiments, you should read the most recent publications about it because they will often show you which older sources of information are still important.
3. **Reliable.** The source must be accurate. A respected newspaper or periodical, such as *The Washington Post* or *Smithsonian*, or a respected scholar can generally be counted on to have facts straight. If in doubt about a source, consult a librarian or expert and look for the authors most often quoted on the topic or listed in the bibliographies of other sources.
4. **Representative.** If there are two opposing viewpoints on your topic, you need to look at sources with information and opinions on both sides of the issue. As a researcher, you must examine and present all relevant information, even if you finally draw a conclusion that one side's position is stronger.

Using Primary and Secondary Sources. A *primary source* is firsthand, original information. It may be a letter, a speech, or a literary work. It may be eyewitness testimony, a personal remembrance, an autobiography, a historical document, or information gathered from firsthand interviews or surveys. For example, in a report on the Iroquois League and the founding of the United States, a letter on the subject written by Benjamin Franklin is a primary source. You will want to use primary sources if they're available on your topic, but remember that the *R's* of *reliable* and *representative* apply to them too. A primary source could be mistaken or show bias. To be able to judge, research widely.

A *secondary source* contains secondhand or indirect information, but that does not mean such sources are unimportant. An encyclopedia entry, an expert's opinion, a magazine article, and a biography are all secondary sources. In fact, the research report you are now working on will be a secondary source about your topic for other researchers, just as the book *The Indians of Northeastern America* is a secondary source for a paper on the Iroquois League. You'll use secondary sources in virtually any research project, with the mix between primary and secondary sources depending mainly on the topic.

Listing Sources of Information.   When people read your research report, they expect answers to the question "How do you know that?" In a *Works Cited* list at the end of your report, you will provide full information about every source you used—in a very precise format. Consequently, always carefully record information about sources *as you use them.* Otherwise, you may find yourself running back to the library or making a hasty, last-minute phone call to track down source information.

A good way to keep track of sources is to make a *source card,* or *bibliography card,* on a 3″ × 5″ index card for every source you decide to examine. You can use notebook paper or computer files, but cards are very easy to handle, add to, and sort into alphabetical order for the Works Cited list. You'll also save time later if you record the information in final format (see the Works Cited examples on pages 476–480).

write down some helpful hints based on their experiences with these early steps. The extent of your debriefing depends on how much time you have.

Ask students to evaluate other students' work so that they might gain better perspective of their own. As each step is completed, students may exchange papers; for example, after you review briefly the criteria for a good topic or thesis, ask students to respond to the exchanged paper by answering specific questions. Ask students to

CRITICAL THINKING

Analysis. After each step in the process of writing a research paper, you may want to ask each student to write a brief expressive paragraph telling why a particular step is done in the way suggested. For example, have students explain why note cards need four kinds of information: page number, source number, notes, and main idea. In this way, students can reinforce their understanding of the process and relate it to other research writing projects.

TECHNOLOGY TIP

Students may need to review how to use microfilm or microfiche. If possible, plan a library trip to explain and demonstrate.

WRITING NOTE

The format for recording source information shown in this chapter is that of the Modern Language Association (MLA). Your teacher may want you to follow a different format; but whatever system you use, pay close attention to *information required, styling* (capitalization, underlining, and so on), and *punctuation*.

GUIDELINES FOR SOURCE CARDS

1. **Number your sources.** To save time during note taking, assign a number to each source. Then you can write the number, rather than author and title, when you are taking notes.
2. **Record all publishing information.** Take down everything you *might* need: title and subtitle, an editor or translator, volume number, original publication year, revised edition year, and so on. You may have more than you need for the Works Cited list, but you won't have to backtrack for a tiny piece of missing information. (See the sample entries on pages 476–480 for the kinds of information required.)
3. **Note the call number or location.** This information will save you time if you must go back to a source later.

SAMPLE SOURCE CARD

8	Source num
Jennings, Francis. *The Ambiguous Iroquois Empire.* New York: Norton, 1984.	Author, book title, publication information in MLA form
E 93 J44 1984	Call numbe (or other location)

elaborate on their answers by suggesting what the changes might be. The writers need to know, however, that it is entirely their own decision whether or not to use those suggestions.

For example, when students have selected topics, you could review the **Checklist for a Suitable Topic** on p. 442 and ask students to answer those specific questions by relating them to the theses the students are evaluating.

☞

Reminder

To develop a research plan

- create a list of questions to guide your research
- gain a quick overview of your topic from general reference sources
- find specific information sources in the library or community
- use the "4R" test to evaluate the sources (pages 447–448)
- record all publishing information about your sources on index cards

| **WRITING** ASSIGNMENT | PART 2: **Finding, Evaluating, and Listing Sources of Information** |

As director of research, you now need to identify sources of information for the topic you selected in the Writing Assignment, Part 1 (page 443). Follow the basic steps listed in the Reminder above, but allow yourself some flexibility to work with your topic. For example, the best overview for your topic may come from some knowledgeable person, not an encyclopedia. Try to find five or six different, acceptable information sources, of whatever type; and when you have a good list together, save it for later use.

A DIFFERENT APPROACH

To help students develop the skill of note taking instead of copying whole parts of sources, provide a change of pace with a quick game. Give students a paragraph from any book or article and ask them to take notes on the paragraph. The object of the game is to get all of the main ideas in the fewest words. After everyone has finished, ask who took notes in fewer than twenty words, fewer than fifteen words, and so on until you've found the winner. Then, ask the winner to read his or her notes aloud to make sure all the information is there. You then could repeat the game several times, on the same day or one game a day for several days. The students can work as individuals or in groups.

TECHNOLOGY TIP

The *Writer's Workshop CD-ROM* composition program provides a **Bibliography Maker** that will automatically arrange the student's bibliographical source information into a standard bibliography format. If students input their source information early in their research, the form on the computer screen will serve as a reminder, should they forget to note important data. Students will still have time, then, to collect the missing information and complete their final bibliography listings.

You might want to expand this activity by asking students to choose topics of concern in the world today, or, even more specifically, in your community. These topics might come from such general subjects as ecological abuse, health care, insurance rates, congestion in the court system, budget allocations, or public education. Or, because some of your seniors are old enough to vote, you can help them become more knowledgeable about current issues by suggesting that they refer to current newspapers and periodicals for ideas. ■

A DIFFERENT APPROACH

Students often don't know how to make use of community resources because they don't know about the sources. Have students look through local telephone books to make lists of museums, historical societies, and government offices.

During class, have students name some of the resources and write their suggestions on the chalkboard. Have students suggest at least one topic for which each resource might be consulted.

Prewriting

Researching Your Topic

The word *search* is three fourths of the word *research*, which is an appropriate proportion: The diligent search for specific information is often the major part of a research project. The time you spend finding the facts, examples, opinions, and quotations you need to produce a strong and convincing report will be time well spent—provided that you take good notes.

Taking Notes

Careful note taking is vital to a good paper. Take notes thoughtfully but sparingly—you can't write down everything. Referring to your research questions will keep you focused on needed information. Use 4″ × 6″ cards, single sheets of paper, or computer files to record the information you collect from your sources. You'll take two main kinds of notes: (1) *summaries or paraphrases* and (2) *direct quotations*.

Summaries and Paraphrases. In most of your notes, you'll use your own words. A *summary* is a very brief statement, in your own words, of a source's main ideas. For example, you might summarize the relevant ideas in a two-page encyclopedia article on a single note card. A *paraphrase* is a restatement that retains more details. Often you'll want to note important details such as names, places, dates, and statistics; they're necessary and effective in a good report. For note-taking purposes, summaries and paraphrases don't have to be written in complete sentences. (See pages 1114–1117 for information on more formal uses of summaries and paraphrases.) You save space and time by using abbreviations, phrases, lists, and sentence fragments.

Direct Quotations. Use a *direct quotation* only when an idea is particularly well phrased or intriguing, or when you want to be sure of technical accuracy. When writing down a direct quotation, copy each word and punctuation mark carefully. *Always* enclose direct quotes in quotation marks on your note card (even if you expect to paraphrase them later) so that when you write your report, you'll remember that these words are the author's, not your own.

GUIDELINES FOR NOTE CARDS

1. **Use a separate note card, sheet of paper, or computer file for each source and for each main idea.** If a card has information about different sources or main ideas, you will have trouble sorting and grouping the notes later.
2. **Write the source number in the upper right-hand corner and the page number(s) at the bottom of the note.** Both numbers are essential for correct documentation. The number you have assigned to the source is your key to all publication data on the source card. And if you use the note's information, you will have to supply the page number(s) in your paper.
3. **Write a label showing the main idea at the top of the card.** The labels will let you see content at a glance.
4. **Reread the note to make sure you understand it.** Abbreviations and other shortcuts are fine, but be sure you can "translate" them. Check for clarity now—not later, when you're trying to draft.

TIMESAVER

You could make the most recent edition of the *MLA Handbook for Writers of Research Papers* available to students. Keep a copy on your desk or at a central location in the classroom. Instruct students to look in the handbook for particular style situations, such as books with editors or translators.

Below is an excerpt from *Native American Heritage* (page 316), by Merwyn S. Garbarino and Robert F. Sasso. On the next page is a sample note card summarizing the information.

Women were important not only because they were cultivators and property owners, but also because they nominated the leader who represented their clan in the tribal political struggle and could recall him if he were unsatisfactory. Each tribe was governed by a council of chiefs, usually called *sachems*. Families within the clans held the rights to clan leadership positions, but competence settled which man would become a sachem. When an old sachem died, the women of his clan nominated his successor. The tribal council and the rest of the tribe had to approve the selection, but approval was almost automatic.

The League had nothing to do with internal affairs within each of the five tribes, but dealt with intertribal, external problems. The League was led by a council of fifty leaders, all sachems of the member tribes.

ANSWERS
Exercise 3

Information on the note cards will vary. An acceptable note card will include the number *2* in the upper right-hand corner, the page number between 90 and 101 at the bottom, the main idea of the note in the upper left-hand corner, and the note in the middle of the card. Here are three sample note cards:

Origin of *hippopotamus*   2

Greeks encountered these animals in the mud of the Nile Delta and called them *hippopotamos,* which means "river horse," because of their size and habits.

                                        90

Nocturnal feeding   2

Hippos feed at night, alone, because they have a very thin outer layer of skin that is easily dehydrated in the sun.

                                        95

Why hippos can stay submerged   2

The hemoglobin in hippos' blood is able to hold onto oxygen in the same way that the hemoglobin in the blood of dolphins, whales, and porpoises does.

                                        100

SAMPLE NOTE CARD

Political Structure   14

— Women played an important role; named and recalled
  representatives in tribal government
— League governed by council made up of fifty leaders
  (sachems) from the member tribes
— League dealt with intertribal problems only, not
  internal problems of individual tribes

                                        p. 316

EXERCISE 3 ▶ **Taking Notes**

The following excerpt is from an article titled "Snatching Scientific Secrets from the Hippo's Gaping Jaws," by David M. Schwartz. It appears on pages 90–101 in the March 1996 issue of *Smithsonian* magazine. Take notes on the article for a research report, answering the questions below. Make a minimum of three note cards (give the source number as 2), and include in your notes at least one direct quotation.

1. What is the origin of the name *hippopotamus*?
2. For what reason do hippos feed at night?
3. Why can hippos stay submerged for long periods?

Three thousand years ago, when the Greeks encountered these massive mammals lolling in the Nile Delta, they named the species *hippopotamos,* or "river horse." With bulls growing up to 15 feet long, 5 feet high and 8,000 pounds in weight, hippos are the second-largest terrestrial mammals. Only elephants are larger.

Gregarious and generally aquatic during the day, hippos are solitary and terrestrial at night, hauling themselves out of the water to feed. They can walk five miles in search of grass and sedge, which they tear from the ground with wide, fleshy lips. One night's take can be 100 pounds, but in light of their size, it is not a particularly gluttonous feast. Nocturnal activity is necessary because hippos have a very thin epidermis (the protective outer layer of skin), leaving them vulnerable to dessication. Hence, they spend the daylight hours in water or mud. The myth that hippos sweat blood derives from a pinkish, oily skin secretion that helps to protect them from the sun's rays.

Although feeding always occurs on land, most everything else—courtship, copulation, birth and nursing—takes place underwater. A hippo can dip below the surface for five minutes at a breath because the hemoglobin in its red blood cells, like that of cetaceans (whales, dolphins and porpoises), latches onto oxygen with unusual tenacity. While hippos appear to be great swimmers, they actually move underwater by walking or running along the bottom. Whether in aquatic or terrestrial mode, their speed belies their bulk: they've been clocked in short dashes at 30 miles per hour.

Herds typically space themselves out at intervals of about a hundred yards, each herd with roughly 10 to 100 animals. Cows are guarded vigilantly by a single highly territorial bull. When a show of tusk is not enough to deter transgressors, a territory holder will lock jaws with a challenger in vicious, sometimes lethal, battles. (In older males, razor-sharp canines can grow more than two feet long.) As a result, the hide of every experienced bull hippo is well gashed, sometimes so badly it looks like Arabic graffiti. The comical, huggable hippo of cartoons and children's books is, in reality, a bellicose beast of murderous temperament.

It is not surprising that hippopotamuses would evolve an ability to speak to one another. It saves energy and even lives to be able to advertise location, social status and

CRITICAL THINKING EXERCISE:
Drawing Conclusions

Graphs, tables, and charts provide a good opportunity to practice drawing conclusions because they present "raw data"—uninterpreted facts. You'll frequently find a graph or chart in your research, and to present its information in your paper, you will have to draw conclusions for readers. Study the three graphs below; then answer the questions following the graphs.

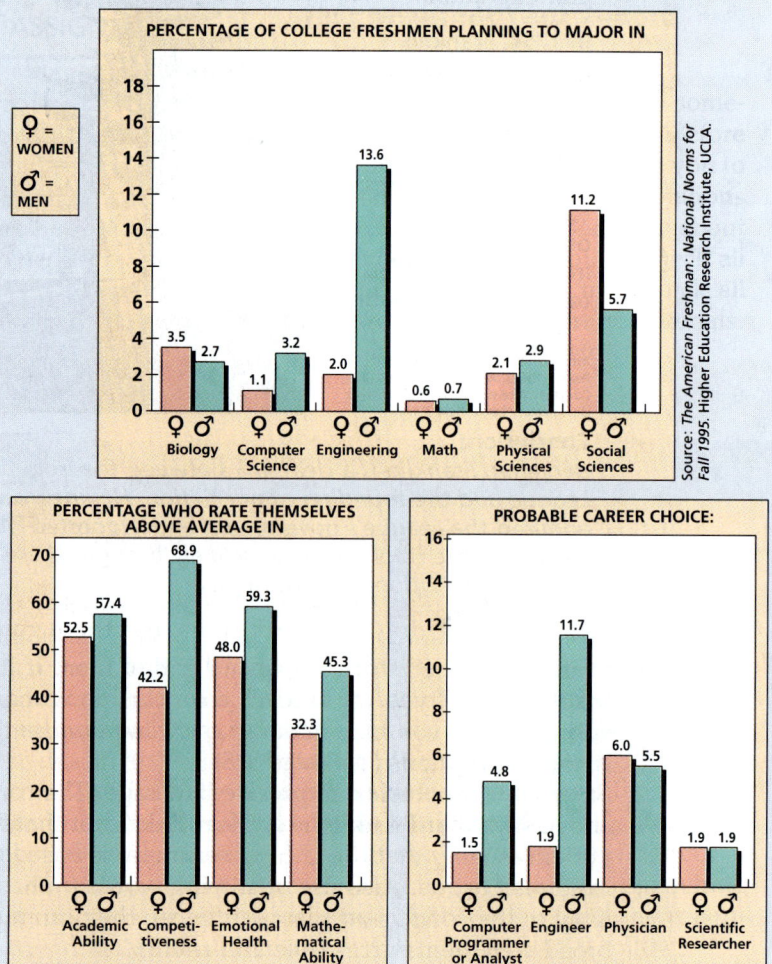

PERCENTAGE OF COLLEGE FRESHMEN PLANNING TO MAJOR IN

♀ = WOMEN
♂ = MEN

Biology: 3.5 / 2.7
Computer Science: 1.1 / 3.2
Engineering: 2.0 / 13.6
Math: 0.6 / 0.7
Physical Sciences: 2.1 / 2.9
Social Sciences: 11.2 / 5.7

Source: *The American Freshman: National Norms for Fall 1995.* Higher Education Research Institute, UCLA.

PERCENTAGE WHO RATE THEMSELVES ABOVE AVERAGE IN

Academic Ability: 52.5 / 57.4
Competitiveness: 42.2 / 68.9
Emotional Health: 48.0 / 59.3
Mathematical Ability: 32.3 / 45.3

PROBABLE CAREER CHOICE:

Computer Programmer or Analyst: 1.5 / 4.8
Engineer: 1.9 / 11.7
Physician: 6.0 / 5.5
Scientific Researcher: 1.9 / 1.9

1. What conclusion(s) could you draw about the differences between men and women regarding the field of engineering?
2. What conclusion(s) could you draw about the self-image of male and female first-year students?
3. Based on the information in these graphs, would the following conclusion be valid? "In their first year of college, men have somewhat greater academic abilities, drive, and emotional health than women have."
4. Should the date of the survey be given when you draw conclusions about these graphs in a paper? Why or why not?

WRITING NOTE Graphs and charts can be useful in research reports because they allow you to condense information into a compact form. Often, putting numerical data or other detailed information into sentences and paragraphs is cumbersome—for you and your readers. Instead, you can refer readers to a chart's data while discussing its meaning in your paper. Whether you use a chart from a source or create your own, check the *MLA Handbook* (or a style guide your teacher specifies) for mechanics of form and of crediting a source.

Writing a Thesis Statement

Your **thesis statement** is a sentence or two telling the main idea of your paper. Like drawing a conclusion, writing a thesis statement is an act of **synthesis,** reviewing and pulling together all your information to say what the paper is about. A thesis statement guides you as you write by helping you focus on information that should directly support or develop the thesis. Of course, a thesis statement at this point is *preliminary:* It may change as you draft and revise the paper.

SAMPLE THESIS STATEMENTS

Because the Iroquois League had an influence on the founders of the United States, important similarities exist between the League and the U.S. government.

COOPERATIVE LEARNING

One way for students to get immediate feedback on their thesis statements and outlines is to let the class meet in groups of no more than four to check one another's work. One student at a time can read his or her thesis statement aloud and then ask the other students to say what information they expect the paper to include. The writer will then know whether or not the thesis is clear.

Then each student can show his or her outline to the others in the group and explain the order of the ideas. The group can again respond by asking questions about anything unclear in the plan. Students might also suggest other information that is needed.

TECHNOLOGY TIP

Remind students that the outline features of some word-processing programs don't use the traditional Roman numerals, uppercase letters, Arabic numerals, etc., of conventional outlines and that students will have to supply these themselves. Also remind them that other conventions of outlining, such as using grammatically parallel expressions for outline items that are equal to one another, still apply.

There are a number of parallels between the lives of the English novelist Jane Austen and the American poet Emily Dickinson.

◀ JANE AUSTEN

EMILY ▶ DICKINSON

☞ **REFERENCE NOTE:** For more information on writing thesis statements, see pages 100–101.

Making an Outline

Even though you've organized many papers before, the mass of information that you collect for a research report may make you dread this necessary step. Don't. Note cards (or notes on single sheets of paper or in computer files) actually help accomplish your main tasks of grouping and ordering.

The labels on your notes allow you to sort notes into sets by main idea. You can go through each set, deciding which ideas to use or set aside, whether subsets are possible, and what order will present the information clearly. Cards make arranging and rearranging information very easy.

However, it is also helpful to make an outline on paper so that you have an overview of your writing plan. You can make an *informal outline* for planning; but after your paper is complete, your teacher may want you to prepare a final outline, which serves as a table of contents. This final *formal outline* must follow standard outline format, as shown in the model on the next page. (The model shows a partial outline. Note that formal outlines often omit the introduction and conclusion.)

COMPUTER NOTE: Use a stand-alone outlining program or your word-processing program's outline feature to organize your prewriting notes into an outline for your first draft.

HERE'S HOW

America's Legacy from the Iroquois League

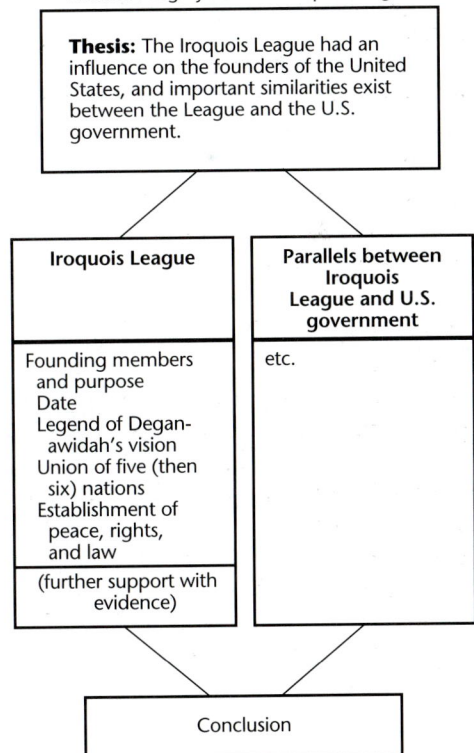

I. Iroquois League
  A. Founding, members, and purpose
    1. Date: before 1600
    2. Legend of Deganawidah
    3. Union of five (then six) nations: Mohawk, Oneida, Onondaga, Cayuga, Seneca (Tuscarora, 1722)
    4. Establishment of peace, rights, and law
  B. Great Law of Peace, or constitution
    1. Joint laws, rules, and customs
    2. Oral transmission
    3. Official written version, about 1900
    4. Drafted in English by John Gibson, a Seneca chief
  C. Council of sachems (chiefs)
    1. Fifty sachems
      a. Influence of clan mothers
      b. Some nations had more sachems
    2. One vote per nation
    3. Unanimous decisions
II. Parallels between Iroquois League and U.S. government
  A. etc.

👉 **REFERENCE NOTE:** To review outline form, see pages 105–106.

WRITING ASSIGNMENT

PART 4:
Writing a Thesis Statement and Outlining

This is a time to look in two directions—back at the information you have collected and ahead to the paper you plan to write. You have been "in the field," as some researchers say, collecting information. Now take a look at what you have and write a preliminary thesis statement, identifying the main thing you want readers to know about your topic. Then decide how to organize and create an informal outline. When you have finished this assignment, you'll be ready to think about drafting.

MEETING individual NEEDS

LEARNING STYLES

Visual Learners. You may want to share with students a type of organizer other than outlining. The following graphic organizer (using the information from the model outline) is a possibility:

America's Legacy from the Iroquois League

Thesis: The Iroquois League had an influence on the founders of the United States, and important similarities exist between the League and the U.S. government.

Iroquois League / **Parallels between Iroquois League and U.S. government**

Founding members and purpose; Date; Legend of Deganawidah's vision; Union of five (then six) nations; Establishment of peace, rights, and law; (further support with evidence)

etc.

Conclusion

WRITING YOUR FIRST DRAFT

- To use quotations effectively
- To summarize source information

OBJECTIVES

- To write a first draft of a research paper that includes proper in-text documentation and a Works Cited

PROGRAM MANAGER

WRITING YOUR FIRST DRAFT

- **Instructional Support** For help with writing a body paragraph, see **Writing** in *Strategies for Writing*, p. 56.

- **Computer Guided Instruction** For additional instruction and practice with procedures and formatting for a research paper, see **Lesson 61** in *Language Workshop CD-ROM*.

MEETING *individual* NEEDS

LEP/ESL

General Strategies. To give extra practice with the Works Cited format, pair students needing practice. Create several versions of the Works Cited on p. 469. One version could have the entries scrambled alphabetically. Another version could have neither book titles nor journal titles underlined. Have students correct the versions by comparing them with the original.

Writing Your First Draft

Source information, sets of notes, a thesis statement, and a preliminary outline—you have everything you need to begin writing. If you've done your work carefully up to this point, you should be able to transform your notes and ideas into sentences and paragraphs with relative ease. The important thing is to dive in.

A research paper does have unique elements, however, as the following chart shows. Notice that a research paper, like many longer pieces of writing, such as most compositions, includes an introduction, body, and conclusion.

ELEMENTS OF A RESEARCH REPORT	
Formal outline (optional)	Some teachers request a formal outline of the final content of the report.
Title	The title of the report, sometimes on a separate page, can be interesting but should also communicate the topic. (Your teacher may recommend a title-page format.)
Introduction	The introduction captures the reader's attention and curiosity.
Thesis statement	A statement of the main idea appears early in the report, usually in the introduction. Its wording may not be the same as the preliminary thesis statement.
Body	The body paragraphs develop the main ideas supporting the thesis statement.
Conclusion	The conclusion brings the paper to a convincing end, usually by restating or summarizing the main idea.
Works Cited list	This list appears on a separate page (or pages) at the end of the report. It provides complete publication information for each source cited in the report.

MOTIVATION

Ask students what they think the value is of the research done so far. They will probably respond that they have learned a lot.

Remind students that painters frequently make preliminary sketches of their ideas before transferring them to the final canvases. Tell students that they will be painting with words and that their rough drafts will be their preliminary sketches. Be sure students know that they don't have to get everything organized and correct at this point. Encourage them to be original in putting together the information they've collected.

☞

Writing Your First Draft **463**

Notice the listed elements in the Writer's Model that follows, as well as the way the writer weaves facts, quotations, and summaries of information into a unified essay. In the paper, you will see source information, or *citations* (covered in detail on pages 471–475), in parentheses.

A WRITER'S MODEL

America's Legacy from the Iroquois League

INTRODUCTION

In 1991, television journalist Bill Moyers interviewed Oren Lyons, chief of the Onondaga nation and a professor of American studies at the State University of New York at Buffalo. Chief Lyons mentioned the upsurge of American-inspired democracy throughout the world and commented,

Author named, TV interview, no pages

Striking quotation

"But America got it from the Indians. America got the ideas of democracy and freedom and peace here."

Thesis statement

Lyons's statement may seem extreme, but he is not alone in believing that Native Americans, particularly the Iroquois, influenced the colonists who founded the United States. In 1988, which was the two hundredth anniversary of the signing of the U.S. Constitution, a joint Congressional resolution stated that

Indented quotation

the confederation of the original Thirteen Colonies into one republic was influenced by the political system developed by the Iroquois Confederacy as were many of the democratic principles which were incorporated into the Constitution itself. (United States)

Despite an official resolution, many people do not know about this influence. What was the Iroquois Confederacy? What parallels between it and the American government have historians found? What contacts did Iroquois and colonial leaders have?

463

You'll probably want to begin this section with an overview of a research paper's main parts by using the **Elements of a Research Report** chart. You may want to point out that a research paper includes the basic elements of any informative composition.

Ask students to read **A Writer's Model,** or read it to them as they follow along. After reading, analyze the organization and form of the model by discussing the side glosses at the left. You will also probably want to give special attention to the **Guidelines for Using Quotations** (pp. 470–471). Stress that these guidelines should not be memorized but should be used as a reference tool. The same attention should also be given to the charts for documenting parenthetical information,

MEETING *individual* NEEDS

LEARNING STYLES

Kinetic Learners. When you analyze **A Writer's Model,** you could involve kinetic learners by making copies of the sample paper so that the students can write on them.

Each time you point out a particular feature of the model, ask the students to underline the sentence or phrase in the model that illustrates that feature—the thesis statement, an indented quotation, a direct quotation, or supporting details. You may want to provide colored pens so the students can underline different kinds of examples in different colors.

---

464   *Writing a Research Paper*

BODY
History of the League

Three sources cited

Principles

Source with two authors
Great Law of Peace

Council
Summary

More than one title in Works Cited

Parallels between League and U.S. government

This Iroquois Confederacy, a union of five (later six) nations, originated more than four hundred years ago. Also known as the League of the Haudenosaunee and the League of the Five Nations, it traces its history to a legendary Huron, called Deganwidah, who is credited with uniting the Iroquois nations that formed it (Powless; Snow 58-59; Grinde and Johansen 28-29).

Deganwidah, along with another man named Ayonhwahthah, is said to have persuaded leaders of the Five Nations (the Seneca, Mohawk, Cayuga, Oneida, and Onondaga) to accept a "code" based on a concern for three principles: righteousness, civil authority, and the health of society (Snow 60). The willingness of the leaders to embrace the code may have had much to do with their desire to end the cycle of self-destructive blood feuds in which many clans were entangled (Grinde and Johansen 28).

The League created an unwritten but detailed "Great Law of Peace," or constitution, that was passed down through the generations. In 1900, the chiefs of the League approved an official written version of the constitution, drafted in English, that had been developed under the guidance of a Seneca chief named John Gibson (Snow 183-184).

The constitution authorized a council of fifty sachems, or chiefs, to make official decisions about affairs among member nations. Originally, these sachems were selected from leaders who had been chosen by powerful clan mothers within each nation; but, eventually, leadership ability began to have more importance than family relationships (Johansen, Forgotten 26). The number of each nation's sachems varied. The Onondaga, for example, had fourteen sachems, while the Seneca had only eight. In League deliberations, however, each nation had just one vote, which was internally decided by its sachems. All of the League's decisions had to be unanimous (Garbarino and Sasso 316).

An obvious parallel between the Iroquois League and the federal government is union itself. The League was a strong confederation of nations

GUIDED PRACTICE

You may want to reinforce the skills used in writing a research paper by using **A Writer's Model.** In class discussion, ask students to identify the elements of a research report in the model.

Work with students to find examples illustrating each of the guidelines for using ☞

that were related by language and culture but had a history of being separate and quarrelsome (Jennings 362-63). The thirteen American colonies were likewise separate and sometimes at odds. First the Articles of Confederation, in 1781, and then the Constitution of the United States created a strong union of these formerly divided colonies.

Unity

Also, the League dealt only with issues concerning all the nations, primarily matters involving safety and defense. It did not interfere in the internal affairs of member nations (Garbarino and Sasso 316). Similarly, the U.S. Constitution spells out the powers delegated to the federal government, including national defense, reserving all other powers to the states' own governments.

Noninterference in nations/states

Common knowledge, no citation

Both the Iroquois and U.S. constitutions established a representative government of delegates, and several historians have noted likenesses between Iroquois and Congressional procedures. Bruce E. Johansen explains in Forgotten Founders that the Great Law of Peace spelled out a "complex system of checks and balances," with the Senecas and Mohawks called the "older brothers," the Cayugas and Oneidas the "younger brothers," and the Onondagas the "firekeepers" (24-25).

Delegates' procedures

Author and title named in text

Negotiation was highly structured, and Johansen compares the younger and older brothers to a "two-house congress" and says, "The Onondagas filled something of an executive role, with a veto that could be overridden by the older and younger brothers in concert" (25).

As members of Congress do when working out compromise bills, League sachems conducted lengthy deliberations designed to overcome disputes and to create accord (Hooker; "Iroquois League"). To achieve unanimity, senior leaders spoke last, so that they could convey a synthesis or union of the opinions expressed by earlier speakers (Snow 61).

Online source, encyclopedia article, no page numbers needed

Finally, scholars have noted the Great Law's provisions for amendments and for accepting other peoples into the union (Johansen, Forgotten 24-25). Like the framers of the U.S. Constitution,

Amendments, nondiscrimination

MEETING *individual* **NEEDS**

ADVANCED STUDENTS

Challenge advanced students by having them raise the level of their research papers to the evaluative level. You could ask them to provide documentation that supports their evaluation of a subject, such as a government project, the administration of Abraham Lincoln, or the polio vaccine. Although students will still need to give factual information, they will also need to formulate opinions that can be supported.

AT-RISK STUDENTS

Stagger the deadlines for completed first drafts to give more time to students who need it. You may need to compensate for home environments that make writing especially difficult. If your schedule allows, set up additional first-draft meetings before or after school or during free periods to give at-risk students extra time to discuss their problems and to write their reports. You also could encourage students to discuss their writings with each other.

quotations and the guidelines for crediting sources.

You may then lead a search for examples in **A Writer's Model** of the types of parenthetical citations listed on p. 473. This practice should help the students to become familiar with the types of citations as well as with the required form. You can follow the same procedure to analyze the Works Cited by using the guidelines on p. 475.

To give students practice with using sources, work with the groups to complete **Exercise 4** as a class activity.

TECHNOLOGY TIP

Computer programs are available to set up tables, charts, and graphs. You may want to ask one or two students who are adept computer operators to demonstrate some software for these purposes.

You may also want to point out the footnoting capabilities of most word-processing programs; these capabilities can save time and reduce frustration.

the Iroquois provided a mechanism for changing their law, and they made "no bars on the basis of race or national origin." Two colonial men were actually given full citizenship in the Iroquois Confederacy (Johansen, Forgotten 24).

Opposing views

Of course, the League and America's new government were not identical, and not everyone agrees that the Iroquois League was a direct model or had an important influence. Michael Newman, a political journalist, maintains that "Western civilization, beginning in Greece" was a closer model for the founders (17). He has pointed out differences in the Iroquois and U.S. systems, also noting that a respected Constitutional scholar, Michael Kammen, does not support the idea that the Iroquois influenced the writing of the Constitution (17). Kammen's books, A Machine That Would Go of Itself: The Constitution in American Culture and The Origins of the American Constitution: A Documentary History, in fact do not discuss the Iroquois League.

Other models

Expert opinion

Entire books cited

Differences in system
Specific examples

The differences Newman highlights are that the sachems were appointed, not elected; that representation on the Council wasn't proportional; and that Council votes had to be unanimous (17).

Historians who support the theory of Iroquois influence, however, do not claim that no differences existed. Grinde and Johansen, among others, have pointed out fundamental ones: The League, for example, had no coercive power to enforce decisions in the areas of military service or taxation (32). As Johansen replied to Newman's article, the point is not that colonial leaders tried to "copy" the Great Law but that Native Americans helped "shape the thoughts of our Founders" (Letter).

One-word quotation
Rebuttal

Transition to new main topic

Newman's position, however, seems even to reject this idea. In his view, the writers of the Constitution had "nothing" to gain by "looking to the New World for inspiration" (17-18). Nevertheless, Newman does not discuss the considerable contact between colonial leaders and the Iroquois.

Contact between Iroquois and founders

INDEPENDENT PRACTICE

You can use **Writing Assignment: Part 5** for instructions on writing first drafts of research papers. You may want to allow one or two periods for students to work in class so they can get a good start and can ask you about any problems that they need help with.

ASSESSMENT

Provide students with a grading scale to attach to their papers. If you use a scale, you will want to go over each criterion so that students can interpret the scale. Having this scale to consult as they write their first drafts will encourage most students to do a better job. Here is a suggested grading scale: ☛

Writing Your First Draft **467**

The 1988 Congressional resolution states that "the original framers of the Constitution, including, most notably, George Washington and Benjamin Franklin, are known to have greatly admired the concepts of the Six Nations of the Iroquois Confederacy" (United States).

Benjamin Franklin's knowledge of Iroquois League

Benjamin Franklin is an especially clear link between the two political systems, as history documents. He was Pennsylvania's representative to the Iroquois Nations and, as clerk of the Assembly, served as recording secretary at a 1744 meeting between leaders of the Six Nations and the Virginia, Maryland, and Pennsylvania colonies (Johansen, Letter). Here sachems advised the colonial governors to join together as the Iroquois had. One chief took a single arrow in his hand and snapped it easily. Then he took five arrows bound together with a deer sinew; they could not be broken.

Franklin's opinions

There is no question that Franklin found the Iroquois League impressive. On March 20, 1750, he wrote to James Parker, his friend and fellow printer:

Primary source

> It would be a strange thing if Six Nations . . . should be capable of forming a scheme for such a union, and be able to execute it in such a manner as that it has subsisted ages and appears indissoluble; and yet that a like union would be impracticable for ten or a dozen English colonies, to whom it is more necessary and must be more advantageous, and who cannot be supposed to want an equal understanding of their interests. (444)

Early plan

In 1754, Franklin proposed his Albany Plan of Union for the American colonies; the plan resulted from a meeting at which Tiyanoga, an Iroquois chief, was an invited adviser (Johansen, Letter).

Native American participation

Franklin's plan called for a Grand Council made up of delegates from the colonies. The number of delegates from each colony would vary, based not on population, but on the amount of tax revenues

INTEGRATING THE LANGUAGE ARTS

Literature Link. If the work is available in your literature textbook, refer students to an excerpt from James Boswell's *Life of Samuel Johnson* to analyze how a researcher incorporates information from a variety of sources into a biography. Ask the students to read the excerpt and identify all sources mentioned by Boswell.

Introduction	1	2	3	4	5
Thesis	1	2	3	4	5
Organization	5	10	15	20	25
Support	5	10	15	20	25
Documentation	2	4	6	8	10
Quotations	1	2	3	4	5
Conclusion	1	2	3	4	5
Works Cited	2	4	6	8	10
Sources	2	4	6	8	10

Using a grading scale such as this one, you will need only to circle the appropriate number, the middle one being average and the highest one being the best. A perfect score will be 100.

MEETING individual NEEDS

LEARNING STYLES

Visual Learners. You may want to put up posters illustrating the forms needed in a research project (note cards, source cards, Works Cited, and parenthetical citations). Students would probably volunteer to make these posters for extra credit.

TECHNOLOGY TIP

Students can use the *Writer's Workshop CD-ROM* composition program, which has a **Bibliography Maker** feature that will automatically format the student's source information into MLA or APA bibliography style. This bibliography-making feature can be very helpful to the student who becomes easily frustrated by the attention to detail that correctly writing a bibliography often requires.

each colony contributed to the general treasury (Grinde and Johansen 107). The Albany Plan failed, but it planted the seeds for the Articles of Confederation and the U.S. Constitution.

Additional evidence of contact and knowledge

Franklin and others who wrote the Constitution and earlier plans for union may not have specified--in historical documents--that they were using Native American political concepts and laws, but they did consider them. Records show that colonial leaders purposely studied many examples of union. Stephen L. Schechter, executive director of the New York State Bicentennial Commission, said,

Quotation from an indirect source

"They contemplated examples from Europe, examples from Greco-Roman times, examples from the Bible. And they also looked at Native American examples, particularly the Iroquois Confederacy" (qtd. in "Iroquois Constitution").

CONCLUSION

Most Americans today have probably heard something about the Iroquois League, but many are only dimly aware of the principles on which the League was based, not realizing that the people of the United States may owe a debt to the Six Nations for America's political heritage. Among our nation's founders, however, were men who were very familiar with the principles of the League--principles of "peace, brotherhood, and unity, a balance of power, the natural rights of all people, and sharing of resources" (Grinde and Johansen 29). It shouldn't be surprising, then, that some historians maintain that our Constitution--which has so inspired the people of other nations--was not necessarily "cut entirely from European cloth" (Johansen, Letter).

Writer's conclusion/ restatement of thesis

Clincher/vivid quotation

Students who have difficulty writing this first draft can probably benefit from working with you while the other students write independently. Because getting started is usually the main problem, let the student describe the paper before the actual writing begins. After that, ask students to write their first paragraphs. Then, ask the students what they think should come next. Ask them to write the next paragraphs. You may have to make suggestions at first, but after following this step-by-step procedure (first planning orally and then writing) students will probably be able to continue independently.

Writing Your First Draft **469**

Works Cited

Franklin, Benjamin. "To James Parker." 20 Mar. 1750. Letter in Benjamin Franklin: Writings. New York: Library of America, 1987.

Garbarino, Merwyn S., and Robert F. Sasso. Native American Heritage. Prospect Heights, IL: Waveland, 1994.

Grinde, Donald A., Jr., and Bruce E. Johansen. Exemplar of Liberty: Native America and the Evolution of Democracy. Los Angeles: Amer. Indian Studies Center, U of California, Los Angeles, 1991.

Hooker, Richard. "The Iroquois League." World Cultures. 1996. Online. Internet. 12 Dec. 1997. Available http://www.wsu.edu:8080/~dee/IroquoisLeague.html.

"Iroquois Constitution: A Forerunner to Colonists' Democratic Principles." New York Times 28 June 1987, sec. 1: 40.

"Iroquois League." New Encyclopaedia Britannica: Micropaedia. 15th ed. 1988.

Jennings, Francis. The Ambiguous Iroquois Empire. New York: Norton, 1984.

Johansen, Bruce E. Forgotten Founders: Benjamin Franklin, the Iroquois and the Rationale for the American Revolution. Ipswich: Gambit, 1982.

---. Letter. New Republic 19 Dec. 1988: 4.

Kammen, Michael. A Machine That Would Go of Itself: The Constitution in American Culture. New York: Knopf, 1987.

---. The Origins of the American Constitution: A Documentary History. New York: Penguin, 1986.

Lyons, Oren. Interview with Bill Moyers. The Faithkeeper. Prod. and Dir. Betsy McCarthy. Videocassette. Mystic Fire, 1991.

Newman, Michael. "Founding Feathers: The Iroquois and the Constitution." New Republic 7 Nov. 1988: 17-18.

Powless, Robert E. "Iroquois Indians." World Book Multimedia Encyclopedia. CD-ROM. Chicago: World Book, 1995.

Snow, Dean R. The Iroquois. Oxford: Blackwell, 1996.

United States. Cong. House Committee on Interior and Insular Affairs. House Report 100-1031. 100th Cong., 2nd sess. H. Res. 331. Washington: GPO, 1988.

INTEGRATING THE LANGUAGE ARTS

Mechanics Link. As you go over **A Writer's Model** with students, review several uses of punctuation that they will need in their papers later. These rules might include the use of quotation marks for whole or partial quotations, capitalization of proper nouns, commas to set off appositives identifying a person, and underlining or quotation marks to indicate a title.

Ask students to take notes and to include sample sentences to illustrate each use. When students have written their first drafts, you can ask them to review their notes and to check their papers for correct usage.

GUIDELINES FOR PREPARING THE WORKS CITED

The MLA calls for a five-space indent. For the typeface used in this book, the five-space indent translates into a printer's measure that is slightly different.

You may want to lead a discussion about how writing a research paper differs from writing other expository or persuasive papers. What additional skills are required for the research paper? Which skills already learned were used for the research paper?

You may want to relate research skills to other academic disciplines by making arrangements with a teacher of another class, such as government or science or math, to make the research paper a joint project. Or, since all of your students may not be together in any other class, you may

Using Quotations

When you use information from sources in your paper, most of it will be summarized. By summarizing, you shape the information to the needs of your own writing *and* avoid boring readers with strings of quotations. However, direct quotations are important for variety and will sometimes make your point better or more vividly than a summary. Following are some ways to use quotations smoothly.

QUOTATION FOR THE DAY

"Taking something from one man and making it worse is plagiarism." (George Moore, 1852–1933, Irish writer)

Write the quotation on the chalkboard and use it to approach the subject of documentation within a research composition. Remind students that properly crediting sources is an important part of drafting a research paper.

A DIFFERENT APPROACH

Students unfamiliar with documentation may have difficulty understanding what the parts of entries in a Works Cited stand for. You could divide the class into groups of three or four and ask the groups to read the **Sample Entries for List of Works Cited** on pp. 476–480 and to identify what each part stands for. You could model by explaining the first entry.

After the groups finish, lead a game. Go around the room asking groups questions about the meanings of parts of the Works Cited entries. For every correct answer, the group receives a point. The group receiving the most points wins.

GUIDELINES FOR USING QUOTATIONS

1. **Quote one or more whole sentences, introducing them in your own words.**

   EXAMPLE   Chief Lyons commented, "But America got it from the Indians. America got the ideas of democracy and freedom and peace here."

2. **Quote part of a sentence within a sentence of your own.**

   EXAMPLE   Bruce E. Johansen explains that the Great Law spelled out a "complex system of checks and balances" (Forgotten 24).

3. **Quote only a few words (or even just one word) within a sentence of your own.**

   EXAMPLE   These historians do not believe the writers of the Constitution tried to "copy" the Great Law (Johansen, Letter).

4. **Use ellipsis points (three spaced periods) to show you've omitted words from a quotation.** You may want to alter a quotation to shorten it or make it fit grammatically into your text. If so, you must use ellipsis points for words deleted within a sentence or for any deletion that makes a partial sentence from the source appear to be a complete sentence.

   EXAMPLE   Johansen explains that "The retention of internal sovereignty within the individual colonies . . . closely resembled the Iroquoian system" (Forgotten 71-72).

(continued)

want to try to make arrangements between departments.

Before making the assignment, you and the other teachers could work out mutual requirements and deadlines; you will also need to agree on which part of the process each teacher will teach. Generally, in joint projects the other subject-area teacher will help students select topics, write thesis statements, and do research. The English teacher usually teaches skills such as writing note cards, organizing material in an outline, and providing clear transitions.

Both teachers need to evaluate the papers, but they can divide the duties by evaluating the different areas suggested in a grading scale similar to the one in **Assessment.** ■

GUIDELINES FOR USING QUOTATIONS *(continued)*

5. **Set off longer quotations as "blocks."** For quotations of four lines or more, start a new line, indent the entire quotation ten spaces from the left margin, continue to double-space, and do not use quotation marks.

   EXAMPLE   See the quotation from Benjamin Franklin's letter on page 467.

Documenting Sources

Documentation, giving credit to your sources, is an important part of writing a research report. How can you tell whether to give credit or not? Here are some *do's* and *don't's.*

GUIDELINES FOR CREDITING SOURCES

1. **Do** credit the source of each quotation (unless it's very widely known, such as George Bush's "Read my lips").

2. **Do** credit the source of information from scientific studies, surveys, and polls and other sources of unique or little-known information. (Doing so also lends credibility to sources of information unfamiliar to your audience. You want your audience to accept the information you present.)

3. **Do** credit any original theory, opinion, or conclusion. You must not present another person's ideas as your own, even if you are paraphrasing them. (See the discussion of plagiarism on the next page.)

4. **Don't** credit facts that appear in standard reference works or several sources. For example, the names of the nations in the Iroquois League are given in most encyclopedias and do not need documentation. And if several history books state that League votes had to be unanimous, you do not need to credit this information.

5. **Don't** credit common, or general, knowledge. For example, you don't have to document the fact that oil spills damage the environment or that Washington, D.C., does not have Congressional representatives.

A DIFFERENT APPROACH

One method to encourage good individual writing is to give students about ten minutes to look over their note cards before they begin writing their first drafts from memory. They should look only at the thesis statements and outlines prepared during prewriting. If they have forgotten some details or can't remember direct quotations they want to use, they can leave blanks to be filled in later.

This procedure helps students to avoid copying from sources. It is almost impossible to write smoothly and creatively while staring first at one card and then at another. Voice will come through much more clearly when students are freed from the monotonous shuffling of note cards; as writers, they will more likely provide transitions and employ logic. As soon as the drafts are finished, students can consult their cards and fill in the parenthetical citations.

Finally, students can use their source cards to compile their Works Cited.

Avoiding Plagiarism. Caution! If you use someone else's *words or ideas* without giving proper credit, you're guilty of *plagiarism.* Plagiarism is a serious offense, and your teacher will view it as such. Be scrupulous about crediting not only direct quotations but also restatements of the original ideas of others. Don't use another person's phrases or exact sentence structure unless you enclose the material in quotation marks. When in doubt about plagiarism, give credit.

Using Parenthetical Citations. The source references in parentheses in the body of the Writer's Model are called *parenthetical citations.* The purpose of a parenthetical citation is to give the reader just enough information to find the full source listing on the Works Cited page. Often, the author's last name and the page numbers are all that is needed, but here are some exceptions to that rule.

- A nonprint source such as a Web page or videotape will not have a page number.
- A print source of fewer than two pages (such as a one-page letter) will not require a page number.
- If you name the author in your sentence, you need give only the page number (for print sources of more than one page) in parentheses: Michael Newman, a political journalist, maintains that "Western civilization, beginning in Greece" was a closer model for the founders (17).
- If the author has more than one work in the Works Cited list, you will also have to give a short form of the title so readers will know which work you are citing: (Johansen, Forgotten 24) or (Johansen, Letter).

The following chart defines and illustrates the basic forms of parenthetical citations.

<table>
<tr><td colspan="2" align="center">**BASIC CONTENT AND FORM OF PARENTHETICAL CITATIONS**</td></tr>
<tr><td colspan="2">These examples assume that the author or work has not been named in introducing the source information.</td></tr>
<tr><td>**Works by one author**
Author's last name and a page reference</td><td>(Farb 97)</td></tr>
<tr><td>**Works by more than one author**
All author's last names (or first author and *et al.* if over three) and a page reference</td><td>(Richter and Merrill 78)
(Spencer et al. 384)</td></tr>
<tr><td>**Multivolume works**
Author's last name plus volume and page(s)</td><td>(Prucha 2: 115-16)</td></tr>
<tr><td>**Works with a title only**
Full title (if short) or a shortened version and a page reference</td><td>(Great Law of Peace 9)
("Iroquois Debate" 5)</td></tr>
<tr><td>**Literary works published in many editions**
Author and title above, but with other identifying information, such as act, scene, and line numbers</td><td>(Shakespeare, Tempest 3. 2. 51-52)</td></tr>
<tr><td>**Indirect sources**
Qtd. in ("quoted in") before the source and a page reference</td><td>(qtd. in Newman 17)</td></tr>
<tr><td>**More than one work**
Citations, with page numbers, separated by semicolons</td><td>(Bjorklund 57; Moquin 20)</td></tr>
</table>

A DIFFERENT APPROACH
Students could engage their imaginations and practice using quotations at the same time. Have students write articles about school life for a community magazine. Have them base their articles on facts or made-up material. They should include quotations from real or made-up sources. Have them include quotation lead-ins such as the following ones:

1. As _____ stated, ". . . ."
2. According to _____, ". . . ."
3. _____ reports that ". . . ."

COOPERATIVE LEARNING

Deciding when to give credit can be difficult even for your best writers. To help students see the difference between general information and information that needs to be documented, divide the class into four groups and assign each group a different author about whom information is widely and readily available.

Each group member should consult reference sources and write down one fact about the assigned author that should be documented and one fact that would not need to be documented, according to the guidelines. Group members should discuss the information to make decisions about documenting.

There are rules of form about placement of citations, too. Again, use both the following chart and the Writer's Model for examples.

PLACEMENT OF CITATIONS

1. Put the citation close to the information it documents, but try not to interrupt sentences. Place it at the end of a sentence or at another point of punctuation.
2. Place the citation *before* the punctuation mark of the sentence, clause, or phrase you're documenting.

   EXAMPLE   The League was a strong confederation of nations that were related by language and culture but had a history of being separate and quarrelsome (Jennings 362-63).

3. For a direct quotation that ends a sentence, place the citation *after* the quotation mark but *before* the end punctuation mark.

   EXAMPLE   The Onondagas were the "firekeepers" (Johansen 24).

4. For an indented quotation, place the citation **two spaces after the final punctuation mark.**

   EXAMPLE   See pages 463 and 467.

WRITING NOTE   An alternative to the parenthetical citation system is citation by numbered *footnotes* or *endnotes.* Footnotes and endnotes are identical, except that a **footnote** goes at the bottom of the page where the source is cited, while **endnotes** are listed together on a separate page at the end of the report.

In using either type of note, place the note number in the text where a parenthetical citation would otherwise appear. The first time a work is cited, give full publication information in the note. Thereafter, use a short form. If your teacher wants you to use footnotes or endnotes, you'll need guidelines showing further examples of form.

EXAMPLE

Number in body of paper In the giant tree a vigilant eagle searched for anyone who threatened to disturb the Great Peace.[7]

Note (full form) [7] Karna L. Bjorklund, The Indians of Northeastern America (New York: Dodd, 1969) 61.

Listing Works Cited. The list of *Works Cited* contains all the sources that you cite in your paper. *Works Cited* is a broader term than *Bibliography,* which refers only to printed information. If your list includes sources that you consulted but did not directly cite in the body of your paper, your teacher may prefer that you title the list *Works Consulted.*

GUIDELINES FOR PREPARING THE WORKS CITED LIST

1. **Center the heading *Works Cited* on a separate page from your report.**
2. **Begin each entry on a separate line.** Start the first line of the entry at the left margin. Then indent the second and subsequent lines five spaces. Use double-spacing.
3. **Alphabetize the sources by the authors' last names.** If a source has no author, alphabetize it by the first word of the title, ignoring an initial *A, An,* or *The.*
4. **If you list two or more sources by the same author, put the author's name only in the first entry.** For subsequent entries, put three hyphens where the author's name would be, followed by a period (- - -.).

EXERCISE 4 ▶ Using Sources

Work with a partner to practice using direct quotations, summaries, and paraphrases of material from sources, as well as parenthetical citations. Using the source information in the directions for Exercise 3 (page 454) and its excerpt about hippopotamuses, complete the tasks that follow on the next page. For each task item, include a parenthetical citation.

directions for Exercise 3 (page 454)

MEETING *individual* **NEEDS**

LESS-ADVANCED STUDENTS

You may want to help students, either individually or in groups, outline **A Writer's Model.** This activity can help them to visualize the concise and logical overall organization of the report. Refer them to **Here's How** on p. 461. Tell students that the side glosses for the body of **A Writer's Model** correspond to the main ideas that follow the Roman numerals and the details that follow the letters and Arabic numerals in the outline. Refer students to the first two Roman numerals in the outline and the side glosses.

ANSWERS
Exercise 4

Sentences and paragraphs will vary.

1. A sentence will be acceptable if it accurately summarizes Schwartz's points, includes a few words of direct quotation, and is followed by a correct parenthetical citation.

2. This sentence or two will be acceptable if it/they show how hippos perform some activities, such as feeding, on land and others, such as bearing and nursing young, underwater. Paraphrased material requires appropriate parenthetical citations.

3. The paragraph will be acceptable if it tells how hippos herd together and how a dominant bull hippo protects the cows, often through warfare with other bulls. Quoted and paraphrased material must have appropriate parenthetical citations.

1. Write a sentence that summarizes David Schwartz's description of the hippopotamus's eating habits. Include a few words of direct quotation in the sentence.
2. Write one or two sentences that contrast a description of the hippo's behavior in water with a description of its behavior on land. You will probably need to paraphrase parts of the third paragraph of the excerpt.
3. Write a short paragraph explaining the role that Schwartz says bull hippos play in hippopotamus herds. Make sure to include at least one direct quotation from the fourth paragraph of the excerpt.

| WRITING ASSIGNMENT | PART 5: **Writing Your First Draft** |

Use your outline and note cards to write a first draft of your research report. Before you begin, recheck the list of elements on page 462, and then concentrate on getting ideas down on paper. *Do* insert parenthetical citations—without stopping your flow too much. You only need to get a basic reference in: You can add, delete, and correct form in the citations later. Finally, draft a Works Cited list of the sources you actually credit in the paper, *using the guidelines that follow to prepare it.*

SAMPLE ENTRIES FOR LIST OF WORKS CITED

These sample entries, which use MLA style, are a reference for preparing your Works Cited list. Notice that you include page numbers only for articles in periodicals or for other works that are part of a whole work, such as one essay in a book of essays.

Standard Reference Works
When an author or editor is credited in a standard reference work, that person's name is written first. Otherwise, the title of the book or article appears first. Page and volume numbers aren't needed if the work alphabetizes entries. For common reference works, the edition year is sufficient publication information.

(continued)

SAMPLE ENTRIES FOR LIST OF WORKS CITED *(continued)*

PRINT ENCYCLOPEDIA ARTICLE

Smith, Whitney. "Great Seal of the United States."
    Encyclopedia Americana. 1990 ed.
"Iroquois League." New Encyclopaedia Britannica:
    Micropaedia. 15th ed. 1988.

ARTICLE IN A BIOGRAPHICAL REFERENCE BOOK

Amacher, Richard E. "Benjamin Franklin." Dictionary
    of Literary Biography. Ed. Emory Elliott. Vol. 24.
    Detroit: Gale, 1984. 125-47.

Books
Use shortened forms of publishers' names. For the words
University **and** *Press* **use** *U* **and** *P.*

ONE AUTHOR

Snow, Dean R. The Iroquois. Oxford: Blackwell, 1996.

TWO AUTHORS

Grinde, Donald A., Jr., and Bruce E. Johansen. Exemplar
    of Liberty: Native America and the Evolution of
    Democracy. Los Angeles: Amer. Indian Studies Center,
    U of California, Los Angeles, 1991.

THREE AUTHORS

Hirschfelder, Arlene B., Mary Gloyne Byler, and Michael A.
    Dorris. Guide to Research on North American
    Indians. Chicago: Amer. Lib. Assn., 1983.

FOUR OR MORE AUTHORS

Lyons, Oren, et al. Exiled in the Land of the Free:
    Democracy, Indian Nations, and the U.S.
    Constitution. Santa Fe: Clear Light, 1992.

NO AUTHOR SHOWN

The Great Law of Peace and the Constitution of the United
    States of America. Akwesasne, NY: Tree of Peace, 1988.

EDITOR OF A COLLECTION OF WRITINGS

Tooker, Elisabeth, ed. An Iroquois Sourcebook: Political
    and Social Organization. New York: Garland, 1985.

(continued)

INTEGRATING THE LANGUAGE ARTS

Paragraph Link. You may want to refer students to the section in **Chapter 2** on connecting ideas within and between sentences in a paragraph. Explain that direct references and transitional expressions are also used to connect ideas between paragraphs in a longer composition. You could display an article from a newspaper or a magazine on an overhead transparency and ask students to find the direct references and transitional expressions that help link ideas between paragraphs.

SAMPLE ENTRIES FOR LIST OF WORKS CITED *(continued)*

TWO OR THREE EDITORS
Foster, Michael, Jack Campisi, and Marianne Mithun, eds. Extending the Rafters: Interdisciplinary Approaches to Iroquoian Studies. Albany: State U of New York P, 1984.

BIBLIOGRAPHY PUBLISHED AS A BOOK
Johansen, Bruce E., comp. Native American Political Systems and the Evolution of Democracy: An Annotated Bibliography. Westport: Greenwood, 1996.

UNPUBLISHED THESIS OR DISSERTATION
Katz, Regina. "Iroquois Diplomacy and the Great Binding Law." Thesis. East Stroudsburg U, 1992.

Selections Within Books

FROM A BOOK OF WORKS BY ONE AUTHOR
Wilson, Edmund. "The Seneca Republic." Apologies to the Iroquois. 1959. Syracuse: Syracuse UP, 1992.

FROM A BOOK OF WORKS BY SEVERAL AUTHORS
Grinde, Donald A., Jr. "Iroquoian Political Concept and the Genesis of American Government." Indian Roots of American Democracy. Ed. José Barreiro. Ithaca, NY: Akwe:kon Press, Cornell U, 1992. 47-66.

INTRODUCTION, PREFACE, FOREWORD, OR AFTERWORD
Barreiro, José. Introduction. The Indian Roots of American Democracy. Ed. José Barreiro. Ithaca, NY: Akwe:kon Press, Cornell U, 1992. 1-9.

Articles from Magazines, Newspapers, and Journals

FROM A WEEKLY MAGAZINE
Adler, Jerry. "The Genius of the People." Newsweek 25 May 1987: 46-47.

FROM A MONTHLY OR QUARTERLY MAGAZINE
Zobel, Hiller B. "How History Made the Constitution." American Heritage Mar. 1988: 54+.

[The + sign means the article isn't on consecutive pages.]

(continued)

SAMPLE ENTRIES FOR LIST OF WORKS CITED *(continued)*

NO AUTHOR SHOWN
"Revenge of the Senecas." Time 2 July 1990: 27.

FROM A SCHOLARLY JOURNAL
Fargnoli, Joseph. "Zuni and Iroquois: Edmund Wilson's 'People's History.'" Clio 25.1 (1995): 21-41.

FROM A DAILY NEWSPAPER, WITH A BYLINE (LINE IDENTIFYING THE WRITER)
Grimes, William. "The Indian Museum's Last Stand." New York Times 27 Nov. 1988, sec. 6: 46+.

FROM A DAILY NEWSPAPER, WITHOUT A BYLINE
"Iroquois Constitution: A Forerunner to Colonists' Democratic Principles." New York Times 28 June 1987, sec. 1: 40.

UNSIGNED EDITORIAL FROM A DAILY NEWSPAPER, NO CITY IN PAPER'S TITLE
"Supreme Injustice." Editorial. Star-Ledger [Newark, NJ] 6 Oct. 1991: 17.

Other Sources

PERSONAL INTERVIEW
Whitecrow, Gloria. Personal interview. 15 Dec. 1997.

TELEPHONE INTERVIEW
Snow, Dean R. Telephone interview. 5 Dec. 1997.

PUBLISHED INTERVIEW WITH TITLE
Johnson, Elias. "Origin of the Five Nations." Cry of the Thunderbird: The American Indian's Own Story. Ed. Charles Hamilton. Norman: U of Oklahoma P, 1972.

BROADCAST OR RECORDED INTERVIEW WITH TITLE
Lyons, Oren. Interview with Bill Moyers. The Faithkeeper. Prod. and Dir. Betsy McCarthy. Videocassette. Mystic Fire, 1991.

(continued)

A DIFFERENT APPROACH

Encourage interested students to provide visuals for their research reports. Students should be thinking of ideas for illustrations as they write and complete their first drafts. You could help students select appropriate visual categories based on their topics. For example, some topics may lend themselves to paintings or drawings, while others may be best illustrated with models or maps. Students could provide original visuals or find appropriate existing visuals. Students can be creative in doing their own artwork, but they can also be creative in selecting visuals.

A DIFFERENT APPROACH

As a review, you may want to give students the following true-or-false test:

1. A Works Cited contains only print material. [false]
2. A parenthetical citation is placed at the bottom of a page. [false]
3. In general, facts that appear in standard reference books are not documented. [true]
4. Use dashes to indicate omissions from quotations. [false]
5. A thesis statement should appear early in the paper. [true]

TEACHING NOTE

Students may be confused when a sentence ends with an Internet address and a period follows the address. Remind students that the final period in such a listing is punctuation for the sentence; the period is not part of the internet address. Although the mark for a period looks the same as the mark used to separate parts of an Internet address, the mark is called a *dot* when it appears in an Internet address.

Also, although MLA style requires listing a city of publication for a CD-ROM database, you may want to allow students to omit the city when the information is not readily available. For example, the city name may be printed on the box that the CD-ROM came in, but the city name and other copyright information may not be available from within the database itself.

SAMPLE ENTRIES FOR LIST OF WORKS CITED *(continued)*

PUBLISHED LETTER
Franklin, Benjamin. "To James Parker." 20 Mar. 1750. Letter in Benjamin Franklin: Writings. New York: Library of America, 1987.

PERSONAL LETTER OR E-MAIL MESSAGE
Hooker, Richard. Letter to the author. 10 Dec. 1997.

SOUND RECORDING
Grinde, Donald A. The Iroquois Influence on July 4, 1776. Audiocassette. Chautauqua Inst.; Audio Magic, 1992.

FILM OR VIDEO RECORDING
The Iroquois. Prod. Henry Nevison. Videocassette. Library Video Co., 1993.
[Always include the title, director or producer, distributor, and year. For video recordings, add a description of the medium (*Videotape* or *Videocassette*) before the distributor's name.]

MATERIAL ACCESSED THROUGH THE INTERNET
Hooker, Richard. "The Iroquois League." World Cultures. 1996. Online. Internet. 12 Dec. 1997. Available http://www.wsu.edu:8080/~dee/IroquoisLeague.html.

ARTICLE FROM A CD-ROM REFERENCE WORK
Powless, Robert E. "Iroquois Indians." World Book Multimedia Encyclopedia. CD-ROM. Chicago: World Book, 1995.

FULL-TEXT MAGAZINE, NEWSPAPER, OR JOURNAL ARTICLE FROM A CD-ROM DATABASE
Leo, John. "The Junking of History." U.S. News & World Report 28 Feb. 1994:17. Middle Search. CD-ROM. EBSCO Publishing, Aug. 1996.

EVALUATING AND REVISING

OBJECTIVES

- To analyze a writer's revisions
- To evaluate and revise a research report

TEACHING THE LESSON

Explain the **Evaluating and Revising Research Reports** chart on p. 482. Be sure students understand how to use the chart and call attention to the three general techniques emphasized throughout the chart—add, replace, and cut.

You could use **Exercise 5** for modeling evaluation and revision. Students might ☞

Evaluating and Revising

Evaluate and revise in steps: First focus on content, then on structure, and finally on clarity. Use the chart on page 482.

EXERCISE 5 ▶ **Analyzing a Writer's Revisions**

Here is the first draft of a paragraph from the model on page 464. Study the revisions and answer the questions.

The constitution authorized a council
of fifty sachems ∧or chiefs∧ to make official decisions   **add**
about affairs among member nations.
Originally, these sachems were selected
from leaders who had been ~~selected~~ *chosen* by   **replace**
powerful clan mothers within each
nation; but, eventually, leadership ability
began to have more importance than
family relationships (Johansen, Forgotten
26). In League deliberations, *however,* ∧each nation   **add**
had ∧*just* one vote. *∧which was internally decided by its sachems* The number of each   **add/reorder**
nation's sachems varied. The Onondaga,
for example, had fourteen sachems, while
the Seneca had only eight. ∧All of the
League's decisions had to be ~~decided~~   **cut**
~~unanimously~~ (Garbarino and Sasso 316).   **cut**

1. Why does the writer add two words to the first sentence?
2. The writer replaces a word in the second sentence. Why?
3. For what reasons does the writer move the third sentence and make several additions to it?
4. Explain why the writer makes cuts to the last sentence.

ANSWERS
Exercise 5

1. In the first sentence, the writer adds two words to identify a term that is unfamiliar to most readers.

also benefit from practice with sentence combining. You can use the examples on varying sentence structure in the **Grammar Hint** for illustration.

Let students work in pairs on the evaluation and revision of their papers for **Writing Assignment: Part 6.** Ask students to evaluate their papers to decide on the revisions to be made. Then each student can explain the plans to his or her partner, who will read the paper and respond to those plans. Urge students to be supportive and encouraging.

continued from p. 481

2. The change is made to avoid using the word *selected* twice in the same sentence.

3. The third sentence offers a contrast to the fact that nations had different numbers of sachems, and the new position makes this contrast clearer. The addition of *however* makes the contrast more explicit, and the relative clause explains how voting worked with different numbers of chiefs in each nation.

4. This sentence is redundant and is inconsistent with the tone of the rest of the essay.

5. The cuts eliminate wordiness.

MEETING *individual* NEEDS

LESS-ADVANCED STUDENTS

Some students may be able to evaluate and revise their papers more effectively if you lead them through the process using the guidelines in **Evaluating and Revising Research Reports.**

For example, first ask students to underline their thesis statements. Ask for volunteers to read their statements for other students to evaluate. If there is a problem, point out the revision technique suggested and ask both the writer and the other students what might be done to improve the paper. Continue with each of the eight points listed.

EVALUATING AND REVISING RESEARCH REPORTS

EVALUATION GUIDE	REVISION TECHNIQUE
1 Does a thesis statement appear early in the report?	**Add** a statement to the introduction that gives your report's main idea.
2 Is the report developed with sufficient sources that are relevant, reliable, recent, and representative?	**Add** facts, examples, or expert opinions. **Cut** or **replace** outdated or questionable information. **Add** sources to balance controversial views.
3 Is the report clear, interesting, and suitable for its audience?	**Add** needed background information and explanations. **Add** interesting, unusual, or surprising details.
4 Is the tone of the report appropriate?	**Replace** words or phrases that make your report sound too casual.
5 Are ideas and information stated mainly in the writer's own words?	**Cut** unnecessary quotations. **Replace** sentences in which your wording is too close to that of the source.
6 Does all the information relate directly to the topic and thesis?	**Cut** information that doesn't develop your main ideas.
7 Has proper credit been given for each source of information?	**Add** proper documentation for quotations, others' ideas, and information that is unique or not general knowledge.
8 Does documentation follow the style recommended by your teacher?	**Replace** and correct as necessary to follow MLA style or another professional style.

Ask each student to write down his or her plans for revision and to turn those plans in with the revised first draft. You can do a quick check to see whether or not the student has evaluated his or her writing carefully and made good revisions.

Have students discuss the revisions they have made in their papers. It will be helpful for students to determine what types of problems are most likely to arise so that they will have fewer revisions to make, especially in content and organization, the next time. ∎

GRAMMAR HINT

Varying Sentence Structure

It's very possible to write a long paper, full of information, that is energetic and easy to read. One way to do that is to vary the types of sentences you use. By paying attention to how your sentences work together and using different sentence structures, you can create variety both in length and in rhythm.

EXAMPLES

Simple sentence: one independent clause. *It did not interfere in the internal affairs of member nations.*

Compound sentence: two or more independent clauses connected by a conjunction or semicolon. *Then he took five arrows bound together with a deer sinew; they could not be broken.*

Complex sentence: one independent clause and one or more subordinate clauses. *As Johansen replied to Newman's article, the point is not that colonial leaders tried to "copy" the Great Law.*

Compound-complex sentence: two or more independent clauses and at least one subordinate clause. *Lyons's statement may seem extreme, but he is not alone in believing that Native Americans influenced the colonists who founded the United States.*

☞ **REFERENCE NOTE:** For more information on sentence structure, see pages 686–687.

COOPERATIVE LEARNING

Divide the class into groups of three or four and ask students to provide enough copies of their first drafts so that each student in the group can read at the same time. (For students who don't have access to computers, you may need to make copies on the school duplicator.)

Ask students to evaluate and suggest revisions for one paper at a time, using as a guideline **Evaluating and Revising Research Reports.**

Assign group members the following roles: discussion leader (keeps the discussion going), timer (makes sure that all papers are discussed in the time allotted), watchdog (keeps the group on task), and writer (takes notes).

TIMESAVER

Instruct students to mark additions, cuts, and replacements on their rough drafts so that you easily can identify intended changes. If they are using word-processing programs, tell students to make printouts of the rough drafts and to mark revisions.

WRITING ASSIGNMENT

PART 6:
Evaluating and Revising Your Report

Ask someone else to read your report, and pay close attention to reactions and suggestions. Using the guidelines on page 482, continue to revise until you're satisfied that your report is tightly organized, well focused, clear, and interesting.

PROOFREADING AND PUBLISHING

OBJECTIVES

- To proofread a research report
- To publish a research report

TEACHING THE LESSON

You may want to instruct students to divide the proofreading stage of the writing process into three parts. First, refer students to standard guidelines for proofreading. Tell them to use the guidelines referring to grammar, usage, and mechanics to proofread the bodies of their papers. Then, have students check the mechanics of their documentation

PROGRAM MANAGER

PROOFREADING AND PUBLISHING

- **Instructional Support** For a chart students may use to evaluate their proofreading progress, see **Proofreading** in *Strategies for Writing,* p. 58.

- **Independent Practice/ Reteaching** For additional practice with language skills, see **Proofreading Practice: Varying Sentence Structure** in *Strategies for Writing,* p. 59.

- **Assessment/Reflection** To assess student work and evaluate progress, see **Portfolio Forms** in *Portfolio Assessment,* pp. 22–25.

TEACHING NOTE

In addition to the questions for reflection in the textbook, you might want to have students compile lists of things they would do differently the next time they undertake research papers. Remind them that these notes might prove very valuable to them in the future.

Proofreading and Publishing

Proofreading. A research paper requires a careful check for accuracy in citations and Works Cited entries. Consult the lists on pages 473 and 476–480 as you work. Peer proofreading will help you catch errors you might otherwise miss.

Publishing. A research paper is a real achievement that deserves to be shared with others. Brainstorm with your class about imaginative publishing, and consider these possibilities:

- Send a copy of your report to a group that has an interest in your subject. The Association on American Indian Affairs, for example, might appreciate a copy of the Writer's Model, "America's Legacy from the Iroquois League."
- Use your research report as a writing sample to accompany a college application or a job application. First, make sure, though, that it fits the requirements given by the college or business.

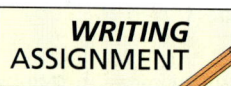

> **WRITING ASSIGNMENT**
>
> PART 7:
> **Proofreading and Publishing Your Report**

When you proofread, do a separate review of your citations and the Works Cited list. Make sure the two *match:* Does every citation have an entry in *Works Cited*? Do authors or titles appear the same way in both places? But don't neglect errors in your writing itself. When you have a clean, professional-looking paper, share it with interested readers.

Reflecting on Your Writing

If you include your research paper in your **portfolio,** date the paper and attach responses to the following questions.

- What resources helped most in preparing your paper? Why? Which did not help much? Why not?
- When you began writing the first draft of your paper, how did your notes and your outline become useful?

by referring to the guidelines in this chapter. Finally, tell students to check the mechanics of their Works Cited against the guidelines in the chapter.

Some class time may be needed to give students special instruction in any areas of grammar, usage, and mechanics in which they are generally weak. You also may want to require students to read **A Student Model** for another example of a polished paper.

After students have proofread their papers, give directions about how their papers should be handed in (directions about cover sheets, folders, and so forth). Then, join students in brainstorming some ways to publish their reports.

"WRITE A THOUSAND-WORD ESSAY ON LOUIS XIV AND HIS ESTABLISHMENT OF THE ACADÉMIE ROYALE de DANSE"

"IDENTIFY REFERENCES AND SOURCE MATERIAL BY CHAPTER AND PAGE"

NO, MA'AM, I'M NOT SLEEPING...

I JUST PASSED OUT!

Peanuts reprinted by permission of United Feature Syndicate, Inc.

A STUDENT MODEL

You can apply your research skills to any topic, as Jennifer Guild—a student at Nashua High School in Nashua, New Hampshire—shows in her research paper on birth order and personality. Notice how the following excerpts both develop support for her thesis and provide a thought-provoking conclusion. And Jennifer has this to say about writing a research paper: "Keep track of where your notes are from!"

Birth Order
by Jennifer Guild

Your birth order, whether you were born first, second or later in your family, has a powerful influence on the kind of person you will be. It also affects the kind of person you will marry, the type of occupation you will choose, and even the

A STUDENT MODEL
Evaluation

1. Jennifer gives the main idea of her report as the last sentence of the introductory paragraph.

2. The sources in Jennifer's report are relevant, recent, reliable, and representative. For example, she refers to five different sources, includes several direct quotations as support, and gives more than one expert's evidence to support her assertions. Dr. Leman's book, *The Birth Order Book,* was published in 1984.

3. How to understand a person's personality through birth order is an interesting and timely topic, one suitable to either Jennifer's peers or her teacher.

4. Jennifer is able to state her ideas and information in her own words because she logically introduces and explains quotations and documented material.

5. All of the information Jennifer includes directly relates to her thesis.

6. Jennifer gives credit for others' ideas and words by properly documenting them within her paper.

Ask students to identify the stages of the writing process that they've used to create their research papers [prewriting, writing first draft, evaluating and revising, proofreading and publishing]. Then, have students briefly discuss what they have found most challenging, difficult, interesting, and enjoyable about writing their research papers. ■

MEETING individual NEEDS

LEP/ESL

General Strategies. Students will benefit more from proofreading if they are instructed to focus on one element of the language at a time. Pair students with peer tutors. Ask English-language learners to underline all verbs in their reports and, with the peer tutors' assistance, to check only for correct tense and agreement. By following this diagnostic process, students can easily identify problem areas relating to verb usage. Assign students study material that will help strengthen their specific areas of weakness.

◆ INTEGRATING THE LANGUAGE ARTS

Speaking Link. Encourage students to present their reports aloud to the class or to other classes or clubs. Tell students to rehearse their presentations on their own. If possible, schedule some time when you can give them pointers on eye contact, facial expressions, gestures, posture, and pronunciation.

486

---

486   *Writing a Research Paper*

type of parent you will be (Leman 11). The patterns set in motion by birth order don't prescribe what must occur; they simply describe tendencies that may need to be recognized or overcome (Withers 58). This paper illustrates what some researchers suggest about how oldest, only, middle, and youngest children are affected by their birth order.

Birth order characteristics appear to be set by age five. They tend to start over with the next child when there exists a large age difference of five or more years between siblings. Birth order traits develop as coping strategies a child uses to feel comfortable in his or her particular position in the family. These coping strategies include to be pleasing, to be perfect, to be strong, or to try hard (Isaacson 5).

Some only children develop birth order characteristics while trying to avoid excessive attention from their parents and while playing alone without the company of siblings. Shy and self-conscious around their peers, onlies are used to considerate treatment from their parents and other adults. Thus, their feelings are easily hurt when other children are rude. Not having siblings to relate to or play with, onlies automatically identify with their parents and come to think of themselves as small adults (Spock 38). Only children tend to pick up characteristics of their same-sex parent. Onlies are often most comfortable alone, yet they tend to be well-adjusted individuals (Withers 59). . . .

Firstborn children tend to be more serious in their approach to life and are likely to be jealous of their younger siblings' easy popularity (Spock 38). Usually the more studious of the children, firstborns may be considered overachievers. Relatively quiet and reserved, self-assured firstborns may become perfectionists and worriers who find it difficult to take criticism or tolerate others' mistakes. They may be slow to make friends, perhaps being content with only one companion (Withers 59). Firstborn children may identify more readily with parental authority because, among other things, they are often put in charge of younger siblings. Through this identification, firstborns absorb the norms and values of society in ways that subsequent children do not. "The older child gets responsibility. He's the company man," says University of Michigan psychologist Robert Zajonc (Denworth 76). . . .

Middle children, in contrast to onlies and oldest children, tend to make friends more quickly. Unlike firstborns, they identify with other children and share their eager playfulness. In fact, they're so eager to make friends that they easily overlook the impolite behavior of other children and win them over with their innate friendliness. Middle children are not generally self-conscious; they tend to be more at ease with themselves and the world (Spock 38). Middle children are less likely to take initiative or achieve the high academic standards of an only or an oldest child. They are more anxious and self-critical than others (Withers 59). "The general conclusion of all research studies done on birth order is that middle children will probably be somewhat opposite of firstborns" (Leman 117). . . .

Lastborn children may carry the yoke of not being taken very seriously, first by their families and then by the world. Lastborns are acutely aware that they are the youngest, smallest, weakest, and least equipped to cope with life. Lastborns instinctively know and understand that their knowledge and ability carry far less weight than that of their older brothers and sisters. The older kids always laugh at the baby who still believes blindly in fantasies like Santa Claus and the Tooth Fairy. It's no wonder the lastborns grow up with an "I'll show them!" attitude (Leman 133-136). . . .

Birth order continues to be revealing when you look at who's in what occupation. All seven astronauts in the original Mercury program were firstborns in their families (Leman 11). James Watson and Francis Crick were the pair of firstborns who won the 1962 Nobel Prize in physiology or medicine, for explaining the makeup of DNA. Fran S. Sullaway, a historian of science at MIT, says, "Nobel Prizes are given for solving clever puzzles. That's something firstborns are good at. Firstborns tackle officially sanctioned puzzles while later borns flock to the untried and novel" (Denworth 76).

Birth order can give great insight and may be helpful in understanding others. Not every aspect of birth order psychology may apply to every individual, but for the most part, birth order does have an effect on people's personalities. Look at the understanding of birth order as a tool, allowing conflicts with others to be an opportunity for growing.

QUOTATION FOR THE DAY

"Success comes to a writer, as a rule, so gradually that it is always something of a shock to him to look back and realize the heights to which he has climbed." (P. G. Wodehouse, 1881–1975, English novelist)

As students finish proofreading and publishing their final versions of research papers, share the quotation with the class. Encourage the students to freewrite for a few minutes about whether their published work is successful research writing. Ask students to look back at their early plans and rough drafts to decide if their writing has improved while working on this project.

COOPERATIVE LEARNING

When students bring their final drafts to class, you may want to encourage one more proofreading check by asking each student to have two other students read the paper for spelling and punctuation errors. Allow the students to correct these errors neatly without retyping the papers.

TEACHING NOTE

You will want to explain to students that although a Works Cited has not been included for **A Student Model**, one was produced. It does not appear in the students' textbooks because of space constraints.

CLOSURE

Put students into groups according to topics and ask each group to select a spokesperson to tell about their unsolved mystery. Other group members could add any information overlooked by the group's representative. ■

⬥ TIMESAVER

You can use a checklist for evaluating students' papers. (You may even want the evaluation to be done by students.) Here's a suggested evaluation form:

Student Evaluation Form
(Circle the number that best assesses students' performance. 5 = best and 1 = worst)

1. This paper is interesting.
  1 2 3 4 5

2. This paper is easy to understand.
  1 2 3 4 5

3. This paper answers most questions about this topic.
  1 2 3 4 5

4. This paper shows that a lot of research has been done.
  1 2 3 4 5

5. This paper is relatively free of errors in punctuation, grammar, and spelling.
  1 2 3 4 5

6. The research is displayed in an interesting way.
  1 2 3 4 5

Scores for evaluation forms can be tabulated and grade equivalents assigned.

TEACHING NOTE

Base evaluation of students' answers on whether they have addressed all the issues raised in the questions listed under **Reflecting on Your Writing**, p. 484.

2. What theory or theories explain the mystery? What evidence do the researchers use to support their ideas?

3. What conclusions, if any, can *you* draw? Is one theory more believable? Why? (This theory *may* be your own.) Does solving the mystery seem probable or not? Why?

Writing, Evaluating, and Revising. At the beginning of your report, give background information for understanding the mystery and the theories about it. This material may include dates, places, statistics, and facts about people important to the research. Then, devote at least one paragraph to each theory. Finally, give and explain your opinion. You might judge one theory more plausible and well supported. You might speculate on the new facts or discoveries needed to *prove* a theory—that is, to change it from theory to fact.

Since this report is informal, it is not necessary to use formal citations and a Works Cited page to credit sources. As in many magazine and newspaper articles, you can simply identify the source within the body of your report. For example, here is the way you might handle a source of information on the Loch Ness monster:

> According to Mary Cardenes of Earth's Mysteries, "The sightings of the Loch Ness monster have increased considerably in the last five years."

You can use the guidelines on page 482 to evaluate and revise your paper. Exchange papers with a partner or small group, and ask your partner-editor to note anything that puzzles him or her and to point out unanswered questions.

Proofreading and Publishing. After proofreading your writing and checking the accuracy of your references to sources, share your report as part of an "Unexplained Mysteries" display in the library or classroom. Presenting your findings in a speech is another good idea.

You might decide to add your informal report to your **portfolio.** If you do, date the report and include responses to these questions: How did you choose a mystery to write about? How did you locate sources for your report?

👉 **REFERENCE NOTE:** See pages 1022–1028 for detailed suggestions on how to prepare and present a speech.

MAKING CONNECTIONS

- To design and conduct scientific experimental research
- To write a report on an experiment

491

MAKING CONNECTIONS

RESEARCH ACROSS THE CURRICULUM

Science: Experimental Research

Generally speaking, the kind of research you've been doing in this chapter involves finding information that other people have discovered using a variety of research methods. You assemble this information into a well-developed report and perhaps add your own conclusions.

Experimental research is different. It involves *designing and conducting* experiments to yield information about specific areas of interest. The researcher first determines what question he or she wants to answer and then carefully structures the experiment, controls its operation, records and tabulates the results (often numerical data), and writes a report.

Experimental research isn't restricted to laboratories. Deborah Tannen, for example, is a language researcher interested in comparing the ways men and women communicate. In her book *You Just Don't Understand: Women and Men in Conversation*, she reports on experimental research that has yielded these findings:

- Women use tag questions far more frequently than men. A tag question is a statement with a brief question tacked on at the end: "She's a fine actress, isn't she?"
- Men sit in relaxed postures (sprawling, taking up room) in both all-male and mixed gender groups; women sit in relaxed postures with other women but draw in to "ladylike" postures in mixed-gender groups.

Do these findings seem accurate? Experiment for yourself to find out—that's what other researchers in a field have done whenever new studies have been published. An important task of experimental research is attempting to verify information by *replicating* a study: performing the same or a similar experiment to see if the same results occur. Working with others, use the steps listed on the next page:

RESEARCH ACROSS THE CURRICULUM

Teaching Strategies

This assignment would work well as a cooperative learning activity. You could divide the class in half to work on this experimental research project—selecting one of the experiments, planning the collection of data, reviewing and compiling data, and writing a report based on the data. Assign the following roles to members of each group: leader, data gatherers (all members), data compilers, table/chart creators, report writers, and typists. If your class hasn't had much cooperative-learning experience, you might want to keep the groups small, with four or five students in each group.

GUIDELINES

To be sure that all members of each group participate, ask all students to keep logs of their work. You can approach evaluation in two ways, by assessing individual performance and by assessing the final product. Individually, students should carry out their assignments. Collectively, the groups should produce reports that describe the experiment, present the data, and draw conclusions about the data.

1. Design and conduct one of the following experiments. Use the directions as a guide, working out details with your group. If possible, consult a teacher familiar with research design. *The participants in the research cannot know what you are studying.*

   a. **Tag questions**: Count male and female tag questions in a mixed-gender group conversation for at least 30 minutes. You might observe a class discussion (with the teacher's permission), a public meeting, or a television talk show. Write *F* or *M* for each speaker, with a check mark for each tag question used.

   b. **Body posture**: Observe—if possible, videotape—three small-group meetings that you arrange: men alone, women alone, both together. You might ask for volunteers for an experimental discussion group on any topic (don't reveal your actual research objective). Devise a labeling system for "relaxed" and more "reserved" postures (again, use *F* and *M*), and take careful notes.

2. Review your data, and create tables or charts to show your findings. Think about different ways to present the information. For example, you may show total "counts" for each gender; you may calculate percentages (what percentages of male and female speakers used tag questions?); you may create comparison charts.

3. Write a report that describes the experiment, presents the data, and draws conclusions based on the data (see the Critical Thinking activity on pages 456–459).

SPEAKING AND LISTENING
OBJECTIVES
• To research a historical figure
• To answer questions in the role of a
  historical figure

493

SPEAKING AND LISTENING

History: Biography in Action

Curiosity about the lives of famous people, whether heroes or villains, is natural. What were they like—in life, not just in the pages of a history book or encyclopedia? What would they have to say if you could talk to them? Use your imagination and research to find out.

Choose a historical figure, from any age and any country, that you would like to learn more about. Read a full-length biography or several detailed articles about that person's life, and, if they are available, use films and videos as sources, too. Then, prepare yourself to appear before the class, not as yourself, but as the famous person you've studied (and become). Costumes and props are fine, but your main purpose is to take questions from the class in an interview format. Here are some basic questions you should be ready to answer about "yourself" as that historical figure:

1. When and where were you born?
2. Who were your parents, and what were they like? (Also, sisters and brothers?)
3. What are some of the unusual or memorable experiences you had as a child and as a young adult?
4. What did you do that made you famous? What was your life like during the period when you achieved your greatest accomplishment?
5. What was your greatest mistake?
6. What about your life isn't generally known?
7. What person in your life had the greatest influence on you?
8. What do you think of the way the world is today? What would you like to change?

Encourage your audience to ask additional questions, and be prepared for imaginative questioning tactics.

SPEAKING AND LISTENING
Teaching Strategies

Begin by asking the class to brainstorm ideas for historical figures that sound interesting to them. A day in the library will help students to get ideas. All students will need to prepare two sets of questions: questions about themselves as historical figures (in addition to the ones on this page) and questions to ask the historical figures.

GUIDELINES

You will want to be sure that each student has read a full-length biography or several detailed articles about his or her subject, compiled a list of questions both to ask and to answer, and participated in each interview as a historical figure or as a questioner.

ENGLISH: HISTORY AND DEVELOPMENT

OBJECTIVES

- To compare and contrast word formation, spelling, word combination, and word order in Old English and Modern English
- To identify original forms and meanings of words
- To draw conclusions about the lives of speakers of Old English and French in early medieval England on the basis of language
- To identify words of Old English and French origin
- To use a dictionary to identify Americanisms

WORKPLACE writing

Dictionaries of Specialized Fields

Suggest that students expand their study of the history and development of language by researching words specific to career fields they are interested in and by creating dictionaries of twenty to twenty-five key words or terms from that profession.

- **Brainstorming** Have interpersonal learners interested in the same field work together, with one student concentrating on a verb dictionary while the other creates a noun glossary. If the career choice is related to a subject area taught in the school, students may consult with the appropriate teacher. When they are conducting research, students should consult librarians, specialized journals and dictionaries, or professionals in the field.

- **Writing** The titles of students' dictionaries should indicate the fields under consideration. The dictionaries should contain the following information:

  - the words correctly spelled and placed in alphabetical order;
  - the definition of the word in nontechnical language, if possible;
  - the etymology or history of the word;
  - the part of speech;
  - one sentence that explains the word's context.

Example:

> **Dictionary Title:** *Film Production Terminology*
> **Montage** n. [French, a mounting or setting together, from *monter*] a) The process of editing; b) the process of editing together a series of images that alternate, are superimposed on one another, or flash in and out of focus to make a single thematic point; c) a segment of a film in which this process is used. *Montage* is a technique developed by Soviet filmmakers in the 1920s, particularly Sergei Eisenstein, who used the series of images to encourage viewers to make certain associations.

- **Evaluating and Revising** Students may wish to enlist the aid of someone in the field to give input before publishing the product.

- **Publishing** Invite students to present their dictionaries to the class. Students may make copies of their dictionaries available in the school library, career counseling office, or appropriate classrooms.

- **Reflecting** Ask students to write a brief statement about the creation of their dictionaries—how they chose their subject matter, selected their words, and researched definitions and sources.

INTEGRATING THE LANGUAGE ARTS

SELECTION	READING AND LITERATURE	WRITING AND CRITICAL THINKING	LANGUAGE AND SYNTAX	SPEAKING, LISTENING, AND OTHER EXPRESSION SKILLS
	• Reading for specific information pp. 499, 500, 502, 506–507, 512–513, 514 • Comparing an Old English conversation with Modern English p. 499 • Using references materials pp. 500, 502, 506–507, 510, 514 • Applying interpretive and creative thinking p. 502	• Identifying changes in English p. 499 • Comparing modern forms of words to their original spelling and meaning pp. 499, 500 • Comparing words derived from Old English and French p. 502 • Making inferences and drawing conclusions pp. 502, 510 • Applying interpretive and creative thinking pp. 502, 509, 512–513 • Writing a dialogue in Future English p. 509 • Identifying words from international varieties of English p. 510 • Identifying differences in dialect pp. 512–513 • Writing a list of sports terms and their origins p. 514	• Comparing Modern English to Old English pp. 499, 500 • Using a dictionary to find etymologies pp. 500, 502, 514 • Recognizing the sociological functions of language p. 502 • Using a dictionary to identify Americanisms pp. 506–507 • Inventing new words and new spellings from old words p. 509 • Hypothesizing about future language changes p. 509 • Using a dictionary to identify words from international varieties of English p. 510 • Identifying differences in dialect pp. 512–513 • Using a dictionary to research sports terms p. 514	• Talking to others to identify differences in dialect pp. 512–513

CHAPTER 12: ENGLISH: HISTORY AND DEVELOPMENT

Use this guide to create an instructional plan that addresses the individual needs of your students. Assignments accompanied by the following symbol (*) may be completed out of class. Times given for pacing lessons are estimated.

CHAPTER PLANNING GUIDE—PUPIL'S EDITION

LESSONS	A VARIOUS LANGUAGE pp. 494–507	ENGLISH AROUND THE WORLD pp. 507–510	DIALECTS OF AMERICAN ENGLISH pp. 510–513
DEVELOPMENTAL PROGRAM	🕐 **90 minutes** • Main Assignment: Looking Ahead p. 494 • A Various Language pp. 494–499 • Exercise 2 p. 500* • Middle English p. 501 • Exercise 3 in pairs p. 502 • Modern English/American English pp. 502–506 • Exercise 4 #2, 4, 6, 8, 10 pp. 506–507	🕐 **50–55 minutes** • English Around the World pp. 507–510 • Exercises 5, 6 in pairs pp. 509, 510	🕐 **30 minutes** • Dialects of American English pp. 510–512 • Exercise 7 as a class pp. 512–513 • Standard English p. 513
CORE PROGRAM	🕐 **60 minutes** • Main Assignment: Looking Ahead p. 494 • A Various Language pp. 494–499* • Exercise 1 as a class p. 499 • Middle English p. 501* • Exercise 3 #1, 3, 5, 7, 9 p. 502* • Modern English/American English pp. 502–506 • Exercise 4 pp. 506–507*	🕐 **30–35 minutes** • English Around the World pp. 507–510* • Exercises 5, 6 pp. 509*, 510 • Exercise 7 as a class pp. 512–513	🕐 **20–25 minutes** • Dialects of American English pp. 510–512 • Dialect Chart p. 511 • Exercise 7 as a class pp. 512–513 • Standard English p. 513
ACCELERATED PROGRAM	🕐 **45 minutes** • Main Assignment: Looking Ahead p. 494 • A Various Language pp. 496–499* • Exercise 1 p. 499* • Middle English p. 501 • Exercise 3 p. 502* • Modern English/American English pp. 502–506 • Exercise 4 pp. 506–507*	🕐 **25–30 minutes** • Exercise 5 pp. 509* • Varieties of International English pp. 509–510 • Exercise 6 p. 510*	🕐 **20 minutes** • Dialects of American English pp. 510–512 • Dialect Chart p. 511 • Exercise 7 as a class pp. 512–513 • Standard English p. 513

CHAPTER PLANNING GUIDE—PROGRAM RESOURCES

	A VARIOUS LANGUAGE pp. 494–507	ENGLISH AROUND THE WORLD pp. 507–510	DIALECTS OF AMERICAN ENGLISH pp. 510–513
PRINT	• Old English, Middle English, *Word Choice and Sentence Style* pp. 1, 2 • Modern English, American English, *Word Choice and Sentence Style* pp. 3, 4 • The Origins of English, *English Workshop* pp. 113–114	• International English, *Word Choice and Sentence Style* p. 5	• Varieties of American English, *Word Choice and Sentence Style* p. 6

ELEMENTS OF WRITING: CURRICULUM CONNECTIONS

Making Connections
• International Games p. 514

ASSESSMENT OPTIONS

Summative Assessment
English: History and Development, Review A and B, *Word Choice and Sentence Style* pp. 7–8
Chapter Review, Exercise A, *English Workshop* p. 123

Reflection
Self-assessment Record, *Portfolio Assessment* p. 19

OBJECTIVES

- To compare and contrast word formation, spelling, word combination, and word order in Old English and Modern English
- To research the original forms and meanings of words

- To research words of Old English and French origin
- To draw conclusions about the lives of speakers of Old English and of French in early medieval England on the basis of language
- To use a dictionary to identify Americanisms

PROGRAM MANAGER

FOR THE WHOLE CHAPTER

- **Review** For exercises on chapter concepts, see **Review Form A** and **Review Form B** in *Word Choice and Sentence Style,* pp. 7–8.

PROGRAM MANAGER

A VARIOUS LANGUAGE

- **Independent Practice/ Reteaching** For practice and reinforcement, see **Old English, Middle English, Modern English,** and **American English** in *Word Choice and Sentence Style,* pp. 1–4.
- **Practice** To help less-advanced students with additional instruction and practice with Old English, Middle English, and Modern English, see **Chapter 9** in *English Workshop, Complete Course,* pp. 113–114.

QUOTATION FOR THE DAY

"Ours is a precarious language, as every writer knows, in which the merest shadow line often separates affirmation from negation, sense from nonsense, and one sex from another." (James Thurber, 1894–1961, American writer)

12 ENGLISH: HISTORY AND DEVELOPMENT

LOOKING AHEAD

Every English word you use—from *aardvark* to *zucchini*—has its own place in the history of the language. This chapter will lead you on a journey through that history, giving you a close look at some people, places, times, and events in the amazing story of English. As you work through the chapter, you will learn

- where English comes from
- how English has grown and developed
- how English is used throughout the world today

A Various Language

Like people and their cultures, languages change and develop over time. English used to sound and look very different from the way it does now. If you had lived in England a thousand years ago, you might have taken part in a conversation like the one on the next page.

A valuable motivational resource for this chapter is the set of videotapes called *The Story of English*, produced for PBS and now widely available from a variety of sources. The tapes in this series consider virtually every aspect of the history, development, and spread of the English language. The second and third programs in the series deal with the history of the language from its beginnings to the settlement of North America. They include readings in Old English, Middle English, and early Modern English.

Forhwi ne fixast þu on sæ?

Hwilon ic do, ac seldon, forþam micel rewyt me ys to sæ.

Wylt þu fon sumne hwæl?

Nic.

Forhwi?

Forþam plyhtlic þingc hit ys gefon hwæl.

That exchange from *Aelfric's Colloquy* is the English half of an English-Latin conversation for use by students of Latin in tenth-century England. The modern equivalent would be this:

Why don't you go fishing on the ocean?
Sometimes I do, but not often, because on the ocean I have to do a lot of rowing.
Would you like to catch a whale?
Not me!
Why?
Because it's a dangerous thing to catch a whale!

The English of a thousand years ago is so different from the language we speak that it is like a foreign tongue to us. However, we can still recognize some similarities between that form (called *Old English* or *Anglo-Saxon*) and our English. If we go back farther, though—say five thousand years—the language would be so different that we would not call it English at all, but give it a different name (*Proto-Indo-European*).

A language changes gradually as it is passed on from one generation to the next. We change the words we use, the way we pronounce and spell them, and the way we put them together to make sentences. One cause of those changes is the fact that we meet speakers of other languages and imitate them. Over the centuries, English speakers have met speakers of Latin, Danish, French, Dutch, Spanish, German, and many other languages, and have taken something from each of those languages to make English marvelously complex and varied.

As a result of English speakers coming into contact with other languages around the world, English itself has grown in different directions in various places. Today, English takes many different forms in countries all over the planet.

MEETING individual NEEDS

LEP/ESL

General Strategies. Few languages have borrowed as much vocabulary from other languages as English has. In fact, no more than a third of Modern English vocabulary is from Old English. Ask students to think of any English words that have been borrowed from other languages.

LEARNING STYLES

Visual and Kinetic Learners. Have students create illustrated time lines to show the development of English from the Old English period through the first English-speaking settlements in North America. Time lines can then be displayed in the classroom.

The history of English can be divided into four main periods: *Pre-English, Old English, Middle English,* and *Modern English.* The following time line shows approximately when English moved from one period to the next. It shows which languages influenced the development of English and when. It also shows a rise in the number of English speakers.

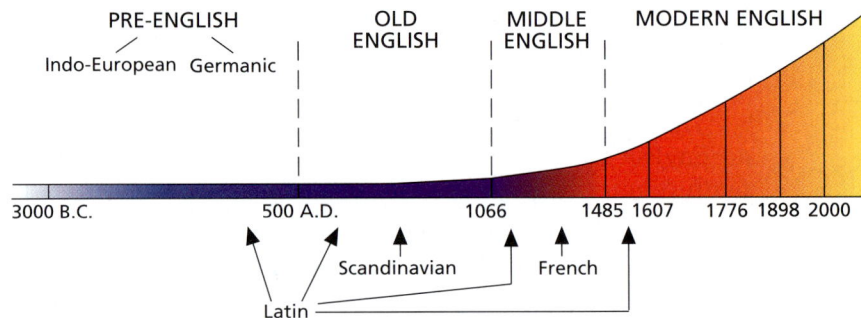

The Origins of English: Pre-English

About five thousand years ago, the language we call **Proto-Indo-European** was spoken in Asia Minor or in southeast Europe—scholars are not sure exactly where. It was the ancestor of most of the languages of Europe and many of those of north India and Iran, and for that reason we name it *Indo–* (for India) and *European.* (*Proto–* means "first or earliest.")

Speakers of Proto-Indo-European migrated over all of Europe and south central Asia. One group of migrants settled along the coast of the North Sea, in what today is northern Germany. They consisted of several tribes—the Angles, Saxons, and Jutes. Their version of Proto-Indo-European, called **Germanic,** is the ancestor of present-day English.

While the Anglo-Saxons (as those tribes are collectively called) were living in northern Europe, they got to know another Indo-European people to their south, the Romans. From the Romans, they borrowed a number of Latin words (along with the things the words name), such as *wine* (*vinum*), *cheese* (*caseus*), *pepper* (*piper*), *kettle* (*catillus*), and *sack* (*saccus*).

Words that one language borrows from another are called **loanwords.** The chart on the next page shows the origins of some present-day English words.

449	Traditional date of Anglo-Saxon invasion	878	King Alfred defeats Norsemen
450–1100	Old English Period	1066	Norman (French) Conquest
c. 700	*Beowulf* composed in its present form	1100–1500	Middle English Period
787	First invasion by Norsemen	c. 1387	Chaucer writes "Prologue" to *The Canterbury Tales*
c. 850	Conquest of Britain by the Norsemen	c. 1477	William Caxton sets up first printing press in England

PROTO-INDO-EUROPEAN

kwon-
"dog"

OLD ENGLISH	GERMAN	WELSH	LATIN	GREEK
hund "dog"	*dachshund* "badger-dog"	*corgi (corr + ci)* "dwarf dog"	*canis, caninus* "of dogs"	*kyon, kynikos* "doglike"
↓	↓	↓	↓	↓
hound	**dachshund**	**corgi**	**canine**	**cynic**

Old English

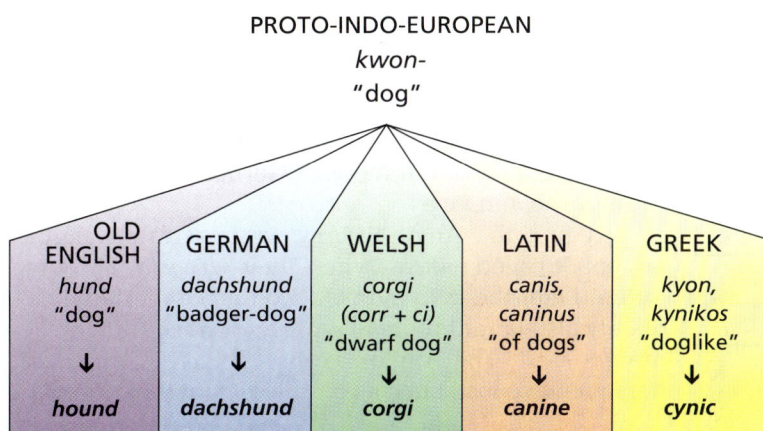

The Anglo-Saxons did not stay in northern Germany. Some of them took jobs with the Roman army, to work as mercenaries in the British Isles. Southern Britain and its native population of Celts had earlier been conquered by the Emperor Claudius and made into a province of the Roman Empire, but the northern part of the island was inhabited by a fierce, independent people called the Picts.

The Picts had a disconcerting habit of stripping naked, painting themselves blue, and howling as they charged down from the hills to raid their southern neighbors. To prevent such unwanted visits, the Roman Emperor Hadrian built a wall across northern England and hired troops, such as the Angles and Saxons, to keep the Picts on the other side. They succeeded in keeping the Picts under control, but in the long run the Anglo-Saxons turned out to be even more of a problem to the Celts than the Picts had been.

After the Romans ceased ruling Britain, the Anglo-Saxons stayed on, and kin of theirs from the Continent arrived to join them. These Germanic peoples took over the south of the main island of Britain and called it after themselves, *Engla land*—the land of the Angles—or as we know it today, England. They also called their language *Englisc;* we call it **Old English.**

The English of the Anglo-Saxons sounded very different from our English. They used sounds we have lost, as in their

1500–present	Modern English Period	
1564	Birth of Shakespeare	
1607	Jamestown, Va., colony founded; first permanent English-speaking settlement in North America	
1611	King James translation of the Bible	

GUIDED PRACTICE

To prepare for **Exercise 1,** guide students through the first two lines. For **Exercise 2** on p. 500, have the whole class look up the first word. Point out where the etymology is and how to interpret it. For **Exercise 3** on p. 502, you may have to help students infer social characteristics by pointing out where (city or country) certain words would

498   *English: History and Development*

INTEGRATING THE LANGUAGE ARTS

Language and Writing. Carved or cut on wood, metal, or stone, rune stones were inscriptions that honored or glorified someone. For example, a stone might have said "Rolf raised this stone to the memory of his father, Gudmond, a brave and strong warrior."

You might want to have your students create their own rune stones. You can find the entire runic alphabet in an encyclopedia. After sharing this alphabet with your students, tell them to write short dedications either to people they know or to fictional characters or historical figures. Students should write first in modern English and then translate their inscriptions into runes.

word *cniht,* which meant "boy" but has come to us with a changed meaning as *knight.* In Old English *cniht* had an initial *c* or *k* sound, which we continue to spell although we do not pronounce it. We also keep an unpronounced *gh* in the spelling, where Old English had an *h* representing a throaty sound like that at the end of the modern German word *ich* (a strong version of the *h* in *huge*).

At first the Anglo-Saxons wrote with an angular-looking alphabet called *runes*—when they wrote at all, which wasn't often. Later the Irish monks who first converted them to Christianity also taught them to write a rounded form of letters called *insular hand.* The Anglo-Saxons' alphabet contained some letters we have lost, such as þ, called *thorn* (today replaced by *th*).

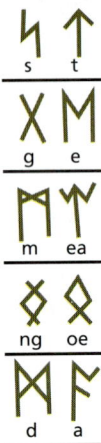

Many Old English words differed in spelling and pronunciation from those we use. For example, in Old English the verb *fish* was spelled *fix, fics,* or *fisc.* The Anglo-Saxons also had some words we have lost completely, such as *fon* or *gefon* for "take" or "catch," and they lacked a great many words we have, such as *dangerous* (instead of which they used *plyhtlic,* that is, "plightly"). Some words have changed meaning, like *cniht* (knight) mentioned earlier.

Old English words also had endings to relate them to other words in a sentence. For example, the verb *fish* took different forms depending on its subject.

ic fixe *or* fisce = I fish
þu fixast *or* fiscast = you fish
we fixiaþ *or* fisciaþ = we fish

(runic alphabet chart:)
f   u
th   o
r   w
h   n
eo   ch
s   t
g   e
m   ea
ng   oe
d   a

likely be used most often. Finally, you can offer guided practice for **Exercise 4** on p. 506 by pointing out to students that the abbreviations and symbols keys in their dictionaries will tell them how their dictionaries denote Americanisms.

INDEPENDENT PRACTICE

All four of the exercises in this lesson are designed to be done independently. These exercises should provide ample independent practice for your students.

☞

Although English has changed over the centuries, many of our most familiar, everyday words are still native English— words that have been used by English speakers as far back in the past as we can see or imagine. Most of these words have changed their pronunciation and spelling, and many have changed their meanings, too. Yet their old forms are recognizable from their modern ones.

OLD ENGLISH	PRESENT-DAY ENGLISH
finger	finger
fot	foot
broþor	brother
hnutu	nut
hlaf (meaning "bread")	loaf
tun (meaning "enclosed place")	town

EXERCISE 1 ▶ **Identifying Changes in Our Language**

Here is a word-by-word translation of the Old English conversation at the beginning of this chapter. Using this literal translation to help you, compare the Old English version with its Modern English equivalent on page 495. What differences do you find in words, spellings, word combinations, and word order? What similarities do you see?

Forhwi ne fixast þu on sæ?
For-why not fishest thou on sea?

Hwilon ic do, ac seldon, forþam micel rewyt me ys to sæ.
Sometimes I do, but seldom, because much rowing to-me is at sea.

Wylt þu fon sumne hwæl?
Wilt thou catch some whale?

Nic.
Not I. [Nic is a contraction of ne ic.]

Forhwi?
For-why?

Forþam plyhtlic þingc hit ys gefon hwæl.
Because dangerous thing it is to-catch whale.

ANSWERS
Exercise 1

Responses will vary. Here are some differences and similarities:
Differences: Some words in Old English don't exist in Modern English, and the spellings of some words are different. Old English uses the equivalent of *for-why* where Modern English uses only *why,* and the Old English contraction for *not I* is unlike any contraction in Modern English. The word order in Old English puts the subject of the sentence after the verb.
Similarities: Some of the words in Old English are the same as words in Modern English, and some words, such as *sae* for *sea,* are obviously related to one another. Except for the subject-verb flip-flop, the word order in Old English is similar to the word order in Modern English.

ANSWERS
Exercise 2

1. *heofon;* meaning hasn't changed
2. *dream;* meaning in Old English was "joy, music"
3. *bread;* meaning in Old English was "crumb, morsel"
4. *elboga;* meaning hasn't changed
5. *steorfan;* meaning in Old English was "to die, perish"

CRITICAL THINKING

Inference. The meanings of words sometimes change over time. Ask your students to look up the following words in a dictionary and compare their original meanings (found in their etymologies) to their present meanings. Then, ask students to make inferences about how meanings can change.

1. slim [useless, bad, weak]
2. nice [strange, lazy, foolish]
3. bully [sweetheart]
4. hound [any dog]
5. girl [any young person]
6. wife [any woman]

[Students might infer that meanings can change from positive to negative (*bully*), from negative to positive (*slim, nice*) and from general to specific (*hound, girl, wife*).]

500

English: History and Development

EXERCISE 2 ▶ Identifying Original Forms of Words

Look up each of the following words in a dictionary that gives etymologies (word origins). What did the word look like in Old English? Has its meaning changed since Old English times? If so, what did it originally mean?

1. heaven	3. bread	5. starve
2. dream	4. elbow	

After they had been converted to Christianity by monks from Rome, the English borrowed many more Latin words. Many of these were for religious matters, but some were for other things. Following are examples of words that came into English from Latin. Notice the changes these words underwent on their way to Modern English.

Latin	Old English	Modern English
presbyter	preost	priest
apostolus	apostol	apostle
schola	scol	school
portus	port	port
butyrum	butere	butter

Old English also formed some compound words by imitation of Latin. Some of these compounds have survived. For example, *gospel* comes from the Old English compound *godspel*, meaning "good story," after Latin *evangelium*, from a Greek word meaning "good news." Other compound words have gone by the wayside, for example, the Old English *leorningcniht* meaning "learning-boy, student, disciple."

England was invaded by Vikings from Scandinavia several times in the ninth to eleventh centuries. Large numbers of these Northmen, or Norse, as they were also called, settled among the English. The Norse introduced into Old English Scandinavian words such as *give, skin, take, want,* and *window* (originally *vindauga,* "wind eye"), as well as the pronouns *they, them,* and *their.* The corresponding Old English words had been *giefan, hyd* (which survives as *hide*), *niman, willan* (which survives as *will*), *eagþyrl* ("eye-hole"), and the pronouns *hie, hem, heora.*

you can reteach the idea of the objective—drawing inferences about how people live by examining their language—by working through **Exercise 3** with students.

CLOSURE

Ask students to name some of the major influences on the development of English. [Answers could include contact with Romans, conquest by Vikings, conquest by Normans, the appearance of the printing press, contact with the indigenous peoples of the New World, and the Industrial Revolution.] ☞

Middle English

In 1066 yet another group of Norse conquered England. Called the Normans ("northern people"), they had earlier settled in France and learned French. The Normans began the process of introducing a great many French words into the English language. *Army, court, government, literature, mirror,* and *service* are a few of those words.

The Norman Conquest marks the beginning of the ***Middle English*** period. During much of the Middle English period, English was used only by the common people for everyday matters. The important languages of the country were French and Latin, in which affairs of government, education, religion, law, and literature were expressed. In the fourteenth century, English began to be used for important purposes again, but by then English speakers had forgotten the native English words for many specialized subjects. And so they found it easiest to borrow large numbers of French and Latin words to use in talking about these matters.

Following are some more examples of French and Latin loanwords from the Middle English period:

FRENCH	cité	contrée	juge	libraire
ENGLISH	city	country	judge	library

LATIN	mercurius	scriba	sub poena ("under penalty")
ENGLISH	mercury	scribe	subpoena

I'm sorry, but I can't sell you one until you give me the correct pronunciation.

authentic French CROISSANTS

David Sipress, *Wishful Thinking.* © 1987, Harper & Row.

INTEGRATING THE LANGUAGE ARTS

Vocabulary Link. A great many French words entered the English vocabulary after 1066, but they didn't always replace the English equivalents. For example, English had the words *ox* and *calf,* while French had *boef* and *veel* as names of the same animals. When these French words entered the English vocabulary, they became the names of these animals' meat (*beef* and *veal*), while the English words continued to be used to name the animals. This is just one of many examples of how English made use of French loanwords to expand its vocabulary without sacrificing its own words. Challenge students to find additional examples of words for types of meat that were borrowed from French words for animals. [Examples include *mutton* and *pork.*]

Speaking and Listening Link. Have volunteers find short passages in Middle English—perhaps from Chaucer's *The Canterbury Tales*—to present orally to the class. After each presentation, ask students if they understood the passage, and then have presenters read modern English translations of the passages.

Language change occurs at all times, and you and your students participate in this process perhaps without realizing it. You can bring home this point to students by enlisting their help to generate a list of words that have entered the language during the last twenty-five years. One place to start is with household appliances. [Answers may include *camcorder, compact disc, call waiting, VHS, auto-drip coffee maker, icemaker,* and *solar cell calculator*.] Other fruitful areas to investigate for new words include social issues and concerns [*ecofeminist, latchkey child, environmentalist*]. You can lead the class in a discussion, based on the new words they generate, of how new words are formed. [Ideas may include compounding,

ANSWERS
Exercise 3

Conclusions will vary. Most of the French words name officials of government and aspects of city life. These categories suggest that the French speakers in medieval England were concerned with governmental and official affairs and lived in towns and cities. The fact that most of the Old English words name things associated with agriculture and country life suggests that English was spoken by people in the countryside—probably peasants.

EXERCISE 3 ▶ **The Origin of Words**

Look up each of the following words in a dictionary that gives etymologies (word origins). Which of the words came from Old English and which from French? What conclusions might you draw about the difference in life between English and French speakers in early medieval England?

1. admiral **1. French**
2. attorney **2. French**
3. fowler **3. Old English**
4. plow **4. Old English**
5. profession **5. French**

6. shepherd **6. Old English**
7. sheriff **7. Old English**
8. soldier **8. French**
9. tailor **9. French**
10. weave **10. Old English**

Modern English

Despite the Scandinavian and Norman French invasions of England, the Anglo-Saxons were relatively protected and isolated in England for nearly 1,200 years. Most of them were illiterate; they had little need to write or read because books were copied by hand and therefore were much too expensive for ordinary people.

Near the end of the fifteenth century, however, printing was introduced to England. The printing press had appeared in Germany in the late 1430s, and by 1455, Gutenberg had printed the Bible in Latin. Around 1475 William Caxton published the first English book on a printing press in Belgium; it was a translation of a French work about the legends of the Trojan War. Two years later, Caxton began publishing books in England. Cheap books became readily available, and, as a result, communication and the English language were forever changed.

Handwritten manuscripts were produced slowly and expensively. Each copy was unique—at least slightly, and often greatly, different from every other. The printing press, on the other hand, allowed many identical copies of the same work to be produced cheaply. For the first time, anyone could have books to read, and many people could read the same text. The mass production of books and the resulting increase in literacy helped standardize the English language and make universal education possible.

ENRICHMENT

One valuable resource to use to trace the history of words in English is the *Oxford English Dictionary*, First or Second Edition. Considered by some the greatest work of scholarship ever undertaken, the *OED* traces the histories of words to their origins in the language by citing quotations of the uses of words throughout history. If your school ☞

In the sixteenth century, while the revolution of the printing press was still fresh, some English people got an itch to travel and see whether they could make their fortunes in foreign lands. The first of these adventurers and explorers were little more than pirates. They were sanctioned by the English government because they directed their piracy against other governments (like that of Spain, with whom Queen Elizabeth I had been feuding).

The Granger Collection, New York.

MEETING *individual* NEEDS

ADVANCED STUDENTS

You may want to ask interested students to do some research on the King James version of the Bible. Ask them to find out why James I ordered a new translation of the Bible, who did it, how widely it was used, and how it affected the English language in America. Students can report to the class on their findings. Other possible topics for research include Noah Webster and his effect on English in America, the development of the *Oxford English Dictionary,* and the Great Vowel Shift.

Eventually, though, some English people traveled abroad for another reason—to settle in new lands. A little more than a hundred years after Columbus had stumbled upon the Western Hemisphere in 1492, the English decided they would try to plant some colonies there, too. They got into the colonial game rather late: Spain, Portugal, and France had all been busy sending out explorers, shipping over settlers, and exploiting the resources of the New World, while the English stayed cozily at home. The first successful English settlement in America was at Jamestown, Virginia, in 1607; the next was at Plymouth, Massachusetts, in 1620.

library doesn't own a full-size twelve-volume set, you may be able to find a copy of the compact edition of the *OED* that comes equipped with its own magnifying glass. A good word to look up and read about is *nice,* which has undergone amazing changes in meaning through the centuries. ■

A DIFFERENT APPROACH

In some formerly colonized countries, especially in the Caribbean, people are gaining a new sense of cultural independence from Great Britain. In many of these countries, people are developing literatures in their own varieties of English. In Jamaica, "dub poetry," which is an outgrowth of reggae music, expresses Jamaican folk culture and ignores the rules and vocabulary of standard English in favor of the variety of English, known as Jamaican creole, spoken by the people of Jamaica.

The following lines of dub poetry were written by Louise Bennet, known as "Miss Lou," the grandmother of dub poetry. Write the lines on the chalkboard and have students volunteer to read them as they imagine they should sound.

Him sey Englan is foreign, an
Afta dis election,
We mus move King pickcha an put
We own Jamaica man.

Initiate a discussion of the meaning of the lines of poetry. Ask students how the language of the poetry supports its subject. [The use of the Jamaican variety of English reinforces the message that Jamaica is now independent of England and wishes to assert its own political and cultural identity.]

LOOKING AT Language

Edibles from the New World

Can you imagine life without french fries or catsup, mashed potatoes or spaghetti sauce? Potatoes and tomatoes, like many other common foods, were unknown in Europe before they were imported from the Americas. More often than not, the words used to name these foods were new to the Europeans, too.

Spanish explorers in the Americas discovered the white, or "Irish," potato among the Incas at the end of the sixteenth century. The English borrowed their name for this vegetable from the Spanish. The Spanish word was *patata,* a variant of the West Indian word for sweet potato.

Tomato comes from the language of the Nahuatl, a native people of Mexico and Central America. The Nahuatl word *tomatl* came into Spanish as *tomate,* and the English adapted the spelling in 1753.

The English colonies in America were the beginning of the British Empire. When those colonies broke away and declared themselves a single, independent nation, that action had two effects on the English language. First, the United States formed its own variety of standard English, different from the standard English of England. This new variety, **American English,** then proceeded to develop in its own direction. Second, deprived of their American colonies, the British were motivated to establish new colonies elsewhere. This colonization process encouraged the growth not only of the British Empire but also of British English.

The British began building an empire around the globe. British settlers and traders went to Canada, the Caribbean, India, Australia, New Zealand, South Africa, and many other places, taking the English language with them wherever they traveled. At the same time, Americans were spreading out into the West, gradually filling the area between the Atlantic and the Pacific that became the forty-eight continental states. As a result of these two expansions, English soon became the most widely dispersed language in the world, as well as one of the most widely used languages.

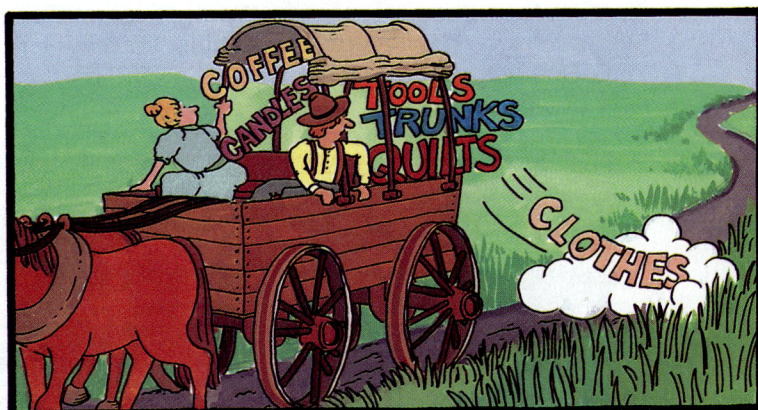

Meanwhile, back in England, the Industrial Revolution of the late eighteenth and early nineteenth centuries introduced more efficient methods of manufacturing. The combination of abundant goods and worldwide commerce helped spread the English language still further and make it into an important international tongue.

American English

The early American settlers, like colonists everywhere, changed their language by necessity. For example, they had to find names for some animals they had never encountered before. One such animal was a nocturnal creature with a ringed, bushy tail and black marks around its eyes that made it look like a bandit wearing a mask. It was a complete novelty to the English settlers, who asked the Algonquians of Virginia what they called it. The answer was something like *ärähkun*, which the settlers imitated as *raccoon*.

The settlers also saw another animal, a large bird with a splendid tail, which seemed very exotic to the English. Because exotic things were associated with the Orient or the Middle East, the colonists called this bird a *turkey fowl* after the country of Turkey. The raccoon has a borrowed name and the turkey an imaginative, invented one.

In other cases, the settlers adapted old words to new uses. In England, the word *creek* was used for a small bay or harbor on the seacoast. When the settlers arrived in the New World, they often landed at creeks, in the older English sense. But

COOPERATIVE LEARNING
Hold a contest in which groups of three or four students work together to compile lists of words that originated from American Indian languages. The only resource students should be allowed to use for the contest is a college dictionary in which they can check the etymologies of words. The group with the longest list wins. [Words that originated from American Indian languages include *hickory, moccasin, moose, skunk, squash, succotash, wigwam,* and the names of many states and cities.]

because those "creeks" were frequently the mouths of streams, the settlers used the word *creek* not just for the inlet by the sea but also for the stream that emptied into it, and for any tributary of a larger river.

The differentiation of American English from British English was greatly accelerated after the Declaration of Independence in 1776 and the success of the American Revolution. The citizens of the new country were proud of their land and wanted to be independent culturally as well as politically. As they set about building a new nation, they were also building a new literature and a new variety of the language.

In the late 1800s, Americans began to turn their attention to areas outside the continental United States. During the twentieth century, the nation has become an increasingly important international power. As a result, American English has exerted increasing influence on other varieties of English and other languages throughout the world. At the same time, these languages have been influencing American English.

Among the words and expressions that America has contributed to the English language are these:

arm-twisting	jalapeño pepper
charge card	maple syrup
fluorescent lamp	possum

EXERCISE 4 ▶ **Identifying Americanisms**

Which of the following words are <u>Americanisms</u>—words that entered the English language in the United States? To find out,

ENGLISH AROUND THE WORLD

OBJECTIVES

- To write an imaginative dialogue emphasizing changes likely to occur in English in the next five hundred years
- To match words from non-American varieties of English with their meanings and origins

☞

look up each word in a dictionary that identifies Americanisms. (A good one is *Webster's New World Dictionary*, which labels each Americanism with a star.)

1. blintz
2. blizzard
3. dishwasher
4. fingerprint
5. ghostwriter
6. motel
7. pretzel
8. smog
9. tom-tom
10. waffle

10. n.: Americanism
v.: not an Americanism

English Around the World

Today, English has three kinds of users. First, there are those who speak it as their native language. They include all or much of the populations of the United States, Canada, the United Kingdom, Ireland, Australia, New Zealand, South Africa, Jamaica, and a number of other countries.

Second, there are those who use English frequently, often every day, as a second language. For example, India has two official languages, Hindi and English, and fourteen regional languages, some of which are completely unrelated to Hindi. Speakers of the latter languages in India prefer to use English for official use, rather than Hindi. English is used as a first or second language more widely around the world than any other language.

Third, some people use English occasionally or for special purposes. It is the main language of international commerce, communication, transportation, entertainment, science, technology, and scholarship around the world. A Norwegian pilot landing an airplane in Greece talks to the airport controller in English. A Japanese businessperson dealing with an Arabian sheik conducts negotiations in English. A Dutch student of physics reads textbooks and journal articles written in English. As a result, almost five hundred million people use English fluently, and about half again as many use it with lesser degrees of fluency.

With so many people using English in so many places around the world, it is inevitable that new varieties and uses of the language should develop. For example, in India, English speakers talk about a *lakh*, which is "a hundred thousand" or loosely "a very large number," and call a popsicle *ice-candy*. They also say things like "Today is hot like anything," meaning "It is very hot today."

PROGRAM MANAGER

ENGLISH AROUND THE WORLD

- **Independent Practice/ Reteaching** For practice and reinforcement, see **International English** in *Word Choice and Sentence Style*, p. 5.

QUOTATION FOR THE DAY

"Our fathers have, in process of centuries, provided this realm, its colonies and wide dependencies, with a speech as malleable and pliant as Attic, dignified as Latin, masculine, yet free of Teutonic guttural, capable of being precise as French, dulcet as Italian, sonorous as Spanish, and captaining all these excellences to its service." (Sir Arthur Quiller-Couch, 1863–1944, English author)

Write Quiller-Couch's description of English on the chalkboard and discuss with students the meanings of any words they don't understand. Then, ask them how the language of the quotation supports the opinion it presents. [Students might say that malleability is exhibited by the use of *captain* as a verb and that precision is exemplified by the highly specific meanings of words such as *guttural* and *sonorous*.]

Have students read this lesson independently, perhaps as homework. After students have read the material, initiate discussion by asking students if they were surprised to learn that English is so widely spoken. You may want to bring a world map or an atlas to class so you can point out to students the many places in which English is spoken as a first or second language. Encourage debate about whether or not English will splinter into many different languages. Have students give reasons to support their opinions.

The two exercises in this lesson can be used for guided and independent practice. You can lead students in discussions of how to complete each exercise and then let them work on the exercises independently.

MEETING individual NEEDS

LEP/ESL

General Strategies. English-language learners in your class might be familiar with non-American varieties of English, such as British, Indian, or Jamaican English. To encourage interest in non-American English, invite students who have heard non-American English to describe differences in pronunciation and vocabulary that they have noticed between American and non-American English.

LEARNING STYLES

Visual and Kinetic Learners. Let your visual and kinetic learners work with an outline map of the world to identify the countries where English is the first or second language. They can color first-language countries green (Australia, Britain, Canada, New Zealand, and the United States) and second-language countries purple (Hong Kong, India, Kenya, Malaysia, Myanmar, Nigeria, Pakistan, Philippines, South Africa, Sri Lanka, Sudan, Tanzania, Uganda, and Zambia, among others).

508

---

508   *English: History and Development*

Some people think that because of such new varieties, English will break up into a number of different and mutually incomprehensible languages. That is exactly what happened to Latin some 1,500 years ago, when Italian, Spanish, French, Portuguese, Romanian, and other Romance languages began to develop out of local dialects of Latin. It also happened to Proto-Indo-European much earlier, and has happened to many other languages throughout history.

However, today circumstances are different. All languages change constantly. They have to, in order to adapt to changes in human knowledge and society. But if speakers of a language communicate with each other freely, their language will change in the same way for all of them over a period of time. The big difference between us and sixth-century speakers of Latin is the improvement in our communication and transportation. We can travel from the United States to Europe overnight, and we can talk with people on the other side of the globe almost instantaneously by means of telephone signals bounced off a satellite.

Local varieties of English are developing and will certainly continue to do so. But an international variety of the language is also developing. Because those who use that international variety communicate frequently with each other, it will stay relatively uniform. And it will influence the local varieties so that they do not turn into separate languages. What we are likely to see in the future is an international English that is pretty much the same all over the earth. Many local subvarieties of English will flourish, but they will be related to the central international variety as planets are to the sun.

Base your assessment of the objectives for this lesson on students' performance on the exercises.

Valuable resources for use with this lesson are the first program ("An English-Speaking World") and the ninth program ("The New Englishes") in the PBS series *The Story of English.*

CLOSURE

Ask students to name three countries besides the United States and Great Britain in which English is spoken. ■

E X E R C I S E 5 ▶ **Speculating on the Future of English**

You are an English-speaking person in the year 2500. What does your language look and sound like? How is it different from the English of the 1990s? Write a dialogue between two people discussing entertainment, sports, business, travel, or a similar subject. Write it in the kind of English you think might be used in the future. For your dialogue you might invent new words, new spellings for words, and new uses for old words.

Varieties of International English

The two major national varieties of English are American English and British English. About two thirds of the native speakers of English are Americans, and the United States and the United Kingdom together account for more than 85 percent of the world's native speakers of the language.

American and British versions differ somewhat in pronunciation or accent. They have quite a few differences in informal and specialized vocabulary but not many important ones in grammar. Americans and Britons have very little difficulty in understanding each other's writing and not much in understanding each other's speech.

Here are some differences in word choice between the two main national varieties of English.

British	American
beetroot	beet
biscuit	cracker or cookie
block of flats	apartment building
cornet	ice-cream cone
drawing pin	thumbtack
fiddle	swindle, cheat
hire (a car)	rent (a car)
jelly	jello
mash	mashed potatoes
polling day	election day
rota	duty roster, work schedule
sister	nurse
toffee-nosed	snobbish, stuck-up
zip	zipper

ANSWERS
Exercise 5

Dialogues will vary. The best dialogues will show imagination and creativity. Their language will be an obvious variety of English, and they will reflect tendencies in contemporary English, such as phonetic spellings (*lite, tho, thru*), the invention of new words by redefining existing words, and the formation of acronyms.

◆ **INTEGRATING THE LANGUAGE ARTS**

Literature Link. The Scotsman Robert Burns wrote in a variety of English other than that spoken in England or the United States. If his poems are available in your literature textbook, ask your students to read his poem "To a Mouse" and to pay attention to the Scottish dialect throughout it. If possible, have students listen to a recording of "To a Mouse." Ask students how Burns's use of Scottish English adds to his poem's effect. [Responses will vary. The Scottish dialect that Burns uses corresponds with the rustic subject matter of the poem. The use of dialect lends authenticity to the poem because the speaker of the poem is a Scottish farmer, and it is unlikely that a Scottish farmer would speak "the King's English."]

DIALECTS OF AMERICAN ENGLISH

OBJECTIVE

• To identify regional dialect differences for common items and expressions

TEACHING THE LESSON

After students have read this lesson independently, initiate a class discussion of regional and ethnic dialects. Ask students for examples of dialect from their regions and ethnic groups. Reinforce the point that every variety of English has value and that different speech forms aren't wrong. Discuss with

Each national variety of English has its own distinctive characteristics. The differences among the varieties are strongest in slang and informal language. In Australia, people say *g'day* for "hello," and they talk about having a *barbie* ("barbecue"), drinking *lollywater* ("a soft drink"), and eating a *sanger* ("sandwich"). In New Zealand, a driver may hit a *judder bar* ("speed-breaker, a bump in the road to slow down traffic") on the way to buy some *kitset furniture* ("ready-to-assemble furniture").

EXERCISE 6 ▶ Identifying Words from Other Varieties of English

Here are some words from other varieties of English around the world. The meanings and origins of these words are given in the second and third columns in jumbled order. See whether you can match each word to its meaning and origin. Try to guess and to use elimination before you look the words up in a dictionary.   Words in each column are matched by number.
Example: 1-colleen; 1-young woman; 1-Irish

Word	Meaning	Origin
1 colleen	8 club	2 Australian
2 dinkum	3 yearly festival	10 Australian
3 eisteddfod	10 food	4 British
4 hols	7 good, first-rate	9 British
5 kraal	9 hideaway, nook	7 Indic
6 loch	6 lake	1 Irish
7 pukka	2 true, genuine	8 Irish
8 shillelagh	4 holiday	6 Scottish
9 snuggery	5 village, stockade	5 South African
10 tucker	1 young woman	3 Welsh

Dialects of American English

The language we use tells much about us—our home locality, ethnic background, education, gender, and age. Language variation that tells such things about us, thus helping to identify who we are, is called *dialect*. The two main types of dialect are *regional dialects* and *ethnic dialects*.

INTEGRATING THE LANGUAGE ARTS

Literature Link. If the short story is in your literature textbook, tell students to read "No Witchcraft for Sale" by Doris Lessing and to note any words that they do not recognize as being from British or American English [*kraal, piccanin, baas, veld, kaffir,* and *mealie*]. Ask students why they think Lessing includes these words in the story and what effect they have on the story. [Responses will vary. Students might say that the inclusion of words from South African English helps to establish the setting. Also, the use of the words *kraal* (a native village), *piccanin* (a native child), *baas* (boss), and *kaffir* (a black African native) serves to describe and emphasize the separation between the white ruling class and the black native people.]

PROGRAM MANAGER

DIALECTS OF AMERICAN ENGLISH

■ **Independent Practice/ Reteaching** For practice and reinforcement, see **Varieties of American English** in *Word Choice and Sentence Style*, p. 6.

students when it is appropriate to use standard English.

For guided practice, model the first item in **Exercise 7**. Students can then do the remainder of the exercise as independent practice.

ASSESSMENT

Assessment of **Exercise 7** on p. 512 can be based on students' efforts to obtain appropriate interviewees.

☛

Regional Dialects. Language varies from place to place. Geographical differences in a major variety of English are called *regional dialects.*

In the United States, there are four main dialect regions in the eastern half of the country: *Northern, North Midland, South Midland, and Southern.* In the West, there is less regional distinctiveness. Within each of the major regions, there are also local dialects. In the North, Bostonians talk differently from New Yorkers; in the South, Charlestonians talk differently from New Orleanians. So too in Britain, there are major regional dialects like those of Scotland, Wales, and Southern England. And there are local variations, too: Liverpudlians (from Liverpool) don't talk like Glaswegians (from Glasgow) or Tynesiders (from Newcastle).

This chart shows some features of pronunciation, vocabulary, and grammar that distinguish one regional dialect in American English from another.

FEATURES OF REGIONAL DIALECTS

		NORTHERN	NORTH MIDLAND	SOUTH MIDLAND	SOUTHERN
PRONUN-CIATION		"greassy"	"greassy"	"greazy"	"greazy"
		"hahg"	"hahg" or hog	hog	"hawg"
		"pahked cah"	parked car	parked car	"pawked caw"
WORD CHOICE		burlap bag or gunny sack	burlap bag	burlap bag	burlap bag or croker sack
		pail	bucket	bucket	bucket
		devil's darning needle	snake feeder	snake doctor	skeeter hawk
GRAMMAR		quarter of/to	quarter to	quarter till	quarter till/to
		you, youse	you	you, you'uns	you, y'all

QUOTATION FOR THE DAY

"If you aren't willing to study language, then you aren't willing to be a writer." (Rita Mae Brown, 1944–   , American poet, writer, educator, and feminist)

Write the quotation on the chalkboard and ask students to speculate about how the study of dialects might be useful to writers. [Writers often use dialect to establish settings and to enhance characterizations.] You could also have students brainstorm titles of short stories and novels that contain dialect.

MEETING *individual* **NEEDS**

LEP/ESL

General Strategies. You may have some students who speak American dialects and some who speak other languages. You can help both groups by emphasizing that nearly all languages have dialects; that dialects are normal; and that many languages, including English, French, and Spanish, have a standard form for writing and for speaking to people who do not speak the same dialect.

EXTENSION

Some students have small children in their households. Encourage these students to keep records of the children's progress in acquiring language. Students could report on the children's language development to the class. The records can include a list of words each child uses, each child's first word

A DIFFERENT APPROACH

One resource that captures the diversity of regional dialects in America is the video program *American Tongues,* produced by the Center for New American Media. This program is available in an appropriate version that is short enough to be used in a single class period. The Center for New American Media also produced *Yeah, You Rite* about the neighborhood and social class dialects of New Orleans. Both of these programs present information about the nature of language as a social institution and about dialect in ways that are amusing and understandable.

Ethnic Dialects.   In addition to regional dialects, there are also *ethnic dialects*—the dialects of special communities that have preserved some of their heritage from the past.

The most prominent ethnic dialect in the United States is that of African Americans. It unites some features of West African languages with others from conservative varieties of early Southern speech and yet others developed by the African American community itself. Some features are *aunt* pronounced "ahnt," "He be sick" (meaning a continuing, rather than a temporary, illness), and *tote,* "carry" (of African origin, but now common in all Southern use).

Clearly, not all African Americans speak in the ethnic dialect associated with their group, and some features of this dialect appear in other speech communities. The boundaries of ethnic dialects, like those of geographical dialects, are fluid.

The second most prominent American ethnic dialect is Hispanic English, with three subvarieties: Mexican-influenced English in the Southwest; Cuban-influenced English in Florida; and Puerto-Rican-influenced English both in New York City and in Puerto Rico. Early Hispanic influence in the West introduced such words as *vamoose* for "leave quickly" (from Spanish *vamos,* "let's go"), *hoosegow* for "jail" (from *juzgado,* "courtroom"), and *mesa* ("table").

Today, Spanish-influenced English sometimes uses English words with the meanings of similar Spanish words. For example, speakers of a Hispanic dialect may use *apple* with the meaning of "city block," since the Spanish word for apple, *manzana,* can also mean "city block." And Hispanic speakers may use *direction* with the meaning of the Spanish word *dirección* ("address").

EXERCISE 7   **Identifying Dialect Differences**

The following descriptions identify things that have different names in different parts of the United States. What word do you use for each thing? Do you know any other words for the same thing? Read each description to a friend, neighbor, or relative who grew up in another part of the United States (or another country) than you did. Note any differences between that person's word choice and your own.

1. a small town or rural area remote from the city
2. a porch or covered entrance outside a house
3. peanuts
4. what you say when you want to claim something as yours
5. a thick drink made of ice cream, milk, and flavoring blended together.

Standard English

Standard English is the most useful and the most widely used variety of English. Unlike a dialect, it is not limited to a particular place or group. It is used all over the United States (and even all over the world) by people of all backgrounds without indicating what place or group they belong to. It is the one variety of English that belongs to everybody.

The term *standard English* applies more to writing than to speech, especially in the United States. Standard English is especially appropriate for communicating with a general audience and with anyone outside a familiar circle of family and friends. It is the language of public affairs and education, publication and television, science and technology, business and government.

Nobody needs to use standard English all the time, but everybody should be able to use it when it is the appropriate variety to use. Dictionaries and grammar handbooks record the rules and guidelines of standard English for ready reference. You can find some of these rules and guidelines in the **Handbook** in this textbook. The **Handbook** uses the labels *standard* and *nonstandard* to identify differences between standard English and other varieties of English. *Nonstandard* doesn't mean wrong language. It means language that is inappropriate in situations where standard English is expected.

👉 **REFERENCE NOTE:** For more about standard English, see page 842.

ANSWERS
Exercise 7

Answers will vary. Some words and expressions students may list include the following:

1. village, borough, hamlet, township
2. gallery, piazza, patio, portico, stoop, veranda
3. goobers, groundnuts
4. It's mine. It belongs to me.
5. malt, malted, malted milk, milkshake

◆ INTEGRATING THE LANGUAGE ARTS

Literature Link. Ask students to read V. S. Naipaul's "B. Wordsworth" and to cite examples of how Naipaul's use of the vernacular helps to create setting and character. Have students consider how the story would differ if Naipaul had used only standard English in his dialogue.

Speaking Link. Let your students hold a debate to argue for and against the proposition "The concept of standard English should be abolished, and people should be encouraged to speak and write in the ways that best express their own cultures." If students need information on how to hold a debate, refer them to **Chapter 33: "Formal Speaking and Debate."**

MAKING CONNECTIONS

INTERNATIONAL GAMES
OBJECTIVE

- To research and identify the origins of sports terms and the sports or games in which the terms are used

INTERNATIONAL GAMES

Teaching Strategies

You may find it helpful to have a sports dictionary or encyclopedia available in the classroom when your students do this exercise. Your school librarian may be able to help you obtain one.

Several students who are interested in the same sport or game may want to work together to complete the second activity. If you allow students to work in groups, you may want to make each student responsible for at least one term.

ANSWERS

1. **a.** skiing—*hotdogging:* American English; *schuss:* German; *slalom:* Norwegian
   b. sailing—*davit:* Middle English and Old French; *luff:* Middle English from Old Dutch; *yaw:* Old Norse
   c. golf—*caddie:* Scottish form of French *cadet; niblick:* Scottish; *par:* Latin
2. Answers will vary. Each term should be a recognized part of the vocabulary of a sport or game.

514

MAKING CONNECTIONS

International Games

Sports terms are as international as the games themselves. Although each nation may specialize in a few sports, many sports are played—and talked about—around the world. As a result, a single sport may use terms from several different languages.

1. What sport or game uses each of the following terms? What language does each term come from? Use a dictionary to help you find out.

   a. hotdogging, schuss, slalom
   b. davit, luff, yaw
   c. caddie, niblick, par

2. Choose a sport or game you are interested in, and write down at least four terms used in it. Where do the terms come from?

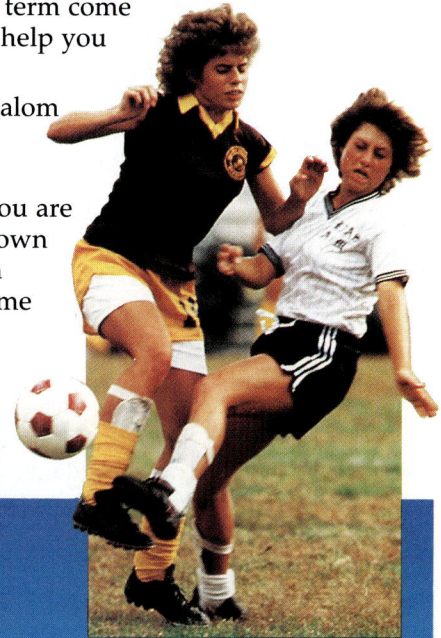

Chapter
13

STYLE IN WRITING

OBJECTIVES

- To identify writing as formal or informal
- To use vivid words to rewrite dull sentences
- To identify and analyze connotations of words
- To replace jargon, tired words, gobbledygook, euphemisms, and clichés in writing
- To use loaded words appropriately
- To use easily confused words in sentences correctly

cross CURRICULUM

Translating Jargon in Psychology

As this chapter explains on pp. 529–530, jargon or specialized vocabulary may prevent readers without specialized knowledge from understanding a text. Being able to explain technical terminology so that a nonspecialist audience can understand is a particularly useful skill for students, especially when they write research papers about specialized topics. As an exercise in awareness of audience and the use of jargon, have students choose three specialized words in the field of psychology and write a short expository essay for nonspecialists that defines the words and explains their significance.

- **Locating and Defining Words** To give students an opportunity to explain specialized words from psychology, offer them the following list to choose from or allow students to skim psychology texts or self-help books for their own list of words.

cognitive learning	*projection*
superego	*environment*
reinforcement	*regression*

- **Audience** The audience for this paper should be an average high-school educated person who wants a broad understanding of some important terms and concepts in psychology.

- **Writing** Suggest to students a framework like the following for their essays.

Introduction
Body Paragraph 1 (Explanation of first word)
Body Paragraph 2 (Explanation of the second word)
Body Paragraph 3 (Explanation of the third word)
Conclusion

- **Publishing** Have students give brief oral presentations of their essays and offer copies of their essay to their psychology teacher.

CHAPTER 13: STYLE IN WRITING

Use this guide to create an instructional plan that addresses the individual needs of your students. Assignments accompanied by the following symbol (*) may be completed out of class. Times given for pacing lessons are estimated.

CHAPTER PLANNING GUIDE—PUPIL'S EDITION

LESSONS	WHAT IS YOUR STYLE?/ FORMAL TO INFORMAL pp. 515–523	LEVELS OF MEANING pp. 523–530	DON'T CRAMP YOUR STYLE pp. 530–537
DEVELOPMENTAL PROGRAM	🕐 **60–65 minutes** • Main Assignment: Looking Ahead p. 515 • What Is Your Style?/Formal to Informal pp. 515–523 • Exercises 1, 2 pp. 519, 523* • Style Note p. 521	🕐 **45–50 minutes** • Levels of Meaning pp. 523–529 • Style Note p. 528 • Exercises 3, 5, 6 pp. 525, 529, 530* • Exercise 4 in pairs p. 527	🕐 **45–50 minutes** • Don't Cramp Your Style pp. 530–536 • Exercises 7, 8, 10 in pairs pp. 531–533, 537
CORE PROGRAM	🕐 **35–40 minutes** • Main Assignment: Looking Ahead p. 515 • Adapting Style to Aim/Voice and Tone pp. 516–518* • Exercises 1, 2 pp. 519, 523* • Charts pp. 519, 520 • Style Note p. 521 • Informal English Usage pp. 521–523*	🕐 **30–35 minutes** • Nonsexist Language/Connotations pp. 525–527* • Exercise 4 in pairs p. 527 • Loaded Words/Jargon pp. 528–529 • Style Note p. 528 • Exercises 5, 6 pp. 529, 530*	🕐 **35–40 minutes** • Misused Words/Tired Words/Clichés pp. 530–533* • Exercises 7, 9, 10 pp. 531–532, 534, 537* • Mixed Idioms and Metaphors/Gobbledygook/Euphemisms pp. 534–536
ACCELERATED PROGRAM	🕐 **30–35 minutes** • Main Assignment: Looking Ahead p. 515 • Voice and Tone pp. 517–518 • Exercises 1, 2 pp. 519, 523* • Charts pp. 519, 520 • Style Note p. 521	🕐 **25–30 minutes** • Charts p. 526 • Exercise 4 p. 527* • Style Note p. 528 • Jargon p. 529 • Exercises 5, 6 pp. 529, 530*	🕐 **20–25 minutes** • Misused Words pp. 530–531* • Exercises 7, 9, 10 pp. 531–532, 534, 537* • Mixed Idioms and Metaphors/Gobbledygook/Euphemisms pp. 534–536

CHAPTER PLANNING GUIDE—PROGRAM RESOURCES

	WHAT IS YOUR STYLE?/ FORMAL TO INFORMAL pp. 515–523	LEVELS OF MEANING pp. 523–530	DON'T CRAMP YOUR STYLE pp. 530–537
PRINT	• Voice and Tone, Formal and Informal English, *Word Choice and Sentence Style* pp. 11–12 • Formal and Informal English, *English Workshop* pp. 115–116	• Vivid Words, Nonsexist Language, Denotation and Connotation, *Word Choice and Sentence Style* pp. 13–15 • Specific and Vivid Words, Levels of Meaning, *English Workshop* pp. 117–120	• Misused Words, Tired Words, and Clichés; Mixed Idioms and Metaphors; Euphemisms and Gobbledygook; *Word Choice and Sentence Style* pp. 16–18 • Unclear Language, *English Workshop* pp. 121–122
MEDIA	• *Language Workshop:* Lesson 35	• *Language Workshop:* Lesson 36	• *Language Workshop:* Lesson 37

Computer disk or CD-ROM   Overhead transparencies

ELEMENTS OF WRITING: CURRICULUM CONNECTIONS

Making Connections
• Aim for Style pp. 538–539

ASSESSMENT OPTIONS

Summative Assessment
Style in Writing, Reviews A and B, *Word Choice and Sentence Style* pp. 19–20
Chapter Review, *English Workshop* pp. 123–124

Reflection
Self-assessment Record, *Portfolio Assessment* p. 19

INTEGRATING THE LANGUAGE ARTS

SELECTION	READING AND LITERATURE	WRITING AND CRITICAL THINKING	LANGUAGE AND SYNTAX	SPEAKING, LISTENING, AND OTHER EXPRESSION SKILLS
• from "**The Names of Women**" by Louise Erdrich p. 518 • *The Consul's File* by Paul Theroux p. 518 • from *Charlotte Sun Herald* p. 521 • "**Then He Goes Free**" by Jessamyn West p. 521 • *Rich in Love* by Josephine Humphreys p. 522 • *The New Yorker* by Philip Booth p. 522 • *The Great Gatsby* by F. Scott Fitzgerald p. 524	• Identifying formal and informal English p. 523 • Interpreting jargon p. 530 • Interpreting gobbledygook and euphemisms p. 537	• Writing a paragraph using neutral language p. 519 • Writing a paragraph using tone to reveal attitude p. 519 • Finding examples of formal and informal language p. 523 • Rewriting sentences using vivid words p. 525 • Applying interpretive and creative thinking pp. 527, 537 • Responding to connotations p. 527 • Writing descriptions using loaded words p. 529 • Revising jargon into plain language pp. 530, 537 • Choosing correct words pp. 531–532 • Replacing clichés and tired expressions p. 533 • Writing an original descriptive paragraph p. 534 • Revising euphemisms and gobbledygook p. 537 • Writing and revising a persuasive speech pp. 538–539 • Writing a letter to describe an emotional response p. 539	• Using tone p. 519 • Identifying formal and informal language p. 523 • Using vivid language p. 525 • Investigating connotation p. 527 • Using loaded words p. 529 • Substituting plain language for jargon pp. 530, 537 • Choosing correct words pp. 531–532 • Identifying tired words p. 533 • Using original language p. 534 • Identifying euphemisms and gobbledygook p. 537	• Working with a classmate to analyze and describe tone p. 519

OBJECTIVE

- To create tone in two written descriptions of a place

MOTIVATION

You can help your students understand the concept of style in writing by comparing it to style of dress. The title of this lesson is **What Is Your Style?** Ask students "What is your style of dress?" and "Does your style of dress ever change?" Point out that just as students' styles of dress change according to what they are doing (jeans for ☞

13 STYLE IN WRITING

LOOKING AHEAD

Behind each effortless-sounding piece of writing is a real person who chose words with care. Professional writers develop style the same way you do—one word at a time. In this chapter, you will work on your style by

- adapting your writing to audience, situation, and aim
- experimenting with voice and tone
- choosing clearer, livelier words
- sidestepping some common obstacles to style

PROGRAM MANAGER

FOR THE WHOLE CHAPTER

- **Review** For exercises on chapter concepts, see **Review Form A** and **Review Form B** in *Word Choice and Sentence Style*, pp. 19–20.

PROGRAM MANAGER

WHAT IS YOUR STYLE?

- **Independent Practice/ Reteaching** For practice and reinforcement, see **Voice and Tone** in *Word Choice and Sentence Style*, p. 11.
- **Computer Guided Instruction** For additional instruction and practice with voice and tone, see **Lesson 35** in *Language Workshop CD-ROM*.

QUOTATION FOR THE DAY

"Style is everything and nothing. It is not that, as is commonly supposed, you get your content and soup it up with style; style is absolutely embedded in the way you perceive." (Martin Amis, 1949–   , English novelist and journalist)

What Is Your Style?

Whether you are applying for a job, writing a history paper, preparing a report about your workplace project, or describing a movie to a friend, you make choices about what words to use

working and fancier clothes for going to parties, for example), their styles of writing should also change according to their purposes.

TEACHING THE LESSON

When teaching this material, you could read aloud to students the example sentences under **Adapting Style to Aim** and the passages under **Voice and Tone**. Because the concept of style is abstract, you may want to supply additional examples of voice and tone and of style adapted to aim. Work with students to answer the

and how to use them. The choices you make define your *style*. *Style* is your way of adapting your language to suit different occasions.

When you speak and write, you adapt your language to

- your aim—the purpose behind your words
- your attitude—the way you feel about your subject
- your audience—the people who will hear or read your words
- your situation—the time and place

Depending on the writing you do, some of these factors may be more important than others. For example, in personal journal entries, you write for yourself without worrying about how other people might react to your words. In a persuasive essay, though, you always keep your audience in mind, choosing words for their likely effects on readers. As you develop style in many different kinds of writing, you'll also develop greater sureness about word choice.

ADAPTING STYLE TO AIM

You can help students see how style is related to purpose by asking them to analyze the language in the passage exemplifying the persuasive aim. Ask students to identify ways in which the language used is persuasive. [Responses will vary. The mood of the sentence is imperative. Words such as *brilliant* and *mastery* are strongly laudatory.]

Adapting Style to Aim

Read the following four sentences about the same event. Notice how in each case, a change in aim brings a change in language.

INFORMATIVE	In a sellout concert at Carnegie Hall last night, popular singer Raul Fisher performed selections from his first album.
PERSUASIVE	By all means, plan to attend this brilliant young musician's demonstration of technical mastery and contemporary showmanship.
EXPRESSIVE	Fisher's got an awesome light show—I felt like I was on another planet. Intense sounds, too—he laid down riffs that made me look to make sure my feet were still on the floor.
LITERARY	Onto the most venerable stage in American music history stepped a young man about to smash the barriers between traditional and contemporary music, bringing listeners to their feet in thunderous approval.

☞ **REFERENCE NOTE:** For more about these four aims of writing, see pages 7 and 19.

two questions that precede the passage by Paul Theroux.

To prepare students for **Exercise 1** on p. 519, help them to write on the chalkboard two sentences describing an object in the room. The first sentence should use neutral language, and the second sentence should use language that creates a certain tone.

☞

Voice and Tone

People have distinctive voices when they write just as they do when they speak. *Voice* in writing is the unique sound and rhythm of a writer's language—a writer's personal way of talking to the reader. Voice is an important part of style because it gives a ring of honesty and authority to writing. It helps the reader imagine a real person speaking from the page.

Your personal voice can shine through in any kind of writing, from a science report to a thank-you note. Most often, you will want to write in a voice that sounds like you. Sometimes, though, you may want to imitate someone else's voice—for example, when you write a short story from the point of view of a particular narrator.

Like your speaking voice, your writing voice can express many different attitudes and feelings, or *tones.* It can sound happy, angry, sad, serious, sentimental, objective, horrified, offhand, sarcastic—however you want it to sound.

When you speak, you raise, lower, and otherwise alter your voice to express how you feel about your subject. But when you write, your words, sentence structure, and punctuation do all the work. That's why careful word choice is the key to creating tone.

In the following passage, Louise Erdrich creates a contemplative tone as she describes the activities of fall.

MEETING *individual* NEEDS

LEARNING STYLES

Visual Learners. Some students may need to see graphic representations of style adapted to purpose. Find and present to students a diagram designed to inform, a magazine advertisement designed to persuade, an image that expresses a thought or emotion, and a work of art that appeals to the senses. Discuss with students how the different purposes for the pictures affect their styles.

Auditory Learners. You can show the effect of style by playing versions of the same song in different musical styles. "Santa Claus is Coming to Town" is available in country, rock, soul, and neutral styles. Point out that the words and melody are the same in each version, but the style of each creates its unique impact.

TIMESAVER

For **Exercise 1**, ask your students to identify at the tops of their papers the tone they're trying to achieve and to underline the words they have chosen to create this tone. You can use this information to determine quickly where students are having problems.

AMENDMENTS TO SELECTIONS
Description of change: excerpted
Rationale: to focus on the concept of style presented in this chapter

518

---

518 *Style in Writing*

> It is autumn in the Plains, and in the little sloughs ducks land, and mudhens, whose flesh always tastes greasy and charred. Snow is coming soon, and after its first fall there will be a short, false warmth that brings out the sweet-sour odour of highbush cranberries. As a descendant of the women who skinned buffalo and tanned and smoked the hides, of women who pounded berries with the dried meat to make winter food, who made tea from willow bark and rosehips, who gathered snakeroot, I am affected by the change of seasons.
>
> Louise Erdrich, "The Names of Women"

Notice how Erdrich creates a quiet, contemplative tone by using words that describe the sights, smells, sounds, feelings, and activities of the season.

Now read a passage with a very different tone from Erdrich's. In this passage, Paul Theroux describes a tree in Malaysia called "The Midnight Horror." (The corolla are the petals of the tree's flowers.) What is the overall feeling of the passage? What words help create the tone?

> During the day the tree looked comic, a tall simple pole like an enormous coatrack, with big leaves that looked like branches—but there were very few of them. It was covered with knobs, stark black things; and around the base of the trunk there were always fragments of leaves that looked like shattered bones, not human bones.
>
> At night the tree was different, not comic at all. It was Ladysmith who showed me the underlined passage in his copy of Professor Corner's *Wayside Trees of Malaya.* Below the entry for *Oroxylum indicum* it read, "Botanically, it is the sole representative of its kind; aesthetically, it is monstrous. . . . The corolla begins to open about 10 P.M., when the tumid, wrinkled lips part and the harsh odor escapes from them. By midnight, the lurid mouth gapes widely and is filled with stink. . . . The flowers are pollinated by bats which are attracted by the smell and, holding to the fleshy corolla with the claws on their wings, thrust their noses into its throat; scratches, as of bats, can be seen on the fallen leaves the next morning. . . ."
>
> Paul Theroux, *The Consul's File*

OBJECTIVE

- To identify writing as formal or informal English

MOTIVATION

Tell students that research shows that people constantly shift their styles from very formal to very informal in specific speaking situations. Ask students if they shift their styles of speaking and, if so, when and why they do so.

☞

EXERCISE 1 ▶ **Creating Tone**

Write two descriptions of a familiar place or scene—for example, a shopping mall, a football game, or a neighborhood park. In the first description, use neutral language that doesn't reveal your feelings about your subject. In the second description, use language that does show your attitude—affection, humor, disdain, or whatever. Ask a classmate to read your two paragraphs and describe the tone of each.

Formal to Informal

Like your clothes, your language can be formal, informal, or somewhere in between. Often, you adapt the level of formality in your language without thinking about it. For example, your language is naturally more formal in an English essay than it is in a note to a friend. Sometimes, though, you must take extra care to be sure that your language is appropriate and consistent. You want to be sure that your words have the effect you intend.

Whether you use formal or informal language depends on the situation. Following are some of the appropriate uses for *formal English* and *informal English.*

WRITING	
Formal	Informal
serious essays, official reports, research papers, some literary criticism, and speeches on serious or solemn occasions	personal letters, journal entries, newspaper and magazine articles, and some nonfiction books, novels, short stories, and plays
SPEAKING	
Formal	Informal
banquets, dedication ceremonies, addresses, presentation ceremonies	everyday conversation at home, school, work, and recreation

ANSWERS
Exercise 1

Descriptions will vary. The description written in a neutral tone should contain words that are devoid of connotation. The description written in a specific tone should contain words that connote meanings that are consistent with that tone. In both descriptions, the tone should be consistent throughout.

PROGRAM MANAGER

FORMAL TO INFORMAL

- **Independent Practice/ Reteaching** For practice and reinforcement, see **Formal and Informal English** in *Word Choice and Sentence Style,* p. 12.

- **Computer Guided Instruction** For additional instruction and practice with formal and informal English, see **Lesson 35** in *Language Workshop CD-ROM.*

- **Practice** To help less-advanced students with additional instruction and practice with formal and informal English, see **Chapter 9** in *English Workshop, Complete Course,* pp. 115–116.

QUOTATION FOR THE DAY
"A good style must, first of all, be clear. It must not be mean or above the dignity of the subject. It must be appropriate." (Aristotle, 384–322 B.C., Greek philosopher and scientist)

As you discuss this lesson with your class, have students help you generate additional examples of situations that call for formal and informal English and examples of the features of formal and informal English. Students will probably enjoy discussing colloquialisms and slang. Ask your class to help you generate additional (perhaps local) examples of colloquialisms and slang.

MEETING individual NEEDS

LEP/ESL

General Strategies. Exercise 2 in this lesson suggests that students find examples of formal and informal writing in newspapers or magazines. Some students may need help in distinguishing between the two types of English. Consequently, you may want to find the material yourself and make handouts labeled as either formal or informal. Look for high-interest reading material that will grab students' attention. The more relevant the reading selections are to students' lives, the more likely the students will be to grasp the concepts presented.

520 *Style in Writing*

The following chart gives some examples of formal and informal English usage.

FEATURES OF FORMAL AND INFORMAL ENGLISH			
WORDS			
FORMAL	EXAMPLE	INFORMAL	EXAMPLE
longer	*intelligent*	**shorter**	*smart*
rare	*incendiarism*	**common**	*arson*
precise	*unimpressive*	**fuzzy**	*so-so*
specialized	*apiarist*	**general**	*beekeeper*
serious	*Please calm down.*	**offhand**	*Cool it!*
restrained	*very commendable*	**exaggerated**	*fantastic*
PRONUNCIATION			
FORMAL	EXAMPLE	INFORMAL	EXAMPLE
slower	*Get out of the way.*	**faster**	*Getouttatheway!*
precise	*How do you know?*	**relaxed**	*How d'ya know?*
SPELLING			
FORMAL	EXAMPLE	INFORMAL	EXAMPLE
in full	*should not*	**contractions**	*shouldn't*
conventional	*though*	**unconventional**	*tho*
GRAMMAR			
FORMAL	EXAMPLE	INFORMAL	EXAMPLE
complex	*The woman who wrote the story was Jamaican.*	**compound**	*The woman was Jamaican, and she wrote the story.*
complete	*It is chilly today.*	**fragmentary**	*Chilly today.*
explicit	*What he just did was amazing.*	**implied**	*Amazing!*

Formal language usually creates a serious tone. For example, notice the tone of the following formal passage.

GUIDED PRACTICE

You can provide guided practice for **Exercise 2**, p. 523, by pointing out the features in the passage by Jessamyn West that make it informal. These include contractions ("don't," "boy's"), fragments ("Hit him?"), figures of speech ("too tender-hearted to hurt a fly"), and nonstandard usage ("What would she want to hit him for?").

INDEPENDENT PRACTICE

Exercise 2 can provide independent practice. You may want to have three or four students read the same article and discuss their findings as a group. You can assess students' abilities to identify formal and informal writing by evaluating their performance on **Exercise 2**.

☛

Benjamin Joshua Baker, Charlotte County's first black educator, had a thousand children but none bearing his name. They were his students who revere his memory through periodic reunions of the Baker Academy of Punta Gorda.

Charlotte Sun Herald

For informal situations, your language will tend to have a friendlier, more personal tone.

"Hit him? What would she want to hit him for?"

"I don't know," said Mr. Delahanty. "I don't know that she did hit him. Maybe she kicked him. Anyway, his mother seems to think the boy's been damaged in some way."

"Damaged," repeated Mrs. Delahanty angrily. "Damaged! Why, Cress is too tender-hearted to hurt a fly. She shoos them outside instead of killing them. And you sit there talking of hitting and kicking."

Jessamyn West, "Then He Goes Free"

STYLE NOTE

Always consider your audience and situation before you "dress up" or "dress down" your language. In informal situations, a formal style may sound stiff or unfriendly. At a formal occasion, casual language may be considered disrespectful.

Informal English Usage

Colloquialisms and *slang* are two kinds of expressions that give flavor to informal English.

Colloquialisms are the everyday words and phrases of conversational language. If you say that the home team "bit the dust" in last night's basketball game, you are using a colloquialism. If you tell a friend that you "couldn't care less" about new fashions, you are using a colloquialism.

Colloquialisms are most common in casual conversation. However, they also have a place in expressive and creative writing. Notice how the writers of the following sentences use colloquialisms to get their points across.

INTEGRATING THE LANGUAGE ARTS

Literature Link. Have students read poetry by one of the Augustan poets, such as Pope or Dryden, and by a Romantic poet, such as Wordsworth, Coleridge, Keats, or Shelley. Afterward, ask students to describe any differences in style that they perceive in the poems. [Augustan poetry tends to be more formal than Romantic poetry. Augustan poetry conforms to strict rhyme and meter and focuses on public issues rather than personal ones.]

AMENDMENTS TO SELECTIONS

Description of change: excerpted
Rationale: to focus on the concept of style presented in this chapter

CLOSURE

Ask students to tell you two situations in which formal English is called for and two in which informal English is appropriate. ■

CRITICAL THINKING

Analysis. Colloquialisms and slang are sometimes used in advertising. Collect ads from newspapers and magazines and ask your students to identify uses of colloquialisms and slang in the ads. Discuss with students why advertisers might choose to use such informal speech. [Colloquialisms and slang can serve to personalize ads and make them more accessible by acting as a form of mass appeal.] Ask your students to analyze the types of ads that use colloquialisms and slang. Do they perceive any patterns?

> We had our irregularities; but every family has something or other out of whack.
>
> Josephine Humphreys, *Rich in Love*
>
> I used to get all revved up.
>
> Philip Booth, *The New Yorker*

When Booth uses the term "revved up," he makes the reader think of fast cars, loud engines, and the exhilaration of racing. Imagining those things helps the reader understand the kind of excitement that Booth is talking about. But if you were writing a letter to a prospective employer, you would not say that you are *"all revved up* about this *really cool* job."

Slang consists of new words, or old words used in new ways, that are vivid and colorful. Almost any group of closely associated people creates slang. For example, students and musicians are constantly devising slang words, some of which are eventually used by the general public. Some slang words have been around for centuries—for example, the slang word *lousy* dates back to the 1600s. However, most slang is short-lived. It rides a crest of popularity and then is quickly replaced.

Here are a few expressions that are considered slang. How many do you recognize? What expressions do you use to mean the same things?

chill out: relax   *stupid money:* money spent
awesome: very good   unwisely
weirdo: a strange person   *lame:* weak, pathetic
nuts: crazy   *zone out:* relax
bummer: disappointing

AMENDMENTS TO SELECTIONS
Description of change: excerpted
Rationale: to focus on the concept of style presented in this chapter

Shoe reprinted by permission: Tribune Media Services.

LEVELS OF MEANING

OBJECTIVES

- To use vivid words to rewrite dull sentences
- To identify and analyze the connotations of words
- To use loaded words in writing
- To replace jargon in sentences

MOTIVATION

Ask students to select from the following pairs the words that they would rather be described as: *fair* or *pale, slender* or *skinny, assertive* or *pushy.* If students choose *fair, slender,* and *assertive,* explain that they've responded to the connotations rather than the literal meanings of the words and that in this lesson they will learn more about these levels of meaning. ☞

Slang is considered highly informal and is inappropriate in most kinds of writing. However, like colloquial language, slang sometimes has a place in expressive and creative writing. For example, in fictional dialogue, slang can help make your characters sound like real people.

EXERCISE 2▶ **Identifying Formal and Informal English** Answers will vary. Each student should give at least five examples.

Read a newspaper or magazine article on a topic that interests you. Is the article written in formal or informal English? What words, expressions, and sentences make the writer's language seem more formal or more informal? Give at least five examples.

Levels of Meaning

The effect that a word has on its audience is part of the meaning of the word. A word can have different meanings for different people and in different situations. Understanding the effects that your words have will help you make better choices when you write.

Specific Words

The English language is full of general nouns and verbs. The word *house* is a general noun that could refer to any number of specific dwellings: a brick row house, an apartment house, a split level, a prefab, an adobe hut, a mobile home, a farmhouse.

General words tend to weaken your writing because they call up only a vague picture in your reader's mind. Take, for example, the sentence "I went to the store." Is it a video store, a hardware store, a grocery, a deli, or a boutique? Even the verb *went* could be more specific—did the speaker *walk, run, dash, meander, fly*? Maybe the speaker *rode* the bus or *drove.*

Compare the following pairs of passages. Notice how the specific words in the second version give readers better, clearer, more interesting information.

TIMESAVER

You can save time grading **Exercise 2** by limiting your students to three or four articles that you familiarize yourself with beforehand. This way you won't have to read and analyze a different article for each student.

PROGRAM MANAGER

LEVELS OF MEANING

- **Independent Practice/ Reteaching** For practice and reinforcement, see **Vivid Words, Nonsexist Language,** and **Denotation and Connotation** in *Word Choice and Sentence Style,* pp. 13–15.

- **Computer Guided Instruction** For additional instruction and practice with vivid words, nonsexist language, and denotation and connotation, see **Lesson 36** in *Language Workshop CD-ROM.*

- **Practice** To help less-advanced students with additional instruction and practice with vivid words, nonsexist language, and denotation and connotation, see **Chapter 9** in *English Workshop, Complete Course,* pp. 117–120.

QUOTATION FOR THE DAY

"I hate false words, and seek with care, difficulty, and moroseness, those that fit the thing." (Walter Savage Landor, 1775–1864, English writer)

The goal of this lesson is to make students conscious of the effects words have on readers. Most people respond intuitively to the emotional appeal of certain words, but students are often unaware of their ability to use words to achieve these responses. Additionally, a conscious awareness of levels of meaning will help make your students better critical readers.

You may want to ask students to read this lesson independently and then to discuss any questions later in class.

If you're using this lesson as part of a concentration on revision, you can have students revise their own writing to make their language more specific and vivid and to

COOPERATIVE LEARNING

When teaching specific and vivid words, you could let your students work in pairs. One member of each pair could write a sentence using general language and then give it to the other member, who could rewrite it using specific, vivid language. After each rewrite, students should switch roles and repeat the activity.

TECHNOLOGY TIP

Some word-processing programs include thesauruses. Encourage your students to use these features, but remind students that not all of the words given in a thesaurus are exact synonyms. Writers have to learn to respond to subtle shades of meaning to avoid misusing words.

SELECTION AMENDMENT
Description of change: excerpted
Rationale: to focus on the concept of style presented in this chapter

---

524   *Style in Writing*

a. If we don't do something, those people will keep putting waste water into the lake.
b. If we don't protest, XYZ Corporation will continue its irresponsible dumping of over one hundred thousand tons of industrial waste water into the once-crystal waters of Rabbit Lake.

a. Add some cloves, some cinnamon, and some vanilla.
b. Add one-quarter teaspoon cloves, one-half teaspoon cinnamon, and one teaspoon vanilla.

a. About half way between West Egg and New York the motor road goes alongside the railroad to avoid an ash dump.
b. "About half way between West Egg and New York the motor-road hastily joins the railroad and runs beside it for a quarter of a mile so as to shrink away from a certain area of land. This is a valley of ashes—a fantastic farm where ashes grow like wheat into ridges and hills and grotesque gardens. . . ."

F. Scott Fitzgerald, *The Great Gatsby*

The more specific a description is, the more realistic it will seem. The more realistic it seems, the more impact it will have on an audience. When Shakespeare wrote *Julius Caesar*, he didn't have a character say that ghosts were *talking* in the streets. The character reported that "ghosts did *shriek* and *squeal* about the streets."

Vivid Words

Vivid words are specific words that appeal to the senses. A well-chosen vivid word can make a dramatic impression on your readers. When your audience can see, hear, touch, taste, and smell what you are describing, your writing will come alive. If you compare writing that does not use vivid words to writing that does, the contrast is like the difference between a black-and-white film and a color film.

The following passages are from Edward Abbey's essay "The First Morning," which is about his job as a park ranger in Utah. Each passage by Abbey is preceded by a passage that says basically the same thing but uses general words that do not create sensory images.

GUIDED PRACTICE

Your students may benefit from seeing how the first sentence in **Exercise 3** could be rewritten by using vivid language. For **Exercise 4** on p. 527, work with students to identify the connotations associated with the first one or two animal names. For **Exercise 5** on p. 529, work with students to identify the loaded words in the second newspaper's ☞

Levels of Meaning   **525**

a. Some birds are near the rock, making noises.
b. "Three ravens are wheeling near the balanced rock, squawking at each other and at the dawn."

a. The birds call and flap their wings. I smell breakfast cooking.
b. "The ravens cry out in husky voices, blue-black wings flapping against the golden sky. Over my shoulder comes the sizzle and smell of frying bacon."

"Birds . . . making noises" does not help you see or hear the birds, but "ravens . . . squawking" does. In the same way, "I smell breakfast cooking" does not call to mind a specific smell, but "Over my shoulder comes the sizzle and smell of frying bacon" creates a specific sensory image of sound and odor.

EXERCISE 3 ▶ **Using Vivid Words**

Here are five dull sentences that don't say much. Rewrite each sentence to express the same idea in specific, vivid language. Add as many words and details as you wish.

1. Xavier's car is full of stuff.
2. I smelled dinner cooking.
3. The dog went after a rabbit.
4. At night I hear the sound of traffic through my window.
5. The cars moved toward the starting line.

Nonsexist Language

Nonsexist language is language that applies to people in general, both male and female. When you are referring to humanity as a whole, nonsexist expressions are more appropriate than gender-specific ones. For example, you might use the nonsexist terms *humanity, human beings,* and *people* instead of the gender-specific term *mankind*.

In the past, many skills and occupations excluded either men or women. Expressions like *seamstress, stewardess,* and *mailman* reflect those limitations. Now that most jobs are held by both men and women, language is adjusting to reflect this change.

SELECTION AMENDMENT
Description of change: excerpted
Rationale: to focus on the concept of style presented in this chapter

account on p. 528 [*exhausted, struggled, and rambling*]. And for **Exercise 6**, model a revision of the first sentence.

INDEPENDENT PRACTICE

All four of the exercises in this lesson offer opportunities for independent practice. The jargon in **Exercise 6**, p. 530, can be found in a college dictionary.

Following are some widely used nonsexist terms that you can use to replace the older, gender-specific ones.

Gender-Specific	Nonsexist
businessman	executive, businessperson
chairman	chairperson
deliveryman	delivery person
fireman	firefighter
foreman	supervisor
housewife	homemaker
mailman	mail carrier
manmade	synthetic
manpower	workers, human resources
may the best man win	may the best person win
policeman	police officer
salesman	salesperson
steward, stewardess	flight attendant
watchman	security guard

Connotations

Before you use a word, you need to know both its denotation and its connotations. *Denotation* is the strict dictionary definition of a word. *Connotations* are the emotions and associations that a word may suggest. Not all words have connotations. For most people, *look, paper, set,* and *table* suggest no particular emotions or associations. But words such as *skinny, slender, glare, gray, intellectual,* and *spring* do.

Connotations become attached to words through everyday usage and common experience. For example, each of the following words for dwellings has similar connotations for many people.

WORDS	CONNOTATIONS
log cabin	simplicity, strength, the pioneer past, Abraham Lincoln
lodge	country retreats, hunting
shack	poverty, shabbiness
chalet	skiing, snow, Switzerland

INTEGRATING THE LANGUAGE ARTS

Usage Link. Some contemporary usage authorities suggest that writers avoid the awkward use of *he or she* and *his or her* whenever possible. Ask your students to rewrite the following sentences to avoid awkward usage:

1. Each student should turn in his or her paper before class begins. [Students should turn in their papers before class begins.]
2. Everyone on the math team had his or her calculator ready for action. [The members of the math team had their calculators ready for action.]
3. Our family will host an exchange student next year; he or she will arrive in January. [Our family will host an exchange student next year; the student will arrive in January.]

COOPERATIVE LEARNING

Group students in pairs. Let each pair work together to rewrite headlines from a newspaper or magazine by replacing neutral words with connotative words.

When you choose your words, be aware of their connotations. Suppose you want to write about someone who is not working. You might refer to that person as *unemployed, out of work, at leisure,* or *between jobs.* None of these terms have strongly negative connotations. However, if you describe the person as a *freeloader* or a *moocher,* your word choice will prompt your readers to associate negative feelings with the person.

Connotations help set the tone of writing. When a writer's attitude changes, his or her word choice changes, too. For example, during the Boer War in South Africa, the British fought the Boers, descendants of the Dutch colonists. During the earlier days of the war, the British press described the Boers as "sneaking and skulking behind rocks and bushes." But when the British forces learned to imitate the Boers' tactics for veld warfare, the press described the British as "cleverly taking advantage of cover."

"Cleverly Taking Advantage of Cover"

"Sneaking and Skulking Behind Rocks and Bushes"

EXERCISE 4 ▶ Responding to Connotations

Many animal names have strong associations for us, whether or not we feel strongly about the animals themselves. What would each of the following names call to mind if it were used to describe a person? Identify the animal habits or mannerisms, real or legendary, that account for each word's effect.

1. owl	5. ox	9. weasel
2. worm	6. skunk	10. wolf
3. lamb	7. cat	
4. mouse	8. fox	

MEETING individual NEEDS

LEP/ESL

General Strategies. Animal names have different connotations in different cultures. If you have students from various cultural backgrounds in your class, expect their responses to **Exercise 4** to vary. Invite students to share their responses with the class to initiate discussion of the similarities and differences among cultures.

ANSWERS
Exercise 4

Responses will vary. Here are some possibilities:

1. wise; Athena's favorite bird
2. lowly; lives underground
3. gentle; biblical references
4. timid; small and skittish
5. strength; strong work animal
6. bad odor; exudes an unpleasant odor when confronted
7. independent; seems to do what it pleases
8. sly; elusive when hunted
9. sneaky; often robs henhouses at night
10. fierce; formidable hunter

EXTENSION

Have students read two or more newspapers' reports of the same event. Tell students to look for connotative and loaded language in the newspaper articles. Then, have students evaluate, on the basis of objectivity, the articles they have read.

INTEGRATING THE LANGUAGE ARTS

Literature Link. Andrew Marvell makes use of loaded words in "To His Coy Mistress," especially in the second stanza. Ask your students to read the poem, which may be found in their literature textbooks. Have students identify the loaded words Marvell uses in the second stanza [*deserts, worms, dust, ashes,* and *grave*]. Discuss with students why he uses this language. [The speaker tries to persuade his beloved through loaded language that her chastity will be of no value after her death.]

CRITICAL THINKING

Analysis. Connotative and loaded words are often used to persuade people to adopt particular political opinions. Bring to class editorials, and ask students to identify the connotative and loaded language used in the editorials.

528 *Style in Writing*

Loaded Words

Words and phrases that have strong connotations, either positive or negative, are called *loaded words.* Because they appeal to emotions, loaded words can bias people for or against something. For example, if prospective car buyers hear a salesperson describe a car as a *roomy luxury sedan*, they might want to test-drive the car. But if they hear someone else describe the car as an *oversized, overpriced gas-guzzler*, they will probably hesitate to consider the purchase.

Advertisers, politicians, salespeople, and writers of newspaper editorials all use loaded words to influence their audiences. Writers of literary works often use loaded words to get readers emotionally involved with situations and characters. Even writers of informative articles and news reports do not always use objective language.

Here are two reports of a trial. If you read these accounts in two different newspapers, what would you guess about each newspaper's point of view?

The first newspaper's account:

> In the courtroom this morning, weary but attentive jurors listened somberly to Tasha Jones's long-awaited testimony. The room was deathly silent as Jones, one of the few witnesses to the robbery, described in detail what she saw.

The second newspaper's account:

> In the courtroom this morning, exhausted jurors struggled to remain attentive through the fourth and last witness's account of the robbery. According to one observer, even the judge, Roland Foster, glanced at his watch several times during Tasha Jones's long, rambling testimony.

STYLE NOTE Use loaded words with care. Intelligent readers recognize them as attempts to manipulate emotions and therefore view them with suspicion. When you do use loaded words, remember that your readers will associate these feelings with your subject. Avoid any words that might leave your audience with the wrong impression.

EXERCISE 5 ▶ **Using Loaded Words**

You have just attended a fancy banquet. Write two descriptions of your seven-course meal. In the first, use language that will make your readers wish they had been there. In the second, use words that will convince them they were better off eating frozen dinners at home.

Jargon

Jargon is language that has a special meaning for a particular group of people. Jargon most often appears in informative writing. However, you will find jargon wherever people share an occupation, a hobby, or a field of study. Military personnel, computer users, editors, truck drivers, doctors, astronauts, and baseball players all have their own specialized vocabularies. Properly used, jargon is a valuable tool because it compresses complex information into a precise word or two.

SAILING	*fox:* several ropes twisted together
HORSE SHOWS	*in and out:* two fences situated twenty-five feet apart over which a horse and rider jump, touching the ground after the first fence
AVIATION	*check the runway:* to fly at high speed with wheels up just above an airstrip
FILM	*cut:* to stop filming
PSYCHOLOGY	*constellation:* several thoughts having a relationship to one another and centered on one idea

Don't use jargon unless you are sure that your audience will understand the terms. Often, jargon might as well be a foreign language to people outside a field of interest. When you write a description of an experiment for your science instructor, you might say that "the compound entered an excited state." However, if you describe the experiment to someone who is not familiar with physics, just say "the water began to boil."

OBJECTIVES

- To use easily confused words correctly in sentences
- To replace tired words in sentences
- To write a description without using clichés
- To revise gobbledygook and euphemisms in a paragraph

530

---

530   *Style in Writing*

EXERCISE 6 ▶   **Revising Jargon**

You're probably more familiar with jargon than you think. Rewrite each of the following sentences, replacing the italicized jargon with clear, plain English that anyone would under- stand. If you're in doubt about the meaning of a word, use a dictionary. (In most dictionaries, jargon uses of words are labeled with the field of interest they apply to.)

1. The poker player cracked a smile as he laid down a *flush*, but he changed his expression when his opponent dis- played a *full house*.
2. The football league drafted two new *backs* from the state university.
3. At the start of the season, with only three *tko's* under his belt, the contender knocked out the reigning champion of five years.
4. When we spotted the school of dolphins, the pilot *peeled off* and *banked right* to give us a closer look.
5. This film is *fast*.

Don't Cramp Your Style

Some kinds of words and expressions get in the way of an effective style. They weaken your writing by boring or confus- ing your reader. You can bring clarity and interest to your writ- ing by eliminating these stumbling blocks to style. First, though, you need to identify the words and expressions that give you trouble. This section of the chapter will help you do just that.

Misused Words

Many words sound so much alike or seem so close in meaning that they're easily confused with one another. For clear writ- ing, it's important to know the differences in meaning between similar words. Don't leave your readers wondering what you meant to say. As you revise and proofread, use a dictionary to check the spellings and meanings of words you're not sure about. Then choose words that say exactly what you mean.

This lesson deals with six topics related to style in writing. The first four topics—misused words, tired words, clichés, and mixed idioms and metaphors—have a direct relationship to your students' writing. The other two topics—gobbledygook and euphemisms—may occasionally need attention during revision, but this information will best serve your students by making them sharper critical readers. Have students read this lesson as homework and discuss the material with them in class the following day.

As you discuss each of these style problems, work with students to generate additional examples. You could write examples on the chalkboard under the textbook 👉

Following are some pairs of easily confused words. Note any words that you've had trouble with, and look them up in a dictionary. You might keep your own list of tricky words and their definitions as a reference for when you revise and proofread.

disinterested	affect	famous	set
uninterested	effect	notorious	sit
principal	allusion	imply	emigrate
principle	illusion	infer	immigrate

👉 **REFERENCE NOTE:** The **Glossary of Usage** on pages 842–862 includes discussions of many easily confused words. Also see the lists and discussions of easily confused words on pages 784–787 and 816–817.

EXERCISE 7 ▶ **Choosing the Correct Words**

For each of the following sentences, choose the <u>word in parentheses that has the correct meaning</u>. Use a dictionary to check the meanings of any words you're not sure about.

1. By constantly (*<u>flouting</u>*, *flaunting*) the rules, Charles ended up thrown out of the game.
2. The model on the magazine cover wore a (*livid*, *<u>vivid</u>*) red dress.
3. The ambassador (*<u>respectfully</u>*, *respectively*) approached the Queen and asked her to read the message from his government.

MEETING *individual* **NEEDS**

STUDENTS WITH SPECIAL NEEDS

Some students have trouble with visual discrimination, which makes it difficult for them to perceive the difference between two words that are similar. You can help by suggesting that students write and pronounce misused words that are similar to one another.

LESS-ADVANCED STUDENTS

One set of words that is often misused is *there, their, they're*. To help students, tell them about the following mnemonic devices:

1. Remember the *here* in *there* in writing about a place.
2. Remember the *heir* in *their* when writing about possession.
3. If *they are* can be substituted, use *they're*.

Encourage students to develop and share additional mnemonics for misused words.

GUIDED PRACTICE

For **Exercise 7**, suggest that students look up both words in a dictionary before they decide which word is correct. You could demonstrate this process for the first item in the exercise and also model completion of the first item in **Exercise 8** on p. 533. For **Exercise 9**, p. 534, guide students by writing a descriptive paragraph on the

MEETING individual NEEDS

LEP/ESL

General Strategies. Students might have a difficult time identifying tired words and clichés because this is an ability that comes with fluency and extensive exposure to the language. To help students, have the class work in groups of three or four to generate clichés and tired words. Each group should generate at least two of each. You could then compile a list of clichés and tired words to be used as a reference.

COMPUTER NOTE

Remind students to use the thesaurus feature carefully to avoid selecting words that do not fit the context of their compositions. Students should use thesauruses to find words they already know but can't recall. This way, they are less likely to use words that are inappropriate for the meaning they want to convey.

532

---

532   *Style in Writing*

4. From the look on his face, I (*inferred, implied*) that the party had been a disaster.
5. By drawing an (*anthology, analogy*) between birds and dinosaurs, he explained the development of the dolphin.
6. The black, swollen clouds gathering over our heads told us that rain was (*immanent, imminent*).
7. If they do not reach a settlement out of court, their lawyers will (*persecute, prosecute*).
8. By milking poisonous snakes for their venom, snake handlers help scientists make (*anecdotes, antidotes*) to snakebites.
9. After hearing Mrs. Abeyto's arguments, the committee (*capitalized, capitulated*) to her demands.
10. The judge agreed to shut down the plant after we presented (*credible, credulous*) evidence that the owners were violating environmental protection laws.

Tired Words

A *tired word* is one that has become vague and bland from overuse. The word *great* is a good example of a tired word. Used to refer to everything from a sandwich to a Nobel Prize winner, it has lost its descriptive power.

Tired words sap the strength from your writing. If you write in a movie review that a movie is *nice,* your readers probably won't hurry to buy tickets and judge for themselves.

With every tired word you use, you lose an opportunity to develop an exact, vivid description of your subject. Keep your readers' attention by using lively, specific words.

COMPUTER NOTE: Use your word-processing program's thesaurus tool to help you find vivid words to replace tired ones.

Clichés

A *cliché* is a tired expression. The word *cliché* comes from a French word for a master printing plate used to print thousands of impressions. Each impression is identical, but each is just a little less sharp than the last. And finally the master plate, the cliché, is so worn down that it is thrown away.

INDEPENDENT PRACTICE

The four exercises in this lesson should provide ample opportunity for independent practice. Have students write drafts of the descriptions required in **Exercise 9** as homework. Later, in class, have students revise their descriptions under your supervision or in the context of peer-response groups. If you use peer-response groups, you ☞

Don't Cramp Your Style **533**

The English language contains thousands of clichés. Many are figures of speech—metaphors, similes, or personifications. Others are hyperboles—exaggerations for special effect. Here are a few clichés based on figurative language.

EXAMPLES clear as crystal   the long arm of the law
          hungry as a horse   Father Time
          a dog's life   wise as an owl

Some clichés come to us so naturally that we use them without thinking. That's the problem with clichés. They keep us from being original—from seeing and describing things in new ways. They may be handy in conversation, but they are too dull to be effective in writing. Watch for clichés as you evaluate and revise your writing. Try to create vivid, unique expressions to replace them.

EXERCISE 8 ▶ **Replacing Tired Words**

For each tired word in italics, suggest two effective replacements. (You may suggest other ways to reword a sentence, too.)

1. For two weeks last summer, we hiked through the mountains of Switzerland and saw all that *great* scenery.
2. After Kito bought the rusted chassis of an old roadster and completely restored the car, no one could doubt that he was a *good* mechanic.
3. My stepmother is a *nice* person who always has time to talk to my sister and me.
4. This computer program is really *neat;* all you have to do is tap a key to bring up dozens of synonyms on the screen.
5. She thought it was a *good* movie because the ending came as a complete surprise.
6. "Look out!" he said as we met the watchful eyes of a tiny tan beast sitting in the corner yard. "That's a *bad* dog!"
7. It was a *nice* day, but all I could think about was the root canal that the dentist said I had to have.
8. The field trips make this a *great* course for anyone interested in botany.
9. Did Mr. Méndez take you up in that *terrific* twin-engined plane of his?
10. He ran *well,* finishing first by over twenty yards.

ADVANCED STUDENTS

Many figurative phrases written by Shakespeare in his plays and sonnets have been reused so often that they have become clichés. The expressions "the milk of human kindness" and "what's done is done," for example, are from *The Tragedy of Macbeth.* Challenge students to find other clichés that originated with Shakespeare, and have the students report their findings to the class.

ANSWERS
Exercise 8

Responses will vary. Here are some possible replacements for the tired words:

1. idyllic, inspiring, picturesque
2. skilled, well-trained, ingenious
3. empathetic, considerate, caring
4. sophisticated, advanced, elegant
5. exciting, arresting, memorable
6. vicious, fierce, ferocious
7. pleasant, enjoyable, gorgeous
8. worthwhile, engaging, rewarding
9. remarkable, extraordinary, amazing
10. swiftly, brilliantly, rapidly

can make students accountable for suggestions by having them write their initials next to their suggestions.

You can use your students' performances on **Exercises 7–10** to determine whether the students have met the objectives for this lesson. If you're using this lesson as part of a study of revision, you can also make a point of evaluating how well students use what they have learned to revise their writing.

ANSWERS
Exercise 9

Responses will vary. The descriptions should employ specific, vivid language that appeals to the reader's senses and should avoid clichés and tired words.

CRITICAL THINKING

Synthesis. Ask your students to brainstorm possible origins of the following idioms:

1. don't look a gift horse in the mouth
2. down the hatch
3. fine as frog's hair
4. on the ball
5. run of the mill

After they have spent ten minutes writing down possible origins, let students share their ideas with the class. Arrive at a consensus about which origin seems to make the most sense for each idiom. You could then challenge students to research the origins of these and other idioms.

EXERCISE 9 ▶   **Writing an Original Description**

You are an alien sent to observe and record the habits and environments of Earth creatures. Write a paragraph describing a person, thing, or event you have witnessed. Some possible topics follow. Use words that will help your readers see, hear, feel, smell, or taste what you are describing. Because you aren't familiar with any of the clichés Earthlings use, you will have to come up with original ways to describe your topic.

1. a cat chasing a squirrel
2. someone mowing a lawn
3. a concert
4. a family eating spaghetti at a restaurant
5. a violent thunderstorm

Mixed Idioms and Metaphors

An *idiom* is an expression that can't be taken literally. It says one thing but means another. For example, if your brother says "I lost my head," you don't expect to see him walking around headless. And if you hear that "Stephanie fell for Carlos," you don't think that Carlos was supposed to fall down but Stephanie did it for him. Like *fall for*, many idioms are also colloquialisms.

A *metaphor* is a figure of speech that describes one thing by comparing it to another, basically different thing. The *roof of the mouth*, the *arm of the chair*, the *foot of the table*, and the *nose of the plane* are all metaphors. William Shakespeare's "All the world's a stage," Emily Dickinson's "'Hope' is the thing with feathers," and "The Lord is my shepherd" from Psalm 23 also are metaphors.

It's important to use idioms and metaphors correctly and consistently. If you mix up idioms or metaphors, you may confuse your readers or create unintentionally funny mental images. For example, if you say "we've been sold up the creek" (a mix of the idioms *up a creek* and *sold down the river*), readers won't know what you mean. And if you say that "the woman flapped her arms and barked for silence," your mixed metaphor will create a picture of somebody who is birdlike and doglike at the same time.

RETEACHING

If the results of your assessment indicate a need for reteaching, you could provide students with some copies of an essay that you have created that contains at least one example of each of the style problems discussed in this lesson. Then, work with students to identify and revise the elements that detract from good style.

CLOSURE

Ask students to name three kinds of words or expressions that can weaken their writing.

☞

Don't Cramp Your Style **535**

Gobbledygook

Gobbledygook is wordy, puffed-up language. Awkward and confusing, it obscures rather than clarifies meaning. You can recognize gobbledygook by its strings of long, complicated words and long, complicated sentences. At first glance, gobbledygook may seem impressive. But on a closer look, it is like a balloon filled with hot air. For example, here is a famous little proverb restated in gobbledygook.

> A plethora of culinary specialists has a deleterious effect upon the quality of purées, consommés, and other soluble pabula.

In plain English this says:

> Too many cooks spoil the broth.

Can you translate the following gobbledygook into the plain English of the original proverb?

> A mobile section of petrified matter agglomerates no bryophytes.

Gobbledygook is an enemy of style because it confuses your audience and buries your natural voice. It can even make readers wonder if, underneath all those words, you have anything real to say. Stick to clear, straightforward language in your writing. Use simple words instead of complicated ones, and use only as many words as you need to make your point.

☞ **REFERENCE NOTE:** For more about reducing wordiness in writing, see pages 588–592.

The reason Verbal SAT scores are at an all-time low.

INCOMPLETE IMPLEMENTATION OF STRATEGIZED PROGRAMMATICS DESIGNATED TO MAXIMIZE ACQUISITION OF AWARENESS AND UTILIZATION OF COMMUNICATIONS SKILLS PURSUANT TO STANDARDIZED REVIEW AND ASSESSMENT OF LANGUAGINAL DEVELOPMENT.

ANY INTERROGATORY VERBALIZATIONS?

A DIFFERENT APPROACH

Your students might enjoy turning common adages into gobbledygook. Let them work independently or in pairs to rewrite the following sayings:

1. Don't kill the goose that laid the golden egg.
2. A stitch in time saves nine.
3. Never put off until tomorrow what you can do today.
4. Loose lips sink ships.
5. A penny saved is a penny earned.

You could sponsor a contest for the best gobbledygook.

INTEGRATING THE LANGUAGE ARTS

Library Link. Arrange for students to spend some time in the school library to look for examples of gobbledygook and euphemisms in government publications and political speeches. You may want to let your students work in pairs during this activity. In class, discuss with your students what the examples might mean and whether they represent intentional attempts to deceive the public.

535

Euphemisms

Euphemisms are indirect, agreeable words used in place of direct words that might seem offensive to people. Most euphemisms are used as a courtesy. For example, instead of saying that your best friend's dog is "hyperactive," you might say the animal is "frisky." During dinner at a neighbor's house, you might refer to a strange dish as "interesting" or "unusual" rather than "odd" or "bizarre."

Following are some of the euphemisms you might hear, read, or use in everyday life:

EUPHEMISM	MORE DIRECT TERM
additional revenues	higher taxes
deceased	dead
correctional institution	prison
offender	criminal
faux	imitation
memorial garden	cemetery
misrepresentation	lie
powder room	toilet

Euphemisms eliminate negative connotations that might interfere with a writer's aim. If government officials want to persuade people to accept higher taxes, they might refer to the proposed plan as "revenue enhancement." If a press agent's job is to announce a nuclear power plant explosion without causing panic, he or she might call the explosion an "energetic disassembly."

Like the examples in the paragraph above, many euphemisms have nothing to do with courtesy. Instead, their purpose is to mislead people by hiding unpleasant truths or misrepresenting important facts.

Euphemisms are appropriate whenever you want to show courtesy and tact. However, keep in mind that their indirectness tends to weaken your writing. Also, euphemisms might cause readers to wonder if you are being honest with them. Use direct language whenever you can. Check your writing for any euphemisms that you can replace with more straightforward terms.

E X E R C I S E **10** ▶   **Revising Gobbledygook and Euphemisms**

How good are you at translating gobbledygook and euphemisms? First, figure out what the writer of the following passage is really saying. (You may need to use a dictionary.) Then, rewrite the passage in plain, straightforward language. You may use either formal or informal English.

> Congratulations! Our office is happy to inform you that your neighborhood has been selected to be the recipient site of a new refuse management facility that will serve the entire county.
>
> This new service center features an ivy-covered brick barrier encompassing the entire campus and rising to a height of over ten feet. Our studies tend to indicate that this buffer will ensure that the center's schedule of ceaseless activities become an almost noiseless and invisible part of your everyday life.
>
> No expense has been spared and every effort has been made to incorporate the latest technology and an elegant design into this modern campus specializing in the rapid oxidation of flammable refuse. We are proud to report that our projections anticipate that residents will enjoy the virtually clean, odorless, and nearly invisible operation of this vital utility not only in the near future but for the next several decades.

■ LESSON 5 *(pp. 538–539)*
MAKING CONNECTIONS
AIM FOR STYLE
OBJECTIVES
- To write a persuasive speech
- To write an expressive letter

AIM FOR STYLE
Teaching Strategies

For the first exercise on p. 539, encourage students to keep the sentences in their speeches relatively short and to avoid using pronouns that might not be clear to listeners. Students should also keep in mind that their speeches should end with a call to action to involve their listeners in the cleanup effort.

If students choose the letter-writing exercise, you may want to spend a few minutes reviewing the characteristics of a friendly letter before they begin this assignment. You can also encourage students to spend a few minutes visualizing what the cleanup process would be like and imagining what feelings they might have during the process.

538

MAKING CONNECTIONS

Aim for Style

You are reading the newspaper one afternoon after school. As you turn the pages to the local section, a photograph catches your eye. You are surprised to see a classmate of yours holding a very dirty seagull. Curious, you read the article that follows.

Volunteers Save Sea Birds

Thursday's oil spill left hundreds of sea birds dead and dying along the coast. Drenched with sticky black oil, the birds that were still alive floundered along the shore, unable to swim or fly. But thanks to the efforts of students, retirees, and dozens of other concerned community members, many of these birds are being saved.

On Friday morning, volunteers chased, coaxed, and captured over one hundred unwilling birds and rushed them to East Side Community Center. There, teams of volunteers helped clean the oil from the birds' wings, using special detergents and other supplies donated by local merchants. About one hundred birds are now recovering in captivity.

Aim: Persuasive

You've decided to recruit volunteers from your school to help save the sea birds. Write a brief speech persuading your classmates to work all weekend capturing and cleaning the injured birds. To gain your friends' help, you will need to stir their emotions. You will also need to offer them reasons why they should sacrifice their free time. Choose your words carefully to make your speech convincing. Then use the following checklist to help you revise your speech for effectiveness and style.

Revision Checklist

- Is your tone appropriate for your aim and your audience?
- Is your language clear and to the point?
- Have you weighed your words for their connotations?
- Have you used specific words that create a vivid picture of the birds' plight?

Aim: Expressive

You are one of the volunteers who helped catch, cage, and wash the oil-soaked sea birds. How do you feel knowing you've saved lives? Do you think all the hard work was worthwhile?

Write a letter to a friend or a relative describing your part in the rescue operation and explaining how you feel about the experience. Help your reader imagine and understand your experiences and feelings. You may use either formal or informal English—whichever you think is appropriate for your audience.

GUIDELINES

You could use the questions in the **Revision Checklist** as criteria for evaluating students' speeches. You'll probably also want students to open their speeches with statements that arouse interest and to end with calls to action.

The letters your students write should be in the correct form for a friendly letter. They should also convey what the experience was like from the participant's point of view. This means using language that expresses feelings.

WRITING CLEAR SENTENCES

OBJECTIVES

- To use coordinating and subordinating conjunctions to sharpen the focus of written sentences
- To use adverb and adjective clauses to achieve clarity
- To express parallel ideas in parallel form
- To recognize and correct sentence fragments and run-on sentences
- To revise sentences to eliminate shifts in verb tense and voice

Workshop on Style in Business Writing

Ask the business teacher at your school to lead a short workshop on sentence style in business writing. The focus should be on the contrast between the sentence style for business writing, such as letters, newsletters, and memos, and the sentence style for academic writing.

- **Procedure** After students have reviewed the contents of Chapter 14, ask the business teacher to bring examples of workplace writing to illustrate issues of sentence style in the business world. Specific points of business writing should include the following:
  - The content, not the style, is what should stand out in business writing.
  - Good style seems effortless and natural on the page. Avoid unnecessary jargon, wordy sentences, and run-on sentences.
  - Present information in a straightforward way. Keep sentences short, place subjects and verbs at the beginning of sentences, and regularly use the normal word order of subject, verb, and direct object.
- Avoid faulty coordination. If two ideas occur in the same sentence, they should be of equal importance. If they are not, de-emphasize the less important idea by placing it in a subordinate clause or phrase.
- Avoid overloading sentences with too many ideas.
- Always use nonsexist, non-biased language. Keep the tone polite.
- Always be aware of the audience. Be aware of what your reader already knows and wants to know.
- **Activity** Have students work in small groups to analyze examples of workplace writing provided by the business teacher. They should use the points above as criteria for their evaluations. Then, ask students to write a brief statement explaining their evaluation and to share their statements with the class.

INTEGRATING THE LANGUAGE ARTS

SELECTION	READING AND LITERATURE	WRITING AND CRITICAL THINKING	LANGUAGE AND SYNTAX
• from **"A Christmas Memory"** by Truman Capote p. 557 • from ***Martin and Meditations on the South Valley*** by Jimmy Santiago Baca p. 563	• Evaluating and identifying relationships within sentences pp. 543–544, 545–546, 550, 554 • Evaluating sentences to identify faulty parallelism pp. 552–553, 554 • Reading to identify sentence fragments pp. 556–557, 562 • Reading to identify run-on sentences pp. 559, 562 • Evaluating sentences for awkward subject-verb shifts pp. 561–562 • Analyzing rhythm and parallel structure in a poem p. 563	• Analyzing relationships to choose appropriate subordinating conjunctions pp. 545–546 • Revising sentences by inserting adverb clauses pp. 546–547 • Applying interpretive and creative thinking pp. 547, 548–549, 554, 563 • Evaluating the effects of rearranging subordinate and independent clauses pp. 548–549 • Revising sentences by correcting faulty coordination pp. 550, 554 • Correcting faulty parallelism pp. 552–553, 554 • Identifying and revising sentence fragments pp. 556–557, 562 • Revising run-on sentences pp. 559, 562 • Revising awkward subject-verb relationships pp. 561–562 • Writing a poem using parallel structure p. 563 • Recalling sensory details p. 563	• Using connectives pp. 543–544 • Using appropriate punctuation pp. 543–544, 546–547, 550 • Using subordinating conjunctions pp. 545–546, 547 • Using adjective clauses to subordinate ideas pp. 548–549 • Using appropriate coordination pp. 550, 554 • Using parallel construction pp. 552–553, 554, 563 • Using correlative conjunctions pp. 552–553, 554 • Identifying sentence fragments pp. 556–557, 562 • Identifying awkward subject-verb relationships pp. 561–562 • Identifying run-on sentences p. 562

CHAPTER 14: WRITING CLEAR SENTENCES

Use this guide for creating an instructional plan that addresses the individual needs of your students. Assignments accompanied by the following symbol (*) may be completed out of class. Times given for pacing lessons are estimated.

CHAPTER PLANNING GUIDE—PUPIL'S EDITION

LESSONS	WAYS TO ACHIEVE CLARITY/ USING PARALLEL STRUCTURE pp. 540–554	OBSTACLES TO CLARITY pp. 555–562
DEVELOPMENTAL PROGRAM	**70–75 minutes** • Main Assignment: Looking Ahead p. 540 • Ways to Achieve Clarity pp. 540–550 • Mechanics Hint p. 542 • Exercises 1–5 pp. 543–550 in groups • Writing Note p. 545	**50–55 minutes** • Obstacles to Clarity pp. 555–561 • Exercises 7, 8 in pairs pp. 556–557, 559 • Style Note p. 557 • Writing Note p. 561 • Exercise 9 pp. 561–562
CORE PROGRAM	**35–40 minutes** • Main Assignment: Looking Ahead p. 540 • Coordinating Ideas/Subordinating Ideas/ Using Parallel Structure pp. 541–548, 550–552 • Mechanics Hint p. 542 • Exercises 1–4, 6 pp. 543–549, 552–553* • Writing Note p. 545	**30–35 minutes** • Obstacles to Clarity pp. 555–561* • Exercises 7, 8, 9 pp. 556–557, 559, 561–562* • Style Note p. 557 • Writing Note p. 561
ACCELERATED PROGRAM	**30–35 minutes** • Main Assignment: Looking Ahead p. 540 • Mechanics Hint p. 542 • Subordinating Conjunctions Chart p. 545 • Correcting Faulty Coordination/ Using Parallel Structure pp. 549–552 • Exercises 5–6 pp. 550, 552–553* • Writing Note p. 545	**25–30 minutes** • Sentence Fragments/Run-on Sentences pp. 555–556, 558* • Style Note p. 557 • Unnecessary Shifts pp. 559–560 • Writing Note p. 561 • Exercise 9 pp. 561–562*

CHAPTER PLANNING GUIDE—PROGRAM RESOURCES

	WAYS TO ACHIEVE CLARITY/ USING PARALLEL STRUCTURE pp. 540–554	OBSTACLES TO CLARITY pp. 555–562
PRINT	• Coordinating Ideas, Subordinating Ideas in Clauses, Faulty Coordination, Parallel Structure, *Word Choice and Sentence Style* pp. 25–28 • Coordinating Ideas, Subordinating Ideas, Using Parallel Structure, *English Workshop* pp. 87–92	• Obstacles to Clarity in Sentences, *Word Choice and Sentence Style* p. 29 • Sentence Fragments and Run-on Sentences, Unnecessary Shifts, *English Workshop* pp. 93–96
MEDIA	• *Language Workshop:* Lesson 34	• *Language Workshop:* Lessons 31–33

Computer disk or CD-ROM

ELEMENTS OF WRITING: CURRICULUM CONNECTIONS

Making Connections
• Parallel Structure in Poetry p. 563

ASSESSMENT OPTIONS

Summative Assessment
Reviews A and B, *Elements of Writing,* Pupil's Edition pp. 554, 562
Writing Clear Sentences, Reviews A and B, *Word Choice and Sentence Style* pp. 30–33
Review Exercise, *English Workshop* pp. 97–98

Reflection
Self-assessment Record, *Portfolio Assessment* p. 19

OBJECTIVES

- To use appropriate connectives to show addition, contrast, choice, and result between coordinated ideas in sentences
- To punctuate compound sentences correctly
- To use appropriate conjunctions in sentences with adverb clauses to show subordination of ideas
- To punctuate introductory adverb clauses correctly
- To rewrite sentences to reverse independent clauses and subordinate clauses
- To recognize and correct faulty coordination in sentences

14 WRITING CLEAR SENTENCES

LOOKING AHEAD

Clear, smooth sentences are basic to any writer's style. In this chapter, you will learn how to improve both the style and the sense of your sentences by

- using sentence structure to show the relationships between ideas
- expressing parallel ideas in parallel form
- recognizing and removing obstacles to clarity in your writing

Ways to Achieve Clarity

You write for many different purposes. Maybe you want to give a friend your recipe for chili, to persuade other students that you're the best choice for class treasurer, to describe how the first crisp day of fall makes you feel, or to summarize the

Write the following questions on the chalkboard:

1. Would you like to see a movie and go dancing?
2. Would you like to see a movie or go dancing?

Ask students to explain the difference between these sentences. Lead students to understand that the sentences are the same except for the conjunctions, and discuss how *and* and *or* create different relationships in the sentences.

☞

results of a workplace project for your supervisor. No matter what your purpose is, you want to communicate your meaning clearly for your readers (or just for yourself).

One of the best ways to bring clarity to your writing is to sharpen the focus of your sentences. You can bring your sentences into focus by *coordinating* and *subordinating* ideas.

Coordinating Ideas

When two or more ideas carry the same weight in a sentence, they are called **coordinate** ideas. (*Coordinate* means "equal-ranked.") To show that two ideas are coordinate, you link them with a connecting word and/or with appropriate punctuation.

He felt some light object fall across his palm, **and** his fingers closed upon a match. [comma and coordinating conjunction]
H. G. Wells, "The Man Who Could Work Miracles"

It was so quiet; the bees hummed and the river water played the pebbles, the rocks, and the hollows. [semicolon]
Maxine Hong Kingston, *The Woman Warrior*

Different connectives show different kinds of relationships between ideas. Following are some connecting words you can use to show *addition, contrast, choice,* and *result.*

ADDITION	CONTRAST	CHOICE	RESULT
also and besides both . . . and likewise	but however nevertheless still yet	either . . . or neither . . . nor nor or otherwise	accordingly consequently hence therefore

You can use connecting words to join words, phrases, independent clauses (clauses that express complete thoughts), or subordinate clauses (clauses that don't express complete thoughts). The result is a compound element in your sentence.

CONTRAST Yolanda **stumbled** over the second hurdle **but recovered** to win the race. [compound verb]
CHOICE **Either Mr. Chávez or Ms. Hutchins** will drive us to the match. [compound subject]

QUOTATION FOR THE DAY
"Ah, the simple rapture of fulfillment at my work being understood that cold morning. What unutterable reward for my labor." (Sylvia Ashton-Warner, 1908–1984, New Zealand educator and writer)

Write the quotation on the chalkboard and ask students to write about a positive experience that occurred when someone understood them or understood their motives or personalities or goals. Explain that good writers strive to create clear, effective sentences.

MEETING individual NEEDS

LEP/ESL

Spanish. Before students can be expected to use connectives or subordinating conjunctions in a correct syntactic manner, they must first understand how these words are used semantically. Pair students and have them use bilingual dictionaries to look up any connectives that they don't understand. Ask them to record Spanish equivalents in the word banks of their writing journals, along with a sample Spanish sentence using the word in context.

AMENDMENTS TO SELECTIONS
Description of change: excerpted
Rationale: to focus on the concept of coordinating ideas presented in this chapter

TEACHING THE LESSON

Write on the chalkboard a few sample sentences that you created or that you picked from the textbook. Have volunteers punctuate each sentence, underline the compound element in each sentence, and then circle the connective or subordinating conjunction in each sentence. Call on students to explain in their own words the relationship between the compound elements that is suggested by the connective in each sentence.

You might want to use a visual aid to help explain the concept of subordination. You could use either a movie, a videotape, or a photo to help prompt ideas and sentences from students. Show students a picture from which a number of sentences can be created. Ask students to suggest simple sentences

542   *Writing Clear Sentences*

ADDITION   Every successful football team has a quarterback who is **strong, quick, and agile.** [compound predicate adjective]

RESULT   Your entire premise is faulty; **therefore,** I cannot accept the rest of your argument. [compound sentence]

Be sure to choose a connective that shows the correct relationship between the linked ideas. Otherwise, your meaning may not be clear to your readers.

UNCLEAR   Hector checked the movie listings, and he couldn't find the show times for *The Slime.*

CLEAR   Hector checked the movie listings, **but** he couldn't find the show times for *The Slime.* [contrast]

UNCLEAR   Keep the stove on low heat, yet the eggs will burn.

CLEAR   Keep the stove on low heat; **otherwise,** the eggs will burn. [choice]

◆ INTEGRATING THE LANGUAGE ARTS

Mechanics and Writing. You may want to let students know that the semicolon is probably the most advanced punctuation mark of all. Choosing a semicolon over a period involves a fairly sophisticated knowledge of relationships between independent clauses. Let students know that they can always split the clauses into two sentences with a period if they are in doubt about the relationship between the independent clauses.

542

MECHANICS HINT

Punctuation in Compound Sentences

When you use a coordinating conjunction to join two independent clauses, put a comma before the conjunction unless the clauses are very short.

> We played volleyball in the back yard for a while, and then we got ready to barbecue.
> Janna cooked and Rico set the table.

When you use a conjunctive adverb to link independent clauses, put a semicolon before the connecting word.

> Kiko did poorly on the midterm; however, she got an A on the final exam.

☞ **REFERENCE NOTE:** For more about punctuating compound sentences, see pages 686, 907, and 928–929.

GUIDED PRACTICE

Use the first two sentences in **Exercises 1–5** as models. You may want to work through the examples first.

☞

EXERCISE 1 ▶ **Using Appropriate Connectives**

Complete each of the following sentences by deciding which connecting word(s) will best fit in the blank(s). Give the correct punctuation to go with the connective you choose.

Answers may vary.

EXAMPLE   **1.** Matthew Henson was a famous African American navigator _____ explorer.
            1. *and*

1. Henson had very little formal education or other advantages _____ he overcame these limitations and became the first explorer to reach the North Pole. **1. , but** Con

2. Admiral Robert E. Peary led the 1909 expedition to the Pole _____ Henson, his assistant, may have been the first to set foot on the Pole. **2. ; however,** con

3. Radio and satellite communications had not yet been invented _____ the world did not learn of the expedition's success until months after the event. **3. ; consequently** result

4. Peary and Henson met in 1888 _____ they worked and traveled together for twenty-three years. **4. , and** add

5. They journeyed first to the tropical climates of Central America _____ then to the frozen lands of the Arctic. **5. and** add

6. When they began their trek to the North Pole, _____ Peary _____ Henson were familiar with the harsh Arctic climate. add.

7. They had already led seven Arctic expeditions _____ their final goal was to reach the Pole. **6. both/and**   **7. , but** con.

INDEPENDENT PRACTICE

Students can independently complete the sentences not used for guided practice. You may want to let them work in pairs on **Exercises 1–3** and then have them complete **Exercises 4** and **5** by themselves.

ASSESSMENT

Exercise 5 is the most comprehensive of the exercises in this lesson. Performance on this exercise will indicate students' ability to recognize and to correct coordination and subordination errors.

A DIFFERENT APPROACH

Constructing incorrect examples may help students develop a better sense of the force of different connectives. Have them work independently or in pairs to come up with sentences in which the meaning is deliberately confused by an inappropriate connective or conjunction. Call on students to read their sentences aloud and to challenge their classmates to suggest a connective or conjunction that would make more sense. [Here is an example: *Because* everything seemed to go wrong, I left feeling I had done as well as I could. *Although* should replace *Because* because the conditional conjunction *Although* makes more sense than the causal conjunction *Because*.]

AMENDMENTS TO SELECTIONS
Description of change: excerpted
Rationale: to focus on the concept of subordinating ideas presented in this chapter

544

---

544   *Writing Clear Sentences*

8. Henson had learned the ways of native Arctic people _____ he knew how to survive in the cold.   **8.** , so *consequence*
9. Fierce winds _____ blinding snow made travel extremely difficult.   **9.** and *add*
10. The explorers returned from their mission exhausted _____ triumphant.   **10.** but *contrast*.

Subordinating Ideas

Sometimes you will want to show that one idea in a sentence is more important than another. To make your main idea stand out, you can downplay the less important ideas. Ideas that are given lower rank in a sentence are called *subordinate* ideas.

One way to subordinate an idea is to place it in a *subordinate clause.* Used as part of a sentence, a subordinate clause elaborates on the thought expressed in an independent clause.

EXAMPLES   James, **who has seen all of the *Star Trek* movies,** chose *The Wrath of Khan* as his favorite.
Sara likes *The Voyage Home* best **because it warns against the extinction of endangered species.**

The kinds of subordinate clauses you will use most often are *adverb clauses* and *adjective clauses.*

👉 **REFERENCE NOTE:** For more about the types of subordinate clauses, see pages 675–683.

Adverb Clauses

An *adverb clause* modifies a verb, an adjective, or another adverb in a sentence. You introduce an adverb clause with a subordinating conjunction such as *although, after, because, if, when,* or *while.* The conjunction shows how the adverb clause relates to the main clause. Usually, the conjunction shows a relationship of *time, cause or reason, purpose or result,* or *condition.*

TIME   **At Bonanza Creek, while our socks dried by the fire, we fished for arctic grayling.**

Barry Lopez, *Crossing Open Ground*

CAUSE OR REASON   **Because we had no other name for her, we called her Baby.**

Jeanne Larsen, *Silk Road*

Write out two simple sentences and ask students to work in pairs or small groups to combine the two in a variety of coordinate and subordinate constructions. Allow students to use their books for reference. [Example sentences: It began to rain. I took a walk. Possible variations: Before it began to rain, I took a walk. It began to rain; nevertheless, I took a walk.]

PURPOSE OR RESULT	Rage made him weak, **so that he stumbled.**

Carson McCullers, *The Heart Is a Lonely Hunter*

CONDITION	He ran so hard that he could feel the sweat fly from his head and arms, **though it was winter and the air was filled with snow.**

N. Scott Momaday, *House Made of Dawn*

The following chart lists subordinating conjunctions you can use to show each kind of relationship.

TIME	CAUSE	PURPOSE	CONDITION
after	as	in order that	although
as	because	so that	provided that
before	even though	that	though
since	since		
until	unless		
when	whereas if		
whenever	while		
while			

WRITING NOTE

You can place an adverb clause at either the beginning or the end of a sentence. Read the sentence aloud with the clause in each position to see which sounds better. When you place an adverb clause at the beginning, be sure to put a comma after the clause.

EXERCISE 2 ▶ **Choosing Appropriate Subordinating Conjunctions**

Answers may vary.

Each of the following sentences is missing a subordinating conjunction. First, decide what the relationship is between the independent clause and the subordinate clause. Then, give a subordinating conjunction that clearly shows the relationship.

1. _____ you buy a rare manuscript, make sure it's authentic.
1. Before

2. William Henry Ireland was a highly successful forger _____ he was only a teenager at the height of his exploits.
2. although

AMENDMENTS TO SELECTIONS
Description of change: excerpted
Rationale: to focus on the concept of subordinating ideas presented in this chapter

CLOSURE

Call on students to identify the relationship suggested by each of the following connectives and subordinating conjunctions: *and, or, but, therefore, after, because,* and *if* [addition, choice, contrast, result, time, cause, and condition].

EXTENSION

To help students realize that there are many different ways to use sentence structure to show the relationships of ideas, have them work in small groups to rewrite **Exercise 4.** Tell the groups that they should keep the basic ideas of the sentences but should revise them so that no adjective clauses are

MEETING *individual* NEEDS

ADVANCED STUDENTS

Select well-written sentences from literary selections and have students write sentences that imitate the structural elements used in these sentences. You could also make it a practice to call attention to matters of style in the literature the class is reading and to read aloud well-written passages.

546

---

546   *Writing Clear Sentences*

3. Ireland started forging Shakespeare manuscripts _____ his father had a keen interest in them.   **3. because**   **4. Before**
4. _____ he forged a document, Ireland had to do careful research on the details that would make it look genuine.

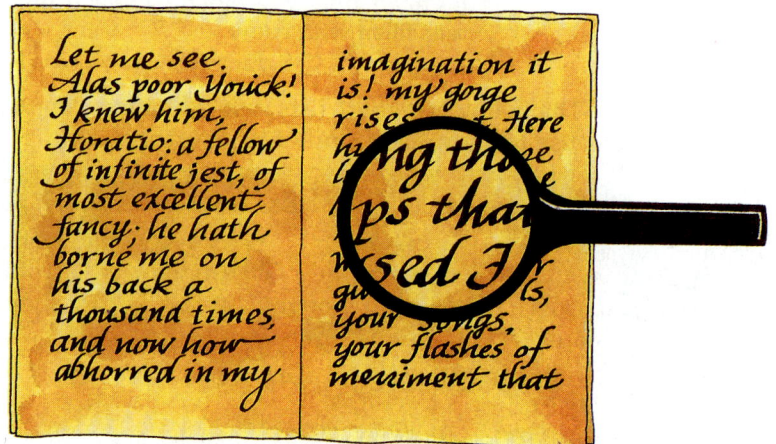

5. He used special blends of ink _____ the forged manuscript would look older than it really was.   **5. so that**   **6. Because**
6. _____ he trusted his son, Ireland's father published a collection of the forged manuscripts.   **7. until**   **8. after**
7. Scholars became more and more skeptical _____ Ireland could no longer defend himself against their accusations.
8. Ireland published a confession _____ the documents were proven to be fraudulent, and his father's health declined.
9. _____ Ireland tried to ease his father's disappointment, the older man died in disgrace in the middle of the scandal.
10. _____ Ireland himself died in 1835, the art of forgery obviously did not die with him.   **9. While**   **10. Although**

EXERCISE 3 ▶ **Revising Sentences by Inserting Adverb Clauses**

Using the photos on the next page to help spark your imagination, revise each of the following sentences by adding an adverb clause at the beginning or the end of the sentence. Use a different subordinating conjunction for each sentence. [Note: Remember to add a comma if you place the clause at the beginning.]

used. Instead, they are to use other forms of coordinate and subordinate constructions.

ENRICHMENT

Have students work in small groups to identify and to analyze the coordinating and subordinating constructions in a short passage from their literature books. Suggest they rewrite the passage in simple sentences and discuss how this rewriting changes the passage.

EXAMPLE 1. White-water rafting is fun.
1. *White-water rafting is fun because it's full of surprises.*

1. We tried some of the calmer rapids.
2. We learned how to maneuver in faster rapids.
3. You should try this exciting sport sometime.
4. The guide describes the high points of the upcoming rapids.
5. Some of the best white-water rapids are in Virginia.

ANSWERS
Exercise 3

Revisions will vary. Here are some possibilities:

1. Before taking on the difficult white water, we tried some of the calmer rapids.
2. We learned how to maneuver in faster rapids after we had mastered basic skills.
3. If you like adventure, you should try this exciting sport sometime.
4. The guide describes the high points of the upcoming rapids in order that we would be fully prepared.
5. Although Wisconsin has a university named "Whitewater," some of the best white-water rapids are in Virginia.

Adjective Clauses

You can also subordinate an idea by placing it in an *adjective clause,* a subordinate clause that modifies a noun or a pronoun in a sentence. An adjective clause usually begins with *who, whom, whose, which, that,* or *where.*

I propped myself against the brick wall of the schoolhouse, **where the school delinquent found me.**

Henry Louis Gates, Jr., "A Giant Step"

Before you use an adjective clause in a sentence, you need to decide which idea in the sentence you want to subordinate. Suppose you want to combine these two ideas in one sentence:

Ishmael Reed helped found the Yardbird Publishing Company in 1971. He considers himself as much a publisher as a writer.

SELECTION AMENDMENT
Description of change: excerpted
Rationale: to focus on the concept of adjective clauses as presented in this chapter

If you want to emphasize that Reed helped found Yardbird, put that information in an independent clause and the other information in an adjective clause.

> Ishmael Reed, **who considers himself as much a publisher as a writer,** helped found the Yardbird Publishing Company in 1971.

If you want to emphasize that Reed is both a publisher and a writer, put the information about Yardbird in an adjective clause.

> Ishmael Reed, **who helped found the Yardbird Publishing Company in 1971,** considers himself as much a publisher as a writer.

👉 **REFERENCE NOTE:** For more about combining sentences by subordinating ideas, see pages 574–577.

🖱 **EXERCISE 4** ▶ **Subordinating Ideas by Using Adjective Clauses**

Change the emphasis in each of the following sentences. Emphasize the idea that is now in the subordinate clause, and subordinate the idea that is now in the independent clause. [Hint: You may have to delete or add some words or change the word order.] Which version sounds better and clearer to you?

1. The word *alphabet,* which comes from the Greek letters *alpha* and *beta,* refers to a series of signs used to write a language.
2. The Egyptians, who developed their alphabet around 3000 B.C., had several hundred signs for words and syllables.

ANSWERS
Exercise 4

Responses will vary. Here are some possibilities:

1. The word *alphabet,* which refers to a series of signs used to write a language, comes from the Greek letters *alpha* and *beta.*
2. The Egyptians, who had several hundred signs for words and syllables, developed their alphabet around 3000 B.C.

3. The Greeks, who borrowed symbols from the Phoenician alphabet, improved on earlier alphabets by using separate signs for vowel sounds.
4. The Roman alphabet, which is the one we use to write English today, comes from the Greek alphabet.
5. Roman stonecutters, who had to make the alphabet practical for carving, simplified the letters and added graceful finishing strokes called serifs.

Correcting Faulty Coordination

In everyday speech, we tend to be casual about stringing together ideas with *and*. In writing, though, it's important to clearly show the relative importance of ideas. If you use a coordinating conjunction to join ideas of unequal importance, you end up with *faulty coordination*.

To avoid faulty coordination, check each compound sentence to make sure the ideas in it are really equal in importance. If they aren't, subordinate the less-important idea by placing it in a subordinate clause or a phrase. You may need to rearrange some words in the sentence.

FAULTY   The tiny sand crab was the same color as the sand, and it could hardly be seen.

BETTER   **Because it was the same color as the sand,** the tiny sand crab could hardly be seen. [adverb clause]

FAULTY   Wild horses are beautiful, inspiring animals, and some them make their home on the islands of Chincoteague and Assateague.

BETTER   Wild horses, **some of which make their home on the islands of Chincoteague and Assateague,** are beautiful, inspiring animals. [adjective clause]

3. The Greeks, who improved on earlier alphabets by using separate signs for vowel sounds, borrowed symbols from the Phoenician alphabet.
4. The Roman alphabet, which comes from the Greek alphabet, is the one we use to write English today.
5. Roman stonecutters, who simplified the letters and added graceful finishing strokes called serifs, had to make the alphabet practical for carving.

MEETING *individual* NEEDS

LEP/ESL

General Strategies. Exercises 4 and 5 require having had a broad and continuous exposure to the English language. You may want to pair English-language learners with English-proficient speakers who can guide them through the revision process. Being able to create smooth transitions is a skill one expects from speakers with advanced proficiency in English.

USING PARALLEL STRUCTURE

OBJECTIVE

• To revise sentences by correcting faulty parallelism

MOTIVATION

Ask students why most people don't wear mismatched socks or shoes. Discuss how the style of each pair may be acceptable and attractive in itself, yet a combination of the two would look out of place. Not only may the wearer appear odd, but also he or she may find it uncomfortable to wear two different shoes. Explain that using parallel

---

FAULTY   The light was at the end of the pier, and it showed us how far we had walked.

BETTER   The light **at the end of the pier** showed us how far we had walked. [prepositional phrases]

FAULTY   Tama was the lifeguard on duty that day, and she saved the drowning child.

BETTER   Tama, **the lifeguard on duty that day,** saved the drowning child. [appositive phrase]

👉 **REFERENCE NOTE:** For more about using phrases in sentences, see pages 652–667.

EXERCISE 5 ▶ **Revising Sentences by Correcting Faulty Coordination**

Faulty coordination blurs the focus in each of the following sentences. Revise each sentence by placing one of the ideas in a subordinate clause or a phrase. [Hint: You may need to add or delete some words or change the punctuation.] Make sure each revised sentence shows the appropriate relationship between the two ideas.

1. Mackinac Island is located in a channel between Lake Michigan and Lake Huron, and it is my favorite place to visit.
2. People get around mostly by bicycle and by horse and carriage, and automobiles are not permitted on the island.
3. It was the first morning of our visit, and we woke to the click-clack of horses' hooves on the street below.
4. I had some mechanical problems with my bike, but I still enjoyed my ride, and the ride was around the island.
5. Mackinac Island's Grand Hotel is one of the oldest hotels in the United States, and the movie *Somewhere in Time* was filmed there.

Using Parallel Structure

For clear meaning and smooth rhythm in a sentence, it's important to place equal ideas in the same grammatical form. For example, pair an adjective with an adjective, a prepositional phrase with a prepositional phrase, and a noun clause with a noun clause. When you use the same grammatical form for equal ideas, you create *parallel structure.*

---

construction in writing is analogous to wearing matching shoes and socks.

He had come to tell his brother **that power corrupts, that a man who fights for justice must himself be cleansed and purified, that love is greater than force.**

Alan Paton, *Cry, the Beloved Country*

He was the **weather-beaten, brown-faced, black-eyed** Cupid of the community.

Jovita González, "The Mail Carrier"

She hadn't expected that, because he was shy and seemed more at home **with his hogs** than **with people.**

Bobbie Ann Mason, "Memphis"

Use parallel structure when you link coordinate ideas.

FAULTY	My favorite camping activities are fishing and to hike. [gerund paired with infinitive]
PARALLEL	My favorite camping activities are **fishing** and **hiking.** [gerund paired with gerund]
FAULTY	Mari's sculpture projects reveal her talent and that she has patience. [noun paired with noun clause]
PARALLEL	Mari's sculpture projects reveal **that she is talented** and **that she has patience.** [noun clause paired with noun clause]

Use parallel structure when you compare or contrast ideas.

FAULTY	Water-skiing no longer interests me as much as to go scuba diving. [gerund contrasted with infinitive]
PARALLEL	**Water-skiing** no longer interests me as much as **scuba diving.** [gerund contrasted with gerund]
FAULTY	In figure skating, style is just as important as that you have technical expertise. [noun paired with noun clause]
PARALLEL	In figure skating, **style** is just as important as **technical expertise.** [noun paired with noun]

Use parallel structure when you link ideas with correlative conjunctions (*both . . . and, either . . . or, neither . . . nor, not only . . . but also*).

FAULTY	The medicine woman was revered not only for her healing abilities but also because she possessed wisdom. [prepositional phrase correlated with adverb clause]
PARALLEL	The medicine woman was revered not only **for her healing abilities** but also **for her wisdom.** [prepositional phrase correlated with prepositional phrase]

the infinitive marker *to,* or the gerund ending *–ing.*

Work through the sentences in **Exercise 6** with students. You may want to identify the unparallel elements, and then you could have volunteers revise the sentences.

Have students test their ability to recognize and revise parallel constructions by doing **Review A** independently.

ASSESSMENT

An important step in producing clear writing is analyzing and revising stylistic features that make the meaning of the writing unclear. Evaluating students' revisions of **Review A** will help you assess whether students can correctly analyze faulty parallelism even if they have difficulty revising.

552 *Writing Clear Sentences*

Be sure to place correlative conjunctions directly before the parallel terms. Otherwise, your sentence may sound awkward and unclear.

UNCLEAR	Those interested in stage acting can either join the drama club or the community theater.
BETTER	Those interested in stage acting can join **either** the drama club **or** the community theater.
UNCLEAR	The team both felt the satisfaction of victory and the disappointment of defeat.
BETTER	The team felt **both** the satisfaction of victory **and** the disappointment of defeat.

When you create parallel structure, you often need to repeat an article, a preposition, or a pronoun before each of the parallel terms to make your meaning clear. Notice how the first version of each of the following sentences might be misread.

UNCLEAR	Before the meeting I talked with the secretary and treasurer.
BETTER	Before the meeting I talked with **the** secretary and **the** treasurer.
UNCLEAR	The old diaries revealed more about that era in history than the man who wrote them.
BETTER	The old diaries revealed more **about** that era in history than **about** the man who wrote them.

Sometimes you will need to add a few words to the second part of the parallel structure to clarify your meaning.

UNCLEAR	We enjoyed the music of the opening band more than the featured band.
BETTER	We enjoyed the music of the opening band more than **that of** the featured band.

EXERCISE 6 ▶ **Revising Sentences by Correcting Faulty Parallelism**

Some of the following sentences are unclear because they lack parallel structure. Revise each faulty sentence by putting parallel ideas into the same grammatical form. Add, delete, and replace words as necessary. [Note: Remember to check the placement of correlative conjunctions.] If a sentence is already in parallel form, write C.

Ways to Achieve Clarity   **553**

1. When Thomas "Fats" Waller was a child, his favorite pastimes were singing for his family and to pretend to play the piano.
2. At the suggestion of Waller's older brother and because an uncle helped to finance it, the family finally got a real piano at home.
3. His parents hired a music teacher for him, but Fats was more interested in learning by ear than to take lessons.

4. After his tour with a vaudeville group and writing the hit tune "Boston Blues," Fats got a job playing the organ at the Lincoln Theater in New York.
5. He became a favorite there, not only for his musical talents but also because he had a sense of humor.
6. James P. Johnson, a well-known Harlem pianist, taught Fats the secrets of symmetry and style.
7. Waller was as successful at writing full-length musical revues as he was as a performer.
8. In 1928, Fats participated in a concert at Carnegie Hall called "Musical History of the Negro," which was a rousing success both artistically and as far as finances.
9. His jazz combo "Fats Waller and His Rhythm Boys" was a hit in both its live performances and on record.
10. Later in his career, Waller received as much praise for his work in film as when he did live performances.

ANSWERS
Exercise 6

Revisions of faulty sentences may vary. Here are some possibilities. The parallel elements are underlined.

1. When Thomas "Fats" Waller was a child, his favorite pastimes were singing for his family and pretending to play the piano.
2. Because his older brother suggested it and because an uncle helped to finance it, the family finally got a real piano at home.
3. His parents hired a music teacher for him, but Fats was more interested in learning by ear than in taking lessons.
4. After touring with a vaudeville group and writing the hit tune "Boston Blues," Fats got a job playing the organ at the Lincoln Theater in New York.
5. He became a favorite there, not only for his musical talents but also for his sense of humor.
6. C
7. Waller was as successful at writing full-length musical revues as he was at performing.
8. In 1928, Fats participated in a concert at Carnegie Hall called "Musical History of the Negro," which was a rousing success both artistically and financially.
9. His jazz combo "Fats Waller and His Rhythm Boys" was a hit both for its live performances and for its records.
10. Later in his career, Waller received as much praise for his work in film as for his live performances.

COOPERATIVE LEARNING

Give students a chance to create pieces of writing with parallelism. Have students work in groups of two or three to compose a "World's Greatest" certificate that declares some person outstanding in some way. Each certificate should employ parallel construction in at least four examples of how the person has earned the distinction.

554

---

554 *Writing Clear Sentences*

R E V I E W A ▶ **Revising Paragraphs for Clarity**

The following paragraphs are confusing because they contain faulty coordination and faulty parallelism. Use the methods you've learned in this chapter to make each faulty sentence smoother and clearer. [Hint: You may need to add, delete, or rearrange some words in the sentences.]

Simon J. Ortiz is an Acoma Pueblo, and he writes eloquently about the experiences of American Indians. His poems and short stories are infused with American Indian history, mythology, and philosophical. Ortiz uses simple, direct language, and his language reflects the oral storytelling tradition of his heritage. Ortiz often employs a sorrowful tone, but he tempers his writings with humor and being optimistic.

Going for the Rain was Ortiz's first full-length collection of poems, and it was published in 1976. Going for the Rain depicts a journey that begins in the traditional American Indian world, goes through present-day America, and returning to its origin. In these poems Ortiz expresses concern not only for his own people but also American society as a whole.

The collection A Good Journey is similar to Going for the Rain both in structure and theme. The poems in A Good Journey describe American Indian history and expressing concern about the environment. But the conclusion of this volume is as hopeful as his other works.

Acoma Pueblo Indian Pottery

OBJECTIVE
- To identify and revise sentence fragments, run-on sentences, and unecessary shifts in subject and verb

MOTIVATION

Write the following word groups on the chalkboard and ask students to identify the complete sentence:

1. When I pounded around the final curve in the road.
2. I was the first.

Obstacles to Clarity

In this part of the chapter, you will learn how to check your writing for some common obstacles to clarity: *sentence fragments*, *run-on sentences*, and *unnecessary shifts*.

Sentence Fragments

A sentence expresses a complete thought. If you punctuate a part of a sentence as if it were a whole sentence, you create a *sentence fragment.* Fragments are usually confusing in writing because the reader has to puzzle out the missing information.

FRAGMENT   Photographed families who were victims of the Great Depression. [missing subject]

SENTENCE   **Dorothea Lange** photographed families who were victims of the Great Depression.

FRAGMENT   After the flood, the barn roof in pieces in the yard. [missing verb]

SENTENCE   After the flood, the barn roof **lay** in pieces in the yard.

FRAGMENT   We observing the bacteria through a powerful microscope. [missing helping verb]

SENTENCE   We **were** observing the bacteria through a powerful microscope.

FRAGMENT   When she won three gold medals in track at the 1960 Olympics. [not a complete thought]

SENTENCE   **Wilma Rudolph became famous** when she won three gold medals in track at the 1960 Olympics.

Phrase Fragments

A *phrase* is a group of words that doesn't have a subject and its verb. If a phrase gets separated from the sentence it belongs with, it becomes a *phrase fragment.*

FRAGMENT   I found my sister in the den. **Making origami swans out of blue and green paper.** [participial phrase fragment]

SENTENCE   I found my sister in the den making origami swans out of blue and green paper.

PROGRAM MANAGER

OBSTACLES TO CLARITY

- **Independent Practice/ Reteaching** For practice and reinforcement, see **Obstacles to Clarity in Sentences** in *Word Choice and Sentence Style,* p. 29.
- **Computer Guided Instruction** For additional instruction and practice with obstacles to clarity, see **Lessons 31–33** in *Language Workshop CD-ROM.*
- **Practice** To help less-advanced students with additional instruction and practice with obstacles to clarity, see **Chapter 8** in *English Workshop, Complete Course,* pp. 93–95.

QUOTATION FOR THE DAY

"The greatest of faults, I should say, is to be conscious of none." (Thomas Carlyle, 1795–1881, Scottish essayist and historian)

Share the quotation with your students and ask them to discuss what they think Carlyle is saying. How can this idea be applied to revising sentence fragments and run-on sentences?

3. The thrilling experience of winning over tough competitors.

Ask students to explain how the shortest item could be the only complete sentence.

TEACHING THE LESSON

Have someone read aloud the first item of the **Motivation** and ask students if it seems complete. Point out that a conjunction like when leaves the reader waiting for more. Do the same with the third item. Then rewrite the three to form a single sentence by changing the first period to a comma, replacing the second period with the phrase *and I*

| FRAGMENT | The Miami chief Little Turtle was born near the Eel River. **In the Midwest.** [prepositional phrase fragment] |
| SENTENCE | The Miami chief Little Turtle was born near the Eel River in the Midwest. |

| FRAGMENT | They got together all the supplies they would need. **To make the canoe trip go smoothly.** [infinitive phrase fragment] |
| SENTENCE | They got together all the supplies they would need to make the canoe trip go smoothly. |

| FRAGMENT | Coretta brought her two favorite kites. **A stunt kite and a parafoil kite.** [appositive phrase fragment] |
| SENTENCE | Coretta brought her two favorite kites, a stunt kite and a parafoil kite. |

Subordinate Clause Fragments

A *subordinate clause* has a subject and a verb but doesn't express a complete thought. Unlike an independent clause, a subordinate clause can't stand on its own as a sentence.

| FRAGMENT | Some lizards used to be killed for their skins. **Which were used to make wallets and handbags.** [adjective clause fragment] |
| SENTENCE | Some lizards used to be killed for their skins, which were used to make wallets and handbags. |

| FRAGMENT | I had nightmares. **After I watched that scary movie.** [adverb clause fragment] |
| SENTENCE | I had nightmares after I watched that scary movie. |

E X E R C I S E 7 ▶ Revising to Eliminate Fragments

Some of the following items contain phrases or clauses that have been separated from the sentences they belong with. Fix each fragment by attaching it to the independent clause. [Note: You may need to move or add some words.] If the item is already correct, just write C. Revisions may vary.

1. Elizabeth Blackwell was born in 1821, and died in 1910.
2. In 1832 her parents immigrated with their eight children to New York, to escape an unpleasant social and political situation in Bristol, England.

realize I will have, and lowercasing the first letter of *The*. Challenge students to explain the two new obstacles to clarity that these changes create. [The changes create a run-on sentence and leave a shift in tense.] Discuss different ways to revise the passage into two or three clearly written sentences.

After students have read the textbook explanations, put several textbook examples of fragments, run-ons, and shifts in tense or voice on the chalkboard, and work with students to suggest ways to correct the faulty sentences. Students then can work independently on **Exercises 7–9**.

3. Because of the financial plight of her family, Blackwell and her mother established a boarding school.
4. A friend of Blackwell's encouraged her to become a doctor. At first, Blackwell totally rejected this suggestion.   **4. C**
5. Eventually, ~~Blackwell became interested~~ in the idea of becoming a doctor, ~~Leading~~ her to investigate the possibility of a woman studying medicine.   **5. Blackwell's interest/led**
6. She became even more determined to follow her friend's advice. After she was told that it would be impossible for a woman to become a doctor.
7. In 1847 Elizabeth Blackwell was granted admission to the Medical Institution of Geneva College, Which is today known as Hobart College.
8. She became the first woman in the United States to earn an M.D. degree, When she graduated in 1849 at the head of her class.
9. Elizabeth was not content with these honors. She spent the next two years doing graduate work in Europe.   **9. C**
10. In 1857 Elizabeth Blackwell established the New York Infirmary for Women and Children, a hospital staffed by women. She opened the hospital on May 12, the birthday of her friend Florence Nightingale.   **10. C**

STYLE NOTE

A complete sentence is usually the best and clearest way to express a thought. However, experienced writers sometimes use fragments for stylistic effect. For example, in the following passage, notice how each fragment creates a single, precise image in your mind. The fragments make sense because they are clearly related to the complete sentence before them.

> Silently, wallowing in the pleasures of conspiracy, we take the bead purse from its secret place and spill its contents on the scrap quilt. Dollar bills, tightly rolled and green as May buds. Somber fifty-cent pieces, heavy enough to weight a dead man's eyes. Lovely dimes, the liveliest coin, the one that really jingles. Nickels and quarters, worn smooth as creek pebbles. But mostly a hateful heap of bitter-odored pennies.
>
> Truman Capote, "A Christmas Memory"

SELECTION AMENDMENT
Description of change: excerpted
Rationale: to focus on the concept of sentence fragments presented in this chapter

ASSESSMENT

Use **Review B** to assess how well students are able to recognize and revise sentence fragments, run-ons, and awkward shifts in voice and tense. A student's errors might indicate a specific problem that needs additional study.

RETEACHING

Reversing the process—having students remove words from sentences to form fragments—might help to illustrate for students the concept of sentence completeness. Write the following sentences on the chalkboard:

1. Hilda bought a new word-processing program for her computer.

INTEGRATING THE LANGUAGE ARTS

Grammar Link. Some students forget that a sentence must complete a thought; they reduce the definition of a sentence to the presence of a subject and a verb. Consequently, students regularly treat subordinating clauses as sentences because they contain both subjects and verbs. You can refer students to **Chapter 20: "The Clause"** to review the difference between subordinate and independent clauses. The chapter also includes a list of subordinating conjunctions that should act as signals that a period should not separate the clause from its main idea.

558 *Writing Clear Sentences*

You can use fragments occasionally in expressive and creative writing such as journal entries and short stories. For example, you might use fragments in dialogue to capture the natural sounds of your characters' speech. You can also use fragments in classified ads and other types of writing where an informal, shorthand style is appropriate. However, avoid fragments in informative writing such as research papers and reports. Because your readers expect formal, straightforward language in this type of writing, fragments may interfere with your aim.

Run-on Sentences

A *run-on sentence* is just the opposite of a fragment. It is made up of two complete sentences run together as if they were one sentence. Like fragments, run-ons usually occur when you're writing in a hurry. Most run-ons are *comma splices*—two complete thoughts that have only a comma between them. Other run-ons, called *fused sentences*, have no punctuation between the two thoughts.

The following examples show four ways to correct run-ons.

RUN-ON   Bill "Bojangles" Robinson worked in motion pictures from 1929–1943, the films he made with Shirley Temple were very popular.

CORRECT   Bill "Bojangles" Robinson worked in motion pictures from 1929–1943. The films he made with Shirley Temple were very popular. [two sentences]

RUN-ON   We were fifteen minutes late, the concert hadn't started yet.

CORRECT   We were fifteen minutes late, but the concert hadn't started yet. [compound sentence with comma and coordinating conjunction]

RUN-ON   Everybody dreams at night, dreaming is a normal part of the sleep cycle.

CORRECT   Everybody dreams at night; dreaming is a normal part of the sleep cycle. [compound sentence with semicolon]

RUN-ON   We struggled to set up the tent the mosquitoes ate us alive.

CORRECT   We struggled to set up the tent; meanwhile, the mosquitoes ate us alive. [compound sentence with semicolon plus conjunctive adverb]

2. The program is supposed to be more versatile.
3. Since she bought the program, Hilda has not had time to install it.

Have students remove words from the first sentence to create a fragment with no verb. Have them use the second sentence to create a fragment with no subject. For the third sentence, have students create a fragment that does not express a complete thought but that does contain a subject and verb.

You could use a similar tactic by having students incorrectly combine two sentences to form a run-on sentence.

☞

E X E R C I S E 8 ▶   Revising Run-on Sentences

The following items are confusing because they're run-ons. Revise each run-on by using one of the methods you've learned in this section. Use each of the four methods at least once.

Revisions will vary.

1. Some friends and I are making a movie, it will be on videotape.
2. We saved up our money, then we rented a camcorder from an electronics store.
3. We're still revising some parts of the script, we've already written most of the scenes.   **3. but**
4. The sets will be simple, most of the scenes will be shot in Joe's back yard.   **4. ; actually,**
5. We want to shoot a pool-party scene at the neighborhood swimming pool, we'll need to recruit some of our friends as "pool-party extras."   **5. so**

COMPUTER NOTE: Some word-processing programs have a tool to check grammatical constructions. This tool can find fragments and run-on sentences for you to revise.

Unnecessary Shifts in Sentences

For clarity, it's usually best to keep the same subject and the same verb form throughout a sentence. Unnecessary shifts in subject or verb forms can make a sentence awkward to read.

COOPERATIVE LEARNING

Take a passage from your students' literature textbook and revise the passage so that it contains no punctuation. Organize students into small groups and give each group a copy of the revised passage. Have each group then replace the punctuation in the passage. The groups should not change the wording of the passage, but they should use correct punctuation to avoid run-ons and fragments as well as any awkward shifts of voice or tense within a sentence. Groups can check their results with the original text.

TECHNOLOGY TIP

Point out to students that even though grammar checking functions of word-processing programs can be a big help in identifying possible sentence fragments and run-on sentences, these functions do not replace the need for students to recognize and correct such faulty sentences. Many word-processing programs merely indicate that a construction might be a fragment or run-on sentence. The writer must make the final judgment. If the writer decides that the construction is a sentence fault, she or he must know how to correct it.

Call on students to define or to give an example of each of the following obstacles to clarity: fragment [a group of words punctuated as a sentence that does not express a complete thought]; run-on sentence [two or more sentences run together as if it were one sentence]; unnecessary shift [a shift in verb tense, subject, or voice in the middle of a sentence].

CRITICAL THINKING

Analysis. Help students see that punctuation is not arbitrary but rather a tool for creating meaning in written language. Write the following sentence on the chalkboard:

Tom felt he could win if he could just pass Geraldo it would be easy.

Point out that merging two thoughts together like this can be confusing for the reader. In fact, the example has two different possible meanings, depending on where the period is inserted. [The period could follow *win* or *Geraldo*.] Discuss how making *it would be easy* a separate sentence would suggest much more confidence on Tom's part than placing the period after *win*. Students might enjoy creating similar sets of clauses.

Shifts in Subject

Sometimes, especially in short compound sentences, a shift in subject is necessary to express your intended meaning. In the following sentence, the shift in subject is natural.

NATURAL SHIFT   I knocked on the door, but no one answered.

Most often, though, a shift in subject is awkward and unnecessary. In the following examples, notice that each sentence is much clearer when it has the same subject throughout.

AWKWARD   Team members should be at the locker room by 5:30 so that you can pick up your uniforms.

BETTER   **Team members** should be at the locker room by 5:30 so that **they** can pick up **their** uniforms.

AWKWARD   Fishers from around the country visit the Ontario lakes, where fish are found in abundance.

BETTER   **Fishers** from around the country visit the Ontario lakes, where **they** find fish in abundance.

Shifts in Verb Tense and Voice

Changing verb tense or voice in mid-sentence can also create awkwardness and confusion. Stick to the tense and voice you start with unless you have a good reason for changing.

AWKWARD   Carl gave us a ten-minute lecture about recycling, but then he tosses his aluminum can into the trash. [shift from past tense to present tense]

BETTER   Carl **gave** us a ten-minute lecture about recycling, but then he **tossed** his aluminum can into the trash. [past tense throughout]

AWKWARD   Volunteers made the dangerous journey after dark, but no wolves were encountered. [shift from active voice to passive voice]

BETTER   Volunteers **made** the dangerous journey after dark but **encountered** no wolves.

A shift in voice usually causes a shift in subject, too. Notice that in the first part of the last example, the shift from active to passive voice results in a shift from the subject *volunteers* to the subject *wolves*.

☞ **REFERENCE NOTE:** If you're not sure about the difference between active and passive voice, see pages 800–804.

Have students look through different sections of the newspaper to see if they can find examples of fragments used stylistically. Discuss where the examples occur. While some may be found in feature articles containing colloquial language or in the comics, very few are likely to occur in the editorials or lead stories. ■

Obstacles to Clarity   **561**

WRITING NOTE

Often, the best way to correct a shift in voice and subject in a compound sentence is to create a compound verb. Just omit the second subject and place the second verb in the same voice as the first. You may also need to delete a comma when you take out the second subject.

AWKWARD   Margaret Walker worked for the Federal Writers' Project for four years, and then graduate studies were pursued at the University of Iowa.

BETTER   **Margaret Walker worked** for the Federal Writers' Project for four years and then **pursued** graduate studies at the University of Iowa.

EXERCISE 9 ▶ **Eliminating Unnecessary Shifts in Subject and Verb**

Most of the following sentences contain unnecessary shifts from one subject to another or from one verb to another. Revise each awkward sentence to make it flow more smoothly. You may need to add, delete, or rearrange some words. If a sentence doesn't need improving, write C.   **Revisions will vary.**

1. *Windwalker* is a 1980 film that ~~portrayed~~ the cultures of the Cheyenne and Crow people.   **1. portrays**
2. Set in the late 1700s, the film informs the viewer about traditional American Indian values.   **2. C**
3. In the film, a dying Cheyenne warrior tells his grandchildren the story of his life.   **3. C**

A DIFFERENT APPROACH

Dictate several sentences for students to write out. Do not identify any punctuation but have students decide on punctuation based on your intonation. Have students exchange papers as you reread the passage and give the correct punctuation. If many students had run-ons or fragments, review the ways in which punctuation reflects spoken language. [Voice rises at the end of a question but is sustained for a declarative sentence. There is a longer pause between sentences than between phrases.] After the review, try another dictation exercise.

4. Before he can die, he must find his long-lost son, and ~~the~~ telling ~~of~~ his story~~,~~ ~~must be finished.~~   **4. he must finish**

5. A Crow warrior, who said he ~~considers~~ Windwalker an enemy for life, kidnapped Windwalker's son.   **5. considered**

6. The Crow warrior developed his vengeful feelings when the woman he ~~wants~~ to marry ~~marries~~ Windwalker instead of him.   **6. wanted/married**

7. Trevor Howard stars as Windwalker, and an excellent performance~~.~~ ~~is delivered by him.~~   **7. he delivers**

8. ~~One~~ will enjoy seeing this film if you like breathtaking cinematography and suspenseful action scenes.   **8. You**

9. Very little dialogue is contained in the film; the visual elements largely speak for themselves.   **9. C**

10. American Indian music helps set the tone for each sequence and for the film as a whole.   **10. C**

REVIEW B ▶ Revising Paragraphs for Clarity

Fragments, run-ons, and unnecessary shifts in subjects and verbs make the following paragraphs awkward and unclear. Using the methods you've learned, revise the sentences to eliminate these obstacles to clarity. Notice how much smoother the paragraphs sound when you're finished.   **Revisions will vary.**

Dorothy West began writing stories when she was seven, and several Boston Post prizes ~~were won by her~~ **she won** while she was a teenager. Opportunity published West's story "The Typewriter," ~~W~~hich later appeared in The Best Short Stories of 1926.

West **was** born in Boston but eventually settled in New York City~~,~~ there West met many writers of the Harlem Renaissance, including Zora Neale Hurston and Langston Hughes. In the early 1930s, she founded Challenge, a magazine that published the works of young African American writers.

After West's magazine ventures failed, she took a job as a welfare investigator in Harlem~~,~~ she later joined the Federal Writers' Project. She became a contributor to the New York Daily News, ~~W~~hich published many of her stories. In 1945, West moved to Martha's Vineyard, where her only novel, The Living Is Easy~~,~~ **she wrote** ~~was written.~~

MAKING CONNECTIONS

PARALLEL STRUCTURE IN POETRY
OBJECTIVE

- To use parallel structure in writing poetry

MAKING CONNECTIONS

Parallel Structure in Poetry

For many professional writers, parallel structure is an important stylistic tool. Parallelism creates natural rhythm and flow in both prose and poetry.

In the following stanza, notice that a string of parallel phrases follows the preposition *between*. How does the parallel structure help form the rhythm of this stanza?

> On visiting days with aunts and uncles,
> I was shuttled back and forth—
> between Chavez bourgeois in the city
> and rural Lucero sheepherders,
> new cars and gleaming furniture
> and leather saddles and burlap sacks,
> noon football games and six packs of cokes
> and hoes, welfare cards and bottles of goat milk.
>
> Jimmy Santiago Baca,
> *Martín and Meditations on the South Valley*

Think of a time that is vivid in your memory. It may be a period from your childhood or a more recent event. Perhaps there is a certain place that you especially like (or even dislike). What are the details surrounding this memory or place? Why does it stand out for you? What objects, smells, or people come to mind when you think about it?

Write a one-stanza poem, modeled after the stanza above, describing the topic you've chosen. Use parallel structure to present the sensory details, and concentrate on making the words and phrases flow smoothly.

PARALLEL STRUCTURE IN POETRY
Teaching Strategies

Have a volunteer read the poem aloud. Allow time for student responses, and then have the poem read again. This time insert the preposition *between* after every comma in lines 4 to 8. Discuss how implying rather than repeating *between* each time allows the writer to recreate the speaker's experience of two contrasting cultures jumbled together in memory.

GUIDELINES

Tell students that their poems should reflect their own experiences. Some students may want to juxtapose varied impressions, as in Baca's poem; others might catalog similar images to develop a single harmonious impression.

Once students have decided on the general focus of their poems, have them brainstorm images with sensory appeal and then develop those images that they feel are most likely to produce the effects they have in mind. Tell students to think about whether verbal repetition of an element such as the preposition *between* will add to the impression they wish to create.

Have students work with partners to revise each other's first drafts.

You can base your assessment on whether students have used parallel construction correctly.

Chapter 15

COMBINING SENTENCES

OBJECTIVES

- To combine sentences by using adjectives and adverbs
- To combine sentences by using prepositional, participial, and appositive phrases
- To combine sentences by coordinating ideas
- To combine sentences by subordinating ideas
- To use a variety of methods to combine sentences and improve style

WORKPLACE writing

Writing an Abstract

An abstract is a short, written summary of a technical paper or report. In the business world, abstracts are written for a reader, usually a supervisor or manager, who needs to know the content of a long technical report but may not have the time to read it. In preparing an abstract, the writer must condense the report into 150 to 200 words—about four or five sentences.

- **Writing** An abstract writer must use sentence-combining strategies to present key and equal ideas in concise, comprehensible sentences. Have students practice sentence-combining strategies by writing an abstract of the research paper they wrote for Chapter 11 or of one they have written for a science or technical class. In preparing to write their abstracts, students should do the following:
  - Read the document once
  - Reread the document and take notes on the following:
    - the subject of the document
    - the purpose of the document
    - the main idea or thesis statement
    - the main points

- Reread notes and brainstorm by writing nonstop about the document for three minutes. (Students will probably find a pattern in their writing; they will probably mention the most important points of the document several times.)
- Use the sentence-combining strategies from this chapter to condense the brainstorming ideas into the four or five sentences of the abstract.
- Work with a partner to evaluate, revise, and proofread the abstract.
- **Publishing and Reflection** Ask students to read their abstracts aloud to the class. Publish the abstracts by displaying them with copies of the abstracted document. Encourage students to read each other's documents and abstracts and to comment on the abstracts.

After students have published their work, have them respond in their journals to two questions.
- What was the most difficult or the easiest part of writing the abstract?
- What did you learn about your reading and writing from this exercise?

INTEGRATING THE LANGUAGE ARTS

SELECTION	READING AND LITERATURE	WRITING AND CRITICAL THINKING	LANGUAGE AND SYNTAX	SPEAKING, LISTENING, AND OTHER EXPRESSION SKILLS
	• Reading a paragraph to decide which sentences need revision p. 572 • Reading pairs of sentences to determine relationships between ideas p. 577	• Combining sentences by inserting single-word modifiers and prepositional phrases p. 567 • Combining sentences by inserting participial phrases p. 569 • Combining sentences by inserting appositive phrases p. 571 • Applying interpretive and creative thinking p. 572 • Improving the style of a paragraph by combining sentences pp. 572, 579 • Combining sentences by coordinating ideas pp. 573, 578 • Combining sentences by subordinating ideas pp. 577, 578 • Writing a children's story p. 580 • Revising a children's story for an audience of peers p. 580	• Changing the forms of words while combining sentences p. 569 • Using correct punctuation pp. 569, 571, 577 • Correctly placing participial phrases in sentences p. 571 • Choosing conjunctions that express relationships clearly pp. 573, 577, 579 • Using a variety of sentence lengths and structures p. 579	

CHAPTER 15: COMBINING SENTENCES

Use this guide for creating an instructional plan that addresses the individual needs of your students. Assignments accompanied by the following symbol (*) may be completed out of class. Times given for pacing lessons are estimated.

CHAPTER PLANNING GUIDE—PUPIL'S EDITION

LESSONS	INSERTING WORDS AND PHRASES pp. 565–572	COORDINATING IDEAS/ SUBORDINATING IDEAS pp. 572–579
DEVELOPMENTAL PROGRAM	🕐 **50–55 minutes** • Main Assignment: Looking Ahead p. 564 • Combining for Variety pp. 564–571 • Exercises 1, 2, 3 in pairs pp. 567–571 • Writing Note p. 569 • Mechanics Hint pp. 570–571	🕐 **50–55 minutes** • Coordinating Ideas pp. 572–573 • Exercise 4 pp. 573–574* • Subordinating Ideas pp. 574–577 • Mechanics Hint p. 575 • Exercise 5 in pairs p. 577
CORE PROGRAM	🕐 **35–40 minutes** • Main Assignment: Looking Ahead p. 564 • Inserting Words and Phrases pp. 565–571* • Exercises 1, 2, 3 pp. 567–571* • Writing Note p. 569 • Mechanics Hint pp. 570–571	🕐 **35–40 minutes** • Coordinating Ideas pp. 572–573* • Exercises 4, 5 pp. 573–574, 577* • Subordinating Ideas pp. 574–577 • Mechanics Hint p. 575
ACCELERATED PROGRAM	🕐 **25–30 minutes** • Main Assignment: Looking Ahead p. 564 • Participial Phrases pp. 568–569 • Writing Note p. 569 • Exercise 2 pp. 569–570* • Mechanics Hint pp. 570–571	🕐 **15–20 minutes** • Subordinating Ideas pp. 574–577* • Mechanics Hint p. 575 • Exercise 5 p. 577*

CHAPTER PLANNING GUIDE—PROGRAM RESOURCES

	INSERTING WORDS AND PHRASES pp. 565–572	COORDINATING IDEAS/ SUBORDINATING IDEAS pp. 572–579
PRINT	• Combining by Inserting Words and Phrases, *Word Choice and Sentence Style* p. 37 • Combining by Inserting Words, Combining by Inserting Phrases, *English Workshop* pp. 99–102	• Combining by Coordinating Ideas, Combining by Subordinating Ideas, *Word Choice and Sentence Style* pp. 38–39 • Combining by Coordination and Subordination, *English Workshop* pp. 103–104
MEDIA	• *Language Workshop:* Lesson 38	• *Language Workshop:* Lesson 39

Computer disk or CD-ROM

ELEMENTS OF WRITING: CURRICULUM CONNECTIONS

Making Connections
• Writing for Different Audiences p. 580

ASSESSMENT OPTIONS

Summative Assessment
Reviews A, B, and C, *Elements of Writing, Pupil's Edition* pp. 572, 578, 579
Writing Clear Sentences, Reviews A and B, *Word Choice and Sentence Style* pp. 40–43

Reflection
Self-assessment Record, *Portfolio Assessment* p. 19

INSERTING WORDS AND PHRASES

OBJECTIVES

- To combine sentences by inserting words and phrases
- To combine sentences by using participial phrases and appositive phrases

MOTIVATION

To interest students in this lesson, begin by writing on the chalkboard the sentence "Variety is the spice of life." Ask students what they associate this old saying with, and encourage them to discuss ways in which variety makes life more interesting. Tell students that sentence variety can add spice to their writing.

PROGRAM MANAGER

FOR THE WHOLE CHAPTER

- **Review** For exercises on chapter concepts, see **Review Form A** and **Review Form B** in *Word Choice and Sentence Style,* pp. 40–43.

PROGRAM MANAGER

INSERTING WORDS AND PHRASES

- **Independent Practice/ Reteaching** For practice and reinforcement, see **Combining by Inserting Words and Phrases** in *Word Choice and Sentence Style,* p. 37.

- **Computer Guided Instruction** For additional instruction and practice with combining sentences by inserting words and phrases, see **Lesson 38** in *Language Workshop CD-ROM.*

- **Practice** To help less-advanced students with additional instruction and practice with combining sentences by inserting words and phrases, see **Chapter 8** in *English Workshop, Complete Course,* pp. 99–102.

15 COMBINING SENTENCES

LOOKING AHEAD

By using sentence-combining techniques, you can add detail to your sentences and variety to your writing style. In this chapter, you will learn how to combine sentences by

- inserting words and phrases
- coordinating ideas
- subordinating ideas

Combining for Variety

Sometimes a short, simple sentence can have just the effect you want. Whether you are writing reflective thoughts in your journal, an analysis of a literary work for your English class, or a research report about a workplace project, you can use short, simple sentences to create emphasis. But if you use only short sentences, you probably won't hold your reader's attention for very long. Notice that the following passage, which contains only short sentences, sounds dull and choppy.

Begin by considering the introductory material under **Combining for Variety.** Ask a student to read the first version of the paragraph about the *Titanic,* and then ask another student to read the second version. Encourage students to discuss and analyze their reactions to the two paragraphs.

You may want to read aloud **Inserting Words and Phrases** as students follow along in their textbooks. If necessary, define and discuss the terms *modifier, prepositional phrase, participial phrase,* and *appositive phrase.* To involve students, enlist their help in generating examples of each type of sentence combination discussed. Encourage ☞

The sinking of the <u>Titanic</u> was one of the worst maritime disasters in history. The <u>Titanic</u> was the largest ship of its time. It was the most luxurious ship of its time. The <u>Titanic</u> was on its maiden voyage. The ship struck an iceberg. The iceberg was located off the Grand Banks of Newfoundland. The accident happened on the night of April 14, 1912. The night was clear and cold. The <u>Titanic</u>'s hull had sixteen watertight compartments. The iceberg punctured five compartments. The ship sank in less than three hours.

When some of the short sentences are combined to create longer, more varied ones, the passage sounds smoother and more interesting.

The sinking of the <u>Titanic</u>, the largest and most luxurious ship of its time, was one of the worst maritime disasters in history. On the clear, cold night of April 14, 1912, the ship, which was on its maiden voyage, struck an iceberg off the Grand Banks of Newfoundland. The iceberg punctured five of the sixteen watertight compartments in the ship's hull, and the ship sank in less than three hours.

Sentence-combining techniques can help you create lively, detailed sentences that read smoothly. You can combine related sentences to improve your style in any kind of writing.

Inserting Words and Phrases

Sometimes a sentence adds only a little information to a more important idea before or after it. Instead of giving the small detail a sentence of its own, you can insert it into the other sentence as a word or phrase. By combining the sentences, you'll eliminate extra words and repeated ideas.

FOUR SENTENCES	The archaeologist agreed to an interview. She agreed readily. She was elated by her discovery. It was a recent discovery. [Notice how many words are repeated.]
ONE SENTENCE	**Elated by her recent discovery,** the archaeologist **readily** agreed to an interview.
	or
	The archaeologist, **elated by her recent discovery, readily** agreed to an interview.

continued on next page

GUIDED PRACTICE

Guide students through one or two possible combinations of the first sets of sentences in **Exercises 1**, p. 567, **2**, p. 569, and **3**, p. 571, before assigning the remaining sets as independent practice.

students have read the material, they can then name and discuss the techniques they originally used to combine the sentences, and they can compare their combinations with the combinations in the textbook.

MEETING *individual* NEEDS

ADVANCED STUDENTS

Achieving sentence variety comes easily to some students. Such students will benefit from experimenting with the effects that various combinations have on style. Students might, for instance, use a variety of sentence-combining techniques to make example sentences from the text seem either more formal or more informal in tone.

You may see several possibilities for the placement of the words or phrases you are inserting. Just make sure your combined sentence sounds smooth and expresses the meaning you intend. Watch out for awkward, confusing combinations like this one: *Readily, the archaeologist agreed, elated by her recent discovery, to an interview.*

Single-Word Modifiers

Before you take a word from one sentence and insert it into another sentence, check to make sure the word can act as a modifier in the second sentence. You may need to change the word into an adverb or adjective before you insert it.

USING THE SAME FORM

ORIGINAL   Angela de Hoyos is a Mexican American poet. She is an award-winning poet.

COMBINED   Angela de Hoyos is an **award-winning** Mexican American poet.

ORIGINAL   De Hoyos has spoken out against racism and social oppression. She has spoken out publicly.

COMBINED   De Hoyos has spoken out **publicly** against racism and social oppression.

CHANGING THE FORM

ORIGINAL   She was involved in the revolution of the 1960s. It was a revolution of the culture.

COMBINED   She was involved in the **cultural** revolution of the 1960s.

ORIGINAL   In her poetry de Hoyos often explores themes through humor. The humor is based on irony.

COMBINED   In her poetry de Hoyos often explores themes through **ironic** humor.

Prepositional Phrases

Usually, you can insert a prepositional phrase without any change in form.

ORIGINAL   Jason likes science fiction novels. He likes the ones with fantastical creatures.

COMBINED   Jason likes science fiction novels **with fantastical creatures.**

ASSESSMENT

Use your evaluations of students' responses to **Exercises 1–3** in conjunction with evaluations of students' writing to assess their understanding of and ability to apply the material covered in this lesson.

RETEACHING

Copy onto the chalkboard a well-written paragraph that includes a variety of sentence structures. Then work with students to write beside it a second version of the paragraph. The second version should convey the same information but should include only short, choppy sentences. Afterward, compare ☞

Sometimes you can change a part of one sentence into a prepositional phrase and then insert it into the other sentence.

ORIGINAL   Science fiction stretches the imagination. It contains thought-provoking concepts.

COMBINED   Science fiction stretches the imagination **with thought-provoking concepts.**

COMPUTER NOTE: Use your word-processing program's Cut and Paste commands to move words or phrases as you combine sentences. If you change your mind, you can always move the text again.

EXERCISE 1 ▶ Combining Sentences by Inserting Adjectives, Adverbs, and Prepositional Phrases

Combine each of the following groups of short sentences by inserting adjectives, adverbs, or prepositional phrases into the first sentence. [Hint: You may need to change the forms of some words before you insert them.] Read your combined sentences aloud to make sure they're clear.   **Revisions will vary.**

EXAMPLE   1. Peregrine falcons soar. They soar gracefully. They soar near their nests.
1. *Peregrine falcons soar gracefully near their nests.*

1. Peregrine falcons ~~became scarce. They~~ became scarce in the United States. ~~They became scarce~~ because of the pesticide DDT.   **2. By 1970,**
2. ∧No breeding ~~pairs remained. No pairs~~ remained in the eastern United States. ~~The breeding pairs were gone by 1970.~~

TECHNOLOGY TIP

Remind students there are usually several ways to accomplish a task in word-processing programs. One example is the Cut and Paste commands. Students can usually find these commands in the Edit menu on the menu bar at the top of the screen, and they can open the menu and its items by clicking on them with the mouse. However, there are usually shortcut keys that accomplish the same things as the menu items. Encourage students to learn the shortcut keys, especially for items they will use frequently.

VISUAL CONNECTIONS

Exploring the Subject. The peregrine falcons are not the only birds seriously harmed by DDT before the ban. Ordinarily DDT did not directly kill the birds. Instead the pesticide interfered with calcium metabolism. The shells of the eggs were thin, and the eggs broke when the birds sat on them.

CLOSURE

Ask students to name three ways in which sentences can be combined and to explain the importance of varying sentence structures. ■

3. ~~Scientists have reintroduced peregrine falcons. These~~ scientists ~~are~~ from the Peregrine Fund. ~~The falcons are wild. The scientists~~ have reintroduced the falcons around the country. ~~They have reintroduced the falcons~~ under controlled conditions.   **3. wild peregrine**

4. A ban on most uses of DDT has helped the falcons. ~~The ban has been effective. It has been a considerable help.~~

5. Peregrines are hatching eggs. ~~The peregrines are~~ in the eastern wilderness. ~~It is~~ the first time ~~they are hatching eggs~~ since the 1950s.   **4. An effective/considerably.**   **5. for**

Participial Phrases

A *participial phrase* contains a participle and its modifiers and complements. Participial phrases act as adjectives in a sentence. They help develop concrete details that elaborate on a sentence's main idea. You can use participial phrases to add interest to your writing.

> Sometimes their mother sat in the room behind them, sewing, or **dressing their younger sister,** or **nursing the baby, Paul.**
>
> James Baldwin, "The Rockpile"

☞ **REFERENCE NOTE:** For more about participles and participial phrases, see pages 657–658.

Often, you can take a participial phrase from one sentence and insert it into another sentence without a change in form.

ORIGINAL	Judy arrived early for the "Syndicated TV Shows" theme party. She was dressed as Alice from *The Brady Bunch.*
COMBINED	Judy, **dressed as Alice from *The Brady Bunch*,** arrived early for the "Syndicated TV Shows" theme party.

Sometimes you can create a participial phrase by changing the verb of a sentence into a participle. Then you can insert the phrase into another sentence.

ORIGINAL	A Gilligan impersonator stumbled in the door a few minutes later. He carried a coconut and a homemade fishing pole.
COMBINED	A Gilligan impersonator, **carrying a coconut and a homemade fishing pole,** stumbled in the door a few minutes later.

INTEGRATING THE LANGUAGE ARTS

Usage Link. Remind students that modifying phrases should be placed as closely as possible to the words they modify. To give students practice placing modifying phrases correctly, write the following sentences on the chalkboard. Have students revise them to eliminate misplaced modifiers.

1. More than 10,000 Hispanics fought in the Civil War, including Loretta Velasquez.
2. In the Confederate Army, Velasquez enlisted disguised as a man.
3. She had fought several battles when the army discharged her discovering she was a woman.

[**1.** More than 10,000 Hispanics, including Loretta Velasquez, fought in the Civil War.

2. Disguised as a man, Velasquez enlisted in the Confederate Army.

3. She had fought several battles when the army, discovering she was a woman, discharged her.]

SELECTION AMENDMENT
Description of change: excerpted
Rationale: to focus on the concept of combining sentences presented in this chapter

WRITING NOTE Place a participial phrase beside the noun or pronoun you want it to modify. Otherwise, you may give your sentence a meaning you don't intend. Notice how the placement of the modifier makes a difference in the meaning of the following sentence.

MISPLACED   **Wrapped in silver paper,** Samantha tried to guess the contents of the box.

CORRECT   Samantha tried to guess the contents of the box **wrapped in silver paper.**

EXERCISE 2 ▶ **Combining Sentences by Using Participial Phrases**

Combine each of the following pairs of sentences by reducing one sentence to a participial phrase and inserting the phrase into the other sentence. In some of the pairs, you'll need to change a verb form into a participle first. You may also have to delete some words from a participial phrase to avoid an awkward combination. Be sure to use correct punctuation.

EXAMPLE   1. Marian Anderson demonstrated her love for music at an early age. She sang in the church choir.
    1. *Singing in the church choir, Marian Anderson demonstrated her love for music at an early age.*

1. Anderson traveled to Europe to study for a year when she was twenty-two. She was awarded a fellowship to do this.
2. Anderson became famous. She was well received by audiences all over Europe.
3. She returned to the United States for a recital in 1935. She won the praise of American opera lovers as well.

ANSWERS
Exercise 2

Answers may vary.

1. Awarded a fellowship, Anderson traveled to Europe to study for a year when she was twenty-two.
2. Well received by audiences all over Europe, Anderson became famous.
3. Returning to the United States for a recital in 1935, she won the praise of American opera lovers as well.
4. Anderson, banned from singing at Constitution Hall because she was black, sang in protest on the steps of the Lincoln Memorial on Easter morning of 1939.
5. Seventy-five thousand people, expressing their disapproval of the discriminatory treatment, came to hear the Easter morning concert.

569

VISUAL CONNECTIONS

Exploring the Subject. After her famous performance at the Lincoln Memorial, Marian Anderson (1902–1993) went on to win the Spingarn Medal that same year. Later, in 1955, she became the first African American singer to perform as a member of the Metropolitan Opera in New York City.

Marian Anderson was made a delegate to the United Nations in 1958 and won the UN peace prize in 1977.

MECHANICS HINT

Some appositives are restrictive and should not be set off by commas. Restrictive appositives are usually one word. You may want to show students the following examples of restrictive appositives:

1. Yoshi's sister Claire went with us. (Yoshi has more than one sister.)
2. I loved Dylan Thomas' poem "Fern Hill." (Dylan Thomas wrote more than one poem.)
3. She always forgets how to spell the word *weird*.

SELECTION AMENDMENT
Description of change: excerpted
Rationale: to focus on the concept of combining sentences presented in this chapter

4. Anderson sang on the steps of the Lincoln Memorial in protest on Easter morning of 1939. She had been banned from singing at Constitution Hall because she was black.
5. Seventy-five thousand people came to hear the Easter morning concert. They expressed their disapproval of the discriminatory treatment.

UPI/Bettman

Appositive Phrases

An *appositive phrase* is made up of an appositive and its modifiers. It adds detail by identifying or explaining a noun or pronoun in a sentence. For clear meaning, insert an appositive phrase directly before or after the noun or pronoun it explains.

> The gang met every morning in an impromptu car-park, **the site of the last bomb of the first blitz.**
>
> Graham Greene, "The Destructors"

MECHANICS HINT

Punctuating Appositive Phrases

Set an appositive phrase off from the rest of the sentence with a comma (or two commas if you place the phrase in the middle of the sentence).

> The town of Canterbury, **the ancient religious center of England,** attracted many pilgrims during the Middle Ages.

☞ **REFERENCE NOTE:** For more about punctuating phrases in sentences, see pages 909–915.

You can combine sentences in a variety of ways by using appositive phrases.

TWO SENTENCES   Hernando De Soto was a Spanish explorer of the 1500s. He led the first European expedition to reach the Mississippi River.

ONE SENTENCE   **A Spanish explorer of the 1500s,** Hernando De Soto led the first European expedition to reach the Mississippi River.

or

Hernando De Soto, **leader of the first European expedition to reach the Mississippi River,** was a Spanish explorer of the 1500s.

In the second combination, the verb *led* was changed into the noun *leader* to create the appositive phrase. Notice that each combination emphasizes a different idea.

EXERCISE 3   **Combining Sentences by Using Appositive Phrases**

To combine the following pairs of sentences, turn one of the sentences into an appositive phrase and insert it into the other sentence. Be sure to check your punctuation. **Revisions will vary.**

EXAMPLE   **1.** Elizabeth Bowen became one of the leading writers in England after World War I. She was a native of Ireland.

1. *Elizabeth Bowen, a native of Ireland, became one of the leading writers in England after World War I.*

1. , one of Bowen's best-known novels,

1. In *The Death of the Heart*ˏthe protagonist is a sensitive teenage girl. ~~*The Death of the Heart* is one of Bowen's best-known novels.~~

2. Bowenˏ~~was~~ a nurse in World War I and an air-raid warden during World War IIˏ ~~Bowen~~ wrote about the psychological effects of war on civilians.

3. ˏWriter Doris Lessing describes people attempting to find meaning in life. ~~She is a sensitive observer of social and political struggles.~~ **3. A sensitive observer of social and political struggles,**

4. In *Going Home,*ˏDoris Lessing writes about a return visit to Rhodesia. ~~*Going Home* is an autobiographical narrative.~~

5. Toni Morrisonˏ~~is~~ one of America's most celebrated novelistsˏ ~~Morrison~~ won the Pulitzer Prize for her best-selling novel *Beloved*.   **4. an autobiographical narrative,**

? CRITICAL THINKING

Analysis. Caution students to be aware of subtle shifts in meaning that sometimes occur when the forms of words are changed. As an example of this, write the following sentences on the chalkboard:

Manuel is studying history.
He is studying the history of Cambodia.

Ask students if these two sentences could be combined as "Manuel is studying historic Cambodia." [No, the combination does not have the same meaning as the original sentences.]

REVIEW A

OBJECTIVE

- To revise a paragraph by combining sentences

LESSON 2 (pp. 572–574)

COORDINATING IDEAS

OBJECTIVE

- To combine sentences by coordinating ideas

REVIEW A ▶ **Combining Sentences**

The following paragraphs sound choppy because they contain many short sentences. Combine some of the sentences by using the methods you've learned. Use your judgment about which sentences to combine and how to combine them. When you're finished, the paragraphs should have a smoother, livelier style.

Revisions will vary.

The surface of the planet Mars can be seen through a telescope, ~~The surface can be seen~~ from Earth. ~~The planet is~~ reddish in color, ~~It~~ was named after the ancient Romans' red god of war. Mars travels in an elliptical orbit, ~~It travels~~ **and** around the sun, ~~It~~ maintains a distance from the sun of at least 128 million miles.

Part of the planet's surface is covered with craters, ~~These craters were~~ caused by meteors. Mars also has canyons and gorges, ~~The gorges are deep.~~ **deep** ~~Such features~~ seem to support **that** the view that large quantities **of some** of water once flowed on the **scientists** planet's surface. ~~This is the view of some scientists.~~ Mars also has plains, ~~The plains are~~ **windblow** ~~windblown. They are~~ covered by sand dunes and rocks. ~~The~~ **jagged** ~~rocks are jagged.~~

Coordinating Ideas

You can join equally important words, phrases, or clauses by using coordinating conjunctions (such as *and, but, or, for, yet*) or correlative conjunctions (such as *both . . . and, either . . . or, neither . . . nor*). When you combine sentences in this way, you will usually create a compound subject, a compound verb, or a compound sentence.

COORDINATING IDEAS

- **Independent Practice/Reteaching** For practice and reinforcement, see **Combining by Coordinating Ideas** in *Word Choice and Sentence Style,* p. 38.

- **Computer Guided Instruction** For additional instruction and practice with combining sentences by coordinating ideas, see **Lesson 39** in *Language Workshop CD-ROM.*

- **Practice** To help less-advanced students with additional instruction and practice with combining sentences by coordinating ideas, see **Chapter 8** in *English Workshop, Complete Course,* pp. 103–104.

MEETING *individual* NEEDS

LESS-ADVANCED STUDENTS

It is important that students be rewarded for successful combinations. If students are able to create good, clear sentences from the materials in **Exercise 4,** you may want to praise their efforts even if the responses do not contain coordinate elements. Help students rewrite such sentences to achieve appropriate responses, but allow the students to designate the versions of the sentences they like best.

TEACHING THE LESSON

You may want to stress that elements joined by coordinating and correlative conjunctions are of equal importance to both the meanings and the structures of sentences.

After discussing the coordinate components of each of the examples in the lesson, guide students through the first two items in **Exercise 4.** Assign the remainder of the exercise as independent practice.

To close, ask students which words, phrases, or clauses can be joined by coordinating and correlative conjunctions [those of equal importance]. ∎

ORIGINAL   Angelo displayed leadership ability at the meeting. Suzanne also displayed leadership ability at the meeting.

COMBINED   **Both Angelo and Suzanne** displayed leadership ability at the meeting. [compound subject]

ORIGINAL   Many people who have cerebral palsy lead active lives. They are productive members of society.

COMBINED   Many people who have cerebral palsy **lead active lives and are productive members of society.** [compound verb]

ORIGINAL   Toshi executed a quick move toward the basket. Her opponent blocked the shot.

COMBINED   Toshi executed a quick move toward the basket, **but** her opponent blocked the shot. [compound sentence]

To form a compound sentence, you can also link independent clauses with a semicolon and a conjunctive adverb or just a semicolon.

Winston had never made the smallest effort to verify this guess; **indeed,** there was no way of doing so.

George Orwell, *1984*

The beautiful church took years to build; thousands of adobe are in those thick walls.

Nina Otero, "The Bells of Santa Cruz"

☞ **REFERENCE NOTE:** You can find a more detailed discussion of coordination on pages 541–542.

EXERCISE 4 ▶ **Combining Sentences by Coordinating Ideas**

Combine each of the following pairs of sentences by creating a compound subject, a compound verb, or a compound sentence. Make sure the connective you use shows the proper relationship between the ideas. **Revisions will vary.**

1. Between 1840 and 1850, Canton Province in China experienced severe economic problems. Large numbers of Chinese peasants emigrated to the United States. **1. , and**

2. During the 1850s, more than 41,000 Chinese made their way to this country. ~~They~~ joined the great "gold rush" of that time. **2. and**

QUOTATION FOR THE DAY

"Word-carpentry is like any other kind of carpentry: you must join your sentences smoothly." (Anatole France, 1844–1924, French novelist and critic)

Use Anatole France's carpentry metaphor to launch a discussion about the various ways to join sentences.

MEETING *individual* NEEDS

LEP/ESL

General Strategies. It may be helpful to students to provide a context in which the uses of the coordinating conjunctions are contrasted. Omitting the italicized words, write the following paragraph on the chalkboard. Have students fill in the blanks with appropriate coordinating conjunctions.

Saul had a job interview early Monday morning, *so* he decided to go to bed early. He knew he would get a good night's sleep, *yet* he went to bed feeling uneasy. The next morning Saul woke up late, *for* he had forgotten to set his alarm clock! Then Saul realized that he had misplaced his driver's license *and* his car keys. He didn't panic, however. Saul realized that he could take the bus *or* walk to the interview.

AMENDMENTS TO SELECTIONS
Description of change: excerpted
Rationale: to focus on the concept of combining sentences presented in this chapter

OBJECTIVE

- To combine sentences by subordinating ideas

TEACHING THE LESSON

To focus students' attention on the lesson, have them write definitions of the terms *adjective clause, adverb clause,* and *noun clause* prior to discussing the material in this lesson. Then read the material aloud to students. Pause after each explanation to discuss any questions students have. You might want to work with students to

---

COMMON ERROR

Problem. Students sometimes use the subordinating conjunction *although* to begin sentences that consist of two independent clauses joined by *but.*

Solution. Explain to students that because the two conjunctions serve a similar function (to contrast elements), it is not necessary or desirable to use both.

PROGRAM MANAGER

SUBORDINATING IDEAS

- **Independent Practice/ Reteaching** For practice and reinforcement, see **Combining by Subordinating Ideas** in *Word Choice and Sentence Style,* p. 39.

- **Computer Guided Instruction** For additional instruction and practice with combining sentences by subordinating ideas, see **Lesson 39** in *Language Workshop CD-ROM.*

- **Practice** To help less-advanced students with additional instruction and practice with combining sentences by subordinating ideas, see **Chapter 8** in *English Workshop, Complete Course,* pp. 103–104.

AMENDMENTS TO SELECTIONS
Description of change: excerpted
Rationale: to focus on the concept of combining sentences presented in this chapter

---

574   *Combining Sentences*

3. Most of these early Chinese immigrants found no gold. They found no well-paying work.   **3. neither/nor**

4. They came seeking prosperity. They found only hard work and discrimination.   **4. but**

5. The transcontinental railroad system was being built in the 1850s. Cheap labor was in great demand.   **5. , and**

6. Ten thousand laborers built the Union Pacific railroad. Nine thousand of them were Chinese.

7. The railroad builders of America initially favored Chinese immigration. The sentiment changed when the railroad system was finished.   **7. ; however,**

8. In 1869, the tracks of the Central Pacific joined those of the Union Pacific in Ogden, Utah. Thousands of Chinese were immediately out of work.   **8. , and**

9. Most new immigrants in the nineteenth century lacked education. They possessed few skills.   **9. skills and**

10. Despite their hardships, many Chinese immigrants stayed in the United States. They began to make it their home.   **10. and**

Subordinating Ideas

When two related sentences contain ideas of unequal importance, you can combine the sentences by placing the less-important idea in a subordinate clause (an *adjective clause,* an *adverb clause,* or a *noun clause*). The use of subordination will help show the relationships between the ideas.

In the following sentences, notice how each subordinate clause begins with a connecting word that shows how the clause relates to the main idea.

> Nettie, **who was quickly bored in those days,** began to break up straw and drop it into her lunch pail. [adjective clause]
>
> Roseanne Coggeshall, "Peter the Rock"

> **As his hearing got fuzzier,** he accused more and more people of whispering. [adverb clause]
>
> John Steinbeck, *The Winter of Our Discontent*

> Brave Orchid thought **that her niece was like her mother, the lovely, useless type.** [noun clause]
>
> Maxine Hong Kingston, *The Woman Warrior*

☞ **REFERENCE NOTE:** For more about subordination, see pages 544–548.

GUIDED PRACTICE

Guide students through the first two items in **Exercise 5** on p. 577. Assign the rest of the exercise as independent practice and use students' responses in conjunction with your evaluations of their writing to assess their understanding of the material in this lesson.

☞

Subordinating Ideas   **575**

Adjective Clauses

An *adjective clause* modifies a noun or pronoun and usually begins with *who, whose, which, where,* or *that.* To combine sentences by using an adjective clause, first decide which sentence you want to subordinate. Then, change that sentence into an adjective clause and insert it into the other sentence.

ORIGINAL   Donner Pass cuts through the Sierra Nevada in eastern California. It lies 2,160 meters above sea level.

COMBINED   Donner Pass, **which cuts through the Sierra Nevada in eastern California,** lies 2,160 meters above sea level.

or

Donner Pass, **which lies 2,160 meters above sea level,** cuts through the Sierra Nevada in eastern California.

MECHANICS HINT

Punctuating Adjective Clauses

Use a comma or commas to set off an adjective clause that is not essential to the meaning of the sentence.

ESSENTIAL   The bicycle **that has the wider tires** is designed for riding on rugged surfaces.

NONESSENTIAL   The bicycle**, which hasn't been well maintained,** has only one working brake.

☞ **REFERENCE NOTE:** For more information on punctuating adjective clauses, see pages 909–910.

QUOTATION FOR THE DAY

"The sentence is where one important, immediate individual experience of literature takes place." (Richard Ford, 1944–   , American novelist)

You may wish to use this quotation to emphasize to students the importance of well-written sentences in their writing. To extend this lesson, you could ask students to skim their favorite literature to locate sentences that students find particularly effective. Ask students to share the sentences with the class.

INTEGRATING THE LANGUAGE ARTS

Literature Link. To help students understand the desirability of varied sentence structures, you could discuss with students the sentence structures used in a selection in your literature textbook. Have students read the selection and then have them analyze a portion of it for compound subjects and verbs, compound sentences, and subordinate clauses. Ask students how the selection would be different if it consisted of only simple sentences.

INTEGRATING THE LANGUAGE ARTS

Usage Link. Students are often troubled by distinctions between *who* and *whom* and between *whoever* and *whomever.* You may want to tell students that the case of the pronoun beginning a subordinate clause is determined by its use in the clause. Give them the following step-by-step strategy for determining which pronoun to use:

1. Isolate the subordinate clause.
2. Determine how the pronoun is used in the clause—subject, predicate nominative, object of a verb, or object of a preposition.
3. Select the correct form of the pronoun. If the pronoun is used as the subject or predicate nominative of the clause, it should be in the nominative case (who, whoever). If the pronoun is used as the object of a verb or as the object of a preposition, it should be in the objective case (whom, whomever).

576

---

576   *Combining Sentences*

Adverb Clauses

An *adverb clause* modifies a verb, an adjective, or an adverb in a sentence. To form an adverb clause, add a subordinating conjunction (*although, after, because, if, when, where, while*) to the beginning of the sentence you want to subordinate. (You may also need to delete or replace some words to form the clause.) You can then attach the adverb clause to the sentence it's related to.

When you combine sentences by using an adverb clause, choose the subordinating conjunction carefully. Make sure it shows the proper relationship between the ideas in the adverb clause and the independent clause.

ORIGINAL   The band played patriotic music. Fireworks burst into brilliant color across the night sky.
COMBINED   The band played patriotic music **as fireworks burst into brilliant color across the night sky.**

ORIGINAL   There may not be any racquetball courts open. In that case, we'll go to the park and play tennis.
COMBINED   **If there are no racquetball courts open,** we'll go to the park and play tennis.

☞ **REFERENCE NOTE:** For lists of subordinating conjunctions, see pages 545, 622, and 682.

Noun Clauses

A *noun clause* is a subordinate clause used as a noun. It usually begins with *that, what, whatever, why, whether, how, who, whom, whoever,* or *whomever.* Here are a few examples of noun clauses in sentences.

Whoever buys that car will be sorry. [noun clause as subject]
Many people don't realize **that the actress Raquel Welch is part Hispanic.** [noun clause as direct object]
We can spend the money on **whatever we like.** [noun clause as object of preposition]

Sometimes you can drop the introductory word *that* from a noun clause without any confusion.

EXAMPLE   My sister told us (that) *Independence Day* **was a fast-paced, exciting movie.**

You can combine sentences by turning one of the sentences into a noun clause and attaching it to the other sentence.

ORIGINAL Cactus plants are able to survive in the desert. The TV documentary explained it.

COMBINED The TV documentary explained **how cactus plants are able to survive in the desert.**

ORIGINAL The actress knew it. The role was right for her.

COMBINED The actress knew **that the role was right for her.**

EXERCISE 5 ▶ **Combining Sentences by Subordinating Ideas**

Revisions will vary.

Combine each of the following pairs of sentences. Change one sentence into a subordinate clause and attach the clause to the other sentence. [Hint: You may need to add, delete, or rearrange some words.] Choose your connectives carefully, and check your combined sentences for correct punctuation.

1. Louise Erdrich writes in lyrical prose about the American Indian experience. ~~She is part Chippewa.~~
   1. , who is part Chippewa,

2. The Turtle Mountain Chippewa Reservation is the setting for her novel *Love Medicine*. ~~Erdrich spent time there as a child.~~
   2. , where Erdrich spent time as a child,

3. Erdrich attended the Bureau of Indian Affairs boarding school. Both ~~of~~ her parents worked ~~there.~~
   3. , where

4. Erdrich had close ties to the Chippewa community. ~~S~~he never really thought about her American Indian heritage.
   4. Although

5. As a young adult Erdrich began to realize ~~something.~~ Her American Indian heritage was important to her.
   5. that

6. Erdrich's writing emphasizes the beauty and universality of the American Indian experience. ~~Critics have noted this about her writing.~~
   6. Critics have noted that

7. Her characters take on a mythic quality. ~~T~~hey struggle to overcome their problems.
   7. as

8. Erdrich met her husband, Michael Dorris. ~~Erdrich~~ was attending Dartmouth College ~~at the time.~~
   8. , while she

9. Dartmouth was founded in 1769 under a charter that stressed the education of American Indians. ~~B~~y 1972 it had graduated only twelve American Indians.
   9. Although

10. Dorris has collaborated closely with Erdrich on her works. ~~He is also part American Indian.~~
   10. , who is also part American Indian,

OBJECTIVES

- To use coordination or subordination to combine pairs of sentences
- To use a variety of methods to combine sentences in a paragraph

578   *Combining Sentences*

R E V I E W B ▶ **Combining Sentences by Coordinating and Subordinating Ideas**

Use either coordination or subordination to combine each of the following pairs of sentences. You may see more than one way to combine a sentence pair. Just write the combination that sounds best to you.

EXAMPLE   1. *Amazing Stories* was the first science fiction magazine. Hugo Gernsback began publishing it in 1926.
1. Amazing Stories, *which Hugo Gernsback began publishing in 1926, was the first science fiction magazine.*

1. Some science fiction contains outlandish speculation. It has to seem somewhat believable in order to be effective.
2. *Frankenstein* is an early example of science fiction. The novel describes the scientific creation of human life.
3. H. G. Wells's *The Time Machine* offers thought-provoking social criticism. *The Time Machine* describes a devastated future world.
4. Some critics did not accept science fiction as serious literature. Major authors in the early twentieth century often included science fiction in their works.
5. Today science fiction has many supporters. They hold annual conventions and present awards for the best writing.

ANSWERS
Review B

Answers may vary.

1. Some science fiction contains outlandish speculation; however, it has to seem somewhat believable in order to be effective.
2. *Frankenstein,* which describes the scientific creation of human life, is an early example of science fiction.
3. H. G. Wells's *The Time Machine,* which describes a devastated future world, offers thought-provoking social criticism.
4. Although major authors in the early twentieth century often included science fiction in their works, some critics did not accept science fiction as serious literature.
5. Today science fiction has many supporters who hold annual conventions and present awards for the best writing.

| REVIEW C ▶ | **Revising a Paragraph by Combining Sentences** |

Here's a chance to put all of your sentence-combining skills to the test. The following paragraph is made up of short, choppy sentences. Using the methods you've learned, combine the short sentences into longer sentences. [Note: In some cases you'll be combining more than just two sentences.] Your combined sentences should add variety and improve the style of the paragraph. Remember to check for correct punctuation.

Mount Saint Helens erupted in May 1980. It is near Vancouver, Washington. The eruption was sudden. The explosion had a force over five hundred times that of an atomic bomb. It tore the top off the mountain. It threw ash high into the air. The explosion and resulting mudslides caused more than thirty deaths. The explosions and mudslides left many people homeless. The mud killed hundreds of deer and elk. The mud turned Spirit Lake into a mudhole. Much of the ash fell to earth within a few days. A cloud of dust remained. This cloud was over much of the Northern Hemisphere. People saw spectacular sunrises and sunsets for years. The sunrises and sunsets were rose-colored. The color was due to solar rays striking microscopic particles of ash.

ANSWERS
Review C

Revisions will vary. Here is a possibility:

Mount Saint Helens, located near Vancouver, Washington, erupted suddenly in May 1980. The explosion, which had a force over five hundred times that of an atomic bomb, tore the top off the mountain and threw ash high into the air. The explosion and resulting mudslides caused more than thirty deaths and left many homeless. The mud killed hundreds of deer and elk and turned Spirit Lake into a mudhole. Although much of the ash fell to earth within a few days, a cloud of dust remained over much of the Northern Hemisphere. For years, people saw spectacular, rose-colored sunrises and sunsets that were due to solar rays striking microscopic particles of ash.

VISUAL CONNECTIONS
Exploring the Subject. Mount Saint Helens serves as a double reminder of how powerful nature can be. The explosion was terrifying and destructive, but nature also possesses great power to heal. By the next spring, some plants were beginning to appear on the mountainside. Soon the entire ecosystem was beginning to heal itself.

LESSON 4 *(p. 580)*
MAKING CONNECTIONS

**WRITING FOR
DIFFERENT AUDIENCES
OBJECTIVES**
• To write a children's story
• To write a story for peers

**WRITING FOR
DIFFERENT AUDIENCES**
Teaching Strategies

Students will find it more profitable to work on only one version of the story at a time. As students work on the children's story, you may need to remind them that writing short sentences does not mean eliminating specific details.

Encourage students to use the stages of the writing process as they write each story. Allow class time for peer feedback and for editing sessions for both stories.

GUIDELINES

Responses to this assignment will vary widely. The first version of the story should contain short, clear sentences, but the language should be lively enough to interest the audience. The second version should contain longer sentences, but clarity should not be sacrificed.

MAKING CONNECTIONS

Writing for Different Audiences

Think back to when you were first learning to read. The books you read in those days used mostly short, simple sentences. Now that you're a more accomplished reader, you'd probably become bored or impatient with that type of writing. You're looking for more richness and variety in what you read as well as in what you write.

Writing a Children's Story

It's a week before an important holiday. You've been working after school at a day-care center. One of the teachers has asked you to plan a special holiday activity for the children. You've decided to have a story hour in which you tell the children a short, simple story about the upcoming holiday. Write a brief, entertaining story to tell the children. Your story might tell about the origin of the holiday, or it might just illustrate the meaning and spirit of the holiday. Feel free to draw from your own memories and experiences as you write the story. (For help with planning and writing a story, see pages 169–199.) Be sure to use clear, short sentences that the children will understand.

Writing a Story for Your Peers

Your high school has caught the holiday spirit, too. The editor of the school newspaper is compiling a special holiday issue. Write a different version of your holiday story to submit for publication in the paper. Revise the story so that it will hold the interest of readers your age. You may want to add or replace details. Use sentence-combining techniques to adapt the style of your writing for an older audience. Craft lively, detailed sentences that are fun to read.

Chapter 16

IMPROVING SENTENCE STYLE

OBJECTIVES
- To vary sentence beginnings
- To vary sentence structure
- To revise for wordiness

Sentence Style in Workplace Writing

Explain to students that sentence length and vocabulary affect readability. Longer sentences require readers to comprehend more and thus to work harder. In the workplace, writers are urged to use short and concise sentences. According to *Effective Business Communication,* sentences should be limited to no more than twenty words each. Short, concise sentences help the busy reader who does not have the time to decipher long sentences and paragraphs. Yet, combining sentences helps to bring ideas together in a single sentence. Other factors that influence readability are contrasted in the chart below.

	Workplace	Academic
Sentence Length	should vary, but should be no more than 20 words. If a longer sentence is necessary, use numbers to highlight key points	varies but can be as high as 60 words
Sentence Structure	should have varied constructions, but most of the time put subject first so that the thought is direct	needs to have varied constructions; subject should not always be put first
Vocabulary	should be simple and serious; should be precise; should put action into verbs	varies according to the audience

- **Practice** Assign students to small groups. Bring to class a descriptive passage from an autobiography and one each of the following examples of workplace writing—instructions for assembling a toy, a memo from a business, and an informational insert from a bottle of aspirin. Randomly assign one example to each group. Ask the groups to use the information in the chart to analyze the sentence style of their example.

- **Strategies** Suggest that students count the words in each sentence in the example and calculate the average sentence length. Then, to analyze sentence structure, they should underline the subjects and verbs in each sentence to see where they are generally placed. Finally, they should examine the vocabulary and circle any high-level vocabulary words or jargon. Students should also decide if the example contains one part of speech significantly more than another; for example, directions use more verbs and nouns than adjectives, and descriptive passages rely heavily on adjectives and adverbs.

- **Reflection** Bring the class together to discuss the results of each group's analysis. Ask students if they think their examples corroborated the information given in the chart. Ask students how they will apply their analyses to their own writing.

CHAPTER 16: IMPROVING SENTENCE STYLE

Use this guide for creating an instructional plan that addresses the individual needs of your students. Assignments accompanied by the following symbol (*) may be completed out of class. Times given for pacing lessons are estimated.

CHAPTER PLANNING GUIDE—PUPIL'S EDITION

LESSONS	REVISING FOR VARIETY pp. 581–593
DEVELOPMENTAL PROGRAM	🕐 **60–65 minutes** • Main Assignment: Looking Ahead p. 581 • Revising for Variety pp. 581–587 • Varying Sentence Beginnings Chart pp. 583–584 • Writing Note p. 584 • Exercise 1 pp. 584–585 in pairs • Exercise 2 p. 587* 🕐 **50–55 minutes** • Revising to Reduce Wordiness pp. 588–592 • Exercise 3 p. 590 in pairs • Exercises 4, 5 pp. 590–591, 592–593* • Reducing Groups of Words pp. 591–592
CORE PROGRAM	🕐 **35–40 minutes** • Main Assignment: Looking Ahead p. 581 • Varying Sentence Beginnings Chart pp. 583–584 • Writing Note p. 584 • Exercise 1 pp. 584–585* • Varying Sentence Structure pp. 585–587 • Exercise 2 p. 587* 🕐 **20–25 minutes** • Eliminating Unnecessary Words p. 589 • Exercise 4 pp. 590–591* • Clauses/Phrases Charts pp. 591–592 • Exercise 5 pp. 592–593*
ACCELERATED PROGRAM	🕐 **25–30 minutes** • Main Assignment: Looking Ahead p. 581 • Varying Sentence Beginnings Chart pp. 583–584 • Writing Note p. 584 • Varying Sentence Structure pp. 585–587* • Exercise 2 p. 587* 🕐 **15–20 minutes** • Eliminating Unnecessary Words p. 589 • Exercise 4 pp. 590–591* • Clauses/Phrases Charts pp. 591–592 • Exercise 5 pp. 592–593*

CHAPTER PLANNING GUIDE—PROGRAM RESOURCES

	REVISING FOR VARIETY pp. 581–593
PRINT	• Varying Sentence Beginnings, Varying Sentence Structure, *Word Choice and Sentence Style* pp. 47–48 • Reducing Wordiness, *Word Choice and Sentence Style* p. 49 • Varying Sentence Beginnings, Varying Sentence Structure *English Workshop* pp. 105–108 • Reducing Wordiness, *English Workshop* pp. 109–110
MEDIA	• *Language Workshop:* Lessons 40–41

Computer disk or CD-ROM

CROSS CURRICULUM — ELEMENTS OF WRITING: CURRICULUM CONNECTIONS

Making Connections
• Writing a College Admissions Essay pp. 594–595

ASSESSMENT OPTIONS

Summative Assessment
Reviews A and B, *Elements of Writing,* Pupil's Edition pp. 588, 593
Improving Sentence Style, Reviews A and B, *Word Choice and Sentence Style* pp. 50–53
Chapter Review, Exercise D, *English Workshop* p. 112

Reflection
Self-assessment Record, *Portfolio Assessment* p. 19

INTEGRATING THE LANGUAGE ARTS

SELECTION	READING AND LITERATURE	WRITING AND CRITICAL THINKING	LANGUAGE AND SYNTAX	SPEAKING, LISTENING, AND OTHER EXPRESSION SKILLS
• from **A Child's Christmas in Wales** by Dylan Thomas p. 582 • from **"The Moustache"** by Robert Cormier p. 584	• Reading paragraphs to determine which sentences need revision pp. 587, 588, 590–591, 593 • Reading sentences to determine wordiness pp. 590, 591, 593	• Varying sentence beginnings pp. 584–585, 588 • Revising sentence structure pp. 587, 588, 592–593 • Rewriting a paragraph pp. 587, 588 • Revising wordy sentences pp. 590, 592–593 • Revising a paragraph by eliminating unnecessary words pp. 590–591, 593 • Applying interpretive and creative thinking pp. 592–593, 594–595 • Revising sentences through reduction pp. 592–593 • Writing a college admissions essay pp. 594–595	• Using appositives, phrases, and clause modifiers to begin sentences pp. 584–585, 588 • Varying sentence structure pp. 587, 588, 592–593 • Eliminating unnecessary words pp. 590–591, 592–593	

REVISING FOR VARIETY

• To evaluate and revise sentences by reduction

OBJECTIVES

• To revise sentences by varying their beginnings
• To revise sentences by varying their structures

16 IMPROVING SENTENCE STYLE

LOOKING AHEAD

This chapter will give you some practice in revising your sentences for style. As you work through the chapter, you will learn ways to

• vary sentence beginnings and sentence structures
• reduce wordiness in sentences

PROGRAM MANAGER

FOR THE WHOLE CHAPTER

■ **Review** For exercises on chapter concepts, see **Review Form A** and **Review Form B** in *Word Choice and Sentence Style,* pp. 50–53.

PROGRAM MANAGER

REVISING FOR VARIETY

■ **Independent Practice/ Reteaching** For practice and reinforcement, see **Varying Sentence Beginnings, Varying Sentence Structure**, and **Reducing Wordiness** in *Word Choice and Sentence Style,* pp. 47–49.

■ **Computer Guided Instruction** For additional instruction and practice with varying sentence beginnings, varying sentence structure, and reducing wordiness, see **Lessons 40** and **41** in *Language Workshop CD-ROM.*

■ **Practice** To help less-advanced students with additional instruction and practice with varying sentence beginnings, varying sentence structure, and reducing wordiness, see **Chapter 8** in *English Workshop, Complete Course,* pp. 105–110.

Revising for Variety

No one likes to read dull writing—not your cousin in Canada to whom you write personal letters, not your social studies teacher for whom you might write an analysis of urban poverty, and not your employer for whom you might write monthly status reports.

As you evaluate and revise your writing, it's important to read your sentences with an eye for style. Notice how the sentences fit together. Do they add up to lively, natural-sounding paragraphs or dull, stilted ones? If your writing sounds dull, you probably need to vary the beginnings and the structures of some of your sentences.

As you read the following passage, notice how the varied sentences work together to form a smooth, effective paragraph.

Begin a class discussion on effective sentences by asking students to consider their own reading experiences. Here are some potential questions:

1. When you pick up something to read, do you want to be able to read quickly and smoothly?

2. Do you want to be able to understand the material the first time without having to reread?

3. What kinds of sentences within the text might allow you to do so?

4. Do you want to be drawn into the reading as if you were a part of it?

Encourage varied responses.

QUOTATION FOR THE DAY

"Once you've finished writing for yourself and begin to write for your *reader,* your mumbo jumbo will start slowly turning into bona fide prose—i.e., sentences that make sense." (John R. Trimble, American writer and professor at the University of Texas at Austin)

Write the quotation on the chalkboard and ask students to reflect on the meaning of Trimble's words and their connection to revising sentences for style. Help students understand that in the revision stage of writing, writers often have to play with sentences and words to create effective writing.

MEETING *individual* NEEDS

LEP/ESL

General Strategies. When assigning **Exercise 1** on pp. 584–585, you may want to group each student with a peer tutor, preferably a student with strong cognitive and communicative skills. Your English-language learners may not have the requisite vocabulary or syntactic knowledge to complete this activity independently.

SELECTION AMENDMENT
Description of change: excerpted
Rationale: to focus on the concept of sentence style presented in this chapter

> Bring out the tall tales now that we told by the fire as the gaslight bubbled like a diver. Ghosts whooed like owls in the long nights when I dared not look over my shoulder; animals lurked in the cubbyhole under the stairs where the gas meter ticked. And I remember that we went singing carols once, when there wasn't the shaving of a moon to light the flying streets. At the end of a long road was a drive that led to a large house, and we stumbled up the darkness of the drive that night, each one of us afraid, each one holding a stone in his hand in case, and all of us too brave to say a word. The wind through the trees made noises as of old and unpleasant and maybe webfooted men wheezing in caves. We reached the black bulk of the house.
>
> Dylan Thomas, *A Child's Christmas in Wales*

Varying Sentence Beginnings

Most sentences begin with a subject followed by a verb.

EXAMPLES   **I sprained** my ankle the first time I went ice-skating.
           That cat is a finicky eater.

There's nothing wrong with this basic subject-verb pattern—except that it begins to sound monotonous after a while. You can improve the style of your writing by beginning some sentences with introductory words, phrases, and clauses instead of with subjects. At the same time, you can make more effective connections between related sentences.

In each example below, the first version of the sentences is clear. But notice that the revision brings the ideas into sharper focus by shifting the emphasis in the second sentence.

BLAND   The lacrosse team qualified for the state finals. The players never stopped practicing from the minute they got the news.

BETTER   The lacrosse team qualified for the state finals. **From the minute they got the news,** the players never stopped practicing.

BLAND   Marion was shy in the classroom. She came into her own, however, on the stage.

BETTER   Marion was shy in the classroom. **On the stage,** however, she came into her own.

Have a volunteer read aloud the excerpt from *A Child's Christmas in Wales.* Ask students to explain why they think the sentences fit so well together to create a unified paragraph. Lead students to understand that the paragraph is effective because of the varied sentence beginnings and structures and the careful choice of words.

Guide students through the strategies in the **Varying Sentence Beginnings** chart on pp. 583–584. Be sure to point out that various introductory elements require punctuation. Continue with the strategies for varying sentence structure discussed on pp. 585–587. You may want to read some of the examples aloud as part of your discussion. Be sure also to discuss the information ☛

Revising for Variety **583**

Sometimes the best way to vary sentence beginnings is to reduce a short sentence to an introductory word, phrase, or clause and attach it to another sentence. Here's where your sentence-combining skills come in handy.

BLAND **The novel put me to sleep after an hour of reading. It is long and dull.**

BETTER **Long and dull,** the novel put me to sleep after an hour of reading.

☛ **REFERENCE NOTE:** For more about combining sentences, see pages 564–577.

You can begin sentences in many different ways. The following chart gives some examples.

VARYING SENTENCE BEGINNINGS
SENTENCE CONNECTIVES
Almost everyone watches television. **But** how many people really know how a television set works?
I don't mind lending you my new book. **However,** you must promise to give it back.
APPOSITIVES
An enormously complex mechanism, the human brain contains between 10 and 100 billion nerve cells.
A merchant sailor for ten years, Jim knew every important port in the world.
SINGLE-WORD MODIFIERS
Methodically, Mrs. Williams worked the calculus problem on the board.
Shivering, we warmed our chapped hands by the fire.
Large and heavy, the water-dwelling manatee can eat over one hundred pounds of plants in a day.
PHRASE MODIFIERS
From the window of the plane, Marisol saw her family waving goodbye.

(continued)

MEETING *individual* NEEDS

STUDENTS WITH SPECIAL NEEDS

The exercises in this chapter require extensive revision, a task that can be extremely tedious and frustrating for students who have trouble writing or transferring written material from one place to another. Word-processing programs, therefore, are very valuable tools for these students. If students are not yet skilled with the keyboard, enter the exercises to be revised and then students can revise. Other word-processing skills that students need to be familiar with include inserting, deleting, and rearranging blocks of text.

LESS-ADVANCED STUDENTS

Students who have not mastered the concept of sentence parts might have problems with the revision techniques in this chapter. You may want to review subjects and verbs to help students identify the sentence base in some of the example sentences. Explain the importance of first locating the sentence base of each clause when students are attempting to add variety to sentences.

ADVANCED STUDENTS

You might want to bring in contracts (lease agreements or contracts for hire) and have students revise them to eliminate wordiness. Encourage students to use dictionaries to help them understand the legal terminology.

about revising to reduce wordiness on pp. 588–592.

Before students apply these strategies to **Exercises 1–5,** model how you would revise the first sentence for each exercise. Students can then work independently to finish the exercises. Ask students to share their sentences. Write several responses on the chalkboard and emphasize the various ways each sentence can be revised.

◆ INTEGRATING THE LANGUAGE ARTS

Literature Link. If the selection is available in your literature textbook, choose an excerpt from Virginia Woolf's "The Death of a Moth" and ask your students to analyze it for variety in sentence structure and beginnings. Explain that Woolf's writing style is very effective because she employs the natural rhythm of speech in her writing. To achieve this rhythm, she varies her sentence lengths. People speak in varying sentence lengths; thus they are automatically bothered when they read something that all sounds the same, even if the message of each sentence varies.

To illustrate this concept, have students analyze a passage by using lines to represent each sentence's length. Their diagrams will look something like this:

_____. _____.
_____. _____? _____
_____, _____. _____
_____.

What students will discover is that Woolf uses short, long, and medium sentences in random order. Explain that authors tend to use short sentences for emphasis, longer sentences for details and intensity, and medium length sentences to balance the rhythm.

SELECTION AMENDMENT
Description of change: excerpted
Rationale: to focus on the concept of sentence connectives presented in this chapter

---

VARYING SENTENCE BEGINNINGS *(continued)*
PHRASE MODIFIERS *(continued)*
Tiring rapidly, Joe decided to save his strength for the final set.
To win the essay prize, Tanya worked late every night.
CLAUSE MODIFIERS
Because no one saw the crash, investigators had to depend on evidence found in the wreckage.
Although the investigators had little to go on, they were successful in uncovering the cause of the crash.

WRITING NOTE Sentence connectives like *and, but,* and *however* can help you make transitions between ideas. Usually, these connecting words link ideas within a sentence. Sometimes, though—especially in informal writing—you may use one at the beginning of a sentence for variety and emphasis. For example, notice how Robert Cormier uses a sentence connective for emphasis in the following passage.

> You drive out in your father's Le Mans doing seventy-five on the pike and all you're doing is visiting an old lady in a nursing home. A duty call. And then you find out that she's a person. She's *somebody.*
>
> Robert Cormier, "The Moustache"

Use sentence connectives sparingly and carefully. Be sure that the connective you use shows the appropriate relationship between your ideas.

EXERCISE 1 ▶ Varying Sentence Beginnings

Here's a chance to practice varying sentence beginnings. Revise each sentence so that it begins with an appositive or with a single-word, phrase, or clause modifier.

ASSESSMENT

Students' performances on **Exercises 1–5** should help you assess mastery of the material of this chapter. However, evaluating students' writing will give an even clearer picture of their sentence style.

CLOSURE

Ask students to help you list the three revision techniques to improve sentence style that this chapter explains.

☞

1. Michael Jordan, one of the most exciting players in the National Basketball Association, is the leading scorer for the Chicago Bulls.
2. He darts aggressively past defensive players and scores basket after basket.
3. Jordan practiced hard to become the star he is today.
4. Jordan had to work to overcome a lack of self-confidence as a teenager, although today he radiates self-assurance.
5. Jordan, self-conscious and shy, began playing sports with the hope of becoming more popular.
6. He was embarrassed by his awkwardness and rarely dated in high school.
7. He chose to attend the University of North Carolina and was determined to succeed in a major college basketball program.
8. Jordan was named All-American Player and College Player of the Year during his years at the University of North Carolina.
9. Jordan acknowledges that his knowledge and ability seemed to come together at the pro level, although his college career was outstanding.
10. Jordan, smiling happily, agrees that he has traveled a long way from his days as a gawky teenager.

Varying Sentence Structure

When you revise your writing for style, it isn't always enough to vary your sentence beginnings. It's also important to vary your sentence structures. That means using a mix of simple, compound, complex (and sometimes compound-complex) sentences.

☞ **REFERENCE NOTE:** For information about the four types of sentence structures, see pages 686–687.

ANSWERS
Exercise 1

1. One of the most exciting players in the National Basketball Association, Michael Jordan is the leading scorer for the Chicago Bulls.
2. Darting aggressively past defensive players, he scores basket after basket.
3. To become the star he is today, Jordan practiced hard.
4. Although today he radiates self-confidence, Jordan had to work to overcome a lack of self-confidence as a teenager.
5. Self-conscious and shy, Jordan began playing sports with the hope of becoming more popular.
6. Embarrassed by his awkwardness, he rarely dated in high school.
7. Determined to succeed in a major college basketball program, he chose to attend the University of North Carolina.
8. During his years at the University of North Carolina, Jordan was named an All-American Player and College Player of the Year.
9. Although his college career was outstanding, Jordan acknowledges that his knowledge and ability seemed to come together at the pro level.
10. Smiling happily, Jordan agrees that he has traveled a long way from his days as a gawky teenager.

585

EXTENSION

You might have each student bring in a factual news article and a human-interest story from a newspaper to compare the kinds of sentences and the variety in sentence structures that are used in each article. Students might also evaluate the word choices of the writers based on purpose and audience. ■

MEETING *individual* NEEDS

LEP/ESL

General Strategies. Your English-language learners will benefit greatly from **Exercise 5** if it is assigned as a small-group activity. This format allows students to dialogue with their peers by using English. Once all groups have completed the exercise, call upon students from each group to describe how they have made the sentences more succinct. Write suggested revisions on the chalkboard and encourage class discussion. Is this the only way to improve the sentence? The best way? Is there a best way? Why or why not? Try to include students in the discussion as much as possible.

COOPERATIVE LEARNING

You might have students work in groups of three on any of the exercises. **Exercises 1, 2,** and **5** will lend themselves well to collaborative discussions on the different ways each student within a group might revise the sentences or paragraphs.

---

586   *Improving Sentence Style*

Read the following short paragraph, which contains only simple sentences.

> Quasars are the brightest, most distant objects in the sky. For decades they have puzzled and intrigued astronomers. Quasars may hold important clues to the birth and formation of galaxies. Astronomers believe this. Astronomers first observed quasars in 1963. Since then, they have discovered over one thousand of these objects. With the help of two segmented-mirror telescopes in Hawaii, astronomers hope to discover the power source of quasars. Some astronomers believe that giant black holes produce the energy.

Now, read the revised version of the paragraph. Notice how the writer has made the paragraph smoother by including a variety of sentence structures.

> Quasars are the brightest, most distant objects in the sky. For decades they have puzzled and intrigued astronomers, who believe quasars may hold important clues to the birth and formation of galaxies. Astronomers first observed quasars in 1963, and since then, they have discovered over one thousand of these objects. With the help of two segmented-mirror telescopes in Hawaii, astronomers hope to discover the power source of quasars, which some scientists believe to be giant black holes.

Complex sentences do more than add variety to your writing. They also help bring your thoughts into focus by emphasizing main ideas and subordinating less important ones. For example, in the revised paragraph, notice how the complex sentence at the end makes a clearer connection between the last two ideas. As a subordinate clause, the information about the potential source of the quasars' energy indicates the objects in the universe that the scientists will be studying.

☞ **REFERENCE NOTE:** For more about subordinating ideas in sentences, see pages 544–548 and 574–577.

EXERCISE 2 ▶ **Varying Sentence Structure**

The writer of the following paragraph wants to make an important point, but too many simple sentences make the writing sound dull. Improve the paragraph by varying the structure of the sentences. You can add, delete, or rearrange words.

I learned recently that companies can pay filmmakers to display name-brand products in films. I was shocked. Commercials shown before a feature film are annoying. Ads sneaked into the films themselves are downright unethical, though. People go to the movies expecting to enjoy a commercial-free film. They see an actor eating Brand X pizza or wearing Brand Y jeans. At the time, they don't realize that they are watching a paid advertisement. Filmmakers have a responsibility to make their audiences aware of these ads. They shouldn't have to interrupt a film to identify an ad. They should be required to list the advertisers in the credits.

ANSWERS
Exercise 2

Paragraphs may vary. Here is a possibility:
   I was shocked when I learned recently that companies can pay filmmakers to display name-brand products in their films. Commercials shown before a feature film are annoying, but ads sneaked into the films themselves are downright unethical. People go to the movies expecting to enjoy a commercial-free film. When they see an actor eating Brand X pizza or wearing Brand Y jeans, they don't realize they are watching a paid advertisement. Filmmakers have a responsibility to make their audiences aware of these ads. They shouldn't have to interrupt to identify an ad, but they should be required to list the advertisers in the credits.

A DIFFERENT APPROACH
Students could check for sentence variety in their own writing by using alternate colored markers to circle the beginning of each sentence. Also, they could put parentheses around repeated words and phrases. Students should then make revisions on the drafts they have colored.

TECHNOLOGY TIP
Remind students that they can change the line spacing and margins after they have typed their drafts. The usual procedure is to select all of the text in the document and make the changes through menu items or by using shortcut keys.

587

ANSWERS
Review A

Paragraphs may vary. Here is a possibility:
A gifted African American playwright, Lorraine Hansberry earned international acclaim for her work. She won the New York Drama Critics' Circle Award for her play, *A Raisin in the Sun,* the first African American playwright to do so. The story of an African American family and of each member's frustration in realizing a dream, the play demonstrates Hansberry's talent for describing social conflict and for portraying complex human relationships.

CRITICAL THINKING

Synthesis. Because models might help students see the folly of inflated diction, have your class read Russell Baker's "Little Red Riding Hood Revisited" or a similar spoof from your literature textbook. Then challenge your students to incorporate inflated diction to write their own satires. They could rewrite a folktale, an article from the school paper, or any other work.

COMPUTER NOTE: When you print out a draft to revise, use double or triple line spacing and wide margins to allow room for handwritten corrections. When you print a final copy, remember to reset the spacing and margins.

REVIEW A ▶ Varying Sentence Beginnings and Sentence Structure

Using what you've learned about varying sentence beginnings and sentence structure, revise the following paragraph for style. Add, delete, and rearrange words wherever necessary to make the sentences more varied. Be careful to keep the original meaning of the paragraph.

Lorraine Hansberry, a gifted African American playwright, earned international acclaim for her work. She won the New York Drama Critics' Circle Award for her play, A Raisin in the Sun. She was the first African American playwright to win this award. The play demonstrates Hansberry's talent for describing social conflict and for portraying complex human emotions and relationships. It tells the story of an African American family and of each member's frustration in realizing a dream.

Revising to Reduce Wordiness

Don't make the mistake of thinking that the more words you use, the better your writing will sound. Extra words don't improve your style; they just get in your reader's way. Your writing is most effective when it is clear and concise—that is, free of the clutter of unnecessary words.

To avoid wordiness, keep these three points in mind.

- Use only the words you need to make your point.
- Avoid complicated words where simple ones will do.
- Don't repeat words unless it's absolutely necessary.

Sometimes you can fix a wordy sentence by taking out whole groups of unnecessary words. At other times you can revise by reducing clauses to phrases and both clauses and phrases to single words.

Eliminating Unnecessary Words

The following paragraph about computer viruses is an example of wordy writing. Lines have been drawn through the unnecessary words. First, read the paragraph aloud with the crossed-through words left in. Then, read the shorter, more concise version. Notice the difference the revisions make in the sound of the paragraph.

> In the 1980s computer experts became aware of a dangerous type of program called a computer virus. A computer virus ~~by its very nature~~ is designed to alter or destroy data and to copy itself into other programs in the same computer or in other computers. Sometimes a virus removes and deletes information, and sometimes it simply inserts a message. Some mischievous programmers ~~who like to play jokes~~ design computer viruses as a joke ~~or a prank~~. Their type of virus might cause a humorous message to appear ~~in a funny way~~ on a computer's screen. However, some people design viruses ~~with the intent~~ to deliberately destroy data. In one well-publicized 1988 incident ~~that made all the newspapers~~, a computer virus crippled sixty thousand computers in a research network ~~in a matter of hours~~ overnight. Since the emergence of computer viruses, the U.S. government has passed strict laws making it illegal to introduce viruses into the computers of unwitting users ~~when they are not aware of it~~.

Following are some more examples of how less can be more when it comes to sentences. Can you see other ways in which the sentences might have been revised to reduce the wordiness?

WORDY   The game is played with tiny, little round balls that, in my opinion, I think, are made of steel.

BETTER   The game is played with tiny balls that, I think, are made of steel.

WORDY   Far away at a great distance, the small, diminutive shapes of the campers' tents were outlined in silhouette against the dark night sky.

BETTER   Far away, the small shapes of the campers' tents were outlined against the night sky.

INTEGRATING THE LANGUAGE ARTS

Listening Link. You may want to point out one of the main differences between the sentence styles of spoken and written language. Written language is more likely to include a long introductory phrase or clause before the main verb of a sentence. For example, the following sentences are characteristic of written and spoken language respectively:

1. Crossing the street at the corner, she then hurriedly walked down the hill.
2. She crossed the street at the corner, and then she walked quickly down the hill.

Write the two sentences on the chalkboard and ask students to determine which one they might read and which one they might hear. Explain that in first drafts writers often write material that mirrors speech. When revising, however, writers can change and combine sentences to create an effective and interesting style.

EXERCISE 3 ▶ Revising Wordy Sentences

For each of the following sentences, ask: Does it have any unnecessary words? Does it repeat any ideas? If you answer "yes" to either of these questions, revise the sentence to reduce the wordiness. If a sentence is already concise, write C.

1. Most people have heard of William Shakespeare, the man many people call the greatest writer of all time.
2. Even though Shakespeare is famous throughout the world everywhere, we can't be certain about his physical appearance—that is, what he looked like.
3. From the portraits of Shakespeare that have survived and withstood the passage of time, he appears to have been a slim man of slight build and average height.
4. Artists rendered Shakespeare with well-proportioned features and expressive eyes.
5. Although we may never learn more about Shakespeare the man himself, we can continue to learn and gain information about Shakespeare the writer by studying his magnificent works.

EXERCISE 4 ▶ Revising a Paragraph by Eliminating Unnecessary Words

Revise the following paragraph to make it more concise. Eliminate unnecessary words, keeping the original meaning of each sentence. [Note: You may need to change some verb forms, too.]

Few athletes earn lasting reputations that endure outside the realm of sports. However, athlete and baseball player Roberto Clemente is remembered not only as a skilled athlete but also as a compassionate human being. A lifelong opponent of injustice and unfairness, Clemente, who was from Puerto Rico, fought prejudice in the major leagues and in every part of his life. In 1972 Clemente died in an accident in a plane crash on his way to help deliver supplies to the victims of a terrible, horrible earthquake in Nicaragua. His courage and bravery live on in the memories of his fans, who still think of him.

Reducing Groups of Words

Writing concisely means using only as many words as you need. You don't want to leave out words that clarify your meaning or add interest to your sentences. However, you do want to make sure that every word counts. The charts on this page and the next page give some examples of how you can trim away excess words from your writing.

CLAUSES REDUCED TO PHRASES

CLAUSE	**When they were trapped by a cave-in,** the miners waited for rescuers.
PARTICIPIAL PHRASE	**Trapped by a cave-in,** the miners waited for rescuers.
CLAUSE	We decided **that we would get an early start.**
INFINITIVE PHRASE	We decided **to get an early start.**
CLAUSE	The teams **that had come from Missouri** were not scheduled to play the first day of the tournament.
PREPOSITIONAL PHRASE	The teams **from Missouri** were not scheduled to play the first day of the tournament.
CLAUSE	Her two dogs, **one of which is a collie and the other a spaniel,** perform different duties on the farm.
APPOSITIVE PHRASE	Her two dogs, **a collie and a spaniel,** perform different duties on the farm.

ANSWERS
Exercise 4

Paragraphs may vary. Here is a possibility:

Few athletes earn lasting reputations outside the realm of sports. However, baseball player Roberto Clemente is remembered not only as a skilled athlete but also as a compassionate human being. A lifelong opponent of injustice, Clemente, who was from Puerto Rico, fought prejudice in the major leagues and in every other part of his life. In 1972, Clemente died in a plane crash on his way to help deliver supplies to the victims of a terrible earthquake in Nicaragua. His courage lives on in the memories of his fans.

PART TWO

HANDBOOK

GRAMMAR

USAGE

MECHANICS

PART TWO: HANDBOOK

The following **Teaching Resources** booklets contain materials that may be used with this part of the Pupil's Edition.

- *Language Skills Practice and Assessment*
- *Practice for Assessment in Reading, Vocabulary, and Spelling* (for Ch. 31)

GRAMMAR

GRAMMAR

GRAMMAR

Liter...

poem...

noun...

"Prelu...

the e...

abstr...

and f...

poem...

have...

stude...

place...

conc...

that...

their...

expe...

evoki...

ANS

Exerc...

1. *do*
   co

2. *la*
   co
   co
   ey
   ab

3. *sa*
   co
   co
   co
   C
   Z
   co

4. co
   co
   co

5. *si*
   co
   ab
   co
   co

MEETING *individual* NEEDS

LEP/ESL

Japanese. There are no definite or indefinite articles in Japanese. Consequently, students might omit *a, an,* and *the* from their speech and writing. If this has been happening, review the material on articles thoroughly with students. Then give them paragraphs from which articles have been deleted and have the students insert the appropriate articles.

602

606

GRAMMAR

606 *The Parts of Speech*

The Adjective

17c. An *adjective* is a word used to modify a noun or a pronoun.

To modify means "to describe or to make more definite." Adjectives modify nouns or pronouns by telling *what kind, which one,* or *how many (how much).*

WHAT KIND?	**ripe** apples **blue** sky	**happy** child **loud** music
WHICH ONE?	**this** book **those** girls	**last** straw **next** step
HOW MANY?	**two** students **several** choices	**both** answers **many** people
HOW MUCH?	**some** news **more** money	**enough** time **less** trouble

An adjective usually precedes the word it modifies.

EXAMPLE   The **tired** and **hungry** hikers straggled into camp.

For emphasis, however, a writer may place an adjective after the word it modifies.

EXAMPLE   The hikers, **tired** and **hungry,** straggled into camp.

A *predicate adjective* is separated from the word it modifies by a linking verb.

EXAMPLES   The hikers were **hungry** and **tired.**
The hikers felt **hungry** and **tired.**

☞ REFERENCE NOTE: See pages 642–643 for more information about predicate adjectives. For guidelines on using adjectives, see Chapter 25.

Articles

The most frequently used adjectives are *a, an,* and *the.* These words are called *articles.*

A and *an* are ***indefinite articles;*** they refer to *any* one of a general group. *A* is used before words beginning with a consonant sound; *an* is used before words beginning with a vowel sound.

EXAMPLES   Felipe added **a** tomato and **an** avocado to the salad.
It's **an** honor to be here.

Notice in the second example above that *an* is used before *honor* because the *h* in *honor* is not pronounced; *honor* is pronounced as though it began with a vowel. Remember that the *sound* of the noun, not the spelling, determines which indefinite article to use.

The is the ***definite article.*** It specifies a particular person, place, thing, or idea.

EXAMPLE   We spent **the** hour discussing **the** revolution of **the** slaves that began in 1791 in Haiti.

Adjective or Pronoun?

In different contexts, a word may be used as different parts of speech. For example, the following words may be used as adjectives or as pronouns.

all	either	much	some	what
another	few	neither	that	which
any	many	one	these	whose
both	more	other	this	
each	most	several	those	

Remember that an adjective *modifies* a noun and that a pronoun *takes the place of* a noun.

ADJECTIVE   **These** books are overdue. [*These* modifies the noun *books.*]

PRONOUN   **These** are overdue. [*These* takes the place of the noun *books.*]

ADJECTIVE   Ntozake Shange wrote **both** poems. [*Both* modifies the noun *poems.*]

PRONOUN   Ntozake Shange wrote **both.** [*Both* takes the place of the noun *poems.*]

INTEGRATING THE LANGUAGE ARTS

Grammar and Writing. Have each student write a one-page expressive/descriptive paper that includes many adjectives. Tell students that their objective is to let their readers see, smell, touch, hear, and taste whatever they're describing. When they have finished, have them circle each adjective and draw an arrow from it to the word it modifies.

607

NOTE: In this book the words *my, your, his, her, its, our,* and *their* are called possessive pronouns. Since they precede nouns and tell *which one* or *whose,* some teachers prefer to call these words possessive adjectives.

EXAMPLES   **my** job, **your** essay, **their** plans

Follow your teacher's instructions in labeling these words.

Nouns Used as Adjectives

Nouns are sometimes used as adjectives.

NOUNS	NOUNS USED AS ADJECTIVES
sofa	**sofa** cushion
hotel	**hotel** lobby
taco	**taco** salad
high school	**high school** senior
Marine Corps	**Marine Corps** cadet

NOTE: Remember that some pairs of nouns form compound nouns.

EXAMPLES   paper clips, cable TV, time capsule, goal line

▶ **EXERCISE 4**   **Identifying Adjectives and the Words They Modify**

Identify the <u>adjectives</u> and the <u>words they modify</u> in the following paragraph. Do not include articles (*a, an,* and *the*).

[1] <u>William Least Heat-Moon's</u> <u>first</u> <u>book</u>, *Blue Highways,* chronicled <u>his</u> journey across the <u>United States</u> in 1978. [2] <u>That</u> <u>book</u> attracted <u>many</u> <u>readers</u> and even made the <u>bestseller</u> <u>lists</u>. [3] In *PrairyErth,* Heat-Moon narrows his focus to a <u>single</u> <u>Kansas</u> <u>county</u>. [4] The <u>book's</u> <u>unusual</u> <u>title</u> comes from the <u>short-hand</u> <u>term</u> scientists use for the <u>unique</u> <u>soils</u> of the <u>nation's</u> <u>central</u> <u>states</u>. [5] Chase County lies in east <u>central</u> <u>Kansas</u>. [6] It is, as Heat-Moon says, "the most <u>easterly</u> <u>piece</u> of the American <u>Far West</u>." [7] A county with a population of 3,013 may seem an <u>unlikely</u> <u>location</u> for an examination of <u>humans'</u> <u>place</u> on <u>this</u> <u>planet</u>. [8] After all, the county has only <u>two</u> <u>towns</u> and

---

EXERCISE 4

Teaching Note. Before students begin this exercise, you may want to discuss with them the fact that possessive nouns function as adjectives. Give students the following examples of possessive nouns used as adjectives:

1. *Faulkner's* home is in Mississippi.
2. The *car's* tire was flat.

Point out that in sentences 1 and 3 of **Exercise 4,** the possessive pronoun *his* could be correctly identified as an adjective.

In sentence 1, *Blue Highways* is a compound noun.

608

REVIEW A

OBJECTIVES
- To identify words in sentences as nouns, pronouns, or adjectives
- To identify the words that adjectives modify

a few villages. [9] In many ways, though, Kansas is a microcosm of America. [10] And in Heat-Moon's proficient hands, Chase County reveals itself to be a microcosm of Kansas.

GRAMMAR

REVIEW A ▸ **Identifying Nouns, Pronouns, and Adjectives**

Identify each italicized word in the following sentences as a *noun*, a *pronoun*, or an *adjective*. If a word is an adjective, give the word it modifies.

EXAMPLE   **1.** *Everyone* in class is writing a poem about an *American* pioneer.
1. *Everyone—pronoun; American—adjective—pioneer*

1. Several students are writing *theirs* about people whose names are familiar to *many;* others have chosen people who they believe merit wider recognition.
2. After *much* thought, I have finally narrowed my choices to two *African American* women whom I admire.
3. Both of *these* women broke *new* ground in their fields—one in the performing arts and the other in the visual arts.
4. The fieldwork *that* Katherine Dunham (right) did as an anthropology student in the West Indies inspired her to incorporate elements of African and Caribbean folk culture into *modern dance.*
5. After touring the world for *several* decades, the dancer and choreographer founded the Katherine Dunham Children's Workshop in *East St. Louis,* Illinois, which she still directs.

REVIEW A

Teaching Note. You may want to remind students to check a dictionary to distinguish between compound nouns and phrases consisting of a noun and an adjective.

GRAMMAR

VISUAL CONNECTIONS
Exploring the Subject. Katherine Dunham was born on June 22, 1910, in Joliet, Illinois, near Chicago. A dancer, choreographer, anthropologist, lecturer, and writer, Dunham could accurately be called a Renaissance woman. As an anthropologist, Dunham studied the roots of African American culture, and as a performer, she interpreted primitive dance in the black dance troupe she formed. Her company, the first black dance troupe of concert caliber, toured the United States and Europe.

WRITING APPLICATION

OBJECTIVES

- To write a paragraph proposing coined words for things that exist but that have no names or are misnamed
- To give the derivation, use, and part of speech for each newly coined word

610 *The Parts of Speech*

6. Tributes to Dunham, [*who*] is now in her eighties, continue to pour in; for she is considered a true *dance* innovator.
7. My other *potential* choice is Barbara Brandon, who in 1991 became the first African American woman cartoonist to achieve syndication in the *mainstream* press.
8. As you can see below, Brandon's *cartoon* strip depicts life from the *perspective* of an African American woman.
9. Brandon pictures only the heads and, occasionally, the hands of her characters, [*all*] of whom are women; for she believes that women's bodies are displayed enough in the *media*.
10. As [*you*] might guess, *my* final *choice* of a subject will not be an easy one. **10.** *or* [my]

Where I'm Coming From copyright 1991 Barbara Brandon.
Reprinted with permission of Universal Press Syndicate. All

VISUAL CONNECTIONS

About the Artwork. In her cartoon strip *Where I'm Coming From,* Barbara Brandon addresses issues of racism and sexism. She explores themes ranging from the universal (female-male relations) to the mundane (doing the laundry). Her aim is to record her experience as an African American woman in the United States.

WRITING APPLICATION

Tell students that although the English language has a large vocabulary, it does not have a word for everything. For example, there is no English equivalent for the Italian word *culacino,* which refers to the ring left on a table by a glass, or for the German word *schadenfreude,* which means "taking delight in the misfortunes of others."

If you have English-language learners in your class, ask them if their languages contain words for which there are no equivalents in English.

610

WRITING APPLICATION

Creating a Dictionary of New Words

There are over 450,000 words in the English language, yet we still don't have a word for everything. What, for instance, do you call your former best friend? or the feeling you have when a word is on the tip of your tongue but you can't quite remember it? What's more, many words in our language seem ill-suited to the things they stand for. For example, why do we drive on parkways and park in driveways? Fortunately for us, our language is readily open to change and adopts new words all the time to meet the needs of those who use it.

WRITING ACTIVITY

For a school project, you and your classmates have decided to create a dictionary of words that should exist but don't. Write a complete dictionary entry proposing a name for something that doesn't have one or that you think could be more aptly named. Give the new word's derivation, use, and part of speech.

Prewriting Use observation, brainstorming, or freewriting to come up with situations, things, places, thoughts, feelings, and qualities that could benefit from a new word. Then choose the one that appeals to you the most and create a word for it. Next, think of the information you will need for your dictionary entry. How is your new word spelled and pronounced? What is its part of speech, and what other forms does it have? What is the word's derivation? its definition(s)? (For more information about the content and form of dictionary entries, see pages 1070–1071.)

Writing Refer to your prewriting notes often as you write your first draft. Don't be concerned about using complete sentences. Consider including an example sentence that gives the word in context.

Evaluating and Revising As you reread your dictionary entry, check to make sure that your organization and tone are appropriate for a dictionary entry. Compare your entry with the sample one found on page 1070. Make any changes that you think will improve your entry.

Proofreading and Publishing Proofread your dictionary entry carefully. You and your classmates may want to gather together all of your dictionary entries and photocopy them or input them on a computer. The entries could then be alphabetized to create a new-word dictionary, which could be photocopied for the entire class.

CRITICAL THINKING

Synthesis. You may want to discuss with students some ways in which new words are commonly formed:

1. compound words—compact disc, roller skates, surfboard
2. blended words—smog (smoke + fog), brunch (breakfast + lunch), motel (motor + hotel)
3. acronyms—radar (radio detecting and ranging), laser (light amplification by stimulated emission of radiation)

Have students use each of these methods to form new words. This activity could be done individually or in small groups.

COOPERATIVE LEARNING

Have students work in groups of three or four to write paragraphs that include words from the class's new-word dictionary. Paragraphs can be on any topic, and new words can be adapted to conform to grammatical rules. For example, new words that are verbs can be conjugated. The groups could compete to see whose paragraph includes the most new words.

OBJECTIVES

- To identify and classify verbs (including verb phrases) as transitive, intransitive, or linking
- To rewrite a dialogue by replacing general verbs with specific ones
- To identify adverbs and the words they modify

The Verb

17d. A *verb* is a word used to express action or a state of being.

Action Verbs

An *action verb* expresses physical or mental activity.

PHYSICAL	speak	sleep	carry	give
MENTAL	think	imagine	dream	believe

(1) A *transitive verb* is an action verb that takes an *object*—a noun or a pronoun that tells *who* or *what* receives the action.

EXAMPLES The rain **lashed** the windows. [*Windows* receives the action of *lashed.*]
We **closed** and **bolted** the shutters. [*Shutters* receives the action of *closed* and *bolted.*]

(2) An *intransitive verb* is an action verb that doesn't take an object.

EXAMPLES The rain **fell.**
My cousin **arrived** before the rain **began.**

Most English verbs can be either transitive or intransitive, depending on the context of the sentence.

EXAMPLES The chorus **sang** patriotic songs. [transitive]
The chorus **sang** beautifully. [intransitive]

NOTE: Most dictionaries group the definitions of verbs according to whether the verbs are used transitively (marked *v.t.* in most dictionaries) or intransitively (*v.i.*).

Linking Verbs

A *linking verb* is a verb that connects the subject with a noun, a pronoun, or an adjective that describes or identifies the subject. The word that is linked to the subject is called the *subject complement.*

PROGRAM MANAGER

THE VERB AND THE ADVERB

- **Independent Practice/ Reteaching** For instruction and exercises, see **Verbs and Verb Phrases** and **Adverbs** in *Language Skills Practice and Assessment,* pp. 15–16.

- **Computer Guided Instruction** For additional instruction and practice with verbs and adverbs, see **Lesson 2** in *Language Workshop CD-ROM.*

- **Practice** To help less-advanced students with additional instruction and practice with verbs and adverbs, see **Chapter 10** in *English Workshop, Complete Course,* pp. 131–134.

QUICK REMINDER

Write the following incomplete sentences on the chalkboard:

1. The '69 Chevy _____ into the garage.
2. The roses _____ lovely.
3. The deer _____ the fence.
4. George _____ sleepily.
5. Their teacher _____ also a poet.

Ask the students to complete each sentence by adding an appropriate verb, to label each verb as action or linking, and to label action verbs as transitive or intransitive.

EXAMPLES Marcy **looks** serious.
[*Serious* describes the subject *Marcy*.]

Wovoka **was** an influential Paiute prophet.
[*Prophet* identifies the subject *Wovoka*.]

👉 **REFERENCE NOTE:** For more about subject complements, see pages 642–643.

NOTE: Linking verbs are sometimes called *state-of-being verbs* because they help make a statement about the subject's condition, or state of being.

COMMON LINKING VERBS

FORMS OF *BE*

am	be	will be	had been
is	can be	could be	shall have been
are	may be	should be	will have been
was	might be	would be	could have been
were	must be	has been	should have been
being	shall be	have been	would have been

OTHERS

appear	grow	seem	stay
become	look	smell	taste
feel	remain	sound	turn

NOTE: The forms of *be* are not considered linking verbs when they're followed by words that tell *where* or *when*.

EXAMPLE You should have been **here yesterday.** [*Here* tells *where*, and *yesterday* tells *when*.]

Some of the other verbs listed above can be either linking verbs or action verbs, depending on the context of the sentence.

LINKING The alarm **sounded** shrill.
ACTION I **sounded** the alarm.

To determine whether a verb is a linking verb or an action verb, substitute a form of *be* or *seem*. If the sentence still makes sense, the verb is probably a linking verb.

LINKING The fabric **felt** soft. [*The fabric was soft* makes sense.]
ACTION I **felt** the fabric. [*I was the fabric* doesn't make sense.]

The Verb Phrase

A *verb phrase* consists of a main verb and at least one *helping verb* (also called an *auxiliary verb*).

EXAMPLES   has played [*Has* is a helping verb; *played* is the main verb.]

will be going [*Will* and *be* are helping verbs; *going* is the main verb.]

COMMON HELPING VERBS			
Forms of *be*	am were is	be are being	was been
Forms of *have*	has	have	had
Forms of *do*	do	does	did
Others	may might must	can shall will	could should would

A helping verb may be separated from the main verb.

EXAMPLES   **Have** you **seen** Lorraine Hansberry's play *A Raisin in the Sun?*

You **should** not **miss** it.

☞ **REFERENCE NOTE:** The word *not* and its contraction, *–n't,* are adverbs telling *to what extent;* they are never part of a verb phrase. See pages 616–617 for more information about adverbs.

▶ EXERCISE 5   **Identifying and Classifying Verbs and Verb Phrases**

Identify the verbs and verb phrases in the following sentences. Then classify each verb or verb phrase as *transitive, intransitive,* or *linking.*

                                                   1. link./link.   2. tr./tr./tr.

1. The Statue of Liberty, which has become a major American landmark, may be the best-known structure in the world.

2. It possesses a twofold appeal: It symbolizes human liberty, and it unfailingly awes the visitor by its colossal size.

3. Moreover, it has withstood the continuous assaults of time and weather. **3. tr.**

4. Although Frédéric Auguste Bartholdi <u>designed</u> the statue, the supporting framework <u>came</u> from the drawing board of Alexandre Gustave Eiffel. **4. tr./itr.**
5. The copper-plated statue <u>has</u> an intricate iron framework that <u>supports</u> Liberty's familiar pose. **5. tr./tr. 6. link./tr.**
6. The statue itself <u>was</u> a gift from the people of France, but Americans <u>paid</u> the construction costs for the pedestal.
7. In newspaper editorials, Joseph Pulitzer <u>persuaded</u> the American people that they <u>needed</u> the statue. **7. tr./tr.**
8. The people <u>agreed</u>, and in 1886 the nation <u>celebrated</u> the dedication of the Statue of Liberty on what <u>was</u> then <u>named</u> Bedloe's Island in Upper New York Bay. **8. itr./tr./tr.**
9. Bartholdi <u>modeled</u> Liberty's face after his mother's features. **9. tr.**
10. Those features (*left,* before the mid-1980s restoration; and *right,* after) <u>have remained</u> symbols of quiet determination. **10. link.**

▶ EXERCISE 6   **Replacing General Verbs with Specific Ones**

Rewrite the following dialogue twice, replacing each italicized verb with two more specific ones to create two different conversations.

1. "Let's *go* downtown after school," said Frank.
2. "I can't," said Aldo. "Tonight's the night I *cook*."
3. "Oh, yeah? What *are* you *making*?"
4. "It's one of my original concoctions; you should *try* it!"
5. "In that case, I have just one more question: When *are* you *serving*?"

GRAMMAR

INTEGRATING THE LANGUAGE ARTS

Grammar and Writing. Have students bring to class compositions they are writing for this or another class. If students are not writing anything at present, they could bring in old papers. Then have students identify all of the verbs in their writing. Tell students to evaluate each verb and to replace overused, dull, and unspecific verbs with interesting, specific ones.

GRAMMAR

ANSWERS
Exercise 6

Responses will vary. Here are some possibilities:

1. drive, stroll
2. bake, jam (play music)
3. are creating, are composing
4. sample, experience
5. are dining, are playing

COOPERATIVE LEARNING

Students often overuse weak adverbs such as *very* and *really,* especially in conjunction with the verb *be,* as in "I am very happy."

Have students work in groups of three or four to compile lists of weak adverbs. Lists might include *very, really,* and *pretty.* Groups can then generate lists of adverbs that could be used to replace the weak ones. Students can refer to their lists during the evaluating and revising stages of the writing process and replace weak adverbs with more effective choices.

The Adverb

17e. An *adverb* is a word used to modify a verb, an adjective, or another adverb.

Most adverbs modify by telling *how, when, where,* or *to what extent.* Adverbs are most commonly used to modify verbs and verb phrases.

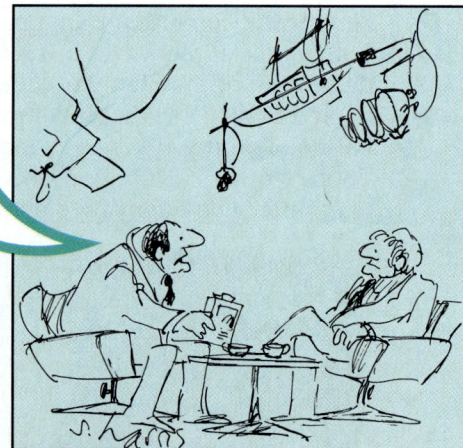

"I've just read your latest book and found it fast moving, full of suspense, and very well written. You're probably just the person who could clear up something that's been puzzling me for years. What's an adverb?"

© 1993 Sidney Harris.

EXAMPLES   She reads **quickly.** [*how*]
She reads **early** and **late.** [*when*]
She reads **everywhere.** [*where*]
She reads **thoroughly.** [*to what extent*]

Adverbs may modify adjectives.

EXAMPLES   She is **quite** creative. [The adverb *quite* modifies the adjective *creative,* telling *to what extent.*]
This species is found on an **extremely** remote island. [The adverb *extremely* modifies the adjective *remote,* telling *to what extent.*]

Adverbs may also modify other adverbs.

EXAMPLES   Florence Griffith-Joyner runs **remarkably** swiftly. [The adverb *remarkably* modifies the adverb *swiftly,* telling *to what extent.*]
It's **too** soon to know the results. [The adverb *too* modifies the adverb *soon,* telling *to what extent.*]

NOTE: The word *not* and its contraction, *–n't,* are classified as adverbs; they tell *to what extent.*

17e

Nouns Used as Adverbs

Some nouns may be used as adverbs.

EXAMPLES **My parents left yesterday.** [The noun *yesterday* is used as an adverb, telling *when.*]
They will return home Saturday. [The noun *home* is used as an adverb, telling *where.* The noun *Saturday* is used as an adverb, telling *when.*]

In identifying parts of speech, label a noun used in this way as an adverb.

👉 **REFERENCE NOTE:** For guidelines on using adverbs, see Chapter 25.

▶ EXERCISE 7 **Identifying Adverbs and the Words They Modify**

Identify the adverbs and the words they modify in the following sentences. Be prepared to tell whether each adverb tells *how, when, where,* or *to what extent.*

1. American physicist Rosalyn Yalow helped develop an extremely sensitive biological technique.
2. Radioimmunoassay, which is now used in laboratories worldwide, readily detects antibodies and hormones.
3. Yalow realized that anyone who proposes a distinctly new idea must always anticipate that it will not likely be readily accepted at first.
4. In other words, most scientists do not leap excitedly from the bath crying "Eureka!" as Archimedes supposedly did.
5. Yalow and her colleague discovered radioimmunoassay accidentally while observing two patients.
6. After they carefully interpreted their observations, they arrived at their exciting discovery.
7. In 1977, though Yalow's collaborator had died, the Nobel Prize Committee awarded Yalow the undeniably prestigious Nobel Prize for medicine.
8. Radioimmunoassay eventually became a basic diagnostic tool in widely different areas of medicine.
9. According to Yalow, the technique was not quickly accepted because people ordinarily resist change.
10. She believes that progress can not be impeded forever and that good ideas are eventually accepted.

ANSWERS
Exercise 7
1. extemely—sensitive—extent
2. now—is used—when
   worldwide—is used—where
   readily—detects—how
3. distinctly—new—extent
   always—must anticipate—when
   not—likely—extent
   likely—will be accepted—extent
   readily—will be accepted—how
4. not—do leap—extent
   excitedly—do leap—how
   supposedly—did—how
5. accidentally—discovered—how
6. carefully—interpreted—how
7. undeniably—prestigious—extent
8. eventually—became—when
   widely—different—extent
9. not—quickly—extent
   quickly—was accepted—how
   ordinarily—resist—how
10. not—can be impeded—extent
    forever—can be impeded—when
    eventually—are accepted—when

OBJECTIVES
- To identify the parts of speech of words in a passage
- To identify the words that adjectives and adverbs modify

GRAMMAR

618 *The Parts of Speech*

GRAMMAR

REVIEW B   Identifying Parts of Speech

Identify the part of speech of each <u>italicized word</u> in the following paragraphs. Tell what <u>word or words each adjective or adverb modifies</u>.   n. = noun   pro. = pronoun   adj. = adjective
v. = verb   adv. = adverb

1. adv./v.
2. adj./pro.
3. pro./adv.
4. adj./n.
5. adv./pro.
6. n./v.
7. pro. [or adj.]/n.
8. pro./pro.
9. adj./adj.
10. pro./n.

[1] Diego Rivera is *chiefly* <u>famous</u> for his murals, but he was a prolific artist who *worked* in a wide variety of styles. [2] *This* <u>landscape</u> is an example of his early work; *it* was painted in 1904. [3] Rivera, *who* was born in Guanajuato, Mexico, in 1886, entered the San Carlos Academy of Fine Arts in Mexico City when he was *only* <u>eleven</u>. [4] In 1907, with the proceeds from his first *art* <u>show</u>, he made the *first* of several lengthy visits to Europe. [5] *There* he <u>experimented</u> with different approaches until he realized it was the fresco process, the art of painting on wet plaster, *that* best suited his artistic vision.

[6] *Two* of Rivera's lifelong interests *were* Mexican history and machinery. [7] *His* <u>murals</u> in the former palace of *Hernán Cortés* in Cuernavaca, in the state of Morelos, depict the history of Morelos from before the conquest by Spain until after the Mexican Revolution of 1910. [8] *One* of the works *that* Rivera created in the United States was a series of twenty-seven murals that the Detroit Arts Commission asked him to paint on subjects related to Detroit and the general theme of industrialization.

[9] <u>Rivera</u> was *controversial* in the United States because he included *political* <u>themes</u> in his work. [10] Ironically, capitalists attacked *him* for his affiliation with Communists, and Communists attacked him for accepting *commissions* from capitalists.

VISUAL CONNECTIONS

Ideas for Writing. Students might be interested in the fact that Rivera was only eighteen when he painted this work. Challenge them to use words to describe the scene depicted in the painting. Students should write an informative descriptive paragraph containing vivid verbs, adjectives, and adverbs to convey the mood evoked by the painting.

LESSON 4 (pp. 619–625)

THE PREPOSITION, THE CONJUNCTION, THE INTERJECTION, and THE SAME WORD AS DIFFERENT PARTS OF SPEECH Rules 17f–17i

OBJECTIVES

- To complete sentences by adding prepositional phrases
- To identify and classify conjunctions in sentences

17f

The Preposition

17f. A *preposition* is a word used to show how a noun or a pronoun is related to some other word in the sentence.

Notice how changing the preposition in the following examples changes the relationship between *swam* and *raft.*

I swam **to** the raft.
I swam **from** the raft.
I swam **around** the raft.
I swam **past** the raft.
I swam **under** the raft.

Object of a Preposition

The *object of a preposition* is a noun or a pronoun that follows a preposition. Together, the preposition, its object, and any modifiers of the object make a *prepositional phrase.*

EXAMPLES   before **lunch**   at the **game**   throughout the **week**

☞ **REFERENCE NOTE:** See pages 652–655 for more information on prepositional phrases.

Commonly Used Prepositions			
about	beside	in	through
above	besides	inside	throughout
across	between	into	to
after	beyond	like	toward
against	but (meaning	near	under
along	"except")	of	underneath
among	by	off	until
around	concerning	on	unto
at	down	out	up
before	during	outside	upon
behind	except	over	with
below	for	past	within
beneath	from	since	without

PROGRAM MANAGER

OTHER PARTS OF SPEECH

- **Independent Practice/ Reteaching** For instruction and exercises, see **Other Parts of Speech** and **Review of the Parts of Speech** in *Language Skills Practice and Assessment,* pp. 17–18.

- **Computer Guided Instruction** For additional instruction and practice with other parts of speech, see **Lessons 3** and **4** in *Language Workshop CD-ROM.*

- **Practice** To help less-advanced students with additional instruction and practice with other parts of speech, see **Chapter 10** in *English Workshop, Complete Course,* pp. 137–141.

QUICK REMINDER

Write the following sentence on the chalkboard. Have students identify the prepositions, the conjunctions, and the interjection in the sentence.

Yikes, Ratman, either jump in the Ratmobile or dive through that window, but don't just stand around.

GRAMMAR

LEP/ESL

Spanish. In Spanish, the equivalents of the verbs *learn, attend, marry, play,* and *leave,* as well as some others, are always followed by certain prepositions. Consequently, students may automatically insert prepositions when they are writing and speaking in English. If you find that students are consistently making mistakes of this kind, acknowledge and discuss the difference between Spanish and English on this point and offer extra practice.

ANSWERS

Exercise 8

Answers will vary. Here are some possibilities:

1. from foreign countries
2. After our shopping expedition
3. at the recreation center
4. In the park
5. across the living room
6. across the road; out of sight
7. in the audience
8. by the long trek; near a stream
9. During the meeting; next to the firehouse; into a storage facility
10. In spite of his reassurances; because of the storm

620

GRAMMAR

620   *The Parts of Speech*

NOTE: Some of the words in this list may also be used as adverbs. Keep in mind that an adverb is a modifier, and it does not take an object.

ADVERB	I'll meet you **outside** at noon. [*Outside* modifies ***meet.***]
PREPOSITION	I'll meet you **outside** the library. [*Outside* introduces a prepositional phrase ending with the object *library.*]

A preposition that consists of two or more words is a *compound preposition.*

EXAMPLES   Tena has been accepted by several private colleges **in addition to** both state universities.
As of today, she hasn't made her final choice.

Commonly Used Compound Prepositions

according to	because of	in spite of
along with	by means of	instead of
apart from	in addition to	next to
aside from	in front of	on account of
as of	in place of	out of

▶ EXERCISE 8   **Completing Sentences by Adding Prepositional Phrases**

Complete the following sentences by replacing each blank with a prepositional phrase.

1. Rob collects postcards ____.
2. ____ we collapsed.
3. We first heard the rumor ____.
4. ____ people had gathered to hear the concert.
5. I tiptoed ____ and listened quietly.
6. The deer darted quickly ____ and raced ____.
7. Everyone ____ applauded Branford Marsalis' solo.
8. Exhausted ____, the explorers pitched their tents ____ and planned the next day's work.
9. ____ the city council has voted to renovate the abandoned building ____ and turn it ____.
10. ____ I thought that something may have gone wrong ____.

17g

The Conjunction

17g. A *conjunction* is a word used to join words or groups of words.

Coordinating Conjunctions

A *coordinating conjunction* connects words or groups of words that are used in the same way.

Coordinating Conjunctions						
and	but	for	nor	or	so	yet

EXAMPLES   In A.D. 711, the Berbers **invaded** and **conquered** Spain. [*And* joins two words.]
We missed the opening scene, **but** we enjoyed the rest of the play. [*But* joins two groups of words.]

Correlative Conjunctions

Correlative conjunctions are pairs of conjunctions that join words or groups of words used in the same way.

Correlative Conjunctions		
both . . . and	either . . . or	whether . . . or
not only . . . but also	neither . . . nor	

EXAMPLES   **Either** Fred **or** Manuela will bring music for the party. [*Either . . . or* joins two words.]
Not only did Garrett Morgan patent the first gas mask, **but** he **also** invented the automatic traffic signal. [*Not only . . . but also* joins two groups of words.]

Subordinating Conjunctions

A *subordinating conjunction* begins a subordinate clause, joining it to an independent clause.

GRAMMAR

COMMON ERROR

Problem. In their writing, students sometimes use coordinating conjunctions to join dissimilar elements. This use results in unparallel writing. For example, "Lucy sauntered toward us and wearing her costume."

Solution. Remind students that coordinating conjunctions should join similar elements. For example, a coordinating conjunction could join two independent clauses, as in "Lucy sauntered toward us, and she was wearing her costume." Or a coordinating conjunction could join two participial phrases, as in "Wearing her costume and grinning triumphantly, Lucy sauntered toward us."

MEETING *individual* NEEDS

LESS-ADVANCED STUDENTS

Some students may need practice to understand the possible relationships that using conjunctions can show. Write the following pairs of sentences on the chalkboard and ask students to combine them by using conjunctions that show the relationship of the two sentences:

1. Harry planned a day of shopping.
   He forgot his money.
2. The two dogs barked loudly.
   A man was walking down the alley.
3. The Raiders missed their starting fullback.
   The Raiders' quarterback was also gone.
4. Latoya goes fishing every Sunday.
   She doesn't go fishing when it is raining.
5. The contractor promised that the house would be ready by March 1.
   We didn't move in until April 15.

Commonly Used Subordinating Conjunctions			
after	because	since	until
although	before	so that	when
as	how	than	whenever
as if	if	that	where
as much as	in order that	though	wherever
as though	provided	unless	while

EXAMPLES   Many Native Americans are reluctant to reveal their traditional names for some places **because** the names have spiritual meaning.
I gasped **when** I saw the headline.

A subordinating conjunction may begin a sentence instead of coming between the groups of words it joins.

EXAMPLE   **When** I saw the headline, I gasped.

☞ **REFERENCE NOTE:** See pages 675–683 for more information about subordinate clauses.

▶ **EXERCISE 9**   **Identifying and Classifying Conjunctions**

Identify the <u>conjunction</u>(s) in each of the following sentences, and tell whether each is a *coordinating conjunction*, a *correlative conjunction*, or a *subordinating conjunction*.

1. corr.   1. Our old car needs <u>either</u> a valve job <u>or</u> a new engine.
2. sub.   2. <u>Before</u> you write your paper, you must submit an outline.
3. corr.   3. Have you decided <u>whether</u> I'll take physics <u>or</u> economics?
4. corr.   4. During the Tang dynasty (618–906), China experienced <u>not only</u> a revival of Confucianism <u>but also</u> the development of specifically Chinese schools of Buddhism.
5. sub.   5. Thomas Hardy found a publisher for his poetry only <u>after</u> he had published more than a dozen novels.
6. coor.   6. Workers here pay city, state, <u>and</u> federal income taxes.
7. corr.   7. José Martí, a hero of the Cuban rebellion against Spain, was <u>both</u> a revolutionary leader <u>and</u> a great poet.
8. sub.   8. Mike enjoyed the movie <u>as much as</u> Sue did.
9. coor.   9. Are you going to the movies <u>or</u> to the concert?
10. sub.   10. <u>When</u> Liberia was founded in 1821, thousands of free African Americans moved there.

PICTURE THIS

Shipwrecked alone on this desert island, you have an ample supply of food and water, but no means of leaving the island. Fortunately, however, you also have a pencil, paper, and four bottles. Write four different messages to place in the bottles, explaining your predicament and requesting rescue. In your messages use a variety of coordinating, correlative, and subordinating conjunctions.

Subject: rescue notes
Audience: whoever finds each of the bottles
Purpose: to explain and persuade

GRAMMAR

PICTURE THIS

As a prewriting activity, suggest that students establish some background information on which to base their messages. To help them get started, you could offer students the following questions:

1. Where is the island?
2. How did you become stranded on the island?
3. Who is your audience? Who would be most likely to find one of the bottles?
4. How can you persuade someone to rescue you? Can you offer a reward?

GRAMMAR

The Interjection

17h. An *interjection* is a word used to express emotion. It has no grammatical relation to other words in the sentence.

EXAMPLES   ah   oh   well   whoops
               hey   ouch   whew   wow

GRAMMAR

▶ EXERCISE 10   **Completing Sentences by Adding Interjections**

Complete the following conversation by replacing each blank with an appropriate interjection. Do not use any interjection more than twice.

Responses will vary. Accept any appropriate interjections.

"[1] ____, Mariana, why are you so edgy tonight?" Mrs. Montero asked her eighteen-year-old daughter.

"[2] ____, Mom, don't you remember? Tonight's the night KHOP announces who won the drawing for a free car."

"[3] ____, yes, how could I forget? You've been talking about it for months."

"[4] ____, Mom, it's only been two weeks, and—wait, that's the phone; I'll get it. Hello? This is Mariana Montero. What? [5] ____, are you kidding me? I did? Really?! [6] ____, you're serious! [7] ____! That's incredible! When can I pick it up? Tonight? [8] ____, that's great! I'll be there in twenty minutes! 'Bye—and thanks! [9] ____, Mom, will you drive me? [10] ____, just think: That's the last time you'll ever hear me say those words!"

The Same Word as Different Parts of Speech

17i.   A word's part of speech is determined by how the word is used in a sentence.

EXAMPLES   This **plant** is native to North America. [noun]
We **plant** tomatoes every year. [verb]
Bacteria cause many **plant** diseases. [adjective]

Marisa led, and we followed **after.** [adverb]
We crossed the finish line **after** Marisa. [preposition]
We crossed it **after** all the other runners did, too. [conjunction]

This pillow is filled with **down** from geese. [noun]
I've always wanted a **down** pillow. [adjective]
Put it **down;** it's too expensive. [adverb]
We can find cheaper pillows at the store **down** the street. [preposition]

REVIEW C

OBJECTIVE

• To identify the parts of speech of words in a passage

REVIEW C   **Identifying Parts of Speech**

Identify the part of speech of each underlined <u>italicized word</u> in the following paragraphs.   n. = noun pro. = pronoun adj. = adjective adv. = adverb
v. = verb conj. = conjunction prep. = preposition itj. = interjection

[1] Did you know that millions of African Americans celebrate a *uniquely* American holiday *whose* roots lie in ancient Africa? [2] *Well*, they do; called Kwanzaa, which in Swahili means "the first fruits of the harvest," the holiday is observed *during* the week between Christmas and New Year's Day.

[3] Kwanzaa isn't a religious holiday or a substitute for Christmas *but* a celebration of black Americans' rich cultural *heritage*. [4] The holiday, which was created by Maulana (Ron) Karenga of California State University in Long Beach in 1966, *synthesizes* elements from a variety of *African* harvest festivals.

[5] Kwanzaa *focuses* on seven basic principles: unity, self-determination, collective work and responsibility, cooperative economics, purpose, *creativity*, and faith. [6] *Among* the symbols of the holiday *are* a straw mat for respect for tradition; an ear of corn for each child in the family; and a candleholder with seven green, red, and black candles for the continent of Africa. [7] *Each* day during the week family members light *one* of the candles and discuss one of the principles. [8] They *also* exchange simple gifts *that* reflect their heritage and eat foods from Africa and from the lands to which their ancestors were taken, such as the Caribbean and South America.

[9] Some families follow Karenga's original program for the holiday strictly, *while* others *freely* adapt it. [10] In some communities families gather for concerts and *dance* performances *like* this one, which took place in Los Angeles.

1. adv./
pro.
[or
adj.]
2. itj./
prep.
3.
conj./n.

4. v./adj.

5. v./n.

6. prep./v.

7. adj./pro.
8. adv./
pro.

9. conj./
adv.
10. adj./
prep.

CRITICAL THINKING

Analysis. Some students may have small children in their households. Ask such students to pay careful attention to the children's first words. Students could keep written records of the words spoken and at what age they were spoken. Have students analyze and compare their records. What parts of speech seem to be used first by most children? [Students may find, as some studies have found, that children generally use nouns and pronouns first, followed by verbs.] Encourage discussion of why children might acquire language in the way students' records indicate.

OBJECTIVES

- To identify parts of speech in sentences
- To identify the parts of speech of words in a passage
- To write sentences that include words as specific parts of speech

Review: Posttest 1

A. Identifying Parts of Speech

For each of the following sentences, identify every word or word group that is the part of speech indicated in parentheses.

1. If anyone calls me while I am out, will you please tell whoever it is that I can be reached at one or the other of these two numbers? (*pronoun*)
2. Although she lost both her sight and her hearing during childhood, Helen Keller later learned to communicate effectively with other people. (*noun*)
3. As much as we all had wanted to eat at the new French restaurant, we could not afford the prices. (*conjunction*)
4. Inca artisans were quite expert; among the works they left behind are elaborate jewelry and colorful tapestries. (*adverb*)
5. At the very beginning of the movie, many people in the audience were startled by the eerie sound effects that came toward them from all directions. (*preposition*)
6. This antique mantel clock chimes a delicate melody every quarter-hour. (*adjective*)
7. Do you think that the weather will finally turn cool once this low-pressure system moves through? (*verb*)
8. I developed extremely painful shin splints when I jogged much farther than I usually do. (*adverb*)
9. Oh, how beautifully Kathleen Battle and Jessye Norman sang in their concert at Carnegie Hall! (*interjection*)
10. Neither the coach nor the team members offered excuses for the loss, for they had done their best. (*conjunction*)

B. Identifying Parts of Speech

Identify the part of speech of each italicized word in the following paragraphs. n. = noun pro. = pronoun adj. = adjective
adv. = adverb v. = verb conj. = conjunction prep. = preposition

11. pro./prep. **[11]** When *it* opened in 1991, the Museum of Television and Radio became New York City's first new major museum *since*
12. n./v. 1966. **[12]** The late William Paley, the *founder* of CBS, *established*

the museum with contributions from the broadcasting industry. **[13]** The museum doesn't contain *everything* ever heard on
radio or seen on TV, *for* many early programs were never
copied, and some of those that were are missing or unplayable.
[14] But *its* collection is *quite* extensive: twenty-five thousand TV
programs, fifteen thousand radio shows, and ten thousand
commercials. **[15]** *Whether* you want to hear Jack Benny in a
comedy sketch from the 1930s *or* watch Billie Holiday in a
live performance from the 1950s, you'll find the recording *here*.
[16] In fact, the earliest material *dates* to 1920, *when* the nation's
first radio station, KDKA in Pittsburgh, went on the air.

    [17] Modern *technology* provides *easy* access to the museum's
collection. **[18]** Simply answer a *few* questions and press a button *on* one of the computers that store the catalog. **[19]** *Instantly*
a museum worker using the computer signals special machines
in the basement, *which* automatically load the tapes. **[20]** Often
by the time you've made *yourself* comfortable in one of the con-
sole rooms, the tape is *ready* for you to enjoy.

13. pro./conj.
14. pro. [or adj.]/adv.
15. conj./adv.
16. v./conj.
17. n./adj.
18. adj./prep.
19. adv./pro.
20. pro./adj.

[15. *Whether/or* is a pair of words that constitutes a correlative conjunction.]

Review: Posttest 2

Writing Sentences Using Words as Specific Parts of Speech

Write two sentences for each numbered item, according to the
following guidelines.

1. Use *right* as a noun and as an adjective.
2. Use *signal* as a noun and as a verb.
3. Use *home* as a noun and as an adverb.
4. Use *few* as a pronoun and as an adjective.
5. Use *that* as a pronoun and as an adjective.
6. Use *around* as an adverb and as a preposition.
7. Use *how* as an adverb and as a conjunction.
8. Use *well* as an adverb and as an interjection.
9. Use *for* as a preposition and as a conjunction.
10. Use *since* as a preposition and as a conjunction.

GRAMMAR

ANSWERS
Review: Posttest 2

Responses will vary. Here are some
possibilities:

1. Have you heard the saying "Two
   wrongs don't make a *right*"? (noun)
   "My *right* ear is killing me." (adjective)

2. The traffic *signal* at the busiest
   intersection in town is broken. (noun)
   The Dolphins' backup quarterback
   signals the plays to the quarterback in
   the huddle. (verb)

3. Most people dream of owning a
   home. (noun)
   The third-base coach waved the
   runner *home*. (adverb)

4. Only a *few* in the crowd realized what
   had happened. (pronoun)
   Jeff had a *few* dollars in his pocket.
   (adjective)

5. Is *that* your grammar book?
   (pronoun)
   That book is mine. (adjective)

6. Terrence was thrilled when his turn
   came *around* again. (adverb)
   Two men were seen hanging *around*
   the mall shortly before it closed.
   (preposition)

7. *How* well do you know the new
   student? (adverb)
   Jamie didn't know *how* his white mice
   escaped from their cage. (conjunction)

8. Ruthie performed *well* in her school
   play. (adverb)
   Well, excuse me! (interjection)

9. Toyoko wrote a haiku *for* her mother.
   (preposition)
   Young Oliver could only stand and
   watch the other children eat, *for* he
   had no food. (conjunction)

10. Jon has had only three hours of sleep
    since Sunday. (preposition)
    Since you are finished with your
    breakfast, let's go. (conjunction)

GRAMMAR

SUMMARY OF PARTS OF SPEECH

Rule	Part of Speech	Use	Examples
17a	noun	names	**Max** has an **idea** for our **party** on **Valentine's Day**.
17b	pronoun	takes the place of a noun or another pronoun	**Who** told **you this** is the **one that I** want for **myself**?
17c	adjective	modifies a noun or a pronoun	**Some nice** people bought **the big** house on **the next** block.
17d	verb	shows action or a state of being	**Are** you warm enough, or **do** you **need** a sweater?
17e	adverb	modifies a verb, an adjective, or another adverb	We need to find a **much** shorter route, or we'll arrive **too late**.
17f	preposition	relates a noun or a pronoun to another word	**As of** today we have only two weeks **of** school **before** graduation.
17g	conjunction	joins words or groups of words	**Both** Maria **and** I hope to be there **if** we can make it.
17h	interjection	shows emotion	**Hey!** What are you doing here?

DIAGNOSTIC TEST

OBJECTIVE

- To identify subjects, verbs, direct objects, indirect objects, objective complements, predicate nominatives, and predicate adjectives

18 THE PARTS OF A SENTENCE

Subject, Predicate, Complement

GRAMMAR

PROGRAM MANAGER

FOR THE WHOLE CHAPTER

- **Review** For exercises on chapter concepts, see **Review Form A** and **Review Form B** in *Language Skills Practice and Assessment,* pp. 33–36.

- **Assessment** For additional testing, see **Grammar Pretests** and **Grammar Mastery Tests** in *Language Skills Practice and Assessment,* pp. 1–7 and pp. 83–92.

GRAMMAR

CHAPTER OVERVIEW

The chapter begins by defining a sentence and distinguishing it from a sentence fragment. The text then discusses the subject and the predicate and the various complements. There is also an analysis of the relationships between the major sentence parts and a discussion of how these parts form sentences. In the **Writing Application,** students use their knowledge of sentence parts to write a college admissions essay.

USING THE DIAGNOSTIC TEST

The **Diagnostic Test** contains two parts: **Part A** asks students to classify one specific part in each of several different sentences as a subject, a verb, or a complement. **Part B** focuses on analysis of the parts of sentences. You may use the results to determine which chapter lessons require special emphasis. Inconsistencies between test results on the two parts (particularly a significantly lower score on **Part B**) may suggest that guessing, rather than understanding, was a determining factor in students' answers.

Diagnostic Test

A. Identifying Subjects, Verbs, and Complements

Identify the <u>italicized word</u> or word group in each of the following sentences as a *subject*, a *verb*, a *direct object*, an *indirect object*, an *objective complement*, a *predicate nominative*, or a *predicate adjective*.

EXAMPLE   **1.** Have *you* seen Jim?
           1. *subject*

1. Many fugitive slaves found *shelter* with the Seminoles of Spanish Florida.   **1.** d.o.
2. The water in the bay feels quite *cold*.   **2.** p.a.
3. Cheryl gave *me* her paper to read.   **3.** i.o.
4. The Great Wall of China *is* one of that nation's oldest structures.   **4.** v.
5. There are two *parts* to this test.   **5.** s.

6. The coach named Yolanda *captain* of the team. **6.** o.c.

you 7. Please put the *dishes* away. **7.** d.o.

8. The mail carrier left *you* this letter. **8.** i.o.

9. From out of the darkness lumbered a huge, shaggy *creature*. **9.** s.

10. Lee Trevino is *one* of America's all-time best golfers. **10.** p.n.

B. Identifying Subjects, Verbs, and Complements

Identify the <u>subject</u> and <u>verb</u> in each sentence in the following paragraph. If a sentence has any complements, identify them as well, and indicate whether each is a *direct object*, an *indirect object*, an *objective complement*, a *predicate nominative*, or a *predicate adjective*.

EXAMPLE [1] Manny and I visited Coney Island last weekend.
1. *subject—Manny, I; verb—visited; direct object—Coney Island*

[11] Along the coast of the Atlantic Ocean in Brooklyn, New York, <u>lies</u> <u>Coney Island</u>, a world-famous amusement park. [12] Until 1654, the <u>island</u> (now a peninsula) <u>was</u> the summer campground of the Canarsie and the Nyack peoples. [13] In that year, the <u>Native Americans</u> <u>sold</u> a group of Dutch settlers the island. [14] The <u>Dutch</u> <u>named</u> the island Conye (Dutch for "rabbit") because of the abundance of wild rabbits in the area. [15] In the 1820s, the <u>island</u> <u>became</u> popular as an ocean resort and throughout the nineteenth and early twentieth centuries <u>grew</u> increasingly lavish. [16] Among its many attractions <u>were</u> the mechanical <u>horses</u> and the 250-foot <u>Parachute Jump</u> of Steeplechase Park and the onion <u>domes</u>, <u>minarets</u>, and Japanese tea <u>gardens</u> of Luna Park. [17] Today, after years of neglect and a series of fires, the amusement <u>area</u> of this once-grand resort <u>is</u> only a five-block strip between Surf Avenue and the 80-foot-wide boardwalk along the ocean. [18] Yet ten million <u>people</u> still <u>visit</u> Coney Island each year. [19] Now <u>Horace Bullard</u>, the founder of a restaurant chain, <u>is planning</u> a major facelift for the area. [20] <u>Bullard</u> <u>holds</u> the rights to the former site of Steeplechase Park and <u>envisions</u> the park spectacularly beautiful once again.

12. p.n.
13. i.o./d.o.
14. d.o./o.c.
15. p.a./p.a.
17. p.n.
18. d.o.
19. d.o.
20. d.o./d.o./ o.c.

LESSON 2 *(pp. 631–632)*
THE SENTENCE Rule 18a

OBJECTIVE

- To write and proofread five complete sentences summarizing information provided on a chart

The Sentence

18a. A *sentence* is a group of words that expresses a complete thought.

A thought is complete when it makes sense by itself.

EXAMPLES   In many ways the development of the microprocessor has revolutionized technology.
When did Mexico achieve independence from Spain?
How quickly this year has passed!

Every sentence begins with a capital letter. The punctuation mark that follows a sentence depends on the purpose of the sentence.

☞ **REFERENCE NOTE:** See pages 689–690 for more information on the purposes of sentences. See pages 899–901 for more on end marks.

A group of words that looks like a sentence but that doesn't make sense by itself is a *sentence fragment.*

SENTENCE FRAGMENT   Students representing sixty-one historically black universities and colleges.
SENTENCE   Students representing sixty-one historically black universities and colleges competed in the knowledge bowl.

SENTENCE FRAGMENT   The graduation ceremony scheduled for June 20.
SENTENCE   The graduation ceremony is scheduled for June 20.

SENTENCE FRAGMENT   Sponsors election-year debates.
SENTENCE   The League of Women Voters sponsors election-year debates.

☞ **REFERENCE NOTE:** For more information about sentence fragments, see pages 555–558.

▶ EXERCISE 1   **Writing Complete Sentences**

Write five sentences summarizing the trends shown in the chart on the next page. Proofread each sentence to make sure that you have not included any sentence fragments.

EXAMPLE   **1.** *The decline in shipments of long-playing records leveled off between 1983 and 1984.*

GRAMMAR

THE SUBJECT AND THE PREDICATE
Rules 18b–18f

OBJECTIVE
- To identify simple subjects and verbs in a paragraph

MEETING individual NEEDS

LEARNING STYLES

Auditory Learners. If students are having trouble recognizing the differences between complete sentences and sentence fragments, you may want to provide oral examples. Some students are better at hearing the differences than they are at recognizing these differences in print. For example, you could read aloud "A picture of the city at night" and "A picture of the city at night won first prize in the photography contest." Ask students which sentence sounds complete.

PROGRAM MANAGER

THE SUBJECT AND THE PREDICATE

- **Independent Practice/ Reteaching** For instruction and exercises, see **Subjects and Predicates** in *Language Skills Practice and Assessment,* p. 28.

- **Computer Guided Instruction** For additional instruction and practice with subjects and predicates, see **Lesson 28** in *Language Workshop CD-ROM.*

- **Practice** To help less-advanced students with additional instruction and practice with subjects and predicates, see **Chapter 11** in *English Workshop, Complete Course,* pp. 145–146.

632

---

632 *The Parts of a Sentence*

Changing Trends in Recorded Music
Numbers of compact discs, cassettes, long-playing records, and singles shipped by manufacturers.

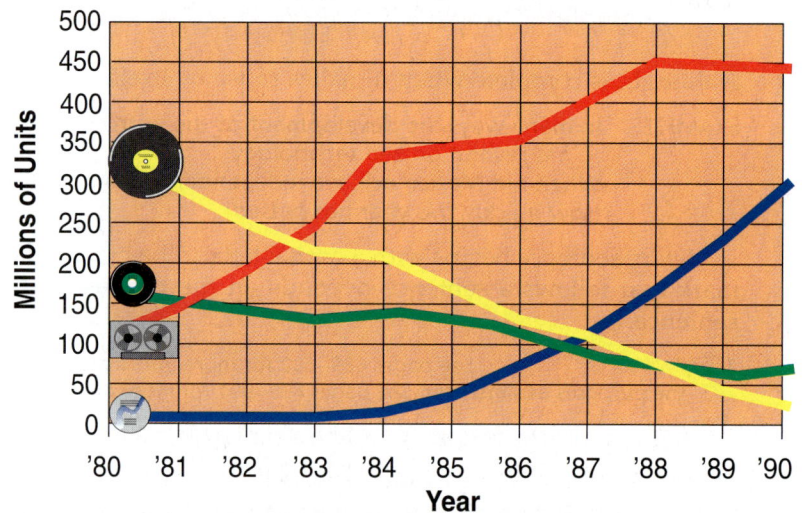

LP's Singles Cassettes CD's

Source: Recording Industry Association of America

The Subject and the Predicate

18b. A sentence consists of two parts: the *subject* and the *predicate*. The **subject** tells *whom* or *what* the sentence is about. The **predicate** tells something about the subject.

Subject	Predicate
EXAMPLES Jenny	laughed.

Subject	Predicate
Rain	pelted the sailors.

Subject	Predicate
Each of the amateur mimes	performed.

Predicate	Subject
Away on the breeze sailed	the dry leaves.

Predicate	Subject	Predicate
When did	Alex Haley	write *Roots?*

As you can see, a subject or a predicate may consist of one word or more than one word. In these examples, all the words labeled subject make up the *complete subject,* and all the words labeled predicate make up the *complete predicate.*

The Simple Subject

18c. The *simple subject* is the main word or group of words that tells *whom* or *what* the sentence is about.

EXAMPLES The **view** from the observatory on the top floor of the building is extraordinary. [The complete subject is *The view from the observatory on the top floor of the building.*]

Lasting for eight days, **Hanukkah** celebrates the rededication of the temple in Jerusalem in 165 B.C. [The complete subject is *Lasting for eight days, Hanukkah.*]

The **Memorial Coliseum** in Los Angeles was filled to capacity. [The complete subject is *The Memorial Coliseum in Los Angeles.*]

☞ **REFERENCE NOTE:** Compound nouns, such as *Memorial Coliseum,* are considered single nouns. Therefore, they may be used as simple subjects. For more about compound nouns, see page 601.

NOTE: In this book the term *subject* refers to the simple subject unless otherwise indicated.

The Simple Predicate

18d. The *simple predicate* is a verb or verb phrase that tells something about the subject.

EXAMPLES The crowd **surged** forward. [The complete predicate is *surged forward.*]

QUICK REMINDER

Have students copy the following sentences in their notebooks. Then, tell them to underline each part that is indicated in parentheses.

1. The tallest woman in the photograph is my grandmother. (complete subject)
2. Tara correctly identified every state capital. (complete predicate)
3. Did the reference section of the library have the information? (complete subject)

MEETING individual NEEDS

LEP/ESL

Asian Languages. In some Asian languages, the verb always appears at the end of a sentence. As a result, speakers of such languages may have difficulty identifying subjects and verbs in English sentences.

Make sure students are aware of the fact that verbs in English can appear at the beginning, middle, or end of sentences. Give students examples of the various possibilities.

ADVANCED STUDENTS

Challenge students to create new sentences by inverting the order of subjects and verbs in existing sentences. Suggest that each student explore various types of writing—novels, poetry, newspapers, and magazines—to find examples of sentences suitable for inversion. Remind students that occasionally reversing the order of the subject and the verb is a good way to add variety to their writing. Encourage students to share their work with the class.

GRAMMAR

GRAMMAR

COMMON ERROR

Problem. Students might mistake the object of a preposition for the subject of a sentence.

Solution. Suggest to students that the first steps in analyzing a sentence should be to find all prepositional phrases and then to put brackets around these phrases. This procedure can be a reminder to students to look outside a prepositional phrase for the subject of a sentence.

The victorious athletes **were** completely **surrounded** by admirers. [The complete predicate is *were completely surrounded by admirers.*]
Felipe **has** not yet **revealed** his plans. [The complete predicate is *has not yet revealed his plans.*]

NOTE: In this book, the term *verb* refers to the simple predicate (a one-word verb or a verb phrase) unless otherwise indicated.

☞ **REFERENCE NOTE:** For more information about verbs and verb phrases, see pages 612–614.

The Compound Subject and the Compound Verb

18e. A *compound subject* consists of two or more subjects that are joined by a conjunction and have the same verb.

Compound subjects are usually joined by *and* or *or.*

EXAMPLES   **East Germany** and **West Germany** have been reunited.
Did **Michelle** or **Chondra** lead the petition drive?
Hokkaido, Honshu, Shikoku, and **Kyushu** are the four main islands of Japan.

18f. A *compound verb* consists of two or more verbs that are joined by a conjunction and have the same subject.

Compound verbs are usually joined by *and, but,* or *or.*

EXAMPLES   Mary McLeod Bethune **founded** Bethune-Cookman College and twice **served** as its president.
I **read** the book but **missed** the movie.
Would you rather **wash** the dishes or **dry** them?

Do not confuse a sentence containing a compound subject or compound predicate with a compound sentence.

EXAMPLES   **Anna** and **Lyle will sing** and **do** a comedy routine. [compound subject and compound predicate]
Anna will sing, and **Lyle will do** a comedy routine. [compound sentence]

☞ **REFERENCE NOTE:** For more information about compound sentences, see pages 686–687.

How to Find the Subject of a Sentence

To find the subject of a sentence, ask *Who?* or *What?* before the verb.

EXAMPLES In the auditorium **friends** and **relatives** of the gradu-ates awaited the ceremony. [Who awaited? Friends and relatives awaited.]
Sharing the island of Hispaniola with Haiti is the **Dominican Republic.** [What is sharing? Dominican Republic is sharing.]

Keep the following four guidelines in mind whenever you are trying to find the subject of a sentence.

(1) The subject of a command or a request is always understood to be *you*, even if the word *you* does not appear in the sentence.

COMMAND Always document the source of a direct quotation. [Who documents? You document.]
REQUEST Please write soon. [Who writes? You write.]

If a command or a request contains a *noun of direct address*—a word naming the one or ones spoken to—the subject is still understood to be *you*.

EXAMPLE Frances, (you) walk the dog.

(2) The subject of a sentence is never in a prepositional phrase.

EXAMPLES A **committee** of students investigated the allegations. [Who investigated? Committee investigated. *Students* is the object of the preposition *of*.]
One of the parks in Austin, Texas, is named for the Mexican general Ignacio Seguín Zaragoza. [What is named? One is named. *Parks* is the object of the preposition *of*. *Austin* is the object of the preposition *in*.]
From the alley came the **wail** of a siren. [What came? Wail came. *Alley* is the object of the preposition *from*. *Siren* is the object of the preposition *of*.]

☞ REFERENCE NOTE: For more information about prepositional phrases, see pages 619–620 and 652–655.

(3) The subject of a question usually follows the verb or comes between the parts of a verb phrase.

INTEGRATING THE LANGUAGE ARTS

Literature Link. Consider giving students different examples of subject-verb order from literature. For example, have the class read and discuss Shakespeare's "When Icicles Hang by the Wall" from *Love's Labor's Lost*. The first five lines of each stanza follow a common subject-verb order. The sixth line reverses the pattern ("Then nightly sings the staring owl").

Other examples of poetry with unusual syntax include Byron's "The Destruction of Sennacherib" and Shelley's "Ode to the West Wind." Discuss with students the effect of an inverted word order. [It produces rhythm and variety, and it shifts the emphasis to different words.]

EXAMPLES   Are these **jeans** on sale? [What are on sale? Jeans are.]
When did **Thurgood Marshall** retire from the United States Supreme Court? [Who did retire? Thurgood Marshall did retire.]

To find the subject of a question, turn the question into a statement.

QUESTION   Have you tasted sushi?
STATEMENT   **You** have tasted sushi. [Who have tasted? You have tasted.]

QUESTION   Is the cold war over?
STATEMENT   The **cold war** is over. [What is over? Cold war is over.]

(4) *There* or *here* is never the subject of a sentence. In the following examples, *there* and *here* are adverbs telling *where*.

EXAMPLES   There goes **Rebecca**. [Who goes? Rebecca goes.]
Here is your **receipt**. [What is? Receipt is.]

> **NOTE:** *There* is not always an adverb. It may instead be an *expletive*—a word that fills out the structure of a sentence but does not add to the meaning.
>
> EXAMPLE   **There** will be a special broadcast on the coup tonight at 11:30 P.M.

▶ **EXERCISE 2**   **Identifying Subjects and Verbs**

Identify each simple subject and verb in the following paragraphs. Include all parts of a compound word and all words in a verb phrase.

EXAMPLE   [1] The miniature Japanese sculptures shown on the next page are called *netsuke*.
     1. *subject—sculptures; verb—are called*

[1] This exquisite art form originated as a practical solution to an everyday problem. [2] During Japan's Tokugawa period (1615–1867), an integral part of the traditional costume of the new merchant class was a set of lacquerware boxes for medicines and spices. [3] The boxes were threaded onto the sash of the kimono and served as pockets for the otherwise pocketless garment. [4] Originally just small, plain toggles of lightweight ivory or wood, the *netsuke* held the boxes in place along the sash.

OBJECTIVES

- To write a descriptive encyclopedia entry that includes direct and indirect objects
- To identify the direct objects, the indirect objects, and the objective complements in paragraphs

18g

GRAMMAR

[5] Under the feudal system then in effect, there <u>were</u> strict <u>laws</u> against any display of wealth by persons below the rank of *samurai.* [6] However, wealthy <u>merchants</u> <u>wanted</u> some obvious symbol of their success. [7] Over time, increasingly elaborate *netsuke* from the nation's finest artisans <u>became</u> that symbol.

[8] Eventually, the <u>Japanese</u> <u>adopted</u> Western clothing, with pockets. [9] As a result, both the small <u>boxes</u> and the *netsuke* <u>became</u> obsolete. [10] Today, <u>collectors</u> all over the world gladly <u>pay</u> large sums for specimens of these beautiful objects with the humble origin.

The Peabody Museum of Salem

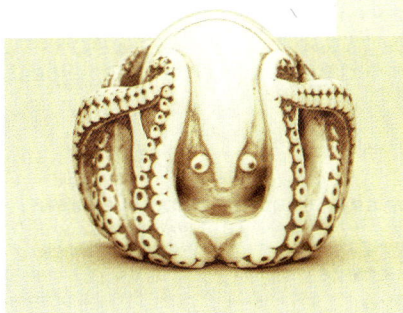

Netsuke

The Peabody Museum of Salem

Complements

18g. A *complement* is a word or word group that completes the meaning of a predicate.

Some sentences are complete with only a subject and a verb.

EXAMPLES
　　　S　　V
　　She won.

　　　　S　　V
　　(You) Look!

VISUAL CONNECTIONS
Ideas for Writing. *Netsuke* may be considered an early example of a fashion accessory worn by a particular group to give the impression of importance or wealth. Today, we refer to such changeable fashion statements as fads. Fads are still prevalent among teenagers and young adults.

Brainstorm with the class to create a list of past and current fads. Ask each student to write an informative paragraph about one fad and how it started. Select several volunteers to read their work and to discuss their opinions with the class.

GRAMMAR

PROGRAM MANAGER

COMPLEMENTS

■ **Independent Practice/ Reteaching** For instruction and exercises, see **Complements, Direct and Indirect Objects, Objective Complements,** and **Subject Complements** in *Language Skills Practice and Assessment,* pp. 29–32.

■ **Computer Guided Instruction** For additional instruction and practice with complements, see **Lesson 29** in *Language Workshop CD-ROM.*

■ **Practice** To help less-advanced students with additional instruction and practice with complements, see **Chapter 11** in *English Workshop, Complete Course,* pp. 151–156.

GRAMMAR

✔ **QUICK REMINDER**

Tell the students that a linking verb is like a mirror. In the linking-verb mirror, the subject sees the complement, which is a reflection of the subject. In contrast, an action verb would break a mirror to impart action to the direct object.

Ask students to create four sentences of their own. Two should use action verbs, and two should use linking verbs.

MEETING *individual* **NEEDS**

LEP/ESL

General Strategies. English uses a subject-verb-object sentence structure. Other languages use subject-object-verb or verb-subject-object structures. For example, if you ask native speakers of Japanese, Korean, or Persian "Whom did Ann call?" and they answer, "Her friend called" or "Her friend did," they are probably trying to tell you that Ann called her friend. Consequently, students may need extra practice in using the English subject-verb-object sentence structure.

GRAMMAR

638   *The Parts of a Sentence*

Other sentences require one or more complements to complete their meaning.

	S V
INCOMPLETE	Judith Baca created
	S V C
COMPLETE	Judith Baca created the mural.
	S V
INCOMPLETE	They mailed
	S V C C
COMPLETE	They mailed me the information.
	S V
INCOMPLETE	The republics declared
	S V C C
COMPLETE	The republics declared themselves independent.
	S V
INCOMPLETE	Who in the world named
	S V C C
COMPLETE	Who in the world named the puppy Cerberus?
	S V
INCOMPLETE	Seiji Ozawa became
	S V C
COMPLETE	Seiji Ozawa became a successful conductor.
	S V
INCOMPLETE	The horse seems
	S V C
COMPLETE	The horse seems skittish.

Complements may be nouns, pronouns, or adjectives. Be careful not to mistake an adverb for a complement.

ADVERB   Hatshepsut ruled **ably.** [The adverb *ably* tells *how* Hatshepsut ruled.]

COMPLEMENT   Hatshepsut ruled **Egypt** during the early fifteenth century B.C. [The noun *Egypt* completes the meaning of *ruled.*]

A complement is never in a prepositional phrase.

EXAMPLE   At first Hatshepsut ruled with her husband. [The noun *husband* is the object of the preposition *with.*]

☞ **REFERENCE NOTE:** See pages 619–620 and 652–655 for more information on prepositional phrases.

**18
h–i**

Direct Objects and Indirect Objects

18h. A *direct object* is a noun or a pronoun that receives the action of the verb or shows the result of the action. A direct object tells *whom* or *what* after an action verb.

EXAMPLES   Mr. Martínez uses **newspapers** as supplements to our history text. [Uses what? Newspapers.]
The tornado leveled the **warehouse**. [Leveled what? Warehouse.]
I miss **you**. [Miss whom? You.]

A direct object may be compound.

EXAMPLES   The concert starred **Wynton Marsalis** and **Marcus Roberts**.
The cat followed **Karen** and **me** home.

NOTE: For emphasis, a writer may place the direct object before the subject and the verb.

EXAMPLE   What an eerie **sound** we heard! [Heard what? Sound.]

18i. An *indirect object* is a noun or a pronoun that comes between an action verb and a direct object. It tells *to whom* or *to what* (or *for whom* or *for what*) the action of the verb is done.

EXAMPLES   The Swedish Academy awarded **Octavio Paz** the 1990 Nobel Prize in literature. [Awarded the prize to whom? Octavio Paz.]
Julie's part-time work experience landed **her** a full-time position. [Landed the position for whom? Her.]

Don't mistake an object of the preposition *to* or *for* for an indirect object.

INDIRECT OBJECT   Clarice wrote **me** a letter.
OBJECT OF PREPOSITION   Clarice wrote a letter to **me**. [*Me* is the object of the preposition *to*.]

An indirect object may be compound.

EXAMPLES   The travel agent gave **Todd** and **Steve** their itinerary.
The incident earned my **sister** and **me** our nicknames.

GRAMMAR

MEETING *individual* NEEDS

LEARNING STYLES

Kinetic Learners. Allow students to act out several sentences that have both direct and indirect objects. For example, they could act out sample sentences given in this lesson or write original sentences to present to the class. For each sentence, you may reinforce the distinction between the direct and indirect objects.

Visual Learners. You may want to ask students to diagram sample sentences to illustrate for students the way parts of a sentence fit together and the relationship between complements and other sentence parts.

GRAMMAR

PICTURE THIS

Before students begin writing this assignment, you may want to have them read encyclopedia entries on basketball. Stress that students should use a formal style and format and should find ideas for describing aspects of the game. Begin by selecting one facet of the game, such as passing, and ask the class to imagine how someone who knows nothing about basketball might interpret this action. Encourage appropriate humor.

COOPERATIVE LEARNING

You could divide the class into groups of three or four to complete the **Picture This** activity. Have each group compile a list of terms associated with basketball. Then, ask the groups to brainstorm for reactions an interplanetary visitor might have to each term. As students write, they can use this list to generate ideas for their encyclopedia entries. Group members can exchange their work, make suggestions to improve sentence structure, and check that direct and indirect objects have been correctly incorporated. Select one student from each group to share his or her revised description with the class. You may wish to display the finished entries.

PICTURE THIS

Now what are the earthlings doing? There's certainly nothing like this on your home planet. You're here to gather information for the "Earth" entry in the new edition of *Encyclopedia Galactica*. Surveillance cameras have shown that the strange activity shown here is highly popular in some areas of the planet. Write a description of what the earthlings are doing, and speculate about the meaning and purpose of their activities. In your encyclopedia entry, use at least three direct objects and two indirect objects.

Subject: a basketball game
Audience: readers of the
               Encyclopedia Galactica
Purpose: to inform

Objective Complements

18j.   An ***objective complement*** is a word or word group that helps complete the meaning of an action verb by identifying or modifying the direct object.

An objective complement may be a noun, a pronoun, or an adjective.

EXAMPLES   France named Miles Davis a **knight** in the Legion of Honor. [The noun *knight* identifies the direct object *Miles Davis.*]
Garfield considers the refrigerator **his**. [The possessive pronoun *his* modifies the direct object *refrigerator.*]
We have painted the house **blue**. [The adjective *blue* modifies the direct object *house.*]

Only a few action verbs take an objective complement. These verbs are *consider*, *make*, and any verbs that can be replaced by *consider* or *make*, such as *call*, *keep*, *name*, *find*, *choose*, *elect*, *appoint*, *paint*, *color*, and *render*.

EXAMPLES   The referee called the line drive **foul**. [or *considered the line drive foul*]
The Supreme Court's 1954 decision rendered public-school segregation **unlawful**. [or *made* public-school segregation unlawful]

An objective complement may be compound.

EXAMPLES   The stockholders elected her **president** and **chief executive officer.**
The lack of ventilation made the room **stuffy** and **uncomfortable.**

▶ EXERCISE 3   **Identifying Direct Objects, Indirect Objects, and Objective Complements**

Identify each *direct object*, *indirect object*, and (objective complement) in the sentences in the following paragraphs.

[1] Recent advances in technology have made interactive television systems a (reality). [2] The system shown here includes a remote-control converter box with a computer inside. [3] The computer gives viewers several options for the content of a program. [4] During a football game, for example, viewers can

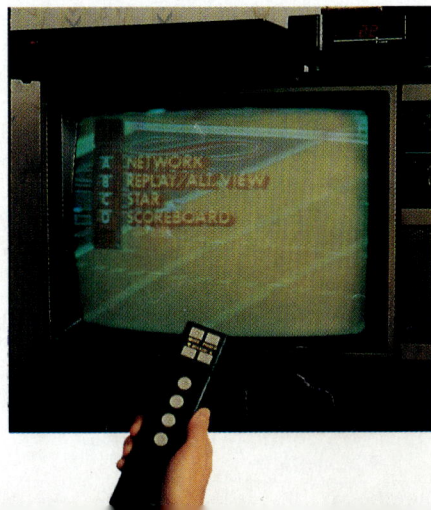

MEETING *individual* **NEEDS**

LEARNING STYLES

Auditory Learners. Because voice inflections can indicate the purpose of various words in a sentence, you may want to read the sentences in **Exercise 3** aloud.

◆ **TIMESAVER**

To facilitate evaluation of **Exercise 3**, you may want to have the students color-code their answers. Indirect objects could be marked in red, direct objects marked in black, and objective complements highlighted in blue.

GRAMMAR

order the network's <u>choice</u> of camera angle, an alternate <u>view</u>, an instant <u>replay</u>, or the <u>scores</u> in other games. [5] The computer records each <u>response</u> made by the viewer. [6] Viewers can also select exercise <u>workouts</u> suited to their needs and can tailor <u>news</u> and comedy <u>programs</u> to their interests. [7] Most viewers have found the new <u>technology</u> quite enjoyable. [8] In addition, advertisers consider <u>it</u> a boon to their business. [9] Viewers' responses give the <u>advertisers</u> valuable demographic <u>data</u>. [10] With that data, they can target <u>commercials</u> to highly specific audiences.

Subject Complements

A *subject complement* is a word or word group that completes the meaning of a linking verb and identifies or modifies the subject.

☞ **REFERENCE NOTE:** For a list of linking verbs, see page 613.

The two kinds of subject complements are the *predicate nominative* and the *predicate adjective.*

18k. A *predicate nominative* is a noun or a pronoun that follows a linking verb and refers to the same person or thing as the subject of the verb.

EXAMPLES   Robert Hayden is my favorite **poet.** [The noun *poet* refers to the subject *Robert Hayden.*]
Those people over there are **several** of my neighbors. [The pronoun *several* refers to the subject *people.*]

A predicate nominative may be compound.

EXAMPLES   The four most populated states are **California, New York, Texas,** and **Florida.**
The last people off the bus were **Julie** and **I.**

18l. A *predicate adjective* is an adjective that follows a linking verb and modifies the subject of the verb.

EXAMPLES   Your lotus-blossom necklace is **lovely.** [The adjective *lovely* modifies the subject *necklace.*]
Does the cottage cheese smell **sour?** [The adjective *sour* modifies the subject *cottage cheese.*]

OBJECTIVE

- To identify the subjects, verbs, and any complements in sentences

18
k–l

A predicate adjective may be compound.

EXAMPLES   Freedom is **precious** and **costly.**
The refugees were **hungry** and **weary.**
The weather turned **cold, wet,** and **foggy.**

NOTE: For emphasis, a writer may place the subject complement before the subject and the verb.

PREDICATE
NOMINATIVE   What an amazing **coincidence** that is! [The noun *coincidence* refers to the subject *that.*]

PREDICATE
ADJECTIVES   **Cruel** and **blue** were the villain's crafty eyes. [The adjectives *cruel* and *blue* modify the subject *eyes.*]

GRAMMAR

▶ EXERCISE 4   Identifying Predicate Nominatives and Predicate Adjectives

Identify the subject complement in each of the following sentences. Indicate whether each one is a *predicate nominative* or a *predicate adjective*.

1. The candidate's campaign speech at last night's rally was both <u>effective</u> and <u>persuasive</u>.
2. Do these strawberries look <u>ripe</u>?
3. Mexican president Porfirio Díaz became more <u>ruthless</u> and <u>dictatorial</u>.
4. Very <u>sleek</u>, very <u>red</u>, and incredibly <u>powerful</u> is Eric's dream car.
5. The dog grew <u>restless</u> just before the storm.
6. Pablo Casals was not only a brilliant <u>cellist</u> but also a sensitive <u>conductor</u>.
7. The sea spray tasted <u>salty</u>.
8. How <u>musty</u> the rooms in this empty house smell!
9. In 1988, George Bush became the fourth <u>president</u> who came from Massachusetts.
10. Kicking Bear was a Sioux <u>warrior</u>, <u>artist</u>, and <u>prophet</u>.

▶ REVIEW   Identifying Subjects, Verbs, and Complements

Identify the <u>subject</u>, the <u>verb</u>, and any (complements) in each sentence in the following paragraphs. Indicate whether each complement is a *direct object,* an *indirect object,* an *objective complement,* a *predicate nominative,* or a *predicate adjective.*

GRAMMAR

MEETING *individual* NEEDS

STUDENTS WITH SPECIAL NEEDS

Some students may have difficulty in reading lengthy blocks of material. You could simplify the **Review** by transferring its paragraphs to individual sheets on which students can write. If possible, double space between the lines of text to make the paragraphs easier to read. Then students can concentrate on the task of identifying subjects, verbs, and complements.

ANSWERS
Review

1. subjects—arabesques, ones; verb—illustrate; direct object—link

2. subjects—Arabs, Berbers; verbs—invaded, occupied; direct object—Spain

3. subject—They; verbs—launched, were called; direct objects—invasion, Moors

4. subject—encouragement; verb—made; direct object—cities; objective complement—wealthy

5. subject—patronage; verb—rendered; direct object—cities; objective complement—centers

6. subject—parts; verb—became; predicate adjective—Christian

7. subjects—Granada, it; verbs—remained, fell; predicate nominative—stronghold

8. subject—Spain; verb—gave; direct object—choice; indirect object—Moors

9. subject—all; verbs—rejected, left; direct object—idea

10. subject—traces; verb—survive

EXAMPLE [1] Arabesques are complex, elaborate designs of flowers, foliage, calligraphy, and geometric patterns.
1. *subject—Arabesques; verb—are; predicate nominative—designs*

[1] The arabesques on the left from the fortress-palace of the Alhambra in Granada, Spain, and the ones on the right from the king's palace in Fez, Morocco, illustrate a historic link

between two cultures. [2] In 711, Arabs and Muslim Berbers from North Africa invaded and occupied Spain. [3] They launched the invasion from Morocco and as a result were called Moors.

[4] The Moors' encouragement of commerce made Spain's major cities wealthy. [5] Meanwhile, the Moors' patronage of art, literature, and science rendered the cities centers of learning for Christian, Jewish, and Muslim scholars.

[6] Through reconquest, parts of Spain became Christian again as early as 1085. [7] At the end of the fifteenth century, Granada remained the Moors' last stronghold, until finally in 1492, it too fell to the forces of Ferdinand V and Isabella I. [8] Spain gave the Moors the choice of conversion to Christianity or expulsion from the country. [9] Nearly all of them rejected the idea of conversion and left. [10] Yet traces of their rich heritage still survive in the architecture, poetry, and music of Spain.

WRITING APPLICATION

OBJECTIVE

- To write a college admissions essay that contains varied elements, structures, and sentence lengths to create rhythm

Using Sentence Variety to Improve Style

Like a song, a piece of writing has rhythm. In addition to your choice of words, the structure and arrangement of your sentences create this rhythm. One way to avoid a monotonous rhythm is to vary the elements in each sentence. For example, try using a mixture of long and short subjects, use one-word verbs as well as verb phrases, or include an assortment of action verbs and linking verbs that require a variety of complements. Once in a while, begin a sentence with a phrase, a clause, or a single-word modifier instead of the subject.

As you read the following paragraph from a student's college admissions essay, notice the rhythm the writer creates by varying her sentences.

EXAMPLE When I tried out for the field hockey team in ninth grade, it was merely because a good friend of mine begged me to do it with her. The idea of spending 3 hours every day running around a field didn't particularly appeal to me, but for a friend I'd do anything. After 2 weeks, my friend quit. Quitting has always been anathema to me, but in this case it never entered my mind anyway. I was having fun. Those 3 hours of practice were the best part of my day. I loved being outside, and being physically active. Most importantly, I loved being with my teammates. Between studying and practicing the piano, I'd spend so much time alone that my time on the field became a welcome and necessary break in my day. Also, coming home at six o'clock every evening helped me to budget my time, since I knew I only had a few hours in which to complete my assignments.

George Ehrenhaft, from *Write Your Way Into College*

▶ WRITING ACTIVITY

You have been looking through a number of college brochures. At last, you have found a school that seems right for you and have decided to apply for admission. Your

---

WRITING APPLICATION

You may want to display sample essay questions from a variety of college application forms and have students discuss how the essay requirements differ from requirements of this assignment.

CRITICAL THINKING

Analysis. After compiling lists of topics, students should analyze these topics to determine their suitability for an essay. Once topics are selected, students should decide on appropriate tones. Have the students jot down facts, details, and examples that might help them develop theses. Students should then analyze their lists and select those details that provide the strongest support for their essays.

MEETING *individual* NEEDS

AT-RISK STUDENTS

Some students might be planning on interim employment before further pursuing their educations. Therefore, for the **Writing Application**, you may want to present an alternative to the college essay. Have interested students compose job résumés. Partners might tape-record modeled questions and verbal responses and then play back the responses and use them as guides to writing personal résumés.

SELECTION AMENDMENT
Description of change: excerpted
Rationale: to focus on the use of sentence structure presented in this chapter

PREWRITING

Before students begin compiling their personal lists, note that many colleges provide a suggested topic but also allow applicants the latitude to select their own subjects. Some of your students will feel more comfortable with an assigned topic; others might appreciate the opportunity to develop an independent idea.

WRITING

Remind students that topic sentences usually set the tone for an essay. Note that attention-grabbing first sentences are usually short. Asking a provocative question is one frequently employed device. However, if a writer uses that device, he or she must provide an answer to the question.

EVALUATING AND REVISING

Remind students that voice inflections can soften the tone of written words but that students will not have the option of reading their essays to admissions officers. When writing humorously, students should be especially careful that none of their statements appear to be sarcastic.

PROOFREADING

Explain to students that admissions officers often suggest that applicants have at least one other person proofread their essays for mistakes in grammar, usage, and mechanics. You could establish proofreading groups to focus on finding certain kinds of errors.

application is complete except for one thing—the admissions essay. The essay instructions are as follows: In a short essay, tell about something that is important to you.

Prewriting First, you'll need to decide on a topic for your essay. Brainstorm a list of issues, ideas, and activities that are important to you. For example, do you especially enjoy (or dislike) a particular sport? Is playing music, writing science fiction, or doing volunteer work a significant part of your life? Choose the most engaging topic from your list. Then, decide whether the tone of your essay will be serious or light-hearted. Jot down facts, details, and examples to help develop your topic.

Writing Begin your essay with an attention-grabber. You might start with a brief anecdote, a thoughtful question, or a surprising statement. Then develop your topic with supporting examples, facts, and details. Explain your feelings and the reasons behind them. Sum up your ideas in a clincher paragraph. (For more about writing a personal essay, see pages 154–156.)

Evaluating and Revising Now that you've gotten your ideas down on paper, you can fine-tune the content, organization, and style of your essay. First, make sure that your thesis statement gives a clear focus to your essay. Then, check to be sure the body of your essay supports that thesis. Do your supporting paragraphs follow a clear, logical sequence? If not, revise or rearrange details. Next, evaluate the tone of your essay. (For a discussion of tone, see pages 32–34 and 517–518.) Although you may write a humorous essay, you'll want to avoid a silly or sarcastic tone that might annoy the members of the admissions committee. Finally, check your sentence style. Have you varied the elements of your sentences to avoid a monotonous rhythm? During the revision process, you can ask a friend to read your essay and give you feedback and suggestions.

Proofreading Using standard English is very important in an admissions essay. Check your writing carefully for errors in usage, spelling, or punctuation. Be sure that you've used only complete sentences.

REVIEW: POSTTEST

OBJECTIVES

- To identify italicized words in sentences as subjects, verbs, and specific types of complements
- To write sentences following guidelines that specify certain sentence parts

Review: Posttest 1

A. Identifying Subjects, Verbs, and Complements

Identify the <u>italicized word or word group</u> in each of the following sentences as a <u>s</u>ubject, a <u>v</u>erb, a <u>d</u>irect <u>o</u>bject, an <u>i</u>ndirect <u>o</u>bject, an <u>o</u>bjective <u>c</u>omplement, a <u>p</u>redicate <u>n</u>ominative, or a <u>p</u>redicate <u>a</u>djective.

EXAMPLE   **1.** We *took* the shortest route.
           1. *verb*

1. The girls' gymnastics team unanimously elected Ming Chin their *captain*.   **1.** o.c.
2. *Carlos Chávez* established the Symphony Orchestra of Mexico.   **2.** s.
3. The antique dresser *was* carefully *moved* to a protected corner of the showroom.   **3.** v.
4. Margaret wants a *set* of luggage for graduation.   **4.** d.o.
5. On Fajada Butte in northwestern New Mexico is an ancient Anasazi solar *calendar*.   **5.** s.
6. The director gave my *grandfather* a part in the play.   **6.** i.o.
7. *Call* me after school.   **7.** v.
8. Exercise keeps me *energetic*.   **8.** o.c.
9. Since she won the Pulitzer Prize in 1983, Alice Walker has become a famous *writer*.   **9.** p.n.
10. My mother is *taller* than any of her four sisters.   **10.** p.a.

B. Identifying Subjects, Verbs, and Complements

Identify each <u>italicized word or word group</u> in the following paragraphs as a <u>s</u>ubject, a <u>v</u>erb, a <u>d</u>irect <u>o</u>bject, an <u>i</u>ndirect <u>o</u>bject, an <u>o</u>bjective <u>c</u>omplement, a <u>p</u>redicate <u>n</u>ominative, or a <u>p</u>redicate <u>a</u>djective.

EXAMPLE   [1] In 1675, Spanish friar Juan Paiva recorded the *rules* of a major sports contest between the Apalachee and the Timucuan peoples of North Florida.
           1. *direct object*

[11] The arrival of a messenger in a raccoon costume was a *challenge* to a ballgame from the loser of the last game. [12] On acceptance of the challenge, *all* of the villagers traveled to meet   **11.** p.n.   **12.** s.

GRAMMAR

their opponents. **[13]** In an all-night vigil before the game, elders of the host village interpreted their dreams and told the home *team* their predictions of the game's outcome. **[14]** Meanwhile, the visitors *made* a stew with rancid food, *mixed* it with decorative clays, and *painted* their bodies with the foul mixture as a deterrent to the other players.

[15] On game day, a village leader started *play* by tossing out a small, hard ball to teams of forty to fifty players on each side. **[16]** Suddenly, eighty to one hundred men *were scrambling* for a ball only about an inch in diameter! **[17]** The goal post in the center of an empty field was a ten- to fifteen-foot *pole* with an eagle's nest on top. **[18]** Teams scored one *point* for each throw of the ball against the pole and two *points* for each basket. **[19]** When one team had scored eleven points, the game was *over*. **[20]** According to historians, these rules probably made the average game a one- to two-hour *contest*.

13. i.o.
14. v./v./ v.
15. d.o.
16. v.
17. p.n.
18. d.o./ d.o.
19. p.a.
20. o.c.

ANSWERS
Review: Posttest 2

Sentences will vary. Students should follow the guidelines provided and underline words used as the italicized sentence parts. Partners might exchange papers and proofread to check that all answers include the required components.

To help them to develop writing skills, encourage students to use the exercise as an opportunity to write an original essay or story on a specific topic of their choosing. Select several students to read their essays to the class.

Review: Posttest 2

Writing Sentences

Write your own sentences according to the following guidelines. In your sentences, underline the words you use as the italicized sentence parts. Use a variety of subjects, verbs, and complements in your sentences.

1. a sentence with a *compound subject*
2. a sentence with a *compound verb*
3. a sentence with a *direct object*
4. a sentence with a *compound direct object*
5. a sentence with an *indirect object* and a *direct object*
6. a sentence with a *compound indirect object* and a *compound direct object*
7. a sentence with a *predicate nominative*
8. a sentence with a *compound predicate adjective*
9. a sentence with a *direct object* and an *objective complement*
10. a sentence with a *direct object* and a *compound objective complement*

SEVEN COMMON SENTENCE PATTERNS

The subject and the verb produce one sentence pattern. The subject, the verb, and the various complements produce the other six sentence patterns.

    S   V
Velma painted.

    S   V   D.O.
Velma painted a landscape.

       S   V   I.O.   D.O.
The judges gave Velma an award.

    S   V   D.O.   Obj. Comp.
                                     (Noun)
They considered her landscape a masterpiece.

    S   V   D.O. Obj. Comp
                               (Adj.)
They called the painting brilliant.

    S   V   P.N.
Velma has become a celebrity.

   S V P.A.
She is famous.

GRAMMAR

INTEGRATING THE LANGUAGE ARTS

Grammar, Writing, and Speaking.
To give practice with the seven common sentence patterns, as well as an opportunity for imaginative writing, have students work on the following project. Ask each student to bring a magazine article to class. Divide the class into groups of three or four. Have each group select one member's article to use as a basis for a dramatic scene they will write. Tell each group to include at least one example of each sentence pattern and a speaking part for each member of the group. Ask each group to perform its scene for the class.

To model this activity, choose a scene from the literature textbook for the class to analyze together by looking for various sentence patterns.

GRAMMAR

DIAGNOSTIC TEST

OBJECTIVE
- To identify prepositional, participial, gerund, infinitive, and appositive phrases in sentences and in a paragraph

FOR THE WHOLE CHAPTER
- **Review** For exercises on chapter concepts, see **Review Form A** and **Review Form B** in *Language Skills Practice and Assessment,* pp. 46–49.
- **Assessment** For additional testing, see **Grammar Pretests** and **Grammar Mastery Tests** in *Language Skills Practice and Assessment,* pp. 1–7 and pp. 83–92.

CHAPTER OVERVIEW
This chapter begins with a definition of *prepositional phrases* and a description of how these phrases are used as either adjective or adverb phrases. Then, the different verbals and verbal phrases are presented, including the participle, the participial phrase, the gerund, the gerund phrase, the infinitive, and the infinitive phrase. The **Picture This** feature asks students to write descriptive paragraphs containing prepositional, participial, and gerund phrases. The final lesson discusses appositives and appositive phrases. Students are given an opportunity to practice using infinitive and appositive phrases in the **Writing Application.**

19 THE PHRASE

Kinds of Phrases and Their Functions

Diagnostic Test

A. Identifying Phrases

For each of the following sentences, identify the italicized phrase as an *adjective phrase,* an *adverb phrase,* a *participial phrase,* a *gerund phrase,* an *infinitive phrase,* or an *appositive phrase.* Do not separately identify a prepositional phrase that is part of a larger phrase.

EXAMPLE **1.** For a split second, the football sat balanced *on the goal-post bar.*
1. adverb phrase

1. *Smiling broadly,* Anthony showed us the sizable amount of interest he has earned on his savings account. **1. part.**
2. Asked about enjoyable ways to both relax and get fit, the librarian recommended the new book *about tai chi.* **2. adj.**
3. Gabriel García Márquez, *the brilliant Colombian novelist,* was awarded the Nobel Prize for literature in 1982. **3. app.**
4. Donya wants to ride her bicycle from Washington, D.C., *to Seattle, Washington.* **4. adv.**

5. Kai's ambition is *to drive a tractor-trailer truck*. **5. inf.**
6. Marnie made an appointment *to audition for a part in the play this morning*. **6. inf.**
7. Many of us in biology class have mixed emotions *about dissecting frogs*. **7. adj.**
8. *Moving their vehicles to the right*, all of the drivers let the ambulance pass. **8. part.**
9. *Watching closed-captioned television programs* is a joy for my cousin, who is hard of hearing. **9. ger.**
10. My friends *Alecca and Leon* sent me a postcard from Rome. **10. app.**

B. Identifying Phrases

For each sentence in the following paragraph, identify the <u>italicized phrase</u> as an *adjective phrase*, an *adverb phrase*, a *participial phrase*, a *gerund phrase*, an *infinitive phrase*, or an *appositive phrase*. Do not separately identify a prepositional phrase that is part of a larger phrase.

EXAMPLE **[1]** *Wondering about different clothing terms*, Marcie went to the library to do some research.
   1. *participial phrase*

[11] After a lively discussion in home economics class, Marcie wanted *to learn more about the history of fabrics, clothes, and clothing parts*. **11. inf.** **[12]** One material *of special interest* to the entire class was Velcro. **12. adj.** **[13]** In her research, Marcie discovered that the idea for Velcro is attributed to Georges de Mestral, *a Swiss hiker and engineer*. **13. app.** **[14]** *During an outing in the 1940s*, de Mestral started thinking about the burrs that stuck to his socks. **14. adv.** **[15]** *Adapting the idea from nature*, de Mestral developed a pair of nylon tapes that fastened together. **15. part.** **[16]** The new material was called *Velcro*, a name that combines the French words *for velvet (velours) and hook (crochet)*. **16. adj.** **[17]** *Patented in 1955*, Velcro is widely used today instead of other fasteners such as zippers. **17. part.** **[18]** However, zippers were once considered high-tech in the fashion industry, and *learning about those devices* was Marcie's next goal. **18. ger.** **[19]** The zipper, she found out, was patented in 1893 *by Whitcomb Judson* of Chicago. **19. adv.** **[20]** The public was reluctant to try the new fasteners until the United States military decided *to use zippers on some uniforms during World War I*. **20. inf.**

USING THE DIAGNOSTIC TEST

The **Diagnostic Test** contains two parts. **Part A** focuses on identifying prepositional, participial, gerund, infinitive, and appositive phrases in sentences. **Part B** asks students to identify these types of phrases in a paragraph.

You may want to use the results of this test to determine whether your students have already mastered phrases or whether they need to study some or all of the related material in this chapter.

OBJECTIVES
- To identify adjective phrases and the words they modify
- To identify adverb phrases and the words they modify

PROGRAM MANAGER

PREPOSITIONAL PHRASES

- **Independent Practice/ Reteaching** For instruction and exercises, see **Adjective and Adverb Phrases** in *Language Skills Practice and Assessment,* p. 41.

- **Computer Guided Instruction** For additional instruction and practice with prepositional phrases, see **Lesson 23** in *Language Workshop CD-ROM.*

- **Practice** To help less-advanced students with additional instruction and practice with prepositional phrases, see **Chapter 12** in *English Workshop, Complete Course,* pp. 159–160.

QUICK REMINDER

Write the following sentences on the chalkboard and ask volunteers to identify the prepositional phrases:

1. Tara wore a hat with a large purple feather. [with a large purple feather]
2. Jamal likes to run near the wildlife preserve. [near the wildlife preserve]
3. Micah's experiment will be performed on the next space shuttle flight. [on the next space shuttle flight]

Point out that each phrase includes a preposition and an object. Then, ask students if these prepositional phrases are adjective or adverb phrases. [(1) adjective, (2) adverb, (3) adverb]

652 *The Phrase*

19a. A *phrase* is a group of words that is used as a single part of speech and does not contain a verb and its subject.

VERB PHRASE	have been waiting [no subject]
PREPOSITIONAL PHRASE	during the storm [no subject or verb]

☞ **REFERENCE NOTE:** A group of words that has a subject and a verb is called a *clause.* For more about independent and subordinate clauses, see pages 674–683.

Prepositional Phrases

19b. A *prepositional phrase* includes a preposition, a noun or a pronoun called the *object of the preposition,* and any modifiers of that object.

EXAMPLES Did officials **of the Smithsonian Institution** recently unveil plans **for a new museum**? [The compound noun *Smithsonian Institution* is the object of the preposition *of.* The noun *museum* is the object of the preposition *for.*]
According to them, the National African-American Museum may open **on the Mall.** [The pronoun *them* is the object of the preposition *According to.* The noun *Mall* is the object of the preposition *on.*]

The object of a preposition may be compound.

EXAMPLE Do you know the Greek myth **about Daedalus and Icarus**?

Prepositional phrases are usually used as adjectives or adverbs. Occasionally, a prepositional phrase is used as a noun.

EXAMPLE **Before lunch** will be convenient. [*Before lunch* is used as a noun; it is the subject of the sentence.]

👉 **REFERENCE NOTE:** For lists of commonly used prepositions, see pages 619–620.

The Adjective Phrase

19c. An *adjective phrase* is a prepositional phrase that modifies a noun or a pronoun.

An adjective phrase tells *what kind* or *which one*.

EXAMPLE One **of my friends** is making a film **about our senior year.** [*Of my friends* modifies the pronoun *one. About our senior year* modifies the noun *film.*]

An adjective phrase always follows the word it modifies. That word may be the object of another preposition.

EXAMPLE The film won't include all **of the students in our class.** [*Of the students* modifies the direct object *all. In our class* modifies *students,* which is the object of the preposition *of.*]

More than one adjective phrase may modify the same word.

EXAMPLE Instead, it will relate the adventures **of five students at school** and **in their neighborhood.** [The three phrases *of five students, at school,* and *in their neighborhood* modify the noun *adventures.*]

▶ **EXERCISE 1** **Identifying Adjective Phrases and the Words They Modify**

The following sentences contain ten adjective phrases. Identify each adjective phrase and the word it modifies.

1. New Guinea rivers, like the one shown on the next page, are popular areas for rafting enthusiasts.
2. As you can see, a series of nearly continuous rapids crisscrosses jungles of primeval beauty. 2
3. The twenty-eight major rapids on the Tua River make it a course for rafters with experience and courage. 3

GRAMMAR

GRAMMAR

653

INTEGRATING THE LANGUAGE ARTS

Literature Link. If your literature text-book contains "Sonnet 43" from *Sonnets from the Portuguese* by Elizabeth Barrett Browning, have students read and discuss the poem. Direct students' attention to the techniques the speaker uses to explain how she loves [prepositional phrases]. Have students identify the prepositional phrases and explain why—with so many similar syntactical constructions—the poem does not seem repetitious and boring. [Browning changes the prepositions and the functions of the phrases in her sentences.]

4. Brilliantly colored butterflies brighten the riverbanks, and the metallic whine of cicadas almost drowns out the roar of the river.

5. The banks are a chaos of tumbled boulders and uprooted trees.

The Adverb Phrase

19d. An *adverb phrase* is a prepositional phrase that modifies a verb, an adjective, or an adverb.

An adverb phrase tells *how, when, where, why,* or *to what extent* (*how long* or *how far*).

An adverb phrase may modify a verb.

EXAMPLE   **After the early 800s,** the Fujiwara family ruled **as regents in Japan for more than three hundred years.** [Each phrase modifies the verb *ruled. After the early 800s* tells *when, as regents* tells *how, in Japan* tells *where,* and *for more than three hundred years* tells *how long.*]

As this example shows, more than one adverb phrase can modify the same word. The example also shows that an adverb phrase, unlike an adjective phrase, can precede the word it modifies.

An adverb phrase may modify an adjective.

EXAMPLE   Then the Minamoto, another family active **in court intrigues,** gained power. [*In court intrigues* modifies the adjective *active.*]

An adverb phrase may modify an adverb.

EXAMPLE   The Fujiwara had ruled too complacently **for their own good.** [*For their own good* modifies the adverb *complacently.*]

▶ EXERCISE 2   **Identifying Adverb Phrases and the Words They Modify**

Each of the following sentences contains at least one adverb phrase. Identify each <u>adverb phrase</u> and the <u>word or words it modifies</u>.

EXAMPLE   **1.** From this map, you can clearly tell the function of the Panama Canal.
          1. *From this map—can tell*

COSTA RICA · Caribbean Sea · Panama Canal · ATLANTIC OCEAN · N W E S · Panama Canal Zone · Panama City · Bay of Panama · PANAMA · Gulf of Panama · 0 100 km · 0 100 mi · PACIFIC OCEAN · COLOMBIA

1. The canal, which is fifty-one miles long, <u>links</u> the Pacific Ocean <u>to the Atlantic Ocean</u>.
2. Ships <u>can travel</u> <u>from ocean</u> <u>to ocean</u> using the canal's elaborate series of locks that raise and lower the water levels.
3. Construction of the canal, an engineering marvel, <u>began</u> <u>in 1904</u> and <u>continued</u> <u>until 1914</u>.
4. Naturally, the builders <u>faced</u> many obstacles <u>during the</u> <u>canal's construction</u>.

VISUAL CONNECTIONS
Exploring the Subject. The Panama Canal stretches 50.72 miles from Limón Bay on the Atlantic Ocean to the Bay of Panama on the Pacific Ocean. Approximately 12,000 ships travel through the canal every year—an average of about 33 vessels per day. The canal cost about 380 million dollars to build.

The original treaty with Panama designated the Canal Zone as a constitutionally acquired territorial possession of the United States, granted in perpetuity, for the construction and perpetual maintenance, operation, and protection of the canal. In 1977, a new treaty was signed that returned territorial jurisdiction of the Canal Zone to Panama in 1979. The new treaty also provides for Panama to take control of the operation of the canal at the end of 1999, although a second new treaty gives the United States the right to defend the canal's neutrality.

5. Mosquitoes <u>posed</u> a major health risk <u>throughout the area</u> and had to be eliminated.

6. <u>For the duration</u> of the canal project, Dr. William C. Gorgas, an army surgeon, <u>fought</u> the mosquitoes.

7. <u>With great efficiency</u>, he <u>drained</u> swamps, <u>fumigated</u> buildings, and <u>installed</u> a pure water supply.

8. <u>After the resignation</u> of two chief engineers, President Theodore Roosevelt <u>in 1907</u> <u>appointed</u> Army Lieutenant Colonel George W. Goethals to be chief engineer.

9. Goethals, <u>active</u> <u>in all phases</u> of canal construction, quickly gained the respect of workers.

10. This photograph shows some of the workers who <u>dug</u> <u>through the mountains</u> along the Isthmus of Panama.

Verbals and Verbal Phrases

A *verbal* is a form of a verb used as a noun, an adjective, or an adverb. The three kinds of verbals are the *participle*, the *gerund*, and the *infinitive*.

A *verbal phrase* consists of a verbal and its modifiers and complements. The three kinds of verbal phrases are the *participial phrase*, the *gerund phrase*, and the *infinitive phrase*.

THE PARTICIPLE and THE PARTICIPIAL PHRASE Rules 19e, 19f

OBJECTIVE

- To identify participial phrases and the words they modify

GRAMMAR

The Participle

19e. A *participle* is a verb form that can be used as an adjective.

Two kinds of participles are the *present participle* and the *past participle*.

Present participles end in *–ing*.

EXAMPLES The **freezing** rain made the road slick. [*Freezing,* a form of the verb *freeze,* modifies the noun *rain.*]
Bowing, the performers acknowledged the applause. [*Bowing,* a form of the verb *bow,* modifies the noun *performers.*]
Did I hear someone **knocking** on the door? [*Knocking,* a form of the verb *knock,* modifies the pronoun *someone.*]

Most past participles end in *–d* or *–ed.* Others are irregularly formed.

EXAMPLES First prize was an **engraved** trophy. [*Engraved,* a form of the verb *engrave,* modifies the noun *trophy.*]
The lab tested samples of water **taken** from wells in the area. [*Taken,* a form of the verb *take,* modifies the noun *water.*]
Rested and **relaxed,** we returned to work. [*Rested,* a form of the verb *rest,* and *relaxed,* a form of the verb *relax,* modify the pronoun *we.*]

☞ REFERENCE NOTE: Because they are verbs, participles have different tenses. In addition to the present and past forms, they also have a present perfect form.

EXAMPLES   having gone   having been gone

For more about present perfect participles, see page 799.

Don't confuse a participle used as an adjective with a participle used as part of a verb phrase.

ADJECTIVE   The Hispanic Association of Colleges and Universities, **founded** in 1986, is based in San Antonio, Texas.
VERB PHRASE   The Hispanic Association of Colleges and Universities, which **was founded** in 1986, is based in San Antonio, Texas.

✔ **QUICK REMINDER**

Write the following sentences on the chalkboard:

1. The water was undulating and looked inviting.
2. The undulating water looked inviting.

Ask students how the use of *undulating* differs in the two sentences. [In the first sentence it is part of the verb; in the second, it is a participle used as an adjective.] Challenge the class to create other pairs of sentences that illustrate this difference.

GRAMMAR

658

GRAMMAR

The Participial Phrase

19f. A *participial phrase* consists of a participle and all of the words related to the participle.

Participles may be modified by adverbs and may also have complements.

EXAMPLES   **Grinning broadly,** Whoopi Goldberg accepted the Oscar. [The participial phrase modifies the compound noun *Whoopi Goldberg.* The adverb *broadly* modifies the present participle *Grinning.*]
Proclaiming his innocence, the candidate denied the charges. [The participial phrase modifies the noun *candidate.* The noun *innocence* is the direct object of the present participle *proclaiming.*]
Puzzled by their behavior, I asked for an explanation. [The participial phrase modifies the pronoun *I.* The adverb phrase *by their behavior* modifies the past participle *Puzzled.*]
Zimbabwe, **formerly named Rhodesia,** is in southern Africa. [The participial phrase modifies the noun *Zimbabwe.* The adverb *formerly* modifies the past participle *named.* The noun *Rhodesia* is the direct object of *named.*]

To prevent confusion, place participial phrases as close as possible to the words they modify.

MISPLACED   **Stalking the squirrel,** I saw the cat out in the yard.
IMPROVED   I saw the cat **stalking the squirrel** out in the yard.

☞ **REFERENCE NOTE:** For more information about misplaced participial phrases, see pages 832–836. For information about the participial phrase as a sentence fragment, see pages 555–556.

▶ EXERCISE 3   **Identifying Participial Phrases and the Words They Modify**

Each of the following sentences contains at least one participial phrase. Identify each <u>participial phrase</u> and the <u>word or words it modifies</u>.

EXAMPLE   **1.** Living far from the city, I developed an interest in nature at an early age.
1. *Living far from the city—I*

1. All of the students trying out for the soccer team have heard from the coach or her assistant.
2. Thanking us several times, the piano teacher returned the chairs borrowed for the recital.
3. Today's newspaper, printed last night, made no mention of the president's announcement.
4. Annoyed by the high prices, Mr. Sims has decided not to shop at that store anymore.
5. Addressing the senior class, the principal praised all of the students for their work on the clean-up campaign.
6. Having studied hard, Karen wasn't surprised that she did well on the Spanish test.
7. The movies showing at that theater are old ones released before 1940.
8. Cheered by the crowd, our school's Special Olympics team rushed onto the field.
9. Looking through the catalog, Earl found a Cajun cookbook.
10. Smiling shyly, Lynn showed us the pictures she had taken.

REVIEW A   **Identifying Prepositional and Participial Phrases and the Words They Modify**

Identify each italicized phrase in the following sentences as a *prepositional phrase* or a *participial phrase*. Then give the word or words each phrase modifies. Do not separately identify a prepositional phrase that is part of a participial phrase.

EXAMPLE   [1] *Visiting friends in Los Angeles last year,* I became interested *in low-riders.*
1. participial—I; prepositional—interested

[1] My friend Jorge told me that this unique form *of folk art* has been popular *for forty years or more.* [2] He said the term *low-rider* refers *to the automobile, its driver, and any passengers.* [3] *Making artistic statements with their automobiles,* many young Mexican American men *in the Southwest* spend both time and money on their cars. [4] First, a car is lowered *by several methods* so that its chassis just skims the pavement. [5] *After the height adjustment,* the car is embellished *with exterior paint and trim work.* [6] *Decorated elaborately,* Jorge's car *shown on the next page,* is a good example *of a low-rider.* [7] When their cars are finished and spotlessly clean, riders drive slowly *through their communities.* [8] *Relaxing behind the steering wheel of his car,* Jorge is proud

INTEGRATING THE LANGUAGE ARTS

Grammar and Mechanics. To familiarize students with punctuation rules concerning participial phrases, write the following sentences on the chalkboard and underline the participial phrases:

1. Bending gracefully, the dancers moved to the music.
2. The groceries packed in the crate are for the local food bank.
3. The twins, laughing loudly, raced to the car.

Explain to students that a participial phrase at the beginning of a sentence is always followed by a comma (first sentence). When the phrase is in the middle of the sentence and the information it presents is essential to the meaning of the sentence, no commas are needed (second sentence). However, if the phrase contains nonessential information, it is surrounded by commas (third sentence). You could reinforce these rules by discussing the use of commas in **Exercise 3.**

COMMON ERROR

Problem. Misplaced and dangling participles often appear in students' writing.

Solution. Suggest that students circle the modified words and check to see that the participial phrases are placed correctly.

THE GERUND and THE GERUND PHRASE
Rules 19g, 19h

OBJECTIVES

- To identify gerund phrases and their functions
- To write a paragraph containing prepositional phrases, participial phrases, and gerund phrases

PROGRAM MANAGER

THE GERUND AND THE GERUND PHRASE

- **Independent Practice/Reteaching** For instruction and exercises, see **Gerunds and Gerund Phrases** in *Language Skills Practice and Assessment,* p. 43.

- **Computer Guided Instruction** For additional instruction and practice with gerunds and gerund phrases, see **Lesson 24** in *Language Workshop CD-ROM.*

- **Practice** To help less-advanced students with additional instruction and practice with gerunds and gerund phrases, see **Chapter 12** in *English Workshop, Complete Course,* pp. 165–166.

QUICK REMINDER

Write the following sentences on the chalkboard:

1. Practicing will improve your discus technique.
2. Her favorite exercise is cycling.
3. Dad hated washing the skunk smell off our dog.

Ask students what the underlined words have in common. [All are verb forms ending in –*ing* and are used as nouns.] Explain that the students have just described gerunds.

---

660 *The Phrase*

when people admire the results *of his hard work.* [9] On sunny days, long caravans *of low-riders* may drive for hours *through the neighborhood.* [10] Low-riders *in some cities* have even formed clubs that work *with charitable organizations.*

The Gerund

19g. A *gerund* is a verb form ending in –*ing* that is used as a noun.

SUBJECT	**Fishing** requires great patience.
PREDICATE NOMINATIVE	Norene's trade is **welding.**
DIRECT OBJECT	Please stop **whispering.**
INDIRECT OBJECT	The team gave **winning** their best effort.
OBJECT OF PREPOSITION	In **answering,** give specific examples.

Don't confuse a gerund with a present participle used as an adjective or as part of a verb phrase.

GERUND	I remember **driving** from Florida to Texas last fall. [direct object of the verb *remember*]
PRESENT PARTICIPLE	**Driving** on long trips, we usually take turns behind the wheel. [adjective modifying the pronoun *we*]
PRESENT PARTICIPLE	We heard mostly country music on the radio while we were **driving.** [main verb in the verb phrase *were driving*]

NOTE: When you use a noun or a pronoun just before a gerund, use the possessive form.

EXAMPLES	**Lee's** pitching won the game.
	What did the teacher say about **your** missing the test yesterday?

The Gerund Phrase

19h. A *gerund phrase* consists of a gerund and all of the words related to the gerund.

Like participles, gerunds may have modifiers and complements.

EXAMPLES **Managing the restaurant efficiently** required lots of hard work. [The gerund phrase is the subject of the verb *required*. The noun *restaurant* is the direct object of the gerund *Managing*. The adverb *efficiently* modifies the gerund *Managing*.]

My cousin enjoys **working as a lifeguard.** [The gerund phrase is the direct object of the verb *enjoys*. The adverb phrase *as a lifeguard* modifies the gerund *working*.]

We were fined for **parking there.** [The gerund phrase is the object of the preposition *for*. The adverb *there* modifies the gerund *parking*.]

Her greatest achievement was **winning three gold medals.** [The gerund phrase is a predicate nominative explaining the subject *achievement*. The noun *medals* is the direct object of the gerund *winning*.]

▶ EXERCISE 4 **Identifying Gerund Phrases and Their Functions**

Identify the gerund phrase in each of the following sentences as a *subject*, a *predicate nominative*, a *direct object*, an *indirect object*, or an *object of a preposition*.

EXAMPLE 1. Learning to type has been one of my most practical accomplishments.
   1. *Learning to type—subject*

1. Solving crossword puzzles is one of Geraldo's favorite pastimes. **1. s.**
2. Sylvia's method of making decisions reveals a great deal about her. **2. o.p.**
3. My grandparents enjoy practicing their square-dance routines with the Nicholsons. **3. d.o.**
4. In making any changes, please notify our secretary, Ms. Erikson. **4. o.p.**
5. Producing a movie for Mr. Matsuyama's cinematography course requires the ability to organize and communicate. **5. s.**
6. Ms. Sanapaw finished writing her paper. **6. d.o.**

MEETING *individual* NEEDS

LEARNING STYLES

Visual Learners. Diagram on the chalkboard the example sentences following **Rule 19g** to illustrate the grammatical functions of gerunds and gerund phrases.

LESS-ADVANCED STUDENTS

To help students learn to identify gerunds, tell the class that if a pronoun can be substituted for the word or phrase in question, the word is a gerund or the phrase is a gerund phrase. Write the following sentences on the chalkboard to illustrate the technique:

1. Hiking is an adventuresome way to exercise.
2. Mercedes excels at playing the oboe.
3. Snoring loudly, Hal continued to sleep.

[The first two sentences contain gerunds because pronouns can be substituted: (1) It is an adventuresome way to exercise; (2) Mercedes excels at it. A pronoun cannot be substituted for *snoring loudly,* which is a participial phrase.]

GRAMMAR

662 *The Phrase*

7. <u>Gaining the vote for women</u> was Susan B. Anthony's
   mission. **7.** s.   **8.** p.n.
8. One of the most interesting characteristics of bees (is) <u>their
   dancing to communicate the location of food sources</u>.
9. Hector earns money on the weekends by <u>giving guitar
   lessons</u>. **9.** o.p.
10. <u>My brother's singing in the shower</u> annoys everyone
    early in the morning. **10.** s.

PICTURE THIS

You are a publicist for Alaska's Division of Tourism. Your current project is to prepare a brochure about Misty Fiords National Monument, a beautiful wilderness reserve. From the many pictures taken by your staff photographer, you've chosen these to use in your brochure. Now, write two or three paragraphs based on the photos, describing some of the things visitors can see and do in the area. In your paragraphs, use at least five prepositional phrases, three participial phrases, and two gerund phrases.

Subject: Misty Fiords National Monument
Audience: readers of a travel brochure
Purpose: to inform; to persuade readers
             that Misty Fiords is a great
             place to visit

PICTURE THIS

You may want to provide some sample brochures from Alaska (or other places) as models for students who are unfamiliar with this type of writing. Encourage students to use their imaginations to provide missing details while staying true to the photographs. You may want to point out that this kind of writing can be written in the second person.

MEETING individual NEEDS

LEP/ESL

Spanish. Students might need extra practice in reviewing gerund and infinitive forms to help them distinguish between the forms. The present participle in Spanish is called *gerundio,* but, unlike the English gerund, it cannot be used as a noun or an adjective. The Spanish infinitive form is normally used where English uses the gerund form.

THE INFINITIVE and THE INFINITIVE PHRASE Rules 19i, 19j

OBJECTIVE

- To identify infinitive phrases, their functions, and the words they modify

The Infinitive

19i. An *infinitive* is a verb form that can be used as a noun, an adjective, or an adverb. An infinitive usually begins with *to*.

NOUNS	**To leave** now would be rude. [subject of *would be*]
	No one wants **to stay.** [direct object of *wants*]
	Her goal is **to win.** [predicate nominative identifying the subject *goal*]
ADJECTIVES	She is the candidate **to watch.** [adjective modifying the noun *candidate*]
	The one **to see** is the class president. [adjective modifying the pronoun *one*]
ADVERBS	We came **to cheer.** [adverb modifying the verb *came*]
	Is everybody ready **to go**? [adverb modifying the adjective *ready*]

NOTE: Don't confuse an infinitive with a prepositional phrase beginning with *to.* Remember that a prepositional phrase ends with a noun or a pronoun.

INFINITIVES	to go	to forget	to graduate
PREPOSITIONAL PHRASES	to them	to the party	to everyone

☞ **REFERENCE NOTE:** Infinitives, like participles, have different tense forms. The preceding examples all contain present infinitives. There is also a present perfect infinitive form.

EXAMPLES	**To have seen** Spike Lee would have pleased Jerome.
	Elsa was disappointed not **to have been chosen.**

For more about present perfect infinitives, see pages 798–799.

The word *to,* the sign of the infinitive, is sometimes omitted.

EXAMPLES	Let's [to] **wait** here.
	The clowns made us [to] **laugh.**
	Help me [to] **wash** the car.

The Infinitive Phrase

19j. An *infinitive phrase* consists of an infinitive and all of the words related to the infinitive.

Infinitives may have modifiers and complements.

PROGRAM MANAGER

THE INFINITIVE AND THE INFINITIVE PHRASE

- **Independent Practice/ Reteaching** For instruction and exercises, see **Infinitives and Infinitive Phrases** in *Language Skills Practice and Assessment,* p. 44.

- **Computer Guided Instruction** For additional instruction and practice with infinitives and infinitive phrases, see **Lesson 24** in *Language Workshop CD-ROM.*

- **Practice** To help less-advanced students with additional instruction and practice with infinitives and infinitive phrases, see **Chapter 12** in *English Workshop, Complete Course,* pp. 167–168.

✔ QUICK REMINDER

Write the following phrases on the chalkboard and ask students to tell whether each is a prepositional phrase or an infinitive:

1. to you [prepositional phrase]
2. to spill [infinitive]
3. to Mars [prepositional phrase]
4. to mark [infinitive]
5. to fiddle [infinitive]

Lead the class to understand that *to* followed by a noun or a pronoun forms a prepositional phrase, while *to* followed by a verb forms an infinitive.

A DIFFERENT APPROACH

To emphasize the different uses of infinitive phrases, use the same infinitive in three different ways—as a noun, as an adjective, and as an adverb—in three different sentences. Write the sentences on the chalkboard and ask students to pick out the infinitive phrases. Then, discuss whether these phrases are used as nouns, adjectives, or adverbs. Here are some examples using the infinitive *to make:*

1. To make puff pastry is a difficult art. *[To make puff pastry—noun]*

2. I have the ability to make whipped cream. *[to make whipped cream—adjective]*

3. To make cheese, Lawanda needs cheesecloth. *To make cheese—adjective]*

COMMON ERROR

Problem. An infinitive sometimes has a subject, and this construction can cause a problem for students.

Solution. The subject of such an infinitive is considered to be in the objective case. Therefore, a predicate pronoun following the infinitive is also in the objective case, as in "Mrs. Ramirez took my younger sister to be me."

EXAMPLES **To become a doctor** is her goal. [The infinitive phrase is the subject of the verb *is.* The noun *doctor* is the predicate nominative of the infinitive *to become.*]

They promised **to return soon.** [The infinitive phrase is the direct object of the verb *promised.* The adverb *soon* modifies the infinitive *to return.*]

We have time **to walk to the concert.** [The infinitive phrase modifies the noun *time.* The adverb phrase *to the concert* modifies the infinitive *to walk.*]

It's important **to be prompt for an interview.** [The infinitive phrase modifies the adjective *important.* The modifier *prompt* is the predicate adjective of the infinitive *to be.* The adverb phrase *for an interview* modifies the adjective *prompt.*]

NOTE: Unlike other verbals, an infinitive may have a subject. Such a construction is called an ***infinitive clause.***

EXAMPLES Everyone expects **Guadalupe to win the election.** [*Guadalupe* is the subject of the infinitive *to win.* The entire infinitive clause is the direct object of the verb *expects.*]

We asked **her to lead the discussion.** [*Her* is the subject of the infinitive *to lead.* The entire infinitive clause is the direct object of the verb *asked.*]

I found **everyone to be friendly.** [*Everyone* is the subject of the infinitive *to be.* The entire infinitive clause is the direct object of the verb *found.*]

Notice that the subject of an infinitive is in the objective case.

EXERCISE 5 **Identifying Infinitive Phrases and Their Functions**

Identify each infinitive phrase in the following sentences as a *noun*, an *adjective*, or an *adverb*. If a phrase is used as a noun, tell whether it is the *subject*, the *direct object*, or the *predicate nominative*. If the phrase is used as a modifier, give the word it modifies.

EXAMPLE **1.** I like to compose music for the guitar.
1. *to compose music for the guitar—noun, direct object*

1. To win an Olympic medal is the dream of every member of the women's ski team. **1. s.**

2. The candidate had the courage to speak on a controversial issue. **2. courage**

3. We went to Italy <u>to see Michelangelo's statue *David*</u>.   **3.** went
4. The Latin and French clubs try <u>to work together on projects</u>.   **4.** d.o.
5. Martin Luther King, Jr., believed that all U.S. citizens should be free <u>to exercise their civil rights.</u>   **5.** free
6. Louis Pasteur experimented for many years <u>to discover a method for preventing rabies</u>.   **6.** experimented
7. The ability (to speak distinctly) is an advantage in job interviews.   **7.** ability
8. <u>To open the box</u> required a hammer and a crowbar.   **8.** s.
9. Alana's hobby is <u>to spend hours each day developing original computer programs</u>.   **9.** p.n.
10. Marvella has always wanted <u>to learn about photography</u>.   **10.** d.o.

▶ REVIEW B

Identifying Prepositional, Participial, Gerund, and Infinitive Phrases

Identify each numbered italicized phrase in the following paragraph as a *prepositional phrase*, a *participial phrase*, a *gerund phrase*, an *infinitive phrase*, or an *infinitive clause*. Do not separately identify a prepositional phrase, a verbal, a verbal phrase, or a clause that is part of a larger phrase.

EXAMPLE   **Actress Marlee Matlin has gained attention for [1]** *championing the rights of people who are hard of hearing,* **and it almost seems she has made a career [2]** *of tackling new challenges.*

   1. *gerund phrase*
   2. *prepositional phrase*

Matlin, who lost her hearing [1] *because of complications from childhood measles,* never let her deafness [2] *stand in her way.* [3] *Learning to sign, to read lips, and to speak* helped the young Matlin [4] *to communicate effectively* [5] *with a wide range* of people. [6] *Interested in acting,* she was soon performing [7] *in a children's theater group.* [8] *After high school,* she started on the road [9] *to Hollywood and stardom* by [10] *winning a supporting role* [11] *in a Chicago revival* of the play <u>Children of a Lesser God</u>. Film producers saw a tape [12] *of Matlin's performance* and wanted [13] *her to audition for a starring role.* [14] *Praised by the critics and the public alike,* Matlin's portrayal of a proud and independent deaf woman was magnificent. [15] *For her stellar performance,* Matlin won the Oscar for Best Actress [16] *at the 1987 Academy Award*

   1. prep.   **2.** inf.
   3. ger.
   4. inf.
   5. prep.
   6. part.
   7. prep.
   8. prep.
   9. prep.
   10. ger.
   11. prep.
   12. prep.
   13. inf.
   14. part.
   15. prep.
   16. prep.

GRAMMAR

COOPERATIVE LEARNING
Divide the class into groups of three and ask the groups to find as many examples of infinitive use as they can. Suggest that the groups look in newspapers, magazines, books, and so on. Ask groups to list the sources with the infinitives and to classify the infinitives according to how they are used.

GRAMMAR

17. part. *ceremonies.* [17] *Turning her abilities to television,* Matlin starred in
18. inf. the movie <u>Bridge to Silence</u>. Later, she decided [18] *to try a full-time TV series* and costarred with Mark Harmon in <u>Reasonable</u>
19. part. <u>Doubt</u>. [19] *Playing the role of a hearing-impaired assistant district*
20. part. *attorney,* Matlin, [20] *shown here in a scene from the show,* usually
signed but sometimes spoke her lines.

Appositives and Appositive Phrases

19k. An *appositive* is a noun or pronoun placed beside another noun or pronoun to identify or explain it.

An appositive usually follows the word it identifies or explains.

EXAMPLES   My cousin **María** is an accomplished violinist.
         Riboflavin, a **vitamin,** is found in leafy vegetables.

For emphasis, however, an appositive may come at the beginning of a sentence.

EXAMPLE   A natural **leader,** Joseph Cinqué led the *Amistad* revolt.

19l. An *appositive phrase* consists of an appositive and its modifiers.

EXAMPLE   My brother's car, **a sporty red hatchback with bucket seats,** has over 100,000 miles on it.

PROGRAM MANAGER

APPOSITIVES AND APPOSITIVE PHRASES

- **Independent Practice/ Reteaching** For instruction and exercises, see **Appositives and Appositive Phrases** in *Language Skills Practice and Assessment,* p. 45.

- **Computer Guided Instruction** For additional instruction and practice with appositives and appositive phrases, see **Lesson 25** in *Language Workshop CD-ROM.*

- **Practice** To help less-advanced students with additional instruction and practice with appositives and appositive phrases, see **Chapter 12** in *English Workshop, Complete Course,* pp. 169–170.

QUICK REMINDER

Write these sentences on the chalkboard and have students combine the sentences by using appositive phrases:

1. Lake Arrowhead is one of my favorite places.
2. Lake Arrowhead is in California.

[Two possibilities are "Lake Arrowhead, one of my favorite places, is in California" and "Arrowhead, a lake in California, is one of my favorite places."]

An appositive phrase usually follows the word it explains or identifies but may precede it.

EXAMPLE **Once a pagan feast,** Valentine's Day is now celebrated as a day of love.

☞ **REFERENCE NOTE:** For information on how to punctuate appositives, see pages 914–915. For a discussion of the use of appositives, see pages 570–571 and 740–741.

WRITING APPLICATION

Using Infinitive and Appositive Phrases in Business Writing

Infinitive and appositive phrases add variety and detail to sentences. Such phrases also help make writing more concise. Often, a writer can reduce a sentence to an appositive or infinitive phrase and insert the phrase into another sentence. As you read the following examples, notice how the writer eliminates unnecessary words by reducing the less-important sentence to a phrase.

ORIGINAL Mr. Jenkins of Jenkins' Sporting Goods donated a valuable, autographed baseball. He made this donation to help our fund-raiser.

COMBINED **To help our fund-raiser,** Mr. Jenkins of Jenkins' Sporting Goods donated a valuable, autographed baseball.

ORIGINAL Lakewood Cineplex donated a month's supply of movie passes. Lakewood Cineplex is the new movie theater in town.

COMBINED Lakewood Cineplex, **the new movie theater in town,** donated a month's supply of movie passes.

▶ **WRITING ACTIVITY**

Every year your school holds a raffle to raise funds for special equipment and activities. This year's goal is to raise enough money for two new computers. As secretary of the student council, you've been asked to contact owners of local businesses and ask them to donate prizes for the raffle. Write a letter explaining the purpose of the raffle and

MEETING *individual* NEEDS

LESS-ADVANCED STUDENTS

You may need to review with students the use of commas with appositives and appositive phrases. Write the following sentences on the chalkboard (without commas) and have the students punctuate them properly:

1. His sister[,] a former NASA engineer [,] is now a teacher.
2. Simón Bolívar[,] a general and revolutionary known as The Liberator[,] freed South America from Spanish rule.
3. Sylvia is reading a book about Catherine the Great. [no commas needed]

WRITING APPLICATION

Because infinitive phrases and appositive phrases can be added to a piece of writing in the revision stage, you may want to suggest that students write their rough drafts without being overly concerned about whether all five phrases (p. 668) are included. Tell students that they can combine sentences to create the phrases or add required phrases in the revision stage.

CRITICAL THINKING

Analysis. Remind students to analyze the intended audience when writing their letters—to consider the audience's desire for promotion and need for advertising at a low cost. The suggestions students make about donating products should be planned both to enhance the fund-raising potential of the raffle and to serve the business community's goals.

667

PREWRITING

Have students develop lists of local businesses that could be recipients of the letters. Lead the students in an open discussion to explore techniques for persuading the businesses to donate. For example, carefully explaining the need for the money the raffle will raise may influence some businesses, while citing the generosity of competitors might entice others to contribute.

persuading the business owners to donate their products or services. You may want to give examples of donated prizes that helped raise money for the school last year. Include at least three infinitive phrases and two appositive phrases in your letter.

Prewriting   First, invent some details about last year's raffle. List three or four interesting items that local businesses donated. Note how much money was raised and what the money was used for. Then, jot down specific information about the upcoming raffle, including when and where it's being held. Think about how you can convince business owners that they should donate prizes. You might explain that the names of contributors will be displayed prominently at the raffle, giving the businesses good publicity.

Writing   Begin your letter by clearly stating your purpose for writing. Then give specific information about the raffle. Explain how local businesses helped make last year's raffle a success. Conclude by restating your request. Also, tell your reader whom to contact to make a donation.

Evaluating and Revising   Make sure your letter says what you want it to say. Have you clearly explained the purpose of the raffle? Have you told your reader everything he or she needs to know about the event? Will your letter convince your reader that the raffle is a worthy cause? Also be sure that the form and the tone of your letter are appropriate for business correspondence. (See pages 1088–1095 for more about business letters.) Note any revisions you will need to make. You may want to ask an adult friend or family member to read your letter and to offer further suggestions for revision. As you revise your letter, look for short, choppy sentences that you could combine into longer, smoother ones. Be sure that you include at least three infinitive phrases and two appositive phrases.

Proofreading   Errors in grammar, usage, spelling, or punctuation won't help your cause, so be sure to proofread carefully. Check that your letter follows the correct form for business letters. Also take care not to count prepositional phrases beginning with *to* as infinitive phrases.

REVIEW C

OBJECTIVE

• To identify prepositional, participial, gerund, infinitive, and appositive phrases in a paragraph

GRAMMAR

⏵ REVIEW C

Identifying Prepositional, Verbal, and Appositive Phrases

Identify each italicized phrase in the following paragraph as a *prepositional phrase*, a *participial phrase*, a *gerund phrase*, an *infinitive phrase*, or an *appositive phrase*. Do not separately identify a prepositional phrase that is part of a larger phrase.

Altamont Pass, [1]*an area of grassy hills* [2]*surrounding San Francisco Bay*, is producing a new cash crop. Energy entrepreneurs are hurrying [3]*to lease wind rights on acreage* [4]*throughout the Altamont*. One rancher owns several hundred acres [5]*dotted with tall white wind machines like the ones shown here*. [6]*Standing in rows on the windswept hills*, these machines are expected [7]*to produce electricity*. [8]*With any luck*, the wind-power industry may soon spread [9]*to other parts* of the country. The temperature differences [10]*between the cool coast and the hot valley* can create air surges [11]*funneling inland through natural gaps* [12]*like the Altamont*. According to some energy experts, there will be several hundred wind machines [13]*producing thirty million kilowatts per year*, the power [14]*used by 4,800 homes*. [15]*An economist and a trained engineer*, John Eckland has advocated [16]*generating electricity* by [17]*using these updated windmills*. Not until the oil shortages of the 1970s did a serious effort begin [18]*in the United States* [19]*to develop a wind industry*. Modern wind turbines may someday become as numerous [20]*in the United States* as windmills were in Holland.

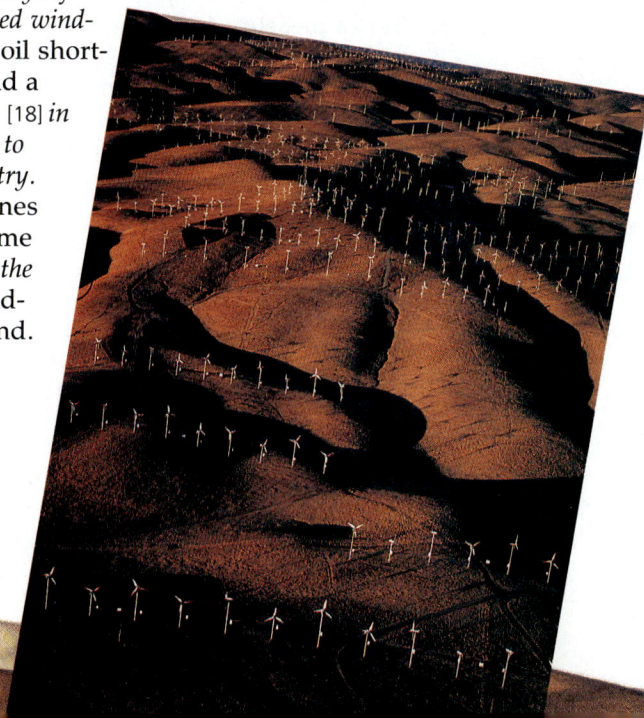

INTEGRATING THE LANGUAGE ARTS

Grammar and Writing. To provide further practice with phrases, have each student write six sentences containing phrases according to the following guidelines:

1. a sentence with a prepositional phrase used as an adjective
2. a sentence with a prepositional phrase used as an adverb
3. a sentence with a participial phrase
4. a sentence with an infinitive phrase
5. a sentence with a gerund phrase
6. a sentence with an appositive phrase

Have those students who finish first write their sentences on the chalkboard while the other students are finishing. Then, have students identify and classify the phrases.

ANSWERS
Review C

1.	appositive	11.	participial
2.	participial	12.	prepositional
3.	infinitive	13.	participial
4.	prepositional	14.	participial
5.	participial	15.	appositive
6.	participial	16.	gerund
7.	infinitive	17.	gerund
8.	prepositional	18.	prepositional
9.	prepositional	19.	infinitive
10.	prepositional	20.	prepositional

GRAMMAR

OBJECTIVES

- To identify prepositional, participial, gerund, infinitive, and appositive phrases in sentences and in a paragraph
- To write sentences containing prepositional phrases, participial phrases, gerund phrases, infinitive phrases, and appositive phrases

670 *The Phrase*

Review: Posttest 1

A. Identifying Phrases

Identify the <u>italicized phrase</u> in each of the following sentences as a *prepositional phrase*, a *participial phrase*, a *gerund phrase*, an *infinitive phrase*, or an *appositive phrase*. Do not separately identify a prepositional phrase that is part of a larger phrase.

EXAMPLE   **1.** The sunlight shimmering *on the lake* was beautiful.
           1. *on the lake—prepositional phrase*

1. Juanita likes <u>*to draw caricatures of her friends*</u>.   **1. inf.** **2. part.**
2. <u>*Arriving late at school*</u>, Bill went to the office to get a pass.
3. <u>*Made in Ireland*</u>, Waterford crystal is admired throughout the world.   **3. part.**
4. By <u>*inventing the telephone*</u>, Alexander Graham Bell assured himself a place in history.   **4. ger.**
5. Luciano Pavarotti, <u>*the great Italian tenor*</u>, received a hearty standing ovation at the end of his concert.   **5. app.** **6. part.**
6. After the concert we saw them <u>*looking in vain for a taxi*</u>.
7. Raúl has the talent <u>*to sculpt and design beautiful objects*</u>.   **7. inf.**
8. "It is a pleasure to be here with you today," remarked the mayor <u>*at the beginning*</u> of her talk.   **8. prep.**
9. A number of pioneer women kept diaries and journals <u>*of their experiences*</u> settling the American wilderness.   **9. prep.**
10. <u>*To speak freely on any issue*</u> is a right guaranteed to all U.S. citizens.   **10. inf.**

B. Identifying Prepositional, Verbal, and Appositive Phrases

Identify each italicized phrase in the following paragraph as a *prepositional phrase*, a *participial phrase*, a *gerund phrase*, an *infinitive phrase*, or an *appositive phrase*. Do not separately identify a prepositional phrase or a verbal phrase that is part of a larger phrase.

EXAMPLE   **[1]** *For more than fifty years,* Thurgood Marshall worked
            [2] *to protect the rights of all people in the United States.*

            1. *prepositional phrase*
            2. *infinitive phrase*

GRAMMAR

[11] *Ranked at the top of his law school class*, Thurgood Marshall   **11.** part.
began law practice in Baltimore; and in 1936, he was selected   **12.** inf.
[12] *to be a counsel for the National Association for the Advancement of*   **13.**
Colored People. From the start of his career, he believed strongly   ger.
in **[13]** *using the U.S. Constitution to fight injustice*. **[14]** *Risking his*   **14.**
life at times, Marshall, **[15]** *the son of a schoolteacher*, won many   part.
civil rights cases **[16]** *before federal and state courts*. His arguments   **15.**
played an important role in **[17]** *convincing the Supreme Court* that   app.
"separate but equal" educational facilities were unconstitu-   **16.**
tional. **[18]** *During the Kennedy administration*, Marshall became a   prep.
federal judge. **[19]** *After a two-year term* as U.S. solicitor general,   **17.**
he was nominated for the Supreme Court by President Lyndon   ger.
Johnson. Marshall was the first African American **[20]** *to serve on*   **18.** prep.
the nation's highest court.   **19.** prep.   **20.** inf.

GRAMMAR

Review: Posttest 2

Writing Sentences with Phrases

Write ten sentences according to the following guidelines.

1. Use *because of the rain* as an adverb phrase.
2. Use *from Puerto Rico* as an adjective phrase.
3. Use *running towards us* as a participial phrase.
4. Use *seen from a distance* as a participial phrase.
5. Use *building a fence* as a gerund phrase that is the object of a preposition.
6. Use *writing résumés* as a gerund phrase that is the subject.
7. Use *to dream* as an infinitive phrase that is the object of a verb.
8. Use *to sell* as an infinitive phrase that is a modifier.
9. Use *to study music* as an infinitive phrase that is the predicate nominative.
10. Use *our local newspaper* as an appositive phrase.

ANSWERS
Review: Posttest 2

Sentences will vary. Here are some possibilities:

1. We stayed inside because of the rain.
2. My aunt from Puerto Rico is a doctor.
3. Running towards us, the children shouted in surprise.
4. Seen from a distance, the city looked majestic.
5. We tried to help our neighbor by building a fence.
6. Writing résumés is an important part of finding jobs.
7. Every night, she likes to dream.
8. In the summer, air conditioners are easy to sell.
9. His dream is to study music.
10. *The Gazette,* our local newspaper, has many subscribers.

OBJECTIVES

- To identify independent and subordinate clauses in sentences and to classify the subordinate clauses as adjective, adverb, or noun clauses
- To classify sentences as simple, compound, complex, or compound-complex

PROGRAM MANAGER

FOR THE WHOLE CHAPTER

- **Review** For exercises on chapter concepts, see **Review Form A** and **Review Form B** in *Language Skills Practice and Assessment,* pp. 58–61.
- **Assessment** For additional testing, see **Grammar Pretests** and **Grammar Mastery Tests** in *Language Skills Practice and Assessment,* pp. 1–7 and pp. 83–92.

CHAPTER OVERVIEW

This chapter defines and discusses the independent clause and the types of subordinate clauses. Subordinate clauses are classified as adjective, noun, or adverb clauses according to their uses in sentences. Sentences are then classified according to structure and purpose. In the **Writing Application**, students are asked to use end marks correctly in writing interviews.

Instead of assigning the entire chapter, you may want to refer to specific sections for problems or questions about writing and about punctuating sentences or clauses. This chapter may be useful when revising and proofreading the writing assignments for **Chapters 4–11.**

20 THE CLAUSE

The Function of Clauses

Diagnostic Test

A. Identifying and Classifying Clauses

Identify the italicized word group in each of the following sentences as an *independent clause* or a *subordinate clause*. Then classify each subordinate clause as an *adjective clause*, an *adverb clause*, or a *noun clause*.

EXAMPLE   **1.** I hope *that the snow will be deep and solid enough for sledding.*
       1. subordinate clause—noun clause

1. The violinist *whom I most enjoy hearing* is Itzhak Perlman.   **1. adj. cl.**
2. This car is more fuel efficient *than the other ones*.   **2. adv. cl.**
3. *The pitcher read the catcher's signals,* and then she struck out the hitter with a fastball.
4. *Where the city will build the new recycling center* has still not been decided.   **4. n. cl.**

5. *When champion golfer Juan Rodríguez was a boy*, he worked on a sugar-cane plantation in Puerto Rico. **5.** adv. cl.
6. Here is the savings bond *that Aunt Ruthie and Uncle Bob gave me for graduation*. **6.** adj. cl.
7. *Because his artwork received wide recognition*, Pablo Picasso became famous and wealthy. **7.** adv. cl.
8. As we walked along the road, *we saw the wheat waving in the wind*.
9. The Kimbell Art Museum, *which was designed by architect Louis Kahn*, is one of the leading attractions in Fort Worth. **9.** adj. cl.
10. During the quiz bowl, *whoever rings the buzzer first* gets to answer the question. **10.** n. cl.

B. Classifying Sentences According to Structure

Classify each sentence of the following paragraph as *simple*, *compound*, *complex*, or *compound-complex* and then as *declarative*, *interrogative*, *imperative*, or *exclamatory*.

EXAMPLE   [1] Walt Disney, who won many awards for his movies and cartoons, received the U.S. Presidential Medal of Freedom in 1964.
          1. *complex—declarative*

[11] What simple beginnings great men and women often have! [12] Consider the life of famed animator Walt Disney, for example. [13] Although he was born in Chicago in 1901, Disney grew up on a farm in Missouri. [14] Disney loved farm life, and he paid particular attention to the animals, which he sketched constantly. [15] Surely you're not surprised that his early drawings were of farm animals! [16] Where do you think he got his ideas for Mickey Mouse, Donald Duck, and the other Disney-animated animals that are now household names? [17] During his school years, Disney and a friend enjoyed acting; indeed, they even performed a short-lived comedy routine together. [18] How fortunate it is that Disney's main interest remained art! [19] He continued to doodle, and later he attended several art institutes where he learned not only about drawing anatomical figures but also about drawing cartoons. [20] Is it any wonder that one of Disney's first jobs was to draw farm animals for an advertising company?

11. excl.
12. imp.
13. decl.
14. decl.
15. excl.
16. int.
17. decl.
18. excl.
19. decl.
20. int.

GRAMMAR

USING THE DIAGNOSTIC TEST

The **Diagnostic Test** contains two parts. **Part A** asks students to identify clauses as independent or subordinate and then to determine how subordinate clauses are used. **Part B** requires students to classify sentences according to structure and purpose.

To prevent needless reteaching, analyze the results of students' tests. For example, assign the section on adjective clauses to students who miss items 1, 6, and 9. If students miss 2, 5, and 7, assign adverb clauses; if they miss 4 and 10, assign noun clauses.

GRAMMAR

THE INDEPENDENT CLAUSE and THE SUBORDINATE CLAUSE Rules 20a–20c

OBJECTIVE

- To label independent and subordinate clauses in sentences

PROGRAM MANAGER

THE INDEPENDENT CLAUSE AND THE SUBORDINATE CLAUSE

- **Independent Practice/ Reteaching** See **Independent and Subordinate Clauses** in *Language Skills Practice and Assessment*, p. 53.
- **Computer Guided Instruction** See **Lesson 26** in *Language Workshop CD-ROM*.
- **Practice** See **Chapter 13** in *English Workshop, Complete Course*, pp. 173–174.

QUICK REMINDER

Tell students that compound sentences can be written in a variety of ways. Write the following patterns on the chalkboard and have students use the patterns to compose three original sentences:

1. independent clause-comma-coordinating conjunction-independent clause [It is late May, but there is still frost in Vermont.]
2. independent clause-semicolon-independent clause [The cold last night killed three of my tomato plants; the weather service predicts that the temperature will be in the twenties tonight.]
3. independent clause-semicolon-conjunctive adverb-comma-independent clause [Usually I'm glad I live in Texas; however, Texas has had many flash floods recently.]

GRAMMAR

---

674 *The Clause*

20a. A *clause* is a group of words that contains a subject and its predicate and is used as part of a sentence.

Every clause has both a subject and a verb. Not every clause expresses a complete thought, however.

SENTENCE   A sitar is an Indian stringed instrument that resembles a lute.

CLAUSE   A sitar is an Indian stringed instrument. [complete thought]

CLAUSE   that resembles a lute [incomplete thought]

There are two kinds of clauses: the *independent clause* and the *subordinate clause*. Standing alone, an independent clause is a complete sentence. Like a word or a phrase, a subordinate clause acts as a single part of speech.

☞ **REFERENCE NOTE:** Another type of clause—the infinitive clause—is discussed on page 664.

The Independent Clause

20b. An *independent* (or *main*) *clause* expresses a complete thought and can stand by itself as a sentence.

EXAMPLES

            S   V

Mexican artist José Guadalupe Posada opposed the dictatorship of Porfirio Díaz. [one independent clause]

    S   V

Posada attacked the Díaz regime in his paintings, and

   S V

he made thousands of inexpensive prints of his work. [two independent clauses joined by *and*]

       S   V

Posada's art helped to stir the social unrest that led to the overthrow of Díaz in the revolution of 1910. [an independent clause combined with a subordinate clause]

By itself an independent clause is simply called a sentence. It is called an independent clause only when it is combined with at least one other clause (independent or subordinate) to form a sentence.

The Subordinate Clause

20c. A *subordinate* (or *dependent*) *clause* does not express a complete thought and cannot stand alone as a sentence.

EXAMPLES   whoever knows the song
which is my favorite song
as we were singing

The meaning of a subordinate clause becomes clear only when the clause is combined with an independent clause.

Whoever knows the song may join in.
We sang "We Shall Overcome," **which is my favorite song.**
As we were singing, we joined hands and formed a circle.

EXERCISE 1   Identifying Independent and Subordinate Clauses

Identify the italicized word group in each of the following sentences as an *independent clause* or a *subordinate clause*.

1. Egyptology is the branch of learning *that is concerned with the language and culture of ancient Egypt*.
2. *Until the Rosetta Stone was discovered in 1799,* the ancient Egyptian language was an enigma to scholars.
3. A man named Bouchard, *who was a captain under Napoleon*, and some of his men found the stone near Rosetta, a city near the mouth of the Nile.
4. As you can see in this photograph of the Rosetta Stone, *it has three different kinds of writing inscribed on it*.

The Rosetta Stone (196 B.C.). British Museum, London. Bridgeman/Art Resource, N.Y., BAL2359.

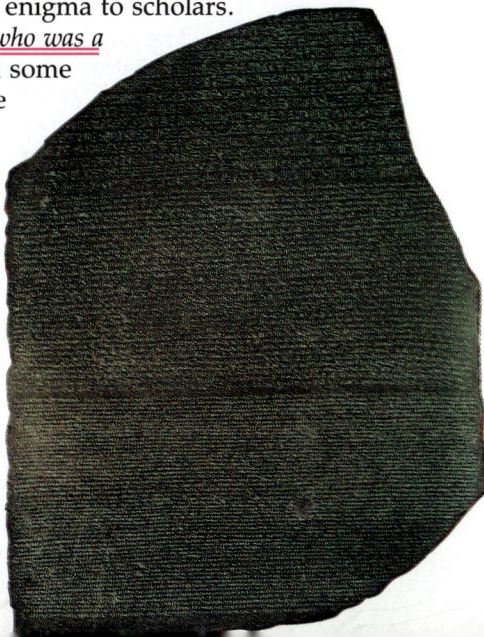

GRAMMAR

LEARNING STYLES

Auditory Learners. You may want to read aloud the examples in this lesson and the italicized clauses in **Exercise 1**. It may be easier for some students to hear the differences between complete and incomplete thoughts than it would be for them to recognize the differences visually.

COOPERATIVE LEARNING

To give students practice with using subordinate clauses, divide the class into groups of four or five. Write on a large piece of poster board the following word groups. Have students complete them with the types of clauses indicated.

1. . . . (subordinate) I spent the summer working.
2. Because I was so young . . . (independent).
3. I had a lot of fun that summer, mainly . . . (subordinate).
4. My best friend works at school . . . (subordinate).
5. I learned a lot . . . (independent plus conjunction).

After groups have finished, two group members can face the class, one holding the poster board and the other reading the story. The listeners will be responsible for determining if the correct clause types have been used. To help students avoid using phrases instead of clauses, ask that each group circle the subject and the verb in each clause they create.

GRAMMAR

675

OBJECTIVES

- To identify adjective clauses and the words they modify
- To label the uses of relative pronouns and relative adverbs in sentences

PROGRAM MANAGER

THE ADJECTIVE CLAUSE

- **Independent Practice/ Reteaching** See **The Adjective Clause** in *Language Skills Practice and Assessment,* p. 54.
- **Computer Guided Instruction** See **Lesson 27** in *Language Workshop CD-ROM.*
- **Practice** See **Chapter 13** in *English Workshop, Complete Course,* pp. 175–176.

GRAMMAR

✓ **QUICK REMINDER**

Write the following sentence pairs on the chalkboard and have students combine the sentences by using the relative pronouns in parentheses. Ask students to underline the adjective clauses in their sentences.

1. I looked at a dog. Its pedigree was flawless. (whose) [I looked at a dog whose pedigree was flawless.]
2. This is the painting. It was recovered last week. (that) [This is the painting that was recovered last week.]
3. Mr. Schwartz is the manager. He does the hiring. (who) [Mr. Schwartz is the manager who does the hiring. or Mr. Schwartz, who does the hiring, is the manager.]

676

GRAMMAR

676   *The Clause*

5. Because the same message was written on the stone in two kinds of Egyptian writing and in Greek script, *it provided the needed key for deciphering the Egyptian language.*
6. *When the Rosetta Stone was found,* part of the hieroglyphic portion was missing.
7. Scholars could easily read the Greek inscription, *which was nearly complete.*
8. *In 1816, Jean François Champollion and Thomas Young isolated several hieroglyphics* that they took to represent names.
9. *The message* that was inscribed on the stone *was not very exciting.*
10. Since the priests of Egypt were grateful for benefits from the king, *they were commemorating the crowning of Ptolemy V.*

The Adjective Clause

20d. An *adjective clause* is a subordinate clause that modifies a noun or a pronoun.

An adjective clause always follows the word or words it modifies and tells *what kind* or *which one.*

EXAMPLES The report **that Diego wrote** was on the Battle of the Little Bighorn. [The adjective clause modifies the noun *report.*]

The Cuban Cultural Heritage Walk, **which is located in Hialeah, Florida,** honors Cuban artists in exile. [The adjective clause modifies the compound noun *Cuban Cultural Heritage Walk.*]

She is someone **whom I admire.** [The adjective clause modifies the pronoun *someone.*]

Relative Pronouns

An adjective clause usually begins with a *relative pronoun*—a word that relates the clause to the word or words the clause modifies.

where
when

Relative Pronouns				
that	which	who	whom	whose

20d

A relative pronoun does three things.

(1) It refers to a preceding noun or pronoun, the antecedent.
(2) It connects the adjective clause with the rest of the sentence.
(3) It performs a function within its own clause by serving as a subject, a direct object, an indirect object, an object of a preposition, or a modifier in the adjective clause.

EXAMPLES   Mr. Mendoza is a good counselor **who never betrays a confidence.** [The relative pronoun *who* relates the adjective clause to its noun antecedent *counselor* and serves as the subject of the verb *betrays.*]
Han-Ling is the one **whose essay took first place.** [The relative pronoun *whose* relates the adjective clause to its pronoun antecedent *one* and modifies the noun *essay* by showing possession.]
Have you practiced the speech **that you will give on Friday**? [The relative pronoun *that* relates the adjective clause to its noun antecedent *speech* and serves as the direct object of the verb *will give.*]
The mariachi band **in which I play** once performed for Governor Ann Richards. [The relative pronoun *which* relates the adjective clause to its noun antecedent *band* and serves as the object of the preposition *in.*]

An adjective clause may also begin with a relative adverb such as *when* or *where*.

EXAMPLES   Dr. Martin Luther King, Jr., dreamed of the day **when freedom and justice would reign in the United States.** [The relative adverb *when* relates the adjective clause to its noun antecedent *day* and modifies the verb *would reign.*]
The site **where Dr. King delivered his great "I Have a Dream" speech in 1963** was the Lincoln Memorial in Washington, D.C. [The relative adverb *where* relates the adjective clause to its noun antecedent *site* and modifies the verb *delivered.*]

The relative pronoun or relative adverb is sometimes not expressed, but its meaning is understood.

EXAMPLES   The vase **[that] my family brought from the Philippines** was made by my great-grandmother.
Do you remember the first time **[when] we met each other?**

MEETING individual NEEDS

LEP/ESL

Spanish. Some students may have difficulty with adjective clauses that end with verbs, as in "I like the book that Maria is reading." In Spanish, it is considered awkward to end a clause with a verb. Spanish speakers may invert the subject and the verb to produce the following sentence: "Me gusta el libro que lee Maria." Inverting the word order in this manner may occur when students write in English.

LESS-ADVANCED STUDENTS

Students may need practice with determining which words are modified by an adjective clause. To help them more readily see the function of adjective clauses, work with students to draw arrows from the adjective clauses to the nouns or pronouns that are being modified.

MEETING individual NEEDS

ADVANCED STUDENTS

Explain to students that an adjective clause may not be needed where a single adjective will do. Ask students to examine previously written paragraphs and to revise them for wordiness by substituting precise adjectives where possible.

LEP/ESL

General Strategies. The use of relative pronouns varies with languages; for example, in Vietnamese, a relative pronoun is placed before an essential clause but after a nonessential clause. Some languages do not even use relative pronouns. Because usage differs so widely, you may want to reinforce the concept that in English a relative pronoun introduces an adjective clause and refers to a noun in the main clause.

▷ **EXERCISE 2** **Identifying Adjective Clauses and the Words They Modify**

Identify the adjective clauses in the following sentences. Then give the noun or pronoun that the adjective clause modifies. Be prepared to tell whether the relative pronoun or relative adverb is used as the subject, the direct object, the object of a preposition, or a modifier in the adjective clause.

1. The Mars of the nonscientist is a planet of the imagination, where an ancient civilization has left its mark and where maps blossom with romantic place names like Utopia and Elysium. **1. mod./mod.**
2. "Earthlings," who were awed by the planet's red glow in the evening sky, looked on Mars as a home for creatures who might someday cross cosmic barriers and visit planet Earth. **2. s./s.**
3. Such thinking was encouraged by an Italian astronomer who observed the planet through a telescope and saw a series of fine lines that crisscrossed its surface.
4. He called the lines *canali*, which is Italian for "channels"; this word was erroneously translated into English as "canals." **4. s.**
5. A planet where there are such canals must, of course, be inhabited by people who are capable of building not only canals but also the cities that presumably sprang up at their intersections. **5. mod./s./s.**
6. Percival Lowell, the astronomer who founded the Lowell Observatory in Flagstaff, Arizona, brought new life to old myths about life on Mars with nonscientific observations most astronomers disputed. **6. s./(that)—d.o.**
7. Lowell reported a total of more than four hundred Martian canals, of which a considerable number were discovered by his own team of astronomers. **7. o.p.**
8. One writer whose interest was drawn to Mars was Edgar Rice Burroughs, whom many people know as the creator of Tarzan. **8. mod./d.o.**
9. In his Martian books, Burroughs recounts the adventures of John Carter, who could get to Mars by standing in a field and wishing. **9. s.**
10. Burroughs' best-known literary successor is Ray Bradbury, who wrote *The Martian Chronicles*, published in 1950. **10. s.**

OBJECTIVES
- To label noun clauses in sentences and to explain their functions
- To distinguish between adjective clauses and noun clauses in sentences

The Noun Clause

20e. A *noun clause* is a subordinate clause used as a noun.

A noun clause may be used as a subject, a predicate nominative, a direct object, an indirect object, or an object of a preposition.

Subject	**How students can apply for college loans** was the speaker's topic.
Predicate Nominative	My suggestion is **that we all meet again tomorrow.**
Direct Object	Many modern historians question **whether Columbus was truly the first European to explore the Americas.**
Indirect Object	Mrs. Romero offers **whoever completes additional assignments** extra credit.
Object of a Preposition	Write about **whomever you admire most.**

Common Introductory Words for Noun Clauses

that	which	whoever
what	whichever	whom
whatever	who	whomever
how	whenever	whether
if	where	why
when	wherever	

REFERENCE NOTE: For more about the use of these words in subordinate clauses, see pages 544–545, 604, 621–622, 675–677, and 681–682.

The word that introduces a noun clause may or may not serve a function in the noun clause.

EXAMPLES Tawana will do well at **whatever she attempts.** [The word *whatever* introduces the noun clause and serves as the direct object of the verb *attempts.*]
Does Luís think **that Puerto Rico will become a state someday?** [The word *that* introduces the noun clause but does not serve a function in its clause.]

679

GRAMMAR

Sometimes the word that introduces a noun clause is not expressed, but its meaning is understood.

EXAMPLES   I think **[that] I. M. Pei is one of the judges of the design contest.**

Did you know **[that] the actor James Earl Jones was once a pre-med student?**

▶ EXERCISE 3   **Identifying Noun Clauses and Their Functions**

Identify each <u>noun clause</u> in the following sentences, and tell whether it is a *subject*, a *direct object*, an *indirect object*, a *predicate nominative*, or an *object of a preposition*.

1. The problem is that my finances don't quite allow me to live in style; in fact, I'm broke! **1. p.n.**
2. Do you know what the referee says to the opponents at the start of a boxing match? **2. d.o.**   **3. s./p.n.**
3. What I like most about Harriet is that she never complains.
4. Scientists disagree about why dinosaurs died out. **4. o.p.**
5. Sometimes I am amused and sometimes I am amazed by what I read in the newspaper's advice column. **5. o.p.**
6. I don't know how they decided who would be the leader.
7. What the dancers Agnes de Mille and Martha Graham did was to create a new form of American dance. **6. d.o./d.o.**   **7. s.**
8. Can you please tell me where the Museum of African Art is located and what time it opens? **8. d.o./d.o.**
9. The radio station will give whoever can answer the next question one hundred dollars. **9. i.o.**
10. Through scientific research, psychologists have learned that everyone dreams during sleep. **10. d.o.**

▶ EXERCISE 4   **Distinguishing Between Adjective and Noun Clauses**

Identify the subordinate clause or clauses in each of the following sentences. Tell whether each subordinate clause is used as an *adjective* or a *noun*. Be prepared to tell what word each adjective clause modifies and whether each noun clause is a subject, a predicate nominative, a direct object, an indirect object, or an object of a preposition.

1. d.o.

1. The person in the photograph on the next page, Athelstan Spilhaus, found that toys are not meant only for children.

THE ADVERB CLAUSE Rules 20f, 20g

OBJECTIVES
- To identify adverb clauses, the words they modify, and their purposes
- To use subordinate clauses to compose a writing journal entry about a dream

2. Spilhaus, an oceanographer, admits he has sometimes been unable to distinguish between his work and his play. **2. d.o.**
3. Some of the toys he collects are simply to be admired; his favorites are those that can be put into action.
4. Some of his collectibles are put into intensive care, where he skillfully replaces parts that have been damaged or lost.
5. Dr. Spilhaus says that a toy is anything that enables us to stop and refresh ourselves during our hectic lives. **5. d.o.**
6. What is appealing about some toys is that they can make us laugh. **6. s./p.n.**
7. I have read that many mechanical principles were first applied to playthings. **7. d.o.**
8. For example, the toy monkey shown here is activated by squeezing a rubber bulb that uses the same principle as the jackhammer that digs up our streets.
9. Only those who have lost touch with childhood question what a toy can be worth to a young boy or girl. **9. d.o.**
10. Ask someone who knows toys what their enchantment is worth. **10. d.o.**

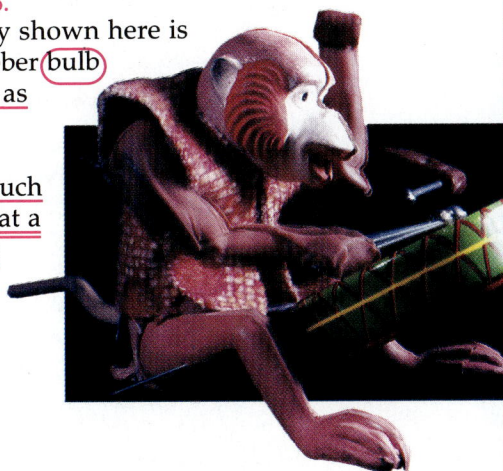

The Adverb Clause

20f. An *adverb clause* is a subordinate clause that modifies a verb, an adjective, or an adverb.

An adverb clause tells *how, how much, when, where, why, to what extent,* or *under what conditions.*

PROGRAM MANAGER

THE ADVERB CLAUSE

■ **Independent Practice/ Reteaching** For instruction and exercises, see **The Adverb Clause** in *Language Skills Practice and Assessment,* p. 56.

■ **Computer Guided Instruction** For additional instruction and practice with the adverb clause, see **Lesson 27** in *Language Workshop CD-ROM.*

■ **Practice** To help less-advanced students with additional instruction and practice with the adverb clause, see **Chapter 13** in *English Workshop, Complete Course,* pp. 177–178.

QUICK REMINDER
Write the following sentences on the chalkboard and ask students to determine if the underlined words are prepositional phrases or if they are used as adverbs or adverb clauses:

1. I will leave for college before Labor Day. [prep. phrase]
2. If I knew Latin, I would enter the contest. [adv. clause]
3. Before you go, look at the great job I did frosting the cake. [adv. clause]
4. I've been practicing this new dance since Monday. [prep. phrase]
5. My dog has been happier since she had her claws clipped. [adv. clause]

MEETING individual NEEDS

LEP/ESL

General Strategies. Most languages have structures similar to adverb clauses; however, often the order of the subject and the verb is inverted. You may want to have students practice saying and writing sentences with adverb clauses by using the **Common Subordinating Conjunctions** list. Emphasize the subject-verb pattern that is most common in English by having students label the subject and the verb of each clause they write.

COMMON ERROR

Problem. Students often hesitate to vary the position of adverb clauses in sentences they write. For example, they may place adverb clauses only at the beginnings of sentences.

Solution. Encourage students to experiment with the placement of adverb clauses. To allow students to see this variety more easily, ask them to bracket any independent clauses in their writing and occasionally to switch the positions of the adverb clauses and the main clauses.

---

682 *The Clause*

EXAMPLES

You look **as though you have a lot on your mind.** [The adverb clause modifies the verb *look,* telling *how* you look.]

Many Western artists were influenced by the Asian art they saw **while they were studying in Paris.** [The adverb clause modifies the verb *saw,* telling *when* the artists saw.]

Miriam Makeba attracts huge audiences **wherever she performs.** [The adverb clause modifies the verb *attracts,* telling *where* she attracts huge audiences.]

The conquest of Cuba was essential to the Spanish **because the island is strategically located at the entrance to the Gulf of Mexico.** [The adverb clause modifies the adjective *essential,* telling *why* the conquest of Cuba was essential to the Spanish.]

Davita likes classical music better **than I do.** [The adverb clause modifies the adverb *better,* telling *to what extent* Davita likes classical music.]

If you want to gain an understanding of Native American culture, read *Voices of Our Ancestors* by Dhyani Ywahoo. [The adverb clause modifies the verb *read,* telling *under what condition* you should read Ywahoo's book.]

Subordinating Conjunctions

An adverb clause is introduced by a *subordinating conjunction*—a word that shows the relationship between the adverb clause and the word or words the clause modifies.

Common Subordinating Conjunctions			
after	as though	since	when
although	because	so that	whenever
as	before	than	where
as if	if	though	wherever
as long as	in order that	unless	whether
as soon as	provided that	until	while

☞ **REFERENCE NOTE:** The words *after, as, before, since,* and *until* may also be used as prepositions. See pages 619–620.

20g

The Elliptical Clause

20g. Part of a clause may be left out when the meaning can be understood from the context of the sentence. Such a clause is called an *elliptical clause.*

Most elliptical clauses are adverb clauses. In the following examples, the word or words in brackets may be omitted because they can be understood from the context.

EXAMPLES   Australia is smaller **than the other continents** [are].
            When [you are] **taking notes,** use your own words.

NOTE: Often the meaning of an elliptical clause depends on the form of the pronoun in it.

> EXAMPLES   I like Anne as much as **she** [likes Anne].
>   I like Anne as much as [I like] **her.**

☞ **REFERENCE NOTE:** For more about the correct use of pronouns in elliptical clauses, see pages 741–742.

EXERCISE 5   **Identifying Adverb Clauses and the Words They Modify**

Identify the <u>adverb clause</u> in each of the following sentences. Give the <u>word or words that the clause modifies</u>. Be prepared to state whether the clause tells *how, how much, when, where, why, to what extent,* or *under what conditions.*

1. <u>Because company was coming for dinner</u>, Lola Gómez and her father <u>prepared</u> a special treat of Cuban-style black beans, one of their specialties.   **1. why**
2. <u>After Lola had soaked a pound of black beans overnight</u>, she <u>drained</u> them and <u>covered</u> them with fresh water to make the beans more easily digestible.   **2. when**
3. <u>Before she lit the stove</u>, she <u>added</u> some chopped onion and green pepper, a bay leaf, cilantro leaves, oregano, and salt pork to the beans.   **3. when**
4. <u>While the beans were simmering</u>, Mr. Gómez <u>prepared</u> the *sofrito*, which is a characteristic ingredient in many Latin American dishes.   **4. when**
5. <u>Whenever a recipe calls for *sofrito*</u>, you finely <u>chop</u> some onion, green pepper, and garlic.   **5. conditions**

MEETING individual NEEDS

LEP/ESL

General Strategies. Some students might have difficulty with the omission of the introductory word *that* in noun clauses. You may want to write the following sentences on the chalkboard and have students read the sentences aloud. Tell the students to omit the word *that* in parentheses.

1. I wish (that) I could be an astronaut.
2. I understand (that) you are building a go-cart.
3. The firefighter said (that) she rescued a baby yesterday.
4. The mayor told us (that) he would be happy to review our petition.

GRAMMAR

GRAMMAR

GRAMMAR

684 *The Clause*

6. Then you <u>fry</u> these vegetables in a little oil <u>until they are tender</u>, and add herbs and spices such as basil, cilantro, cumin, and black and white pepper. **6. extent**

7. <u>As soon as the *sofrito* was ready</u>, Mr. Gómez <u>added</u> it to the bean mixture. **7. when**

8. He then <u>crushed</u> some of the beans against the side of the pot <u>so that the bean mixture would become thicker</u>. **8. why**

9. <u>When the mixture was thick</u>, Lola <u>put</u> in a blend of vinegar and sugar, <u>which gives the beans that extra "tang."</u> **9. when**

10. No one at the dinner table was more <u>eager</u> <u>than I</u> to enjoy a large helping of the Gómezes' special black beans.
10. (was eager) — extent

▶ REVIEW A   **Identifying and Classifying Subordinate Clauses**

Identify the <u>subordinate clause</u> or clauses in each of the following sentences. Tell whether each one is used as an *adjective*, a *noun*, or an *adverb*.

1. <u>When a group of scholars first applied computer science to the study of literature</u>, their colleagues expressed <u>what can only be described as polite skepticism</u>. **1. adv./n.**

2. <u>What</u>, they asked, <u>would the computer do</u>? **2. n.**

3. Scornful scholars argued <u>that measuring the length of Hemingway's sentences was dreary enough</u> <u>when it was done without computers</u>. **3. n./adv.**   **4. n.**

4. Would precise mathematical analyses of style determine <u>whether Thomas More wrote one of Shakespeare's plays</u>?

5. Initial studies made along these lines fueled controversy <u>that raged for years</u>. **5. adj.**

6. Researchers now use computers <u>whenever their projects involve such mechanical tasks as compiling an index or a bibliography</u>. **6. adv.**   **7. adv./adj.**

7. <u>Since all of ancient Greek is now stored on computers</u>, scholars can make analyses <u>that shed light on etymology</u>.

8. There are some features of literary works <u>that computers can identify faster</u> <u>than human readers can</u>. **8. adj./adv.**

9. Of course, nowadays many students take advantage of computer technology <u>when writing research papers about literature</u>. **9. (they are) adv.**

10. After writing their first drafts, students may then revise their papers using software programs <u>that check spelling, grammar, and style</u>. **10. adj.**

684

PICTURE THIS

In your creative writing class, you've been experimenting with *magical realism*, a technique of fiction writing that interweaves fantastical details with realistic narrative. Since some of your most imaginative story ideas come from dreams, you've also been keeping a dream journal. You just woke from a dream in which you visited this mysterious city. Write a journal entry describing what you saw and experienced there. Include both realistic and fantastical details. In your journal entry, use at least five subordinate clauses.

Subject: a dream city
Audience: yourself
Purpose: to record a dream; to collect imaginative details
            for a story

El Greco (Domenikos Theotocopoulos), *View of Toledo* (1610–1614). Oil on canvas, 47 3/4" × 42 3/4". H. O. Havemeyer Collection, Bequest of Mrs. H. O. Havemeyer, 1929. (29.100.6) © 1992 The Metropolitan Museum of Art.

GRAMMAR

PICTURE THIS

This exercise asks students to write about an assigned topic as if they had dreamed it themselves. Some students may be unable to generate ideas for a topic given in this way. Let students use the content of an actual dream rather than this suggested one, but do require that they each include at least five subordinate clauses in the final product. *Remind students to choose examples they would not mind sharing with the class.*

GRAMMAR

686 *The Clause*

Sentences Classified According to Structure

20h. Sentences are classified according to their structure as *simple, compound, complex,* or *compound-complex.*

(1) A *simple sentence* has one independent clause and no subordinate clauses.

EXAMPLES Great literature stirs the imagination.
Located on an island in Lake Texcoco, Tenochtitlán was the capital of the Aztec empire and may have had more than 100,000 inhabitants in the 1500s.

(2) A *compound sentence* has two or more independent clauses but no subordinate clauses.

Independent clauses may be joined either by a comma and a coordinating conjunction (*and, but, for, nor, or, so,* or *yet*); by a semicolon; or by a semicolon and a conjunctive adverb or transitional expression.

EXAMPLES In 1528, the Spanish explored the area near present-day Tampa, but Europeans did not begin settling there until 1823. [two independent clauses joined by a comma and the coordinating conjunction *but*]
The Aswan High Dam is on the Nile River in Egypt; it is one of the world's largest dams. [two independent clauses joined by a semicolon]
We should leave early; otherwise, we will miss our bus. [two independent clauses joined by a semicolon and the conjunctive adverb *otherwise*]

Common Conjunctive Adverbs		
also	incidentally	next
anyway	indeed	nonetheless
besides	instead	otherwise
consequently	likewise	still
finally	meanwhile	then
furthermore	moreover	therefore
however	nevertheless	thus

20h

Common Transitional Expressions		
after all	even so	in fact
as a result	for example	in other words
at any rate	for instance	on the contrary
by the way	in addition	on the other hand

NOTE: Don't confuse a simple sentence that has a compound subject or a compound predicate with a compound sentence.

EXAMPLES   The 1991 eruption of Mount Pinatubo destroyed many homes and led to the closing of Clark Air Base. [simple sentence with compound predicate]
The 1991 eruption of Mount Pinatubo destroyed many homes, and it led to the closing of Clark Air Base. [compound sentence]

(3) A *complex sentence* has one independent clause and at least one subordinate clause.

EXAMPLES   Yiddish, which is a West Germanic language, is now spoken by millions of people all over the world. [The independent clause is *Yiddish is spoken by millions of people all over the world.* The subordinate clause is *which is a West Germanic language.*]
After Napoleon I was defeated at Waterloo, he was exiled to Saint Helena. [The independent clause is *he was exiled to Saint Helena.* The subordinate clause is *After Napoleon I was defeated at Waterloo.*]

(4) A *compound-complex sentence* has two or more independent clauses and at least one subordinate clause.

EXAMPLES   The interest that you pay on a car loan will increase the actual cost of the car, so be sure to shop for the lowest interest rate. [The two independent clauses are *The interest will increase the actual cost of the car* and *be sure to shop for the lowest interest rate.* The subordinate clause is *that you pay on a car loan.*]
Hong Kong had been a crown colony of Britain since 1898; however, it reverted to China when the lease expired in 1997. [The two independent clauses are *Hong Kong had been a crown colony of Britain since 1898* and *it reverted to China.* The subordinate clause is *when the lease expired in 1997.*]

MEETING *individual* NEEDS

LEP/ESL

General Strategies. You may wish to remind students that in English a clause contains both a subject and a verb. (In some languages, clauses do not always require subjects.) As practice, have students locate the subject and verb combinations in the example sentences on p. 689.

MEETING *individual* NEEDS

STUDENTS WITH SPECIAL NEEDS

Because of the length and format of **Exercise 6,** some students might lose their places. You could adapt the activity by providing index cards or rulers for students to use as horizontal guides. The guides will help students concentrate on one line at a time.

COMMON ERROR

Problem. Students often have trouble with punctuating two independent clauses within the same sentence.

Solution. Ask students to study carefully the correct combinations of independent clauses shown on p. 686. Summarize the three methods of linking independent clauses: a comma and a coordinating conjunction, a semicolon, or a semicolon and a conjunctive adverb.

688

EXERCISE 6   **Classifying Sentences According to Structure**

Classify each sentence of the following paragraphs as *simple,* *compound, complex,* or *compound-complex.*

EXAMPLE   [1] **H. J. (Henry Jackson) Lewis is generally regarded as the first African American political cartoonist.**
     1. *simple*

1. cx.
2. cd.

3. cd.-cx.

[1] During the late 1800s, H. J. Lewis drew political cartoons for *The Freeman,* which was the first illustrated African American newspaper. [2] Through his cartoons, Lewis frequently criticized the U.S. government's racial policies; however, he also produced nonpolitical ink drawings, sketches, and chalk plates. [3] If you examine this self-portrait of Lewis, you can see evidence of his artistic versatility, and you can get a sense of the atmosphere in which he worked.

Henry Jackson Lewis, *Self-Portrait.* Courtesy of the DuSable Museum of African American History, Chicago, Illinois.

4. cd.

5. cx.
6. cx.

7. cx.

[4] Lewis had to overcome many difficulties to achieve success as an artist, and parts of his life are shrouded in mystery. [5] Lewis was born into slavery in Mississippi and was badly burned and blinded in one eye when he was a toddler. [6] As a young man, he worked at various menial jobs until a Little Rock newspaper artist taught him how to draw. [7] It is known that Lewis made sketches for archaeological studies in Arkansas, Mississippi, Tennessee, and Louisiana in 1882 and 1883.

OBJECTIVE

• To classify sentences according to structure and purpose

8. cx.

[8] The Smithsonian Institution now has most of these sketches, which include drawings of prehistoric Native American burial mounds. [9] Throughout his life, Lewis produced drawings for various publications. [10] Upon Lewis' death in 1891, *The Freeman*, the newspaper that had made him famous, praised his talent and mourned his loss.

9. simp.

10. cx.

20i

GRAMMAR

Sentences Classified According to Purpose

20i. Sentences are classified according to purpose as *declarative, imperative, interrogative,* or *exclamatory.*

(1) A *declarative sentence* makes a statement. All declarative sentences end with periods.

EXAMPLE   Homes should be made more accessible for people who have disabilities.

(2) An *imperative sentence* gives a command or makes a request. Imperative sentences usually end with periods, but a very strong command may end with an exclamation point.

EXAMPLES   Please pay attention.
Stop what you're doing and listen!

(3) An *interrogative sentence* asks a question. Interrogative sentences end with question marks.

EXAMPLES   What is the name of that song?
Have you seen Alma?

NOTE: Any sentence may be spoken in such a way that it is interrogative. If so, it should end with a question mark.

EXAMPLES   Rex came back yesterday? [Declarative becomes interrogative.]
Ask Ed? [Imperative becomes interrogative.]
What great news I got? [Exclamatory becomes interrogative.]

GRAMMAR

MEETING *individual* NEEDS

LEP/ESL

General Strategies. Review the punctuation of the four sentence types. Because not all languages use the same marks of punctuation or punctuate exclusively at the end of sentences, students will benefit from instruction in this area.

GRAMMAR

(4) An *exclamatory sentence* expresses strong feeling. Exclamatory sentences end with exclamation points.

EXAMPLES   How happy you look!
            What a surprise to see you here!

NOTE: Any sentence may be spoken in such a way that it is exclamatory. If so, it should end with an exclamation point.

EXAMPLES   You're home early! [Declarative becomes exclamatory.]
            Stop that racket! [Imperative becomes exclamatory.]
            How do you expect me to react! [Interrogative becomes exclamatory.]

▶ EXERCISE 7   **Classifying Sentences According to Structure and Purpose**

Classify each of the following sentences first according to its structure and then according to its purpose.   decl. = declarative
int. = interrogative   imp. = imperative   excl. = exclamatory   simp. = simple
EXAMPLE   **1.** Look at this article I'm reading.   cx. = complex
           1. *complex—imperative*   cd. = compound
                                          cd.-cx. = compound-complex

1. Are you aware that there is a huge worldwide demand for butterflies?   **1.** cx.—int.
2. Millions are caught and sold each year to entomologists, museums, private collectors, and factories.   **2.** simp.—decl.
3. The plastic-encased butterflies that are used to decorate ornamental objects such as trays, tabletops, and screens are usually common varieties, many of which come from Taiwan, Korea, and Malaysia.   **3.** cx.—decl.
4. There is a difference, though, between collection practices used there and those used in Papua New Guinea.   **4.** cx.—decl.
5. Papua New Guinea, which was administered by Australia until 1975, has taken advantage of a growing interest in tropical butterflies.   **5.** cx.—decl.
6. The butterfly rancher shown on the next page gathers, raises, and markets high-quality specimens, which are accompanied by scientific data.   **6.** cx.—decl.
7. Because biologists have not yet determined the life cycles of all of these butterflies, local villagers have become the experts; as a result, butterfly ranching has improved the country's economy.   **7.** cd-cx.—decl.
8. Some butterfly specimens are quite small, but others are larger than an adult human hand.   **8.** cd.—decl.

9. cx.—decl. **10.** simp.—excl.

9. The middle photograph shows butterflies emerging from cocoons that the rancher had gathered.
10. What rich, vibrant colors these butterflies have!

▶ REVIEW B **Classifying Sentences**

Classify each of the following sentences first as *simple*, *compound*, *complex*, or *compound-complex* and then as *declarative*, *interrogative*, *imperative*, or *exclamatory*.

1. Have you discovered that imaginative teachers who are enthusiastic about their work can make school enjoyable for their students? **1.** cx.—int.
2. Last year, when I took a social studies elective, Law and Order, I found myself looking forward to fourth period each day. **2.** cx.—decl.
3. What our teacher, Ms. Klein, did to make our course more interesting was to bring the outside world into the classroom. **3.** cx.—decl.
4. In addition to having us watch the TV news and read the local newspaper, she invited guest speakers to share their experiences with us. **4.** simp.—decl.
5. By the end of three months, the class had heard from a defense attorney, a prosecutor, and several local police officers; and we had interviewed the first FBI agent any of us had ever met. **5.** cd.-cx.—decl.
6. Ms. Klein also arranged to have four prisoners, escorted by police, tell us about prison life. **6.** simp.—decl.

WRITING APPLICATION

OBJECTIVES

- To use speaking and listening skills to interview someone about a chosen vocation
- To use end marks to reflect attitude in a write-up of an interview

692 *The Clause*

7. cx.—excl.

7. After we had listened to their descriptions of their experiences, we all agreed that crime definitely does not pay!

8. In addition to bringing these people into the classroom, Ms. Klein set up a schedule of field trips, and she then took the classroom out into the world. **8. cd.—decl.**

9. For example, on one of our trips, we visited the local jail; and on another, when we observed a jury trial, we spoke personally with the judge. **9. cd.-cx.—decl.**

10. I am glad that I was in Ms. Klein's class, and I was very pleased when she was voted "Outstanding Educator of the Year." **10. cd.-cx.—decl.**

WRITING APPLICATION

It is important not to record speech peculiarities in a way that the subject of the interview would find offensive. Point out that people may feel trivialized by a style of reporting that they feel is hypercritical of their ability to use standard English. Discuss how students can show sensitivity in making decisions about how they record their interviews.

CRITICAL THINKING

Analysis. Asking good questions can require background research. Lead an analytical discussion focusing on what types of information about a profession would help interviewers ask good questions. Students might suggest that knowledge of production processes, managerial structure, daily schedules, and so forth would provide background that could lead to good questions. As a follow-up, have students find some background information that is applicable to their topics—they might even ask their interviewees for some materials to read, if any such materials are available.

WRITING APPLICATION

Using End Marks to Reflect Attitude in an Interview

The main purpose of an interview is to gather information. However, unlike an encyclopedia or other reference source, people who are interviewed provide more than information on a subject—they provide their own unique and personal perspective on the subject. Often that perspective is reflected in the way a person speaks. A good interviewer, therefore, records not only *what* a person says but also *how* he or she says it—colloquial expressions, slang, and technical terms included.

Recording a person's exact words is easy enough with a tape recorder, but transcribing, or writing down, those words is a little more complicated. The interviewer must choose end marks that accurately reflect the speaker's attitude. In addition, it is the interviewer's job to decide where and how to break the flow of ideas into sentences. As you read the example below, notice how an interviewer recorded the speech of cowboy Jack Pate.

"I think cowboys is as good a class a people as any. They might not have as much money as some but money don't mean everything. It's just whatever you're happy doing. I'll tell you one thing. Most cowboys—if they've got a dollar and you need it—you can shore get four bits of it.

692

"Would I recommend it? Well, really I don't guess I would—but I wouldn't change my own life. Do what you're happy doing. It's poor pay and hard work but I think living outside and eating cow meat and gravy keeps you young!"

Eliot Wigginton, Editor, from *"I wish I could give my son a wild raccoon."*

The passage above records both what Mr. Pate said and how he said it. The writer chose to use dashes to join some ideas together, but that is not the only way the passage could be punctuated. How might you punctuate the passage differently?

▶ WRITING ACTIVITY

Is there a job you've always dreamed of doing? Maybe it's driving a truck, being an attorney, designing computer software, running a day-care center, practicing medicine, or even being a cowboy like Jack Pate. Well, now's your chance to learn what that "dream job" is all about. For a class project, you are to interview someone employed in a field that interests you. Find out what kind of training the person needed for his or her job and what a typical day on the job is like. If possible, arrange to visit the person's workplace. When you write your interview, use end marks to accurately reflect your interviewee's tone and attitude.

Prewriting First, brainstorm a list of interesting jobs. Choose the one that most appeals to you, and start looking for someone to interview. You may need to use the Yellow Pages or ask friends and family members to help you find a person working in the area you've chosen. Ask the person if he or she will grant you an interview either in person or over the phone. Be sure to explain the purpose of the interview. Set up a date and time to conduct it.

Next, prepare for your interview. Jot down a number of questions that you might ask about the person's job. Make your questions clear and specific, but avoid questions that could be answered with a simple yes or no. Instead, use the 5W–How? questions listed on page 25.

When you conduct the interview, be friendly and polite. If you're planning to use a tape recorder, be sure to get the person's permission before you begin recording. Feel free

PREWRITING

Provide a list of local sources of possible candidates for interviews, sources beyond those mentioned in the students' textbooks. Some possible sources are local colleges, universities, and vocational schools; sources reachable by telecommunication; and local armed-forces facilities.

SELECTION AMENDMENT
Description of change: excerpted
Rationale: to focus on the concept of writing an interview presented in this chapter

to redirect or add to your original questions as the interview progresses. Remember, an interview should have a personal flavor. Encourage your interviewee to tell any interesting anecdotes that reveal what his or her job is really like.

Writing Begin with a brief paragraph introducing your interviewee and telling the date and location of the interview. In writing the interview itself, you'll need to record the interviewee's responses exactly. You can leave out selected portions of the interview, but be sure to use ellipsis points to mark the omissions. (See pages 941–943 on the use of ellipses.) Don't "correct" the speaker's grammar or usage as you write. Instead, try to capture the actual sound of the person's speech. Use contractions wherever the speaker used them. If you think a spoken sentence won't be clear to readers, paraphrase it in brackets. As you write, choose end marks that accurately reflect the speaker's pauses, questions, and exclamations.

Evaluating and Revising Evaluate the written version of your interview for accuracy and clarity. Keep in mind the purpose of the interview—to gather information about an interesting job. With that aim in mind, you may want to omit some passages from the interview. However, don't change the meaning of any quoted material. If you are lacking needed information, you may have to call your interviewee and conduct a brief telephone interview.

Proofreading and Publishing Check your writing carefully against your tape or notes. Be sure that you've quoted the person exactly and that your punctuation accurately reflects contractions, pauses, questions, and exclamations. Check your end marks to make sure that they show the intended purpose of each sentence.

You and your classmates may want to collect the interviews in a booklet. Work together to write a brief introduction explaining the nature and purpose of the interviews. Also include an acknowledgment page thanking each of the contributors.

EVALUATING AND REVISING

Different people have different views on showing the final product of an interview to the subject. Though some people think it is unnecessary, others consider it a courteous thing to do, and still others think it is a moral obligation. Raise the question with the class and help students develop strategies to deal with this issue.

REVIEW: POSTTESTS 1 and 2

OBJECTIVES

- To identify independent and subordinate clauses in sentences
- To classify subordinate clauses in sentences as noun, adjective, or adverb clauses
- To classify sentences according to structure and purpose
- To write sentences with a variety of sentence structures

Review: Posttest 1

GRAMMAR

A. Identifying and Classifying Clauses

Identify the italicized clause in each of the following sentences as an *independent clause* or a *subordinate clause*. If a clause is subordinate, tell whether it is an *adjective clause*, an *adverb clause*, or a *noun clause*.

EXAMPLE   **1.** *While we were talking on the telephone,* my call-waiting light flashed.
     1. subordinate clause—adverb clause

1. *Tamara applied for the job last Monday,* and each day since then she has been waiting for a call from the company.
2. *The band played calypso and reggae music from the West Indies.*
3. Serious hikers know *that a topographical map is often useful in unfamiliar territory.* **3.** n. cl.   **4.** n. cl.
4. Amelia Earhart, *who was the first woman to fly solo over both the Atlantic Ocean and the Pacific Ocean,* had great courage.
5. Mr. Benoit was the best coach at Northeast High School, *even though he had become paraplegic because of injuries sustained in an auto accident.* **5.** adv. cl.
6. As you wait, concentrate on *what you have to do to win.* **6.** n. cl.
7. Since last year Erin and Jim have been rotating household tasks, and *as a result, each has become more understanding and more helpful.*
8. *Renowned underwater explorer Jacques-Yves Cousteau was ten years old* when he made his first dive.
9. How was I ever going to get the parts of the engine put back together *before my father got home*? **9.** adv. cl.
10. Lawrence, who transferred to our school last month, is taller *than the other boys on the team.* **10.** (are) adv. cl.
11. Tired after a long day in the summer sun, the lifeguard reported *that there had been no accidents.* **11.** n. cl.
12. In high school, Lori Garcia set an all-city scoring record in basketball, and *she later went to college on a scholarship.*
13. Can you tell me *why there is still famine in parts of the world*? **13.** n. cl.
14. After World War II, President Harry Truman authorized the Marshall Plan, *which was a massive program designed to speed economic recovery in Europe.* **14.** adj. cl.

696 *The Clause*

15. The Vietnam Veterans Memorial, a black granite wall engraved with the names of those *who died in the war in Vietnam*, was designed by Maya Ying Lin when she was a student at Yale University. **15. adj. cl.**

B. Classifying Sentences

Classify each of the following sentences first according to its structure and then according to its purpose.

simp. = simple   cx. = complex   cd. = compound   cd.-cx. = compound-complex

EXAMPLE   **1.** Did you know that some of the best-preserved Anasazi dwellings are at Mesa Verde National Park in Colorado?

1. *complex—interrogative*

decl. = declarative   int. = interrogative   imp. = imperative   excl. = exclamatory

16. *Anasazi* means "ancient ones," and that term accurately describes these cliff dwellers. **16. cd.—decl.   17. simp.—decl.**

17. The Anasazi had a thriving culture around A.D. 1100.

18. They lived primarily in an area now called the Four Corners, where the states of New Mexico, Colorado, Utah, and Arizona converge. **18. cx.—decl.**

19. These remarkable people built dwellings, some of which were several stories high, in the cliffs. **19. cx.—decl.**

20. What unusual villages they created, and what views they had over the canyons! **20. cd.—excl.   21. cx.—imp.**

21. Don't assume, however, that this fascinating civilization lasted as long as the Mayan and Aztec civilizations did.

22. The Anasazi disappeared completely around A.D. 1300.

23. Do you know why they disappeared? **22. simp.—decl.**

24. Nobody does for sure, but anthropologists have several theories that may explain the disappearance. **23. cx.—int.**

25. A drought that lasted many years is one good possibility, but the Anasazi may have been driven from their villages by enemies or by changes in climate. **24. cd.-cx.—decl.**
25. cd.-cx.—decl.

Review: Posttest 2

Writing a Variety of Sentence Structures

Write ten sentences according to the following guidelines.

1. Write an exclamatory simple sentence.

MEETING *individual* NEEDS

LESS-ADVANCED STUDENTS

You may want to simplify **Review: Posttest 2** by rewording the instructions so that there is only one requirement for each sentence.

ANSWERS

Review: Posttest 2

Answers will vary, but students should meet the requirements in each sentence. You may want students to highlight or label each required element in their sentences.

2. Write a simple sentence with a compound verb.
3. Write an interrogative compound sentence.
4. Write an imperative sentence.
5. Write a complex sentence with an adjective clause beginning with the relative adverb *where*.
6. Write a complex sentence with a noun clause used as the object of the main verb of the sentence.
7. Write a complex sentence with an adjective clause beginning with the relative pronoun *who*.
8. Write a complex sentence with an adverb clause beginning with the subordinating conjunction *because*.
9. Write a compound-complex sentence.
10. Write a complex sentence with an elliptical clause.

OBJECTIVES

- To identify verbs that agree in number with their subjects
- To identify pronouns that agree with their antecedents
- To proofread for subject-verb agreement
- To proofread for pronoun-antecedent agreement

USAGE

PROGRAM MANAGER

FOR THE WHOLE CHAPTER

- **Review** For exercises on chapter concepts, see **Review Form A** and **Review Form B** in *Language Skills Practice and Assessment,* pp. 110–113.
- **Assessment** For additional testing, see **Usage Pretests** and **Usage Mastery Tests** in *Language Skills Practice and Assessment,* pp. 95–101 and 179–185.

CHAPTER OVERVIEW

After reviewing grammatical number, this chapter addresses the idea of subject-verb agreement and discusses intervening phrases and clauses, indefinite pronouns, compound subjects, and special problems in subject-verb agreement. The last part of the chapter is concerned with the agreement of pronouns and their antecedents.

Students can apply the rules and examples to solving specific problems they encounter in proofreading their writing. You can also introduce chapter concepts to English-language learners or as a general review for the whole class.

USAGE

21 AGREEMENT

Subject and Verb, Pronoun and Antecedent

Diagnostic Test

A. Identifying Verbs That Agree in Number with Their Subjects and Pronouns That Agree with Their Antecedents

Choose the <u>word</u> in parentheses <u>that correctly completes each of the following sentences</u>.

1. Neither of the pitchers (*was, were*) able to stop the Hawks from winning the baseball game.
2. "(*Is, Are*) mumps contagious?" I asked when my sister got the disease just two days before I was to star in our high school play.
3. Martin's greatest problem before a race (*is, are*) nerves.

4. One of the girls left (*her, their*) camera when she got off the train in Wyoming.
5. Coach Ruíz says that a team with too many superstars (*has, have*) trouble working as a unit.
6. Both of your answers (*is, are*) correct.
7. An adventure novel by French writer Alexandre Dumas, *The Three Musketeers* (*has, have*) been made into a movie many times.
8. When we got to the picnic grounds, we discovered that neither Josh nor Brandon had brought (*his, their*) radio.
9. My mother thought that twenty-five dollars (*was, were*) too much to pay for the designer T-shirt.
10. Our city is proud of (*its, their*) cultural activities.

B. Proofreading for Subject-Verb Agreement and Pronoun-Antecedent Agreement

Most of the sentences in the following paragraph contain errors in agreement between subjects and verbs or between pronouns and their antecedents. If a sentence contains an error, give the correct form. If a sentence is correct, write *C.*

[11] Most of us has some knowledge of the periods in European history known as the Middle Ages and the Renaissance. [12] Those times is the special interest of the Society for Creative Anachronism. [13] Members of this society, who is found all over the world, do more than study the Middle Ages and the Renaissance. [14] Every member takes a name and becomes a character appropriate to the society's historical period (A.D. 500 to A.D. 1500). [15] Popular characters in the society includes princes, princesses, lords, and ladies. [16] After joining, everyone is free to choose a new name and to re-create his or her favorite aspect of medieval life. [17] Each person can pursue their own interests. [18] For example, some people enjoys costuming, armor-making, calligraphy, and woodworking. [19] There is also some members who compete in tournaments to become monarchs of the society's kingdoms. [20] If you want to learn more about such historical activities in your area, the society usually displays their brochures at public Renaissance festivals.

11. have
12. are
13. are
14. C
15. include
16. C
17. his or her
18. enjoy
19. are
20. its

USING THE DIAGNOSTIC TEST

If you notice that some students are having problems with agreement in their compositions, you can use the **Diagnostic Test** to pinpoint error patterns and specific strengths and weaknesses. **Part A** assesses students' understanding of subject-verb agreement, and **Part B** concentrates on proofreading for subject-verb and pronoun-antecedent agreement. Assessing students' responses will help you determine which rules of agreement students need to review.

AGREEMENT OF SUBJECT AND VERB
Rules 21b–21i

OBJECTIVES

- To identify in sentences subjects and verbs that agree in number
- To revise subject-verb agreement in sentences
- To choose in sentences verbs that agree with compound subjects

---

PROGRAM MANAGER

AGREEMENT OF SUBJECT AND VERB

- **Independent Practice/ Reteaching** See **Agreement of Subject and Verb A** and **Agreement of Subject and Verb B** in *Language Skills Practice and Assessment,* pp. 105–106.

- **Computer Guided Instruction** See **Lesson 5** in *Language Workshop CD-ROM.*

- **Practice** See **Chapter 14** in *English Workshop, Complete Course,* pp. 187–188.

✔ QUICK REMINDER

Write these two nonsense sentences on the chalkboard:

1. The shink (*grimp* or *grimps*) the vork. [grimps]
2. The shinks (*grimp* or *grimps*) the vork. [grimp]

Ask students to select the correct verbs and to explain how they were able to make the correct choices. [Answers may vary, but the basic idea is that students recognized the subject-verb-object pattern of the sentences and that they knew how to choose the correct verbs by the presence or absence of an –s on the end.] Point out that not all sentences are as obvious as these, but that the same rule applies to all sentences.

700

Number

Number is the form of a word that indicates whether the word is singular or plural.

21a. A word that refers to one person or thing is *singular* in number. A word that refers to more than one is *plural* in number.

| SINGULAR | employer | theory | woman | that | either | it |
| PLURAL | employers | theories | women | those | both | they |

Most nouns that end in *s* are plural; most present-tense verbs that end in *s* are singular. Past-tense verbs (except *be*) have the same form in both the singular and the plural.

NOTE: The singular pronouns *I* and *you* almost always take plural verbs. The only exceptions are the forms *I am* and *I was*.

Agreement of Subject and Verb

21b. A verb should agree with its subject in number.

(1) Singular subjects take singular verbs.

EXAMPLES   The **child takes** an afternoon nap.
She cleans and **restores** old paintings.

(2) Plural subjects take plural verbs.

EXAMPLES   The **children take** an afternoon nap.
They clean and **restore** old paintings.

A verb phrase, like a one-word verb, agrees in number with its subject. The number of a verb phrase is indicated by the form of its first auxiliary (helping) verb.

EXAMPLES   The **Vietnam Veterans Memorial was** designed by Maya Lin. [singular subject and verb phrase]
The **Vietnam Veterans Memorial** and the **Civil Rights Memorial were** designed by Maya Lin. [plural subject and verb phrase]

Intervening Phrases and Clauses

21c. The number of the subject is not changed by a phrase or a clause following the subject.

EXAMPLES   The **short stories are** by various contemporary Native American writers.

The **short stories** in this anthology **are** by various contemporary Native American writers. [The prepositional phrase *in this anthology* does not affect the number of the subject, *short stories.*]

Edmonia Lewis was the first African American woman to achieve renown for her sculpture.

Edmonia Lewis, whose subjects included John Brown and Abraham Lincoln, **was** the first African American woman to achieve renown for her sculpture. [The adjective clause *whose subjects included John Brown and Abraham Lincoln* does not affect the number of the subject, *Edmonia Lewis.*]

The number of the subject is also not affected when the subject is followed by a phrase that begins with an expression such as *along with, as well as, in addition to,* and *together with.*

EXAMPLES   The **man** in the next apartment, as well as the people across the hall, **has lived** in the building since the mid-1970s. [singular subject and verb]

The **people** across the hall, as well as the man in the next apartment, **have lived** in the building since the mid-1970s. [plural subject and verb]

grade on Monday.

▶ EXERCISE 1   **Identifying Subjects and Verbs That Agree in Number**

For each of the following sentences, identify the <u>subject</u> of the verb in parentheses. Then choose the <u>verb form that agrees in number with the subject.</u>

1. The <u>theory</u> of plate tectonics (*has, have*) explained causes of earthquake activity throughout the world.
2. Enormous <u>plates</u> of rock (*is, are*) shifting constantly far beneath the earth's surface.
3. The <u>movements</u>, in addition to the pressure of molten rock, (*causes, cause*) the plates to collide.

USAGE

LEP/ESL

General Strategies. Some languages do not show number in nouns or verbs. Students should be reminded that in written English, proper agreement is essential in every sentence—not just in the first sentence in a series.

General Strategies. In some languages, objects can appear before their verbs. For example, the English sentence "Jack sees runners often" might have the order "Runners often Jack sees" or "Often Jack runners sees." Therefore, some English-language learners may try to make the verb agree with the object. Stress that students should concentrate primarily on writing English sentences in the order of subject-verb-object until they feel more comfortable with English. Remind them that they should always make the verb agree with the subject.

USAGE

4. The <u>pressure</u> of colliding plates (*forces, force*) the rock to bend until it breaks.
5. A <u>ridge</u> of these breaks (*is, are*) called a fault.
6. The <u>cause</u> of most earthquakes (*is, are*) the sudden release of stress along a fault.
7. The Richter <u>scale</u>, as well as other measurements, (*has, have*) been used to record the magnitude of earthquakes.
8. The <u>tremors</u> of the great San Francisco earthquake that occurred in 1906 (*was, were*) estimated to have measured 8.3 on the Richter scale.
9. <u>California</u>, with two major fault lines, (*has, have*) about ten times the world average of earthquake activity.
10. A <u>map</u> of the earth's plates, such as the one shown here, (*gives, give*) you a pretty good idea of why California has so many quakes.

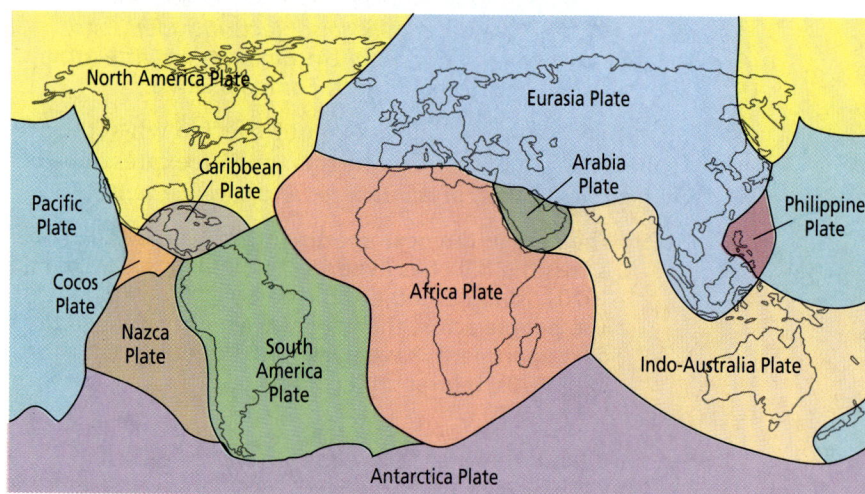

North America Plate
Eurasia Plate
Caribbean Plate
Arabia Plate
Pacific Plate
Philippine Plate
Cocos Plate
Africa Plate
Nazca Plate
South America Plate
Indo-Australia Plate
Antarctica Plate

Indefinite Pronouns

21d. The following indefinite pronouns are singular: *anybody, anyone, anything, each, either, everybody, everyone, everything, neither, nobody, no one, nothing, one, somebody, someone,* and *something.*

EXAMPLES   **Is anyone** in the audience a medical doctor?
            Each of the boys **does** his own cooking.
            Either of these videos **is** suitable for a four-year-old.

USAGE

21e. The following indefinite pronouns are plural: *both, few, many,* and *several.*

EXAMPLES   **Both** of the universities **offer** degrees in forestry.
Few on the committee ever **miss** a meeting.
Several of the students **have transferred.**

21f. The following indefinite pronouns may be singular or plural: *all, any, most, none,* and *some.*

These pronouns are singular when they refer to singular words. They are plural when they refer to plural words.

EXAMPLES   **All** of the workout **seems** simple. [*All* refers to the singular noun *workout.*]
All of the exercises **seem** simple. [*All* refers to the plural noun *exercises.*]

Is any of the salad left? [*Any* refers to the singular noun *salad.*]
Are any of the vegetables left? [*Any* refers to the plural noun *vegetables.*]

Most of the plan **was** new to me. [*Most* refers to the singular noun *plan.*]
Most of the plans **were** new to me. [*Most* refers to the plural noun *plans.*]

None of the deck **is** missing. [*None* refers to the singular noun *deck.*]
None of the cards **are** missing. [*None* refers to the plural noun *cards.*]

Some of the show **was** hilarious. [*Some* refers to the singular noun *show.*]
Some of the acts **were** hilarious. [*Some* refers to the plural noun *acts.*]

▶ EXERCISE 2   **Identifying Subjects and Verbs That Agree in Number**

For each of the following sentences, identify the subject of the verb in parentheses. Then choose the verb form that agrees in number with the subject.

1. Each of the pictures (*was, were*) in a silver frame.
2. One of my friends (*play, plays*) the tuba.

COMMON ERROR

Problem. The pronouns *everybody* and *everyone* cause problems because they're singular in form but might imply more than one person.

Solution. Tell students to focus on the second part of each of these compound words (*one* and *body*) to remind themselves that these words take singular verbs.

MEETING *individual* NEEDS

LEP/ESL

General Strategies. Some English-language learners may be confused by the meaning of the word *agreement.* They might expect that when the subject ends in –s, the verb must also end in –s. It may be wise to emphasize that for agreement, a singular subject requires a singular verb, ordinarily one ending in –s. Point out that *singular* starts with an s and singular verbs usually end in –s.

INTEGRATING THE LANGUAGE ARTS

Dictionary Skills. Some words are plural in form and meaning, but many people use the words as if they were singular. Some words of Latin and Greek origin are in this group: *media, data, criteria,* and *phenomena.* Ask students to look in a dictionary to find the singular forms of these words [*medium, datum, criterion,* and *phenomenon*]. Remind students to use plural verbs with plural subjects of sentences.

3. (All) of our belongings (*is, are*) carefully unpacked.
4. Some of these rare books (*has, have*) leather covers.
5. None of the people in the theater (*was, were*) sitting in the first two rows.
6. Every one of these computer games (*is, are*) on sale.
7. A few in my class (*was, were*) asked to help out.
8. The lack of funds (*present, presents*) a problem.
9. Everybody living in Lewis Heights (*go, goes*) to George Washington Carver High School.
10. A band with two trumpet players and thirty-five clarinetists (*sound, sounds*) terrible.

📕➡ EXERCISE 3 **Revising Subject-Verb Agreement in Sentences**

Revise each of the following sentences according to the instructions in brackets after each sentence. Make any needed changes in the form of the verb.

EXAMPLE **1.** Each of the contestants was confused by the question. [Change *Each* to *Several*.]
1. *Several of the contestants were confused by the question.*

1. All of the ~~fruit has~~ been picked. [Change *fruit* to *oranges*.]   **1. oranges have**
2. ~~Each~~ of us ~~was~~ angry about the election. [Change *Each* to *Many*.]   **2. Many/were**
3. ~~Has anybody~~ joined the choir? [Change *anybody* to *any of the new students*.]   **3. Have any of the new students**
4. The ~~committee~~ leaves today for Washington, D.C. [Add *representing the farmers* after *committee*.]   **4. committee representing the farmers**
5. Our team ~~is~~ going to Austin for the debate tournament. [Add *Three members of* before *Our team*.]   **5. Three members of/are**
6. ~~Most~~ of the classrooms were equipped with new microcomputers. [Change *Most* to *None*.]   **6. None**
7. The pitcher was disappointed in the coach's decision. [Add *as well as the other players* after *pitcher*. Set off the addition with commas.]   **7. , as well as the other players,**
8. ~~Every one~~ of the smoke detectors ~~works~~ fine. [Change *Every one* to *All but two*.]   **8. All but two/work**
9. ~~Both of them~~ usually ~~hope~~ that things will turn out for the best. [Change *Both of them* to *Everyone*.]   **9. Everyone/hopes**
10. Some of her ~~plan has~~ been adopted. [Change *plan* to *ideas*.]   **10. ideas have**

REVIEW A

OBJECTIVE

- To proofread a paragraph for subject-verb agreement

21g

▶ REVIEW A **Proofreading for Subject-Verb Agreement**

Most of the sentences in the following paragraph contain errors in subject-verb agreement. If a sentence contains an error, give the correct form. If a sentence is correct, write *C*.

[1] The history of the Hawaiian Islands tell of some interesting rulers. [2] Of course, none of these rulers is more amazing than King Kamehameha I. [3] This powerful leader, together with his followers, are credited with uniting the numerous islands into a kingdom in 1795. [4] Kamehameha I, whose family ruled the islands until 1872, was sometimes called the Napoleon of the Pacific. [5] Few of his descendants was more influential than King Kamehameha III. [6] No one deny that he helped the common people by permitting them to own land and by issuing a democratic constitution. [7] The musical interest of Hawaii's last two royal rulers, King Kalakaua I and Queen Liliuokalani, are fascinating. [8] Both of these monarchs was known as songwriters. [9] The queen, whose regal bearing is evident in this photograph, has several claims to fame. [10] One of these are having written the famous song "*Aloha Oe*" ("Farewell to Thee").

1. tells
2. are
3. is
4. C
5. were
6. denies
7. is
8. were
9. C
10. is

USAGE

Compound Subjects

A *compound subject* is two or more subjects that have the same verb.

21g. Subjects joined by *and* usually take a plural verb.

EXAMPLES **Spanish** and **Quechua are** the official languages of Peru.
Hannah and **Dot have been** friends for years.

MEETING *individual* NEEDS

LEP/ESL

Spanish.   Be aware that the rules for subject-verb agreement with compound subjects in Spanish are complex. Whether the Spanish verb should be singular or plural can be influenced by three things—the applicability of the verb to both elements of the compound subject, the relative distance of the subject and the object from the verb, and the importance of the predicate nominative, if there is one.

USAGE

NOTE: Subjects joined by *and* may be considered a single item or may refer to the same thing. In such cases, a compound subject takes a singular verb.

EXAMPLES   My next-door **neighbor** and best **friend is** from Mexico. [one person]
Macaroni and **cheese is** a nutritious main course. [one dish]

21h. Singular subjects joined by *or* or *nor* take a singular verb.

EXAMPLES   A **jacket** or a **sweater is** warm enough for tonight.
Neither the **coach** nor the **trainer knows** the umpire.
Either **Soledad** or **Chen writes** the weekly editorial.

21i. When a singular subject and a plural subject are joined by *or* or *nor,* the verb agrees with the subject nearer the verb.

EXAMPLES   Either the **musicians** or the **singer is** off-key. [The singular subject *singer* is nearer the verb.]
Either the **singer** or the **musicians are** off-key. [The plural subject *musicians* is nearer the verb.]

Whenever possible, revise the sentence to avoid this awkward construction.

EXAMPLE   Either the singer is off-key, or the musicians are.

NOTE: Formal usage requires a singular verb after a singular subject. Informal usage, however, often permits the use of a plural verb if the meaning is clearly plural.

FORMAL   The director, as well as the star and several stage hands, was trapped in the theater fire.
INFORMAL   The director, as well as the star and several stage hands, were trapped in the theater fire.

☞ **REFERENCE NOTE:** For a discussion of formal and informal English, see pages 519–523. As you work the exercises in this chapter, follow the rules of formal standard usage.

▶ EXERCISE 4   **Identifying Verbs That Agree with Compound Subjects**

Choose the verb form in parentheses that correctly completes each of the following sentences.

21
h–i

1. Del Rio and San Angelo (*is*, *are*) two Texas cities that have names of Spanish origin.
2. My books and tennis racket barely (*fit*, *fits*) in the locker.
3. Either my cat or the raccoons always (*eat*, *eats*) all the food by morning.
4. That blouse and scarf (*is*, *are*) a good combination.
5. Neither Mariah Carey nor Gloria Estefan, I believe, (*sing*, *sings*) that song.

▶ REVIEW B   **Correcting Errors in Subject-Verb Agreement**

grade on Thursday

Most of the following sentences contain verbs that do not agree with their subjects. If a verb does not agree with its subject, give the correct form of the verb. If a sentence is correct, write C.

1. One of the most precious resources in the nation is water.
2. The abundance and use of water vary greatly among the regions of the United States.
3. The water supply in every region comes from either surface water or underground water.
4. Unfortunately, neither overuse nor contamination of our water supplies has stopped completely.
5. After years of study, the pollution of lakes, rivers, and streams continue to be a serious problem.
6. Lake Erie, as well as the Potomac River and the Cuyahoga River, have been saved by clean-up efforts.

7. As you can see in the picture above, Lake Erie, which is bounded by several large, industrial cities, sparkle again.

USAGE

A DIFFERENT APPROACH

Tell your students that they will write expressive paragraphs together. Have the student at the beginning of each row write a topic sentence with a compound subject and verb. If students have trouble getting started, suggest topics for their paragraphs, such as music, sports, or clothes. As the first writer finishes writing, he or she will pass the paper back to the next student, who will compose a sentence with another compound subject and verb and then pass the paper on. When all rows have finished writing, the papers will be returned to the first student in each row, who will read the paragraph aloud.

ANSWERS
Review B
1. C
2. C
3. C
4. C
5. continues
6. has
7. sparkles

USAGE

OBJECTIVE
- To identify in sentences subjects and verbs that agree in number

USAGE

8. is
9. are
10. are
11. comes
12. C
13. C
14. causes
15. contaminate
16. C
17. is
18. C
19. is
20. has

PROGRAM MANAGER

SPECIAL PROBLEMS IN SUBJECT-VERB AGREEMENT

- **Independent Practice/ Reteaching** For instruction and exercises, see **Other Problems in Agreement A** and **Other Problems in Agreement B** in *Language Skills Practice and Assessment,* pp. 107–108.

- **Computer Guided Instruction** For additional instruction and practice with subject-verb agreement, see **Lessons 6** and **7** in *Language Workshop CD-ROM.*

- **Practice** To help less-advanced students with additional instruction and practice with subject-verb agreement, see **Chapter 14** in *English Workshop, Complete Course,* pp. 189–200.

8. The government, in addition to environmentalists, are also worried about the quality and abundance of ground water.
9. Aquifers, a source of ground water, is layers of rock, sand, and soil that hold water.
10. Billions of gallons of water is pumped out of the ground each day.
11. In some regions, drinking water for thousands of people come from aquifers.
12. Every one of the recent studies of aquifers has revealed contamination to some degree.
13. The causes of contamination are varied.
14. Salt for melting ice on city streets cause pollution.
15. The chemicals that sometimes leak out of a sewer system or waste dump contaminates aquifers.
16. Fertilizers and pesticides used widely all over the country also add pollutants to the water.
17. The extent of the damages from pollution are not known.
18. Another problem, according to scientists, is uncontrolled use of water sources.
19. Ground water in some areas are being used faster than the supply can be renewed.
20. Each one of the fifty states have a stake in preserving sources of water.

Special Problems in Subject-Verb Agreement

21j. When the subject follows the verb, as in questions and in sentences beginning with *here* and *there*, identify the subject and make sure that the verb agrees with it.

The verb usually comes before the subject in sentences beginning with *Here* or *There* and in questions.

EXAMPLES   Here **is** the **book** you reserved.
Here **are** the **books** you reserved.

There **was** a **detour** on the interstate.
There **were** no **detours** on the interstate.

When **is Passover** this year?
When **are Passover** and **Easter** this year?

NOTE: Contractions such as *Here's, There's, When's,* and *Where's* incorporate the verb *is.* Use such contractions only with subjects that are singular in meaning.

NONSTANDARD	When's your finals?
STANDARD	When **are** your **finals**?

NONSTANDARD	Here's your gloves.
STANDARD	Here **are** your **gloves**.
STANDARD	Here**'s** your **pair** of gloves.

21k. Collective nouns may be either singular or plural.

A *collective noun* is singular in form but names a group of persons or things.

Common Collective Nouns			
army	club	flock	squadron
assembly	committee	group	staff
audience	crowd	herd	swarm
band	family	jury	team
class	fleet	public	troop

A collective noun takes a singular verb when the noun refers to the group as a unit. A collective noun takes a plural verb when the noun refers to the parts or members of the group.

SINGULAR The **class meets** Monday, Wednesday, and Friday. [The class meets as a unit.]

PLURAL The **class** usually **bring** their calculators with them. [The members of the class bring separate calculators.]

SINGULAR The **team has won** the semifinals. [The team won as a unit.]

PLURAL The **team have voted** twenty-one to nothing to buy new uniforms. [The members of the team voted individually.]

SINGULAR A **herd** of cattle **was stranded** by the flood. [The herd was stranded as a unit.]

PLURAL The **herd** of cattle **were grazing** in the clover. [The cattle were grazing individually.]

USAGE

USAGE

QUICK REMINDER

Write the following sentences on the chalkboard. Ask students to choose the correct form of the verb in parentheses (underscored). You may want to have volunteers explain why choosing the correct verb is a challenge.

1. The team (is, are) meeting in the locker room. [*Team* refers to a group and needs a singular verb.]
2. The team (is, are) putting on their helmets. [*Team* refers to individuals and needs a plural verb.]
3. In that tree (live, lives) two chipmunks. [The subject follows the verb.]
4. He (doesn't, don't) like this music. [Incorrect usage is reinforced orally.]

MEETING individual NEEDS

LEP/ESL

General Strategies. Many languages have variations in the rules governing agreement between collective-noun subjects and verbs. For example, British English, which many students learn, uses the plural more frequently than American English, as in "The Government have decided to . . . ." You may wish to give English-language learners additional examples of sentences with collective nouns and to explain whether each reference is to a unit or to its members.

STUDENTS WITH SPECIAL NEEDS

A helpful strategy for some students is for them to hear the material, then to say it, then to see it, and finally to involve the motor processes. Have students work in groups to make up examples for each noun in the box.

USAGE

Peanuts reprinted by permission of United Feature Syndicate, Inc.

21l. An expression stating an amount (such as a measurement, a statistic, or a fraction) may be singular or plural.

An expression stating an amount is

- singular when the amount is thought of as a unit
- plural when the amount is thought of as separate parts

EXAMPLES **Twenty-seven dollars is** all we've raised so far. [The amount refers to one unit. Notice that the entire expression *Twenty-seven dollars* is the subject.]
Twenty-seven **dollars were** counted out by the teller. [The amount refers to separate dollars. Notice that only the noun *dollars* is the subject. *Twenty-seven* is an adjective telling how many.]

Eight hours is now the standard workday throughout the United States. [one unit]
Eight **hours were** set aside for that miniseries about the Civil War. [separate hours]

☞ **REFERENCE NOTE:** For information on using hyphens in expressions stating an amount, see page 953.

A fraction or a percentage is singular when it refers to a singular word and plural when it refers to a plural word.

EXAMPLES **Two thirds** of my bibliography **has been typed.** [The fraction refers to the singular noun *bibliography*.]
Two thirds of my references **have been typed.** [The fraction refers to the plural noun *references*.]

Forty-two percent of the senior class **is planning** to go to college. [The percentage refers to the singular noun *class*.]
Forty-two percent of the seniors **are planning** to go to college. [The percentage refers to the plural noun *seniors*.]

Expressions of measurement (length, weight, capacity, area) are usually singular.

EXAMPLES **Two and fifty-four hundredths centimeters equals** one inch.
Seven pounds was the baby's weight at birth.
Ninety miles is the distance between Florida and Cuba.

☞ **REFERENCE NOTE:** For information on when to spell out numbers and when to use numerals, see pages 973–974.

▶ EXERCISE 5 **Identifying Subjects and Verbs That Agree in Number**

Choose the word in parentheses that correctly completes each of the following sentences.

1. Forty dollars (*is, are*) too much to pay for those jeans.
2. (*Where's, Where are*) my coat and boots?
3. There (*seems, seem*) to be something for everyone.
4. The newspaper staff (*has, have*) turned in all their stories.
5. One half of the receipts (*was, were*) found in a shoe box.
6. (*Here's, Here are*) the notes you took about the history and symbolism of Japanese pagodas.
7. Two thirds of the students (*intend, intends*) to go to trade school or college.
8. The orchestra (*specialize, specializes*) in the Big Band music of Count Basie and Duke Ellington.
9. A number of us (*think, thinks*) the test was hard.
10. Fifty miles (*is, are*) a long way to drive to work every day.

INTEGRATING THE LANGUAGE ARTS

Usage and Writing. Because **Rules 21j–21t** each address a different aspect of agreement, you may want to discuss the rules individually during the school year as each one applies to the class's writing or speech activities. The fact that titles of books, poems, and stories are treated as singular, for instance, could be addressed when students are preparing for their literary-analysis assignments in **Chapter 10.**

Usage and Vocabulary. Rule 21o deals with nouns that may be singular or plural and nouns that seem plural in form but that take singular verbs. Students can apply a simple test to decide whether such a noun is plural or singular. A word that ends in *–ics* is singular if it refers to the science or study of something. For example, *acoustics* means "the science that deals with the way sound behaves in an enclosed area." The same word is used in a plural sense if it refers to the individual kinds of sound behavior within an area.

In the sentence "The acoustics in the new auditorium are excellent," it is clear that science cannot be described as "excellent." In this usage, *acoustics* must be plural.

USAGE

USAGE

21m. The title of a creative work (such as a book, song, film, or painting) and the name of a country (even if it is plural in form) take a singular verb.

EXAMPLES *Dust Tracks on a Road* **is** Zora Neale Hurston's autobiography.

Vermilion Lotuses **was** among the paintings by Chinese artist Chang Dai-chien exhibited at the Smithsonian Institution.

The **United Arab Emirates generates** most of its revenue from the sale of oil.

The **United States of America belongs** to both the United Nations and the Organization of American States.

21n. The name of an organization usually takes a singular verb even if it is plural in form.

EXAMPLES **The United Nations has** its headquarters in New York City.

Is Benson Motors where you bought your car?

The names of some organizations may take singular or plural verbs. When the name refers to the organization as a unit, it takes a singular verb. When the name refers to the members of the organization, it takes a plural verb.

EXAMPLES The **Veterans of Foreign Wars was founded** in 1899. [The organization was founded in 1899.]

The **Veterans of Foreign Wars are leading** the parade. [The members of the organization are leading the parade.]

21o. Some nouns that are plural in form are singular in meaning.

(1) The following nouns always take singular verbs.

civics	genetics	mumps
economics	mathematics	news
electronics	measles	physics

EXAMPLES **Mumps is** usually more severe in adults than in children.

Economics was my mother's major in college.

(2) The following nouns always take plural verbs.

binoculars	pliers	shears
eyeglasses	scissors	trousers

EXAMPLES   The **binoculars are** on the screened porch.
                     Have these **shears** ever **been sharpened**?

NOTE: Many nouns ending in *–ics,* such as *acoustics, athletics, ethics, politics, statistics,* and *tactics,* may be singular or plural in meaning. Generally, such a noun takes a singular verb when it names a science, a system, or a skill. It takes a plural verb when it names qualities, operations, or activities.

> EXAMPLES   Who said, "**Politics is** the art of the possible"?
>   **Are** your **politics** like those of your parents?

If you don't know whether a noun that is plural in form is singular or plural in meaning, check a dictionary.

21p. A verb should always agree with its subject, not with its predicate nominative.

EXAMPLES   Quick **reflexes are** one requirement for becoming an astronaut.
                     One **requirement** for becoming an astronaut **is** quick reflexes.

                     The **highlight** of the evening **was** the compositions by Quincy Jones.
                     The **compositions** by Quincy Jones **were** the highlight of the evening.

21q. Subjects preceded by *every* or *many a* take singular verbs.

EXAMPLES   **Every takeoff** and **landing is cleared** with the tower.
                     Many a runner finishes a marathon long after the winner.

21r. *Doesn't,* not *don't,* is used with singular subjects except *I* and *you.*

Remember that *doesn't* is the contraction for *does not* and that *don't* is the contraction for *do not.*

NONSTANDARD   He don't live here anymore.
        STANDARD   **He doesn't** [does not] live here anymore.

USAGE

USAGE

713

CRITICAL THINKING

Analysis. Tell students the use of *do* as a support for yes-or-no questions and negation is relatively new in the English language. In Shakespeare's time, the usual way to ask a yes-or-no question was to put the verb first in the sentence, as in "Want you some pie?" Negative statements were formed by adding *not* after the verb, as in "I want not any pie." Write those two examples of sixteenth-century usage on the chalkboard and have students copy them and write the modern usage next to them. Tell students there is a general belief that changes in language always simplify grammar. Ask students if they think the modern form is simpler or more complicated. [Some will say that "Want you some pie?" is simpler than "Do you want some pie?" and that "I want not any pie" is simpler than "I don't want any pie."]

USAGE

USAGE

| NONSTANDARD | It don't look like rain. |
| STANDARD | **It doesn't** [does not] look like rain. |

| NONSTANDARD | Ruth don't know about the surprise party for her. |
| STANDARD | **Ruth doesn't** [does not] know about the surprise party for her. |

21s. When a relative pronoun (*that, which,* or *who*) is the subject of an adjective clause, the verb in the clause should agree with the word that the relative pronoun refers to.

EXAMPLE   San Juan, **which is** the capital of Puerto Rico, is a major tourist destination. [*Which* refers to the singular noun *San Juan.*]
I know some people **who own** a Christmas-tree farm. [*Who* refers to the plural noun *people.*]

NOTE: When the relative pronoun is preceded by *one of those* [or *these* or another plural word] it takes a plural verb. When it is preceded by *the only one of those* [or *these* or another plural word] it takes a singular verb.

EXAMPLES   Egypt is **one of the nations that border** the Red Sea.
Quebec is **the only one of the Canadian provinces that has** a majority of French-speaking citizens.

21t. The word *number* when followed by the word *of* is singular when preceded by *the*; it is plural when preceded by *a*.

EXAMPLES   **The number** of volunteers **is** surprising.
A number of volunteers **are** signing up now.

EXERCISE 6   **Identifying Subjects and Verbs That Agree in Number**

For each of the following sentences, identify the <u>subject</u> of the verb in parentheses. Then choose the <u>verb form that agrees in number with the subject</u>.

1. Many a gymnast (*dreams, dream*) of winning a medal in the Olympic games.
2. Bao (*doesn't, don't*) remember what year her grandparents moved here from Vietnam.
3. Many critics agree that *Boyz N the Hood* (*offer, offers*) movie watchers a realistic look at inner-city life.

4. The Chicago Cubs is a team that (*rallies*, *rally*) in the late innings.
5. Civics (*is*, *are*) supposed to be his best subject.
6. The Society of Procrastinators (*has*, *have*) postponed its annual meeting.
7. That was one of those jokes that (*offends*, *offend*) everyone.
8. The kitchen scissors (*was*, *were*) not on the counter this morning.
9. My favorite part of the movie (*was*, *were*) scenes in New York's Adirondack Mountains.
10. Every volunteer in the regional hospitals (*is*, *are*) being honored at the banquet.

REVIEW C | **Correcting Errors in Subject-Verb Agreement**

Most of the sentences in the following paragraph contain verbs that do not agree with their subjects. If a verb does not agree with its subject, give the correct form of the verb. If a sentence is correct, write C.

[1] The White House, which has been home to all U.S. presidents since John Adams, is a national treasure. [2] The public, as you can see in this picture, like to view the White House and grounds when visiting Washington, D.C. [3] How many people actually tours the White House each year? [4] One million are a conservative estimate. [5] There's more than 130 rooms in the White House. [6] Of course, a tourist don't get to see all the rooms. [7] In fact, only seven rooms, including the State Dining Room, is open to the public on the official tour. [8] Many a party have been given in the East Room, another large reception area. [9] The White House chefs, who works in two kitchens, sometimes prepare food for more than one hundred people in a single day. [10] The presence in the White House of recreational facilities, such as a movie theater and a bowling alley, usually surprises some visitors.

USAGE

ANSWERS
Review C
1. C
2. likes
3. tour
4. is
5. There are
6. doesn't
7. are
8. has
9. work
10. C

USAGE

WRITING APPLICATION

OBJECTIVE

- To use correct subject-verb agreement in writing an original letter of recommendation

WRITING APPLICATION

Using Correct Subject-Verb Agreement in Formal Writing

By now you've learned that a word can mean different things in different contexts. For example, the same word can be a singular subject in one sentence and a plural subject in another. To determine the number of a collective noun, a plural noun, an expression of an amount, and a relative pronoun, you need to look at how each word is used. As you read the following paragraph, notice which subjects take singular verbs and which take plural ones.

> Ten years is a long time to stay friends with someone. Shawn Popovich, who has applied for a position at your summer camp, has been my best friend since the second grade. In addition to being a loyal friend, he is also a natural leader and athlete. Four years ago Shawn was the only freshman who made the cut for the varsity football team. This year, as a senior and captain of the team, he led us to victory in the state championship. But athletics isn't the only area in which Shawn stands out from the crowd. Last year he singlehandedly recruited more than a dozen volunteers from our school for the Big Brother/Big Sister program, which he and I still participate in. An openhearted, fun-loving person, Shawn earns the trust and admiration of children and adults alike. I know that the majority of the senior class share my high opinion of him.

What effect does this writer's careful use of subject-verb agreement have on you as a reader? What is your general impression of the writer? of his friend Shawn?

WRITING ACTIVITY

A friend of yours is applying for a summer job as a camp counselor and has asked you to write a letter of recommendation. Because you think highly of this person, you've agreed to write a letter explaining why he or she would make an excellent counselor. Write the letter of recommendation that you will send to the director of the summer camp. In your letter, follow the rules of formal standard English and pay particular attention to subject-verb agreement.

Prewriting Take a few minutes to jot down a list of your friend's positive qualities and outstanding abilities. Focus on traits that you think would make your friend a good camp counselor. For example, does he or she work well with children? excel at a particular sport, craft, or academic subject? exhibit enthusiasm and team spirit? have a responsible attitude toward work? Think of specific examples that illustrate the qualities you've listed.

Writing Begin your letter by introducing yourself and stating your purpose. Tell how long you've known the person you're recommending. Then express your positive opinion of the person and his or her abilities. Be specific. You may want to give two or three brief examples to illustrate your friend's qualities. Or you may want to tell one interesting anecdote that achieves the same result. Resist the temptation to exaggerate your friend's achievements or abilities. Nobody expects him or her to be perfect, and an employer may become suspicious if an applicant sounds "too good to be true."

Evaluating and Revising Read through your letter once before you begin to revise it. Does it have the effect you want? Will it help your friend get the job? On a second reading, identify specific parts of the letter that need revising. Note any examples that don't illustrate your friend's qualities as well as they could. Also delete overly general statements such as "He's a great guy" or "She's a nice person." Replace colloquialisms or slang words with more formal expressions. (For help identifying colloquialisms and slang, see pages 521–523.) During your revision process, you may wish to ask a friend to read your letter and offer suggestions. Check to be sure you've followed the standard form for a business letter. (See pages 1088–1095.)

Proofreading Correct grammar, usage, punctuation, and spelling are extremely important in a letter of recommendation. Be sure to proofread your letter carefully. When you check for errors in subject-verb agreement, take extra care with collective nouns, plural nouns, expressions of an amount, and relative pronouns.

CRITICAL THINKING

Analysis. Have students analyze the methods of persuasion used in the sample recommendation. Students may cite the firsthand knowledge of the writer, the example of the subject's success and persistence, the example of his initiative and ability to persuade others, and the opinions of others as being convincing elements.

PREWRITING

You could point out that the writer of a letter of recommendation often asks the subject what experiences, talents, or abilities to emphasize. You may want students to consult their chosen subjects for material to emphasize.

USAGE

USAGE

OBJECTIVES

- To correct errors in pronoun-antecedent agreement in sentences
- To plan an original skit
- To use correct pronoun-antecedent agreement in an original informative/persuasive letter

718 *Agreement*

Agreement of Pronoun and Antecedent

A pronoun usually refers to a noun or another pronoun. The word to which a pronoun refers is called its *antecedent.*

21u. A pronoun should agree with its antecedent in number and in gender.

(1) Singular pronouns refer to singular antecedents. Plural pronouns refer to plural antecedents.

EXAMPLES   **Arthur Mitchell** founded **his** own ballet company.
Many **Native Americans** live **their** lives in harmony with the natural world around **them.**

(2) A few singular pronouns indicate gender. The singular pronouns *he, him, his,* and *himself* refer to masculine antecedents. The singular pronouns *she, her, hers,* and *herself* refer to feminine antecedents. The singular pronouns *it, its,* and *itself* refer to antecedents that are neuter (neither masculine nor feminine).

EXAMPLES   **Rudolfo** stated **his** position clearly.
Maxine has already prepared **her** acceptance speech.
The **river** overflowed **its** banks.

21v. Singular pronouns are used to refer to the following antecedents: *anybody, anyone, anything, each, either, everybody, everyone, everything, neither, nobody, no one, nothing, one, somebody, someone,* and *something.*

These words do not indicate gender. To determine their gender, look in phrases following them.

EXAMPLES   **Each** of these **women** runs **her** own business.
One of the **men** in the audience forgot **his** coat.

If the antecedent may be either masculine or feminine, use both the masculine and feminine pronouns to refer to it.

EXAMPLES   **Everyone** should learn how to manage **his or her** money.
Each of the participants in the contest paid **his or her** own entry fee.

You can often avoid the awkward *his or her* construction by substituting an article (*a, an,* or *the*) for the construction or by rephrasing the sentence, using the plural forms of both the pronoun and its antecedent.

EXAMPLES **Each** of the participants in the contest must pay **an** entry fee.
All of the **participants** in the contest must pay **their** own entry fees.

In conversation, plural pronouns are often used to refer to singular antecedents that can be either masculine or feminine.

EXAMPLES **Everyone** remembered **their** first day of school.
Each of the students read **their** poems.

This usage is becoming increasingly popular in writing. One reason for the growing use of this form is that using a singular pronoun with a singular antecedent that is clearly plural in meaning may be awkward or misleading.

MISLEADING **No one** failed the pop quiz because **he or she** had done **his or her** homework. [Since *no one* is clearly plural in meaning, the singular pronouns, though grammatically correct, are awkward.]
IMPROVED **No one** failed the pop quiz because **they** had done **their** homework.

MISLEADING **Everyone** in the band was so tired from the long bus ride that **he or she** did not play well.
IMPROVED **Everyone** in the band was so tired from the long bus ride that **they** did not play well.

21w. A plural pronoun is used to refer to two or more singular antecedents joined by *and*.

EXAMPLES **Hilda** and **Lupe** presented **their** reports.
After **Ethel, Jared,** and **Cam** ate lunch together, **they** went to **their** next class.

21x. A singular pronoun is used to refer to two or more singular antecedents joined by *or* or *nor*.

EXAMPLES Either **Paul** or **Diego** is willing to drive **his** car.
Neither **Sue** nor **María** brought **her** vacation photos with **her**.

USAGE

MEETING *individual* NEEDS

LEP/ESL

General Strategies. English-language learners whose native languages do not use pronouns in the same way as English does may have difficulty with this lesson. For example, in Korean, pronouns are not differentiated by gender. The Japanese and Turkish languages have no number agreement. In the languages of Vietnam and Laos, there are no neuter pronouns. To prevent any confusion, you can explain which personal pronouns refer to which sorts of antecedents, with special emphasis on the use of *he, she,* and *it.* If someone mentions that in Spanish it is possible to identify the gender of a group—as in *ellos hablan* (*they speak,* masculine), *ellas hablan* (*they speak,* feminine)—note that English uses the third-person plural pronoun *they* for males, females, and mixed-gender groups.

USAGE

INTEGRATING THE LANGUAGE ARTS

Usage and Vocabulary. Ask your students to find *antecedent* in a dictionary and to read its etymology. The word consists of two parts, both from Latin. *Ante–* means "before," while *cedent,* derived from *cedere,* means "go." Ask students how the etymology of the word can help them remember how its meaning is applied in grammar. [An antecedent usually comes before the pronoun that refers to it.]

ANSWERS

Exercise 7

1. his or her

2. C

3. his or her

4. his or her *or* an opinion

5. his or her *or* a camera

6. their

7. their

8. he or she

720

21y. When a singular and a plural antecedent are joined by *or* or *nor*, the pronoun usually agrees with the nearer antecedent.

EXAMPLES   Neither the **puppies nor** our full-grown **dog** likes **its** new toys.

Neither our full-grown **dog nor** the **puppies** like **their** new toys.

Whenever possible, revise the sentence to avoid such an awkward construction.

EXAMPLE   The **puppies** don't like **their** new toys, and our full-grown **dog** doesn't like **its** new toys either.

NOTE: Sometimes following the rules results in another type of awkward or misleading sentence.

MISLEADING   Either Anthony or Dolores is bringing her guitar. [The pronoun agrees in gender with the nearer of the two antecedents; however, the antecedents are of different genders.]

REVISED   Either **Anthony** is bringing **his** guitar, or **Dolores** is bringing **hers.**

EXERCISE 7 Correcting Errors in Pronoun-Antecedent Agreement

Most of the following sentences contain pronouns that do not agree with their antecedents. If a pronoun does not agree with its antecedent, write the correct form of the pronoun. If a sentence is correct, write *C*.

EXAMPLE   **1.** Neither Elena nor Barbara made any errors on their test.
   1. *her*

1. Each of the skiers waxed their skis every morning.
2. All of the senior citizens enjoyed their trip to Boston, where they walked the Freedom Trail.
3. Every one of the reporters at the press conference asked their questions too quickly.
4. I think that anybody should be free to express their opinion.
5. No one brought their camera to the party.
6. Both of the male soloists pronounced his words clearly.
7. Did any of the newborn kittens seem steady on its feet?
8. If anyone gets lost while exploring Salt Lake City, they should use the street maps available from the tour guide.

REVIEWS D–F

OBJECTIVES

- To proofread sentences for pronoun-antecedent agreement
- To proofread sentences for correct subject-verb agreement
- To revise subject-verb agreement in sentences

Agreement of Pronoun and Antecedent **721**

21y

9. As far as I could see, each of the speakers made a mistake while presenting their argument during the debate.
10. One of the interesting quirks of American history is that neither President Gerald Ford nor Vice President Nelson Rockefeller was elected to his high office.

▶ REVIEW D **Proofreading Sentences for Pronoun-Antecedent Agreement**

Most of the following sentences contain errors in pronoun-antecedent agreement. If a sentence contains an error in agreement, supply the correct form of the pronoun. If a sentence is correct, write *C*.

1. Each of the men says that they will help deliver the gift packages to the families.
2. One of those cars has their own factory-installed stereo.
3. The factory of the future will have robots working on its assembly line.
4. Either the Wilsons or Mrs. Kim will bring their camera.
5. Has either of the new students been assigned his locker?
6. Anyone who speaks a foreign language increases their chance for a high-paying job.
7. When the bank's computer breaks down, every one of the tellers holds their breath.
8. No one in the crowd had noticed the pickpocket stealing his wallet.
9. Neither Jason nor Maggie bought their shoes on sale.
10. Brenda and Charlene read her report about Rosa Parks and the civil rights movement.

▶ REVIEW E **Proofreading for Correct Subject-Verb Agreement**

Most of the following sentences contain errors in subject-verb agreement. If a sentence contains an error, supply the correct form of the verb. If a sentence is correct, write *C*.

EXAMPLE **1.** This great book called *Games of the World* not only describe all kinds of games but also explain how to make and to play them.
1. *describes; explains*

1. Although customs and language differs across continents, people worldwide enjoy playing games.

REVIEW D

Teaching Note. To encourage students to avoid awkward constructions, suggest that they revise some sentences rather than just change the pronouns.

ANSWERS
Review D

9. his or her
10. C
1. he
2. its
3. C
4. her *or* a camera
5. his or her *or* a locker
6. his or her *or* the chance
7. his or her
8. his or her *or* a wallet
9. his or her *or* "Jason didn't buy his shoes on sale, and Maggie didn't either."
10. their

USAGE

721

USAGE

ANSWERS
Review E

1. differ
2. is
3. discovers
4. require
5. C
6. were
7. There are('re)
8. requires
9. thrill
10. Doesn't

ANSWERS
Review F

1. Many a famous sports star has made television commercials.
2. Where are my book and my pen?
3. Neither of the candidates has promised to cut taxes.
4. She is one of those people who write neatly.
5. Neither our soccer team nor our basketball team has won the city championship.

USAGE

2. The game of dominoes are a popular pastime throughout Europe and Latin America.
3. Many a player discover winning a game of dominoes takes skill and strategy rather than luck.
4. One of the games that requires even more strategy than dominoes is chess.
5. Scholars believe the earliest version of chess originated in India during the seventh century.
6. As chess became popular throughout Asia and Europe, its rules and appearance was transformed.
7. There's a number of skills a chess player needs; among these are imagination, concentration, and foresight.
8. Like many other games, marbles require physical skills in addition to strategy and concentration.
9. Children from the schoolyards of Israel to the sidewalks of Tahiti thrills to "knuckling down outside the circle."
10. Don't the number of different games that can be played with marbles seem limitless?

▶ REVIEW F   **Revising Subject-Verb Agreement in Sentences**

Revise each of the following sentences according to the directions given in brackets after each one. Make any needed changes in the forms of verbs.

1. A number of famous sports stars have made television commercials. [Change *A number of famous sports stars* to *Many a famous sports star*.]
2. Where's my book? [Add *and my pen* after *book*.]
3. Both of the candidates have promised to cut taxes. [Change *Both* to *Neither*.]
4. She writes neatly. [Add *is one of those people who* after *She*.]
5. Our basketball team has won the city championship. [Add *Neither our soccer team nor* at the beginning of the sentence.]

6. Nearly all people need at least one friend to confide in. [Change *all people* to *everyone*.]
7. A complete copy of your high school transcript is required by the state university. [After *transcript* add *together with a completed application form and an autobiographical essay*. Put a comma before *together* and after *essay*.]
8. The tigers are growling ferociously. [At the beginning of the sentence, add *Either the lion or*.]
9. The movie screen is hard to see. [At the beginning of the sentence, add *The captions on*.]
10. A day in the library is all the time I will need to finish my research. [Change *A day* to *Two days*.]

PICTURE THIS

You and two other aspiring comedians want to volunteer to perform a clown skit at the local children's hospital. To spark some ideas for your skit, you and your friends went to the circus to watch this clown troupe. Plan a skit that you and your friends could perform. Then, write a letter proposing the skit to the program director at the hospital. Tell what happens in the skit and what props are required. Also describe any audience participation that you think will make the show more fun for the children. In your description, use each of the following words at least once as the antecedent of a pronoun: *each, either, all, one,* and *somebody.*

Subject:	a clown skit
Audience:	the director of the comedy show
Purpose:	to inform; to persuade

USAGE

6. Nearly everyone needs at least one friend to confide in.
7. A complete copy of your high school transcript, together with a completed application form and an autobiographical essay, is required by the state university.
8. Either the lion or the tigers are growling ferociously.
9. The captions on the movie screen are hard to see.
10. Two days in the library is all the time I will need to finish my research.

INTEGRATING THE LANGUAGE ARTS

Usage and Writing. Students may be unfamiliar with the correct pronoun constructions to apply when the gender of an antecedent isn't clear. For example, they may see *he/she* or *(s)he* used in some publications. Explain that even though gender-neutral constructions are a relatively recent development in the English language, the prevailing trend seems to be the one described in the textbook.

PICTURE THIS

You may want to suggest to your students that they write first drafts in which they concentrate on ideas and not on pronouns. After they've written the drafts, encourage students to revise sentences as necessary. Students should make sure they use the pronouns specified in the assignment. Let students work in pairs or groups of three as they revise to make sure they satisfy the requirements of the assignment.

In assessing the letters, you may want to rate the persuasiveness of the writing. You can have students number their pronouns to save grading time.

USAGE

723

OBJECTIVES
- To proofread sentences for subject-verb and pronoun-antecedent agreement
- To correct errors in subject-verb and pronoun-antecedent agreement in a paragraph

USAGE

USAGE

724 *Agreement*

Review: Posttest

A. Proofreading Sentences for Subject-Verb and Pronoun-Antecedent Agreement

Most of the following sentences contain errors in agreement. If a sentence contains an error, supply the correct form of the verb or pronoun. If a sentence is correct, write C.

1. One of the South's most precious ecological treasures are the flatlands and estuary of Galveston Bay.
2. In September, the new teacher was delighted because the class were enthusiastic and cooperative.
3. One junior, as well as four seniors, have been invited to attend the Milford Youth Council next month.
4. The number of investors in companies that manufacture robots is increasing.
5. Twenty miles are quite far for someone to walk without stopping and resting.
6. Neither Charlotte nor Tyrone answered their telephone yesterday.
7. Anyone earning such a small salary will have difficulty paying their bills.
8. You may be surprised to know that many a city dweller grows vegetables in a backyard garden.
9. A completed application, in addition to a full financial statement, are required of all students seeking college scholarships.
10. Every file cabinet, bookcase, and desk drawer have been stuffed with books and papers.
11. Doesn't the boys get bonuses for their work?
12. Where there's people and excitement, you're sure to find Kazuo and Yori.
13. Public relations and advertising is exciting but frequently stressful work.
14. Do you know whether the Lesser Antilles are nearer to Puerto Rico or to Cuba?
15. Did you know that the city of Savannah, Georgia, has their own spectacular parade on Saint Patrick's Day?

B. Correcting Errors in Subject-Verb and Pronoun-Antecedent Agreement

Most of the sentences in the following paragraph contain errors in agreement. If a verb or pronoun is incorrect, give the correct form. If a sentence is correct, write C.

[16] There's a number of people and programs making life safer for endangered and threatened animals. [17] For example, many a preservation effort have been directed at saving eagles. [18] What, you may ask, is the biggest threats to eagles? [19] Most of the danger comes from hunters and expanding civilization. [20] Fortunately, eagles is one of the world's most admired animals. [21] As a result, many governments have passed laws to protect eagles and their habitats. [22] The United States, for example, have created sanctuaries for bald eagles and golden eagles. [23] The Philippine eagle, which are the rarest of these magnificent birds, receives special protection on the Philippine island of Mindanao. [24] Ethiopia, as well as some other countries, has planted trees for their eagles to use as nesting places. [25] Anybody who wants to know more about these and other preservation programs for eagles should consult their local library or conservation club.

USAGE

ANSWERS
Posttest: Part B
16. There are
17. has
18. are
19. C
20. are
21. C
22. has
23. is
24. its
25. his or her *or* the local library

USAGE

OBJECTIVES

- To select the correct forms of pronouns in sentences
- To proofread a paragraph for correct pronoun forms

PROGRAM MANAGER

FOR THE WHOLE CHAPTER

- **Review** For exercises on chapter concepts, see **Review Form A** and **Review Form B** in *Language Skills Practice and Assessment,* pp. 124–127.
- **Assessment** For additional testing, see **Usage Pretests** and **Usage Mastery Tests** in *Language Skills Practice and Assessment,* pp. 95–101 and pp. 179–185.

USAGE

CHAPTER OVERVIEW

Concentrate on helping less-advanced students and English-language learners master the sections on nominative- and objective-case pronouns. Advanced students who make few errors in pronoun usage in written work might focus on the section entitled **Special Pronoun Problems.** The conventions taught in this section should challenge even accomplished writers.

The **Writing Application** (p. 738) and **Picture This** (p. 747) activities lead students to focus on the correct use of pronouns within informative writing. These assignments may be adapted according to your students' needs and abilities.

USAGE

22 CORRECT PRONOUN USAGE

Case Forms of Pronouns; Special Problems

Diagnostic Test

A. Selecting Correct Forms of Pronouns

For each of the following sentences, choose the <u>correct pronoun form</u> in parentheses.

EXAMPLE **1.** José and (*her, she*) completed the math test first.
               1. *she*

1. Greg and (<u>*I*</u>, *myself*) both got our driver's licenses on the same day.
2. My Uncle Bill, (*who*, <u>*whom*</u>) I greatly admire, worked in the Peace Corps for two years after he had finished college.
3. As we waited at the starting line, I knew in my heart that the race was really going to be between Ted and (*I*, <u>*me*</u>).
4. At the town meeting, Ellen McCarthy asked, "If (<u>*we*</u>, *us*) citizens don't vote, how can we expect the situation to change?"

5. I thought Manuel was in Kansas City; so when he walked into the restaurant, I could hardly believe it was (*he*, *him*).

6. Even though we are twins, Janice has always been taller than (*I*, *me*).

7. Does anyone in this group know (*who*, *whom*) was using the computer after school yesterday?

8. Sometimes my parents have a low tolerance for (*me*, *my*) playing rock music, even though I play it in my room with the door closed.

9. "Does anyone dance better than (*she*, *her*)?" I wondered, as I watched Twyla Tharpe on the stage.

10. (*Who*, *Whom*) can describe the different shapes of Navajo hogans?

B. Proofreading a Paragraph for Correct Pronoun Usage

Most of the sentences in the following paragraph contain an error in pronoun usage. Identify each error, and then give the correct pronoun form. If a sentence is correct, write *C*.

[11] Jim Henson's gifts to all of we puppet fans were some of the most beloved characters in show business—Kermit the Frog, Miss Piggy, and the Cookie Monster, to name a few. **[12]** You probably know that Henson was the puppeteer who created the Muppets. **[13]** In the history of television, few puppeteers have been as successful as him. **[14]** Henson's associate Frank Oz and himself operated many of the Muppets. **[15]** Whom do you think spoke for Kermit on *Sesame Street* and *The Muppet Show* and in such movies as *The Muppets Take Manhattan?* **[16]** As you may have guessed, us Kermit fans were listening to Henson's voice. **[17]** Kermit and him started performing together in 1956 when Henson introduced his frog to the audience of the late-night TV show *Sam and Friends* in Washington, D.C. **[18]** Henson, whom originally fashioned Kermit out of an old coat and a split Ping-Pong ball, revolutionized puppetry. **[19]** Henson's ability to give each of his puppets a life of its own earned himself international renown and many awards. **[20]** When Henson died in 1990, people throughout the world mourned his passing.

11. us
12. C
13. he
14. he
15. Who
16. we
17. he
18. who
19. him
20. C

USAGE

USAGE

MEETING
individual
NEEDS

LEP/ESL

General Strategies. Although English pronouns have three cases, other languages vary in their number of cases. Students who speak languages that use several cases may wonder what cases to use in English. Those who speak caseless languages may have trouble understanding what case is and why it is important. You may wish to hold individual or small group sessions with students to field any questions they might have.

728 *Correct Pronoun Usage*

Case

Case is the form that a noun or a pronoun takes to indicate its use in a sentence. In English, there are three cases: *nominative, objective,* and *possessive.*

The form of a noun is the same for both the nominative case and the objective case. For example, a noun used as a subject (nominative case) will have the same form if used as an object (objective case).

NOMINATIVE CASE   The **ghost** of Banquo suddenly appeared. [subject]

OBJECTIVE CASE   Only Macbeth saw the **ghost**. [direct object]

A noun changes its form for the possessive case, usually by adding an apostrophe and an *s*.

POSSESSIVE CASE   What effect did the **ghost's** appearance have on Macbeth?

☞ **REFERENCE NOTE:** For more information about forming possessive nouns, see pages 944–947.

Case Forms of Personal Pronouns

Unlike nouns, most personal pronouns have three forms, one for each case. The form a pronoun takes depends on its function in a sentence.

NOMINATIVE CASE   **We** enjoyed reading *Macbeth.* [subject]

OBJECTIVE CASE   Some of **us** had seen a performance of the play on PBS. [object of the preposition *of*]

POSSESSIVE CASE   **Our** next assignment is to read *Othello.*

Within each case, the forms of the personal pronouns indicate *number, person,* and *gender.* **Number** is the form of a word that indicates whether it is *singular* or *plural.* **Person** is the form a word takes to indicate the one(s) speaking (*first person*), the one(s) spoken to (*second person*), or the one(s) spoken of (*third person*). **Gender** is the form of the word that indicates whether it is *masculine, feminine,* or *neuter* (neither masculine nor feminine).

LESSON 3 *(pp. 729–731)*
THE NOMINATIVE CASE Rules 22a, 22b

OBJECTIVE

- To replace nouns in sentences with nominative-case pronouns

PERSONAL PRONOUNS			
SINGULAR			
PERSON	NOMINATIVE CASE	OBJECTIVE CASE	POSSESSIVE CASE
FIRST	I	me	my, mine
SECOND	you	you	your, yours
THIRD	he, she, it	him, her, it	his, her, hers, its
PLURAL			
PERSON	NOMINATIVE CASE	OBJECTIVE CASE	POSSESSIVE CASE
FIRST	we	us	our, ours
SECOND	you	you	your, yours
THIRD	they	them	their, theirs

Notice in the chart that *you* and *it* have the same forms for the nominative and the objective cases. All other personal pronouns have different forms for each case. Notice also that only the third-person singular pronouns indicate gender.

WHY AM I LEAVING YOU? BECAUSE YOU'RE A POSSESSIVE PRONOUN AND YOU'VE ALWAYS BEEN A POSSESSIVE PRONOUN.

Mother Goose & Grimm reprinted by permission: Tribune Media Services.

The Nominative Case

The personal pronouns in the nominative case—*I, you, he, she, it, we, they*—are used as subjects of verbs and as predicate nominatives.

USAGE

QUICK REMINDER

Write the following sentences on the chalkboard and ask students which sentences are incorrect:

1. Me will go to the mall tomorrow.
2. Crystal and me are giving a party.
3. Her got herself a new hairstyle.
4. Randall and him both got new sneakers.

[Some students will say that numbers 1 and 3 sound incorrect, while numbers 2 and 4 sound all right. Point out that all four sentences incorrectly use objective pronouns as subjects.] Have students substitute nominative pronouns for the objective pronouns in the sentences.

USAGE

LEP/ESL

General Strategies. You may want to emphasize to students that the English subject pronoun is an essential part of the sentence. Point out that in some languages (Spanish, for example) the subject pronoun is used for stress or clarification.

Ask students to create charts of pronouns found in their native languages. Then, have the students write the English equivalents beside the words from their first languages. If you have a difficult time checking these, you could try extending this assignment beyond the classroom. Offer students extra credit, perhaps, if they can have an adult who speaks their first language verify their work.

AT-RISK STUDENTS

As an alternative to one of the exercises, or as a supplementary activity, have students bring articles from their favorite magazines or newspapers to class. Then, ask students to identify the nominative and objective pronouns used in the articles. (If the articles are long, assign smaller portions.)

USAGE

730

---

730 *Correct Pronoun Usage*

22a. **The subject of a verb is in the nominative case.**

EXAMPLES **They** are playing backgammon.
We think that **she** deserves the Most Valuable Player award.

A subject may be compound, with a pronoun appearing in combination with a noun or another pronoun. To help you choose the correct pronoun form in a compound subject, try each form as the simple subject of the verb.

CHOICES: Erin and (*he, him*) built a scale model of the Pyramid of the Magician. [*He built* or *him built*?]
ANSWER: Erin and **he** built a scale model of the Pyramid of the Magician.

CHOICES: (*She, Her*) and (*I, me*) made all of the Aztec costumes for the pageant. [*She made* or *her made*? *I made* or *me made*?]
ANSWER: **She** and **I** made all of the Aztec costumes for the pageant.

22b. **A predicate nominative is in the nominative case.**

A predicate nominative follows a linking verb and explains or identifies the subject of the verb.

A pronoun used as a predicate nominative always follows a form of the linking verb *be: am, is, are, was, were, be,* or *been.*

EXAMPLES The one that you should appoint chairperson is **she.** [*She* follows *is* and identifies the subject *one.*]
The first speaker will be **he.** [*He* follows *will be* and identifies the subject *speaker.*]

As you can see, the predicate nominative and the subject of the verb indicate the same individual(s). To help you choose the correct pronoun form to use as a predicate nominative, try each form as the subject of the verb.

CHOICES: The best clog dancers are (*they, them*). [*They are* or *them are* the best clog dancers?]
ANSWER: The best clog dancers are **they.**

CHOICES: The composer of the sonata is (*she, her*). [*She is* or *her is* the composer?]
ANSWER: The composer of the sonata is **she.**

THE OBJECTIVE CASE   Rules 22c, 22d

OBJECTIVES

- To use pronouns in the objective case to complete sentences
- To select pronouns as objects of prepositions

Like a subject, a predicate nominative may be compound.

EXAMPLES   The only seniors who volunteered were **Elia** and **I**. [*Elia* and *I* follow *were* and identify the subject *seniors.*]
The managers of the new Thai restaurant are **she** and **he**. [*She* and *he* follow *are* and identify the subject *managers.*]

NOTE: Expressions such as *It's me, This is her,* and *It was them* are examples of informal usage. Though acceptable in everyday situations, such expressions should be avoided in formal speaking and writing.

☞ **REFERENCE NOTE:** For more about predicate nominatives, see page 642.

EXERCISE 1   Using Pronouns in the Nominative Case

For each of the following sentences, give a personal pronoun that can be substituted for the word or words in brackets.

EXAMPLES   1. Carl and [*Sue Ann*] are always happy.
   1. *she*
   2. Terri and [*first person singular*] were at the picnic.
   2. *I*

1. Jorge and [*Mike*] are tied for third place.   **1. he**
2. [*Donna*] and her parents have moved to San Antonio.   **2. She**
3. [*First-person plural*] will take the exam on Friday.   **3. We**
4. Can it be [*some choir members*] in that picture?   **4. they**
5. Either Ellen or [*Sally*] will be in charge.   **5. she**
6. The team and [*Mr. Knight*] have chartered a bus.   **6. he**
7. [*First-person plural*] earned our trophies.   **7. We**
8. Neither [*Carolyn*] nor Michele has change for the bus.   **8. she**
9. Did you know that Greg and [*first-person singular*] are leaving?   **9. I**
10. I am sure it was [*Ed*] and you on the dance floor.   **10. he**

The Objective Case

The personal pronouns in the objective case—*me, you, him, her, it, us, them*—are used as objects of verbs and as objects of prepositions.

COMMON ERROR

Problem. Because students frequently hear people use objective pronouns rather than nominative pronouns in compound subjects and in predicate nominatives, the incorrect usage may sound correct to them.

Solution. Tell students that they can rely on their ear if they strip the sentence so that only one pronoun remains as the subject. (Sample: "Tami and me worked hard" is stripped to become "Me worked hard." Replace *me* with *I*.) To test predicate nominative pronouns, suggest flipping the pronoun so that it's in front of the verb. (Sample: "The singer was her" flipped becomes "Her was the singer." Replace *her* with *she*.) As a reminder you might post the rule "Check your pronoun: Strip it or flip it." Working as a class or in small groups, students can practice stripping and flipping sentences in **Exercise 1**.

PROGRAM MANAGER

THE OBJECTIVE CASE

- **Independent Practice/ Reteaching** For instruction and exercises, see **The Objective Case** in *Language Skills Practice and Assessment*, p. 119.
- **Computer Guided Instruction** For additional instruction and practice with the objective case, see **Lesson 15** in *Language Workshop CD-ROM*.
- **Practice** To help less-advanced students with additional instruction and practice with the objective case, see **Chapter 15** in *English Workshop, Complete Course*, pp. 213–214.

Remind students that objective-case pronouns can receive the action of verbs or can function as objects of prepositions. Write the following sentences on the chalkboard. Have students identify the objective pronouns and tell how they are used in each sentence.

1. Suki helped me for two hours. [me—direct object]
2. Eduardo gave us a homemade loaf of bread. [us—indirect object]
3. When LaTanya got the message, she passed it to me. [it—direct object; me—object of preposition]

USAGE

MEETING *individual* NEEDS

LEP/ESL

General Strategies. To help English-language learners perform well on **Exercises 2** and **3**, give them the option of making small pronoun charts, such as the one on p. 729, that they can refer to as they work. If they feel ready to sort out the forms without using a chart, encourage them to do so.

732

USAGE

22c. An object of a verb is in the objective case.

The object of a verb may be a *direct object* or an *indirect object*. A **direct object** follows a transitive verb and tells *whom* or *what* receives the action of the verb.

EXAMPLES   Carmen has invited **me** to the fiesta. [*Me* tells *whom* Carmen has invited.]
The kittens were asleep until the sudden noise woke **them**. [*Them* tells *what* the noise woke.]

An **indirect object** comes between a transitive verb and a direct object and tells *to whom or what* or *for whom or what* the action of the verb is performed.

EXAMPLES   His uncle brought **him** a poncho from Mexico. [*Him* tells *to whom* his uncle brought a poncho.]
Because the engine was running rough, Uncle Theo gave **it** a tune-up. [*It* tells *to what* Uncle Theo gave a tune-up.]

An object of a verb may be compound. To help you choose the correct pronoun form in a compound object, read the sentence, using each form as a single object.

CHOICES: Mr. Osaka gave Karl and (*she, her*) the job. [*Mr. Osaka gave she* or *gave her*?]
ANSWER: Mr. Osaka gave Karl and **her** the job.

CHOICES: Celia showed (*he, him*) and (*I, me*) photographs of her vacation in Hawaii. [*Celia showed he* or *showed him*? *Celia showed I* or *showed me*?]
ANSWER: Celia showed **him** and **me** photographs of her vacation in Hawaii.

☞ **REFERENCE NOTE:** For more information about objects of verbs, see pages 639–641.

▶ EXERCISE 2   Using Pronouns in the Objective Case

For each of the following sentences, give a personal pronoun that can be substituted for the word or words in brackets.

EXAMPLES   1. I helped [*Rod*] and her with their projects.
            1. *him*

            2. Sonia and Molly sent [*first person singular*] a get-well card.
            2. *me*

OBJECTIVES

- To select correct forms of personal pronouns in sentences
- To proofread a paragraph for correct pronoun usage

22c

1. Did you tell the superintendent or [*Ms. Marshall*]?   **1. her**
2. [*Carla*] and [*Dave*] I would never doubt.   **2. Her/him**
3. Leave [*first-person plural*] alone for a while.   **3. us**
4. Carmen will be inviting both you and [*first-person singular*] to the recital.   **4. me**
5. Did you see Lois or [*Andy*] today?   **5. him**   **6. her [*or* him]**
6. I sent the admissions director and [*her assistant*] a letter.
7. The coach chose Joan and [*Michelle and me*].   **7. us**
8. The principal should have notified [*Sven*] and Gail.   **8. him**
9. Ron just passed Tina and [*first-person singular*] in the hall.   **9. me**
10. Please don't ask [*the athletes*] about today's game.   **10. them**

▶ REVIEW A   **Selecting Correct Forms of Personal Pronouns**

For each of the following sentences, choose the <u>correct pronoun form</u> in parentheses.

EXAMPLE   **1.** Paulo and (*her, she*) are my lab partners.
            1. *she*

1. The guests thanked Rita and (*she,* <u>*her*</u>).
2. Gloria and (<u>*I*</u>, *me*) are giving a report on the relationship between the Shoshone people and the Mormon settlers in the 1800s.
3. That's (<u>*he*</u>, *him*) standing on the corner.
4. (<u>*We*</u>, *Us*) are learning about Hendrick Arnold, a scout who helped Texas win independence from Mexico.
5. What were you telling Chuck and (*we,* <u>*us*</u>) earlier?
6. Of course, I remember Monica and (*she,* <u>*her*</u>).
7. We knew the first guests to arrive would be (<u>*they*</u>, *them*).
8. Give (*we,* <u>*us*</u>) the message as soon as possible.
9. Jana and (<u>*she*</u>, *her*) are active members.
10. It's either you or (<u>*he*</u>, *him*) in the runoff.

▶ REVIEW B   **Proofreading a Paragraph for Correct Pronoun Usage**

Most sentences in the following paragraph contain errors in pronoun usage. Identify each error, and then give the correct pronoun form. If a sentence is correct, write *C*.

[1] At the start of track season, our coach told Sarah and I   **1. me**
the story of famous sprinter Evelyn Ashford. [2] During high

USAGE

EXERCISE 2

Teaching Note. In this and other exercises in this chapter, some students may have difficulty recognizing whether the names used are male or female. You may wish to identify male and female names prior to assigning the exercises so that the students can focus on using the correct pronouns.

USAGE

MEETING *individual* NEEDS

LEP/ESL

Spanish. Most Spanish personal pronouns have the same form for both the nominative and objective cases, as in "She spoke to she," or "They spoke to they." Therefore, Spanish-speakers are unaccustomed to making a distinction between nominative- and objective-case personal pronouns. Have students practice by reading aloud the sentences for the written exercises. Oral repetition will help students establish a correct nominative-objective system for personal pronouns.

USAGE

---

734 *Correct Pronoun Usage*

USAGE

2. them
3. C

4. she

5. him
6. C

7. she

8. her

9. she

10. C

school, Ashford had started running races against the boys at lunchtime, and eventually she beat ~~they~~. [3] Later, champion coach Pat Connolly recognized the young runner as a great talent when she saw Ashford race at the University of California at Los Angeles in 1976. [4] In 1983 and 1984, Ashford set records in the women's 100-meter event, and ~~her~~ became the fastest woman in the world. [5] Our coach said that Ashford's speed—10.76 seconds for the 100-meter dash in 1984—amazed even ~~he~~. [6] At the 1988 Olympic games Ashford hoped that she could better her record time. [7] The other competitors knew that the runner to beat that year was ~~her~~. [8] Ashford's talent, hard work, and determination earned ~~she~~ a gold and a silver medal, but set no new records, at those games. [9] The athlete in this picture is ~~her~~ carrying the flag for the American team at the 1988 Olympics. [10] Don't you think she looks like a winner?

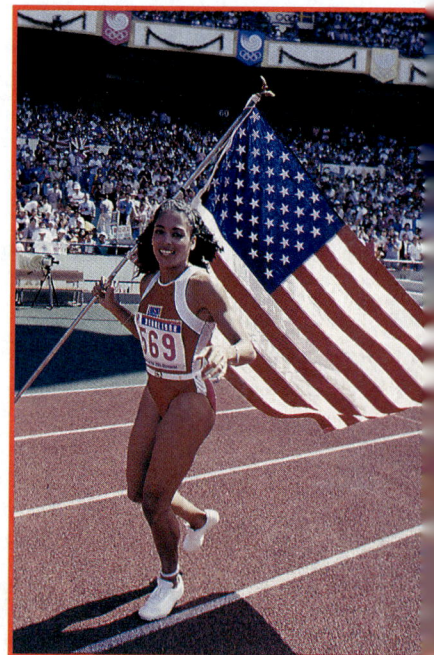

22d. The object of a preposition is in the objective case.

An *object of a preposition* comes at the end of a phrase that begins with a preposition.

EXAMPLES	for **me**	after **her**	next to **them**
	with **us**	beside **him**	between **you** and **me**

☞ **REFERENCE NOTE:** For lists of prepositions, see pages 619–620.

An object of a preposition may be compound, such as in the phrase *between you and me.* To help you determine the pronoun form to use, read each form separately with the preposition.

CHOICES: Dwayne sat behind Norman and (*I, me*) at the jazz concert. [*Behind I or behind me?*]
ANSWER: Dwayne sat behind Norman and **me** at the jazz concert.

734

OBJECTIVES

- To select correct forms of personal pronouns in sentences
- To proofread a paragraph for correct pronoun usage

CHOICES: Give the extra tickets to (*he, him*) and (*she, her*). [*To he or to him? To she or to her?*]

ANSWER: Give the extra tickets to **him** and **her**.

EXERCISE 3 — Selecting Pronouns as Objects of Prepositions

For each of the following sentences, choose the correct pronoun form in parentheses.

EXAMPLE 1. This letter is addressed to you and (*I, me*).
1. *me*

1. The chess team sent a challenge to Don and (*he, him*).
2. The slide show was presented by my sister and (*I, me*).
3. We are planning to leave with (*they, them*) and Alice.
4. I dedicated my poem to both Marcia and (*she, her*).
5. Frank arrived right after Juanita and (*I, me*).
6. The responsibility has fallen upon (*we, us*).
7. Were you sitting near Tony and (*she, her*)?
8. The matter is strictly between Ms. James and (*they, them*).
9. Consuelo has been asking about you and (*she, her*).
10. Would you draw a cartoon for the girls and (*we, us*)?

REVIEW C — Selecting Correct Forms of Personal Pronouns

For each of the following sentences, choose the correct pronoun form in parentheses. Then identify its use in the sentence—*subject of a verb, predicate nominative, direct object, indirect object,* or *object of a preposition.*

EXAMPLE 1. Leave the pamphlets with Kim and (*he, him*).
1. *him—object of a preposition*

1. The coach chose Darrell and (*he, him*).   **1.** d.o.
2. Luckily, the Smiths and (*we, us*) got tickets to Kathleen Battle's concert.   **2.** s.
3. I haven't heard from Mark and (*she, her*) in ages.   **3.** o.p.
4. It could be (*they, them*) across the street.   **4.** p.n.
5. Ms. Grant, the Dodges, and (*she, her*) went to the Palos Verdes Peninsula for the day.   **5.** s.
6. The mayor granted (*they, them*) an interview.   **6.** i.o.
7. (*She, Her*) and Heather always sit in the last row.   **7.** s.

Usage and Writing. Students often use the indefinite *you* in writing. Sometimes this is in an effort to avoid using the pronoun *I*. However, second-person pronouns should be used only in specific situations, such as when a writer directly addresses the reader or uses dialogue.

You can use the following examples to illustrate vague uses of *you* in writing:

1. The book makes you feel sad and dreary. Revision: The book makes me feel sad and dreary.

2. My English teacher always wants you to type your homework. Revision: My English teacher always wants us to type our homework.

Usage and Grammar. As your class studies pronouns used as objects of prepositions, you may want to help students review prepositions. Begin by giving students this definition: A preposition is a word that shows the relationship between a noun or a pronoun and some other word in the sentence.

Write the following sentences on the chalkboard. Ask students to identify the prepositions and to explain which words in each sentence they relate to.

1. Norman ran to the track. [*To* shows the relationship between *Norman* and *track.*]

2. The puppy in the cage is hungry. [*In* shows the relationship between *puppy* and *cage.*]

USAGE

USAGE

8. d.o.   **8.** Would you please stop bothering Simon and (*I*, *me*)?

9. o.p./o.p.   **9.** Adele painted a picture for (*they*, *them*) and (*we*, *us*).

10. d.o./d.o.   **10.** Jim Bob visited (*she*, *her*) and (*I*, *me*) in the hospital.

▶ REVIEW D   **Proofreading a Paragraph for Correct Pronoun Usage**

Most of the sentences in the following paragraph contain errors in pronoun usage. Identify each error, and then give the correct pronoun form. If a sentence is correct, write *C*.

1. I
2. them
3. us
4. he
5. C
6. him
7. C
8. him
9. me
10. them

[1] Looking through an old history book, Larry and ~~me~~ found this fascinating picture of four famous men. [2] Do you recognize any of ~~they~~? [3] Of course, most of ~~we~~ are familiar with Thomas Edison and his inventions. [4] The man standing on the left is ~~him~~. [5] Beside him on the old mill wheel are John Burroughs, Henry Ford, and Harvey Firestone. [6] Burroughs was an American naturalist and author; such books as *Birds and Poets* and *Field and Study* were written by ~~he~~. [7] Ford, as you probably know, gave us the Model T in 1908 and helped usher in the age of the automobile. [8] Standing next to ~~he~~ is Firestone, who was head of the world's largest rubber company. [9] It surprised Larry and ~~I~~ to see these four noted Americans together. [10] Wouldn't it have been great to meet and talk with ~~they~~ at the old mill?

THE POSSESSIVE CASE Rules 22e–22g

OBJECTIVE

- To complete sentences by using possessive pronouns

The Possessive Case

The personal pronouns in the possessive case—*my, mine, your, yours, his, her, hers, its, our, ours, their, theirs*—are used to show ownership or relationship.

22e. The possessive pronouns *mine, yours, his, hers, its, ours,* and *theirs* are used in the same ways that the pronouns in the nominative and objective cases are.

SUBJECT OF VERB	**Mine** has a flat tire.
PREDICATE NOMINATIVE	This floppy disk is **hers.**
OBJECT OF VERB	We haven't received **ours** yet.
OBJECT OF PREPOSITION	My mother wants to talk to **yours.**

22f. The possessive pronouns *my, your, his, her, its, our,* and *their* are used as adjectives before nouns.

EXAMPLES   The subject of **my** report is the Inuit of Canada.
Her first novel was published in 1960.
Do you have **their** telephone number?

22g. A noun or a pronoun preceding a gerund is in the possessive case.

A *gerund* is a verb form that ends in *–ing* and functions as a noun.

EXAMPLES   John objected to his **sister's** using his new computer. [*Sister's,* not *sister,* is used because John objected to the using, not to his sister.]
Their winning the Stanley Cup surprised us ice hockey fans. [*Their,* instead of *them* or *they,* is used because the winning, not they, surprised us.]

Do not confuse a gerund with a present participle, which also ends in *–ing.* A gerund serves as a noun, whereas a present participle serves as an adjective. A noun or a pronoun before a present participle is not in the possessive case.

EXAMPLES   Suddenly, her Chihuahua started chasing a **boy** riding on a skateboard. [*Riding* is a participle that modifies the noun *boy.*]
We heard **them** talking in the hallway. [*Talking* is a participle that modifies the pronoun *them.*]

USAGE

USAGE

PROGRAM MANAGER

THE POSSESSIVE CASE

- **Independent Practice/ Reteaching** For instruction and exercises, see **The Possessive Case** in *Language Skills Practice and Assessment,* p. 120.

- **Computer Guided Instruction** For additional instruction and practice with the possessive case, see **Lesson 16** in *Language Workshop CD-ROM.*

- **Practice** To help less-advanced students with additional instruction and practice with the possessive case, see **Chapter 15** in *English Workshop, Complete Course,* pp. 215–216.

QUICK REMINDER

Write the following sentences on the chalkboard and have students choose the correct pronoun forms:

1. I hate (him, his) playing the tuba at night. [his]
2. Mr. Jarvis won't mind (me, my) feeding his rabbit a carrot top. [my]

Explain that the pronouns should be possessive, not objective, because they are not the objects of the verbs (the gerunds are) but rather modifiers of the gerunds.

MEETING *individual* **NEEDS**

LESS-ADVANCED STUDENTS

Remind students of the correct forms of possessive personal pronouns and stress that possessive personal pronouns do not take apostrophes. Only indefinite pronouns have –'s endings to show possession.

Because they might have problems with forming the possessive case of pronouns, students need to understand that while an apostrophe or an –'s is added to a noun to show possession, an apostrophe or an –'s added to a first-person pronoun forms a contraction. (For instance, *who's* means "who is"; *whose* is a possessive pronoun.)

USAGE

WRITING APPLICATION

Before students begin this **Writing Application**, you may want to review the information on gerunds and participles in **Chapter 19.** This review will help students clear up any confusion they may have about the verbals, enabling them to focus on the use of pronouns as they write and revise.

738

USAGE

738 *Correct Pronoun Usage*

The form of a noun or a pronoun before an *–ing* word often depends on the meaning you want to express. If you want to emphasize the *–ing* word, use the possessive form. If you want to emphasize the noun or pronoun preceding the *–ing* word, avoid the possessive form. Notice the difference in meaning between the following sentences.

EXAMPLES   Can you imagine **Dena's** riding a camel and **my** riding an elephant? [emphasis on *riding*]
Can you imagine **Dena** riding a camel and **me** riding an elephant? [emphasis on *Dena* and *me*]

👉 **REFERENCE NOTE:** For more about present participles, see page 657. For more about gerunds, see page 660.

EXERCISE 4   Using Possessive Pronouns

Complete each of the following sentences with an appropriate possessive pronoun. Do not use the same pronoun twice.

Answers will vary for numbers 2 and 5.

1. I admire the work of Edmonia Lewis; ____ sculptures of famous people are outstanding.   **1. her**   **2. mine**
2. His car looks great, but ____ is in better running condition.
3. Nathan is a dedicated student, but ____ winning the science contest was a surprise.   **3. his**
4. If you let me, I'd like to borrow ____.   **4. yours**
5. ____ rescuing the kitten certainly was a humane act.   **5. Their**

WRITING APPLICATION

Using Possessive Pronouns with Gerunds

Most of the time, you probably can read a sentence aloud and "hear" which pronoun form is correct to use. Sometimes, though, you may need to examine the sentence more closely. Be especially careful with pronouns preceding an *–ing* word. Use the possessive case before a gerund and the objective case before a participle.

EXAMPLES I saw him studying for his American government exam this morning. [The sentence emphasizes *him*, not the studying. *Studying* is a participle modifying *him*.]
Emma teased Larry about his studying for exams at the last possible minute. [The sentence emphasizes the act of studying. The possessive pronoun *his* modifies the gerund *studying*.]

▶ WRITING ACTIVITY

Exam week is approaching fast, and soon everyone will be busy studying for finals. To help students cope with test anxiety, the editor of your school's newspaper has decided to devote an entire issue to that subject. Write an article to submit for publication in the paper. In your article, present some helpful tips for students studying for exams. Your article may be humorous or serious. Use at least two pronouns preceding gerunds and three pronouns preceding participles. Be sure to check your writing for correct pronoun usage.

Prewriting Brainstorm a list of strategies that have helped you stay calm and collected through exams. If you wish, poll a number of other students about their "survival" strategies. From your notes, choose several of the most practical suggestions. Next, decide how you will present the information. You may want to give straightforward lists of "do's" and "don'ts" preceded by a brief introduction. Or you may want to tell a humorous story about an imaginary student preparing for exams. Whatever approach you use, be sure to organize your information in a rough outline.

Writing Refer to your prewriting notes and outline as you write your first draft. Begin with a lively, attention-grabbing opener. Remember: You want to inform as well as to entertain the reader. Even if you take a lighthearted tone, be sure to present some helpful information.

Evaluating and Revising Ask a friend or classmate to read your article. Is it helpful and interesting? Does it address the concerns of students preparing for exams? If not, add, cut, and revise details. Be sure you've used at least two gerunds and three participles preceded by pronouns.

? CRITICAL THINKING

Predicting. Since all the students in the class will be focusing on an identical topic, students may want to give some thought to making their contributions unique. To help students generate original ideas, have them predict what information will be most common and what information is most likely to be used by more than one person (for example, "Get a good night's rest" or "Study over a period of several days"). Students can either leave out information that they feel will be redundant, treat it minimally ("Of course, everyone knows that you're supposed to get a good night's sleep, but that's not always realistic"), or find an interesting slant that gives new life (perhaps framing an essay as a countdown: "T minus 48 hours—Ask any questions about test material in class").

WRITING

Because each article is one part of a whole work that focuses on the same topic, students may want to give more attention than usual not only to having lively, attention-getting openers but also to keeping their writing lively and engaging throughout. You could suggest that students focus especially on the first sentence in each paragraph to give a quick-moving pace to their writing.

LESSON 6 (pp. 740–749)
SPECIAL PRONOUN PROBLEMS Rules 22h–22l

OBJECTIVES
• To select pronouns to use as appositives in sentences
• To complete elliptical constructions by adding groups of words that include appropriate pronoun forms
• To use reflexive, intensive, and personal pronouns in sentences

INTEGRATING THE LANGUAGE ARTS

Grammar and Library Skills. You may wish to integrate the study of appositives with learning how to use the library. Have students familiarize themselves with biographies by locating, in the library, the biography/autobiography section and any biographical dictionaries or encyclopedias.

Have each student write the name of a person who is unfamiliar to his or her partner. Tell partners to exchange names, to find information in the library, and to each write a short paragraph about the person. The paragraph should contain at least three sentences with appositives. Have partners exchange paragraphs for evaluation.

740

Proofreading and Publishing Read through your article once, checking for errors in pronoun usage. Then proofread for other errors in grammar, usage, punctuation, and spelling. To publish your articles, you and your classmates may want to create a bulletin-board display for your classroom or for a widely trafficked area in your school.

Special Pronoun Problems

Appositives

An *appositive* is a noun or a pronoun placed next to another noun or pronoun to explain or identify it.

22h. An appositive is in the same case as the word to which it refers.

EXAMPLES Both teachers, **Mr. Petrakis** and **she,** have agreed to coach the academic team. [*Mr. Petrakis* and *she* are in apposition with the subject *teachers.* Since a subject is always in the nominative case, an appositive to the subject is also in the nominative case.]
For two of the major roles in *Purlie Victorious,* the director chose us, **Joel** and **me.** [*Joel* and *me* are in apposition with the direct object *us.* Since *us* is in the objective case, an appositive to *us* is also in the objective case.]

To help you choose which pronoun form to use in a compound appositive, try each form in the position of the word it refers to.

CHOICES: Two seniors, Theo and (*she, her*), gave the speeches. [The appositive refers to *seniors,* the subject of the verb *gave. She gave* or *her gave*?]
ANSWER: Two seniors, Theo and **she,** gave the speeches.

CHOICES: The speeches were given by two seniors, Theo and (*she, her*). [The appositive refers to *seniors,* the object of the preposition *by. Were given by she* or *by her*?]
ANSWER: The speeches were given by two seniors, Theo and **her.**

Special Pronoun Problems **741**

22 h–i

Sometimes the pronoun *we* or *us* is followed by a noun appositive. To determine which pronoun form to use, try each form without the noun appositive.

CHOICES: (*We, Us*) senior citizens are in charge of the paper drive. [*We are in charge* or *us are in charge*?]

ANSWER: **We** senior citizens are in charge of the paper drive.

CHOICES: Coach Klein talked to (*we, us*) players about sportsmanship. [*Coach Klein talked to we* or *talked to us*?]

ANSWER: Coach Klein talked to **us** players about sportsmanship.

👉 **REFERENCE NOTE:** For more information about appositives, see pages 666–667.

▶ **EXERCISE 5** **Selecting Pronouns to Use as Appositives**

For each of the following sentences, choose the <u>correct pronoun form</u> in parentheses.

1. The bus driver greeted (*we, <u>us</u>*) students with a smile.
2. Owen said that for the first time the basketball team had elected co-captains, Mario and (*he, <u>him</u>*).
3. Two students, Angela and (*<u>she</u>, her*), toured the Frederick Douglass National Historic Site in Washington, D.C.
4. Should (*<u>we</u>, us*) members of the fitness club sponsor the walk-a-thon?
5. The new mural in the cafeteria was painted by two seniors, Chad and (*he, <u>him</u>*).

Elliptical Constructions

An *elliptical construction* is a clause from which words have been omitted. The word *than* or *as* often begins an elliptical construction.

22i. A pronoun following *than* or *as* in an elliptical construction is in the same case as it would be if the construction were completed.

ELLIPTICAL The tenor sang louder **than he.**
COMPLETED The tenor sang louder **than he sang.**

ELLIPTICAL The accident hurt Tim as much **as her.**
COMPLETED The accident hurt Tim as much **as the accident hurt her.**

MEETING *individual* **NEEDS**

STUDENTS WITH SPECIAL NEEDS

Oral practice can be useful when you are teaching students to develop an ear for recognizing standard and nonstandard usage. Recording the corrected exercises provides a set of model sentences for students to hear repeatedly, without having to struggle with reading aloud.

✔ **QUICK REMINDER**

You may want to tell your students that it is common to use elliptical constructions, but that one way to assure correct pronoun usage is to finish elliptical clauses in sentences mentally. Write the following sentence on the chalkboard:

At dinner last night, Mom served Alice more green beans than me.

Ask students what the sentence means. [Students will probably say that it means the mother gave a larger portion of green beans to Alice than to the speaker.] Ask students how the sentence should be changed to mean that the speaker served Alice less food than the mother did. [At dinner last night, Mom served Alice more green beans than I.] Tell them that to check this construction, they can complete the sentence:

"At dinner last night, Mom served Alice more green beans than I (served her)."

741

Suggest that students complete sentences softly to themselves before choosing correct answers in **Exercise 6** and when using elliptical constructions of their own. Also, point out that the words omitted in an elliptical construction do not have to be omitted; it would be correct to include them.

USAGE

---

742 *Correct Pronoun Usage*

Be sure to use the pronoun case form that expresses the meaning you intend. Notice how the meaning of each of the following sentences depends on the form of the pronoun in the elliptical construction.

EXAMPLES I think I helped Macaulay more **than she.** [I think I helped Macaulay more *than she helped Macaulay.*]
I think I helped Macaulay more **than her.** [I think I helped Macaulay more *than I helped her.*]

▶ EXERCISE 6 **Selecting Pronouns for Elliptical Constructions**

For each of the following sentences, add words to the elliptical clause to make its meaning clear. Include in the clause the <u>correct pronoun form</u>. [Note: In several sentences, either pronoun form may be correct, depending on how the elliptical clause is completed. Give both correct forms.]

EXAMPLE **1.** I don't know Brenda as well as (*she, her*).
1. *as well as she knows Brenda*
or
as well as I know her

1. Have you and the rest of your family lived in this area as long as (*they, them*)? **1. have lived in this area**
2. Nolan has worked longer than (*he, him*)‸ **2. has worked.**
3. Eva is shorter than (*I, me*)‸ **3. am short.**
4. The senior class scored higher than (*they, them*)‸ **4. scored.**
5. The field trip next week will probably benefit Roger more than‸(*I, me*). **5. it will benefit**
6. Is she six months older than (*I, me*)? **6. am old**
7. The results show that I do better on essay tests than (*he, him*)‸ **7. does.**
8. Do they play handball as often as (*we, us*)? **8. play handball**
9. I understand him better than‸(*she, her*)‸
10. Can Ms. Edwards tutor Paula as well as‸(*I, me*)?
    9. (she) understands him./I understand (her).
    10. (I) can tutor Paula/she can tutor (me)

Reflexive and Intensive Pronouns

Reflexive and intensive pronouns (sometimes called *compound personal pronouns*) have the same forms.

REFLEXIVE AND INTENSIVE PRONOUNS		
PERSON	SINGULAR	PLURAL
FIRST SECOND THIRD	myself yourself himself herself itself	ourselves yourselves themselves

A *reflexive pronoun* directs the action of the verb back to the subject.

EXAMPLES   I hurt **myself.** [*Myself* refers to *I.*]
Clarice and Jane should be proud of **themselves.**
[*Themselves* refers to *Clarice and Jane.*]

An *intensive pronoun* emphasizes its antecedent, a noun or another pronoun.

EXAMPLES   Simon **himself** developed both rolls of film. [*Himself* emphasizes *Simon.*]
Jorge and Kim installed the tape player in the car **themselves.** [*Themselves* emphasizes *Jorge* and *Kim.*]

NOTE: Unlike a reflexive pronoun, an intensive pronoun may be omitted from a sentence without a significant change in meaning.

EXAMPLE   Tamisha herself washed and waxed the car.
Tamisha washed and waxed the car.

☞ REFERENCE NOTE: The words *hisself* and *theirselves* are nonstandard usage. See page 854.

22j.   A pronoun ending in *–self* or *–selves* should not be used in place of a simple personal pronoun.

Avoid using a pronoun ending in *–self* or *–selves* when there is no word that it can refer to or emphasize.

NONSTANDARD   Mariah and myself went to the rodeo.
STANDARD   Mariah and **I** went to the rodeo.

NONSTANDARD   I know I can depend on Katrina and yourself.
STANDARD   I know I can depend on Katrina and **you.**

COOPERATIVE LEARNING

Divide the class into groups of three or four. Tell each group to think of a person about whom the group can write questions using *who* and *whom*. For example, a group that chooses Elvis Presley might ask, "Who has been called the king of rock and roll?" Each group member should write and initial at least one question.

When the questions have been formulated, ask a representative from each group to read the group's questions to the class. Students should try to guess the names of the other groups' subjects.

MEETING *individual* NEEDS

LEP/ESL

General Strategies. Some languages, such as Japanese, Korean, Turkish, and Vietnamese, do not normally use the relative pronouns *who, whom, which,* and *that.* For example, the phrase *the boy who is reading the book* would be rendered as *boy reading book* in Japanese, Korean, and Turkish, and *boy read book* in Vietnamese. To help students, give numerous oral and written examples of these relative pronouns.

Spanish. It may be helpful to simply point out the lack of a parallel, in the Spanish language, to the *who/whom* distinction and to suggest that special attention be given to this particular concept.

USAGE

USAGE

Correct Pronoun Usage

▶ EXERCISE 7 **Using Reflexive, Intensive, and Personal Pronouns**

Complete each of the following sentences with an appropriate pronoun. Label each pronoun you use as *reflexive, intensive,* or *personal.* **Answers will vary.**

1. Will the principal ____ preside at the academic awards ceremony? **1. herself—its.**
2. After the test I will wait for Linda and ____. **2. him—pers.**
3. I bought ____ a Scottish kilt at the import store.
4. Mark and Ginger should be ashamed of ____ for forgetting your birthday. **3. myself—refl. *or* him—pers. 4. themselves—refl.**
5. Evelyn and ____ raked the leaves in the front yard. **5. we—pers.**

Who and Whom

Like most personal pronouns, the pronoun *who* (*whoever*) has three case forms.

NOMINATIVE	who	whoever
OBJECTIVE	whom	whomever
POSSESSIVE	whose	whosever

These pronouns may be used in two ways: to form questions and to introduce subordinate clauses. When they are used to form questions, they are called ***interrogative pronouns.*** When they are used to introduce subordinate clauses, they are called ***relative pronouns.***

22k. The form an interrogative pronoun takes depends on its use in the question.

Who is used as a subject of a verb or as a predicate nominative. *Whom* is used as an object of a verb or as an object of a preposition.

NOMINATIVE **Who** plays the part of Peter Pan in the film *Hook*? [*Who* is the subject of the verb *plays.*]
Who could it be? [*Who* is the predicate nominative identifying the subject *it.*]

OBJECTIVE **Whom** did Ella choose? [*Whom* is the direct object of the verb *did choose.*]
With **whom** did Aaron Neville sing the ballad? [*Whom* is the object of the preposition *with.*]

NOTE: In informal situations, *who* is often used in place of *whom* as an interrogative pronoun. In formal speaking and writing, however, the distinction between *who* and *whom* should be observed.

INFORMAL **Who** did you call?
FORMAL **Whom** did you call? [direct object]

INFORMAL **Who** is he baking the pita bread for?
FORMAL For **whom** is he baking the pita bread? [object of a preposition]

22l. The form a relative pronoun takes depends on its use in the subordinate clause.

When choosing between *who* and *whom* in a subordinate clause, follow these steps:

CHOICES: Nadine Gordimer, *(who, whom)* is famous for writing novels and short stories set in South Africa, won the Nobel Prize for literature in 1991.

STEP 1: Find the subordinate clause. In the sentence above, the subordinate clause is *(who, whom) is famous for writing novels and short stories set in South Africa.*

STEP 2: Decide how the relative pronoun is used in the clause—*subject, predicate nominative, object of the verb,* or *object of a preposition.* In the example sentence the relative pronoun serves as the subject of the verb *is.*

STEP 3: Determine the case for this use of the relative pronoun. A subject of a verb is in the nominative case.

STEP 4: Select the correct form of the relative pronoun. The nominative form of the relative pronoun is *who.*

ANSWER: Nadine Gordimer, **who** is famous for writing novels and short stories set in South Africa, won the Nobel Prize for literature in 1991.

CHOICES: Harry Houdini, *(who, whom)* audiences adored, performed daring escape tricks.

STEP 1: The subordinate clause is *(who, whom) audiences adored.*

STEP 2: The relative pronoun serves as the direct object of the verb *adored.*

STEP 3: A direct object is in the objective case.

STEP 4: The objective form of the relative pronoun is *whom.*

ANSWER: Harry Houdini, **whom** audiences adored, performed daring escape tricks.

USAGE

COMMON ERROR

Problem. In an attempt to write more formally, students might use *whom* in their writing, even when *who* is correct.

Solution. One simple trick that might help students determine the correct form is to substitute other nominative-case pronouns (such as *I, she,* or *they*) for the word *who* or *whom.* If a nominative-case pronoun is grammatically correct, then the nominative form *who* is needed. If a nominative-case pronoun is not correct, then the objective form *whom* is needed.

COOPERATIVE LEARNING

A team race will help students become more familiar with the correct use of *who* and *whom* in sentences. Put the following clauses on the chalkboard:

1. whom we admire
2. who trusted us
3. who trotted past
4. who asked directions
5. whom we comforted

Have each team write as many sentences as possible in five minutes. Teams should use each clause at least once. Award a point for each correct sentence.

You can continue the game by having teams write clauses beginning with *who* and *whom* and then exchanging their clauses with other teams. Again, give the teams a time limit.

USAGE

Remember that the case of a relative pronoun is not affected by any word outside the subordinate clause.

CHOICES: A plaque will be given to (*whoever, whomever*) catches the most fish.

STEP 1: The subordinate clause is (*whoever, whomever*) *catches the most fish.*

STEP 2: The relative pronoun serves as the subject of the verb *catches,* not as object of the preposition *to.* The entire subordinate clause is the object of *to.*

STEP 3: A subject of a verb is in the nominative case.

STEP 4: The nominative form of the relative pronoun is *whoever.*

ANSWER: A plaque will be given to **whoever** catches the most fish.

☞ **REFERENCE NOTE:** For more about subordinate clauses, see pages 675–683.

When choosing between *who* and *whom* to begin a question or a subordinate clause, do not be misled by a parenthetical expression consisting of a subject and a verb, such as *I think, he feels,* or *they believe.* Select the pronoun form you would use if the parenthetical expression were not in the sentence.

EXAMPLES **Who** do you suppose will win the election? [*Who* is the subject of the verb *will win.*]

Roberta is the student **who** Mr. Hines thinks should be a chemist. [*Who* is the subject of the verb *should be.*]

☞ **REFERENCE NOTE:** For more information about parenthetical expressions, see pages 914–915.

▶ **EXERCISE 8**   **Using *Who* and *Whom* Correctly**

For each of the following sentences, choose the correct pronoun form in parentheses. Then identify its use in the subordinate clause—*subject, predicate nominative, object of a verb,* or *object of a preposition.*

EXAMPLE **1.** Can you tell me (*who, whom*) wrote *Bury My Heart at Wounded Knee?*
1. *who—subject*

1. The two people (*who, whom*) I like most are Will and Rosa. **1.** o.v.

2. Someone called, but I don't know (*who, whom*) she was. **2.** p.n.

3. Be sure to talk to (*whoever, whomever*) is in charge. **3.** s.

4. Several of the women (*who, whom*) had served on other committees were considered for the position. **4.** s.

5. Did (*whoever, whomever*) called leave a message? **5. s.**
6. Allen is the only person in school (*who, whom*), I believe, has lived in a foreign country. **6. s.**
7. I never found out (*who, whom*) the driver was. **7. p.n.**
8. It does not matter (*who, whom*) wins, as long as you do your best. **8. s.**
9. Was he the person to (*who, whom*) this package belongs? **9. o.p.**
10. Ralph Bunche was a man (*who, whom*) many people respected for helping to found the United Nations. **10. o.v.**

PICTURE THIS

These behind-the-scenes volunteers worked hard to make the senior-class dance a success. As chair of the Dance Committee, you were responsible for recruiting the volunteers and organizing their efforts. Now, you'd like to thank the volunteers for their help. Write an open letter to your school's newspaper. In your letter, name each volunteer and explain the role he or she played in the preparations. Use the pronouns *who* and *whom* at least twice each in subordinate clauses and use *who* or *whom* in a question.

Subject:	senior-class dance
Audience:	readers of the school newspaper
Purpose:	to inform; to express your thanks

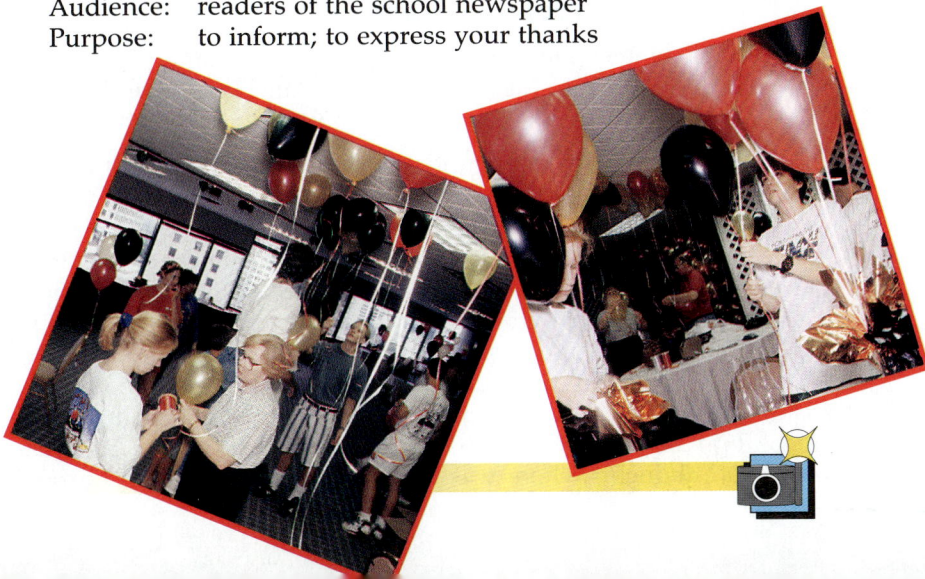

USAGE

PICTURE THIS

If students are having a hard time getting started, suggest that they ignore the specifications for using pronouns as they write their first drafts. Students can then revise their drafts to include the specified pronouns. Assess students' letters on the basis of how well the directions were followed. Give extra points for creativity. To save grading time, you could have students underline pronouns and identify their uses.

USAGE

MEETING *individual* NEEDS

LEARNING STYLES

Auditory Learners. Read students a paragraph or a brief excerpt from an article or a composition after you have changed some of the pronouns in the excerpt to incorrect forms. Students should listen and write down any incorrectly used pronoun forms that they hear. Then, you can read through the selection again to discuss and correct each incorrect pronoun usage.

COOPERATIVE LEARNING

Assign students to mixed-level groups of three or four and have the groups compete to complete **Reviews E and F.** Let the groups know that their final scores will depend both on time and on accuracy. Nonstandard usage and incorrect identifications will be penalized. Add another twist by having teams exchange papers for evaluation. Then, review both the originals and the evaluations to add or subtract group credits for mismarked items. (Thus, if a group marks an item wrong when it is right, the group that mismarked the item loses a point, while the other group gains two points.)

748

REVIEWS E and F

OBJECTIVES

- To proofread sentences for correct pronoun usage
- To proofread a paragraph for correct pronoun usage

▶ **REVIEW E**   **Proofreading Sentences for Correct Pronoun Usage**

Each of the following sentences contains an error in pronoun usage. Identify the error, and then give the correct pronoun form, according to the rules of formal standard usage.

1. Do you know ^who they gave the money to?   **1.** whom
2. "We sprinters are better than the ones on Central High's team," Phillip said. "So why aren't we doing better than ^them?"   **2.** they
3. Oscar, ^whom I believe is the most adventurous member of our family, is backpacking in the Appalachians.   **3.** who
4. When Anna and I were young, ^us children loved to ride on the tractor with my father.   **4.** we
5. John and ^myself wish we could excel in both baseball and football like Bo Jackson.   **5.** I
6. ^Who did the teacher choose to give the first speech?   **6.** Whom
7. When Andrew and I study together, nobody else in our class does better than ^us.   **7.** we
8. Kyle was here looking for Josh and ^yourself.   **8.** you
9. When we heard that Ms. Cohen was going to retire, all three of ^we seniors felt sad.   **9.** us
10. The two people ^who you can always rely on are Dave and she.   **10.** whom

▶ **REVIEW F**   **Proofreading a Paragraph for Correct Pronoun Usage**

Each sentence in the following paragraph contains an error in pronoun usage. Identify each error, and then give the correct pronoun form.

1. who   [1] Satoshi Yabuuchi is a modern Japanese sculptor ^whom works with wood. [2] Critics generally agree that few sculptors today are as inventive as ^him. [3] For example, look at the works by ^he on the following page. [4] ^Them are children's heads representing the seven days of the week. [5] Working with simple tools, Yabuuchi created ^they out of cypress. [6] ^Who do you know that could resist these engaging faces? [7] As you can see, Yabuuchi's imagination and sense of humor are important to ^himself. [8] Other modern Japanese wood sculptors and ^him use techniques that date back more than 1,500 years. [9] Yabuuchi, ^whom was born in 1953, first studied European

2. he
3. him
4. They
5. them
6. Whom
7. him
8. he
9. who

REVIEW: POSTTEST

OBJECTIVES

- To select correct forms of pronouns in sentences
- To proofread a paragraph for correct pronoun usage

art but then became interested in wood carving and sculpture. [10] A number of works by ~~himself~~ also incorporate elements of American pop art.   **10.** him

Satoshi Yabuuchi/Courtesy of Gallery Kitano, Tokyo, Japan.

USAGE

Review: Posttest

A. Selecting Correct Forms of Pronouns

For each of the following sentences, choose the correct pronoun form in parentheses.

EXAMPLE   **1.** After a pause, I heard Megan say into the phone, "Yes, this is (*she, her*)."
   1. *she*

1. Last summer my friend Megan and (*I, me*) worked in a factory that produces microchips for computers.
2. Before we began, we made a pact that (*we, us*) teenagers would show the adults that we were responsible workers.

USAGE

MEETING individual NEEDS

STUDENTS WITH SPECIAL NEEDS

Students with visual-processing deficits might have trouble reading the twenty sentences of the **Review: Posttest** in a limited amount of time. To ensure that the testing situation is fair to these students, engage student helpers to read the sentences aloud. Student helpers should read the sentences slowly and should pause after each sentence to allow their partners to record their answers. Student helpers should reread sentences if asked to do so.

Literature Link. If it is available in your literature textbook, have students read and discuss D. H. Lawrence's poem "Snake." Then, ask them to reread it and to pay special attention to Lawrence's use of first-person pronouns. Ask students what effect the speaker's frequent use of the first person has in the poem. [Answers will vary. Students may suggest that it shows the speaker's self-centeredness, that it shows humankind as the center of the universe, or that it shows the separation of humans and nature.] Explain to students that this poem is an example of how the proper use of pronouns can relay meaning beyond that of the words themselves.

3. For the first two weeks, everything ran smoothly because our supervisor, Mr. Karas, was a person (*who, whom*) we thought was firm and just.
4. In fact, we were surprised by (*him, his*) showing interest in our progress and going out of his way to train us.
5. When Mr. Karas went on vacation, we doubted that his assistant, Ms. Sullivan, would be as firm as (*he, him*).
6. Our first mistake was in thinking that Mr. Karas and (*she, her*) would have different sets of standards.
7. We started giving (*us, ourselves*) ten extra minutes during our morning break a week after Ms. Sullivan took over.
8. One afternoon Ms. Sullivan walked up to us at our job stations and said, "Megan and Rick, until recently I had thought you were employees (*who, whom*) took pride in your work."
9. "If you're late again," she said calmly, "we, Mr. Karas and (*I, me*), will be looking for two new trainees for this station after he gets back."
10. The experience has really taught (*we, us*) some valuable lessons.
11. First, (*us, our*) deliberately taking extra time at the break was wrong.
12. Second, we had let Mr. Karas down because it was (*he, him*) who had hired us, trained us, and trusted us.
13. Third, we had mistakenly presumed that Ms. Sullivan wouldn't do her job as well as (*he, him*).
14. Fourth, we had let (*us, ourselves*) down by failing to do our best.
15. (*Who, Whom*) do you think were model employees the rest of the summer?

B. Proofreading a Paragraph for Correct Pronoun Usage

Most of the sentences in the following paragraph contain errors in pronoun usage. Identify each error, and then give the correct pronoun form. If a sentence is correct, write *C*.

16. who
17. C
18. We

[16] Do you know ~~whom~~ Tiberius Claudius Nero Germanicus was? [17] Such a long, elegant name certainly seems fitting for a Roman emperor, and that's exactly what he was. [18] Us

modern readers and television watchers, as well as historians, know him simply as Claudius. **[19]** Robert Graves wrote about ~~he~~ in the popular novel *I, Claudius.* **[20]** Claudius, ~~whom~~ had a severe speech impediment, lived from 10 B.C. to A.D. 54. **[21]** ~~Him~~ becoming emperor in A.D. 41 troubled many Romans because they thought he was a fool and would be a weak ruler. **[22]** Claudius had not been an important government figure during the reigns of emperors Tiberius and Caligula, but he outlived both of ~~they~~. **[23]** He was a more stable ruler than Caligula and accomplished more than ~~him~~. **[24]** Claudius, ~~who~~ historians now generally praise, initiated many building programs, such as the huge Claudian Aqueduct. **[25]** In addition, many Roman civil and military accomplishments of the time are credited to ~~himself~~.

19. him
20. who
21. His
22. them
23. he
24. whom
25. him

USAGE

USAGE

OBJECTIVE

• To revise sentences to correct faulty pronoun usage

FOR THE WHOLE CHAPTER

■ **Review** For exercises on chapter concepts, see **Review Form A** and **Review Form B** in *Language Skills Practice and Assessment,* pp. 133–136.

■ **Assessment** For additional testing, see **Usage Pretests** and **Usage Mastery Tests** in *Language Skills Practice and Assessment,* pp. 95–101 and pp. 179–185.

CHAPTER OVERVIEW

This chapter helps students become aware of four pronoun reference problems: ambiguous reference, general reference, weak reference, and indefinite reference.

The **Picture This** activity leads students to incorporate clear pronoun reference in a letter. For more help with letters, see **Chapter 39: "Letters and Forms."**

ANSWERS

Diagnostic Test: Part A

Answers may vary. Here are some possibilities:

1. Dana is afraid of large dogs, but she doesn't let her fear show.
2. The subway system in Washington is modern and efficient.
3. When James was ten years old, he saw Michael Jordan play basketball.

752

23 CLEAR REFERENCE

Pronouns and Antecedents

Diagnostic Test

A. Revising Sentences to Correct Faulty Pronoun References

Revise each of the following sentences to correct ambiguous, general, weak, or indefinite pronoun references.

1. Dana is afraid of large dogs, but she doesn't let it show.
2. In Washington they have a subway system that is modern and efficient.
3. James saw Michael Jordan play basketball when he was ten years old.

4. My cousins showed a video of their trip to Puerto Rico, which made me want to go there.
5. In some classes you are given additional time to finish semester tests.
6. After the choir director asked Larry to sing the solo, he left the rehearsal room.
7. I think James Michener is a fine novelist; unfortunately, I don't own any of them.
8. In the program it describes the play as a lighthearted look at a serious subject.
9. The larger school won the geography competition at the convention, which didn't surprise us.
10. Beth wanted Laura to see the movie because she is a fan of Lou Diamond Phillips.

B. Revising Sentences to Correct Faulty Pronoun References

Revise the following sentences to correct each weak, general, ambiguous, or indefinite pronoun reference.

11. In the city library, they have a videotape about Martha Washington's early life and first marriage to a wealthy Virginia planter.
12. After Aaron Burr played matchmaker for Dolley Payne Todd and James Madison, she married Madison.
13. Abigail Adams is the only woman who was the wife of one president and mother of another, which is an interesting bit of First Lady trivia.
14. Julia Tyler supported her husband John Tyler's causes, especially the annexation of Texas, and that gave him strength.
15. In one book I read, it says that people accused Mary Todd Lincoln, who was from Kentucky, of opposing the Union, but she actually was a strong Unionist.
16. In addition to all of her social duties as First Lady, Edith Roosevelt, wife of Theodore Roosevelt, had to attend to her six children and the family's many pets, including cats, dogs, and snakes. It must have been a wild place.
17. Helen Taft was a determined woman who wanted her husband William Howard Taft to be president, and it paid off.

4. After seeing my cousins' video of their trip to Puerto Rico, I wanted to go there.
5. In some classes students are given additional time to finish semester tests.
6. Larry left the rehearsal room after the choir director asked him to sing the solo.
7. I think James Michener is a fine novelist, but, unfortunately, I don't own any of his books.
8. The program describes the play as a lighthearted look at a serious subject.
9. That the larger school won the geography competition at the convention didn't surprise us.
10. Because Laura is a fan of Lou Diamond Phillips, Beth wanted Laura to see the movie.

Diagnostic Test: Part B

Answers may vary. Here are some possibilities:

11. A videotape about Martha Washington's early life and first marriage to a wealthy Virginia planter is in the city library.
12. Dolley Payne Todd married James Madison after Aaron Burr played matchmaker.
13. That Abigail Adams is the only woman who was the wife of one president and the mother of another is an interesting bit of First Lady trivia.
14. Julia Tyler's support for her husband John Tyler's causes, especially the annexation of Texas, gave him strength.
15. One book I read says that people accused Mary Todd Lincoln, who was from Kentucky, of opposing the Union, but she was actually a strong Unionist.

16. The White House must have been a wild place when Theodore Roosevelt was president; in addition to all of her social duties as First Lady, Edith Roosevelt had to attend to her six children and the family's many pets, including cats, dogs, and snakes.

17. Helen Taft's determination to help her husband William Howard Taft become president paid off.

18. The newspaper article tells all about the "birthday calendar" that Mamie Eisenhower kept on her White House employees and about the presents and cakes she gave to them.

19. Jacqueline Kennedy's later career as a book editor was foreshadowed in the help she gave her husband John Kennedy as he researched and organized his book *Profiles in Courage*.

20. One of the many similarities between Lady Bird Johnson and Eleanor Roosevelt is that in the 1960s Mrs. Johnson championed the rights of United States citizens living in poverty.

DIAGNOSTIC TEST

Teaching Note. Students may need additional information for items 16 (*It* is the White House) and 20 (Lady Bird Johnson was a First Lady in the 1960s).

18. In the newspaper article it tells all about the "birthday calendar" that Mamie Eisenhower kept on her White House employees and about the presents and cakes she gave to them.

19. Jacqueline Kennedy helped her husband John Kennedy research and organize his book *Profiles in Courage*. This foreshadowed her later career as a book editor.

20. One of the many similarities between Lady Bird Johnson and Eleanor Roosevelt is that in the 1960s she championed the rights of United States citizens living in poverty.

One cause of ambiguity in writing is the use of pronouns without clear antecedents. A pronoun has no definite meaning in itself. Its meaning is clear only when the reader knows which word the pronoun refers to. This word is called the *antecedent* of the pronoun.

☞ **REFERENCE NOTE:** For more information about pronouns and antecedents, see pages 602–605 and 718–720.

23a. A pronoun should refer clearly to its antecedent.

In the following examples, arrows point from the pronouns to their antecedents.

EXAMPLES   Amy promised Brandon she would help him clean up the kitchen.

The Sánchezes have a new sailboat on which they intend to cruise to the Bahamas.

Handing Shina the novel, the librarian told her, "This won the Pulitzer Prize."

Often, an unclear pronoun reference is due to a lack of agreement between a pronoun and its antecedent.

UNCLEAR   Eli is always thinking about computers. It seems to be his only interest.

CLEAR   Eli is always thinking about computers. **They** seem to be his only interest.

☞ **REFERENCE NOTE:** For more about agreement between pronouns and their antecedents, see pages 718–720.

USAGE

USAGE

AMBIGUOUS REFERENCE and GENERAL REFERENCE Rules 23a–23c

OBJECTIVES

- To revise sentences to correct ambiguous pronoun references
- To revise sentences to correct general pronoun references

Ambiguous Reference

23b. Avoid an *ambiguous reference,* which occurs when a pronoun can refer to either of two antecedents.

A simple way to correct some ambiguous pronoun references is to replace the pronoun with an appropriate noun.

AMBIGUOUS   The partnership between Jones and Potter ended when he drew the firm's money from the bank and flew to Brazil. [To whom does *he* refer: *Jones* or *Potter*?]

CLEAR   The partnership between Jones and Potter ended when Jones [*or* Potter] drew the firm's money from the bank and flew to Brazil.

If replacing the pronoun with a noun results in awkward repetition, rephrase the sentence to eliminate the ambiguous pronoun reference.

AMBIGUOUS   The mayor appointed Ms. Vásquez chairperson of the committee because she was convinced of the need for an environmental study. [To whom does *she* refer: the *mayor* or *Ms. Vásquez*?]

CLEAR   Convinced of the need for an environmental study, the mayor appointed Ms. Vásquez chairperson of the committee.

CLEAR   Because Ms. Vásquez was convinced of the need for an environmental study, the mayor appointed her chairperson of the committee.

EXERCISE 1 Revising Sentences to Correct Ambiguous Pronoun References

Revise each of the following sentences to correct the ambiguous pronoun reference. [Note: A sentence may be correctly revised in more than one way.]

EXAMPLE   **1.** As soon as Lucinda and Gwen arrived, we asked her to tell us about her trip to the Yukon.
     1. *As soon as Lucinda and Gwen arrived, we asked Lucinda to tell us about her trip to the Yukon.*

1. Leta offered Molly a bowl of plantain porridge, which she thoroughly enjoyed.
2. One of the passengers told the bus driver that she didn't know the route very well.

PROGRAM MANAGER

AMBIGUOUS REFERENCE AND GENERAL REFERENCE

- **Independent Practice/ Reteaching** For instruction and exercises, see **Ambiguous and General Reference** in *Language Skills Practice and Assessment,* p. 131.

- **Computer Guided Instruction** For additional instruction and practice with ambiguous reference and general reference, see **Lesson 18** in *Language Workshop CD-ROM.*

- **Practice** To help less-advanced students with additional instruction and practice with ambiguous reference and general reference, see **Chapter 16** in *English Workshop, Complete Course,* pp. 223–224.

ANSWERS
Exercise 1

Answers may vary.

1. Leta offered Molly a bowl of plantain porridge, a meal that Molly thoroughly enjoyed.

2. One of the bus passengers accused the bus driver of not knowing the route very well.

USAGE

USAGE

3. The accountant became very much alarmed right after she sent in a report to the treasurer.
4. Always apply varnish with a soft-bristle brush, and allow the varnish to dry thoroughly before applying the next coat.
5. We washed the bottles after removing their labels.

A DIFFERENT APPROACH
Have students search newspapers and magazines for ambiguous pronoun references to share with the class. The class can then work together to correct any errors that students find.

ANSWERS
Exercise 2

Answers may vary. Here are some possibilities:

1. The emergence of Spanish-language newspapers in the Southwest in the 1800s helped many Mexican Americans maintain ties to their culture.
2. Clarissa shrieked when her four-year-old sister brought a frog inside and let it loose.
3. My enjoyment of the author's style and characterization made me want to read her other books.
4. A sturdy friendship grew out of Rabbi Meyer's daily visits to the house.
5. The success of the undertaking resulted from the effort that went into planning the expedition, hiring the right people, and anticipating every emergency.

756

---

3. Right after the accountant sent in a report to the treasurer, she became very much alarmed.
4. Always apply varnish with a soft-bristle brush, and allow it to dry thoroughly before applying the next coat.
5. We removed the labels from the bottles and washed them.

General Reference

23c. Avoid a *general reference,* which occurs when a pronoun refers to a general idea rather than to a specific word or group of words.

The pronouns commonly used in making general references are *it, that, this, such,* and *which.* To correct a general pronoun reference, either replace the pronoun with an appropriate noun or rephrase the sentence.

GENERAL   Great ships were moving slowly up the harbor; tugs and ferryboats scurried in and out among them; here and there a white cabin cruiser sliced through the blue water under the suspension bridge. It was thrilling to a young farmer. [*It* has no specific antecedent.]

CLEAR   The sight was thrilling to a young farmer.

GENERAL   In her act Mariana told jokes, did impersonations, and sang comic songs. This amused her audience. [*This* has no specific antecedent.]

CLEAR   Mariana amused her audience by telling jokes, doing impersonations, and singing comic songs.

▶ EXERCISE 2   **Revising Sentences to Correct General Pronoun References**

Revise the following sentences to correct each general pronoun reference.

EXAMPLE   1. Carla was declared the winner of the debate, which didn't surprise me.
           1. *That Carla was declared the winner of the debate didn't surprise me.*

1. In the 1800s, Spanish-language newspapers sprang up throughout the Southwest. This helped many Mexican Americans maintain ties to their culture.

REVIEW A

OBJECTIVE

- To revise ambiguous and general pronoun references in sentences

2. Clarissa's four-year-old sister brought a frog inside and let it loose, which made Clarissa shriek.
3. I enjoyed the author's style and the type of characters she wrote about. It made me want to read her other books.
4. Rabbi Meyer came to the house daily, from which a sturdy friendship grew.
5. A great deal of effort went into planning that expedition, hiring the right people, and anticipating every emergency, which accounts for the success of the undertaking.

▶ REVIEW A **Revising Ambiguous and General Pronoun References**

Revise the following sentences to correct each ambiguous or general pronoun reference.

1. Benito Pablo Juárez was a liberal reformer and president of Mexico during the 1860s and early 1870s, and he helped mold Mexico into a nation. That established Juárez as Mexico's foremost national hero.
2. Juárez, of Zapotec ancestry, was a serious, hard-working man, which is suggested in this photograph.
3. A professor who obviously had researched Juárez' life described his childhood in Oaxaca, his interest in law and social reforms, and his military successes. This kept the students' attention.
4. One of the students told the professor that he hoped he would write a biography of Juárez someday.
5. Juárez, a state governor in 1855, and General Santa Anna were on opposing sides, and he was exiled.
6. Juárez later returned to Mexico and joined the revolution to overthrow Santa Anna, who had seized control of the government. It was a brave and risky endeavor.

USAGE

REVIEW A

Teaching Note. Review A presents an opportunity for students to practice good test-taking skills, such as recognizing relationships between details in a reading passage. You may want to refer students to **Chapter 40: "Reading, Studying, and Test Taking."**

ANSWERS
Review A

Answers may vary. Here are some possibilities:

1. Benito Pablo Juárez was a liberal reformer and president of Mexico during the 1860s and early 1870s. His help in molding Mexico into a nation established him as Mexico's foremost national hero.

2. This photograph suggests that Juárez, who was of Zapotec ancestry, was a serious, hard-working man.

3. A professor who obviously had researched Juárez' life kept the students' attention by describing Juárez' childhood in Oaxaca, his interest in law and social reforms, and his military successes.

4. One of the students told the professor that he hoped the professor would write a biography of Juárez someday.

5. Juárez, who was a state governor in 1855, was exiled when he opposed General Santa Anna.

6. Bravely taking risks, Juárez later returned to Mexico and joined the revolution to overthrow Santa Anna, who had seized control of the government.

USAGE

7. Because France installed Maximilian as emperor of Mexico in 1864, Juárez moved his capital from Mexico City, but Maximilian was not popular.
8. The collapse of Maximilian's government in 1867 opened the way for Juárez to be reelected president.
9. Juárez' interest in education and his help in establishing free public schools in Mexico had a major impact on Mexico's people.
10. The government of José de la Cruz Porfirio Díaz, who overthrew Juárez' successor and governed Mexico longer than any other person, was certainly a contrast to Juárez' government.

PROGRAM MANAGER

WEAK REFERENCE AND INDEFINITE REFERENCE

■ **Independent Practice/ Reteaching** For instruction and exercises, see **Weak and Indefinite Reference** in *Language Skills Practice and Assessment,* p. 132.

■ **Computer Guided Instruction** For additional instruction and practice with weak reference and indefinite reference, see **Lesson 18** in *Language Workshop CD-ROM.*

■ **Practice** To help less-advanced students with additional instruction and practice with weak reference and indefinite reference, see **Chapter 16** in *English Workshop, Complete Course,* pp. 225–226.

WEAK REFERENCE AND INDEFINITE REFERENCE Rules 23d, 23e

OBJECTIVES
- To revise sentences to correct weak pronoun references
- To revise sentences to correct indefinite pronoun references

758 *Clear Reference*

7. France installed Maximilian as emperor of Mexico in 1864, and Juárez moved his capital from Mexico City, but he was not popular.
8. Maximilian's government collapsed in 1867, which opened the way for Juárez to be reelected president.
9. Juárez was interested in education and helped to establish free public schools in Mexico. This, of course, had a major impact on Mexico's people.
10. José de la Cruz Porfirio Díaz overthrew Juárez' successor and governed Mexico longer than any other person. It was certainly a contrast to Juárez' government.

Weak Reference

23d. Avoid a *weak reference,* which occurs when a pronoun refers to an antecedent that has not been expressed.

To correct a weak pronoun reference, either replace the pronoun with an appropriate noun or give the pronoun a clear antecedent.

WEAK   The people want honest public servants, but many voters think that is not a virtue of any of the candidates. [The antecedent of *that* is not expressed.]

CLEAR   The people want honest public servants, but many voters think that honesty is not a virtue of any of the candidates.

WEAK   We spent the day on a fishing boat, but we didn't catch a single one. [The antecedent of *one* is not expressed.]

CLEAR   We spent the day on a fishing boat, but we didn't catch a single fish.

CLEAR   We spent the day on a fishing boat, trying to catch some fish, but we didn't catch a single one.

▶ EXERCISE 3 **Revising Sentences to Correct Weak Pronoun References**

Revise each of the following sentences to correct the weak pronoun reference.

EXAMPLE   **1.** We went to the card shop but didn't buy any.
1. *We went to the card shop but didn't buy any cards.*

23d

1. I take many photographs with my camera and consider it an enjoyable hobby.
2. Being neighborly is important because you may need their help someday in an emergency.
3. Nguyen has become a virtuoso violinist, but he has never owned a valuable one.
4. Luisa is highly intelligent, but she hides it from people she doesn't know well.
5. Our guide said the Pueblo village was well worth seeing, but it would take three hours.

USAGE

PICTURE THIS

What is it like to see the earth from space? to float free of gravity? to open a spacecraft hatch and gaze at the stars? You are one of the few people who know. A short while ago, you had your first mission in space. Now that you're back on earth, you're eager to answer everyone's questions. You've decided to write a letter describing some of the experiences you had on your mission. You'll send copies of the letter and of this picture of yourself in space to all your friends and relatives. In your letter, make sure that each pronoun you use clearly refers to its proper antecedent.

Subject: your first space mission
Audience: friends and relatives
Purpose: to inform; to express your thoughts and feelings

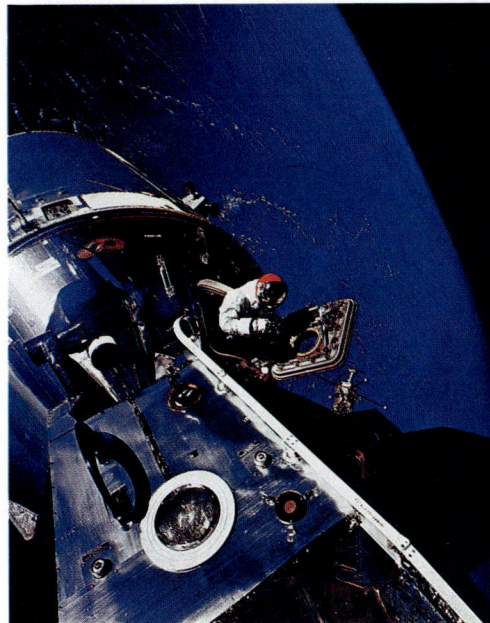

ANSWERS
Exercise 3

Answers will vary. Here are some possibilities:

1. I consider photography an enjoyable hobby, and I take many pictures with my camera.
2. Being neighborly is important because neighbors may someday need each other's help in an emergency.
3. Nguyen has become a virtuoso violinist, but he has never owned a valuable violin.
4. Luisa is highly intelligent, but she hides her intelligence from people she doesn't know well.
5. Our guide said the Pueblo village was well worth seeing but that a proper tour of it would take three hours.

USAGE

PICTURE THIS

The audience for this assignment may be particularly diverse in age, experience, interest, knowledge, and even cultural background. Discuss with students how they might approach the diversity of their audience. One possibility is to choose a particular person or small group to focus on and to let the others "eavesdrop." Another possibility is to address certain individuals directly in their own special parts of the letter, as in the following example:

Sally, it may be hard for you to imagine, but think of the earth appearing as a blue and green beachball in the sky. Grandpa, you would have appreciated the instrumentation in the spacecraft—everything was carefully crafted and comfortable to use.

Indefinite Reference

23e. In formal writing, avoid the indefinite use of the personal pronouns *you, it,* and *they.*

An *indefinite reference* occurs when *you, it,* or *they* has no specific person or thing as its antecedent. To correct an indefinite reference, rephrase the sentence, eliminating the personal pronoun.

INDEFINITE   In some countries, you don't dare express political views openly. [*You* does not refer to any specific person.]

CLEAR   In some countries, people don't dare express their political views openly.

INDEFINITE   In the magazine article, it describes the aftermath of the eruption of Mount Pinatubo. [*It* does not refer to any specific thing.]

CLEAR   The magazine article describes the aftermath of the eruption of Mount Pinatubo.

INDEFINITE   Each summer in Cherokee, North Carolina, they present the historical drama *Unto These Hills* outdoors.

CLEAR   Each summer in Cherokee, North Carolina, the historical drama *Unto These Hills* is presented outdoors.

NOTE: The indefinite reference of *it* in expressions such as *it is raining, it seems,* and *it's late* is acceptable.

▶ EXERCISE 4   **Revising Sentences to Correct Indefinite References**

Revise each of the following sentences to correct the indefinite references of personal pronouns.

1. In many households in India, they serve a flat, pancake-like bread called a *chapati.*
2. In large cities you often don't feel comfortable calling the mayor about problems.
3. In the newspaper article, it calls this presidential election the closest race in many years.

USAGE

ANSWERS
Exercise 4

Answers will vary. Here are some possibilities:

1. A flat, pancake-like bread called a *chapati* is served in many households in India.
2. People in large cities often don't feel comfortable calling the mayor about problems.
3. According to the newspaper article, this presidential election is the closest race in many years.

760

OBJECTIVE

- To revise sentences to correct weak and indefinite pronoun references

23e

4. Each summer in Round Top, Texas, they have an international music festival that is extremely popular.
5. In the telephone book, it lists only five music stores in the city.

REVIEW B

Revising Sentences to Correct Weak and Indefinite Pronoun References

Revise each sentence of the following paragraph to correct weak pronoun references and indefinite references of personal pronouns.

[1] Irish author Christy Brown (1932–1981) was extremely talented, but he had to overcome great physical challenges for it to be recognized. [2] In Brown's autobiography, *My Left Foot*, it tells about his lifelong struggle with cerebral palsy. [3] In some biographies, you don't become emotionally involved, but Brown's autobiography is very personal. [4] The public likes accurate film biographies, and that is a strong point of the movie *My Left Foot*. [5] In this scene from the movie, it shows actor Daniel Day-Lewis portraying Christy Brown. [6] In the movie, they show how Brown learned to write and type with his only functioning limb—his left foot. [7] Brown married in 1972 and her help contributed to Brown's improved muscular control. [8] Brown excelled as a writer, but it is sometimes difficult to locate them in libraries and bookstores in the United States. [9] Brown was acclaimed as a poet as well as a novelist, but I never read one. [10] In the card catalog it lists these books by Brown: *My Left Foot*, *Down All the Days*, *A Shadow on Summer*, and *Wild Grow the Lilies*.

USAGE

4. Each summer, citizens in Round Top, Texas, hold an extremely popular international music festival.
5. Only five music stores in the city are listed in the telephone book.

ANSWERS
Review B

Answers will vary. Here are some possibilities:

1. Irish author Christy Brown (1932–1981) was extremely talented, but he had to overcome great physical challenges for his talent to be recognized.

2. Brown's autobiography, *My Left Foot*, tells about his lifelong struggle with cerebral palsy.

3. Some biographies don't invite readers' emotional involvement, but Brown's autobiography is very personal.

4. The public likes accurate film biographies, and accuracy is a strong point of the movie *My Left Foot*.

5. This scene from the movie shows actor Daniel Day-Lewis portraying Christy Brown.

6. The movie shows how Brown learned to write and type with his only functioning limb—his left foot.

7. Brown married in 1972, and his wife's help contributed to Brown's improved muscular control.

8. Brown excelled as a writer, but locating his books in libraries and bookstores in the United States is sometimes difficult.

9. Brown was acclaimed as a poet as well as a novelist, but I have never read any of his poetry.

10. The following books by Brown are listed in the card catalog: *My Left Foot*, *Down All the Days*, *A Shadow on Summer*, and *Wild Grow the Lilies*.

USAGE

OBJECTIVE
- To revise sentences to correct faulty pronoun references

ANSWERS

Review: Posttest Part A

Answers may vary. Here are some possibilities:

1. Golf wouldn't cost me so much if I didn't lose so many balls in the rough.
2. The radiator was leaking badly; the fluid ran all over the garage floor.
3. In the cabin he checked the fuel. In those days the amount of fuel remaining might have meant the difference between life and death.
4. She overcame her hip injury, although doctors had said recovery was impossible.
5. Her spelling and sentence variety are not good, but most of her errors are due to carelessness.
6. When Ruth was in town last week, she saw Julie.
7. Yesterday's editorial says that the mayor has failed to live up to his campaign promises.
8. The witness testified to having seen the accused eating dinner in the dining car. This testimony convinced the jury that the accused had been on the train.
9. Because the library has an insufficient number of copies of the books most needed for writing research papers, students have difficulty finding the information they need.
10. In Washington, politicians are skeptical about the success of the new farm program. (Allow any reasonable replacement for *they*.)

---

762 *Clear Reference*

Review: Posttest

A. Revising Sentences to Correct Faulty Pronoun References

The following sentences contain ambiguous, general, weak, and indefinite references of pronouns. Revise the sentences to correct each faulty pronoun reference.

EXAMPLE   1. On this cruise, they serve meals without charge.
           1. *On this cruise, meals are served without charge.*

1. Golf wouldn't cost me so much if I didn't lose so many in the rough.
2. The radiator was leaking badly; it ran all over the garage floor.
3. In the cabin he checked the fuel. In those days this might mean the difference between life and death.
4. She overcame her hip injury, which doctors had said was impossible.
5. Her spelling and sentence variety are not good, but most of it is due to carelessness.
6. Ruth saw Julie when she was in town last week.
7. In yesterday's editorial, it says that the mayor has failed to live up to his campaign promises.
8. The witness testified that she had seen the accused when she was eating dinner in the dining car, which convinced the jury that she had been on the train.
9. The library does not have enough copies of some of the books in greatest demand by students writing research papers, which makes it difficult to find the information you need.
10. In Washington they are skeptical about the success of the new farm program.

B. Revising Sentences to Correct Faulty Pronoun References

Revise the following sentences to correct each ambiguous, general, weak, or indefinite pronoun reference.

11. Scientist Carl Sagan wrote and lectured extensively about the possibility of life on other planets, which contributed to his appeal to the general public.
12. Johnny Carson liked Sagan's informal science lectures so much that he appeared many times on *The Tonight Show* after his first appearance in 1972.
13. Sagan came to be known as an expert in the study of extraterrestrial life, even though he had never seen one.
14. In Daniel Cohen's book *Carl Sagan: Superstar Scientist*, it tells about Sagan's childhood in Brooklyn and about his early fascination with the stars and planets.
15. As a boy, Sagan discovered the genre of science fiction, and he read them regularly.
16. At the University of Chicago, they had a highly regarded astronomy department, so Sagan enrolled there in 1951.
17. Sagan served as a consultant for many of NASA's major programs, including the *Mariner, Viking,* and *Voyager* planetary expeditions. This resulted in such awards as the NASA Medal for Distinguished Public Service and the NASA Medal for Exceptional Scientific Achievement.
18. When my father saw Sagan on the popular television series *Cosmos*, he was greatly impressed.
19. Sagan's novel *Contact* explores a number of scientific and social issues that arise when extraterrestrial life makes contact with earthlings. Of course, this made me want to read some of his nonfiction books.
20. In this magazine, it says Sagan believed that the public's understanding of science is necessary for the good of the planet.

USAGE

ANSWERS
Review: Posttest Part B
Answers may vary. Here are some possibilities:

11. Scientist Carl Sagan's extensive writing and lecturing about the possibility of life on other planets contributed to his appeal to the general public.
12. Because Johnny Carson liked Sagan's informal science lectures so much, Sagan appeared many times on *The Tonight Show* after his first appearance in 1972.
13. Sagan came to be known as an expert in the study of extraterrestrial life, even though he had never seen such life.
14. Daniel Cohen's book *Carl Sagan: Superstar Scientist* tells about Sagan's childhood in Brooklyn and his early fascination with the stars and planets.
15. As a boy, Sagan discovered and read widely in the genre of science fiction.
16. Because the University of Chicago had a highly regarded astronomy department, Sagan enrolled there in 1951.
17. Sagan served as a consultant for many of NASA's major programs, including the *Mariner, Viking,* and *Voyager* planetary expeditions. His involvement with these expeditions resulted in such awards as the NASA Medal for Distinguished Public Service and the NASA Medal for Exceptional Scientific Achievement.
18. My father was greatly impressed when he saw Sagan on the popular television series *Cosmos*.
19. That Sagan's novel *Contact* explores a number of scientific and social issues that arise when extraterrestrial life makes contact with earthlings made me want to read some of Sagan's nonfiction books.
20. This magazine says Sagan believed that the public's understanding of science is necessary for the good of the planet.

USAGE

OBJECTIVES
- To choose the correct verb form to complete a sentence
- To revise sentences by correcting verb forms

PROGRAM MANAGER

FOR THE WHOLE CHAPTER
- **Review** For exercises on chapter concepts, see **Review Form A** and **Review Form B** in *Language Skills Practice and Assessment,* pp. 146–149.
- **Assessment** For additional testing, see **Usage Pretests** and **Usage Mastery Tests** in *Language Skills Practice and Assessment,* pp. 95–101 and pp. 179–185.

CHAPTER OVERVIEW

The material in this chapter will clarify for students the sometimes confusing nature of verbs. Principal parts of regular and irregular verbs, verb tense, active and passive voice, and mood are all discussed. Additional explanation for troublesome verbs such as *lie* and *lay, sit* and *set,* and *rise* and *raise* is provided and is reinforced by multiple exercises. The **Writing Application** will give students the opportunity to use verb tenses correctly when writing paragraphs describing what special events helped make their senior year memorable.

A quick review of the usage of verbs before the revision stage can provide students the help they need to make their papers clear and effective.

24 CORRECT FORM AND USE OF VERBS

Principal Parts, Tense, Voice, Mood

Diagnostic Test

A. Choosing the Correct Verb Form

For each of the following sentences, choose the correct form of the verb in parentheses.

EXAMPLE **1.** In a hurry to go to work, I couldn't remember where I had (*laid, lain*) my keys.
1. *laid*

1. During the political rally, many of the balloons filled with helium (*burst, bursted*) as they rose from the ground.
2. Whenever Joan watches television, her Samoyed puppy (*lies, lays*) down at her feet.
3. If I (*was, were*) president, I would make world peace my first priority.
4. Mary Louise (*swam, swum*) the hundred-meter race in record time.

5. If I (*had, would have*) told the truth in the first place, the situation would have been much easier to handle.
6. (*Cooking, Having cooked*) a delicious Thanksgiving meal together, the newlyweds received many compliments from their guests.
7. The members of the second-place math team were upset because they (*hoped, had hoped*) to take first place.
8. Because we did not add the proper amount of yeast, the loaves of bread failed to (*raise, rise*).
9. The tree died after it (*was hit, had been hit*) by lightning.
10. The five riders are pleased (*to qualify, to have qualified*) for the equestrian team.
11. After I had (*wrote, written*) my autobiographical essay for my college application, I heaved a sigh of relief.
12. I wished that there (*was, were*) a good movie playing in town.
13. Because he had starred in four high school productions, David hoped (*to pursue, to have pursued*) an acting career.
14. (*Lie, Lay*) your work aside and relax for a few minutes.
15. In 1984, Joaquim Cruz, whose right leg is slightly shorter than his left leg, was overjoyed when he (*won, had won*) Brazil's first gold medal in the 800-meter run.

B. Revising Sentences by Correcting Verb Forms

Revise each sentence in the following paragraph by correcting any incorrect verb forms.

[16] For at least five thousand years, people been eating popcorn. [17] If you are like most of them, you probably falled in love with popcorn when you were a child. [18] The ancient Aztecs thought so highly of popcorn that they even use to wear it around their necks. [19] Centuries ago adult Native Americans probably would have been remembering popcorn as a source of delight and excitement in their childhoods. [20] After all, at that time popcorn was often simply throwed into a fire or roasted on a stick. [21] What a stir there must have been among the children when the kernels began to have popped clear of the fire! [22] Like children today, they probably would not be too bothered by the sand or dirt that the popcorn must have picked up. [23] Still, these early popcorn lovers were not plagued by duds, which can have broken your teeth and which

16. have
17. fell
18. wore
19. remembered
20. thrown
21. pop
22. have been
23. break

USAGE

USING THE DIAGNOSTIC TEST

This test will reveal any problems students have with using correct verb forms in sentences. Some students will make errors because they do not recognize the auxiliary verbs that determine verb forms. Other students will have problems with using the correct forms of the irregular verbs and the six troublesome verbs discussed in this chapter.

USAGE

USAGE

had been the scourge of the popcorn industry until the 1950s. **[24]** That was when Orville Redenbacher and Charles Bowman

24. grew successfully ~~growed~~ a variety of corn that just did not have very many duds. **[25]** When the big popcorn manufacturers rejected the new corn, Redenbacher went into business for himself, and as you probably know, the company he founded

25. has ~~had~~ experienced phenomenal success ever since.

The Principal Parts of a Verb

24a. Every verb has four basic forms called its *principal parts:* the *base form,* the *present participle,* the *past,* and the *past participle.* All other verb forms are derived from these principal parts.

The following examples include *is* with the present participle and *have* with the past participle forms to indicate that helping verbs (forms of *be* and *have*) are used with those forms.

BASE FORM	PRESENT PARTICIPLE	PAST	PAST PARTICIPLE
live	(is) living	lived	(have) lived
talk	(is) talking	talked	(have) talked
run	(is) running	ran	(have) run
rise	(is) rising	rose	(have) risen
hit	(is) hitting	hit	(have) hit

NOTE: Some teachers refer to the base form as the infinitive. Follow your teacher's directions in labeling these forms.

All verbs form the present participle in the same way: by adding *–ing* to the base form. Not all verbs form the past and past participle in the same way, however. The way in which a verb forms the past and past participle determines whether it is classified as *regular* or *irregular.*

☞ **REFERENCE NOTE:** For more discussion about the different kinds of verbs, see pages 612–614.

OBJECTIVE
• To use the past and past participle forms of verbs correctly

Regular Verbs

24b. A *regular verb* forms the past and past participle by adding *–d* or *–ed* to the base form.

BASE FORM	PRESENT PARTICIPLE	PAST	PAST PARTICIPLE
care	(is) caring	cared	(have) cared
remove	(is) removing	removed	(have) removed
suppose	(is) supposing	supposed	(have) supposed
match	(is) matching	matched	(have) matched
offer	(is) offering	offered	(have) offered
push	(is) pushing	pushed	(have) pushed

A few regular verbs have alternate past and past participle forms ending in *–t.*

BASE FORM	PRESENT PARTICIPLE	PAST	PAST PARTICIPLE
burn	(is) burning	burned *or* burnt	(have) burned *or* burnt
dream	(is) dreaming	dreamed *or* dreamt	(have) dreamed *or* dreamt
leap	(is) leaping	leaped *or* leapt	(have) leaped *or* leapt

NOTE: The regular verbs *deal* and *mean* always form the past and past participle by adding *–t: dealt, (have) dealt; meant, (have) meant.*

When forming the past and past participle of regular verbs, don't make the common mistake of leaving off the *–d* or *–ed* ending. Pay particular attention to the forms of the verbs *ask, attack, drown, prejudice, risk, suppose,* and *use.*

NONSTANDARD	We use to live in Bakersfield.
STANDARD	We **used** to live in Bakersfield.

NONSTANDARD	I was suppose to be home by now.
STANDARD	I was **supposed** to be home by now.

☞ **REFERENCE NOTE:** For more about standard English, see pages 513 and 842.

PROGRAM MANAGER

REGULAR VERBS AND IRREGULAR VERBS

■ **Independent Practice/ Reteaching** For instruction and exercises, see **Principal Parts of Regular Verbs** and **Principal Parts of Irregular Verbs** in *Language Skills Practice and Assessment,* pp. 139–140.

■ **Computer Guided Instruction** For additional instruction and practice with regular and irregular verbs, see **Lesson 9** in *Language Workshop CD-ROM.*

■ **Practice** To help less-advanced students with additional instruction and practice with regular and irregular verbs, see **Chapter 17** in *English Workshop, Complete Course,* pp. 229–234.

MEETING individual NEEDS

LEP/ESL

General Strategies. Some strategies for creating verb forms in English require familiarity with vowel sounds. For example, forming the present participle by doubling final consonants before adding *–ing* necessitates recognizing short vowel sounds. Some students might not be able to distinguish some of these sounds, especially vowels that sound similar, such as short *e* and short *a.* Try reviewing the long and short vowels, the stress patterns in words, and the sound pairs that seem problematic for students.

INTEGRATING THE LANGUAGE ARTS

Usage and Dictionary Skills. Point out to students that when they have questions about the principal parts of verbs, they can look the verbs up in a dictionary. Explain that the entry word in a dictionary is the base form and that the past, past-participle, and present-participle forms are listed following the entry word. For example, if students look up *sing,* they will find *sang, sung,* and *singing* listed after *sing.* Have each student choose two or three irregular verbs to look up in a dictionary. Students should write each verb's principal parts.

COMMON IRREGULAR VERBS *(continued)*			
GROUP I			
BASE FORM	**PRESENT PARTICIPLE**	**PAST**	**PAST PARTICIPLE**
pay	(is) paying	paid	(have) paid
say	(is) saying	said	(have) said
seek	(is) seeking	sought	(have) sought
sell	(is) selling	sold	(have) sold
send	(is) sending	sent	(have) sent
sit	(is) sitting	sat	(have) sat
spend	(is) spending	spent	(have) spent
spin	(is) spinning	spun	(have) spun
stand	(is) standing	stood	(have) stood
sting	(is) stinging	stung	(have) stung
swing	(is) swinging	swung	(have) swung
teach	(is) teaching	taught	(have) taught
tell	(is) telling	told	(have) told
think	(is) thinking	thought	(have) thought
win	(is) winning	won	(have) won

▶ EXERCISE 1   **Using the Past and Past Participle Forms of Verbs Correctly**

Most of the following sentences contain errors in the use of the past or past participle forms of verbs. If a verb form is incorrect, give the correct form. If a sentence is correct, write C.

1. Before the festival last Sunday, the Conchero dancers ~~had meet~~ behind the church to practice.   **1. met**
2. By some unlucky chance, I ~~winned~~ the door prize—a full-grown Leghorn rooster.   **2. won**
3. The accomplishments of Maggie Lena Walker, the first woman bank president in the United States, ~~layed~~ a firm financial foundation for the African American community of Richmond, Virginia.   **3. laid**
4. The macaw, happy to see its owner, ~~hop~~ to the door of its cage and shrieked excitedly.   **4. hopped**

5. After a few hesitant steps, we ~~swinged~~ into the rhythm of the foxtrot. **5.** swung

6. For all those years, the old man had ~~keeped~~ the dog-eared photograph of his childhood home in Hawaii. **6.** kept

7. While in Arizona, Uncle Arthur ~~boughten~~ a magnificent storm-pattern Navajo rug by Shirley Tsinnie. **7.** bought

8. How could you have ~~spended~~ all of your allowance before Saturday afternoon! **8.** spent

9. A green velvet ribbon ~~binded~~ the large white box on the dining room table. **9.** bound

10. The cool skin of the chameleon ~~feeled~~ dry, not wet. **10.** felt

11. Her strokes were sure and steady, for she had ~~swam~~ out to the little island many times. **11.** swum

12. No one said a word as the big yellow arrow was ~~spinned~~ to determine who would take the first turn. **12.** spun

13. Haven't you ~~sayed~~ enough? **13.** said   **14.** fought

14. On the front porch that very afternoon, the two second-graders had ~~fighted~~ furiously over the only blue crayon.

15. In modern China, Qiu Jin ~~leaded~~ the way for women's emancipation. **15.** led

16. Have you ~~selled~~ the mare with the three white feet and white mane? **16.** sold   **17.** C *or* dreamed

17. For some reason, I have dreamt for two nights in a row of two bottles on a huge round table.   **18.** prejudiced

18. Unfortunately, her rash remarks had ~~prejudice~~ the jury.

19. We should have sat in the shade of a towering oak tree on the university's front lawn. **19.** C

20. That colorful painting by the Haitian artist Euguerrand Gourgue ~~lended~~ a cheery touch to the room. **20.** lent

▶ **EXERCISE 2**   **Using the Past and Past Participle Forms of Irregular Verbs Correctly**

Complete each of the following sentences, using the correct past or past participle form of the italicized verb.

1. sought

1. *seek*   Spanish explorers had ____ gold in the Americas.
2. *find*   The gold that they ____, however, was in golden ears of corn. **2.** found
3. *leave* Spanish ships ____ carrying these precious kernels back to Europe. **3.** left

USAGE

USAGE

4. *bring*   The holds of the ships _____ a cheap, new food source into a world of recurrent famine.   **4. brought**

5. *lead*   A diet of corn _____ many of the world's poor to suffer from pellagra, a disease that affects the stomach, mind, and skin.   **5. led**   **6. built**

6. *build*   Yet the peoples of Mexico and Central America had _____ healthy bodies on a steady diet of corn.

7. *make*   When the women of Mexico and Central America _____ tortillas, they added some lime or ashes to the dough.   **7. made**

8. *stand*   Then, after the mixture of corn, water, and lime or ashes had _____ for a few hours, the tortillas were shaped and cooked.   **8. stood**

9. *have*   Heated, this alkali solution _____ the ability to release not only corn's niacin but also its protein and calcium.   **9. had**

10. *lose*   In European and African methods of preparation, corn had unfortunately _____ much of its essential nutrient value.   **10. lost**

COMMON IRREGULAR VERBS

GROUP II:	Each of these irregular verbs has a different form for its past and past participle.		
BASE FORM	**PRESENT PARTICIPLE**	**PAST**	**PAST PARTICIPLE**
arise	(is) arising	arose	(have) arisen
be	(is) being	was, were	(have) been
bear	(is) bearing	bore	(have) borne
beat	(is) beating	beat	(have) beaten *or* beat
become	(is) becoming	became	(have) become
begin	(is) beginning	began	(have) begun
bite	(is) biting	bit	(have) bitten
blow	(is) blowing	blew	(have) blown
break	(is) breaking	broke	(have) broken
choose	(is) choosing	chose	(have) chosen
come	(is) coming	came	(have) come
dive	(is) diving	dove *or* dived	(have) dived

(continued)

COMMON IRREGULAR VERBS *(continued)*			
GROUP II			
BASE FORM	PRESENT PARTICIPLE	PAST	PAST PARTICIPLE
do	(is) doing	did	(have) done
draw	(is) drawing	drew	(have) drawn
drink	(is) drinking	drank	(have) drunk
drive	(is) driving	drove	(have) driven
eat	(is) eating	ate	(have) eaten
fall	(is) falling	fell	(have) fallen
fly	(is) flying	flew	(have) flown
forbid	(is) forbidding	forbade *or* forbad	(have) forbidden
forgive	(is) forgiving	forgave	(have) forgiven
forget	(is) forgetting	forgot	(have) forgotten *or* forgot
forsake	(is) forsaking	forsook	(have) forsaken
freeze	(is) freezing	froze	(have) frozen
get	(is) getting	got	(have) gotten *or* got
give	(is) giving	gave	(have) given
go	(is) going	went	(have) gone
grow	(is) growing	grew	(have) grown
hide	(is) hiding	hid	(have) hidden
know	(is) knowing	knew	(have) known
lie	(is) lying	lay	(have) lain
ride	(is) riding	rode	(have) ridden
ring	(is) ringing	rang	(have) rung
rise	(is) rising	rose	(have) risen
run	(is) running	ran	(have) run
see	(is) seeing	saw	(have) seen
shake	(is) shaking	shook	(have) shaken
shrink	(is) shrinking	shrank *or* shrunk	(have) shrunk
sing	(is) singing	sang	(have) sung
sink	(is) sinking	sank *or* sunk	(have) sunk

(continued)

USAGE

COOPERATIVE LEARNING

To help students remember verb forms, have them conjugate verbs to a rhythmic beat. Divide the class into groups of three or four students. Assign each group ten irregular verbs and have the groups prepare rhythmic oral presentations that include the present, past, and past-participle forms of the verbs. The presentations can be poems, songs, stories, chants, or recitations, and students can use movement to keep the beat or to act out their verbs.

USAGE

USAGE

COMMON IRREGULAR VERBS *(continued)*			
GROUP II			
BASE FORM	**PRESENT PARTICIPLE**	**PAST**	**PAST PARTICIPLE**
slay	(is) slaying	slew	(have) slain
speak	(is) speaking	spoke	(have) spoken
spring	(is) springing	sprang *or* sprung	(have) sprung
steal	(is) stealing	stole	(have) stolen
strike	(is) striking	struck	(have) struck *or* stricken
strive	(is) striving	strove *or* strived	(have) striven *or* strived
swear	(is) swearing	swore	(have) sworn
swim	(is) swimming	swam	(have) swum
take	(is) taking	took	(have) taken
tear	(is) tearing	tore	(have) torn
throw	(is) throwing	threw	(have) thrown
wake	(is) waking	woke	(have) woke, waked, *or* wakened
wear	(is) wearing	wore	(have) worn
weave	(is) weaving	wove	(have) woven
write	(is) writing	wrote	(have) written

EXERCISE 3   Using the Past and Past Participle Forms of Irregular Verbs Correctly

For each sentence in the following paragraphs, choose the <u>correct one of the two verbs</u> in parentheses.

[1] Years ago in Africa, languages like Bantu had no alphabet; therefore, nothing was (*wrote, written*) in these languages. [2] In fact, the musical quality of many African languages (*gived, gave*) them an intricacy unsuitable for written alphabets. [3] Consequently, drums (*sung, sang*) these languages throughout equatorial and southern Africa, and these songs acted as a kind of musical writing. [4] According to Janheinz Jahn, the use of

drums (*arose*, *arisen*) for communication at a distance. [5] Young Africans learned to "read" the different sounds of the drums and (*knew*, *known*) the meaning of these sounds in combinations, just as you were taught to read using the alphabet.

[6] The wide acoustic range of drums like the Yorubas' *dundun* (*gived*, *gave*) quick and easy access to a complex language. [7] By varying tone, pitch, and modulation, a skillful drummer (*striven*, *strove*) to re-create the sounds of his language. [8] With this meaningful music, he (*wove*, *woven*) the news of the day into an informative report. [9] At the speed of sound, his warnings, invitations, and other messages (*flew*, *flown*) over miles of jungle and plain. [10] With drum scripts that had been (*beat*, *beaten*) for decades, he sent information to interested listeners. [11] Many of the drum scripts eventually (*became*, *become*) classic epics. [12] As you can see, drummers were not just musicians; they (*been*, *were*) also teachers and historians. [13] Through them, generations of young Africans (*drank*, *drunk*) in the history of their ancestors.

[14] When European missionaries came to Africa, however, they (*forbidden*, *forbade*) the playing of drums. [15] Their prohibitions (*struck*, *stricken*) at the hearts of many African cultures. [16] Today, through disuse, almost all of the old drum scripts have been (*forgot*, *forgotten*). [17] Scholars, however, have (*maked*, *made*) recordings of many of the remaining scripts. [18] Sadly, many listeners have not (*spoke*, *spoken*) their native language in their whole lives; consequently, even verbal translations of the drum songs are meaningless to many Africans. [19] The power of the drums has (*went*, *gone*). [20] Like so much of ancient knowledge and wisdom, this marvelous system of communication has been (*forsaken*, *forsook*).

EXERCISE 4   **Using the Past and Past Participle Forms of Irregular Verbs Correctly**

Most of the following sentences contain incorrect past or past participle forms of verbs. If a verb form is incorrect, give the correct form. If a sentence is correct, write *C*.

1. Benjamin Franklin may have gotten many of his ideas for the structure of our government from his observations of the League of the Iroquois.   **1. C**
2. She should not have ~~drew~~ a beard on that poster.   **2. drawn**

776 *Correct Form and Use of Verbs*

3. Why would anyone have ~~stole~~ your notebook?   **3.** stolen

4. I have ~~ran~~ too far to turn back now.   **4.** run

5. Tommy has ~~growed~~ two inches taller than I.   **5.** grown

6. After 1922, other ancient treasures ~~shrunk~~ in significance when compared to the discoveries made in the tomb of Tutankhamen.   **6.** shrank [*or* C]

7. Last night, the noise from the party ~~waked~~ up the whole neighborhood.   **7.** woke

8. I ~~seen~~ that movie several times.   **8.** saw

9. Who ~~throwed~~ out my old comic books?   **9.** threw   **10.** C

10. They have frozen a peck of green beans for next winter.

11. Henry ~~done~~ his best yesterday.   **11.** did

12. In the courtroom, the young man was ~~sweared~~ in to give testimony.   **12.** sworn

13. Jesse Owens' spectacular run at the 1936 Olympic games ~~shaked~~ the world.   **13.** shook   **14.** dived

14. Have you ever ~~dove~~ from the high board?   **15.** blew

15. Thunder crashed, and wind ~~blowed~~ the candles out.

16. We should have ~~chose~~ seats closer to the stage.   **16.** chosen

17. Why have they ~~tore~~ up the newspapers?   **17.** torn

18. How the ancient Mexicans' multicolored garments made of feathers must have ~~shined~~ in the sunlight!   **18.** shone

19. He always ~~rid~~ the bus to school.   **19.** rode

20. Has the bell rung yet?   **20.** C

▶ **REVIEW A**   **Proofreading for Correct Verb Forms**

For each sentence in the following paragraphs, find and correct any errors in verb forms. If a sentence is correct, write C.

1. forsaken

2. come

3. led

4. supposed

5. found

6. sought

[1] Many cultures have not ~~forsaked~~ their traditional ceremonies that mark the significant stages in a person's life. [2] For instance, when an Apache girl has ~~came~~ of age, she sometimes receives a Sunrise Ceremonial. [3] Through this ceremony, the young woman is forever separated from her girlhood and ~~lead~~ into womanhood. [4] Everything in the ceremony is ~~suppose~~ to remind the young woman of the deep spiritual meaning of her life. [5] Perhaps part of that meaning can be ~~founded~~ in the glad hearts of her many friends and family members who come to participate in the ceremony.

[6] Not long ago, Carla, the young woman in the photograph on the next page, and her mother ~~seeked~~ the blessings of a traditional Sunrise Ceremonial. [7] Complex preparations

had ~~began~~ months in advance. [8] During the winter, Carla's mother ~~choose~~ a campsite where Carla, her family, and her friends would live for two weeks according to the ways of their ancestors. [9] The crucial choice of godparents for the young woman also had been ~~maked~~ by Carla's mother. [10] Not surprisingly, she chose a couple who had ~~keeped~~ to the traditional Apache way of life. [11] By summer, Carla's mother and godparents had ~~builded~~ enough shelters at the campsite to house at least eight families.

7. begun
8. chose
9. made
10. kept
11. built

[12] During Carla's ceremonial, many traditional songs were ~~sang~~, thirty-two of them by one group of dancers alone. [13] The two cows that had been ~~slew~~ for the feasting were eaten. [14] In addition, Carla and her family gave away all of the gifts they had ~~brung~~ for the godparents and other friends. [15] Although young women used to dance all night, Carla danced for six hours at a time at her ceremonial. [16] Then she ~~standed~~ for seemingly endless hours in the burning sun. [17] Through it all, she ~~worn~~ a hot, heavy buckskin dress. [18] Surely, these tests of self-discipline ~~teached~~ Carla and everyone who ~~attend~~ the ceremony something about the endurance and strength that a woman needs to live as a proper Apache. [19] Finally, after offering a blessing, a medicine man ~~gived~~ Carla a cane, a reminder that she will not always be young. [20] In her old age, when the cane has ~~became~~ her constant companion, it will, no doubt, remind her of the strength of her youth.

12. sung
13. slain
14. brought
15. C
16. stood
17. wore
18. taught/attended
19. gave
20. become

USAGE

USAGE

A DIFFERENT APPROACH

Ask your students to think of examples of irregular verbs that form their past tenses and past participles in one of the following ways:

1. changing a vowel [sit, begin]
2. adding –*en* [take, give]
3. changing the complete word [fly, go]
4. making no change [set, bid]

Students can use the **Common Irregular Verbs** charts if necessary.

MEETING *individual* NEEDS

General Strategies. Ask students to think of a rite of passage or an initiation ceremony similar to the one in the photograph. Then, have each student write an informative paragraph that includes at least five irregular verb forms to describe the event.

COMMON IRREGULAR VERBS			
GROUP III:	Each of these irregular verbs has the same form for its base form, past, and past participle.		
BASE FORM	**PRESENT PARTICIPLE**	**PAST**	**PAST PARTICIPLE**
burst	(is) bursting	burst	(have) burst
cost	(is) costing	cost	(have) cost
cut	(is) cutting	cut	(have) cut
hit	(is) hitting	hit	(have) hit
hurt	(is) hurting	hurt	(have) hurt
let	(is) letting	let	(have) let
put	(is) putting	put	(have) put
read	(is) reading	read	(have) read
set	(is) setting	set	(have) set
spread	(is) spreading	spread	(have) spread

▶ EXERCISE 5 **Using the Past and Past Participle Forms of Irregular Verbs Correctly**

Most of the following sentences contain errors in the use of verbs. If a verb form is incorrect, give the correct form of the verb. If a sentence is correct, write *C*.

1. During the freeze last March, the water pipes at school bursted.   **1. burst**
2. That dog would not have hurted a fly.   **2. hurt**
3. Yesterday evening, I had just putted dinner on the table when the phone rang.   **3. put**   **4. spread**
4. Shaka Zulu led his warriors into battle, and soon news of Shaka's victory had spreaded throughout Zululand.
5. Have you ever cutted out a pattern before?   **5. cut**
6. Have you read the assignment yet?   **6. C**
7. After art class, Jeremy and I setted our pottery out in the sun to dry.   **7. set**
8. The drought hitted the spring crops hard.   **8. hit**
9. One chance remark had costed her the election.   **9. cost**
10. Wisely, Francisca Henrique de Ribera letted the Andean natives treat her malaria attack with a powerful bark, now known as quinine.   **10. let**

USAGE

USAGE

REVIEW B

OBJECTIVE

- To proofread for correct verb forms and usage

> **REVIEW B**   **Proofreading for Correct Verb Forms and Usage**

Most of the sentences in the following paragraphs contain errors in verb usage. If a verb is incorrect, give the correct form of the verb. If a sentence is correct, write *C*.

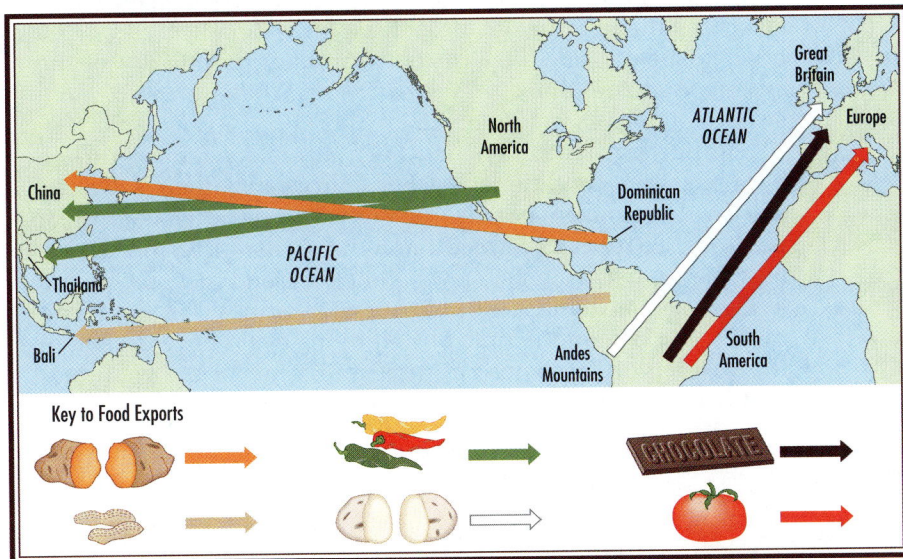

Key to Food Exports

[1] Now that you've readed the map shown above, are you surprised by where these food products originated? [2] Perhaps you have ate some of these foods. [3] Like naturalized citizens, many food products have became vital, even characteristic, parts of their adopted nations. [4] Consequently, most people have forgot that key ingredients, such as tomato sauce on pizza, come from the Americas.

[5] Reports from early explorers putted cooks all over Europe into a creative frenzy. [6] When the explorers returned home, dozens of strange and exotic foods were suddenly maked available to Europeans. [7] Some of the foods that the explorers sended home include sweet potatoes, white potatoes, corn, peppers, tomatoes, avocados, vanilla, maple sugar, chocolate, peanuts, all sorts of beans (kidney, lima, snap, string, butter, pole, and navy), and a host of other welcome additions to a chef's larder. [8] So many new spices, fruits, vegetables, meats, and grains hitted the market that this period in history can be called a "Food Revolution."

1. read
2. eaten
3. become
4. came
5. put
6. made
7. sent/ included
8. hit

USAGE

LEP/ESL

General Strategies. Some languages, such as Indonesian, Japanese, Korean, Turkish, and Vietnamese, have few or no irregular verbs. Give students a comprehensive list of irregular verbs. Leave blank spaces for the past-tense forms. Tell students to write the past-tense forms of the verbs in the blanks and to keep this list as a reference in their notebooks.

USAGE

780 *Correct Form and Use of Verbs*

9. found
10. used
11. lost
12. arose
13. C
14. put
15. grown
16. C
17. lay
18. fought
19. lent
20. C

[9] In these unfamiliar foods, many peoples also ~~founded~~ new hope. [10] For example, the Chinese ~~use~~ to experience severe famine. [11] Countless lives had been ~~losed~~ due to the failure of rice crops. [12] However, with the introduction of the sweet potato, an alternative to rice ~~arisen~~. [13] Sweet potatoes cost little and did well in poor soil. [14] Soon, cooks had ~~putted~~ sweet potato flour into Chinese dumplings, noodles, and many other dishes. [15] Because of the continuing popularity of the sweet potato in China, Chinese farmers have ~~growed~~ more sweet potatoes than farmers in any other country.

[16] Europe, too, often had been struck by famine due to poor weather conditions. [17] For Europeans, their salvation ~~lain~~ in the Andean potato. [18] With harvest after harvest of potatoes, Europeans ~~fighted~~ famine and also rang in a whole new menu. [19] In soups, stews, pancakes, and pies, the potato ~~lended~~ its substance and nutrition to a host of European dishes. [20] Who in the time of Columbus could have dreamt of the vast variety of American food sources or of the vital roles they would play in the world's fight against famine?

WRITING APPLICATION

The writing assignment helps students understand the importance of standard usage in formal writing. Ask students to think of reasons that published materials must be accurate. [Possible responses are that correcting errors is expensive or that errors detract from the credibility of the written work.]

WRITING APPLICATION

Using Standard Verb Forms in Writing

Often, writers make errors in using the past and past participle forms of verbs because many nonstandard verb forms sound quite natural. When you proofread your writing for incorrect verb forms, don't rely on how a form sounds. Always check the sentence to determine which form—past or past participle—is called for.

EXAMPLES By April, the Eastside High Choir had (*gave, given*) four excellent performances at the town auditorium. [The helping verb *had* signals that the past participle form is called for.]

By April, the Eastside High Choir **had given** four excellent performances at the town auditorium.

USAGE

USAGE

The new telescope (*cost, costed*) almost exactly as much as we had raised at the school raffle. [The sentence requires the simple past form of *cost.*] The new telescope **cost** almost exactly as much as we had raised at the school raffle.

To save time, identify the verbs that give you trouble and memorize their forms. Keep a dictionary handy to check any forms you're not sure about.

▶ WRITING ACTIVITY

The editor of your school's yearbook is planning a seniors-only feature. Interested seniors may submit one-paragraph descriptions of school or special events that helped make this year memorable. Selected descriptions, along with photographs, will be published as part of the feature. Write a paragraph to submit for publication. In your paragraph, include at least five irregular verbs from the lists on pages 769–770, 772–774, and 778. Be sure that you've used the correct past and past participle forms of verbs.

Prewriting   Brainstorm a list of memorable moments in the school year. Focus on events in which a number of students participated. From your list choose the one event that you remember most vividly. What was the high point of the event? What made the moment special?

Writing   As you write your first draft, name the event and give the time at which it occurred. Then describe the event, capturing the feeling or mood it inspired in your school. Include vivid sensory details to hold the reader's interest. Mention some of the people who helped make the event memorable.

Evaluating and Revising   Ask a classmate who took part in the event to read your paragraph. Have you described the event clearly and captured its special flavor? Will your description help students remember the event in years to come? Note down your reader's comments and suggestions. Then add, cut, and revise details as necessary to improve your description. Replace bland adjectives, adverbs, and verbs with livelier, more expressive ones. Be sure that you've used at least five irregular verbs from the lists.

USAGE

CRITICAL THINKING

Analysis. Ask students to make copies of their paragraphs to place in a time capsule. Ask students also to include available photographs or articles that reflect the written descriptions. After students have collected all the items, ask them to work together to vote on the ten articles that most adequately reflect the school year and that will provide future readers with insight into the past.

PREWRITING

Briefly remind students that sensory details of sight, sound, taste, smell, and touch make readers feel as if they are part of the described event. Encourage students to use as many sensory words as possible because the sensory words will help them recreate the experiences in their minds.

EVALUATING AND REVISING

As students revise their paragraphs, ask them to circle all verbs. Ask each student to exchange papers with a partner for evaluation. You may also want to recommend that students circle all adjectives and adverbs so that their partners can help them think of livelier, more expressive ones.

USAGE

781

USAGE

REVIEWS C and D

OBJECTIVES

- To use correct past and past participle forms
- To proofread for correct verb forms and usage

Proofreading and Publishing Read through your paragraph several times, checking for any errors in grammar, usage, spelling, or punctuation. Take extra care with the past and past participle forms of verbs. To publish your descriptions, you and your classmates can compile them in a mini-yearbook. You may want to include photographs or drawings to accompany the descriptions. Leave a few blank pages for future events.

USAGE

▶ REVIEW C   Using the Past and Past Participle Forms

For each of the following sentences, write the correct past or past participle form of the italicized word.

1. *creep*   While the children were asleep, their father ____ into their room to kiss them good night.   **1.** crept
2. *let*   After breakfast, I ____ the cat go outside.   **2.** let
3. *visit*   Many Cheyenne, Arapaho, Shoshone, Blackfoot, Crow, and Sioux pilgrims have ____ the Bighorn Medicine Wheel in Wyoming, a ceremonial site for perhaps two thousand years.   **3.** visited
4. *fling*   Joyfully, he ____ his cap into the air.   **4.** flung
5. *sting*   Where had the bee ____ her?   **5.** stung   **6.** won
6. *win*   The baby's trusting smile ____ our hearts.   **7.** thought
7. *think*   At last, I had ____ of the perfect present for Amy.
8. *bear*   We could not have ____ another moment of that awful music.   **8.** borne   **9.** swam
9. *swim*   The frantic cat ____ desperately to the shore.
10. *blow*   Even before the whistle had ____, they had seen the train coming.   **10.** blown
11. *sink*   After our long voyage, we gratefully ____ into the plush velvet chairs.   **11.** sank   **12.** hidden
12. *hide*   Someone had ____ one of my birthday presents at the back of the top shelf in a kitchen cabinet.
13. *set*   That afternoon, we hurriedly ____ the table for the party.   **13.** set
14. *lie*   During World War II, the success of England's military blood bank ____ in the capable hands of Dr. Charles Drew.   **14.** lay

15. *hold* Only that morning, I had ____ the trembling bird in my hands. **15.** held

16. *bite* The injured whale had obviously been ____ many times by sharks. **16.** bitten

17. *lead* Boadicea, a queen in ancient Britain, ____ her people in a revolt against the Romans. **17.** led

18. *cut* With one sure stroke, he had ____ his ties to his native country. **18.** cut

19. *throw* That horse has ____ everybody who has tried to ride her. **19.** thrown

20. *break* The death of Mao Zedong ____ the rigid rule that had governed China for many years and opened the way for somewhat greater freedom for the Chinese people. **20.** broke

REVIEW D

Proofreading for Correct Verb Forms and Usage

Most of the sentences in the following paragraphs contain errors in the use of verbs. If a verb form is incorrect, give the correct form. If a sentence is correct, write *C*.

[1] For over thirty years, my aunt has had a lacquerware plate similar to the one in this picture. [2] When I been a child, she displayed the plate on a low table in her living room in Tacoma, Washington. [3] Naturally, she forbidded me to touch her prized plate, and I respected her wish. [4] One day, however, my younger brother runned through the living room. [5] As he zoomed past the table, his foot accidentally hitted the leg. [6] In the blink of an eye, my aunt's beautiful plate falled.

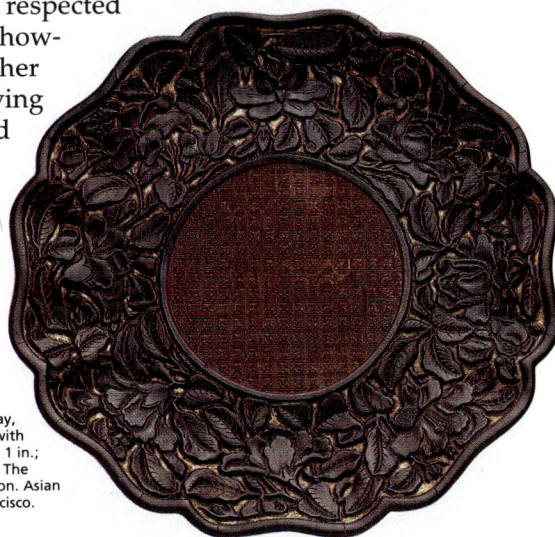

1. C
2. was
3. forbade
4. ran
5. hit
6. fell

Song-Yuan dynasties. Tray, brown and red lacquer with gilt background. Height, 1 in.; diameter, 9 in. #B83M9. The Avery Brundage Collection. Asian Art Museum of San Francisco.

VISUAL CONNECTIONS
Ideas for Writing. Students probably will be impressed with the artist's diligence in applying lacquer to the pictured plate. Ask students to write an informative paragraph explaining the steps they used to complete a school or home project. You may want students to present their paragraphs orally to the class.

783

OBJECTIVES

- To choose the correct forms of *lie* and *lay*
- To choose the correct forms of *sit* and *set*
- To choose the correct forms of *rise* and *raise*

USAGE

QUICK REMINDER

Write the following chart on the chalkboard:

Pres.	Past	Past Part.	Meaning
lie	lay	(have) lain	to rest
lay	laid	(have) laid	to put

Stress to students that although these two verbs are similar in appearance, they have two different meanings. Then, have students determine which of these words belongs in the blank in each of the following sentences. Have students give reasons for their choices.

1. I _____ the book on the table yesterday. [laid]

2. The dog _____ beside the fireplace last night. [lay]

784

USAGE

784 *Correct Form and Use of Verbs*

6. spun
7. sat

8. told
9. made
10. began/ spread
11. kept
12. C

13. sold

14. C

15. left
16. took
17. chosen
18. devoted
19. felt

20. paid

and ~~spinned~~ wildly on the floor. [7] After that, the plate, which was miraculously unbroken, ~~sitted~~ on the top shelf of my aunt's china closet.

[8] Ever since I first expressed an interest in lacquerware, my aunt has ~~telled~~ me more and more about its history and production. [9] Lacquerware has been ~~make~~ since around 300 B.C. [10] The art ~~begun~~ in China and later ~~spreaded~~ to Japan and then to the Western world. [11] To protect their trade, the tappers of lacquer in ancient China ~~keeped~~ their valuable knowledge of lacquer production secret. [12] Now we know that they drew the sap from lacquer trees, filtered it, and dried it to a thick, syrupy consistency. [13] Then they ~~selled~~ it to artists for its beauty and for its waterproofing ability.

[14] In the finer pieces of lacquerware, like this one, some two hundred coats of lacquer might have been spread over the plate. [15] For each coat, a thin film of lacquer was applied and then was ~~leaved~~ to dry thoroughly. [16] Consequently, the whole lacquering process sometimes ~~taked~~ as long as a year to complete. [17] Then, when the artist had ~~chosed~~ a design, the carving began. [18] Would you have ~~devote~~ a year's work to such an intricate design? [19] What confidence these artists must have ~~feeled~~! [20] My aunt bought her plate years ago for only a few dollars; now, it has brought offers of many, many times the price that she ~~payed~~.

Six Troublesome Verbs

Lie and *Lay*

The verb *lie* means "to rest" or "to stay, to recline, or to remain in a certain state or position." *Lie* never takes an object. The verb *lay* means "to put [something] in a place." *Lay* usually takes an object.

BASE FORM	PRESENT PARTICIPLE	PAST	PAST PARTICIPLE
lie *(rest)*	(is) lying	lay	(have) lain
lay *(put)*	(is) laying	laid	(have) laid

EXAMPLES   Your car keys **are lying** on the kitchen counter. [no object]
The servers **are laying** a napkin on each diner's plate. [*Napkin* is the object of *are laying.*]

The valedictorian spoke of the challenges that **lay** before the graduates. [no object]
Last winter we **laid** seed on the ground for the wild birds. [*Seed* is the object of *laid.*]

The clothes to be ironed **have lain** in the basket all week. [no object]
The state legislators **have laid** the matter before the voters. [*Matter* is the object of *have laid.*]

> ■▶ EXERCISE 6   **Choosing the Forms of *Lie* and *Lay***

For each of the following sentences, choose the correct present participle, past, or past participle form in parentheses.

1. If you are sick, you should be (<u>lying</u>, laying) down.
2. They (lay, <u>laid</u>) the heavy crate on the handcart.
3. Lucia's mother has always (lain, <u>laid</u>) a great deal of emphasis on bilingual education.
4. Amy (<u>lay</u>, laid) down for a while.
5. I left my gloves (<u>lying</u>, laying) on the counter.
6. She had just (<u>lain</u>, laid) down when the doorbell rang.
7. They (lay, <u>laid</u>) their plans before the committee.
8. The calf (<u>lay</u>, laid) on a pile of straw.
9. Kiyoshi (lay, <u>laid</u>) his paintbrush down and added more blue to his palette.
10. Don't leave your shoes (<u>lying</u>, laying) under the table.

Sit and *Set*

The verb *sit* means "to rest in an upright, seated position." *Sit* seldom takes an object. The verb *set* means "to put [something] in a place." *Set* usually takes an object.

BASE FORM	PRESENT PARTICIPLE	PAST	PAST PARTICIPLE
sit (*rest*)	(is) sitting	sat	(have) sat
set (*put*)	(is) setting	set	(have) set

MEETING *individual* NEEDS

LEP/ESL

General Strategies. Many speakers will use confusing verbs incorrectly because they hear the verbs spoken incorrectly. Students, therefore, may think that standard usage sounds incorrect. You could emphasize that writers use standard English because it is clear to all and that speakers can use either formal or informal English, depending on the audience. Stress that it is important for students to know both standard and nonstandard English in order to have options.

CRITICAL THINKING

Analysis. Have each student choose two television shows to view and analyze. Tell each student that he or she should watch one scene and write down the verbs that one of the characters uses. Students should repeat this activity with another scene and character. Then, have each student use the following questions as the basis for a summary of his or her findings:

1. Were the characters' choices standard or nonstandard?
2. Why are these characters appealing?
3. Describe the scenes in which these verbs were used.
4. Is there a connection between the scenes and the choice of language?

LESS-ADVANCED STUDENTS

Have students work in pairs to use the problem verbs in original cartoon strips. One person in each pair could be the illustrator, while the other partner could write the dialogue. These comic strips could be displayed on a bulletin board to highlight the troublesome verbs for other students.

ADVANCED STUDENTS

You may want to have students develop rules for using additional verb pairs that frequently cause problems—verbs such as *learn* and *teach* or *leave* and *let*. Ask students to write explanations of each of the verbs and to include sentences as examples of correct usage.

EXAMPLES   Where **should** we **sit**? [no object]
Where **should** I **set** this bag of groceries? [*Bag* is the object of *should set*.]

We **sat** in the bleachers behind the end zone at last night's game. [no object]
Liang **set** the platter of egg foo yong on the table. [*Platter* is the object of *set*.]

▶ **EXERCISE 7**   **Choosing the Forms of *Sit* and *Set***

For each of the following sentences, choose the <u>correct verb form</u> in parentheses.

1. After he had struck out, Pete (*sat*, *set*) on the bench.
2. Part of San Francisco's Chinatown (*sits*, *sets*) on an incline that overlooks the San Francisco Bay.
3. Where were the packages (*sitting*, *setting*) this morning?
4. We had (*sat*, *set*) the cushions on the plush chairs.
5. In Japan people often (*sit*, *set*) on tatami instead of chairs.
6. They were (*sitting*, *setting*) placemats on the table.
7. It makes no difference to me where you (*sit*, *set*).
8. We (*sat*, *set*) down our packs and got out our map.
9. Mr. Carr told me to (*sit*, *set*) the equipment on his desk.
10. I may never know who had (*sat*, *set*) on my glasses.

Rise and Raise

The verb *rise* means "to go up" or "to get up." *Rise* never takes an object. The verb *raise* means "to cause [something] to rise" or "to lift up." *Raise* usually takes an object.

BASE FORM	PRESENT PARTICIPLE	PAST	PAST PARTICIPLE
rise (*go up*)	(is) rising	rose	(have) risen
raise (*lift up*)	(is) raising	raised	(have) raised

EXAMPLES   Una **rose** from her desk and walked to the front of the classroom. [no object]
The players **raised** the coach onto their shoulders. [*Coach* is the object of *raised*.]

REVIEW E

OBJECTIVE

- To choose the correct forms of *lie* and *lay*, *sit* and *set*, and *rise* and *raise*

The number of women who work outside the home **has risen** steadily during the past decade. [no object]
The reporters **have raised** that issue at several press conferences. [*Issue* is the object of *have raised*.]

EXERCISE 8   Choosing the Forms of *Rise* and *Raise*

For each of the following sentences, choose the correct verb form in parentheses.

1. Air bubbles have been (*rising, raising*) to the surface.
2. Increasing the import duty will (*rise, raise*) retail prices.
3. The speaker (*rose, raised*) from her chair and took the mike.
4. This month, the star has been (*rising, raising*) in the east.
5. The rooster (*rises, raises*) early.
6. Before and during the Revolutionary War, many colonists worked hard to (*rise, raise*) public sentiment against King George III.
7. Balloons can (*rise, raise*) because they contain heated air, which is less dense than the surrounding air.
8. At the tribal council meeting, someone (*rose, raised*) the issue of land ownership within reservation boundaries.
9. Mist was (*rising, raising*) from the ground.
10. To make traditional challah, braid the bread dough after it has (*risen, raised*) for an hour.

REVIEW E   Choosing the Forms of *Lie* and *Lay,* *Sit* and *Set,* and *Rise* and *Raise*

For each of the following sentences, choose the correct verb form in parentheses.

1. All week that box has (*lain, laid*) unopened on the desk.
2. We (*rose, raised*) our hats to salute the astronauts.
3. The injured deer (*lay, laid*) motionless in the road.
4. Our applications were (*lying, laying*) in front of the file.
5. Would you like to (*sit, set*) with us at the powwow?
6. I always (*lie, lay*) the phone book on this table.
7. We arrived late and had to (*sit, set*) at the top of the bleachers.
8. Kathy sang as she (*lay, laid*) the baby in the crib.
9. Clean up the mess that's (*lying, laying*) on your floor.
10. Last night's victory really (*rose, raised*) the team's spirit and confidence.

MEETING individual NEEDS

LEARNING STYLES

Visual Learners. Have students make collages of pictures that illustrate the six troublesome verbs. Students could look in magazines for pictures of people performing the actions of the verbs, arrange their pictures on poster board, and write under each picture a sentence using the appropriate verb.

COOPERATIVE LEARNING

Have students work in pairs to write short verses using forms of *lie* and *lay*, *sit* and *set*, and *rise* and *raise*.

[Lying under summer skies,
I try to lay my troubles aside.
It would have been fun
if I could have laid them aside
before they troubled me.
Instead, though, I'll sit up,
set my priorities straight,
raise my spirits,
and rise to the occasion.]

OBJECTIVES

- To identify verb tense and to explain differences in meaning in pairs of sentences
- To identify the tenses that correctly express given meanings in sentences
- To use tenses correctly in writing an informative paragraph

11. Our potbellied pig Oscar often (*lies*, *lays*) in my lap when I watch TV.
12. Fred should (*lie*, *lay*) on his side to stop snoring.
13. After the fire, the museum (*lay*, *laid*) in a heap.
14. Tempers (*rose*, *raised*) as the debate progressed.
15. In Washington, D.C., we will (*lie*, *lay*) flowers at the Vietnam Veterans Memorial.
16. Mrs. Nasser (*sat*, *set*) the tabbouleh and kibbe next to other traditional Lebanese foods.
17. If you (*sit*, *set*) the pie on the ledge, it may vanish.
18. Billows of dust (*rose*, *raised*) up from the field.
19. Haven't they (*sat*, *set*) down the piano yet?
20. You should (*lie*, *lay*) on a padded surface to do exercises.

Tense

24d. The *tense* of a verb indicates the time of the action or state of being expressed by the verb.

Every verb has six tenses: *present, past, future, present perfect, past perfect,* and *future perfect.* These six tenses are formed from the principal parts of the verb. Listing all of the forms of a verb according to tense is called *conjugating* a verb.

CONJUGATION OF THE VERB *GIVE*			
PRINCIPAL PARTS			
BASE FORM	**PRESENT PARTICIPLE**	**PAST**	**PAST PARTICIPLE**
give	(is) giving	gave	(have) given
PRESENT TENSE			
SINGULAR		*PLURAL*	
I give		we give	
you give		you give	
he, she, it gives		they give	

(continued)

USAGE

PROGRAM MANAGER

TENSE

■ **Independent Practice/ Reteaching** For instruction and exercises, see **Tense** in *Language Skills Practice and Assessment,* p. 142.

■ **Computer Guided Instruction** For additional instruction and practice with verb tense, see **Lesson 10** in *Language Workshop CD-ROM.*

■ **Practice** To help less-advanced students with additional instruction and practice with verb tense, see **Chapter 16** in *English Workshop, Complete Course,* pp. 239–242.

QUICK REMINDER

Write the following sentences on the chalkboard and have students rewrite them by changing the verb to the tense indicated in parentheses:

1. Kilroy runs faster than anyone else in his class. (past) [ran]
2. Samantha is a lifeguard at the beach. (future) [will be]
3. Keesha wants to be a doctor. (present perfect) [has wanted]
4. The weight lifter really pressed fifty pounds. (past perfect) [had pressed]
5. Stopping that oil-well fire cost over a billion dollars. (future perfect) [will have cost]

24d

CONJUGATION OF THE VERB *GIVE* (continued)

PAST TENSE

SINGULAR	PLURAL
I gave	we gave
you gave	you gave
he, she, it gave	they gave

FUTURE TENSE
(*will* or *shall* + base form)

SINGULAR	PLURAL
I will (shall) give	we will (shall) give
you will give	you will give
he, she, it will give	they will give

PRESENT PERFECT TENSE
(*have* or *has* + past participle)

SINGULAR	PLURAL
I have given	we have given
you have given	you have given
he, she, it has given	they have given

PAST PERFECT TENSE
(*had* + past participle)

SINGULAR	PLURAL
I had given	we had given
you had given	you had given
he, she, it had given	they had given

FUTURE PERFECT TENSE
(*will have* or *shall have* + past participle)

SINGULAR	PLURAL
I will (shall) have given	we will (shall) have given
you will have given	you will have given
he, she, it will have given	they will have given

USAGE

Each tense has an additional form called the *progressive form,* which expresses continuing action or state of being. In each tense, the progressive form of a verb consists of the appropriate tense of *be* plus the verb's present participle. Some tenses also include one or more helping verbs.

MEETING *individual* NEEDS

LEP/ESL

General Strategies. To help students with the present-perfect verb form, you might use the following oral exercise. Give each student a question to ask the other members of the class. Have each student use one of the following questions:

1. Have you ever ridden a horse?
2. Have you ever been to Canada?
3. Have you ever slept outside?
4. Have you ever seen a flamingo?
5. Have you ever had the mumps?

The rhythmic repetition of a phrase is a key method of language acquisition and will help students fix this construction in their minds.

Asian Languages. Some languages, such as Chinese, Lao, Indonesian, and Vietnamese, do not use verb tenses to indicate time. Instead, a speaker will use either context or an adverb to establish the time of the events being discussed. The idea of specifying tense in every sentence might seem redundant to some students; therefore, they might use only the present tense. Emphasize that in English, the correct tense must be used in every sentence if the reader is to understand what has been written.

USAGE

Literature Link. Students are told to be consistent in their use of verb tense and are often confused when they read a short story that incorporates several tenses. Tell students to read a short story and to identify the various tenses it incorporates. Ask students why they think short stories often include so many different verb tenses. [A short story is a fictional narrative that relates a series of events. In order to show the sequence of events, several tenses often must be used.]

USAGE

USAGE

Present Progressive	**am, is, are giving**
Past Progressive	**was, were giving**
Future Progressive	**will (shall) be giving**
Present Perfect Progressive	**has been, have been giving**
Past Perfect Progressive	**had been giving**
Future Perfect Progressive	**will (shall) have been giving**

Only the present and the past tenses have another form called the *emphatic form,* which shows emphasis. In the present tense, the emphatic form of a verb consists of *do* or *does* plus the verb's base form. In the past tense, the emphatic form consists of *did* plus the verb's base form.

Present Emphatic	I **do** not **intend** to give up.
	Although the grass is green, the lawn **does need** watering.
Past Emphatic	The explorers suffered many hardships, yet they **did** finally **reach** their destination.

The conjugation of the verb *be* is somewhat different from that of other verbs. Notice that only the present and past tenses of *be* have the progressive form and that none of the tenses has the emphatic form.

CONJUGATION OF THE VERB *BE*			
PRINCIPAL PARTS			
BASE FORM	**PRESENT PARTICIPLE**	**PAST**	**PAST PARTICIPLE**
be	(is) being	was, were	(have) been
PRESENT TENSE			
SINGULAR		*PLURAL*	
I am		we are	
you are		you are	
he, she, it is		they are	
Present Progressive: am, is, are being			
PAST TENSE			
SINGULAR		*PLURAL*	
I was		we were	
you were		you were	
he, she, it was		they were	
Past Progressive: was, were being			

(continued)

USAGE

USAGE

CONJUGATION OF THE VERB *BE* (continued)	
FUTURE TENSE (*will* or *shall* + base form)	
SINGULAR	*PLURAL*
I will (shall) be	we will (shall) be
you will be	you will be
he, she, it will be	they will be
PRESENT PERFECT TENSE (*have* or *has* + past participle)	
SINGULAR	*PLURAL*
I have been	we have been
you have been	you have been
he, she, it has been	they have been
PAST PERFECT TENSE (*had* + past participle)	
SINGULAR	*PLURAL*
I had been	we had been
you had been	you had been
he, she, it had been	they had been
FUTURE PERFECT TENSE (*will have* or *shall have* + past participle)	
SINGULAR	*PLURAL*
I will (shall) have been	we will (shall) have beer
you will have been	you will have been
he, she, it will have been	they will have been

The Uses of the Tenses

24e. Each of the six tenses has its own special uses.

(1) The *present tense* is used mainly to express an action or state of being that is occurring now.

EXAMPLES   Ashley and Ira **wait** patiently for the bus. [present]
Ashley and Ira **are waiting** patiently for the bus.
[present progressive]
Ashley and Ira **do wait** patiently for the bus. [present emphatic]

COOPERATIVE LEARNING

Have students work in groups of three or four to engage in a game of writing roulette. Ask one student in each group to begin a short story relating a series of events. When you call time, the student will pass his or her paper to another student in the group, and the student who receives the paper will begin adding to the narrative. However, when you call time, also call out the new tense for the next writing period. Tell students to begin a new paragraph with this new tense. Have groups continue passing papers until students have written in all tenses. Encourage students to make the shift in tense smoothly and logically. You may want students to read their stories to the class.

792 *Correct Form and Use of Verbs*

The present tense is also used

- to show a customary or habitual action or state of being
- to state a general truth—something that is always true
- to summarize the plot or subject matter of a literary work (such use is called the *literary present*)
- to make a historical event seem current (such use is called the *historical present*)
- to express future time

EXAMPLES   After school I **wash** the breakfast dishes and **start** supper. [customary action]
In the Northern Hemisphere the summer solstice **occurs** when the sun is farthest from the equator. [general truth]
Countee Cullen **uses** traditional verse forms to explore African American themes. [literary present]
In 1520, Ferdinand Magellan **rounds** the southern tip of South America and **names** the ocean that **lies** before him the Pacific Ocean. [historical present]
The movie that **opens** tomorrow **runs** through next week. [future time]

(2) The *past tense* is used to express an action or state of being that occurred in the past but did not continue into the present.

EXAMPLES   I **stayed** at the library until closing time. [past]
I **was researching** the life of Timothy Thomas Fortune, a civil rights advocate in the 1800s. [past progressive]
My research **did provide** me with enough information for my paper on Fortune. [past emphatic]

NOTE: A past action or state of being may also be shown in another way.
EXAMPLE   She **used to collect** stamps.

(3) The *future tense* is used to express an action or a state of being that will occur. The future tense is formed with *will* or *shall* and the verb's base form.

EXAMPLES   I **will attend** the University of Iowa in the fall. [future]
I **will be attending** the University of Iowa in the fall. [future progressive]

NOTE: A future action or state of being may also be expressed by using

- the present tense of *be* with *going to* and the base form of a verb

- the present tense of *be* with *about to* and the base form of a verb
- the present tense of a verb with a word or phrase that expresses future time

EXAMPLES   My aunt and uncle **are going to visit** the Philippines.
Mr. Campos **is about to open** the time capsule.
Finals **begin next Monday.**

(4) The *present perfect tense* is used mainly to express an action or a state of being that occurred at some indefinite time in the past. The present perfect tense always includes the helping verb *have* or *has*.

EXAMPLES   I **have written** to the governor, but I **have** not **received** a reply. [present perfect]
Who **has been playing** my cassettes? [present perfect progressive]

NOTE: Avoid the use of the present perfect tense to express a *specific* time in the past. Instead, use the past tense.

NONSTANDARD   *Prairie Schooner* has published a new short story by Louise Erdrich last month.
STANDARD   *Prairie Schooner* **published** a new short story by Louise Erdrich last month.

The present perfect tense is also used to express action (or a state of being) that began in the past and continues into the present.

EXAMPLES   The International Sister City program **has existed** for more than thirty-five years. [present perfect]
The program **has been pairing** cities in the United States with cities in other nations since 1956. [present perfect progressive]

(5) The *past perfect tense* is used mainly to express an action or a state of being that was completed in the past before some other past occurrence. The past perfect tense always includes the helping verb *had*.

EXAMPLES   I finally remembered where I **had seen** a copy of Rufino Tamayo's mural *Nature and the Artist.* [The seeing occurred before the remembering.]
I **had been looking** through dozens of old magazines before I finally remembered to check the latest issue of *Smithsonian.* [past perfect progressive]

USAGE

? CRITICAL THINKING
Synthesis. Have students apply what they have learned about future and future perfect tenses by writing literary paragraphs that describe what they think school will be like two hundred years from now. After students finish their drafts, tell them to underline their verbs, to check their papers for correctness, and to write final drafts to share with the class.

USAGE

USAGE

ANSWERS
Exercise 9

1. past tense—indicates that Margo's stay in Brazil began and ended at a specific time; present perfect tense—indicates that Margo still lives in Brazil

2. past perfect tense—indicates an action that was completed before some other past occurrence; present perfect progressive tense—indicates an action that began at some indefinite time in the past and that is continuing at the present time

3. present perfect tense—indicates that the directions were explained at some indefinite time in the past; past perfect tense—indicates that the directions were explained in the past before some other past occurrence

4. past progressive tense—indicates an action that began and ended at a specific time; past perfect progressive tense—indicates that she was driving in the past before some other past occurrence

5. future perfect tense—indicates that taxes will be raised in the future before some other future occurrence; future progressive tense—indicates that the action of raising taxes will occur and is continuous

ANSWERS
Exercise 10

1. a. present perfect
   b. past perfect

2. a. present progressive
   b. future progressive

3. a. present perfect progressive
   b. past

4. a. present
   b. present progressive

5. a. past perfect
   b. past

---

(6) The *future perfect tense* is used to express an action or a state of being that will be completed in the future before some other future occurrence. The future perfect tense always includes *will have* or *shall have.*

EXAMPLES By the time I leave Chicago, my letter **will have arrived** in Pittsburgh. [The letter's arriving will occur before my leaving.]
By then, you **will have been waiting** for it for more than a week. [future perfect progressive]

EXERCISE 9   Understanding the Uses of the Six Tenses

Identify the tenses of the verbs in each of the following pairs of sentences. Be prepared to explain how these differences in tense alter the meanings of the sentences.

1. Margo lived in Brazil for eight years.
   Margo has lived in Brazil for eight years.
2. Why had she gone to the theater?
   Why has she been going to the theater?
3. Have the directions been explained clearly?
   Had the directions been explained clearly?
4. Was she driving?
   Had she been driving?
5. As of June 30, they will have raised taxes twice this year.
   As of June 30, they will be raising taxes twice this year.

EXERCISE 10   Understanding the Uses of the Six Tenses

Identify which sentence in each pair correctly expresses the meaning given. Be prepared to name the tenses used in each sentence.

1. *Meaning:* John still works for Mr. Porzio.
   a. John has worked for Mr. Porzio for a year.
   b. John had worked for Mr. Porzio for a year.
2. *Meaning:* Ann Rosine could be on her way to Worcester right now or could be going later.
   a. Ann Rosine is moving to Worcester, Massachusetts.
   b. Ann Rosine will be moving to Worcester, Massachusetts.
3. *Meaning:* Jaime is still studying physics.
   a. Jaime has been studying physics since last summer.
   b. Jaime studied physics last summer.

4. *Meaning:* Alison takes a bus to work on a regular basis.
   (a.) Alison takes the bus to work.
   b. Alison is taking the bus to work.
5. *Meaning:* Ray was a bank officer at the age of twenty-four.
   (a.) When Ray turned twenty-five, he had been promoted to the position of bank officer.
   b. When Ray turned twenty-five, he was promoted to the position of bank officer.

PICTURE THIS

The year is 2993. Due to a computer error, certain historical records have been erased from the World Archives. You are a member of the task force whose job is to travel back in time to collect factual information that will fill in the gaps in the record. Because you have a special interest in twentieth-century entertainment, you've slipped into this movie audience and put on a pair of the optical devices they're wearing. Take careful notes for your records. Describe the experience of viewing a movie, and also explain the purpose of wearing the strange devices. Compare this experience to one that you're familiar with in the thirtieth century. Be sure to use verb tenses that accurately express your meaning.

Subject: viewing a movie through 3-D glasses
Audience: people in the thirtieth century
Purpose: to inform

PICTURE THIS

Tell students it probably will be easier to write their informative paragraphs if they concentrate first on content. After they complete first drafts, they can check to make sure they have used each of the six verb tenses. You could have students work in pairs during the revision stage as they check for correct use of tenses.

USAGE

USAGE

SPECIAL PROBLEMS IN THE USE OF TENSES Rules 24f–24k

OBJECTIVE

- To identify and correct errors in the use of verb tenses

PROGRAM MANAGER

SPECIAL PROBLEMS IN THE USE OF TENSES

- **Independent Practice/Reteaching** For instruction and exercises, see **Special Problems in the Use of Tenses** in *Language Skills Practice and Assessment,* p. 143.

- **Computer Guided Instruction** For additional instruction and practice with special problems in the use of tenses, see **Lesson 12** in *Language Workshop CD-ROM.*

- **Practice** To help less-advanced students with additional instruction and practice with special problems in the use of tenses, see **Chapter 17** in *English Workshop, Complete Course,* pp. 243–246.

USAGE

QUICK REMINDER

Write the following sentences on the chalkboard. Have students correct the tenses of the underlined verbs.

1. The bus stops, and the driver <u>opened</u> the door. [present tense: *opens*]
2. The singer wept and <u>will leave</u> the stage. [past tense: *left*]

USAGE

Special Problems in the Use of Tenses

Sequence of Tenses

24f. Use tense forms carefully to show the correct relationship between verbs in a sentence.

(1) When describing events that occur at the same time, use verbs in the same tense.

EXAMPLES The bell **rings,** and the classroom **empties.** [present tense]
The bell **rang,** and the classroom **emptied.** [past tense]

(2) When describing events that occur at different times, use verbs in different tenses to show the order of events.

EXAMPLES I **play** football now, but I **played** basketball in junior high. [Because I am playing football now, the present tense form *play* is correct. My playing basketball occurred in the past and did not continue into the present; therefore, the past tense is correct.]
Sabrena **mentioned** that she **had invited** some of her neighbors to the party. [Because Sabrena made the statement in the past, the past tense form *mentioned* is correct. She invited the neighbors before she made the statement; therefore, the past perfect form *had invited* is correct.]

The tense you use depends on the meaning you want to express.

EXAMPLES I **believe** they **own** the Flamingo Cafe. [Both verbs are in the present tense to indicate that both actions are occurring now.]
I **believe** they **owned** the Flamingo Cafe. [The change to the past tense in the second verb implies that they no longer own the Flamingo Cafe.]

Joan **said** that she **worked** at the textile mill. [Both verbs are in the past tense to indicate that both actions no longer occur.]
Joan **said** that she **will work** at the textile mill. [The change in the second verb implies that Joan did not work at the textile mill when she made the statement but that she planned to work there.]

24g. **Avoid the use of *would have* in "if clauses" that express the earlier of two past actions. Use the past perfect tense.**

NONSTANDARD	If he would have taken more time, he would have won.
STANDARD	If he **had taken** more time, he would have won.
NONSTANDARD	I would not have been late if I would have had a watch.
STANDARD	I would not have been late if I **had had** a watch.
NONSTANDARD	If you would have stopped by, you could have met my cousin.
STANDARD	If you **had stopped** by, you could have met my cousin.

▶ EXERCISE 11   **Using Tenses Correctly**

Each of the following sentences contains an error in the use of tenses. Identify the error, and then give the correct form of the verb.

1. Pam finally appreciated the old saying that every cloud ~~had~~ a silver lining.   **1. has**
2. By the time we graduate in June, Ms. Vargas will ~~be~~ teaching Spanish for twenty-four years.
3. Although Denny's skill ~~was~~ demonstrated during the season, he was not chosen to play in the All-Star game.
4. If they ~~would have~~ called sooner, we would have given them a ride.   **4. had**
5. When Jeremy finally got to the dentist, his tooth already stopped hurting.   **5. had**
6. The company hired Ms. Littmann because she lived for many years in Japan.   **6. had**
7. By the time I presented my report before the committee, the members ~~have~~ already studied several other reports on nuclear waste disposal.   **7. had**
8. Mr. Frey already complained to the neighbors many times before he called the police.   **8. had**
9. By then I will ~~receive~~ my first paycheck.
10. If she ~~forgot~~ the directions, we could have been lost.
11. Hiram R. Revels, the first African American senator, ~~was~~ a minister and teacher before he entered politics.   **11. had been**

2. have been

3. had been

9. have received

10. had forgotten

USAGE

USAGE

COMMON ERROR

Problem. Students sometimes make inappropriate shifts in tenses.

Solution. Remind students of the following rules to help them with the present perfect tense, the past perfect tense, and the future perfect tense.

1. *Have* and *has* are present tense. Combining either of these verbs with a past participle will form the present perfect tense.

2. *Had* is the past tense. It is combined with the past participle of a verb to create the past perfect tense.

3. *Will have* is future tense, and it is combined with the past participle of a verb to create the future perfect tense.

USAGE

USAGE

12. If they had enough money, they could have taken a taxi to the opening of that new musical. **12.** had
13. As I thought about our argument, I was sure you lost your temper first. **13.** had
14. Next Saturday is a very important anniversary for Mai's family; they will be living in the United States for exactly one year. **14.** have been
15. When we reviewed the videotapes of the game, we saw that the other team committed the foul. **15.** had
16. The clerk remembered that the manager has ordered the new shipment last Tuesday. **16.** had   **17.** includes
17. How could I have forgotten the United Kingdom included England, Wales, Scotland, and Northern Ireland?
18. We estimate that when we're in our forties, we will be working more than twenty years. **18.** have been   **19.** had
19. If Gary would have read the ad more carefully, he could have saved more than fifty dollars on his new camera.
20. J.D. would have done much better on the art history exam if he reviewed the chapter on Aztec stonework.

20. had

The Present Infinitive and the Present Perfect Infinitive

PRESENT INFINITIVE	to be	to discover
PRESENT PERFECT INFINITIVE	to have been	to have discovered

24h. The *present infinitive* is used to express an action or a state of being that occurs after another action or state of being.

EXAMPLES Charlotte had expected **to go** with us. [The action expressed by *to go* follows the action expressed by *had expected*.]

Charlotte had planned **to ask** her boss for time off. [The action expressed by *to ask* follows the action expressed by *had planned*.]

24i. The *present perfect infinitive* is used to express an action or a state of being that occurs before another action or state of being.

EXAMPLES   My little brother pretended **to have read** my diary. [The action expressed by *to have read* precedes the action expressed by *pretended*.]
I would like **to have gone** to the movie with you. [The action expressed by *to have gone* precedes the action expressed by *would like*.]

☞ **REFERENCE NOTE:** For more information about infinitives and how they are used, see pages 663–664.

The Present Participle and the Present Perfect Participle

PRESENT PARTICIPLE	being	discovering
PRESENT PERFECT PARTICIPLE	having been	having discovered

USAGE

24j.   The *present participle* is used to express an action or a state of being that occurs at the same time as another action or state of being.

> **Receiving** word of their freedom in June 1865, former slaves in Texas created the Juneteenth holiday. [The action expressed by *receiving* occurs at the same time as the action expressed by *created*.]
> **Celebrating** Juneteenth this year, my family gathered at my grandmother's house on June 19. [The action expressed by *celebrating* occurs at the same time as the action expressed by *gathered*.]

24k.   The *present perfect participle* is used to express an action or a state of being that comes before another action or state of being.

EXAMPLES   **Having missed** the midterm exam, I took a makeup test. [The action expressed by *having missed* precedes the action expressed by *took*.]
Having been accepted by several colleges, Rosa chose one. [The action expressed by *having been accepted* precedes the action expressed by *chose*.]

☞ **REFERENCE NOTE:** For more information about participles and how they are used, see pages 657–658.

CRITICAL THINKING

Synthesis. Ask students to work in pairs to apply the rules they have learned in this lesson. Ask one student in each group to write an "if clause" that uses the past perfect tense, and ask their partners to write the second half of the sentence. After students have written three sentences, ask them to switch roles.

USAGE

ACTIVE VOICE AND PASSIVE VOICE Rules 24l, 24m

OBJECTIVE

• To revise sentences in the passive voice

EXERCISE 12 Using Tenses Correctly

Each of the following sentences contains an error in the use of verbs. Identify the error and then give the correct form of the verb.

1. ~~Spending~~ three hours on a review of chemistry, we then worked on irregular French verbs. **1.** Having spent
2. Tutankhamen, Helen of Troy, and Shakespeare are the three people I would have most liked to ~~have met~~. **2.** meet
3. To ~~have written~~ about Pueblo ceremonies, I would have to do more research. **3.** write (see below for alternative answer)
4. ~~Flying~~ from Missouri to California before, we remembered to set our watches back. **4.** Having flown
5. We wanted to ~~have avoided~~ any controversy. **5.** avoid
6. ~~Having attempted~~ to travel across the African continent, the explorers encountered both vast deserts and dense swamp forests. **6.** Attempting
7. Native Arctic peoples learned to ~~have survived~~ in a harsh environment. **7.** survive
8. They were hoping to have ~~had~~ a multiple-choice test in history instead of an essay exam.
9. If you ~~want~~ to go shopping, I would have driven you to the mall. **9.** had wanted (see below for alternative answer)
10. ~~Standing~~ in line for more than two hours, Tamisha finally got tickets to the Pam Tillis concert. **10.** Having stood

3. To have written about Pueblo ceremonies, I would have had to do more research.
9. If you want to go shopping, I will drive you to the mall.

Active Voice and Passive Voice

24l. *Voice* is the form a transitive verb takes to indicate whether the subject of the verb performs or receives the action.

☞ **REFERENCE NOTE:** For more information about transitive verbs, see page 612.

Transitive verbs may be in the *active voice* or the *passive voice*. When the subject of a verb performs the action, the verb is in the **active voice.** When the subject receives the action, the verb is in the **passive voice.**

As the examples on the next page show, verbs in the active voice take objects, and verbs in the passive voice do not.

USAGE

ACTIVE VOICE AND PASSIVE VOICE

■ **Independent Practice/ Reteaching** For instruction and exercises, see **Active and Passive Voice** in *Language Skills Practice and Assessment*, p. 144.

■ **Computer Guided Instruction** For additional instruction and practice with active and passive voice, see **Lesson 13** in *Language Workshop CD-ROM.*

■ **Practice** To help less-advanced students with additional instruction and practice with active and passive voice, see **Chapter 17** in *English Workshop, Complete Course*, pp. 247–248.

✔ QUICK REMINDER

Write the verbs *terminate, build,* and *adopt* on the chalkboard. Ask students to compose for each verb one sentence in the active voice and one sentence in the passive voice.

ACTIVE VOICE	Mark Riley **anchors** the local evening news. [*News* is the direct object.]
PASSIVE VOICE	The local evening news **is anchored** by Mark Riley.
ACTIVE VOICE	Han **took** many of the photos in the yearbook. [*Many* is the direct object.]
PASSIVE VOICE	Many of the photos in the yearbook **were taken** by Han.
ACTIVE VOICE	The firefighters **have extinguished** the blazing fire. [*Fire* is the direct object.]
PASSIVE VOICE	The blazing fire **has been extinguished** by the firefighters.
PASSIVE VOICE	The fire **has been extinguished.**

From these examples, you can see how an active construction can become a passive construction.

- The object of the verb in the active voice becomes the subject of the verb in the passive voice.
- The subject of the verb in the active voice becomes an object of the preposition *by*. (As the last example shows, this prepositional phrase is not always necessary.)

The Retained Object

A verb in the active voice often has an indirect object as well as a direct object. When such a verb is put into the passive voice, either object can become the subject. The other object then serves as a complement called a *retained object.*

	S V IO DO
ACTIVE	Mrs. Platero gives each new employee a tour of the plant.
PASSIVE	Each new employee is given a tour of the plant (by Mrs. Platero). [The indirect object *employee* becomes the subject, and the direct object *tour* becomes the retained object.]
PASSIVE	A tour of the plant is given each new employee (by Mrs. Platero). [The direct object *tour* becomes the subject, and the indirect object *employee* becomes the retained object.]

A verb in the passive voice always includes a form of *be* and the verb's past participle. The form of *be* and the helping verb, if any, indicate the tense of the verb phrase.

USAGE

ADVANCED STUDENTS

Tell students that although, as a general rule, they should avoid using the passive voice, there are times when it is effective. For example, the passive voice can be used to neutralize the sense of action, to create a sense of evasiveness, or to create suspense in writing. Have students look in magazines or newspapers for examples of effective use of the passive voice. You may want to ask students to share their examples of passive voice with the class and to explain why those examples are effective.

USAGE

LEP/ESL

General Strategies. Some students have difficulty in forming the passive voice because several helping verbs must be correctly sequenced. Using the conjugation of the verb *give* as a model, have students practice changing active-voice sentences with transitive verbs to passive-voice sentences.

COMMON ERROR

Problem. Students might over-use passive voice and thus produce weak writing.

Solution. Have students circle passive-voice forms in their writing assignments and then determine which could be changed to make the writing more lively and forceful.

USAGE

USAGE

802 *Correct Form and Use of Verbs*

CONJUGATION OF THE VERB *GIVE* IN THE PASSIVE VOICE	
PRESENT TENSE	
SINGULAR	*PLURAL*
I am given	we are given
you are given	you are given
he, she, it is given	they are given
Present Progressive: am, are, is being given	
PAST TENSE	
SINGULAR	*PLURAL*
I was given	we were given
you were given	you were given
he, she, it was given	they were given
Past Progressive: was, were being given	
FUTURE TENSE (*will* or *shall be* + past participle)	
SINGULAR	*PLURAL*
I will (shall) be given	we will (shall) be given
you will be given	you will be given
he, she, it will be given	they will be given
Future Progressive: will (shall) be being given	
PRESENT PERFECT TENSE (*have* or *has been* + past participle)	
SINGULAR	*PLURAL*
I have been given	we have been given
you have been given	you have been given
he, she, it has been given	they have been given
PAST PERFECT TENSE (*had been* + past participle)	
SINGULAR	*PLURAL*
I had been given	we had been given
you had been given	you had been given
he, she, it had been given	they had been given
FUTURE PERFECT TENSE (*will* or *shall have been* + past participle)	
SINGULAR	*PLURAL*
I will (shall) have been given	we will (shall) have been given
you will have been given	you will have been given
he, she, it will have been given	they will have been given

☞ **REFERENCE NOTE:** The conjugation of *give* in the active voice is on pages 788–789.

24m

The Uses of the Passive Voice

24m. Use the passive voice sparingly.

Choosing between the active voice and the passive voice is a matter of style, not correctness. In general, however, the passive voice is less direct, less forceful, and less concise than the active voice. In fact, the passive voice may produce an awkward effect.

AWKWARD PASSIVE	The final event was completed when a triple somersault was done by Mario.
ACTIVE	Mario **completed** the final event by doing a triple somersault.
AWKWARD PASSIVE	Steady rains were hoped for by all of us, but a hurricane was wanted by none of us.
ACTIVE	All of us **hoped** for steady rains, but none of us wanted a hurricane.

A string of passives is particularly awkward.

STRING OF PASSIVES	I was invited by Ms. Long to visit her animal shelter. Rows of cages had been placed along two sides of a large storage shed. Dozens of cats, dogs, hamsters, and guinea pigs were held in the cages. A large parrot was even spotted by me. In one corner of the noisy building, a scrawny, brown puppy was being hand-fed by an assistant. Ms. Long said so many unwanted pets had been brought to her by people, homes could not be found for all of them. It was agreed by us that the responsibility of owning a pet should be understood by people before one is bought.
ACTIVE	Ms. Long **invited** me to visit her animal shelter. She **had placed** rows of cages along two sides of a large storage shed. The cages **held** dozens of cats, dogs, hamsters, and guinea pigs. I even **spotted** a large parrot. In one corner of the noisy building, an assistant **was hand-feeding** a scrawny, brown puppy. Ms. Long said people **had brought** her so many unwanted pets that she **could** not **find** homes for all of them. We agreed that people **should understand** the responsibility of owning a pet before they **buy** one.

USAGE

INTEGRATING THE LANGUAGE ARTS

Grammar and Writing. Ask your students to write brief narratives in the passive voice about experiences they have had. Ask volunteers to read their papers aloud. The class should listen carefully to the readers. Then, have students change their narratives to the active voice. Have volunteers read the revised narratives aloud. Discuss the differences that the use of the active voice makes.

TECHNOLOGY TIP

There are computer programs that can check writing for overuse of the passive voice. You may want to encourage students to use such programs, if the equipment is available.

COOPERATIVE LEARNING

To help students understand the difference between active and passive voice, ask students to work in groups of three to rewrite news articles that use the passive voice. After students have finished, ask groups to list reasons that the active-voice versions of the articles are more effective.

USAGE

Passive voice constructions are not always awkward. In fact, the passive voice is useful in the following situations:

(1) when you do not know who performed the action

EXAMPLE   All of the tickets **had been sold** weeks before the concert.

(2) when you do not want to reveal the performer

EXAMPLE   Shoddy work **was done** on the building.

(3) when you want to emphasize the receiver of the action rather than the performer

EXAMPLES   Lasers **are used** in industry, communications, and medicine.
Ivy Swan **has been emulated** by many young singers.

▶ **EXERCISE 13**   **Revising Sentences in the Passive Voice**

Revise the following sentences by changing verbs in the passive voice to active voice wherever you think the change is desirable. If you think the passive is preferable, write *C*. For each sentence, be prepared to explain why you kept or changed the passive voice verb.

1. After the new computers had been installed by the service reps, a training session was given to us by them.
2. If the children had been enchanted by Mr. Wright's tales before, they would be even more enthralled by his new story of a fantasy kingdom.
3. A community meeting was held by the area homeowners to discuss the landfill project, which had been proposed by the City Council.
4. The value of storytelling is explained in an ancient Seneca myth.
5. While the decorations are being created by Clarence, the buffet will be prepared by Edna.
6. Potatoes had been cultivated by the Incas for more than twenty centuries before they were grown by Europeans.
7. The 1539 expedition of Francisco Vásquez de Coronado was guided by Estevanico, a well-known black explorer.
8. The chapters on constitutional amendments, which had been assigned to us last week by Mrs. Robinson, were reviewed by us before the test.

ANSWERS
Exercise 13

Answers will vary. Here are possibilities.

1. The service reps gave us a training session after they had installed the computers.
2. C
3. Area homeowners held a community meeting to discuss the landfill project, which had been proposed by the City Council.
4. C
5. While Clarence creates the decorations, Edna will prepare the buffet.
6. The Incas had cultivated potatoes for more than twenty centuries before the Europeans grew them.
7. Estevanico, a well-known black explorer, guided the 1539 expedition of Francisco Vásquez de Coronado.
8. Before the test, we reviewed the chapters on constitutional amendments, which Mrs. Robinson had assigned to us last week.
9. C
10. If Mike Smith had demonstrated the practicality of home robots, the committee would not have rejected his request for funding.

OBJECTIVE

- To use the subjunctive mood correctly

9. Shinae Chun is admired and respected by her colleagues.
10. If the practicality of home robots had been demonstrated by Mike Smith, his request for funding would not have been rejected by the committee.

Mood

Mood is the form that a verb takes to indicate the attitude of the person using the verb. Verbs may be in one of three moods: *indicative, imperative,* or *subjunctive.*

24n. The *indicative mood* is used to express a fact, an opinion, or a question.

EXAMPLES   Heitor Villa-Lobos **was** a composer who **became** known for his use of Brazilian folk music.
Amy Tan **is** a gifted writer.
Can you **tell** me when the United States **entered** World War I?

☞ **REFERENCE NOTE:** For examples of all of the tense forms in the indicative mood, see the conjugations on pages 788–789 and 790–791.

24o. The *imperative mood* is used to express a request or a command.

A verb in the imperative mood has only one form. That form is the same as the verb's base form.

EXAMPLES   **Tell** me when the United States entered World War I.
Please **pass** the salsa.

24p. The *subjunctive mood* is used to express a suggestion, a necessity, a condition contrary to fact, or a wish.

In the subjunctive mood, only the present tense and the past tense have distinctive forms. The other tense forms are the same as those in the indicative mood.

PROGRAM MANAGER

MOOD

- **Independent Practice/ Reteaching** For instruction and exercises, see **Mood** in *Language Skills Practice and Assessment,* p. 145.

- **Computer Guided Instruction** For additional instruction and practice with mood, see **Lesson 14** in *Language Workshop CD-ROM.*

- **Practice** To help less-advanced students with additional instruction and practice with mood, see **Chapter 17** in *English Workshop, Complete Course,* pp. 249–250.

✔ QUICK REMINDER

Ask students to determine the mood of each of the following sentences:

1. I am writing an essay. [indicative; this sentence expresses a fact]
2. Write an essay about careers in medicine. [imperative; this sentence expresses a command]
3. If I were writing about careers in medicine, I would have selected surgical nursing. [subjunctive; this sentence expresses a condition contrary to fact]

USAGE

USAGE

INTEGRATING THE LANGUAGE ARTS

Usage and Writing. Remind students that the imperative mood relies on an implied *you* to achieve a command. Provide students with the following examples to help them understand the implied *you.*

1. (You) Turn off the radio immediately.
2. (You) Draw a circle around the verb phrase.

Notice in the following partial conjugation of *be* how the present tense and the past tense in the subjunctive mood differ from those in the indicative mood. [Note: The use of *that* and *if,* which are shown in parentheses, is explained on this page and on page 807.]

PRESENT INDICATIVE		PRESENT SUBJUNCTIVE	
SINGULAR	*PLURAL*	*SINGULAR*	*PLURAL*
I am	we are	(that) I be	(that) we be
you are	you are	(that) you be	(that) you be
he is	they are	(that) he be	(that) they be
PAST INDICATIVE		PAST SUBJUNCTIVE	
I was	we were	(if) I were	(if) we were
you were	you were	(if) you were	(if) you were
he was	they were	(if) he were	(if) they were

The present subjunctive form of a verb is the same as its base form. *Be* is the only verb whose past subjunctive form is different from its past form.

Miss Peach courtesy of Mell Lazarus and Creators Syndicate. © 1991, Mell Lazarus.

(1) The *present subjunctive* is used to express a suggestion or a necessity.

The verb in a subordinate clause beginning with *that* is usually in the subjunctive mood when a word in the independent clause indicates a suggestion (such as *ask, request, suggest,* or *recommend*) or a necessity (such as *necessary* or *essential*).

EXAMPLES We recommended that Marva Collins **be invited** to speak.
The students have urged that John **be reinstated.**
I move that the motion **be approved.**
It is essential that she **have** a chance to compete.

(2) The *past subjunctive* is used to express a condition contrary to fact or to express a wish.

A clause beginning with *if*, *as if*, or *as though* often expresses a condition contrary to fact—something that is not true. In such a clause, use the past subjunctive.

EXAMPLES   If I **were** you, I'd be pleased.
            If she **were** to apply, she would undoubtedly be admitted.
            My friend Doris teases me as though she **were** my sister.

Similarly, use the past subjunctive to express a wish.

EXAMPLES   I wish I **were** on a Caribbean island.
            Jaime wishes that his mother **weren't** feeling ill.

▶ **EXERCISE 14   Using the Subjunctive Mood Correctly**

Some of the following sentences contain errors in the use of the subjunctive mood. If a sentence is incorrect, give the correct form of the verb. If a sentence is correct, write *C*.

1. Willis had insisted that every employee is invited to the company's Juneteenth picnic.   **1.** be
2. I'd be a lobster fisherman if I was living on Cape Cod.   **2.** were
3. Gloria was confused all day because it seemed as though it was Friday, but it was only Thursday.   **3.** were
4. Striking out again, Katie moaned, "I wish I was a better hitter!"   **4.** were
5. Vernon lost many of his friends when he began acting as if he were better than they.   **5.** C
6. If bowling was an elective at our school, Lisa and Joshua would be at the front of the line to sign up for it.   **6.** were
7. "I wish this book was a little shorter," sighed Sabrena as she turned to page 378.   **7.** were
8. We often complain about working too many hours; but if we were to work fewer, we would be complaining about smaller paychecks.   **8.** C
9. I wish I was able to go to the sneak preview of the new Spike Lee movie, but I have to work.   **9.** were
10. "I wish this was next year so that I would already be in college," Takala said.   **10.** were

USAGE

REVIEWS F and G

OBJECTIVE

• To proofread sentences and a paragraph for errors in the form and use of verbs

▶ **REVIEW F**

Proofreading Sentences for Errors in the Form and Use of Verbs

For each of the following sentences, correct the error in the form or use of the verb.

1. If we ~~would have~~ checked, we'd have known the library was closed.   **1.** had
2. ~~The movie was especially liked by~~ Kira and her brother, because of the beautiful nature photography.   **2.** especially liked the movie
3. If I ~~was~~ Luís, I would have argued with the umpire.   **3.** were
4. Cindy retraced her steps and found the cafe at which she left her credit card.   **4.** had
5. I never realized that hurricanes and typhoons ~~were~~ really the same thing.   **5.** are
6. As he slowly turned the key, the door suddenly ~~swings~~ wide open.   **6.** swung
7. Last week, the school newspaper ~~has~~ printed Kim's story.
8. ~~Winning~~ the medal, she revised her practice schedule and gave herself more free time.   **8.** Having won
9. By the time the next presidential election comes up, I will ~~be~~ in the United States for six years.   **9.** have been
10. Mr. Washington wanted to ~~shown~~ them his collection of African sculptures, but he was suddenly called away on business.   **10.** show

▶ **REVIEW G**

Proofreading a Paragraph for Errors in the Form and Use of Verbs

Most of the sentences in the following paragraph contain errors in the form and use of verbs. If a verb is incorrect, give the correct form. If a sentence is correct, write *C*.

1. were

2. are

3. experience

4. you will return

5. C

6. C

7. Staring

[1] Have you ever seen a band of light shimmering over a hot road, as though a pool of water ~~was~~ lying just ahead? [2] Mirages ~~have been~~ just one of many types of illusions that ~~will~~ fool the average observer. [3] The simple illustration shown on the next page will allow you to ~~have experienced~~ another kind of illusion. [4] In a few minutes, the flying bird ~~will be returned~~ to its cage ~~by you.~~ [5] However, to do so, it is essential that you are calm and give the experiment your full attention. [6] Fix your stare on the bird for a minute or two, then focus on the white space in the center of the cage that stands next to the bird. [7] ~~Having stared~~ at the white space, you will, at the same

→ REVIEW: POSTTEST

OBJECTIVE

- To proofread sentences and a paragraph for correct verb usage

time, see the bird slowly appear. [8] However, when the bird appears, you will probably ~~have noticed~~ something strange—its feathers will be green and purple. [9] Although you ~~have~~ no longer ~~been~~ looking at the bird, its image (or, rather, its afterimage) ~~has remained~~ on your retina. [10] The afterimage is composed of colors opposite to the bird's original red and yellow colors.

8. notice

9. are/remains

10. C

USAGE

Review: Posttest

A. Proofreading Sentences for Correct Verb Usage

Some of the following sentences contain errors in the use of verbs. If a sentence is incorrect, revise it, using the correct verb. If a sentence is correct, write *C*.

1. They were ~~setting~~ on the bench and feeding the ducks.   **1.** sitting
2. She thought the runner had ~~broke~~ the world record.   **2.** broken
3. We would have preferred to ~~have eaten~~ Chinese food.   **3.** eat
4. Mrs. Ames was pleased that when the driver's test ~~was taken by her son,~~ he passed easily.   **4.** her son took
5. The shoppers laid down their purchases carefully.   **5.** C
6. We cheered when the movie finally ~~begun.~~   **6.** began.

REVIEW: POSTTEST

Teaching Note. There are some verbs that have alternative past-tense forms. Some of these are *dived* or *dove, shone* or *shined, rang* or *rung,* and *shrank* or *shrunk.* Explain that these alternatives have recently evolved in the language and that students may encounter them on this **Posttest** and other tests. If students give alternative forms, have them show dictionary evidence of the forms' acceptability.

USAGE

809

7. were   8. have interviewed

7. If I ~~was~~ Anne, I would ask for a promotion and a raise.
8. They would have liked to ~~interview~~ the astronauts.

9. go

9. On vacation they plan to ~~have gone~~ deep-sea fishing.
10. Yesterday I ~~swum~~ in the Millers' new pool.

10. swam

11. The rate of inflation has ~~raised~~ steadily.

11. risen

12. When they returned to the scene, they discovered that the weapon ~~was~~ taken.

12. had been

13. When I enter college, my parents will ~~be~~ married thirty years.

13. have been

14. had/broken

14. When we saw the group perform, Julia, the lead vocalist, just ~~broke~~ her contract with a big recording company.
15. If we had the chance, we would have stopped by your house.

15. had

B. Proofreading for Correct Verb Usage

Revise each sentence in the following paragraph by correcting any incorrect verb forms. If a sentence is correct, write *C*.

16. were

17. is

18. had

19. slide.

20. it has taken

21. do

22. Having mastered

23. beaten

24. done

25. remain

[16] When you were a child, you may have played with an abacus as though it ~~was~~ a toy. [17] Possibly, a teacher told you that the abacus ~~was~~ a device for counting—for adding and subtracting. [18] If you ~~would have~~ spent the time, you might have learned to calculate on this simple device. [19] An abacus consists of a series of wooden bars on which beads ~~have slided.~~ [20] Because the abacus has been widely used for hundreds of years, many forms ~~have been taken by it.~~ [21] For example, on a Chinese abacus, you move beads toward a crossbar to add a sum, while other types of abacuses ~~did~~ not even have a crossbar. [22] ~~Mastering~~ the appropriate technique, operators calculate quickly and accurately. [23] In fact, on any number of occasions, people using abacuses have ~~beat~~ people using calculators in speed trials. [24] Consequently, an abacus sits beside many tradespeople all over Asia, just as it has ~~did~~ for centuries. [25] A century from now, the abacus will probably ~~have remained~~ practical, rugged, portable, fast, accurate, and comparatively inexpensive.

OBJECTIVES
- To select modifiers to complete sentences
- To proofread for correct use of modifiers

PROGRAM MANAGER

FOR THE WHOLE CHAPTER
- **Review** For exercises on chapter concepts, see **Review Form A** and **Review Form B** in *Language Skills Practice and Assessment,* pp. 158–159.
- **Assessment** For additional testing, see **Usage Pretests** and **Usage Mastery Tests** in *Language Skills Practice and Assessment,* pp. 95–101 and pp. 179–185.

25 CORRECT USE OF MODIFIERS

Forms of Adjectives and Adverbs; Comparison

USAGE

USAGE

CHAPTER OVERVIEW

This chapter begins with a discussion of the forms and uses of modifiers. It then discusses four pairs of troublesome modifiers: *bad* and *badly, good* and *well, real* and *really,* and *slow* and *slowly.* Comparison of modifiers is also discussed, including regular and irregular comparisons and the uses of comparative and superlative forms. A **Picture This** feature asks students to write descriptions that include adjectives and adverbs, and the **Writing Application** has students use comparative and superlative forms of modifiers in writing informative paragraphs. The chapter ends with a **Review: Posttest** for determining students' mastery of the correct use of modifiers.

Diagnostic Test

A. Selecting Modifiers to Complete Sentences

For each of the following sentences, select the <u>correct modifier</u> from the pair given in parentheses.

EXAMPLE   **1.** The hurricane hit the town very (*sudden, suddenly*).
          1. *suddenly*

1. The music sounds (<u>*strange*</u>, *strangely*) on this old record player.
2. The rehearsals for *Porgy and Bess* are going as (*good*, <u>*well*</u>) as can be expected at this point.

USING THE DIAGNOSTIC TEST

The **Diagnostic Test** is designed to be used in conjunction with your assessments of students' writing to detect any problems students might be having with using adjectives and adverbs. Evaluation of students' responses to the **Diagnostic Test** can indicate which sections of the chapter students need to concentrate on for help with any confusion they have about the use of modifiers.

USAGE

USAGE

3. Jeanne looked (*casual, casually*) in my direction.
4. My stepbrother Dylan is younger than (*anyone, anyone else*) in his class.
5. The coast road is more scenic, but Route 180 is usually (*quicker, quickest*).
6. "These aerobic exercises seem (*easier, more easier*) to do than the exercises I have been doing," Audrey said.
7. Have you seen a (*friendlier, more friendlier*) spaniel than mine?
8. "Olympia Dukakis was (*real, really*) outstanding in the movie *Moonstruck*," Chris said.
9. The close of the letter read, "With our (*most sincerest, sincerest*) thanks."
10. When you get to the stop sign, turn (*sharp, sharply*) to the left.

B. Proofreading a Paragraph for Correct Use of Modifiers

Most of the sentences in the following paragraph contain errors in the use of modifiers. If a sentence is incorrect, revise the sentence to correct the error. If a sentence is correct, write *C*.

11. other
12. peaceful
13. slowly
14. most
15. really
16. steadily
17. C
18. C
19. carefully
20. bad

[11] Making a pot on a potter's wheel, or "throwing" a pot, is more relaxing than any artistic activity I know of. [12] I feel peacefully as the wheel spins and I shape the ball of clay with my fingers. [13] Sometimes I plan what to make, but other times a pot takes shape slow, almost by itself. [14] To me, kneading the clay to get rid of air bubbles is the more difficult of the dozen or so steps in throwing a pot. [15] The real exciting part is pulling up on the clay to form a cone and then pressing a hole in the center. [16] To prevent the pot from becoming lopsided, I have to work steady and keep the wheel spinning. [17] I'm happiest while gently pressing the clay and forming the walls of a pot. [18] This stage is more pleasant than any other stage because I can daydream as my fingers seem to do the work almost automatically. [19] Most of the time, though, I have to concentrate careful to make a perfect pot. [20] I usually don't feel too badly if a pot doesn't turn out right the first time; part of the fun is starting over.

FORMS AND USES OF MODIFIERS
Rules 25a, 25b

OBJECTIVE

• To select the correct modifiers to complete sentences

25a

Forms of Modifiers

A *modifier* is a word that limits the meaning of another word. The two kinds of modifiers are the *adjective* and the *adverb*.

An *adjective* limits the meaning of a noun or a pronoun.

EXAMPLES   a **perfect** score   an **eager** participant
           a **clear** night   the **last** one

An *adverb* limits the meaning of a verb, an adjective, or another adverb.

EXAMPLES   walks **briskly**   **gradually** appeared
           completely innocent   working **remarkably** hard

Most modifiers with an *–ly* ending are used as adverbs. Many adverbs, in fact, are formed by adding *–ly* to an adjective.

ADJECTIVES	usual	calm	brief	absurd	appropriate
ADVERBS	usually	calmly	briefly	absurdly	appropriately

Some modifiers ending in *–ly* may be used as adjectives.

EXAMPLES   **monthly** budget   **early** indication   **likely** outcome

A few modifiers have the same form whether they are used as adjectives or as adverbs.

ADJECTIVES	ADVERBS
a **fast** train	moves **fast**
a **little** speech	spoke **little**
an **early** start	starting **early**

Uses of Modifiers

25a. Use an adjective to modify the subject of a linking verb.

The most common linking verbs are the forms of *be: am, is, are, was, were, be, been,* and *being.* A linking verb is often followed by a *predicate adjective*—a word that modifies the subject.

EXAMPLES   The company's training program is **rigorous.**
           The baby soon became **tired** and **cranky.**

USAGE

USAGE

QUICK REMINDER

Write the following sentences on the chalkboard. Tell students to choose the modifier that correctly completes each sentence.

1. The greens tasted (<u>bitter</u>, bitterly).
2. George's dog, King, is (<u>nervous</u>, nervously).
3. Betty catapulted (easy, <u>easily</u>) over the fence.

25b. Use an adverb to modify an action verb.

An action verb is often modified by an adverb—a word that explains *how, when, where,* or *to what extent* the action is performed.

EXAMPLES   The world's population is increasing **rapidly.**
The astronaut spoke **enthusiastically** about her successful mission in space.

Some verbs may be used as linking verbs or action verbs.

EXAMPLES   Carlos looked **happy.** [*Looked* is a linking verb. Notice that the modifier following it, *happy,* is an adjective.]
Carlos looked **happily** at his latest design. [*Looked* is an action verb. Notice that the modifier following it, *happily,* is an adverb.]

To determine whether to use an adjective or an adverb after a verb, replace the verb with the appropriate form of the linking verb *seem.* If *seem* makes sense in the sentence, the original verb is being used as a linking verb, which calls for an adjective. If *seem* is absurd in the sentence, the original verb is being used as an action verb, which calls for an adverb.

EXAMPLES   Carlos looked happy. [Since *Carlos seemed happy* makes sense, *looked* is being used as a linking verb and calls for the adjective *happy.*]
Carlos looked happily at his latest design. [Since *Carlos seemed happily at his latest design* is absurd, *looked* is being used as an action verb and calls for the adverb *happily.*]

☞ REFERENCE NOTE: See pages 612–613 for more information about linking verbs and action verbs. For more about predicate adjectives, see pages 642–643.

▶ EXERCISE 1   **Selecting Modifiers to Complete Sentences**

Select the correct modifier from the pair given in parentheses in each of the following sentences.

1. The sled's runners slid (*smooth, smoothly*) over the ice.
2. The weather outside looks (*miserable, miserably*).
3. Neka embroidered the rain-bird symbol (*perfect, perfectly*), checking each stitch as she worked.

4. Doesn't the official explanation of the budget cut sound (*incredible*, *incredibly*) to you?
5. Why was she looking at me (*suspicious*, *suspiciously*)?
6. This apple tastes (*peculiar*, *peculiarly*) to me.
7. Mike smiled (*proud*, *proudly*) when he told us about his West African heritage.
8. Dawn goes jogging (*regular*, *regularly*).
9. He disappeared (*silent*, *silently*) into the underbrush.
10. The conference room smelled (*stuffy*, *stuffily*).

▶ EXERCISE 2   **Selecting Modifiers to Complete Sentences**

For each sentence in the following paragraph, select the correct modifier from the pair given in parentheses.

[1] In this picture, Debbie Allen dances (*energetic*, *energetically*) in a scene from the TV series *Fame*. [2] You might say that fame itself looks (*comfortable*, *comfortably*) on her. [3] Allen, who grew up in Houston, Texas, has danced (*continual*, *continually*) since the age of three. [4] She attended the Houston Ballet School, graduated from Howard University, and then headed (*confident*, *confidently*) to New York City. [5] On Broadway, she was (*triumphant*, *triumphantly*) in the revivals of the musicals *West Side Story* and *Sweet Charity*. [6] Later, she (*successful*, *successfully*) choreographed *Fame* and won two Emmy Awards for her work on that show. [7] Allen looks (*natural*, *naturally*) in a director's chair, too, and has directed episodes of such TV shows as *A Different World* and *Quantum Leap*. [8] Through the

USAGE

MEETING *individual* **NEEDS**

LEARNING STYLES

Auditory Learners. You may want to have students work in pairs to complete **Exercise 2** orally. Have one student in each pair read each sentence aloud twice, first including one of the modifiers in parentheses, and then including the other. The other student in each pair should listen to decide which modifier correctly completes each sentence.

USAGE

EIGHT TROUBLESOME MODIFIERS

OBJECTIVE

- To correct errors in sentences in the use of *bad* and *badly*, *good* and *well*, *real* and *really*, and *slow* and *slowly*

---

years, she has worked (*diligent*, <u>*diligently*</u>) and has battled racism and sexism to succeed. [9] Never one to accept second best, Allen has risen (*steady*, <u>*steadily*</u>) to the top in her profession. [10] In interviews, Debbie Allen seems (<u>*proud*</u>, *proudly*) of her achievements but ready for new challenges, too.

Eight Troublesome Modifiers

Bad and Badly

Bad is an adjective. *Badly* is an adverb. In standard English, only the adjective form should follow a sense verb, such as *feel*, *see*, *hear*, *taste*, or *smell*, or other linking verb.

NONSTANDARD	This leftover chicken smells badly.
STANDARD	This leftover chicken smells **bad.**

NOTE: The expression *feel badly* has become acceptable in informal situations, but use *feel bad* in formal speaking and writing.

Good and Well

Good is an adjective. *Well* may be used as an adjective or an adverb. Avoid using *good* to modify an action verb. Instead, use *well* as an adverb meaning "capably" or "satisfactorily."

NONSTANDARD	The track team did good at the meet.
STANDARD	The track team did **well** at the meet.

NONSTANDARD	Bao performs good even under pressure.
STANDARD	Bao performs **well** even under pressure.

As an adjective, *well* means "in good health" or "satisfactory in condition."

EXAMPLES	Yes, I feel quite **well,** thank you.
	The new car seems to run **well.**
	All is **well** with us.

Real and Really

Real is an adjective. *Really* is an adverb meaning "actually" or "truly." Although *real* is commonly used as an adverb meaning "very" in everyday situations, avoid its use in formal speaking and writing.

PROGRAM MANAGER

EIGHT TROUBLESOME MODIFIERS

- **Independent Practice/ Reteaching** For instruction and exercises, see **Troublesome Modifiers A** and **Troublesome Modifiers B** in *Language Skills Practice and Assessment,* pp. 154–155.

- **Computer Guided Instruction** For additional instruction and practice with troublesome modifiers, see **Lesson 21** in *Language Workshop CD-ROM.*

- **Practice** To help less-advanced students with troublesome modifiers, see **Chapter 18** in *English Workshop, Complete Course,* pp. 255–256.

✔ QUICK REMINDER

Write the following sentences on the chalkboard. Have students fill in the blanks with either *good* or *well.*

1. I can't roller-skate very _____. [well]
2. You can skate as _____ as I can. [well]
3. Maybe we both need a _____ teacher. [good]

| INFORMAL | Your new car is real nice. |
| FORMAL | Your new car is **really** nice. |

| INFORMAL | He played real well in the tryouts. |
| FORMAL | He played **really** well in the tryouts. |

Slow and *Slowly*

Slow is an adjective. *Slowly* is an adverb. Although *slow* is also labeled as an adverb in many dictionaries, this usage applies only to informal situations and colloquial expressions, such as *drive slow* and *go slow*.

| INFORMAL | She eased slow out of the cockpit. |
| FORMAL | She eased **slowly** out of the cockpit. |

Fox Trot copyright 1989 Bill Amend. Reprinted with permission of Universal Press Syndicate. All rights reserved.

▶ **EXERCISE 3**

Revising Sentences to Correct Errors in the Use of *Bad—Badly, Good—Well, Real—Really,* and *Slow—Slowly*

For each of the following sentences, if a modifier is incorrect, give the correct form. If the sentence is correct, write C.

EXAMPLE **1.** After a long rehearsal, the dance troupe performed good.
1. *well*

1. After she had lost the election, Bernadette felt very bad.   1. C
2. Charlotte seemed real happy about getting an A on her history test.   2. really
                                                                          3. C
3. Ms. Stein is a good teacher who prepares her lessons well.
4. Some shades of blue and green go good together.   4. well

INTEGRATING THE LANGUAGE ARTS

Usage and Vocabulary. Students often overuse the modifier *really* in their speech and writing. Explain that overuse of a word dulls it in the same way that repeated washing of a shirt fades its color. Work with students to generate a list of vivid words that could be used in place of *really.* [Possibilities include *genuinely, extremely, certainly, positively, sincerely,* and *extraordinarily.*]

MEETING *individual* NEEDS

LEP/ESL

General Strategies. When English-proficient speakers are asked how they are doing, they often respond by saying "Good" rather than "Well." Because most English-language learners put a great deal of faith in the spoken forms they hear, they appreciate knowing why these forms often deviate from those in the textbook. You could tell these students that the use of *good* in response to the greeting "How are you doing?" is a casual, informal use of English and that it is acceptable in everyday speech.

817

OBJECTIVES
- To determine the correct use of modifiers in sentences
- To proofread for correct use of modifiers in a paragraph

818   *Correct Use of Modifiers*

5. Chen tried to teach me to use chopsticks, but the lesson didn't go very ~~good~~.   **5.** well
6. "I'm positive I did ~~good~~ on that test," Anzu confidently remarked.   **6.** well
7. Since it is very sweet, the Turkish candy halvah should be served in small pieces and eaten slowly.   **7.** C
8. Everyone wondered whether the stone he found was a real diamond.   **8.** C   **9.** slowly
9. "Remember to speak ~~slow~~ when you give your speech," Mr. Schmidt advised the nervous candidate.   **10.** badly
10. "Life can't be treating you all that ~~bad~~," I told Walker.

REVIEW A   **Determining the Correct Use of Modifiers**

Each of the following sentences contains an <u>italicized modifier</u>. If the modifier is incorrect, give the correct form. If the modifier is correct, write *C*. Then identify the <u>word that each modifier describes</u>.

EXAMPLE   **1.** Something sounds *strangely* next door.
          1. *strange*

1. The players <u>did</u> *good* in the fourth quarter.   **1.** well
2. The bread dough <u>rose</u> too *quick*.   **2.** quickly
3. We <u>walked</u> *slow* on the icy sidewalk.   **3.** slowly
4. <u>Sam</u> feels *bad* about forgetting your birthday.   **4.** C
5. <u>She</u> sounded very *angrily* on the phone.   **5.** angry
6. These new jeans <u>do</u> not fit me *good* at all.   **6.** well
7. Rita <u>answered</u> the questions *precisely*.   **7.** C
8. Fortunately, no one <u>was hurt</u> *bad* in the accident.   **8.** badly
9. Mr. Tate's company <u>can do</u> the job *efficiently*.   **9.** C
10. The judge <u>rapped</u> her gavel *sharp* to restore order.
                                                          10. sharply

REVIEW B   **Proofreading for Correct Use of Modifiers**

Most of the sentences in the following paragraph contain errors in the use of modifiers. Identify each incorrect modifier and give the correct form. If a sentence is correct, write *C*.

1. tremendously
2. exclusively
3. nearly
4. recent

[1] The popularity of country and western music (C & W) has grown ~~tremendous~~ in the last twenty-five years. [2] In fact, many radio stations all over the nation are playing C & W ~~exclusive~~. [3] Nowadays, country music appeals to fans of ~~near~~ all ages and occupations. [4] For example, one ~~recently~~ American

A DIFFERENT APPROACH Divide the class into two teams and create sentences that call for choices between troublesome modifiers (you could use the sentences in **Exercise 3**).
        Read a sentence to one team and give the team thirty seconds to respond by supplying the correct modifier. Then, give the other team a chance to choose the correct modifier to complete the sentence. Teams receive a point for each correct answer and lose a point for each incorrect answer.

TIMESAVER Because **Reviews A** and **B** cover the same material, you could use **Review A** as oral practice and then assign **Review B** as independent practice.

USAGE

- To write the comparative and superlative forms of modifiers
- To write a descriptive paragraph containing at least three adjectives and two adverbs
- To correctly use the comparative and superlative forms of modifiers in sentences

Comparison of Modifiers **819**

25c

president, George Bush, officially declared his fondness for country music when he attended the Country Music Awards ceremony. [5] Top country stars, such as Clint Black, Reba McEntire, and Garth Brooks, not only have best-selling albums but play to ~~increasing~~ large numbers of fans. [6] In the photo below, for example, Garth Brooks looks ~~cheerfully~~ as he acknowledges his fans' enthusiastic applause. [7] Many C & W performers, such as Brooks, are known for their wildly successful music videos. [8] Some country singers feel ~~badly~~ about the problems in America and have started taking musical stands on social issues. [9] Others do ~~real~~ well singing songs on the traditional country themes of love and heartache. [10] Veteran performer Loretta Lynn, country music's own "Coal Miner's Daughter," is shown here singing movingly before an admiring crowd.

5. increasingly
6. cheerful
7. C
8. bad
9. really
10. C

USAGE

Comparison of Modifiers

25c. *Comparison* refers to the change in the form of an adjective or an adverb to show increasing or decreasing degrees in the quality that the modifier expresses.

There are three degrees of comparison: *positive, comparative,* and *superlative.*

USAGE

QUICK REMINDER

Write the following sentences on the chalkboard. Have students supply the correct forms of the words in parentheses.

1. I like the red hat (good) than the blue one. [better]
2. Of the three comedians, I think Dot is (funny). [funniest]
3. Carla is (confident) than I am. [more confident]

Remind students that the *–er* suffix or *more* is used to compare two things, while the *–est* suffix or *most* is used to compare three or more things.

MEETING *individual* NEEDS

ADVANCED STUDENTS

Some adjectives don't have comparative or superlative forms because the adjectives express absolute qualities. Challenge students to list at least five of these adjectives. You may want to allow students to work together on this activity. [Some possibilities are *perfect, wooden, opposite, legal, newborn, misspelled,* and *last.*]

	POSITIVE	COMPARATIVE	SUPERLATIVE
Adjectives	big	bigger	biggest
	eager	more eager	most eager
	good	better	best
Adverbs	late	later	latest
	swiftly	more swiftly	most swiftly
	well	better	best

Regular Comparison

(1) Most one-syllable modifiers form the comparative and superlative degrees by adding *–er* and *–est*.

POSITIVE	COMPARATIVE	SUPERLATIVE
neat	neater	neatest
warm	warmer	warmest
fast	faster	fastest
straight	straighter	straightest

(2) Some two-syllable modifiers form the comparative and superlative degrees by adding *–er* or *–est*. Other two-syllable modifiers form the comparative and superlative degrees by using *more* and *most*.

POSITIVE	COMPARATIVE	SUPERLATIVE
gentle	gentler	gentlest
lively	livelier	liveliest
agile	more agile	most agile
clearly	more clearly	most clearly

If you are not sure how a two-syllable modifier is compared, check a dictionary.

☞ **REFERENCE NOTE:** For guidelines on spelling modifiers with *-er* and *-est*, see pages 966–968.

(3) Modifiers of more than two syllables form the comparative and superlative degrees by using *more* and *most*.

POSITIVE	COMPARATIVE	SUPERLATIVE
expensive	more expensive	most expensive
delightful	more delightful	most delightful
quietly	more quietly	most quietly
poetically	more poetically	most poetically

(4) To show a decrease in the qualities they express, all modifiers form the comparative and superlative degrees by using *less* and *least*.

POSITIVE	COMPARATIVE	SUPERLATIVE
weak	less weak	least weak
useful	less useful	least useful
contentedly	less contentedly	least contentedly
urgently	less urgently	least urgently

Irregular Comparison

Some modifiers do not follow the regular methods of forming the comparative and superlative degrees.

POSITIVE	COMPARATIVE	SUPERLATIVE
bad	worse	worst
good	better	best
well	better	best
little	less	least
many	more	most
much	more	most

USAGE

◈ INTEGRATING THE LANGUAGE ARTS

Literature Link. If your students' literature textbook contains Samuel Taylor Coleridge's *The Rime of the Ancient Mariner,* have students read and discuss the poem. Direct students' attention to Part IV of the poem and discuss with them the contrast between the Mariner's description of living creatures in line 238 and the description in lines 274 through 283. Ask students to write paragraphs contrasting the two descriptions and relating this contrast to the theme of the poem. Have students use at least two comparative forms of modifiers in their paragraphs. For an example of a paper about literature, refer students to **A Student Model** on pp. 424–425.

USAGE

ANSWERS
Exercise 4
1. tinier, tiniest
2. more ill, most ill
3. more wistful, most wistful
4. more modest, most modest
5. more curious, most curious
6. more proudly, most proudly
7. thinner, thinnest
8. better, best
9. more gently, most gently
10. more abruptly, most abruptly

◆ INTEGRATING THE LANGUAGE ARTS

Usage and Mechanics. Comparative and superlative degrees often are formed according to three spelling rules for adding suffixes. As students proofread their writing, remind them of the following rules:

1. With words ending in *–y* preceded by a consonant, change *–y* to *i* before any suffix not beginning with *i.* (For example, *dry* becomes *drier* or *driest.*)
2. Double the final consonant before a suffix that begins with a vowel if the word has only one syllable or is accented on the last syllable and ends in a single consonant preceded by a single vowel. (For example, *thin* becomes *thinner* or *thinnest.*)
3. Drop the final *–e* before a suffix beginning with a vowel. (For example, *safe* becomes *safer* or *safest.*)

822

▶ EXERCISE 4 **Writing the Comparative and Superlative Forms of Modifiers**

Give the comparative form and the superlative form of each of the following modifiers. Use a dictionary to check any words you are unsure of.

EXAMPLE   **1.** flat
        1. *flatter, flattest*

1. tiny	3. wistful	5. curious	7. thin	9. gently
2. ill	4. modest	6. proudly	8. good	10. abruptly

Uses of Comparative Forms and Superlative Forms

25d. Use the comparative degree when comparing two things. Use the superlative degree when comparing more than two.

COMPARATIVE   Although both Laura and Justin wrote about the development of the Swahili culture, Laura's paper was **longer.** [comparison of two papers]
After listening to both candidates, we concluded that Ms. García was the **more highly** qualified. [comparison of two candidates]

SUPERLATIVE   Of the four major river-valley cultures that arose long ago in Africa and Asia, the Huang He was probably the **most fully** isolated from the others. [comparison of four civilizations]
I bought this model of car because it gets the **best** mileage. [comparison of many models]

NOTE: In informal situations, the superlative degree is sometimes used to emphasize the comparison of only two things. Avoid such use of the superlative degree in formal speaking and writing.

INFORMAL   Which park did you enjoy most, Yellowstone or Hot Springs?
FORMAL   Which park did you enjoy **more,** Yellowstone or Hot Springs?

The superlative degree is also used to compare two things in some idiomatic expressions.

EXAMPLE   Put your best foot forward.

PICTURE THIS

Until now, you never imagined that chemistry could be so fascinating! Viewing this image through a microscope, you realize that science can, indeed, be stranger than fiction. This beautiful "landscape" is actually a magnified piece of agate (a semiprecious stone). Since your chemistry teacher expects your lab report to include careful, precise notes on what you see, write a clear, accurate description of this microscopic image. In your description, use at least three adjectives and two adverbs.

John I. Koivula/Courtesy of Nikon Small World Photo Competition

USAGE

Subject: a piece of agate seen through a microscope
Audience: yourself and your chemistry teacher
Purpose: to record information; to inform

PICTURE THIS

This activity could be expanded to include comparative and superlative forms of modifiers. If possible, ask a science teacher in your school to supply microscopes and slides for students to use (two or three students per microscope). Students then could compare the image of agate to some other microscopic image.

USAGE

25e. Include the word *other* or *else* when comparing one member of a group with the rest of the members.

NONSTANDARD   Diamond, a crystalline form of carbon, is harder than any mineral in the world. [The diamond is one of the minerals of the world. Logically, the diamond cannot be harder than itself.]

STANDARD   Diamond, a crystalline form of carbon, is harder than any **other** mineral in the world.

INTEGRATING THE LANGUAGE ARTS

Usage and Writing. To give students practice using comparisons, ask them to act as movie critics. They should choose two movies and then write reviews that compare and contrast them. Suggest categories of evaluation for students to use, such as plot, acting, special effects, and music. Encourage students to include as many comparative and superlative forms of modifiers as possible.

824 *Correct Use of Modifiers*

NONSTANDARD	Pete has won more races than anyone in his club. [Pete is a member of the club. Logically, he cannot have won more races than himself.]
STANDARD	Pete has won more races than anyone **else** in his club.

25f. Avoid double comparisons.

A *double comparison* is the result of using two comparative forms (usually –*er* and *more*) or using two superlative forms (usually –*est* and *most*) to modify the same word.

NONSTANDARD	Alice is a more faster swimmer than you.
STANDARD	Alice is a **faster** swimmer than you.

NONSTANDARD	She is the most smartest girl in school.
STANDARD	She is the **smartest** girl in school.

▶ EXERCISE 5   **Using the Comparative and Superlative Forms of Modifiers**

Revise the following sentences by correcting the errors in the use of the comparative and the superlative forms of modifiers. If a sentence is correct, write *C*.

EXAMPLE   **1.** That was the most highest grade Oscar ever earned on a Spanish test.
1. *highest*

1. worse   1. Colleen thought nothing could be as bad as the snow; but when the ice storm hit, she said, "This is even worser!"

2. darker   2. Both twins, Holly and Julie, have brown eyes, but Holly's are darkest.

3. other   3. In each graduating class, the valedictorian is the student whose academic average is higher than that of any senior.

4. most   4. Thomas Jefferson is generally regarded as one of the more important Americans in United States history.

5. clearer   5. To gain a more clear understanding of the problems in the Middle East, people need to learn more about the history of that region.

6. C   6. Suzanne made the mistake of buying less paint than she needed for the small room.

7. other   7. Performing better than all the gymnasts, Mary Lou Retton was the first American to win an Olympic gold medal in her sport.

OBJECTIVES
- To revise sentences to correct errors in the use of modifiers
- To proofread a paragraph for correct use of modifiers

8. Myles is taking more classes than I.   **8.** C
9. Dividing the pumpkin pie in two, Felicia gave me the ~~largest~~ portion.   **9.** larger   **10.** other
10. According to my friend Juan, Houston, Texas, is more interesting and more exciting than any city in that state.

REVIEW C Using Modifiers Correctly

Some of the following sentences contain errors in the use of modifiers. Revise each incorrect sentence to correct the error. If a sentence is correct, write C.

1. I am ~~least~~ prepared to take the test than you.   **1.** less
2. Jim speaks Portuguese more fluently than anyone in our class.   **2.** else
3. You cheered more often than anyone at the concert.   **3.** else
4. Mr. Brown is many pounds ~~more~~ heavier than I.
5. The picture looks much ~~more~~ clearer on this television set than on that one.
6. We thought Patti was the most talented of all the actors in the community play.   **6.** C
7. I read the ~~shorter~~ of the three books for my report.   **7.** shortest
8. I have narrowed my choices to two colleges, and I want to visit them to see which I like ~~best~~.   **8.** better
9. She was less determined to win than her sister was.   **9.** C
10. Modeling her mother's silk kimono, Toshi seemed even ~~gracefuller~~ than usual.   **10.** more graceful

REVIEW D Proofreading for Correct Use of Modifiers

Most of the sentences in the following paragraph contain errors in the use of modifiers. If a sentence is incorrect, revise the sentence to correct the error. If a sentence is correct, write C.

[1] Of all the world's movie directors, Akira Kurosawa of Japan is considered one of the ~~greater~~. [2] He is certainly better known in the United States than any Japanese director. [3] In addition to directing, the multitalented Kurosawa has edited and written many of his films. [4] Acclaimed by critics, his films not only look ~~beautifully~~, but they also contain serious moral themes. [5] Among the ~~more~~ popular of his dozens of films is *Ran*, which blends Shakespeare's *King Lear* with a Japanese folk tale. [6] Kurosawa made the story more ~~forcefuler~~ for his

1. greatest
2. other
3. C
4. beautiful
5. most
6. forceful

Have students work in groups of three or four to create sentences in which the comparisons are unclear. Then, have the groups exchange sentences for correction. Encourage students to make unclear comparisons as funny as possible. Here is an example:

The Smiths enjoy roasting corn even more than their neighbors. [The Smiths enjoy roasting corn even more than their neighbors do.]

826 *Correct Use of Modifiers*

Japanese audience by having the conflict be between a father and three sons instead of three daughters. [7] That conflict is

7. really ~~real~~ apparent in this scene from *Ran*. [8] Moviegoers in the United States also enjoyed Kurosawa's film *Dersu Uzala*, which

8. best won an Academy Award for ~~bestest~~ foreign film. [9] The stark

9. fierce scenery in that film certainly shows how ~~fiercely~~ the Siberian wilderness can be. [10] If you have the chance to see these two

10. better films, you can decide which one you like ~~best~~.

WRITING APPLICATION

This assignment gives students practice writing clear comparisons to inform others. Students must consider their audience (their peers) and their purpose (to inform their peers how various products or services compare with one another).

WRITING APPLICATION

Using Comparisons in a Consumer's Guide

Each day, you make choices about how to spend your time and money. You decide which movies to see, which products to buy, which clubs and sports to participate in. Often, you arrive at a decision by comparing two or more alternatives. You express such comparisons by using adjectives and adverbs in comparative and superlative forms.

EXAMPLE   I buy Pimple-Go acne medication because it works **more quickly** than No-Blemish. Pimple-Go also has the **strongest** formula available over the counter.

▶ WRITING ACTIVITY

With so many products and services claiming to be the "best," how do you know which ones to choose? You and your classmates have decided to compile an informal consumer's guide to some everyday products and services available in your community. Choose a product, such as sandwiches or jeans, or a service, such as car washing or hair cutting. Write a paragraph or two comparing at least three different choices for the product or service and telling which, if any, you think is best. In your writing, use at least three comparative and two superlative forms of modifiers.

Prewriting You and your classmates may want to work together to compile a list of products and services. Then decide which type of product or service each person will write about. Jot down notes on at least three alternatives, judging the quality, effectiveness, and cost of each. Use your notes to help you compare the brands. Be sure to judge each by the same criteria. You may wish to look in some reliable consumer guides to see the kinds of criteria their evaluators use.

Writing Begin your draft by identifying the type of product or service you are evaluating and listing the brands you will focus on. Then give a detailed comparison of the brands. Rate the alternatives on quality, effectiveness, and value. Give specific, objective reasons for your opinions.

Evaluating and Revising Ask a classmate to read your draft. Have you evaluated each alternative thoroughly? Have you stated your opinion clearly? Are the reasons for your opinion clear? If not, add, cut, or revise information. Be sure that you've used at least three comparative and two superlative forms of modifiers.

Proofreading and Publishing Check your writing for errors in grammar, usage, punctuation, and spelling. Pay special attention to modifiers, and revise any double comparisons. You and your classmates may wish to publish a consumer's guide by compiling your evaluations in a booklet. You can then use the booklet as a handy reference for choosing local products or services.

USAGE

? CRITICAL THINKING

Evaluation. To evaluate the products or services in question, students will need to develop lists of criteria by which the products or services can be rated. These criteria will depend, of course, on the kinds of products and services being evaluated. Work with students to develop criteria by which to evaluate a specific product, such as a camera.

PREWRITING

Remind students to consider their audience as they compile lists of products and services. Students should decide which products and services their classmates might be interested in learning more about. Encourage students to take short, informal surveys to determine which products or services might be appropriate for their audience.

USAGE

LESSON 5 (*pp. 828–829*)
REVIEW: POSTTEST

OBJECTIVES
• To identify and correct errors in the use of modifiers in sentences
• To select modifiers to complete sentences

USAGE

USAGE

828   *Correct Use of Modifiers*

Review: Posttest

A. Using Modifiers Correctly

Most of the following sentences contain errors in the use of modifiers. If a sentence is incorrect, revise the sentence to correct the error. If a sentence is correct, write *C*.

EXAMPLE   **1.** Among my three brothers and sisters, my sister Giselle has the better sense of humor.
    1. *best*

1. Which is ~~widest~~, the Mississippi River or the Colorado River?   **1.** wider

2. When the temperature reached 103 degrees in August, the board of health warned people not to go outdoors unless they absolutely had to.   **2.** C

3. That is the ~~most~~ palest shade of blue I have ever seen.

4. Because the drummer played ~~bad~~, the band's melody line was drowned out.   **4.** badly

5. Pointing to the two glasses partially filled with water, the magician asked, "Which glass has ~~the least~~ water?"   **5.** less

6. When you dress for a job interview, you should wear the styles and colors of clothing that look ~~attractively~~ on you.

7. If Mark keeps pedaling his bike that ~~slow~~, he'll never get home before dark.   **6.** attractive   **7.** slowly

8. Has Thomas been saving money ~~regular~~ for his trip to the Yucatán?   **8.** regularly

9. Philadelphia and Atlantic City are the largest cities near my home, but Philadelphia is the ~~closest~~.   **9.** closer

10. Even though they can't play their guitars too ~~good~~, their albums sell well.   **10.** well

11. "Nurse López, I feel remarkably well today, better than I have ever felt before," said Mr. Parker.   **11.** C

12. "Sharon has been working harder than anyone here," I said.   **12.** else

13. My brother William became the strongest player on the wheelchair basketball team.   **13.** C

14. You can adjust the control on the television set to make the picture a little less ~~brighter~~.   **14.** bright

15. The cheese smells ~~badly~~ but tastes good.   **15.** bad

B. Selecting Modifiers to Complete Sentences

For each sentence in the following paragraph, select the <u>correct</u> <u>modifier</u> from the pair given in parentheses.

[16] It's (*real*, <u>*really*</u>) amazing what house movers can accomplish! **[17]** One of the (*more*, <u>*most*</u>) interesting house-moving feats involved the Queen Anne Mansion in Eureka Springs, Arkansas. **[18]** Built in 1891, the three-story home, with a tower and wrap-around porch, was moved (*efficient*, <u>*efficiently*</u>) from Carthage, Missouri. **[19]** Beginning in May, 1984, crews worked (*quick*, <u>*quickly*</u>) to dismantle the mansion. **[20]** They used special tools and worked (*careful*, <u>*carefully*</u>) to cut and pry the building apart. **[21]** The contractor had planned (*good*, <u>*well*</u>), and the first pieces of the home arrived in Eureka Springs in October of that year. **[22]** The ninety-mile move, the (*larger*, <u>*largest*</u>) ever seen in that area, required thirty-seven long flatbed trucks and three storage vans. **[23]** The new owners looked on (*happy*, <u>*happily*</u>) as workers reassembled the mansion's more than two thousand exterior stones, its wooden walls and floors, its hand-beveled windows, and its central oak staircase. **[24]** The restored Victorian mansion, which opened for tours in 1985, has a more unusual history than (*any*, <u>*any other*</u>) house in the city. **[25]** It now looks (<u>*impressive*</u>, *impressively*), set atop a hill near downtown Eureka Springs.

DIAGNOSTIC TEST

OBJECTIVE

- To revise sentences by correcting faulty modifiers

PROGRAM MANAGER

FOR THE WHOLE CHAPTER

- **Review** For exercises on chapter concepts, see **Review Form A** and **Review Form B** in *Language Skills Practice and Assessment,* pp. 165–166.
- **Assessment** For additional testing, see **Usage Pretests** and **Usage Mastery Tests** in *Language Skills Practice and Assessment,* pp. 95–101 and pp. 179–185.

USAGE

CHAPTER OVERVIEW

This chapter contains lessons on misplaced modifiers and dangling modifiers. The lessons contain rules, many examples, and exercises.

USING THE DIAGNOSTIC TEST

If students seem to be having problems with placement of modifiers in their writing, you can use the **Diagnostic Test** to identify error patterns and specific strengths and weaknesses. Assessment of the test can help you determine which parts of the chapter students need to review.

USAGE

26 PLACEMENT OF MODIFIERS

Misplaced and Dangling Modifiers

Diagnostic Test

A. Revising Sentences by Correcting Faulty Modifiers

Revisions may vary.

The following sentences contain misplaced, dangling, and two-way modifiers. Revise each sentence so that its meaning will be clear on first reading.

1. The Kovaks gave a toy robot ~~to one of their children~~ with a square glass head and flashing red eyes. **1. to one of their children.**

2. ~~Pounding the piano keys with all her might,~~ the chords of the prelude resounded through the concert hall.

3. ~~We saw a herd of sheep~~ on the way to our hotel in Wales. **3. , we saw a herd of sheep.**

4. To succeed in college, a great deal of time ~~must be spent~~ studying. **4. you must spend**

5. ~~Topped with yogurt,~~ many people love fresh strawberries. **5. topped with yogurt.**

2. as she pounded the piano keys with all her might.

6. when I was only five years old.

6. ~~When only five years old,~~ Dad took me camping on the Fort Apache Reservation in Arizona.

7. ~~Hungry,~~ our bait had barely hit the water before the fish grabbed it.   **7. hungry**

8. Elaine told Joanne ~~after the first act~~ the drama gets more exciting.   **8. that/after the first act.**

9. ~~By putting money aside regularly,~~ a small savings account will grow steadily larger.   **9. if you put money aside regularly.**

10. A tarantula ~~bit one of the dock workers that had a hairy,~~ huge body as big as a man's hand.

10. with a/, hairy/bit one of the dock workers.

B. Revising Sentences by Correcting Faulty Modifiers

The following sentences contain misplaced, dangling, and two-way modifiers. Revise each sentence so that its meaning will be clear on first reading.

11. Jody said on Saturday Fred should go to the antique and classic car show.

12. Seeing a red 1928 Hispano-Suiza motorcar, his family's minivan seemed bulky and drab to Rick.

13. The Volkswagen "Beetle" remains one of the world's most popular cars first made in Germany in 1938.

14. Captivated by the Italian sports cars, the 1938 Alfa Romeo impressed Mark.

15. Mr. Reynolds showed a Model T Ford to his daughter that came off the assembly line in 1924.

16. Would you please tell Thelma after lunch Mary Beth plans to watch the documentary about the history of European and American motorcars?

17. To keep a classic car in excellent condition, much money and patience often are needed.

18. I got a chance to ride in a 1929 Rolls-Royce Continental that the Arnolds restored yesterday.

19. After writing a report about classic luxury motorcars, the 1940 Packard and 1938 Lagonda De Ville were of special interest to me.

20. Looking at the various exhibits, it is easy to see why very early cars were called horseless carriages.

USAGE

ANSWERS
Diagnostic Test: Part B

Revisions may vary.

11. Jody said Fred should go to the antique and classic car show on Saturday.

12. His family's minivan seemed bulky and drab to Rick after he saw a 1928 Hispano-Suiza motorcar.

13. The Volkswagen "Beetle," first made in Germany in 1938, remains one of the world's most popular cars.

14. Captivated by the Italian sports cars, Mark was impressed with the 1938 Alfa Romeo.

15. Mr. Reynolds showed his daughter a Model T Ford that came off the assembly line in 1924.

16. Would you please tell Thelma that after lunch Mary Beth plans to watch the documentary about the history of European and American motorcars?

17. Much money and patience often are needed to keep a classic car in excellent condition.

18. Yesterday I got a chance to ride in a 1929 Rolls-Royce Continental that the Arnolds restored.

19. The 1940 Packard and 1938 Lagonda De Ville were of special interest to me after I wrote a report about classic luxury motorcars.

20. Looking at the various exhibits, one can easily see why very early cars were called horseless carriages.

USAGE

OBJECTIVES
• To revise sentences by correcting misplaced modifiers
• To write a persuasive paragraph that includes at least five modifying words, phrases, and clauses

PROGRAM MANAGER

MISPLACED MODIFIERS

■ **Independent Practice/Reteaching** For instruction and exercises, see **Misplaced Modifiers** in *Language Skills Practice and Assessment,* p. 163.

■ **Computer Guided Instruction** For additional instruction and practice with misplaced modifiers, see **Lesson 22** in *Language Workshop CD-ROM.*

■ **Practice** To help less-advanced students with misplaced modifiers, see **Chapter 19** in *English Workshop, Complete Course,* pp. 263–264.

USAGE

✔ QUICK REMINDER

Ask students to revise the following sentences to eliminate errors in the placement of modifying phrases and clauses:

1. With its cute, curly tail, Tad loved his pet pig.
2. Carla's Deli delivered two submarine sandwiches to Keesha wrapped in foil.
3. Forrest read that Ernie Benchpress's new movie was opening in the newspaper.

USAGE

832 *Placement of Modifiers*

Misplaced Modifiers

A modifying word, phrase, or clause that is placed too far from the word it sensibly modifies is called a *misplaced modifier.*

26a. Avoid using a misplaced modifier.

To correct a misplaced modifier, place the word, phrase, or clause as close as possible to the word you intend it to modify.

MISPLACED	We plan to go to the antique auto show that we read about in the paper tomorrow. [Did we do the planning before reading the paper?]
CORRECT	**Tomorrow,** we plan to go to the antique auto show that we read about in the paper.
MISPLACED	I finished reading the book that Alice Walker wrote about Langston Hughes during spring break. [Did Alice Walker write the book about Langston Hughes during spring break?]
CORRECT	**During spring break** I finished reading the book that Alice Walker wrote about Langston Hughes.
MISPLACED	The thief tried to run away from the police officer abandoning the stolen car and dashing into the woods. [Was the police officer abandoning the stolen car and dashing into the woods?]
CORRECT	**Abandoning the stolen car and dashing into the woods,** the thief tried to run away from the police officer.
MISPLACED	I bought a small computer for the accounting staff, which gave everyone a great deal of trouble. [Did the staff give everyone a great deal of trouble?]
CORRECT	I bought the accounting staff a small computer, **which gave everyone a great deal of trouble.**

Avoid placing a word, phrase, or clause so that it seems to modify either of two words. Such a misplaced modifier is often called a *two-way,* or *squinting, modifier.*

MISPLACED	Mary said during rehearsal Lori acted nervous. [Did Mary say this about Lori during rehearsal, or did Lori act nervous during rehearsal?]
CORRECT	**During rehearsal** Mary said Lori acted nervous.
CORRECT	Mary said Lori acted nervous **during rehearsal.**

26a

MISPLACED	Tell Marco before he goes to his karate class I want to see him.
CORRECT	**Before he goes to his karate class,** tell Marco I want to see him.
CORRECT	Tell Marco I want to see him **before he goes to his karate class.**

☞ **REFERENCE NOTE:** For information about using commas with modifying words, phrases, and clauses, see pages 909–913.

▶ EXERCISE 1 **Revising Sentences by Correcting Misplaced Modifiers**

The following sentences contain misplaced modifiers. Revise each sentence so that its meaning is clear and correct.

Revisions may vary.

EXAMPLE   1. Recently vetoed by the president, Congress is amending the tax bill.
   1. *Congress is amending the tax bill recently vetoed by the president.*

1. in the Union Army

1. Captain Andre Callioux was one of many heroic African American soldiers who fought during the Civil War ~~in the Union Army~~.

2. that

2. Mrs. Rodríguez announced at the end of the period she would treat the students to a real Mexican fiesta.

3. a plane

3. One of our observers sighted ~~a plane~~ through binoculars that she could not identify.

4. , from which all fishing is prohibited,

4. The causeway has a drawbridge to permit the passage of large boats ~~from which all fishing is prohibited~~.

5. Please tell Terry ~~when he gets home from the mall~~ Mom wants him to make dinner.   **5. that/when he gets home from the mall.**

6. At Tuesday's meeting, the mayor discussed the enormous cost of draining Buskill Swamp ~~with city council members~~.

7. According to the hieroglyphics, the mummy had ~~nearly~~ been buried for nearly four thousand years.   **7. nearly**

8. Li Hua inherited that antique fan ~~from her great-aunt~~ that has a mother-of-pearl handle.   **8. from her great-aunt**

9. Ms. Steinberg, the explorer, described her trips through the jungle ~~in our social studies class~~.   **9. In our social studies class**

10. Uncle Jim said after reading all the consumer guides and asking his friends for advice he would decide what kind of personal computer to buy.   **10. that**

6. with city council members

MEETING *individual* **NEEDS**

LESS-ADVANCED STUDENTS

To place a modifier correctly in a sentence, a student must determine which word the modifier is intended to modify. Work with students to identify the words being modified in the example sentences in this lesson.

You could write the sentences on the chalkboard. Use one color to underline the modifiers and another color to underline the words they modify.

LEP/ESL

General Strategies. In languages such as Korean and Turkish, nearly all modifiers precede the words modified. In other languages, such as Indonesian, Spanish, and Tagalog, nearly all modifiers follow the words modified. Errors may occur as students confuse other languages' rules for placement of modifiers with those of English. You may wish to give students extra practice with correct placement of English modifiers.

LEARNING STYLES

Kinetic Learners. To reinforce the concept that modifying phrases and clauses need to be as close as possible to the words they modify, write sentences on strips of paper. For each sentence, write a modifying phrase or clause that could be added to the sentence without any rewording. Ask students to cut the sentence strips where appropriate and to insert the corresponding phrase and clause strips.

USAGE

USAGE

833

USAGE

PICTURE THIS

You may want to borrow a painting from your school's library or art department and model this activity for students before they begin. You may want to suggest that students first look at the painting and then brainstorm their impressions for several minutes before they begin writing. Remind students that there is no one correct evaluation for a work of art, but that they should support their opinions with reasons.

USAGE

PICTURE THIS

You are a writer for the magazine *Art Notes,* and you're reviewing a new exhibit of abstract paintings. At the exhibit, this painting, called *Untitled,* by Tony Da immediately catches your attention. Write a paragraph or two about the painting to include in your review of the exhibit. First describe the painting, and then give your opinion of it. If your readers visit the exhibit, should they make a special point of seeing this painting? Tell why or why not. In your review, use at least five modifying words, phrases, and clauses.

Subject: an abstract painting
Audience: readers of an art magazine
Purpose: to evaluate a painting in an exhibit; to persuade

Tony Da, *Untitled* (1979). Oil on canvas, 24" × 36". Courtesy of the Artist/The Heard Museum of Phoenix (Arizona).

DANGLING MODIFIERS Rule 26b

OBJECTIVE

- To revise sentences by correcting dangling modifiers

Dangling Modifiers

A modifying word, phrase, or clause that does not sensibly modify any word or group of words in the sentence is called a *dangling modifier.*

26b. Avoid using a dangling modifier.

You may correct a dangling modifier by adding a word that the word, phrase, or clause can sensibly modify, by adding words to the modifier so that its meaning is clear, or by rewording the sentence.

DANGLING   Foggy, we couldn't see eight feet in front of us. [Were we foggy?]

CORRECT   **In the fog,** we couldn't see eight feet in front of us.

CORRECT   We couldn't see eight feet in front of us **in the foggy weather.**

DANGLING   After reading the article "Keeping America Beautiful," a recycling program was organized in their neighborhood. [Who read the article?]

CORRECT   **After reading the article "Keeping America Beautiful," Luís and Olan** organized a recycling program in their neighborhood.

CORRECT   **After Luís and Olan read the article "Keeping America Beautiful,"** they organized a recycling program in their neighborhood.

DANGLING   To win the election, your support will be needed. [Is your support trying to win the election?]

CORRECT   **To win the election, I** will need your support.

CORRECT   **If I am to win the election, I** will need your support.

DANGLING   Convicted of stealing a loaf of bread for his sister's seven starving children, Jean Valjean's sentence was five years in prison. [Was Jean Valjean's sentence convicted?]

CORRECT   **Convicted of stealing a loaf of bread for his sister's seven starving children, Jean Valjean** was sentenced to five years in prison.

CORRECT   **Jean Valjean was convicted of stealing a loaf of bread for his sister's seven starving children** and was sentenced to five years in prison.

USAGE

USAGE

PROGRAM MANAGER

DANGLING MODIFIERS

- **Independent Practice/ Reteaching** For instruction and exercises, see **Dangling Modifiers** in *Language Skills Practice and Assessment,* p. 164.

- **Computer Guided Instruction** For additional instruction and practice with dangling modifiers, see **Lesson 22** in *Language Workshop CD-ROM.*

- **Practice** To help less-advanced students with additional instruction and practice with dangling modifiers, see **Chapter 19** in *English Workshop, Complete Course,* pp. 265–266.

QUICK REMINDER

Ask students to rewrite the following descriptions so that each modifier clearly and sensibly modifies a word in the sentence:

1. Lifting the trophy high over her head, the photographer snapped her picture.
2. After becoming frustrated his essay was hurled into the wastebasket.
3. Without food and water for weeks, her survival was miraculous.

USAGE

USAGE

NOTE: A few dangling modifiers have become standard idiomatic expressions.

EXAMPLES   **Judging from the audience's response,** the band's new number will be a big hit.
Relatively speaking, the cost of living remained static for several years.
To be perfectly frank, the rate of inflation is still too high.

☞ **REFERENCE NOTE:** For more information about idiomatic expressions, see page 534.

▶ **EXERCISE 2**   **Revising Sentences by Correcting Dangling Modifiers**

The following sentences contain dangling modifiers. Revise each sentence so that its meaning is clear and correct.

Revisions will vary.

EXAMPLE   **1. Before moving to San Angelo, Miami had been their home.**
1. *Before they moved to San Angelo, Miami had been their home.*

1. Listening to his grandfather's stories, ~~it~~ was ~~amazing~~ to learn that several of their ancestors had worked with the Underground Railroad.   **1.** he/amazed
2. ~~Architecturally striking,~~ everyone is impressed by the new building's size and elegance.   **2.** architecturally striking
3. When selecting a college, a number of factors ~~should be considered.~~   **3.** you are/you should consider
4. While talking with some friends of mine, the topic of careers in dentistry came up.   **4.** I was   **5.** we found
5. After searching all over the bookstore, Amy Tan's novel ~~was found~~ in the "Best-seller" section.   **6.** you should cover
6. To keep the guacamole dip from turning brown, its surface ~~should be covered~~ with a thin layer of lemon juice.
7. After working in the fields all day, little energy ~~was~~ left for social activities.   **7.** we had
8. ~~To understand~~ many of the allusions in modern literature, a knowledge of Greek and Roman myths is essential.
9. ~~Thirsty and weary,~~ the oasis was a welcome sight to the dusty travelers.   **9.** thirsty, weary,
10. Riding in the glass-bottomed boat, hundreds of beautiful tropical fish ~~could be seen.~~   **10.** they could see

8. A knowledge of Greek and Roman myths is essential/understanding

REVIEW

Revising Sentences by Correcting Faulty Modifiers

The sentences in the following paragraph contain misplaced and dangling modifiers. Revise each sentence so that its meaning will be clear on first reading.

USAGE

Major Cultural Areas and Native Peoples of North America

[1] I found a fascinating book at the library book sale that includes this map showing where Native Americans traditionally lived on the Plains. [2] You can see the homelands of the major Plains peoples, looking at the map. [3] The size of the Great Plains especially surprised me, extending farther north and south than I had thought. [4] While thumbing through the

CRITICAL THINKING

Analysis. Ask students to analyze the following sentences to determine whether the modifiers are dangling or misplaced:

1. Walking down the street, the car was admired. [dangling modifier]
2. On leaving the office, the radio was heard. [dangling modifier]
3. Under the sofa, we saw a pair of beady little eyes. [misplaced modifier]

USAGE

ANSWERS
Review

Revisions may vary.

1. At the library book sale I found a fascinating book that includes this map showing where Native Americans traditionally lived on the plains.

2. Looking at the map, you can see the homelands of the major Plains peoples.

3. The size of the Great Plains area, extending farther north and south than I had thought, especially surprised me.

4. This picture of a Sioux encampment caught my attention while I was thumbing through the book.

5. Farming was the main activity of most of these peoples, who lived much of the year in villages.

6. I read, however, that they hunted buffalo during the summer.

7. They followed the buffalo, which provided them with food and clothing, across the plains.

8. Characterized by a strong sense of independence, the Plains peoples practiced a form of democracy.

9. To make key decisions, they cast votes at council meetings.

10. Having read this fascinating book about the peoples of the Plains, I'm going to find out more about such peoples as the Crow and Cheyenne.

USAGE

ANSWERS
Review: Posttest Part A

Revisions may vary.

1. We chose the Adirondacks as our vacation spot because we preferred the mountains to the seashore.

2. After working in Washington for more than twenty years, I was familiar with the methods of lobbyists.

3. To qualified individuals, this bank approves car loans of any size.

4. The signs warned that the animals, because they were untamed, were dangerous.

838

REVIEW: POSTTEST

OBJECTIVE

- To revise sentences by correcting faulty modifiers

USAGE

838 *Placement of Modifiers*

book, this picture of a Sioux encampment caught my attention. [5] Living much of the year in villages, farming was the main activity of most of these peoples. [6] However, I read during the summer they hunted buffalo. [7] They followed the buffalo across the plains, which provided them with food and clothing. [8] Characterized by a strong sense of independence, a form of democracy was practiced by the Plains peoples. [9] To make key decisions, votes were cast at council meetings. [10] I'm going to find out more about such peoples as the Crow and Cheyenne, having read this fascinating book about the peoples of the Plains.

Review: Posttest

A. Revising Sentences by Correcting Faulty Modifiers

The following sentences contain misplaced and dangling modifiers. Revise each sentence so that its meaning will be clear on first reading.

1. Preferring the mountains rather than the seashore, the Adirondacks were chosen as our vacation spot.
2. After working in Washington for more than twenty years, the methods of lobbyists were familiar.
3. This bank approves car loans to qualified individuals of any size.
4. Because they were untamed, the signs warned that the animals were dangerous.

5. One can see more than a hundred lakes, flying at an altitude of several thousand feet.
6. Jack bought a book of shorthand lessons along with his new typewriter, which he read and studied diligently.
7. The people in line only had to stand out in the cold for a few minutes.
8. We followed several routes that early Spanish explorers took on vacation last year.
9. Salvador said after the game the referee explained his unpopular decision to the two team captains.
10. Rounding a sharp curve on El Camino del Rio on the way to Big Bend, a detour sign warned us of danger.

B. Revising Sentences by Correcting Faulty Modifiers

Revisions may vary.

The following sentences contain misplaced and dangling modifiers. Revise each sentence so that its meaning will be clear on first reading.

11. ~~Among popular mystery writers,~~ the novels of Agatha Christie continue to lead sales. **11. of books by famous mystery writers.**
12. Phoebe said ~~in the summer~~ Karl is planning to read all of Christie's novels about the Belgian detective Hercule Poirot. **12. in the summer**
13. Pat said ~~tonight~~ the performance of Christie's whodunit play *The Mousetrap* is sold out. **13. tonight**
14. ~~Concluding~~ the play, the audience is always told by the cast not to give away the surprise ending. **14. After**
15. After reading all of Christie's novels, our library received many requests for books by another great mystery writer, Dorothy L. Sayers. **15. I heard that**
16. While still in junior high school, Mom bought me my first Sayers mystery. **16. I was**
17. ~~A British nobleman and amateur detective,~~ there are few criminal investigators who rival Lord Peter Wimsey. **17. , British nobleman and amateur detective.**
18. After ~~reading~~ a detective story by Ngaio (pronounced Ny-o) Marsh, New Zealand became an interest of mine. **18. I read**
19. ~~One of my favorite mysteries,~~ I have read Marsh's *Died in the Wool* three times. **19. , one of my favorite mysteries,**
20. Fond of mysteries, novels such as *Devices and Desires* by British author P. D. James keep ~~Ben~~ spellbound. **20. Because Ben is/him**

---

5. Flying at an altitude of several thousand feet, one can see more than a hundred lakes.
6. Along with his new typewriter, Jack bought a book of shorthand lessons, which he read and studied diligently.
7. The people in line had to stand out in the cold for only a few minutes.
8. While on vacation last year, we followed several routes that early Spanish explorers took.
9. Salvador said that after the game the referee explained his unpopular decision to the two team captains.
10. Rounding a sharp curve on El Camino del Rio on the way to Big Bend, we saw a detour sign warning us of danger.

A DIFFERENT APPROACH

Have students look in newspapers and magazines for sentences with misplaced or dangling modifiers. Then, ask students to read the sentences to the class and to suggest revisions.

PROGRAM MANAGER

FOR THE WHOLE CHAPTER

- **Review** For exercises on chapter concepts, see **Review Form A** and **Review Form B** in *Language Skills Practice and Assessment,* pp. 174–175.
- **Assessment** For additional testing, see **Usage Pretests** and **Usage Mastery Tests** in *Language Skills Practice and Assessment,* pp. 95–101 and pp. 179–185.

USAGE

CHAPTER OVERVIEW

This chapter consists of instruction on words and expressions that are commonly confused or misused. Standard, nonstandard, formal, and informal usage are discussed.

A **Picture This** feature asks students to write informative/descriptive paragraphs that correctly use some often misused words. The **Writing Application** feature asks students to use standard and nonstandard English in original fictional narratives.

The chapter concludes with a **Review: Posttest** for checking students' mastery of common usage problems.

USAGE

27 A GLOSSARY OF USAGE

Common Usage Problems

Diagnostic Test

A. Identifying Correct Usage

For each of the following sentences, choose the <u>correct word or words</u> in parentheses.

EXAMPLE **1.** We were (*kind of, rather*) disappointed with the results.
1. *rather*

1. After Shirley had starred in our spring play, she acted (*like, <u>as if</u>*) she were a famous movie star.
2. When we need the tape, we never know where (*it's at, <u>it is</u>*).
3. At the restaurant where I work, all four of us divide the tips evenly (*between, <u>among</u>*) ourselves.
4. As I was about to pay for my new jeans, I discovered that I (<u>*had,*</u> *hadn't*) scarcely any money in my wallet.
5. (*Accept, <u>Except</u>*) for Carlos and Glenn, everyone went to the fair.

6. The reason we are moving is (*because, that*) our parents have always wanted to live in Oregon.
7. Although we do the same type of work, Hasina and I are (*affected, effected*) differently by it.
8. (*Bring, Take*) the dog with you when you go for a walk.
9. Looking at the crisp green beans, Rosa said, "(*This, Those*) kind of bean has always been my favorite."
10. Both of Emily's grandmothers (*immigrated, emigrated*) here from Poland.

B. Identifying Correct Usage

For each sentence in the following paragraph, choose the correct word or words in parentheses.

EXAMPLE   **[1]** (*Don't, Doesn't*) a hot summer day make you long for an ice-cold drink?
   1. *Doesn't*

[11] Even during ancient times, people (*which, who*) were sweltering in the heat found ways to cool off. **[12]** Around 3000 B.C., the Egyptians beat the heat when they (*discovered, invented*) the cooling effect of evaporation. **[13]** The Egyptians poured water into shallow trays made of clay; (*than, then*) they put the trays on a layer of straw. **[14]** As the temperature dropped during the night, the water quickly evaporated, forming a thin layer of ice, (*which, and which*) was eagerly gathered early the next morning. **[15]** Because more ice forms in very dry air, the (*amount, number*) of ice crystals depended on the dryness of the air. **[16]** A thousand years later, wealthy Babylonians would use the (*effects, affects*) of evaporation to cool their homes. **[17]** At twilight, they had the exterior walls and interior floors doused with water; as it evaporated from (*these, said, such, same*) surfaces, the houses cooled down dramatically. **[18]** In ancient India, the same (*type, kind of*) system was adapted for home cooling. **[19]** Wet grass mats hung in windward windows were (*liable, likely*) to create a considerable, as much as thirty-degree, drop in temperature inside the house. **[20]** To maintain cooling, either someone kept the mats wet during the night, or (*a, an*) reservoir over the windows slowly dripped water on the mats.

USAGE

USING THE DIAGNOSTIC TEST

This test will provide information about each student's ability to recognize common usage problems and to use standard formal language. After reviewing students' performances, you may decide to have students work selectively on specific expressions with which they have had difficulty.

USAGE

OBJECTIVE

- To identify correct usage in sentences

PROGRAM MANAGER

A, AN—AT

- **Independent Practice/ Reteaching** For instruction and exercises, see **Common Usage Problems A** in *Language Skills Practice and Assessment,* p. 169.

- **Computer Guided Instruction** For additional instruction and practice with common usage problems, see **Lesson 59** in *Language Workshop CD-ROM.*

- **Practice** To help less-advanced students with common usage problems, see **Chapter 20** in *English Workshop, Complete Course,* pp. 269–270.

✔ QUICK REMINDER

Write the following sentences on the chalkboard. Ask students to rewrite them in standard, formal English.

1. She received <u>a</u> honorable discharge. [an]

2. Bring scissors, thread, measuring tape, <u>and</u> etc. [omit *and*]

3. Where are the reference materials <u>at</u>? [omit *at*]

842

---

842 *A Glossary of Usage*

A *glossary* is an alphabetical list of special terms or expressions with definitions, explanations, and examples. You'll notice that some examples in this glossary are labeled *standard*, *nonstandard*, *formal*, or *informal*. The label *standard* or *formal* identifies usage that is appropriate in serious speaking and writing situations (such as in speeches and in compositions for school). The label *informal* indicates standard usage common in conversation and in everyday writing such as personal letters. The label *nonstandard* identifies usage that is suitable only in the most casual speaking situations and in writing that attempts to re-create casual speech. In doing the exercises in this chapter, be sure to use only formal standard English.

☞ **REFERENCE NOTE:** See page 513 for more about standard English. Problems in spelling, such as the difference between *already* and *all ready*, are discussed on page 977.

a, an These *indefinite articles* refer to one of the members of a general group. Use *a* before words beginning with a consonant sound. Use *an* before words beginning with a vowel sound.

> EXAMPLE It was **an** honor and **a** surprise to receive **an** award for my work as **a** hospital volunteer. [Notice that *an* is used before *honor* because *honor* begins with a vowel sound even though the first letter is the consonant *h*. The article *a* is used before *hospital* because *hospital* begins with a consonant sound.]

accept, except *Accept* is a verb meaning "to receive." *Except* may be either a verb or a preposition. As a verb, *except* means "to leave out." As a preposition, *except* means "excluding."

> EXAMPLES Did you **accept** the gift?
> Did the new census **except** homeless people? [verb]
> We were busy every evening this week **except** Tuesday. [preposition]

adapt, adopt *Adapt* means "to change or adjust something in order to make it fit or to make it suitable." *Adopt* means "to take something and make it one's own."

> EXAMPLES The play was **adapted** from a popular book.
> My aunt and uncle **adopted** a nine-year-old boy from Guatemala.

affect, effect *Affect* is a verb meaning "to influence." As a verb, *effect* means "to bring about" or "to accomplish." As a noun, *effect* means "the result [of an action]."

EXAMPLES   Try not to let unkind remarks **affect** you.
The school board **effected** drastic changes in the budget. [verb]
The **effects** of the hurricane were evident the next day. [noun]

all the farther, all the faster These expressions are used informally in some parts of the United States. In formal situations, use *as far as* or *as fast as*.

INFORMAL   Thirty miles per hour was all the faster the first airplane could travel.
FORMAL   Thirty miles per hour was **as fast as** the first airplane could travel.

allusion, illusion An *allusion* is an indirect reference to something. An *illusion* is a mistaken idea or a misleading appearance.

EXAMPLES   Amy Tan's writings include numerous **allusions** to Chinese mythology.
At one time, many people shared the **illusion** that the earth was flat.
The movie's special effects created the **illusion** of space travel.

alumni, alumnae *Alumni* (ə lum′nī) is the plural of *alumnus* (a male graduate). *Alumnae* (ə lum′nē) is the plural of *alumna* (a female graduate). As a group, the graduates of a coeducational school are usually called *alumni*.

EXAMPLES   Both men are **alumni** of Harvard University.
All of my sisters are **alumnae** of Hollins College.
My parents went to their **alumni** reunion.

among   See **between, among.**

amount, number Use *amount* to refer to a singular word. Use *number* to refer to a plural word. (See also **number,** page 858.)

EXAMPLES   The **amount** of research on stress has increased.
[*Amount* refers to the singular word *research.*]
A large **number** of studies have been conducted.
[*Number* refers to the plural word *studies.*]

USAGE

MEETING *individual* NEEDS

LEP/ESL

General Strategies. English-language learners often learn English by communicating with classmates who may sometimes use nonstandard English. You may want to give students more examples of the correct use of commonly misused words and phrases. Also, keep in mind that while it is important for students to learn standard English usage, it is more important that students become conversant in English and able to make themselves understood.

INTEGRATING THE LANGUAGE ARTS

Usage and Diction. To reinforce the concept that English usage varies depending on the occasion, have students make lists of slang expressions they commonly use. Then, work with students to make a list of more formal phrases that could be used in place of the slang phrases when writing or speaking formal English. Discuss with your class how to determine when to use formal English. This activity will help reinforce the connection between audience and choice of vocabulary.

A DIFFERENT APPROACH

To reinforce correct usage, have students compose sentences that include the words and phrases discussed in this lesson. Then, have students exchange papers and evaluate each other's sentences.

USAGE

and etc. *Etc.* is an abbreviation of the Latin words *et cetera*, meaning "and others" or "and so forth." Consequently, *and* should not be used before *etc.*

> EXAMPLE   This unit discusses writers associated with the Harlem Renaissance: Countee Cullen, Langston Hughes, Zora Neale Hurston, **etc.** [not *and etc.*].

and which, but which The expressions *and which, but which* (*and who, but who*) should be used only when a *which* (or *who*) clause precedes them in the sentence.

> NONSTANDARD   Our jazz band was pleased with the fans' enthusiastic response and which was even greater than we had expected.
> STANDARD   Our jazz band was pleased with the fans' response, **which** was enthusiastic **and which** was even greater than we had expected.
> STANDARD   Our jazz band was pleased with the fans' enthusiastic response, **which** was even greater than we had expected.

anyways, anywheres Omit the final *s* from these words and others like them (*everywheres, nowheres, somewheres*).

> EXAMPLE   I couldn't find my keys **anywhere** [not *anywheres*]; I looked **everywhere** [not *everywheres*], but they were **nowhere** [not *nowheres*] in the house.

as See **like, as.**

as if See **like, as if, as though.**

at Avoid using *at* after a construction beginning with *where.*

> NONSTANDARD   Where do most Navajo live at now?
> STANDARD   **Where** do most Navajo live now?

▶ EXERCISE 1   **Identifying Correct Usage**

For each of the following sentences, choose the <u>correct word or words</u> in parentheses.

1. Some pets find it hard to (*adapt, adopt*) to city life.
2. I own a large (*number, amount*) of campaign buttons.
3. During my travels in Mexico, I met a group of Canadian students (*somewhere, somewheres*) in Jalisco.

TIMESAVER

You may want to use **Exercises 1** and **2** as guided practice. Discuss and analyze with students only the even-numbered sentences. You will save time and will be able to assess students' progress quickly. If students need additional practice, assign the odd-numbered sentences as independent practice.

4. Everyone I know likes peanut butter (*accept, except*) you.
5. One line appears to be longer because the drawing is an optical (*allusion, illusion*).
6. Do you know whether or not Anderson Boulevard will be turned into (*a, an*) one-way street?
7. The committee's job is to analyze the possible long-term (*affects, effects*) of acid rain on European forests.
8. Four hundred miles is (*all the farther, as far as*) this car will go on one tank of gas.
9. Were any crops (*affected, effected*) by this year's dry spell?
10. The expression "lock, stock, and barrel" is an (*allusion, illusion*) to the parts of a flintlock rifle.

▶ EXERCISE 2   Identifying Correct Usage

For each sentence in the following paragraph, choose the correct word or words in parentheses.

[1] At one time, the name Madame C. J. Walker was known by black women just about (*everywhere, everywheres*) in America and Europe. [2] Walker's likeness, (*and which, which*) you can see in this photo of her driving a car, was familiar, too, because it appeared on each of the millions of packages of beauty products that she manufactured. [3] For eighteen years Walker washed clothes for a living, but she never believed people who

USAGE

VISUAL CONNECTIONS
Exploring the Subject. Sarah McWilliams (1869–1919) was born near Delta, Louisiana. Not much is known of her early life except that she was orphaned at age seven, married at age fourteen, and was left a widow with a small child at age twenty.

After moving to St. Louis, McWilliams married Charles J. Walker. Under the name of Madame C. J. Walker, she began manufacturing her hair preparations. She later added a complete line of toiletries and cosmetics and established the Walker beauty schools. Walker was the first African American woman to become a millionaire.

OBJECTIVES

- To write a description that contains correct usage of selected words
- To identify correct usage in sentences
- To revise sentences to correct errors in usage

USAGE

USAGE

846 *A Glossary of Usage*

said she had gone (*all the farther*, *as far as*) a black woman could in business. [4] Eventually, she invested in a sizable (*number*, *amount*) of oils, shampoos, and lotions and began experimenting with them in a washtub. [5] When she was done, Walker had a formula that softened coarse hair; later, she would patent (*an*, *a*) hair-straightening comb that gave users soft, manageable coiffures. [6] The public, however, was reluctant to (*accept*, *except*) Walker's new products, and she had to go door-to-door, selling her system of hair care. [7] The success of her dynamic personal demonstrations enabled Walker to purchase (*a*, *an*) additional office. [8] Before long, her offices, laboratory, manufacturing plant, (*and etc.*, *etc.*), took up a whole city block, and thousands of Walker's sales representatives canvassed not only America but also Europe, where the performer Josephine Baker used the Walker method to obtain her sleek hairstyle.

[9] A pioneer in the development, sales, and marketing of cosmetics, Madame Walker insisted that her salespeople (*adopt*, *adapt*) a strict program of hygiene, a requirement that later became part of state cosmetology laws. [10] As a wealthy older woman, she did not forget her years of poverty and toil, and many (*alumnae*, *alumni*) of Tuskegee Institute and Palmer Memorial Institute were grateful for the scholarships that Walker funded for young women.

bad, badly See page 816.

because In formal situations, do not use the construction *reason . . . because*. Instead, use *reason . . . that*.

> INFORMAL   The reason I'm late is because my car had a flat tire.
>
> FORMAL   The reason I'm late is **that** my car had a flat tire. [This sentence can also be revised to make the statement more directly: *I'm late because my car had a flat tire.*]

being as, being that Avoid using either of these expressions for *since* or *because*.

> EXAMPLE   **Because** [not *Being as*] Elena lived in Mexico until she was almost eight years old, she can speak both Spanish and English quite fluently.

beside, besides *Beside* is a preposition meaning "by the side

---

PROGRAM
MANAGER

BAD, BADLY—GOOD, WELL

- **Independent Practice/ Reteaching** For instruction and exercises, see **Common Usage Problems B** in *Language Skills Practice and Assessment,* p. 170.

- **Computer Guided Instruction** For additional instruction and practice with common usage problems, see **Lesson 59** in *Language Workshop CD-ROM.*

- **Practice** To help less-advanced students with common usage problems, see **Chapter 20** in *English Workshop, Complete Course,* pp. 269–272.

of" or "next to." *Besides* may be used as either a preposition or an adverb. As a preposition, *besides* means "in addition to" or "except." As an adverb, *besides* means "moreover."

EXAMPLES   Who sits **beside** you in English class?
Besides my homework, I still have chores to do. [preposition]
It's too cold to go camping; **besides,** the forecast calls for rain. [adverb]

between, among   Use *between* when referring to only two items or to more than two when each item is being compared individually to each of the others.

EXAMPLES   The final chess match was **between** Anne and Lisa.
Don't you know the difference **between** mambo, salsa, and merengue? [*Between* is used because each dance is compared individually to each of the other dances; in other words, the dances are compared two at a time.]

Use *among* when you are referring to more than two items and are not considering each item in relation to each other item individually.

EXAMPLE   College admissions offices must decide **among** thousands of qualified applicants.

bring, take   *Bring* means "to come carrying something." *Take* means "to go carrying something."

EXAMPLES   I'll **bring** my collection of Black Heritage postage stamps for the Black History Month display.
Please **take** the recycling bin out to the curb when you leave for school.

bust, busted   Avoid using these words as verbs. Use a form of *break* or *burst,* depending on the meaning.

EXAMPLES   How did your glasses get **broken** [not *busted*]?
My car's radiator hose **burst** [not *busted*].

but, only   See **The Double Negative,** pages 864–865.

can't hardly, can't scarcely   See **The Double Negative,** pages 864–865.

could of   See **of.**

QUICK REMINDER

Write the following sentences on the chalkboard. Ask students to revise the sentences so that they contain formal, standard English.

1. The referee <u>busted up</u> that fight. [broke up]
2. <u>Being as</u> the team won, the players celebrated. [Because]
3. The camaraderie <u>between</u> the many players was evident. [among]
4. There were <u>less</u> spectators at Saturday's game, due to the inclement weather. [fewer]

MEETING *individual* NEEDS

LEP/ESL

Spanish. Students whose first language is Spanish may need further explanation of the difference between *among* and *between* because no such distinction is made in Spanish.

Usage and Writing. Instruct students to write paragraphs that include common errors in usage in every sentence. Paragraphs should contain between five and ten sentences. Then, have students exchange papers and attempt to find the errors in each other's paragraphs.

Usage and Speaking and Listening. Have students work in pairs to create dialogues or raps that contain nonstandard usage. Have students perform their dialogues or raps for the class. As students listen to their classmates, they should take note of any nonstandard usage.

USAGE

---

848 *A Glossary of Usage*

USAGE

credible, creditable, credulous *Credible* means "believable."

> EXAMPLE The children gave a **credible** excuse for breaking the vase.

Creditable means "praiseworthy."

> EXAMPLE Her quick thinking and competent action were **creditable.**

Credulous means "inclined to believe too readily."

> EXAMPLE The **credulous** listeners thought that the Martians really had invaded Earth.

data *Data* is the plural form of the Latin *datum*. In standard informal English, *data* is frequently used, like a collective noun, with singular pronouns and verbs. In formal usage, *data* takes plural pronouns and verbs.

> INFORMAL As soon as the census data was published, it was immediately challenged.
> FORMAL As soon as the census **data were** published, **they** were immediately challenged.

discover, invent *Discover* means "to learn of the existence of [something]." *Invent* means "to bring something new into existence."

> EXAMPLES Engineers **discovered** oil deposits in Michigan.
> Sequoyah **invented** a written Cherokee language based on the spoken Cherokee language.

done *Done* is the past participle of *do*. When used as a main verb, *done* requires an auxiliary, or helping, verb. Avoid using *done* for *did*, which does not require an auxiliary verb. [Note: When used as a gerund or a participle, *done* does not always require an auxiliary verb.]

> NONSTANDARD We done all our chores today.
> STANDARD We **have done** all our chores today.
> STANDARD We **did** all our chores today.

don't, doesn't *Don't* is the contraction of *do not*. *Doesn't* is the contraction of *does not*. Use *doesn't*, not *don't*, with singular subjects except *I* and *you*.

> EXAMPLES Franklin **doesn't** [not *don't*] ever skip school.
> Our local grocery store **doesn't** [not *don't*] carry mangoes.

PICTURE THIS

You are working in the physics lab after school. While doing some routine tests to learn about the properties of convex surfaces, you hold this crystal ball up to your face. You can scarcely believe your eyes! Instead of seeing your own reflection, you see this mysterious man peering out at you from an unfamiliar room. You quickly stifle your impulse to shout, and your scientific curiosity takes over. With your free hand, jot down a detailed description of the image that you see. Hypothesize about the source of the image. In your description, use correctly at least five of the following words. As you revise what you've written, consult the **Glossary of Usage** to check any usages you're not sure about.

affect	illusion	beside	among
effect	as if	besides	don't
allusion	like	between	doesn't

Subject: unexpected image in a crystal ball
Audience: yourself; your physics teacher
Purpose: to record information; to form a hypothesis

M. C. Escher (1898–1972), *Hand with Reflecting Sphere* (1935). Lithograph.
M. C. Escher/Cordon Art-Baarn-Holland.

USAGE

PICTURE THIS

You may want to specify whether you want students' descriptions to be written in paragraph form or in the form of a set of notes. You could also take this opportunity to discuss mood with your students. Tell them that the mood or atmosphere of a piece of writing is established in part by the words that the author chooses to use. As an example, write the following two sentences on the chalkboard:

1. The rose was scarlet, and its scent was sweet.
2. The rose was a dark, dull red, and its smell was cloying.

Have students discuss any differences in mood they discern between the two sentences.

Challenge students to use in their descriptions words that establish a particular mood.

USAGE

849

USAGE

COOPERATIVE LEARNING
Divide the class into groups of three and ask the groups to find printed examples of uses of the words and phrases presented in this lesson. Students might look in newspapers, magazines, short stories, and advertisements. Have a spokesperson from each group report on the group's findings.

effect See **affect, effect.**

emigrate, immigrate *Emigrate* means "to leave a country or a region to settle elsewhere." *Immigrate* means "to come into a country or a region to settle there."

> EXAMPLES   The war forced people to **emigrate** from their homeland.
> Marie's grandparents **immigrated** to the United States in 1960.

etc. See **and etc.**

everywheres See **anyways, anywheres.**

except See **accept, except.**

famous, notorious *Famous* means "widely known." *Notorious* means "widely but unfavorably known."

> EXAMPLES   Gloria Steinem is a **famous** leader of the women's movement in the United States.
> In the 1920s, Al Capone was a **notorious** gangster.

farther See **all the farther, all the faster.**

fewer, less Use *fewer,* which tells "how many," to modify a plural noun. Use *less,* which tells "how much," to modify a singular noun.

> EXAMPLES   I worked **fewer** hours this week than last week.
> I worked **less** time this week than last week.

good, well See page 816.

▶ EXERCISE 3   **Identifying Correct Usage**

Choose the correct word or words in parentheses.

1. (*Being that, Because*) Eric is shy, he doesn't say much.
2. When the car broke down, they had only thirteen dollars (*between, among*) the six of them.
3. (*Beside, Besides*) our volunteer work, our club sponsors an annual ski trip.
4. Please (*bring, take*) your guitar when you come to my party.
5. Jon is so (*credulous, credible, creditable*) that he believed your crazy story.
6. They sold (*fewer, less*) new cars than used cars.
7. In what year was the transistor (*invented, discovered*)?

8. Their reason for being late to the rehearsal was (*because*, *that*) they missed their bus.
9. Did Carla (*bring*, *take*) her camera on her trip to Panama?
10. Basketball is his favorite sport (*beside*, *besides*) tennis.
11. All the critics praised Gene Wilder's (*creditable*, *credulous*) performance in his most recent movie.
12. They (*done*, *did*) well in the playoffs.
13. Angie forgot to (*bring*, *take*) her homework assignment when she went to school this morning.
14. (*Among*, *Between*) the four of us, we can paint the house.
15. The dog ate all of the leftovers (*accept*, *except*) the okra.
16. Lupe's family (*emigrated*, *immigrated*) from the Philippines when she was nine years old.
17. I had (*fewer*, *less*) cavities than my sister.
18. Alan Shepard, Jr., became (*famous*, *notorious*) as the first American in space.
19. Kristine decided to (*invent*, *discover*) a computer game of her own.
20. Cold weather (*don't*, *doesn't*) bother him very much.

EXERCISE 4   **Correcting Errors in Usage**

Most of the following sentences contain errors in usage. If a sentence contains any errors in usage, revise the sentence. If a sentence is correct, write *C*.

EXAMPLE   **1. We excepted the telegram nervously.**
          1. *We accepted the telegram nervously.*

1. Frank has ~~less~~ hobbies than his friend.   **1. fewer**
2. ~~Being as~~ Bernard Malamud is my favorite writer, I was excited to find one of his novels at the yard sale.   **2. Because**
3. Would you please take this monstrosity out of here?   **3. C**
4. Sue Ellen plays and enjoys many sports: baseball, tennis, bowling, field hockey, volleyball, ~~and~~ etc.
5. One of the main reasons for the widespread concern for eagles is ~~because~~ many are dying from lead poisoning.   **5. that**
6. The manager divided the work ~~between~~ the four of us.   **6. among**
7. The Chinese ballet dancer ~~immigrated~~ from his homeland to find creative freedom.   **7. emigrated**
8. Have any of you ~~did~~ your research for your report yet?   **8. done**
9. To prepare her report, Judy used current data that were published by the Department of the Treasury.   **9. C**
10. Roy said it ~~don't~~ matter, but I can see that he is angry.   **10. doesn't**

USAGE

852

REVIEW A

OBJECTIVE

• To identify and correct the usage errors in a paragraph

USAGE

▶ **REVIEW A**   **Proofreading for Correct Usage**

Most sentences in the following paragraphs contain usage errors. If a sentence is incorrect, correct each error in usage. If a sentence is correct, write *C*.

1. anywhere

[1] One of the most powerful works of art ~~anywheres~~, the bull shown below was painted some fifteen thousand years ago in Lascaux, France. [2] The painting remained hidden until 1940, when a dog named Robot darted down a hole and the four young men following him accidentally ~~invented~~ these marvelous cave paintings. [3] According to one of these adventurous boys, Marcel Ravidat, it was he who painstakingly enlarged the hole and wriggled down into the now ~~notorious~~ caverns. [4] With only a weak light to guide him, he soon tripped and fell; luckily, his flashlight did not ~~bust~~. [5] When Ravidat aimed the light at the walls, ~~an~~ herd of animal figures leapt into view. [6] As the other boys joined him, the sight of the giant bulls, cows, elk, stags, ~~and~~ etc., filled the young men with joy and wonder, prompting them to celebrate with a wild dance. [7] With difficulty, the boys got out of the cavern, promising to return and admonishing each other, "Don't tell anyone about this!"

2. discovered

3. famous

4. break
5. a

7. C

8. took

[8] When they left home the next day, the boys ~~brought~~ a stronger light with them. [9] Impatiently, they investigated the cave until they found a passage that was so deep and dark that no one ~~accept~~ Ravidat would enter it. [10] Using a rope, the boys lowered him down the dangerous vertical passage ~~all the farther~~ he could go. [11] At the bottom, Ravidat hardly knew

9. except
10. as far as

HAD OF—MYSELF, OURSELVES

OBJECTIVE

- To identify correct usage in sentences

where he was at, but gradually he began to explore this new area. [12] Soon, a picture of a human body with a bird's head appeared, and though it spanned ~~less~~ feet than the great bulls, it was just as awesome. [13] One by one, each of the other boys came down to glimpse the image of the strange creature, ~~and~~ which is shown being knocked over by a bison. [14] This eerie figure ~~effected~~ the boys differently than the bull did; instead of feeling triumphant, they were left shaken and pale.

[15] For Ravidat and his friends, these days were joyous and exciting ~~beside~~ being sometimes frightening. [16] Quite possibly, the artists who ~~done~~ the paintings hoped to instill these very emotions in viewers long ago. [17] Despite all the ~~datum~~ that scientists have since collected about the age and meaning of the paintings, much about them remains uncertain. [18] Some scientists believe that the purpose of the paintings was to initiate young hunters; other theorists think that the paintings were meant to magically increase the ~~amount~~ of game animals; but most scientists agree that the paintings were considered sacred and were kept secret. [19] The reason they have survived for so long is ~~because~~ they were secreted away in dark caves, protected from light and kept at a constant humidity. [20] ~~Being as~~ modern-day tourists have introduced destructive microorganisms into the Lascaux caverns, the caves are now, unfortunately, closed to the public.

12. fewer

14. affected

15. besides

16. did

17. data

18. number

19. that

20. Because

had of See **of.**

had ought, hadn't ought Do not use *had* or *hadn't* with *ought.*

| NONSTANDARD | You had ought to be more patient. |
| STANDARD | You **ought** to be more patient. |

| NONSTANDARD | I hadn't ought to spend any more money. |
| STANDARD | I **ought not** to spend any more money. |

hardly See **The Double Negative,** pages 864–865.

he, she, it, they Do not use an unnecessary pronoun after its antecedent when the antecedent is a subject. Such an error is called the *double subject.*

| NONSTANDARD | Faith Ringgold, who was recently featured in a one-woman show, she designs remarkable story quilts. |
| STANDARD | Faith Ringgold, who was recently featured in a one-woman show, designs remarkable story quilts. |

USAGE

MEETING *individual* NEEDS

LEP/ESL

Asian Languages. Several Asian languages, such as Chinese, Japanese, and Korean, have common sentence forms in which one first states the topic (usually a noun) and then comments on it, as in the nonstandard English sentence "My aunt, she's coming to visit tomorrow." It is very natural for speakers of such languages to transfer this structure into English sentences. The result is sentences with double subjects. Acknowledge that you are aware of this potential difficulty and offer students extra written or oral practice, as necessary.

USAGE

1. The soup tastes salty, (<u>as if</u>, like) someone salted it twice.
2. Marian looks (kind of, <u>rather</u>) sleepy.
3. She (hadn't ought, <u>ought not</u>) to be late.

USAGE

USAGE

hisself, theirselves Avoid using these words for *himself* and *themselves*.

  EXAMPLE   Lou built the shed **himself** [not *hisself*].

illusion See **allusion, illusion.**

immigrate See **emigrate, immigrate.**

imply, infer *Imply* means "to suggest something indirectly." *Infer* means "to interpret" or "to get a certain meaning from a remark or an action."

  EXAMPLES   Mayor Hanson **implied** during yesterday's press conference that she would run for reelection.
  I **inferred** from the mayor's comments that she would run for reelection.

in, into *In* means "within." *Into* means "from the outside to the inside." In formal situations, avoid using *in* for *into.*

  INFORMAL   Feeling nervous, Jim opened the door and walked in the personnel office.
  FORMAL   Feeling nervous, Jim opened the door and walked **into** the personnel office.

invent See **discover, invent.**

it See **he, she, it, they.**

kind(s), sort(s), type(s) With the singular form of each of these nouns, use *this* or *that*. With the plural form, use *these* or *those*.

  EXAMPLES   **This kind** of package is recyclable, but **those kinds** are not.
  These types of examples are helpful.

kind of, sort of In formal situations, avoid using *kind of* for the adverb *somewhat* or *rather*.

  INFORMAL   You look kind of worried.
  FORMAL   You look **rather** [or **somewhat**] worried.

kind of a, sort of a In formal situations, omit the *a.*

  INFORMAL   What kind of a car is that?
  FORMAL   What **kind of** car is that?

lay, lie See pages 784–785.

learn, teach *Learn* means "to gain knowledge." *Teach* means "to provide with knowledge."

> EXAMPLE   If you will **teach** me how to play the guitar, I will **learn** some traditional Mexican folk songs.

leave, let *Leave* means "to go away." *Let* means "to permit" or "to allow." Avoid using *leave* for *let*.

> EXAMPLES   **Let** [not *leave*] us finish our dinner.
> I knew I shouldn't have **let** [not *left*] them borrow my car.

less See **fewer, less.**

liable See **likely, liable.**

lie, lay See pages 784–785.

like, as *Like* is a preposition. In formal situations, do not use *like* for the conjunction *as* to introduce a subordinate clause.

> INFORMAL   The plan worked like they thought it would.
> FORMAL   The plan worked **as** they thought it would.

👉 **REFERENCE NOTE:** See pages 675–683 for more information about subordinate clauses.

like, as if, as though In formal situations, avoid using the preposition *like* for the conjunction *as if* or *as though* to introduce a subordinate clause.

> INFORMAL   I feel like I have the flu.
> FORMAL   I feel **as if** [or **as though**] I have the flu.

likely, liable In formal situations, use *likely* to express simple probability and *liable* to express probability with potential harm or misfortune.

> EXAMPLES   Ginny is **likely** to arrive any minute.
> The children playing in the abandoned building are **liable** to get hurt.

Liable is also used to mean "responsible" or "answerable."

> EXAMPLE   The Smiths are **liable** for the damages that their dog caused.

might of, must of See **of.**

MEETING *individual* **NEEDS**

ADVANCED STUDENTS

Some students will benefit from exposure to usage errors not covered in this chapter. Have students review other grammar textbooks or manuals of style. Encourage students to identify additional information concerning errors in usage that might help them or their classmates.

To present the information they discover, students can compile a booklet of examples and explanations.

USAGE

USAGE

855

856 *A Glossary of Usage*

myself, ourselves Avoid using pronouns ending in *–self* or *–selves* to replace personal pronouns as subjects or objects.

EXAMPLES   Amy and **I** [not *myself*] appreciate your help.
          Could you do a favor for Wanda and **us** [not *ourselves*]?

☞ **REFERENCE NOTE:** For more information about the kinds of pronouns, see pages 602–605. For more about how personal pronouns are used as subjects and objects, see pages 728–735.

EXERCISE 5   Correcting Errors in Usage

For each of the following sentences, choose the <u>correct word or words</u> in parentheses.

1. In his address to Congress, the president (<u>*implied*</u>, *inferred*) that an economic reversal might occur soon.
2. When you have time, will you (*learn*, <u>*teach*</u>) me to sew?
3. He slipped on the wet deck and fell (*in*, <u>*into*</u>) the water.
4. We (<u>*ought*</u>, *had ought*) to have asked Allison to give us her chimichanga recipe.
5. You look (*like*, <u>*as if*</u>) you've just seen a ghost!
6. Doyle and (<u>*I*</u>, *myself*) worked together on this project.
7. If you (<u>*had*</u>, *had of*) asked me, I would have told you.
8. Have you been changing the oil and filter every 3,000–5,000 miles (<u>*as*</u>, *like*) you're supposed to?
9. (*Leave*, <u>*Let*</u>) them stay if they don't want to go with us.
10. Her recordings of West African folk tales are (*liable*, <u>*likely*</u>) to become classics.

REVIEW B   Correcting Errors in Usage

Most of the following sentences contain errors in usage. If a sentence contains an error in usage, revise the sentence. If a sentence is correct, write *C*.

1. The magician dazzled us with flawless ~~allusions~~.   **1. illusions**
2. Without any warning, the cat jumped from the chair and leaped ~~in~~ my arms.   **2. into**   **3. themselves**
3. The children helped ~~theirselves~~ to more vegetable curry.
4. Your room looks ~~like~~ it's been hit by a tornado.   **4. as if**
5. What can you infer from the refrain in Paul Laurence Dunbar's poem?   **5. C**

USAGE

USAGE

6. You ~~hadn't ought~~ to complain so much.   **6.** ought not
7. Jane and ~~myself~~ are the editors of our yearbook.   **7.** I
8. What sort of ~~a~~ CD player does Margaret plan to buy with her Christmas bonus?
9. I asked my boss if he would let me have next Wednesday afternoon off.   **9.** C   **10.** are
10. Some people ~~they're~~ always making a fuss about nothing.

REVIEW C   Proofreading for Correct Usage

Each sentence in the following paragraph contains an error in usage. Correct each error.   Revisions may vary.

[1] Georges Seurat ~~he~~ spent his short career studying the mysteries of the human eye, light, and color. [2] One of the results of his study is this painting, which is composed of thousands, perhaps millions, of ~~kind of~~ small dots. [3] This sort of ~~a~~ technique is called pointillism, a name derived from the small

2. rather

points of color on the canvas. [4] Rather than mix paint ~~theirselves~~, artists using this technique let the viewer's eyes blend the colors. [5] Seen from a certain distance, the small points of color flow together and become solid ~~like~~ the pixels on a computer screen or the dots of a printed photograph do. [6] In fact, some critics believe that observations of modern printed

4. themselves

5. as

VISUAL CONNECTIONS
About the Artist. Georges Seurat (1859–1891) was an artist who integrated art with science. Seurat used the latest scientific discoveries about the perception of color and light to develop his artistic technique, called pointillism. Incredibly, Seurat produced a number of masterpieces during his short lifetime. He died at the age of thirty-one. The painting reproduced here is considered Seurat's greatest work and one of the landmarks of modern art.

OBJECTIVE
• To revise sentences to correct errors in usage

858 *A Glossary of Usage*

6. taught photographs ∧learned̶ Seurat all about pointillism. [7] However, these critics h̶a̶d̶ ought to examine Seurat's painting more closely. [8] Unlike some of his contemporaries, Seurat was, indeed, interested in the new photographic technology; however, the dots that make up his paintings are rather large, and **8. types** obviously these ∧t̶y̶p̶e̶ of points are not meant to appear com- **9. kinds** pletely solid. [9] If you go to a museum to see one of these ∧k̶i̶n̶d̶ of paintings, estimate the diagonal length of the picture and then step back about three times that distance. [10] From this **10. likely** viewpoint, a pointillist painting is ∧l̶i̶a̶b̶l̶e̶ to flicker or shimmer with the very vibrancy of life itself.

nauseated, nauseous *Nauseated* means "sick." *Nauseous* means "disgusting" or "sickening."

> EXAMPLES After riding the roller coaster, the child became **nauseated.**
> The chemical reaction gave off a **nauseous** odor.

no, nobody, none, no one, not, nothing, nowhere See **The Double Negative,** pages 864–865.

nor See **or, nor.**

notorious See **famous, notorious.**

nowheres See **anyways, anywheres.**

number Use a singular verb after the expression *the number of.* Use a plural verb after the expression *a number of.*

> EXAMPLES **The number of** candidates **was** surprising.
> **A number of** candidates **were** nominated by the committee.

number See **amount, number.**

of *Of* is a preposition. Do not use *of* in place of *have* after verbs such as *could, should, would, might, must,* and *ought [to].* Also, do not use *had of* for had.

> NONSTANDARD You could of told me that you were going to be late.
> STANDARD You **could've** told me that you were going to be late.

> NONSTANDARD You ought to of seen the look on his face.
> STANDARD You **ought to have** seen the look on his face.

NONSTANDARD	If I had of known that the party was casual, I wouldn't of worn this dressy outfit.
STANDARD	If I **had** known that the party was casual, I **wouldn't have** worn this dressy outfit.

Avoid using *of* after other prepositions such as *inside, off,* and *outside.*

EXAMPLE Leslie turned **off** [not *off of*] the parkway.

off, off of Do not use *off* or *off of* for *from.*

NONSTANDARD	I got some good advice off that mechanic.
STANDARD	I got some good advice **from** that mechanic.

or, nor Use *or* with *either;* use *nor* with *neither.*

EXAMPLES	**Either** Celia Cruz **or** Gloria Estefan will host the awards show.
	Neither Gwen **nor** Lily has been absent this term.

ought See **had ought, hadn't ought.**

ought to of See **of.**

persecute, prosecute *Persecute* means "to attack or annoy someone constantly." *Prosecute* means "to bring legal action against someone for unlawful behavior."

EXAMPLES	The dictator **persecuted** those who opposed him.
	The district attorney **will prosecute** any person caught looting.

phenomena *Phenomena* is the plural form of the word *phenomenon.* Do not use *phenomena* as a singular noun.

PLURAL	We studied **those phenomena** of nature, which **are** quite rare.
SINGULAR	We studied **that phenomenon** of nature, which **is** quite rare.

reason . . . because See **because.**

Reverend, Honorable Do not use these titles before a person's last name alone. Do use the word *the* before the title.

NONSTANDARD	Reverend King, the Reverend King, Honorable Inouye
STANDARD	the Reverend Martin Luther King, Jr., the Reverend M. L. King, Jr., the Reverend Dr. King, the Honorable Daniel Inouye

USAGE

USAGE

rise, raise See pages 786–787.

same, said, such In business or legal writing, these words are sometimes used in the following kinds of constructions. Avoid such uses in general writing.

LEGAL   The artist had worked hard on the sculptures and had same fully insured.

GENERAL   The artist had worked hard on the sculptures and had **them** fully insured.

LEGAL   The said sculptures were fully insured.

GENERAL   **Those** [or **The artist's**] sculptures were fully insured.

LEGAL   Someone suggested that the artist overstate the value of the sculptures; however, the artist didn't approve of such.

GENERAL   Someone suggested that the artist overstate the value of the sculptures; however, the artist didn't approve of **such dishonesty.**

says Do not use *say* after a past-tense verb. *Said* is the past-tense form.

NONSTANDARD   Then she glared at me and says, "Where have you been?"

STANDARD   Then she glared at me and **said,** "Where have you been?"

scarcely See **The Double Negative,** pages 864–865.

she See **he, she, it, they.**

should of See **of.**

sit, set See pages 785–786.

slow, slowly See page 817.

some, somewhat In formal situations, avoid using *some* to mean "to some extent." Use *somewhat.*

INFORMAL   Tensions between East and West began to ease some.

FORMAL   Tensions between East and West began to ease **somewhat.**

somewheres See **anyways, anywheres.**

sort(s) See **kind(s), sort(s), type(s)** and **kind of a, sort of a.**

sort of See **kind of, sort of.**

take See **bring, take.**

than, then *Than* is a conjunction used in comparisons. *Then* is an adverb telling *when.*

EXAMPLES   Tyrone is more studious **than** I am.
Take your diploma in your left hand and shake hands with the principal; **then** leave the stage and return to your seat.

that See **who, which, that.**

them Do not use *them* as an adjective. Use *those.*

EXAMPLE   Have you seen **those** [not *them*] murals by Judith Baca at the art museum?

they See **he, she, it, they.**

this here, that there Avoid using *here* or *there* after *this* or *that.*

EXAMPLE   **This** [not *This here*] magazine has an article about Japanese koto player Kazue Sawai.

this, that, these, those See **kind(s), sort(s), type(s).**

type(s) See **kind(s), sort(s), type(s).**

type, type of Avoid using *type* as an adjective. Add *of* after *type.*

NONSTANDARD   That's the type job I'd like to have.
STANDARD   That's the **type of** job I'd like to have.

ways Use *way,* not *ways,* when referring to distance.

INFORMAL   At dusk we were still a long ways from home.
FORMAL   At dusk we were still a long **way** from home.

well, good See page 816.

when, where Do not use *when* or *where* to begin a definition.

NONSTANDARD   A hurricane is when a tropical cyclone has winds greater than 75 miles per hour.
STANDARD   A hurricane is **a tropical cyclone that has winds greater than 75 miles per hour.**

NONSTANDARD   An implosion is where something bursts inward.
STANDARD   An implosion is an **inward burst.**

USAGE

COMMON ERROR

Problem. Students often confuse the conjunction *than* with the adverb *then.*

Solution. Explain to students that they should use *then* only when an expression tells when. Write the following reminder on the chalkboard:

THE̲N = WHE̲N

At all other times, students should use *than,* which compares or contrasts. Write this reminder on the chalkboard:

THA̲N = COMPA̲RE or CONTRA̲ST

USAGE

where Do not use *where* for *that*.

> EXAMPLE   I read **that** [not *where*] the Smithsonian Institution has preserved more than one thousand of William H. Johnson's paintings.

where . . . at See **at.**

who, which, that *Who* refers to persons only. *Which* refers to things only. *That* may refer to either persons or things.

> EXAMPLES   Shah Jahan was the Indian ruler **who** [or **that**] built the Taj Mahal.
> The monument, **which** is the tomb of the ruler's wife, is adorned with verses from the Koran.
> Have you seen any pictures of the building **that** symbolizes India for so many people in other lands?

who, whom See pages 744–745.

would of See **of.**

▶ EXERCISE 6   Correcting Errors in Usage

Most of the following sentences contain errors in usage. If a sentence contains an error in usage, revise the sentence. If a sentence is correct, write *C.*

1. Backlighting is when the main source of light is placed in back of the subject being photographed.   **1.** occurs
2. I never saw that type camera before.   **2.** of
3. Why don't you borrow some change off of Rhoda?   **3.** from
4. A number of unusual themes has already been proposed for the senior prom.   **4.** have
5. Neither Chico or Robert has any albums by Tish Hinojosa.   **5.** nor
6. Sharon turned to me and says, "Did you see the beautiful sari that woman was wearing?"   **6.** said
7. You should of seen *Young Soul Rebels,* which was directed by Isaac Julien.   **7.** have
8. The aurora borealis is a spectacular phenomena of nature in the northern sky.   **8.** phenomenon
9. We stayed up to watch the late-night horror movie, which wasn't worth the loss of sleep.   **9.** C
10. It's a long ways to Memphis, but we may reach northern Tennessee by morning.   **10.** way

---

USAGE

USAGE

A Glossary of Usage **863**

▶ REVIEW D   **Proofreading for Correct Usage**

Most of the sentences in the following paragraphs contain errors in usage. If a sentence is incorrect, correct the error. If a sentence is correct, write *C*.   Responses will vary.

1. the/John **2.** phenomenon

[1] Several years ago, I accompanied Reverend Kemp and his wife Angela on a sightseeing trip to Alaska in July. [2] On our flight to Fairbanks, we saw a double rainbow—a marvelous phenomena that we felt was a lucky sign. [3] At the hotel, we began to plan what we would do the next day, but the number of possibilities were huge, and we didn't know where to start. [4] Finally, we decided that we would neither stay in our rooms or eat dinner at the hotel; instead, we would go for a drive that evening. [5] As we headed for the car, I saw on a poster where the World Eskimo-Indian Olympics were being held that very day. [6] "Doesn't this sound like fun?" I asked, showing Mrs. Kemp the advertisement for the games.

3. was
4. nor
5. that
6. C

[7] The Kemps agreed, and as soon as we arrived at the fairgrounds, we introduced ourselves to a Mrs. McBride. [8] She was a friendly woman which was happy to tell us about the games. [9] I was surprised some at the many different events that had been scheduled. [10] Said games included tests of skill, such as the Alaskan high kick, and tests of strength, such as drop-the-bomb.

7. C
8. who
9. somewhat
10. The

11. performed by/trying

[11] The Alaskan high kick is where a person sitting on the ground tries to kick a ball suspended in midair. [12] An event requiring exceptional balance, the Alaskan high kick is an example of the type skills that were traditionally needed by Native Alaskans. [13] The drop-the-bomb competition begins when three men lift another man off of the ground. [14] The man who is held by his wrists and ankles must remain perfectly horizontal while them three other men carry him. [15] The contestant who is carried the longest ways without sagging wins the event.

12. of
14. the
15. way

[16] As Mrs. McBride finished describing the games, she smiled and says, "This is the thirty-first year we've held these Olympic games." [17] Than she proudly pointed out Cecelia Chanerak, who was sailing through the air during the blanket toss. [18] This event is when a group of people stretch out a hide blanket and throw a man or a woman as high as possible; the winner must jump the highest and keep the best balance. [19] I must confess that I got a bit nauseous watching people fly

16. said
17. Then
18. In
19. nauseated

863

OBJECTIVE

- To identify correct usage in sentences

864 *A Glossary of Usage*

up so far in the air, but I managed to snap a picture anyway. [20] That ~~there~~ day was one of the best of our trip, and when I got back home, I eagerly described the Eskimo-Indian Olympics to my family and friends.

PROGRAM MANAGER

THE DOUBLE NEGATIVE

- **Independent Practice/ Reteaching** For instruction and exercises, see **The Double Negative** in *Language Skills Practice and Assessment,* p. 173.

- **Computer Guided Instruction** For additional instruction and practice with the double negative, see **Lesson 60** in *Language Workshop CD-ROM.*

- **Practice** To help less-advanced students with additional instruction and practice with the double negative, see **Chapter 20** in *English Workshop, Complete Course,* pp. 275–276.

The Double Negative

A *double negative* is a construction in which two negative words are used where one is enough. Double negatives were acceptable during Shakespeare's time, but they are now considered nonstandard.

Common Negative Words		
barely	never	not (n't)
but (meaning "only")	no	nothing
	nobody	nowhere
hardly	none	only
neither	no one	scarcely

NONSTANDARD	She has never missed none of Toni Morrison's books.
STANDARD	She has **never** missed **any** of Toni Morrison's books.
STANDARD	She has missed **none** of Toni Morrison's books.

NONSTANDARD	I have not said nothing about your plans.
STANDARD	I have **not** said **anything** about your plans.
STANDARD	I have said **nothing** about your plans.

NONSTANDARD	I hadn't never heard Estonian music before.
STANDARD	I **hadn't ever** heard Estonian music before.
STANDARD	I had **never** heard Estonian music before.

Winthrop reprinted by permission of Newspaper Enterprise Association, Inc.

NOTE: Avoid the common error of using *n't*, the contraction of *not*, with another negative word, such as *barely*, *hardly*, or *scarcely*.

| NONSTANDARD | I can't hardly see anything in this fog. |
| STANDARD | I can **hardly** see anything in this fog. |

| NONSTANDARD | Our lunch break was so short that we didn't scarcely have time to eat. |
| STANDARD | Our lunch break was so short that we **scarcely** had time to eat. |

The words *but* and *only* are negative when they are used as adverbs meaning "no more than." In such cases, the use of another negative word with *but* or *only* is considered informal.

INFORMAL	I don't have but one pair of dress shoes.
FORMAL	I have **but** one pair of dress shoes.
FORMAL	I have **only** one pair of dress shoes.

QUICK REMINDER

Write the following sentences on the chalkboard. Have students revise them by deleting one word from each sentence. Words that should be deleted are underscored.

1. I don't have no good reason for leaving early.
2. Without his glasses, he could not hardly see.
3. None of the teenagers could not remember.

MEETING *individual* NEEDS

LEP/ESL

General Strategies. The use of double and triple negatives is standard in many languages. Therefore, you may need to work closely with some students to help them avoid using double negatives in their writing in English.

REVIEW E

OBJECTIVE

- To identify and correct the usage errors in sentences

▶ **EXERCISE 7** **Identifying Correct Usage**

Choose the <u>correct word</u> from the pair given in parentheses.

EXAMPLE **1.** I don't have (*any, none*) left.
1. *any*

1. Benjamin will never get (*nowhere,* <u>*anywhere*</u>) until he starts believing in himself.
2. Luís (<u>*can,*</u> *can't*) hardly keep from being proud of you.
3. I was so sleepy that I (<u>*could,*</u> *couldn't*) hardly keep my eyes open.
4. The detectives (*haven't,* <u>*have*</u>) no clues in the case.
5. There (<u>*is,*</u> *isn't*) no good reason for your being late.
6. We hadn't (<u>*ever,*</u> *never*) tasted papaya before.
7. Neither of them wants (*nothing,* <u>*anything*</u>) to do with the preparations for the dance.
8. We (<u>*had,*</u> *hadn't*) but one choice to make.
9. The candidates (<u>*have,*</u> *haven't*) only three minutes each to state their positions.
10. The manager insisted that there wasn't (<u>*any,*</u> *no*) reason for making the customers wait so long.

▶ **REVIEW E** **Correcting Errors in Usage**

Most of the following sentences contain errors in usage. If a sentence contains an error, revise the sentence. If a sentence is correct, write *C*. **Revisions may vary.**

1. C

1. We had to adapt the stage lighting for the rock concert.
2. The professor made an ~~illusion~~ to Ralph Ellison's novel *Invisible Man*. **2.** allusion
3. The organization helped a large ~~amount~~ of Asian refugees find work. **3.** number
4. Where did you stay ~~at~~ over Thanksgiving? **5.** accepted
5. Everyone except Tim has ~~excepted~~ the invitation. **6.** Between
6. ~~Among~~ the two performers, I like Quincy Jones better.
7. The data on acid rain ~~is~~ not complete. **7.** are **8.** emigrated
8. My parents ~~immigrated~~ from Cuba before I was born.
9. Have you ever read about the pirate Bluebeard, who was ~~famous~~ for his cruelty? **9.** notorious **10.** C
10. Were you credulous enough to believe the fortuneteller?
11. My sister ~~she~~ attends Iowa State University. **12.** inferred
12. We ~~implied~~ from Rudy's comment that the movie was dull.
13. The Coopers grew all the vegetables ~~theirselves~~. **13.** themselves

USAGE

14. I ~~had~~ ought to spend more time with my friends.
15. He has been the catcher for every game this year, and he is beginning to look ~~kind of~~ tired.   **15.** rather   **16.** taught
16. Ms. Robinson ~~learned~~ me all I know about public speaking.
17. What kind of ~~a~~ car is that?
18. At the school assembly yesterday, the Honorable Murphy encouraged students to register to vote as soon as they turn eighteen.   **18.** Shannon   **19.** who
19. There were four freshmen ~~which~~ made the basketball team.
20. A number of suggestions have been submitted to the prom decorations committee.   **20.** C

WRITING APPLICATION

Using Standard English in a Story

English usage varies from place to place and from group to group. However, standard English is familiar to almost all people who speak English, no matter what their background. Following the rules of standard usage in writing helps to ensure that the widest possible range of readers will understand what you have to say.

In literature, writers sometimes break the rules of standard English to achieve a particular effect. In writing a story, an author might use nonstandard English in dialogue to capture the sound of a speaker's language. In the rest of the story, however, the writer would probably use standard English to appeal to as diverse an audience as possible. As you read the excerpt below, notice how the writer uses both standard and nonstandard English in his short story.

> She still held him. But she bent down enough to permit him to stoop and pick up her purse. Then she said, "Now ain't you ashamed of yourself?"
> Firmly gripped by his shirt front, the boy said, "Yes'm."
> The woman said, "What did you want to do it for?"
> The boy said, "I didn't aim to."
> She said, "You a lie!"
>
> Langston Hughes, from "Thank You, M'am"

USAGE

USAGE

WRITING APPLICATION

If students don't keep writing journals, they may need some prompting to help them choose experiences on which to base their stories. You might ask them to think about personal experiences, such as their most embarrassing moments or strange events that they have witnessed, to get them started.

Because this writing activity is to be based on personal experience, students may write their narratives in the first person without considering other possibilities. Remind students that their narratives are to be fictional; therefore, any point of view is valid. You may want to discuss literary points of view with students and tell them that third-person omniscient or third-person limited omniscient point of view may be better suited to their stories.

SELECTION AMENDMENT

Description of change: excerpted
Rationale: to focus on the concept of the use of standard and nonstandard English in a short story

CRITICAL THINKING

Synthesis. To help them to create three-dimensional, nonstereotypical characters in their short stories, ask students to develop character sketches in the prewriting stage. Have students brainstorm for details that describe their characters. You may want to provide the following questions for students to answer about each of the characters in their narratives:

1. How big are the character's feet?
2. Does the character cry during sad movies?
3. What is the character's favorite color?
4. What is the character's favorite food?
5. Is the character afraid of anything?

Tell students that they will not necessarily include all of these details in their narratives.

WRITING ACTIVITY

Some experiences are so strange, moving, or funny that they just beg to be told in a story. Recently you heard about or had such an experience and wrote about it in your journal. Now, you've decided to develop the journal entry into a short story. Write a fictional narrative based on your journal entry. Use both true and imaginary details to create an entertaining story. You may use nonstandard English in dialogue, but be sure to write the rest of the story in standard English. Use the **Glossary of Usage** to check any words or phrases you're not sure about.

Prewriting Think about something strange, inspiring, or funny that happened to you or to someone you know. If you keep a journal, you may want to skim through it for ideas. Think about how to develop one particular experience into a short story. Decide on the characters and the setting of the story, and determine your narrator's point of view. Finally, create a brief plot outline. Be sure to include a *conflict*, a problem that the main character or characters must solve. (For help with developing a short-story plot, see pages 171–172.)

Writing Using your prewriting notes, write a first draft of your story. As you write, you will want to expand on your original ideas. Add interest to your story by inventing vivid details. In writing dialogue, you may find it useful to include some colloquial or nonstandard expressions to make your characters' speech sound more natural. You may use as many or as few details from real life as you wish. However, do not use real names of people.

Evaluating and Revising Ask a friend or a relative to read your draft. Is the story interesting and believable? Can your reader picture the setting and characters? Jot down your reader's suggestions, and decide which, if any, to use in your story. Also, add any details that you think will improve the plot, setting, or characterization. Next, focus on your writing style. Revise your sentences to make them clearer and more concise. As you revise, be sure to use the **Glossary of Usage** to help you find and correct nonstandard usages.

Proofreading Read over your story to find any errors in grammar, usage, spelling, or punctuation. Be sure that

OBJECTIVE

- To identify and revise usage errors in sentences

you've placed quotation marks around dialogue. (See pages 935–939 for more about using quotation marks.) Check to be sure that any nonstandard usages are intentional, not accidental.

Review: Posttest

A. Correcting Errors in Usage

Most of the following sentences contain errors in usage. If a sentence contains an error, revise the sentence. If a sentence is correct, write *C*. **Revisions may vary.**

EXAMPLE
1. I was surprised to learn that Roberto's parents are wealthy, because he doesn't act like he's rich.
1. *I was surprised to learn that Roberto's parents are wealthy, because he doesn't act as if he's rich.*

1. Please enclose a copy of your birth certificate, and we will return said document at a later date. **1. C (legal or business writing)**
2. You ~~hadn't~~ ought to be so careless with your new watch. **2. not**
3. The Student Council's arguments had little ~~affect~~ on the faculty's vote on the new dress code for school dances. **3. effect**
4. Theo ~~don't~~ care what others think; he has the courage to say what he believes. **4. doesn't**
5. Tricia, Angelo, and ~~myself~~ have tickets to the White Sox game next Saturday. **5. I**
6. Whenever I feel sad, I ~~can't~~ hardly wait to talk with my friend Marcus, who always cheers me up. **6. can**
7. Arthur Fiedler ~~he~~ made the Boston Pops' concerts popular with millions of people all over America.
8. The reason we're so late is ~~because~~ our car battery was dead and we had to get a jump-start. **8. that**
9. We didn't know whether the light was a ~~phenomena~~ of nature or a UFO. **9. phenomenon**
10. I have never seen this kind of insect before. **10. C**
11. Because Eula made a mistake when she put the film ~~in~~ the camera, none of her pictures could be developed. **11. into**

USAGE

USAGE

USAGE

12. We plan to visit Tim at Christmas, ~~being as~~ we haven't seen him in three years. **12. because**
13. She asked Tom if he was going to the dance, and he ~~says~~, "Maybe I'll go and maybe I won't." **13. said**
14. Where was Beth ~~at~~ last night when all of us went to the game? **15. did**
15. Our teacher said we ~~done~~ a creditable job on our project.

B. Proofreading for Correct Usage

For each sentence in the following paragraph, correct the error in usage.

16. any
17. everywhere
18. that
19. adapts
20. data
21. that
22. persecuted
23. notorious
25. these

[16] There are hardly ~~no~~ tales in the world that are as popular as the story of Cinderella. [17] Almost ~~everywheres~~, people tell some version of this folk tale. [18] The reason for the story's popularity is probably ~~because~~ its themes of love and wealth appeal universally. [19] However, each culture ~~adopts~~ the tale by changing the heroine's name and other details. [20] According to the ~~datum~~ collected by folklorists, almost seven hundred versions of the Cinderella story exist. [21] In the English version, Cinderella is granted a wish by her fairy godmother; in Scotland, Rashin Coatie wishes on a dead calf's bones; and in Italy, it is a magic date tree ~~who~~ grants Zezolla's wish. [22] In the Chinese version, perhaps the oldest Cinderella story, the main character is Yeh-hsien, who is ~~prosecuted~~ by her stepmother. [23] In this version, the stepmother, ~~famous~~ for her cruelty, gives Yeh-hsien the dangerous task of drawing water from very deep wells. [24] As in other Cinderella stories, a slipper drops off ~~of~~ Yeh-hsien's foot on her way back from a festival. [25] The ending of ~~said~~ stories is always the same—the mistreated heroine, no matter what her name is, finds love and happiness with the man who searches for the owner of the slipper.

LESSON 1 *(pp. 871–873)*

LESSON 1 *(pp. 871–873)*
DIAGNOSTIC TEST

OBJECTIVES
- To identify standard uses of capital letters
- To proofread a paragraph for correct capitalization

28 CAPITALIZATION

Standard Uses of Capital Letters

PROGRAM MANAGER

FOR THE WHOLE CHAPTER
- **Review** For exercises on chapter concepts, see **Review Form A** and **Review Form B** in *Language Skills Practice and Assessment,* pp. 203–207.
- **Assessment** For additional testing, see **Mechanics Pretests** and **Mechanics Mastery Tests** in *Language Skills Practice and Assessment,* pp. 189–196 and pp. 259–267.

CHAPTER OVERVIEW

This chapter presents rules for capitalizing the first words of sentences, the pronoun *I,* the interjection *O,* proper nouns, proper adjectives, specific course names, names of languages, and titles.

In the **Writing Application,** students will apply the rules of capitalization in this chapter to writing letters.

Students could refer to this chapter when proofreading any writing assignment. The **Summary Style Review** chart (pp. 894–896) may be a useful reference tool.

MECHANICS

Diagnostic Test

A. Identifying Standard Uses of Capital Letters

For each of the following pairs of items, select the letter of the item that is correctly capitalized according to standard usage.

EXAMPLE **1. a.** a Movie starring Lena Horne
    b. a movie starring Lena Horne
    1. *b*

1. **a.** in honor of Secretaries Day
   b. in honor of Secretaries day
2. **a.** one of the nations in the middle east
   b. one of the nations in the Middle East
3. **a.** took courses in English, Spanish, and chemistry
   b. took courses in English, Spanish, and Chemistry

If some students are having problems with capitalization in their writing, the **Diagnostic Test** can help you to identify particular areas in which students need instruction and practice. The test assesses understanding of all the rules of capitalization that are presented in this chapter. You can assess students' responses to determine which rules students need to review.

872 *Capitalization*

4. a. the crew of the Space Shuttle *Columbia*
    b. the crew of the space shuttle *Columbia*
5. a. at the intersection of Sixth avenue and Market street
    b. at the intersection of Sixth Avenue and Market Street
6. **a.** a trip to Yosemite National Park
    b. a trip to Yosemite national park
7. a. fought the Battle of Saratoga during the Revolutionary war
    b. fought the Battle of Saratoga during the Revolutionary War
8. a. enjoyed Toni Morrison's *the Bluest Eye*
    b. enjoyed Toni Morrison's *The Bluest Eye*
9. a. a visit to the world Trade Center
    b. a visit to the World Trade Center
10. **a.** a biography of the American novelist James Baldwin
    b. a biography of the american novelist James Baldwin

B. Proofreading a Paragraph for Correct Capitalization

Proofread the following paragraph, changing capital letters to small letters and small letters to capitals where necessary. If a sentence is correct, write *C*. Words that should be capitalized or lowercased are underscored.

EXAMPLE [1] The National Museum Of American History is a branch of the Smithsonian institution.
1. *of, Institution*

[11] Popularly known as "the Nation's attic," the Museum grew out of the U.S. National Museum, which was built to
12. C house the collections of the U.S. Patent office. [12] Today, many Americans seem to consider the museum an extension of their own attics. [13] Each year hundreds of items arrive at the museum unsolicited, many of them addressed simply "Smithsonian, Washington, d.c." [14] According to Katherine Neill Ridgley, Manager of public-inquiry mail at the Smithsonian, the packages are often accompanied by wistful letters stating, "i want this to go to a place where it will be appreciated." [15] Staff historian Ellen Roney Hughes considers the offerings evidence that Americans have a strong sense of His-
16. C tory. [16] "They realize the importance," she says, "of both ordinary things and extraordinary things." [17] "Extraordinary" is an

apt description for one recent donation—a rubber chicken that had accompanied an <u>Expedition</u> to Antarctica. **[18]** Other packages contain less-startling objects; one would-be donor sent his <u>Great</u>-grandmother's wedding dress, and another submitted a <u>polaroid</u> snapshot of a stuffed alligator. **[19]** People from both the <u>north</u> and the South regularly contribute letters and other memorabilia dating from the Civil <u>war</u>. **[20]** Most of the items **20. C** are returned to their owners, yet the contributions continue; perhaps the senders reason that since the museum welcomed Archie Bunker's armchair from the television series *All in The Family*, it will welcome their treasures, too.

In your reading, you may notice variations in the use of capital letters. Most writers, however, follow the rules presented in this chapter. In your own writing, following these rules will help you communicate clearly.

28a. **Capitalize the first word of every sentence.**

EXAMPLES   **R**eading the article, I learned about the Blessingway and other traditional Navajo ceremonies.
What is the formula for converting degrees Celsius to degrees Fahrenheit?

(1) Capitalize the first word of a sentence following a colon.

EXAMPLE   The committee issued the following statement: **I**n light of these statistics, we recommend that four-way stop signs be installed.

(2) Capitalize the first word of a resolution following the word *Resolved*.

EXAMPLE   Resolved: **T**hat government support of the arts be increased.

(3) Capitalize the first word of a direct quotation.

EXAMPLE   When he surrendered in 1877, Chief Joseph declared, "**F**rom where the sun now stands I will fight no more forever."

LESSON 2 *(pp. 873–883)*
FIRST WORDS, THE PRONOUN *I*, THE INTERJECTION *O*, PROPER NOUNS, AND PROPER ADJECTIVES Rules 28a–28c

OBJECTIVES
- To identify standard uses of capitalization
- To use standard capitalization

PROGRAM MANAGER

FIRST WORDS, THE PRONOUN *I*, THE INTERJECTION *O*, PROPER NOUNS, AND PROPER ADJECTIVES

- **Independent Practice/ Reteaching** For instruction and exercises, see **First Words, *I* and *O*; Proper Nouns and Adjectives A;** and **Proper Nouns and Adjectives B** in *Language Skills Practice and Assessment,* pp. 199–201.

- **Computer Guided Instruction** For additional instruction and practice with capitalization, see **Lessons 54** and **55** in *Language Workshop CD-ROM.*

- **Practice** To help less-advanced students with additional instruction and practice with capitalization, see **Chapter 21** in *English Workshop, Complete Course,* pp. 279–288.

MEETING *individual* NEEDS

LESS-ADVANCED STUDENTS
To prevent students from being overwhelmed by capitalization rules, teach only the rules pertaining to situations that occur frequently in everyday writing.

MECHANICS

✔ QUICK REMINDER

Write the following sentences on the chalkboard. Have students copy them and correct errors in capitalization. Letters that should be capitalized or lowercased are underscored.

1. <u>t</u>he rain came in my window, and my bed got soaked.
2. <u>i</u>f you see her before <u>i</u> do, tell her <u>i</u>'ll be there soon.
3. My mother read me the poem "<u>o</u> Captain, My Captain!"
4. What she asked was, "<u>w</u>ho has the remote control?"
5. We now have accurate pictures showing the landscape on <u>m</u>ars.

◆ INTEGRATING THE LANGUAGE ARTS

Literature Link. You may want to direct students to poems that use conventional capitalization and poems that do not. You can find many suitable examples in literature anthologies. For example, poets sometimes capitalize internal words to emphasize them or to use them as proper nouns or adjectives. Students might want to read "When I Have Fears" by John Keats, "Ode to the West Wind" by Percy Bysshe Shelley, or either version of William Blake's "The Chimney Sweeper" for examples of internal capitalization. Discuss with students how this style difference affects their sense of the poetry.

MECHANICS

SELECTION AMENDMENT
Description of change: excerpted
Rationale: to focus on the concept of capitalization presented in this chapter

---

874 *Capitalization*

When quoting from another writer's work, do not capitalize the first word of the quotation unless the other writer has capitalized it.

EXAMPLE   In his speech of surrender in 1877, Chief Joseph declared that he would "fight no more forever."

☞ **REFERENCE NOTE:** For more information about using capital letters in quotations, see pages 935–936.

Traditionally, the first word in a line of poetry is capitalized.

EXAMPLE   He clasps the crag with crooked hands;
Close to the sun in lonely lands,
Ringed with the azure world, he stands.

The wrinkled sea beneath him crawls;
He watches from his mountain walls,
And like a thunderbolt he falls.

Alfred, Lord Tennyson, "The Eagle"

For reasons of style, however, some writers do not follow this rule.

EXAMPLE   The art of losing isn't hard to master;
so many things seem filled with the intent
to be lost that their loss is no disaster.

Elizabeth Bishop, "One Art"

When quoting from another writer's work, always follow the style of the writer.

(4) Capitalize the first word of a statement or question inserted in a sentence without quotation marks.

EXAMPLE   My question is, **W**ill this action solve the problem?

28b. **Capitalize the pronoun *I* and the interjection *O*.**

The interjection *O* is usually used for invocations and is followed by the name of the person or thing being addressed. Don't confuse *O* with the common interjection *oh*, which is capitalized only when it appears at the beginning of a sentence and is usually followed by a mark of punctuation.

EXAMPLES   Where could **I** have put my book report?
Rejoice in the Lord, **O** ye righteous!
He was driving, **oh,** about thirty-five miles an hour.

28c. Capitalize proper nouns and proper adjectives.

A *common noun* names any one of a group of persons, places, or things. A *proper noun* names a particular person, place, or thing. A *proper adjective* is formed from a proper noun.

COMMON NOUNS	PROPER NOUNS	PROPER ADJECTIVES
king	King Arthur	Arthurian legend
country	Thailand	Thai restaurant
city	Moscow	Muscovite voters
people	Algonquians	Algonquian customs
religion	Buddhism	Buddhist shrine

In proper nouns made up of two or more words, do not capitalize

- articles (*a, an, the*)
- short prepositions (those with fewer than five letters, such as *at, of, for, with*)
- coordinating conjunctions (*and, but, for, nor, or, so, yet*)

EXAMPLES   Alfred **the** Great
               Gulf **of** Oman
               International Union **for the** Conservation **of** Nature
                   and Natural Resources

Some proper nouns and proper adjectives have lost their capitals after long usage.

EXAMPLES   a cardigan (sweater)   china (dishes)
               morocco leather   creole sauce

Others may be written with or without capitals.

EXAMPLES   Roman (roman) numerals   Venetian (venetian) blinds
               plaster of Paris (paris)   Gothic (gothic) style

If you're not sure whether to capitalize a word, check an up-to-date dictionary.

👉 **REFERENCE NOTE:** For more information about common and proper nouns, see page 600. For more about proper adjectives, see page 953.

MECHANICS

MEETING *individual* NEEDS

LEP/ESL

General Strategies. In some languages such as French, Spanish, and Vietnamese, days of the week, months, and nationalities used as proper adjectives begin with lowercase letters, as in "On the first monday in april, we're going to watch a french film." Acknowledge the fact that students are being asked to reverse rules they have already mastered in their native language. You could involve students in the lesson by giving them the opportunity to be the experts. Ask them to teach you and the class the words in their first languages for the days of the week.

MECHANICS

TIMESAVER

If you feel that students have a good understanding of the basic rules of capitalization, you may want to have them review the rules on their own so that you can devote class time to discussing the **Notes** under some of the textbook rules.

INTEGRATING THE LANGUAGE ARTS

Mechanics and Writing. To reinforce the rules for capitalizing geographical names, ask students to write informative paragraphs describing dream trips they would like to take.

Have students tell why they would like to make the trips. Students should include the names of places they would like to visit on their way to their destinations. If possible, provide maps of the world, the United States, and your state for students to consult.

(1) Capitalize the names of persons.

GIVEN NAMES	**Jamal**	**Christina**	**Yoshi**	**Alicia**	**Marco**
SURNAMES	**Tseng**	**Youngblood**	**Johnson**	**Martínez**	**Costner**

NOTE: Some names may contain more than one capital letter. If you are not sure about the spelling of a name, check with the person or consult a reference source.

EXAMPLES	**De La Renta**	**de la Renta**
	Von Ryan	**von Ryan**
	Morning Star	**Morningstar**
	La Fontaine	**Lafontaine**
	Dupont	**du Pont**
	MacKenzie	**Mackenzie**

Capitalize the abbreviations *Jr.* and *Sr.* following a name.

EXAMPLES   Martin Luther King, **Jr.**   John D. Rockefeller, **Sr.**

☞ **REFERENCE NOTE:** The abbreviations of other titles such as *Mr., Dr., Gen., RN,* and *Ph.D.* are also capitalized. For more about punctuating abbreviations, see page 903.

(2) Capitalize geographical names.

TYPE OF NAME	EXAMPLES	
Towns and Cities	**Campbellsville** **Manila**	**Pigeon Forge** **San Juan**
Counties and Townships	**Maricopa County** **Concord Township**	**Orleans Parish** **Lawrence Township**
States	**Alaska**	**South Carolina**
Regions	**the South** **Great Plains**	**Western Hemisphere** **New England**

NOTE: Words such as *north, eastern,* and *southwestern* are not capitalized when indicating direction.

EXAMPLES   flying **s**outh for the winter
living in the **w**estern part of the state

☞ **REFERENCE NOTE:** The abbreviations of names of states are always capitalized. For more about using and punctuating such abbreviations, see page 903.

TYPE OF NAME	EXAMPLES	
Countries	Zimbabwe	Saudi Arabia
Continents	Antarctica	North America
Islands	Isle of Wight	Solomon Islands
Mountains	Mount St. Helens Pobeda Peak	Sierra Madre Sugarloaf Mountain
Other Land Forms and Features	Painted Desert Palo Duro Canyon Dismal Swamp	Keweenaw Peninsula Ouachita National Forest
Bodies of Water	Indian Ocean Lake Huron Dead Sea	Amazon River Persian Gulf Guanabara Bay

Parks	Lake Clark
	  National Park
		Ozark National
		  Scenic Riverways

Roads, Streets, and Highways	Route 66 Interstate 10 Quail Briar Drive East Third Street	Raintree Road Bluegrass Parkway Fifth Avenue Gulf-to-Bay Boulevard

☞ **REFERENCE NOTE:** In addresses, abbreviations such as *St., Blvd., Ave., Dr.,* and *Ln.* are capitalized. For more about abbreviations, see page 903.

NOTE: The second word in a hyphenated number begins with a lowercase letter.

EXAMPLE   Twenty-**s**econd Street

A word such as *city, lake, park,* or *street* is capitalized only when it is part of a proper noun.

PROPER NOUNS	COMMON NOUNS
in **Sioux City**	in the **c**ity
near **Lake Okeechobee**	near the **l**ake
through **Mesa Verde National Park**	through the **p**ark
on **Dunbar Street**	on the next **s**treet

MECHANICS

COOPERATIVE LEARNING
Divide the class into groups of three or four students. Ask each group to write a tourist brochure for a specific local geographical region; each brochure should include information about at least one town or city and about geographical features such as lakes, rivers, mountain ranges, and caves. The brochure could mention specific historical sites, as well as recreational and entertainment facilities. You also could have groups provide directions to each attraction. Remind students to capitalize geographical names correctly. Students could publish their brochures by displaying them at a local tourist-information center.

MECHANICS

877

MEETING *individual* NEEDS

LEARNING STYLES

Visual and Kinetic Learners. To help students learn capitalization rules, assign two capitalization rules to each student. Then, ask students to find examples and to use them to assemble a bulletin board display of capitalization rules and examples.

While searching for examples, students might find examples that contradict the capitalization rules they have learned. Explain that newspapers and magazines sometimes use styles of their own, which may differ from the standard use.

▶ **EXERCISE 1** **Identifying Standard Uses of Capitalization**

For each of the following pairs of items, select the letter of the item that is correctly capitalized.

1. a. the Nile river
    b. the Nile River
2. **a.** She said, "Tell me, too."
    b. She said, "tell me, too."
3. a. Bering strait
    b. Bering Strait
4. a. Fifty-Second Street
    b. Fifty-second Street
5. **a.** Hoover Dam
    b. Hoover dam
6. **a.** Charles Adams, Jr.
    b. Charles Adams, jr.
7. **a.** New Jersey Turnpike
    b. New Jersey turnpike
8. a. austin, Texas
    b. Austin, Texas
9. a. an American Citizen
    b. an American citizen
10. **a.** Los Angeles County highways
    b. Los Angeles County Highways

11. **a.** east of the river
    b. East of the river
12. a. the Iberian peninsula
    b. the Iberian Peninsula
13. **a.** people of the Far East
    b. people of the far east
14. **a.** the Brooklyn Bridge
    b. the Brooklyn bridge
15. **a.** an Irish setter
    b. an Irish Setter
16. a. Billy The Kid
    b. Billy the Kid
17. **a.** We heard him say he was "pleased to be here."
    b. We heard him say he was "Pleased to be here."
18. a. Eastern seaports
    b. eastern seaports
19. a. Plum county
    b. Plum County
20. a. the grand Canyon
    b. the Grand Canyon

▶ **EXERCISE 2** **Using Standard Capitalization**

Write each of the following items, using capital letters where they are needed. **Words that should be capitalized are underscored.**

1. <u>cook county</u>
2. an <u>african</u> village on the <u>atlantic</u> coast
3. four miles south of <u>route</u> 10
4. ranching in the <u>south</u>
5. <u>forty</u>-ninth <u>street</u>
6. <u>olympic national park</u>
7. a city like <u>new orleans</u>, <u>louisiana</u>
8. a popular <u>spanish</u> singer
9. a beautiful gray <u>arabian</u> stallion
10. <u>james o'toole</u>, <u>jr</u>.

PICTURE THIS

The year is 1925, and you are visiting a cousin in New York City. Earlier today, you and your cousin were walking down Centre Street when you saw this surprising sight—all traffic on a busy city street brought to a standstill by a cat carrying her kitten. You're still so amused by the scene that you've decided to write to your best friend back home. Write a letter describing the Centre Street traffic jam. In your letter, use at least six proper nouns and four proper adjectives.

Subject: a cat holding up traffic
Audience: your best friend
Purpose: to inform; to entertain

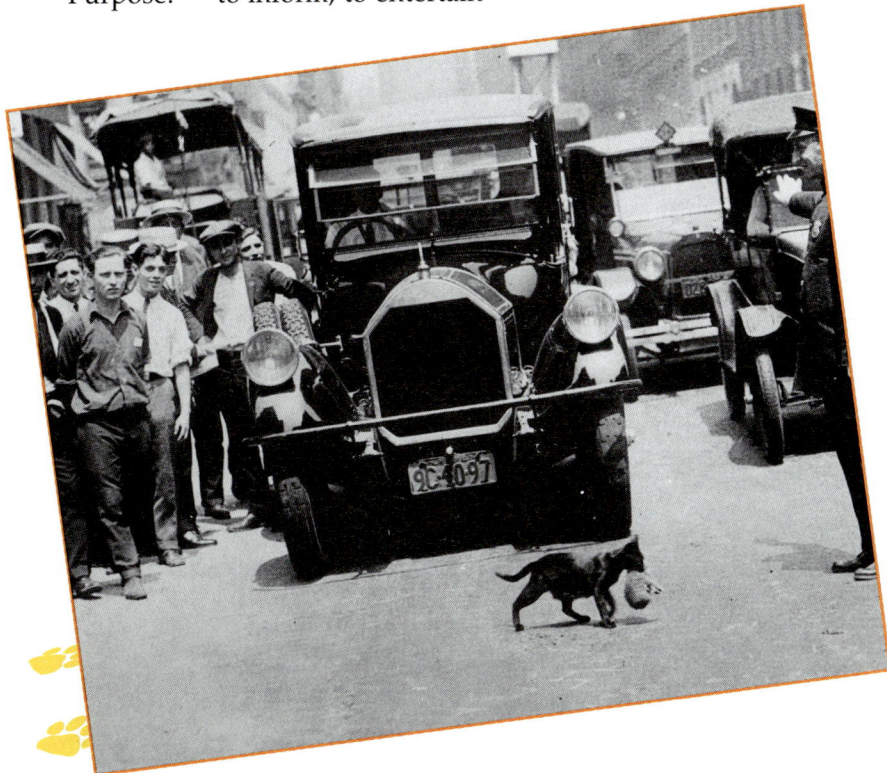

MECHANICS

PICTURE THIS

As a prewriting activity, have the class discuss traffic jams they have either been in or witnessed.

You may want to refer students to **Chapter 39: "Letters and Forms"** for the correct format for the letters they are to write.

MECHANICS

MEETING
individual
NEEDS

LEARNING STYLES

Auditory Learners. Some students might benefit from an oral exercise in which they generate proper nouns from common nouns. Begin with a general category and ask a volunteer to name a specific example in that category. If you were to say "building," for example, a student might say "Empire State Building." Repeat this exercise until you think students understand the difference between common and proper nouns.

MECHANICS

(3) Capitalize the names of organizations, teams, business firms, institutions, buildings, and government bodies.

TYPE OF NAME	EXAMPLES
Organizations	National Collegiate Athletic Association League of Women Voters Humane Society of Austin National Forensic League
Teams	Detroit Red Wings San Antonio Spurs Seattle Seahawks Oak Ridge Rangers
Business Firms	Procter and Gamble Company International Business Machines Pan American Airlines Uptown Discount Shoe Store
Institutions	Beverly Hills High School Catawba Valley Technical College Smithsonian Institution Massachusetts General Hospital
Buildings	Shubert Theater Plaza Hotel Leaning Tower of Pisa Grand Central Station
Government Bodies	House of Representatives Federal Aviation Administration Department of Commerce Peace Corps

NOTE: The names of organizations, businesses, and government bodies are often abbreviated to a series of capital letters.

EXAMPLES	National Organization for Women	NOW
	American Telephone & Telegraph	AT&T
	National Science Foundation	NSF

Usually the letters in such abbreviations are not followed by periods, but always check an up-to-date dictionary or other reliable source to be sure.

☞ **REFERENCE NOTE:** For more information about abbreviations, see page 903.

"After working all day on my MBA, I hop into my BMW and race home to watch PBS on my VCR—OK?"

© 1990; reprinted courtesy of Bunny Hoest and *Parade Magazine.*

Do not capitalize a word such as *hotel*, *theater*, *church*, or *school* unless it is part of a proper noun.

PROPER NOUNS	COMMON NOUNS
Chelsea Hotel	at the hotel
Webster High School	a nearby high school
Fox Theater	a crowded theater
First Baptist Church	in the church

Do not capitalize words such as *democratic* and *republican* when they refer to principles or forms of government. Capitalize such words only when they refer to the political parties.

EXAMPLES   a democratic policy   the Democratic Party (or party)

Notice that the word *party* in the name of a political party may begin with a capital letter or a small letter.

(4) Capitalize the names of historical events and periods, special events, and holidays and other calendar items.

TYPE OF NAME	EXAMPLES	
Historical Events and Periods	Renaissance Vietnam War	Elizabethan Age American Revolution
Special Events	Super Bowl Special Olympics	Conference on World Hunger
Holidays and Other Calendar Items	Labor Day Monday December	Fourth of July Hispanic Heritage Month

NOTE: Do not capitalize the name of a season unless it is part of a proper noun or unless the season is being personified.

EXAMPLES an early winter
the Suncoast Summer Festival

"O wild West Wind, thou breath of Autumn's being, . . ."

Percy Bysshe Shelley, "Ode to the West Wind"

(5) Capitalize the names of nationalities, races, and peoples.

EXAMPLES **Asian Caucasian Norse Ojibwa**
Zulu Hispanic Aztec African American

(6) Capitalize the names of religions and their followers, holy days and celebrations, holy writings, and specific deities.

TYPE OF NAME	EXAMPLES	
Religions and Followers	Christianity Buddhist Hinduism	Judaism Methodist Taoist
Holy Days and Celebrations	Christmas Purim	Ramadan Potlatch
Holy Writings	Talmud Veda	New Testament Koran
Specific Deities	Allah God	Jehovah Brahma

The words *god* and *goddess* are not capitalized when they refer to deities of ancient mythology. The names of specific mythological deities are capitalized, however.

EXAMPLE   Cassandra could foretell the future but was condemned by the **g**od **A**pollo never to be believed.

NOTE: Some writers always capitalize pronouns that refer to the Deity. Other writers capitalize such pronouns only if necessary to prevent confusion.

EXAMPLE   The priest asked God to bring peace to **H**is people.

(7) Capitalize the brand names of business products.

EXAMPLES   **P**olaroid camera   **X**erox copier
          Nintendo video game   **J**if peanut butter

Notice that the names of the types of products are not capitalized.

(8) Capitalize the names of ships, trains, aircraft, spacecraft, monuments, awards, planets, and any other particular things, places, or events.

TYPE OF NAME	EXAMPLES	
Ships	*Merrimac*	*Cunard Princess*
Trains	*Orient Express*	*North Coast Limited*
Aircraft	*Spirit of St. Louis*	*Air Force One*
Spacecraft	*Atlantis*	*Apollo 11*
Monuments	Lincoln Memorial	Statue of Liberty
Awards	Academy Award	Pulitzer Prize
Planets, Stars, Constellations	Neptune Sirius Big Dipper	Mercury Canis Major Cassiopeia

NOTE: The words *sun* and *moon* are rarely capitalized. Do not capitalize the word *earth* unless it is used along with the name of another heavenly body that is capitalized.

EXAMPLES   gazing at the **s**un, **m**oon, and stars
          below the surface of the **e**arth
          the distance between **V**enus and **E**arth

INTEGRATING THE LANGUAGE ARTS

Mechanics and Vocabulary. Some brand names have been used so often that they have come to stand for the products themselves and have become common nouns. You may want to read the following clues to your class and ask students to identify the nouns:

1. a moving stairway [escalator]
2. a synthetic material [nylon]
3. a bran cereal with raisins [raisin bran]
4. a device used to fasten two edges of material together [zipper]
5. a commonly used pain-relieving medicine [aspirin]

Have students generate a list of other brand names that they think will eventually become common nouns.

MEETING *individual* NEEDS

AT-RISK STUDENTS

Provide for students a questionnaire that personalizes the application of capitalization rules governing proper nouns. Here are some sample questions:

1. What are the names of your favorite movie stars?
2. What is your favorite holiday?
3. Which state, county, and city do you live in?
4. What are the names of some shops or restaurants that you like to visit?
5. In what month were you born?
6. What brands of cereal do you like?

Students could also record the responses of family members or friends.

LANGUAGES, SPECIFIC COURSE NAMES, AND TITLES   Rules 28d, 28e

OBJECTIVE

• To use standard capitalization rules to correctly capitalize words

✔ QUICK REMINDER

Tell students to write as many titles as they can in two minutes. You may want to remind them of the kinds of things that have titles—books, songs, movies, poems, plays, reports, and people. Then, take a count to see who wrote the most titles. Ask that student to write some of his or her correctly capitalized titles on the chalkboard.

MECHANICS

---

884   *Capitalization*

28d.   Do not capitalize the names of school subjects, except for course names followed by a number and for the names of languages.

EXAMPLES
art	algebra	chemistry
Art 102	Algebra I	Chemistry II
English	Spanish	German

NOTE: As a rule, nouns identified by a number or letter are capitalized.

EXAMPLES   **Room 31   Parlor B   School District 18   Chapter 4**

Do not capitalize the class name *senior, junior, sophomore,* or *freshman* unless it is part of a proper noun.

EXAMPLES   The **j**uniors and the **s**eniors will hold their talent show on May 4.
The **J**unior-**S**enior Revue will be held on May 4.

▶ EXERCISE 3   Using Standard Capitalization

Rewrite each of the following items, using capital letters where they are needed. If an item is correct, write *C.*
Words that should be capitalized are underscored.

1. itawamba junior college
2. a hotel across town   **2. C**
3. central high school
4. She is a junior.   **4. C**
5. medal of freedom
6. a royal typewriter
7. winter blizzard   **7. C**
8. the barclay hotel
9. trigonometry   **9. C**
10. physics I
11. labor day
12. history class   **12. C**
13. apple computer   **14. [or C]**
14. the senior class picnic
15. bureau of the census
16. zephyr (train)
17. the crusades
18. the world series
19. newport athletic club
20. the rings of saturn

▶ REVIEW A   Proofreading a Paragraph for Correct Capitalization

Proofread the following paragraph, changing capital letters to small letters or small letters to capitals where necessary. If a sentence is correct, write *C.* Words that should be capitalized or lowercased are underscored.

EXAMPLE   [1] Only well-educated, highly skilled candidates are chosen as mission specialists with Today's National Aeronautics and Space administration (NASA).

1. *today's, Administration*

REVIEW A

OBJECTIVE

- To proofread a paragraph for correct capitalization

[1] A physician who speaks four languages and is trained in modern dance, dr. Mae Jemison (above) is one of NASA's most sought-after speakers. [2] Jemison, the first African american woman astronaut, grew up in Chicago and won a scholarship to Stanford university in northern California. [3] At Stanford she turned her attention to chemical engineering and African and Afro-american studies. [4] Later, while earning her Medical degree at Cornell University in Ithaca, new York, she worked at a refugee camp in Thailand. [5] After obtaining her m.d. degree, she served as a Peace corps medical officer in the west African nations of Sierra leone and Liberia. [6] Jemison joined NASA in 1987 while working as a general practitioner and attending graduate Engineering classes in Los angeles. [7] With her first spaceflight on *Endeavor* in the Fall of 1992, she sought to bring people "A view of the space program they may not [otherwise] get." [8] As the United States gets closer to building a space station and sending crews to the Moon and Mars, the number of mission specialists is expected to increase dramatically. [9] As a result, more opportunities will be available to female and minority candidates who excel in research, science, and engineering. [10] "everyone has skills and talents," Jemison emphasizes, "and no one has a lock on scientific ability or physical ability."

9. C

MECHANICS

MECHANICS

28e.   Capitalize titles.

(1) Capitalize a title belonging to a particular person when it comes before the person's name.

EXAMPLES   **Captain Valdés   Justice O'Connor
Senator Inouye   President White Feather**

Generally, do not capitalize a title used alone or following a person's name.

EXAMPLES   the **c**aptain of the ship
every **j**ustice of the U.S. Supreme Court
Daniel Inouye, a **s**enator from Hawaii
Uta White Feather, the class **p**resident

For clarity or special emphasis, you may capitalize a title used alone or following a person's name. In addition, a few titles are always capitalized. If you are unsure of whether to capitalize a title, check in a dictionary.

EXAMPLES   Both the **P**resident and the **V**ice **P**resident met with
Yitzhak Shamir, the **P**rime **M**inister of Israel.
The **S**urgeon **G**eneral explained HIV testing to us.

Generally, capitalize a title when using it alone in direct address.

EXAMPLES   Goodbye, **P**rofessor.
Thank you, **S**ir [or sir].

NOTE: Do not capitalize *ex–, –elect, former,* and *late* when using them with titles.

EXAMPLES   governor-elect   ex-President Reagan

(2) Capitalize a word showing a family relationship when the word is used with a person's name but *not* when it is preceded by a possessive.

EXAMPLES   **U**ncle Juan   **C**ousin Denisa   **G**randfather Ewing
your **m**other   my **a**unt Eunice   Jay's **c**ousin Ramón

NOTE: A word showing a family relationship is capitalized when used in place of a person's name.

EXAMPLE   I think that someone must have told **G**randma about the surprise party.

MECHANICS

(3) Capitalize the first and last words and other important words in titles and subtitles of books, periodicals, poems, stories, plays, historical documents, movies, radio and television programs, works of art, and musical compositions.

Unimportant words within titles are

- articles (*a, an, the*)
- short prepositions (those with fewer than five letters, such as *in, of, to, for, from, with*)
- coordinating conjunctions (*and, but, for, nor, or, so, yet*)

TYPE OF TITLE	EXAMPLES
Books	*A Portrait of the Artist as a Young Man* *Modern Poetry: American and British*
Periodicals	*The San Diego Tribune* *People Weekly*
Poems	"Ode on a Grecian Urn" *I Am Joaquín*
Stories	"The Old Man at the Bridge" "The Train from Rhodesia"
Plays	*The Merchant of Venice* *A Land Beyond the River*
Historical Documents	Declaration of Independence Magna Carta
Movies	*It's a Wonderful Life* *Dances with Wolves*
Radio and TV Programs	*Billboard's Top 40 Countdown* *The Tonight Show*
Works of Art	*Nike of Samothrace* [sculpture] *I and the Village* [painting]
Musical Compositions	*Ragtime Dance* "The Sky Is Crying"

NOTE: The article *the* is often written before a title but is not capitalized unless it is the first word of the title.

EXAMPLES   **the** *Science Digest*   **the** *St. Louis Dispatch*
                 The Count of Monte Cristo   *The Spectator*

MECHANICS

MEETING *individual* NEEDS

LEP/ESL

General Strategies. In some languages, only the first letter of the first word of the title of a book, article, or movie is capitalized, as in the title of the Mexican novel *Los de abajo (The Ones from Below).* Consequently, when they are writing in English, some students might have difficulty determining which words in titles to capitalize. Help students by showing them a variety of titles, so that the students get a sense of which words in titles are capitalized in English.

MECHANICS

MECHANICS

INTEGRATING THE LANGUAGE ARTS

Mechanics and Listening. Have students interview at least five people to get answers to the following questions:

1. What is your favorite book?
2. What is your favorite magazine?
3. What is your favorite song?
4. What is your least favorite song?
5. What is your favorite television show?

Remind students to capitalize titles correctly as they record responses.

A DIFFERENT APPROACH

Some students may be confused about when to use italics (underlining) with titles and when to use quotation marks with titles. Be sure that students understand that they should use italics (underlining) for titles of books, periodicals, movies, television programs, and works of art, and that they should use quotation marks to enclose the titles of short works such as articles, short stories, poems, and songs.

OBJECTIVES

- To use standard capitalization rules to correctly capitalize words in sentences
- To proofread a paragraph for correct capitalization

888 *Capitalization*

EXERCISE 4   Using Standard Capitalization

Write each of the following items, using capital letters where they are needed. If an item is correct, write C. **Words that should be capitalized are underscored.**

1. <u>captain</u> Ahab
2. <u>guernica</u> (painting)
3. a sergeant in an army   **3. C**
4. the club president   **4. C**
5. <u>aunt</u> Betty
6. <u>senator</u> Campbell
7. <u>mayor</u> Fulton of Nashville
8. <u>down</u> and <u>out</u> in <u>paris</u> and <u>london</u> (book title)
9. the <u>speaker</u> of the House of Representatives
10. Rabbi Klein, a military chaplain   **10. C**
11. ex-<u>president</u> Reagan   **12. C**
12. the leader of a brass band
13. Ms. Solomon, the center director   **13. C**
14. the mayor-elect   **14. C**
15. the <u>bill</u> of <u>rights</u>
16. your aunt   **16. C**
17. the *Los Angeles* <u>times</u>
18. duties of a legislator   **18. C**
19. Mildred Zaharias, former national golf champion   **19. C**
20. "<u>the</u> <u>world</u> is <u>too</u> <u>much</u> with <u>us</u>" (poem)

REVIEW B   Using Standard Capitalization

Write in order the <u>words that should be capitalized</u> in each of the following sentences, and capitalize the words correctly.

1. In their <u>english</u> classes this term, the juniors have read <u>o</u> <u>pioneers!</u>, a novel written by <u>willa</u> <u>cather</u> about <u>swedish</u> immigrants in <u>nebraska</u>.
2. A recent report from the <u>secretary</u> of <u>labor</u> included the following statement: <u>most</u> of the new jobs in the next decade will be in service fields.
3. According to professor De La Rey, the first of Alfred, <u>lord</u> Tennyson's *idylls of the king* was published in 1859, the same year as the publication of Charles Darwin's *the origin of species*, George Eliot's *adam bede*, and Charles Dickens's *a tale of two cities*.
4. In "<u>canto</u> I" the poet Ezra Pound describes an ominous sea voyage to the same mythical land of the dead visited by the hero Odysseus in the *Odyssey*, an epic by the <u>greek</u> poet Homer.
5. Speaking to a reporter from the *Tri-County Clarion*, <u>coach</u> Sheila Smith explained the drafting of a team resolution, which read, in part, "Resolved: <u>that</u> we will win all of our games next year."

6. In ancient <u>egypt</u> the people worshiped many gods equally until the sun god Ra became the principal deity.
7. Dr. Bruce Jackson, <u>jr.</u>, principal of the high school, formerly taught <u>mathematics</u> I classes and an introductory class in computer science offered to freshmen and sophomores.
8. From the St. Croix <u>island</u> <u>national</u> <u>monument</u> in Maine to the Huleia <u>wildlife</u> <u>refuge</u> in Hawaii, public lands managed by the federal government, including the military, equal a large percentage of the nation's total acreage.
9. Suzanne <u>o'</u>Rourke, president of the jogging club, has an exercise route that takes her three times a week through Myers <u>park</u>, down Carriage <u>street</u>, and then back west to Dean <u>avenue</u>.
10. The will of the <u>swedish</u> industrialist and inventor of dynamite, Alfred Nobel, established the Nobel <u>prize</u> to honor those who have benefited the world in the areas of literature, medicine, physics, chemistry, and peace; a prize in economics was added in 1969.

▶ REVIEW C **Proofreading a Paragraph for Correct Capitalization**

Proofread the following paragraph, changing capital letters to small letters and small letters to capitals where necessary. If a sentence is correct, write *C*. Words that should be capitalized or lowercased are underscored.

EXAMPLE [1] An intriguing museum in Western Oklahoma celebrates the diversity and vitality of American Indian Culture.
  1. *western, culture*

[1] The Southern Plains Indian Museum on Highway 62 <u>East</u> of Anadarko, Oklahoma, was founded in 1947. [2] Administered by the Indian <u>arts</u> and <u>crafts</u> <u>board</u>, an agency of the U.S. <u>department</u> of the Interior, the museum showcases the creative achievements of the Kiowa, Comanche, Kiowa-Apache, Southern Cheyenne, Southern Arapaho, Wichita, Caddo, Delaware, and Ft. Sill Apache. [3] The display of several authentically detailed traditional costumes, shown on the next page, highlights the <u>Museum's</u> permanent collection. [4] Also on permanent display are four dioramas and a mural by nationally renowned <u>Artist</u> and sculptor Allen Houser, a Ft. Sill Apache; these exhibits illustrate the traditional social and ceremonial

MECHANICS

A DIFFERENT APPROACH

Your students might enjoy a capitalization bee. Following the rules of a spelling bee, divide the class into two teams and present words and phrases to each team alternately. Have a student from either team tell which of the given words should be capitalized and why. Give each team a point for a correct response and no score for an incorrect response. Continue the game until one team has scored thirty points.

CRITICAL THINKING

Application. Give your class practice in using the rules of capitalization presented in this chapter by having the students write letters to imaginary pen pals abroad. Students should tell where they are from, who the members of their families are, what subjects they are studying in school, and what their ambitions are for the future.

MECHANICS

5. C customs of the region's peoples. [5] The museum also offers changing exhibits of contemporary arts and crafts, including painting, beadwork, metalwork, and featherwork. [6] These displays, as well as frequent one-person shows and demonstrations, are held in cooperation with the Oklahoma Indian Arts and Crafts <u>cooperative</u>, an independent business owned and operated by American <u>indian</u> artists and craftworkers. [7] The <u>Cooperative</u> operates the museum's gift shop and certifies the authenticity of all products sold there. [8] One special attraction during the <u>Summer</u> is a display on the museum grounds of full-scale tepees, like these, painted by contemporary artists. [9] Another attraction is the week-long American Indian Expo held each August at the Caddo <u>county</u> Fairgrounds adjacent to the museum. [10] The largest gathering of <u>native</u> American peoples in the <u>State</u> of Oklahoma, the exposition features dance contests, a pageant, horse races, and parades.

Southern Plains Indian Museum, Anadarko, Oklahoma

Southern Plains Indian Museum, Anadarko, Oklahoma

MECHANICS

MECHANICS

890

WRITING APPLICATION

Using Standard Capitalization in a Letter

Following the rules of capitalization is not just a matter of correctness. By choosing a capital letter or a small letter to begin a particular word, a writer indicates how the reader should interpret that word. How do the differences in the use of capitals and small letters affect the meaning of the following pair of sentences?

EXAMPLES   From my informal survey, I found that the harpers, the bishops, the kings, and the knights feel that you should purchase a passage to India.

From my informal survey, I found that the Harpers, the Bishops, the Kings, and the Knights feel that you should purchase *A Passage to India.*

Notice in the examples above that italics also affect the meaning of a sentence. For more about how to punctuate titles, see pages 933–934 and 938–939.

▶ **WRITING ACTIVITY**
Your school's library has received funding to expand its collection, and now students and teachers have been invited to make suggestions for new materials. Write a letter to the librarian naming five titles—books, periodicals, or videocassettes—that you think the library should acquire. Give a brief description of each title, and tell why you think each would be a worthwhile addition to the library. Be sure to use correct capitalization in your note.

Prewriting   Jot down a list of novels, biographies, how-to manuals, reference books, newspapers, literary journals, educational videocassettes, and other materials that you think would be helpful additions to the library. Choose five titles from your list. Note whether each title is fiction or nonfiction; a book, a periodical, or a videocassette; one volume or several volumes. Briefly describe the subject matter of each title. You may want to visit the public library to collect or confirm information.

MECHANICS

WRITING APPLICATION
If students have trouble remembering the form for a letter, refer them to **Chapter 39: "Letters and Forms."**
Remind students that this is to be a persuasive letter and that keeping their audience (the librarian) in mind is essential to achieving their writing objective. For examples of persuasive writing done by their peers, refer students to the student models on pp. 333–334.

CRITICAL THINKING
Analysis. To help students decide which materials to choose as additions to the library, have students analyze and evaluate their peers' reading and viewing interests. You may want to suggest to students that they poll their peers outside class for help in deciding which materials would be appropriate to suggest in the letter. Students then will need to evaluate the materials suggested by their peers to decide which materials are most worthwhile and appropriate.

MECHANICS

OBJECTIVES

- To use standard capitalization rules to correctly capitalize words in sentences
- To proofread a paragraph for correct capitalization

---

892 *Capitalization*

Writing   Use your notes to help you write your first draft. Give clear, specific information about each book, periodical, or video. Convince the librarian that each would make a useful addition to the library. Explain why it's important for students to have easy access to these materials.

Evaluating and Revising   Put your first draft aside for a few hours or overnight. Then, read it critically. Is your letter persuasive? Does it follow the proper form for a business letter? (For more about business letters, see pages 1088–1095.) Be sure that all of your information is accurate and complete. Check your draft against your prewriting notes to see if you've left out any important details.

Proofreading and Publishing   Use this checklist to help you proofread your letter. Have you

- spelled each title correctly?
- followed the rules of standard capitalization?
- underlined each title or enclosed it in quotation marks correctly?
- corrected any errors in grammar, usage, spelling, and punctuation?

You and your classmates may want to compile your information and write a group letter to the librarian suggesting needed additions to the library's collection.

Review: Posttest

A. Using Standard Capitalization

Many of the following sentences contain errors in standard capitalization. For each error, write the standard form of the word. If the sentence does not contain any errors, write *C*.

Words that should be capitalized or lowercased are underscored.

EXAMPLE   **1.** Manolo Cruz will be attending Stanford university in the Fall.

1. *University, fall*

MECHANICS

MECHANICS

1. I am studying <u>russian</u>, English, and <u>Art</u> this <u>Semester</u>.
2. Go north for two <u>Streets</u> and then turn east on Central Avenue.
3. In the <u>History</u> of the United States, only one person, Gerald R. Ford, has held the nation's highest office without being elected president or <u>Vice</u> <u>President</u>.
4. Last summer I enjoyed reading *To Kill <u>A</u> Mockingbird* by Harper Lee, a <u>southern</u> writer.
5. HOMES is an acronym for the five <u>great</u> <u>lakes</u>: Huron, Ontario, Michigan, Erie, and Superior.
6. The first American woman in space, Sally Ride, was a member of the crew aboard the space shuttle *<u>challenger</u>* launched from <u>cape</u> Canaveral, Florida, on June 18, 1983.
7. The <u>Mountain</u> <u>Ranges</u> in the <u>Western</u> states offer a variety of hiking experiences for those who love the outdoors.
8. Despite their political differences, my mother, a Democrat, and my father, a Republican, worked together to increase voter registration. **6. C**
9. Because Michael's letter was addressed to 730 Lexington Place instead of to 730 Lexington Court, it was delayed. **9. C**
10. America's political and economic interests are closely tied to those of its northern neighbor, Canada, and to those of its southern neighbors, Mexico and the <u>central</u> American countries.

B. Proofreading a Paragraph for Correct Capitalization

Proofread the following paragraph, changing capital letters to small letters and small letters to capitals where necessary. If a sentence is correct, write C. **Words that should be capitalized or lowercased are underscored.**

EXAMPLE   **[1]** Chattanooga, Tennessee, is the seat of Hamilton county.

   1. *County*

   [11] Chattanooga, on the Georgia border in <u>Southeast</u> Tennessee, is building its future by inviting visitors to explore its past. **[12]** The city has been welcoming tourists since at least **12. C** 1866, when an ad in the *Chattanooga Times* invited northerners to visit with the assurance that the Ku Klux Klan had no power in Chattanooga. **[13]** Today a multimillion-dollar plaza on the banks of the Tennessee <u>river</u> marks the city's original site, a landing established about 1815 by a trader named <u>john</u> Ross. **[14]** <u>exhibits</u> throughout the plaza depict the city's history, including the forced removal of the Cherokee to Indian Territory (now Oklahoma) in 1838. **[15]** Ross, who was himself part Cherokee and who vehemently protested the removal, led that tragic journey, which became known as the <u>trail</u> of Tears. **[16]** The city of Chattanooga plans to build a trolley system to connect the plaza at Ross' <u>landing</u> to the restored Chattanooga Choo-Choo Terminal and Station on Market Street, where visitors can see a car and an engine from the first train that provided passenger service between the <u>north</u> and the South. **[17]** Chattanooga's status as a rail center made the <u>City</u> strategically important to both sides during the Civil War. **[18]** As the junction point for railroads to Atlanta, Georgia, and Memphis, Nashville, and Knoxville in Tennessee, Chattanooga provided a vital link for the movement of <u>confederate</u> troops and equip-

19. C ment. **[19]** In fact, the struggle for control of the railroads in the fall of 1863 led to a series of battles in and around the city that may have determined the outcome of the war. **[20]** For it was the Union general William Tecumseh Sherman's victory in the last of those confrontations, the Battle of Missionary Ridge on November 24–25, that cleared the way for his devastating march through Georgia to the <u>Sea</u>.

SUMMARY STYLE REVIEW

Names of Persons

Margot Fonteyn	a dancer
Mr. David G. DeLotto, Jr.	a teacher
William the Conqueror	an English king

Geographical Names

Kansas City	a city in Kansas
Cuyahoga County	a county in Ohio
in the **N**orth, **S**outhwest, **Middle East**	heading **n**orth, **s**outh, **e**ast, west
Argentina	a country in South America
Isle Royale	an island in Lake Superior
Mount Ararat	a mountain in Turkey
Mississippi River	a river flowing into the Gulf of Mexico
East Sixty-first Street	across the street

(continued)

MECHANICS

SUMMARY STYLE REVIEW *(continued)*

Names of Organizations, Teams, Business Firms, Institutions, Buildings, Government Bodies

the Toastmasters Club	a public-speaking club
San Diego Padres	a baseball team
Boeing Company	an aircraft company
Lakeland High School	a large high school
Black Hawk College	four years in college
the Chrysler Building	a tall building
Department of Education	a department of government

Names of Historical Periods and Events, Special Events, Calendar Items

the Bronze Age	a prehistoric age
the American Civil War	a civil war
the World Series	a series of baseball games
Thanksgiving Day	a national holiday
March, June, September, December	spring, summer, autumn, winter

Names of Nationalities, Races, Peoples

Egyptian	a native of Egypt
Caucasian	a race
Native Americans	indigenous peoples of the Western Hemisphere

Names of Religions, Their Followers, Holy Days, Celebrations, Holy Writings, Specific Deities

Islam	the religious faith of Muslims
Ash Wednesday	the first day of Lent
Hanukkah	a Jewish festival
Holy Bible	a holy book
God	Zeus, a Greek god

Brand Names

Levi's	blue jeans
Kleenex	facial tissues

Names of Languages, Specific Courses

French, Spanish, Latin	languages
Home Economics 101	my home economics class
American History II	a course in American history

(continued)

TECHNOLOGY TIP

There are video and computer games available that move the player closer to achieving a given goal each time he or she correctly capitalizes a word. Such games can be useful learning tools for students.

You also may want to have students call up information on capitalization with a style- and grammar-checking computer program. As students ask questions and receive information from the program, point out how the information in the computer program reinforces the rules in the textbook. Discuss possible reasons for any differences between the two.

MECHANICS

MECHANICS

SUMMARY STYLE REVIEW *(continued)*

Names of Other Particular Things, Places, Events

Santa Maria	a ship
Riverina XPT	a train
Concorde	an aircraft
Columbia	a spacecraft
Tomb of the Unknowns	a monument
George Peabody Award	an award
Little Dipper	a group of stars in the constellation Ursa Minor
Earth, Jupiter, Saturn	the surface of the earth
Room 212	the second room on the left
Oakdale Senior Prom	a group of seniors
Biosphere II	a scientific study of the biosphere

Titles

Governor Richards	a governor
President Kennedy	the president of the club
Aunt Elena	Sonia's aunt
a message from **Mother**	a message from my **m**other
Portraits of the Valley and Other Works	a book
"Kubla Khan"	a poem
"The Secret Sharer"	a short story
Androcles and the Lion	a play
The Wall Street Journal	a newspaper
the Bill of Rights	a document
Robin Hood: Prince of Thieves	a movie
The Wonder Years	a television program
Mona Lisa	a work of art
"America the Beautiful"	a musical composition

OBJECTIVES

- To revise sentences for correct use of end marks and commas
- To revise a paragraph for correct use of end marks and commas

29 PUNCTUATION

End Marks and Commas

Diagnostic Test

A. Correcting Errors in the Use of End Marks and Commas in Sentences

Add, delete, or change end marks or commas to correct any of the following sentences that are incorrectly punctuated. If a sentence is correct, write C.

EXAMPLES **1.** Well I think it's a good idea.
 1. *Well, I think it's a good idea.*

 2. We went to the mall, to the movies, and to our favorite restaurant, this afternoon
 2. *We went to the mall, to the movies, and to our favorite restaurant this afternoon.*

 1. Mr. Stanton‚will you please give me a reference?
 2. Students who do well in academic subjects should‚in my opinion‚be commended by their school administrators.
 3. No‚Sandy will not leave until the fifth of August.
 4. Hoping to meet Arsenio Hall‚we got tickets to a taping of his show.

CHAPTER OVERVIEW

This chapter contains the rules for using commas and end marks in punctuating sentences. You may want to refer to this chapter throughout the year, especially as students work on proofreading their writing.

The first lesson presents the use of end marks with the four types of sentences—declarative, interrogative, exclamatory, and imperative—and the use of periods with abbreviations. Although twelfth-grade students may have little trouble with end marks, they may need frequent reviews of the comma rules in the third lesson of this chapter. This lesson explains three basic uses of commas: to separate a series of nouns or adjectives; to set off independent clauses, nonessential clauses, or participial phrases; and to clarify introductory or interrupting elements. The lesson also presents the conventional use of commas in dates, in addresses, in letters, and in abbreviations after names.

MECHANICS

MECHANICS

897

You may want to use the results of the **Diagnostic Test** in conjunction with assessment of students' papers to determine whether students need to review the rules for using end marks and commas in punctuating sentences.

MECHANICS

MECHANICS

898 *Punctuation*

5. Look at the size of the fish I caught**!**
6. On Jan**.** 1**,** 2000**,** my niece will celebrate her twenty-first birthday.
7. Mom or Dad or Uncle Paul will cook dinner tonight. **7. C**
8. On the last day of school**,** the juniors will prepare juice, toast, and ham, and eggs for the seniors.
9. Please address all complaints to Dr**.** Joseph Redwing**,** Jr**.,** Department of Consumer Affairs**,** 4749 Prospect Street**,** Eugene**,** OR 97401.
10. My grandmother**,** a housekeeper all her life**,** saved her money**,** invested wisely**,** and put both of her children through college.

B. Correcting Errors in the Use of End Marks and Commas in Paragraphs

Add, delete, or change end marks or commas in the following paragraphs to correct sentences that are incorrectly punctuated. If a sentence is correct, write *C*.

EXAMPLE   **[1]** When I wrenched my back playing basketball I consulted a doctor, who specializes in sports medicine.

    1. *When I wrenched my back playing basketball, I consulted a doctor who specializes in sports medicine.*

[11] Sports medicine is a branch of medicine concerned with preventing and treating injuries suffered during participation in sports. **[12]** Initially practiced by doctors working with professional sports teams, the practice of sports medicine has grown rapidly as interest in amateur sports and physical-fitness programs has increased.

12. C

[13] One ailment that doctors who specialize in sports medicine frequently encounter is tendinitis**,** the inflammation of a tendon. **[14]** Tendons are the tough**,** fibrous**,** inelastic tissues that connect muscles to bones or other body parts. **[15]** "Tennis elbow," for example**,** is a form of tendinitis caused by straining the tendons that attach the muscles of the lower arm at the elbow.

[16] You don't have to be active in sports to benefit from advances in sports medicine**,** for those advances are now being

OBJECTIVES

- To correct a passage by adding appropriate end marks
- To use end marks and abbreviations correctly in a writing journal entry on the topic of personal challenges

End Marks **899**

applied in the workplace. **[17]** Repetitive strain injury (RSI), caused by tendinitis, can afflict anyone whose job requires performing the same motion hundreds or even thousands of times a day. **[18]** In fact, RSI strikes workers as varied as meatpackers, word processors, fruit pickers, supermarket checkout clerks, and musicians. **[19]** Because permanent disability can set in if RSI is left untreated, physicians are teaming up with ergonomists, scientists who adapt working conditions or the work itself to prevent injuries. **[20]** Employers, are finding that the preventive measures are a sound investment, not a waste of money, paying for themselves many times over in increased productivity, reduced turnover, and lower medical costs.

End Marks

Sentences

An *end mark*—a *period*, a *question mark*, or an *exclamation point*—is used to indicate the purpose of a sentence. A period is also used at the end of many abbreviations.

☞ **REFERENCE NOTE:** For more information on how sentences are classified according to purpose, see pages 689–690.

29a. A statement (or declarative sentence) is followed by a period.

EXAMPLES   Mexico City is the home of the Ballet Folklórico.

My words are like the stars that never change.
Chief Seattle, "Speech of Chief Seattle"

29b. A question (or interrogative sentence) is followed by a question mark.

EXAMPLES   When will Terrell prepare the wild rice?

Have you read Lorraine Hansberry's *To Be Young, Gifted, and Black*?

PROGRAM MANAGER

END MARKS

- **Independent Practice/ Reteaching** For instruction and exercises, see **Using End Marks** in *Language Skills Practice and Assessment*, p. 211.

- **Computer Guided Instruction** For additional instruction and practice with using end marks, see **Lesson 46** in *Language Workshop CD-ROM.*

- **Practice** To help less-advanced students with additional instruction and practice with end marks, see **Chapter 22** in *English Workshop, Complete Course*, pp. 293–294.

QUICK REMINDER

Write on the chalkboard the following passage. Have your students correct it by adding end marks.

Have you seen Spike Lee's movie about Malcolm X I found it thought-provoking, especially the part about Malcolm's trip to Mecca I loved it You will too

After students have copied and corrected the passage independently, have a volunteer make the necessary corrections to the paragraph on the chalkboard.

SELECTION AMENDMENT
Description of change: excerpted
Rationale: to focus on the use of end marks presented in this chapter

MECHANICS

MECHANICS

MEETING *individual* NEEDS

LEP/ESL

General Strategies. Punctuation marks differ from language to language. For example, a period is represented by a vertical line in Hindi and by a circle in Japanese. In languages such as Greek, Korean, Persian, and Arabic, the period is slightly raised. The Greek question mark looks like an English semicolon, and Spanish interrogative and exclamatory sentences have end marks at both ends of the sentence, with the first mark inverted. Encourage students to discuss differences in punctuation between their native languages and English. Such discussion will aid some students in remembering English punctuation rules and may increase other students' awareness of such variations among languages.

900 *Punctuation*

(1) Do not use a question mark after a declarative sentence containing an indirect question.

INDIRECT QUESTION   Mariana wants to know in what year Junko Tabei climbed Mount Everest.

QUESTION   In what year did Junko Tabei climb Mount Everest?

(2) Polite requests in question form may be followed by either a question mark or a period.

EXAMPLE   Would you please return these books and videotapes to the media center?

or

Would you please return these books and videotapes to the media center.

(3) A question mark should be placed inside the closing quotation marks when the quotation is a question. Otherwise, it should be placed outside the closing quotation marks.

EXAMPLES   Cara asked, "Did Scott Joplin compose the opera *Treemonisha*?" [The quotation is a question.]
Do you agree with the Spanish proverb "Whoever gossips to you will gossip about you"? [The entire sentence, not the quotation, is a question.]

☞ **REFERENCE NOTE:** For more information about the placement of end marks with closing quotation marks, see pages 936–937.

29c.   An exclamation is followed by an exclamation point.

EXAMPLES   What a talented artist Frida Kahlo was!
I can't stand that noise!

(1) An interjection at the beginning of a sentence is usually followed by a comma but may be followed by an exclamation point.

CUSTOMARY   Ah, there you are!

RARE   Ah! There you are! [Notice that an exclamation point may be used after a single word as well as after a sentence.]

(2) An exclamation point should be placed inside the closing quotation marks when the quotation is an exclamation. Otherwise, it should be placed outside the closing quotation marks.

EXAMPLES   "What a good movie!" exclaimed Natalie as she left the theater. [The quotation is an exclamation.]
How quickly she said, "You'll love it"! [The entire sentence, not the quotation, is an exclamation.]

29d.   **An imperative sentence may be followed by either a period or an exclamation point.**

A request is usually followed by a period; a command is usually followed by an exclamation point.

EXAMPLES   Please write me a letter. [a request]
Hold that line! [a command]

Hi and Lois reprinted with special permission of King Features Syndicate, Inc.

▶ EXERCISE 1   **Correcting a Passage by Adding End Marks**   Some answers may vary.

Many periods and all exclamation points and question marks have been omitted from the following passage. Write each <u>word that should be followed by an end mark</u>, and add the appropriate end mark. If a new sentence begins after the end mark, capitalize the first word of the sentence. For any quotation requiring an end mark, include the closing quotation mark to show the proper placement of the end mark.

MECHANICS

Literature Link. If "The Tyger" by William Blake is available to students, have them read the poem. After students have read the poem, discuss Blake's use of exclamation points and question marks. Ask students to consider, for example, how the poem would be different without the exclamation points in its first line. [Students might point out that the exclamation points serve to show the emphatic nature of the speaker's address and that they heighten the sense of energy and tension in the poem. Students might find that the numerous question marks in the poem serve to underscore the speaker's wonder and inability to comprehend the tiger.]

MECHANICS

COOPERATIVE LEARNING

Have students work in groups of three or four to write short skits or raps that each include at least two questions, two exclamations, and two commands. After they have written their pieces, ask students to perform them for the class. Tell students to use intonation, body language, and facial expressions to convey the sense of each sentence.

MECHANICS

EXAMPLES [1] Dr. Lynn Block, director of research for the Larson Soap Company, looked at her appointment book
[2] "oh, no" she groaned

1. *book.*
2. *"Oh, no!"; groaned.*

[1] Today she must conduct interviews to hire a new secretary. [2] "how nerve-racking it is when an applicant is unprepared" [3] nonetheless, she was ready for the 9:00 A.M. interview.

[4] At 9:35 A.M., the receptionist ushered in the late arrival. [5] "Oh, dear" thought Dr. Block as she surveyed the young man's torn jeans, unironed T-shirt, and shaggy hair. [6] to questions about his qualifications, the young man answered only yes or no instead of mentioning specific details, and he did not apologize for his lateness. [7] "Well," Dr. Block puzzled, "this person has good experience and typing skills, but he certainly doesn't seem to want the job"

[8] The next applicant, Ms. Smith, entered wearing a professional tool belt with well-cared-for carpentry tools around her waist. [9] she said, "I'm so sorry to disturb you. [10] I'm interested in the maintenance position being advertised" [11] I must have taken a wrong turn when I got off the elevator.

[12] "I'll say" exclaimed Dr. Block. [13] she directed the woman to the maintenance office on the other side of the building and wished her luck. [14] To herself, she mused, "Whew! at this rate, I may never get a secretary" [15] By then the next interviewee had arrived—on time. [16] "Now what" wondered Dr. Block. [17] Looking up to see a neatly dressed young man, she asked, "Are *you* sure you're in the right place? [18] it's been a highly unusual morning so far"

[19] he replied, "Oh, yes I'm applying for the secretarial position. [20] he gave brief, helpful explanations and asked appropriate questions about the job. [21] About his career plans, he said, "I would someday like to be an office manager. [22] I like office work and believe good management is vital to a smooth operation"

[23] "You're right about that" exclaimed Dr. Block. [24] After the interview ended, Dr. Block pondered her choices. [25] she thought, "Well, he doesn't have as much experience or quite as high a typing rate as the first interviewee, but I know whom I'm going to hire"

2. !
5. !
7. .
10. .
12. !
14. !
16. ?
18. .
19. .
22. .
23. !
25. .

29e

Abbreviations

29e. An abbreviation is usually followed by a period.

Names of Persons	Ida B. Wells E. M. Forster
Titles Used with Names	Mr. Mrs. Ms. Dr. Jr. Sr.
Kinds of Organizations	Co. Inc. Corp. Assn. Ltd.

NOTE: Commonly known abbreviations for the names of organizations and services in areas such as government, education, and broadcasting media are written without periods. Each letter of the abbreviation is capitalized.

EXAMPLES   FBI   HUD   ZIP   ROTC   PTA   MTV   BBC   PBS

Times	A.M. P.M. B.C. A.D.
Parts of Addresses	Ave. St. Rd. Blvd. P.O. Box
Names of States	Ala. Del. Neb. Ky. S. Dak.

NOTE: A two-letter state abbreviation without periods is used when it is followed by a ZIP Code. Each letter of the abbreviation is capitalized, and no comma separates the abbreviation from the ZIP Code.

EXAMPLE   Tampa, **FL** 33624

NOTE: Abbreviations for units of measurement are usually written without periods. However, do use a period with the abbreviation for *inch* (*in.*) to prevent confusing it with the word *in*.

EXAMPLES   mm, kg, ml, tsp, doz, yd, ft, lb

When an abbreviation with a period is written at the end of a sentence, another period is not used as an end mark. However, a question mark or an exclamation point is used as needed.

EXAMPLES   The Méndezes are moving to Broken Arrow, Okla.
Are the Méndezes moving to Broken Arrow, Okla.?

☞ **REFERENCE NOTE:** For information on capitalizing abbreviations, see pages 876, 877, and 880.

MECHANICS

INTEGRATING THE LANGUAGE ARTS

Mechanics and Writing. You may want to remind students to avoid most abbreviations in formal writing. Titles used with names can be abbreviated, but students should avoid abbreviating parts of addresses, the names of states, and units of measure.

Literature Link. Few poems include abbreviations; however, "The Unknown Citizen" by W. H. Auden does include one. Have students read the poem, which can be found in some literature textbooks, and ask them to consider Auden's use of an abbreviation, *Inc.* Ask students what they think is the theme of the poem and how the use of an abbreviation supports that theme. [The theme of the poem can be seen as the anonymity of the individual in a bureaucratic, impersonal world in which people are valued on the basis of productivity, conformity, consumption, and complacency. The use of the abbreviation supports this theme because abbreviations—shortened for the sake of efficiency—are seen as impersonal and result from the desire to enhance speed and, therefore, productivity.]

MECHANICS

PICTURE THIS

This assignment allows students to explore their feelings and attitudes toward taking risks. You may need to initiate a discussion about different kinds of risks—physical (as in the example), intellectual, and emotional. The questions posed in the text provide a good starting place. You could also review the characteristics of expressive writing. Remind students that expressive writing consists of thoughts and personal feelings conveyed in informal language, including slang. You could encourage students to look for other pictures that convey a sense of risk and challenge. Take this opportunity to encourage students to keep writing journals in which they explore personal topics.

PICTURE THIS

While reading the Sunday newspaper, you come upon this amazing photograph. The man in the picture is performing a bungee jump, a carefully supervised free fall from a height of several hundred feet. The special elastic cord will stop his fall before he can reach the ground. Seeing this photograph starts you thinking. Why do people set mental and physical challenges for themselves? What purpose do such challenges serve? What sorts of challenges do you set for yourself? Write a journal entry on the topic of personal challenges. In your entry, use each of the three types of end marks at least once, and include at least two abbreviations.

Subject: personal challenges
Audience: yourself
Purpose: to express your opinion; to record your thoughts

Brian Van Leeuwen, 28, a Sandia Labs engineer who is paraplegic, takes a daring plunge from a platform in Albuquerque, N.M., as part of a bungee-jumping experiment., Van Leeuwen said he made the jump strapped to his wheelchair because the chair is part of him.

OBJECTIVES

- To correct sentences by adding commas
- To identify essential and nonessential clauses and phrases and to add commas in sentences where needed

Commas **905**

29f

Commas

Items in a Series

29f. Use commas to separate items in a series.

EXAMPLES She had been a correspondent for the wire service in London, Paris, Rome, and Madrid. [words]
I studied for the test on the way to school, during homeroom, and in study hall. [phrases]
The reporter wanted to know who I was, where I went to school, and how I felt about getting my driver's license. [clauses]

NOTE: Do not place a comma before the first item or after the final item in a series.

INCORRECT The students in auto mechanics class learned, to replace the spark plugs, check the fluid levels, and change the oil, in several makes of cars.
CORRECT The students in auto mechanics class learned to replace the spark plugs, check the fluid levels, and change the oil in several makes of cars.

(1) When *and, or,* **or** *nor* **joins the last two items in a series, you may omit the comma before the conjunction. Never omit the final comma, however, if such an omission would make the sentence unclear.**

EXAMPLES Soccer, basketball and lacrosse are my best sports. [The sentence is clear without the final comma.]
Joetta, Lucia and Ben are rehearsing a scene from the musical *Grease.* [The sentence is unclear without the comma. It appears that Joetta is being addressed.]
Joetta, Lucia, and Ben are rehearsing a scene from the musical *Grease.* [The sentence clearly states that all three people are rehearsing.]

Some writers prefer always to use the comma before the conjunction in a series. Follow your teacher's instructions on this point.

NOTE: Words customarily used in pairs are set off as one item in a series, such as *bag and baggage, law and order,* and *macaroni and cheese.*

EXAMPLE For supper they served a tossed salad, spaghetti and meatballs, garlic bread, milk, and fruit.

MECHANICS

QUICK REMINDER

Write the following sentences on the chalkboard and ask students to add commas where necessary:

1. In 1787 in Saint Augustine Florida the first integrated public school in the United States was founded.
2. The school was founded by Father Thomas Hassett an Irish priest.
3. The school was free and it was open to children of all races.
4. It is believed however that the school did not admit girls.

MECHANICS

905

INTEGRATING THE LANGUAGE ARTS

Mechanics and Dictionary Skills.
The word *comma* has an interesting etymology. Have students look up *comma* in a dictionary to discover its origin. [*Comma* comes from the Greek word *komma,* meaning "that which is cut off," from the Greek word *koptein,* meaning "to cut or split."] Discuss with students how the origin of the word *comma* relates to the function of the comma in writing.

MECHANICS

(2) If all the items in a series are joined by *and, or,* or *nor,* do not use commas to separate them.

EXAMPLE   Derrick **and** Han **and** Jina will represent the senior class.

(3) Short independent clauses may be separated by commas.

EXAMPLE   Kelly plays the electric guitar, Diego plays the piano, and Chee sings.

☞ **REFERENCE NOTE:** Independent clauses in a series are usually separated by a semicolon. For more about this use of the semicolon, see pages 928–929.

29g.   **Use a comma to separate two or more adjectives preceding a noun.**

EXAMPLES   Katherine Dunham is a creative, talented dancer and choreographer.
Did you see that boring, silly, worthless movie?

Do not use a comma before the final adjective in a series if the adjective is thought of as part of the noun.

EXAMPLES   Lawanda hung colorful, delicate Chinese lanterns around the patio. [*Chinese lanterns* is regarded as a single compound noun.]
It was a crisp, clear fall day. [*Fall day* is considered one item.]

You can use two tests to determine whether an adjective and a noun form a unit.

TEST 1:   Insert the word *and* between the adjectives. If *and* fits sensibly between the adjectives, use a comma. In the first example above, *and* fits logically between the first two adjectives (*crisp* and *clear*) but not between *clear* and *fall.*

TEST 2:   Change the order of the adjectives. If the order of the adjectives can be reversed sensibly, use a comma. *Clear, crisp fall day* makes sense, but *clear, fall, crisp day* does not.

NOTE: If one of the words in a series modifies another word in the series, do *not* separate them with a comma.

EXAMPLE   Why did he wear a **bright red** cap?

29 g–h

▶ **EXERCISE 2** **Correcting Sentences by Adding Commas**

For each of the following sentences, write each <u>word that should be followed by a comma</u>, and place a comma after it. If a sentence is correct, write *C*.

EXAMPLE **1.** The firefighters arrived promptly extinguished the blaze and returned to the station.
  1. *promptly,; blaze,*

1. She is a <u>bright</u>⁁charming young woman.
2. Albert Cunningham prepared a tossed green <u>salad</u>⁁ham and cheese <u>sandwiches</u>⁁and iced tea.
3. Armando <u>sang</u>⁁<u>danced</u>⁁and juggled in the talent show.
4. My parents always ask me where I'm <u>going</u>⁁who'll be <u>there</u>⁁ and when I'll be home.
5. Should we go to the mall or to the park or to Yoko's house? **5.** C

Independent Clauses

29h. Use a comma before *and, but, or, nor, for, so,* and *yet* when they join independent clauses.

EXAMPLES The sky looks clear, yet rain has been forecast.
  I saw a performance of August Wilson's *Fences*, and now I am eager to read his other plays.

NOTE: Always use a comma before *for, so,* or *yet* joining independent clauses. You may omit the comma before *and, but, or,* or *nor* whenever the independent clauses are very short and the sentence will not be confusing or awkward without the comma.

EXAMPLES We didn't enjoy the film but you might. [clear without comma]
  I will work with Emma and Josh will help Madison. [awkward without comma]
  I will work with Emma, and Josh will help Madison. [clear with comma]

Don't confuse a compound sentence with a simple sentence that has a compound verb.

COMPOUND SENTENCE Ashley and I looked everywhere for the sheet music, but we couldn't find it. [two independent clauses]

SIMPLE SENTENCE Ashley and I looked everywhere for the sheet music but couldn't find it. [one independent clause with a compound verb]

MECHANICS

MEETING *individual* NEEDS

LEP/ESL

Spanish. In Spanish, commas often are used between independent clauses, as in "The rain was falling steadily, it looked as if the game would be canceled." Using the comma in this way in English constitutes a mechanical error, a comma splice. Suggest that students proofread for such errors and that they replace the commas with periods or add coordinating conjunctions after the commas.

MECHANICS

907

INTEGRATING THE LANGUAGE ARTS

Mechanics and Grammar. Students may need a quick review of some grammatical terms used in this lesson, such as *independent clause, participial phrase, prepositional phrase,* and *adverb clause.*

Divide the class into groups and assign each group one of the terms that you feel students may need to review. Each group should provide a brief definition of its term, along with five examples. You could then have groups make presentations to the class. Encourage groups to use colorful visual aids in their presentations.

908 *Punctuation*

▶ **EXERCISE 3**   **Correcting Sentences by Adding Commas**

For each of the following sentences, write the <u>word that should be followed by a comma</u>, and place a comma after it.

1. We're eating dinner <u>now</u>,but I'll call you back as soon as we finish.
2. Are you busy Friday <u>night</u>,or would you like to go to the movies with me?
3. Don't forget to take your history book home this <u>weekend</u>, for the test is Monday.
4. The recipes in *Spirit of the Harvest: North American Indian Cooking* are adapted for modern <u>cooks</u>,yet the ingredients listed are all traditional.
5. Quilting is a practical folk <u>art</u>,and it is also a relaxing and enjoyable pastime.

▶ **REVIEW A**   **Correcting Errors in the Use of End Marks and Commas in a Paragraph**

Add, delete, or change end marks or commas in the following paragraph to correct sentences that are incorrectly punctuated. If a sentence is correct, write *C*.

EXAMPLE   [1] Do you know what the second-largest city in Russia is.

1. *Do you know what the second-largest city in Russia is?*

[1] In 1697, Czar Peter I of Russia toured Western Europe, liked what he saw,and determined to remodel his nation along Western lines. [2] Six years later he decreed that a whole, new city be built at the eastern end of the Gulf of Finland on land recently reconquered from Sweden. [3] Peter hired leading Russian,French, and Italian architects to create a city with planned squares, wide avenues, and extensive parks, and gardens. [4] He named the city St. Petersburg and in 1712 moved the capital there from Moscow. [5] The German name of the capital was kept for two centuries but in Aug. 1914, was Russianized to *Petrograd* by Czar Nicholas II. [6] Three years later the city witnessed both the abdication of Nicholas and the return from exile of the Russian, Marxist revolutionary V. I. Lenin. [7] Petrograd served as the first capital of Soviet Russia after the Communist Revolution of Nov. 1917 but lost that

status to Moscow early the following year. [8] Then in Jan. 1924 the Second Congress of the Soviets of the USSR, changed the city's name to Leningrad to honor the recently deceased Lenin. [9] Further, name changes seemed unlikely once the Communist system became firmly entrenched. [10] Yet in 1991 the Russian people went to the polls, repudiated the name Leningrad, and reclaimed their beautiful historic city's original name— St. Petersburg.

Nonessential Elements

29i. Use commas to set off nonessential clauses and nonessential participial phrases.

A *nonessential* (or *nonrestrictive*) clause or participial phrase contains information that is not necessary to the meaning of the sentence.

NONESSENTIAL CLAUSES	Carla Harris, **who was offered scholarships to three colleges,** will go to Vassar in the fall.
	The word *telethon*, **which is a combination of the words** *television* **and** *marathon*, is an example of a portmanteau word.
NONESSENTIAL PHRASES	Antonio, **following his grandmother's recipe,** prepared *arroz con pollo* for his home economics class.
	Both of the kittens, **frightened by the thunder,** jumped into my lap.

Each nonessential clause or phrase in the examples above can be omitted without changing the main idea expressed in the rest of the sentence.

EXAMPLES	Carla Harris will go to Vassar in the fall.
	The word *telethon* is an example of a portmanteau word.
	Antonio prepared *arroz con pollo* for his home economics class.
	Both of the kittens jumped into my lap.

An *essential* (or *restrictive*) clause or participial phrase is not set off by commas because it contains information that is necessary to the meaning of the sentence.

MECHANICS

ESSENTIAL CLAUSES	Carla Harris is the only senior **who was offered scholarships to three colleges.**
	Mercury is the planet **that is closest to the Sun.**
ESSENTIAL PHRASES	Any student **wanting to learn about the new reference database** should sign up in the library by Friday.
	The lines **cited at the beginning and the end of the speech** are from Omar Khayyám's *Rubáiyát.*

Notice how the omission of the essential clause or phrase affects the main idea of the sentence.

EXAMPLES   Carla Harris is the only senior.
Mercury is the planet.
Any student should sign up in the library by Friday.
The lines are from Omar Khayyám's *Rubáiyát.*

NOTE: Adjective clauses beginning with *that* are usually essential.

Some clauses and participial phrases may be either essential or nonessential. The presence or absence of commas tells the reader how the clause or phrase relates to the main idea of the sentence.

ESSENTIAL	Dave took his problem to the librarian **who is an authority on children's literature.** [The library has more than one librarian, but only one is an authority on children's literature.]
NONESSENTIAL	Dave took his problem to the librarian**,** **who is an authority on children's literature.** [The library has only one librarian.]

☞ REFERENCE NOTE: See pages 674–683 for more information on clauses and pages 657–658 for more information on participial phrases.

▶ EXERCISE 4   **Identifying Essential and Nonessential Clauses and Phrases**

In the following sentences, identify each italicized phrase or clause as *essential* or *nonessential*. Add commas where they are needed.

1. Employees *who always have a ready smile* make the job seem easier.
2. She is wearing the shirt *that she received for her birthday*.

3. A chile relleno, *consisting of a stuffed, breaded green chile,* is Eduardo's favorite appetizer.
4. People *who are overly nervous* may not make good drivers.
5. Adults, *whose development has been studied and recorded as they grow older,* continue to mature, usually in predictable stages, after the age of eighteen.
6. Cities *that seem alike* bear a closer look.
7. Lake Chad, *covering an area of about six thousand square miles,* is West Africa's largest body of water.
8. The Federal Reserve System, *serving as the central bank of the United States,* monitors money and credit growth.
9. That law, *which may have met a real need one hundred years ago,* should be repealed or rewritten to deal with today's situation.
10. The Suez Canal, *extending more than a hundred miles,* links the Mediterranean Sea and the Red Sea.

▶ REVIEW B

Correcting Errors in the Use of Commas in a Paragraph

Add or delete commas in the following paragraph to correct sentences that are incorrectly punctuated. If a sentence is correct, write C.

EXAMPLE [1] **Rona asked me, when the Old Spanish Days fiesta is.**
1. *me*

[1] Each August visitors are welcomed to the Old Spanish Days fiesta sponsored by the city of Santa Barbara in California. [2] The festival, which lasts five days, attracts nearly half a million people. [3] It honors the Spaniards, who colonized the area, beginning in the early 1700s. [4] The festivities start on Wednesday with blessings and singing and dancing at *La Fiesta Pequeña,* which is Spanish for "Little Festival," outside Mission Santa Barbara on E. Los Olivos and Laguna streets. [5] The mission, founded in 1786, is one of the best preserved of the twenty-one missions, that the Spanish established in California between 1769 and 1823. [6] Costumed dancers and colorful floats enliven Thursday's *Desfile Histórico* ("Historic Parade"), which recounts how Spanish conquistador Sebastian Vizcaino sailed into the nearby bay in 1602, why he named the bay Santa Barbara, and what drew settlers to the area. [7] A free, variety show that begins later in the day and continues nightly features Spanish flamenco dancers and Mexican folkloric dancers like those,

1. C
2. C

VISUAL CONNECTIONS

Ideas for Writing. Ask students to consider the various metaphors that have been used to describe American society. One compares American society to a melting pot, emphasizing the blending of ethnic and national groups into a homogeneous America. Other metaphors compare American society to a salad bowl or stew, in which separate ingredients retain their qualities yet combine to form a whole. Another metaphor compares American culture to a mosaic, in which pieces that are different from one another are put together to form a picture.

After discussing the ideas about unity and diversity suggested by these metaphors, ask students to write persuasive paragraphs that state and support students' opinions as to which of these metaphors is most appropriate. For models of persuasive writing, refer students to the student models on pp. 333–334.

pictured here. [8] On the weekend artists and craftworkers set up booths along Cabrillo Blvd. and State St. and sell handmade items. [9] Fiesta-goers needn't go hungry for authentic Latin foods such as tortas, tacos, enchiladas, *flautas*, and tamales are sold in the two open-air markets. [10] What an eventful, fun-filled five days Old Spanish Days provides!

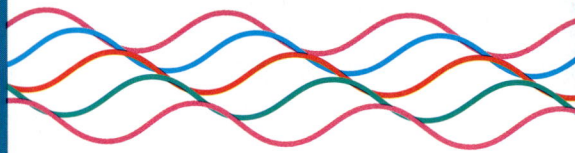

Introductory Elements

29j. Use a comma after certain introductory elements.

(1) Use a comma after *yes, no,* or any mild exclamation such as *well* or *why* at the beginning of a sentence.

EXAMPLES   Yes, you are welcome to join us.
Well, what do you think?
Why, the whole story sounds suspicious!

(2) Use a comma after an introductory participial phrase.

EXAMPLES   **Proofreading my report,** I saw that I had written *gorilla,* instead of *guerrilla, warfare.*
Almost hidden by the dense brush, the tiny, brown rabbit sat absolutely still.

NOTE: Do not confuse a gerund phrase used as the subject of a sentence with an introductory participial phrase.

GERUND PHRASE   **Planting the Japanese quinces along the fence** took several hours.

PARTICIPIAL PHRASE   **Planting the Japanese quinces along the fence,** I stepped on a mound of fire ants.

29j

(3) Use a comma after two or more introductory prepositional phrases.

EXAMPLES **At the end of the block just beyond the new railroad station,** my grandparents own and operate a small restaurant.
Near the beginning of the trail alongside the lake, the scout leader found an overturned canoe.

NOTE: A single introductory prepositional phrase does not require a comma unless the phrase is parenthetical or unless the sentence is confusing or awkward without the comma.

EXAMPLES **During spring break** we're going camping in the mountains. [clear without comma]
By the way, you're late. [The comma is needed because the phrase is parenthetical. See pages 914–915.]
From Laura, Lee had borrowed a sleeping bag, a canteen, and a flashlight. [The comma is needed to avoid reading "Laura Lee."]

(4) Use a comma after an introductory adverb clause.

EXAMPLES **While the orchestra tuned their instruments,** the stagehands checked the curtain.
As soon as we finished eating, we cleared the table for a game of mah-jongg.

▶ **EXERCISE 5   Correcting Sentences by Adding Commas**

For each of the following sentences, write each <u>word that should be followed by a comma</u>, and place a comma after it.

1. When they had finished <u>playing,</u>the musicians moved their instruments offstage to make room for the dancers.
2. By the end of the second day of <u>school,</u>nearly all of the students seemed to have found their assigned <u>classrooms,</u> <u>teachers,</u>and lockers.
3. <u>Oh,</u>I meant to ask Gloria if she had watched the Chinese New Year parade.
4. In the second half of the third <u>period,</u>Johnson caught a twenty-yard pass and raced into the end zone.
5. After a lengthy discussion of the <u>options,</u>the committee voted to reject both of the themes proposed for the prom and to seek fresh ideas.

MECHANICS

CRITICAL THINKING

Analysis. To emphasize the importance of commas in making meaning clear, write the following sentences on the chalkboard and ask students to explain how the meanings of the sentences would be different if the commas were deleted:

1. No, children are allowed to see movies that carry a PG rating. [The comma indicates that *no* is an introductory element. If the comma were deleted, the sentence would state that children are not permitted to see movies rated PG.]
2. The officer, who works with street gangs, coaches a soccer team in his spare time. [The commas set off a nonessential clause. If the commas were deleted, it would be understood that the clause was needed to distinguish the particular officer being discussed from other officers.]

MECHANICS

MECHANICS

MEETING *individual* NEEDS

LEARNING STYLES

Visual Learners. To help students visualize some of the uses of commas, show examples of comma usage in four columns on the chalkboard. Label the columns *independent clauses, nonessential clauses, introductory elements,* and *interrupters.* Then, work with students to generate examples of each usage; write the examples under the appropriate headings on the chalkboard.

Interrupters

29k. Use commas to set off elements that interrupt a sentence.

(1) Appositives and appositive phrases are usually set off by commas.

An *appositive* is a noun or a pronoun placed beside another noun or pronoun to identify or explain it. An *appositive phrase* consists of an appositive and its modifiers.

EXAMPLES   An interview with Florence Cohen, **the well-known landscape architect,** will appear in the *Herald.*
Sipa, **a game similar to volleyball,** is a popular sport in the Philippines.

Sometimes an appositive is so closely related to the word or words preceding it that it should not be set off by commas. Such an appositive is called a *restrictive appositive.*

EXAMPLES   the landscape artist **Fernando Amorsolo**
the novel ***Go Tell It on the Mountain***
the preposition **with**

(2) Words used in direct address are set off by commas.

EXAMPLES   Will you explain to the class, **Lena,** how you solved the last problem?
Dexter, please help your brother set the table.
You seem upset, **my friend.**

(3) Parenthetical expressions are set off by commas.

Parenthetical expressions are remarks that add incidental information or relate ideas to each other.

Commonly Used Parenthetical Expressions		
after all	I believe	naturally
at any rate	incidentally	nevertheless
by the way	in fact	of course
consequently	in general	on the contrary
for example	in the first place	on the other hand
for instance	meanwhile	that is
however	moreover	therefore

EXAMPLES   The train will**, I am sure,** be on time.
On the contrary, exercise is relaxing.
Jameson was the first to solve the puzzle**, naturally.**

Some of these expressions are not always parenthetical. When an expression is not used parenthetically, it is not set off by commas.

EXAMPLE   My grandfather**, by the way,** created these colorful sand paintings. [parenthetical, meaning "incidentally"] We could see **by the way** Melinda worked that she wanted to do her best. [not parenthetical, meaning "by the manner in which"]

Frequently, your intention determines the punctuation you use. If you want your reader to pause for a parenthetical expression, set it off with commas; if not, leave it unpunctuated. Sometimes, though, the placement of the expression in a sentence determines the punctuation.

EXAMPLES   That is **indeed** startling news. [no pause]
That is**, indeed,** startling news. [pause]
Indeed, that is startling news. [comma required by placement of expression]

        I hope this report will clarify the situation for you. [no comma because of placement]
This report will**, I hope,** clarify the situation for you. [commas required by placement of expression]

NOTE: A contrasting expression introduced by *not* is parenthetical and should be set off by commas.

    EXAMPLE   Frank Robinson**, not Jackie Robinson,** was the first African American to manage a major league baseball team.

☞ REFERENCE NOTE: Parentheses and dashes are sometimes used to set off parenthetical expressions. See pages 955–956.

▶ EXERCISE 6   **Correcting Sentences by Adding Commas**

For each of the following sentences, write each <u>word that should be followed by a comma</u>, and place a comma after it. If a sentence is correct, write C.

EXAMPLE   **1.** My take-home pay at any rate is less than yours.
        1. *pay, . . . rate,*

916 *Punctuation*

1. The Red Sea, not the Black Sea, separates Northeast Africa and the Arabian Peninsula.
2. My father's youngest sister, Aunt Pilar, is an architect in New Orleans.
3. The future, of course, is largely in your hands.
4. Naturally, well-nourished babies have a better chance of surviving infancy.
5. Call Felipe as soon as you can, Hope.
6. A rose window, by the way, resembles an open rose.
7. In 1901 Chiricahua Apache leader Geronimo took part in President Theodore Roosevelt's inaugural procession. **7. C**
8. In college, however, students arrange their own schedules.
9. Alex Haley, the author of *Roots*, attributed his interest in writing to stories his grandmother and great-aunts told.
10. The fairy tale "Cinderella," I believe, originated in ninth-century China.

▶ **REVIEW C**   **Correcting Sentences by Adding Commas**

For each of the following sentences, write each word that should be followed by a comma, and place a comma after it. If a sentence is correct, write *C*.

1. The plot of that book, a murder mystery, is, in my opinion, far too complicated.
2. If you give us your application now, our office will process it before the deadline, which is this afternoon.
3. Ancient Mayan ruins, tropical rain forests, and beautiful mountains are just a few of the sights I saw in Guatemala, where my cousins live.
4. Please understand, friends, that as much as I would like to, I cannot be at the picnic, the game, and the track meet all at the same time.
5. The people riding in the front seat of the roller coaster were the ones who screamed the loudest. **5. C**
6. Hiroshi, whom you met last night, is an exchange student from Kyoto, a large city in Japan.
7. Looking for economical transportation, Harry, who had never bought a car before, nervously investigated all of the possibilities at Country Motors.
8. Before you start putting that jigsaw puzzle together, Rosa, make sure that all of it will fit on the table.

9. When Jamie had <u>finished</u>⌃the chicken and salad were all <u>gone</u>⌃and the <u>beans</u>⌃<u>carrots</u>⌃and potatoes had been left untouched.
10. In my <u>opinion</u>⌃*Coming to America*⌃not *Beverly Hills Cop*⌃is Eddie Murphy's best movie.

Conventional Uses

29l. Use a comma in certain conventional situations.

(1) Use a comma to separate items in dates and addresses.

EXAMPLES   Hawaii achieved statehood on August 21, 1959, becoming the fiftieth state.
Write to me at 423 Twentieth Street, Salt Lake City, UT 84101, after the first of May.

Notice that a comma also separates the final item in a date (*1959*) and in an address (*84101*) from the words that follow it. Notice also that a comma does *not* separate the month from the day (*August 21*), the house number from the street name (*423 Twentieth Street*), or a state abbreviation from the ZIP Code (*UT 84101*).

NOTE: Do not use a comma when writing

- the day before the month
EXAMPLE   The Hubble Space Telescope was launched on **25 April** 1990.

- only the month and the day
EXAMPLE   We began rehearsals on **June 20.**

- only the month and the year
EXAMPLE   A severe storm hit Luzon in **October 1991.**

- a preposition between the items in a date or an address
EXAMPLE   Joanna lives at **301 Green Street in San Diego.**

(2) Use a comma after the salutation of a friendly letter and after the closing of any letter.

EXAMPLES   Dear Angela,   Sincerely yours,

☞ **REFERENCE NOTE:** For more on punctuating the salutation in a business letter, see pages 931 and 1089–1090.

918 *Punctuation*

(3) Use a comma after a name followed by an abbreviation such as *Jr., Sr.,* or *Ph.D.*

EXAMPLES   Peter Grundel, Jr.   Lorraine Henson, Ph.D.

NOTE: Within a sentence, these abbreviations are followed by a comma as well.

EXAMPLE   Hazel Sellers, M.D., will be the guest speaker.

Unnecessary Commas

29m. **Do not use unnecessary commas.**

Use a comma only when a rule requires one or when the meaning would be unclear without one.

INCORRECT   Amy, and I put a videocassette, and a fashion catalog in the time capsule.
CORRECT   Amy and I put a videocassette and a fashion catalog in the time capsule.

▶ REVIEW D   **Correcting Sentences by Adding End Marks and Commas**

Write the following sentences, adding end marks and commas where needed.

1. Stalled in the traffic jam, the motorcyclists Carl and Lou, who were on their way home, settled in to wait.
2. In A.D. 1238 the Thai people created the first Thai nation, named *Sukothai*, which means "dawn of happiness" **2.** .
3. Our new apartment at 310 Columbia Avenue, Fort Wayne, Indiana, is comfortable, but I wish we were still living at 2125 West Third Street in Omaha, Nebraska.
4. Jay Carson, Jr., a senior with excellent organizational skills, arranged for the benefit concert, setting the date and ticket sales, hiring the musical talent, and handling the publicity.
5. In 1936 the library staff at the *Tribune* began recording the newspaper on microfilm, and now the library contains microfilm copies of every issue from October 14, 1858, up to the most recent one.
6. Our company, which we started as high school seniors, provides home, office, and factory cleaning services.

REVIEW D

Teaching Note. You may want to point out to students that a dash could be used between the words *concert* and *setting* in the fourth sentence. You could take this opportunity to discuss the functions of dashes: to mark sudden turns in thought and to set off parenthetical elements for emphasis or for clarity.

29m

7. When the doctor informed me that, on the one hand, only a very small percentage of people suffer a bad reaction to the vaccine and that, on the other hand, the disease that it prevents is nearly always fatal, what could I do but agree to have the shot?
8. How good it was to see Aunt Marissa, Uncle Bill, and all of our cousins back in Tennessee!
9. The island of Tierra del Fuego, named the Land of Fire by Ferdinand Magellan because of the many bonfires he saw there, lies off the southern tip of South America in a cold, windy climate.
10. Benjamin Banneker, the noted inventor, astronomer, and mathematician, served on the commission that surveyed and laid out Washington, DC.

▶ REVIEW E   **Correcting Errors in the Use of End Marks and Commas in a Paragraph**

Add, delete, or change any end marks or commas in the following paragraph to correct each sentence that is incorrectly punctuated. If a sentence is correct, write *C*.

EXAMPLE   [1] **The Japan America Theatre is the performing arts stage of the Japanese American Cultural and Community Center in Los Angeles Cal..**

1. *The Japan America Theatre is the performing arts stage of the Japanese American Cultural and Community Center in Los Angeles, Cal.*

[1] Since it opened in 1984, the theater, which you can see on the next page, has won worldwide acclaim for the quality and scope of its productions. [2] Those productions range from **2. C** all-male casts (such as the one shown) performing works in the sixteenth-century Grand Kabuki tradition to American premieres of contemporary works by leading Japanese choreographers. [3] The theater doesn't just book productions, but, rather, works closely with the artists, whom it presents. [4] In fact, according to managing director for programs, Cora Mirikatani, between 60 and 70 percent of the theater's presentations are developed in partnership with the artists. [5] In 1988, for example, the theater staged the first, Broadway-style Japanese musical, *Utamoro: The Musical,* Tako Izumi's story of eighteenth-century woodcut artist Utamoro. [6] To make the work more

---

MEETING *individual* **NEEDS**

LEARNING STYLES

Visual and Kinetic Learners. Have students find, in newspapers and magazines, examples of each type of comma usage discussed in this lesson. Students then could cut out the sentences that contain the examples and use those sentences to create charts. On their charts, students should label each comma according to which usage rule it exemplifies.

accessible to American audiences, the Los Angeles production pared down the slang in the Tokyo version, emphasized movement and gesture more, and provided narration, and supertitles in English. [7] It also used more elaborate costumes, wigs, and masks, to convey the splendor of the Edo period. [8] Recognizing that outstanding art transcends national boundaries, the theater features performing artists of all nationalities. [9] In recent years, for example, both New York City's Theater of the Open Eye and the Los Angeles Chamber Ballet have performed there. [10] In addition, a few years ago Indian sitar player Ravi Shankar, working with American musicians, created an original composition incorporating classical Japanese instruments into an Indian musical form.

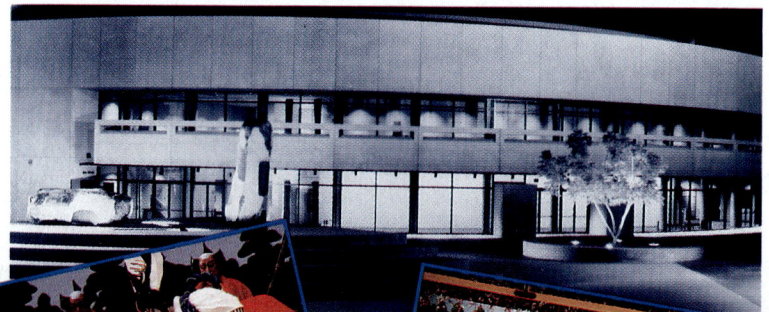

9. C

WRITING APPLICATION

This activity challenges students to integrate information about another subject with grammar and mechanics. Organization and writing skills are important because students will need to write game rules that can be easily followed. You may want to provide the playing rules from several popular board games.

WRITING APPLICATION

Using Commas Correctly to Make Your Writing Clear

In many writing situations, you will find it helpful to express your ideas concisely. Often, you can combine short sentences by turning one sentence into an adverb clause and attaching it to the other sentence. The subordinating conjunction at the beginning of the clause shows the relationship between the two ideas. The relationship may be one of time, cause or reason, purpose or result, or condition. What relationship does the subordinating conjunction show in the following combined sentences?

ORIGINAL   I read the instructions to the players. Mary and Jerome pass out the game pieces.

COMBINED   Mary and Jerome pass out the game pieces while I read the instructions to the players.

or

While I read the instructions to the players, Mary and Jerome pass out the game pieces.

Notice in the combined sentences above that the adverb clause may be placed at either the beginning or the end of a sentence. The placement of the clause determines what punctuation you should use. Notice also that a comma is placed after the adverb clause used as an introductory element.

WRITING ACTIVITY
You and some friends are planning to study together for an important final exam. To make the study sessions more interesting, you've decided to create a game using the information to be covered on the exam. Invent a game based on a subject you are studying in school—perhaps history, chemistry, or English. Then write a set of instructions for playing the game. In your instructions, use at least five adverb clauses. Be sure to use commas correctly.

Prewriting   First, jot down several ideas for a game based on one of your school subjects. For example, you might have ideas for a geographical or historical trivia game or a word game using literary terms. If you wish, team up with a few classmates for a brainstorming session. Then, decide which idea you want to develop. What are the rules of the game? What, if any, game pieces are needed? Take notes for your instructions. Arrange the information in an easy-to-follow order.

Writing   Begin your draft by giving a brief, general description of the game. Then give complete, step-by-step

MECHANICS

CRITICAL THINKING
Analysis and Classification.
In order to write step-by-step instructions, students will need to analyze their games. Categorizing the information may help students. Information could be categorized into the following groups:

1. necessary equipment
2. necessary information from a school subject
3. rules of a game
4. criteria for winning

MECHANICS

LESSON 4 *(pp. 922–925)*
REVIEW: POSTTEST

OBJECTIVES
- To correct sentences by adding or deleting end marks and commas
- To correct a paragraph by adding, deleting, or changing end marks and commas

922 *Punctuation*

instructions for playing the game. Add rules and steps that occur to you as you write, keeping your audience in mind. Be sure to explain the game clearly so that a reader can play it from your instructions.

Evaluating and Revising To help you evaluate your instructions, ask a friend to read them. Can your reader follow the instructions easily? Are any of the rules confusing? Does the game seem like an enjoyable as well as a helpful study tool? Ask your friend to suggest improvements. As you revise, try to combine sentences to make the instructions more concise. (For more about sentence combining, see pages 564–577.) Be sure to use at least five adverb clauses. (For a list of subordinating conjunctions, see page 682.)

Proofreading and Publishing Read your instructions carefully to find any errors in grammar, usage, punctuation, or spelling. Pay special attention to punctuation. Be sure that you've used commas correctly with introductory elements, interrupters, and items in a series. You may want to publish your game by distributing the instructions to your classmates as a study tool.

Review: Posttest

A. Correcting Errors in the Use of End Marks and Commas in Sentences

Write the following sentences, adding, deleting, or changing end marks and commas as necessary. If a sentence is correct, write *C*.

EXAMPLE **1.** My best friend has moved to 9782, Revere Avenue, New York NY 10465

1. *My best friend has moved to 9782 Revere Avenue, New York, NY 10465.*

1. Marilyn and Antonio, who both work at a nearby child-care center, greatly enjoy inventing, and playing games with the children.
2. Unfolding the solar panels, placing satellites into orbit, and conducting medical experiments had kept the space shuttle crew busy.
3. Because we had to rekindle the fire twice, our cookout was delayed.
4. Well, if you apply to all eight colleges, Paul, you will pay a sizable sum in application fees.
5. "It is my pleasure to introduce Vernon K. Foster, Jr., who has recently returned from a visit to Nairobi, Kenya," said Adele Peters, president of our school's Student Foreign Exchange League.
6. The diplomats, both educated at American University in Washington, DC, were assigned posts in Athens, Greece, and Nicosia, Cyprus.
7. "The house is on fire," shouted my father. "Everyone get out right now," *7. !/!*
8. On the far wall to the right of the main entrance, you will see a striking oil painting done in matte black, ash white, and neutral gray.
9. Studying *Beowulf* for the first time, the class particularly enjoyed Grendel, the grim, gruesome monster.
10. The treasurer's report did, I believe, make it clear that the senior class has been very successful in its fund-raising activities this year.
11. Interrupting his friends, Philip asked, "Are you ready to leave," *11. ?*
12. We spent the morning cleaning the basement and sorting boxes, but in the afternoon we rode our bikes along lovely country roads.
13. We have already decided to hold our first class reunion on July 4, 2003, at the Bollingbroke Hotel in San Francisco, California.
14. Using hyperbole, the store claimed in a colorful full-page newspaper ad that it will be having the "World's Most Spectacular Labor Day Sale."
15. When they went to the prom, did Martha wear a lavender lace gown with blue satin ribbons, and did George wear a light blue tuxedo?

MECHANICS

MECHANICS

B. Correcting Errors in the Use of End Marks and Commas in a Paragraph

Add, delete, or change any end marks and commas in the following paragraph to correct sentences that are incorrectly punctuated. If a sentence is correct, write *C*.

EXAMPLE [1] In looking through a United States atlas have you ever been tempted to use it, as a menu to serve a meal of places named for foods.

        1. *In looking through a United States atlas, have you ever been tempted to use it as a menu to serve a meal of places named for foods?*

[16] For an appetizer, that will take the edge off your family's hunger, without filling them up, serve a relish tray assembled from Pickleville in Utah, Olive in Montana, and Pepperton in Georgia, along with Rolls from Arizona and Indiana and Butters from North Carolina. [17] You might follow that opener with a salad made with Tomato from Mississippi, dressed with Mayo from Maryland, Thousand Island from New York, or French from New Mexico, or Wyoming. [18] Seafood-loving families won't be disappointed, for you can find Whitefish in Washington, Salmon in Idaho, Haddock in Georgia, and Trout in Louisiana. [19] Families that enjoy red meat can savor selections from Rib Lake in Wisconsin, Lambs Junction in South Carolina, Rabbithash in Kentucky, or, indeed, Beef Island in the Virgin Islands. [20] If your family prefers poultry, on the other hand, consider Chicken from Alaska, or Duck or Turkey from North Carolina. [21] You'll want to serve some vegetables, too, so choose your family's favorites from Corn in Oklahoma, Bean City in Florida, Greens in Kansas and Michigan, and Pea Patch Island in Delaware. [22] For a delicious, nourishing side dish, look no further than Noodle in Texas, Rice in Minnesota or Virginia, or Wild Rice in North Dakota. [23] Naturally, Milk River in Montana, Goodwater in Alabama, and Tea in South Dakota will remind you to include a beverage or two. [24] Round out your satisfying meal with Oranges, which you'll find in, among other places, California and Vermont, and Almonds from Alabama and Wisconsin. [25] And when your kid brother raves about the meal, but complains about having to do the dishes, simply suggest that he get out the atlas and see how far it is to Soap Lake, Washington.

SUMMARY OF USES OF END MARKS AND COMMAS

29a	Use a period at the end of a statement.
29b	Use a question mark at the end of a question.
29c	Use an exclamation point after an exclamation.
29d	Use either a period or an exclamation point at the end of an imperative sentence.
29e	Use a period after most abbreviations.
29f	Use commas to separate items in a series.
29g	Use a comma to separate two or more adjectives preceding a noun.
29h	Use a comma before *and, but, or, nor, for, so,* and *yet* when they join independent clauses.
29i	Use commas to set off nonessential clauses and nonessential participial phrases.
29j	Use a comma after certain introductory elements. (1) After a word such as *yes, no,* or any mild exclamation at the beginning of a sentence (2) After an introductory participial phrase (3) After two or more introductory prepositional phrases (4) After an introductory adverb clause
29k	Use commas to set off elements that interrupt a sentence. (1) Appositives and appositive phrases (2) Words in direct address (3) Parenthetical expressions
29l	Use a comma in certain conventional situations. (1) Between items in dates and addresses (2) After the salutation of a friendly letter and the closing of any letter (3) After a name followed by an abbreviation such as *Jr., Sr.,* or *Ph.D.*

MECHANICS

OBJECTIVE

- To proofread sentences and paragraphs for correct use of punctuation

PROGRAM MANAGER

FOR THE WHOLE CHAPTER

- **Review** For exercises on chapter concepts, see **Review Form A** and **Review Form B** in *Language Skills Practice and Assessment*, pp. 236–241.

- **Assessment** For additional testing, see **Mechanics Pretests** and **Mechanics Mastery Tests** in *Language Skills Practice and Assessment*, pp. 189–196 and pp. 259–267.

CHAPTER OVERVIEW

Although students might know the uses of semicolons, colons, and quotation marks, they may need to refer to the material in this chapter for information on the use of other punctuation marks.

This chapter explains correct use of less common marks: italics (underlining), ellipsis points, hyphens, dashes, parentheses, and brackets. In addition, the **Writing Application** exercise offers an opportunity for students to practice using the apostrophe to form the possessive case of nouns and pronouns in informative/descriptive reports.

Have students refer to this chapter during the proofreading and publishing stages of writing.

MECHANICS

30 PUNCTUATION

Other Marks of Punctuation

Diagnostic Test

A. Proofreading Sentences for Correct Punctuation

The following sentences contain errors in the uses of semicolons, colons, dashes, parentheses, brackets, italics (underlining), quotation marks, apostrophes, and hyphens. Rewrite each sentence, correcting each error. *Hyphens are indicated by the ⌃ symbol.*

EXAMPLE **1.** I just saw Paulas picture's of Washington, D.C.
  1. *I just saw Paula's pictures of Washington, D.C.*

1. Traffic was stopped for the city's Martin Luther King, Jr., Day parade; consequently, a huge traffic jam developed.
2. One of my favorite Biblical passages is the story of Jesus and the Samaritan woman in John 4:5–42.
3. Since Bethany visited Europe last summer, she has been using foreign expressions such as <u>bonjour</u> and <u>ciao</u>.
4. "How long will it take for these three rolls of film to be developed?" I asked.
5. Our English class agrees that James Baldwin's short story "The Rockpile" is one of the best we have ever read.
6. Please turn down the radio; I'm getting a headache.

7. The confusion occurred because I thought that the brief-
   case was your's, not Dorothy's.
8. Very successful people, whether they excel in politics, the
   arts, or sports, share a common trait: self-motivation.
9. We might and according to the tour schedule should have
   a free afternoon in Rome, the first city on the tour.
10. The newspaper quoted Mr. Busch as saying, "People who
    take it [Auto Mechanics I] usually are glad they did."

B. Proofreading Paragraphs for Correct Punctuation

Rewrite the following paragraphs, adding and deleting punctuation as needed.   Hyphens are indicated by the $_\wedge$ symbol.
Answers may vary.

[11] The National Museum of American History (formerly
the National Museum of History and Technology) is a fascinating place, it's part of the Smithsonian Institution in Washington,
D.C. [12] You may ask—I know I did—what makes the museum so
fascinating. [13] The museum offers changing displays on various themes represented by extremely diverse artifacts of the
United States' culture. [14] When we visited the three-story
building, we saw the actual flag that inspired Francis Scott Key
to write "The Star Spangled Banner" and a pair of ruby slippers
that Judy Garland wore in the film The Wizard of Oz (1939)
[15] Another crowd pleaser was the museum's collection of First
Ladies' gowns. [16] Children shouldn't miss the Hands-On History Room, they can explore our history and culture there in
well-planned, creative ways.

[17] We spent all day looking for such cultural keepsakes as
the Fonz's jacket from the television show Happy Days, however, there were also many scientific and technological displays
to see. [18] One of these displays—the Foucault Pendulum—was
almost impossible to overlook upon entering the building.
[19] Some of the other scientific treasures were: Henry Ford's
Model T car, our country's oldest working steam engine, cotton
gins, and Samuel Morse's telegraph. [20] We also allowed time
for such interesting displays as the National Philatelic Collection, which was especially popular with stamp collectors like
my dad; a country store post office, which came from a West
Virginia town; and a variety of other wonderful exhibits.

USING THE DIAGNOSTIC TEST

The **Diagnostic Test** has two parts. **Part A** involves editing sentences for the correct use of semicolons, colons, dashes, parentheses, brackets, italics, quotation marks, apostrophes, and hyphens. **Part B** involves the same skills but is organized in paragraph form.

The results of this test will indicate students' skill levels by identifying which students have mastered the use of less common punctuation marks and which students need a rule-by-rule explanation.

MECHANICS

MECHANICS

MECHANICS

932

REVIEW A

OBJECTIVE

- To correct paragraphs by adding semicolons and colons

▶ EXERCISE 2   **Correcting Sentences by Adding Colons**

Rewrite the following sentences, adding colons where they are needed.

1. Not surprisingly, my mom, who was a big fan of *Star Trek* during the '60s, now regularly watches *Star Trek: The Next Generation.*
2. Two of my favorite stories from the Bible are the battle between David and Goliath in I Samuel 17:4–58 and the story of the good Samaritan in Luke 10:25–37.
3. Groups of art students, all going to see Egyptian, Greek, and Assyrian exhibits, boarded the buses at 8:30 A.M. and arrived at the museum at 10:00 A.M.
4. She revised her report three times: she looked first at the content, then she considered organization, and then she read the report for style.
5. Our local paper is divided into the following five sections: news, features, business, sports, and classified advertising.

▶ REVIEW A   **Correcting Paragraphs by Adding Semicolons and Colons**

Rewrite the following paragraphs, adding semicolons and colons where they are needed.

[1] Arthur Mitchell blazed new trails in the world of ballet: he became the American Ballet Theater's first African American male principal dancer, and he founded the Dance Theater of Harlem. [2] As a young man, Mitchell studied tap dance, modern dance, and ballet at a special high school for the performing arts; the challenges of ballet especially appealed to him. [3] After graduation from high school in 1952, Mitchell enrolled in the School of American Ballet, part of the New York City Ballet; however, he continued modern dancing in other companies.

[4] Mitchell's fine technique and commanding style, evident in the photograph on the next page, were impressive; consequently, he was invited to join the New York City Ballet in 1955. [5] Director George Balanchine admired Mitchell; as a result, Balanchine choreographed dances for Mitchell and cast him in many leading roles. [6] Among the New York City Ballet productions featuring Mitchell were these: *Agon, Arcade, The Nutcracker,* and *Creation of the World.* [7] The company was often

criticized for showcasing an African American dancer; nevertheless, Balanchine remained adamant in his support for Mitchell.

[8] During his years with the New York City Ballet, Mitchell broke racial barriers, received much praise on foreign tours, and helped organize ballet companies in many countries; but in 1968 Mitchell decided to form his own ballet company and school, which became the Dance Theater of Harlem. [9] The all-black ballet company quickly established a name for itself; in fact, it is acclaimed throughout the world. [10] Critics and audiences have responded enthusiastically to such productions as the following: *Creole Giselle*, *Fancy Free*, and *Firebird*.

OBJECTIVE

- To underline in sentences words that should be italicized

PROGRAM MANAGER

ITALICS (UNDERLINING)

- **Independent Practice/ Reteaching** For instruction and exercises, see **Italics and Underlining** in *Language Skills Practice and Assessment*, p. 229.

- **Computer Guided Instruction** For additional instruction and practice with using italics, see **Lesson 49** in *Language Workshop CD-ROM*.

- **Practice** To help less-advanced students with additional instruction and practice with italics, see **Chapter 23** in *English Workshop, Complete Course*, pp. 315–316.

QUICK REMINDER

Take a survey of students' favorite movies, books, and television series for the year. Write the titles on the chalkboard and underline each. Ask students what they notice about how you wrote the titles [underlining]. Have them brainstorm for other titles that receive the same treatment [plays, works of art, newspapers, ships].

MECHANICS

MECHANICS

Italics (Underlining)

Italics are printed characters that slant to the right. To indicate italics in handwritten or typewritten work, use underlining.

PRINTED **The Once and Future King** was written by T. H. White.

TYPED The Once and Future King was written by T. H. White.

NOTE: If you use a personal computer, you may be able to set words in italics. Most word-processing software and many printers are capable of producing italic type.

933

LEP/ESL

General Strategies. Students sometimes make mistakes using the verbs *said* and *told,* which results in sentences such as "He said me, 'Look out!'" Give the following examples of how these verbs differ and draw attention to the idea that *told* usually takes an indirect object:

1. He said "Look out!" (He told me to look out.)
2. Maria said, "This is a good book." (Maria told us that this is a good book.)

◈ INTEGRATING THE LANGUAGE ARTS

Literature Link. If the selection is available, have students read and discuss "I Fall into Disgrace," the fourth chapter of *David Copperfield.* Refer them to the first two pages of the story in which the characters are clearly differentiated through dialogue.

Point out that much of the story is told by narration. Ask students why the author might have chosen to include the direct quotations. [The direct quotations give the reader a direct and immediate experience of the characters' personalities. The quotations add a dimension not possible to achieve through description and narration.]

936

When the quotation is only a part of a sentence, do not begin it with a capital letter.

EXAMPLE   A film critic has called the movie **"a futile attempt by the director to trade on his reputation as a creator of blockbusters."**

(2) When an expression identifying the speaker interrupts a quoted sentence, the second part of the quotation begins with a small letter.

EXAMPLE   **"When we do the best that we can,"** explained Helen Keller, **"we never know what miracle is wrought in our life, or in the life of another."** [Notice that each part of a divided quotation is enclosed in quotation marks.]

When the second part of a divided quotation is another sentence, it begins with a capital letter.

EXAMPLE   **"Please don't open the door,"** he shouted. **"We're developing film."**

(3) A direct quotation is set off from the rest of the sentence by a comma, a question mark, or an exclamation point, but not by a period.

EXAMPLES   **"For tomorrow, please read the article about the Sherpas of Nepal,"** requested Ms. Estevan.

"Who is the president of the Philippines?" asked Nathan.

"The Wildcats have upset the Rockets!" exclaimed the sportscaster.

NOTE: If the quotation is only a word or a phrase, do not set it off by commas.

EXAMPLE   In his speech, Enrique said that "one for all and all for one" is the key to a successful club.

(4) When used with quotation marks, the other marks of punctuation are placed according to the following rules:

■ Commas and periods are always placed inside the closing quotation marks.

EXAMPLE   **"Generosity,"** said Nathaniel Hawthorne, **"is the flower of justice."**

- Semicolons and colons are always placed outside the closing quotation marks.

EXAMPLES   "Eva," my grandmother said, "you should keep up with your chores"; then she reminded me that it was my turn to vacuum.

Gail Sloan described the following as "deserted-island reading": *An Encyclopedia of World History,* the complete works of Shakespeare, and *Robinson Crusoe.*

- Question marks and exclamation points are placed inside the closing quotation marks if a quotation is a question or an exclamation. Otherwise, they are placed outside.

EXAMPLES   The teacher asked me, "Where did you find this information about José Rizal?"

Someone behind me shouted, "Watch out!"

Did Franklin Roosevelt say, "The only thing we have to fear is fear itself"?

How proud and happy Colleen was when her supervisor told her, "You deserve a raise"!

NOTE: In a sentence that ends with a quotation, only one end mark is necessary.

INCORRECT   Have you ever asked yourself, "Where will I be ten years from now?"?

CORRECT   Have you ever asked yourself, "Where will I be ten years from now?"

(5) When writing dialogue, begin a new paragraph every time the speaker changes, and enclose each speaker's words in quotation marks.

EXAMPLE   "Don't stand chattering to yourself like that," Humpty Dumpty said, looking at her for the first time, "but tell me your name and business."

"My *name* is Alice, but—"

"It's a stupid name enough!" Humpty Dumpty interrupted impatiently. "What does it mean?"

"*Must* a name mean something?" Alice asked doubtfully.

"Of course it must," Humpty Dumpty said with a short laugh: "*my* name means the shape I am—and a good handsome shape it is, too. With a name like yours, you might be any shape, almost."

Lewis Carroll, from *Through the Looking-Glass*

COOPERATIVE LEARNING

Divide the class into groups of three or four. Have students create imaginary situations in which they have been defrauded, deceived, or shortchanged in a consumer transaction. Have each group role-play the encounter. Then, have group members collaborate on writing a complaint letter to a consumer protection agency, a newspaper consumer column, or the consumer advocate of a local TV station. Have them write the letter using both direct and indirect quotations to describe the transaction.

COMMON ERROR

Problem. When a direct quotation appears in a sentence that begins with an attribution, students might fail to capitalize the first word of the quotation.

Solution. Have students read each direct quotation in their writing without the attribution. This exercise will help them to decide whether the quotation needs capitalization.

MECHANICS

MECHANICS

SELECTION AMENDMENT
Description of change: excerpted
Rationale: to focus on the concept of quotation marks presented in this chapter

A DIFFERENT APPROACH

Instead of having students read all the rules and examples and then take a test on them, you may wish to present the material in this chapter in a different way. Assign students the rules you wish them to master. Review them as a class and use the textbook for reference, or model the rules with examples related to a form of writing you are currently studying. Then, have each student write a composition in which he or she uses an example of each rule assigned. For easier grading, have students label each rule in their compositions.

QUICK REMINDER

To emphasize how quotation marks help understanding, write on the chalkboard the following dialogue between two students, Julio and Martha, as a single paragraph without quotation marks. Have students read the passage and try to figure out who is saying what. Then, show them where the correct divisions occur. Have them talk about the conventions for making dialogue easier to read and understand.

"Hello," said Julio. "Where are you going? I'm going to gym class."

"I'm going to study hall. Have you done your algebra homework?"

"Sure."

"When did you do it?" Martha asked. "I finished mine this morning."

SELECTION AMENDMENT
Description of change: excerpted
Rationale: to focus on the concept of quotation marks presented in this chapter

(6) When quoting a passage that consists of more than one paragraph, place quotation marks at the beginning of each paragraph and at the end of only the last paragraph in the passage.

EXAMPLE   "The engine cuts again, and then catches, and each time it spurts to life I climb as high as I can get, and then it splutters and stops and I glide once more toward the water, to rise again and descend again, like a hunting sea bird.

"I find the land. Visibility is perfect now and I see land forty or fifty miles ahead. If I am on my course, that will be Cape Breton. Minute after minute goes by. The minutes almost materialize; they pass before my eyes like links in a long slow-moving chain, and each time the engine cuts, I see a broken link in the chain and catch my breath until it passes."

Beryl Markham, from *West with the Night*

NOTE: A long passage quoted from a printed source is often set off from the rest of the text. The entire passage may be indented or set in smaller type. The passage is sometimes single-spaced instead of double-spaced. (Modern Language Association [MLA] guidelines, however, call for double-spacing.) When a quotation is set off in any of these ways, no quotation marks are necessary.

(7) Use single quotation marks to enclose a quotation within a quotation.

EXAMPLES   Mrs. Winters said, "Cristina, please tell us what you think Alexander Pope meant when he said, 'To err is human, to forgive divine.' " [Notice that the period is placed inside the single quotation mark.]

Mrs. Winters asked, "Do you think the moral of the story could be 'To err is human, to forgive divine'?" [The question mark is placed between the double quotation marks and the single quotation mark because only Mrs. Winters' words, not Pope's, are a question.]

30j. Use quotation marks to enclose titles of short works, such as short stories, short poems, essays, articles, songs, episodes of television series, and chapters and other parts of books.

TYPE OF TITLE	EXAMPLES	
Short Stories	"Raymond's Run"	"Chee's Daughter"
	"The Necklace"	"A Worn Path"
Poems	"My Mother Pieced Quilts"	
	"A Black Man Talks of Reaping"	
Essays	"A Child's Christmas in Wales"	
	"Fenimore Cooper's Literary Offenses"	
Articles	"How to Choose a Career"	
	"Water: Not as Cheap as You Think"	
Songs	"We Are the World"	
	"The Star-Spangled Banner"	
TV Episodes	"The Trouble with Tribbles"	
	"Secret of the Dead Sea Scrolls"	
Chapters	"The War in the Persian Gulf"	
	"Biology: The Study of Life"	

☞ **REFERENCE NOTE:** For examples of titles that are italicized, see page 934.

30k. Use quotation marks to enclose slang words, invented words, technical terms, dictionary definitions of words, and any expressions that are unusual in standard English.

EXAMPLES   In the drama club's latest production, Dylan plays the role of Lyndon, a "nerd."

The running of the bulls through the streets (one might say "bullevards") of Pamplona, Spain, is an annual event.

What do you mean by "looping" the computer instructions?

The name *Arkansas* is derived from the Sioux word for "downstream people."

What do Southerners mean when they say they are "fixing to" do something?

NOTE: Avoid using slang words in formal speaking and writing whenever possible. When using technical terms, be sure to explain their meanings. If you are not sure whether a word is appropriate or its meaning is clear, consult an up-to-date dictionary.

◆ **INTEGRATING THE LANGUAGE ARTS**

Mechanics and Writing. Have students create guides they can keep in their notebooks to use for reference when punctuating titles in their writing. List on the chalkboard all the categories of names and titles in the examples for **Rules 30g** and **30j.** Have students copy the lists and illustrate their guides with pictures or icons.

> **EXERCISE 4**

Correcting Sentences by Adding Quotation Marks, Other Punctuation Marks, and Capitalization

Revise the following sentences by adding quotation marks, other marks of punctuation, and capitalization.

EXAMPLE 1. Jim asked have you read James Alan McPherson's story Why I Like Country Music.

1. *Jim asked, "Have you read James Alan McPherson's story 'Why I Like Country Music'?"*

1. "How many of you, Mrs. Martínez asked, have studied a foreign language for more than two years?"
2. "Nice try, Donna, was what the coach said.
3. "We should have started our homework earlier, said Beth. "we have answered only three questions so far."
4. "Where have you been? she asked.
5. Someone once asked Jonathan Swift how old he was, and he answered, "I'm as old as my tongue and a few years older than my teeth."
6. "Can you tell me, asked Mrs. Ross, how many syllables are in a haiku?"
7. "Was it Elizabeth Barrett Browning, asked Lani, who wrote the poem 'Shall I Compare Thee to a Summer's Day?'"
8. "Cast off, shouted the captain, "we're bound for Panama."
9. "Would you let us hand in our research papers next week, Ms. Lewis? we asked, "none of the books we need are in the library."
10. Alice whispered, "thank you for lending me the article 'Is There Life on Other Planets?'"

PICTURE THIS

Sometimes the most challenging part of writing a story is creating natural-sounding dialogue between characters. To practice your dialogue-writing skills, you've come to the restaurant shown on the next page to watch people having casual conversations and to write what you imagine they are saying. Taking your cues from their body language and facial expressions,

PICTURE THIS

You may want to have students work in small groups to brainstorm before writing. The brainstorming sessions should be devoted to creating possible story lines and developing the characters involved. Encourage students to create characters that are diverse in interests, motivations, or heritage.

write down an imaginary dialogue between two of the people in this picture. In your dialogue, try to capture the people's personalities and moods. Change speakers at least four times, being sure to use quotation marks and paragraph breaks correctly.

Subject:　a conversation between two people
Audience:　yourself
Purpose:　to practice writing dialogue; to be creative

Ellipsis Points

30l. Use ellipsis points (. . .) to mark omissions from quoted material and pauses in a written passage.

ORIGINAL　At Lincoln, making us into Americans did not mean scrubbing away what made us originally foreign. The teachers called us as our parents did or as close as they could pronounce our names in Spanish or Japanese. No one was ever scolded or punished for speaking in his native tongue on the playground. Matti told the class about his mother's down quilt, which she had made

---

PROGRAM MANAGER

ELLIPSIS POINTS

■ **Independent Practice/ Reteaching** For instruction and exercises, see **Ellipsis Points** in *Language Skills Practice and Assessment,* p. 232.

■ **Computer Guided Instruction** For additional instruction and practice with ellipsis points, see **Lesson 53** in *Language Workshop CD-ROM.*

■ **Practice** To help less-advanced students with additional instruction and practice with ellipsis points, see **Chapter 23** in *English Workshop, Complete Course,* pp. 313–314.

QUICK REMINDER

Write the following sentence on the chalkboard and ask students to replace the underlined part with ellipsis points:

When I go to college, I plan to <u>take many interesting courses, join a service fraternity, play intramural sports, and</u> experience as much as I can.

[When I go to college, I plan to . . . experience as much as I can.]

Ask students to think of at least two reasons why ellipsis points might be used [space constraints, deleting unnecessary material].

OBJECTIVE

• To use ellipsis points correctly in sentences

MECHANICS

SELECTION AMENDMENT
Description of change: excerpted
Rationale: to focus on the concept of quotation marks presented in this chapter

942

MECHANICS

in Italy with the fine feathers of a thousand geese. Encarnación acted out how boys learned to fish in the Philippines. I astounded the third grade with the story of my travels on a stagecoach, which nobody else in the class had seen except in the museum at Sutter's Fort. After a visit to the Crocker Art Gallery and its collection of heroic paintings of the golden age of California, someone showed a silk scroll with a Chinese painting. Miss Hopley herself had a way of expressing wonder over these matters before a class, her eyes wide open until they popped slightly. It was easy for me to feel that becoming a proud American, as she said we should, did not mean feeling ashamed of being a Mexican.

Ernesto Galarza, from *Barrio Boy*

(1) If the quoted material that comes before the omission is not a complete sentence, use three ellipsis points with a space before the first point.

EXAMPLE   In his autobiography, Galarza recalls, "It was easy for me to feel that becoming a proud American, . . . did not mean feeling ashamed of being a Mexican."

(2) If the quoted material that comes before the omission is a complete sentence, keep the end mark and add the ellipsis points.

EXAMPLE   Galarza remembers that his teachers encouraged him and his classmates to share stories about their families and backgrounds: "Matti told the class about his mother's down quilt, which she had made in Italy. . . . Encarnación acted out how boys learned to fish in the Philippines. I astounded the third grade with the story of my travels on a stagecoach. . . ."

(3) If one or more than one sentence is omitted, the ellipsis points follow the end mark that precedes the omission.

EXAMPLE   About Lincoln School, Galarza writes, "At Lincoln, making us into Americans did not mean scrubbing away what made us originally foreign. . . . It was easy for me to feel that becoming a proud American, as she [the principal] said we should, did not mean feeling ashamed of being a Mexican."

Notice in the last example that the words *the principal* are included to identify *she*. The words are enclosed in brackets to show that they have been inserted into the quotation and are not the exact words of the speaker.

☞ **REFERENCE NOTE:** For more on using brackets, see page 957.

(4) To show that a full line or more of poetry has been omitted, use an entire line of spaced periods.

ORIGINAL
> I dream of Hanoi:
> Co-ngu Road
> ten years of separation
> the way back sliced by a frontier of hatred.
> I want to bury the past
> to burn the future
> still I yearn
> still I fear
> those endless nights
> waiting for dawn.
>
> Nguyen Thi Vinh, from "Thoughts of Hanoi"

WITH OMISSION
> I dream of Hanoi:
> . . . .
> ten years of separation
> . . . .
> still I yearn
> still I fear
> those endless nights
> waiting for dawn.

Notice that the line of periods is as long as the line of poetry above it.

(5) To indicate a pause in a written passage, use three ellipsis points with a space before the first point.

EXAMPLE   "Well, . . . I don't know what to say," Sarah answered.

▶ EXERCISE 5   **Using Ellipsis Points Correctly**

Omit the italicized parts of the following passages. Use ellipsis points to correctly punctuate each omission.

1. It was nearly the time of full moon, *and on this account, though the sky was lined with a uniform sheet of dripping cloud,* ordinary objects out of doors were readily visible.

   1. moon, . . . ordinary   Thomas Hardy, "The Three Strangers"

MECHANICS

MECHANICS

OBJECTIVES

- To use apostrophes in forming possessive nouns and pronouns
- To proofread sentences and phrases for correct use of apostrophes

944 *Punctuation*

2. **stood, . . . balanced**

2. The old native stood, *breath blowing out the skin between his ribs, feet tense,* balanced in the sand, smiling and shaking his head.

Nadine Gordimer, from "The Train from Rhodesia"

3. In the world's broad field of battle,
In the bivouac of Life,
Be not like dumb, driven cattle!
Be a hero in the strife!

3. **In the world's broad field of battle,**
. . . .
Be a hero in the strife!

Henry Wadsworth Longfellow, from "A Psalm of Life"

4. Remember, I am not recording the vision of a madman. *The sun does not more certainly shine in the heavens, than that which I now affirm is true. Some miracle might have produced it, yet the stages of the discovery were distinct and probable.* After days and nights of incredible labor and fatigue, I succeeded in discovering the cause of generation and life; nay, more, I became myself capable of bestowing animation upon lifeless matter.

4. **madman. . . . After**

Mary Shelley, from *Frankenstein*

5. When the lights went on, little boys like a bevy of flies assembled around the lamppost for gossip and stories. *Elsewhere in a similar manner men gathered to throw dice or cut cards or simply to talk.* The spectacle repeated itself at each crossing where there was a street lamp ringed to a post.

5. **stories. . . . The**

George Lamming, from *In the Castle of My Skin*

Apostrophes

Possessive Case

The *possessive case* of a noun or a pronoun shows ownership or relationship.

OWNERSHIP	RELATIONSHIP
Alice Walker's poetry the **student's** suggestions **your** opinion	**Crowfoot's** family **five dollars'** worth **my** grandparents

---

PROGRAM MANAGER

APOSTROPHES

- **Independent Practice/ Reteaching** For instruction and exercises, see **Apostrophes** in *Language Skills Practice and Assessment,* p. 233.

- **Computer Guided Instruction** For additional instruction and practice with apostrophes, see **Lessons 47** and **48** in *Language Workshop CD-ROM.*

- **Practice** To help less-advanced students with additional instruction and practice with apostrophes, see **Chapter 23** in *English Workshop, Complete Course,* pp. 317–318.

QUICK REMINDER

Write the following words on the chalkboard:

1. their, they're
2. theirs, there's
3. who's, whose
4. it's, its
5. you're, your

Then, have volunteers use the words correctly in sentences. Ask students to explain how these words are different. [They can be classified into two groups: possessive pronouns and contractions.]

AMENDMENTS TO SELECTIONS
Description of change: excerpted
Rationale: to focus on the concept of ellipsis points presented in this chapter

30m.

30m. **Use an apostrophe in forming the possessive of nouns and some pronouns.**

(1) To form the possessive of a singular noun, add an apostrophe and an –s.

EXAMPLES   the senator's comments   Charles's grades
           tennis racquet's size   player's turn

NOTE: When forming the possessive of a singular noun ending in an *s* sound, add only an apostrophe if the noun has two or more syllables and if the addition of 's will make the noun awkward to pronounce. Otherwise, add 's.

        EXAMPLES   the seamstress' work
                   for goodness' sake
                   Achilles' battles
                   Mr. Martinez' article

(2) To form the possessive of a plural noun ending in *s*, add only the apostrophe.

EXAMPLES   the girls' team   the Millses' back yard
           the winners' trophy   the governors' conference

The few plural nouns that do not end in *s* form the possessive by adding an apostrophe and an –s.

EXAMPLES   women's tournament   children's playground

NOTE: Do not use an apostrophe to form the plural of a noun.

        INCORRECT   Two of the novel's that Jean Rhys wrote are *Wide Sargasso Sea* and *Voyage in the Dark.*
        CORRECT   Two of the **novels** that Jean Rhys wrote are *Wide Sargasso Sea* and *Voyage in the Dark.*

(3) Do not use an apostrophe with possessive personal pronouns or with the possessive pronoun *whose*.

INCORRECT   We thought the top score was her's.
CORRECT   We thought the top score was **hers.**

INCORRECT   I have witnessed democracy at it's best.
CORRECT   I have witnessed democracy at **its** best.

INCORRECT   Who's notebook is this?
CORRECT   **Whose** notebook is this?

MECHANICS

LEP/ESL

Spanish. Spanish has a possessive form for pronouns but not for other nouns; therefore, students may be confused about the use of apostrophes. For example, in Spanish the possessive is "the book of José." Students will need extra practice using the possessive form. You may want to give them a series of statements that they can change by using the possessive form of the noun. An example is "This book belongs to José. It is _____."

◆ INTEGRATING THE LANGUAGE ARTS

Mechanics and Writing. You could have students write short poems using possessive case/contraction homophones such as *their/they're, whose/who's,* and *your/you're.* Tell students to begin a new line each time they use a homophone. You may want to write the following example on the chalkboard:

You're too quick to give up
Your dreams. Trust
Your visions to be
Your guide.
Who's going to reach
Your dreams if not you?
Whose dreams will you reach if not
Your own?

MECHANICS

> **Possessive Personal Pronouns**
>
> | | |
> |---|---|
> | my, mine | our, ours |
> | your, yours | their, theirs |
> | his, her, hers, its | |

☞ **REFERENCE NOTE:** Do not confuse the possessive pronouns *your, their, theirs, its,* and *whose* with the contractions *you're, they're, there's, it's,* and *who's.* See pages 985, 984, 950, and 980.

(4) To form the possessive of an indefinite pronoun, add an apostrophe and an –s.

EXAMPLES **Everyone's** vote counts equally.
She consented to **everybody's** request for a class meeting.

NOTE: In such forms as *anyone else* and *somebody else,* the correct possessives are *anyone else's* and *somebody else's.*

☞ **REFERENCE NOTE:** For a list of indefinite pronouns, see page 605.

(5) Form the possessive of only the last word in a hyphenated word, in the name of an organization or a business firm, or in a word group showing joint possession.

EXAMPLES father-in-law**'s** hobby
the Economic and Social Council**'s** members
Lewis and Clark**'s** expedition

When a possessive pronoun is part of a word group showing joint possession, each noun in the word group is also possessive.

EXAMPLE **Lusita's, Joshua's,** and **my** report

(6) Form the possessive of each noun in a word group showing individual possession of similar items.

EXAMPLE **Maria Bethania's** and **Aster Aweke's** albums

(7) Use an apostrophe in possessive forms of words that indicate time, such as *minute, hour, day, week, month,* and *year,* and possessives indicating an amount in cents or dollars.

MECHANICS

◆ **INTEGRATING THE LANGUAGE ARTS**

Mechanics and Writing. Ask students to select eight of the possessive phrases in **Exercise 6** and to incorporate them in original paragraphs. Students should underline the phrases and exchange their paragraphs for proofreading. Ask volunteers to read their paragraphs aloud.

EXAMPLES a **minute's** work five **minutes'** work
a **day's** rest three **days'** rest
one **cent's** worth five **cents'** worth

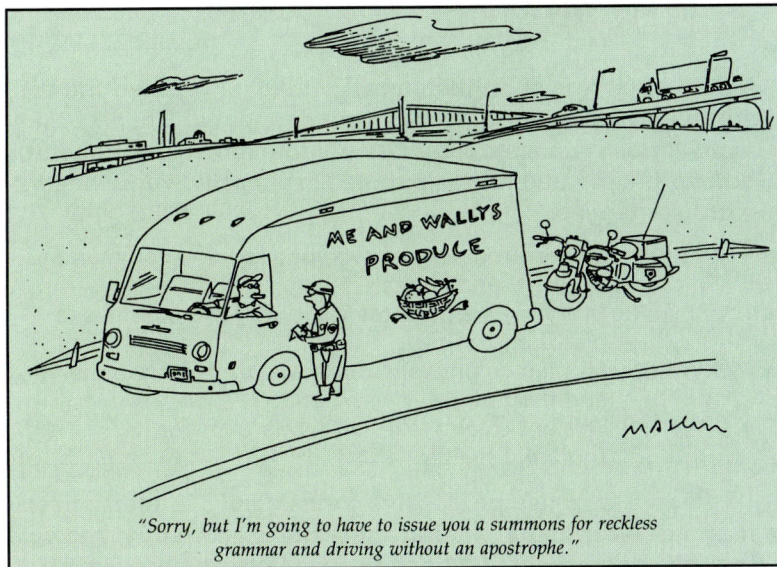

ME AND WALLYS PRODUCE

"Sorry, but I'm going to have to issue you a summons for reckless grammar and driving without an apostrophe."

Drawing by Maslin; © 1987 The New Yorker Magazine, Inc.

MECHANICS

▶ **EXERCISE 6** **Forming Possessive Nouns and Pronouns**

Each of the following groups of words expresses a possessive relationship by means of a prepositional phrase. Revise each word group so that a possessive noun or pronoun will express the same relationship.

EXAMPLE **1.** a vacation of two weeks
1. *a two weeks' vacation*

1. hats of the firefighters
2. dressing room of the star
3. job of my sister-in-law
4. character of a person
5. business of Jorge and her
6. speech of the mayor-elect
7. a pause of a moment
8. owner of the Doberman pinscher
9. highlights of the film
10. kimonos of the women
11. costumes of the matadors
12. worth of four dollars
13. admission prices of adults and children
14. prize of Ralph Bunche
15. sides of it
16. remarks of the judges
17. trip of Maria and Cam
18. a wait of an hour
19. responsibility of everyone
20. CD of the group Genesis

ANSWERS
Exercise 6

1. the firefighters' hats
2. the star's dressing room
3. my sister-in-law's job
4. a person's character
5. Jorge's and her business
6. the mayor-elect's speech
7. a moment's pause
8. the Doberman pinscher's owner
9. the film's highlights
10. the women's kimonos
11. the matadors' costumes
12. four dollars' worth
13. adults' and children's admission prices
14. Ralph Bunche's prize
15. its sides
16. the judges' remarks
17. Maria and Cam's trip
18. an hour's wait
19. everyone's responsibility
20. the group Genesis' CD

MECHANICS

MECHANICS

WRITING APPLICATION

Using Apostrophes Correctly in Writing

Native speakers of English usually take for granted the possessive case forms of nouns and pronouns. These handy word forms help speakers not only to express relationships among people and things but also to simplify wordy or awkward sentences.

WORDY	The environment of everyone includes communities of plants and animals.
BETTER	**Everyone's** environment includes communities of plants and animals.
AWKWARD	This ant colony relies on acacia trees for the shelter and food of it.
BETTER	This ant colony relies on acacia trees for **its** [not *it's*] food and shelter.

People who use possessive forms easily in their speech may have difficulty writing these forms correctly because they are unsure about when apostrophes are necessary and where they should be placed. To determine whether a noun is in the possessive case, try converting it into a prepositional phrase. For example, *the **boy's** cap* becomes *the cap **of the boy.*** If the noun can't be converted into a prepositional phrase, the noun is not possessive.

▶ WRITING ACTIVITY

In biology class you have learned that a *community* is a group of living things that forms a system of production, consumption, and decomposition. Now your biology teacher wants each person in your class to observe a community and write a report on his or her findings. Your assignment:

- Identify a community of organisms and form a hypothesis about how the members of that community interact.
- Observe the interactions of plants and animals in the community for at least ten minutes a day for several days.
- Take notes on your observations.
- Decide whether the data you've collected support your hypothesis.

- Write up your hypothesis, observations, and conclusions in a brief report. (Be sure to use apostrophes correctly to form the possessive case of nouns and pronouns.)

Prewriting Almost any place can house a living community—a decaying log, an aquarium, a garden, a tree, a crack in the sidewalk, a compost heap, a pond, a window box of plants, even your own room. Choose a community that you can observe easily. Be sure to record the date and time of each observation. If possible, use a magnifying glass or microscope to discover organisms not visible to the naked eye. After you have completed your observations, review your notes carefully. How does the information you've gathered compare with your original hypothesis? What tentative conclusions can you draw about how the community functions?

Writing Write a draft of your report. Begin by describing the setting of the community and identifying the organisms that live there. State your hypothesis, and clearly present your observations. Then, state your conclusions. Explain how they differ from or support your original hypothesis. Finally, write your report in the formal English appropriate for scientific writing. (For more about formal English, see pages 519–523.)

Evaluating and Revising Check your draft against your notes. Be sure that you do not state your own opinions as if they are factual observations. (For more about the difference between facts and opinions, see pages 68 and 302–303.) Do your conclusions follow clearly from your observations? Have you left out any important information? Have you included any unnecessary information? Revise your report as necessary. Be sure that you've used only formal English. Use possessive case forms of nouns and pronouns to revise wordy or awkward sentences.

Proofreading Proofread your report for errors in grammar, usage, spelling, and punctuation. Take special care with possessive forms, using apostrophes only where they belong.

TECHNOLOGY TIP
Tell students who are using word-processing programs to take advantage of the global search function when they are proofreading. By searching for the apostrophe, for example, students can check each usage for correctness.

MECHANICS

MECHANICS

COMMON ERROR

Problem. Because some contractions and possessive pronouns sound alike (*who's/whose; it's/its; you're/your; they're/their*), students often confuse the pairs.

Solution. You may want to make a list of confusing contraction/possessive pronoun pairs. Suggest that students read all contractions and all possessive pronouns as if they were two words. If the expanded phrase makes sense, then the word is a contraction and should have an apostrophe.

Contractions

30n. Use an apostrophe to show where letters, numbers, or words have been omitted in a contraction.

A *contraction* is a shortened form of a word, word group, or number in which an apostrophe takes the place of the letters, numbers, or words that are omitted.

EXAMPLES

I am	I'm	they had	they'd
he has	he's	where is	where's
let us	let's	we are	we're
of the clock	o'clock	we have	we've
1950s	'50s	you will	you'll

The word *not* can be shortened to *n't* and added to a verb, usually without any change in the spelling of the verb.

EXAMPLES

is not	isn't	has not	hasn't
does not	doesn't	should not	shouldn't
do not	don't	were not	weren't

EXCEPTIONS

will not	won't	cannot	can't

Do not confuse contractions with possessive pronouns.

CONTRACTIONS	POSSESSIVE PRONOUNS
It's [*It is*] time to go. **It's** [*It has*] been snowing since noon.	**Its** diameter is almost 2,290 kilometers.
Who's [*Who is*] the captain? **Who's** [*Who has*] been using the computer?	**Whose** umbrella is this?
You're [*You are*] late.	**Your** skates are in the attic.
They're [*They are*] in the gym. **There's** [*There is*] only one left.	We are learning about **their** customs. This equipment is **theirs**.

NOTE: Contractions are perfectly acceptable in most writing and speaking situations. However, in formal writing, such as in essays for school and in business letters, avoid using nearly all contractions of verb forms, years, and the word *not*.

**30
n–o**

Plurals

30o. Use an apostrophe and an –s to form the plurals of all lowercase letters, some uppercase letters, and some words referred to as words.

EXAMPLES   *Hawaii* ends with two *i*'s. [Without the apostrophe, the plural of *i* would spell *is.*]
Not many names begin with *U*'s, but the names of my favorite bands do—U2 and UB40. [Without the apostrophe, the plural of *U* would spell *Us.*]
Jeremy's *No want to*'s are just a sign that he's a normal two-year-old.

You may add only an –s to form the plurals of such items—except lowercase letters—if the plural forms cannot be misread.

EXAMPLE   Most of his grades this term are **Cs.**

Be sure to use apostrophes consistently.

EXAMPLE   The printed *T*'s look like *I*'s. [Without the apostrophe, the plural of *I* would spell *Is.* The apostrophe in the plural of *T* is included for consistency.]

NOTE: To form the plurals of abbreviations that end with a period, add 's.

EXAMPLES   Ph.D.'s   M.A.'s

To form the plurals of abbreviations not followed by periods, add either 's or –s.

EXAMPLES   VCR's *or* VCRs
CD's *or* CDs

▶ EXERCISE 7   **Proofreading for the Correct Uses of the Apostrophe**

Proofread the following phrases and sentences, adding apostrophes where needed. If an item is correct, write C.

1. men's sports cars   **2. C**
2. statements of a mayor-elect
3. It's a pagoda, isn't it?
4. sand in its gears   **4. C**
5. She's wearing a sari, I'm sure.
6. If he lets us, we'll go too.
7. Her cousin's choices were the same as hers.   **7. *or* cousins'**
8. Let's see what's going on.
9. I've found it's no help.
10. office of the rabbi   **10. C**

MECHANICS

MECHANICS

OBJECTIVE
• To hyphenate words correctly

952 *Punctuation*

11. What's its title?
12. on a minute's notice **13. C**
13. party of Frank and Carlos
14. Who's on Vicky's bicycle?
15. this taco's ingredients
16. How many *i*'s are there in *Mississippi*?
17. mice's nest
18. His grades in French are all A's.
19. musicals of Rodgers and Hammerstein **19. C**
20. practice of Olmos and Ramírez **20. C**

Hyphens

30p. Use a hyphen to divide a word at the end of a line.

When dividing a word at the end of a line, remember the following rules:

■ Do not divide a one-syllable word.

| INCORRECT | Alicia chose to write her report about the pli-ght of the homeless. |
| CORRECT | Alicia chose to write her report about the plight of the homeless. |

■ Divide a word only between syllables.

| INCORRECT | Isn't Ethan running for student council presid-ent this year? |
| CORRECT | Isn't Ethan running for student council presi-dent this year? |

NOTE: When you are not sure about the syllabication of a word, look in a dictionary.

■ Divide a hyphenated word at the hyphen.

| INCORRECT | Hirohito was the emperor of Japan for six-ty-three years. |
| CORRECT | Hirohito was the emperor of Japan for sixty-three years. |

■ Do not divide a word so that one letter stands alone.

| INCORRECT | Proofreading my report, I saw that I had o-mitted an important quotation. |
| CORRECT | Proofreading my report, I saw that I had omitted an important quotation. |

PROGRAM MANAGER

HYPHENS

■ **Independent Practice/Reteaching** For instruction and exercises, see **Hyphens** in *Language Skills Practice and Assessment,* p. 234.

■ **Computer Guided Instruction** For additional instruction and practice with hyphens, see **Lesson 52** in *Language Workshop CD-ROM.*

QUICK REMINDER

Write the following words on the chalkboard and ask students to divide them by using hyphens as they would if the words were at the end of a line in writing:

1. apple [ap-ple]
2. strength [can't be divided]
3. doctor [doc-tor]
4. yearlong [year-long]

Point out to students that using hyphens to divide words isn't always a matter of common sense. They will have to study the rules in this chapter to discover some of the standard ways words can be divided.

30q. Use a hyphen with compound numbers from *twenty-one* to *ninety-nine* and with fractions used as modifiers.

EXAMPLES **forty-two** applicants
a **two-thirds** majority [*Two-thirds* is an adjective modifying *majority.*]
about **three-fourths** empty [*Three-fourths* is an adverb modifying *empty.*]
two thirds of the voters [*Two thirds* is not an adjective. *Thirds* is a noun modified by the adjective *two.*]

30r. Hyphenate a compound adjective when it precedes the word it modifies.

EXAMPLES **well-liked** author — an author who is **well liked**
world-renowned composer — a composer who is **world renowned**

NOTE: Some compound adjectives are always hyphenated.

EXAMPLE a **well-balanced** meal — a meal that is **well-balanced**

If you are unsure about whether a compound adjective is hyphenated, look up the word in a dictionary.

Do not use a hyphen if one of the modifiers is an adverb ending in *–ly*.

EXAMPLE a **highly polished** surface

30s. Use a hyphen with the prefixes *ex–, self–,* and *all–,* with the suffix *–elect,* and with all prefixes before a proper noun or proper adjective.

EXAMPLES **ex-**mayor **non-**European
self-control **anti-**Fascist
all-star **pro-**Canadian
president**-elect** **Pan-**American

NOTE: Although you may see a variety of spellings for some words (*reelect, re-elect, reëlect*), the preferred style today is to close up most prefixes not listed in rule 30s.

EXAMPLES biannual reevaluate semiarid miniseries

MEETING *individual* NEEDS

LEP/ESL

General Strategies. Students sometimes do not know how to divide an English word into syllables, and this problem leads students to hyphenate improperly at the end of a line. Let students know that there are some basic rules for the division of words (one vowel sound per syllable; divide between a double consonant) and that they can always check in a dictionary for correct word divisions.

TECHNOLOGY TIP

Because most computer programs simply move words that are too long to the next line or automatically insert hyphens to divide words, students may question the purpose of studying the rules for hyphens. Point out that in order to proofread computer-generated text accurately, and in order to be able to write by hand when computers are not available, students need to know the rules for dividing words.

VISUAL CONNECTIONS
Cow's Skull: Red, White and Blue

About the Artist. Georgia O'Keeffe's paintings were first shown in New York City at an art gallery established by Alfred Stieglitz, an American photographer. O'Keeffe and Stieglitz married in 1924, and for many years he displayed her work at galleries he operated in New York City. O'Keeffe settled near Abiquiu, New Mexico, in 1949.

REVIEW B

OBJECTIVE

- To correct paragraphs by adding italics, quotation marks, ellipsis points, apostrophes, and hyphens

954 *Punctuation*

30t. Use a hyphen to prevent confusion or awkwardness.

EXAMPLES   re-collect [prevents confusion with *recollect*]
            anti-icer [avoids the awkwardness of *antiicer*]

EXERCISE 8   Using Hyphens

Revise the following groups of words by adding hyphens where they are needed. If a word group is correct, write *C*.
Placement of hyphens is indicated by carets.

1. almost two‸thirds full
2. pre‸Columbian artifact
3. well‸spoken individual
4. a highly motivated employee   4. C
5. anti‸imperialism

REVIEW B   Correcting Paragraphs by Adding Italics (Underlining), Quotation Marks, Ellipsis Points, Apostrophes, and Hyphens

Rewrite the following paragraphs, adding italics (underlining), quotation marks, ellipsis points, apostrophes, and hyphens where they are needed.   Hyphens are indicated by the ‸ symbol.

[1] "This painting, <u>Cow's Skull: Red, White and Blue</u>, really intrigues me; I'm sure it's extremely symbolic," Darla said. [2] "What do you think of it?"

[3] "You've asked the right person," replied Anthony, "because Georgia O'Keeffe is one of my favorite painters. [4] One biography of her, which is simply titled <u>Georgia O'Keeffe</u>, tells how she'd collect horses' and cows' skulls in New Mexico and then paint pictures of them. [5] This well-known work, which she painted in 1931, *is* symbolic; the painting's colors represent O'Keeffe's pro-American feelings."

Georgia O'Keeffe (1887–1986), *Cow's Skull: Red, White and Blue* (1952). Oil on canvas, 39 7/8" x 35 7/8". The Metropolitan Museum of Art, The Alfred Stieglitz Collection (52.203). © 1997 The Georgia O'Keeffe Foundation/Artists Rights Society (ARS), New York.

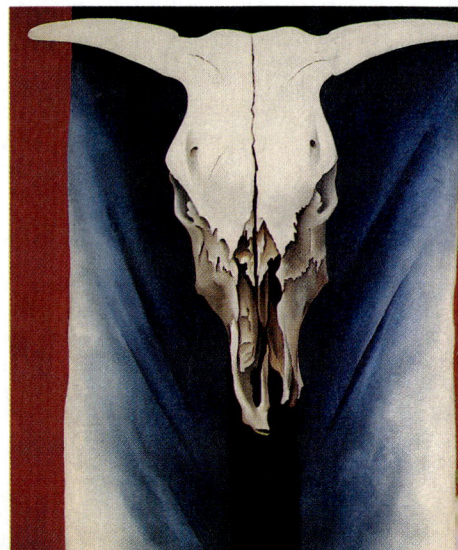

OBJECTIVE

- To correct sentences by adding dashes, parentheses, and brackets

[6] "I like this photograph of O'Keeffe, too," Darla added. [7] "Don't you think she looks extremely self-reliant and self-assured?"

[8] "Well, ... that's probably an understatement," chuckled Anthony. [9] "O'Keeffe, who was born in Wisconsin in 1887, developed her own independent style in art and life. [10] She's best known for her abstract paintings, especially the ones of flowers and of New Mexico desert scenes, such as her painting Ranchos Church—Taos."

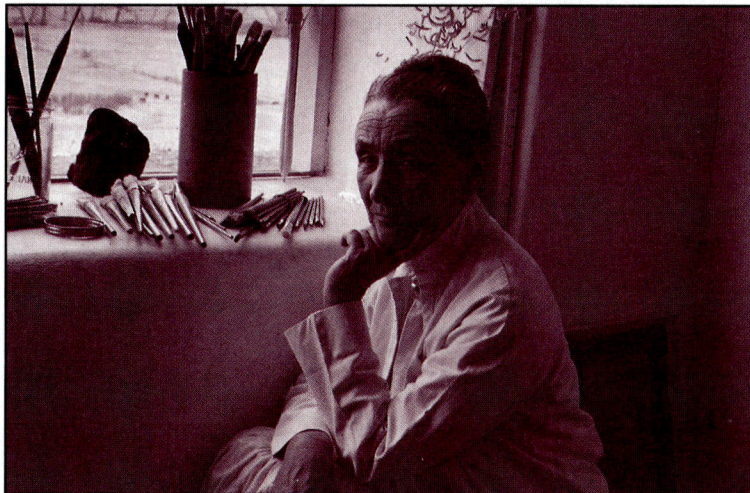

Laura Gilpin, Photographer, *Georgia O'Keeffe* (January 15, 1953). 3¼" x 4¼" saf. neg. Laura Gilpin Collection, Amon Carter Museum, Fort Worth, Texas.

MECHANICS

Dashes

30u. Use a dash to indicate an abrupt break in thought.

EXAMPLES The director of the film—I can't recall his name—said that there would be a sequel.
The truth is—and you probably already know this—we can't finish the project on time.

30v. Use a dash to mean *namely, in other words,* or *that is* before an explanation.

EXAMPLES It was a close call—the sudden gust of wind pushed the helicopter to within inches of the power line.
The early Native American civilizations—the Mayan, the Incan, and the Aztec—depended mainly on farming for their livelihood.

MECHANICS

QUICK REMINDER

Write the sentence "My brother third from the left in the picture made the team this year" on the chalkboard.

Ask students to answer these questions:

1. What's the most important idea in the sentence? [My brother made the team this year.]
2. Does the basic meaning change when the rest of the sentence is added? [No]

Explain to students that the extra part of the sentence is called a parenthetical element and that it should be set off from the rest of the sentence. Dashes can be used for this, but before students can learn to use dashes correctly, they will need to have a clear idea of what a parenthetical element is.

LEP/ESL

General Strategies. Some students may occasionally use a topic-comment subject. For example, the construction, "My mother, she . . ." is a topic (mother) and comment (she . . .) on the topic. Students who use this feature may have trouble telling the difference between the topic-comment subject and a parenthetical element. Point out that these sentences are correct with either the topic or the comment, but not with both.

LEARNING STYLES

Auditory Learners. Encourage students to read sentences aloud and to listen for the drop in their voices when they read parenthetical expressions.

COOPERATIVE LEARNING

Tell students that good writing is smooth writing; having too many parenthetical expressions interrupts the flow of ideas. Have students work in small groups to write five sentences that contain too many parenthetical expressions. Then, have the groups exchange papers and rewrite the sentences to make them smoother without losing any of the information in the parentheses.

---

956 *Punctuation*

Parentheses

30w. **Use parentheses to enclose informative or explanatory material of minor importance.**

EXAMPLES   As a state representative, Barbara Jordan **(**Texas**)** served on that committee.
The length of the Mekong River is 4,186 kilometers **(**about 2,600 miles**)**.

Be sure that the material within parentheses can be omitted without changing the basic meaning or structure of the sentence.

IMPROPER USE   Tina had been shopping (in that store) most of
OF PARENTHESES   her life. [The idea in parentheses is important to the meaning of the sentence.]

A sentence enclosed in parentheses may fall within another sentence or may stand by itself.

(1) A parenthetical sentence that falls within another sentence
- should not begin with a capital letter unless it begins with a word that should always be capitalized
- should not end with a period but may end with a question mark or an exclamation point

EXAMPLES   The largest island of the Solomon Islands **(see the map on page 453)** is Guadalcanal.
I hope I persuaded Alex **(is he a senior?)** to help us.

(2) A parenthetical sentence that stands by itself
- should begin with a capital letter
- should end with a period, a question mark, or an exclamation point

EXAMPLES   The largest island of the Solomon Islands is Guadalcanal. **(See the map on page 453.)**
Alex asked me if he could help us. **(What do you think I said?)**

NOTE: When parenthetical material falls within a sentence, punctuation never comes before the opening parenthesis but may follow the closing parenthesis.

INCORRECT   According to this article about Grandma Moses, (1860–1961) she began to paint in her seventies.
CORRECT   According to this article about Grandma Moses (1860–1961), she began to paint in her seventies.

Brackets

30x. Use brackets to enclose an explanation within quoted or parenthetical material.

EXAMPLES Ms. Grayson was quoted as saying in her acceptance speech: "I am honored by this **[**the award**]**, and I would like to share the recognition with those who made my work possible."

By a vote of 5 to 4, the Supreme Court overturned the lower court's ruling. (See page 149 **[**Diagram A**]** for a chronology of the case.)

> **EXERCISE 9** **Correcting Sentences by Adding Dashes, Parentheses, and Brackets**

Add dashes, parentheses, and brackets where they are needed in each of the following sentences.

1. Dr. Percy Lavon Julian, who was born in Montgomery, Alabama, is noted for developing helpful drugs from—this surprised me, too—soybeans.
2. My cousin Matthew (my father's brother's son) plans to open an aerobics and yoga center on the north side of town.
3. Some offspring of famous performers (Michael Douglas, Liza Minnelli, Jeff and Beau Bridges, and Jane Fonda, for example) have established award-winning careers for themselves.
4. Christine was quoted as saying in her valedictory speech: "We seniors are not at an ending but a beginning, and it [graduation] marks an exciting time of change in our lives."
5. For the new course in government and society, students are required to analyze the nonfiction writings of Ayn Rand (1905–1982) and to read her novel *Anthem*.

> **REVIEW C** **Proofreading a Paragraph for Correct Punctuation**

Rewrite the following paragraph, adding semicolons, colons, dashes, parentheses, brackets, italics (underlining), quotation marks, apostrophes, and hyphens where they are needed.

Hyphens are indicated by the ‸ symbol.

[1] As you can see in the pictures on the next page, Jim Thorpe (his American Indian name was <u>Wa-tho-huck</u>) looked exactly like what he was—a strong athlete. [2] No discussion of

MECHANICS

> **TIMESAVER**
> You could provide keys for **Exercise 9** and allow students to check their answers independently and to correct their errors. Then, use **Review C** to evaluate students' mastery of the material in this lesson.

MECHANICS

America's outstanding sports figures would be complete without reference to Thorpe, who in 1950 was voted the greatest athlete of the century's first half. [3] His feats in football, track, and baseball remain unique, and his strength and speed are legendary.

4. C

[4] Born of Irish, French, and American Indian heritage and reared in Prague, Oklahoma, Thorpe began earning honors early in his life. [5] He was an all-American halfback for two years while playing for the local school and broke all previous records in winning the gold medals for the pentathlon and the decathlon at the 1912 Olympic Games, where he was hailed as the greatest athlete in the world. [6] Because he'd already begun playing professional baseball, however, he was forced to return his medals a year later. [7] (They were restored posthumously

7. .

in 1982.) [8] Thorpe spent six outstanding years in professional baseball, but he became best known as a football player who could do everything well: run, pass,

9. C

catch, punt, and more. [9] He played professional football for more than ten years. [10] In 1969, sixteen years after his death—and on the National Football League's fiftieth birthday, Thorpe was named to football's all-time all-professional team.

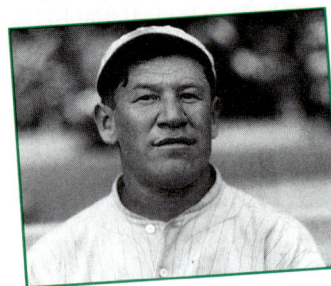

MECHANICS

MECHANICS

> REVIEW D

Proofreading a Dialogue for Correct Punctuation and Capitalization

Rewrite the following dialogue, adding commas, semicolons, quotation marks, apostrophes, and capital letters where they are needed. If a sentence is correct, write *C*.

[1] Roger Morton sat back for a moment, feeling proud of himself.

OBJECTIVE

- To proofread sentences and a paragraph for correct punctuation

[2] "Have you finished those sample business letters yet?" asked Ms. Zimsky, the typing teacher.

[3] "Yes," Roger replied. [4] "I think I've improved on the format, too. [5] Look how much space I've saved on each page!"

[6] Ms. Zimsky glanced down. [7] "These aren't done the way they are in the book. [8] Just do them that way for now. [9] You need to finish this chapter today, or you'll be way behind. [10] There's no time to talk about format."

    6. C

    8. C

[11] Embarrassed and tired, Roger later told his friend Annette about the incident.   **11. C**

[12] "Your problem," she explained, "isn't that you improved the letters; it's that you didn't get Ms. Zimsky's permission first. [13] I learned that any time you want to change a procedure, no matter how great an improvement the change will make, you should first talk your idea over with the person who will need to approve it. [14] Try discussing your suggestions again when Ms. Zimsky has more time."

    13. C

[15] Roger went back to the typing classroom after school, and Ms. Zimsky listened to his ideas.   **15. C**

[16] "Oh, I see what you're doing," she said. [17] "It's really a very good idea; in fact, I think I'll share it with the whole class. [18] See you tomorrow, Roger."

[19] "See you tomorrow," said Roger, "and thanks for listening, Ms. Zimsky. [20] If I think of any other improvements, I'll be sure to discuss them with you first."

MECHANICS

Review: Posttest

A. Proofreading Sentences for Correct Punctuation

Each of the following sentences contains at least one punctuation error in the use of semicolons, colons, dashes, parentheses, brackets, italics (underlining), quotation marks, apostrophes, or hyphens. Rewrite each sentence, punctuating it correctly. **Hyphens are indicated by the ‸ symbol.**

EXAMPLE **1.** Why did you wait until the last minute asked my friend Tanya when I told her my problem?

      1. *"Why did you wait until the last minute?" asked my friend Tanya when I told her my problem.*

AT-RISK STUDENTS

You may want to simplify the **Review: Posttest** by telling students how many errors are in each sentence and identifying the kinds of errors.

1. When I read The Hobbit, my favorite chapter was the one in which Bilbo meets Gollum.

2. Among the members of the Fine Arts Commission who met in New York City were some very talented people: Diane Keaton, actress; Paul McCartney, musician; Paul Taylor, choreographer; and Lee Krasner, artist.

3. My brothers and sisters and I have been encouraged to be self-reliant since we were children.

4. The rapid spread of the bacterial infection (see the time line and the map below) posed a grave puzzle to the medical experts.

5. "We're going to win this game!" said the soccer coach to the newspaper sportswriter.

6. Paulette sent in my application before the deadline; however, she neglected to put a stamp on the envelope.

7. When a graduate of our high school recently appeared on television playing Scott Joplin's "Maple Leaf Rag," a new interest in ragtime music blossomed at Franklin High School.

8. "The packages sitting over there are yours, aren't they?" asked Tamala. **8. ?**

9. Although the oil contract had not been renewed, the oil company had made a delivery; the customers complained when they received the bill.

10. The mayor-elect met for two hours yesterday afternoon with members of the Allentown Youth Council (see the picture on page 17). **10.** ⊙

11. At Book Lore—the bookstore where I work—we sold twenty-seven copies of that book in one day.

12. "I'll never forget the first time I read Walt Whitman's poem 'When Lilacs Last in the Dooryard Bloom'd,'" said Megan. "It made me feel the tragedy of Abraham Lincoln's death."

13. Within the next three week's, new television stations will begin broadcasting from the following cities: Kalamazoo, Michigan; Salinas, California; and Fairbanks, Alaska.

14. Helena knew the day would be less than perfect when she heard herself saying, "Don't forget to dot your i's and cross your t's."

15. The article I read in Travel Today began, "Come to the Galápagos Islands—six hundred miles west of Ecuador—and see blue-footed birds and green iguanas."

B. Proofreading a Paragraph for Correct Punctuation

Rewrite the following paragraph, punctuating each sentence correctly.   Hyphens are indicated by the ∧ symbol.

[16] When you hear the word *composer,* you probably think of the world‿renowned musical masters of long ago∧Mozart, Bach, Beethoven, and Chopin, among others. **[17]** However, you don't really have to think that far back‿the twentieth century also has produced some outstanding talents. **[18]** You'll probably recognize at least one of these modern composers∧George Gershwin, Benjamin Britten, Leonard Bernstein, Richard Rodgers, or Paul McCartney. **[19]** Yes, McCartney and other rock musicians have produced many memorable compositions‿for example, McCartney and his long‿time composing partner John Lennon gave us such popular ballads as "Yesterday" and "Michelle." **[20]** Richard Rodgers worked with lyricist Oscar Hammerstein, II, on many projects including the following musical plays∧<u>Oklahoma</u>, <u>South Pacific</u>, <u>The King and I</u>, and <u>The Sound of Music</u>. **[21]** Leonard Bernstein, too, was involved in many musical productions, but perhaps his most famous is <u>West Side Story</u>. **[22]** Both Bernstein and Rodgers are known primarily for their Broadway musicals‿however, much of their music has become standard outside the theater. **[23]** Benjamin Britten, on the other hand, is often ranked as England's greatest technical composer‿his difficult operas, such as <u>Death in Venice</u>, are performed only by highly-skilled musicians and vocalists. **[24]** George Gershwin (1898–1937) was one of America's finest and best‿loved composers. **[25]** He wrote the opera <u>Porgy and Bess</u>, which contains the all‿time classic song "Summertime."

TECHNOLOGY TIP

Typewriters and some word-processing programs are not capable of making dashes. Instead, dashes are keyed by using two hyphens without any spacing before, between, or after them. If students are unaware of this convention, point it out to them and remind them of it when they proofread.

Some programs use a series of commands to create dashes. You may want to make sure students know the commands for dashes if their word-processing programs have that capability.

OBJECTIVE

• To divide words into syllables

PROGRAM MANAGER

FOR THE WHOLE CHAPTER

■ **Review** For exercises on chapter concepts, see **Review Form A** and **Review Form B** in *Language Skills Practice and Assessment,* pp. 252–255.

■ **Assessment** For additional testing, see **Mechanics Pretests** and **Mechanics Mastery Tests** in *Language Skills Practice and Assessment,* pp. 189–196 and pp. 259–267.

■ **Extension/Enrichment** For additional instruction and exercises, see **Spelling Masters 1–8** in *Practice for Assessment in Reading, Vocabulary, and Spelling,* pp. 23–30.

MECHANICS

CHAPTER OVERVIEW

This chapter focuses on spelling rules and strategies that students can use if they are uncertain about the correct spelling of a word. The chapter also clarifies distinctions between words whose spellings and meanings are often confused. In addition, the chapter provides a list titled **300 Spelling Words** that students can study and master over the course of a semester or year.

The material in this chapter can serve as a useful reference for students when they are studying dictionary skills, the principal parts of verbs, or any of the writing chapters.

MECHANICS

31 SPELLING

Improving Your Spelling

Good Spelling Habits

Using the following techniques will improve your spelling:

1. **Pronounce words carefully.**

   EXAMPLES   ath • let • ic   [not *a • the • let • ic*]
               soph • o • more   [not *soph • more*]
               jew • el • ry   [not *jew • le • ry*]

2. **Spell by syllables.** A *syllable* is a word part that can be pronounced by itself.

   EXAMPLES   prob • a • bly   [three syllables]
               dip • lo • ma • tic   [four syllables]
               co • in • ci • den • tal   [five syllables]

3. **Use a dictionary.** Don't guess about correct spelling. Look up any words you are unsure of. Using a dictionary to check the spelling of one word may help you spell other words. For example, by checking the spelling of *criticism*, you will see that the word ends in –*ism*, not –*isim*. Learning this spelling may help you spell other words ending in –*ism*, such as *patriotism*, *skepticism*, and *socialism*.

4. Proofread for careless spelling errors. Always reread what you have written so that you can eliminate careless spelling errors, such as typos (*trail* for *trial*), missing letters (*goverment* for *government*), and the misuse of words that sound the same (*except* for *accept*).

5. Keep a spelling notebook. Divide each page into four columns.

COLUMN 1   Write correctly any word you find troublesome.
COLUMN 2   Write the word again, dividing it into syllables and marking the stressed syllable(s). (You may need to use a dictionary.)
COLUMN 3   Write the word again, circling the part(s) causing you trouble.
COLUMN 4   Jot down any comments that will help you remember the correct spelling.

SAMPLE NOTEBOOK ENTRIES

Correct Spelling	Syllables and Accents	Trouble Spot	Comments
emperor	em•per•or	emper(or)	Pronounce clearly
awfully	aw′•ful•ly	awfu(ll)y	Study rule 31e.

Becoming a careful speller takes a little practice, but the results are certainly worth the effort. Because readers constantly make assumptions about writers based on their writing, looking good on paper is important. If, for example, a written passage contains misspellings, a reader may suspect that the writer was careless about other information in the passage. Also, the writer appears too lazy to look up the misspelled words or too ignorant to recognize that the words were misspelled. By correcting misspelled words, the writer helps to focus the reader's attention on what is being said.

NOTE: Word-processing software that checks spelling is a valuable tool for improving your writing. If you have access to such software, be sure to use it whenever possible to help you proofread your writing.

MECHANICS

PROGRAM MANAGER

GOOD SPELLING HABITS

■ **Independent Practice/ Reteaching** For instruction and exercises, see **Proofreading for Spelling Errors** in *Language Skills Practice and Assessment,* p. 247.

■ **Computer Guided Instruction** For additional instruction and practice with good spelling habits, see **Lesson 56** in *Language Workshop CD-ROM.*

GOOD SPELLING HABITS

Here are some additional spelling strategies that you could suggest to students:

1. Periodically review spelling notebooks for duplicate entries. Duplicate entries might suggest that particular spelling rules should be reviewed.
2. Write particularly troublesome spelling words on index cards to post in prominent places.
3. Generate mnemonics. For example, students might use the sentence *We are weird* to help them remember that the word *weird* begins with *we.*

MECHANICS

SPELLING RULES   Rules 31a–31o

OBJECTIVES

- To spell correctly *ie* and *ei* words
- To spell correctly words with prefixes and suffixes
- To spell correctly the plural forms of nouns
- To use numbers in sentences

MEETING *individual* NEEDS

LEP/ESL

General Strategies. A review of dictionary and glossary skills may be helpful to students. To ensure that they understand dictionary abbreviations and other keys to pronunciation and meaning, you can create a simple key as a handout.

PROGRAM MANAGER

SPELLING RULES

- **Independent Practice/Reteaching** For instruction and exercises, see **Spelling Rules A** and **Spelling Rules B** in *Language Skills Practice and Assessment,* pp. 248–249.

- **Computer Guided Instruction** For additional instruction and practice with spelling rules, see **Lesson 56** in *Language Workshop CD-ROM.*

- **Practice** To help less-advanced students with additional instruction and practice with spelling rules, see **Chapter 24** in *English Workshop, Complete Course,* pp. 327–336.

✓ QUICK REMINDER

Read the following words to students and have them write the words on notebook paper: *yield, vein, recede, unnecessary, easily, occurrence,* and *allies.* Then, write the words on the chalkboard so that students can check the spellings. Tell students to watch for the spelling rules that govern the words they misspelled.

MECHANICS

964 *Spelling*

▶ EXERCISE 1   Spelling Words by Syllables

Divide each of the following words into syllables, inserting a hyphen between syllables. Be sure that the division of each word includes all of the letters of the word. **Vertical lines indicate syllable division.**

EXAMPLE   **1. evacuate**
        1. *e-vac-u-ate*

1. mod|ern	8. em|bar|rass|ing	15. rep|re|sent|a|tive
2. sim|i|lar	9. per|spi|ra|tion	16. en|trance
3. li|bra|ry	10. bound|a|ry	17. ac|ci|den|tal|ly
4. sur|prise	11. can|di|date	18. mis|chie|vous
5. priv|i|lege	12. e|quip|ment	19. gov|ern|ment
6. dis|as|trous	13. rec|og|nize	20. un|nec|es|sa|ry
7. qui|et	14. busi|ness	

Spelling Rules

ie and *ei*

31a.   Write *ie* when the sound is long *e*, except after *c*.

EXAMPLES   th**ie**f   bel**ie**ve   f**ie**ld   **cei**ling   re**cei**ve   de**cei**ve
EXCEPTIONS   s**ei**ze   **ei**ther   w**ei**rd   l**ei**sure   n**ei**ther

31b.   Write *ei* when the sound is not long *e*, especially when the sound is *a*.

EXAMPLES   forf**ei**t   n**ei**ghbor   fr**ei**ght   h**ei**ght   w**ei**gh
EXCEPTIONS   anc**ie**nt   consc**ie**nce   misch**ie**f   fr**ie**nd   v**ie**w

▶ EXERCISE 2   Spelling *ie* and *ei* Words

Spell each of the following words correctly by supplying *ie* or *ei*.

1. for.**ei**.gn	6. n.**ie**.ce	11. counterf.**ei**.t	16. w.**ei**.rd
2. br.**ie**.f	7. sl.**ei**.gh	12. ach.**ie**.ve	17. rec.**ei**.pt
3. rel.**ie**.ve	8. gr.**ie**.f	13. handkerch.**ie**.f	18. bel.**ie**.f
4. s.**ie**.ge	9. p.**ie**.ce	14. perc.**ei**.ve	19. f.**ie**.nd
5. v.**ei**.l	10. retr.**ie**.ve	15. conc.**ei**.ve	20. ch.**ie**.f

I'M IN A DITHER ABOUT THE 'I AND E' SPELLING RULE!

IT'S REALLY QUITE SIMPLE,.. JUST REMEMBER:

'I' BEFORE 'E' EXCEPT AFTER 'C'

'OR WHEN SOUNDED LIKE 'A' AS IN NEIGHBOR AND WEIGH.

EXCEPT FOR EIGHT EXCEPTIONS:

WEIRD, HEIGHT AND FOREIGN, LEISURE, NEITHER, SEIZE NOR FORFEIT, EITHER

I THINK I'LL JUST MEMORIZE THE DICTIONARY

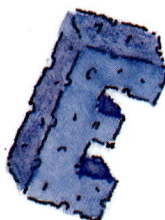

B.C. by Johnny Hart. By permission of Johnny Hart and Creators Syndicate.

–cede, –ceed, and –sede

31c. The only English word that ends in *–sede* is *supersede.* The only words ending in *–ceed* are *exceed, proceed,* and *succeed.* Most other words with this sound end in *–cede.*

EXAMPLES   ac**cede**   con**cede**   inter**cede**   pre**cede**   re**cede**   se**cede**

Adding Prefixes

A *prefix* is one or more than one letter or syllable added to the beginning of a word to create a new word that has a different meaning.

31d. When adding a prefix, do not change the spelling of the original word.

EXAMPLES   a + moral = **a**moral   il + legal = **il**legal
           mis + spell = **mis**spell   in + elegant = **in**elegant
           re + print = **re**print   im + movable = **im**movable
           over + run = **over**run   un + necessary = **un**necessary

VISUAL CONNECTIONS

Related Expression Skills. Have each student create a cartoon that interprets one spelling rule. Drawings could incorporate popular cartoon characters, or students might use original ideas.

MEETING *individual* NEEDS

LEARNING STYLES

Auditory Learners. Auditory learners will benefit from hearing words pronounced and spelled aloud. Encourage students to create rhymes about particular spelling rules. You could provide the following rhyme as an example:

> Write *i* before *e*
> Except after *c*
> Or when sounded like *ay*
> As in *neighbor* and *weigh.*

QUICK REMINDER

Ask each student to list five to ten words that he or she has trouble spelling. Students should write each word as they think it should be spelled, then look up each of their words in a dictionary to find the correct spelling. Any incorrectly spelled words can serve as the first entries in students' spelling notebooks.

INTEGRATING THE LANGUAGE ARTS

Mechanics and Vocabulary. To help students expand their vocabularies, categorize prefixes that modify the meanings of words. The following prefixes are grouped according to meaning:

Prefixes that show quantity

| half | *semi*circle |
| one | *uni*cycle |

Prefixes that show negation

not, lack of	*un*happy
	*dis*respect
opposite or against	*anti*war

Prefixes that show time

before	*fore*cast
	*pre*date
after	*post*war
again	*re*view

Prefixes that show direction or position

above, over	*super*vise
across, over	*trans*port
together	*co*exist

You may want to ask students to generate lists of words that include these prefixes.

TIMESAVER

Before assigning **Exercises 2–6,** you might give students a pretest that includes words exemplifying rules in this lesson. The results of the pretest will tell you which rules you will need to emphasize and which ones you can review quickly. You can compile the words for such a pretest by selecting a few words from the examples that follow each rule.

Adding Suffixes

A *suffix* is one or more than one letter or syllable added to the end of a word to create a new word with a different meaning.

31e. When adding the suffix *–ness* or *–ly*, do not change the spelling of the original word.

EXAMPLES	mean + ness = mean**ness**	final + ly = final**ly**
	open + ness = open**ness**	social + ly = social**ly**
EXCEPTIONS	For most words ending in *y*, change the *y* to *i* before adding *–ness* or *–ly*:	
	heavy + ness = heav**iness**	ready + ly = read**ily**
	happy + ness = happ**iness**	busy + ly = bus**ily**

NOTE: One-syllable adjectives ending in *y* generally follow rule 31e.

| EXAMPLES | dry + ness = dry**ness** | shy + ly = shy**ly** |

EXERCISE 3 **Spelling Words with Prefixes and Suffixes** Except for numbers 10 and 20, the correct spelling of each word is formed by adding the prefix/suffix to the root word. Spell correctly each of the following words as indicated.

1. over + rate
2. habitual + ly
3. green + ness
4. im + material
5. dis + appoint
6. mis + apprehend
7. practical + ly
8. un + abated
9. un + natural
10. silly + ness   **10. silliness**
11. il + legible
12. in + appropriate
13. dis + appear
14. mis + step
15. re + construct
16. in + animate
17. dis + similar
18. keen + ness
19. un + avoidable
20. merry + ly   **20. merrily**

31f. Drop the final silent *e* before a suffix beginning with a vowel.

EXAMPLES	care + ing = car**ing**	use + able = us**able**
	active + ity = activ**ity**	large + er = larg**er**
EXCEPTIONS	Keep the final silent *e*	

- in a word ending in *ce* or *ge* before a suffix beginning with *a* or *o*: noti**ce**able, coura**ge**ous
- in *dye* and in *singe* before *–ing*: dye**ing**, singe**ing**
- in *mile* before *–age*: mil**eage**

31g. Keep the final silent *e* before a suffix beginning with a consonant.

EXAMPLES	use + less = use**less**	care + ful = care**ful**
	nine + ty = nine**ty**	amuse + ment = amuse**ment**
EXCEPTIONS	nine + th = nin**th**	argue + ment = argu**ment**
	true + ly = tru**ly**	judge + ment = judg**ment**
	awe + ful = aw**ful**	acknowledge + ment =
	whole + ly = whol**ly**	acknowledg**ment** *or*
		acknowledg**ement**

31h. For words ending in *y* preceded by a consonant, change the *y* to *i* before adding any suffix that does not begin with *i*.

EXAMPLES	funny + er = funn**ier**	twenty + eth = twent**ieth**
	reply + ed = repl**ied**	reply + ing = repl**ying**

NOTE: Some one-syllable words do not follow rule 31h.

EXAMPLES	dryness	slyly

31i. For words ending in *y* preceded by a vowel, keep the *y* when adding any suffix.

EXAMPLES	gray + est = gray**est**	convey + ing = convey**ing**
	pay + ment = pay**ment**	employ + ed = employ**ed**
EXCEPTIONS	lay—la**id** pay—pa**id**	say—sa**id** day—da**ily**

31j. Double the final consonant before adding a suffix that begins with a vowel if the word (1) has only one syllable or has the accent on the final syllable and (2) ends in a single consonant preceded by a single vowel.

EXAMPLES	slim + er = slim**mer**	prefer + ing = prefer**ring**
	excel + ed = excel**led**	forget + able = forget**table**

Do not double the final consonant unless the word satisfies both of the conditions.

EXAMPLES	benefit + ed = benefit**ed** [*Benefit* ends in a single consonant preceded by a single vowel but does not have the accent on the final syllable.]
	select + ing = selec**ting** [*Select* has the accent on the final syllable but does not end in a single consonant.]

MEETING *individual* **NEEDS**

LESS-ADVANCED STUDENTS

The number of rules in this chapter may seem overwhelming. Explain that students don't have to remember all the rules at once. Remind students to focus on one rule at a time. Give students positive reinforcement each time a rule is mastered.

When a word satisfies both conditions but the addition of the suffix causes the accent to shift, do not double the final consonant.

EXAMPLES   refer + ence = **reference**
              prefer + able = **preferable**
EXCEPTIONS   excel—**excellent, excellence, excellency**

NOTE: The final consonant of some words may or may not be doubled. Either spelling is acceptable.

EXAMPLES   cancel + ed = **canceled** *or* **cancelled**
              travel + ing = **traveling** *or* **travelling**
              program + er = **programer** *or* **programmer**

If you are not sure whether you should double the final consonant, consult a dictionary.

▶ EXERCISE 4   Spelling Words with Suffixes

Spell out each of the following words, as indicated.

1. defer + ed
2. defer + ence
3. hope + ing
4. approve + al
5. discover + er
6. safe + ty
7. prepare + ing
8. obey + ing
9. spicy + er
10. propel + ing
11. desire + ed
12. control + ed
13. hope + less
14. green + er
15. due + ly
16. run + ing
17. singe + ing
18. remote + est
19. name + less
20. red + est

▶ REVIEW A   Proofreading a Paragraph to Correct Misspelled Words

Proofread the following paragraph, correcting any misspelled words. If all the words in a sentence are spelled correctly, write *C*.

EXAMPLE   [1] Accordding to legend, Jean-Jacques Dessalines created the Haitian flag by removeing the white panel from the French flag.
       1. *according; removing*

[1] When news of the French Revolution reached the colony of Saint Dominigue on the Caribbean island of Hispaniola, the African slaves and the freed islanders of mixxed ancestry rebeled against the French colonists. [2] Uniting the two rebel

---

MECHANICS

MECHANICS

ANSWERS
Exercise 4

1. deferred
2. deference
3. hoping
4. approval
5. discoverer
6. safety
7. preparing
8. obeying
9. spicier
10. propelling
11. desired
12. controlled
13. hopeless
14. greener
15. duly
16. running
17. singeing
18. remotest
19. nameless
20. reddest

groups, the man on the left below, General Pierre Dominique Toussaint L'Ouverture, conquerred the entire island and abolished slavery in 1802. [3] The next year, however, Toussaint was siezed by the French and deported to France, where he dyed a prisoner. [4] General Jean-Jacques Dessalines then declared the island independent and renamed it Haiti. [5] Declaring himself emperor, Dessalines ordered that this fortress, the Citadelle, and a series of smaller fortresses be built to prevent the Europeans from restablishing power on the island. [6] Dessalines' breif reign lasted only until 1806, when he was assassinated in an uprising believed to have been ploted by his cheif rival, General Henri Christophe, shown below on the right. [7] Christophe, unable to control the legislature, in 1807 set up a separate state in northern Haiti and had himself crowned Henri I, King of Haiti. [8] Convinced that imposing structures such as the Citadelle would boost his nation's stature, Christophe launched an extensive building program carried out by forced labor. [9] Hospitals and schools sprang up, and work on the Citadelle progressed steadyly, but eventualy the people rebeled. [10] In 1820, having sufferred a series of strokes, Christophe, the last of the revolution's three great generals, took his own life.

MECHANICS

MECHANICS

ANSWERS
Review A
1. mixed; rebelled
2. conquered
3. seized; died
4. C
5. reestablishing
6. brief; plotted; chief
7. C
8. carried
9. steadily; eventually; rebelled
10. suffered

VISUAL CONNECTIONS
Ideas for Writing. Using the library as a resource, students could research and write short biographies about any of the three generals who influenced the development of Haiti. Have students exchange rough drafts to proofread for any errors in spelling. Ask partners to cite the spelling rules that apply to errors they have discovered.

969

MEETING individual NEEDS

LEP/ESL

General Strategies. Some of your students might speak languages that have no plural forms. Others might speak languages that have very regular plurals. Remind students of the importance of the rules governing plurals in English.

A DIFFERENT APPROACH

Students might be wondering why there has been no attempt to make English spelling more consistent. Tell students that several campaigns have been mounted to simplify English spellings. One of the most famous proponents of a simplified spelling system was Bernard Shaw (1856–1950). He felt that time and effort were wasted in spelling and campaigned for a new alphabet. Challenge interested students to discover more about Shaw's ideas for reform. Students could then present their findings to the class.

---

970 *Spelling*

Forming the Plural of Nouns

31k. Remembering the following rules will help you spell the plural forms of nouns.

(1) For most nouns, add –s.

SINGULAR	artist	song	lake	flower	muscle	Wilson
PLURAL	artists	songs	lakes	flowers	muscles	Wilsons

(2) For nouns ending in s, x, z, ch, or sh, add –es.

SINGULAR	dress	box	waltz	birch	bush	Ruíz
PLURAL	dresses	boxes	waltzes	birches	bushes	Ruízes

(3) For nouns ending in y preceded by a vowel, add –s.

SINGULAR	monkey	journey	essay	decoy	alley	Friday
PLURAL	monkeys	journeys	essays	decoys	alleys	Fridays

(4) For nouns ending in y preceded by a consonant, change the y to i and add –es.

SINGULAR	fly	enemy	lady	trophy	ally	theory
PLURAL	flies	enemies	ladies	trophies	allies	theories

For most proper nouns, add –s.

EXAMPLES Brady—Bradys Mallory—Mallorys

(5) For some nouns ending in f or fe, add –s. For others, change the f or fe to v and add –es.

SINGULAR	roof	chief	carafe	knife	loaf	wharf
PLURAL	roofs	chiefs	carafes	knives	loaves	wharves

For proper nouns, add –s.

EXAMPLES Cardiff—Cardiffs Wolfe—Wolfes

NOTE: If you are not sure about how to spell the plural of a noun ending in f or fe, look in a dictionary.

(6) For nouns ending in o preceded by a vowel, add –s.

SINGULAR	radio	studio	cameo	stereo	igloo	Matsuo
PLURAL	radios	studios	cameos	stereos	igloos	Matsuos

31k

(7) For many nouns ending in _o_ preceded by a consonant, add _–es._

SINGULAR	tomato	potato	hero	veto	torpedo	echo
PLURAL	tomato**es**	potato**es**	hero**es**	veto**es**	torpedo**es**	echo**es**

For some common nouns, especially those referring to music, and for proper nouns, add _–s._

SINGULAR	burrito	silo	photo	piano	soprano	Navajo
PLURAL	burrito**s**	silo**s**	photo**s**	piano**s**	soprano**s**	Navajo**s**

NOTE: For some nouns ending in _o_ preceded by a consonant, you may add either _–s_ or _–es._

SINGULAR	motto	tornado	mosquito	zero	banjo
PLURAL	motto**s**	tornado**s**	mosquito**s**	zero**s**	banjo**s**
	or	*or*	*or*	*or*	*or*
	motto**es**	tornado**es**	mosquito**es**	zero**es**	banjo**es**

If you are in doubt about the plural form of a noun ending in _o,_ check the spelling in a dictionary.

(8) The plural of a few nouns is formed irregularly.

SINGULAR	mouse	woman	tooth	goose	foot	child
PLURAL	m**ice**	w**o**men	t**ee**th	g**ee**se	f**ee**t	child**ren**

(9) For most compound nouns, form the plural of only the last word of the compound.

SINGULAR	seatbelt	bookshelf	two-year-old	baby sitter
PLURAL	seatbelt**s**	bookshel**ves**	two-year-old**s**	baby sitter**s**

(10) For compound nouns in which one of the words is modified by the other word or words, form the plural of the word modified.

SINGULAR	sister-in-law	runner-up	passer-by	senior citizen
PLURAL	sister**s**-in-law	runner**s**-up	passer**s**-by	senior citizen**s**

NOTE: Some compound nouns have two acceptable plural forms.

SINGULAR	attorney general	court-martial	notary public
PLURAL	attorney general**s**	court-martial**s**	notary public**s**
	or	*or*	*or*
	attorney**s** general	court**s**-martial	notar**ies** public

Check an up-to-date dictionary whenever you are in doubt about the plural form of a compound noun.

INTEGRATING THE LANGUAGE ARTS

Mechanics and Dictionary Skills. Have students look up the etymologies of the words *alumnus, vertebra, parenthesis,* and *datum.* [Three of these words have Latin origins and one of the words, *parenthesis,* entered English from Greek via Latin.] Students might also be interested in finding the etymologies of some other groups of words in order to detect any patterns. For example, students might research the etymologies of several nouns that form their plurals in irregular ways—such as *child, ox, woman, tooth, mouse,* and *foot*—to discover whether any of these words have similar origins.

(11) For a few nouns, the singular and the plural forms are the same.

SINGULAR AND PLURAL   sheep   deer   species   trout
   moose   aircraft   Chinese   Sioux

(12) For some nouns borrowed from other languages, the plural is formed as in the original language.

SINGULAR	alumnus [male]	alumna [female]	phenomenon
PLURAL	alumni [male]	alumnae [female]	phenomena

A few nouns borrowed from other languages have two acceptable plural forms. For each of the following nouns, the plural form preferred in English is given first.

SINGULAR	index	appendix	formula	cactus
PLURAL	indexes	appendixes	formulas	cactuses
	or	*or*	*or*	*or*
	indices	appendices	formulae	cacti

NOTE: Whenever you are in doubt about which spelling to use, remember that a dictionary lists the preferred spelling first.

(13) To form the plural of numerals, most uppercase letters, symbols, and most words referred to as words, add an –s or both an apostrophe and an –s.

SINGULAR	5	1990	B	+	and
PLURAL	5s	1990s	Bs	+s	ands
	or	*or*	*or*	*or*	*or*
	5's	1990's	B's	+'s	and's

To prevent confusion, add both an apostrophe and an –s to form the plural of all lowercase letters, certain uppercase letters, and some words referred to as words.

EXAMPLES   The word *Philippines* contains three *p*'s and three *i*'s. [Both letters are lowercase.]
Most of her grades are ***A***'s. [Without an apostrophe the plural of *A* could be confused with the word *As*.]
In the last paragraph of your story, I can't tell which women the ***her***'s refer to. [Without an apostrophe the plural of the word *her* could be confused with the word *hers*.]

👉 **REFERENCE NOTE:** For more information about forming these kinds of plurals, see page 951.

OBJECTIVE

• To explain the spellings of words

EXERCISE 5 — Spelling the Plural Forms of Nouns

Spell the plural form of each of the following nouns.

1. candy   **1.** candies
2. sheep   **2.** sheep
3. hairdo**s**
4. turkey**s**
5. medium
6. video**s**
7. torch**es**

8. belief**s**
9. embargo**es**
10. gas**es**
11. fly   **11.** flies
12. alto**s**
13. poncho**s**
14. shelf   **14.** shelves

15. radish**es**
16. editor**s** in chief
17. spoonful**s**
18. twelfth-grader**s**
19. Gomez**es**
20. goose   **20.** geese

5. media *or* mediums

REVIEW B — Explaining the Spellings of Words

By referring to the rules on the preceding pages, explain the spelling of each of the following words.

1. misstate
2. stubbornness
3. peaceable

4. ladies
5. alumnae
6. leisure

7. occurred
8. writing

9. roofs
10. weigh

Writing Numbers

31l. Spell out a *cardinal number*—a number that states how many—that can be expressed in one or two words. Otherwise, use numerals.

EXAMPLES   **thirteen** seniors   **forty-four** days   **one thousand** books
            346 seniors   **365** days   **1,345** books

Do not spell out some numbers and use numerals for others in the same context. If numerals are required for any of the numbers, use numerals for all of the numbers.

INCONSISTENT   The Congress of the United States is composed of one hundred senators and 435 representatives.
CONSISTENT   The Congress of the United States is composed of **100** senators and **435** representatives.

However, to distinguish between numbers appearing beside each other, spell out one number and use numerals for the other.

EXAMPLE   We bought **seven 15**-pound sacks.

ANSWERS

Review B

1. *misstate:* **Rule 31d.** When adding a prefix, do not change the spelling of the original word.

2. *stubbornness:* **Rule 31e.** When adding the suffix *–ness* or *–ly,* do not change the spelling of the original word.

3. *peaceable:* exception to **Rule 31f.** Keep the final silent *–e* in a word ending in *–ce* or *–ge* before a suffix beginning with *a* or *o.*

4. *ladies:* **Rule 31k(4).** For nouns ending in *–y* preceded by a consonant, change the *–y* to *–i* and add *–es.*

5. *alumnae:* **Rule 31k(12).** For some nouns borrowed from other languages, the plural is formed as in the original languages.

6. *leisure:* exception to **Rule 31a.** Write *ie* when the sound is long *e,* except after *c.*

7. *occurred:* **Rule 31j.** Double the final consonant before adding a suffix that begins with a vowel if the word (1) has only one syllable or has the accent on the final syllable and (2) ends in a single consonant preceded by a single vowel.

8. *writing:* **Rule 31f.** Drop the silent *–e* before a suffix beginning with a vowel.

9. *roofs:* **Rule 31k(5).** For some nouns ending in *f* or *fe,* add *–s.*

10. *weigh:* **Rule 31b.** Write *ei* when the sound is not long *e,* especially when the sound is *a.*

CRITICAL THINKING

Synthesis and Evaluation. Ask each student to choose five of the rules in the chapter and to write an expressive/narrative paragraph using five words that exemplify those rules but that are intentionally misspelled. (You may wish to substitute series of sentences for paragraphs if time is limited.)

Have students trade papers to underline each word that is misspelled in their partners' paragraphs. Then, they should give the number of the rule that applies to the word and correct the spelling in their partners' papers.

974

31m. Spell out a number that begins a sentence.

EXAMPLE   **Four hundred twenty-one** students participated in the contest.

If a number appears awkward when spelled out, revise the sentence so that it does not begin with the number.

AWKWARD   Two hundred twenty-three thousand six hundred thirty-one votes were cast in the election.
IMPROVED   In the election, **223,631** votes were cast.

31n. Spell out an *ordinal number*—a number that expresses order.

EXAMPLES   Junko Tabei, the **first** [not *1st*] woman who climbed Mount Everest, was born in Japan in 1939.
Of the fifty states, Tennessee ranks **thirty-fourth** [not *34th*] in total land area.

31o. Use numerals to express numbers in conventional situations.

TYPE OF NUMBER	EXAMPLES		
Identification Numbers	Room 12 Channel 4	pages 246–315 State Road 541	Model 19-A lines 3–19
Measurements/ Statistics	72 degrees 14 percent	$6\frac{1}{2}$ yards 84 years old	32.7 ounces ratio of 6 to 1
Dates	July 4, 1776	1200 B.C.	A.D. 2000
Addresses	345 Lexington Drive Tampa, FL 33628-4533		
Times of Day	8:20 P.M. (*or* p.m.)		7:35 A.M. (*or* a.m.)

NOTE: Spell out a number used with *o'clock.*

EXAMPLE   **ten** o'clock

REVIEW C

OBJECTIVE

- To proofread a paragraph to correct misspelled words

EXERCISE 6 Using Numbers in Sentences

Each of the following sentences contains at least one error in the use of numbers. Revise each sentence.

1. When you go to Washington, D.C., visit the Frederick Douglass National Historic Site, which is located at ~~One Thousand Four Hundred Eleven~~ W Street, SE. **1. 1411**
2. Since he was 15, my brother's 1st choice as a college major has been computer science, and his second choice has been mathematics. **2. fifteen/first**
3. 590 people attended the play on opening night, September fourth, setting an attendance record for the community theater. **3. Five hundred ninety/4**
4. Did you realize that ninety-seven percent of the earth's water supply is salt water? **4. 97**
5. According to the chart on page three, only fifty-one of the company's 360 products are sold in this region. **5. 3/51**

REVIEW C Proofreading a Paragraph to Correct Misspelled Words

Proofread the following paragraph, correcting any misspelled words. If all the words in a sentence are spelled correctly, write *C*.

EXAMPLE [1] Did you see the Channel Seven report on the new system for assigning areas code?

1. *7; area codes*

[1] As the map on the next page shows, some area codes in the United States have zeros, ones, or twos as the middle digit; this 2nd digit signals the computerized telephone switching equipment that the call is long distance. [2] When large citys such as Los Angeles use up the supply of potential numbers within a code, the city is simply divided into two parts, and each part is assigned a new code. [3] By August 1991, however, only three area codes were still unassigned, not nearly enough to meet the growing demand for numbers for cellular phones, fax machines, pocket pagers, and computer modems. [4] Yet those 3 codes had to handle all of the load until July 1995, because it took until then for all of the nation's telephone switchs to be reprogrammed for a new system devised by

1. second

2. cities

3. C

4. three/switches

VISUAL CONNECTIONS

Ideas for Writing. Have students research and write brief reports on the ways in which local telephone service has changed over the last fifty years. Ask students to interview older relatives and neighbors who can offer information and personal opinions about these innovations. Students might share their findings with the class.

5. twenty-three/640/6 billion

6. C

Bellcore, the telephone industry research organization. [5] Already in effect in 23 area codes, the new system adds six hundred forty codes to the previous supply of 152 and increases the number of potential phone numbers to approximately 6,000,000,000. [6] In many areas, however, the Bellcore

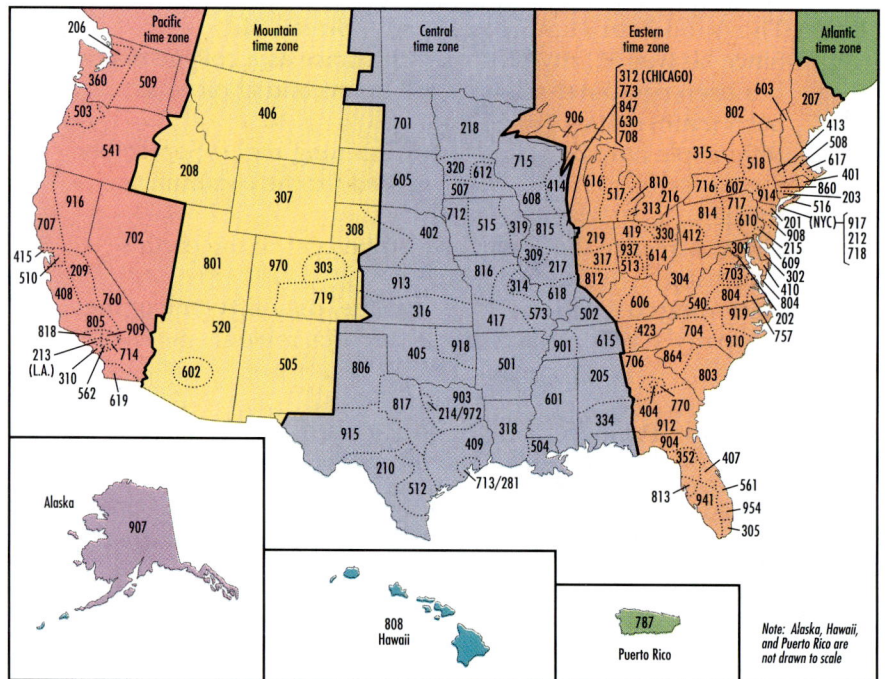

Reference provided by CCMI, Rockville, MD

7. executives/ their/ companies

8. leading

9. four

10. determined/utilities/changes

system may require callers to dial the area code on all long-distance calls, even those to numbers within their own area code. [7] Some telephone company executivs object to the new system, saying that it creates problems not only for thier companys but also for other businesses. [8] The president of one telephone company even characterized Bellcore's plan as leadding telephone users "like lambs to the slaughter." [9] He proposed a system of 4-digit area codes, which would increase the potential number of codes tenfold but would require assigning every telephone customer a new number. [10] In the end, decisions regarding area codes are determinned by the state agencies that regulate public utilitys, for Bellcore can only recommend changs, not enforce them.

→ WORDS OFTEN CONFUSED

OBJECTIVE

- To distinguish between words whose spellings or meanings are often confused

Words Often Confused

all ready	*all prepared* Give the signal when you are *all ready*.
already	*previously* I had *already* read several articles about the customs of the Micmac people of Canada.
all right	[Although the spelling *alright* appears in some dictionaries, it has not become standard usage.]
all together	*everyone in the same place* We were *all together* for the holidays.
altogether	*entirely* Her reaction was *altogether* different from what I had expected.
altar	[noun] *a table or stand at which religious rites are performed* The priest was standing beside the *altar*.
alter	[verb] *to change* If we are late, we will *alter* our plans.
born	*given birth* Where was Zora Neale Hurston *born*?
borne	*carried; endured* The people there have *borne* their hardships bravely.
brake	[verb] *to slow down or stop;* [noun] *a device for slowing down or stopping* *Brake* cautiously on wet roads. A defective *brake* caused the accident.
break	[verb] *to cause to come apart; to shatter;* [noun] *a fracture* Try not to *break* any dishes. The X-ray shows a *break* in your left fibula.

MECHANICS

PROGRAM MANAGER

WORDS OFTEN CONFUSED

- **Independent Practice/Reteaching** For instruction and exercises, see **Words Often Confused A** and **Words Often Confused B** in *Language Skills Practice and Assessment,* pp. 250–251.

- **Computer Guided Instruction** For additional instruction and practice with words often confused, see **Lesson 58** in *Language Workshop CD-ROM.*

✓ QUICK REMINDER

Give students the following dictation to evaluate their ability to distinguish between words that are often confused:

Counselors advise that correct spelling is important. You may fear that it's already too late, that your skills are too weak to be improved. But if you're willing to learn a few basic principles, you can break the failure pattern and you can effect quite a change in your life. The compliments you receive will lift your morale, and success often leads to more success.

MECHANICS

MEETING *individual* NEEDS

LEP/ESL

General Strategies. If available, software that teaches spelling can be very helpful for students. Pair English-language learners with English-proficient speakers so that the English-proficient speakers can model pronunciation, an integral part of spelling ability.

TECHNOLOGY TIP

Remind students that spell-checking features in word-processing programs cannot distinguish between homonyms and cannot identify words that have been confused with other words. For example, a spell-checker will not indicate when *affect* has been confused with *effect,* since *affect* is a correctly spelled word in other contexts. Although they are helpful, spell-checkers do not eliminate the need to learn spelling skills and to proofread carefully.

capital	[spelling used in all cases except when referring to a building in which a legislature meets]
	Washington, D.C., is the *capital* of the United States. [*city*]
	Do they have enough *capital* to start their business? [*wealth*]
	In most states, murder is a *capital* offense. [*punishable by death*]
	That is a *capital* idea. [*of major importance*]
capitol	*a building in which a legislature meets* [capitalized when it refers to a building for a national legislature]
	The *capitol* faces a park.
	On our visit to Washington, D.C., we toured the *Capitol.*
clothes	*wearing apparel*
	Should these *clothes* be dry-cleaned?
cloths	*pieces of fabric*
	Use these *cloths* to dust the furniture.

EXERCISE 7   **Distinguishing Between Words Often Confused**

From the choices in parentheses, select the <u>correct word or words</u> for each of the following sentences.

1. Mother was (*all together,* <u>*altogether*</u>) too surprised to protest.
2. We have (*born,* <u>*borne*</u>) more than our share of the burden.
3. What was the Supreme Court decision on (<u>*capital*</u>, *capitol*) punishment?
4. When you are (*already,* <u>*all ready*</u>), I will help you.
5. We polished the car with (<u>*cloths*</u>, *clothes*).
6. They will (*altar,* <u>*alter*</u>) the building to suit tenants.
7. The dome on the (*capital,* <u>*capitol*</u>) is illuminated at night.
8. The club members were (<u>*all together*</u>, *altogether*) only once.
9. If you (*brake,* <u>*break*</u>) a window, you will pay for it.
10. Are the sandwiches (<u>*already*</u>, *all ready*) prepared, or do we need to make them?

coarse	[adjective] *rough; crude* This fabric is as *coarse* as burlap.
course	[noun] *path of action; part of a meal; series of studies* [also used after *of* to mean *naturally* or *certainly*] What *course* should I follow to find a job overseas? Soup was the first *course*. I am taking a *course* in creative writing. Of *course* I'll help you set the table.

complement	[noun] *something that makes whole or complete;* [verb] *to make whole or complete* The *complement* of a 50° angle is a 40° angle. [The two angles complete a 90° angle.] Their part of this job *complements* mine. [Together the parts complete the job.]
compliment	[noun] *praise; a courteous act or expression;* [verb] *to express praise or respect* Thank you for the *compliment*. The tennis coach *complimented* me on my backhand.

consul	[noun] *a person appointed by a government to serve its citizens in a foreign country* The American *consul* in Quito helped us during our visit.
council, **councilor**	[noun] *a group called together to accomplish a job* [noun] *a member of a council* The *council* met to vote on the proposal. Did each *councilor* vote in favor of the proposal?
counsel, **counselor**	[noun] *advice;* [verb] *to advise* [noun] *one who gives advice* I accepted the wise *counsel* of Ms. Ariyoshi. Ms. Ariyoshi had *counseled* me to take Algebra II. Ms. Ariyoshi is my guidance *counselor*.

MECHANICS

MEETING *individual* NEEDS

ADVANCED STUDENTS

Many of the word groups that are often confused have similar etymologies or origins. *Counsel* and *council,* for example, both come from the Latin word *concilium,* meaning "group of people" or "meeting."

Have students use dictionaries to discover which of the pairs or groups of often-confused words have similar etymologies. Afterward, ask students to present their findings to the class.

MECHANICS

COMMON ERROR

Problem. *Its* and *it's* continue to confuse many students and often appear on lists of commonly misspelled words.

Solution. This confusion can be avoided if you encourage students to substitute *it is* for *it's* to see if *it is* sounds right. Remind students that an apostrophe is not needed when they are using *its* to indicate possession.

980 *Spelling*

des′ert	[noun] *a dry region* The Sahara is the world's largest *desert*.
desert′	[verb] *to leave or abandon* She would never *desert* her friends in their time of need.
dessert′	[noun] *the final course of a meal* For *dessert* we had strawberry yogurt.
formally	*in a proper or dignified manner, according to strict rules* The Nobel prizes are *formally* presented on December 10.
formerly	*previously; in the past* Katherine Davalos Ortega was *formerly* the treasurer of the United States.
its	[possessive form of *it*] The community is proud of *its* school system.
it's	[contraction of *it is* or *it has*] *It's* a symbol of peace. *It's* been a long time since your last visit.
later	[adjective; adverb] *more late* We will send the package at a *later* time. I will help you *later*.
latter	[adjective] *the second of two* (as opposed to *former*) When given the choice of a volleyball or a tennis racket, I chose the *latter*.
lead	[verb, pronounced "leed"] *to go first; to guide* Who will *lead* the parade?
led	[verb, past tense of *lead*] She *led* the team to victory.
lead	[noun, pronounced "led"] *a heavy metal; graphite in a pencil* The magician truly believed that he could transform *lead* into gold. I bought new *leads* for my mechanical pencil.

▶ EXERCISE 8   **Distinguishing Between Words Often Confused**

From the choices in parentheses, select the <u>correct word</u> for each of the following sentences.

1. These supplies will (*complement*, *compliment*) those that you already have.
2. What did you order for (*dessert*, *desert*)?
3. Why does he use such (*course*, *coarse*) language?
4. I do not enjoy parties conducted as (*formally*, *formerly*) as this one.
5. We are not sure which (*course*, *coarse*) to follow.
6. Are you sure (*its*, *it's*) not too late?
7. I worked last summer as a camp (*councilor*, *counselor*).
8. He spoke to both the mayor and the superintendent, and the (*later*, *latter*) was more helpful.
9. Last season, Albert (*lead*, *led*) the team to a championship.
10. Our (*consul*, *counsel*) in China has returned to Washington.

loose	[adjective, pronounced "loos"] *free; not close together; not firmly fastened* The *loose* chickens roamed the barnyard. They stumbled in the *loose* sand. Some of the shingles on the roof are *loose*.
lose	[verb, pronounced "looz"] *to suffer loss of* When did you *lose* your books?
miner	[noun] *a worker in a mine* Her father is a coal *miner*.
minor	[noun; adjective] *a person under legal age;* [adjective] *less important* A *minor* cannot marry without a parent's or guardian's consent. They raised only *minor* objections.
moral	[adjective] *good; virtuous;* [noun] *a lesson of conduct* His conduct showed him to be a *moral* person. The class understood the *moral* of the story.
morale	[noun] *spirit; mental condition* The victory boosted the team's *morale*.

TECHNOLOGY TIP

You may want to mention that some word-processing programs have rhyming dictionaries. Students who are interested in writing poetry or song lyrics might find rhyming dictionaries useful for locating words that rhyme and for learning how to spell these words. Students can indicate the words for which they need rhymes, determine how many syllables they wish to rhyme, and let the computer suggest possible words.

MECHANICS

MECHANICS

MEETING *individual* NEEDS

LEARNING STYLES

Kinetic and Visual Learners. Have each student choose a group of often-confused words to illustrate on poster board. For example, a student might illustrate *peace* and *piece* by drawing a large *peace* symbol and a *piece* of pie.

passed	[verb, past tense of *pass*] *went beyond* The red car *passed* me at the finish line.
past	[noun] *time gone by;* [adjective] *of a former time;* [preposition] *beyond* To understand the present, you need to study the *past*. For some people, *past* events are much more interesting than present ones. After you drive *past* the shopping mall, turn right at the first traffic light.
peace	*calmness* (as opposed to *war* or *strife*) Doesn't everyone prefer *peace* to war?
piece	*a part of something* I fed the dog a boneless *piece* of turkey as a special treat.
personal	[adjective] *individual; private* The celebrity declined to answer any *personal* questions.
personnel	[noun] *a group of people employed in the same work or service* The *personnel* of the company ranged in age from sixteen to sixty-four.
plain	[adjective] *not fancy; clear;* [noun] *an area of flat land* The tourist cabin was small and *plain* but quite comfortable. Our problem is *plain* to see. The *plain* stretched before them for miles.
plane	[noun] *a flat surface; a tool; an airplane* Geometry is the study of imaginary flat surfaces, or *planes*. The carpenter used a *plane* to smooth the edge of the board. Waiting for the fog to lift, the *plane* circled the airport for an hour.

principal	[noun] *the head of a school;* [adjective] *main or most important*
	Jorge's mom, Mrs. Pacheco, is the assistant *principal* at our school.
	The *principal* cause of accidents is carelessness.
principle	[noun] *a rule of conduct; a fact or a general truth*
	The plaintiff accused the defendant of having no *principles*.
	We have been studying many of the *principles* of aerodynamics.
quiet	[adjective] *still; silent*
	The library is usually *quiet*, but it wasn't today.
quite	[adverb] *completely; rather; very*
	I had *quite* forgotten her advice.
	Angela's report on the lifestyle of the Amish was *quite* interesting.

EXERCISE 9 **Distinguishing Between Words Often Confused**

From the choices in parentheses, select the correct word for each of the following sentences.

1. All three nations signed a (*peace*, *piece*) treaty.
2. Do these printed instructions seem (*plain*, *plane*) to you?
3. This store's sales (*personal*, *personnel*) are very helpful.
4. The (*principal*, *principle*) of solar energy is not too difficult to understand.
5. If you (*loose*, *lose*) your concentration, you might (*loose*, *lose*) the tennis match.
6. What are the four (*principal*, *principle*) parts of the verb "to shrink"?
7. Mrs. Wilson insists that students remain absolutely (*quiet*, *quite*) during study period.
8. Does every fable have a (*moral*, *morale*)?
9. On my way to school every day, I always walk (*passed*, *past*) the bakery.
10. Now that he is officially no longer a (*miner*, *minor*), he can vote in the upcoming election.

COOPERATIVE LEARNING
All of the often-confused words on this page are homophones—they sound alike but have different spellings and meanings. Have students work in groups of three or four to generate as many homophones as possible in a given period of time. Then, have groups compare lists and delete any homophones that two or more groups have in common. The group with the greatest number of homophones remaining wins.

984 *Spelling*

stationary	[adjective] *in a fixed position* The rabbit remained *stationary* as the hawk circled above.
stationery	[noun] *writing paper* I received a box of *stationery* at Christmas.
than	[conjunction, used for comparisons] Jupiter is larger *than* any other planet.
then	[adverb] *at that time; next* First, make an outline; *then* write the composition according to the outline.
their	[possessive form of *they*] The performers made *their* own costumes.
there	[adverb] *at that place;* [expletive, used to begin a sentence—see page 636] We were *there* at two o'clock. *There* were four of us in the final round of competition.
they're	[contraction of *they are*] *They're* going with us to the jazz festival.
to	[preposition; part of the infinitive form of a verb] Are you going *to* Puerto Rico this summer? My father showed me how *to* prepare sushi.
too	[adverb] *also; more than enough* Lamont is a senior, *too*. It is *too* late to go now.
two	[adjective] *totaling one plus one;* [noun] *the number between one and three* We had only *two* dollars. *Two* of my favorite singers are Linda Ronstadt and Tracy Chapman.
waist	[noun] *the midsection of the body* She wore a colorful obi around her *waist*.
waste	[noun] *unused material;* [verb] *to squander* Pollution can be caused by industrial *wastes*. Don't *waste* your time.

OBJECTIVES

- To distinguish between words whose spellings or meanings are often confused
- To proofread paragraphs to correct misspelled words

who's	[contraction of *who is* or *who has*]
	Who's in charge of the recycling program?
	Who's been using my computer?
whose	[possessive form of *who*]
	Whose castanets are these?
your	[possessive form of *you*]
	Is this *your* car?
you're	[contraction of *you are*]
	You're a true friend.

EXERCISE 10   Distinguishing Between Words Often Confused

From the choices in parentheses, select the <u>correct word</u> for each of the following sentences.

1. They had neglected to close (*there, their*) lockers.
2. I wanted to go to camp, (*to, two, too*).
3. Tie the rope around your (*waist, waste*).
4. The platform, we discovered when we tried to move it, was (*stationary, stationery*).
5. No one could remember (*whose, who's*) name had been drawn first.
6. As soon as (*their, they're*) printed, we will ship the books.
7. Write your letters on business (*stationary, stationery*).
8. (*Your, You're*) lucky to have such a good job.
9. I cannot do any more (*then, than*) I have done.
10. I was surprised at (*you're, your*) taking that attitude.

REVIEW D   Distinguishing Between Words Often Confused

From the choices in parentheses, select the <u>correct word or words</u> for each of the following sentences.

1. Columbia is the (*capital, capitol*) of South Carolina.
2. Have you discussed this problem with your guidance (*councilor, counselor*)?
3. The vegetation in the (*dessert, desert*) surprised us.
4. My companion (*lead, led*) me down a dark passage.

◆ INTEGRATING THE LANGUAGE ARTS

Literature Link. If possible, have volunteers read aloud different stanzas of Lewis Carroll's poem "Jabberwocky." Note that in creating original words, Carroll followed the logic of the English language. For example, *brillig* and *slithy* are portmanteaus—blends of two words. *Brillig* combines *brilliant* and *light*. *Slithy* is a blend of *slimy* and *slither*. Carroll also followed this logic in other word formations. Note that *toves* is a plural noun. Ask volunteers to apply spelling rules to other original words in the poem. For example, ask "How would you spell the present participle of the verb *gimble* [gimbling] . . . the comparative form of the adjective *mimsy* [mimsier] . . . the plural of *bandersnatch* [bandersnatches]?"

MECHANICS

MECHANICS

INTEGRATING THE LANGUAGE ARTS

Literature Link. If possible, play for the class all or selected scenes from a professional recording of Bernard Shaw's satire *Pygmalion.* You also could use the film version starring Wendy Hiller and Leslie Howard. Include Act I, the first part of Act II (in which Eliza visits Higgins at home), and Act III (the garden party). Discuss with the class Shaw's notion of the link between proper diction and success. Have the class discuss the relationships between speaking (pronunciation) and writing skills (spelling).

You could also bring a copy of *Pygmalion* to class. Note that Shaw insisted his plays be printed according to his own views on simplifying spelling. Help the students find examples such as his refusal to use apostrophes in contractions and dropping the silent *e* from *Shakespeare* (near the end of Act III). You might also note his use of phonetic spelling to convey accents (Act I). Have students discuss whether Eliza's pronunciation might have had any effect on the spelling skills she exhibits.

5. We were (<u>all ready</u>, *already*) to start before dawn.
6. Try not to (<u>lose</u>, *loose*) your keys.
7. Each success helps to build (*moral*, <u>morale</u>).
8. Members of the (*counsel*, <u>council</u>) are elected annually.
9. My red tie (<u>complements</u>, *compliments*) my blue suit.
10. The mission was accomplished without loss of (*personal*, <u>personnel</u>).

▶ **REVIEW E**

Proofreading Paragraphs to Correct Misspelled Words

Proofread the following paragraphs, correcting any misspelled words. If all the words in a sentence are spelled correctly, write *C.*

EXAMPLE　[1] **We spent this passed weekend in San Francisco.**
　　　　　　1. *past*

1. their

2. course/ all together

3. its

4. it's

5. believed

6. altar

7. to/later

8. two/ quiet

9. there

10. It's/ quite/ too/ their

[1] Many of the more than 100,000 Hispanics who live in San Francisco make they're homes in the Mission District. [2] They come from many different countries, of coarse, but altogether they've created one of San Francisco's most inviting areas. [3] Comprising twenty square blocks on the city's south side, the District takes it's name from the mission founded in 1771 by Franciscan missionary Junípero Serra.

[4] The whitewashed adobe mission is formerly named Mission San Francisco de Asís, but its popularly known as Mission Dolores after the name of a nearby stream. [5] One of the few structures that survived the devastating earthquake of 1906, it's beleived to be the oldest intact building in the city. [6] Its gilded alter was among the most ornate in the twenty-one Spanish missions Fray Junípero founded in what is now California. [7] The basilica, the grander church next door too the original mission, was demolished in the 1906 earthquake but was latter rebuilt. [8] Nestled between the to buildings, a small park invites visitors to spend a quite moment resting before exploring further.

[9] Even the most unobservant visitor can't fail to notice the striking outdoor murals, like the one on the left on the next page, which brighten walls throughout the neighborhood; all together, their are forty-five of these murals. [10] Its not surprising that quiet a few well-known Hispanic artists, including Amalia Mesa-Bains, Enrique Chagoya, and to many others to list here, launched they're careers there.

MECHANICS

300 Spelling Words

The following list contains three hundred words that are commonly misspelled. The words are grouped so that you can study them ten at a time.

abundant	allegiance	biscuit
academically	alliance	blasphemy
accelerator	allotting	boulevard
accessible	annihilate	buffet
accidentally	anonymous	bureaucrat
acclimated	apologetically	burial
accommodation	apparatus	business
accompaniment	apparent	calculation
accomplishment	arrangement	camouflage
accuracy	atheistic	capable
acknowledge	atmosphere	capitalism
acquaintance	attendance	carburetor
adequately	awfully	caricature
admission	background	catastrophe
admittance	ballet	cellar
adolescence	bankruptcy	cemetery
advantageous	barbarian	changeable
advertisement	beggar	chassis
aerial	beneficial	Christianity
allege	bibliography	circumstantial

VISUAL CONNECTIONS
Related Expression Skills.
Ask students to create murals depicting important locations in their communities. After dividing the class into small groups, provide each group with a roll of drawing paper and colored markers. Ask students to write captions that are spelled correctly. You could display the projects in the classroom, lunchroom, or hallway.

MEETING *individual* NEEDS

ADVANCED STUDENTS

Some students will not have any problems with spelling the words in the **300 Spelling Words** list. Allow such students to generate original lists of words, encountered in outside reading or in other classes, that have proved troublesome. You may group students to compare lists and suggest strategies for mastering these words.

LEARNING STYLES

Visual and Kinetic Learners. Have students create a large chart for each group of ten spelling words. You could have students work in groups to develop a collaborative chart or assign the creation of one chart to each student. As you assign each group of words to be studied, hang the corresponding chart at the front of the classroom.

987

A DIFFERENT APPROACH

Challenge each student to write a paragraph that includes one of the groups of ten words from the **300 Spelling Words** list. Encourage humorous narratives when appropriate. Ask several volunteers to read their paragraphs to the class.

MECHANICS

MECHANICS

colossal	enthusiastically	innocent
commercial	entrance	institution
communist	environment	intellectual
competition	especially	interference
complexion	espionage	irrelevant
conceivable	exercise	irresistible
connoisseur	exhaustion	irritating
conscientious	exhibition	kerosene
consciousness	expensive	laborious
consistency	familiarize	larynx
controlling	fascination	license
controversy	fascism	liquor
courtesy	feminine	livelihood
cruelty	financier	luxurious
curriculum	fission	magistrate
deceitful	forfeit	magnificence
decision	fulfill	maintenance
definitely	fundamentally	malicious
descendant	galaxy	manageable
desirable	gauge	maneuver
despair	government	marriageable
desperately	grammatically	martyrdom
detrimental	guaranteed	materialism
devastation	guidance	meadow
devise	harassment	mediocre
dilemma	hereditary	melancholy
diligence	hindrance	melodious
disagreement	horizontal	metaphor
disastrous	hygiene	miniature
disciple	hypocrisy	mischievous
discrimination	ideally	misspelled
dissatisfied	immediate	mortgage
ecstasy	incidentally	mosquito
efficiency	independent	municipal
embarrassment	indispensable	mysterious
emperor	inevitable	naive
emphasize	inexperienced	necessary
endeavor	influential	neurotic
enormous	ingenious	noticeable
entertainment	initiative	nucleus

nuisance
nutritious
obedience
occasionally
occurrence
omitting
opportunity
orchestra
outrageous
pageant

pamphlet
paralysis
parliament
pastime
peasant
pedestal
penicillin
perceive
permanent
permissible

persistent
perspiration
petition
phenomenon
physician
picnicking
playwright
pneumonia
politician
precede

presence
prestige
presumption
prevalent
privilege
probably
procedure
propaganda
prophesy
psychoanalysis

pursue
quietly
rebellion
receive
recommendation
recruit
reference
referred
refrigerator
rehearsal

relieve
reminiscent
representative
responsibility
restaurant
safety
seize
separation
sergeant
siege

significance
souvenir
specimen
sponsor
statistics
straight
strategic
stubbornness
succeed
succession

summed
superintendent
supersede
suppress
surprise
surroundings
susceptible
symbolic
symmetrical
synonymous

tariff
temperament
temperature
tendency
theoretical
tolerance
tomorrow
tortoise
traffic
tragedy

transcend
transparent
tried
twelfth
tyranny
undoubtedly
universal
unmistakable
unnatural
unnecessary

unscrupulous
vaccine
vacuum
variation
vaudeville
vegetable
vehicle
vengeance
versatile
vigilance

villain
vinegar
visage
welcome
whisper
whistle
withhold
yacht
yawn
yield

MECHANICS

MECHANICS

PROGRAM MANAGER

FOR THE WHOLE CHAPTER

- **Computer Guided Instruction** For additional instruction and practice with concepts often used as indicators of verbal skills on standardized tests, see the **Core Lessons** in *Language Workshop CD-ROM.*

- **Practice** To help less-advanced students who need additional practice with concepts and activities related to this chapter, see specific relevant topics in *English Workshop, Complete Course.*

- **Assessment/Practice** To help students practice marking standardized test answers and as an answer sheet for the **Grammar and Usage Tests** on pp. 1006–1009 and the **Mechanics Tests** on pp. 1016–1019, see the **Standardized Test Answer Sheet** in *Language Skills Practice and Assessment,* p. 271.

CHAPTER OVERVIEW

This chapter provides review of some aspects of grammar, usage, and mechanics that cause students difficulty. You may find the exercises in this chapter useful as diagnostic tests, judging by student scores which topics need greatest attention; you could use them as a resource for reteaching, providing extra practice for concepts you feel need extra emphasis; you could use them as a review of key concepts to help students prepare for standardized tests of language skills mastery; or you could use them in any combination of these ways.

32 CORRECTING COMMON ERRORS

Key Language Skills Review

This chapter reviews key skills and concepts that pose special problems for writers.

- Sentence Fragments and Run-on Sentences
- Subject-Verb and Pronoun-Antecedent Agreement
- Clear Pronoun Reference
- Verb Forms
- Comparison of Modifiers
- Misplaced and Dangling Modifiers
- Capitalization
- Punctuation—Commas, Semicolons, Colons, Quotation Marks, and Apostrophes
- Spelling
- Standard Usage

Most of the exercises in this chapter follow the same format as the exercises found throughout the grammar, usage, and mechanics sections. You will notice, however, that two sets of review exercises are presented in standardized test formats. These exercises are designed to provide you with practice not only in solving usage and mechanics problems but also in dealing with these kinds of problems on such tests.

EXERCISE 1
OBJECTIVE
- To identify and revise sentence fragments and run-on sentences

EXERCISE 2
OBJECTIVE
- To revise a paragraph to correct sentence fragments and run-on sentences

Grammar and Usage **991**

EXERCISE 1 — Identifying and Correcting Sentence Fragments and Run-on Sentences

Each numbered item below is a sentence fragment, a run-on sentence, or a complete sentence. First, identify each by writing *F* for a fragment, *R* for a run-on, or *S* for a complete sentence. Then, rewrite each fragment or run-on to make a complete sentence.

EXAMPLE
  1. Rice and potatoes, two food staples of the world.
  1. *F—Rice and potatoes are two food staples of the world.*

1. Enjoying a bounty harvested from the apple orchards on the coast near here.
2. Tame canaries are generally yellow, they may be bright orange if red peppers are part of their diet.
3. One of the fastest runners and usually the winner in races.
4. Because the fertile land in the river valley had never been farmed before.
5. To go home was all Dorothy wanted.
6. The huge gears had long ago become rusty, they groaned as the blades of the windmill turned.
7. After twenty years, he no longer recognized the prince.
8. An old oak grew there, it had survived being struck by lightning.
9. The Black Hills are in southwest South Dakota, southeast of the Black Hills are the Badlands.
10. Calamity Jane, born in 1852 near Princeton, Missouri, about whom many wild stories are told.

EXERCISE 2 — Revising Sentence Fragments and Run-on Sentences in a Paragraph

The paragraph below contains complete sentences, sentence fragments, and run-on sentences. Rewrite the paragraph to correct each fragment and run-on.

EXAMPLE
  [1] Sculptors in Benin create extremely detailed statues, they use the lost-wax process of bronze casting to do so.
  1. Using the lost-wax process of bronze casting, sculptors in Benin create extremely detailed statues.

[1] To begin the process, a core figure is formed from loamy soil and water, after drying, the figure is coated with beeswax.

ANSWERS
Exercise 1
Answers will vary.

1. F—We enjoy a bounty harvested from the apple orchards on the coast near here.
2. R—Tame canaries are generally yellow, but they may be bright orange if red peppers are part of their diet.
3. F—Noelle is one of the fastest runners and usually the winner in races.
4. F—The fertile land in the river valley had never been farmed before.
5. S
6. R—The huge gears had long ago become rusty, and they groaned as the blades of the windmill turned.
7. S
8. R—An old oak grew there; it had survived being struck by lightning.
9. R—The Black Hills are in southwest South Dakota; southeast of the Black Hills are the Badlands.
10. F—Calamity Jane, born in 1852 near Princeton, Missouri, is someone about whom many wild stories are told.

CORRECTING COMMON ERRORS

CORRECTING COMMON ERRORS

CORRECTING COMMON ERRORS

ANSWERS
Exercise 2

Revisions will vary. Accept reasonable responses. A sample response is given below.

To begin the process, a core figure is formed from loamy soil and water. After drying, the figure is coated with beeswax, which is quite easy to shape. The sculptor can then add detail to the wax figure with knives and modeling tools. When the design is complete, it must be sealed, so a smooth coating of soil is pressed into place all over the beeswax. Then the figure is left to dry. After three such layers have been applied, the sealed figure is heated in a fire. The wax melts and runs out of a channel formed in the base, creating a hollow mold, which is buried upside-down. Next, bronze is heated until it liquefies. Pouring molten bronze into the upside-down mold, the sculptor fills the hollow area left by the "lost" wax. Once the mold is cool, it is broken with a hammer, and the finished bronze figure is cleaned and polished.

CORRECTING COMMON ERRORS

[2] Which is quite easy to shape. [3] The sculptor can then add detail to the wax figure. [4] With knives and modeling tools. [5] When the design is complete, it must be sealed, a smooth coating of soil is pressed into place all over the beeswax, then the figure is left to dry. [6] After three such layers have been applied. [7] The sealed figure is heated in a fire, and the wax melts and runs out of a channel formed in the base. [8] Creating a hollow mold, which is buried upside down. [9] Next, bronze is heated until it liquefies, pouring molten bronze into the upside-down mold, the sculptor fills the hollow area left by the "lost" wax. [10] Once the mold is cool, it is broken with a hammer, the finished bronze figure is cleaned and polished.

EXERCISE 3 — Choosing Verbs That Agree in Number with Their Subjects

Choose the word in parentheses that correctly completes each of the following sentences.

EXAMPLE   1. (*Has, Have*) you or your sister ever been in a play?
          1. *Have*

1. My friend and I (*takes, take*) an English literature course every semester.
2. Charles Dickens's *Great Expectations* (*is, are*) the novel that we are studying now.
3. Our class, lucky enough to have several talented drama students, (*plans, plan*) to dramatize Dickens's novel.
4. We hope that raising enough funds (*don't, doesn't*) prove too difficult.
5. Do you think four dollars (*is, are*) too much for an advance ticket?
6. We're going to see if the PTA (*has, have*) any resources to contribute to a project like this.
7. Hawkins Lumber and Tools (*has, have*) promised to donate some building supplies.
8. One thing we have all learned in producing this play is that economics (*need, needs*) to be considered carefully.
9. Even scissors (*costs, cost*) three dollars apiece, and we need six pairs.
10. Everyone helping put on the show (*has, have*) been working to make the production well worth the time and resources our class and community have been investing in it.

EXERCISE 4
OBJECTIVE

• To correct errors in subject-verb agreement

EXERCISE 5
OBJECTIVE

• To correct errors in pronoun-antecedent agreement

Grammar and Usage **993**

EXERCISE 4 — Correcting Errors in Subject-Verb Agreement

Most of the following sentences contain verbs that do not agree with their subjects. Identify each verb that does not agree with its subject, and give the correct form of the verb. If a sentence is correct, write *C*.

EXAMPLE **1.** Don't he want to go to the Renaissance Fair?
1. *Don't—Doesn't*

1. Admission to most movie theaters now <u>cost</u> more than one hundred times the price of attending a nickelodeon movie theater in 1905.
1. costs
2. The Schomburg collection of books and other materials about Africa and Africans <u>are</u> owned by the New York Public Library.
2. is
3. Pilot-training programs that incorporate virtual-reality technology have recently emerged.
3. C
4. The writers and painters of the Pre-Raphaelite Brotherhood <u>was</u> determined to reform English art.
4. were
5. There <u>are</u> among many peoples all over the world a great respect for the elderly.
5. is
6. A number of brightly colored fish <u>swims</u> among the coral and kelp.
6. swim
7. Mr. Blake said that *Elemental Odes* <u>contain</u> many of Pablo Neruda's most eloquent poems.
7. contains
8. The class president or the members of the key club usually <u>announces</u> the results of the election at the assembly. **8. announce**
9. Each of these men <u>know</u> my uncle Louis. **9. knows**
10. The red doors along the hallway <u>opens</u> into classrooms. **10. open**

EXERCISE 5 — Correcting Errors in Pronoun-Antecedent Agreement

Most of the following sentences contain errors in pronoun-antecedent agreement. If a pronoun does not agree with its antecedent, rewrite the sentence to correct the error. [Note: You may need to revise the wording, especially in sentences that are awkward or misleading.] If a sentence is correct, write *C*.

EXAMPLE **1.** Jim Gatacre founded the Handicapped Scuba Association (HSA), which opened their doors in 1981.
1. *Jim Gatacre founded the Handicapped Scuba Association (HSA), which opened its doors in 1981.*

CORRECTING COMMON ERRORS

COOPERATIVE LEARNING

If you would like to give students extra practice with subject-verb agreement before assigning **Exercise 4,** you could write a list of subjects and a list of verbs on the chalkboard. Ask students to work in pairs to compose sentences showing combinations of various subjects and verbs. Tell the paired students to write sentences showing two verb choices (one correct, one incorrect). Students' sentences should include sentences with compound subjects, sentences with phrases between the subjects and verbs, and sentences with the subjects following the verbs. Then, have the student pairs present their sentences as a challenge to other class members.

CORRECTING COMMON ERRORS

CORRECTING COMMON ERRORS

ANSWERS
Exercise 5

Answers will vary. Sample answers are given.

1. Currently, more than a dozen diver-certification agencies exist, and each of them makes sure that its divers meet rigorous standards.

2. In addition to getting regular certification, HSA students and instructors agree to make sure their dives meet HSA standards.

3. However, neither an instructor nor students are required by law to make their dives in accordance with those standards.

4. HSA has set these standards to help ensure that its members have safe and rewarding dives. [Note: Students may omit *their* instead of changing *their* to *its*.]

5. Everyone who becomes certified through HSA learns to plan dives according to the level of assistance that he or she requires from team members.

6. No divers, not even Level A divers, go on their dives alone.

7. Additionally, each Level B or Level C diver is required to take extra precautions; for example, he or she must be part of a three-person team.

8. A Level C diver always has a trained Rescue Diver as one of his or her team members.

9. Divers must have great control over their movements.

10. Most people who have had physical therapy know how to focus their effort and attention; this ability can be of great importance in disorienting underwater environments.

994 *Correcting Common Errors*

1. Currently, more than a dozen diver-certification agencies exist, and each of them makes sure that their divers meet rigorous standards.
2. In addition to getting regular certification, HSA students and instructors agree to make sure his or her dives meet HSA standards.
3. However, neither an instructor nor students are required by law to make his or her dives in accordance with those standards.
4. HSA has set these standards to help ensure that their members have safe and rewarding dives.
5. Everyone who becomes certified through HSA learns to plan dives according to the level of assistance that they require from team members.
6. No one, not even a Level A diver, goes on their dives alone.
7. Additionally, Level B and Level C divers are required to take extra precautions; for example, he or she must be part of a three-person team.
8. A Level C diver always has a trained Rescue Diver as one of their team members.
9. Every diver must have great control over their movements.
10. Most people who have had physical therapy know how to focus his or her effort and attention; this ability can be of great importance in disorienting underwater environments.

EXERCISE 6 Correcting Errors in Pronoun-Antecedent Agreement

Most of the following sentences contain errors in pronoun-antecedent agreement. If a pronoun does not agree with its antecedent, rewrite the sentence to correct the error. [Note: You may need to revise the wording, especially in sentences that are awkward or misleading.] If a sentence is correct, write *C*.

EXAMPLE 1. Ellen is organizing our class picnic, and she needs somebody to bring their grill.
1. *Ellen is organizing our class picnic, and she needs somebody to bring his or her grill.*
   or
   Ellen is organizing our class picnic, and she needs somebody to bring a grill.

1. Nobody wanted to be left out, so they all called Ellen and volunteered to help with the preparations.

EXERCISE 7
OBJECTIVE
- To identify and correct errors in the use of pronoun forms

2. Everyone wants to do their part to make the class picnic a success.
3. Michael or Don has offered to spend their afternoon today planning the schedule and assigning the teams for the volleyball tournament.
4. Ellen is bringing a stereo, and each of the Mullaney girls will bring their favorite CDs.
5. All of the members of the art club said that he or she will help make a banner for the occasion.
6. Mr. Johnston and Miss Sidney say that he or she both can chaperon our picnic.
7. By the way, the park commission has already given their permission.
8. If anybody wants to play music, they are welcome to bring an instrument.
9. All seven drivers will be at the school by 10:30 A.M. this Saturday to pick up their passengers.
10. Anyone in the class can attend and bring their friends, too.

▶ **EXERCISE 7** **Correcting Errors in the Use of Pronouns**

For each of the following sentences, identify and correct each error in the use of pronoun forms.

EXAMPLE **1.** John is going to let me know when Greg and him are planning to go hiking in Big Bend National Park.
1. *him—he*

1. Did he say the guest of honor will be seated near Ann and <u>I</u>? 1. me
2. Which members of the chorus, besides <u>they</u>, do you want to invite? 2. them
3. In the story, the butler interrupts at the worst possible moment and says, "Pardon, Madame, are you expecting Mr. Forster? It is <u>him</u> at the door." 3. he
4. When large drops began to pelt Christy and <u>I</u>, we ran for cover. 4. me
5. Mrs. Blair gave Richard and <u>he</u> several fifty-cent pieces to take with them. 5. him
6. Did Scott remember to write down directions for her and <u>I</u>, or should we remind him? 6. me
7. Don sent her and <u>we</u> postcards from Moscow. 7. us
8. Was it <u>them</u> who arranged the interview with her? 8. they

ANSWERS
Exercise 6

Answers will vary. Sample responses are given.

1. Nobody wanted to be left out, so everyone called Ellen and volunteered to help with the preparations. [*or* All of the class members wanted to be included, so they all . . .]
2. Everyone wants to do his or her part to make the class picnic a success.
3. Michael or Don has offered to spend his afternoon today planning the schedule and assigning the teams for the volleyball tournament.
4. Ellen is bringing a stereo, and each of the Mullaney girls will bring her favorite CDs.
5. All of the members of the art club said that they will help make a banner for the occasion.
6. Both Mr. Johnston and Miss Sidney say that they can chaperon our picnic.
7. By the way, the park commission has already given its permission.
8. Anybody who wants to play music is welcome to bring an instrument.
9. C
10. Anyone in the class can attend and bring friends, too.

CORRECTING COMMON ERRORS

9. her and them

9. Here's a picture of <u>she and they</u> standing in front of the entrance to the New Orleans World's Fair.

10. We

10. <u>Us</u> soloists need another practice session before we have the dress rehearsal.

EXERCISE 8 · Revising Sentences to Correct Faulty Pronoun References

Rewrite the following sentences to correct each ambiguous, general, weak, or indefinite pronoun reference.

EXAMPLE
1. Kaitlin gave Lynda the photographs just before she went to lunch.
1. *Just before Kaitlin went to lunch, she gave Lynda the photographs.*

                        or

Just before Lynda went to lunch, Kaitlin gave her the photographs.

1. Although the delegates discussed the issues, it didn't settle anything, and no agreement was reached.
2. Jonathan likes watching archaeological films and hopes to become one someday.
3. The singing was so loud that they were heard three blocks away.
4. In this article, it describes the Genroku Era in Japan.
5. When my mom and Aunt Lil spend the afternoon baking, they usually let us have some, if it's not too close to our suppertime.
6. Reporters mobbed the jurors until the police led them away.
7. In some museums, you can see tapestries from the Middle Ages.
8. Amber spoke with Mrs. Davison about her plans for the summer.
9. Last Saturday, we pulled weeds in the garden, but it took longer than we had planned.
10. Clowns were performing acrobatics on the median, and that slowed traffic all morning.

EXERCISE 9 · Rewriting Sentences to Correct Faulty Pronoun References

Rewrite the following items to correct each ambiguous, general, weak, or indefinite pronoun reference.

CORRECTING COMMON ERRORS

ANSWERS
Exercise 8

Revisions may vary. The following are sample responses.

1. Although the delegates discussed the issues, nothing was settled, and no agreement was reached.
2. Jonathan likes watching archaeological films and hopes to become an archaeologist someday.
3. Those singing were so loud that they were heard three blocks away.
4. This article describes the Genroku Era in Japan.
5. When my mom and Aunt Lil spend the afternoon baking, they usually let us have some of what they make, if it's not too close to our suppertime.
6. Reporters mobbed the jurors until the police led the jurors away. [*or* Reporters mobbed the jurors until the police led the reporters away.]
7. Some museums display tapestries from the Middle Ages.
8. Amber spoke with Mrs. Davison about Amber's plans for the summer. [*or* Amber spoke with Mrs. Davison about Mrs. Davison's plans for the summer.]
9. Last Saturday, pulling weeds in the garden took us longer than we had planned.
10. Traffic was slow all morning because clowns were performing acrobatics on the median.

EXERCISE 10
OBJECTIVE
• To use the correct past or past participle forms of irregular verbs

EXAMPLE **1.** Good roads promote communication and trade. This was well understood by many ancient peoples.
1. *Many ancient peoples understood well that good roads promote communication and trade.*

1. In the Roman Empire, they had some 50,000 miles of road connecting the distant points of their domain.
2. Some of these roads, which once stretched from Scotland to North Africa, can still be seen, and this is a testament to the skill of the builders.
3. As the Romans discovered, sound foundations and good drainage are critical features of a good roadway. It ensures longevity.
4. Without drainage, water collects on a road, which causes the surface to deteriorate and creates hazards for travelers.
5. The Roman roads were constructed to bear heavy chariot and cart traffic, but in the Incan civilization, they did not use such vehicles.
6. One of the most famous Incan roads ran more than 2,200 miles along the coast, while another snaked through the Andes, which tied together their far-flung empire.
7. In relays, Incan runners would cover distances of up to 1,200 miles, which sometimes took as few as five days.
8. In various civilizations, roads paved with stone slabs withstood much wear from wheeled carts and wagons, and they are still sometimes used.
9. Improperly designed roads are soon marred by puddles and ruts, and this causes travelers much inconvenience.
10. Layers of sand, gravel, and concrete used in modern road construction help make its foundation strong and stable.

▶ EXERCISE 10 **Using Past and Past Participle Forms of Irregular Verbs Correctly**

For each of the following sentences, fill in the correct past or past participle form of the italicized verb.

EXAMPLE *bind* **1.** Libraries existed long before books were printed and ____.
1. *bound*

1. *hold* Ancient libraries in Mesopotamia and Egypt ____ collections of inscribed clay tablets and papyrus scrolls. **1. held**

ANSWERS
Exercise 9

Revisions may vary. The following are sample responses.

1. The Roman Empire had some 50,000 miles of road connecting the distant points of its domain.
2. Some of these roads, which once stretched from Scotland to North Africa, can still be seen, and their durability is a testament to the skill of the builders.
3. As the Romans discovered, sound foundations and good drainage are critical features of a good roadway and ensure longevity.
4. Without drainage, water collects on a road, causing the surface to deteriorate and creating hazards for travelers.
5. The Roman roads were constructed to bear heavy chariot and cart traffic, but the Incas did not use such vehicles.
6. Two roads tied together the Inca's far-flung empire: one famous road that ran more than 2,200 miles along the coast and another that snaked through the Andes.
7. In relays, Incan runners would cover distances of up to 1,200 miles in as few as five days.
8. In various civilizations, roads paved with stone slabs withstood much wear from wheeled carts and wagons, and such stone slabs [*or* such roads] are still sometimes used.
9. Improperly designed roads are soon marred by puddles and ruts that cause travelers much inconvenience.
10. Layers of sand, gravel, and concrete used in modern road construction help make road foundations strong and stable.

COMMON ERROR

Problem. Students sometimes use the regular *–d* or *–ed* endings for irregular verbs and thus create words such as *runned, catched, gived,* and *shaked.*

Solution. Because students learn to speak by hearing and imitating, they will benefit from oral drills of irregular forms. Try holding a conjugation bee, or let students conjugate verbs to a beat. These activities will help students develop an ear for correct verb forms.

MEETING *individual* NEEDS

LESS-ADVANCED STUDENTS

As they work through **Exercises 10** and **11,** have students list irregular verbs that are problematic for them. Students could make charts with the base, past, and past participle forms of the verbs and keep the charts in their notebooks for reference when they are completing writing assignments.

---

998 *Correcting Common Errors*

2. saw	**2.** *see*	The Alexandrians, whose library was famous, ____ the library at Pergamum as a threat to their prestige.
3. forbade [or forbad]	**3.** *forbid*	Therefore, the Alexandrians ____ the export of any papyrus to Pergamum.
4. made	**4.** *make*	The citizens of Pergamum substituted parchment, which they ____ from dried animal skins, for the papyrus.
5. lost	**5.** *lose*	The world ____ a great storehouse of knowledge when the library at Alexandria was destroyed in 47 B.C.
6. kept	**6.** *keep*	One of the greatest manuscript collections in the Americas was ____ at Maní, in what is now Mexico.
7. left	**7.** *leave*	Unfortunately, most of the manuscripts at Maní were burned; today, only three are ____ .
8. written	**8.** *write*	Prior to the invention of the printing press, monks copied by hand what scholars had ____ .
9. struck	**9.** *strike*	Before they ____ Monte Cassino by air in 1944, the Allied forces warned the monks, thereby affording them the chance to protect the manuscripts at the monastery.
10. told	**10.** *tell*	My grandmother, who has seen the manuscripts at Monte Cassino, ____ me they are very ornate.

EXERCISE 11 **Correcting Errors in the Use of Past and Past Participle Verb Forms**

Identify the incorrect verb form in each of the following sentences, and then provide the correct verb form.

EXAMPLE   **1.** The brothers had ran all the way to the ballpark before they found out that the game had been canceled.
     1. *ran—run*

1. frozen	**1.**	The snow that fell in early spring had <u>froze</u> the blossoms.
2. bore	**2.**	He <u>beared</u> his burdens with such great dignity that the emperor finally forgave him.
3. stolen	**3.**	His terrier has <u>stole</u> a dog biscuit and run out the door.
4. lain	**4.**	The tomb had <u>laid</u> undisturbed for centuries before the archaeologist found it.
5. did	**5.**	After she won the first race, she <u>done</u> her best to win the next two and succeeded.
6. sprung	**6.**	Have they <u>sprang</u> the trap and caught the thief yet?

7. The goldfish they bought at the fair <u>swum</u> round and round in its new home.
   7. swam
8. I met Mr. Russell last fall when he <u>teached</u> math at my brother's middle school.
   8. taught
9. Before the sun had <u>rose</u>, we had already driven many miles toward Ontario.
   9. risen
10. Someone <u>set</u> on my sunglasses, which were on the couch.
    10. sat

▶ EXERCISE 12   **Correcting Errors in the Use of Past and Past Participle Verb Forms**

Identify the incorrect verb form in each of the following sentences, and then provide the correct form.

EXAMPLE   **1. By the time the Spanish come to the desert country of the Southwest, the Navajo had already been living there for at least a hundred years.**
          1. come—came

1. The Navajo learned to weave from the Pueblo people, many of whom had <u>chose</u> to live among the Navajo in northern New Mexico.
   1. chosen
2. The Spanish, Navajo, and Pueblo cultures influenced one another, but each one also <u>keeped</u> its own traditions.
   2. kept
3. The Spanish had <u>brung</u> with them a breed of sheep, the churro, that thrived in the high deserts of New Mexico.
   3. brought
4. Woven from the wool of these sheep, the Navajo blanket was often <u>wore</u> as a robe.
   4. worn
5. Wide blankets, known as *chief's blankets*, could also be <u>lain</u> on the ground and used as rugs.
   5. laid
6. While we often think of blankets as ordinary household items, these blankets were greatly valued and sometimes <u>costed</u> as much as twenty horses.
   6. cost
7. Since the mid-1800s, the Navajo have <u>maked</u> weaving a major commercial enterprise.
   7. made
8. The Navajo <u>drawed</u> on new markets for designs and soon found ways to incorporate trains, flags, and other elements into their traditional designs.
   8. drew
9. In the last century and a half, the market for these useful and durable blankets has <u>growed</u> rapidly.
   9. grown
10. Navajo blankets and rugs are <u>buyed</u> by art lovers, craftspeople, and others who admire things that have both beauty and utility.
    10. bought

CORRECTING COMMON ERRORS

INTEGRATING THE LANGUAGE ARTS

Usage and Dictionary Skills. Point out to students that when they have questions about the principal parts of verbs, they can look the verbs up in a dictionary. Explain that the entry word in a dictionary is the base form and that the past, past participle, and present participle forms are listed following the entry word. For example, if students look up *sing*, they will find *sang*, *sung*, and *singing* listed after *sing*. Have each student choose two or three irregular verbs to look up in a dictionary. Students should write each verb's principal parts.

CORRECTING COMMON ERRORS

EXERCISE 13
OBJECTIVE
• To revise a paragraph to correct errors in consistency of verb tenses

EXERCISE 14
OBJECTIVE
• To use verb tenses correctly in sentences

ANSWERS
Exercise 13

Answers may vary. The following paragraph shows the sentences revised into consistent use of the present tense.

1. Haiti's natural resources—ranging from mahogany forests and Caribbean coral reefs to mountain slopes where farmers grow coffee and cacao—are remarkably diverse.
2. Today, Haiti's environment is under serious threat.
3. Only 10 percent of Haiti's once-lush forests remain.
4. Similarly, waters that teemed with fish no longer yield rich catches.
5. However, efforts are now underway to protect and restore Haiti's lands and waters.
6. For instance, several groups have supported the creation of a marine conservation park at Les Arcadins Bank.
7. Also, fine-mesh nets that harvest young fish before they reproduce [or have reproduced] have already been outlawed.
8. Fishing boats are working in deeper waters now so that fish can grow and spawn in shallow waters.
9. Schoolchildren are being taught about the value of the forests and waters.
10. These efforts and others, it is hoped, will help to conserve and restore Haiti's natural resources.

EXERCISE 13 **Revising a Paragraph for Consistent and Logical Use of Tenses**

The verb tenses in the following paragraph are not used consistently and logically. Rewrite the paragraph to correct errors in the use of tense.

EXAMPLE [1] The name *Haiti* came from the Arawak word *Ayiti,* which means "land of high mountains."
1. *The name* Haiti *comes from the Arawak word* Ayiti, *which means "land of high mountains."*

[1] Haiti's natural resources—ranging from mahogany forests and Caribbean coral reefs to mountain slopes where farmers grow coffee and cacao—have been remarkably diverse. [2] Today, Haiti's environment has been under serious threat. [3] Only 10 percent of Haiti's once-lush forests were remaining. [4] Similarly, waters that have been teeming with fish no longer yielded rich catches. [5] However, efforts were now underway to protect and restore Haiti's lands and waters. [6] For instance, several groups had supported the creation of a marine conservation park at Les Arcadins Bank. [7] Also, fine-mesh nets that will harvest young fish before they have reproduced had already been outlawed. [8] Fishing boats were working in deeper waters now so that fish can grow and spawn in shallow waters. [9] Schoolchildren were being taught about the value of the forests and waters. [10] These efforts and others, it is hoped, will have helped to conserve and restore Haiti's natural resources.

EXERCISE 14 **Using Tenses Correctly**

Each of the following sentences contains an error in the use of tenses. Rewrite the sentences to correct the errors.
Answers may vary. Sample answers are given.
EXAMPLE 1. Once the rain stopped, we had a picnic.
1. *Once the rain had stopped, we had a picnic.*

1. had 1. The project would have been more profitable if they ~~would have~~ consulted the experts.
2. sanded 2. While I ~~sand~~ one board, Kathy stained the other.
3. Walking 3. ~~Having walked~~ through the park, Debra saw a nest of red squirrels near the ranger station.
4. had 4. If you ~~would have~~ asked me, I would have helped you.
5. had 5. Even though we already bought the tickets, we waited in line for almost an hour.

Grammar and Usage **1001**

6. My mom and I just finished painting the boat when the
rain started to fall.   **6. had**
7. Because fire ants' stings were painful, we were especially
careful to avoid ant mounds when we worked in the yard
yesterday.   **7. are**
8. Reading the novel last year, I am eagerly awaiting the film
version of it.   **8. Having read**
9. After detectives had examined the evidence left at the
crime scene, they decided that the butler couldn't commit
the crime.   **9. have committed**
10. On the first of next month, Nelson's Deli will be open for
forty years.   **10. have been**

▶ EXERCISE 15 **Using Modifiers Correctly**

Some of the following sentences contain errors in the use of
modifiers. Revise each incorrect sentence to correct the error. If a
sentence is correct, write *C*.   **Answers may vary.**
                                            Sample answers are given.

EXAMPLE   **1.** Of the McDonald twins, Jessica is the best basketball player.
          1. *Of the McDonald twins, Jessica is the better basket-
ball player.*

1. Try to be carefuller the next time you stack dishes in the
sink.   **1. more careful**
2. For almost two days the sea had been more calmer than
the captain had thought it would be.
3. Which is least expensive—the tall vase on the right or the
music box on the left?   **3. less**
4. After watching the litter awhile, we chose the more playful
of the three kittens.   **4. most**
5. The speech you gave today was better than any I've heard
this week.   **5. other**
6. My stepsister thinks it's real easy to put together a jigsaw
puzzle.   **6. really   7. most narrow [or narrowest]**
7. Is this the most narrowest stretch of the trail?
8. Joshua usually finishes his work faster than anyone in his
math class.   **8. else**
9. We tried green lampshades, but I like the warm look of the
red ones better.   **9. C**
10. During the dinner hour, a number of our customers prefer
lighting that is less brighter.   **10. bright**

CORRECTING COMMON ERRORS

QUICK REMINDER
Write the following sentences on
the chalkboard. Have students decide
which choice offered in parentheses better completes each sentence.

1. The singing contest will determine
the (better, best) voices in the large
chorus. [best]
2. That is the (most beautiful, beauti-
fulest) song of the night. [most beau-
tiful]
3. He has the (most deep, deepest)
voice in the bass section. [deepest]

You may want to remind stu-
dents that the number of syllables in the
modifier can help them determine
whether to add –er or –est or to use
more or *most*.

EXERCISE 16
OBJECTIVE
• To revise sentences to correct misplaced and dangling modifiers
EXERCISE 17
OBJECTIVE
• To revise sentences by correcting faulty modifiers

ANSWERS
Exercise 16

Answers will vary. Sample answers are given.

1. Since I had seen the video before, it didn't seem very exciting.
2. On the way to the mall in San Jose, we saw a flock of geese.
3. Even buses seemed small as I looked down from the thirtieth story.
4. Several meetings have been scheduled so that we can adequately discuss these issues.
5. Pulling twelve cars, the train sped past the van.
6. Absolute silence is required of bystanders while others are recording in the studio.
7. To assign priorities, you must have clear goals.
8. Your idea is even more practical than mine.
9. While performing a routine safety check, the inspector found a leak in the duct.
10. The ivy, growing at a remarkable rate, soon covered the fence.

CORRECTING COMMON ERRORS

CORRECTING COMMON ERRORS

1002 *Correcting Common Errors*

> **EXERCISE 16** **Revising Sentences to Correct Misplaced Modifiers and Dangling Modifiers**

Each of the following sentences contains a misplaced or a dangling modifier. Revise each sentence so that its meaning is clear and correct.

EXAMPLE
1. When training animals, firm and consistent commands should be used.
1. *When training animals, a person should use firm and consistent commands.*
                         or
   A person who is training animals should use firm and consistent commands.

1. Having seen the video before, it didn't seem very exciting.
2. We saw a flock of geese on the way to the mall in San Jose.
3. Looking down from the thirtieth story, even buses seemed small.
4. To adequately discuss these issues, several meetings have been scheduled.
5. The train sped past the van pulling twelve cars.
6. While recording in the studio, absolute silence is required of bystanders.
7. To assign priorities, your goals must be clear.
8. Your idea is more practical even than mine.
9. While performing a routine safety check, a leak was found in the duct.
10. Growing at a remarkable rate, the fence was soon covered with ivy.

> **EXERCISE 17** **Revising Sentences to Correct Misplaced Modifiers and Dangling Modifiers**

Each of the following sentences contains a misplaced or dangling modifier. Revise each sentence so that its meaning is clear and correct.

EXAMPLE
1. There was only one glitch in this computer program that we could find.
1. *There was only one glitch that we could find in this computer program.*

1. Mr. Smith's class watched a movie about how electricity was first used last week.

EXERCISE 18
OBJECTIVE
• To correct sentences with errors in usage

Grammar and Usage **1003**

2. To maintain our debate schedule, your rebuttal will only be limited to three minutes.
3. Practicing for the piano recital, the out-of-tune key was very bothersome.
4. When conducting an experiment, precise notes should be kept.
5. The boom swung wildly over the crowd hanging from the crane at the top of the building.
6. Mrs. Chamberlin said on Thursday my assignment is due.
7. While pondering how to proceed, my neighbor's advice came to mind.
8. You should only dial 911 in an emergency.
9. After having studied all week, the test was easy for me.
10. The ranger told us not to feed the bears before we drove into the park.

EXERCISE 18 Correcting Errors in Usage

Most of the following sentences contain an error in usage. If a sentence contains an error, revise the sentence. If a sentence is correct, write *C*.

EXAMPLE   **1.** Where were you at when I called?
　　　　　1. *Where were you when I called?*

1. There are ~~less~~ ingredients in these recipes than you think there are.　　　　　　　　　　　　**1. fewer**
2. ~~Being as~~ you have studied programming, could you help us install the new software?　　　　**2. Since**
3. I did ~~good~~ on the quiz because I've been paying attention in class.　　　　　　　　　　　　　　**3. well**
4. We ~~had~~ ought to take a map with us.
5. Several dinosaur skeletons have been discovered ~~besides~~ the river near here.　　　　　　　　**5. beside**
6. Few stores specialize in these ~~kind~~ of programs.　　**6. kinds**
7. Douglas is more skillful at flying model airplanes ~~then~~ John is.　　　　　　　　　　　　　　　**7. than**
8. No one knows how the World Wide Web will ultimately ~~effect~~ our culture.　　　　　　　　　　**8. affect**
9. Many a traveler has been fooled by the type of ~~allusion~~ known as a mirage.　　　　　　　　　**9. illusion**
10. A team of three writers will adapt the novel for a three-part miniseries.　　　　　　　　　　　**10. C**

CORRECTING COMMON ERRORS

ANSWERS
Exercise 17

Answers will vary. Sample answers are given.

1. Last week Mr. Smith's class watched a movie about how electricity was first used.
2. To maintain our debate schedule, your rebuttal will be limited to only three minutes.
3. Practicing for the piano recital, Sara was bothered by the out-of-tune key.
4. When conducting an experiment, you should keep precise notes.
5. Hanging from the crane at the top of the building, the boom swung wildly over the crowd.
6. Mrs. Chamberlin said my assignment is due on Thursday.
7. My neighbor's advice came to mind while I was pondering how to proceed.
8. You should dial 911 only in an emergency.
9. After I had studied all week, the test was easy for me.
10. Before we drove into the park, the ranger told us not to feed the bears.

CORRECTING COMMON ERRORS

1003

EXERCISE 19
OBJECTIVE
• To revise sentences by correcting errors in usage

EXERCISE 20
OBJECTIVE
• To identify and correct errors in usage

ANSWERS
Exercise 19

1. I read that the settlement that became St. Paul, Minnesota, used to be known as "Pig's Eye," which was the nickname of Pierre Parrant, the settlement's founder.

2. Ice floats on water because water expands and becomes less dense as it freezes.

3. A number of penguins dove from the chunk of floating ice. [or . . . dove off the . . .]

4. Among the thirty theories, there were only three that gave credible explanations for those phenomena.

5. Lisa and I were just wondering when the scholarship committee would begin accepting applications.

6. Rita inferred from Avi's letter that he had decided to stay somewhere in Montana for the summer.

7. As Mr. Faust indicated, the eruption of Mount Vesuvius covered the city of Pompeii not with lava but with ashes.

8. Amy said that fewer people visit the gallery on Thursdays than on Fridays.

9. Neither the first nor the last person in line knew when the tickets were supposed to go on sale.

10. Joey ought to have written the address on the notepad beside the phone.

CORRECTING COMMON ERRORS

CORRECTING COMMON ERRORS

1004 *Correcting Common Errors*

EXERCISE 19 Rewriting Sentences to Correct Errors in Usage

Each of the following sentences contains an error in usage. Rewrite each sentence to correct the usage error.

EXAMPLE 1. Both the French franc and the Spanish peseta serve as legal tender in Andorra, an European country between France and Spain.
1. *Both the French franc and the Spanish peseta serve as legal tender in Andorra, a European country between France and Spain.*

1. I read where the settlement that became St. Paul, Minnesota, used to be known as "Pig's Eye," which was the nickname of Pierre Parrant, the settlement's founder.
2. The reason ice floats on water is because water expands and becomes less dense as it freezes.
3. A number of penguins dove off of the chunk of floating ice.
4. Between the thirty theories, there were only three that gave credible explanations for those phenomena.
5. Lisa and myself were just wondering when the scholarship committee would begin accepting applications.
6. Rita implied from Avi's letter that he had decided to stay somewhere in Montana for the summer.
7. Like Mr. Faust indicated, the eruption of Mount Vesuvius covered the city of Pompeii not with lava but with ashes.
8. Amy said that less people visit the gallery on Thursdays than on Fridays.
9. Neither the first or the last person in line knew when the tickets were supposed to go on sale.
10. Joey ought to of written the address on the notepad beside the phone.

EXERCISE 20 Correcting Errors in Usage

Each of the following numbered items contains an error in usage. Identify and correct each error.

EXAMPLE 1. Has that phenomena ever been explained?
1. *phenomena—phenomenon*

1. said 1. Then, right after both of us had lost our passports, Erin says, "I just knew this would happen."

1004

2. Richard looked ~~everywheres~~ for Maria and Laura and then asked the information clerk to page them.   **2. everywhere**
3. A number of trout ~~was~~ feeding on the minnows under the lights at the end of the pier.   **3. were**
4. Simone and ~~myself~~ will narrate the tale while Nicole and Peter present it in pantomime.   **4. I**
5. Be careful that you don't ~~bust~~ that mirror.   **5. break**
6. The mechanic told my brother Tim that we ~~had~~ ought to change the oil every three thousand miles.
7. The papers must ~~of~~ blown off the table.   **7. have**
8. If you go to the library tomorrow afternoon, will you ~~bring~~ these videotapes back for me?   **8. take**
9. The reason Jackson Street is closed to vehicles is ~~because~~ a parade will be passing there soon.   **9. that**
10. Where was the Hope Diamond found ~~at~~?

▶ EXERCISE 21   **Correcting Double Negatives and Other Errors in Usage**

Eliminate the double negatives and other errors in usage in the following sentences. Although some sentences can be corrected in more than one way, you need to give only one revision.

Answers may vary. Sample answers are given.

EXAMPLE   **1. Megan doesn't want no more mashed potatoes.**
          1. *Megan doesn't want any more mashed potatoes.*

1. You ~~can't~~ never tell what will happen.   **1. can**
2. I still haven't had a chance to see ~~none~~ of this summer's blockbuster movies yet.   **2. any**
3. The travelers walked a long ~~ways~~ before they reached their destination.   **3. way**
4. We looked all over, but neither my books nor my papers were ~~nowhere~~ in the library.   **4. anywhere**
5. After working outside all morning in the wind and rain, he isn't feeling ~~good~~.   **5. well**
6. Mr. Lee ~~hadn't~~ hardly started class before the bell rang for a fire drill.   **6. had**
7. The power outage couldn't ~~of~~ lasted longer than a minute or so.   **7. have**
8. I did well on every test ~~accept~~ this last one.   **8. except**
9. Were you in the kitchen when the china teapot fell off ~~of~~ the counter?
10. None of the clerks remembered ~~nothing~~ about our order.   **10. anything**

CORRECTING COMMON ERRORS

MEETING *individual* NEEDS

LEP/ESL

General Strategies. The double negative is perfectly acceptable in Spanish, as it is in Russian and a number of other languages. Your observation of your students will help you identify those who are transferring this usage to English, especially with words such as *nothing, none,* or *nobody.* Begin by asking questions that call for the negative form, such as "Did you see anyone who was late to class today?" or "Did you go anywhere special last weekend?" Give additional written practice to students who are having trouble.

CORRECTING COMMON ERRORS

OBJECTIVES

- To practice responses similar to those required on standardized tests of mastery of language skills and concepts
- To select from among given choices the phrasing that is grammatically correct and best expresses the intended meaning

TEACHING NOTE

Using the Grammar and Usage Tests. You may prefer to have students regard the **Grammar and Usage Tests** as review exercises instead of using them as practice with standardized test taking. If so, have students number blank sheets of paper and write their answers there instead of filling in the **Standardized Test Answer Sheet** provided in *Language Skills Practice and Assessment*, p. 271.

CORRECTING COMMON ERRORS

CORRECTING COMMON ERRORS

1006 *Correcting Common Errors*

Grammar and Usage Test: Section 1

DIRECTIONS   Read the paragraph below. For each numbered blank, select the word or group of words that best completes the sentence. Indicate your response by shading in the appropriate oval on your answer sheet.

EXAMPLE

Have you ever wondered __(1)__ systems for classifying fingerprints?

1. (A) who discovered the first
   (B) whom discovered the first
   (C) who invented the first
   (D) whom invented the first
   (E) who first invented the

SAMPLE ANSWER   1. (A) (B) ● (D) (E)

Fingerprinting __(1)__ a significant role in investigative work ever since the late nineteenth century, when Sir Francis Galton, a British anthropologist, determined that __(2)__ identical fingerprints. Building upon the research of Galton, Juan Vucetich of Argentina and Sir Edward R. Henry of Great Britain __(3)__ fingerprint classification systems during the 1890s. Fingerprints are one of the __(4)__ of identification because a person's fingerprints are unlikely to change during __(5)__ lifetime. Thus, when working to solve crimes, __(6)__ find fingerprints that identify people and place them at crime scenes. Sometimes such fingerprints are clearly visible, but other times __(7)__ cannot be seen. Most latent, or hidden, fingerprints __(8)__ detected until they have been covered with colored powder or special chemicals. Moreover, there are some types of latent fingerprints __(9)__ with a laser beam. Fingerprints, which are also used to identify victims of tragedies such as fires and plane crashes, __(10)__ to be an invaluable tool for more than a century.

1. A 1. (A) has played
          (B) played
          (C) plays
          (D) had played
          (E) will have played

2. E 2. (A) no two people never have
          (B) people they never have
          (C) two people don't have no
          (D) no two people don't have
          (E) no two people have

3. B 3. (A) introduced his
          (B) introduced their
          (C) were introducing their
          (D) had introduced their
          (E) have introduced their

4. D 4. (A) more useful types
          (B) usefuller types
          (C) most usefullest types
          (D) most useful types
          (E) usefullest types

Grammar and Usage **1007**

5. C **5.** (A) his
(B) her
(C) his or her
(D) their
(E) they're

6. C **6.** (A) investigators they try and
(B) investigators try and
(C) investigators try to
(D) investigators they try to
(E) those investigators try to

7. A **7.** (A) they
(B) no fingerprints
(C) these here fingerprints
(D) these kind of fingerprints
(E) those type of fingerprints

8. C **8.** (A) can't hardly be
(B) can't in no way be
(C) can hardly be
(D) they can't hardly be
(E) can't scarcely be

9. B **9.** (A) that only can be seen
(B) that can be seen only
(C) which can be seen only
(D) that can only be seen
(E) which only can be seen

10. B **10.** (A) has proven
(B) have proven
(C) will have proven
(D) proved
(E) proves

Grammar and Usage Test: Section 2

DIRECTIONS In the following sentences, either part or all of each sentence is underlined. Using the rules of standard written English, choose the answer that most clearly expresses the meaning of the sentence. If there is no error, choose A. Indicate your response by shading in the appropriate oval on your answer sheet.

EXAMPLE

1. Gail told Wendy that the tryout had gone so <u>well that she was sure she got</u> the part of Emily in *Our Town.*

   (A) well that she was sure she got
   (B) good that she was sure Wendy had got
   (C) well that she was sure Wendy had got
   (D) well that Wendy was sure she had got
   (E) good that Gail was sure she had got

SAMPLE ANSWER   1. Ⓐ Ⓑ ⬤ Ⓓ Ⓔ

1. C **1.** On the other side of <u>these here mountains lie</u> some of the richest farmland in the world.

   (A) these here mountains lie
   (B) these mountains lie
   (C) these mountains lies
   (D) these mountains lay
   (E) these mountains lays

TEACHING NOTE
Using the Grammar and Usage Tests. A Standardized Test Answer Sheet that students may use for this Grammar and Usage Test is provided in *Language Skills Practice and Assessment,* p. 271.

CORRECTING COMMON ERRORS

CORRECTING COMMON ERRORS

1007

2. D   **2.** The myelin sheath which surrounds nerve cells and helps to speed up nerve impulses.

   (A) The myelin sheath which surrounds nerve cells and helps to speed up nerve impulses.
   (B) The myelin sheath surrounding nerve cells, which helps to speed up nerve impulses.
   (C) The myelin sheath surrounding nerve cells and helping to speed up nerve impulses.
   (D) The myelin sheath, which surrounds nerve cells, helps to speed up nerve impulses.
   (E) Helping speed up nerve impulses, the myelin sheath surrounding nerve cells.

3. C   **3.** Arnie carves soapstone beautifully; he plans to give them to his friends at Christmas.

   (A) them
   (B) these
   (C) carvings
   (D) it
   (E) these here

4. D   **4.** Beaming proudly, a medal hung around her neck at the ceremony.

   (A) Beaming proudly, a medal hung around her neck at the ceremony.
   (B) At the ceremony, a medal hung around her neck, beaming proudly.
   (C) At the ceremony, she wore a medal around her neck beaming proudly.
   (D) Beaming proudly at the ceremony, she wore a medal around her neck.
   (E) Beaming proudly at the ceremony, a medal hung around her neck.

5. B   **5.** Each of the athletes in the Olympics wore their nation's jersey.

   (A) Each of the athletes in the Olympics wore their
   (B) Each of the athletes in the Olympics wore his or her
   (C) Every athlete in the Olympics wore their
   (D) All of the athletes in the Olympics wore their
   (E) All of the athletes in the Olympics wore his or her

6. E   **6.** I can't hardly believe that less people than we had predicted turned out for today's carnival.

   (A) I can't hardly believe that less people than
   (B) I can hardly believe that fewer people then
   (C) I can hardly believe that less people then
   (D) I can't hardly believe that fewer people than
   (E) I can hardly believe that fewer people than

7. C **7.** In 1824, I read that a fifteen-year-old student who was blind, Louis Braille, developed a system of reading that used raised dots.

(A) In 1824, I read that a fifteen-year-old student who was blind, Louis Braille, developed a system of reading that used raised dots.
(B) I read in 1824 that a fifteen-year-old student who was blind, Louis Braille, developed a system of reading that used raised dots.
(C) I read that in 1824 a fifteen-year-old student who was blind, Louis Braille, developed a system of reading that used raised dots.
(D) I read that Louis Braille, a fifteen-year-old student who was blind in 1824, developed a system of reading that used raised dots.
(E) I read that a fifteen-year-old student who was blind, Louis Braille, developed a system of reading that used raised dots in 1824.

8. D **8.** In golf, a "mulligan" is when a player is given a free shot after having made a poor shot.

(A) when a player is given a free shot after having made
(B) where a player is given a free shot after having made
(C) when a player is given a free shot after he or she has made
(D) a free shot given to a player after he or she has made
(E) that a player is given a free shot after having made

9. C **9.** Skimming through the magazine, there were two articles I found for my report on Marcus Garvey.

(A) Skimming through the magazine, there were two articles I found for my report on Marcus Garvey.
(B) While skimming through the magazine, there were two articles I found for my report on Marcus Garvey.
(C) Skimming through the magazine, I found two articles for my report on Marcus Garvey.
(D) I found two articles for my report on Marcus Garvey skimming through the magazine.
(E) Two articles for my report on Marcus Garvey were found skimming through the magazine.

10. C **10.** The contract between he and they is quite complex.

(A) between he and they
(B) between him and they
(C) between him and them
(D) among him and them
(E) among he and they

MEETING *individual* NEEDS

LEP/ESL

General Strategies. In some languages, days of the week, months, and nationalities used as adjectives are lowercase, as in "On the first monday in april, we're going to watch a french film." Your acknowledgment to students that they are being asked to reverse rules they may already have mastered in their native languages may help them deal with this change independently.

✓ QUICK REMINDER

Write the following sentences on the chalkboard without commas, and have students tell where commas should be added:

1. We need to ride to the stadium [,] buy our tickets [,] and find our seats before the show starts.

2. The show starts at noon [,] but the bus leaves at 9:00.

3. Reginald [,] the band's drummer [,] grew up in my hometown.

4. Running for the bus [,] Jefferson dropped his backpack.

5. In addition to losing his tickets [,] he lost his bus fare.

EXERCISE 22
OBJECTIVE
• To correct errors in capitalization

EXERCISE 23
OBJECTIVE
• To correct sentences by adding or deleting commas

▶ EXERCISE 22 Using Standard Capitalization

For each of the following items, correct any errors in capitalization by changing lowercase letters to capital letters or capital letters to lowercase letters as necessary. If an item is correct, write C.

EXAMPLE   **1.** tests in Physics, history IV, and spanish
           1. *tests in physics, History IV, and Spanish*

1. business in latin America
2. the middle ages
3. a book called *Everyday life of The Aztecs*
4. on Lake Texcoco 4. C
5. the north American Free Trade Agreement
6. American broadcasting company, inc.
7. my uncle Matthew 7. C
8. Carol Williams, m.d.
9. ancient toltec peoples
10. the gobi desert
11. the university of Michigan
12. the organization habitat for humanity
13. dr. j. s. ramírez, jr.
14. a roman catholic church
15. East of the Jordan River
16. the Nobel Prize 16. C
17. at aunt Susan's house
18. queen Elizabeth I
19. 87 Thirty-Third street
20. a Bakery in New York city

▶ EXERCISE 23 Correcting Errors in the Use of Commas

For each of the following sentences, add or delete commas to correct each error in the use of commas. If a sentence is correct, write C.   **Underscore marks optional commas.**

EXAMPLE   **1.** Wearing a gorilla suit Joe put aside his stage fright and stepped into the spotlight.
           1. *Wearing a gorilla suit, Joe put aside his stage fright and stepped into the spotlight.*

1. Thunder clapped, lightning flashed, and rain pounded the roof.
2. Lewis, having read the book, was especially eager to see the film adaptation.

3. The conference, Mr. Cherensky, will focus on technological advances in medicine, and I hope you'll be able to attend.
4. Scheduled to employ some 1,200 people, the factories will open in Dayton, Ohio, and Phoenix, Arizona.
5. Copies of the videotape have been sent to Michael Tanner, M.D., and Cindy Lowe, Ph.D.
6. Yes, we still need people to play the roles of Diana and Pan and Apollo in next month's production.
7. Actually, John Adams, not Thomas Jefferson, was the second president of the United States.
8. Hey, have you ever read about the African American leader Malcolm X?   **8. C**
9. Robert Penn Warren, who was a poet, novelist, and essayist, was the first official U.S. poet laureate.
10. That is one of the oldest, most valuable antique boxes in the collection, isn't it?

▶ **EXERCISE 24** **Correcting Errors in the Use of Commas**

Rewrite the following sentences, adding or deleting commas as necessary.   **Underscore marks optional commas.**

EXAMPLE   **1.** "Wow" said Ms. Gage "just listen to those, African drummers!"
1. *"Wow," said Ms. Gage, "just listen to those African drummers!"*

1. The oldest musical instrument, the drum, is a percussion instrument.
2. Of the musical instruments that have come from Africa, percussion instruments are probably the most common.
3. Percussion instruments, those that are tapped, shaken, or struck, include drums, bells, and xylophones.
4. The banjo, which was brought to this country from Africa, is a modified percussion instrument.
5. Although the banjo is generally considered to be a string instrument, its body is actually a small drum with a tightly stretched skin on one side.
6. Maurice, have you noticed that African drums have many different shapes and sizes?
7. Drums are often shaped like cones or cylinders, and some, such as ceremonial drums, are decorated with complex, fanciful carvings.

MEETING *individual* NEEDS

LEARNING STYLES

Visual Learners. You may want to help students visualize some of the uses of commas by showing examples of comma usage. On the chalkboard draw six columns. Label the columns *independent clauses, nonessential clauses, introductory elements, interrupters, items in a series,* and *conventions (dates and addresses).* Work with students to generate examples; write the examples under the appropriate headings.

You may then want to assign **Exercise 24** for homework and go over the answers with students in class. Survey the class for error patterns and review those rules of comma usage that seem to be giving students problems.

TEACHING NOTE

Exercise 24. In item 1, if "the drum" is viewed as an appositive that interrupts the independent clause, the second comma is essential. If "the drum" is viewed as the subject of the independent clause, the second comma must be omitted.

MEETING individual NEEDS

LESS-ADVANCED STUDENTS

Some students might confuse the colon with the semicolon or think that they are interchangeable. Tell your class that ordinarily a colon is a kind of sign or pointer to the part of a sentence the writer wants to emphasize, whereas a semicolon helps the reader avoid confusion by separating ideas or items.

A DIFFERENT APPROACH

If students need additional practice with semicolon use, collect a few sentences from several essays and have students correct some of the comma splices and other punctuation errors by inserting semicolons.

1012 *Correcting Common Errors*

8. Reserved for special occasions;ceremonial drums,can be quite elaborate.
9. Drums can be made from many simple objects;for instance; a hollow log,a cooking pot,a tin can,or even an oil drum.
10. I once saw a drum that was shaped like a human torso, and had legs that looked like human legs.

EXERCISE 25 **Correcting Sentences by Adding Semicolons and Colons**

Rewrite the following sentences, replacing commas with semicolons and colons or adding semicolons and colons where they are needed.

EXAMPLE **1.** The house is in need of very few cosmetic repairs, futhermore, the foundation is sound.
1. *The house is in need of very few cosmetic repairs; futhermore, the foundation is sound.*

1. Three books sat on Ethan's desk;his journal, a dictionary, and a copy of *Middlemarch:A Study of Provincial Life.*
2. Leather car seats require upkeep;for instance, they should be cleaned regularly and kept out of direct sunlight.
3. The prizes are as follows:first prize, $500; second prize, $200; and third prize, $100.
4. This setback doesn't mean that the project is over; on the contrary, we'll be reorganizing it and redoubling our efforts.
5. Here are our next reading assignments:pages 51–67, pages 110–130, and pages 185–200.
6. Baby-sitting can be profitable and enjoyable; however, it entails a great deal of responsibility.
7. The following students should report to the front office: Kyle Werner, Brian Weber, and Amanda Lawrence.
8. The unconscious mind is said to contain all the forgotten experiences of a person's lifetime;psychologists are seeking ways to tap that knowledge.
9. Performances will be given in several major cities: Atlanta, Georgia; Orlando, Florida; San Francisco, California; and Seattle, Washington.
10. One of the most well-known of Shakespeare's soliloquies includes these three lines: "Tomorrow, and tomorrow, and tomorrow / Creeps in this petty pace from day to day, / To the last syllable of recorded time."

EXERCISE 26
OBJECTIVE
• To punctuate and capitalize written dialogue correctly

EXERCISE 27
OBJECTIVE
• To correct errors in the use of quotation marks, other marks
of punctuation, and capitalization

Mechanics **1013**

EXERCISE 26   Proofreading a Dialogue for Correct Punctuation and Capitalization

Rewrite the following dialogue, adding or deleting paragraph indents, commas, end marks, and quotation marks where necessary. You may also need to replace some lowercase letters with capital letters.

EXAMPLE   [1] Hey, Annie, look at this sari my aunt brought me from India" Irene said.

    1.   *"Hey, Annie, look at this sari my aunt brought me from India," Irene said.*

[1] "Wow, how do you put it on? Annie asked." [2] "You just wrap it around yourself and put the end over your shoulder," Irene answered.

[3] "It's beautiful! Annie declared. What was your aunt doing in India"?

[4] "She's a professor, and she's studying ancient Hindu texts and manuscripts." "She translated some of her favorite passages and wrote them in a little book for me".

[5] Annie said, "Oh, how nice of her! [6] "Yes," it was Irene replied "and she brought back a number of other interesting things—earrings, wooden carvings, clothes, and recipes." [7] "I'd love to see them." Annie remarked.

[8] Sure, Irene said, and tonight she's going to teach me how to cook a whole Indian dinner.

Have you ever had Indian food? [9] "No" Annie answered. [10] "Well, stay for dinner tonight! You can help us cook and eat!

EXERCISE 27   Proofreading for the Correct Use of Quotation Marks, Other Marks of Punctuation, and Capitalization

For each of the following sentences, correct any error in the use of quotation marks, capitalization, commas, or end marks.

EXAMPLE   1. "Since it's sunny, she said Let's take a walk?"
    1. *"Since it's sunny," she said, "let's take a walk."*

1. Did the flight attendant just say, "This is the last call for passengers boarding Flight 304?"
2. "Next week's story," Ms. Sorvino said "will be "The Ring."
3. Mr. Keith posted Christine's latest essay, Reading for Life, outside the classroom.

ANSWERS
Exercise 26

1. "Wow, how do you put it on?" Annie asked. [*or* "Wow! How do you put it on?" Annie asked.]
2. "You just wrap it around yourself and put the end over your shoulder," Irene answered.
3. "It's beautiful!" Annie declared. "What was your aunt doing in India?"
4. "She's a professor, and she's studying ancient Hindu texts and manuscripts. She translated some of her favorite passages and wrote them in a little book for me."
5. Annie said, "Oh, how nice of her!"
6. "Yes, it was," Irene replied, "and she brought back a number of other interesting things—earrings, wooden carvings, clothes, and recipes."
7. "I'd love to see them," Annie remarked.
8. "Sure," Irene said, "and tonight she's going to teach me how to cook a whole Indian dinner. Have you ever had Indian food?"
9. "No," Annie answered.
10. "Well, stay for dinner tonight! You can help us cook and eat!"

ANSWERS
Exercise 27

1. Did the flight attendant just say, "This is the last call for passengers boarding Flight 304"?
2. "Next week's story," Ms. Sorvino said, "will be 'The Ring.'"
3. Mr. Keith posted Christine's latest essay, "Reading for Life," outside the classroom.

CORRECTING COMMON ERRORS

1013

4. What are "green bytes" in a computer file, Dawn?

5. "Are you really going to write music for Robert Frost's poem 'Fire and Ice'?" Paul asked.

6. Didn't he say that there's a test this Friday?

7. Jethro always called the swimming pool behind his house the "cement pond."

8. Yesterday's review called the novel "immature"; however, I think the novel is fresh and spontaneous.

9. Jonathan asked me if I knew the lyrics to the second verse of "America the Beautiful."

10. The next chapter, "Healthy Teeth and Gums," details basic dental hygiene.

A DIFFERENT APPROACH

To help students become more familiar with the uses of apostrophes, divide the class into groups of three and have each group search through newspapers, magazines, or other texts for different uses of apostrophes. After an allotted time, spokespersons from each group can report on their findings.

EXERCISE 28
OBJECTIVE
- To correct errors in the use of apostrophes
EXERCISE 29
OBJECTIVE
- To correct sentences with errors in spelling

4. What are 'green bytes' in a computer file, Dawn?

5. "Are you really going to write music for Robert Frost's poem "Fire and Ice"? Paul asked.

6. Didn't he say that "There's a test this Friday"?

7. Jethro always called the swimming pool behind his house the 'cement pond.'

8. Yesterday's review called the novel "immature;" however, I think the novel is fresh and spontaneous.

9. Jonathan asked me if I knew the lyrics to the second verse of America the Beautiful.

10. The next chapter, Healthy Teeth and Gums, details basic dental hygiene.

EXERCISE 28 Using Apostrophes Correctly

Add or delete apostrophes to correct each error in the following phrases and sentences. [Note: You may need to change the spelling of some words.] If an item is correct, write C.

EXAMPLE
1. a boys' trousers
1. *a boy's trousers*

1. my sister Angela's room
2. mice's exercise wheel
3. Our's are here, but yours are missing.
4. anybody's suggestion   4. C
5. somebody else's turn
6. her two brothers-in-laws' dogs
7. There's the bell!
8. Susie's and Bill's share of the chores
9. both gymnasts' routines
10. Don't say *can't* to me!
11. Dot your *i's* so that they don't look like *l's*.
12. It's six o'clock.
13. You're right again.
14. We're ready to go!
15. Who's next on the tryout list?
16. You'd need two Ph.D.'s to program these VCRs. 16. or VCR's
17. twenty-five cents' worth
18. a friend of theirs'
19. Lisa's and Tom's uniforms
20. The blouse is her's.

EXERCISE 29 Proofreading Sentences to Correct Misspelled Words

Proofread the following sentences, correcting any misspelled words. If all the words in a sentence are spelled correctly, write C.

EXAMPLE
1. Do you have a reciept for the loafs of bread?
1. *receipt, loaves*

1. If you are still ~~mispelling~~ many words, study your spelling rules more ~~carefuly~~. **1. misspelling/carefully**
2. With ~~3~~ of the ~~bookshelfs~~ almost completed, our job was nearly finished. **2. three/bookshelves**
3. "Julia has always ~~exceled~~ at math," her mother ~~replyed~~.
4. How many solos will there be in tonight's recital? **3. excelled/replied**
5. ~~Dishs~~ filled with ~~appetizeing~~ foods of all kinds covered the banquet table. **4. C 5. Dishes/appetizing**
6. The ~~Welchs~~ looked at several ~~stereoes~~ and chose the one with the ~~bigest~~ speakers. **6. Welches/stereos/biggest**
7. ~~Approximatly~~ 65 percent of the precincts have already reported election results. **7. Approximately 8. editor-in-chief**
8. My uncle Bill is ~~editor-in-cheif~~ of the local newspaper.
9. "~~Ladys~~ and gentlemen," the speaker said, "we have a tie for ~~3rd~~ place!" **9. Ladies/third**
10. Let's cook five or six ~~potatos~~ to serve with the sea ~~trouts~~ Timothy caught. **10. potatoes/trout**

EXERCISE 30 ## Distinguishing Between Words Often Confused

Choose the correct word from each pair in parentheses in the following sentences.

EXAMPLE **1.** Yesterday we borrowed (*their, they're*) bicycles to go to the movies.
　　　　1. *their*

1. The (*principals, principles*) of calculus are generally more difficult to master than those of algebra.
2. I have (*already, all ready*) told them that we are ready to go.
3. (*Your, You're*) performance in the play was terrific!
4. In order to obtain water, a mesquite tree in a (*desert, dessert*) may extend its roots more than 250 feet into the ground.
5. Rather (*then, than*) reading a report, they're going to give a demonstration.
6. Can you tell me (*who's, whose*) in charge of personnel?
7. Do you expect that the team will break the record for this (*coarse, course*)?
8. The scout leader (*lead, led*) our troop to the mountain top.
9. Have you decided (*weather, whether*) you're going to the gym?
10. We must have (*past, passed*) twenty motels before we found one with a Vacancy sign.

COMMON ERROR

Problem. Students might have problems spelling words that sound alike (homophones) but that are different in meaning.

Solution. The quickest way to master these troublesome pairs (or threesomes) is to memorize the words and their spellings. Mnemonics can sometimes work. For example, the *–er* in *letter* and *paper* could help the student remember *stationery* (writing paper), as opposed to *stationary* (not moving). The *o* in *dome* may be associated with the *o* in *capitol* (a government building that often has a dome).

TEACHING NOTE

Using the Mechanics Tests. A Standardized Test Answer Sheet that students may use for these **Mechanics Tests** is provided in *Language Skills Practice and Assessment,* p. 271.

1016 *Correcting Common Errors*

Mechanics Test: Section 1

DIRECTIONS   Each of the following sentences contains an underlined group of words. Choose the answer that shows the correct capitalization, punctuation, and spelling of the underlined part. If there is no error, choose answer E (Correct as is). Indicate your response by shading in the appropriate oval on your answer sheet.

EXAMPLE

1. The nearest mailbox is on Twenty-First Street.

   (A) Twenty-first street
   (B) Twenty first Street
   (C) Twenty First Street
   (D) Twenty-first Street
   (E) Correct as is

SAMPLE ANSWER   1. (A) (B) (C) ● (E)

1. D 1. Have you ever been to my brother-in-laws repair shop, Gus's Garage?

   (A) brothers-in-law's repair shop, Gus's garage
   (B) brother-in-law's repair shop, Gus' Garage
   (C) brother in law's repair shop, Gus' garage
   (D) brother-in-law's repair shop, Gus's Garage
   (E) Correct as is

2. D 2. Please read the next chapter Filing Your Income Tax.

   (A) chapter, *Filing your Income Tax.*
   (B) chapter "Filing Your Income Tax."
   (C) chapter, "Filing your Income Tax."
   (D) chapter, "Filing Your Income Tax."
   (E) Correct as is

3. D 3. Volunteers should bring: hammers, wrenches, and screwdrivers.

   (A) bring, hammers,
   (B) bring—hammers,
   (C) bring; hammers,
   (D) bring hammers,
   (E) Correct as is

4. B 4. Mrs. Hendrix said that "The Chemistry II exam will be next Wednesday."

   (A) said, "The Chemistry II exam will be next Wensday."
   (B) said that the Chemistry II exam will be next Wednesday.
   (C) said that the chemistry II exam will be next Wednesday.
   (D) said that "The chemistry II exam will be next Wednesday."
   (E) Correct as is

5. B **5.** "Next we will visit the Moody <u>Museum of Art." said</u> Mr. Singh.

    (A) Museum Of Art,"
    (B) Museum of Art,"
    (C) Museum of Art"
    (D) Museum of Art",
    (E) Correct as is

6. A **6.** "I don't want to hear any <u>*if*'s, *and*'s, or *but*'s," my Aunt Marjorie</u> said to my cousin and me.

    (A) *if*'s, *and*'s, or *but*'s," my aunt Marjorie
    (B) *if*'s *and*'s or *but*'s," my Aunt Marjorie
    (C) *if*s', *and*s', or *but*s'," my aunt Marjorie
    (D) *if*s, *and*s, or *but*s" my Aunt Marjorie
    (E) Correct as is

7. B **7.** Honeybees live and work <u>together, however, the</u> majority of the world's bees are solitary.

    (A) together, however the
    (B) together; however, the
    (C) together however, the
    (D) together; however the
    (E) Correct as is

8. B **8.** "Didn't," said Tom, "the television <u>movie Gulliver's Travels</u> come out in 1996?"

    (A) movie "Gulliver's Travels"
    (B) movie *Gulliver's Travels*
    (C) movie, "Gulliver's Travels,"
    (D) movie, *Gulliver's Travels*,
    (E) Correct as is

9. D **9.** The state of Michigan borders all of the <u>Great Lakes except lake Ontario.</u>

    (A) Great lakes except lake Ontario
    (B) great lakes except Lake Ontario
    (C) great Lakes except lake Ontario
    (D) Great Lakes except Lake Ontario
    (E) Correct as is

10. C **10.** More than eight million <u>people live in Mexico City one</u> of the largest cities in the world.

    (A) More than 8 million people live in Mexico City, one
    (B) More than 8 million people live in Mexico city one
    (C) More than eight million people live in Mexico City, one
    (D) More then eight million people live in Mexico City, one
    (E) Correct as is

TEACHING NOTE

Using the Mechanics Tests. A Standardized Test Answer Sheet that students may use for these **Mechanics Tests** is provided in *Language Skills Practice and Assessment,* p. 271.

1018 *Correcting Common Errors*

Mechanics Test: Section 2

DIRECTIONS   Each numbered item below contains an underlined group of words. Choose the answer that shows the correct capitalization, punctuation, and spelling of the underlined part. If there is no error, choose answer E (Correct as is). Indicate your response by shading in the appropriate oval on your answer sheet.

EXAMPLE

[1] New York NY, 10023

1. (A) New York NY 10023
   (B) New York, NY 10023
   (C) New York, New York 10023
   (D) New York, New York, 10023
   (E) Correct as is

SAMPLE ANSWER   1. Ⓐ ● Ⓒ Ⓓ Ⓔ

New York, NY 10023
[1] Feburary 3, 1997

Ms. Annelise Wilson
Widgets and Gadgets, Inc.
[2] 8723 Forty-Third Street
New York, NY 10027

[3] Dear Ms. Wilson

Thank you for coming to speak to our chapter of the Young Entrepreneurs [4] club and for sharing your guidelines on [5] principals of good business management. At our meeting the following [6] week, we had a very, lively discussion about the information you had given us. It is always helpful for our group to hear from someone who has [7] already succeded in doing what we hope to accomplish. We especially appreciated your insights about [8] government agencies and their regulations regarding business practices.

We are looking forward to seeing you again at the upcoming Small Business Association Summer Conference at [9] the Leicester hotel and, of course, would be happy to have you speak to our chapter in the future.

[10] Yours sincerely,

Rodney Alvarez

Rodney Alvarez
President, Young Entrepreneurs Club

---

1. D **1.** (A) Febuary 3, 1997
(B) Feburary 3rd, 1997
(C) Febuary 3 1997
(D) February 3, 1997
(E) Correct as is

2. A **2.** (A) 8723 Forty-third Street
(B) 8723 Forty third Street
(C) 8723 Forty Third Street
(D) 8723 Forty-third street
(E) Correct as is

3. A **3.** (A) Dear Ms. Wilson:
(B) Dear Ms. Wilson,
(C) Dear Ms Wilson:
(D) Dear Ms Wilson,
(E) Correct as is

4. D **4.** (A) club and for sharing
you're
(B) Club and for sharing
you're
(C) club and for shareing your
(D) Club and for sharing your
(E) Correct as is

5. B **5.** (A) principals of good
business managment
(B) principles of good
business management
(C) principals of good
busyness management
(D) principles of good
business managment
(E) Correct as is

6. C **6.** (A) week we had a very lively
(B) week we had a very, lively
(C) week, we had a very lively
(D) week, we had a very livly
(E) Correct as is

7. D **7.** (A) all ready suceded
(B) all ready succeeded
(C) already suceded
(D) already succeeded
(E) Correct as is

8. E **8.** (A) goverment agencies and
they're
(B) goverment agencys and
their
(C) government agencies and
they're
(D) government agencys and
their
(E) Correct as is

9. C **9.** (A) The Leicester hotel and, of
course
(B) the Leicester Hotel and, of
coarse,
(C) the Leicester Hotel and, of
course,
(D) the Leicester hotel and, of
coarse,
(E) Correct as is

10. E **10.** (A) Your's sincerely:
(B) Yours' sincerely,
(C) Yours sincerely:
(D) Yours sincerly,
(E) Correct as is

CORRECTING COMMON ERRORS

CORRECTING COMMON ERRORS

PART THREE

RESOURCES

PART THREE: RESOURCES

The following **Teaching Resources** booklets contain materials that may be used with this part of the Pupil's Edition.

- *Academic and Workplace Skills*
- *Portfolio Assessment* (for Chs. 33, 34, 38)
- *Practice for Assessment in Reading, Vocabulary, and Spelling* (for Ch. 38)

OBJECTIVES

- To prepare and give a speech
- To use critical listening skills as a method of evaluating a speech
- To prepare a brief debate
- To conduct a debate

PROGRAM MANAGER

FORMAL SPEAKING AND DEBATE

- **Independent Practice/ Reteaching** For additional practice and reinforcement, see **The Extemporaneous Speech, Listening Critically, The Debate Proposition, Building a Brief,** and **Building a Rebuttal** in *Academic and Workplace Skills,* pp. 1–5.

- **Additional Instruction** For more information on chapter concepts, see **Chapters 4, 9, 13,** and **18** in *Speech for Effective Communication.*

- **Assessment/Reflection** To assess student work and evaluate progress, see **Portfolio Forms** in *Portfolio Assessment,* pp. 36–39.

- **Review** For exercises on chapter concepts, see **Review Form A** and **Review Form B** in *Academic and Workplace Skills,* pp. 6–7.

CHAPTER OVERVIEW

This chapter provides strategies that can be used for effective speaking and critical listening. The chapter also presents the rules of debate. The first part of the chapter focuses on planning, practicing, and delivering a formal speech. The next part of the chapter presents techniques for active listening. The chapter concludes with instruction in the rules, format, and craft of formal debate. The **Review** exercises present opportunities to apply the skills and strategies addressed in the chapter.

RESOURCES

RESOURCES

33 FORMAL SPEAKING AND DEBATE

Skills and Strategies

In most cases, a formal speech takes place at a predetermined time and location. Whether you are speaking at a student rally, delivering an oral interpretation for a speech contest, making a toast at a wedding, or presenting a workplace proposal, you can prepare in advance the particular message that you want to convey to the audience at the prearranged time.

As you prepare for any type of formal speaking, you can use specific techniques and strategies to help you communicate your intended message to your audience. You can also learn techniques to help you evaluate a speech effectively when you are a member of an audience.

Becoming an Effective Speaker

If you plan, prepare, and practice your speech, you are more likely to be successful in accomplishing your purpose for speaking. There are several important factors that you should consider when you plan your speech, including

- your purpose for speaking
- the topic you are speaking about
- the occasion for your speech and the audience you will be speaking to

Preparing a Speech

Preparation is the key to a good speech. The first step is to consider your purpose for speaking. For example, some of the most common purposes are to inform, to persuade, and to entertain.

PURPOSE	DESCRIPTION OF SPEECH	EXAMPLES OF SPEECH TITLES
To inform	gives facts *or* explains how to do something	Job Opportunities for the Year 2000 How to Make a Silk-Screened Poster
To persuade	attempts to change an opinion *or* attempts to get listeners to act	Why Our Town Should Fine Polluters How Violence on Television Affects Children
To entertain	relates an amusing story or incident	My Most Awkward Moment

Selecting a Topic

Although your speech topic will sometimes be assigned to you, often you can choose your own topic. If you are able to choose your topic, be sure to select something you're interested in. If you aren't interested in your subject, you can't expect your audience to be very enthusiastic either. To plan effectively, you will need to answer the following questions as you select your topic.

- *What is your overall purpose in speaking?* Do you want to inform, persuade, or entertain your listeners?
- *What is the occasion for the speech?* Will the topic you are considering fit the occasion?
- *How much time will you have?* Can your speech topic be limited so that you can cover it effectively in the time allowed?

QUICK REMINDER

Write several topics for impromptu speeches such as *educational goals, community service, popular music trends,* and *favorite movies* on the chalkboard. Select a topic and explain to students that you are going to give a one-minute talk. After you finish, explain to students the difference between this kind of impromptu speech and formal methods.

CRITICAL THINKING

Synthesis. You may wish to involve your class in a brainstorming session to generate topics for speeches. Ask students to make lists of current issues that are discussed in the news. As students name topics, help them to see how purpose, audience, and method of delivery are interrelated. For example, discuss how the President might talk about global warming at a staff meeting (impromptu), at a presidential debate (extemporaneous), and at a policy address to the United Nations (memorized).

RESOURCES

RESOURCES

Analyzing Your Audience

As you plan your speech and limit your topic, you will also need to consider the needs and interests of your audience.

AUDIENCE CONSIDERATIONS		
QUESTIONS ABOUT AUDIENCE	EVALUATION	YOUR SPEECH WILL NEED TO
What does the audience already know about this subject?	very little	provide background or details to inform your listeners more completely
	a little	include some background details
	a lot	focus on interesting issues or aspects of the topic
How interested will the audience be in this subject?	very interested	maintain your listeners' interest
	somewhat interested	focus on aspects of the topic that most interest them
	uninterested	focus on persuading your listeners that this topic is very important

Organizing Speech Notes and Materials

After you have focused your speech topic so that it suits your overall purpose as well as your audience's needs and interests, gather and organize the information that you plan to present in your speech.

👉 **REFERENCE NOTE:** For more information about researching information, see pages 435–493 and 1051–1067.

Most experienced public speakers prefer to use a method of speaking that allows them to speak comfortably to their audience. An *extemporaneous speech* is prepared but not memorized. For an extemporaneous speech, you usually write out a complete outline of your speech, and then you prepare note cards to guide you when you are presenting your speech. This method of speaking gives you an opportunity to use the most natural way of speaking and looking at your audience.

GUIDELINES FOR SPEECH NOTE CARDS

1. Write only one key idea, possibly accompanied by a brief example or detail, on each card.
2. Make a special note card for a quotation or a series of dates or statistics that you plan to read word for word.
3. Make a special note card to indicate when you should pause to show a visual, such as a chart, diagram, graph, or model.
4. Number your completed cards to keep them in order.

Practicing Your Speech

Once you have developed your outline and written your stack of note cards, you're ready to practice your speech. Failure to rehearse the presentation sufficiently is the most common reason for awkwardness and ineffectual delivery by inexperienced speakers. As experienced speakers know, you have to practice your speech thoroughly in order to make it sound spontaneous. Remember that there are only three aspects by which your audience can judge your speech, and that you can improve all of these with practice:

1. *Your ideas:* Your written speech outline that you have now transferred onto your speech note cards contains your central message. Rehearse until you are comfortable and familiar with the entire speech that you plan to deliver. Try to use expressive words that help your listeners visualize clearly the ideas you want them to understand.

2. *Your body:* Your "body language" should reinforce the message you intend to convey to your audience. The way

RESOURCES

COMMON ERROR

Problem. Students often have difficulty distinguishing between notes and a detailed script. Reading notes verbatim spoils the spontaneity that is so effective in extemporaneous speaking.

Solution. Stress that key ideas on note cards should be represented by signal words or short phrases, not by complete sentences. Suggest that students use a highlighter to make these words or phrases stand out. Encourage students to use note cards that contain just enough information to jog the memory.

RESOURCES

LEARNING STYLES

Visual Learners. You might suggest that students develop and use visuals whenever possible. Charts, diagrams, or illustrations shared with the audience become integral parts of speeches and keep students from relying on notes.

TECHNOLOGY TIP

Statistical information is best presented visually. You may want to encourage students to use computers to develop simple charts or graphs. The graphs could be similar to those used by many newspapers and magazines.

you stand at the podium, the way you move as you talk, and the way you interact with the audience all make a definite impression on your listeners.

- *Stand confidently.* Look alert and interested in what you're saying.
- *Use natural gestures.* Use relaxed, normal gestures as you speak.
- *Make eye contact with your audience.* Looking directly at many different people in your audience makes it seem as though you are speaking conversationally with them.

3. *Your voice:* Speak loudly and clearly to ensure that everyone in your audience can hear you. Try to make sure your voice is interesting to listen to; use a normal variety of vocal patterns.

- *Volume.* Be loud enough to be heard; however, you can raise and lower your volume for emphasis as you speak.
- *Pitch.* Use the natural rise and fall of your voice to emphasize various ideas; avoid a monotone.
- *Stress.* Give emphasis to important words or phrases.
- *Rate.* Speak at a comfortable, relaxed pace; however, you can vary your rate, or you can pause briefly for emphasis where such a pause would be effective.

Delivering a Speech

Several different methods can be used to present your speech. The type of speaking occasion usually dictates the most suitable method.

METHODS OF DELIVERING A SPEECH		
TYPE OF SPEECH	ADVANTAGES	DISADVANTAGES
Manuscript speech (read to audience word for word from a prepared script)	provides exact words you wish to say; less chance of errors or omissions	doesn't permit audience feedback; tends to be dull

(continued)

METHODS OF DELIVERING A SPEECH *(continued)*		
TYPE OF SPEECH	ADVANTAGES	DISADVANTAGES
Memorized speech (memorized word for word from script and recited to audience)	gives speaker freedom to move around and look at audience	may not sound natural; requires much practice and memorization; risk of forgetting speech
Extemporaneous speech (outlined and carefully prepared, but not memorized; note cards often used)	sounds natural; allows speaker to respond to audience in a natural manner	requires practice and preparation
Impromptu speech (given on the spur of the moment, without notes or preparation)	sounds very natural	can sound disorganized; is not suitable for a formal speech

On radio or television, speakers often use manuscripts so they can stay within rigid time limits. For speech contests or for formal programs, speeches are often memorized. Whenever a speaker must give an unexpected short speech, it's usually impromptu.

However, for a formal speech that is delivered to a live audience, the extemporaneous method is usually preferred. Audiences respond more enthusiastically to extemporaneous speeches because they usually sound more natural and also provide the best opportunities for response and interaction between the speaker and the audience.

Speaking Effectively

Before you give your speech, you may feel nervous. This feeling is normal. However, it's important for you not to allow

RESOURCES

A DIFFERENT APPROACH

Speakers often think they are using more vocal variety than they actually are. Encourage students to record their speeches and evaluate how they sound. Have them exaggerate their use of volume, pitch, stress, and rate.

MEETING *individual* NEEDS

LEP/ESL

General Strategies. Giving English-language learners an opportunity to demonstrate their proficiency in their native languages can provide a boost to their self-esteem and can change the way their fellow students perceive them. If they want to, allow students to give presentations in both English and their native languages.

COMMON ERROR

Problem. Inexperienced speakers often fail to make eye contact with their audiences, sometimes staring at the back wall or delivering their speeches to only one person.

Solution. Tell students that they can look at people's foreheads or at the tops of their heads. To help remind students to direct their speeches to the entire audience, suggest that they write notations on their note cards to look at specific people in different areas of the room.

RESOURCES

COOPERATIVE LEARNING

Ask students to try the LQ2R study method in one of their classes. Later, divide the class into small groups. Members of each group should take turns reporting their success in applying the LQ2R method. Each group should compile a list of the difficulties it encountered and brainstorm for possible remedies. Afterward, have each group share its results with the entire class.

nervousness to distract you to the extent that it affects your speaking. Here are some suggestions that can help.

1. *Be prepared.* Avoid excessive nervousness by carefully organizing your speech and becoming familiar with your note cards and any visuals you plan to use.
2. *Practice your speech.* Rehearse as if you're giving the actual presentation.
3. *Focus on your purpose for speaking.* Concentrate on what you want your listeners to feel, believe, or do as a result of your speech.

Active Listening

Hearing and listening aren't the same. If you can detect sounds, hearing just happens; however, listening requires you to think about and analyze what you hear. There are a number of techniques that you can use, enabling you to listen well and to evaluate a speech effectively.

Listening and Responding Politely

When you are listening to a speaker, be sure to give the speaker a chance to express his or her complete message before you respond. Here are some tips for listening and responding politely.

1. Pay attention. Don't distract others.
2. Respect the speaker and keep an open mind. Try to understand the speaker's point of view. Be aware that your own point of view affects the way you evaluate the opinions and values of others.
3. Wait to hear the speaker's whole message before you make judgments or ask questions.
4. Ask appropriate questions loudly enough for all to hear. For better understanding, summarize or paraphrase the speaker's point you are questioning.
5. Use polite, effective language and gestures that are appropriate to the situation.

Using the LQ2R Method

The LQ2R study method is especially helpful when you are listening to a speaker who is giving information—for example, a teacher giving a lecture in class.

L   *Listen* carefully to all of the material as it is being presented to you. Focus your attention on the speaker's words and the meaning of the speaker's message.

Q   *Question* yourself as you listen. Make a list, either mentally or by taking notes, of the most important questions that occur to you as you listen to the speaker's presentation.

R   *Recite* in your own mind the information as you hear it being presented. Mentally summarize the information or jot down notes as you listen.

R   *Relisten* as the speaker concludes the presentation. Major points may be reemphasized.

Listening Critically

Listening critically means evaluating and analyzing while you listen. Critical listening is particularly important whenever you are listening to information that is new to you or whenever you are listening to a speaker who is trying to persuade you to feel, believe, or do something.

Some persuasive speakers may use propaganda devices to influence their listeners. *Propaganda devices* are statements, sometimes based on invalid arguments, that are used to convince listeners to believe in something or to take some action. For example, the mass media—such as television, radio, and newspapers—carry many paid advertisements that try to influence you by using propaganda or persuasive devices. You will be better able to evaluate a speaker's message without being misled by unfair appeals if you learn to recognize some of the common propaganda devices. (See pages 291–343 for more about persuasive methods.)

You can't possibly remember every word a speaker says when you listen to a speech. However, if you listen critically, you'll be able to identify and analyze the most important parts of the speaker's message.

RESOURCES

CRITICAL THINKING

Analysis. Ask students to distinguish between the experience of hearing news over the radio and seeing and hearing it on television. Ask students to name the medium they prefer and to give reasons for their preference. Lead students into a discussion of how propaganda devices are used on both the radio and television.

Tell students that persuasive techniques, or propaganda devices, are used not only in the media, but also in everyday situations. Have students listen for persuasive techniques in conversations they hear throughout the day; ask students to identify the techniques and discuss them in class.

TECHNOLOGY TIP

If it is possible, record TV commercials on a VCR. Show them in class and discuss the persuasive techniques employed in each. Have students decide whether or not the music and the visual images are related to the product and the intended audience. For each ad, ask students to comment on the effectiveness of the message.

RESOURCES

INTEGRATING THE LANGUAGE ARTS

Literature Link. Responding effectively to an essay that is read aloud tests all aspects of critical listening. John Donne's "Meditation 17" and selections from Elie Wiesel's *Night* and from Sir Richard Steele and Joseph Addison's *The Spectator* are all suitable for such an exercise. After reading a selection to your students, have a class discussion to analyze it by using the **Guidelines for Listening Critically.**

GUIDELINES FOR LISTENING CRITICALLY	
Find main ideas.	What are the most important points? Listen for clue words a speaker might use, such as *major, main, most important,* or similar words.
Identify significant details.	What dates, names, or facts does the speaker use to support the main points of the speech? What kinds of examples or explanations are used to support the main ideas?
Distinguish between facts and opinions.	A fact is a statement that can be proved to be true. An opinion is a belief or a judgment about something; it cannot be proved to be true.
Identify the order of organization.	What kind of order is the speaker using to arrange the details in his or her presentation—time sequence, spatial order, order of importance?
Note comparisons and contrasts.	Are some details compared or contrasted with others?
Understand cause and effect.	Do some of the events that the speaker mentions relate to or affect others?
Predict outcomes and draw conclusions.	What can you reasonably conclude from the facts and evidence that you have gathered from listening to the speech?

☞ **REFERENCE NOTE:** For more information about interpreting and analyzing information, see pages 1104–1107.

Debating

A formal debate involves two teams who discuss a controversial topic publicly in a systematic manner. The discussion topic is called the *proposition.* The *affirmative team* argues that the proposition should be accepted. The *negative team* argues that the proposition should be rejected. To win, the affirmative side must present enough proof to establish its case, while the negative side must refute the affirmative case by defending the status quo or by presenting a counterplan.

Stating a Debate Proposition

The central issue in a debate is a proposition that is stated as a resolution and limited to a specific idea. The proposition should be an issue that is actually debatable, and should offer each side an equal chance to build a reasonable case. The proposition should be clearly stated in language that is understandable to the debaters and to the audience.

DEBATE PROPOSITIONS		
TYPE	**DEFINITION**	**EXAMPLE**
Proposition of fact	determines what is true or false	*Resolved:* That pollution is endangering the world's oceans.
Proposition of value	states the value of a person, place, or thing	*Resolved:* That the American system of education offers learning opportunities to the majority of citizens.
Proposition of policy	determines what action should be taken	*Resolved:* That some form of compulsory public service should be required of all citizens.

A DIFFERENT APPROACH

If possible, arrange for members of your school's debating team to present a mock debate for the class. Have students make a chart like the one on p. 1035 that shows the order of speaking for this debate. Tell the class to take careful notes on points made by each side. Following the debate, allow time for the class to ask the participants questions about debating strategies and techniques. Have the class vote for a winner.

RESOURCES

RESOURCES

INTEGRATING THE LANGUAGE ARTS

Speaking and Writing. Students should carefully record all their sources as they research their propositions. While in informal classroom debates it may be acceptable not to cite sources, in formal debates, debaters are expected to document their sources. Explain that failure to provide documentation would result in the loss of a debate.

COMMON ERROR

Problem. Debate propositions that contain emotional language or loaded words may unfairly skew the debate in favor of one side. For example, "Resolved: That drug dealers are scum who should be locked up for good."

Solution. Tell students to use objective, unemotional language. For example, "Resolved: That convicted drug dealers should receive mandatory life sentences." Have students show their propositions to an objective person such as another teacher and ask that person to look for any nonobjective language or emotional language.

Preparing a Debate Brief

A debate requires preparation. Each of the opposing teams must first research the proposition, and then plan a strategy for the debate.

1. *Research the proposition carefully.* Refer to books, newspapers, periodicals, and the Internet to glean useful information. Record on note cards the facts and evidence that you find.

2. *Identify specific issues.* The **issues** in a debate are the specific differences between the affirmative and the negative positions. List the most significant arguments you have for supporting your side of the proposition and the most important arguments you think your opponents will use.

3. *Support your arguments.* Based on the information that you have gathered during your research, identify evidence that will support your arguments and will refute your opponents' probable arguments. You might use examples, quotations, statistics, expert opinions, analogies, or logic.

4. *Build a brief.* A **brief** is an outline for a debate. It contains a logical arrangement of all the arguments needed to prove or disprove a proposition, as well as the evidence you have gathered to support your arguments. (See the model brief on page 1033.)

COMPUTER NOTE: Use the outline feature of your word-processing program to organize your prewriting notes into outline form when you build your brief.

Refuting the Opposing Arguments

In addition to building a strong case for or against the proposition, each team must argue against, or refute, its opponents' case. To refute your opponents' arguments, you should

- state clearly the arguments you are going to refute
- tell the audience how you plan to refute each argument
- present proof to refute each argument by using facts, statistics, quotations, and so on
- explain how the proof you have presented effectively refutes your opponents' arguments

EXCERPT OF A BRIEF—OPPOSING ARGUMENTS

Resolved: That law enforcement agencies should be given greater freedom in investigation and prosecution of crime.

Affirmative

I. Restrictive Supreme Court rulings on law enforcement have resulted in continued increase of major crime.
    A. Violent crime has increased; it has shown an increase of 200% since 1961.
    B. The general crime rate has increased by 25% during the last 5 years, an increase that was considerably greater than the increase in population over the same period.

II. Removing the restrictions on law enforcement agencies would improve protection for all citizens.
    A. Law enforcement officials would be free to perform their work more effectively.
    B. Because they would be able to work with fewer restrictions, law enforcement officials would be able to collect more evidence and solve more crimes.
    C. The crime rate would decrease as people recognized that they did not have the legal loopholes to escape the law.

III. Giving law enforcement agencies greater freedom is the best solution to the problem of crime in the United States.
    A. Other solutions, like citizens' crime watches, are only partially effective. Law enforcement agencies still have to have the freedom to investigate and prosecute.
    B. It would reduce crime; and because fewer crimes would be committed, it would reduce the number of victims.

Negative

I. The current restrictions are not necessarily the cause of the increase in the crime rate.
    A. There is no evidence of a direct link between the rulings of the Supreme Court and an increase in crime.
    B. The rise in the crime rate is directly related to an increase in population.

II. Giving greater freedom to law enforcement agencies would not improve the protections for citizens.
    A. Removal of safeguards to citizens would lead to abuse of authority.
    B. Rather than decreasing, the crime rate would increase as more people were arrested for minor infractions.

III. Giving greater freedom to law enforcement agencies is not the best solution to the problem of the growing crime rate because it would create other problems.
    A. It would lead to a loss of civil liberties and threaten every citizen's right to freedom from harassment.
    B. The increase in arrests for minor crimes would increase the backlog in the court system.

COMMON ERROR

Problem. Students will tend to favor one side of a proposition and may neglect to build arguments for the opposite side.

Solution. Emphasize that the successful debater ignores personal biases and is prepared to argue either side with equal effectiveness.

Building a Rebuttal

A rebuttal is a restatement or a rebuilding of your case. (The word *rebuttal* is related to the word *buttress,* both meaning "something that supports or reinforces.") During this part of the debate, each side gets a chance to repair or rebuild the arguments that have been attacked by the opposing team. An effective rebuttal should

- restate your original arguments
- state your position on your opponents' attacks
- present proof that supports your arguments
- point out any weaknesses in your opponents' arguments
- summarize your original arguments and present any additional evidence you have gathered that supports your position

Debating Courteously

A debate should always be won or lost on the basis of reasoned argument and convincing delivery. Traditionally, debaters treat one another courteously. Even when debaters cross-examine or refute an opponent, ridicule, sarcasm, or personal attacks are not acceptable. In addition, debaters should never deliberately misquote their opponents or attempt to distract or disturb them.

As a courtesy, it is customary to refer to participants by terms such as "The first negative speaker," "My worthy opponent," "My colleague," or "My teammate."

Speaking Order for a Debate

Most debates are divided into two parts. During the first part, both teams make *constructive speeches,* attempting to "build" their cases by presenting their arguments for or against the proposition, and attempting to refute, or disprove, the points that they believe will be raised by the opposing team. After a brief intermission, the second part of the debate begins, and both teams make *rebuttal speeches,* replying in their closing speeches to damaging arguments that have been raised by the opposing team.

ORDER OF SPEAKING FOR A STANDARD DEBATE

1. CONSTRUCTIVE SPEECHES	2. REBUTTAL SPEECHES
a. First affirmative	a. First negative
b. First negative	b. First affirmative
c. Second affirmative	c. Second negative
d. Second negative	d. Second affirmative

Cross-Examination Debate Format. The opposing teams in a cross-examination debate question their opponents' major points immediately after each constructive speech, requiring the debaters to think critically and respond quickly.

ORDER OF SPEAKING FOR A CROSS-EXAMINATION DEBATE

1. CONSTRUCTIVE SPEECHES
   a. First affirmative constructive
   b. Cross-examination by second negative
   c. First negative constructive
   d. Cross-examination by first affirmative
   e. Second affirmative constructive
   f. Cross-examination by first negative
   g. Second negative constructive
   h. Cross-examination by second affirmative
2. REBUTTAL SPEECHES
   a. First negative rebuttal
   b. First affirmative rebuttal
   c. Second negative rebuttal
   d. Second affirmative rebuttal

Lincoln-Douglas Debate Format. In a Lincoln-Douglas debate there is only one speaker on each team. Also, propositions in this type of debate are always propositions of value rather than propositions of fact or policy. This one-on-one format is often used when opposing political candidates debate each other. It is named for a series of debates between Abraham Lincoln and Stephen Douglas, rival candidates in a senatorial election in 1858.

A DIFFERENT APPROACH

Though the cross-examination format has now largely replaced the standard format in contests, you may wish to start novice debaters with the standard format. After students have developed some debating skill, they will be ready for a more aggressive debate.

Explain to students that during cross-examination, questions should be brief and should attempt to elicit brief responses. In order to avoid unpleasant surprises, skilled debaters normally ask only questions to which they can anticipate the answers.

RESOURCES

RESOURCES

1035

A DIFFERENT APPROACH

You may wish to have the speaker conduct a short question-and-answer session after each speech in **Exercise 1.** This practice keeps the class involved and permits speakers to experience immediate verbal feedback, thus reinforcing the communication cycle. This practice also helps develop confidence, as students tend to forget their nervousness while fielding questions.

MEETING individual NEEDS

LEARNING STYLES

For **Exercise 2,** you can give students opportunities to develop the note-taking styles that work best for them. Auditory learners might need to record only key words, while visual learners might need to highlight their notes as they study.

ANSWERS
Exercise 1

Speeches will vary. You may prepare a checklist that includes every skill and strategy discussed in this segment. Use this as a guide for evaluating each speaker.

**ORDER OF SPEAKING
FOR A LINCOLN-DOUGLAS DEBATE**

1. CONSTRUCTIVE SPEECH
    a. Affirmative constructive
    b. Cross-examination by negative
    c. Negative constructive
    d. Cross-examination by affirmative
2. REBUTTAL SPEECHES
    a. Affirmative rebuttal
    b. Negative rebuttal
    c. Affirmative rebuttal

Conducting and Judging a Debate

A chairperson often presides during a debate. A speaker may appeal to the chairperson if any debating procedures or time limits have been violated by the opposing team.

The most common method of determining the winner of a debate is by decision of three appointed judges. The judges are expected to base their decision on the merits of the debate and not on their own views about the proposition. Occasionally, the audience may be invited to determine the winning team.

Review

▶ EXERCISE 1   **Preparing and Giving a Speech**

Choose a topic for a three- to five-minute speech to be presented to your English class. Consider the occasion, the interests of the listeners in your classroom audience, and your own interests when selecting a topic. Write down—in sentence form—your purpose for speaking. Do research to gather material, make an outline, and prepare note cards. Include at least one visual. Then, deliver your speech, using effective speaking techniques as outlined on pages 1025–1028.

EXERCISE 2   Listening Critically

Listen to a short speech presented by a classmate, by your teacher, or on television or radio. Take brief notes. Then answer the following questions about the speech.

1. Identify the purpose of the speech: to inform, to persuade, or to entertain.
2. What are the main ideas expressed in the speech?
3. What details are used to support or explain the key ideas in the speech?
4. In what ways did the speaker's voice (and body language, if seen) contribute to the message of the speech?
5. Did the speaker achieve the purpose he or she intended? Explain why or why not.

EXERCISE 3   Preparing a Debate Brief

Working in groups of four or six, write a proposition for debate. Each group will then divide into affirmative and negative teams, research the topic, and prepare written debate briefs, using the example on page 1033 as a model. Select one of the following suggested topics, or select an alternate topic. Write the chosen topic in the correct debate-proposition style (see page 1031).

1. Minimum wage laws
2. Patents for genetic engineering
3. Unemployment benefits
4. Student input on curriculum for schools
5. Violence on television
6. Value-added tax for resale of artwork
7. National health insurance
8. Recycling programs
9. Prisoners' rights
10. Uniforms in public schools

EXERCISE 4   Conducting a Debate

Stage a debate, using the affirmative and negative teams, the debate proposition, and the briefs developed for Exercise 3. Select one of the debate formats discussed on pages 1034–1035, and assign specific time limits. Appoint a chairperson to preside over the debate. Select judges for the debate, or create a ballot for use by the whole class when deciding the outcome.

RESOURCES

ANSWERS
Exercise 2

Answers will vary. Each student should present complete answers to the five questions.

ANSWERS
Exercise 3

The briefs should be judged in terms of logical arrangement, identification of all the relevant issues, and completeness of supporting evidence. Sources should be adequately documented.

ANSWERS
Exercise 4

Debate content will vary. All debates must follow established rules set forth in this chapter. Remind students that your evaluation is not contingent on your own opinions about each proposition, but is determined by the effectiveness with which each side presents its arguments.

RESOURCES

OBJECTIVES

- To prepare for an informational interview
- To prepare for a job interview
- To prepare for and practice participating in a college entrance interview
- To present a group discussion
- To present an oral interpretation adapted from a literary work

CHAPTER OVERVIEW

This chapter develops the communication skills that are a natural extension of the reading and writing skills developed in English instruction. It explains the communication cycle and provides suggestions for giving and receiving information. The chapter discusses techniques for conducting an interview and for being interviewed.

Both informal and formal group discussions are included, with responsibilities for participants, rules of order, and basic concepts of parliamentary

continued on next page

34 COMMUNICATION SKILLS

Speaking, Listening, and Analyzing Media

To communicate effectively, you need skills for speaking, for listening, and for analyzing media. Because people spend so much time engaged in these activities, it seems that communication is simple; but true communication takes effort. This chapter covers specific techniques to help you improve your communication skills. These skills will help you achieve the purposes of communication: sharing your ideas, emotions, and information, and analyzing what others communicate to you.

The Communication Cycle

Communication occurs in a cycle. A speaker expresses feelings or ideas, and listeners respond; the *mass media* (television, radio, movies, videos, and others) broadcast ideas, and viewers respond. This response, called *feedback,* may be verbal (words) or nonverbal (facial expressions, body language, or actions).

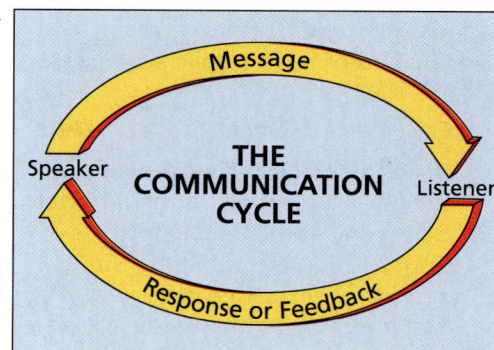

THE COMMUNICATION CYCLE

Message
Speaker
Listener
Response or Feedback

Giving and Receiving Information **1039**

Giving and Receiving Information

The purpose of some of the simplest communication situations is to convey information. In these circumstances, the communication is successful when the speaker gives the information clearly and precisely and when the listener interprets and understands the information correctly. One common example of this type of communication is giving or receiving instructions or directions. Look at the following chart for suggestions to improve your effectiveness whether you are the speaker or the listener in a situation that involves instructions.

GIVING AND RECEIVING DIRECTIONS	
Giving	**Receiving**
Divide the instructions into steps, making each step as simple and easy to understand as possible. Explain the steps in an order that makes sense.	Listen to each step. Look for words—such as *first, second, next, then,* and *last*—that tell you when each step ends and the next one begins.
Remember to include each step or all the necessary information for completing the process.	Listen for the number of steps and the order of steps. Picture yourself doing each step. Take notes if necessary.
Check to see if your listener understands the instructions. If necessary, repeat all directions or instructions so that the other person can remember them.	Make sure you have all the necessary information and understand the directions. Ask questions if you are unclear about any step.

On the following page are some suggestions for improving your communication when you are giving or receiving telephone messages.

procedure given. The section on oral interpretation shows students how to choose, adapt, and present works of literature.

The chapter also gives students an opportunity to apply critical-thinking skills to analyze and interpret information from the full spectrum of the media.

MEETING *individual* NEEDS

LEP/ESL

General Strategies. Understanding related ideas, distinguishing word boundaries, and detecting sentence parts are just a few of the listening skills that students might have trouble with. Strategies that will improve these skills include small group discussions, exposure to visuals related to the topic, giving questions that will be answered after listening, answering multiple-choice questions while students listen a second time, and answering true-false questions after a third listening.

STUDENTS WITH SPECIAL NEEDS

Some students need visual cues to help them listen carefully. Before asking students to listen, write a set of questions on the chalkboard that will help them focus on specific information while they listen.

RESOURCES

RESOURCES

1039

COMMON ERROR

Problem. Even after listening carefully to instructions, students often forget crucial steps.

Solution. Tell students that after listening to instructions, they should repeat the instructions aloud to ensure that all steps have been remembered. If there are more than three steps, they should be written down.

COOPERATIVE LEARNING

Have students imagine receiving the following telephone message: "Tell him I'll meet him in the park at 7:30." Ask students what further information would be needed to make this message clear [the caller's name, who is being called, where in the park, A.M. or P.M., the caller's telephone number].

Group students in pairs and have the pairs practice creating messages. Have partners switch messages to determine if the messages are complete. Ask volunteers to share their examples with the class.

TECHNOLOGY TIP

Remind students that the rules for telephone messages also apply when a caller reaches an answering machine. Callers should identify themselves clearly, give their return number, and leave a brief but complete message. If they reach a wrong number, they should simply say so and apologize.

1040

GIVING AND RECEIVING TELEPHONE MESSAGES	
MAKING CALLS	**RECEIVING CALLS**
If you reach the wrong number, tell the person who answers that you are sorry for the disturbance.	Be understanding if someone dials your number by error. Everyone makes mistakes.
Avoid calling early in the morning, late at night, or at mealtimes.	If someone calls at an inconvenient time, ask if you may return the call later.
Say who you are as soon as the person answers. If the person you're calling is not there, leave your name and number and perhaps a short message.	Say hello when you answer. Take a message if the call is for someone who is out. Repeat the message to make sure you wrote it correctly.
Don't stay on the phone too long. If you place the call, it's your responsibility to end it.	If you need to end the call, say politely that you need to go. You might offer to call back at another time.

Interviews

The purpose of an interview is to communicate by exchanging ideas or information. You might take part in an interview when you gather information, apply for a job, or apply for admission to a college.

Conducting an Interview

You may need to interview certain people for firsthand information when you are preparing a research paper, a class report, a speech, or a newspaper article. Here are suggestions about how to be an effective interviewer.

Preparing for the Interview

- Make arrangements well in advance. Set up a time that is convenient for the other person to meet with you.
- Make a list of questions to ask. Make sure the questions are arranged in a logical order and require more than *yes* or *no* answers.

Participating in the Interview

- Arrive on time.
- Be polite and patient.
- With the other person's permission, take notes or use a tape recorder.
- Avoid argument. Be tactful and courteous. Remember, the interview was granted at your request.
- Listen carefully and ask follow-up questions if you do not understand an answer or if you feel that you need more information.
- Follow up the interview. Review your notes to refresh your memory, and summarize the material you have gathered. Send a note expressing your appreciation for the interview.

Interviewing for a Position

You can usually expect to be interviewed when you apply for a position. For example, a prospective employer will usually interview you before deciding whether to hire you. Other situations that call for interviews include entering college, joining a club or organization, and applying for a scholarship or grant.

<table>
<tr><td>

HOW TO INTERVIEW FOR A JOB

1. *Arrange an appointment.* Write a business letter of application (see pages 1093–1095) in which you request an interview for the job. If you are granted an interview, be prompt for your appointment.
2. *Bring a résumé.* If you haven't already submitted it, take your résumé (see page 1095) to the interview and give it to the interviewer.

</td></tr>
</table>

(continued)

RESOURCES

COOPERATIVE LEARNING

You may wish to have students interview each other about a topic of interest: hobbies, a question of national concern, or aspects of school life. Pair students and allow them time to go over the guidelines, compose questions, and organize their thoughts about the topic. Next, each student should take a turn at interviewing and at being interviewed. After students finish, they should work alone to summarize the interview in their notes. Then have students use their notes to give brief oral reports to the class about the people they interviewed.

RESOURCES

TECHNOLOGY TIP

To ensure that key statements are remembered accurately, professional interviewers sometimes use tape recorders. If tape recorders are available, have students use them for practice interviews with classmates.

A DIFFERENT APPROACH

Invite a guidance counselor to give the class advice on preparing for job interviews. Then have a potential employer as a guest speaker. Conduct short practice interviews in front of the class between two or three students and this speaker. Students should use the guidelines for interviewing for a position on pp. 1041–1042.

HOW TO INTERVIEW FOR A JOB *(continued)*

3. *Be neat and well-groomed.* It's important to look your best when applying for any type of job.

4. *Answer questions clearly and honestly.* Answer the questions the interviewer asks, adding any additional information that might inform the employer that you are the right person for the job.

5. *Ask questions.* Job applicants often ask for information about work hours, salary, or chances for advancement. By your questions, show that you know something about the company or organization.

6. *Be prepared to be tested.* The employer may require you to take tests that demonstrate your skills or intelligence or reflect your personality.

7. *Follow up the interview.* After the interview, it's polite to write a short thank-you note (see page 1093). Tell the interviewer that you appreciated the opportunity for the interview and that you look forward to hearing from the organization in the near future.

☞ **REFERENCE NOTE:** For more about writing business letters and completing application forms, see pages 1088–1097.

Group Discussions

Group discussions are common in all types of gatherings, such as cooperative learning groups, school clubs, community organizations, workplace teams, or legislative assemblies. An effective group discussion always has a specific purpose. Some of the most common purposes for group discussions are

- to share ideas
- to suggest solutions for solving a problem
- to make an evaluation, decision, or recommendation

Whenever a group is deciding on the purpose to be accomplished by its discussion, an important factor is the time available. If there's a specific time limit, the group will need to consider this when deciding on its goal.

Informal Group Discussions

An informal group discussion is one that takes place between members of a small group and that has no formal rules or procedures. Every group discussion should have a clear purpose. In some groups, the discussion follows a prepared outline of topics, or an *agenda.* The agenda may be set by the chairperson, or it may be established by a preliminary discussion and agreed upon by the group.

In order for group discussions to be effective, all participants must play a role. Here are some of the responsibilities of members of a group discussion.

A Chairperson's Responsibilities

1. Announce the topic to be discussed, identify the goal, and explain the agenda.
2. Follow the agenda, keeping the discussion focused.
3. Encourage active participation by each group member.
4. Avoid disagreements by being objective and settling conflicts or confusions fairly.

A Secretary's or Reporter's Responsibilities

1. Make notes of significant information, decisions, findings, or actions of the group.
2. Prepare a final report.

A Participant's Responsibilities

1. Take part in the discussion.
2. Cooperate with other members, being fair and considerate of others' opinions and suggestions.

Formal Group Discussions

Groups that meet on a regular basis often conduct their discussions of important issues following an established set of rules known as *parliamentary procedure.* The single most authoritative source is a book called *Robert's Rules of Order, Revised* by Henry Robert.

The basic principles of parliamentary procedure as found in *Robert's Rules of Order* protect the rights of individual members of the group while providing a systematic means for dealing with issues that come before the group for a decision.

RESOURCES

A DIFFERENT APPROACH

Invite a local businessperson to talk to your class about group discussions at his or her workplace. Ask the speaker to tell why group discussions are important and to give some tips for holding successful group discussions.

MEETING *individual* NEEDS

LEARNING STYLES

Visual Learners. You may wish to videotape informal and formal group discussions. Have the students watch the videos and then compare and contrast the two types of discussions. Ask the class to suggest appropriate forums for each. Suggestions might include planning session—informal; PTA and school board meetings—formal.

RESOURCES

A DIFFERENT APPROACH

Students might want to establish a public interest group, such as an ecology club that is devoted to recycling in and around the school. Have them follow parliamentary procedure in club meetings while defining problems and offering solutions. Point out that discussions may go more smoothly and efficiently if students realize that it is possible to amend a motion. If an amendment is considered, it must be voted on separately before voting on the main motion.

COMMON ERROR

Problem. Negative motions tend to confuse the voting procedure.

Solution. Clarify motions before they are voted on and remind students to state motions only in the affirmative.

Here are some of the basic principles of parliamentary procedure:

- The majority decides.
- The minority has the right to be heard.
- Decisions are made by voting.

The benefits of a system of parliamentary procedures are that it allows a group to deal in an orderly, organized way with issues that are raised and decisions that need to be made about those issues.

ORDER OF BUSINESS

A formal group meeting usually follows the standard order of business suggested in *Robert's Rules of Order.* The words spoken may vary slightly, but the general idea is shown in the examples below.

1. *Call to order:* The chairperson says, "The meeting will come to order."
2. *Reading and approval of the minutes:* The chairperson says, "The secretary (or recorder) will read the minutes from our last meeting." The secretary reads these minutes, and the chairperson inquires, "Are there additions or corrections to the minutes?" The minutes are then approved, or they are corrected and then approved.
3. *Officer's reports:* The chairperson calls for a report from other officers by saying, for example, "Will the treasurer please give us a report?"
4. *Committee reports:* The chairperson may ask the presiding officer of standing committees and then of special committees to make reports to the group.
5. *Old business:* Any issues that were not resolved at the last meeting may now be discussed. The chairperson may ask, "Is there any old business to be discussed?"
6. *New business:* Any new issues that have not previously been discussed may now be addressed.
7. *Announcements:* The chairperson may ask the members, "Are there any announcements?"
8. *Adjournment:* The chairperson ends the meeting, saying, "The meeting is now adjourned."

PROCEDURES FOR DISCUSSION OF BUSINESS

The meeting follows specific procedures for discussion of business.

1. Anyone who wishes to speak must be recognized by the chairperson.
2. A participant may introduce a motion, or proposal, for discussion, by beginning "I move that. . . ."
3. To support the motion, another member must second it, saying "I second the motion." A motion that is not seconded is dropped.
4. A motion that has been seconded may be discussed by the group.
5. Other motions made by members may amend the motion under consideration; may limit, extend, postpone, or set time limits on debate; or may refer the motion to a committee.
6. After discussion, the group votes on the motion. The chairperson usually votes only in the case of a tie.

Oral Interpretation

An *oral interpretation* is the presentation of a work of literature to a group of listeners in order to express the meaning contained in the literary work. Acting and speaking skills—vocal techniques, facial expression, body language, and gestures—are used to convey the overall meaning of the literary work.

Choosing and Adapting Material

It's easier to select material for an oral interpretation if you have a specific purpose and audience in mind. Factors you will need to consider include the length of time that will be allowed for your presentation and your audience's interests. Props or costumes are not usually used for oral interpretations; instead, the audience uses its imagination.

An abbreviated version, or *cutting*, of a work of fiction or nonfiction, a long poem, or a play is usually prepared for an oral interpretation. Here are some ways to make a cutting.

RESOURCES

MEETING *individual* NEEDS

LEP/ESL

General Strategies. You may want to have English-language learners present oral interpretations in their native languages. Require that their interpretations be followed by English translations. This procedure will allow students to express themselves in languages in which they are fluent and will give the rest of class the chance to hear languages other than English.

Students could find literature that has already been translated into English or they could translate selections themselves.

LEARNING STYLES

Auditory Learners. To give students a better idea of what is involved in an oral interpretation, play a recording of a celebrity reading a famous story, prepare a presentation of one of your favorite short works of fiction, or ask a drama teacher to have a student present an oral interpretation.

If possible, before the presentation, students might read the source work. After the presentation, discuss the performance with the class. You could use the following questions to guide the discussion:

1. Was the selection well chosen?
2. Was the adaptation effective?
3. Did the person presenting the oral interpretation use voice and movement variations to convey the meaning of the selection?

RESOURCES

INTEGRATING THE LANGUAGE ARTS

Literature Link. Shakespearean soliloquies such as "The Seven Ages of Man," found in *As You Like It,* Act II, scene 7, provide many opportunities for changes in voice, facial expression, and body language. You could show students how to convey the seven ages through variations in volume, pitch, rate, and tone of voice. Then assign each student a short passage from soliloquies given by other Shakespearean characters such as Hamlet, Ophelia, Macbeth, or Lady Macbeth. Allow students to rehearse their passages in pairs before they present the passages to the class.

ANALYZING INFORMATION FROM THE MEDIA

Tell students that the purpose of analyzing different media sources is to help select the best source or sources for particular types of information. Remind students that they must think critically about the impact of a medium's unique features both on presentation and on content. Students should pay close attention to how media present opinions as well as facts. Students also should be able to recognize biased information, loaded words and images, and faulty reasoning.

1046

1. Follow the story line in chronological order.
2. Delete dialogue tags such as *he responded grumpily.* Instead, use these clues to tell you how to interpret the character's words as you express them.
3. Delete passages that don't contribute to the overall effect or general impression you intend to create.

Presenting an Oral Interpretation

When you prepare your oral interpretation, you may need to write an introduction that sets the scene, tells something about the author, or gives some necessary background details.

When presenting an oral interpretation, you may want to prepare a *reading script,* which is usually typed (double-spaced) and can be marked to help you during your presentation. For example, you might mark a slash (/) to indicate a dramatic pause, or underline words to show emphasis.

When you have developed your reading script, rehearse several interpretations. Use your body and your voice to portray characters in distinctive ways. Use body language and gestures to emphasize the meaning of the selection or to reveal the character's personality as you narrate and act out the story.

COMPUTER NOTE: Use your word-processing program to prepare the reading script for your oral presentation. You can use bold, italic, and underline formatting to indicate presentation directions and notes to yourself. You can even change the type size and style for more emphasis.

Analyzing Information from the Media

When you look for up-to-date news and comprehensive information about the world today, you can choose from broadcast media (television, radio, movies, and videotapes), print media (newspapers, magazines, and books), and electronic sources (the Internet, databases, and CD-ROMs). Within each medium, you can choose from thousands of titles and sources. To make these choices intelligently, you need to know how the ways in which the different media prepare and distribute information affect the content of what you read, view, and hear.

Each medium has unique features that determine what you see and hear and that provide different capabilities. Depending on the type of news or information you seek, the unique features can be either strengths or weaknesses.

Broadcast Media

The messages delivered by broadcast media exist only as long as it takes to say them. Unless you have a videotape or audiotape of the program, you cannot reexamine the program's message or analyze it at length. Most important, whatever you see or hear has been carefully chosen and edited to reflect the editor's or producer's idea of what should be broadcast.

Television engages viewers in a way that print does not. TV news programs present an instant, visual history of each day's news as it happens. But these programs report only the news events that producers select as the most important and only as many as fit in the programmed time. Reports, live interviews, and images are selected and edited tightly to provide maximum impact in a short time. These time constraints make complete, balanced coverage very difficult. Even extended coverage, which documentaries and some cable stations provide, is subject to time constraints.

Radio news reports are limited by the same time constraints as television. Radio also lacks images to provide clarification. Some radio talk shows analyze subjects in greater depth, but listeners should be careful to seek those programs whose speakers are experts with solid credentials.

Movies and **videotapes** based on true stories let viewers hear conversations and see actions that *might* have taken place. If a movie is well done, if the characters seem real and their motivations are clear, viewers may learn a lot. Movies based on historic events can provide factual information and entertainment at the same time. Remember, though, you are viewing the director's, writer's, and editor's ideas about characters and events, which may be quite different from others' views of what happened.

Print Media

Newspapers, magazines, and books allow you to read all or just a part of the material, and to reread. You have time to analyze and verify the information.

RESOURCES

RESOURCES

Newspapers give readers more details (facts, statistics, charts, full texts of speeches and documents) than most TV or radio news broadcasts provide, but the printed information is at least several hours old because of the time it takes to create and deliver the newspaper. As with broadcast media, writers, editors, and publishers choose the information to be printed, decide on its placement, and select the accompanying images. Newspapers often devote two full pages to editorials and columns that offer opinions and analyses of the news.

Newsmagazines review some of the week's important events. The magazines also include color photos and feature stories of people in the news. As with newspapers, editors and publishers choose which story and image should be on the cover and what other stories should be reported.

Books take a long time to research, write, and publish. A nonfiction book about a current topic is at least a year out-of-date by the time it is published. Most almanacs and encyclopedias are updated annually. Despite their lack of timeliness, books usually are reliable sources of information.

Electronic Sources

Electronic sources are often the primary choice for information today because the information is up-to-date and easy to obtain.

The Internet gives users access to late-breaking news and thousands of sources of information, both current and historical. As with other media sources, the accuracy and reliability of information obtained from the Internet depend on the provider.

Databases and **CD-ROMs** are similar to books in that they take a long time to write, edit, and produce. Once the primary source has been created, however, updates are much faster than updates of books. Databases and CD-ROMs are generally reliable sources of information.

Analyzing the Media Critically

Here are some suggestions for analyzing the media critically.

1. *Be aware.* Remember that all media have *gatekeepers,* information gatherers (reporters, editors, publishers, directors), who select what you see and hear. Be wary of accepting the media version as being complete and accurate.

2. *Evaluate.* Distinguish facts from opinions, and, as best you can, judge the accuracy of what you are viewing. Is the information unbiased, or does it present only one viewpoint? If a person is presented as an expert, what are his or her qualifications? Be on the lookout for faulty reasoning and for conclusions based on insufficient evidence. Look for *loaded images,* photographs or video clips chosen to manipulate viewers' emotions and opinions.

3. *Compare coverage or information.* Whose news coverage or information on a subject is best? Sample the various sources available to you, and choose the ones you find most reliable and accurate.

4. *Speak up.* Make your own views known. Send a letter or e-mail to the editor of a newspaper or magazine. If you have suggestions for TV or radio programming, write to the director of programming or the station president.

5. *Think of the medium.* Remember that each medium has strengths and weaknesses that affect the type and amount of information and the way it is presented.

Review

▶ EXERCISE 1   Preparing for an Informational Interview

Select a topic that requires firsthand information from an individual. Design a checklist that includes setting up the interview, doing research, and preparing questions to ask the person being interviewed.

▶ EXERCISE 2   Preparing for a Job Interview

Check the classified section of a local newspaper, and find a job that you might like and for which you are qualified. List the questions that you would expect an interviewer to ask you and the answers you would provide. Also, make a list of questions you would ask the interviewer about the job or position.

▶ EXERCISE 3   Practicing a College Entrance Interview

Working with a partner, make a list of questions you might be asked by a college admissions officer. Then, make a list of questions you might ask this representative. Have one person act as

RESOURCES

GUIDELINES
Exercise 1

Information will vary. Each student should follow the procedure stated in the text when designing a checklist. All questions should relate to the topic selected.

GUIDELINES
Exercise 2

Each student should select a job that matches his or her interests and abilities. Anticipated interviewer questions should relate to specific qualifications associated with that position. Personal questions about the job should reflect the student's priorities but should be phrased in ways that demonstrate desire to obtain that position.

GUIDELINES
Exercise 3

Questions and answers will vary. Partners should collaborate in compiling interviewer and applicant questions. However, individuals should design responses that reflect personal interests and strengths.

RESOURCES

GUIDELINES
Exercise 4

Discussions will vary. Groups should follow the guidelines in the text for conducting an informal discussion.

GUIDELINES
Exercise 5

Presentations will vary. Students should prepare suitable introductions for their selections, make cuttings that meet the time limit, and retain narrative coherence. Reading scripts might include marginal notations or other devices that remind the speaker when to vary voice and body language to convey different characters.

GUIDELINES
Exercise 6

Reports will vary. Students should compare and contrast the coverage provided by different media, note any biased coverage, analyze the use (or non-use) of images in the coverage, and state a clear opinion of which medium or outlet provided the most thorough coverage.

the interviewer and the other as the person being interviewed. Present the interview in class.

EXERCISE 4 Presenting a Group Discussion

Working with a small group, select and discuss a topic from the following list or find your own topic. Phrase the topic as a specific, focused statement or question. Select a reporter to report the group's findings to the class.

1. Training for a job
2. Ecology
3. Television violence
4. Choosing a college

EXERCISE 5 Presenting an Oral Interpretation

Select a portion of a literary work suitable for a short, oral presentation to your class. Adapt the material, prepare a reading script, and present your interpretation.

EXERCISE 6 Following a Story in Different Media

Working with a small group, choose one national news story. Compare treatment of the story by (a) two national television networks, (b) two different newspapers, (c) two radio stations, and (d) two different weekly newsmagazines. After you answer the following questions, summarize your findings, and report them to the class.

1. How is coverage by the different media similar? different?
2. Did any of the reports give just one side of the story? If so, why do you think that was done?
3. How did the images (or lack of them) affect the coverage?
4. Which report(s) provided the most thorough coverage?

OBJECTIVES

- To locate specific books by using the card catalog and online catalog
- To answer various questions by using the *Readers' Guide*
- To research a specific topic by using a computer
- To draw and label a diagram of the school library

35 THE LIBRARY/ MEDIA CENTER

Finding and Using Information

Libraries contain information in many forms. Written materials include manuscripts, books, pamphlets, and newspapers. In recent years, information has also been stored in other forms, such as audio and video recordings, compact and laser discs, computer databases, and various connections to the Internet. The library is now often called a media center or media resource center because of the wide variety of information resources it contains.

The libraries and media centers that exist in schools and communities are very similar to those found in many businesses. If you understand the arrangement of your school or community library, you will probably be able to use the library in your workplace with very little assistance.

The Librarian

Don't overlook one of the most valuable resources found in a library—your librarian. A librarian is a trained professional who can be your guide in locating and using the library's stored information. Your librarian may even be able to help you find information available from other libraries or information services.

PROGRAM MANAGER

THE LIBRARY/MEDIA CENTER

- **Independent Practice/ Reteaching** For additional practice and reinforcement, see **Online Catalog and Card Catalog, The Library of Congress System,** and **The** *Readers' Guide* in *Academic and Workplace Skills,* pp. 21–24.

- **Review** For exercises on chapter concepts, see **Review Form A** and **Review Form B** in *Academic and Workplace Skills,* pp. 25–28.

CHAPTER OVERVIEW

This chapter describes the components, contents, and effective use of the modern library/media center. After stressing the librarian's value as a resource, the text provides an overview of traditional library systems. The Dewey decimal and Library of Congress systems are explained; the organization of card catalogs is examined. Explanations of the *Readers' Guide* and the vertical file as well as explanations of technological innovations such as the online catalog, microforms, databases, and audiovisual materials are provided.

RESOURCES

RESOURCES

QUICK REMINDER

To help students think about how to find information in the library, ask them to create a list of college- and job-related subjects they would like to explore. List these on the chalkboard. Then, ask students how they would go about finding information concerning these subjects. Lead students to understand that the sources in a library have been arranged so that people can more easily locate information.

MEETING *individual* NEEDS

LEP/ESL

General Strategies. Some of your students might be accustomed to using library classification systems other than the Dewey decimal and Library of Congress systems, both of which were developed in and are primarily used in the United States. For example, some students may have been exposed to the Universal Decimal Classification system, which is popular in Europe. You may wish to spend extra time when introducing the two American systems to make sure English-language learners understand both systems.

ADVANCED STUDENTS

Have small groups of students prepare oral reports about libraries. Possible topics include the history of public libraries in the United States, services offered by public libraries, library careers, or famous libraries.

Finding Books in the Library

The Call Number

The contents of a library are classified and arranged using an organized system of ***call numbers,*** identification codes that are usually found printed on the book's spine. Call numbers are assigned according to one of two classification systems: the *Dewey decimal system* or the *Library of Congress system*.

The Dewey Decimal System

Nonfiction. The Dewey decimal system groups nonfiction books and some works of literature into ten broad categories, numbered according to their subject matter. Each of these broad subject areas covers a wide range of subdivisions.

Fiction. The Dewey decimal system arranges works of fiction alphabetically according to the authors' last names. Works by the same author are arranged alphabetically according to the first important word of the title (excluding *A, An,* and *The*). Some libraries shelve short story collections separately.

The Library of Congress System

Subject categories are identified by a letter code in the Library of Congress system. The first letter of a book's call number always shows the general category; the second letter tells the subcategory. Your library's reference desk will have a complete list of letter codes for Library of Congress categories.

Types of Card Catalogs

There are two types of card catalogs: the traditional card catalog and the online catalog. The traditional ***card catalog*** is a cabinet of drawers filled with alphabetically arranged cards. All books have *title cards* and *author cards*. Nonfiction books also have *subject cards* and sometimes *cross-reference cards*.

Catalog cards give the book's title, author, and call number; they may also give publication facts, indicate the book's page count, and show that it contains illustrations or diagrams.

INFORMATION IN THE CARD CATALOG

① 378.3 RAG Winning scholarships for college: an insider's guide.   **Title Card**

② **Ragins, Marianne**
Winning scholarships for college: an insider's guide/by Marianne Ragins.
NY: H. Holt [© 1994]
158 p.

Author Card

378.3 RAG **Ragins, Marianne**
③ Winning scholarships for college: an insider's guide/by Marianne Ragins.
④ NY: H. Holt [© 1994]
158 p.

Subject Card

378.3 RAG SCHOLARSHIPS—UNITED STATES
⑤ **Ragins, Marianne**
Winning scholarships for college: an insider's guide/by Marianne Ragins.
NY: H. Holt [© 1994]
⑥ 158 p.
ISBN 0805030727
⑦ 1. Scholarships—United States
2. Student aid—United States

1. **Call Number** . . . . .The number assigned to a book by the Dewey decimal or Library of Congress classification system
2. **Author** . . . . .Author's full name, last name first
3. **Title** . . . . .Full title and subtitle of a book
4. **Publisher** . . . . .Place and date of publication
5. **Subject** . . . . .General subject of a book; may show specific headings
6. **Physical Description** . .Description of the book, such as its size and number of pages, and whether it is illustrated
7. **Cross-references** . . . . .Lists titles of subject cards that can refer you to books on the same or related topics

RESOURCES

COOPERATIVE LEARNING
To expose students to card catalog and online catalog information found in the library, have the class generate a list of subjects. Then, combine these subjects randomly so that each student receives a different list of books to locate (fiction and nonfiction). Pair students and take them to the school library. Each pair should use the card catalog or online catalog to identify general categories for titles listed.

RESOURCES

1053

CRITICAL THINKING

CRITICAL THINKING

Analysis and Evaluation. Ask students to suggest the possible advantages of using an online catalog as opposed to the traditional card catalog [greater speed, smaller physical space requirements, capability of retrieving sources beyond your library database services, printouts]. Then, ask students to suggest disadvantages [possible temporary system failures or mechanical breakdowns, fewer people able to access the catalog at any given time].

1054

The ***online catalog*** is a computerized version of the card catalog. The online catalog can locate information quickly and may tell you if a book you are looking for is checked out or if it is available at another library. To see a catalog listing on the library's computer, you type in an author's name, a title, or a subject. The computer then displays the results of your search request. When you choose a title from the list of search results, the computer displays information about the book similar to that in the following example.

Online Catalog Record
AUTHOR: Ragins, Marianne
TITLE: Winning scholarships for college: an insider's guide
EDITION: 1st
PLACE: New York
PUBLISHER: H. Holt
YEAR: 1994
FORMAT: xv, 158 p.; 21 cm
ISBN: 0805030727
SUBJECT: Scholarships—United States.
Student aid—United States.

Using Reference Materials

The *Readers' Guide*

When you need to find a magazine article, use the *Readers' Guide to Periodical Literature.* It indexes articles, poems, and stories from more than one hundred magazines. The *Readers' Guide* provides a great amount of information in a very compact space.

Paperback editions of the *Readers' Guide* are published throughout the year, with each issue listing materials published in the previous two to four weeks. At the end of the year, these paperback issues are then bound into a single, hardcover volume.

As the sample entries on page 1055 show, magazine articles are listed by subject and by author but not by title. The *Readers' Guide* also gives cross-references, indicated by the words *"see"* or *"see also."* A key at the front of the *Readers' Guide* explains abbreviations used in the entries.

Printed *Readers' Guide*

(1) ARCTIC NATIONAL WILDLIFE REFUGE (ALASKA)
(2) The Arctic National Wildlife Refuge: the best of the
last wild places. J. Doherty. il *Smithsonian* v26
(3) p32–41 Mr '96
ARCTIC PEOPLES
See also
(4) Eskimos
ARCTIC REGIONS
See also
North Pole
Nunavut
Oceanography—Arctic regions
Wildlife—Arctic regions
ARENA STAGE (THEATER COMPANY)
(5) Resident theater hopes. R. Brustein. *The New
Republic* v214 p28–30 My 20 '96
(6) ARENOFSKY, JANICE
Pump up your personal integrity. il *Current Health 2*
(7) v22 p20–2 My '96
ARGENTINA
Armed Forces
Forces in Croatia
Argentine troops join the peacekeeping mission in
Croatia [remarks, February 29, 1996]
(8) W. Christopher. *US Department of State
Dispatch* v7 p89 Mr 4 '96
(9)

(1) **Subject entry**
(2) **Name of magazine**
(3) **Page references**
(4) **Subject cross-
reference**
(5) **Title of article**
(6) **Author entry**
(7) **Volume number of
magazine**
(8) **Author of article**
(9) **Date of magazine**

Some libraries subscribe to an online, or computerized, version of the *Readers' Guide*. To use this version, you enter a search word or phrase into the computer and choose the records that interest you from the search results. The record below was selected from a list of seventy-seven articles found by a researcher using the search phrase *Arctic National Wildlife Refuge.*

Online *Readers' Guide* Record

AUTHOR:	Doherty, Jim.
TITLE:	The Arctic National Wildlife Refuge: the best of the last wild places.
SOURCE:	Smithsonian v. 26 (Mar. '96) p. 32–41 il.
DATE:	1996
RECORD TYPE:	art
CONTENTS:	feature article
SUBJECT:	Arctic National Wildlife Refuge (Alaska).

INTEGRATING THE LANGUAGE ARTS

Library Skills and Writing. To combine use of the *Readers' Guide* with writing for a real audience, suggest that each student write a letter to a favorite celebrity. First, have each student read the articles indexed in the *Readers' Guide* that pertain to the person chosen. Then, ask each student to write a letter to the celebrity. The letter should incorporate pertinent information about the person's career.

After they have carefully edited and proofread their letters, suggest that students mail them. If any celebrities answer, you might want to display the responses in a glass case.

TECHNOLOGY TIP

If your school library has an online catalog, demonstrate its use and give students class time to find information. You may suggest that students keep note cards with instructions explaining how to use the computer to locate books.

RESOURCES

RESOURCES

COOPERATIVE LEARNING

Divide the class into four or five groups and have each group generate a list of four or five subjects. Topics can include anything from politicians or sports figures to possible professions or hobbies.

When the lists are complete, have each group trade lists and go to the library to find one magazine article and one newspaper story about each item on the exchanged lists. Students should record the title, author(s), magazine, date, and page numbers for each magazine article and the title, byline (if given), newspaper, date, and page number(s) for each newspaper article.

The Vertical File

Most libraries contain a collection of various up-to-date materials, such as pictures, pamphlets, newspaper clippings, government publications, and catalogs. These materials are usually organized by subject and stored in a special file cabinet called the *vertical file.* Your librarian will be able to tell you where the vertical file is located in your library.

Microforms

Many libraries save space by photographically reducing some categories of periodicals, such as newspapers and magazines, and storing them on *microforms.* The microforms most commonly found in a library are *microfilm* (a roll or reel of film) and *microfiche* (a sheet of film). Ask your librarian if your library stores periodicals on microforms, where they are kept, and how you can view them.

Computers

Computers provide researchers with efficient methods of obtaining information. Many libraries use *databases*—collections of information that are stored on a computer, CD-ROMs, or diskettes for easy retrieval. Libraries that are linked to the *Internet,* an international network of computers, have access to thousands of information sources. You search for a specific topic by typing a *keyword* or key phrase, just as you would search the online catalog. Your librarian can assist you with wording a search, using various World Wide Web search engines, and navigating the Internet.

Recorded Materials

Audiovisual materials are often available through your library. They can be a valuable source of research information. These may include videotapes—containing documentaries or other educational programs about specific topics—or audiocassettes of speeches or lectures by experts discussing topics related to their particular specialty.

Review

EXERCISE 1   Using the Card Catalog

For each of the following numbered descriptions, use the card catalog or the online catalog to find a specific book. Write each book's title, author or editor, and call number.

1. a collection of essays about ecology
2. a guide to career choices
3. a recent book on a specific sport
4. a book by each of the following authors: Sandra Cisneros, John Cheever, or James Baldwin
5. a biography of a particular scientist

EXERCISE 2   Using the *Readers' Guide*

Answer the following questions about the *Readers' Guide*.

1. Where are the *Readers' Guide* volumes kept in your library?
2. What is the date of the most recent monthly issue?
3. In the *Readers' Guide,* find a subject heading for popular music. List any *"see"* or *"see also"* references that you find under this heading.
4. Check in the *Readers' Guide* under the subject heading of *health.* Write down the title, author, magazine, date, and page numbers for three articles listed.
5. Find an entry for a review of a book that interests you. Write down the information given in the entry, spelling out any abbreviations.

EXERCISE 3   Using Computers for Research

Complete one of the following exercises, using a computer in your school or public library or in your home. Print out the information you find.

1. Use a CD-ROM reference source, or log on to the Internet to find biographical information about Martin Luther King, Jr.
2. Log on to the Internet, and use a hierarchical directory that organizes information on the World Wide Web to find facts about Blackfriars Theater, managed by William Shakespeare.

RESOURCES

TECHNOLOGY TIP

To acquaint students with microforms, show the class a microfilm or microfiche of an issue of a major newspaper or magazine. Point out that the original paper will deteriorate quickly, but the microform will last up to one hundred years. If your school has microfilm or microfiche viewers, your librarian can show students how to use either.

ANSWERS
Exercise 1

Answers will vary. Each answer must include all the information requested. Partners might exchange completed exercises to check for errors or missing elements.

ANSWERS
Exercise 2

Answers will vary according to the library, but students should follow the directions in the exercise.

ANSWERS
Exercise 3

Answers will vary according to the reference source used, but students should follow the directions in the exercise.

RESOURCES

1057

3. Log on to the Internet, and search a Web-based library catalog to locate *The Women of Shakespeare's Family* by Mary Rose, published in London in 1905. Include information stated about the availability of the book, such as where the book can be used and whether it is available for interlibrary loan.

4. Log on to the Internet, and use an online newspaper to find information about two national political activities that occurred yesterday.

5. Use a CD-ROM reference source, or log on to the Internet to find information about entrance requirements for two colleges or universities that interest you.

▶ EXERCISE 4   **Learning the Arrangement of Your Library**

Draw a diagram of your school library, and label the areas where the following resources are found. [Note: Below your diagram, list any of these resources that your library does not have.]

1. the card catalog (or online catalog)
2. the fiction section
3. the reference section
4. the *Readers' Guide*
5. current issues of magazines

6. the librarian's desk
7. the vertical file
8. microforms
9. computers
10. the checkout and return desk

RESOURCES

RESOURCES

OBJECTIVES

- To identify the principal uses of specified reference sources
- To select appropriate reference sources to find specified information
- To find examples of reference works and to list the call number, title, contents, arrangement, and appropriate uses for each

PROGRAM MANAGER

REFERENCE SOURCES

- **Independent Practice/ Reteaching** For additional practice and reinforcement, see **Books of Synonyms; Encyclopedias; Biographical Reference Works; Atlases, Almanacs, and Yearbooks;** and **Other Reference Works** in *Academic and Workplace Skills,* pp. 31–35.

- **Review** For exercises on chapter concepts, see **Review Form A** and **Review Form B** in *Academic and Workplace Skills,* pp. 36–39.

36 REFERENCE SOURCES

Principal References and Their Uses

In the library you will find a special, separate section known as the *reference section*. Reference sources contain facts and information organized to assist you in finding whatever details you need. If you are familiar with your library's reference books and other resources, you will have a wealth of information at your disposal. This information will allow you to obtain the answer to almost any question you may have at home, at school, or in the workplace.

The Reference Section of the Library

The most common sources in the reference section are books, but your library may also provide reference sources in other forms, such as microfilm or microfiche, compact or laser discs, computer databases, or various links on the Internet. The Internet can be especially valuable as a source of up-to-date information. Ask your librarian for assistance in using any of the sources that may be new to you. Learn to be a resourceful researcher, able to use a variety of sources to find information.

COMPUTER NOTE: You can search computer databases very easily by entering a search word or phrase.

CHAPTER OVERVIEW

This chapter provides students with a guide to the kinds of reference sources available in a library. Specific examples are given for each category, along with a description of the contents of each reference source. Although some of the reference sources are especially useful for research reports or literary research papers, others are useful for everyday situations such as homework assignments, writing journals, and so on. The final group of reference sources includes a variety of guides for institutions of higher learning (both colleges and vocational schools) as well as several career guides.

RESOURCES

RESOURCES

QUICK REMINDER

Have each student write a question about a famous or well-known person, place, or thing. Tell students that many of their questions probably can be answered by using a reference source listed in this chapter. Have students share their questions. For each question, suggest an appropriate type of reference source.

MEETING *individual* NEEDS

LEP/ESL

General Strategies. Some students might be overwhelmed by the number of reference tools available. They might even become frustrated and give up. To keep this from happening, schedule a special trip to the library. Carefully show and explain to students how each kind of reference tool is used. You may want to stress that students won't necessarily need to use all of these tools for each assignment; for most assignments, two or three reference tools will be sufficient.

LEARNING STYLES

Visual Learners. You may want each student to draw a floor plan of the reference section of the school library and to label the location of important reference material. Emphasize that although all libraries have a reference section, not all reference sections will be arranged in exactly the same configuration.

Common Reference Sources

BOOKS OF SYNONYMS	
EXAMPLES	**DESCRIPTION**
Funk & Wagnall's Standard Handbook of Synonyms, Antonyms, & Prepositions	lists entries alphabetically, as in a dictionary
The New Roget's Thesaurus in Dictionary Form	alphabetical listing of synonym entries
Roget's International Thesaurus	uses a categorized index system of synonyms; words grouped into categories and subcategories
Webster's New Dictionary of Synonyms	alphabetical listings; explains differences in meaning between variety of synonyms

ENCYCLOPEDIAS	
EXAMPLES	**DESCRIPTION**
Collier's Encyclopedia *The Encyclopedia Americana* *The Encyclopaedia Britannica* *The World Book Multimedia Encyclopedia*™	common multivolume works; articles arranged alphabetically by subject; may contain an index in a separate volume; may have an annual supplement of up-to-date information
Lincoln Library of Essential Information *The New Columbia Encyclopedia* *The Random House Electronic Encyclopedia*	single-volume works; articles are briefer and less comprehensive in coverage than in multivolume encyclopedias

GENERAL BIOGRAPHICAL REFERENCE SOURCES

EXAMPLES	DESCRIPTION
Biography and Genealogy Master Index CD-ROM	tells where to find books and periodicals with biographical information about four million current/historical persons
Current Biography Yearbook	monthly issues, bound at year-end; often has photographs
The Dictionary of American Biography	profiles famous deceased Americans; multiple volumes
The Dictionary of National Biography	profiles famous deceased British people; multiple volumes
The International Who's Who Webster's New Biographical Dictionary	profile famous people of many nationalities; have details about their births, careers, and accomplishments
Who's Who in America	famous living Americans; same kind of information as *Who's Who*; one volume
Who's Who Among Black Americans	famous African Americans; one volume

LITERARY BIOGRAPHIES

EXAMPLES	DESCRIPTION
American Authors 1600–1900 *American Women Writers* *British Authors of the Nineteenth Century* Magill's *Cyclopedia of World Authors* *Dictionary of Literary Biography* *Contemporary Authors®* on CD-ROM	profiles of authors; usually have details such as dates of authors' birth and death, titles of major works and dates when they were published, awards or honors won; some contain brief critiques of selected authors' works

INTEGRATING THE LANGUAGE ARTS

Library Skills and Speaking. Have each student present an oral report on a different reference book available in the school library. Encourage students to prepare for their reports by studying their books' various parts—preface, table of contents, chapter headings and sub-headings, appendices, glossary, index, and so forth. During their presentations, students should show their books, explain how to use them, and tell the class how the information in the books might be useful.

Literature Link. Remind students that events and places from writers' lives often influence their works. For example, if your literature textbook contains an excerpt from Charles Dickens's *David Copperfield,* have students read and discuss the passage. Point out that biographical information indicates that Dickens felt that he was abandoned by his family at a very young age. Ask students to identify details from the selection that may be based loosely on this youthful experience [Copperfield's forced removal from his mother and his home].

   Tell students that when a work is known to be autobiographical or semi-autobiographical, relating incidents, characters, or themes from the work to similar details in the life of the author is often very revealing.

A DIFFERENT APPROACH

Instead of having students read the charts in this chapter, provide a list of about ten questions that can be answered by using several reference tools that are available in the school library. The questions should cover a wide variety of types of sources. Students should both answer the questions and record the sources they have used. (Some questions may be answered with more than one source.) Completing the assignment will help students gain familiarity with the location, organization, and scope of the reference tools available in the library.

TECHNOLOGY TIP

To familiarize students with finding reference works by using the online catalog, help them develop a simple step-by-step list of instructions.

SPECIAL FIELD BIOGRAPHIES	
EXAMPLES	DESCRIPTION
American Men and Women of Science (database) Biographical Dictionary of American Sports (series) A Biographical Dictionary of Film Vasari's Lives of the Most Eminent Painters, Sculptors, and Architects	profiles of individuals known in specific field or career

ATLASES	
EXAMPLES	DESCRIPTION
Goode's World Atlas Hammond Medallion World Atlas National Geographic Atlas of the World The New York Times Atlas of the World	maps; may also contain statistics about industries, raw materials, exports and imports, or climate

HISTORICAL ATLASES	
EXAMPLES	DESCRIPTION
The American Heritage Pictorial Atlas of United States History Atlas of World Cultures Heyden's Atlas of the Classical World Rand McNally Atlas of World History Rand McNally World Facts & Maps Shepherd's Historical Atlas	graphic representation of historical changes, such as the rise and fall of empires, movement of peoples, and spread of cultures

ALMANACS AND YEARBOOKS

EXAMPLES	DESCRIPTION
The World Almanac and Book of Facts	summary of year's notable events; index usually found in front
Information Please Almanac, Atlas & Yearbook	less formal and complete than *World Almanac;* articles may be longer, more comprehensive
The International Year Book and Statesmen's Who's Who	facts about international organizations, nations of the world, and sketches of world leaders
Statistical Abstract of the United States	statistics on many topics, such as population, health and nutrition, education, and age distribution

INDEXES AND BIBLIOGRAPHIES

EXAMPLES	DESCRIPTION
The New York Times Ondisc *The National Geographic Magazine Cumulative Index* *Art Index* *Biography Index* *Social Sciences Index* *General Sciences Index*	provide information as a guide to articles in periodicals or other information sources
A Biographical Guide to the Study of Western American Literature *Three Centuries of English and American Plays: A Checklist* *World Historical Fiction Guide*	lists of books or articles; grouped by subject, author, or time period; annotated bibliographies include descriptions and notes

MEETING *individual* NEEDS

LESS-ADVANCED STUDENTS

Students may be confused by the dates on yearbooks and almanacs. Point out that almanacs tell about the preceding year: Data for 1991 will be found in the 1992 issue. Students should know, however, that some sections of almanacs list information for more than just the previous year; for example, an almanac might list sports records and the names of prize winners, such as the winners of Nobel Prizes. Students should also be aware that an almanac might have its index in the front of the book rather than in the back.

AT-RISK STUDENTS

Because some students may not see the relevance of many of these reference sources to their needs, you may want to take a different approach to this chapter. One way to begin is by focusing on particular information students need for their current courses. Almanacs and encyclopedias may provide information that will help students complete assignments. Other students may find the career guides useful when they are making vocational decisions. Students who are interested in popular culture might enjoy some of the sports and awards listings in almanacs. You may want either to limit students' instruction to a few of the more useful and interesting reference sources or, if it seems appropriate, to use a select number of sources as a basis on which to build knowledge of other reference sources.

RESOURCES

RESOURCES

INTEGRATING THE LANGUAGE ARTS

Library Skills and Writing. When students are working on composition structure and focusing on main ideas, they may want to include quotations to add emphasis to their writing. One reference that may prove particularly helpful is Bartlett's *Familiar Quotations.* Students can use it when they want to know the author of a quotation, the work in which a quotation appears, or the complete or correct version of a particular quotation. They could also use *Familiar Quotations* when they want to find a quotation by a particular author or on a particular subject. Explain to students that if they are writing papers or speeches, they can find their topics in the index and see what published authors have had to say about their subjects.

SOURCES OF QUOTATIONS	
EXAMPLES	DESCRIPTION
Bartlett's *Familiar Quotations* Flesch's *The New Book of Unusual Quotations* *A New Dictionary of Quotations on Historical Principles from Ancient and Modern Sources* *Gale's Quotations: Who Said What?*™ (CD-ROM)	famous quotations; usually indexed by subject; some are arranged by author or time period; often tell author, source, and date of quotation

REFERENCES TO LITERATURE	
EXAMPLES	DESCRIPTION
The Columbia Granger's® World of Poetry (CD-ROM)	tells where to find specific poems; indexed by subject, title, and first line
Subject Index to Literature	tells where to find short stories and poems; entries are indexed by subject
Benét's Reader's Encyclopedia	contains information about works of literature, such as plots, main characters, summaries of poems, descriptions of artworks and music, etc.
Book Review Digest *Book Review Index* *Brewer's Dictionary of Phrase and Fable* *Essay and General Literature Index* *An Index to One-Act Plays* *Play Index* *Short Story Index*	guides to book reviews, essays, short stories, plays, poems, and other literary works that may be found in periodicals or in collections or anthologies

LITERATURE AND AUTHOR DIRECTORIES

EXAMPLES	DESCRIPTION
Gale Literary Index CD-ROM *The Cambridge History of American Literature* *Harper's Dictionary of Classical Literature and Antiquities* *The Oxford Companion to American Literature* *The Oxford Companion to English Literature*	contain information about authors and their major works; may include brief critiques

SPECIAL REFERENCES FOR SPECIFIC SUBJECTS

EXAMPLES	DESCRIPTION
The Encyclopedia of American Facts and Dates *The Encyclopedia of Religion* *The International Encyclopedia of the Social Sciences* *Facts on File* (series of books and yearbooks) *The New Grove Dictionary of Music and Musicians* (series) *McGraw-Hill Encyclopedia of Science & Technology* *The Sports Encyclopedia* *Webster's New Geographical Dictionary*	contain information related to specific topics or of interest to researchers in specific fields; may include short biographies of major figures or evaluations of major contributions to the particular field

CURRENT EVENTS RESOURCE

EXAMPLES	DESCRIPTION
Social Issues Resources Series (SIRS) (audiotapes, video-tapes, reprints of newspaper and magazine articles, photographs, letters, and posters)	up-to-date information on many important subjects, such as crime, family issues, scientific discoveries, or data from the National Archives

CRITICAL THINKING

Analysis and Evaluation. Ask students to suggest the possible advantages of a student's browsing in a reference section as opposed to using an online catalog or a card catalog. [If the reference section is small, or if the student already knows the location of some references, time can be saved; by browsing, a student might also get to know the available resources.] Then, encourage students to discuss the disadvantages of browsing. [Time may be spent looking for an item that is not available; a source that would serve the student's purposes just as well may be overlooked; the student might fail to consider sources outside the library.]

RESOURCES

RESOURCES

COOPERATIVE LEARNING
Encourage students who are planning to continue their educations to check a variety of sources that rate institutions of higher learning and vocational schools. Have students form groups to compare the entries on several institutions of their choice. They should have an opportunity to discuss any biases or other patterns that they encounter and to draw conclusions about the importance of using more than one rating source.

COLLEGE REFERENCE SOURCES	
EXAMPLES	DESCRIPTION
Barron's Index of College Majors	arranged by state, highlights majors offered at each school
Barron's Profiles of American Colleges on CD-ROM *Peterson's Guide to Two-Year Colleges* *Peterson's Guide to Four-Year Colleges*	cover many accredited four-year colleges; include articles on choosing a college, preparing applications, taking entrance exams; contain information on student life, application deadlines, financial aid, computer facilities, etc.
College Admissions Data Handbook	four volumes; arranged by regions; covers mostly same information as *Barron's*
The Directory of Educational Institutions	covers business schools that offer programs in secretarial science, business administration, accounting, etc.
Technical, Trade, and Business School Data Handbook	divided into regional volumes; includes community and junior colleges; index of programs and index of schools

COLLEGE ENTRANCE EXAM GUIDES	
EXAMPLES	DESCRIPTION
Barron's Basic Tips on the SAT *Barron's How to Prepare for the American College Testing Program* *Official Guide to the ACT Assessment*	contain specific information relating to performing well on college entrance exams

COLLEGE FINANCIAL GUIDES	
EXAMPLES	**DESCRIPTION**
Peterson's College Money Handbook *Meeting College Costs* *The College Cost Book* *Directory of Financial Aids for Women* *Directory of Financial Aids for Minorities*	contain information about grants, scholarships, and loans that may be available through colleges and universities

CAREER GUIDES	
EXAMPLES	**DESCRIPTION**
Encyclopedia of Careers and Vocational Guidance (CD-ROM) *The Dictionary of Occupational Titles* *Occupational Outlook Handbook* *Career Opportunities Series* *Guide to Federal Jobs*	contain information about various industries and occupations, such as job descriptions, projected figures for employment for specific occupations, and job-related education requirements

Review

▶ **EXERCISE 1** **Finding Specific References**

Explain the principal uses of each of the following resource works.

1. *The International Who's Who*
2. *Shepherd's Historical Atlas*
3. *A Biographical Guide to the Study of Western American Literature*
4. *Subject Index to Literature*
5. *The Oxford Companion to English Literature*

RESOURCES

ANSWERS
Exercise 1

Answers will vary. Here are some possibilities:

1. *The International Who's Who* profiles famous people of many nationalities and contains details about their births, careers, and accomplishments.
2. *Shepherd's Historical Atlas* is a graphic representation of historical changes, such as the rise and fall of empires, the movement of peoples, and the spread of cultures.
3. *A Biographical Guide to the Study of Western American Literature* gives lists of books or articles grouped by subject, author, or time period. The annotated bibliographies include descriptions and notes.
4. The *Subject Index to Literature* tells where to find short stories and poems; entries are indexed by subject.
5. *The Oxford Companion to English Literature* contains information about authors and their major works and may include brief critiques.

RESOURCES

1067

ANSWERS
Exercise 2

Answers will vary. Accept any source that provides the necessary information. Here are some possibilities:

1. almanac; recent encyclopedia
2. almanac; recent encyclopedia; *The International Year Book and Statesmen's Who's Who*
3. *The Mythology of All Races; Harper's Dictionary of Classical Literature and Antiquities*
4. *Biography and Genealogy Master Index CD-ROM*
5. almanac; recent encyclopedia; recent atlas

ANSWERS
Exercise 3

Answers will vary. Students' selections should all be sources from the reference section. Students should describe the scope and the categories used in the sources, and descriptions of the usefulness of the sources also should include information on the date(s) and the frequency with which the sources are published or updated.

▶ EXERCISE 2   **Selecting Reference Sources**

Name the reference source you would use to find each of the following items of information.

1. names of the U.S. senators from your state
2. facts about the Secretary General of the United Nations
3. the special power possessed by Clothe, a mythological character
4. titles and authors of biographies of the presidents of the United States
5. the second most important export of Pakistan

▶ EXERCISE 3   **Finding Reference Books**

Find and list three sources in your library from one of the following categories. Describe the contents and arrangement of the information in each source, and explain when students should use it. If the source is a book, give the call number and title.

biographical reference sources	information about authors
literature reference sources	
guides to colleges and universities	sources of quotations
history or science reference sources	reference sources on art or music
almanacs	

37 THE DICTIONARY

Arrangement and Contents

A dictionary is a record of the ways in which words are used. In a dictionary, you can find the meaning and spelling of a word as well as the way the meaning changes in different contexts. Some dictionaries provide information about the history of a word and list its synonyms and antonyms. Most dictionaries tell how a word should be pronounced and how it changes its spelling or meaning as it is used for different parts of speech.

Types of Dictionaries

Many different versions of dictionaries are available for the English language. Each version contains different kinds and amounts of information. The two types of dictionaries used as references about word usage by most speakers of the English language are *unabridged dictionaries* and *abridged* (or *college*) *dictionaries*. Unabridged dictionaries are large books that are usually found in libraries. Abridged dictionaries are likely to be found in homes, classrooms, and workplaces.

COMPUTER NOTE: Some spell-checking programs allow you to create a personalized user dictionary. You can add the special terms and proper nouns you use often.

RESOURCES

RESOURCES

PROGRAM MANAGER

THE DICTIONARY

■ **Independent Practice/ Reteaching** For additional practice and reinforcement, see **Unabridged Dictionaries, Specialized Dictionaries, Dictionary Entries,** and **Etymology and Usage Labels** in *Academic and Workplace Skills,* pp. 43–46.

■ **Review** For exercises on chapter concepts, see **Review Form A** and **Review Form B** in *Academic and Workplace Skills,* pp. 47–48.

CHAPTER OVERVIEW

This chapter offers a brief description of the types of dictionaries available and a ten-part treatment of the standard dictionary entry. The types of information found in various dictionaries are also discussed. Review exercises at the end of the chapter offer students the opportunity to test their mastery of dictionary use.

MEETING *individual* NEEDS

LEARNING STYLES

Visual Learners. You may want to give each student a copy of an enlarged, less-complicated dictionary entry. If possible, reproduce the same entry on an overhead transparency. As you explain each aspect of the model entry, have students use highlighters or colored pencils to identify each aspect on their copies.

LEP/ESL

General Strategies. Some students may have already learned the usefulness of bilingual dictionaries, but others may not know such dictionaries exist. If English-language learners don't know how to use bilingual dictionaries, work with them individually or in small groups to model the necessary skills.

ADVANCED STUDENTS

To illustrate how different dictionaries offer different levels of information, ask students to use the *Oxford English Dictionary* and a collegiate dictionary to look up three words of their choice. Then, have students write short explanations of how the entries differ in the two sources.

COOPERATIVE LEARNING

Divide the class into groups of three and have each group create a dictionary of slang words. (If the members of a group have a common interest, such as a sport or hobby, they may want to create a dictionary of jargon specific to that interest.) You will probably want to specify the number of entries and the type of information needed in each entry. Encourage creativity (illustrations, a clever cover, or an unusual format).

RESOURCES

RESOURCES

1070

Contents of a Dictionary Entry

empty (emp'tē) *adj.* -ti·er, -ti·est ⟦ME *emti* & (with intrusive *-p-*) *empti* < OE *æmettig*, unoccupied, lit., at leisure < *æmetta*, leisure (< *æ-*, without + base of *motan*, to have to: see MUST¹) + *-ig*, -Y²⟧ **1** containing nothing; having nothing in it **2** having no one in it; unoccupied; vacant *[an empty house]* **3** carrying or bearing nothing; bare **4** having no worth or purpose; useless or unsatisfying *[empty pleasure]* **5** without meaning or force; insincere; vain *[empty promises]* **6** [Colloq.] hungry —*vt.* -tied, -ty·ing **1** to make empty **2** *a)* to pour out or remove (the contents) of something *b)* to transfer (the contents) *into, onto,* or *on* something else **3** to unburden or discharge (oneself or itself) —*vi.* **1** to become empty **2** to pour out; discharge *[the river empties into the sea]* —*n., pl.* -ties an empty freight car, truck, bottle, etc. —empty of lacking; without; devoid of —emp'ti·ly *adv.* —emp'ti·ness *n.* SYN.—empty means having nothing in it *[an empty box, street, stomach, etc.]*; vacant means lacking that which appropriately or customarily occupies or fills it *[a vacant apartment, position, etc.]*; void, as discriminated here, specifically stresses complete or vast emptiness *[void of judgment]*; vacuous, now rare in its physical sense, suggests the emptiness of a vacuum See also VAIN —*ANT.* full

From *Webster's New World College Dictionary,* Third Edition. Copyright © 1996, 1994, 1991, 1988 by Simon & Schuster, Inc. Reprinted by permission of Macmillan USA, a Simon & Schuster Macmillan Company.

1. **Entry word.** The boldfaced entry shows how the word is spelled and its division into syllables. The entry word may also show the word's capitalization and alternate spellings.
2. **Pronunciation.** A word's pronunciation is shown by diacritical marks and phonetic respelling. A pronunciation key explains the sounds represented by these symbols. Accent marks show which syllables receive greater stress.
3. **Part-of-speech labels.** These labels (usually abbreviated) show how the entry word is to be used in a sentence. Because some words may be used as more than one part of speech, a part-of-speech label is given in front of each numbered (or lettered) series of definitions.
4. **Other forms.** Spellings may be shown for other forms of the word. These may include complete or partial spellings of the comparison forms of adjectives and adverbs, a variety of verb tenses, or plural forms of nouns.
5. **Etymology.** The etymology of a word is its origin and history. Many word entries tell how the word (or its parts) came into English, tracing it from its earliest known form and indicating the language it came from.
6. **Examples.** Context phrases or sentences may illustrate how the entry word is used.

7. **Definitions.** If there are multiple meanings, the definitions are numbered or lettered to differentiate them. Most dictionaries arrange definitions in order of the frequency of their current use; however, some list definitions in historical order, arranged according to the date of their entry into the English language. Consult your dictionary; its introduction will explain the system it uses in arranging definitions.

8. **Special usage labels.** A definition may be restricted to certain forms of speech (such as [colloquial] or [archaic]). Or, a definition may be used only in a certain field, such as *Physics, Bot.* (botany), or *Chess.* Your dictionary contains a key to explain abbreviations used.

9. **Related word forms.** These are various forms of the entry word, usually created by adding suffixes or prefixes.

10. **Synonyms and antonyms.** At the end of some word entries, synonyms or antonyms may be included.

Information in Dictionaries

Unabridged Dictionaries

An *unabridged dictionary* is a valuable source of information about most words in the English language. Unabridged dictionaries offer thousands of word entries, including words that are rarely used. They usually give more information about their entry words, such as fuller word histories or longer lists of synonyms or antonyms, than abridged dictionaries.

The largest unabridged dictionary is *The Oxford English Dictionary,* or the *OED,* as it is often called. Because the *OED* attempts to define every word used in the English language, it is the world's largest dictionary, consisting of many volumes. The *OED* identifies the approximate date of a word's first appearance in English and illustrates, in a quotation, the way the word was used at that time. The *OED*'s entries also show the changes in spelling or meaning that a word has had over the centuries. Because it features information about the history and changes of a word rather than a word's current meanings, the *OED* is not usually used for ordinary reference purposes.

TECHNOLOGY TIP
Have students compare and contrast dictionaries and spell-checking features that are available in word-processing programs. What can each one do that the other cannot? What are the advantages and disadvantages of each?

MEETING individual NEEDS

LEP/ESL

General Strategies. English-language learners may need help using English-language dictionaries. Dictionaries in many languages lack pronunciation sections because the pronunciation is obvious from the spelling, so you may want to spend extra time explaining diacritical markings. Because English pronunciations are more varied than those in many other languages, students might be confused at first to find that some words may be correctly pronounced in more than one way.

Another difference that may cause students to be confused is that many dictionaries in other languages lack etymological sections because their words do not come from the variety of sources that English words do. Also, English-language learners may need help with part-of-speech labels because their languages might not have the same parts of speech that English does.

A DIFFERENT APPROACH

To familiarize students with the abbreviations used in dictionaries, make and display a chart listing all of the abbreviations that students might encounter in dictionary entries. Include those abbreviations used in etymologies and in usage labels.

ANSWERS
Exercise 1

Answers may vary depending on the dictionary used. These are from *Webster's New World College Dictionary,* Third Edition:

1. zoology
2. *pinochle*
3. Massachusetts
4. The first is a noun that refers to cloth or to tents or sails made of that cloth. The second is a verb that means "to examine evidence or gather votes."
5. *Vide supra* means "see above." It's used to refer a reader to parts of a text.
6. fifteen
7. money exacted for political purposes; a clumsy or stupid fellow
8. myo͞o si laj'ən əs
9. analyses
10. the same as *inert;* resistant to corrosion

Unabridged dictionaries other than the *OED* most often take the form of a single, large volume. *Webster's Third New International Dictionary,* for example, is one well-known, single-volume unabridged dictionary. It is called *international* because it includes words that vary in spelling or meaning as they are used in several English-speaking countries. Most of its entries, however, are in current use in the United States. Another well-known unabridged dictionary is the *Random House Dictionary of the English Language.*

Abridged Dictionaries

The most commonly used reference book in the United States is an *abridged,* or *college, dictionary.* **Abridged dictionaries** contain fewer word entries than unabridged dictionaries, and they do not give as much information about their words. However, abridged dictionaries are frequently updated, so they are the most valuable portable reference for the current meanings and uses of words. In addition to word entries, most abridged dictionaries contain tables or appendixes with other types of reference information, such as lists of commonly used abbreviations, charts of weights and measures, or brief listings of the rules of grammar and punctuation.

Specialized Dictionaries

A **specialized dictionary** limits its entries to those that are related to a specific subject or field. For example, you can find specialized dictionaries for terms used in sports, art, science, medicine, literature, and many other subjects.

Some specialized dictionaries contain terms or phrases not included in a general dictionary, such as idiomatic expressions or slang words. Other specialized dictionaries contain ordinary words that have been grouped or arranged to suit a particular purpose. For example, dictionaries for crossword-puzzle fans group words according to alphabetical combinations. This arrangement would allow you to find quickly many five-letter words with *-ha-* as the second and third letters.

A foreign-language dictionary is another type of specialized dictionary; it contains foreign words and phrases. It may also contain conjugations for a language's irregular verbs or a summary of its rules of grammar or punctuation.

Review

RESOURCES

EXERCISE 1 **Finding Information in the Dictionary**

Using an abridged, or college, dictionary, find the following information.

1. What restrictive label, if any, is given for the word *cryptic*?
2. Which is the correct spelling—*penuchel, pennucckle, pinochle,* or *pinnoccle*?
3. What is *Bay State* the nickname for?
4. How do *canvas* and *canvass* differ in meaning?
5. What is the meaning of the Latin phrase *vide supra*?
6. How many different meanings are given in your dictionary for the word *shuffle*?
7. Give the slang meaning or meanings for the word *lug*.
8. Copy the correct pronunciation for *mucilaginous*, including diacritical marks. Be able to pronounce it correctly.
9. Write the plural of *analysis*.
10. What meaning does the word *passive* have in chemistry?

EXERCISE 2 **Finding the Etymologies of Words**

Using an abridged, or college, dictionary, find the etymologies of the following words. (Refer to the guide at the front of your dictionary for the meanings of abbreviations and symbols.)

EXAMPLE **1.** car
  1. *comes from Middle English and Norman French* carre, *derived from the Latin word* carrum *or* carrus, *originally a name for a two-wheeled Celtic war chariot (*carros, *in Gallic); may be traced to the Indo-European base word* *kers–, *meaning "to run"*

1. churn	6. elope
2. hedge	7. maneuver
3. pedigree	8. theorem
4. fang	9. library
5. rigid	10. sauce

ANSWERS
Exercise 2

Answers may vary depending on the dictionary used. These are from *Webster's New World College Dictionary*, Third Edition:

1. churn < ME *chirne* < OE *cyrne;* akin to *cyrnel*

2. hedge < ME *hegge* < OE *hecg;* akin to Ger *hecke* < IE *kagh* "wickerwork, wickerwork pen"

3. pedigree < ME *pedegru* *pe + de + gre* < MFr *pié de grue* "crane's foot" < L *pes* "foot" + *grus* "crane"

4. fang < ME *fang* "that which is seized" < OE *fon* "to take or catch" < IE *pak* or *pag* "to fasten or tie"

5. rigid < L *rigidus* < *rigere* "to be stiff or numb" < IE (*s*)*rig* "cold"

6. elope < AngloFr *aloper* < ME *aleapen* "to leap up" or "to run away" < OE *ahleapen*

7. maneuver < Fr *manoeuvre* "hand labor" < VL *manuopera* < L *manu operare* "to work by hand" < *manus* "a hand" + *opus* "a work"

8. theorem < Fr *théorème* < L *theorema* < Gr *theōrēma* < *theōrein* "to look at" or "to view" < *theoros* "spectator"

9. library < ME *librarie* < OFr *libraire* "copyist" < L *librarius* "transcriber of books" < *liber* "book"

10. sauce < OFr *sause, saulse* < L *salsa* "salted food" < *salsus, salire* "to salt"

RESOURCES

OBJECTIVES

- To use context clues to determine the meanings of words in sentences and in a paragraph
- To identify Latin and Greek roots in words and to give the current meanings of the words
- To investigate the relationships between the meanings of words and the meanings of prefixes in the words

PROGRAM MANAGER

VOCABULARY

- **Independent Practice/ Reteaching** For additional practice and reinforcement, see **Context Clues, Using Context Clues, Base Words and Roots, Prefixes and Suffixes, New Words from Old, Choosing the Right Synonym,** and **Answering Analogy Questions** in *Academic and Workplace Skills,* pp. 51–57.

- **Reinforcement/Reteaching** For additional instruction and exercises, see **Vocabulary Masters 1–10** in *Practice for Assessment in Reading, Vocabulary, and Spelling,* pp. 13–22.

- **Assessment/Reflection** To assess student work and evaluate progress, see **Portfolio Form** in *Portfolio Assessment,* p. 26.

- **Review** For exercises on chapter concepts, see **Review Form A** and **Review Form B** in *Academic and Workplace Skills,* pp. 60–63.

CHAPTER OVERVIEW

The chapter discusses methods for determining the meanings of new words—using context clues and using word parts—and investigates how words can be formed by shortening, combining, blending, and shifting existing words. In addition, there are sections on choosing synonyms by using denotative and connotative meanings as a guide and on choosing words to complete analogies. Review exercises at the end of the chapter give students the opportunity to test their mastery of these skills.

RESOURCES

RESOURCES

38 VOCABULARY

Learning and Using New Words

Your vocabulary is a valuable resource, giving you the tools with which you can express your ideas and feelings effectively. The larger and more developed your vocabulary, the more likely you are to find success in high school, in college, and in the workplace. Because of this correlation, standardized tests such as college entrance examinations and job placement tests contain vocabulary sections.

Develop a Word Bank

One way to improve your vocabulary is to collect a treasury of words. With each addition to your word bank, you will add to your knowledge and command of words. Every time you encounter new words in your reading or in conversation, write these words in your notebook along with their definitions. Check your dictionary to ensure that you understand the meaning and the use of each word.

COMPUTER NOTE: You may want to create a vocabulary file on your computer. Add new words and their definitions to the end of the file. Then, use the Sort command to arrange the words in alphabetical order. Review the words frequently.

- To identify suffixes and to guess the meanings of words
- To complete analogies

Using Context Clues

You can often perceive the meaning of new words that you hear in conversation or discover in reading passages by examining the way that these unfamiliar words are used. The words, phrases, or sentences that surround a word and contribute to an understanding of its meaning are called its *context*.

You can use **context clues** to decipher the meaning of many unfamiliar words. The following chart shows examples of some of the most common types of context clues.

TYPES OF CONTEXT CLUES	
TYPE OF CLUE	**EXPLANATION**
Definitions and Restatements	Look for words that define or restate the meaning of a word. ■ Samantha owned several *serigraphs*, original silk-screen color prints, which she framed and hung on the wall behind the sofa.
Examples	A word may be accompanied by an example that illustrates its meaning. ■ The plane was full of *garrulous* passengers, including a child that prattled during the entire flight.
Synonyms	Look for clues that indicate an unfamiliar word is similar in meaning to a familiar word. ■ As the *gonfalon* that welcomed the conventioneers to the arena waved lazily over the speaker's lectern, the slow swing of the banner began to lull the bored audience to sleep.
Comparisons	Sometimes an unknown word may be compared to more familiar words. ■ Three soldiers *bivouacked* alongside the creek at twilight, making a campfire and staking out tents before darkness fell.

(continued)

RESOURCES

QUICK REMINDER

Write the word *somniloquist* on the chalkboard. Ask students to break the word into word parts. Then, ask the students to look up the word parts in a dictionary and to share the definitions. Have students try to determine the word's meaning from the meanings of its word parts.

MEETING *individual* NEEDS

LEP/ESL

General Strategies. For students who have very limited English vocabularies, you may want to order *The Oxford Picture Dictionary* and workbook. The book presents colorful illustrations of 2,400 words. Editions come in English/Spanish, Chinese, Japanese, Korean, Vietnamese, Khmer, or Navajo.

COMMON ERROR

Problem. Students may infer incorrect definitions when they use context clues.

Solution. Suggest that if students have used the context to infer the meaning of a word, they should jot down the word in a vocabulary notebook or on an index card and verify the word's meaning later in a dictionary.

RESOURCES

CRITICAL THINKING

Analysis. Students can learn new words from context clues found in song lyrics or raps. Have students work in pairs to find in song lyrics words with meanings that students are unsure of. Then, tell students to analyze the lyrics to determine the meanings of the words. (Remind students that the lyrics should be appropriate for classroom use.) You may want to have students share with the class examples of word meanings inferred from context in songs or raps.

TYPES OF CONTEXT CLUES *(continued)*	
TYPE OF CLUE	EXPLANATION
Contrast	An unfamiliar word may sometimes be contrasted with a more familiar word. ■ The Chihuahua is *minuscule* compared with a huge dog like the Great Dane.
Cause and Effect	Look for clues that indicate an unfamiliar word is related to the cause or is the result of an action, feeling, or idea. ■ Because of the *epeirogeny* that has gradually uplifted parts of the California coast, there are places where steep mountains border the sea.

Determining Meanings from the General Context

Context clues may not be obvious within the immediate surroundings of an unfamiliar word. Sometimes the meaning of a word may not become clear to you until you have read an entire passage. In such cases, you can often infer the meaning of the unfamiliar word by analyzing general context clues, drawing on your own knowledge of the topic, and evaluating the relationship between the unfamiliar word and information in the reading passage.

Using Word Parts

English words can be classified into two types: those that cannot be subdivided into parts, and those that can. Words that cannot be subdivided, like *pride, able,* and *life,* are called **base words.** Words that can be subdivided, like *impersonal, represent,* and *hypersensitive,* are made up of **word parts.** The three types of word parts are

- roots
- prefixes
- suffixes

Knowing the meanings of word parts can help you determine the meanings of many unfamiliar words.

Roots

The *root* is the foundation on which a word is built. It carries the word's core meaning, and it is the part to which prefixes and suffixes are added. For example, the root *–voc–* means "call, voice." This root can be combined with prefixes and suffixes to make new words such as *vocalize*.

Some roots come from base words, such as *–honor–* in *dishonorable*, and are easy to define. Others are more difficult to define, such as *–clam–* ("shout") in *exclamation*.

COMMON WORD ROOTS

ROOT	MEANING	EXAMPLES
GREEK		
–astr(o)–	star	astronaut, astronomy
–bio–	life	biosphere, biometry
–chrom–	color	polychromatic, chromograph
–cycl(o)–	circle, wheel	cyclone, bicycle
–dem–	people	democracy, demographics
–graph–	write, writing	graphologist, lithograph
–hydr–	water	dehydrate, hydroplane
–log–, –logy–	study, word	epilogue, ecology
–phil–	like, love	photophilous, bibliophile
–phono–	sound	symphony, cacophony
–zo–	life, animal	zoological, zoophobia
LATIN		
–aud–, –audi–	hear	audition, audit
–ben–, –bene–	good	benefactor, benevolent
–cent–	hundred	percent, centenarian
–cogn–	know	incognito, cognate
–duc–, –duct–	draw, lead	introduce, induce

(continued)

MEETING *individual* NEEDS

LESS-ADVANCED STUDENTS

You may want to stretch the study of roots, prefixes, and suffixes over the course of a year or a semester. Students probably will experience greater success in increasing their vocabularies if they are assigned a limited number of word parts to learn each week.

LEP/ESL

Spanish. Remind Spanish-speakers that many English words have the same Latin roots as similar words in Spanish.

You may want to have your Spanish-speaking students compose a list of English words and their Spanish counterparts that share the same Latin roots.

A DIFFERENT APPROACH

Students who are studying foreign languages might be better equipped for the study of word parts than students who are only familiar with English. Ask any students who are taking Latin, French, Spanish, or Italian (or English-language learners who speak these languages) to identify additional Latin prefixes, suffixes, and roots that appear in English words. You can also ask the students to identify cognates in other languages that employ the same word parts used in English words.

COMMON WORD ROOTS *(continued)*		
ROOT	MEANING	EXAMPLES
LATIN *(cont'd)*		
–loc–	place	local, circumlocution
–magn–	large, grand	magnificent, magnanimous
–man–	hand	maneuver, mandate
–mater–, –matr–	mother	maternity, matrilineal
–mor–, mort–	death	immortal, mortuary
–omni–	all	omnipotent, omnivorous
–pater–, –patr–	father	patriot, paternity
–prim–	early, first	primordial, primer
–solv–	loosen, accomplish	absolve, dissolve
–spir–	breath	spirit, conspire
–uni–	one	unison, unification
–vid–, –vis–	see	videotape, visualize

Prefixes

A *prefix* is a word part that is added to the beginning of a root. The word that is created from a prefix and a root reflects the meanings of both of its parts.

COMMON PREFIXES		
PREFIX	MEANING	EXAMPLES
GREEK		
a–	lacking, without	amoral, atypical
anti–	against, opposing	antibody, antisocial
dia–	through, across	diagram, dialectic
hyper–	excessive	hyperactive, hyperbole
hypo–	under, below	hypoallergenic, hypodermic
mon–, mono–	one	monarchy, monochromatic

(continued)

COMMON PREFIXES *(continued)*		
PREFIX	**MEANING**	**EXAMPLES**
neo–	new	neonatal, neoclassic
para–	beside, beyond	parallel, paramilitary
peri–	around	periscope, peripheral
psych–, psycho–	mind	psychoanalysis, psyche
sym–	with, together	symbolic, symptom
LATIN AND FRENCH		
ab–	from, away	abduct, abhor
contra–	against	contrast, contraband
de–	away, from, off	depart, deflate
dif–, dis–	away, not, opposing	difficult, discomfort
e–, ef–, ex–	away, from, out	eject, efface, expiration
inter–	among, between	intersect, interval
intra–	within	intravenous, intramolecular
per–	through	permeate, periscope
post–	after, following	postoperative, postpone
pre–	before	predict, predisposition
pro–	forward, favoring	propel, promise
re–	back, backward, again	refrain, reverse, refit
retro–	back, backward	retroactive, retrospective
semi–	partly, half	semisweet, semiserious
ultra–	beyond, excessively	ultrasonic, ultramodern

(continued)

COOPERATIVE LEARNING
Divide the class into groups of three or four and have students explore the history of some of the prefixes listed in this chapter. One group could research five Greek prefixes, a second group could research five Latin and French prefixes, and a third group could research Old English prefixes. Using dictionaries to look up the prefixes, groups should record the information they find on the original meanings and spellings of the prefixes. Each group then could report its most interesting findings to the class.

RESOURCES

RESOURCES

LEARNING STYLES

Kinetic Learners. Have each student write ten prefixes, ten suffixes, and ten word roots on separate slips of paper. Next, have students combine the slips of paper to see how many words they can create. Have the students make lists of their combinations. Finally, have students check in dictionaries to verify that their combinations are actually words.

LEP/ESL

General Strategies. Some students will be tempted to look up every word they do not understand when reading a passage of literature. Encourage students to read whole blocks of text without stopping at every unknown word. Students should try to comprehend the main idea, just as they do in conversation. Students then can go back and look up the new words.

COMMON PREFIXES *(continued)*		
PREFIX	**MEANING**	**EXAMPLES**
OLD ENGLISH be– for– mis– over– un–	around, about away, off, from badly, not, wrongly above, excessively not, reverse of	begrime, befriend forbid, forsake misadventure, miscopy oversee, overbite unquestionable, unsound

☞ **REFERENCE NOTE:** For guidelines on spelling when adding prefixes, see page 965.

Suffixes

A *suffix* is a word part that is added to the end of a root. There are two main kinds of suffixes: those that provide a grammatical signal of some kind but do not greatly change the basic meaning of the word (*–s, –ed, –ing*), and those that create new words. The suffixes listed below are primarily those that create new words.

COMMON SUFFIXES		
NOUN SUFFIXES	**MEANING**	**EXAMPLES**
GREEK, LATIN, AND FRENCH –ance, –ence –cy –er, –or –ism –tude –ty, –y –ure	act, condition state, condition doer, action act, doctrine, manner quality, state quality, state, action act, result, means	radiance, excellence advocacy, redundancy banker, inheritor criticism, ostracism attitude, fortitude subtlety, reality pleasure, measure

(continued)

COMMON SUFFIXES *(continued)*

NOUN SUFFIXES	MEANING	EXAMPLES
OLD ENGLISH		
—dom	state, rank, condition	officialdom, martyrdom
—hood	state, condition	likelihood, childhood
—ness	quality, state	kindness, craziness

ADJECTIVE SUFFIXES	MEANING	EXAMPLES
GREEK, LATIN, AND FRENCH		
—able, —ible	able, likely	likable, legible
—ate	having, characteristic of	desperate, irate
—esque	in the style of, like	arabesque, statuesque
—fic	making, causing	horrific, scientific
—ous	marked by, given to	glorious, laborious
OLD ENGLISH		
—en	like, made of	golden, frozen
—ful	full of, marked by	restful, wonderful
—less	lacking, without	fearless, restless
—some	apt to, showing	irksome, handsome
—ward	in the direction of	upward, skyward

VERB SUFFIXES	MEANING	EXAMPLES
GREEK, LATIN, AND FRENCH		
—ate	become, cause to be	punctuate, alleviate
—esce	become, grow, continue	coalesce, effervesce
—fy	make, cause to have	magnify, falsify
—ize	make, cause to be	energize, agonize
OLD ENGLISH		
—en	cause to be, become	strengthen, lighten

👉 **REFERENCE NOTE:** For guidelines on spelling when adding suffixes, see pages 966–968.

A DIFFERENT APPROACH
Have students use the lists of prefixes and suffixes in the chapter to make up a story. Choose a student to begin the exercise and have the student start with the first prefix on the list of prefixes, *a–*. That student must use the prefix in a word and use the word in a sentence that starts the story. Then each student, in turn, should provide a sentence that elaborates on the story and that contains the prefix or suffix that is next on the list. You may want to allow students to use the example words given in the charts.

COOPERATIVE LEARNING
Divide the class into groups of three or four and give each group a list of five word roots. Then, give the groups five to seven minutes to create as many words as they can by adding prefixes, suffixes, or both to their word roots.

RESOURCES

CRITICAL THINKING

Analysis. Have students read "Jabberwocky" from *Through the Looking Glass* by Lewis Carroll. Then, tell students to analyze the poem to determine which words seem to have been created by adding affixes and which ones seem to have been blended. For the blended words, have students guess the words they were blended from.

Point out to students that the words *beamish* (*beam + –ish*), *galumph* (*gallop + triumph*), and *chortle* (*chuckle + snort*) entered the English language via Carroll's poem.

Other Ways to Form New Words

The English language continuously grows and changes, adding new words frequently. Most new words that are added to English are formed by combination when *affixes* (prefixes or suffixes) are added to a base word or to a word root to make a new word. However, in some cases two base words are combined or put together with a hyphen to make a new word. Here are some of the most common ways new words are made.

PROCESS	DESCRIPTION	EXAMPLES
combining	two base words combined to make a compound *or* a word combined with an affix	eggshell, bird's-eye unbend, masterful
shortening	omitting part of the original word to shorten it or to change it to another part of speech	cabriolet → cab burglar → burgle nuclear → nuke
blending	combining and shortening two words	breakfast + lunch = brunch smoke + fog = smog
shifting	changing the meaning or usage of a word	host (n.) → host (v.) farm (n.) → farm (v.)

Choosing the Appropriate Word

Using the Dictionary

Whenever you express your ideas or feelings by writing or speaking, the words you choose need to match your purpose. At times this can be tricky, since most words in the English language can have more than one meaning. If you consult a dictionary for the definition of a word, look at *all* the definitions given. Remember the context in which you first saw or heard the word. Then, match the various definitions to this context until you find the one that is best suited.

Dictionaries often give sample contexts to help you pinpoint the appropriate definition. Compare the sample contexts in the dictionary with the context in which you first saw or heard the word to be sure you've identified the correct meaning.

Choosing the Right Synonym

Synonyms are words with the same or almost the same meaning. However, there are often subtle shades of difference in the meanings of synonyms. Consult a dictionary or thesaurus to be sure you understand exact meanings of words.

Many words have two kinds of meaning: *denotative* and *connotative*. The **denotative** meaning of a word is the meaning given by a dictionary. The **connotative** meaning of a word is the feeling or tone associated with it. For example, the words *snicker* and *chuckle* both mean "to laugh." However, the word *chuckle* has a more positive connotation than *snicker,* which suggests a sly, derisive laugh.

☞ REFERENCE NOTE: For more information about denotative and connotative meanings, see pages 526–527.

Analogies

Analogies provide a special type of context in which you are asked to analyze the relationship between one pair of words in order to identify or to complete a second pair of words that has the same relationship.

Analogy questions frequently appear on standardized tests because they measure your command of vocabulary as well as your ability to identify relationships and patterns between words. On standardized tests, analogies are frequently presented in multiple-choice form similar to the following example.

EXAMPLE: 1. THERMOMETER : TEMPERATURE : : _____
A speedometer : car
B snow : cold
C barrel : rain
D ruler : length

HOW TO ANSWER ANALOGY QUESTIONS	
Analyze the first pair of words.	Identify the relationship between the first two items. In the example given, a *thermometer* is an instrument that is used to measure *temperature*.
Express the analogy in sentence or question form.	The example given above could be read as "A *thermometer* has the same relationship to *temperature* as . . . (what other pair of items among the choices given?)."
Find the best available choice to complete the analogy.	■ If you are given multiple choices, select the pair of words that has the same type of relationship as the first pair given in the question. (In the example given, only choice *D* shows the same relationship, which is that of a measuring tool to the thing it measures.) ■ If you are required to fill in the blank to complete the analogy, you are often given one word of the second pair of items. Then you are expected to supply the final word that fits the relationship.

Although there are many different relationships that can be represented in analogies, a smaller number of specific relationships are fairly common. Examples of these common types are shown in the following chart.

TYPES OF ANALOGY RELATIONSHIPS

TYPE	EXAMPLE
Word to synonym	JUMP : LEAP :: slide : skid
Word to antonym	SERENE : AGITATED :: groggy : alert
Cause to effect	MATCH : HEAT :: water : wetness
Part to whole	TALON : HAWK :: tentacle : octopus
Whole to part	FOREST : TREES :: swarm : bees
Item to category	ZINC : MINERAL :: neon : gas
Time sequence	ACORN : OAK :: cocoon : butterfly
Object to function	JEWELRY : ADORNMENT :: umbrella : protection
Action to object	ADHERE : GLUE :: pry : crowbar
Action to performer	COOKING : CHEF :: shaving : barber

Review

▶ **EXERCISE 1   Using Context Clues**

For the italicized word in each of the following sentences, write a short definition based on the clues you find in the context. Check your definitions against those in the dictionary. **Answers may vary.**

1. The group *propagated* their ideas through television, billboards, and word of mouth.   **1.** spread
2. The medicine was supposed to be *lenitive*, but instead it made the pain worse.   **2.** soothing; able to lessen pain
3. By his *oscitancy*, I see he didn't get enough sleep last night.
4. It would be a better world if people were always judged by inner beauty instead of *pulchritude*.   **4.** physical beauty
5. Since he had a talent for making hats, he became the town's *milliner*.   **5.** hat maker

3. tiredness; drowsiness

MEETING *individual* NEEDS

ADVANCED STUDENTS

Students may benefit by seeing samples of other analogical relationships.

defining characteristic
pouched : marsupial :: iambic hexameter : alexandrine
relationship of degree
tome : book :: mansion : house
tool and worker
chainsaw : logger :: plane : carpenter

Other types include group and member (pride : lion), degree of intensity (breeze : gale), manner (smirk : smile), age (kid : goat), and symbol and quality represented (lamb : gentleness). Give students a chance to practice creating their own analogies.

◆ INTEGRATING THE LANGUAGE ARTS

Vocabulary and Literature. Analogies can also be used to illustrate ideas in literature. For example, you could have students create analogies that reflect the characters' relationships in Shakespeare's tragedy *Macbeth*. (Duncan : Macbeth :: good : evil, or Banquo : Fleance :: Siward : Young Siward)

ANSWERS
Exercise 2

Answers may vary. Here are some possibilities:

1. calefaction—heating
2. analogous—comparable; similar
3. decelerate—slow
4. permeates—enters and spreads throughout
5. detained—held back
6. superfluous—extra
7. primary—main; chief
8. incineration—burning
9. decimation—destruction
10. repercussions—effects

ANSWERS
Exercise 3

Definitions may vary. Here are some possibilities:

1. –astro–; study of measurements of the distances and positions of stars
2. –chrom–; highly colored; [music] progressing by semitones or using tones not in the key of a work
3. –litho–; –graph–; a printing technique using a flat stone
4. –hydro–; –graph–; study of the locations of bodies of water
5. –lat–; affecting one side only
6. –vis–; part of headgear that shades or protects the eyes
7. –dem–; –graph–; statistical science that studies populations
8. –log–; –gram–; letter, character, or symbol used to represent an entire word
9. –prim–; the state of being first
10. –duct–; pliant, stretchable

EXERCISE 2 — Using the General Context to Determine Meaning

For each italicized word in the paragraph that follows, write your own definition or synonym. Then, check the definitions of each word in a dictionary. If you guessed incorrectly, check the context in the passage again to look for clues you might have missed.

The greenhouse effect is the trapping of the sun's heat in the atmosphere, which results in the [1] *calefaction* of the earth's surface. This process is [2] *analogous* to the heating of a greenhouse. When the sun's rays penetrate the glass exterior of a greenhouse, the interior heats up. Glass walls and roof allow the sun's energy to enter at the speed of light, but they [3] *decelerate* the escape of the resulting heat. Similarly, sunlight [4] *permeates* and heats Earth's atmosphere. Much of the heat escapes, but some is [5] *detained* in the atmosphere, absorbed by gases such as carbon dioxide, ozone, and water vapor. These gases then release [6] *superfluous* heat, warming the earth's surface. Growing amounts of carbon dioxide in the atmosphere intensify the effect. The [7] *primary* reason for this increase is the [8] *incineration* of fossil fuels, which release carbon dioxide when they are burned. Also, the [9] *decimation* of forests, whose vegetation absorbs carbon dioxide, reduces the likelihood of a decrease in carbon dioxide levels. Some of the possible [10] *repercussions* of an intensified greenhouse effect are higher ocean levels, raised temperatures, and shifted rainfall patterns.

EXERCISE 3 — Learning New Words with Latin and Greek Roots

Underline the root or roots in each of the following words. Using your dictionary, write a brief definition of the word.

EXAMPLE **1.** cognizant
1. *cognizant—being knowledgeable or aware; informed*

1. astrometry
2. chromatic
3. lithograph
4. hydrography
5. unilateral
6. visor
7. demography
8. logogram
9. primacy
10. ductile

▶ **EXERCISE 4**   **Understanding the Meanings of Prefixes**

Give the meaning of each of the following words. Then identify the prefix in each word and its meaning. Be prepared to explain the link between the meaning of the prefix and the meaning of the whole word.

EXAMPLE   **1.** antithesis
> **1.** *meaning: direct contrast or opposition of ideas*
> *prefix: anti (against, opposing)*

1. paramount   **4.** forgo
2. abscond   **5.** retrocede
3. monocular

▶ **EXERCISE 5**   **Identifying Suffixes and Defining Words**

For each word, identify the suffix and guess what the whole word means. Use a dictionary to check your answers.

EXAMPLE   **1.** novelty
> **1.** *suffix: –ty (quality, state); meaning: the state or*
> *condition of being novel (new or unusual)*

1. wisdom   **4.** liquefy
2. innocence   **5.** realize
3. Romanesque

▶ **EXERCISE 6**   **Completing Analogies**

In the following items, choose the pair of words whose relationship is most similar to that of the pair in capital letters.

1. STAPLER : ATTACH ::   **(a)** paper : tape
(b) blowtorch : weld   **(c)** needle : cloth
(d) define : dictionary
2. MAST : BOAT ::   **(a)** column : ceiling   **(b)** mane : horse
(c) sail : anchor   **(d)** neck : body
3. TRAIN : TRANSPORTATION ::   **(a)** wheel : car
(b) steam : engine   **(c)** rose : flower   **(d)** boat : canoe
4. PERFECT : DEFECTIVE ::   **(a)** pure : clean
(b) cracked : molded   **(c)** bleached : dyed
(d) interested : intrigued
5. INTENTION : PURPOSE ::   **(a)** end : means
(b) dedication : goal   **(c)** flavor : smell
(d) dedication : devotion

RESOURCES

ANSWERS
Exercise 4

1. *meaning:* chief; highest ranking
prefix: para– *(beside, beyond)*

2. *meaning:* to run away and hide
prefix: ab– *(from, away)*

3. *meaning:* one-eyed; to be used by only one eye
prefix: mon(o)– *(one)*

4. *meaning:* to do without; abstain from
prefix: for– *(away, off, from)*

5. *meaning:* to recede; go back
prefix: retro– *(backward, back)*

ANSWERS
Exercise 5

Definitions may vary. Here are some possibilities:

1. *suffix:* –dom *(state, condition);*
meaning: state of being wise

2. *suffix:* –ence *(quality, state);*
meaning: unknowing

3. *suffix:* –esque *(in the style of);*
meaning: (architecture) in the style of Rome

4. *suffix:* –fy *(make, cause to have);*
meaning: to make into a liquid

5. *suffix:* –ize *(make, cause to have);*
meaning: to make real

RESOURCES

LETTERS AND FORMS *(pp. 1088–1099)*

OBJECTIVES
- To write business letters
- To write a résumé
- To complete a form
- To write a personal letter of regret, thanks, or invitation

CHAPTER OVERVIEW

This chapter offers instruction on the form, tone, and content of business and personal letters. Directions for addressing envelopes and filling out forms also are included. A special section gives instructions for completing a personal résumé.

RESOURCES

RESOURCES

39 LETTERS AND FORMS

Style and Contents

For many purposes, well-written letters are the most effective means of communication. For example, you may want to ask for information, order products, make a complaint, express your appreciation, or apply for a job. You may also want to write certain kinds of social correspondence. Whether you are writing for personal or business purposes, the overall success of your letters and completed forms will depend not only on their content but also on their appearance.

The Appearance of a Business Letter

There are certain standards of style and format that are generally followed for business letters.

- Use plain paper ($8\frac{1}{2}''$ x 11").
- Type your letter if possible (single-spaced, leaving an extra line between paragraphs). Otherwise, write legibly, using black or blue ink.
- Center your letter on the page with equal margins, usually one inch, on all sides.
- Use only one side of the paper. If you need a second page, leave a one-inch margin at the bottom of the first page and carry over at least two lines to the second.
- Avoid mark-outs, erasures, or other careless marks. Check for typing errors and misspellings.

Writing Business Correspondence

The Parts of a Business Letter

A business letter contains six parts:

(1) the heading
(2) the inside address
(3) the salutation
(4) the body
(5) the closing
(6) the signature

Two styles are commonly used for business letters. With the **block form,** every part of the letter begins at the left-hand margin, and paragraphs are not indented. In the **modified block form,** the heading, the closing, and the signature are aligned along an imaginary line just to the right of the center of the page. The other parts of the letter begin at the left-hand margin. All paragraphs are indented.

Block Style

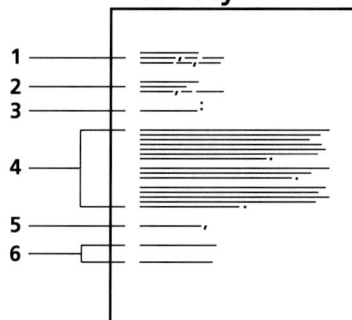

Modified Block Style

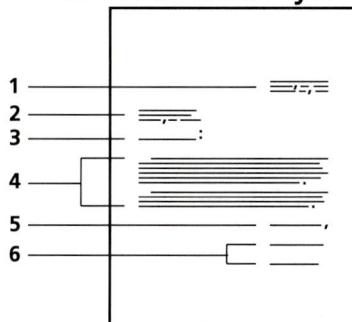

The Heading.   The heading usually consists of three lines:

- your street address (or post office box number)
- your city, state, and ZIP Code
- the date that you wrote the letter

The Inside Address.   The inside address indicates the name and address of the person or organization you are writing. If you're writing to a specific person, use a courtesy title (such as *Mr., Ms., Mrs.,* or *Miss*) or a professional title (such as *Dr.* or *Professor*) in front of the person's name. After the person's name, include the person's business or job title (such as *Editor* or *Admissions Officer*), followed by the name and address of the company or institution.

QUICK REMINDER

Have students brainstorm for reasons they might have for writing letters. Write students' responses on the chalkboard in two columns with the headings *Business Letters* and *Social Letters.*

MEETING *individual* **NEEDS**

LEP/ESL

General Strategies. You may find that some English-language learners already have learned to write letters in their native languages by using formats different from those in this chapter. You could ask students what formats they have been using and discuss with them how the formats differ from the standard form for a business letter in the United States. You could take this opportunity to initiate class discussion on the variance of conventions from region to region. Emphasize that no convention is better or worse than another.

LESS-ADVANCED STUDENTS

Students need to be able to see and copy specific phrases that traditionally appear in business letters, particularly openings and closings such as *I am writing in regard to, It has come to my attention that, Thank you for your cooperation in this matter,* and so on. You may want to create a list of expressions that can be inserted at the beginnings or ends of letters. Give copies to students to keep for future reference.

COMMON ERROR

Problem. Students may have difficulty achieving the correct tone in their business letters.

Solution. Emphasize to students that most business letters will be received by busy people who need straightforward but complete presentations of the writers' intentions. Tell students to pretend they are the recipients of the letters. Then, have students revise their letters with this new perspective in mind.

COOPERATIVE LEARNING

Copy the information from the **Guidelines for the Contents of a Business Letter** onto the chalkboard. Then, split the class into groups of three or four students and ask each group to write five examples of sentences or phrases that illustrate one of the four guidelines. Give the groups a time limit and afterward have them read aloud what they have written.

The Salutation. The salutation is your greeting. If you are writing to a specific person, begin with *Dear,* followed by a courtesy title or a professional title and the person's name. End the salutation with a colon.

If you don't have the name of a specific person, you can use a general salutation, such as *Dear Sir or Madam* or *Ladies and Gentlemen.* You can also use a department or a position title, with or without the word *Dear.*

The Body. The body, or main part, of your letter contains your message. If the body of your letter contains more than one paragraph, leave a space between paragraphs.

The Closing. The closing should end your letter courteously. Several closings that are often used in business letters include *Yours truly, Sincerely,* and *Regards.* Capitalize only the first word of the closing.

The Signature. Your signature should be written in ink, directly below the closing. Sign your full name. Do not use a title. If you type your letter, type your name neatly below your signature.

GUIDELINES FOR THE CONTENTS OF A BUSINESS LETTER

Here are a few valuable suggestions for your business letters.

- *Use a courteous, positive, and professional tone.* Maintain a respectful, constructive tone—even if you're angry. Rude or insulting letters are nonproductive.
- *Use formal, standard English.* Avoid slang, dialect, contractions, or abbreviations. Business letters are usually formal in tone and use of language.
- *State your purpose clearly and quickly.* Assume that the person reading your letter is busy, and tell why you are writing in the first or second sentence of the letter.
- *Include all necessary information.* Provide all the information your reader needs to understand and respond appropriately to your letter.

Types of Business Correspondence

Memos

Memos are standard forms of communication in many businesses. They are concise messages, generally covering only one topic. While they do not include all parts of a letter, they still tell the reader *who, what, when, where, why*, and *how*. Most memos are meeting notices, summaries of meetings, or requests for action or information. Electronic mail (e-mail) is used in many businesses for memos because of the speed of communication and the ease of record keeping.

DATE: February 27, 1998
TO: Shipping Department Staff
FROM: Ella Jones, Shipping Manager, ext. 7890
CC: Chet Park, Director, Distribution
SUBJECT: Missed shipping dates

There will be a meeting Friday, March 6, from 2:00–3:00 P.M., in Room 3A to discuss missed shipping dates. Please bring any ideas you may have regarding this subject.

Here are some tips to help you prepare a memo:

1. Use the words *DATE, TO, FROM,* and *SUBJECT* to guide you as you write your memo.
2. State your request clearly and briefly.
3. If you are asking for action or information, include a deadline.
4. Include your phone number so the recipient can call you if there are any questions.
5. Send a copy (CC) of the memo to people who need to know about the meeting but do not need to attend.

Request or Order Letters

A *request letter* asks for something. For example, you might write a college to request a course catalog or a city's chamber of commerce for a brochure about business opportunities. An *order letter* is a request letter that is written to order merchandise by mail when a printed order form is not available.

TECHNOLOGY TIP

When students write business letters to request information from several sources, they can simplify the task by using computers. Many word-processing programs include well-designed business letter templates. Students need only type in the correct information. Suggest that they plan the bodies of their letters with all the different recipients in mind. Then, have students copy their letters into several new files and change the inside address and salutation for each letter. Remind students to use the preview command, if available, to see how the letters will look when they are printed.

RESOURCES

RESOURCES

CRITICAL THINKING

Evaluation. After showing students a variety of business letters and memos, have them evaluate each using the guidelines given for that type of correspondence. Students should evaluate the correspondence for both correct form and appropriate content and tone.

A DIFFERENT APPROACH

Have students write letters to the editor of a local newspaper. You may want to conduct a brainstorming session for possible topics for students' letters. Emphasize that students need to use an acceptable form and a respectful tone in their letters.

Here are the body and the closing of a sample request letter.

> I am a senior in high school and am interested in applying for admission to your university's undergraduate program.
>
> I would like to know more about the courses you offer in sociology, my area of interest. Please send me your general catalog.
>
> Sincerely yours,
>
> *Greg Nolanski*
>
> Greg Nolanski

When you are writing a request or order letter, follow these guidelines.

1. State your request clearly.
2. If you're asking for something to be sent to you, enclose a self-addressed, stamped envelope.
3. For a special request, make sure your request is reasonable and that it's submitted well in advance.
4. If you're ordering something, include all important details, such as the size, style, and price. Include information about the magazine or paper in which you saw the item advertised. Compute correctly if there are costs involved, including any necessary sales tax or shipping charges.

Complaint or Adjustment Letters

A *complaint* or *adjustment letter* is written to point out errors that require attention and correction.

When you are writing a complaint or adjustment letter, follow these suggestions.

1. Register your complaint as soon as possible.
2. Explain exactly what is wrong. Necessary information might include
   - what product or service you ordered or expected
   - why you are not satisfied (damaged goods, incorrect merchandise, bad service)

- how you were affected (lost time or money)
- what you want the company to do about it
3. Keep the tone of your letter calm and courteous.

Here is a sample adjustment letter.

8511 Callo Ct.
Pueblo, CO 81005
June 4, 1998

Customer Service Dept.
Haley Clothing Co.
535 7th Ave.
Orange, CA 92667

Dear Sir or Madam:

On May 25, I sent an order to you that included requests for several items of clothing, including two red T-shirts, No. 86, size 36, @ $10.00. When the shipment arrived, I found that these shirts were missing from the package.

I assume that this was merely an oversight and would appreciate your sending the two shirts as soon as possible.

Sincerely,

Dwayne Patterson

Dwayne Patterson

Appreciation or Commendation Letters

An *appreciation* or *commendation letter* compliments or expresses appreciation to a person, a group, or an organization. For example, you might write to a restaurant, telling how much you liked the food or the service.

Letters of Application

The purpose of a letter of application is to provide a possible employer or a selection committee with information that will convince them that you are a good candidate for a position. The position you are applying for may be membership in an organization, a scholarship, a job, or a similar type of position.

RESOURCES

◆ INTEGRATING THE LANGUAGE ARTS

Literature and Writing Link. If the selection is available, have students read Samuel Johnson's "Letter to Lord Chesterfield." Ask students to identify elements of the letter that correspond to the elements of a modern business letter [formal language]. Then, ask students to identify the ways in which Johnson's letter is not an appropriate model for modern business correspondence. [Johnson's letter has an ironic tone that is not especially courteous. He does not state his purpose clearly and quickly; instead, he uses elaborate language and literary allusions to make his point.]

After discussing the context in which Johnson wrote this letter, you could have students write responses from Lord Chesterfield. Challenge students to employ an ironic tone similar to that in Johnson's letter.

RESOURCES

A DIFFERENT APPROACH

Ask each student to think about the job he or she would like to have in five years. Then, tell students that they are going to write letters of application for those jobs. Students can make up any necessary information, including their work experience and education.

To make this activity more fun for students, encourage them to use humor in their letters. For example, students might use hyperbole in their descriptions of their qualifications.

1094 *Letters and Forms*

Here is a sample of an application letter.

4974 King Terrace
Rockford, IL 61103
June 8, 1998

Mr. Lyle Walzell
Walzell and Reid Architecture
96 Manor Drive
Rockford, IL 61104

Dear Mr. Walzell:

Please consider me an applicant for the position of summer intern advertised in Sunday's Sentinel.

I am a graduate of Lincoln High School. In addition to college preparatory courses with emphasis on math, I have taken courses in art history, mechanical drawing, and computer science. I will be entering Illinois Institute of Technology this fall, and I plan to major in architecture.

Last summer I worked at The Drawing Board, where I made requested changes to mechanical drawings and created a computer file of stock home plans. I also was given an opportunity to work with the artists producing computer-assisted designs.

I believe my education and summer work experience qualify me for the summer intern position. My résumé, which includes references, is enclosed. Please call me at 555-9263 to set an appointment for an interview. I am home after 4:30 on weekdays. I look forward to hearing from you.

Sincerely,

Marty Castellano

Marty Castellano

Enclosure

Follow these points when you write a letter of application.
1. Identify the job or position you are applying for. Tell how you heard about it.
2. Depending on the position, you might include
   - your grade in school or grade-point average
   - your experience; or your activities, awards, and honors
   - personal qualities or characteristics that make you a good choice for the position
   - the date or times you are available

3. Offer to provide references. Your references should include two or three responsible adults (usually not relatives) who have agreed to recommend you. Be prepared to supply their addresses and telephone numbers.

The Personal Résumé

A *résumé* is a summary of your background and experience often used as part of an application for a position. When you apply for a job, it is common to submit a résumé along with your letter of application. There are many different ways to arrange the information on a résumé. Whatever arrangement you select, be sure your résumé looks neat and businesslike.

A SAMPLE RÉSUMÉ

MARTY E. CASTELLANO   4974 King Terrace
                                             Rockford, IL 61103
                                             (815) 555-9263

EDUCATION: Linclon High School
                    Major studies: College preparatory, computer,
                        and art courses
                    Grade-point average: 3.5 (B+)

WORK   Summer 1997   Design assistant
EXPERIENCE: The Drawing Board
                                     Rockford, IL
                    Summer 1996   Junior lifeguard
                                     YMCA
                                     Rockford, IL

SKILLS: Mechanical drawing; personal computers

EXTRACURRICULAR   Secretary, Student Council of Lincoln High
ACTIVITIES: School; member, Junior Jaycees

REFERENCES: Dr. Mary Ellen Wells, Principal (815) 555-1195
                    Lincoln High School
                    Rockford, IL 61105

                    Mr. Micah Stein, Teacher   (815) 555-0643
                    Lincoln High School
                    Rockford, IL 61105

                    Mr. Carlos Ramirez, Director   (815) 555-9543
                    The Drawing Board
                    Rockford, IL 61101

RESOURCES

RESOURCES

Addressing an Envelope

You should send a business letter in a plain business envelope. Write or type your name and address in the upper left-hand corner of the envelope. Then, write or type the name and address of the person or organization to whom you are writing (the addressee) just to the right of an imaginary line in the center of the envelope. The addressee's name and address should exactly match the inside address on the letter. Use the two-letter postal service abbreviations for state names, and be sure to include each correct ZIP Code.

Completing Printed Forms and Applications

As you begin applying to colleges or applying for jobs, you'll be asked to fill out a variety of forms and applications. The information on your form or application can be processed by the person or organization if you fill the form out neatly, completely, and legibly.

GUIDELINES FOR COMPLETING FORMS

1. Always read the entire form to make sure you understand exactly what items of information you are being asked to supply.
2. Type neatly or print legibly, using a pen or pencil as directed.
3. Include all information requested. If a question does not apply to you, write *N/A* or *not applicable* instead of leaving the space blank.
4. Keep the form neat and clean. Avoid cross-outs.
5. When you have completed the form, proofread it carefully, and correct any spelling, grammar, punctuation, or factual errors.
6. Submit the form to the correct person, or mail it to the correct address.

APPLICATION FOR COLLEGE ADMISSION
■ PERSONAL INFORMATION ■

1. Last name *Yee* First *Elizabeth* Middle *Marie*   2. Phone *(617) 555-6929*

3. Weight *110*   4. Height *5'2"*   5. Birthdate *7/10/81*

6. Address   *812 Ashland Drive, Newton, MA 02161*

7. Siblings: Name   Age   Current Occupation

   Robert Yee   *12*   *Student*

8. Father's occupation *Teacher (4th Grade)*   9. Mother's occupation *School Nurse*

10. Will you apply for financial aid? *Yes*

■ ACADEMIC INFORMATION ■

11. List schools attended (Grades 7–12)

Name	City, State, ZIP	Dates	Principal/Head
Newton High School	*Newton, MA 02165*	*9/95–Now*	*Dr. Albert Souza*
Altamonte Jr. High	*Boston, MA 02116*	*9/92–6/95*	*Mrs. Susan Yamoto*

12. Prizes, honors, awards *Science Fair prize, '96, '97*

13. Rank in high school graduating class *6th in class of 612*

14. If you have been out of high school for more than one year, describe your activities, employment, classes and colleges attended *N/A*

15. Possible major *Chemistry*   16. Career goal *Medical Research*

■ EXTRACURRICULAR ACTIVITIES ■

17. List school, community, and church activities

Activity	Achievements
Piano Accompanist for school	*Accompanied choir for 4 years, toured New England, Feb. '97*
Volunteer Coordinator at	*Coordinated student volunteers at placement home*
Elmwood Children's Home	*for children waiting for foster care*

18. Other activities, hobbies, interest *Reading; Music (piano lessons for 11 years); Computers and computer programming; Hiking; Pets; Babysitting*

19. Which three books that you read during the past year most impressed you?

   List title and author. *Things Fall Apart by Chinua Achebe; Sense and Sensibility by Jane Austen; Ender's Game by Orson Scott Card*

■ EMPLOYMENT EXPERIENCE ■

20. List jobs held, including part-time work

Employer	Type of Work	Hours Weekly	Dates
Newton Public Lib.	*Library Aide*	*10 (approx.)*	*Summers '96–'97*
Mrs. Carla Perez	*Babysitting*	*6*	*Every Saturday, '97*

■ RECOMMENDATIONS ■

21. List the names and addresses of three people (including one teacher and one employer)

   Mr. Alonzo Hernandez, Head, Science Dept, Newton H.S., Newton, MA 02165

   Mr. Robert Ryan, Supervisor, Children's Room, Newton Public Library, Newton, MA 02162

   Ms. Sylvia Brown, 5960 Apple Tree St., Boston, MA 02116

THE INFORMATION ON THIS APPLICATION IS TRUE AND COMPLETE

   Date *1/10/98*   Signature *Elizabeth M. Yee*

MEETING *individual* NEEDS

LEP/ESL

General Strategies. A date sequence of day/month/year is used in many countries. Remind students that the usual date sequence in the United States is month/day/year.

RESOURCES

INTEGRATING THE LANGUAGE ARTS

Writing Letters and Revising. Have students work in pairs to evaluate and revise their items of correspondence for **Exercise 1.** Provide the following checklist for evaluation:

1. Does the correspondence follow the forms presented in this chapter?
2. Is the tone polite and professional?
3. Is the correspondence written in standard, formal English?
4. Is the purpose for writing stated at the beginning of the correspondence?
5. Is all important information included in the correspondence?

ANSWERS
Exercise 1

Each item of correspondence should follow the guidelines presented in this chapter. The body of each letter or memo should be courteous in tone and should be written in formal, standard English. Letters or memos should state their purposes quickly and clearly and should contain all necessary information.

Writing Informal or Social Letters

Sometimes the most appropriate way to communicate with people you know personally is through the mail. When you want to thank someone formally, congratulate someone for an accomplishment, send an invitation, or respond to an invitation, you should write a personal letter.

Personal letters are much less formal in style than business letters. For example, social letters don't include an inside address and most use the modified block form.

Thank-you Letters. The purpose of a thank-you letter is to express appreciation for special effort or a gift. Try to include more than just "thank you." Say how the person's gift or efforts were particularly helpful or appreciated.

Invitations. An informal invitation should contain specific information about a planned event, such as the occasion, the time and place, and any other details your guests need to know.

Letters of Regret. If you have been invited to a party or a specific social function and will be unable to attend, it's polite to send a letter of regret. A written reply is especially appropriate if you were sent a written invitation with the letters *R.S.V.P.* (in French, these letters are an abbreviation for "please reply").

Review

▶ EXERCISE 1   Writing Business Correspondence

Complete any two of the following items of business correspondence, using the forms shown earlier in this chapter. Use your own return address (when appropriate) and today's date, but make up any other information you need to compose the correspondence.

1. Write a letter to any company you want, ordering at least three items for your own company. Order more than one of some of these articles. Include prices.
2. Write a letter of adjustment to a business firm, asking why you have received a bill for an order for which you have already paid. Give all important dates and details.
3. Write a memo to your staff, complimenting them on their high-quality work on a project they just completed and inviting them to a company celebration.
4. Write a letter of complaint or appreciation to an elected official responding to this person's position on an issue. Explain why you agree or disagree. Request a response.
5. From your local newspaper, select a help-wanted advertisement and answer it with a letter of application.

EXERCISE 2   Writing a Résumé

Choose a job that interests you. Then, write a personal résumé that shows you are qualified for such a position. Also, write a short cover letter that explains how you heard about the job and requests a personal interview. Proofread the final versions.

EXERCISE 3   Completing Forms

Choose one of the following activities.

1. Complete an auto insurance application form, using information about your car or a car owned by a friend or relative.
2. Locate a mail-order catalog and select several items to order. Complete the mail-order form in the catalog, indicating the items you have chosen.
3. Complete an application form for employment with a company.

EXERCISE 4   Writing Social Correspondence

Write a personal letter for one of the following situations.

1. Write a letter of regret explaining that you will not be able to attend an event to which you have been invited.
2. Write a thank-you letter expressing appreciation for a gift or favor you have received.
3. Write an invitation letter for an event you are planning.

RESOURCES

ANSWERS
Exercise 2

Résumés should be appropriately spaced on the page and should include correctly spelled and punctuated information in the proper order. Letters should be brief and to the point, should include appropriate information, and should follow the block or modified block form.

ANSWERS
Exercise 3

Forms should be neatly and carefully filled out. Information should be accurate and easy to read.

ANSWERS
Exercise 4

Students should use the modified block form and maintain a polite, friendly tone in their letters. The tone should be appropriate to the occasion and to the relationship between writer and recipient.

RESOURCES

OBJECTIVES

- To choose appropriate reading rates for given situations
- To use the SQ3R method to formulate and to answer questions about reading material
- To analyze details in a reading passage

PROGRAM MANAGER

FOR THE WHOLE CHAPTER

- **Review** For exercises on chapter concepts, see **Review Form A** and **Review Form B** in *Academic and Workplace Skills,* pp. 90–93.

CHAPTER OVERVIEW

Because the information in this chapter can prove immediately useful to students and can help them grasp the material covered in other chapters, you may want to cover this section during the first week or two of class. In addition to helping students academically, a review of reading and study skills and test-taking strategies can give you insight into students' abilities and attitudes.

This chapter discusses and reinforces reading strategies, writing as a tool for learning, reasoning skills, study methods, and test-taking skills.

RESOURCES

RESOURCES

40 READING, STUDYING, AND TEST TAKING

Using Skills and Strategies

As you conclude your high-school studies and prepare for college or a career, you will need skills and strategies to help you read, analyze, evaluate, and apply information for a variety of purposes. The ability to handle information effectively will be useful to you in many different situations, both in the classroom and in the workplace.

Implementing a Study Plan

Productive study habits are crucial to success. To help you improve your study routine, here are a few methods that have proven to be effective.

- keep track of your assignments and due dates
- select a time and place to study free from distractions
- divide large assignments into manageable steps, and then schedule time to complete each step
- allow a reasonable amount of study time to complete each of your assignments

COMPUTER NOTE: Check with your school counselor or the library to see if you can borrow admissions-test or skill-building software to help you prepare for standardized examinations.

- To take study notes and to use a variety of note-taking strategies
- To paraphrase a poem
- To write a précis

Improving Reading and Study Skills

Reading and Understanding

You read many different types of materials, but how you read these materials depends on your purpose for reading them.

READING RATES ACCORDING TO PURPOSE		
READING RATE	**PURPOSE**	**EXAMPLE**
Scanning	Reading for specific details or points of reference	Hunting for the atomic number of einsteinium in the periodic table
Skimming	Reading for main points	The night before an economics test, studying your notes on how to calculate compound interest
Reading for mastery	Reading to understand and remember	Reading the manual for your printer to find out how to load the paper

Writing to Learn

Writing helps you clarify thoughts, react to ideas, evaluate plans, and analyze and recall information. Different types of writing help you in various learning situations.

TYPE OF WRITING	PURPOSE	EXAMPLE
Freewriting	To help you focus your thoughts and identify key ideas	Writing notes on the Industrial Revolution before writing an essay

(continued)

PROGRAM MANAGER

IMPROVING READING AND STUDY SKILLS

- **Independent Practice/ Reteaching** For additional practice and reinforcement, see **Tracking Assignments and Due Dates, Varying Your Reading Rate, Finding Relationships Among Details, Analyzing Graphics, Taking Notes,** and **Writing a Paraphrase or Summary** in *Academic and Workplace Skills,* pp. 81–86.

QUICK REMINDER

Ask students to tell you three purposes for reading and what *SQ3R* stands for [for details, for main points, to understand and remember; survey, question, read, recite, review].

INTEGRATING THE LANGUAGE ARTS

Studying and Writing. To demonstrate that writing can be a valuable learning tool, ask students to keep learning logs for classes of their choice. Encourage the students to include observations, descriptions, questions, problems, answers or solutions, explanations, or personal responses to what they are learning in class.

RESOURCES

RESOURCES

TYPE OF WRITING	PURPOSE	EXAMPLE
Autobiographical Dictionaries	To help you examine the meaning of important events in life	Recording your impressions of your visit to a prospective college
Diaries, Autobiographical Notes	To help you recall your impressions and express your feelings	Writing about an argument and reconciliation with your best friend
Journals and Learning Logs	To help you record your observations, descriptions, solutions, and questions	Writing down each step in the process of an experiment on wave motion
	To help you present a problem, analyze it, and propose a solution	Writing ideas for improving your school to discuss at a planning meeting

Using Word-Processing Tools for Writing

A word processor or a computer word-processing program can help you plan, draft, and edit your writing. These tools can make every step of the writing process easier.

Prewriting. It's easy to freewrite and brainstorm ideas on the computer. Later you can fill in notes or outlines without having to retype them.

Writing First Drafts. With a little practice, you can compose your thoughts fluently and rapidly on the word processor.

Evaluating. The word processor is great for analyzing work in progress. If you save a copy of your document, you can insert and delete text freely. If you later decide that you don't like the changes, your original document is retrievable from its original file.

MEETING *individual* **NEEDS**

LESS-ADVANCED STUDENTS

The information concerning word-processing tools will be of little practical use unless students can have hands-on, one-to-one instruction. Arrange a field trip to your school's computer lab or to a similar facility in the community. Students will probably need individual guidance in the basic steps of opening a file and naming it, creating a document and saving it, and printing a hard copy. Before the trip, discuss with students the terminology that will be used.

Revising.   A word processor can be a great timesaver when you're revising. You can easily insert, move, or delete text wherever you wish. When you're finished, you can print out a clean copy.

Proofreading.   Many word processors have a spell-checking function that can help you find spelling errors. You may also find a search-and-replace function that you can use to correct a specific type of error wherever it occurs throughout a document.

Publishing.   When you have made all of your revisions and have proofread and made all of your corrections, you can quickly produce one or multiple final copies on your printer.

Using the SQ3R Reading Method

Francis Robinson, an educational psychologist, developed a reading method called *SQ3R.* This method is made up of five simple steps.

S   *Survey* the entire study assignment to get an overview of the material. Read all titles, headings, subheadings, and terms in boldface and italic type. Also, look over any charts, outlines, and summaries.

Q   *Question* yourself. What should you know after completing your reading? Make a list of questions to be answered. Also, look at any questions provided at the end of a reading selection.

R   *Read* the material carefully. Think of answers to your questions as you read.

R   *Recite* in your own words the answers to each of the questions that you identified earlier.

R   *Review* the material by rereading quickly, looking over the questions, and recalling the answers.

☞ **REFERENCE NOTE:** For study techniques to help with listening skills, see pages 1028–1030.

For study techniques to help with listening skills, see pages 1028–1030.

TECHNOLOGY TIP
As students use computers to prewrite, have them try invisible writing. Before they begin, have them turn down the brightness until letters no longer appear on the screen. This technique will enable students to enter ideas freely without thinking about grammar, usage, or mechanics. After they have entered their ideas in this way, students can revise.

CRITICAL THINKING
Analysis.   There are variations of the SQ3R reading method. The PQ6R method, developed by Francis Robinson and adapted by Norma Kahn in *More Learning in Less Time,* includes the following steps: preview, question, read, recite, write, review, reflect, and review. Have students compare the two methods to decide which one they think would be more helpful to them.

RESOURCES

RESOURCES

1103

Interpreting and Analyzing What You Read

Finding the Main Idea

To get the meaning out of a passage you are reading, you will need to be able to identify how the information it contains fits together. An important first step is to determine the main idea of the selection.

Stated Main Idea.   The main idea of a passage is often stated directly in one or two specific sentences that express the thesis of the passage.

Implied Main Idea.   At times the main idea of a passage is not stated directly but is implied, or suggested, instead. In this case, you will need to find the main idea by analyzing all of the supporting details of the passage to decide what overall meaning these details express.

HOW TO FIND THE MAIN IDEA

- Identify the overall topic. (What subject is the passage, as a whole, about?)
- Identify what the passage reveals about the topic. (What is the real message of the passage, when it is taken as a whole?)
- Sum up the meaning of the passage in one clear sentence.
- Review the passage. (If you have correctly identified the main idea, all of the other details included in the passage will support it.)

☞ REFERENCE NOTE: For additional information on finding the main idea, whether stated or implied, see pages 64–65.

Reading to Find Relationships Among Details

After you have identified the main idea of a reading passage, the next step is to identify the supporting details and analyze how these items of information are related to each other and to the main idea.

RESOURCES

RESOURCES

FINDING RELATIONSHIPS AMONG DETAILS	
Identify specific details.	What details answer specific questions such as *Who? What? When? Where? Why?* and *How?* (*5W-How?* questions)?
Distinguish between fact and opinion.	What information can be proved true (facts) or false? What statements express a personal belief or attitude? (opinions)
Identify similarities and differences.	Are there any details that are shown to be similar to or different from one another?
Understand cause and effect.	Do prior events impact or affect later events?
Identify an order of organization.	In what kind of order are the details arranged—chronological order, spatial order, order of importance, or any other organizing pattern?

Reading Passage

During the sixteenth and seventeenth centuries, Europeans experienced a dramatic change in their ideas about the universe. Today, historians call this period the Scientific Revolution.

Although the new worldview in Europe during the 1500s and 1600s had its roots in the work of scientists and philosophers during the Middle Ages, the kind of science performed by Nicolaus Copernicus, Galileo Galilei, and Isaac Newton was strikingly new. Medieval science had relied on natural, individual observation and blind faith to authority, but the new science differed from the older science in three unique ways.

Sample Analysis

DETAIL: Where and when did the Scientific Revolution take place?

ANSWER: *It occurred in Europe during the sixteenth and seventeenth centuries.*

DETAIL: What were the central beliefs of medieval philosophers?

ANSWER: *Medieval philosophers relied on individual observation and blind faith in authority.*

RESOURCES

MEETING individual NEEDS

LESS-ADVANCED STUDENTS

This reading passage may prove difficult for some students to follow. To aid comprehension, have students work in pairs to read the passage aloud. To help them focus, you could have students create preview material. The following questions could serve as examples:

1. What vocabulary words should be introduced before the passage?
2. What prior knowledge is assumed?
3. What title or added headings would facilitate reading?
4. What kind of organization would give students an idea of the passage's structure before they begin to read?

RESOURCES

RESOURCES

1106

First, this new science was very methodical. Exact observations were made about the universe through mathematical reasoning. Because mathematics is rigorously logical, there followed careful attention to what we now call the scientific method: stating an experimental aim, forming a hypothesis, conducting an experiment, gathering the results, and forming conclusions.

Second, the new science relied upon technology. The telescope, for example, let scientists see the cosmos in the kind of detail that, in turn, allowed mathematical descriptions to be made. The role played by the printing press is also very important. By 1500, there were over a thousand printers in Europe, who had published several million books. This spread of knowledge through books allowed scientists to explain their work and compare it with the work of others.

Third, the new science was conducted in communities dedicated to learning. By the end of the seventeenth century, universities had established centers for scientific study. Learned societies were also formed by governments. The government of England formed the Royal Society in 1660, and the French government set up the Academy of Sciences in 1666. Through the new technology of printing, these societies also established journals to circulate information on scientific discoveries. Both the French *Journal des Savants* and the English *Philosophical Transactions* began in 1665.

Nicolaus Copernicus (1473–1543) may be said to have begun the movement with publication of his book *On the Revolutions of the Heavenly Spheres.* This Pol-

---

FACT: Who were the leaders of the Scientific Revolution?
ANSWER: *They were Nicolaus Copernicus, Galileo Galilei, and Isaac Newton.*

OPINION: What is the author's opinion of the relationship of science during the Middle Ages to science during the 1500s and 1600s?
ANSWER: *While the author believes that the Scientific Revolution was influenced by medieval science, the author also believes that medieval science was limited by natural observation and blind faith in authority.*

SIMILARITY: What is the similarity between the telescope and the printing press?
ANSWER: *Both are technologies that influenced scientists.*

DIFFERENCE: What is a main difference between medieval science and science of the 1500s and 1600s?
ANSWER: *Medieval scientists worked individually; new scientists worked in communities.*

ish astronomer and mathematician challenged the widespread view that the sun revolved around the earth. Instead, he proposed that the sun was the center of the universe and that all the planets, including the earth, revolved around it. Because it was feared that Copernicus's ideas were controversial, the publication of his book was delayed until his death.

Galileo Galilei (1564–1642), an Italian mathematician, was the first scientist to make use of the telescope. He is best known for illustrating that the universe can be understood by mathematical reasoning. Many contemporaries of Galileo thought that his ideas were disturbing and too controversial; a number of his fellow scientists condemned his work.

Isaac Newton (1642–1727) is best known for his work *Mathematical Principles of Natural Philosophy* (1687). An English mathematician, Newton began investigations that led him to believe that the universe was a uniform machine that operated according to mechanistic, regular laws. His worldview greatly influenced scientific belief until the German scientist Albert Einstein (1879–1955) proposed the theory of relativity in the twentieth century.

CAUSE: Why was the publication of Copernicus's book delayed until his death?
ANSWER: *Because it was feared that Copernicus's ideas were too controversial.*

EFFECT: What was the effect of Newton's work?
ANSWER: *His view of the universe predominated until Einstein introduced his theory of relativity in the twentieth century.*

ORGANIZATION: Why are Copernicus, Galileo, and Newton profiled at the end of the passage?
ANSWER: *The tenets of the Scientific Revolution are discussed first, then the major contributors (logical order).*

Applying Reasoning Skills to Your Reading

You draw conclusions and make inferences by evaluating, interpreting, and analyzing the facts and evidence presented in a reading passage. A *valid conclusion* is one firmly grounded in evidence or logic. Based on your analysis of the reading passage on pages 1105–1107, you might make the following conclusions or inferences about the Scientific Revolution.

RESOURCES

RESOURCES

1107

A DIFFERENT APPROACH

You may want to compare the process of drawing conclusions based on reading to the process of drawing conclusions based on scientific experiments. Ask a student volunteer to describe an experiment he or she performed in a science class and the conclusion that resulted from the experiment.

CRITICAL THINKING

Analysis. To give students practice with analyzing the process of drawing conclusions, have them find texts of speeches that interest them. Ask students to identify the conclusions drawn in the speeches and to list the supporting evidence. Then students should analyze the evidence to determine whether or not it logically leads to the conclusions.

Controversial ideas were not often published in Copernicus's time. (Evidence: Copernicus's book was not published until after his death because of its controversial ideas.)

Newton's view of the universe working as a machine was eventually proven to be limited. (Evidence: The passage states that Newton's views influenced science only until Einstein offered his theory of relativity, meaning that Einstein's ideas displaced Newton's because Einstein's theory was an improvement over Newton's.)

An *invalid conclusion* is one that is not consistent with the evidence presented. For example, it would be invalid to conclude that the Scientific Revolution meant that Europe led the world in scientific knowledge. The passage speaks only of Europe; it omits mention of technology achieved by civilizations such as those in the Middle East and China.

HOW TO DRAW CONCLUSIONS AND MAKE INFERENCES	
Gather all the evidence.	What facts or details have you learned about the subject?
Evaluate the evidence.	Do you know enough to make a few observations based on facts or reasonable assumptions?
Make appropriate connections.	What can you reasonably conclude or infer from the evidence you have gathered and evaluated?

Reading Graphics and Illustrations

Reading materials frequently include graphics, such as diagrams, maps, and charts. Graphics visually organize bodies of information. For example, look at the chart on the next page.

This chart quickly shows you a comparison of the various audiences who watch different types of television programs.

Suppose you are an advertiser for a company selling clothing for teens. Would you place your advertising with adventure programs or with sports specials? One look at the chart tells you that you should advertise on adventure programs, and perhaps on situation comedies and movies.

Estimated Television Audience Composition¹ by Selected Program² Type

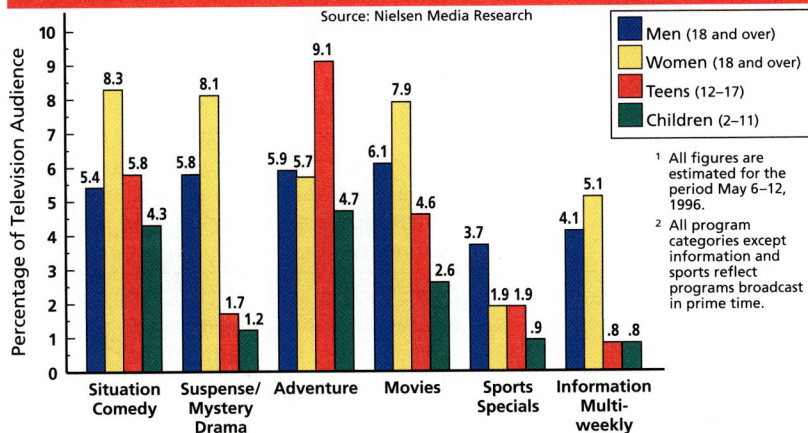

Source: Nielsen Media Research

Program Type	Men (18 and over)	Women (18 and over)	Teens (12–17)	Children (2–11)
Situation Comedy	5.4	8.3	5.8	4.3
Suspense/Mystery Drama	5.8	8.1	1.7	1.2
Adventure	5.9	5.7	9.1	4.7
Movies	6.1	7.9	4.6	2.6
Sports Specials	3.7	1.9	1.9	.9
Information Multi-weekly	4.1	5.1	.8	.8

Percentage of Television Audience

¹ All figures are estimated for the period May 6–12, 1996.
² All program categories except information and sports reflect programs broadcast in prime time.

If you are producing an educational product for young children, you want to advertise it where the most parents will see it. The chart shows that the suspense/mystery drama and movie programs have the largest percentages of men and women viewers over 18, and sports specials have the smallest percentage. This type of information helps you to make your final choice of where to place the ads.

Charts such as the one shown, therefore, help you make decisions more easily because you can quickly see complex relationships between items of data.

Applying Study and Reading Strategies

There are several study and reading strategies for organizing and processing information. Among the most common are

- taking notes
- classifying
- organizing information visually
- outlining
- paraphrasing
- summarizing
- writing a précis
- memorizing

INTEGRATING THE LANGUAGE ARTS

Study Skills and Speaking. Encourage students to incorporate visuals when they make speeches. Remind them that a speaker's ideas can be much clearer when visuals are used; for example, newscasts frequently display lists or symbols linked to a story to emphasize important points made by the commentator. Students can use graphics ranging from simple lists to more complicated graphs to make their speeches more effective.

COOPERATIVE LEARNING

Pair students and have them find statistical data that can be presented graphically. Possible topics include the growth in revenues for college athletic programs and the growth or decline in the birthrates of other countries. Students could use almanacs, encyclopedias, or specialized reference sources to find such data. Have students make and present to the class graphs that represent their information.

A DIFFERENT APPROACH

You may wish to assign the material in **Applying Study and Reading Strategies** as a group activity. Organize students into groups of seven and assign one student in each group the task of examining one of the seven study methods. When students have completed their studies, have members of different teams who have worked on the same topics meet to discuss their topics. Each original group should then reconvene, and each expert should present his or her special topic.

MEETING *individual* NEEDS

LEP/ESL

General Strategies. Taking lecture notes can be especially difficult for some students. Because they cannot ask the speaker to slow down, they are likely to miss information. Furthermore, students often have to concentrate so much on the meanings of individual words that they are unable to absorb broader concepts.

You may want to provide situations in which students can practice their note-taking skills. Suggest that students tape-record lectures. Taped lectures allow students to stop and look up unfamiliar words or to replay portions of the tape whenever necessary.

Taking Notes

If you take careful notes, they can be a valuable tool for remembering what you hear or read. Notes also organize your information for studying, taking tests, and writing research papers.

HOW TO TAKE STUDY NOTES	
Recognize and record main points.	Set off main points as headings in your notes. ■ In a lecture, key words and phrases such as *major* or *most important* and similar clues may indicate key points. ■ In a textbook, chapter headings and sub-headings are usually reliable indicators of main ideas.
Summarize.	Don't record every detail. Summarize or abbreviate, using single words or phrases to record key ideas and supporting details.
Note important examples.	A few vivid examples can help you recall the main ideas.

The following example shows study notes about the reading passage on pages 1105–1107. Notice that the main points in the passage are listed in groups. Then each of these groups of main points is given a heading that identifies the key idea.

Characteristics of Scientific Revolution

• *mathematical and methodical (scientific method)*

• *relied on technology—telescope (helped observation), printing press (spread knowledge)*

• *conducted in communities—ideas exchanged in universities, learned societies (English—Royal Society, French—Academy of Sciences); journals established—Journal des Savants (1665, France), Philosophical Transactions (1665, England)*

Major Figures of the Scientific Revolution
- Nicolaus Copernicus (1473-1543), Polish
  wrote On the Revolutions of the Heavenly Spheres;
  proposed sun as center of universe; ideas
  controversial (book not published until he died)
- Galileo Galilei (1564-1642), Italian
  first to use telescope; showed universe describable
  through mathematics
- Isaac Newton (1642-1727), English
  wrote Mathematical Principles of Natural Philosophy; theory: universe a machine with regular laws
  (eventually replaced by Einstein's theory of relativity)

Classifying

Classifying is a method of organizing items by arranging them into categories or groups. When you group these items, you are identifying the relationships or patterns among the various items.

EXAMPLE   **What characteristics do each of the following people have in common?**

Robert Browning; Elizabeth Barrett Browning; Matthew Arnold; Alfred, Lord Tennyson; William Wordsworth; Samuel Taylor Coleridge

ANSWER   **All of these people were British poets who lived during the nineteenth century.**

You also use classifying when you identify patterns. For example, look at the relationship between the following sequence of numbers.

RESOURCES

MEETING *individual* NEEDS

LEP/ESL

General Strategies. Some students may have difficulty understanding the explanation of classification. To make the concept more accessible, organize students into mixed-ability groups of five or six. Ask the groups to make lists of all the ways they can classify items in the classroom. When they finish, the groups should report to the class and explain the categories they chose. You may want to explain that classifying is a way of showing how people, things, or events relate to each other.

RESOURCES

Study and Reading Strategies and Writing. Relate three of the study skills described in **Applying Study and Reading Strategies**—taking notes, classifying, and outlining—to the prewriting process, and emphasize the connection between organizing information for writing and organizing information for study. Organization helps writers understand and communicate their ideas. It also helps students learn and recall new information.

What's the next number in the sequence below?

| 48 | 53 | 43 | 58 | 38 | **?** |

ANSWER   To the first number (48), *5* is added to produce 53. From this number, *10* is subtracted to produce 43. To this number, *15* is added to produce 58; then *20* is subtracted to produce 38. The pattern is to add, then subtract, by increments of five. Therefore, to produce the next number in the series, you should add *25* to produce *63*.

Organizing Information Visually

The techniques of visually organizing information are valuable as study methods; you can use them to make the information in some types of written passages easier to understand. These techniques include charting, mapping, or diagraming. For example, the passage that follows compares and contrasts the storytelling elements of film and fiction.

The storytelling elements of fiction are also found in film. Both fiction and film, for example, use plot to move a story along; in both media the action rises, builds to a climax, and is finally resolved. Characterization is another shared element; both fiction and film show characters who change over time or whose personalities and relationships to one another affect the action of the story. Theme is also used in film and fiction; the central idea of the story is expressed as clearly in a short story by Doris Lessing as it is in a film by Orson Welles. Setting, too, is a common element.

Film and fiction also share similarities in structure; in both media a completed work is made up of smaller, cohesive structural units. A shot, the basic unit of a film, can be compared to a sentence, the basic meaningful unit of writing. Just as paragraphs link groups of related sentences, so scenes link up various related shots. Sequences in a film may be compared to the chapters of a book. Taken as a whole, the completed book may therefore be compared to the final version of a film.

However, because film relies on moving, visual images, the techniques it uses are different from those of printed, verbal fiction. For instance, fiction often relies on the author's point of view, the relationship the author creates to his or her fictional world. In film, however, the relationship of author to idea is often conveyed by the way one moving image is joined to the next in editing: the fade, dissolve, wipe, and cut help the viewer understand the attitude the filmmaker has toward the subject. In addition, while atmosphere in a work of fiction must be conveyed through verbal description, filmmakers use technical devices such as lighting, camera angle, focus, and a variety of special lenses to give a motion picture its mood.

It would be difficult to read this passage and recall each detail. However, if you organize the information visually in a chart such as the one that follows, you will find the material easier to understand and remember.

FICTION	FILM

Storytelling Elements
  plot
  characterization
  theme
  setting
	Storytelling Elements
	  same
	  same
	  same
	  same

Structural Parts
  sentence
  paragraph
  chapter
  book
	Structural Parts
	  shot
	  scene
	  sequence
	  film

Techniques
  verbal
  point of view expressed
    through language
  atmosphere achieved by
    language
	Techniques
	  visual
	  point of view achieved by
	    editing: fade, dissolve,
	    wipe, cut
	  atmosphere achieved by
	    technical devices: lighting,
	    camera angle, focus, lenses

RESOURCES

MEETING *individual* NEEDS

LEARNING STYLES

Visual Learners. Some students find it helpful to use color to organize information. Give students copies of the passage comparing film and fiction on this page and have them sort the information in the paragraph by using two highlighters. For example, students could use yellow to highlight information pertaining to film and blue to highlight information about fiction.

RESOURCES

1113

A DIFFERENT APPROACH

Ask students to think about a time when they have read a novel or a short story and have visualized the characters and scenes in the story. Then, ask students to speculate about whether the same kind of visualization and sensory involvement might help them learn new material. Point out to students that when studying science material, a student might visualize an experiment, perhaps by recalling the smell of a chemical. When studying history notes, a student might visualize the events being studied, as if she or he were watching a movie. When studying any subject, a student can practice recalling a teacher's lecture by recalling the sounds, smells, and sights of the classroom.

Outlining

An *outline* records only the most important information and ideas. In addition, an outline puts key ideas together, showing their relationship to one another and their order of importance.

However, if you are taking lecture notes, you may want to use an informal outline form. This method can help you to organize information quickly. (See the sample notes shown on pages 1110–1111.)

FORMAL OUTLINE FORM

1. Main Point
   A. Supporting Point
      1. Detail
         a. Information or detail

INFORMAL OUTLINE FORM

Main Idea
   Supporting detail
   Supporting detail
   Supporting detail

Paraphrasing

A *paraphrase* is a restatement of someone's ideas in your own words. A paraphrase can help you analyze the meaning of a poem or complex prose passage. Since a paraphrase is often approximately the same length as the original, this technique is not often used for long passages of writing.

Paraphrasing a Literary Selection.   This type of paraphrase is intended to express in simpler terms the meaning of a work that is written in complex language, such as a poem. For example, you might be asked to paraphrase a poem like the following.

Sonnet 25
by William Shakespeare

Let those who are in favor with their stars
Of public honor and proud titles boast,
Whilst I, whom fortune of such triumph bars,
Unlooked for joy in that I honor most.
Great princes' favorites their fair leaves spread
But as the marigold at the sun's eye,
And in themselves their pride lies burièd,
For at a frown they in their glory die.

> The painful warrior famousèd for fight,
> After a thousand victories once foiled,
> Is from the book of honor razèd quite,
> And all the rest forgot for which he toiled.
>   Then happy I, that love and am beloved
>   Where I may not remove nor be removed.

As an example, here is a possible paraphrase of this poem.

> Although some people enjoy renown and recognition, the speaker has neither. Instead, the speaker hints at a quiet enjoyment of something valued highly. The speaker says that, after all, those popular at court enjoy only temporary regard; without noble favor, they close up like a flower without sunlight. Royal disfavor withers them. Even the hero of a thousand victories needs only one defeat to lose the prestige for which he fought so long. Therefore, the speaker finds fulfillment in love, which is a shared happiness that—once present—cannot be destroyed.

Paraphrasing Prose.   Sometimes you may need to paraphrase a portion of an essay, an article, or another type of prose work. For instance, in writing an essay, you may need to paraphrase another person's ideas in order to support your opinion.

For example, here is an excerpt from "Self-Reliance," an essay by Ralph Waldo Emerson.

> What I must do is all that concerns me, not what the people think. This rule, equally arduous in actual and in intellectual life, may serve for the whole distinction between greatness and meanness. It is the harder, because you will always find those who think they know what is your duty better than you know it. It is easy in the world to live after the world's opinion; it is easy in solitude to live after our own; but the great man is he who in the midst of the crowd keeps with perfect sweetness the independence of solitude.

The following shows how you might paraphrase this passage and incorporate your paraphrase into a composition.

INTEGRATING THE LANGUAGE ARTS

Study Skills and Mechanics. You may want to remind students that while paraphrased material does not contain direct quotations from the original source, credit for the ideas is still given to the original writer. If words or phrases from the original source are used verbatim, they must be enclosed in quotation marks.

SELECTION AMENDMENT
Description of change: excerpted
Rationale: to focus on the concept of paraphrasing presented in this chapter

1115

INTEGRATING THE LANGUAGE ARTS

Literature Link. To give students practice in paraphrasing, have them work as a class to paraphrase a poem. Then, have one student read the paraphrase aloud and have another student present the poem. Lead a discussion of how the students' paraphrase differs from the poem. Students might notice that the paraphrase does not have the same mood, tone, or even meaning as the poem.

> Nonconformists of all types have always attracted a certain approval in American culture. The heroes of American songs, legends, novels, and movies are typically the strong, independent types who persist in doing things their way despite all opposition. Ralph Waldo Emerson stated the credo of the rugged individualist in his essay "Self-Reliance." Emerson proclaimed his conviction that he alone was responsible for doing what he thought was right, not what everyone else believed was right. This obligation, he felt, was true both for real life and the life of the mind; he said this quality was the single most important means of differentiating between superior and inferior persons. Emerson admitted that it is difficult to hold to your own when you are surrounded by others who think they know better than you. He said that when you are among others, conformity is the simplest course of action; when you are alone, it is not difficult to do as you think best. However, only truly remarkable persons are able to live constantly surrounded by others and yet follow their own unique vision happily and pleasantly, as if they were alone.

HOW TO PARAPHRASE

1. Read the entire selection to get the overall meaning before you begin writing your paraphrase. Look up any unfamiliar words or phrases.
2. Identify the main idea of the selection. Keep it in mind while you write your paraphrase.
3. Identify the speaker in fictional material and poetry. (Is the poet or a narrator speaking?)
4. Write your paraphrase in your own words, using complete sentences and standard paragraph form.
5. Review the selection to be sure that your paraphrase expresses the essential ideas of the original.

Summarizing

Summarizing is restating the main ideas of written or spoken material in condensed form. A summary can help you record the basic meaning of a selection you are studying. It can also help you to think critically about what you have read, since writing a summary forces you to analyze material, identify the most important ideas, and then select ideas important enough to be included in the summary, eliminating less significant ideas.

HOW TO SUMMARIZE

1. Review the material carefully, identifying main ideas and supporting details.
2. Condense the material. Focus only on key ideas, deleting unnecessary details. Write a sentence in your own words about each main idea.
3. Use your list of main ideas to write your summary in paragraph form. Add transitional words as necessary to connect the ideas.
4. Revise your summary. Make sure that the information is expressed clearly and that you have remained faithful to the original ideas.

Here is a sample summary of the article on pages 436–438.

> If you observe elephants, you sometimes see whole herds responding to something invisible and inaudible. The answer to this mystery may lie in an aerial throbbing often felt in the vicinity of elephants, a thrumming similar to one accompanying the lowest sound on a pipe organ. This throbbing may signal the presence of infrasound, sounds too low to be heard by humans. Infrasound can travel long distances unaffected by forests or grasslands. Infrasound communication could explain many previously unexplained actions of elephants.

Writing a Précis

When you write a ***précis,*** you shorten a piece of writing—an article, a chapter, a passage, a report—to its bare essentials. Summarizing skills are used in writing a précis. (See pages 1116–1117.) In addition, there are certain standard practices specifically related to précis writing.

RESOURCES

RESOURCES

CRITICAL THINKING

Evaluation. You may want to illustrate the differences between *summary* and *evaluation*. Write the words on the chalkboard and have the class choose a well-known movie to discuss. Ask a volunteer to summarize the movie very briefly. Then, ask a volunteer to evaluate the movie and to give reasons for her or his judgments. Discuss with students the differences between the summary and the evaluation. Are there any value judgments included in the summary? Does the evaluation include a recounting of the movie's plot?

GUIDELINES FOR WRITING A PRÉCIS

1. *Be brief.* A précis is seldom more than a third as long as the material being summarized, often less.
2. *Don't paraphrase.* A paraphrase is often the same length as the original.
3. *Stick to key points.* Cut details and descriptions.
4. *Use your own wording.* Don't just take phrases or sentences from the original.
5. *Be faithful to the author's points and views.* Don't add your own ideas or comments.

Here is a sample paragraph.

> What is particularly strange about this new passivity regarding travel is that not so very long ago the reverse was considered to be the norm; once upon a time, flying was a highly participatory activity—as was automobile driving. As recently as forty years ago, the driver of an ordinary car expected to be intimately involved with the event of driving by means of direct access to the steering wheel, brakes, transmission, and the outside environment. Since then, however, the automobile driver has given up any direct involvement with his or her vehicle in favor of power controls, automatic transmissions, on-board computerized readouts, and sealed-in passenger interiors. Nowadays, only the most adventurous people insist on direct participation in the act of driving by means of sports cars, the last vestige of the old ways. (134 words)

Here are major errors to be avoided in a précis.

COMMON ERRORS IN PRÉCIS-WRITING

TYPE OF ERROR	EXAMPLE
uses words taken directly from original	Until the 1950s, travel by air or auto was a <u>highly participatory activity</u>.

(continued)

COMMON ERRORS IN PRÉCIS-WRITING *(continued)*	
misses the point of the original; emphasizes unimportant points	Makers of modern vehicles have really <u>improved many models</u> by adding devices <u>that make driving much less complicated.</u>
writer of précis injected own ideas	Today, however, most cars insulate their drivers, and <u>that detachment decreases the full enjoyment of travel.</u>

As an example, here is a précis of the paragraph on page 1118 that is an acceptable length and is stated in the writer's own words.

> Detachment from the act of traveling is recent. Until mid-century, air or auto travelers interacted directly with the vehicles and surroundings. Today, however, most cars insulate drivers from direct contact with their machinery or the environment; only the boldest demand hands-on driving, still found in sports cars. (47 words)

Memorizing

When you memorize important information, you are more likely to remember what you need if you practice frequently in short sessions than if you try to cram at the last minute. Use the guidelines in the following chart.

HOW TO MEMORIZE

1. *Condense the information.* Information found in a textbook chapter, for example, can often be outlined, summarized, or condensed.
2. *Rehearse the material in several different ways.* Use several different senses as you commit the material to memory. Write or copy the material so you can see it and use touch and muscle movements. Recite the material aloud or walk back and forth while reciting the material to help "set" it in your mind.

(continued)

MEETING *individual* NEEDS

ADVANCED STUDENTS

Some students may want to create mnemonic devices as study tools. A mnemonic such as "Columbus sailed the ocean blue in fourteen hundred and ninety-two" can be used as an example.

STUDENTS WITH SPECIAL NEEDS

You may want to make available for students calendar forms based on your school's grading cycle, such as a calendar showing six weeks. Have students fill in correct dates. Then, assist students as they plot out assignments for all their classes. For example, if students have long papers to write or novels to read, help students determine how to break the assignments into manageable segments. Have students record test dates and plan time to study and review in advance.

IMPROVING TEST-TAKING SKILLS

OBJECTIVES

- To recognize errors in standard English
- To revise sentences to correct errors
- To prepare a list of questions based on a reading passage to use as a test
- To use critical reading skills to answer test questions

1120   *Reading, Studying, and Test Taking*

HOW TO MEMORIZE   (continued)

3. *Use memory games.* Use the first letter of each word to form a new word. Make a rhyme or associate the information with some particularly vivid mental image.
4. *Repeat the material.* Recite the material frequently in short sessions.

Improving Test-Taking Skills

Preparing for Different Kinds of Tests

You can improve your performance on all types of tests if you learn various test-taking strategies and prepare carefully. For instance, your attitude is one of the most important factors that affect your performance on a test. If you believe you can do well and know that you have prepared as well as you can, you are more likely to concentrate your attention on doing well and focus on the test questions. It's common to feel somewhat anxious before a big test; however, you can learn to convert your nervous energy into concentrated attention and excellence in performance on the test.

Kinds of Tests

Classroom Tests.   The typical classroom test is intended to measure your ability to use important academic skills or to show your knowledge of particular academic subjects. For example, in a Spanish class, your teacher might give you a test to see how well you have learned to conjugate the list of thirty irregular verbs that you were supposed to have covered in an assigned chapter of your textbook.

Frequently, classroom tests combine several types of test questions. For example, your teacher might prepare a test made up of thirty true/false questions worth three points each and an essay question worth ten points. There are any number of combinations of test questions and scoring methods that may be used.

PROGRAM MANAGER

IMPROVING TEST-TAKING SKILLS

- **Independent Practice/ Reteaching** For additional practice and reinforcement, see **Taking Essay Tests; Synonyms, Antonyms, Sentence Completion;** and **Reading Comprehension** in *Academic and Workplace Skills,* pp. 87–89.

QUICK REMINDER

Ask students to name three things they do to prepare themselves for tests. Write responses on the chalkboard and discuss each one. Afterward, fill in any gaps you see in their responses. Then, have students determine the best study methods for different types of tests.

No matter the number or the type of questions, the purpose of classroom tests is always the same: to assess how much you know about a particular subject you have studied or to evaluate your ability to use a specific skill you have practiced. Thus, the best way to prepare for a typical classroom test is to be sure that you are familiar with the assigned material or that you have practiced the skill until you are proficient at it before it is time to take the test. If you review and use the study skills outlined earlier in this chapter, you can generally improve your performance on ordinary classroom tests.

Standardized Tests. On standardized tests, your score is evaluated according to a "standard" or "norm" that has been compiled from the scores of a great number of other students who have taken the same test. Some types of standardized tests may be developed by specific school districts or by your particular state. The best-known standardized tests are those that are given to numerous students across the United States:

- the *National Merit Scholarship Qualifying Test (NMSQT)*
- the *Scholastic Aptitude Test (SAT-I Reasoning Test)*
- the *Scholastic Aptitude Test (SAT-II Subject Test)*
- the *American College Testing Program (ACT)*

Among these examples of the most common standardized tests, there are two basic types of tests administered: aptitude and achievement tests.

TYPES OF STANDARDIZED TESTS	
Aptitude (or Reasoning) Tests	■ intended to evaluate basic skills or reasoning abilities that are needed in various general areas of higher-level study ■ often cover material and skills you have learned during many years of study (such as verbal expression skills and critical thinking ability)
Achievement (or Academic Subject) Tests	■ intended to measure knowledge of specific subjects (such as history, literature, sciences, mathematics, or foreign languages)

RESOURCES

RESOURCES

MEETING *individual* NEEDS

LESS-ADVANCED STUDENTS

You may want to give students the following additional tips for taking objective tests:

1. **multiple choice**—Cover the answer choices as you read the questions. An answer may pop into your mind. Check to see if the answer that came to you is among the answer choices. If so, it is probably correct.
2. **true/false**—Do not go back and change any answers unless you have a good reason to do so. Studies show that people's first responses to true/false questions are usually correct.
3. **matching**—Mark through items you have already matched.
4. **short answer**—Use other parts of the test to find information and to check the spellings of words.

STUDENTS WITH SPECIAL NEEDS

Standardized tests must be given according to specified procedures that include time limits, directions, and the use of calculators or dictionaries. Some state and national standardized tests, such as the SAT, permit deviations from the standardized administration procedures for students with special needs. You probably can obtain detailed information about permitted modifications from guidance counselors. You can discuss these modifications with the students, their parents, test administrators, and others involved in the testing process to make sure that the modifications in test procedures are used.

In general, the best strategies for preparing to take either one of these types of standardized tests include

- keeping up with your schoolwork during the year
- reading and writing often (in addition to regularly assigned material and classwork)
- steadily increasing your vocabulary

A specific suggestion for improving your performance is to become familiar with the types of test questions you will be expected to answer on the test you are scheduled to take. On pages 1123–1135 is information about the types of questions that the best-known standardized tests use when evaluating verbal expression and critical analysis. The following chart contains general suggestions about taking standardized tests.

HOW TO PREPARE FOR STANDARDIZED TESTS

1. *Learn what specific abilities will be tested.* Study any information booklets that are provided. Practice with these or with study guides found in bookstores or libraries.
2. *Know what materials you will need.* On the day of the test, you may need to bring specific materials, such as your official test registration card, number 2 pencils, or lined paper for writing an essay answer.
3. *Determine how the test is evaluated.* If there is no penalty for wrong answers, make your best guess on all questions possible. However, if wrong answers are penalized, make guesses only if you are fairly sure of the correct answer.

Taking Standardized Aptitude Tests

One key reason for standardized aptitude tests is to make a prediction of how likely you are to succeed in going on to a higher educational environment. College work requires large amounts of independent reading and writing, so one of the best indicators of how well you might perform at the college level is your ability to identify and correct problems with verbal expression as well as your ability to analyze and interpret the meaning, purpose, and organization of reading passages.

Kinds of Test Questions

Most test questions can be classified as either limited-response questions or open-response questions.

Limited-Response Questions. Limited-response questions give you a limited number of choices from which you must select the most appropriate answer. These include

- multiple-choice questions
- true/false questions
- matching questions

Open-Response Questions. Open-response questions ask you to provide a written response. These include

- fill-in-the-blank questions
- short answer questions
- essay questions

Tests of Verbal Expression

Standardized tests of verbal expression measure your ability to understand the meaning expressed in written passages and the grammatical correctness or clarity of written expression.

MATERIAL COVERED ON VERBAL EXPRESSION TESTS	
Grammar Questions	You identify the most correct answer, using standard grammar and usage rules. Test items often cover correct use of <ul><li>subject-verb agreement (700–714)</li><li>principal parts of verbs (766–787)</li><li>pronouns (728–746)</li></ul>
Punctuation Questions	You identify use of correct punctuation. Test items often cover correct use of <ul><li>end marks and commas (897–925)</li><li>semicolons and colons (928–931)</li><li>apostrophes, hyphens, dashes, and parentheses (944–956)</li><li>quotation marks (935–939)</li></ul>

(continued)

COOPERATIVE LEARNING

You may want to give students an opportunity to create tests. Have students work in groups of four or five. Have the groups work with textbooks they are currently using to prepare a list of twelve key terms on which they might be tested. Each group should then use the information to write objective test questions.

COMMON ERROR

Problem. Sometimes without even reading the questions, some students routinely guess at answers on standardized tests.

Solution. To minimize guessing, some standardized multiple-choice tests have a guessing factor built into scoring formulas. Typically, if one point is awarded in the scoring formula for each correct answer, a quarter of a point is subtracted for each wrong answer. On most standardized tests, points are neither awarded nor subtracted for items a student leaves blank.

The conventional wisdom of test-taking is that students should guess only when they can eliminate as incorrect all but two answer choices. If students guess between only two choices, they have a fifty percent chance of guessing the right answer. In a hypothetical case in which a student can eliminate all but two choices on four questions, if the student guesses correctly on one question and incorrectly on the other three, he or she is still ahead by a quarter of a point.

MATERIAL COVERED ON TESTS OF VERBAL EXPRESSION *(continued)*	
Sentence Structure Questions	You demonstrate knowledge of what is (and what is not) a complete sentence. Test items often cover correction of ■ fragments and run-on sentences (555–558) ■ combining sentences (564–577) ■ modifiers (813–824) ■ verb tense (788–799) ■ parallel structure (550–552) ■ transitional words (75–77)
Revision-in-Context Questions	You show appropriate revision of a part or a whole composition. Test items often cover correct use of ■ composition structure (95–123) ■ unity and coherence (71–77) ■ tone (32–34) ■ arranging ideas (35–38)
Rhetorical Strategies Questions	You show an understanding of strategies writers use to express ideas and opinions. Test items often cover ■ strategies of development (79–87) ■ sequence of ideas (35–38) ■ style and tone (31–34)

On the best-known standardized tests, these multiple-choice verbal expression test questions are not presented as isolated questions. Instead, they appear in the context of a reading passage. You are given a sample passage, usually a long paragraph, with several words and phrases underlined and numbered. Then you are given a series of test items related to the passage. You are expected to pick, from among the choices given, the answer that best expresses the meaning, is most grammatically correct, or is most consistent with the style and tone of the passage.

Following is a sample test passage with sample questions.

Sample Verbal Expression Test Passage

Everyone has fears. Young children are often terrified of being left alone in the dark, trembling in their beds at night. With a slightly queasy stomach—a passenger momentarily grips the seat arms as the
<u>1</u>
huge jet lumbers up the runway for a takeoff. A high school student is faced with a three-minute speech in front of classmates. She feels weak-kneed and dry-mouthed as the moment approaches. These fears are normal; everyone has them, or is in danger of suffering such fears,
<u>2</u>
at some time. For most people, however, the moment passes and so do
<u>3</u>
the fear and its accompanying physical reactions. The child grows older and becomes less afraid of the dark; the traveler continues to fly; the student survives the speech.

SAMPLE VERBAL EXPRESSION QUESTIONS	
1. A. NO CHANGE ⒝ stomach, a C. stomach. A D. stomach; a	[This is a question about punctuation; it requires you to know which mark of punctuation is appropriate here.]
2. Which of the following is the best revision of the portion of the passage indicated by the number 2? A. fears to be similar to them, B. everyone feels fears like these, Ⓒ fears that are similar to them, D. fears like them—	[This is a revision-in-context question; it requires you to use revision skills to best express the ideas in the passage.]
3. Ⓐ NO CHANGE B. did C. does D. would do	[This is a question about grammar; it requires you to know the correct subject-verb agreement.]

(continued)

A DIFFERENT APPROACH

One widely used test of verbal expression skills is the Test of Standard Written English (TSWE) that is given as part of the SAT. Scores on the TSWE aren't used to calculate a student's total verbal score on the SAT, but TSWE scores are reported along with SAT scores.

Every year the College Board publishes a free booklet that contains a sample SAT and TSWE that students can use for practice. These booklets are usually available from guidance counselors. You can obtain a classroom set of these booklets and let your students work with the TSWE to familiarize themselves with the test's format and with the kinds of skills the test covers. If your students seem to need review or instruction in a particular skill covered on the test, you can provide help before they take the test.

LESS-ADVANCED STUDENTS

Since logic questions are increasingly included on standardized tests, you may want to give students plenty of practice with them. Get a book of brain teasers and have students work in pairs to complete the problems. Or, obtain several Graduate Record Examination study guides that teach techniques for doing logic problems, and teach students these strategies.

ADVANCED STUDENTS

You can use the free booklets published by the College Board for the SAT and by the American College Testing Service for the ACT to obtain additional sample passages and questions for your students to use for practice. In addition, the College Board publishes collections of old tests (for example, *Five SAT's*) that can be used for additional practice.

RESOURCES

RESOURCES

MATERIAL COVERED ON CRITICAL READING TESTS *(continued)*	
Evaluation Questions	You analyze and evaluate the effectiveness of specific techniques used by the author of a reading passage. Test items often cover identification of ■ the author's opinion—directly or indirectly expressed—in the passage (1104–1108) ■ the author's intended audience (31–34) ■ the author's tone or point of view (31–34) ■ the author's purpose (31–34)
Interpretation Questions	You draw conclusions or make inferences about the meaning of information presented in a reading passage. Test items often cover identification of ■ ambiguities in information (540–561) ■ conclusions or inferences based on material given in a passage (1108) ■ specific conclusions or inferences that can be drawn about the author or the topic of a passage (1104–1108)
Synthesis Questions	You show your understanding of how each part of a passage fits together into a whole. Test items often cover interpretation of ■ techniques used to unify details (71–73) ■ the cumulative meaning of details in a passage (1104–1108)
Vocabulary-in-Context Questions	You infer the meaning of an unfamiliar word by an analysis of its context. Test items often cover determination of ■ the meaning of a passage to learn the definition of a word (1075–1076) ■ the meaning of an unfamiliar word, using context clues (1075–1076)

(continued)

MATERIAL COVERED ON CRITICAL READING TESTS *(continued)*	
Style Questions	You analyze a passage to evaluate the author's style. **Test items often cover** ■ the author's style (515–523) ■ the author's voice and tone (517–518) ■ the appropriateness of the author's style for the author's intended audience (31–34)

Here is a sample critical reading test passage with sample questions.

Sample Critical Reading Passage

During the period from 1660 through 1800, Great Britain became convinced of its place as the world's leader. Beginning with the restoration of Charles II to the throne, this period in England's history is best described as a period of authority.

Language itself became submitted to rules during this period. This need to "fix" the English language is best illustrated in the making of the *Dictionary of the English Language* by Samuel Johnson. Guides to the English language had been in existence before Johnson began his project in 1746. These, however, were often little more than lists of hard words. When definitions of common words were supplied, they were often unhelpful. For example, a "horse" was defined in an early dictionary as "a beast well known."

Johnson changed all that, but the task was not an easy one. Renting a house at 17 Gough Square, Johnson began working in the worst of conditions. Supported only by installments from his publisher, Johnson worked on the *Dictionary* with five assistants. Compared to the French Academy's dictionary, which took forty workers fifty-five years to complete (1639–1694), Johnson's dictionary was completed by very few people very quickly.

Balanced on a chair with only three legs, Johnson sat propped against a wall in a room scattered with books. Johnson would read widely from these books, mark quotations illustrating the use of a particular word, and give the book to his assistants so that they could copy the passage on slips of paper. These slips were then pasted in

CRITICAL THINKING

Analysis. One useful procedure for students to use in taking standardized tests is to look over the questions before they read the reading comprehension passages. By looking over the questions, students can figure out what kinds of information the questions expect them to obtain from the passage. It will probably be necessary for students to go back to the passage as they answer the questions, but a quick analysis of the questions before reading can alert students about how to read the passage.

RESOURCES

RESOURCES

Suggest to students that they work in groups of three or four to make up sentence-correction questions. Each group could begin with a list of errors to be studied for the test. Then group members could make up the four sentences needed for each numbered item. Students should make sure that there is only one correct answer, and they should record those answers in a separate key. When the groups have finished, copy the tests and give each student copies of all the tests he or she did not create. Students can then take these tests, and each group can grade the test it made.

1130 *Reading, Studying, and Test Taking*

eighty large notebooks under the key words that Johnson had selected. "Fixing" the word by this method, Johnson could record a word's usage and its definition. To help the reader of the *Dictionary* gain a sense of the history of the word, Johnson also arranged the passages chronologically.

How many passages were used? According to Johnson's modern biographer Walter Jackson Bate, the original total number could have been over 240,000. How many words were defined by the lexicographer? Over 40,000 words appeared in two folio volumes in April of 1755. Did Johnson fully understand the enormous task he was undertaking when he began? As he told his contemporary biographer James Boswell, "I knew very well what I was undertaking—and very well how to do it—and have done it very well."

SAMPLE CRITICAL READING QUESTIONS

1. According to the passage, in which order (from earliest to latest) did the following events occur?
   I. Johnson published his *Dictionary*.
   II. The French Academy's dictionary was published.
   III. Johnson rented a house at 17 Gough Square.
   IV. Charles II was restored to the throne.

   A. II, III, IV, I
   B. IV, II, III, I
   C. IV, I, II, III
   D. IV, III, II, I

   [This is an organization question; it requires you to identify the time sequence of each of these events and to arrange them in the correct historical time order.]

2. Shortly before the publication of the *Dictionary*, Johnson wrote a famous letter to the noble and wealthy Lord Chesterfield, who had been Johnson's sponsor during the project. The following lines are an excerpt from that letter.

   Seven years, my Lord, have passed since I waited in your outward rooms, or was repulsed from your door; during which time I have been pushing on my work through difficulties, of which it is useless to complain, and have brought it, at last, to the verge of publication, without one act of assistance, one word of encouragement, or one smile of favor. Such treatment I did not expect, for I never had a Patron before. . . .

(continued)

SAMPLE CRITICAL READING QUESTIONS *(continued)*

You could assume that Johnson is
A. critical of the lack of assistance from Chesterfield.
B. critical of the conditions under which he had to work.
C. critical of royalty.
D. critical of patrons.

[This is an evaluation question; it requires you to recognize the main point of the original passage and to analyze the second passage to identify which of these main points fits with Johnson's complaint.]

3. The word *fixing* in paragraph four is best taken to mean
A. repairing.
B. correcting.
C. standardizing.
D. augmenting.

[This is an interpretation question; you are asked to examine the context of the word noted in order to explain its meaning in the passage.]

4. It can be inferred from the description of Samuel Johnson that he was
A. a man who represented the eighteenth century.
B. a man who worked inconsistently.
C. a man who had never worked under impoverished conditions.
D. a man who was jealous and petty.

[This is a synthesis question; after reading in the passage about the details of the eighteenth-century preoccupation with standardization, you can conclude that Johnson's attempt to standardize English was in keeping with the times he lived in.]

5. The word *lexicographer* in paragraph five means
A. a maker of dictionaries.
B. a biographer.
C. a scholar.
D. a harmless fellow.

[This is a vocabulary-in-context question; it requires you to examine the context of the passage in which the word appears in order to determine the appropriate definition.]

(continued)

RESOURCES

RESOURCES

General Strategies. You can point out to students that context clues are clues within a passage that hint at the meaning of an unfamiliar word. Sometimes the clue consists of a definition of the unfamiliar word either before or after the word, as in "The next step is to elutriate, or purify, the liquid by straining it." Sometimes the clue consists of a synonym for the unknown word in another clause or sentence, as in "They had to elutriate the solution before it could be used, and they decided to purify it by straining it."

Ask your students to find sentences that contain unfamiliar words and to work with those sentences to demonstrate how readers can use context to obtain the meanings of the unknown words.

SAMPLE CRITICAL READING QUESTIONS *(continued)*

6. Readers of this passage are likely to describe it as
   A. informal.
   B. confessional.
   C. historical.
   D. biographical.

   [This is a question of style; you analyze the way the passage is written to determine the type of writing it represents.]

Tests of Critical Analysis

Standardized critical analysis tests measure your ability to use logic and reasoning to evaluate the context of a passage.

MATERIAL COVERED ON CRITICAL ANALYSIS TESTS

Analogy Questions	■ You analyze the relationship between a pair of words and use reasoning skills to identify a second pair of words with the same relationship (1083–1085).
	EXAMPLE: **1.** ANIMAL : CAT :: _____
	   A. speak : sneeze
	   B. room : kitchen
	   C. cold : ice cube
	   D. match : flame

Logic Questions	You analyze the meaning of a sentence or a brief passage to fill in one or more blanks with the most appropriate words given.
	EXAMPLE: Since Johnson's huge task was so _____, he never did receive fair _____ for compiling the *Dictionary*.
	   A. minimal . . . criticism
	   B. herculean . . . remuneration
	   C. banal . . . remuneration
	   D. equivocal . . . compensation

Essay Tests

An *essay test* is intended to measure your ability to express your understanding of selected material in an organized, written form. Writing an essay for a test calls for critical thinking and writing skills. A well-written essay answer must always be a complete response to the question asked and must always contain a sufficient amount of information to demonstrate thorough knowledge of the material.

Essay questions usually ask you to perform specific tasks, each of which is expressed with a verb. Each task requires a specific response that you can prepare for by becoming familiar with the key terms and the kinds of information called for.

ESSAY TEST QUESTIONS		
KEY VERB	TASK	SAMPLE QUESTION
analyze	Take something apart to see how each part works.	Analyze the process of amending the U.S. Constitution.
argue	Take a viewpoint on an issue and give reasons to support this opinion.	Argue whether or not students who fail a class should repeat it.
compare	Point out likenesses.	Compare Mel Gibson and Laurence Olivier in *Hamlet*.
contrast	Point out differences.	Contrast the processes of fission and fusion.
define	Give specific details that make something unique.	Define the term *gouache* as an artistic medium.
demonstrate (also illustrate, present, show)	Provide examples to support a point.	Demonstrate the advantages of using a word processor.

(continued)

MEETING *individual* **NEEDS**

LESS-ADVANCED STUDENTS

To help students understand the **Essay Test Questions** chart, give students examples for each key verb of several questions that relate to something that students are familiar with. For example, you could create sample questions related to something students have been studying in class or related to a popular television show, movie, or entertainer.

COOPERATIVE LEARNING

Group students in threes or fours and give each group one of the key verbs listed on the **Essay Test Questions** chart. Ask each group to choose three topics and to use their key verb to write an essay question for each topic. Then, when the whole class is meeting together, have a representative from each group read the questions and explain how to answer them.

RESOURCES

RESOURCES

TIMESAVER

To save time when grading essay tests, list the main details that should be included in each answer, attach points to each detail, and grade each essay according to the completeness of the answer. You may also want to make a list of acceptable alternative details and assign point values to each.

INTEGRATING THE LANGUAGE ARTS

Test Taking and Writing. An essay written during a test should have the same qualities in its content as an essay written outside the class. Have students generate a checklist of qualities that a well-written essay should have. You might list students' suggestions on the chalkboard and add any qualities students forget. After completing and organizing the list, have students copy it to use as a future reference.

ESSAY TEST QUESTIONS *(continued)*		
KEY VERB	**TASK**	**SAMPLE QUESTION**
describe	Give a picture in words.	Describe the storm scene in *King Lear*.
discuss	Examine in detail.	Discuss the end of the Soviet Union.
explain	Give reasons.	Explain tidal waves.
identify	Point out specific persons, places, things, or characteristics.	Identify the major political figures in the Watergate scandal.
interpret	Give the meaning or significance of something.	Interpret the meaning of the Monroe Doctrine in terms of American foreign policy.
list (also outline, trace)	Give all steps in order or all details about a subject.	List events leading to the invasion of Kuwait by Iraq.
summarize	Give a brief overview of the main points.	Summarize the plot of Bernard Shaw's *Pygmalion*.

When you begin an essay test, scan the questions to see how many answers you are expected to write. If you have a choice between several items, pick those you can answer best. Plan how much time to spend on each answer; then stay on schedule.

Read the question carefully. There may be several parts to the answer.

Pay attention to important terms in the question. Pay attention to each key verb and identify the tasks that you need to accomplish in your essay.

Take a moment to use prewriting strategies. Make notes or a simple outline on scratch paper to help you plan your response.

Evaluate and revise as you write. You will not be able to redraft your whole essay, but you can edit to strengthen your essay.

QUALITIES OF A GOOD ESSAY ANSWER

- The essay is well organized.
- The main ideas and supporting points are clearly presented.
- The sentences are complete and well written.
- There are no distracting errors in spelling, punctuation, or grammar.

Review

▶ EXERCISE 1   **Using Reading and Study Skills**

The following numbered items suggest ways for you to practice using the reading and study skills discussed on pages 1100–1120.

1. In a brief paragraph, identify the circumstances in which you use each of the rates of reading noted on page 1101 to accomplish different purposes.
2. Choose a magazine article or a textbook chapter, and use the SQ3R reading method outlined on page 1103 to list at least five questions. Write brief answers to each one.
3. Write a list of critical reading questions and answers about Isaac Asimov's "The Villain in the Atmosphere" (pages 363–369), using the sample analysis of the reading passage on pages 1105–1107 as a model.
4. Select a chapter from one of your textbooks that you have been assigned as homework, and take study notes, using the strategies explained on pages 1110–1111.
5. Find a passage in a textbook, a magazine, or a newspaper that gives information that you can express in graphic form. Using the information and example on pages 1112–1113 as a model, make a visual representation of pertinent information from the passage.

RESOURCES

ANSWERS
Exercise 1

1. Paragraphs will vary. Students might list their personal reading preferences as the material they will read for mastery, or they might include textbook reading in this category. Newspapers and magazines could be in the scanning category.

2. Students' questions should deal with significant facts or ideas in their selections. The answers should be complete and accurate.

3. Students' questions should reflect analysis, interpretation, and evaluation. They should not require simple details or translation of a passage into different words.

4. Students' study notes should include all of the main ideas and sufficient details to support the main ideas. The notes should be concise.

5. Each student's graphic should include a title that tells readers what they're reading. The information in the graphic should be accurate and pertinent.

RESOURCES

ANSWERS
Exercise 2

Answers will vary. Each paraphrase should be in the student's own words, and each should use complete sentences and standard paragraph form. The paraphrase should identify the speaker of the poem and should contain the same ideas as the poem.

ANSWERS
Exercise 3

Each student's précis should include the central point of the excerpt, and it should be brief while also including the student's own words.

ANSWERS
Exercise 4

Students' questions will vary, but they should cover a variety of common errors in grammar, punctuation, revision, and sentence structure.

▶ **EXERCISE 2**   **Reading: Paraphrasing a Poem**

Write a paraphrase of "The Bear" by Nina Cassian (page 207), following the guidelines on pages 1114–1116.

▶ **EXERCISE 3**   **Reading: Writing a Précis**

Write a précis of the excerpt by Judith Ortiz Cofer, from *Silent Dancing: A Partial Remembrance of a Puerto Rican Childhood* (pages 140–143), following the guidelines on pages 1117–1119.

▶ **EXERCISE 4**   **Preparing for Tests of Verbal Expression**

Working in groups, find a passage in a nonfiction book or magazine article, and write a list of questions to test your classmates' verbal expression skills. Use the sample passage and sample questions on pages 1125–1126 as a model. Use the chart on pages 1123–1124 as a reference guide to sections in this textbook that you can consult for suggestions and as a resource to check your answers.

▶ **EXERCISE 5**   **Preparing for Tests of Critical Reading**

Using the sample test passage on pages 1129–1130, answer the following questions.

1. Which of the following techniques does the author use in concluding the passage?
   A. restating the main idea.
   B. closing with a final, new thought.
   C. asking, then answering rhetorical questions.
   D. referring to the introduction.

2. The word *installments* in the third paragraph may be defined as
   A. ceremonial assignments of personnel.
   B. a series of payments.
   C. a number of permanent fixtures.
   D. a group of chapters of a book.

3. The author's predominant attitude about the subject seems to be
   A. approval of eighteenth-century political change.
   B. criticism of Johnson's writing and research methods.
   C. criticism of Johnson's ideas about language use.
   D. admiration of Johnson's achievements.

RESOURCES

RESOURCES

4. Which of the following interpretations is suggested by the last paragraph?
   A. Johnson was a self-confident, proud man.
   B. Johnson was a humble, self-effacing man.
   C. Johnson should never have tried his project.
   D. Johnson's health was ruined by the project.

5. This passage most probably has the purpose of
   A. classifying kinds of dictionaries.
   B. entertaining the reader.
   C. expressing the author's personality.
   D. informing the reader.

Glossary of Terms

A

Action verb Expresses physical or mental activity. (See page 612.)

Active voice The voice a verb is in when it expresses an action done *by* its subject. (See page 800.)

Adjective Modifies a noun or a pronoun. (See page 606.)

Adjective clause A subordinate clause that modifies a noun or a pronoun. (See page 676.)

Adjective phrase A prepositional phrase that modifies a noun or a pronoun. (See page 653.)

Adverb Modifies a verb, an adjective, or another adverb. (See page 616.)

Adverb clause A subordinate clause that modifies a verb, an adjective, or an adverb. (See page 681.)

Adverb phrase A prepositional phrase that modifies a verb, an adjective, or an adverb. (See page 654.)

Agreement The correspondence, or match, between grammatical forms. (See Chapter 21.)

Aim One of the four basic purposes, or reasons, for writing. (See pages 7 and 19.)

Ambiguous reference Occurs when a pronoun refers to either of two antecedents. (See page 755.)

Antecedent The word that a pronoun stands for. (See page 718.)

Appositive A noun or a pronoun placed beside another noun or pronoun to identify or explain it. (See page 666.)

Appositive phrase Consists of an appositive and its modifiers. (See page 666.)

Articles *A, an,* and *the,* the most frequently used adjectives. (See page 606.)

B

Base form The base form, or infinitive, is one of the four principal, or basic, parts of a verb. (See page 766.)

C

Case The form of a noun or pronoun that shows how it is used in a sentence. (See page 728.)

Cause-and-effect essay A form of writing in which a writer explains the causes and/or effects of a situation. (See Chapter 7.)

Chronological order A way of arranging ideas in a paragraph or composition according to when events happen. (See pages 35 and 74.)

Classification A strategy of development: looking at a subject as it relates to other subjects in a group. (See page 79.)

Clause A group of words that contains a subject and its predicate and is used as part of a sentence. (See page 674.)

Coherence A quality achieved when all the ideas in a paragraph or composition are clearly arranged and connected. (See pages 74 and 117.)

Comparison Refers to the change in the form of an adjective or an adverb to show increasing or decreasing degrees in the quality the modifier expresses. (See page 819.)

Comparison/Contrast essay A form of writing in which a writer discusses similarities or differences (or both) between two subjects. (See page 247.)

Complement A word or group of words that completes the meaning of a verb. (See page 637.)

Complex sentence Has one independent clause and at least one subordinate clause. (See page 687.)

Compound-complex sentence Has two or more independent clauses and at least one subordinate clause. (See page 687.)

Compound sentence Has two or more independent clauses but no subordinate clauses. (See page 686.)

Conjunction Joins words or groups of words. (See page 621.)

Critical analysis A form of writing in which a writer examines and responds to a piece of literature critically. (See Chapter 10.)

D

Dangling modifier A modifying word, phrase, or clause that does not clearly and sensibly modify a word or a group of words in a sentence. (See page 835.)

Declarative sentence Makes a statement and is followed by a period. (See page 689.)

Description A strategy of development: using sensory details and spatial order to describe individual features of a specific subject. (See page 79.)

Direct object A word or word group that receives the action of the verb or shows the result of the action, telling *whom* or *what* after a transitive verb. (See page 639.)

Direct reference Connects ideas in a paragraph or composition by referring to a noun or pronoun used earlier. (See page 74.)

Double negative The use of two negative words when one is enough. (See page 864.)

E

Elliptical construction A clause or phrase from which words have been omitted. (See pages 683 and 741.)

Essential clause/Essential phrase Also called restrictive: is necessary to

the meaning of a sentence; not set off by commas. (See page 909.)

Evaluating A stage in the writing process: making judgments about a composition's strengths and weaknesses in content, organization, and style. (See pages 6 and 20.)

Evaluation A strategy of development: making judgments about a subject in an attempt to determine its value. (See page 79.)

Exclamatory sentence Expresses strong feeling and is followed by an exclamation point. (See page 690.)

Expository writing Aims at being informative, explanatory, or exploratory. (See pages 7 and 19.)

F

Feasibility report A feasibility report is a report that identifies the need to change the current state of affairs. A typical feasibility report identifies alternative courses of action, establishes criteria to evaluate each possible course of action, and, finally, determines the best course of action. (See Chapter 6.)

G

General reference Occurs when a pronoun refers to a general idea rather than to a specific noun. (See page 756.)

Gerund A verb form ending in *–ing* that is used as a noun. (See page 660.)

Gerund phrase Consists of a gerund and its modifiers and complements. (See page 661.)

I

Imperative mood Used to express a direct command or request. (See page 805.)

Imperative sentence Gives a command or makes a request and is followed by either a period or an exclamation point. (See page 689.)

Indefinite reference Occurs when the pronoun *you, it,* or *they* refers to no particular person or thing. (See page 760.)

Independent clause Also called a main clause: expresses a complete thought and can stand by itself as a sentence. (See page 674.)

Indicative mood Used to express a fact, an opinion, or a question. (See page 805.)

Indirect object A word or word group that comes between a transitive verb and its direct object and tells *to whom* or *to what* or *for whom* or *for what* the action of the verb is done. (See page 639.)

Infinitive A verb form, usually preceded by *to,* used as a noun, an adjective, or an adverb. (See page 663.)

Infinitive phrase Consists of an infinitive and its modifiers and complements. (See page 663.)

Interjection Expresses emotion and has no grammatical relation to the rest of the sentence. (See page 623.)

Interrogative sentence Asks a question and is followed by a question mark. (See page 689.)

Intransitive verb An action verb that does not take an object. (See page 612.)

L

Linking verb Connects the subject with a word that identifies or describes the subject. (See page 612.)

Literary writing Aims at creating imaginative works. (See pages 7 and 19.)

Logical order A way of arranging details in a paragraph or composition according to what makes sense. (See pages 35 and 74.)

M

Misplaced modifier A word, phrase, or clause that makes a sentence awkward by seeming to modify the wrong words. (See page 832.)

Modifier A word that limits the meaning of another word. (See page 813.)

Mood (1) The general feeling in a short story or other literary work. (See page 174.) **(2)** The form a verb takes to indicate the attitude of the person using the verb. (See page 805.)

N

Narration A strategy of development: relating events or actions over a period of time, usually using chronological order. (See page 79.)

Nonessential clause/Nonessential phrase Also called nonrestrictive: adds information not necessary to the main idea in the sentence and is set off by commas. (See page 909.)

Noun Names a person, place, thing, or idea. (See page 599.)

Noun clause A subordinate clause used as a noun. (See page 679.)

Number The form of a word that indicates whether the word is singular or plural. (See page 700.)

O

Objective complement A word or word group that helps complete the meaning of a transitive verb by identifying or modifying the direct object. (See page 640.)

Object of a preposition The noun or pronoun that ends a prepositional phrase. (See page 619.)

Order of importance A way of arranging details from least to most important or from most to least important. (See pages 35 and 74.)

P

Participial phrase Consists of a participle and its complements and modifiers. (See page 658.)

Participle A verb form used as an adjective. (See page 657.)

Passive voice The voice a verb is in when it expresses an action done *to* its subject. (See page 800.)

Persuasive essay A form of writing in which a writer supports an opinion and tries to persuade an audience. (See Chapter 8.)

Persuasive writing Aims at convincing people to accept an idea or to take action. (See pages 7 and 19.)

Phrase A group of related words that does not contain a verb and its subject and is used as a single part of speech. (See page 652.)

Point of view The vantage point, or position, from which a writer tells a story or describes a subject. (See page 174.)

Predicate The part of a sentence that says something about the subject. (See page 632.)

Predicate adjective An adjective that follows a linking verb and modifies the subject of the verb. (See page 642.)

Predicate nominative A noun or pronoun that follows a linking verb and refers to the same person or thing as the subject of the verb. (See page 642.)

Preposition Shows the relationship of a noun or a pronoun to some other word in a sentence. (See page 619.)

Prepositional phrase A group of words beginning with a preposition and ending with an object (a noun or a pronoun). (See page 652.)

Prewriting The first stage in the writing process: thinking and planning, deciding what to write about, collecting ideas and details, and making a plan for presenting ideas. (See pages 6 and 20.)

Problem-solution essay A form of exploratory writing in which a writer explains a problem and proposes an effective solution. (See Chapter 9.)

Pronoun Is used in place of a noun or more than one noun. (See page 602.)

Proofreading A stage of the writing process: carefully reading a revised draft to correct mistakes in grammar, usage, and mechanics. (See pages 6 and 20.)

Publishing The last stage of the writing process: making a final, clean copy of a paper and sharing it with an audience. (See pages 6 and 20.)

Purpose A reason for writing or speaking. (See pages 19 and 31.)

R

Reflective essay A form of writing in which an author explores and shares the meaning of an experience that was especially important to him or her. (See Chapter 4.)

Research paper A form of writing in which a writer presents factual information discovered through exploration and research. (See Chapter 11.)

Revising A stage of the writing process: making changes in a composition's content, organization, and style in order to improve it. (See pages 6 and 42.)

S

Self-expressive writing Aims at expressing a writer's feelings and thoughts. (See pages 7 and 19.)

Sentence A group of words that contains a subject and a verb and expresses a complete thought. (See page 631.)

Simple sentence Has one independent clause and no subordinate clauses. (See page 686.)

Spatial order A way of arranging details in a paragraph or composition according to location. (See pages 35 and 74.)

Style A writer's unique way of adapting language to suit different occasions. (See Chapter 13.)

Subject Tells whom or what a sentence is about. (See page 632.)

Subject complement A word or word group that completes the meaning of a linking verb and identifies or modifies the subject. (See page 642.)

Subjunctive mood Used to express a suggestion, a necessity, a condition contrary to fact, or a wish. (See page 805.)

Subordinate clause Also called a dependent clause: does not express a complete thought and cannot stand alone as a sentence. (See page 675.)

Supporting sentences Give specific details or information to develop the main idea. (See page 67.)

T

Tense Indicates the time of the action or state of being expressed by the verb. (See page 788.)

Theme The underlying meaning or message a writer wants to communicate to readers. (See pages 404 and 405.)

Thesis statement Announces the limited topic of a composition and states the main, or unifying, idea about that topic. (See page 100.)

Tone The feeling or attitude a writer conveys about a topic. (See page 32.)

Topic sentence Expresses the main idea of a paragraph. (See page 64.)

Transitional expressions Words and phrases that indicate relationships between ideas in a paragraph or composition. (See page 75.)

Transitive verb An action verb that takes an object. (See page 612.)

U

Unity A quality achieved when all the sentences or paragraphs in a composition work together as a unit to express or support one main idea. (See pages 71 and 117.)

V

Verb Expresses an action or a state of being. (See page 612.)

Verbal A form of a verb used as a noun, an adjective, or an adverb. (See page 656.)

Verbal phrase Consists of a verbal and its modifiers and complements. (See page 656.)

Verb phrase Consists of a main verb preceded by at least one helping verb. (See page 614.)

Voice (1) The unique sound and rhythm of a writer's language. (See page 517.) **(2)** The form a transitive verb takes to indicate whether the subject of the verb performs or receives the action. (See page 800.)

W

Weak reference Occurs when a pronoun refers to an antecedent that has not been expressed. (See page 758.)

Writing A stage in the writing process: putting ideas into words, following a plan that organizes the ideas. (See pages 6 and 20.)

Writing process The series of stages, or steps, that a writer goes through to develop ideas and to communicate them clearly in a piece of writing. (See pages 6 and 20.)

Glossary

This glossary is a short dictionary of words found in the professional writing models in this textbook. The words are defined according to their meanings in the context of the writing models.

Pronunciation Key

Symbol	Key Words	Symbol	Key Words
a	asp, fat, parrot	b	bed, fable, dub, ebb
ā	ape, date, play, break, fail	d	dip, beadle, had, dodder
ä	ah, car, father, cot	f	fall, after, off, phone
e	elf, ten, berry	g	get, haggle, dog
ē	even, meet, money, flea, grieve	h	he, ahead, hotel
i	is, hit, mirror	j	joy, agile, badge
ī	ice, bite, high, sky	k	kill, tackle, bake, coat, quick
ō	open, tone, go, boat	l	let, yellow, ball
ô	all, horn, law, oar	m	met, camel, trim, summer
σο	look, pull, moor, wolf	n	not, flannel, ton
σ̄ο	ooze, tool, crew, rule	p	put, apple, tap
yσ̄ο	use, cute, few	r	red, port, dear, purr
yσο	cure, globule	s	sell, castle, pass, nice
oi	oil, point, toy	t	top, cattle, hat
ou	out, crowd, plow	v	vat, hovel, have
u	up, cut, color, flood	w	will, always, swear, quick
ʉr	urn, fur, deter, irk	y	yet, onion, yard
ə	a in ago	z	zebra, dazzle, haze, rise
	e in agent	ch	chin, catcher, arch, nature
	i in sanity	sh	she, cushion, dash, machine
	o in comply	th	thin, nothing, truth
	u in focus	*th*	then, father, lathe
ər	perhaps, murder	zh	azure, leisure, beige
		ŋ	ring, anger, drink

Abbreviation Key

adj.	adjective	*vi.*	intransitive verb
adv.	adverb	*vt.*	transitive verb
n.	noun		

A

ab·solve [ab zälv'] *vt.* To free.

a·but [ə but'] *vt.* To border on.

a·do·be [ə dō'bē] *n.* Sun-dried clay brick.

al·lo·cate [al'ō kāt'] *vt.* To allot; to designate and distribute.

am·bro·sia [am brō'zhə] *n.* The legendary food of Greek and Roman gods; anything deliciously satisfying.

an·neal·ment [ə nēl'mənt] *n.* A strengthening.

ap·er·ture [ap'ər chər] *n.* A hole.

ar·chi·vist [är'kə vist] *n.* A person in charge of archives (a place where records are kept). *adj.* Relating to a person in charge of archives.

B

bar·ri·o [bär'ē ō] *n.* A Spanish-speaking city district or neighborhood.

be·grudge [bē gruj'] *vt.* To resent; to be reluctant to give.

bel·ly [bel'ē] *vi.* To swell out.

break·wa·ter [brāk'wôt'ər] *n.* A barrier to protect the shore from strong waves.

C

ca·fé con le·che [kä fe' côn le'che] *n.* Coffee with milk.

caf·tan [kaf'tən] *n.* A long, loose dress or robe with wide sleeves.

car·i·ca·ture [kar'i kə chər] *vt.* To imitate in an exaggerated or distorted manner.

ca·thar·sis [kə thär'sis] *n.* Lessening one's fears by indirectly feeling them through drama.

cir·cum·lo·cu·tion [sur' kəm lō kyoo'shən] *n.* A roundabout way of saying something.

con·cur·rent [kən kur'ənt] *adj.* Occurring at the same time; converging.

cri·te·ri·on [krī tir'ē ən] *n.* A standard by which something is judged.

crone [krōn] *n.* An old, wrinkled, ugly woman.

cum lau·de [koom lou'dā] *adj.* Indicating above-average grades in college.

D

dis·cord [dis'kôrd'] *n.* Conflict; also, lack of musical harmony.

E

ebb [eb] *n.* Low tide, when water flows back to the sea.

e·dict [ē'dikt'] *n.* An official order.

ef·faced [ə fāst'] *adj.* Erased.

F

feign [fān] *vt.* To pretend.

fil·i·al [fil'ē əl] *adj.* Of or like a son or daughter.

fore·fend [fôr fend'] *vt.* To forbid.

H

ham·let [ham'lit] *n.* A tiny village.

He·gi·ra [hi jī'rə] *n.* Mohammed's flight from Mecca; a journey or escape.

hel·ter-skel·ter [hel'tər skel'tər] *adj.* Confused; hurried and hectic.

I

in·ex·o·ra·bly [in eks'ə rə blē] *adv.* Continuously, with no chance of being stopped.

in·ex·pli·ca·ble [in eks'pli kə bəl] *adj.* Unexplainable.

in·tern·ment [in tʉrn'mənt] *n.* Confinement.

in·tone [in tōn'] *vt.* To speak in a dull manner.

in·tu·it [in tōo'it] *vt.* To know without conscious reasoning.

J

jan·gling [jaŋ'gliŋ] *adj.* Sounding harsh and out of tune.

L

lean-to [lēn'tōo'] *n.* A shelter whose roof rests on some object.

le·thar·gic [li thär'jik] *adj.* Sluggish and dull.

loathe [lō*th*] *vt.* To hate.

lu·gu·bri·ous [lə gōo'brē əs] *adj.* Ridiculously sad.

M

man·date [man'dāt'] *vt.* To command with authority.

mat·ri·cide [mat'rə sīd'] *n.* Murder of one's mother.

min·is·ter [min'is tər] *vi.* To give help to or take care of.

mo·nad [mō'nad'] *n.* A separate, complete unit.

N

nar·cis·sis·tic [när'sə sis'tik] *adj.* Self-centered.

O

o·paque [ō pāk'] *adj.* Not letting light, heat, electricity, etc., pass through.

P

pal·pa·ble [pal'pə bəl] *adj.* Capable of being felt, as air movement or pressure.

par·ry [par'ē] *vt.* To reply evasively.

pa·tri·cian [pə trish'ən] *adj.* Proud; noble.

pe·riph·er·al [pə rif'ər əl] *adj.* Incidental; supplementary; away from central part.

pe·ter·ing [pēt'ər iŋ] *adj.* Gradually becoming weaker, then stopping.

phil·is·tine [fi lis'tin] *adj.* Narrow-minded; unable to appreciate the beauty or finer qualities of.

pla·cat·ed [plā'kāt'id] *adj.* Pacified.

plum·met [plum'it] *vi.* To decrease rapidly.

pro·di·gious [prō dij'əs] *adj.* Of great size or number.

R

rep·ro·ba·tion [rep'rə bā'shən] *n.* Disapproval.

S

she·nan·i·gan [shi nan'i gən] *n.* Nonsensical behavior.

short shrift [shôrt shrift] *n.* Very little attention.

smarm·y [smärm'ē] *adj.* Flattering but insincere.

spear·head [spir'hed'] *vt.* To take the lead in a group effort

spec·ter [spek'tər] *n.* A ghost or anything causing fear.

spec·trum [spek'trəm] *n.* The entire extent of a subject, category, etc.

straits [strāts] *n.* Condition or situation of distress.

su·per·sede [sōo'pər sēd'] *vt.* To replace; to supplant.

T

tan · gi · ble [tan′jə bəl] *adj.* Having physical form; that can be touched.

tiered [tird] *adj.* Layered.

U

un · can · ny [un kan′ē] *adj.* Weird.

un · ob · tru · sive [un əb trōō′siv] *adj.* Not noticeable.

V

ve · he · ment [vē′ə mənt] *adj.* Violent; passionate.

ve · neer [və nir′] *n.* An attractive but shallow appearance.

vis · age [viz′ij] *n.* A face, with emphasis on the facial expressions.

Index

J

K

INDEX

N

Q

R

INDEX

INDEX

1169

dictionary as aid, 962
and formal English, 520
good habits, 962–63
homonyms, 977–85
ie, ei, 964
and informal English, 520
numbers (numerals), 973–74
plurals of nouns, 970–72
prefixes, 965
pronunciation as aid, 962
proofreading as aid, 963
rules of, 964–74
spelling notebook as aid, 963
suffixes, 966–68
syllables as aid, 962
word-processing software as aid, 963
words commonly misspelled, 987–89
words often confused, 977–85
Spend, principal parts, 770
Spin, principal parts, 770
Spread, principal parts, 778
Spring, principal parts, 774
SQ3R reading method, 1103
Squinting modifier, 832
Stand, principal parts, 770
Standard English, 513, 842
Standardized tests, 1121–35
achievement tests, 1121
aptitude tests, 1121
critical analysis, tests of, 1132–35
critical reading, tests of, 1127–32
limited-response questions, 1123
open-response questions, 1123
preparing for, 1122
sample questions, 1125–26, 1129–32
taking, strategies for, 1122
verbal expression, tests of, 1123–26
State-of-being verb, 613
Stationary, stationery, 984
Statistics, 68, 302
Steal, principal parts, 774
Sting, principal parts, 770
Story ideas, 169–70
Storytelling, in narration, 81
Strategies for writing
classification, 79, 83–85
description, 79–80
evaluation, 79, 86–87
narration, 79, 80–82
Stratton, Joanna L., 69
Strike, principal parts, 774

Strive, principal parts, 774
Strong, George A., 427
Study skills, 1101–20. *See also* Reading; Reading skills.
classification, 1111–12
graphics and illustrations, 1108–1109
identifying main idea, 1104
interpreting and analyzing information, 1104–1107
memorizing, 1119–20
note taking, 1110–11
organizing information visually, 1112–13
outlining, 1114
paraphrasing, 1114–16
reading and understanding, 1101–1103
reasoning skills, 1107–1108
relationships among details, 1104–1105
routine, 1100
SQ3R method, 1103
study methods, 1109–20
summarizing, 1116–17
word processor use, 1102–1103
writing a précis, 1117–19
writing to learn, 1101–1102
Style, 515–23. *See also* English language; Meaning of a word; Sentence style.
adapting to aim, 516, 538–39
cliché, 532–33
connotation, 526–27
defined, 516
denotation, 526
euphemisms, 536
formal English, 312, 519
informal English, 312, 519, 521–23
jargon, 529
levels of meaning, 304, 523–29
loaded words, 528
misused words, 530–31
mixed idioms, 534
persuasive essay, 301, 310–12
reading for, 42
repetition, 312
rhythm, 312
sentence fragment, 312, 557–58
tired words, 532
and tone, 517–18
vivid words, 524–25
voice, 517–18
Subject cards, 1052–53
Subject complement, 642–43

T

Y

Z

Acknowledgments

For permission to reprint copyrighted material, grateful acknowledgment is made to the following sources:

Arte Público Press: From "Primary Lesson" from *Silent Dancing: A Partial Remembrance of a Puerto Rican Childhood* by Judith Ortiz Cofer. Copyright © 1990 by Judith Ortiz Cofer. Published by Arte Público Press–University of Houston, 1990.

The Asia Society: "Thoughts of Hanoi" by Nguyen Thi Vinh, translated by Nguyen Ngoc Bich from *A Thousand Years of Vietnamese Poetry.* Copyright © 1975 by The Asia Society.

The Estate of Isaac Asimov, c/o Ralph M. Vicinanza, Ltd.: "The Villain in the Atmosphere" by Isaac Asimov from *Past, Present, and Future.* Copyright © 1968 by Isaac Asimov.

Associated Press: From "Astronauts wanted: everyone can apply" by Marcia Dunn from *Tallahassee Democrat,* September 22, 1991. Copyright © 1991 by the Associated Press.

Ballantine Books, Inc., a division of Random House, Inc.: From "Life Is Not A Television Show" from *My Teacher Is Driving Me Crazy* by Joyce L. Vedral, Ph.D. Copyright © 1991 by Joyce L. Vedral, Ph.D.

Barron's Educational Series, Inc.: From *How to Teach Your Old Dog New Tricks* by Ted Baer. Copyright © 1991 by Barron's Educational Series, Inc. From "Angela C" from *Composing a Successful Application Essay: Write Your Way Into College* by George Ehrenhaft. Copyright © 1987 by Barron's Educational Series, Inc.

The Boston Globe: "Out, out, telltale spot!" by Susan Trausch from *The Boston Globe,* October 3, 1990, p. 19. Copyright © 1990 by The Boston Globe.

BPI Communications: "Film Preservation: Whose responsibility should it be?" by Wolf Schneider from *American Film,* August 1991, p. 2. Copyright © 1991 by BPI Communications. From "Vitreography: Making Prints with Glass Plates" by Emily Gaul from *American Artist,* vol. 58, no. 626, September 1994, p. 52. Copyright © 1994 by BPI Communications.

Carol Publishing Group: From "Valedictorian speech to Rutgers University, graduating class, 1919" by Paul Robeson from *The Whole World In His Hands* by Susan Robeson. Copyright © 1981 by Susan Robeson. A Citadel Press Book.

Eugenia W. Collier: From "Marigolds" by Eugenia Collier from *Negro Digest,* November 1969. Copyright © 1969 by Johnson Publishing Company, Inc.

The Darhansoff & Verrill Literary Agency: From "The World in Its Extreme" by William Langewiesche from *The Atlantic,* vol. 268, no. 5, November 1991. Copyright © 1991 by William Langewiesche.

Discover: From "Clever Kanzi" by Frederic Golden from *Discover,* vol. 12, no. 3, p. 20, March 1991. Copyright © 1991 by Discover Magazine. From "Large Pizza, Hold the Microchips" by Carl Zimmer from *Discover,* vol. 12, no. 4, April 1991, p. 12. Copyright © 1991 by Discover Magazine.

Dutton Signet, a division of Penguin Books USA Inc.: From *China Boy* by Gus Lee. Copyright © 1991 by Augustus S.M.S. Lee.

Louise Erdrich, c/o Rembar & Curtis: From "The Names of Women" by Louise Erdrich. Copyright © 1992 by Louise Erdrich. Originally appeared in *Granta,* Issue #41, Autumn 1992.

Farrar, Straus & Giroux, Inc.: From "One Art" from *The Complete Poems 1927–1979* by Elizabeth Bishop. Copyright © 1979, 1983 by Elizabeth Bishop.

Burton Goodman, agent for Manuela William Crosno: "The Precious Stones of Axolotyl" by Manuela Williams Crosno, edited by Burton Goodman. Copyright © 1987 by Manuela Williams Crosno.

Blanche C. Gregory, Inc.: From "To Fashion A Text" from *Inventing the Truth* by Annie Dillard. Copyright © 1987 by Annie Dillard.

Harcourt Brace & Company: From *Problem-Solving Strategies for Writing* by Linda Flower. Copyright © 1981 by Harcourt Brace & Company. From "Then He Goes Free" from *Cress Delahanty* by Jessamyn West. Copyright 1948 and renewed © 1976 by Jessamyn West.

Suzan Shown Harjo: From "I Won't Be Celebrating Columbus Day" by Suzan Shown Harjo from *Newsweek*, Columbus Special Issue, Fall/Winter 1991. Copyright © 1991 by Newsweek, Inc.

HarperCollins Publishers Inc.: From "Dog Training" from *One Man's Meat* by E. B. White. Copyright © 1941 and renewed © 1969 by E. B. White.

The Harvard Common Press: From *Forgotten Founders* by Bruce Johansen. Copyright © 1982 by Bruce Johansen. Published by The Harvard Common Press, 535 Albany Street, Boston, MA 02118.

August Hecksher: "Doing Chores" by August Hecksher.

Egyirba High: From "The Lion Sleeps Tonight" by Egyirba High from *Tight Spaces* by Kesho Scott, Cherry Muhanji, and Egyirba High. Copyright © 1987 by Kesho Scott, Cherry Muhanji, and Egyirba High.

Higher Education Research Institute, Graduate School of Education, UCLA: From "The Cooperative Institutional Research Program of the American Council on Education Research Institute, UCLA" from *The American Freshman: National Norms for Fall 1995,* by L. J. Sax, A. W. Astin, W. S. Korn, K. M. Mahoney. Copyright © 1995 by the Regents of the University of California.

Hill and Wang, a division of Farrar, Straus & Giroux, Inc: From "Thank You M'am" from *Short Stories* by Langston Hughes. Copyright © 1996 by Ramona Bass and Arnold Rampersad.

Henry Holt and Company, Inc.: From *Escalante: The Best Teacher in America* by Jay Matthews. Copyright © 1988 by Jay Matthews.

Houghton Mifflin Company: From *Silent Spring* by Rachel Carson. Copyright © 1962 by Rachel Carson; copyright renewed © 1990 by Roger Christie. All rights reserved. From "Almost a Family" from *Farewell to Manzanar* by Jeanne Wakatsuki Houston and James D. Houston. Copyright © 1973 by James D. Houston. All rights reserved.

IMG Literary: Review of *Back to the Future* from *The Complete Guide to Videocassette Movies*, edited by Steven H. Scheuer. Copyright © 1986 by Steven H. Scheuer.

The Heirs to the Estate of Martin Luther King, Jr., c/o Writers House, Inc., as agent for the proprietor: From "I Have A Dream" by Martin Luther King, Jr. Copyright © 1963 by Martin Luther King, Jr.; copyright renewed © 1991 by Coretta Scott King.

Stephen King: From "Now You Take 'Bambi' and 'Snow White'—That's Scary" by Stephen King from *TV Guide® Magazine*, June 13, 1981. Copyright © 1981 by News America Publications Inc.

CHAPTER 5: Page 169(tr), MGM Studios/SuperStock; 169(cl), Everett Collection; 169(br), Shooting Star International; 176, C. Simms/SuperStock; 178, Albano Guatti/The Stock Market; 180, C. Orrico/SuperStock; 202, Archive Photos.

CHAPTER 6: Pages 219–223, Michelle Bridwell/HRW Photo; 224, Mary Kate Denny/PhotoEdit; 225–227, Michelle Bridwell/HRW Photo; 227, Jim Shippee/Unicorn Stock Photos; 230, Michelle Bridwell/HRW Photo; 231, Robert Wolf/Robert Wolf Photography; 233–238, Michelle Bridwell/HRW Photo; 249, Visual Communications Archives/Asian American Studies Central, Inc.

CHAPTER 7: Page 258(tl), Shooting Star International; 258(tr), Brian Lovell/Nawrocki Stock Photo; 258(bc), P. Cantor/SuperStock; 260, James D. Wilson/Woodfin Camp & Associates; 264, SuperStock; 267, Jim Zuckerman/Westlight; 269, Nathan Benn/Woodfin Camp & Associates; 271, Alon Reininger/Unicorn Stock Photos; 273, Alan Oddie/PhotoEdit; 274, Mary Kate Denny/PhotoEdit; 276, Tony Freeman/PhotoEdit; 278, W. Strode/SuperStock; 280(tl), Michael Heron/Woodfin Camp & Associates; 280(tr), St. Gil & Associates/The Image Bank; 280(c), Elizabeth Zuckerman/PhotoEdit; 282, Craig Aurness/Westlight; 285, Manfred Kage/Peter Arnold, Inc.; 286, G. Glod/SuperStock.

CHAPTER 8: Page 293, Thomas Kristich/Retna Ltd.; 298, A. Koropp/SuperStock; 299, Everett Collection/CSU; 302, Gary Braash/Woodfin Camp & Associates, Inc.; 303, Erich Hartmann/Magnum Photos; 304, Graham/Nawrocki Stock Photo; 310, Mark Richards/PhotoEdit; 311(bl), R. King/SuperStock; 311(bc), David R. Frazier Photolibrary; 311(br), Joe Sohm/Nawrocki Stock Photo; 313, Photofest; 314(cl), Shooting Star International; 314(cr), Shooting Star International; 315, 316(tl), Photofest; 316(tr), Shooting Star International; 317, Jeffrey Hunter/The Kobal Collection; 318(all), Shooting Star International; 320–321, Bob Daemmrich Photography; 322, Tom Stoddart/Woodfin Camp & Associates, Inc.; 326, Paul Conklin/Uniphoto Picture Agency; 327, Alan Oddie/PhotoEdit; 336, Wally McNamee/Woodfin Camp & Associates; 341(tc), HRW Photo; 341(bc), Robert Brenner/PhotoEdit.

CHAPTER 9: Page 347, Nawrocki Stock Photo; 350–353, Michelle Bridwell/HRW Photo/Del Valle Schools, Del Valle, Texas; 355, Photo courtesy of Teach for America, New York, New York; 358, David Young-Wolff/PhotoEdit; 360, Catherine Karnow/ Woodfin Camp & Associates, Inc.; 361, Paul Conklin/PhotoEdit; 364, Bill Ross/Woodfin Camp & Associates, Inc.; 365, C. M. Fitch/SuperStock; 366, David Muench/David Muench Photography; 367, Mike Kirkpatrick/ProFiles West/Index Stock; 369, David Falconer/David R. Frazier Photolibrary; 371, W. Rosseau/SuperStock;

373(tl), P. R. Production/SuperStock; 373(tr), Tony Freeman/PhotoEdit; 374, Michelle Bridwell/HRW Photo/Popham Elementary School, Del Valle, Texas; 383, Bob Adelman/Magnum Photos; 384, FPG International; 387(cl), Everett Collection; 387(cr), Shooting Star International.

CHAPTER 10: Page 390, Shooting Star International; 391(all), Everett Collection; 392, Shooting Star International; 395, Svenkst Pressfoto/Archive Photos; 408, Skjold/Nawrocki Stock Photo; 413(cl), David R. Frazier Photolibrary; 413(cr), Mark Antman/The Image Works; 421, T. Rosenthal/SuperStock; 427, HRW Photo Research Library/New York State Museum Albany, New York; 430(bl), Everett Collection; 430(br), Larry Busacca/Retna Ltd.; 433(cr), Michelle Bridwell/HRW Photo/Laredo Independent School District's Instructional Television Studio, Laredo, Texas.

CHAPTER 11: Page 436, Robert Semeniuk/The Stock Market; 437, David Woods/The Stock Market; 438, Niki Mareschal/The Image Bank; 441(tr), Peter E. Beney/The Image Bank; 441(cl), K. Gibson/SuperStock; 441(bc), Art Kane/The Image Bank; 444, Cameramann International, Ltd.; 449, Gabe Palmer/The Stock Market; 451, Jeffrey W. Myers/Nawrocki Stock Photo; 455, M. Denis-Huot/Liaison International; 460(tl), Culver Pictures, Inc.; 460(tr), Archive Photos; 472, Strauss/John Curtis/The Stock Market; 489(cl), R. Llewellyn/SuperStock; 489(cr), FPG International; 492, Michelle Bridwell/HRW Photo/United High School and Laredo High School, Laredo, Texas.

CHAPTER 12: Page 498(cl), Charlene Smith/ProFiles West/Index Stock; 498(cr), The Book of Durrow. The Beginning of the Gospel of Saint Mark. The Board of Trinity College, Dublin/Photo by The Green Studio Limited, Dublin; 503, The Granger Collection/ New York; 514(bl), Richard Price/Westlight; 514(bc), W. Morgan/Westlight; 514(br), Lewis Portnoy/The Stock Market.

CHAPTER 13: Page 529, Michelle Bridwell/HRW Photo/J. W. Nixon High School, Laredo, Texas.

CHAPTER 14: Page 543, Culver Pictures, Inc.; 547(cl), Australia Picture Library/L & B Hemmings/Westlight; 547(cr), Janear, Inc./The Image Bank; 548, Bridgeman Collection/ SuperStock; 549, Steve Vidler/Nawrocki Stock Photo; 553(cl), Culver Pictures, Inc.; 553(cr), Everett Press Collection/CSU; 554(all), Michelle Bridwell/ HRW Photo/Courtesy of the Texas Memorial Museum; 559, Michelle Bridwell/HRW Photo/ McCallum High School, Austin, Texas; 561, Photofest.

CHAPTER 15: Page 567(all), David H. Ellis/Visuals Unlimited; 570, UPI/Bettmann; 572(all), NASA/Peter Arnold, Inc.; 575, Richard C. Reed/Unicorn Stock Photos; 578, The Everett Collection; 579, Roger Werth/Woodfin Camp & Associates.

CHAPTER 16: Page 585, Paul J. Sutton/Duomo; 86, The Stock Market; 590, Culver Pictures, Inc.; 593, Michelle Bridwell/HRW Photo/McCallum High School, Austin, Texas.

CHAPTER 17: Page 602, AP/Wide World Photos; 609, FPG International; 615(cl), Norman Owen Tomalin/Bruce Coleman, Inc.; 615(cr), The Image Works; 623, Kevin Schafer/Peter Arnold, Inc.; 625, Mpinduzi Khuthaza/African American Cultural Center, Los Angeles.

CHAPTER 18: Page 637(all), The Peabody Museum of Salem; 640(all), Michelle Bridwell/HRW Photo/McCallum High School, Austin, Texas; 641, Ira Wyman/Sygma Photo News; 644(all), Bruno Barbey/Magnum Photos.

CHAPTER 19: Page 654(c), David Austen 1991/Woodfin Camp & Associates; 654(cr), Frank Perkins/Profiles West/Index Stock; 656, Everett Press Collection, CSU; 660, Joe Jaworski/HRW Photo; 662(cl), Chip Porter/Allstock/Tony Stone Images; 662(c), Tom Bean/Allstock/Tony Stone Images; 662(cr)(bl), Alaska Division of Tourism; 666, Everett Collection; 669, Kevin Schaffer/AllStock/Tony Stone Images.

CHAPTER 20: Page 681(all), Courtesy of Dr. Athelstan Spilhaus; 691(all), Insect Farming & Trading Agency. Unitech Development & Consultancy PTY LTD, Morobe Province, Papua New Guinea.

CHAPTER 21: Page 705, Culver Pictures, Inc.; 707, SuperStock; 715, Roddey E. Mims/Uniphoto Picture Agency; 722(cl), Margot Granitsas/Photo Researchers, Inc.; 722(cr), Rommel/Masterfile; 723, L. Berger/SuperStock.

CHAPTER 22: Page 734, Ken Regan/Camera 5; 736, Collection of Henry Ford Museum & Greenfield Village; 747(all), Mavournea Hay/Frontera Fotos; 749, Satoshi Yabuuchi/Courtesy of Gallery Kitano, Tokyo, Japan.

CHAPTER 23: Page 757, Culver Pictures, Inc.; 759, NASA/Broadcast Images; 761, Miramax/Shooting Star International.

CHAPTER 24: Page 777, Fred Hirschmann; 795, J. R. Eyerman/Life Magazine © 1952 Time Inc.

CHAPTER 25: Page 815, Everett Collection, Inc.; 819(cl), William Campbell/Time; 819(cr), Ken Regan/Camera 5; 826, Everett Collection.

CHAPTER 26: Page 837, Courtesy of Harcourt, Brace, Jovanovich, Inc.; 838, The Bettmann Archive.

CHAPTER 27: Page 845, Schomburg Center for Research in Black Culture. The New York Public Library. The Astor, Lennox, and Tilden Foundations; 852, © Sylvian Julienne 1983/Woodfin Camp & Associates, Inc.; 864, Lawrence Migdale.

CHAPTER 28: Page 879(c), from *Great News Photos & the Stories Behind Them* by John Faber, Historian. National Press Photographers Association; 885, NASA/HRW Photo; 890(cr), Stan Byers; 890(bl, br), Southern Plains Indian Museum, Anadarko, Oklahoma.

CHAPTER 29: Page 904, AP/Wide World Photos; 912(both), Gale Gaona/South Coast Enterprises; 920(cl), Michael Yamashita; 920(c), Japanese American Cultural & Community Center; 920(cr), Michael Yamashita.

CHAPTER 30: Page 933, AP/Wide World Photos; 941, Michelle Bridwell; 958(both), UPI/Bettmann.

CHAPTER 31: Page 969(c), Richard Steedman/The Stock Market; 969(bl), Schomburg Center for Research in Black Culture. The New York Public Library. Astor, Lennox, and Tilden Foundations; 969(br), Corbis-Bettmann; 987(both), Karen Preuss.

ILLUSTRATION CREDITS

Linda Blackwell—159, 268, 339

Rondi Collette—xxv, 209, 555, 556, 656, 675, 676, 809

Tom Gianni—722

Mary Jones—64, 295, 587, 965

Brian Karas—212–215

Linda Kelen—81, 505, 506, 508, 527, 537, 569

Susan Kemnitz—xviii, 34, 80, 184, 186, 187, 190, 192, 397, 398, 401, 417, 517

Rich Lo—419, 623, 885

Pamela Paulsrud—173, 379, 425

Precision Graphics—231, 655, 702, 779, 976

Doug Schneider—ix, xxiv, 131, 433, 669

Jack Scott—546

Steve Shock—x, 2, 60, 97, 163, 164, 166, 426

Troy Thomas—xii, 254, 255, 256

Nancy Tucker—207

Acknowledgments

For permission to reprint copyrighted material in the Annotated Teacher's Edition, grateful acknowledgment is made to the following sources:

Algonquin Books of Chapel Hill: From *Daughters of Memory* by Janis Arnold. Copyright © 1991 by Janis Arnold.

Gwendolyn Brooks: From "Memorial to Ed Bland" from *Blacks* by Gwendolyn Brooks. Copyright © 1991 by Gwendolyn Brooks. Reissued by Third World Press, Chicago, 1991.

Will Hobbs: From "Bringing Your Words to Life" by Will Hobbs from *R & E Journal,* Spring 1996. Copyright © 1996 by Will Hobbs.

W.W. Norton and Company, Inc.: From "The Bear" from *Life Sentence: Selected Poems* by Nina Cassian, edited by William Jay Smith, translated by Laura Schiff. Copyright © 1982 by Nina Cassian.

People Weekly: From "Hell on Wheels" from the "Up Front" section of *People Weekly,* vol. 36, no. 10, September 16, 1991. Copyright © 1991 by People Weekly.

Random House, Inc.: From "Why Do We Read Fiction?" from *New and Selected Essays* by Robert Penn Warren. Copyright © 1989 by Robert Penn Warren.

Sangster's Book Stores Ltd.: From "Jamaica Ant'em" from *Jamaica Labrish* by Louise Bennett. Copyright © 1966 by Louise Bennett.

PHOTO CREDITS *(Annotated Teacher's Edition)*

Abbreviations used: (t) top, (c) center, (b) bottom, (l) left, (r) right, (bckgd) background

COVER: Ralph J. Brunke Photography

TABLE OF CONTENTS: Page T7(tr), HRW Photo Library; T7(cr),(br), Culver Pictures, Inc.; T8(tr), V.Englebert/Leo de Wys, Inc.; T8(br),©Dr. Tom Hester/Texas Archaeological Research Laboratory/The University of Texas; T9, © Nathan Bilow Photography; T10, Don King/Lightwaves/The Image Bank; T12, HRW Photo/Michelle Bridwell; T14, David R. Frazier Photolibrary; T15, Nawrocki Stock Photo; T16, Skjold/Nawrocki Stock Photo; T17, John Curtis/The Stock Market; T18(tr), Rhoda Sidney/PhotoEdit; T19, Courtesy of the Texas Memorial Museum/HRW Photo/Michelle Bridwell; T20(l), Paul J. Sutton/Duomo; T20(br), © 1985 Roger Werth/Woodfin Camp & Associates; T21, AP/World Wide Photos; T22, African American Culture Center, Los Angeles, CA.; T23(all photos), Bruno Barbey/Magnum; T26, Culver Pictures, Inc.; T28, Gale Gaona/South Coast Enterprises; T29, AP/ Wide World Photos; T30(tr), © 1978 Karen R. Preuss; T30(br) Crandall/The Image Works; T31,Tony Freeman/PhotoEdit; T33, Todd Powell/ProFiles West/Index Stock Photography; T34, Bob Daemmrich/The Image Works.

PROFESSIONAL ESSAYS: Page T36-T77, border by M. Angelo/Westlight; T36(t), Dennis Carlyle Darling; T36(c), (b), T37(tl), Larry Ford; T37(tr), J. Alexander Newberry; T37(cl), Larry Ford; T37(cr), Dennis Carlyle Darling; T37(bl), (br), James Newberry; T38, T39, T42, Dennis Carlyle Darling; T45, T47, T48, Larry Ford; T51, Dennis Carlyle Darling; T53, T55, Larry Ford; T57, Dennis Carlyle Darling; T62, T65, J. Alexander Newberry; T66, Courtesy of Judith Irvin; T67, James Newberry; T68, Courtesy of Joyce Armstrong Carrol; T69, James Newberry; T72, Jonathan Lock, T73; Larry Ford.

ILLUSTRATION CREDITS: *(Annotated Teacher's Edition)*

Jane Thurmond Design— Page 13A, 61A, 103A, 131A, 165A, 201A, 247A, 283A, 321A, 361A, 405A, 420A, 440A

Edd Patton—Page T39, T40, T41, T44, T46, T49, T50, T53, T54, T57, T58, T59, T60, T61, T63, T64, T66, T67, T69, T71, T72, T74, T75, T76, T77

Front Matter Design—Maeder Design

Icons—Leslie Kell
Mike Krone

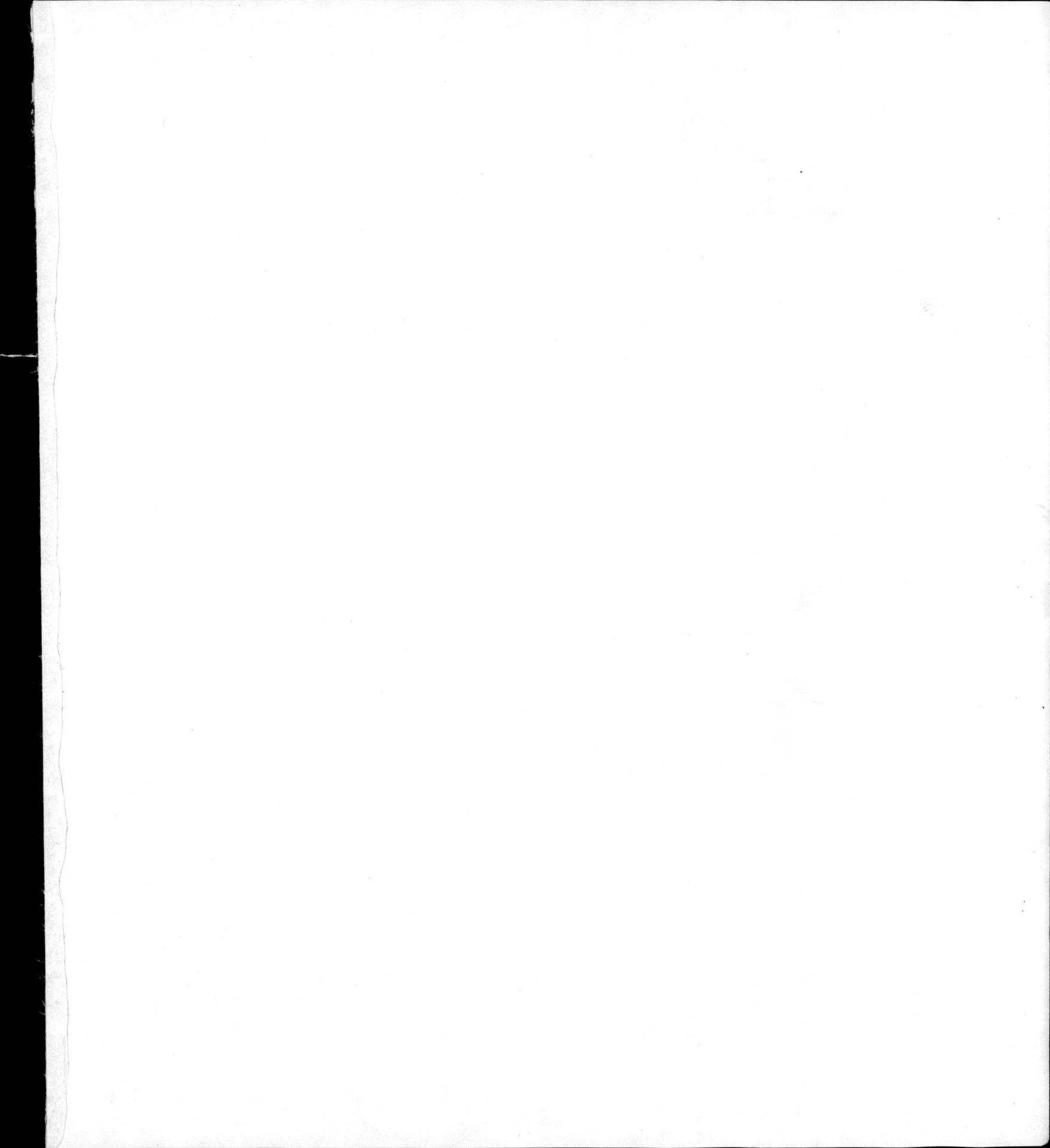